Microprocessors and Microcomputer Systems

Microprocessors and Microcomputer Systems

Second Edition

Guthikonda V. Rao, Ph.D.

Senior Member, Technical Staff
System Sciences Division (Space Applications)
Computer Sciences Corporation
Silver Spring, Maryland

VNR
VAN NOSTRAND REINHOLD COMPANY
NEW YORK CINCINNATI TORONTO LONDON MELBOURNE

To my parents,

Venkatchelm and Rathnama

Van Nostrand Reinhold Company Regional Offices:
New York Cincinnati

Van Nostrand Reinhold Company International Offices:
London Toronto Melbourne

Library of Congress Catalog Card Number: 80-29510
ISBN: 0-442-25626-4

Manufactured in the United States of America

Published by Van Nostrand Reinhold Company
135 West 50th Street, New York, N.Y. 10020

Published simultaneously in Canada by Van Nostrand Reinhold Ltd.

15 14 13 12 11 10 9 8 7 6 5 4 3 2

Library of Congress Cataloging in Publication Data

Rao, Guthikonda V.
Microprocessors and microcomputer systems.

Includes index.
1. Microprocessors. 2. Microcomputers. I. Title.
QA76.5.R36 1981 001.64'04 80-29510
ISBN 0-442-25626-4

Preface

This topical state-of-the-art analysis is an integrated digest of the large volume of information presently available on the subject of digital computers as oriented toward the latest innovations, microprocessor and microcomputer.

With an unpredictably short learning phase covering more than 25 years of changing technology, the digital computer has swiftly moved at an accelerated pace of development, from the relay to the vacuum tube, from the tube to the discrete solid-state temperature-sensitive germanium transistor, parametrics and tunnel diode, from the discrete transistor to the stable silicon monolithic individual integrated circuit (IC), then from the IC to the small- and medium-scale integration (MSI) of the minis, and finally from the MSI to the high-technology of the mass-produced *very large-scale* integrated form of microelectronics, VLSI, to present eventually a dedicated powerful Microcomputer-on-a-chip that performs at speeds enhanced by 4 to 6 orders of magnitude—as compared to the original vacuum-tube versions. Chapter 12 presents a brief exposition of the escalating popularity of the application of low-cost CRT-keyboard microcomputer systems in Personal Computing, by using available BASIC and PASCAL programs on tape cassettes and mini floppy diskettes.

With each advance in the reduction of size, the digital computer has achieved progressively higher reliability in operation. With regard to its flexibility and its computation capacity, the microcomputer is more powerful than the first- and second-generation digital computers built during the 1950s to occupy oversized rooms.

The author presents this analysis on the presently available microprocessors and microcomputer systems, and the associated LSI hardware and firmware, at a time when the technology of microelectronics is fairly well established. The various topics in the text are chosen in order to facilitate communication between not only hardware and software specialists, but also marketing and training personnel. In view of the unavoidable terminology involved, two complete readings are recommended for a better grasp of the hardware and software terms.

The author extends his sincere appreciation to Dr. D. W. C. Shen of the Moore School of Electrical Engineering; Dr. C. N. Weygandt, former chairman, Graduate Group Committee (E. E.), University of Pennsylvania; Dr. Des R. Sood and Dr. Thomas C. Brown of Computer Sciences Corporation; Samuel Weber, Editor-in-Chief of McGraw-Hill's *Electronics* magazine; and Tyler G. Hicks, Editor-in-Chief, Engineering, Science, and Management of the McGraw-Hill Book Company, for their expression of interest and encouragement during the course of this project. Sincere thanks to Maxine Yackman for typing the manuscript in record time. Grateful acknowledgments are due to the many authors who originally presented the information on these new devices in *Electronics*, *IEEE Spectrum*, and several other professional magazines and product brochures.

Guthikonda V. Rao, Ph.D.
Beltsville, Maryland

Contents

1
Introduction to Microprocessors and Microcomputer Systems

1-1. SCOPE

New digital computer systems under stored program control, using microprocessors and programmable read-only memories (PROM) and random-access read/write memories (RAM), allow greater capacity and flexibility at low cost and minimum requirements of space and power. Even seemingly small desk-sets have a capability to turn into interactive computer terminals. And, with the introduction of optical links via fiber-optic mini-waveguide cables, high-capacity, interoffice or intersystem data exchange is a feasible proposition today in business, defense, and communications systems. A **microcomputer on a single-chip** is indeed a new powerful microtool that is comparable in performance to many of the original versions of minicomputers.

The **microprocessor** enables:

1. **A bus-oriented architecture**, thus requiring a minimum of hardware for peripheral support.
2. **Cost effectiveness** through built-in auxiliary features without any elaborate extra hardware, by replacing existing voluminous disk, drum, and core random-access memory designs with extendable, high-density, fast-access, large-scale integrated (LSI), and very-large-scale integrated (VLSI) semi-conductor RAMs as working memory.
3. **Achievement of a "smart" or "intelligent" terminal** that can execute a sequence of instructions under the command of a built-in, extendable read-only memory (ROM).

The latest developments in the following **real-time and off-line digital computer applications** demand expedited progress in improved techniques of solid-state LSI and VLSI.

1. Large-network data communications.
2. Small-scale or large-scale, coded information exchange by radio, satellite, cable and land lines, and associated message-switching systems.

3. Transportation and navigation; dedicated mobile digital computers: and personal computing in home and business.
4. Automated process and numerical control; instrumentation in manufacturing and production; computer simulation; and interactive graphics/color portraits.
5. General-purpose digital computer systems in defense applications and government administration.
6. Business, statistics, and related data-processing systems.
7. Medical care, chemical analyses, medical diagnosis, and decisionmaking.
8. Education, recreation, printing, word processing, and video games.
9. Research in energy and pollution; prediction and optimization/pattern recognition.
10. Research in academic establishments, such as implementation of mathematical models for complex problems in Operations Research, etc.

LSI and **VLSI**, in turn, are enabling the evolution of more and more sophisticated microprocessors and programmable logic arrays (PLAs) and high-density, high-speed, semiconductor memories. The PLAs replace the previous and present hard-wired logic using small- and medium-scale integrated circuits. These new LSI/VLSI components simply outperform and undersell the older alternative technologies in the relevant fields, and considerably extend the scope of their performance and create large-scale usage in yet newer areas of applications. Fairly low-priced, low-power, desktop microcomputer systems have an equivalent capability, via suitable interface, to replace at least some of the previous simpler, leased, high-priced, medium-scale, general-purpose digital computer operating systems. These new systems incidentally enable greater flexibility, by means of plug-in firmware, to meet routine software requirements. Some microprocessors in instrumentation provide not only internal and external controls, but also reduce maintenance costs by furnishing auxiliary internal fault-diagnosis, self-test, and self-calibration. The latest dedicated single-chip microcomputer can be squeezed onto a 200-mil-square substrate, requiring not more than a few hundred milliwatts. And all this happened within an amazingly short span of 15 years; a **silicon monolithic substrate**, less than a quarter of an inch on an edge can incorporate well over 100,000 solid-state components. The cost of each functional component has dropped by a factor of more than 1,000 or so—from several dollars, to 30 cents, to presently a small fraction of a cent.

In fact, it is the so-called desktop **central processing unit (CPU)** of the minicomputer of the 1960s that started the revolution of the microelectronics by way of hybrid and medium-scale integration (MSI). They were based on the relevant thin-film and monolithic solid-state technologies. Today, the turnover has arrived for the less-complex full-fledged minicomputer operating systems, which use built-in assemblers and compilers for high-level languages (as plug-in tape cassettes or random-access floppy-disk auxiliary-memory libraries) and mini-CRT display and keyboard along with an adjoining mini-printer as peripherals. The latest IBM-5120 portable computer, using a built-in mini-CRT and associated keyboard and TV adapter, and the Digital Equipment Corporation's PDP-11/2 and 11/23 microcomputer systems occupy the high-end of these microcomputer operating systems from the viewpoints of cost and on-line operating facility. Brief data on these systems and other microcomputer systems presently available are included in this analysis for a comparative study of their architecture and facilities. The cross-reference tables in Chapter 9 for the various microprocessor types present a comparative set of reference data on their performance and capability. Chapter 12 is devoted to the large-scale application of microprocessors and microcomputer systems to personal computing in small-business and home hobby applications.

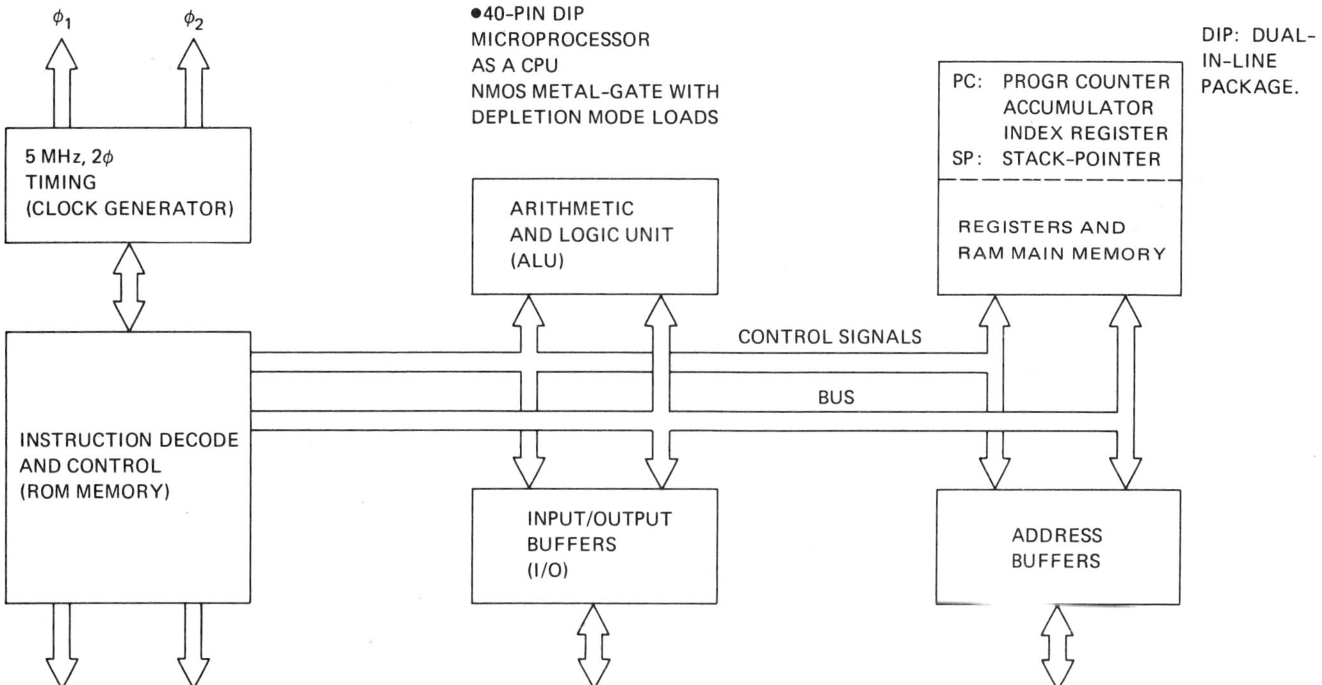

Fig. 1-1. Architecture of a typical microprocessor.

1-2. ARCHITECTURE

The typical architecture of a single-chip microprocessor as a CPU, and the support that goes with it presently on a single printed-circuit board as a dedicated microcomputer system, are shown in Figs. 1-1 and 1-2. The term **main frame** is commercially used for the CPU in the case of the **general-purpose digital computers** of the previous classifications, namely,

1. Large-scale central computer systems
2. Medium-scale leased computer systems
3. Minicomputers.

Instructions from the stored control memory program from a ROM are decoded by the decode-and-control unit and executed by circuits in one or more of the other areas. A **crystal-controlled clock generator** supplies timing and synchronization to most parts of the system. The **arithmetic and logic unit (ALU)** performs arithmetic and logic operations. The **registers** serve as easily accessible working memory-stack for manipulating programs and data transferred from a tape or a floppy-disk to the **internal temporary data storage.** This function is furnished by the **fast-access read/write random-access memory (RAM),** which in some cases may be part of the microprocessor chip. **I/O (input-output) buffers** provide timing and multiplexing. They are bidirectional, that is, they can either read-in instructions and data into the built-in RAM of the microprocessor from the keyboard or a PROM, or write data or instructions on the RAM (or an extended external large-scale RAM) and thence to an external cassette tape or a floppy-disk, or a CRT-display, or a teletype (TTY)-printer, according to the peripheral in use. The **microprocessor** can be generally identified as ALU plus Control (both making it a CPU), while the **microcomputer** will, in addition, have the complement of Input, Output, and ROM/RAM memory sections to make it a dedicated computer system. The internal RAM is usually considered as the main memory of the microcomputer.

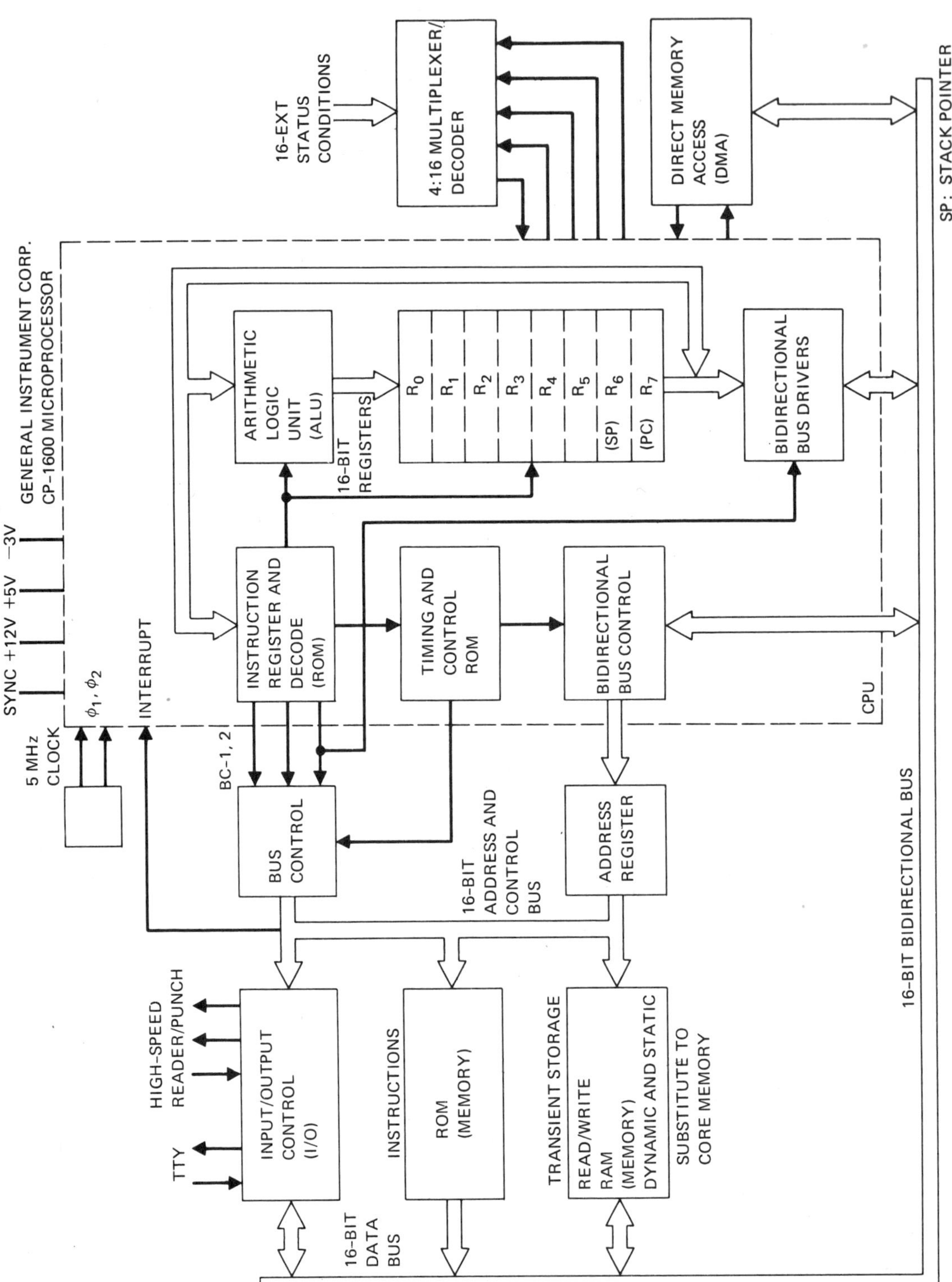

Fig. 1-2. A typical microcomputer system. *(Courtesy of General Instrument Corp.)*

The **accumulator** is a special-purpose register closely associated with the ALU, and it is one of the sources of data for ALU and an immediate temporary destination for the ALU's results. For example, in a dedicated Hughes Avionics microcomputer, the eight programming registers are organized as two **index-registers**; four accumulators; a **stack-pointer** for first-in, first-out (FIFO) or last-in, first-out (LIFO) for four accumulator registers; and a **program-counter**. The **address-buffers** make the memory-interface to supply the control-memory RAM with the address from which to fetch the next instruction. Some microprocessor systems provide **interface adapters** for various types of I/O operations. In some cases, additional ICs may be required to interrupt CPU operation for service requests, for changing program-flow, and for handling special modes of operation. Sometimes, a single microcomputer system may span several technologies such as PMOS, NMOS, CMOS, Bipolar TTL, ECL, and I^2L; then, special interface chips will be required to meet such problems as voltage levels and propagation times. In some systems, for example, 80 instructions programmed on a ROM can manipulate I/O data just like memory in internal or external RAMs. External mass memory is provided by tape cassettes/cartridges, mini-floppy diskettes, and magnetic-bubble memories.

The computation in the ALU is performed in binary arithmetic machine language, and the well-defined procedure of computation for a solution of a problem in finite number of steps is usually designated as an "algorithm." Assembly program coding, however, is commonly done in octal or mostly hexadecimal binary-coded decimal digits.

1-2.1. An Introductory Example of the Architecture of a Microprocessor. The CP-1600 NMOS microprocessor of General Instrument Corporation (as shown in Fig. 1-1) and its adjoining support system for either a teleprinter or a high-speed paper-tape reader/punch constitute a microcomputer system (as shown in Fig. 1-2). It was the first powerful single-chip 16-bit CPU produced, and it is designed with a third-generation minicomputer architecture, using eight high-speed general-purpose 16-bit registers. It is priced at $38.50. The 16-bit word-length and four addressing modes permit efficient access to 64-K bytes of memory; this could be accomplished with programs on ROM, and data storage on RAM or peripheral devices. I/O data can be manipulated like that of memory by its 87 instructions in 1.6 to 4.8 μs. The 16-bit addition from memory takes 3.2 μs. The non-erasable ROM memory can be extended up to 64-K bits with a single 5-V supply, and readily available static RAMs are limited to a capacity of 16-K bits. The microcomputer system is fully compatible with a cross-software package that was developed for an earlier minicomputer version. The on-line debug program to aid in checkout, the text editor, the assembler, the relocating linking-loader, the memory-dump program, the monitor and utility routines, the microprocessor and language-generation package, and a library of subroutines are all available. These additional software packages make a few extra cards in the desktop microcomputer unit. Although the ALU is 8-bit functionally, this particular microprocessor presents a 16-bit architecture to the programmer.

1-3. MICROCOMPUTER ARCHITECTURE COMPARED TO MINICOMPUTER ARCHITECTURE

The following hardware and software features of a microcomputer system are generally compatible with those of an earlier minicomputer system from the same manufacturer. That is, the task of interfacing more expensive peripherals from the same manufacturer becomes much easier.

1. Third-generation minicomputer architecture
2. High-speed general-purpose 16-bit registers

3. 16-bit word-length (32-bit with latest VLSI microprocessors)
4. Four addressing modes permit access to 64 kilo-bytes of memory in any combination of program, data storage, or peripheral devices
5. I/O is manipulated like memory
6. Approximately 100 instructions
7. Unlimited depth of stack-storage or program-interrupts
8. External ROMs of capacity from 4-K to 64-K bits provide 16-bit computing power at 8-bit density
9. Static RAMs of capacity from 1-K to 16-K bits or dynamic and static RAMs of 64-K bits as working memory
10. Programmable interface-controller LSI chips for TTY, high-speed paper-tape, serial line-printer, and cassette-tape peripherals
11. Extensive resident software
12. Cross-software package for compatibility with manufacturer's present minicomputers
13. On-line debug program
14. Text-editor
15. Relocating linking-editor
16. Memory-dump program
17. Monitor and utility routines
18. Microprocessor and language-generation package
19. Expanding library of application subroutines.

As a direct comparison, the functional architecture of a typical average minicomputer is shown in Fig. 1-3 to indicate how identically it is organized around a microprogrammed controller and a two-bus data-and-instruction-exchange structure. The functional elements of the CPU, I/O, and the main-memory accept, interpret, and process and return data from/to the primary bus, whereas the secondary bus simultaneously provides a communication path for transfer of memory between the ALU and the various registers. It

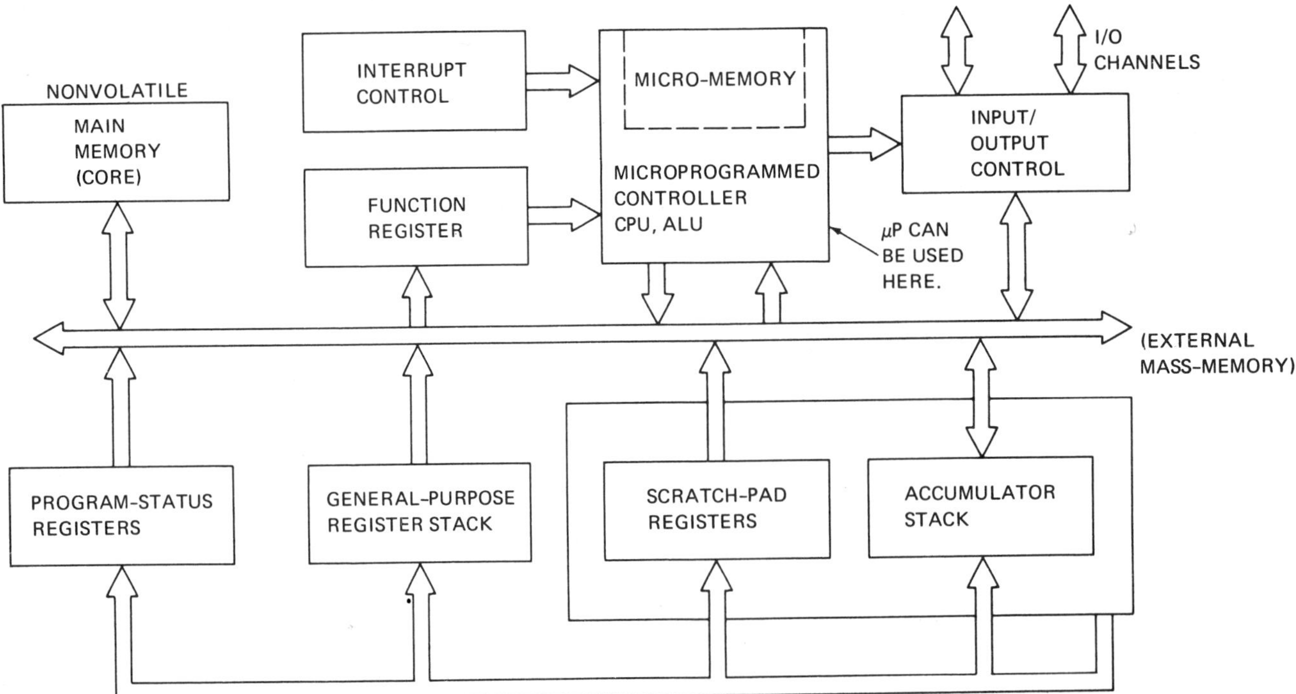

Fig. 1-3. Organization of a typical minicomputer.

may be noted from the commonality of their architecture how similar and powerful the modern microcomputer systems are, compared to the previous higher-cost minicomputer operating systems. Facilities such as a prototyping system, time-share assembler, stand-alone assembler and editor, time-share simulator/debugger, stand-alone debugger, and a minimum of 64-K word-addressing capability, full environmental capability to meet rigorous standards (at extra cost), a single supply voltage at 5 V and minimum operating power, and on-chip direct memory access (DMA)/interrupt/direct program-load capability, all make the microcomputer systems as powerful as the minicomputer operating systems in a variety of systems applications. Even a peripheral, such as an interactive CRT-terminal that includes a 64-character ASCII keyboard and a 16-line display of 40/80 characters per line, and a 2 · 4-K baud/sec "modem" for data applications, is available in a 16" X 19" X 6" case at $1,650 (Digi-Log), to convert a microcomputer system into a full Operating System by using for Interface a few additional MSI integrated circuits on a single card or, as an alternative, an additional custom LSI-chip.

The **performance specifications of a typical high-cost minicomputer** follow. They indicate that the microcomputer system designs presently available are slowly approaching such standards, if they have not already done so, by special multichip system-design and bit-slice techniques. (In general, a CPU designed with about three LSI microprocessor chips enables such a capability. A single VLSI chip has a comparable computational capability.)

1. Main frame (CPU): this corresponds to the actual microprocessor.
2. Internal or external I/O control.
3. Main memory: 64-K bytes of magnetic core as nonvolatile memory. (In the case of microcomputers, for a majority of applications, nonvolatile core at higher cost/power consumption, and comparatively large size is incompatible. Static main-memory RAMs, in conjunction with a mass memory, such as a random-access floppy-disk or an off-line tape-cartridge system, are more appropriate. Latest LSI metal-nitride-oxide semiconductor memories are nonvolatile for years, and they may serve this purpose in the near future in *some* applications—due to their slow write-time in ms.)
4. 16-bit or 32-bit double-length words; 8-bit bytes. 77-instruction repertoire. Math-pack: 1 X 24 (16 ROMs). Microprogrammed ROM: 512 words of 32 bits each (16 ROMs, 1,024 bits each).
5. Five instruction-word formats, using 4-bit literals, 8-bit bytes, and 16- or 32-bit words.
6. Execution time for single word: 65 ns. (Instruction: Read/Interrupt; operand; Read/Perform.)
7. Main-memory cycle-time: 750 ns, Read/Restore time. Macroinstruction: 2.25 to 0.75 μs.
8. Floating-point arithmetic in 4-bit hexadecimal digits. Bootstrap addresses: ROM with a capacity of 192 words.
9. I/O control: 16-word program. Addressable **asynchronous** parallel I/O channels: 16, at 4-MHz clock. (Variations in start pulse-width prevented by sync circuits.)
10. General-purpose registers: 18; serial I/O channels: 4.
11. Internal clock: 1 kHz for slow-speed interface. One and 4 MHz for high-speed interface. External clock: 0.55 kHz.
12. Data load (output); microprocessor interrupt; clock-pulse priority, and then DMA port.

In view of their susceptibility to replacement by microcomputers in a majority of their former applications, the latest high-speed real-time minicomputers have a tendency to attain the performance and versatility standards of the former medium-scale digital computers.

1-4. PRESENT STATUS OF DIGITAL COMPUTERS

Table 1-1 presents a comparative status of the various classes of digital computers. Since the microcomputer takes a midway position in cost and capabilities, it has the inimitable potential to command an outstanding status in a large diversity of applications.

Microprocessors permit software design changes to be made simply by changing the program (partly or whole) as a new ROM plug-in; this firmware change thus involves just a few components. As compared to hardwired logic, microprocessors facilitate implementation of logic in terms of sequences of program steps (as microprogramming) in the ROMs concerned. This naturally increases instruction cycle-time and slows up the execution-time in larger data-processing applications, if the instruction set is limited. So, for higher throughput, microprocessors, providing a larger repertoire of instructions, are already available to minimize the problem of slower execution times. For example, earlier 16-bit add-times of 15 to 20 μs are presently reduced to 3 to 5 μs in some new types of microprocessors. The microprocessors were originally limited to a few applications because of their low speed due to the use of the slower P-channel metal-oxide semiconductor (PMOS) substrate. Now that the higher-speed N-channel metal-oxide semiconductor (NMOS) microprocessors and the fairly high-speed and milliwatt power-consuming CMOS-on-Sapphire (complementary symmetry metal-oxide semiconductor) microprocessors are readily available at competitive prices, they will start replacing minicomputers at the low and lower mid-end of their applications, while incidentally creating more and more "intelligent" consumer products. The upcoming high-speed and high-density low-voltage bipolar integrated-injection logic (I^2L) microprocessor chip gives the system designer a new building-block for both new and old data-processing systems in a truly competitive

TABLE 1-1. Present status of digital computers

Status of:	Hardwired Logic	Logic-Array (FPLA)	Calculator	Micro-computer	Mini-computer	Large-Scale Computers
Cost ($)	10 to 100	10 to 500		50 to 3,500	5,000 to 100,000	100,000 to 3 million
Word-length	1-bit	2-, 4-bit	4-bit	32-, 16-, 8-, and 4-bit	16-, 32-, 64-bit (variable)	64-bit (variable) and above
Program	Read-only (ROM)	Read-only	Read-only and program	Read-only, relocatable	Read-only, relocatable	Mostly relocatable
Speed (cycle-time)	Real-time	Medium-speed real-time	Slow	Medium-speed, real-time (100 ns)	Medium-speed, real-time (25 ns)	High-speed, real-time, throughput oriented (10 ns)
Design	Logic	Logic and microprogram		Micro- and macro, HLL* programs	Micro- and macro, HLL programs	Macro and high-level software
Application and memory	Control, etc.: 10 words	Control, etc.: 2 to 20 words, or more		Dedicated 10 to 2×10^6 words (16/32)	Dedicated 1,000 to 10^9 words (16/32)	High-performance, 1 million to several billion words (64-bit to 128-bit)

HLL* = High Level Languages.

way. Wristwatches using an I^2L-chip and low-power liquid-crystal displays are presently available. Customized single-chip microcomputers are currently being introduced; they will dominate the scene in mass consumer-product applications.

Among manufacturers of large- and medium-scale general-purpose digital computers, IBM Corp. is the top contender. In 1979, IBM had an international sales volume of $18 billion in both hardware and software—almost 50% of the world's computer business. The other 10 or so major computer manufacturers shared the remaining business.

During the 1960s, high-priced, IBM System 360-series computers dominated the international market, on a combined sales and lease basis, with about 85% of the computer business. During the first half of the 1970s, the more advanced IBM System 370-series main-frame computers had to compete for the first time with the MSI-based minicomputers. The lower-cost PDP-series main-frame general-purpose minicomputers of the Digital Equipment Corporation (DEC) took the lead in international medium- and small-scale computer operations.

During the second half of the 1970s, the lower-cost minicomputers and currently low-cost microcomputers qualitatively and quantitatively expanded the computer business a hundredfold. These general-purpose computers are based on high-technology solid-state MSI/LSI silicon monolithic integrated circuits in both main-frame (central processing unit) and memory aspects. The Intel Corporation in the San Francisco Bay area (the "silicon valley") took the lead in the powerful LSI/VLSI silicon monolithic microcomputer technology. The logic per chip is, on an average, boosted from about 100 to 100,000 functions—as are the full-fledged computer business applications at an investment level of under $10,000. The minicomputer business by itself commands a $4 billion market worldwide.

IBM has oriented itself to lower-cost, direct-sale, highly powerful, 4300-series main-frame computers priced at approximately $70,000, compared to the $500,000 price tag on the preceding System 370-series and the subsequent 3033 computers. For distributed processing in data communications networks, IBM markets a special model 8100 main-frame computer. For medium- and small-business applications, IBM turned its emphasis from its System 3-series computers to the Superminis, such as 4331 and 4341, in order to compete with the minicomputer manufacturers on a more or less equal footing. The Superminis have RAM/ROM memory capacities of approximately 18 megabytes in regular hard-disk operating systems.

The other contenders in the general-purpose digital-computer business are listed here in the order of their 1979 sales volume:

1. NCR Corp.
2. Burroughs Corporation
3. Sperry Univac
4. Control Data Corporation (CDC)
5. Digital Equipment Corporation (DEC)
6. Honeywell Information Systems (HIS)
7. Hewlett-Packard Co. (H-P)
8. Texas Instruments Incorporated (TI)
9. Nippon Electric Co., Ltd. (NEC)
10. Three or four major European manufacturers

In view of the low cost of LSI/VLSI chips in mass production, microcomputer manufacturers obviously have not achieved these ranks on a billion-dollar scale. However, the situation will change as the powerful parallel multimicroprocessing systems of the 1980s take the lead because they will gradually replace the large-scale and minicomputer systems. The major contenders in the minicomputer area are DEC, Hewlett-Packard Co., Data General Corp., and Honeywell Information Systems; the other manufacturers share a smaller percentage of this business.

Desk-Top Personal Computers. Some of the major users of the desk-top personal computers are:

1. Computer Services and original equipment manufacturers (OEMs)
2. Insurance
3. Transportation
4. Federal, state, and city governments
5. Retail and point of sale (POS)
6. Durable manufacturing
7. Education and scientific applications
8. Utilities
9. Nondurable manufacturing
10. Wholesale
11. Agriculture, mining, and construction

In the personal computing applications with "canned" BASIC programs, even at consumer-product cost levels, there is bound to be some initial resistance, as happened in the case of color television (until Japanese manufacturers came along with superior assembly quality control). However, small business and professional applications and scientific and hobby usage account for the present sales volume of about half a million microcomputers annually. The worldwide shipments will multiply tenfold during the 1980s. For a discussion of the manufacturers of microcomputers, see Chapter 12.

Most of the currently available low-priced microprocessors handle 4 or 8/16 bits in parallel; since 4 bits can represent a decimal digit, the microprocessors can do decimal arithmetic in serial mode and binary arithmetic in parallel mode. The 8-bit devices can handle both binary and alphanumerical data in either 7- or 8-bit format in "intelligent" terminals for the processing of common Extended Binary-Coded Decimal Interchange Code (EBCDIC) and American Standard Code for Information Interchange (ASCII). Some units can now handle longer 32- and 24-bit words by both direct and "bit-slice" techniques. Software in high-level languages such as BASIC or PASCAL or PL/- is a common feature in the latest microcomputer systems. Where assembly language in the form of mnemonics is mandatory, hexadecimal coding is an invariably popular feature.

The 16/32-bit VLSI microprocessors are establishing themselves in routine signal processing and systems design, and stand-alone single-chip microcomputers are gaining recognition as more than mere microcontrollers. Nonvolatile megabit magnetic bubble memories are simultaneously replacing bulky, power-consuming CORE memory of the main frame in mini- and large-scale computers. In microcomputer systems, the current inimitable rotating mass-memory software systems, four-drive using 5.25-in. mini-floppy diskettes (350-K bytes), moving-head disk (3-M bytes), 8-in. floppy disks (5-to-10-M bytes), and 8/14-in. hard-disk (20-to-50-M bytes) with fixed and moving heads will be gradually replaced by economical, high-density, magnetic-bubble memory systems. For limited rapid-access mass storage up to 0.5-M bytes, 64-K bit EPROM and ROM memory board systems will be preferred. However, for portable program material, off-line 0.25-in. cassette/cartridge drive and $\frac{1}{2}$-in. tape-drive systems will remain as permanent features for the foreseeable future.

Word Processing (or text editing), for the general purpose of adding "intelligence" to a typewriter, is one of the major applications the microcomputer is involved in. 4-K to

16-K bytes of RAM memory is commonly used for elaborate program and buffer text storage. For example, word processing permits typing of letters and reports, correction of mistakes, justification of text, and rearranging of sentences and paragraphs with just a few key strokes.

Automation, including robots, will eventually make life more interesting to the majority of the labor force around the world by eliminating dull, tedious, *repetitive* automaton-like routine manual tasks. The ubiquitous LSI/VLSI microprocessor is gaining recognition as a tool for programmable universal machine assembly attractive to replace high-cost, bulky, power-consuming, and less flexible mechanical, pneumatic, and random logic technologies. If the present rate of advance in microcomputer technology continues, the main frame large-scale and mini computers will soon be realized by VLSI microprocessors working in a parallel/pipeline or "hypercube" fashion. A variety of architectures ranging from shared-memory multiprocessors to "search-tree" modular multicomputer systems are on the drawing board. They offer such potential advantages as increased performance-to-cost, uniform extendability, and management of complexity via standardized plug-in modules. These hierarchical multicomputer system organizations are often supported by simultaneous simulation studies.

Myriad smart and *intelligent* products such as low-cost educational aids, hand-held language translators, home and small-business computers in the field of personal computing, enterprising hobby microcomputers, robotics, and CRT video games are rapidly advancing in popularity. Audio cassette, mini-floppy diskette, and magnetic-bubble memory play an important role for the provision of software. Prewritten "canned" programs in BASIC or PASCAL are readily available at low cost to meet the software requirements.

The microprocessor is currently advancing a new branch of computer science—namely, artificial intelligence (AI). This science is devoted to the programming of microcomputers, in a high-level language, to automatically carry out tasks that would normally require skill and intelligence on the part of a person manually performing those tasks. Automatic programming, computational logic, pattern recognition, memory management associated with information storage and retrieval, and control of robots are examples of AI. The program designed must first work out a step-by-step procedure by extracting *clues* from the significant aspects of the problem; then it must successfully carry out those steps in specific time intervals. Of course, this is an enormously complicated task in problems such as pattern recognition, and hence a long-term proposition well into the next century, as far as the development of the highly sophisticated software for such problems is concerned. The implications of AI, involving superior, instantaneous, and self-learning intelligence via firmware, that would control complex digital control systems, are therefore conceptually futuristic, although the microcomputer has certainly opened the prospects (especially through the channels of probability and statistics) to achieve for itself a significant role in making this proposition slowly feasible on a gradual basis. We have just scratched the surface of the fantastic field of AI. This is not science fiction any more. The scientific and industrial developments during the second half of the twentieth century could have appeared as science fiction during the nineteenth century.

Figures 1-4 through 1-6 present a comparative idea of the original general-purpose digital computers of the 1960s and the revolutionary microcomputers of the second half of the 1970s.

Fig. 1-4a. General-purpose digital computers of the 1960s.

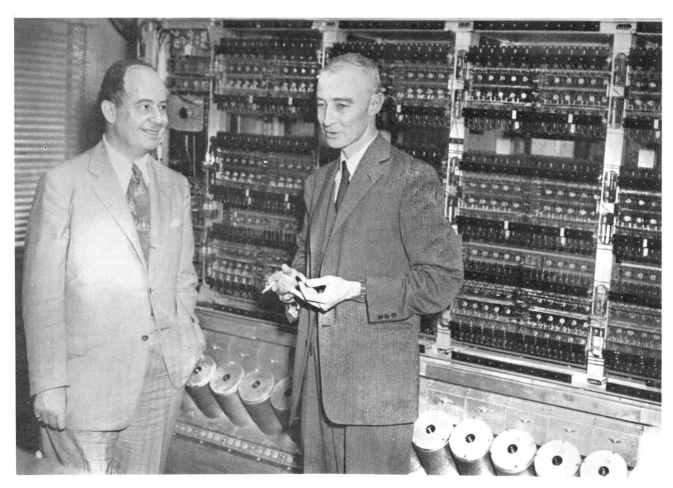

Fig. 1-4b. Von Neumann's computer with CRT storage cylinders. The modern microcomputer is at least 10,000 times more powerful and reliable. (*Courtesy of the Institute for Advanced Study, Princeton, New Jersey*)

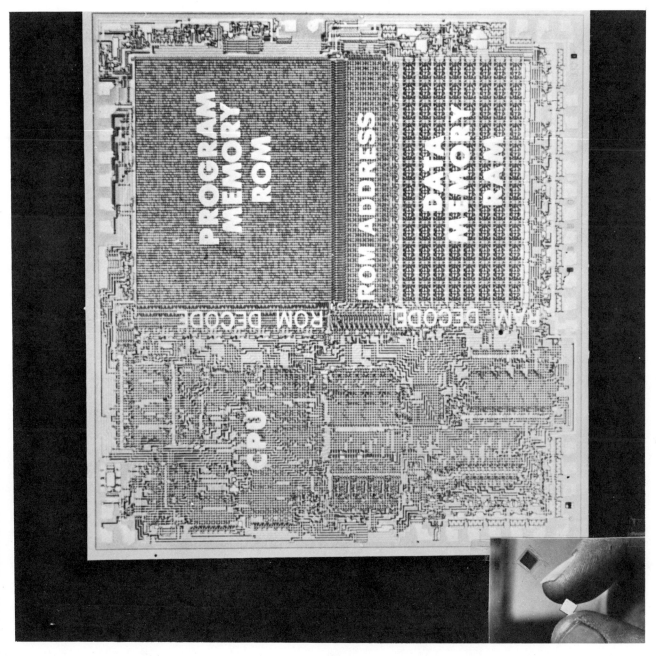

Fig. 1-5. A magnified microcomputer on a chip. (*Courtesy of Rockwell International Corporation*)

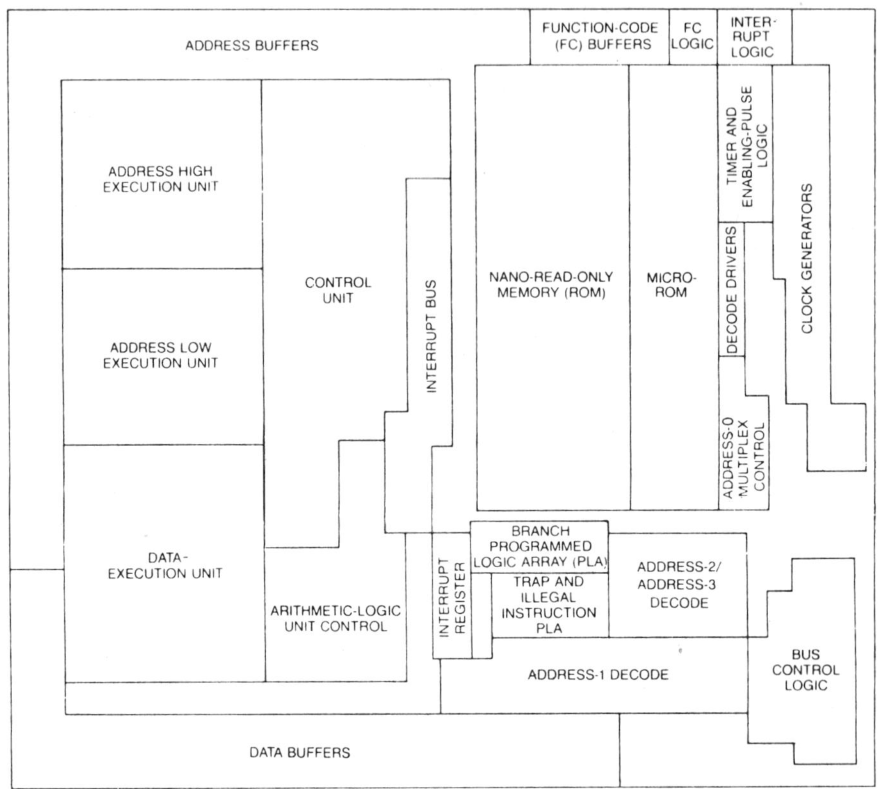

MICROPROCESSOR CHIP made by Motorola Inc., one of a new generation of chips that incorporate special features for implementing high-level programming languages, is shown in the micrograph on the opposite page. A functional map of the microprocessor is shown above. A microprocessor performs the same processing functions as a larger computer, and so it is organized into areas for storing and retrieving strings of binary digits (0's and 1's) representing data and instructions (address high execution unit, address low execution unit) and for performing arithmetical and logical operations (arithmetic-logic unit control, data execution unit). There

Fig. 1-6. The VLSI microcomputer layout (Motorola 68000) and the micrograph.

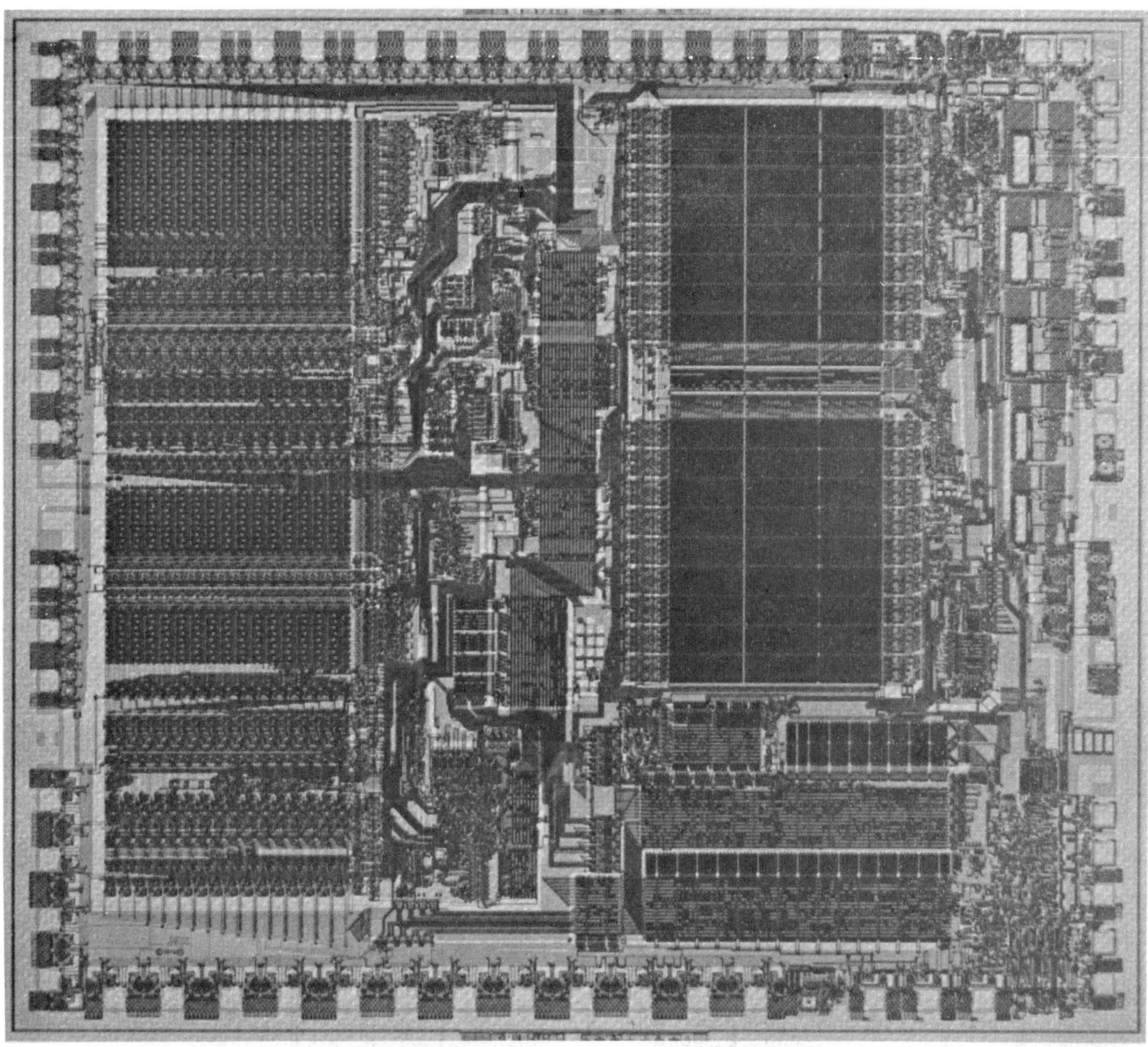

are additional units for carrying out control operations that determine the order in which the statements of stored programs are executed (control unit, programmed logic array units) and for providing interfaces with the large-scale memory and the input and output devices that complete the hardware of the computer system (buffers, decoders and so on). The statements of a high-level programming language are intended to facilitate the user's formulation of computing problems and must be translated by a complex program called a compiler into instructions that are directly executable by the computer. The instructions are (in this chip) themselves further broken down into parts according to fixed microprograms stored in the read-only memories (micro-ROM and nano-ROM). Organization of the chip contains several features to support high-level programming languages, including codes for frequent computations and flexible addressing.

Fig. 1-6 (*Continued*)

2
Large-Scale and Very-Large-Scale Integration (LSI/VLSI)

2-1. FUNDAMENTALS IN BRIEF: SEMICONDUCTOR PHYSICAL CHEMISTRY

2-1.1. Quantum Theory and Electron. Materials like silicon and germanium that exhibit intermediate resistivity, as compared to low-resistivity conductors and high-resistivity insulators or dielectrics, are termed *semiconductors.* According to the general *Periodic Classification of Elements*, diamond (carbon), silicon, and germanium come under group-4A of nonmetals (see Table 2-1).

The dynamics of electrical conduction in crystalline semiconductors are concerned with the movement of electrons, the negative electric charges, and "holes," defined as *the vacancies left behind in the crystalline atomic congregation by the moving electrons under the external stresses imposed.* The so-called hole, although abstract by semantics, exhibits equivalent positive electric charge and moves at a lower rate of mobility compared to the electron, as quantitatively interpreted by quantum mechanics. The quantum theory, in explaining the microscopic atomic-scale phenomena discrete quanta-wise, merely specifies the probability that a moving electron with wavelike properties will be found in a specific volume interval, as the atom concerned assumes a particular energy state, either "normal," "excited," or "transitional resonance," under the environmental conditions imposed. The energy level is specified in electron volts (eV). The energy levels of an atom are determined by spectroscopy, by measuring the wavelengths of the spectra lines emitted when the atom proceeds from one energy level to another. *Photon* is a quantum of electromagnetic radiation that is emitted during this transition.

Since quantum theory, with its involvement of probability and statistics, is mathematically too cumbersome for explaining the dynamics of charge-carriers in semiconductor crystals, a bilateral mix of quantum and Newtonian classical mechanics is generally applied to understand the phenomena. The tunneling effect of the carriers of a semiconductor PN-junction tunnel diode having a negative-resistance characteristic is a typical example in this respect—that, if the potential barrier is thin enough, "a small but non-zero probability" allows an electron, having insufficient energy for climbing the barrier, to pass through it by tunneling.

2-1.2. Periodic Classification of Elements and Silicon. An updated version of Mendeleyev's original periodic classification of 63 elements (1869) contains 103 elements. The **periodic table** is arranged according to the **atomic number** of each element—as defined by the number of electrons surrounding the nucleus of an atom in several shells, varying from one to seven primary shells and from one to four secondary shells within each primary shell. The nucleus in turn consists of an equal number of **protons** (Z) with positive charge plus an **equal number or mostly surplus number** of neutral **neutrons ('N')** to make up the atomic-weight or the integral **mass-number** A(='N' + Z) of the element, as it occurs in the form of the most stable isotope. The elements—starting with hydrogen (1), helium (2), . . . carbon (6), . . . silicon (14), . . . germanium (32), . . . uranium (92; exhibiting fission or the spontaneous disintegration of the unstable nucleus), . . . lawrencium (103)—are divided according to physical and chemical properties and periods into 18 groups (2 of light metals, 10 of heavy metals, 5 of nonmetals, and 1 of inert gases). The elements encountered in semiconductor technology are shown in Table 2-1 under groups 3A through 5A; they take their place under the classification of nonmetals. Table 2-2 gives additional data of interest on the atomic structure of the elements under consideration.

2-1.3. Carbon and Diamond. In their intrinsic form, the elements are electrically neutral. The elements with lower atomic numbers toward left columns and upper rows in the periodic table are progressively more stable and more predictable in physical and chemical properties. The elements are all generally classified as "inorganic" with carbon as the exception. Carbon, the "organic" element that evolutionary processes have chosen, is the "key" element governing the biochemical or life processes, by way of the two side-chains of the carbon atom, namely, the amine group (NH_2), carbon, and the carboxyl group (COOH). The three grouped together in several combinations, in conjunction with other compatible atoms, make the amino acids as a step of transition from the "inanimate" to the "animate." Nineteen of these amino acids are identified in the large-scale-integrated molecules, proteins that regenerate and sustain life. Bacteria start the cycle of molecular evolution with single-cell microorganisms.

Genes, the transmitters of heredity, are the constituent parts of the 23 pairs of chromosomes in the ultimate highly complex and regenerative human cell; the genes number in tens of thousands. The gene is actually half protein and half nucleic acids. The latter are well-known as DNA/RNA. These, in turn, contain a four-letter coded message of nucleotides consisting of five-carbon sugar molecules of H—C—OH chains of atoms, and this coded heredity is a *double-helix* of about 10 billion atoms. The constituent parts of the colossal protein molecules in the microuniverse of the atomic scale can be photographed by X-ray diffraction techniques; the atoms can thus be viewed in one of the layers as a pattern of bright dots. The microdimensions of the molecules are an amazing contrast to the dimensions of the galaxies in the macrouniverse. The complex organic molecule at the microlevel is analogous to a galaxy of the universe, whereas the atoms correspond to the solar systems, with spinning electrons orbiting around nuclei as planets. And, a scale of continuity can be visualized between the two extremes. The basic movements of charge-carriers in the microprocessor take place at the atomic levels in micro- and nanoseconds of timings, as physically measured by the electron beam of the cathode-ray tube (CRT) oscilloscope.

TABLE 2-1. A "window" on the periodic table[a]

Nonmetals							Light Metals		Inert Gas[b]
Period	3A	4A	5A	6A	Period	1A	2A	. . .	-0-
2	11 B 5	12 C 6	14 N 7	16 O 8	1	2 **H** 1			4 **He** 2
3	27 Al 13	28 Si 14	31 P 15	32 S 16	2				20[b] **Ne** 10
4	70 Ga 31	72 Ge 32	75 As 33		3		24 **Mg** 12	*"Key" elements: 5 solid, 5 gaseous*	
5	115 In 49	119 Sn 50	121 Sb 51		4		40 **Ca** 20		

B: Boron
Al: Aluminum
Ga: Gallium
In: Indium
S: Sulfur

C: Carbon (with mass number of 12)
Si: Silicon (SiO_2, silica of *sand* is an insulator); silicon energy levels stable and optimum for processing LSI.
Ge: Germanium (atomic energy levels not stable enough)
Sn: Tin (atomic energy levels too unstable)
As, B, Al, P, Ga are the "impurities" (doping agents) used in semiconductor processing.

N: Nitrogen
P: Phosphorus
As: Arsenic
Sb: Antimony
Mg: Magnesium
Ca: Calcium

Carbon-14: Half-life of 5,600 years. All living organisms absorb carbon-14 via carbon dioxide; hence, organic remains are accurately dated by the isotope (radio) carbon-14 left. Radio carbon has two surplus neutrons, and it can be used as a radioactive tracer.

Carbon-14 incidentally presents a clear proof to the feature of ultra-stability in the case of the "key" elements. In high-speed gallium arsenide FET technology, silicon takes the role of the "impurity."

The three *isotopes* of Hydrogen:
H: Hydrogen $_{1}H^{1}$
HH: Heavy hydrogen $_{1}H^{2}$ (separated from seawater, H_2O)
Tritium $_{1}H^{3}$; (not stable)
He: Helium $_{2}He^{4}$ **O: Oxygen** **Ne: Neon**

Other examples of evidence:
1. A **Helium-Neon** laser has an MTBF (minimum time before failure) of 12,000 hours–compared to only 1,500 hours in the case of a helium-cadmium laser.
2. A (plastic) PROM of Fairchild with a normal 2,000-hour MTBF gains an MTBF of 13,000 hours when **Silicon-Nitride** (Si_3N_4) is used as a protective insulating layer against possible contamination in a low-cost plastic package.

Ten "key" elements: (Z = *1, 2, 6, 7, 8, 10, 12, 14, 16, 20*)*
Note: octaves are emphasized in bold face among the above 10 atomic numbers.
Proton: $_{1}H^{1}$ (nucleus of atomic hydrogen)

Z = Atomic Number (the number of electrons in orbit)
left suffix
A = Mass Number
= 'N' + Z (where 'N' = number of neutrons in the nucleus of the atom.
right index

Note: The author suggests the replacement of the isotope Hydrogen, $_{1}H^{1}$ (which is identically the same symbol for proton too) by the Heavy-Hydrogen, $_{1}H^{2}$ as the regular first element in the periodic table under group 1A. The Hydrogen presently used in the table is unique cosmic fundamental building-block unlike all the other elements in the table; it does not possess any "neutron" in its nucleus, and naturally occurring, highly stable Heavy-Hydrogen does.

[a]See Appendix D for the complete periodic table.
*This amazing interrelationship between the atomic numbers of the elements concerned, discovered by the author, reminds one of the fundamental and second-harmonic oscillations of the enigmatic electrons in the plasma of a split-anode magnetron radar pulse generator working at microwave frequencies in the presence of the surrounding magnetic field. The second-harmonic, orbital electron-octave interrelationship supports modern cosmology from the viewpoint of the fusion of atomic nuclei at supernova temperatures, and release of all the implied superenergy during the fusion processes—the missing mass of the fusion products appears as energy in $E = mc^2$.

TABLE 2-2. "Free valence electrons" of the atoms of interest†

	H	HH	He	O*	B	C	N	Al	Si	P	Ga	Ge	As	In
Atomic number, Z	1	1	2	8	5	6	7	13	14	15	31	32	33	49
Mass number, A	1	2	4	16	11	12	14	27	28	31	70	72	75	115
Shell-K, electrons‡	1	1	2	2	2	2	2	2	2	2	2	2	2	2
Shell-L, electrons	–	–	–	6	3	4	5	8	8	8	8	8	8	8
Shell-M, electrons	–	–	–	–	–	–	–	3	4	5	18	18	18	18
Shell-N, electrons	–	–	–	–	–	–	–	–	–	–	3	4	5	18
Shell-O, electrons	–	–	–	–	–	–	–	–	–	–	–	–	–	3
Surplus "N" neutrons	–	0	0	0	1	0	0	1	0	1	8	8	9	17
Atomic stability: ←														

The following conclusions are drawn from Table 2-2 regarding the semiconductor silicon:

1. From atomic stability and reliability point of view, Boron, Nitride, and Phosphorus should be preferred as "doping" agents for the semiconductor Silicon. For example, metal-nitride-oxide semiconductor (MNOS) memories may eventually prove successful as nonvolatile random-access-memories (RAM).

2. The absence of surplus neutrons in the nucleus of the Silicon atom, with an equal number of protons and neutrons in equilibrium, makes it unique and significant for reliable solid-state transistor operation among the family of semiconductors; the only other alternative is the ultrastable synthetic diamond, but it cannot be processed like other semiconductors at this time owing to the very high energy-level required (5.3 eV as compared to 1.1 eV of silicon) to remove electrons from covalent-bonds.

3. PMOS: Only "acceptor" impurities are involved, with holes as the majority carriers from B, Al, Ga, In (in that order) to Si. Only one-way passage of holes is feasible as a unipolar device. Hole: 3 − 4: −1 (positive charge). See Table D-3 (Appendix D) for the significance of −1.

4. NMOS: Only "donor" impurities are involved, with electrons as the majority carriers from P, As, and nitride to Si. Only one-way passage of electrons is feasible as a unipolar device. Electron: 5 − 4: 1 (negative charge)

5. I^2L: Bipolar. Both acceptor and donor impurities are involved, with the majority carriers holes from B, Al, Ga, and In, and majority carrier electrons from P and As to Si, respectively. Faster simultaneous two-way passage of electrons and holes makes it superior.

*Oxygen (O) is moved to the front from the column next to Nitrogen (N).
†Atoms of interest are set in bold face.
‡Shells: *Energy state* levels at *quantum numbers* 1, 2, 3, 4 · · · .

Diamond, the intrinsic cubic-lattice crystal form of carbon, is the hardest and stablest structure in nature; as semiconductor, it has an electron mobility of 1,800 cm^2/volt-second as compared to 1,500 cm^2 in the silicon cubic-lattice crystal. In the very distant future, the synthetic diamond wafers might be perhaps processed like the present grown-silicon crystal wafers, by doping with the 3-and-5 free valence-electron "impurities" in a controlled technology, to produce artificial diamond microprocessors as potential implants for parts of damaged brain and its terminal functions in the body. They might be naturally more compatible with evolution's own 10-billion neuron "super-computer network," the human brain and its neural communications system throughout the body.

Both analog and time-modulated digital signal processing are involved in **the neural system of switching logic,** which uses sodium and potassium ions along with other complex electrochemical processes. The normally negative-charged individual multifunction brain cell, the *neuron*, with its own wraparound, myelin-insulated, spinal-cord axon and fibrous dendrites, is nonregenerative once destroyed—like any damaged microprocessor and unlike the regenerative body cells. Each stand-alone neuron communicates with its neighbor neurons by the passage of proteins carrying sodium ions piggyback across extremely minute synaptic gaps. The neuron is isolated from the oxygen-carrying bloodstream and is sustained by the six-carbon glucose-sugar $C_6H_{12}O_6$ via its own 10 to 20 or so glucose-feeding glial cells in the regular blood-circulation system. These cells are isolated from the data point of view of neural logic. The switching processes take place mostly in parallel at a slow speed under a millisecond. If, due to the effect of intoxicants or harmful drugs, the glial cells become inactive and stop feeding glucose, the neuron is destroyed within a few minutes. Its function must then be carried on by a redundant neuron in the vicinity, at additional dissipation of energy and effort on the part of the brain itself, depending on whether it is sensory (receptor) or motor (effector), or the more abundant communication and data-processing-type inter-neuron. The brain's primary short-term and permanent long-term mass-memory systems, consisting of layers of coded molecular chains, are reminiscent, respectively, of the present RAM and PROM/ROM solid-state memories of the microcomputer systems. As a result of this new awareness of the highly complex digital processes in the neural system, electroencephalography (EEG), states of consciousness, hypnosis, and biofeedback are some of the present subjects under research—which incidentally could use microcomputer chips for parallel processing of data in a multiprogramming effort. (The modern electron microscope enables the observation of most of the above phenomena. Recent scientific research has gradually transplanted these findings from the realms of speculation and conjecture to the living world of basic facts.)

2-2. SILICON, THE CHOICE SEMICONDUCTOR MATERIAL

The previous incidental reference to the diamond as a semiconductor operating device is purely a hypothetical case, although it is theoretically true. Diamond, Silicon, and Germanium have one and the same cubic crystal-lattice structure of unit-crystal cells. Every atomic nucleus is "covalent-bonded" to four others by the sharing of one pair of valence-electrons with the atomic nuclei of the neighbor cells inside the lattice structure (called *tetrahedral bond structure*). The ideal Silicon single-crystal wafers have gradually displaced during the last decade the previously used, less stable Germanium crystal wafers. The Ge atom occurs farther down in the Periodic Table at a comparatively lower degree of atomic stability in "energy levels." Actually, the problematic Ge atom can occur with a varying number of neutrons (42, 40, or 38) in three isotopes. The nucleus-wise well-balanced silicon is physically and electrically stable and reliable at very high and low temperatures; it furnishes the present high standards of performance and reliability. In fact, the successes of present space technology may be attributed to the choice of silicon in space electronics, coincidentally at the right moment.

In a single-crystal format, **silicon's atomic structure and its unique placement in the periodic table** establish and guarantee a permanent status as the standard source-element, as far as the computer technology is concerned in the foreseeable future. Gallium-arsenide (using silicon atoms as the dual "acceptor-donor" "doping" agent) may be suitable for a limited set of device applications, such as GaAs FET, to achieve greater electron mobility at higher microwave frequencies. But, the silicon's single-crystal semiconductor status, like that of the carbon in biochemical molecular evolution, is unique and indispensable in the unlimited field of linear and digital system applications for many decades to come, since it is rated next only to diamond in stability. Silicon-on-Sapphire, for example, is merely an improved processing technique for high speed in the case of complementary-symmetry metal-oxide–semiconductor microprocessors. The gem sapphire is actually "corundum"—basic Al-oxide.

2-2.1. Ten Key Elements. Silicon, the basic semiconductor used in microcomputer technology, is one of 10 key elements. Elements that have a balanced nucleus in their atomic structure, by their natural endowment of an equal number of positive-charge protons and neutral-charge neutrons in exact equilibrium, are the **outstanding 10** among the latest total of 103 elements. A neutron has the same mass as a proton but no charge. In the order of ascending atomic numbers, the 10 key elements of this special group are heavy-hydrogen, helium, carbon, nitrogen, oxygen, neon, magnesium, silicon, sulfur, and calcium. The atomic numbers of the 10 key elements signify a pattern of pairs of octaves: 1-2, 6-12, 7-14, 8-16, 10-20 (heavy hydrogen–helium, carbon-magnesium, nitrogen-silicon, oxygen-sulfur, neon-calcium). The second harmonic (octave) is the most dominant secondary component when a system, such as the atomic structure of an element, goes into oscillation at a certain fundamental frequency. A similar phenomenon occurs during the original transmutational evolution of the *key* elements to produce this amazing pattern. Also, 2 nuclei of nitrogen can fuse to evolve a silicon nucleus. The cosmic source-element hydrogen is unique because it consists of a single-proton and a single-shell electron. The first key element, heavy-hydrogen, is extracted from heavy-water. Seawater has a small content of heavy-water: 1 part per 6000. The proton is balanced by a neutron in the nucleus of heavy-hydrogen. The neutron has a primary role in cementing the nucleus of a stable element.

The periodic table provides the basis for the exposition of **modern cosmology**. It highlights the *fusion* and *fission* processes and the cycle of transmutation of elements. The proton-proton chain reaction for the release of superenergy by the thermonuclear "fusion" of hydrogen and heavy-hydrogen (or deuterium) into helium, proves the two key elements, heavy-hydrogen and helium, to be the stablest of all. They are the sole occupants of the topmost row of the periodic table, and they together constitute the working basis for a universe of galaxies and their constituent billions of solar systems. Collapsing gravitational forces, electromagnetic radiations, and high-energy cosmic rays are closely involved in this cosmic process. The transmutation of the various elements out of heavy-hydrogen and helium occurs in the plasma of the solar furnace at the time of the penultimate, potential "supernova" explosive phase after an estimated lifetime of about 10-billion years. Subsequent to the explosion, it enters the phase of an invisible radio star. The cosmic dust of the explosion results, aeons later, in the formation of planets orbiting around new stars. These stars generate anew as the result of proton-proton chain reactions under the stresses of collapsing gravitational forces that generate a spherical "magnetic bottle" to maintain a gaseous plasma at core temperatures of millions of degrees. In 1976, American astronomers have photographed a condensing solar system in a gaseous environment in space. It appeared as a disk of concentric rings, with the sun at the center as a bright star. This phenomenon presents noncontroversial evidence to the foundations of modern cosmology—which includes the discovery of (cosmic) infrared radiation at 2.7°K (of the black-body curve) above the absolute zero in the deep interstellar space.

Toward the bottom of the atomic scale in the periodic table occurs the least stable radioactive fissionable uranium atom with an atomic number of 92. Its nucleus can be disintegrated by fast neutrons to radioactive plutonium (94), and positively charged Alpha particles, negatively charged Beta-particles, and Gamma rays. The Alpha particles (helium nuclei), the Beta particles (high-speed electrons), and Gamma rays are all released as Energy out of Matter. The penetrating Gamma rays (10^{-11} to 10^{-12} meters), beyond the *infrared* heat waves (300 to 0.7 microns) and the "visible" light of 0.7 to 0.4 microns, are harmful as electromagnetic radiation at Gamma-ray wavelengths. Energy, mass, and velocity of light are interrelated by Einstein's equation: $E = mc^2$. In nuclear chain reactions, a large number of particles are generated, most with very short half-lifetimes. For example, a neutron can break up into a proton, and electrons and antineutrinos; and a mu-meson can break up into electrons and neutrinos etc. The neutrino has the same mass as an electron but no charge. A negative mu-meson (muon) has the same charge as an electron, but 207 times heavier. A positive muon is an antiparticle like the positron; they both belong to *anti-matter*. The neutrino, which nothing can stop, is theoretically associated with the angular momentum of the spin of the electron. While astronomers with radiotelescopes come up with cosmic phenomena such as nebulae (galaxies), quasars, pulsars, neutron stars, black holes from which light cannot escape, and black holes with central white holes, the nuclear physicist, with his billion electron-volt synchrotrons, comes up with such subnuclear particles as quarks and charms.

The 10 key elements, which are chemically very reactive and versatile, occur in abundance. **Silicon**, the indispensable semiconductor substrate used in microcomputer technology, is next to carbon in abundance in oxide form as silica. Silicon combines easily with calcium and aluminum to form various silicates; in combination with carbon and nitrogen, silicone polymer products such as lubricants and special-purpose rubbers are synthesized. Silicon plays a prominent role (1) as a substrate in compact nonvolatile magnetic bubble-memory technology and (2) as a dual doping agent in superfast semiconductor gallium-arsenide field-effect transistor technology of microwave and digital electronics circuits, presently effective up to 18 GHz.

Calcium occurs in nature mostly as carbonates. Calcium plays a vital function as a clotting agent in the human circulatory system. Any imbalance in the percentage of calcium content in the blood can be fatal; it is therefore metabolically feedback-controlled via the parathyroid hormone for maintaining a balanced concentration. Moreover, as calcium phosphate it is a major component of the skeletal bones. **Magnesium**, which is combustible with a brilliant glow, makes up 1% of the solvents in seawater; hence it is available in large quantities. Magnesium is also found in botanical plant-life as chlorophyll, which enables photosynthesis in the carbon dioxide–oxygen cycle in nature. **Sulfur** is a 1% constituent of human anatomy. As an ingredient of sulfa drugs, it destroys the bacterium of virus infections. And, as stated earlier, **carbon**, is the fundamental organic element that governs the biochemical or life processes. It is well-known that the subject of organic chemistry at this time runs into volumes.

The role of **heavy-hydrogen** and **helium** in cosmology explains their intrinsic importance in the evolution of stars and their planetary systems. The predominant and stable isotope hydrogen is one of the basic building-blocks of the Universe and of water in particular. The muscle tissues and cells of the human body are sustained by proteins, carbohydrates, and fats in a balanced diet. Along with the oxygen inhaled, they make the fuel for slow combustion (or metabolism) and production of energy. The atmospheric **oxygen** and **nitrogen** are of course essential as a life-support system of air. Nitrogen, as an exclusive constituent of fertilizing agents, is responsible for the agricultural production of food. Eleven amino acids, which furnish the organic building-blocks for proteins, consist of the key elements *carbon*, hydrogen, *oxygen*, and *nitrogen*; 10 other such amino acids are essential in a balanced diet (along with several vitamins and minerals) for proper maintenance of sound health. For rigorous nutrition in this connection, the human body requires vitamins such as A, B, C, folic acid, and niacin, and minerals such as **magnesium**, **sulfur**, **calcium**, sodium, potassium, iron, zinc, manganese, copper, iodine, cobalt, chlorine, fluorine, and traces of a few other elements. As a typical example, the *simplified* molecular structure of the *folic acid*, required for the regeneration of the oxygen-carrying red corpuscles of blood in bone marrow, takes the form:

$$HO_2C(CH_2)_2CH(CO_2H)NHC_6H_4NHCH_2C_6N_4H(OH)(NH_2)^*$$

These are *all key elements*. **Neon gas**, classified in the periodic table as an inert gas, is actually not inert because it is extensively used for neon-lighting by electric gas-discharge. Neon gas, in conjunction with helium in the most reliable helium-neon gas laser, plays a prominent role in modern industrial and optical aerospace applications.

The 10-billion-neuron masterpiece of evolution, the human brain, its neural communications supernetwork, and the glandular hormones and enzymes form the most complex bioelectrochemical digital feedback control system in nature. As a parallel state-of-the-art achievement, 1 to 10 million functional building blocks of microelectronics can be incorporated on a minute chip. High-technology VLSI currently fabricates 100,000 functions on a silicon monolithic microcomputer chip!

With some effort the brain-complex can be *self-controlled* and optimized in performance (or behavior) by positive constructive education and training via audio and visual aids. The resultant strength of character is the vital step toward achieving long-term stability in thought and/or action, as a precondition to maturity and inner psychological tranquility. Self-discipline with a broad perspective (as opposed to excesses of gain or unrestrained greed) is a simulation equivalent to the negative-feedback control systems of a stable and effective broad-band system organization. In particular, an instigator of problems is the addictive life-style of indulgence in drug- and alcohol-induced "highs," which interfere with the normal gain and sensitivity of the metabolism. (Metabolism is both involuntarily and voluntarily, through learning and/or iterative programming, controlled by complex and fragile bioelectrochemical processes in the system-architecture of the brain.) The "addicted" behavior is synonymous with disturbing the most important parameter "gain" of an otherwise optimally stable combined analog and digital feedback control system.

The above analogy is merely an obvious extension of the science generally referred to as *cybernetics*.

The specific atomic structure of an element and its place in the periodic table determines its chemical and physical properties; the requisite semiconductor characteristics for the solid-state transistor operation are naturally limited to a set of transitional elements between conductors and nonconductors in the periodic table. One element in this group of transitional elements must be optimally suitable for the reliable transistor function; that specific element is silicon. Nature is a systematic manifestation of a cyclic continuity in Eternity. Occasional spontaneous "jumps" in continuity are inevitable according to the theory of evolution, as a result of the mutational effects of radiation, as based on probability and statistics. There is not even a clear demarcation between matter and energy since the basic electron(s), as a particle under crowded conditions, could phase itself into a wave (or electron-pair waves under special conditions) in the expanse of space; for example, an electron in collision with a positron, results in mutual annihilation and a Gamma ray. An electron-positron pair could be naturally created out of a Gamma ray. That is, matter and energy are mutually interchangeable; hence, they can also coexist dualistically in the cosmic environment of the spacewise uniform, unknowable third force ("ether," "gravitation," or "hole-distribution" whatever one calls this third force in the universe). The positive-charge hole-distribution can be appropriately defined as a *negative-*

*In 1980 the author was accidentally exposed to a heavy dose of X-ray (or electron-beam) radiation in a laboratory. The exposure dangerously destroyed the *bone marrow*, and he was seriously ill with macrocytic anemia. Treatment with hydrochlorothiazide (to dilute the kidney blood vessels and lower the blood pressure) and *folic acid* for a period of *5 months* gradually restored him to normal health.

mass electron distribution in space to enable the propagation of radio waves, electrons, cosmic rays, etc. This analogy of negative-mass is merely a corresponding interpretation like the well-known mathematical concept of a function "-1" along the *negative real-axis* of complex s-plane, or the abstract "*negative-resistance*" effect in an oscillator. The concept of a "hole" is derived from the semi-conductor theory of micro-processors.

Investigators of neutron wave interference have established that the laws of quantum theory apply in the presence of the gravitational fields. The gravitational waves or the hole-distribution of negative-mass electrons in space as positive-charge waves is naturally subject to a dynamic changing wave pattern in the immediate vicinity of a rotating massive object, such as a star or a large planet—hence, the bending effect of the electromagnetic radiation (light waves) predicted by Einstein. The radiation and the negative-charge electrons merely follow the gravitational wave propagation of the hole-distribution in space in the presence of a massive galaxy with its star systems. The astronomer's "black holes" might be interpreted as the corresponding concentrations of positive-charge hole-distributions—as a macrodimension of the majority-carrier hole representation in semiconductor theory. Relativity, according to this new conceptual understanding, can be interpreted as the mutual relative behavior pattern of the positive-mass electrons of matter and the negative-mass holes within the confines of a solar system. No wonder that no moving object can exceed the velocity of light in the restricted space of a star (Sun) in space. That is, the electrons and the waves of the electromagnetic spectrum cannot propagate in the vicinity of a star at a velocity greater than the velocity of light—just as the velocity of sound is determined by the density of the air medium. This conceptual approach thus unifies "gravitational force" and the "energy-versus-mass" of electromagnetism and matter as a unified field theory! It is obvious that the three inherent basic forces of the cosmos—matter, energy, and gravitation—cannot be separated. Theoretical physics, with the aid of solid-state physics, quantum theory, and modern computers, might come up with a mathematical interpretation of the basic concept unifying matter, energy, and gravitation, which Einstein failed to prove. Thermodynamics has the unit, electron-volt, for energy; quantum theory has the electron and neutrino as its basic particles for mass; and gravitation has the positive-charge carrier, "negative-mass electron or hole," according to this new conceptual explanation. Hence, these three forces make the trinity for science/nature/evolution, as a parallel to previous theological interpretations.

Regarding silicon, PMOS and NMOS semiconductor processing allow only *one-way* movement of the valence holes or conduction electrons as "majority carriers." However, the bipolar semiconductor LSI process, using the I^2L technique at voltages as low as 1.5 volts, allows the simultaneous *two-way* movement of both the above majority carriers; hence, the Schottky I^2L in particular has the potential to outperform the presently faster NMOS LSI technology in speed, density, and flexibility. It is quite likely that mW-power-consuming I^2L and CMOS-on-sapphire VLSI microprocessors, using 16/32-bit bus architecture and 64-K bit VLSI memories with access-times of 100 to 200 ns, will dominate the scene during the 1980s at comparatively low prices. The 64-K bit ROMs and dynamic RAMs are recent additions to the VLSI semiconductor memory technology.

2-2.2. Valence and Conduction Bands. For an atom of any element, depending upon its atomic number, there is an integral number of "orbits" or *energy levels* in a number of shells to which electrons can belong (K, L, M, N, O, P, and Q). Each level signifies a certain energy in electron volts (eV). The higher the energy of the electron, as is the case in the upper orbits, the less the attraction or "capture" by the nucleus. The highest-level electrons are called the *free-valence* electrons; they participate in covalent-bonds with those of the adjacent atoms as shown in Fig. 2-1. For atoms congregated in a solid or

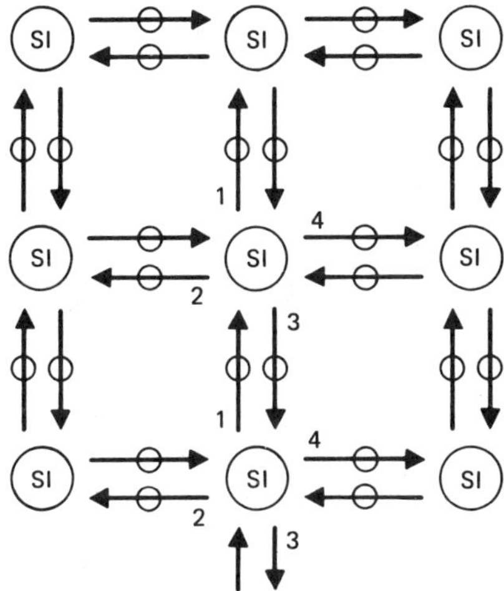

Fig. 2-1. Nuclei of silicon atoms (with inner K and L shells of electrons) in intrinsic single-crystal silicon. Covalent bonds are formed by the four free-valence electrons of adjacent atoms. Controlled "doping" of an atom of impurity will introduce either a "donor" electron or an "acceptor" hole amid the covalent bonds for NMOS and PMOS, respectively.

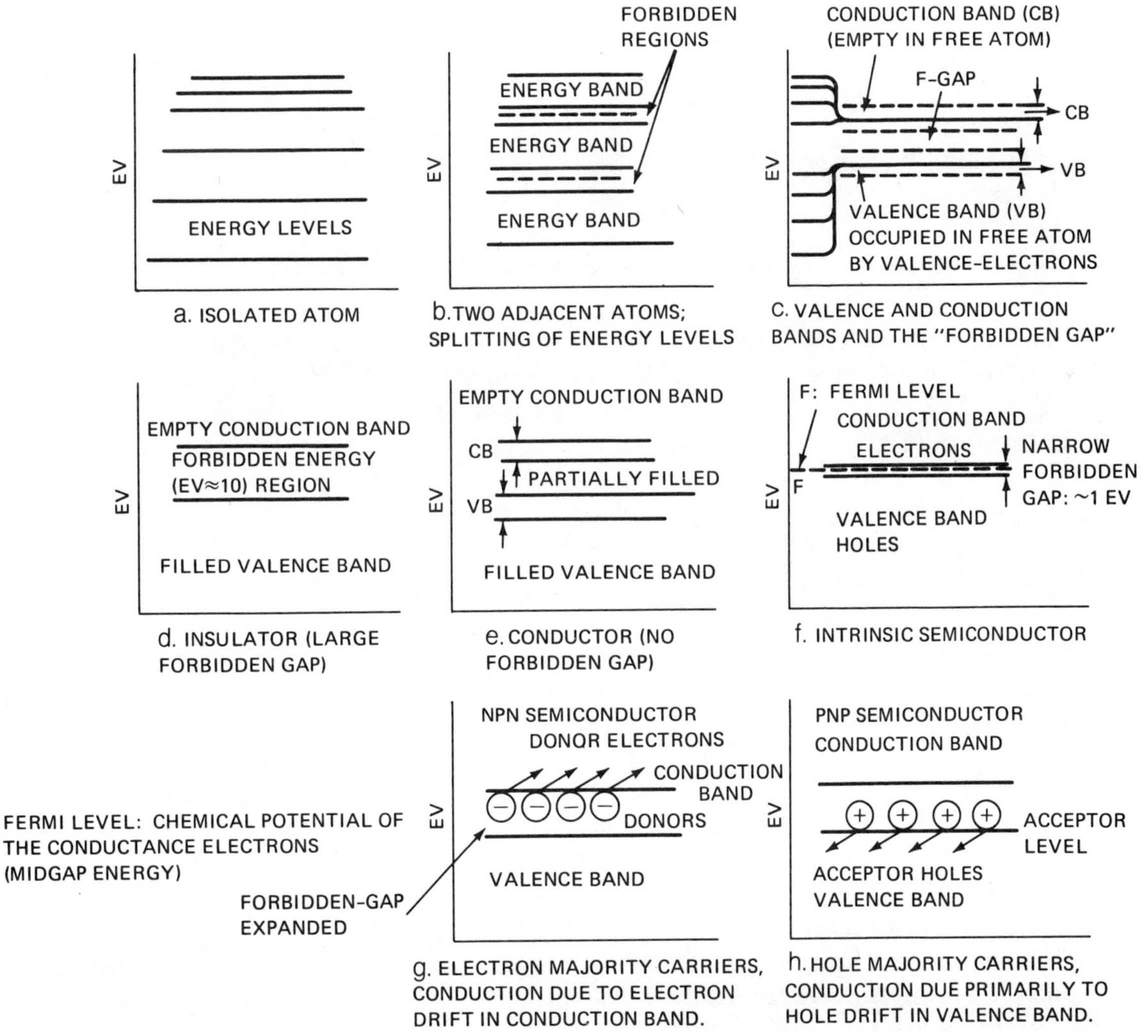

a. ISOLATED ATOM

b. TWO ADJACENT ATOMS; SPLITTING OF ENERGY LEVELS

c. VALENCE AND CONDUCTION BANDS AND THE "FORBIDDEN GAP"

d. INSULATOR (LARGE FORBIDDEN GAP)

e. CONDUCTOR (NO FORBIDDEN GAP)

f. INTRINSIC SEMICONDUCTOR

g. ELECTRON MAJORITY CARRIERS, CONDUCTION DUE TO ELECTRON DRIFT IN CONDUCTION BAND.

h. HOLE MAJORITY CARRIERS, CONDUCTION DUE PRIMARILY TO HOLE DRIFT IN VALENCE BAND.

Fig. 2-2. Energy levels in semiconductors.

crystalline structure, the number of energy levels is large, and they group themselves into *energy bands*. Each band is separated from the adjacent bands by "forbidden gaps," as shown in Fig. 2-2b. In a single-crystal silicon, the electron energy levels thus broaden into energy bands. For germanium, the forbidden gap is so narrow that even at room temperatures, a number of interatomic covalent-bonds are broken up by thermal energy; the resulting drift of electrons is much worse. The drift is much less and comparatively stable for the silicon atom with an optimum width of the forbidden gap. A number of electrons acquire sufficient energy to move from the filled valence band to the empty conduction band of the crystal.

The **energy levels** required to remove electrons from **covalent bonds** illustrated in Fig. 2-1 are specified below for the relevant semiconductors.

Si = 1.1 eV.
Ge = 0.7 eV.
Sn (tin crystal) = 0.1 eV (too unstable).
C (graphite form of carbon) = 7 eV.
C (diamond form of carbon) = 5.3 eV.
1 eV = 1.6×10^{-19} joules or watt-seconds.
GaAs: 1.4 eV.
Electron mobility, cm^2/volt-sec.
Si: 1,400.
Ge: 3,900.
GaAs: 6,800.
Hole mobility, cm^2/volt-sec.
Si: 500.
Ge: 1,900.
GaAs: 680.

Electrons with conduction-band energies leave holes in valence band because of broken interatomic bonds (Fig. 2-2h). The **"donor" impurity with five free valence electrons** adds an electron only, but in so doing it introduces new energy levels into the energy-band picture (Fig. 2-2g). The location of these new levels is just below conduction band for pure "intrinsic" silicon or germanium. Then, if a pentavalent donor impurity is present (N-type semiconductor), the electron from the donor impurity, on ionization at room temperature even, can reach conduction band with 0.04 eV in the case of silicon (dielectric constant is 12; phosphorus is the donor impurity); the ionization energy is much less in the case of germanium 0.012 eV (dielectric constant of Ge is 16). Thus, all electrons from donor atoms acquire conduction-band energies, as shown in Fig. 2-2g.

Similarly, insertion of the **trivalent "acceptor" impurity** with energy levels in the gap just at the top of the valence band results in apparent movement of holes from acceptor levels to the valence band, when temperature ionizes most of the acceptors. This is the case of the P-type semiconductor with hole-drift or conduction in the valence band at approximately the same ionization level, if acceptor boron is used as the impurity for semiconductor silicon. This is shown in Fig. 2-2h.

In the case of the **"intrinsic" semiconductor**, the free valence electrons in the crystal are tightly bound in covalent bonds between adjacent atoms. The semiconductor then acts as a nonconductor without any free charge-carriers. The case of the intrinsic semiconductor is represented in Fig. 2-2f. The preceding NPN/PNP transistor processing cases represent **"extrinsic" semiconductors** in which the charge carriers, electrons, and holes are generated as a result of the impurities or "dopants" introduced into the intrinsic crystal-wafers by a precisely controlled "doping" process. The other plots in Fig. 2-2 are self-explanatory. When atoms share electrons with each other, they are called *homopolar*; when they form covalent bonds in the absence of impurities, the intrinsic atoms are called *heteropolar*.

2-2.3 Summary

1. The specific placement of the element Silicon as one of the 10 key elements in the periodic table establishes its uniqueness and its indispensability in VLSI semiconductor technology for decades to come.

2. The semiconductor material silicon, in its intrinsic form, has four free valence electrons in the outermost shell to form covalent bonds with adjacent atoms in the cubic-lattice crystalline structure. The doping process inserts an impurity such as phosphorus or arsenic (the next higher in the periodic table) with five free valence electrons to make the silicon material N-type. The impurity acts as a donor and furnishes the higher-mobility electron charge-carriers as the majority carriers in the unipolar NMOS technology.

3. If, on the other hand, the doping process inserts an impurity such as boron or aluminum (next lower to silicon in the periodic table) with only three free valence electrons in the outermost shell of the impurity, the unavailability of the fourth electron to form covalent bonds with the adjacent silicon atoms results in an acceptor-hole as a majority carrier. The Si-semiconductor using this acceptor impurity is called P-type semiconductor. It provides the lower-mobility hole majority charge-carriers in the unipolar PMOS technology.

4. In the case of MSI bipolar TTL/ECL and LSI/VLSI bipolar I^2L technologies, potentially higher-speed switching and access-times are feasible by using both electrons and holes simultaneously as majority carriers in a combination of P- and N-semiconductor structures.

5. The semiconductor *silicon* atom has finally established the latest computer technology on a firm basis for decades to come. Silicon is one of the 10 key elements (five solid and five gaseous) that possess nuclei with equal number of protons and neutrons in equilibrium. These 10 ultrastable elements, which exhibit highly reliable physical and chemical properties, occur in the following sequence according to their atomic numbers: heavy hydrogen (1), helium (2), *carbon* (6), nitrogen (7), oxygen (8), neon (10), magnesium (12), *silicon* (14), sulfur (16), and calcium (20). Both carbon and silicon are semiconductors.

In turn, the atomic numbers are constrained within a framework of fundamentals (1, 6, 7, 8, 10) and octaves (2, 12, 14, 16, 20). Carbon as a third-harmonic electron-multiple of helium (during the process of fusion and transmutation of elements) is unique as the basis of life-processes, and silicon, as the octave of nitrogen, is the appropriate element as a silicon-cell, or as an amorphous thin-film in combination with chalcogenide glasses, to enable the storage of the abundance of solar energy in the electrical form. Life, as we know, it not viable without the carbon atom, neither is the art of microcomputer technology possible without the silicon atom. Even the latest superfast, superconductivity Josephson junction microcomputers of IBM use silicon as a substrate.

2-3. MONOLITHIC FABRICATION (SMALL-, MEDIUM-, AND LARGE-SCALE INTEGRATION)

The **integrated circuit** is fabricated by extending previous semiconductor manufacturing processes to include a large number of transistors, diodes, and resistors on a common substrate in one or more functional circuits. The **"monolithic"** construction as a "single structure" is done by the planar process that uses an inherent protective structure for critical junction areas sensitive to surface exposure. All diffusions take place under a passivating layer of pure silicon dioxide, except for a small doping cutout, through which donor and acceptor impurities are introduced for forming NP and PN junctions, respectively.

In monolithic integrated circuits, both active and passive circuit elements are formed on a single substrate of silicon by the planar-diffusion technique, which involves combination photolithography, diffusion, heating and baking, vaporizing and depositing, and ion implantation. Wafers obtained by processing slices of grown ingots of refined silicon sequentially go through such steps of fabrication as photo mask, photo resist, etchant, and molecular processing by diffusion/oxidation/epitaxy/ion-implantation, and then circuit-metallization by evaporation and sputtering, and finally lead-bonding, packaging, and encapsulation. On each silicon slice, the same circuits may be repeated a large number of times. A silicon-substrate chip, less than a quarter of an inch on an edge, can incorporate well over 250,000 semiconductor components. Exclusive costlier ICs produced for meeting Defense Standards are hermetically sealed in dual-in-line (DIP) or Flatpac ceramic (cerpac) packages. These devices are operationally "burned-in" for the equivalent of 168 hours at 125°C before delivery to the user.

Resistors are fabricated by (1) omitting N-type emitter-diffusion used in forming transistors and (2) making two ohmic contacts to a P-type region that is simultaneously formed with the base diffusion of the transistor. Capacitors, limited to a few hundred picofarads, are formed in each case by using the top layer of oxide as the dielectric, the metallized area as one plate, and the N-type material as the other plate. Single NP junctions and the metallized connection patterns make the diodes.

Beam-Lead Bonding of LSI/VLSI Integrated Circuits to Provide Terminal Pins: Process Compliant Bonding (KLB-2000, Keller Machine Co., Buffalo, New York). A thick aluminum tape, with compliant characteristics and a clearance for the thin integrated circuit, is superimposed over the thin-film substrate Si-chip. It is then pressed over the beam-leads of the minute chip and aligned with the substrate bonding pattern by means of an appropriately well-isolated heated ram at 300°C. The aluminum tape yields and flows around the beam-leads of the chip, producing controlled deformation of the beam-leads to enable a reliable and uniform high-quality bond.

Since the aluminum forms an oxide, it does not stick to the internal beam-lead gold contacts of the DIP integrated circuit during bonding. The tape is advanced from one chip to the next by the automatic compliant bonding machine. A prism-type beam-splitting mirror furnishes an in-line vertical view of the lighted device-superimposition on the face of the substrate, which is magnified 10 to 30 times through a horizontal microscope.

COMPUTER ASSISTED DESIGN (CAD). Computer assisted design systems available at high cost on the order of $200,000 from the largest producers such as Calma Inc. of Sunnyvale, Calif., and Applicon Inc. of Burlington, Mass., have a number of limitations, lack of computing power, and limited-scope system design, since artwork is feasible at the basic level of design only, viz., *polygon* level. The topology of the LSI chip is manually created by drawing shapes, polygon-by-polygon, on layers of *Mylar.* The layout is then digitized point-by-point and entered into the memory. The power of the computer is thereupon not helpful to perform tasks such as design-role or interconnection checking, logic, or circuit simulation. (CAD: *aided* is preferred to *assisted*).

Most of the LSI/VLSI manufacturers substitute these methods by artwork techniques totally based on CRT-display, and proprietary software for individual stages of design.

For example, in one case the logic cells stored in the computer memory are retrieved to construct a larger array of logic. The entire chip-composition is methodically automated stage-by-stage to complete the design of the high-density microprocessor or memory; the latter incidentally presents less problems compared to the complex patterns of the microprocessor interconnections.

CAD as a commercial product is not advanced far enough, especially for VLSI. They seem to be experimenting with concepts such as "stretchable cells," "spacing synthesis," and "iterative simulation processing" for both logic and timing. Uncoordinated university software projects make a limited contribution in the generation of ideas only.

Hewlett-Packard Co. uses interactive computer graphics with light-pen to draw the schematic level of the design on the screen with the aid of multi-level polygon representations and then continue the rest of the design with company confidential algorithm's of software. Rockwell International extend the CAD-level design to a level of matrix representation. In one case structured cell-based symbolic technique is used in interconnecting the various logic cell patterns.

Japanese CAD production techniques appear to be slightly advanced in symbolic design; software programs that generate layouts replace manual drawing and digitizing. However, compared to the American production equipment suppliers, Japan uses more powerful computers to run CAD design, simulation, and debugging of software. Nippon Electric Company has a program to perform logic-checking from a layout by comparing circuits with drawn simulated circuitry. Hitachi Ltd. of Japan uses its own improved versions of American basic CAD production equipment. There is better coordination in meticulous manual and CAD roles of circuit design, logic and fault simulation, generation of art from digitized output and checking of art and topology.

The leading computer manufacturers in America, such as IBM, Digital Equipment Corporation, RCA Corporation, Motorola Inc., Hewlett-Packard Co., and Intel Corp., do not appear to wait for usable overall CAD systems from production equipment suppliers. Instead they successfully use their individual proprietary CAD processing software for VLSI on a stage-by-stage basis. IBM designates its computer aided engineering design system, EDS, for the manufacture of the 4341-series of mainframe computers. EDS is based on various computer assisted simulation and verification routines. A metal interconnection layer for gate-array master-slice chips is one exclusive technique in EDS.

Calma Inc. has, however, come up in 1981 with a Vector Memory Display design system which presents the designer with a split-screen display of chip layout, one side zeroing in on a detailed part, and the other on a overall view for fitting in the detailed parts. GDS-II color display system is another new CAD system that allows a finer grid-pattern with 32-bit data points instead of the previous 16-points by using a more powerful minicomputer. A new company, Avera Inc., of Scotts Valley, Calif., has introduced in 1980 a GT-I microprocessor-based graphics input and editing work station for spreading the CAD procedural steps in processing at several work stations.

A single CAD program of TRW Inc. in 10,000 lines of modular PASCAL combines several separate routines for a faster turnaround of the design of VLSI chips. Designated as DRCCL-3D, it can be used for triple-diffusion bipolar process, CCDs, and NMOS circuit design. CAD programs are on the march (undergoing development); highyield Super VLSI, 250-K/500-K/1-M bit ROMs and RAMs will be available before 1985.

OPTICAL, ELECTRON-BEAM, AND X-RAY LITHOGRAPHIC PROCESSING OF LSI, VLSI, AND SUPER-VLSI INTEGRATED CIRCUITS. Ultraviolet (UV) optical direct-step-on-wafer lithographic processing, single and dual electron-beam (E-beam) lithography, and X-ray/X-ray-imaging are the three processing technologies available for mass production of LSI, VLSI, and super VLSI integrated circuits. Especially the E-beam and X-ray techniques, will reach the goal of 0.5- and 1-micron super-VLSI status for 256-K, 512-K, and 1-M bit ROM and RAM memories, etc., before 1985.

UV-optical and X-ray/X-ray imaging lithographic processing technologies are in common use for 5- to 1-micron silicon-substrate channel-widths in the U.S.A. The submicron technology of X-ray-imaging is further advancing at the present stage. Direct-stepping-on-wafer UV-optical, and direct E-beam-on-wafer lithographics, and a combination of the two, are successfully used in Japan at the Nippon Telegraph and Telephone Co. and Japan's VLSI Cooperative Laboratory. One regularly used E-beam lithographic technique (EBMF II) of Cambridge Scientific Instruments Ltd., and a research Dual-E-beam technique (CUMMS II) at the Cambridge University are fully active in this field. CUMMS II, Cambridge University microfabrication and mask-making system, employing the regular E-beam and a special registration E-beam projected on the underside of the wafer, is successfully advancing toward the 1- and 0.5-micron super-VLSI goal. The progress in West Germany, France, and several other countries is not available in American electronics literature at this time.

Optical direct-step-on-wafer and X-ray lithographic processing systems consist of a radiation source (usually aluminum or copper for X-ray), radiation mask, and the silicon crystal wafer disk (4 to 5 in. diam.) coated with a special photo-resist, as shown in the simple configuration of the accompanying diagram, part a. X-rays used must be moderately soft within the range of the hard and soft X-rays, viz., 2 Å and 50 Å. X-rays do not consistently present the diffraction problem as optical and E-beams do at high resolution, and they are not absorbed in the thin window and the mask substrate, if an optimized trade-off is observed in the choice of the exact X-ray wavelength. (Electron-beams generate a trace of X-rays also.) In most cases, only about 25% of the X-ray radiation is actually effective for lithographic processing. X-ray systems are used by Bell Laboratories, General Instrument Corporation, Hughes Research Laboratories (includes CMOS-on-Sapphire), RCA Corporation (CMOS), IBM Corporation (for magnetic bubbles), Philips Electronic Systems Inc. (Mahwah, New Jersey, a subsidiary of Netherlands Philips), and several other LSI/VLSI manufacturers in the U.S.A. Philips Electronic Instruments is marketing a $2 million Vector-scanning E-beamwriter Lithography System, capable of 0.4- to 1-micron resolution in 1981. Other mass production systems available from production equipment manufacturers are steppers, wirebonders, and wafer handlers. However, X-ray systems, using CAD (computer-assisted design) software for the high-precision alignment of the wafer on the table-mounting to 0.1- and 0.2-micron registration accuracy, are not available yet. American semiconductor manufacturers presently use their own proprietary CAD alignment systems with successful results. Single-mask devices such as magnetic bubble and CCD manufacturing systems do not need critical-alignment CAD programs.

X-ray-imaging technique enables the production of lines as fine as 0.16 microns. This technology is already used for the upcoming revolutionary nonvolatile magnetic bubble memories (to replace former indispensable high-power CORE memory) and surface acoustic wave (SAW) filters, which both technically require a single-mask processing approach. X-ray-imaging is also downward-compatible in device geometry as an advantage; systems that use 1-micron geometries can easily transfer the technology to reach the super-VLSI status in transistor density-area toward 1-M bit integrated circuits in the near future. Solid-state ROM and RAM memories are the first to take advantage of 1-micron high-density processing.

Presently used exclusive LSI lithographic techniques such as (1) contact printing and (2) optical direct-step-on-wafer imaging will be slowly phased in to convert most of the present SSI and MSI technology to custom programmable logic-arrays (PLAs).

The resist film-on-wafer used for X-rays and positive/negative E-beams are usually proprietary with undisclosed acronyms of complex organic molecules. For example, Japan's VLSI Cooperative Laboratories has processed for the electron-beam a highly sensitive photo-resist EBR-9, which is molecular-engineered for the substitution of a chlorine atom in the alpha position in polytriofluoro-α-chloroacrylate with a high sensitivity of 8^{-7} coulombs/cm^2 and a 0.1 micron resolution. (Genetic engineering is much more complex and unpredictable in results, because the recombinant double-helix colossal DNA molecule is *beyond* human understanding in its scope and atomic-complexity.) The Lincoln Laboratories of Massachusetts Institute of Technology uses a copper X-ray source and a polymethylmethacrylate (PMMA) photo-resist, which is effective for both X-ray and E-beam patterning; some new photo-resists are capable of allowing resolutions on the order of 0.16-micron channel-widths.

Direct E-beam-on-wafer lithography systems are best for mask-making. Patterns can be directly written on the wafer with satisfactory production yield-rate. Nippon Electric Company is successfully using the E-beam technique. On the other hand, Cambridge University, U.K., has a fully developed successful system, using a dual E-beam lithographic process, as introduced earlier; the upper surface of the wafer on a mounting table faces the main E-beam, and its registration accuracy is maintained with the aid of wafer-underside, extra-fine, registration marks in silicon-nitride. Four L-shaped chip corners of these markings facilitate the automatic positioning of the registration beam. (Haroon Ahmad of Cambridge University developed the system with G. A. C. Jones and R. A. McMahon.) The second E-beam, projected from below, maintains the registration for the final metallization layer of the logic array-pattern, in conjunction with the registration facility of the silicon-nitride markings—without wafer zapping. The silicon-nitride markings provide excellent optical contrast. The process is suitable for producing MNOS VLSI memory integrated circuits. A master mask is used for producing the masks. The effects of wafer distortions such as bowing and warping are cancelled by the registration E-beam. The advantage of this is that a high-precision laser interferometer-controlled wafer-alignment system is not required since the task is taken over by the square-perimeter registration E-beam. See the accompanying diagram, part b. Drift errors are cancelled by using only one set of deflection amplifiers and beam accelerators for both the main and registration E-beams. Larger chips with field dimensions of 6.5 X 6.5 mm and 2 or more field-of-views can be processed by sticking them together with a high-precision registration-grid. The current step-increment in high-precision registration alignment is maintained at 10 MHz, but an advanced model using a higher processing rate, and a beam cross section of variable rectangular dimensions is on the drawing boards.

The direct-writing electron-beam lithography for submicron logic patterns is used at Japan's VLSI Cooperative Laboratories. Minimum line-channel-widths of 1 micron on 4-in.-diam. wafers (or masks up to 5-in.-diam. on a 100 X 100 mm area) are produced in 12 minutes. See the accompanying diagram, part c; it is a typical microphotograph of the 1-micron logic pattern. Increased production rates are expected by raster vector-scanning and variable-dimension beam-cross sections. Lower-detail areas on the logic-patterns can be skipped or advanced with reduced number of scans to boost speed of production. The electron is deflected across a frame of 250 square-microns along X-Y axes. The wafer alignment on the table is optimized by step-and-repeat-and-return scan procedure along the Y-axis. The CAD programming system uses 160-M bytes of disk-memory and 2-M bytes of RAM buffer-memory for pattern information up to 5-M bits/square-cm, as used in digital facsimile systems.

Increased density of microprocessor circuits on a systematic basis is accomplished by integrating raw materials such as oxide, nitride, and polysilicon. Layered structural compositions with combined MOS and bipolar technologies make it feasible to produce complex sensors and hybrid focal-plane image arrays, and high-density nonvolatile RAM memories with 50-nsec write-erase times. Rockwell International Corporation is already working on a 1-M bit ROM by using a planar, fully self-aligned, NMOS structure; a cell size of 24 square microns and an estimated die size of 200 X 260 mils are used. Self-alignment permits features beyond the lithographic capabilities by using new semiconductor processing techniques. New charge-injection diode arrays are advancing in performance along with charge-coupled devices. A simplified 488 X 385-element CCD imager has been fabricated for television cameras by using only two levels of polysilicon. Toshiba Ltd. of Japan developed in 1980 a 492 X 400-pixel color television camera, using the CCD imager technology!

With the advances described in X-ray and E-beam lithographic processing techniques, mass production of low-cost 256-K, 512-K, and 1-M bit super-VLSI integrated circuits is assured during the 1980s.

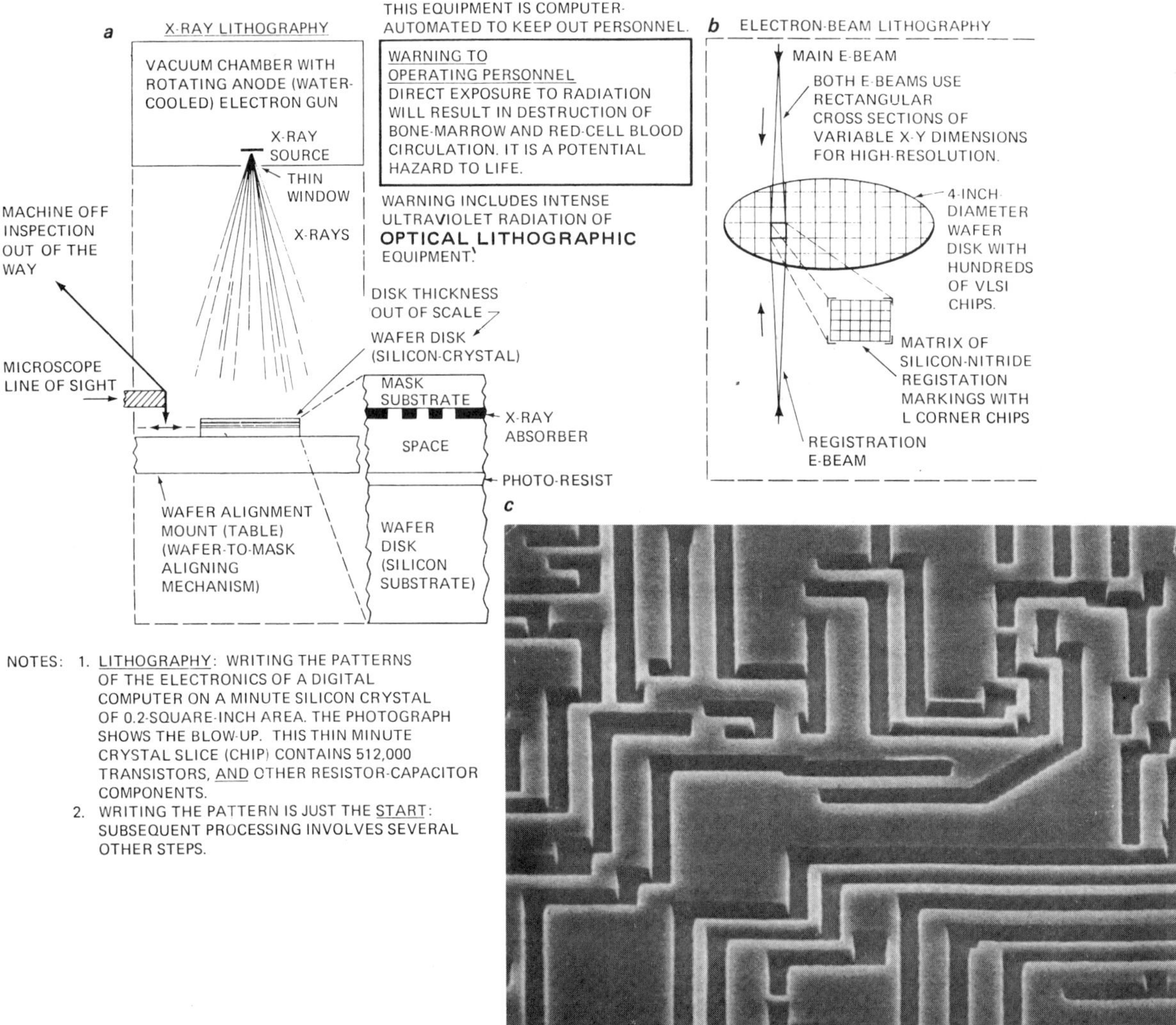

NOTES: 1. LITHOGRAPHY: WRITING THE PATTERNS OF THE ELECTRONICS OF A DIGITAL COMPUTER ON A MINUTE SILICON CRYSTAL OF 0.2-SQUARE-INCH AREA. THE PHOTOGRAPH SHOWS THE BLOW-UP. THIS THIN MINUTE CRYSTAL SLICE (CHIP) CONTAINS 512,000 TRANSISTORS, AND OTHER RESISTOR-CAPACITOR COMPONENTS.

2. WRITING THE PATTERN IS JUST THE START: SUBSEQUENT PROCESSING INVOLVES SEVERAL OTHER STEPS.

2-4. ANALOG/LINEAR INTEGRATED CIRCUITS (ICs)

The operational amplifier and the balanced differential-amplifier readily lend themselves to monolithic fabrication techniques. These amplifiers are also frequently fabricated by hybrid methods for close tolerances; however, where broad tolerances permit, mass-production monolithic techniques are applicable in most cases for video (pulse) bandwidths from DC to 100 MHz, and corresponding propagation-delays down to 5 ns at this time, because the use of capacitors and high-value resistors can be restricted to a minimum in fabrication. Exceptional input-balance afforded by inherent match between differential transistor pairs, and close match in temperature-coefficients of components fabricated from the same material, assure stable electrical characteristics and noise immunity over a broad temperature range. Since ratios are held constant and absolute values take a secondary place, excellent output-to-input isolation is feasible. Also, simplified feedback configurations contribute to higher performance ratings. I^2L (integrated injection logic) processing, in particular, can be adapted by balanced differential amplifier approach in monolithic fabrication techniques.

2-5. THIN-FILM FABRICATION

A substrate-wafer of silicon dioxide is used with a 0.25- to 1-inch-square area. Thin films, with a thickness from 0.1 to 0.001 mil, are deposited by evaporating or sputtering methods. Thin-film resistors of values of 10 to 10^6 ohms are fabricated by evaporating nichrome or tantalum to form strips between terminals; the value is controlled by the composition of the film used, and its length, width, and thickness. Thin-film capacitors are fabricated by applying the requisite conducting areas to both sides of a thin-film of dielectric such as tantalum oxide, aluminum oxide, and silicon dioxide. Most manufacturers use, for example, tantalum for resistor and capacitor fabrication, by photoetching patterns of sputtered tantalum-film over the substrate. The film is then oxidized to the desired depth to form the dielectric for capacitors. Gold or platinum deposits then make the conducting electrodes and interconnections.

2-6. THICK-FILM FABRICATION

The ceramic alumina (0.5 inch by 60 mils thick) is a typical substrate of thick-film fabrication technique. The thick films are applied to the substrate by the silk-screen process. A metallized-ink interconnection pattern by the silk-screen process is followed by firing at 700°C. Resistors are formed by using a metal-glass slurry via the silk-screen process and the desired pattern; firing is repeated. Capacitors are often miniature components soldered or welded into the circuit for higher values; films are fabricated on the substrate for lower values. Deposited ceramic-and-glass paste makes the dielectric. After firing, a top electrode of platinum is applied. The interconnection pattern is coated with 2 to 3 mils of solder. The passive components (in both thick and thin films) can be dynamically trimmed by laser techniques for close tolerances such as 0.05 to 0.001 percent.

2-7. HYBRID TECHNOLOGY

Hybrid technology combines the techniques of monolithic, discrete, thick and thin films for devising the most suitable practical solution (from the viewpoint of cost and performance) to a particular hardware design problem in a system.

In applications where special close-tolerances, temperature-stability, higher power-handling capability, and wider bandwidth are specified, straight monolithic fabrication using diffusion and ion-implantation processing have a limitation. As in the case of the monolithic circuits, active components are mostly formed on separate wafers of silicon by using planar methods; but passive components such as resistors, inductors, and capacitors are fabricated by using the thick- and thin-film techniques. Thus, the hybrid techniques are, in principle, an extension of the previous discrete-component designs, because they are system-wise interconnected assemblies of separate components, formed on or affixed to an insulating base; the semiconductor "substrate" material meeting the desired specification makes this base.

The preceding monolithic, thin-film, thick-film, and hybrid fabrication techniques are the four general semiconductor hardware processing terms used in microelectronics. The monolithic fabrication technique is by far the most specialized and preferred processing system for the grown-ingots of intrinsic silicon, as far as the present LSI microprocessors and microcomputer technology are concerned. The variations in processing, as they stand, are presently well known as PMOS, NMOS, I^2L, CMOS, CMOS-on-Sapphire, CCD, and avalanche MNOS. For large quantity requirements of specialized custom circuits in I^2L or MOS, some custom-LSI design houses offer "master-slice" circuits at prices ranging from 2 to 10 thousand dollars.

2-8. THE LSI SOLID-STATE TECHNOLOGY APPLICABLE TO THE MICROCOMPUTER SYSTEMS

When the number of gates in a silicon monolithic integrated-circuit chip exceeds 100, the term *medium-scale integration (MSI)*, used previously in the case of the minicomputer systems, gives its place to *large-scale integration (LSI)*; a 3,000-gate calculator/microprocessor LSI-chip, at the present high-yield rate, will sell for 2 dollars (less than 0.1 cents/gate), while a 4,096-bit memory-chip will sell for 4 dollars (less than 0.1 cents/bit). High density, unipolar, bulk P-channel silicon metal-oxide semiconductor technology (PMOS) was the first to achieve this status at a fairly low speed (less than 1-μs/gate), and the consumer calculator market was the first to reap the benefit. The faster high-density N-channel MOS and the high-density low-power complementary CMOS or COSMOS have now reached the standards of real-time processing speed (less than 25 ns), formerly attainable by only the low-density, high-power, high-cost, bipolar LSI-TTL (transistor-transistor logic) and by the higher-power and highest-speed LSI-ECL (emitter-coupled logic) technologies. The fairly **recent LSI development of high-speed I^2L (integrated injection logic)** in the bipolar medium is the leading contestant in competition against the unipolar CMOS in respect to both high density and low power—and hence low cost—at higher yields because of simpler processing technology. A brief description of these various LSI techniques is given below to indicate the present status of the highly sophisticated technology behind the microprocessors and the microcomputer systems. See Fig. 2-3a–d for the basic switching circuit, **the "Inverter," used as a building-block** for the digital logic in each LSI technique. Incidentally, the bipolar technique I^2L is, in the form of differential amplifiers, adaptable to analog circuits and large-scale integration for linear signal processing. Each version of these circuits is accompanied by the respective semiconductor substrate structure used in each case for actual material process.

2-8.1. PMOS/NMOS. The basic LSI switching circuits for PMOS and NMOS, shown in Fig. 2-3a, are static P- and N-channel, enhancement, saturation-type, MOS ratio-inverters, with one MOS operating as a static signal-driver (maintaining logic indefinitely) and the other operating as the load. Both PMOS and NMOS operate in **enhancement-mode**; only the supply polarities differ, being negative for PMOS with its low-mobility "hole" charge-carriers and positive for NMOS with its faster "electron" charge-carriers. The term *ratio* stands for *beta-ratio* (approximately 20), which is the ratio of transconductances of the MOS transistors used for the driver and the load in the inverter-circuit shown; the load MOS is operated in **depletion-mode** for a single power-supply version of PMOS and NMOS. The slower PMOS LSI microprocessors presently available at lower cost from most manufacturers, have a gate propagation-delay less than 1 μs. In the past, the production yields for NMOS LSI on a monolithic silicon-chip were low; presently, the faster NMOS microprocessors, with gate-delays less than 2.5 ns and instruction-time close to 1 μs, are making their appearance competitive to the high-speed (less than 2.5 ns), but high power-consuming, bipolar MSI/LSI technology. For the NMOS LSI, the density is high (8,000 MOSFETs on a single-chip), and hence the previous PNP/NPN bipolar-LSI cannot compete with the new N-MOS microprocessors (bipolar I^2L does). Reduced size naturally increases speed-power product, reliability, and mean-time-before-failure (MTBF). Better manufacturing techniques, as they evolve, are also hastening the yields and reliability.

Dynamic, Ratio-less, PMOS/NMOS, LSI, used for the random-access memory (RAM), operate at still lower power dissipation without a load-MOSFET and hence occupy smaller chip-area than the static ones. However, operation of a dynamic inverter, used for the logic, requires two or more common, Refresh/Read and Write/Refresh, clock-pulse drive-MOSFETs for charge transfer. In the case of the dynamic RAM memory cell, the **clock pulse serves the function of Refresh** to continuously maintain the charge or memory when the computer is turned on and operated. That is, the dynamic MOS memory of RAMs is volatile, unlike the conventional nonvolatile CORE memory, unless the memory is maintained by the refresh clock pulses by means of a battery during the computer OFF-time. It may be noted, however, that the registers (serial or parallel shift-registers) used in a PMOS or NMOS microprocessor are **static and Ratio-types,** and hence do not need the refresh circuitry of the above multiphase clocking during operation.

2-8.2. CMOS (Complementary-Symmetry MOSFET). In most microprocessor applications, low power-dissipation is of overriding importance, which led to development of CMOS (or COSMOS by RCA, Fig. 2-3a), since the gate-current of an insulated-gate field-effect transistor (IGFET or MOS) can be in negligible picoampere range. Since only one transistor of the two complementary-symmetry transistors is turned on at any instant, the quiescent power dissipation is determined by the leakage currents and by the load current in the output. Propagation-delays are primarily determined by stray capacitances of less than 5 pF and by the currents available to charge them. By devising special processing techniques using silicon-on-sapphire (CMOS-SOS)—a thin film of sapphire and ion-implantation—the gate propagation-delay is brought down from less than 100 ns to less than 25 ns, and instruction time from 5 to 1 μs. This refined technique allows CMOS LSI microprocessors applicable to low-power real-time processing applications (which previously employed minicomputers using faster TTL/ECL bipolar MSI).

2-8.3. Transistor-Transistor Logic and Schottky Transistor-Transistor Logic. Transistor-transistor logic (TTL) is the bipolar, medium-speed workhorse of the slower real-time minicomputer systems in demand hitherto. The standard NPN, TTL circuit shown in Fig. 2-3b has a typical gate propagation-delay of about 10 to 25 ns and a power dissipation of 10 mW/gate (as compared to 10 nW/quiescent-gate of CMOS). The lower-power 1 mW/gate, TTL has a larger propagation-delay of about 30 ns, whereas the Schottky-diode clamped transistor-transistor logic (STTL), with multiemitter NAND gating, has a mini-

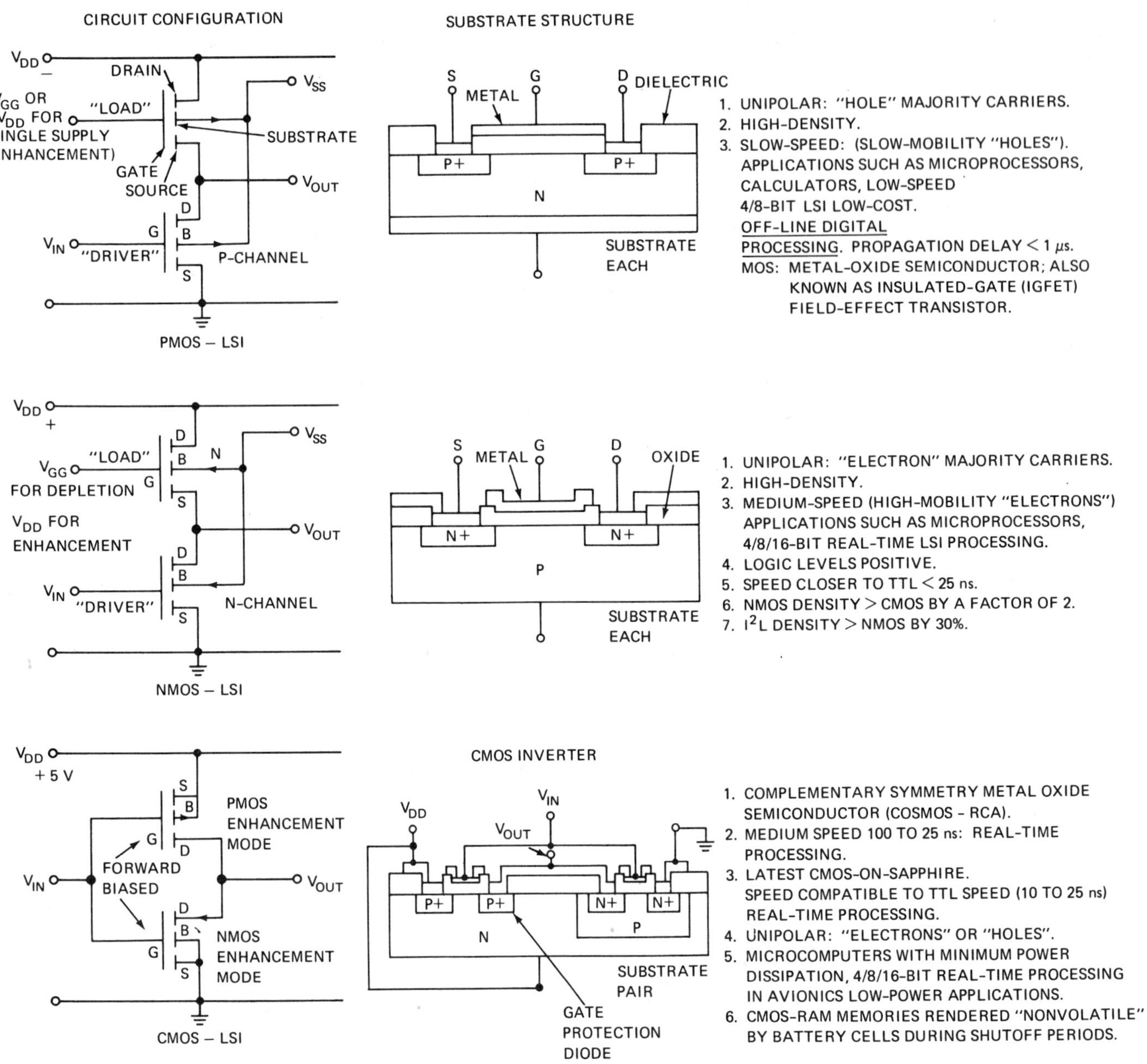

Fig. 2-3a. PMOS, NMOS, CMOS–The basic logic building block, "inverter" of LSI.

mum of delay/gate, such as 3 to 5 ns at a dissipation of 20 mW/gate. In view of the large power-dissipation in TTL-LSI, the density of circuits on a monolithic silicon chip has got to be low, as in MSI. The predominant high-speed Schottky-TTL or ECL (emitter-coupled-logic) technology, so successful in larger minicomputer systems, cannot compete with current NMOS or CMOS in the area of the low-power LSI microprocessors and the high-density LSI memories, unless a radically different alternative **high-density technique** is forthcoming (and it *is* available in I^2L technology).

2-8.4. Emitter-Coupled-Logic (ECL). The shortest propagation-delays can be acquired by the use of emitter-coupled-logic (ECL), as shown in Fig. 2-3b. These circuits operate all their transistors in their forward-active or cutoff regions, thus avoiding saturation and its effective time-delay due to stored charge. A delay/gate of 1 ns is effective in the case

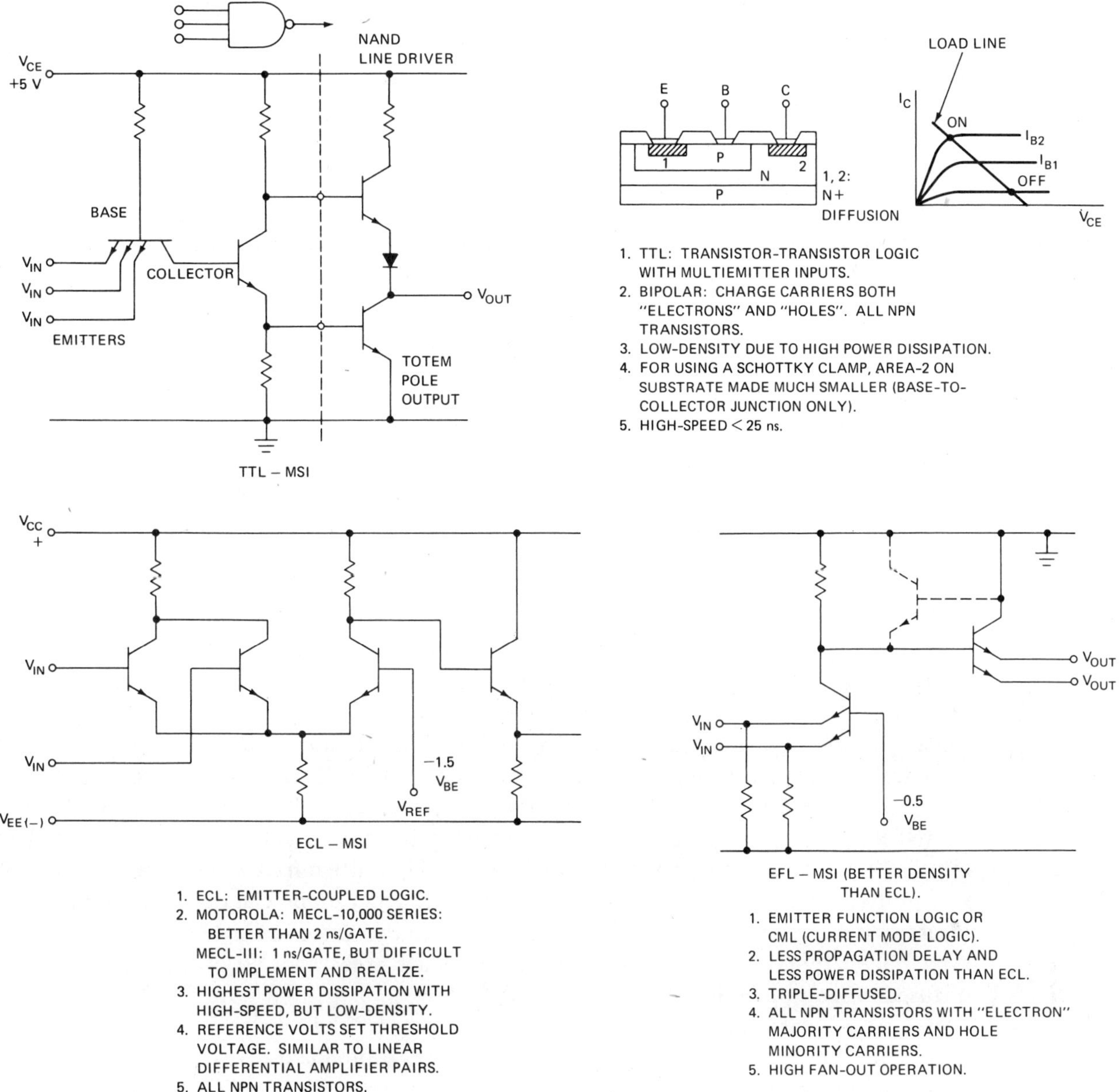
NAND
LINE DRIVER
VCE
+5 V
BASE
VIN
VIN
VIN
COLLECTOR
EMITTERS
VOUT
TOTEM
POLE
OUTPUT
TTL – MSI
LOAD LINE
E B C
P
1 N 2
P
1, 2:
N+
DIFFUSION
IC
ON
IB2
IB1
OFF
VCE
1. TTL: TRANSISTOR-TRANSISTOR LOGIC WITH MULTIEMITTER INPUTS.
2. BIPOLAR: CHARGE CARRIERS BOTH "ELECTRONS" AND "HOLES". ALL NPN TRANSISTORS.
3. LOW-DENSITY DUE TO HIGH POWER DISSIPATION.
4. FOR USING A SCHOTTKY CLAMP, AREA-2 ON SUBSTRATE MADE MUCH SMALLER (BASE-TO-COLLECTOR JUNCTION ONLY).
5. HIGH-SPEED < 25 ns.
VCC
+
VIN
VIN
VEE(–)
–1.5
VBE
VREF
ECL – MSI
1. ECL: EMITTER-COUPLED LOGIC.
2. MOTOROLA: MECL-10,000 SERIES: BETTER THAN 2 ns/GATE. MECL-III: 1 ns/GATE, BUT DIFFICULT TO IMPLEMENT AND REALIZE.
3. HIGHEST POWER DISSIPATION WITH HIGH-SPEED, BUT LOW-DENSITY.
4. REFERENCE VOLTS SET THRESHOLD VOLTAGE. SIMILAR TO LINEAR DIFFERENTIAL AMPLIFIER PAIRS.
5. ALL NPN TRANSISTORS.
VOUT
VOUT
VIN
VIN
–0.5
VBE
EFL – MSI (BETTER DENSITY THAN ECL).
1. EMITTER FUNCTION LOGIC OR CML (CURRENT MODE LOGIC).
2. LESS PROPAGATION DELAY AND LESS POWER DISSIPATION THAN ECL.
3. TRIPLE-DIFFUSED.
4. ALL NPN TRANSISTORS WITH "ELECTRON" MAJORITY CARRIERS AND HOLE MINORITY CARRIERS.
5. HIGH FAN-OUT OPERATION.

Fig. 2-3b. TTL, ECL/EFL–The basic logic building block, "inverter" of MSI.

of the MECL-III logic of Motorola ECL, at a power-dissipation of 60 mW/gate; 2 ns at 25 mW/gate is the corresponding figure for the MECL-10,000 logic. The hitherto low-density MSI is currently the ultimate for high-speed in such large-scale computers as the IBM 370/165 and such minicomputers as DEC-PDP-11/40, for both data-processing and memories. Incidentally, the ultrafast MECL-III has not proved successful in MSI work, since the hard-wired logic design, requiring specialized 50-ohm transmission-line techniques on PC boards, is hard to accomplish in practice.

Emitter Function Logic (EFL) is an improved version of ECL, using multiemitter-drive NPN transistors at slightly lower power-dissipation. As far as the bipolar, MSI-level, low-power Schottky-TTL microprocessors are concerned, the bit-size of the CPU has continued to stay put at a 4-bit slice, in view of the inherent temperature-constrained low-density requirement, as compared to the 8- to 16-bit words of the CPUs under the

PMOS, NMOS, and CMOS microprocessor classifications. Examples of the bipolar CPUs of the 4-bit slice class are Fairchild-9400, Motorola (MECL)-10800, Raytheon RF-16; these all have an address capacity of 64-K bits, consisting of the commercial 4-K bit bipolar or NMOS RAMs with an access time of 200 ns.

2-8.5. Integrated Injection Logic, Philips (Netherlands), and IBM (Germany) as Merged Transistor Logic. Integrated injection logic (I^2L) is the latest high-density, high-speed, low-power, bipolar technique that promises to dominate the technology of the real-time microprocessors and the semiconductor memories in the immediate future.* The clock frequency may go up gradually from 3 to 20 MHz in view of the lower speed-power product, 0.8 picojoule (about 25 times lower than that of low-power Schottky-TTL). A single chip of 100 square mil can accommodate up to 1,000 I^2L gates—higher density than CMOS, but comparable to P or NMOS. Gate propagation-delay down to as low as 1 ns is achieved by using ion implantation and pure-metal Schottky clamps. Thus, MSI technology based especially on the difficult higher-power MECL-III will gradually phase out, as Motorola will introduce C^3L (complementary-constant-current logic, a version of I^2L) to produce, along with other manufacturers, the coming third generation of microprocessors and semiconductor memories (PMOS and NMOS being classified under the first- and second-generation microprocessing techniques). The LSI I^2L processing is flexible enough that, in watch applications, it could dissipate microwatts at slower speeds (as already achieved). In microprocessor and memory applications, it could dissipate only milliwatts at eventual speeds as high as approximately 2 ns/gate in real-time processing. Texas Instruments was the first to announce a 4-bit I^2L microprocessor with an address capacity of 64-K words. The simplicity of the basic switching circuit as an inverter is evident from Fig. 2–3c. The base drive to a multicollector NPN transistor is provided from a lateral PNP transistor, which functions as a hole injector for the fast-mobility electrons of the NPN transistor. No resistive loads are used to require any space on the chip. The multicollector NPN transistor corresponds to a TTL multiemitter transistor, but the NPN is operated inversely. In the latest designs, the Schottky diode clamps are included to increase switching speed. The I^2L actually reduces to the size of a single transistor on an N-type silicon monolithic chip, in which P-type base areas and N-type emitter areas are diffused. (See Appendix B.)*

Merged Transistor Logic (IBM Corp.'s MTL, one of the versions of bipolar I^2L for VLSI): At the Thomas J. Watson Research Center, White Plains, New York, high-density VLSI circuits have been fabricated for VLSI, using modified MTL/I^2L. High-speed switching rates of 0.8 ns/gate are achieved at a 2.5-micron processing level. Power-delay factors on the order of 0.1 picojoules are predicted. So, the higher-speed bipolar I^2L processing technology is closely following the competitive low-power CMOS VLSI processing technology for battery-operated microcomputer systems (See Figure 2-3c, No. 3).

2-8.6. Comparison of TTL and Upcoming I^2L, High-Speed Bipolar LSI Technology. The following table compares the performance and requirements of TTL and I^2L:†

In process complexity, I^2L, built nonisolated with a 4-mask 2-diffusion bipolar process at high yields, with thousands of gates per circuit, and fabricated on a wafer for complex circuit requirements, is simpler than all the other LSI techniques except the low-performance PMOS. The popular NMOS processing requires an additional masking step and two ion-implantation steps as compared to none for I^2L.

*A corresponding discrete PNP/NPN pair was originated by the author in 1959 and regularly used during the 1960s in both linear and digital circuit design.
†Courtesy of *Electronics* magazine.

Performance and Requirements	TTL	I^2L
Packing density (7-μm mask)	10 to 20 gates/mm^2	120 to 200 gates/mm^2
Speed-power product	200 to 100 pj/gate	2 to 0.2 pj/gate
Gate delay	20 to 10 ns	10 to 50 ns at constant speed-power product
Power dissipation	50 to 10 mW	6 nW to 70 μW
Supply voltage	3 to 73 V	1.5 to 15 V
Logic voltage swing	5 V	0.6 V
Current range/gate	5 to 2 mA	1 nA to 1 mA
Interconnect processing	Double-level	Single level

Compared to TTL's seven masks and four diffusions, and CMOS's six masks and three diffusions, I^2L processing is much simpler. At the same time, the gate-electrode is less than one-tenth the area of that of TTL or CMOS. I^2L is presently applicable to 5-to-25-ns real-time processing of main-frame controller systems. The next generation of Schottky-I^2L designs are expected to reach the practical performance standards of the fastest 2-ns ECL-10K technology; added with the high-density advantage for both digital and linear LSI, the I^2L is forecast as a dominating LSI technology in the near future.

2-8.7. Tristate TTL. The common TTL integrated-circuits have low output impedance with totem-pole collector-output configuration (unless they are intermediate **open-collector output** versions for provision of external common pull-up resistors). However, in regard to performance, faster high-impedance "wired-OR" TTL circuits are possible for connecting TTL outputs in parallel, as long as at least one inhibit output is "low" (effectively "high" after inversion), as shown in the logic diagram for each TTL "NAND" inverter. For Tristate TTL operation, the "wired-OR" configuration requires an additional INHIBIT input as shown. The "Tristate" facility allows extension of TTL-compatible RAM/ROM memories by directly paralleling similar external memory chips in the usual bus oriented architecture. (See Chapter 3, Section 3-2, Fig. 3-1c.)

2-8.8. Silicon-on-sapphire CMOS. Silicon-on-sapphire (SOS) CMOS technique has the advantage of high-density (150 gates/mm^2), low speed-power product of about 0.25 picojoules and delay/gate of 1 to 4 ns, and reliable noise margins at 4-volt amplitude. Currently, Hewlett-Packard and RCA are the contenders in this sapphire-insulator silicon technology. Hewlett-Packard has developed a 16-bit CPU microprocessor chip with a 100 to 300 ns cycle-time at a higher price-level to give two to five times better performance than the previous NMOS microprocessors. RCA's 4-K bit SOS-CMOS memories and microprocessors are in the works, and they are expected to join the third-generation microprocessors, in succession to the original PMOS and the present successful silicon-gate NMOS generations. Four 1,024-bit SOS static CMOS RAMs are presently available with an access time of 150 ns and dissipation of 4 mW at 5 V, as compared to 300 mW with NMOS and 800 mW with TTL. Although sapphire is much more expensive than silicon, silicon-on-sapphire processing is in practice much easier for higher yields than the bulk silicon processing. The CMOS 1-K bit SOS-RAM memory can provide better access-time, about 90 ns, if the higher 10-V power supply version is used.

Further information on the various LSI processing techniques is presented in Chapter 3.

2-9. VLSI (VERY-LARGE-SCALE INTEGRATION)

Advanced high-density n-channel silicon-gate MOS technology (HMOS) has an enormous potential for increasing the number of gates on a chip to as many as 250,000. This

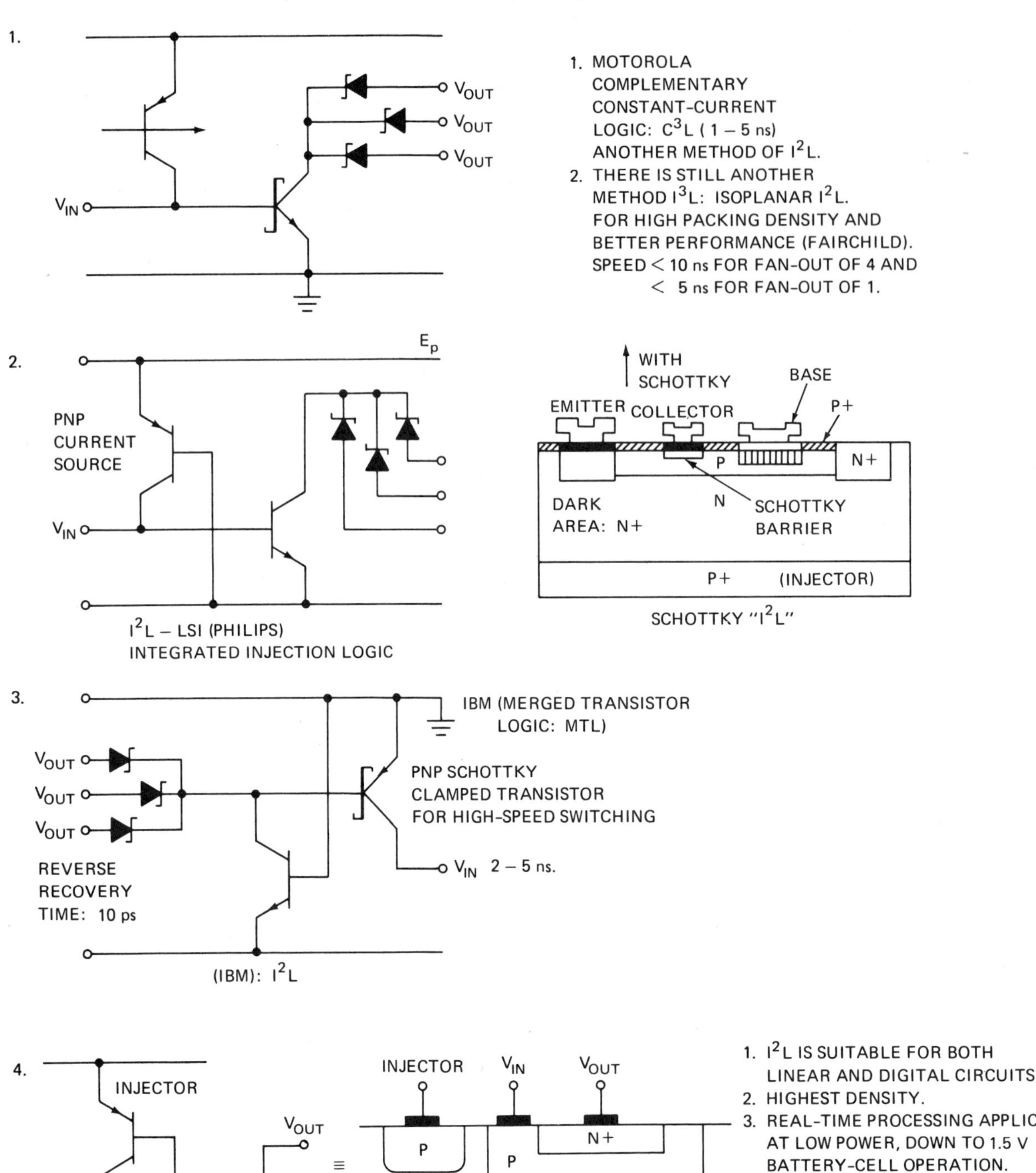

Fig. 2-3c. I^2L, different versions—The basic logic building block, "inverter."

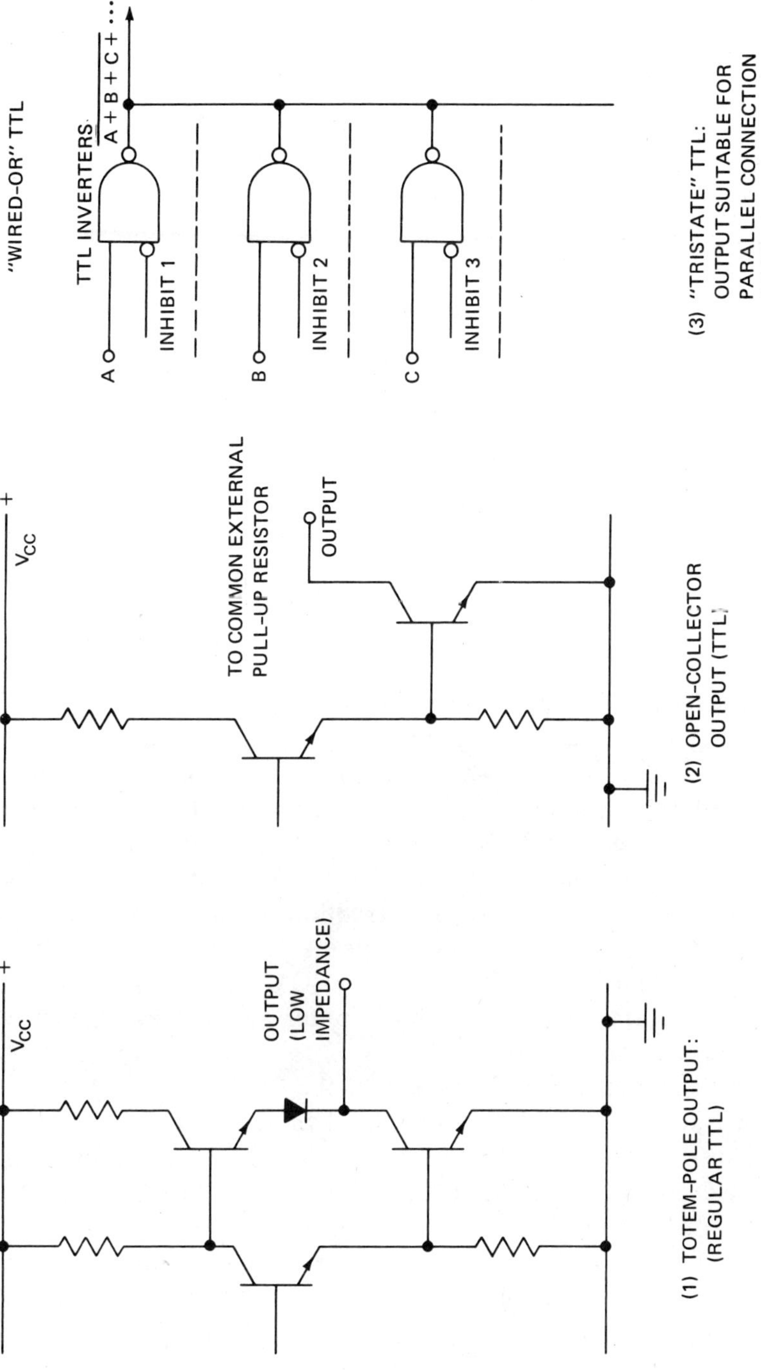

The above TTL output circuits refer to Sections 2-8.7 and Fig. 3-1c.

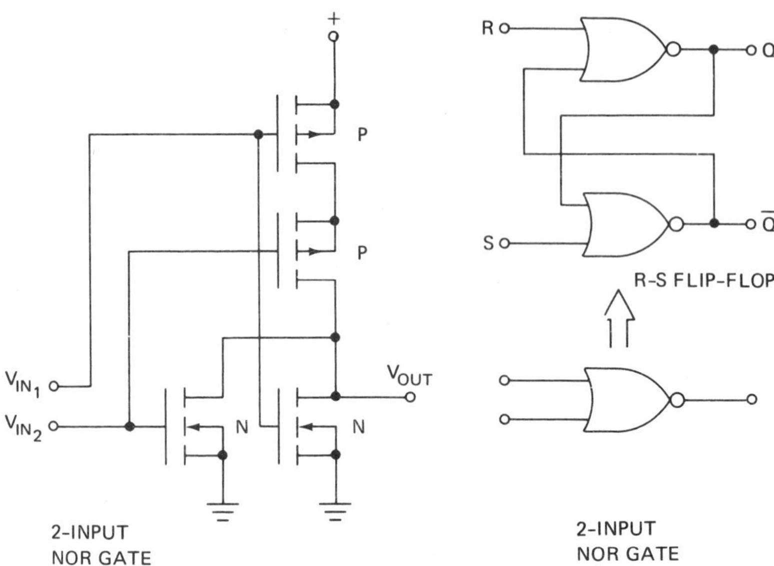

Fig. 2-3d. Extension of a two-input complementary MOSFET NOR-Gate as a building block to R-S storage flip-flop. (*Courtesy of RCA Solid State Division*)

shrinking of IC patterns naturally brings forward the possibility of increasing switching speeds and reducing the chip power consumption. The U.S. Department of Defense calls this technology "VHSIC" (very-high-speed integrated circuits). The chip architecture of the Motorola MC68000, an example of this new VLSI technology, enables the microprocessors to advance into the area of the former high-end minicomputers, by using a 32-bit architecture that supports many instruction and data types and data word sizes. A more effective and simpler instruction set, a multilevel vectored interrupt structure, and a fast asynchronous, nonmultiplexed bus architecture allow these VLSI microprocessors and solid-state 64-K bit RAM/ROM memories to successfully enter into the area of the former high-end minicomputer applications at low cost and low power consumption.

A revolutionary breakthrough is occurring in the "silicon-valley" high-technology in respect to materials; anisotropic plasma etching of thin films for VLSI; pattern transferring lithographic techniques that generate the mask on thin films. Automatic processing and computer-aided circuit design (CAD) and testing are being introduced at the VLSI high-densities of chip architecture. VLSI technology is already established because of the amazing capability of a few manufacturers to make uncontaminated and accurate exposures of high-resolution circuit patterns on resist-covered silicon wafers. High resolutions of circuit patterns extend to the incredible minimum line-widths of 2 microns to 1 micron due to a wide variety of lithographic techniques such as contact, proximity, 1 : 1 projection, step-and-repeat projection, X-ray, and electron-beam projections. As one of the 10 key elements, the silicon atom displays its ultrastable physical characteristics in allowing the present mass-production electronics technology to benefit people all over the world. Contact printing, the original technique for a resolution of up to 5 micron-wide lines, requires: (1) alignment of a glass mask bearing an emulsion or chromium-film pattern on a resist-coated wafer, (2) direct pressing at an even optimum pressure, and (3) exposure of the pattern to ultraviolet light at 3600 to 4600 angstroms. Higher frequency X-ray lithographic techniques are more common for 1-micron line-width VLSI. Scanning and 1 : 1 optical projection is the least expensive technology for resolutions of up to 2.5 to 3 microns for a throughput of 60 wafers/hour (each wafer producing about 50 VLSI chips). The technology of direct wafer-scanning by an electron-beam for a submicron level resolution of wafers is currently at least 10 times more expensive than the lower resolutions, since the finer resolution may result in aborting half the number of wafers processed.

Nikon and Canon Inc. in Japan and Philips Industries in the Netherlands use competing technologies in the VLSI area. IBM uses the scanning electron-beam technology for up to 25 wafers/hour, while Bell Laboratories employs a computer-controlled electron-beam and a laser interferometer feedback technique for a fine alignment within a tolerance of 0.1 micron.

Some of the high-technology lithography equipment suppliers are:

1. Computervision Corp's Cobilt Division, $42K
2. Canon Inc., PLA-520A
3. Perkin-Elmer Corp., 140, Optical Micralign
4. Cobilt CA3000, 5-in. wafers
5. GCA Corporation
6. Electro-Mask
7. Optimetrix, a subsidiary of Cutler-Hammer, Inc.
8. Ultratech
9. Philips Industries, SIRE-2
10. CEA, France
11. Electron-beam machines: IBM Corp. (EL-1), Texas Instruments Incorporated, Bell Laboratories, Hughes Research Labs.

A potentially popular application device is a color graphics CRT terminal that enables home color-television receivers to take the color graphics role as indicated in the following case. Motorola, Inc. has a single VLSI chip that carries all color-graphics circuitry except the video display generator and its display RAM memory (each of these 2 functions presently requires one available LSI chip). These three Motorola chips cost $100; if included on the mass-production scale of the color television receivers, the future home color-television receivers will be produced all set for a microprocessor-controlled color graphics terminal—keyboard and all—at an additional cost of approximately $150 over that of the current color television receiver.

Dr. Gordon Moore, who originated the microprocessor, came up with the idea of "a doubling of IC fabrication densities every year," which is generally termed "Moore's law." ("VLSI: Scoping its future," *IEEE Spectrum*, April, 1979). He is optimistic about the VLSI as a technology that will soon extend the fabrication densities to a million logic gates per chip. When this stage is reached, there will be many possible application areas: the EVLSI (extra-very-large-scale integration) chips will find ready usage in consumer and utility electronics such as telecommunications, electronic telephone exchanges, headsets, video and mobile telephones, home computers, radio/television sets, and telephone subscriber lines with over 10,000 logic gates plus megabits of memory. (In fact, in a *limited* area of the data applications, optical video disks are extending into the 10 billion-bit area with the latest laser-beam technology.) One new development is already on the drawing boards: the extension of the use of the minicomputers employing multimicroprocessor-system architectures into large-scale central computer applications to replace the former large-scale computers. The EVLSI 32-bit microcomputers will then take over the tasks of the present minicomputers. (The term EVLSI is used here as an alternative to "super VLSI" for densities of up to 1-M logic functions.)

2-10. VLSI DEVELOPMENTS

NMOS. A 64-K bit dynamic RAM of Texas Instruments and Intel's 16-K bit static RAM are the present VLSI achievements, with 2-to-3-micron minimum geometrics. Channel lengths of 3 to 5 microns are used in the present VLSI 16/32-bit microprocessors. By using computer-aided design (CAD) and "scaling-down" (or shrinking) individual circuits, 1-micron minimum geometrics are projected within a few years. Larger substrates for growth in chip size are projected. Hitachi has produced 64-K bit static RAM.

HMOS-II RAM is a scaled-down version of the NMOS 3.5-micron gate-length processing with a gate delay of 1 nsec. When the gate-lengths are minimized to 2 microns, the gate-delays are expected to reach 0.4 nsec (40 psec) in order to be competitive with other bipolar and MOS technologies. The limits to scaled-down miniaturization are set at 0.2-micron geometrics, as imposed by the breakdown of dielectrics by electric fields and lithography/processing difficulties, unless chip sizes are increased enormously and voltage is reduced from 5 volts to 2 or 3 volts. The power delay product in HMOS-II is reduced by an inversely proportional scaling-factor, k. The gallium-arsenide MESFETs, as a limited special breed, are expected to serve the demands in the gigahertz or GHz-bit/sec application areas such as waveform synthesizers, time multiplexers, and multi-PSK modems in digital, video, and radar systems. The GaAs MESFETs/(Section 2-14) are n-channel majority carrier devices (junction FETs) with higher electron-mobility, more favorable energy-band gap, and no charge-storage effects. They use a semi-insulating substrate (chromium-doped substrate) and a depletion region for gate lengths on the order of 0.5 to 2 microns. The silicon atoms act as the doping impurity, as a reverse of the normal MOS technology. The very-high-resistive substrate reduces the stray capacitances to lower capacitive time-constants and hence boosts speed. It must be noted that GaAs technology will never replace the ultra-stable silicon-gate NMOS technology.

Schottky-diode FET logic (SDFET) uses low power-depletion mode (normally ON) MESFETs. Direct-coupled FET logic using enhancement-mode MESFETs are termed ENFETs. According to Rockwell International designers, both these versions have been fabricated to exhibit delays on the order of 150 to 300 psec, but no economically reliable processing is in sight for regular production.

SUPER CMOS. The Mitel Corp.'s CMOS, with a 5-micron separation between the n and p types (gate-length), achieves a gate-delay slightly under 2 nsec and a power-delay product of 6 pJ. The next step will be to scale down to a 4-micron separation for a 3-nsec gate-delay at 0.2 pJ power-delay product. When the scaling-down is increased to a 2-micron separation, the gate-delay is expected at 0.5 to 1 nsec with a 0.1-pJ power-delay product, as perhaps the ultimate in the super CMOS technology. American Micro-devices is expected to break the 1-nsec barrier in gate-delay with a scale-down to 3.5 microns, to produce the next generation of low-cost memories and microprocessors at a comparatively low power consumption. The fabrication for the 3.5-micron scale-down will employ a "selective-oxide" approach, with exclusive oxide isolation only between the n^+ type of polysilicon devices. The "ubiquitous P-Well" is implanted under the field oxide; soft errors caused by *alpha particles* are eliminated by the immersion of the n-channel core in a P-type well. High-speed bulk-CMOS 5-micron devices can compete well with the more expensive silicon epitaxy CMOS-on-sapphire. However, RCA has postponed CMOS-on-sapphire fabrication. The standby power consumption of memories and microprocessors during the long nonprocessing intervals is much lower in the case of the bulk-CMOS chips, whereas the NMOS and other chips draw continuous power. So, the original bulk-CMOS is a successful and competing processing technology in VLSI fabrication also.

The American Microsystems VLSI, high-density, common-source, 5-micron line, **V-groove MOS** has produced a single 5-volt-supply 64-K bit ROM (S4264) that packs 8-K bytes of memory into a chip less than 175 mils square. It is comprised of on-chip memory-array and sensors, without any need of an external chip-enable pulse. By replacing four 16-K bit ROMs the 64-K bit ROM saves more than half of power consumption. It is internally organized in four 16-K quadrants; only one quadrant is activated during chip-select, and the other three quadrants are put on a standby mode essentially dissipating no power. The S4264 has a fast access-time of 250 nsec with TTL-compatible inputs and outputs.

The Texas Instruments 5-volt, 16-pin TMS4164, 2.5 micron-channel **VLSI dynamic RAM** uses a 0.8-volt threshold bias for TTL compatibility. (Most other VLSI RAMs require two supply voltages.) The chip uses a single-transistor cell, NMOS double-level polysilicon, and scaled-down technology; it achieves its high performance of 100 to 150 nsec access-time and 200-mW power consumption with a small storage cell, adequate storage-capacitance and charge-capacity, a highly sensitive low-power sense amplifier, and peripheral circuitry. It is insensitive to random data patterns to provide a high-density 64-K bit dynamic RAM at a refresh period of 4 msec.

Status of VLSI in 1980s. The trend toward scaled-down LSI microprocessor and memory geometrics is expected to continue for two or three generations of VLSI chips, until they reach a limit in velocity saturation and increased channel capacitances. The scaling-down of the NMOS Intel HMOS-I and HMOS-II (high performance) chips has respectively reached 0.7 and 0.4 (against 1) in channel-lengths, oxide-thickness, and junction-depths. By the mid-1980s, they are expected to reach a scale-down factor of 0.2 for the ultimate high density of the number of transistors—for example, in a possible 32-bit VLSI microprocessor or 1-M bit ROM/dynamic RAM memories. At the scaling factor of 0.2, the individual transistor will have a channel-length of 1 to 0.5 micron and a gate-oxide thickness of 200 Å as compared to 5 microns and 1000 Å, respectively, in previous LSI microprocessors and memories.

High-performance low-power-consuming CMOS microprocessors and memories processed with computer-aided design (CAD) for higher clock-rates up to 10-MHz will be available in the early 1980s. The processing will be much less expensive and predictable by using CAD for minimum reject ratio, as compared to scale-down optical shrinking procedures. For example, CMOS, the 80C48 microcomputer chip of Nippon Electric Company Ltd., requires only 0.5 mW under standby conditions as compared to Intel's NMOS, 8048's original 75 mW power consumption on standby. However, Intel's low-power HMOS 8048L microcomputer chip consumes a minimum of 200 mW at a clock rate of 4 MHz (and 400 mW at a clock rate of 8 MHz).

2-11. CHARGE-COUPLED DEVICES (CCD)

The basic principle of the charge-coupled device (CCD) and its processing in fabrication are comparatively simple enough. The storage of charge as an electric field, by means of positive "hole" minority-carriers, takes place under a metal plate in a geometrically defined "depletion region" or "potential well" near the surface of the N-type silicon semiconductor when a negative potential is applied to the metal plate. A typical three-phase device using a three-phase clock is shown in Fig. 2-4a–c. The device, used as a shift-register, contains and manipulates individual packets of charge by use of electric fields; adjacent wells interact, and the charge-packet Q is shifted automatically in three phases. (1) depletion mode, (2) storage mode, and (3) transfer mode.

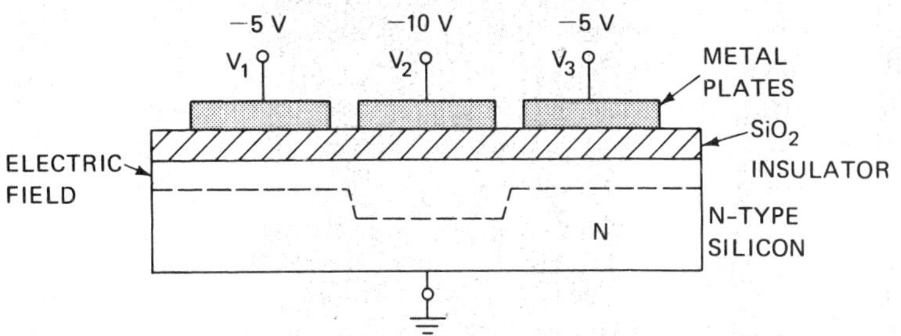

- STORAGE OF MINORITY CARRIER CHARGE IN A GEOMETRICALLY DEFINED "DEPLETION REGION" OR "POTENTIAL WELL" NEAR THE SURFACE OF SEMICONDUCTOR BELOW THE METAL PLATE.
- LARGE ENOUGH NEGATIVE VOLTAGE TO ALL METAL ELECTRODES TO FORM A CHARGE INVERSION LAYER.
- CHARGE DRAINS IN A FEW SECONDS.

Fig. 2-4a. Three-phase CCD "depletion" condition (three-phase clock pulses applied).

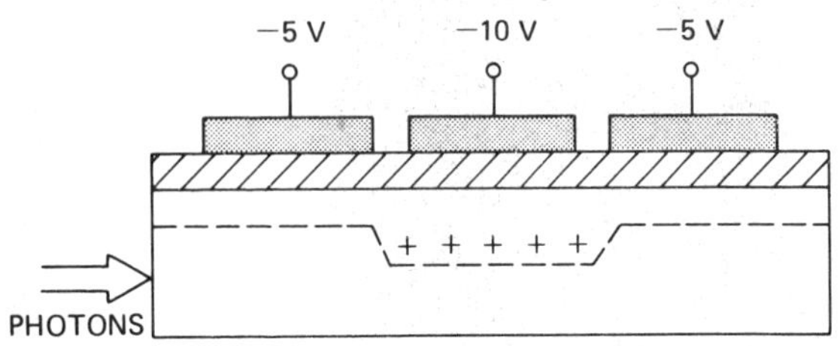

- PHOTON-GENERATED "HOLES" (MINORITY CARRIERS) COLLECT IN "WELL" UNDER PLATE 2.

Fig. 2-4b. CCD: "Storage" condition.

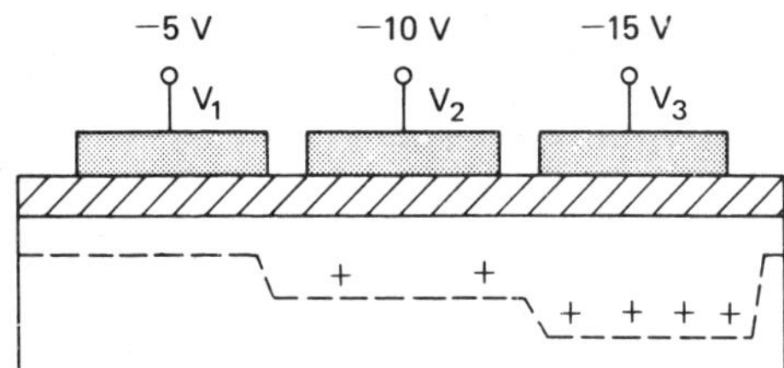

- EXCESS HOLES UNDER 2 WILL FLOW TO "WELL" UNDER 3. CCD HAS NO PREFERRED DIRECTION OF TRANSFER. THE CLOCK-PULSE AMPLITUDES AT V_1, V_2, V_3 DETERMINE THE DIRECTION OF TRANSFER. (TRANSFER TO RIGHT OR LEFT ACCORDING TO CLOCK PULSES).

Fig. 2-4c. CCD: "Transfer" mode.

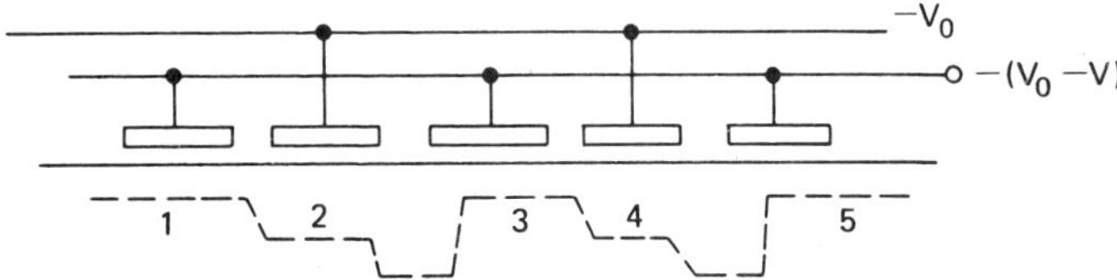

- THE UNIDIRECTIONALITY OF CHARGE IN BOTH THE CASES IS DETERMINED BY THE THICKNESS OF THE SILICON DIOXIDE INSULATOR TO SET UP PROPER POTENTIAL.

Fig. 2-4d. CCD: Two-phase device; charge transfer.

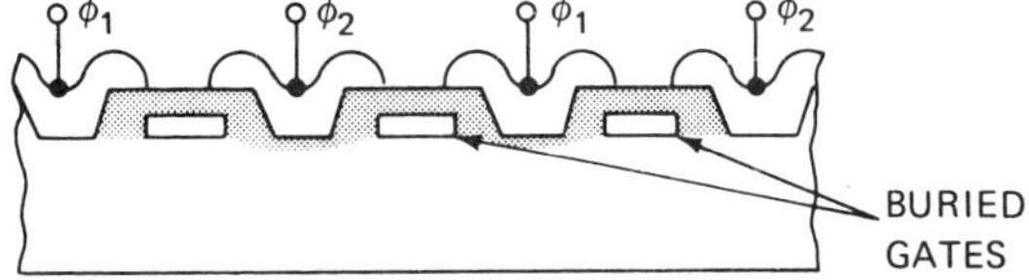

- TWO-PHASE OPERATION CAN BE REALIZED BY ALSO DC-BIAS OR CAPACITIVE COUPLING TO A BURIED GATE.

Fig. 2-4e. Buried-gate CCD.

Fig. 2-4. Charge-coupled devices (CCD). (*Courtesy of the Office of Naval Research, Virginia*)

The magnitude of the applied multiphase clock pulses determine the direction of transfer, left or right. A two-phase device is shown in Fig. 2-4d. The unidirectionality of the charge in both cases is determined by the thickness of the silicone-dioxide insulator to set up the appropriate potential. Two-phase operation can also be implemented by DC-bias or capacitive-coupling to a buried-gate electrode, shown in Fig. 2-4e.

The devices make highly efficient **shift-registers for memory or delay** with a storage-transfer efficiency as high as 99.9%. As minute charge-packets, CCDs make analog sampled-data devices. The function allows either analog or digital version of output. Charge or absence of charge can be introduced selectively as 1s and 0s, respectively, at the input of the metal-oxide semiconductor chain of CCDs by, for example, radiation-generated electron-hole pairs.

A **full-adder** can be easily implemented by using a sophisticated organization of three cells as shown in Fig. 2-4f. A charge packet with a magnitude of 0, 1, 2, and 3 amounts of charge Q, inserted at left, will turn out as a full-adder output at right. The contents of the three "wells" are equivalent to a binary addition, and the adder provides the sum and carry. A CCD adder dissipates well under 20 times less power than equivalent NMOS LSI circuits.

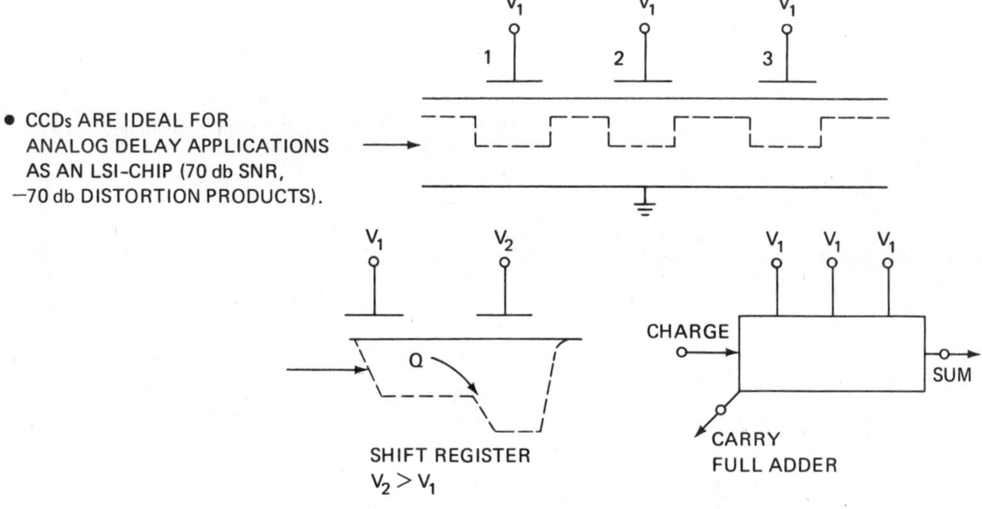

• INSERT AT LEFT A CHARGE-PACKET WITH MAGNITUDE OF 0, 1, 2, OR 3 AMOUNTS OF CHARGE.

SUM OF CONTENTS OF 3 "WELLS" IS EQUIVALENT TO BINARY "ADD".

• ADJACENT WELLS INTERACT, AND THE CHARGE-PACKET Q IS MANIPULATED AUTOMATICALLY.

CHARGE INSERTED	WELL-FILLED			
	NONE	1	2	3
0: 00	X			
1Q: 01		X		
2Q: 10		X	X	
3Q: 11		X	X	X

Fig. 2-4f. CCD as a sophisticated full-adder and shift register. (*Courtesy of the Office of Naval Research, Virginia*)

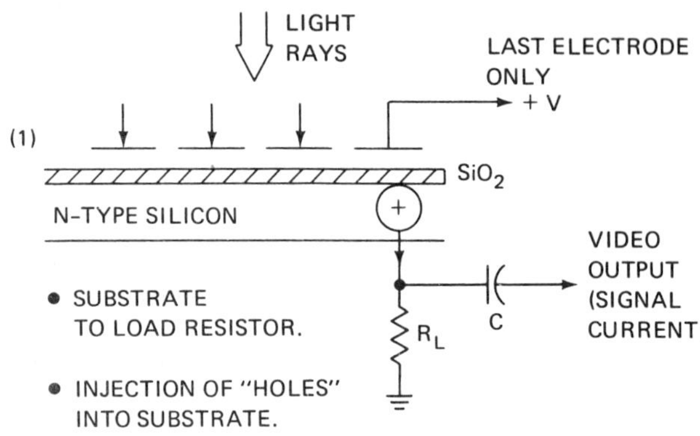
LIGHT
RAYS
LAST ELECTRODE
ONLY
+V
(1)
SiO_2
N-TYPE SILICON
VIDEO
OUTPUT
(SIGNAL
CURRENT)
• SUBSTRATE
TO LOAD RESISTOR.
R_L
C
• INJECTION OF "HOLES"
INTO SUBSTRATE.

• THE CCD IMAGE SENSOR ELIMINATES SMEARING DUE TO ILLUMINATION DURING TRANSFER OF CHARGE HORIZONTALLY.
• CHARGE PATTERN FORMS ON 4 X 4 OPTICAL IMAGE ARRAY WHILE THE PREVIOUS IMAGE IS READ OUT OF CAMERA.
• DURING VERTICAL RETRACE TIME OF TELEVISION, CHARGE PACKETS ARE TRANSFERRED VERTICALLY.

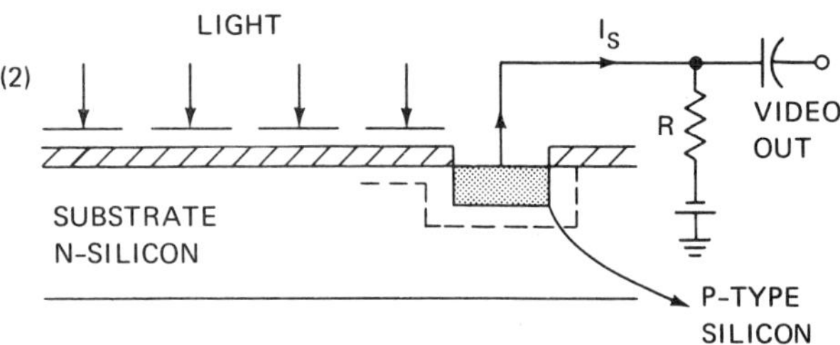
LIGHT
I_S
(2)
R
VIDEO
OUT
SUBSTRATE
N-SILICON
P-TYPE
SILICON
• PN JUNCTION OR SCHOTTKY-BARRIER REVERSE-BIASED DIODE FORMED BY P-DIFFUSION INTO SUBSTRATE. IT CONDUCTS WHEN CHARGE CARRIERS ARE INSERTED FROM PREVIOUS STAGE TO PRODUCE SIGNAL CURRENT IN R.

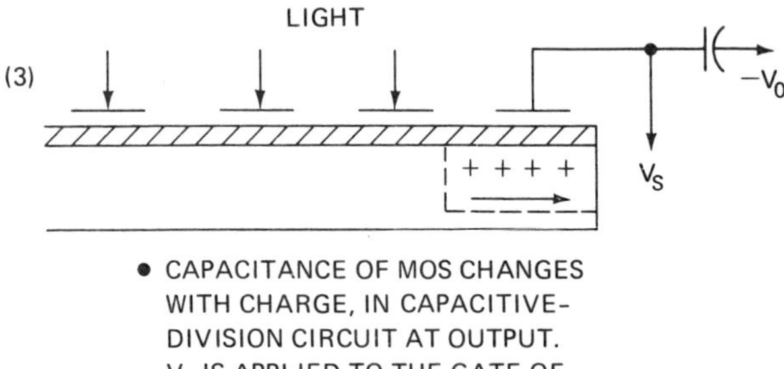
LIGHT
(3)
$-V_0$
+ + + +
V_S
• CAPACITANCE OF MOS CHANGES WITH CHARGE, IN CAPACITIVE-DIVISION CIRCUIT AT OUTPUT. V_S IS APPLIED TO THE GATE OF AN IGFET VIDEO AMPLIFIER.

Fig. 2-4g. CCD as an image-sensing device for television (three versions). (*Courtesy of Bell Laboratories*)

CCDs have the following advantages:

a. High density
b. Good noise-immunity
c. Electronically reprogrammable facility
d. Compatability with TTL and other analog and digital components.

Figure 2-4g illustrates one version of CCD as an **imaging device** to obtain a microamp of video output at 75 ohms. The capacitance of the metal-oxide semiconductor changes with charge; this principle is used in a capacitive-division circuit, where voltage V_s may be connected to the gate of an IGFET video preamplifier. A transfer efficiency of 95% along with a transfer time-constant and a diffusion constant are involved in the design. The fringe field-effects are minimized by reducing gaps between metal plates. Figure 2-4h illustrates the principle of a solid-state (CCD) television camera developed by Bell

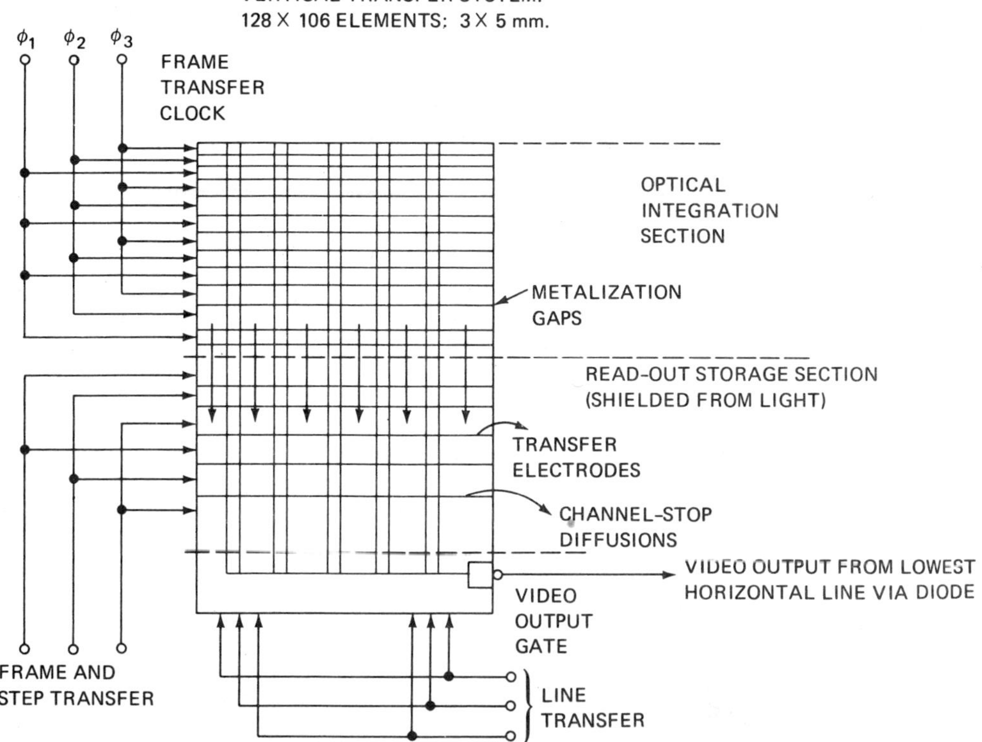

Fig 2-4h. Bell Laboratories CCD video camera. Research version: vertical transfer system; 128 X 106 elements, 3 x 5 mm (*Courtesy of Bell Laboratories*)

Laboratories for imaging purposes. Both black-and-white and color camera operation are demonstrated by RCA by using a faceplate of 525 X 525 elements. The image sensor eliminates lag and "smearing" due to illumination during transfer of charge horizontally. During vertical retrace time of television, the charge packets are transferred vertically. Clock pulses used should be two or three times the highest video frequency generated by photons. The lowest horizontal line gives the direct video readout, while simultaneously some horizontal lines are designated for prereadout storage. The optical array section is then logically activated to read out the next image formation.

CCDs in LSI format are presently used in the following research-and-development applications:

1. Digital correlators in spread-spectrum communications systems, and voice-processing by fast fourier transform (FFT)
2. Matched filters, etc., in sonar, weather, radar and infrared systems
3. LSI arithmetic-chip containing 16 X 16 multipliers, 16-bit adders, gates, and delay; LSI I/O multiplexers
4. An FFT chip, used as a variable delay-line with programmable delay
5. CCD solid-state video cameras
6. High-capacity memory chips of 64-K bits (with 1-mil^2 RAM-cell) in digital computers to replace disk, drum, and tape memory systems
7. Telecommunications

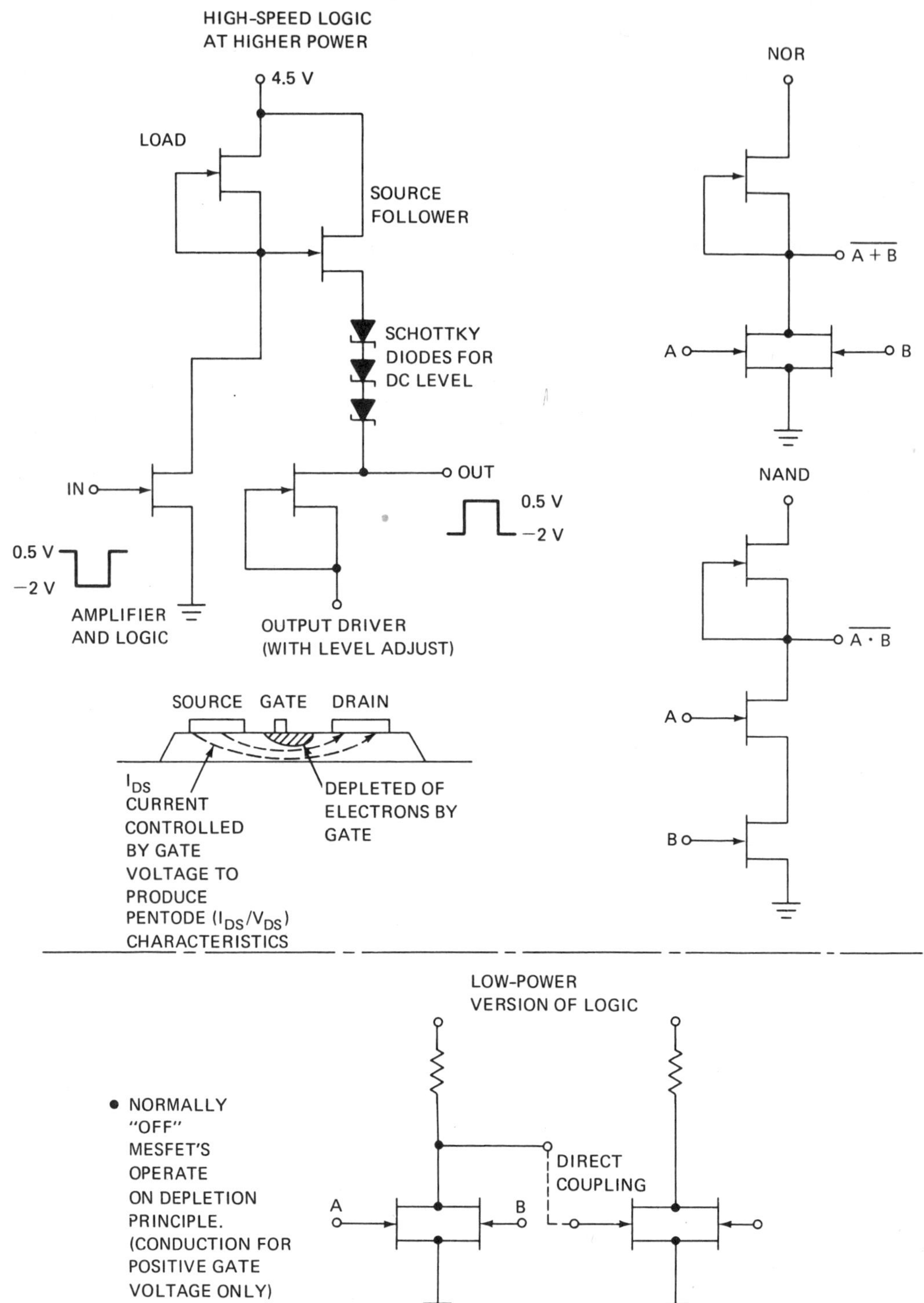

Fig. 2-5. MESFET (metal semiconductor field-effect transistor): High-speed and low-power versions. (*Courtesy of IEEE Spectrum*)

2-12. GALLIUM ARSENIDE FET RF MICROWAVE AMPLIFIERS

GaAs FET RF Microwave amplifiers of the hybrid technology, first commercially developed with successful results in Japan by Nippon Electric for low-noise, low-power, miniature solid-state microwave applications, are currently replacing power-consuming large-size traveling-wave tube amplifiers (TWTAs) in radar and other microwave receiver applications. The amplifiers of Amplica Inc. can handle radar pulse-widths of approximately 50 to 100 ns at frequencies in the range 2 to 18 GHz.

At one octave bandwidth, thin-film low- or high-gain amplifiers extending in frequency range to 12 GHz are commonplace at noise figures under 5 dB and output power to +16 dBm at 1 dB compression to provide ample dynamic range and comparatively higher sensitivity figures. Noise figures may raise utmost to 7 dB at 10 to 18 GHz (as compared to 14 dB for low-noise TWTAs) at power outputs of 9 dBm. At 12 to 14 V dc, they draw 100 to 800 mA depending on the linear power output required (+8 to +26 dBm). Power outputs can reach +30 dBm for 10 to 30% bandwidth.

GaAs FET amplifiers at power outputs to 1 W in the frequency range of 2 to 4 GHz, with a low noise figure of 2.5 dB, presently replace the former hybrid bipolar transistor amplifiers of comparatively higher noise figures. GaAs FET amplifiers at 2.5 dB noisc figures include the input limiter for RF power protection at a high MTBF under the most stringent operating conditions. For higher powers up to 3 W, high-efficiency GaAs Impatt diodes can presently compete with TWTAs in the 6-to-12-GHz range.

At 300°K, electron mobility in GaAs FET crystal structure is 8,600–11,000 cm^2/volt-sec (hole mobility is 3,000) at an energy-band gap of 1.43 eV, as compared to a figure of 1,500 cm^2/volt-sec (hole mobility is 480) in silicon at an energy-band gap of 1.1 eV. The principles of operation of the basic field-effect transistors are explained in Appendix A; the substrate and processing are of course different.

2-13. Bi-FET MONOLITHIC SAMPLE-AND-HOLD IC (BIMOS)

National Semiconductors has developed a MSI single-chip IC for the Bi-FET monolithic sample-and-hold function, in the place of several hybrid chips. It is a Bi-FET linear process that combines bipolar and ion-implanted junction field-effect transistors on one and the same monolithic chip. This particular processing technique produces low input-offset currents (a few hundred nanoamps) for the hold-capacitance, to give high-accuracy measurements. The sample-and-hold IC gives droop-rates as low as 5 mV/minute with 1-μF external hold-capacitor; the low-noise of the JFET contributes to high accuracy and long-range temperature stability. The acquisition-time specification is 5 μs with 1,000 pF; the accuracy is 0.005% at unity-gain, at an off-set voltage of 3 mV and an input bias current of 25 nA.

2-14. MESFET (METAL SEMICONDUCTOR FIELD-EFFECT TRANSISTOR)

MESFET digital and microwave analog circuits extend the performance of the Ga-As technology in the multigigabit area for special applications. This processing, however, is not suitable at the level of LSI; however, MSI is feasible as in the case of the ECL.

The Ga-As MESFET is a version of junction field-effect transistor, which is effective for fabrication on the high electron-mobility gallium arsenide. It can presently function as a microwave amplifier, operating at 10 GHz with a gain of 10 dB, or as a sub-nanosecond logic switch. A propagation delay of about 1 nsec to 300 psec is feasible at a low power of 0.3 mW, while operating in the depletion mode. (Short-channel NMOS is also

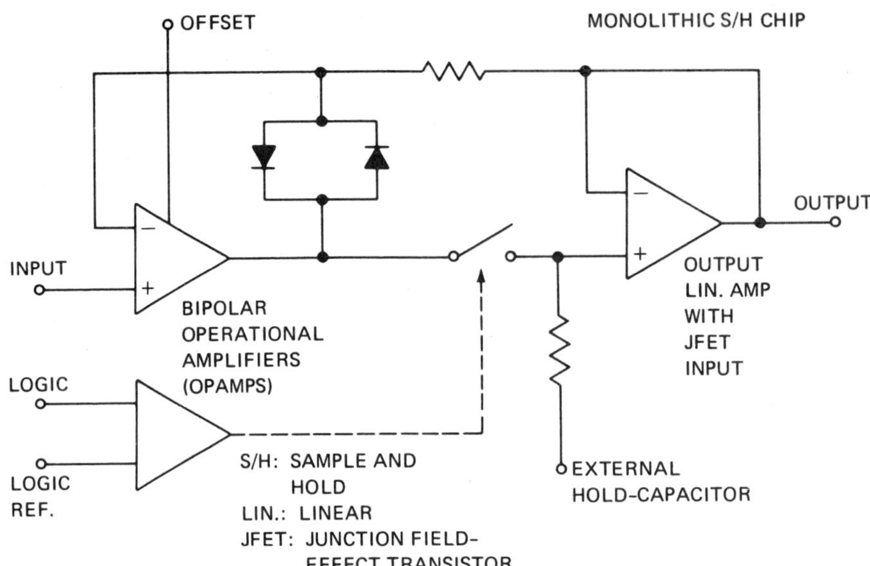

(Courtesy of National Semiconductor Corp.)

capable of this high-speed performance.) Figure 2–5 illustrates the structure of the semiconductor device, and the basic high-speed and low-power logic gates.

2-15. JOSEPHSON JUNCTION CIRCUITS (JJC'S)—IBM CORP.

For use in special-purpose compact, ultrafast computers, 10-psec switching-speed Josephson junction circuits (JJCs), operating at superconductivity temperatures *near* absolute zero (−273°C/−459°F), are attractive with power/delay-time products of the order of 100×10^{-18} joules (100 attojoules). Logical and latch-functions are built with low-capacitance interferometer building blocks consisting of three common-conductor-inductance coupled junctions. Logical gate speeds range from 50 to 110 psec with unlimited fan-out ratio. The 5-micron-diameter switch electrodes are fabricated with lead-alloy, indium, and gold, and a fine 50-angstrom "tunnel" oxide insulating layer. So Josephson junction circuits are, in principle, superfast superconductivity tunnel diodes, as building-blocks. The latest JJCs reach switching speeds *under* 2 psec!

In 1979, IBM fabricated a 4500-junction array with dual-junction cells for main-memory applications. A 16-K bit nonvolatile JJC-RAM is feasible at an operating power-dissipation of 40 μW, 15-nsec access-time, and 20-nsec read/write cycle-time. Standby power-dissipation is practically zero. A memory location is termed "single flux-quantum" (SFQ) cell. Using 16-K bit chips with 2.5-micron line-widths, a 2-M byte superconducting nonvolatile memory would require an area of 5 in.^{2} in a JJC computer incorporating an ultra-high-speed catche memory. See Appendix D.

Thus we see that ultra-high speed subminiature supercomputers, based on the Josephson Junction Interferometer concept at the superconductivity temperature of liquid helium (4° above the absolute zero Kelvin), is already an established achievement. However, it will take several years before the marketable models of this microcomputer from IBM materialize for certain defense and aerospace applications. The microphotograph of an experimental superconductivity computer chip is shown in Figure 2-6.

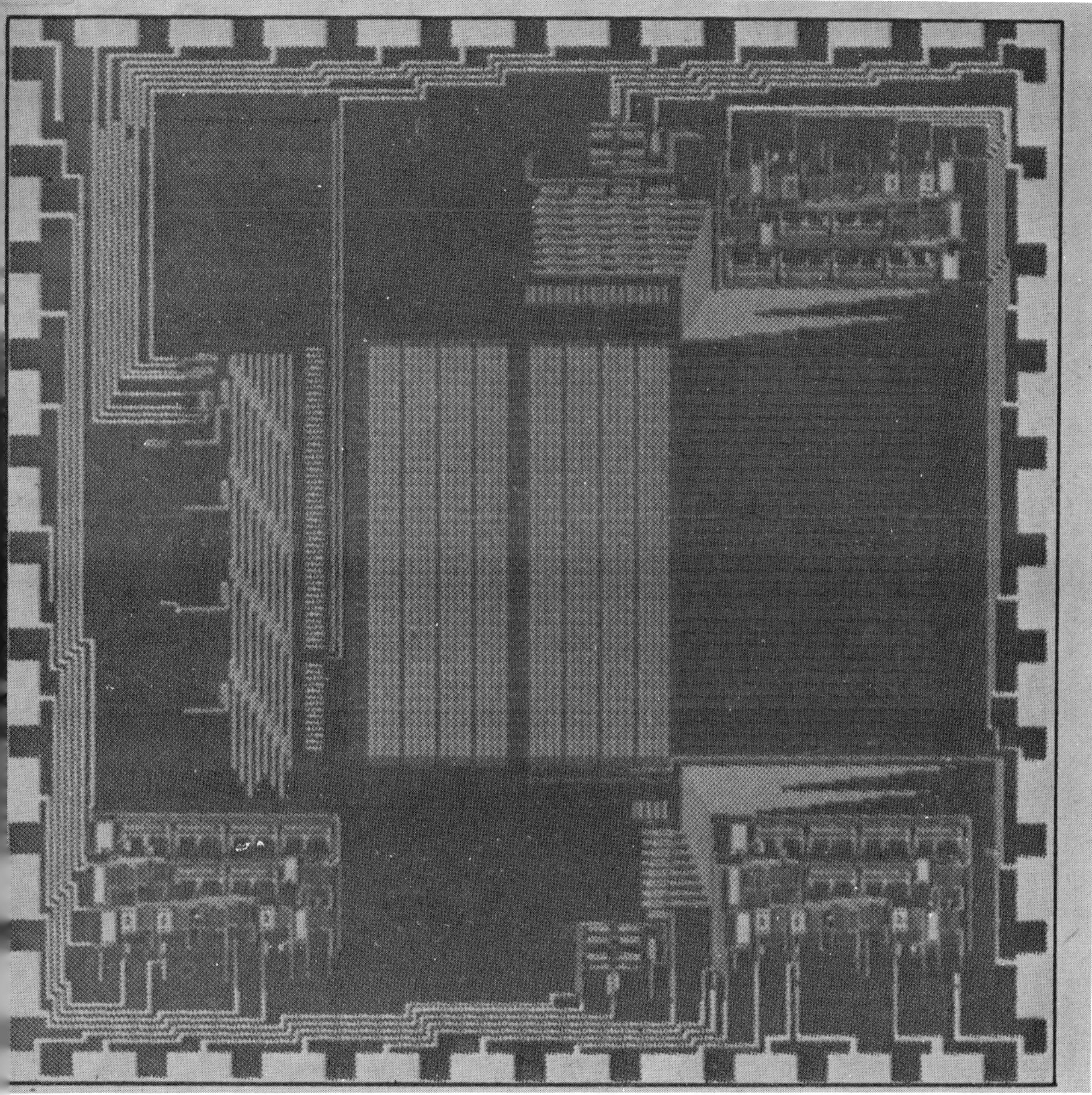

Fig. 2-6. The microphotograph of an experimental IBM superconductivity microcomputer chip. (*Courtesy of IBM Corporation*)

2-16. SOLAR CELLS—PHOTOVOLTAICS

Commercial solar cell arrays, based on mature, conversion-efficient technologies of single-crystal silicon ingots, polycrystalline silicon, cadmium sulfide, gallium arsenide, and concentrators, assure automated mass production of photovoltaics in the near future at consumer prices of approximately $1/watt. They will find a lucrative market among the power-hungry nations of the world. Electric power can be extracted by *insolation* (solar radiation over a given area) more cheaply than it can be produced by conventional generators using fossil fuels. During the next 20 years, annual installed photovoltaics capacity is expected to rise from the 1980 level of 1 MW to at least 5000 MW to minimize dependence on such alternate energy resources as nuclear fission and exorbitantly priced fuel oil. American solar-cell technology, based on the production of polysilicon material, the formation of large crystalline sheets, amorphous silicon, large-grained macrocrystalline ribbons, cell fabrication, and encapsulation, leads the worldwide effort in research and development in this field.

Single-crystal silicon in one of three forms, ingots by the conventional *Czochralski* crystal-growing method, fabricated ribbons or sheets, is processed to produce photovoltaic PN junction solar-cells. It is then assembled and encapsulated by automated mass production techniques to market a competitive solar-cell framework assembly for direct installation on homes, etc., as a consumer utility product. Motorola, Inc., RCA Corp., Texas Instruments Incorporated, Solarex, Spectrolab Inc., Sensor Technology Inc., Centrede Recherches Nucleaires, Heliotronics, Mobil Tyco, Westinghouse Electric Corp., Honeywell Inc., Silicon Technology, Sanyo, and Fuji Electric are some of the manufacturers that will be meeting the huge demand during the 1980s.

Ovshinsky Energy Conversion Devices, RCA Corp., Spear's Group in Great Britain, and Sanyo are engaged in amorphous-silicon research to improve the efficiency of a 1-micron-thick amorphous-silicon cell as a strong absorber of light on a substrate such as glass or plastic. At a much lower conversion efficiency, amorphous silicon cells are more cost-effective.

Solar cells, equipped with low-cost optical mirror *concentrator* systems, are in use. An individual Fresnel-lens/cell is used to intensify the sunlight reaching the solar cells. Sandia Labs in New Mexico is experimenting with solar heliostat thermal energy towers as central 1.5-MW powerhouse systems. The sun's rays (at a concentration of 1100 to 1) are focused against a thick steel plate on a tower by means of an elaborate computer-aided mirror-tracking system. Electric solar-cell-equipped automobile transportation in conjunction with a battery system is another optimistic sign. Presently, active satellites with astronauts and worldwide data communications and television broadcasting are state-of-the-art achievements because of the practicality of extensive panels of solar-cell arrays on satellites in geosynchronous/geostationary orbits. A round-the-clock satellite powerhouse, using *beamed* microwave energy to DC-conversion on the ground is also feasible by enforcing aircraft traffic off-limits.

3
Solid-State LSI Memories

A microcomputer system on one or two chips—that is where the LSI memories are leading the microprocessors to. As indicated in Fig. 1-2, the solid-state LSI memory for the main-memory storage up to 64-K bits, as RAM and PROM, is a common practice. Various types of internal main and external mass-storage memories will eventually replace the present internal CORE main-memory and the external disk and drum electro-mechanical memories, from the viewpoints of cost, size, power, reliability, maintenance, and performance as measured by cycle and access times. These types include:

ROM (read-only memory)
PROM (programmable ROM)
EAROM (electrically alterable ROM)
RAM (bipolar and MOS/CMOS random-access memory, both static and dynamic)
FPLA (field programmable logic array)
CCD memory (charge-coupled device) or fast-access Fairchild LARAM (line-addressable RAM)
EBAM (electron-beam addressable memory) or BEAMOS (beam-addressable MOS memory of General Electric Company)
CAM (content-addressable memory)
Nonvolatile MNOS (metal-nitride-oxide semiconductor memory)
FET memory of IBM, using electron-beam lithographic and ion-implantation techniques
Magnetic-bubble mass-memory

3-1. ROM/PROM/EAROM/EPROM

A ROM LSI is generally an array of semiconductor devices such as diodes or bipolar transistors or MOSFETs, which are connected and/or programmed to perform specific switching functions on command. The ROM memory provides a fixed set of listing of words, either data or instructions, that can be accessed by their corresponding addresses. Data or instructions can be altered using an electrical or mechanical process in the case of EAROM. A ROM is characterized by the number of words ($N = 2^n$) and the number of bits in a word; each word can be accessed by a unique address in a relatively short access time via n address bits applied to an internal decoder having 2^n outputs. The device is ideal for lookup tables in which the address may be an independent variable while the word at that address may contain a function such as x, log x, e^y, etc. For complicated functions, full adders of CCD on an LSI chip may be used to reduce the ROM-bits required by several orders—as in applications like fast fourier transform digital processing. In general, ROMs are used for code conversion (BCD-to-binary, Gray or unit-distance-code to binary, etc.), microprogramming of several instructions (or a subroutine) by using a simple code, character generation, process control, and lookup tables for mathematical functions. (The disk memory too, as a RAM in principle, is too slow for access, and a RAM is considered relatively expensive for the preceding functions in view of the additional logic involved.) In the case of ROMs, a permanent bit pattern of 1s and 0s will be written during the fabrication process; a ROM carrying a fixed set of instructions of program or control in a microprocessor is a common example.

The PROMs, on the other hand, allow users to do their own field-programming of their control memory and a part of the main memory. In one method, a metallic link at one of the electrodes of a specific cell is fused to effect an open circuit by application of a high-current pulse of a fixed duration to form one binary state. Alternatively, "avalanche induced migration" is used to pass a programming current to create one logic-state in a specific cell, by starting with a ROM of all uncommitted cells. In the case of EAROMs, erasure is accomplished nonelectrically by sealing the used ROM with a quartz window, which transmits only ultraviolet light to discharge all the cells to the "0" state. The new programming is done by a large voltage at the selected output terminals, while addressing the requisite word by the use of an x–y coincidence selection scheme. In READ operation, a word is selected using the same address circuit to present the bit-pattern at the output data terminals. Dynamic mode of operation with shorter access time is mandatory in some devices for the decoding circuitry only, and not to the actual memory cells. This procedure may be repeated to arrive at the final debugged program; then, the conventional ROMs may be permanently fabricated with the finalized pattern. PROMs available today in 4-K bit chips are mostly bipolar, NMOS, CMOS, and I^2L.

At this time, 4-K bit NMOS ROMs with an access time of 150 ns, cycle-time of 400 ns, and power dissipation per bit of 100 μW are easily available. As a matter of comparison, 1-K bit bipolar TTL or ECL ROMs have a density-wise, proportionately lower, access and cycle times (ECL is slightly better), but power dissipation is 0.5 mW/bit. And the corresponding 1-K bit CMOS has a power dissipation of only 20 μW/bit at a comparable access time. For a charge coupled device (CCD), the highest so far in density, a 16-K bit chip has an access time from 80 to 250 ns, and its power dissipation is only 10 μW/bit. The 16-K bit NMOS ROMs are commercially available and highly attractive in microcomputer systems. The NMOS PROMs of Westinghouse are more suitable for reprogramming than the MOS EAROMs of National Semiconductors. If NMOS-ROM bit densities continue to climb, simplifying software program development, prices for large MOS-ROM chips will reach 0.1 to 0.5 cents per bit. An entire microcomputer's assembler or compiler for a high-level language like FORTRAN/APL would then be available off a few precoded ROM chips.

The EAROM is field-programmable, in or out of system; its reprogrammable, erase/write-in system is word-alterable, nonvolatile, and available off the shelf (ER2401, 1024 × 4, alterability by block, GI Corporation, Micro Electronics Division. Price: $25).

EPROM (electronically programmed ROM memory) is an ultraviolet erasable PROM. It is field-programmable, reprogrammable, and nonvolatile, but not erase/write-in and word-alterable as EAROM. (A series-90 PROM-programmer is available, for programming MOS or bipolar PROMs, directly from master-PROM, TTY, paper-tape reader, and keyboard from the PRO-LOG Corp.)

3-2. RANDOM-ACCESS MEMORIES (RAMs), STATIC AND DYNAMIC

Random-access memories may be either static or mostly dynamic. A static memory (or gate) is one in which logic levels are maintained indefinitely within each storage cell—when one binary state is inputted, the other binary state is outputted. In the case of the **dynamic memory** (or gate), the memory elements are usually electrode charge-storage capacitances; however, they must be **refreshed periodically** by appropriate clocking or

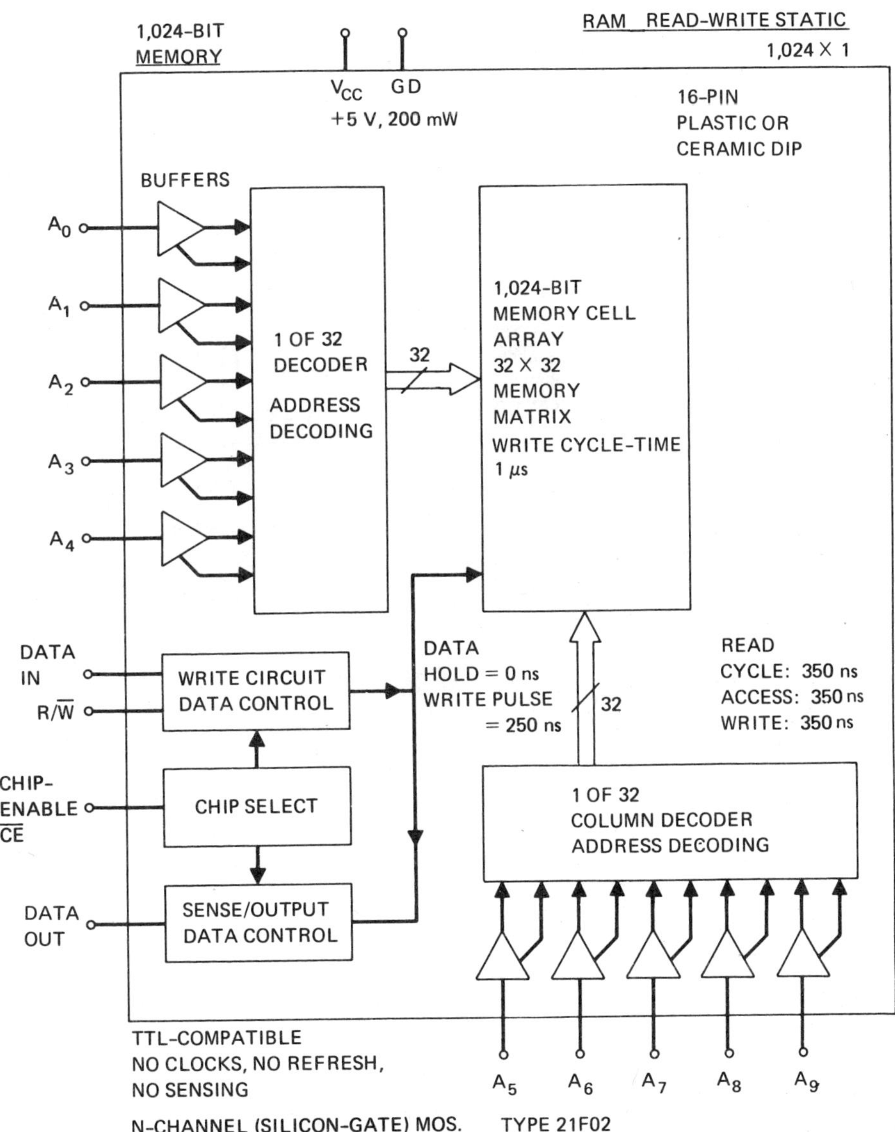

EX. 2: 2112-2: N – CHANNEL, SI-GATE; + 5 V ONLY; RAM (256 X 4) 1,024-BIT STATIC NMOS ROM: I/O TTL-COMPATIBLE READ CYCLE: 650 ns; ACCESS TIME: 650 ns. WRITE CYCLE: 650 ns; WRITE DELAY: 150 ns.

Fig. 3-1a. Static random-access read/write RAM memory. (*Courtesy of Signetics*)

"refresh" circuitry. Single-phase, 2-phase, and 4-phase clock-pulses are generally used for refresh circuitry of dynamic shift-registers; minimum clock-frequency is specified to prevent loss of data due to discharge of capacitances by leakage current. In the case of dynamic MOS-RAMs, since data is "volatile" unless refresh clocks are maintained on a continuous basis with power ON/OFF, nonvolatile memory CORE is the usual alternative. So, in most mini- and micro-computer systems, the use of the less expensive, low-power NMOS-RAMs is mostly a measure of a day-to-day temporary storage function. Some microcomputer systems make additional battery provision for the more expensive static NMOS-RAM memory-chip to allow nonvolatile storage of some residual or halfway data inside the control or main memory of the microprocessor chip or the microcomputer system on a single PC board. A MOS static-memory cell would require address-select

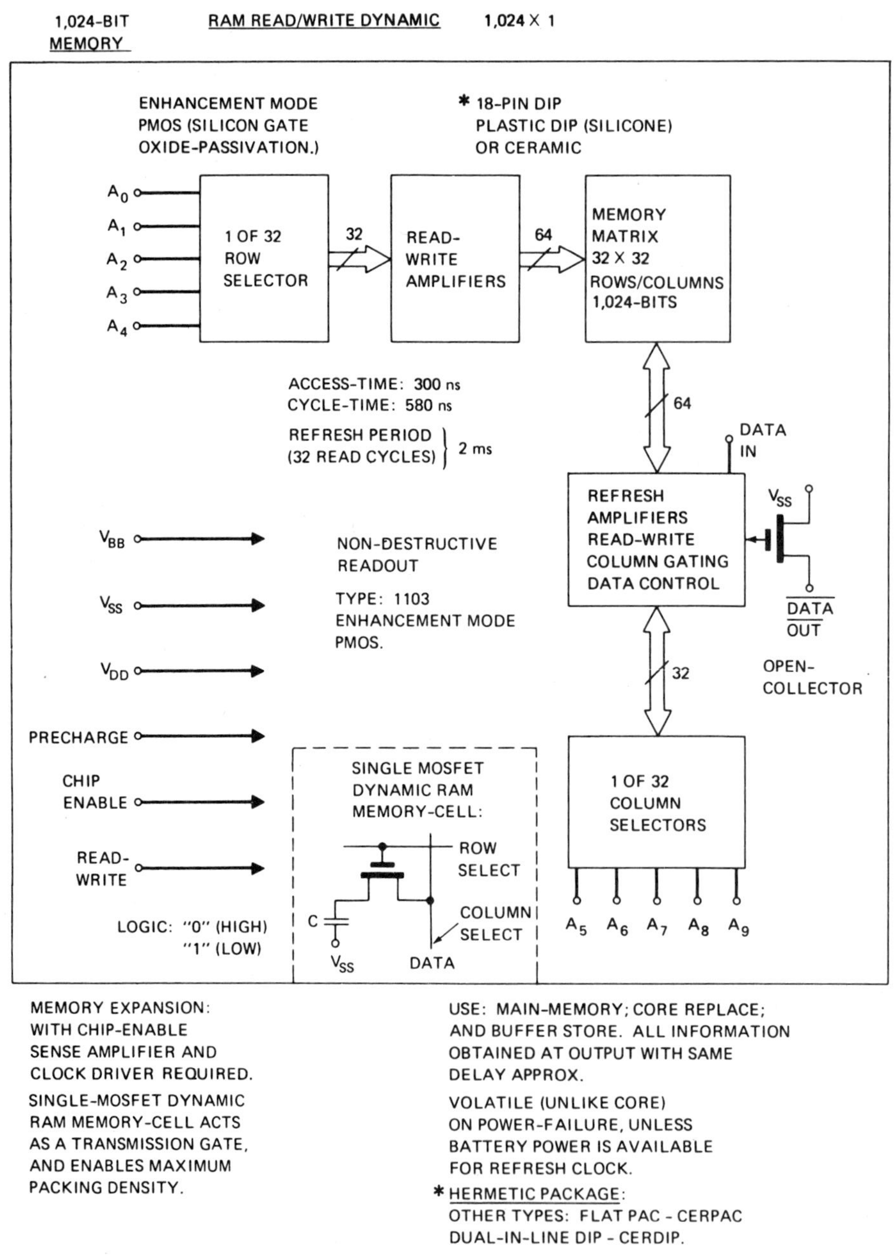

Fig. 3-1b. Dynamic random-access read/write RAM memory. (*Courtesy of Signetics*)

lines and data lines along with special transistor geometrics; for example, eight transistors are required as compared to three to one for a dynamic memory cell. Since the static MOS-RAM and the nonvolatile CORE memory used in most minicomputer systems are expensive and power-consuming, the software used in microcomputer systems may for some time regard the main memory on the card as a temporary storage medium; that is, it cannot be effectively accessed via the direct-memory-access (DMA register) during the

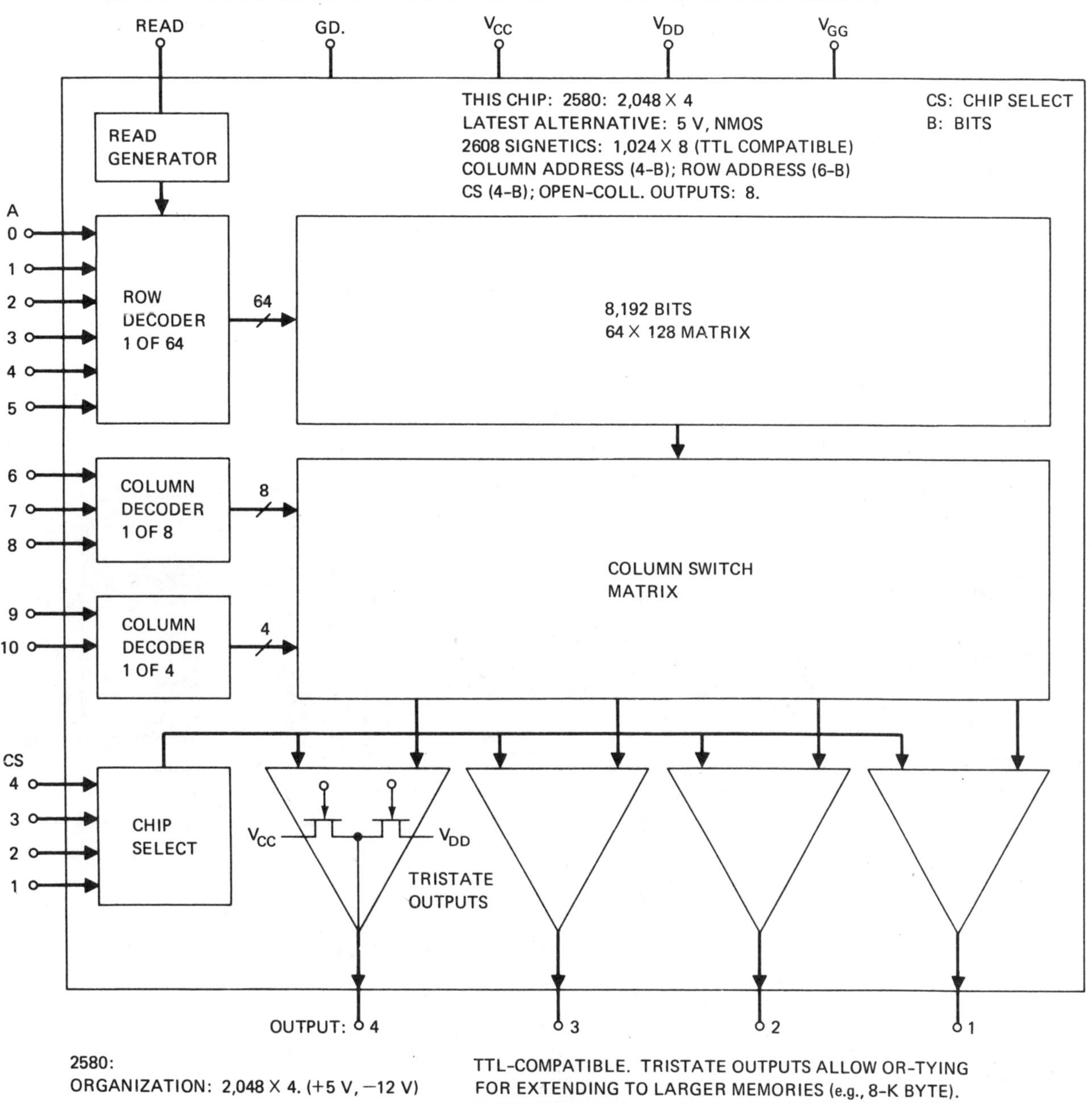

Fig. 3-1c. 8,192-bit static read-only memory (ROM). (*Courtesy of Signetics*)

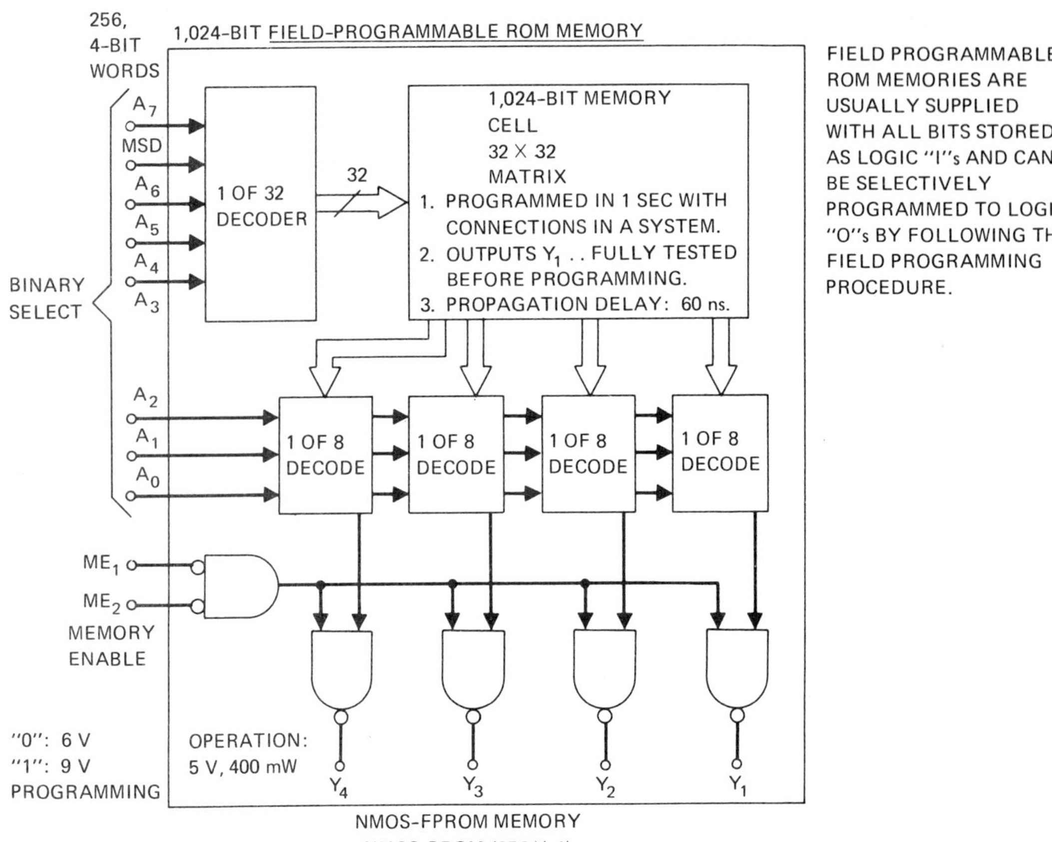

NMOS-FPROM MEMORY
NMOS-PROM (256 X 4)

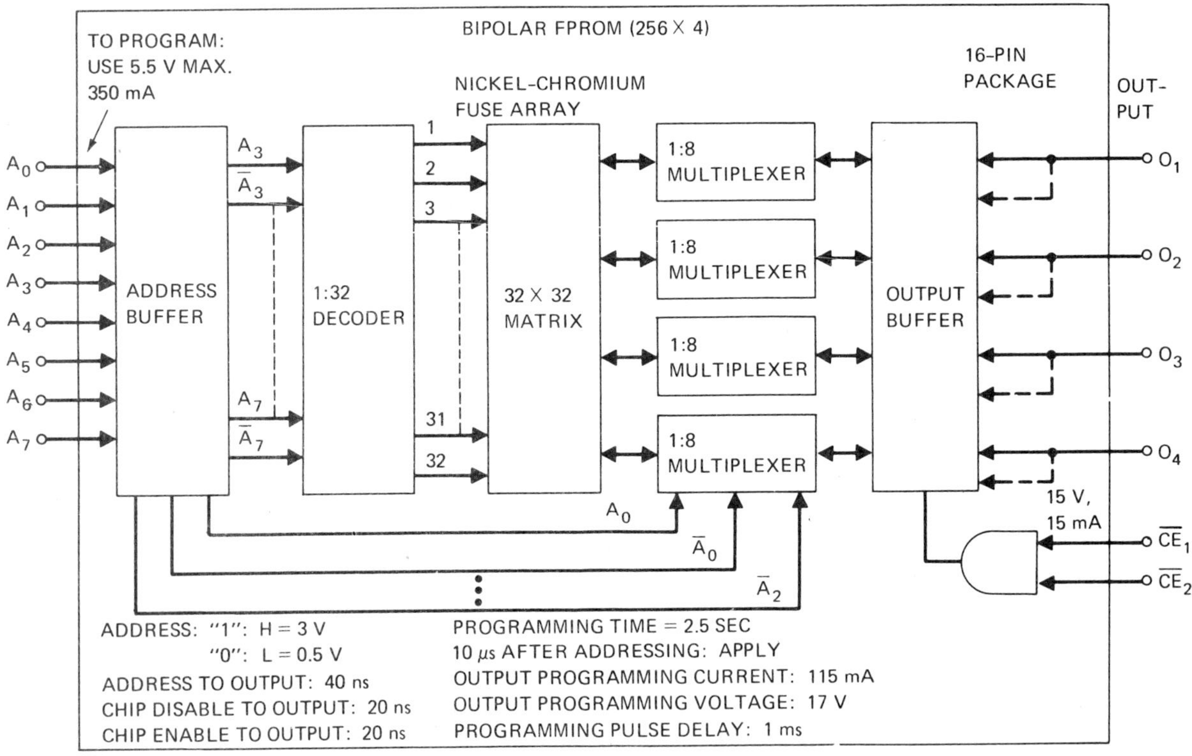

Fig. 3-1d. Bipolar PROM (1,024-bit: 256 X 4). (*Courtesy of Signetics*)

off-time of the system. Meanwhile, by using standby battery cells, low-power 1,024-bit static CMOS-RAM chips are being evaluated and used at this time to replace the power-consuming higher-cost CORE memory. (See Fig. 3-1 for data on RAMs and ROMs.)

MOS-LSI RAMs incorporate the following on-chip circuitry:

1. An address-decoder to select the desired cell(s) within the chip
2. A chip-select CS input signal, which activates the LSIs addressing and/or read/write circuitry
3. A write-amplifier to insert data into the address-selected memory cells
4. Provision to read or sense amplifiers to nondestructively read data out of the selected cells
5. "Open-collector" or "3-state" output buffers. (See Fig. 3-2 and p. 28.)

Static and dynamic RAMs need standby/"refresh" battery power only during computer off-time intervals; precharge signals and logic are also necessary to start operation. This facility will enable nonvolatility like the CORE memory.

Recent efforts in the memory field have accomplished the following tasks:

1. The bit-density of the leading NMOS dynamic RAMs is extended to 16-K bits at the traditional 200-to-300-ns access time
2. New 1,024-bit NMOS RAMs with 50-ns access time are introduced as a substitute to 50-ns high-power ECL RAMs
3. The available low-power CMOS, 4,096-bit static RAMs as a substitute to the previous CORE memory, since they require just a little power from a standby battery.
4. I^2L, low-power high-density RAMs (both static and dynamic) are introduced as an alternative to NMOS, CMOS, and previous bipolar dynamic RAMs.

The 4,096-bit dynamic NMOS RAMs are priced at 0.2 cents/bit, as compared to 0.5 cents/bit of CORE price. The static 1-K bit CMOS RAM is the most attractive memory because it consumes on standby 100 μW against 150 mW for a 1-K bit NMOS static RAM. A 1-K bit CMOS/SOS (silicon-on-sapphire) static RAM, with a 100-ns access-time and just 1 mW of standby power, is available from RCA. Even a dynamic CMOS-RAM regains memory for weeks by activating the "refresh" circuits with a backup of four penlight batteries.

16-K bit RAM for main memory. The low-power, high-density, silicon-gate NMOS technology is developing further to reach the bipolar performance standards. Single and double polysilicon gate, V-notch, double diffusion, and charge coupling are the various techniques. (Polysilicon is the "metal" in the place of Aluminum gate.)

TI's TMS-4070 is the first 0.5 watt, 16,384-bit dynamic RAM that employs the simpler NMOS silicon-gate single-level poly-silicon approach. A 16-pin, single-chip, 16-K bit memory array requiring 1 sq mil/cell is no larger than the previously available 4-K bit RAM. The 16-K bit RAM will become the most favorite memory component in microcomputer systems. The double poly-silicon approach with two separate poly-silicon levels for transistors and capacitances, is the preferred production approach by other manufacturers, since it is a direct extension of the 4-K bit RAM process, and promises still higher memory capacity in a single chip. The high-density, double-poly technique approaches TTL performance in speed at a significant gain of three in power-delay product.

CMOS-on-sapphire, SOS RAM. The presently popular N-MOS RAMs are expected to run against an alternative preference for static CMOS-on-sapphire, where high speed and micropower are the criteria. RCA's NWS-5001 (1-K $\times$ 1 bit) at 150-ns access time at 5 V, and its NWS-5040 (256 $\times$ 4 bit) at 120 ns are two examples for applications in point-of-sales terminals, and automotive and telecommunications applications. A CMOS-on-sapphire, 512 $\times$ 8 bit ROM is also available from RCA for high-density memory applica-

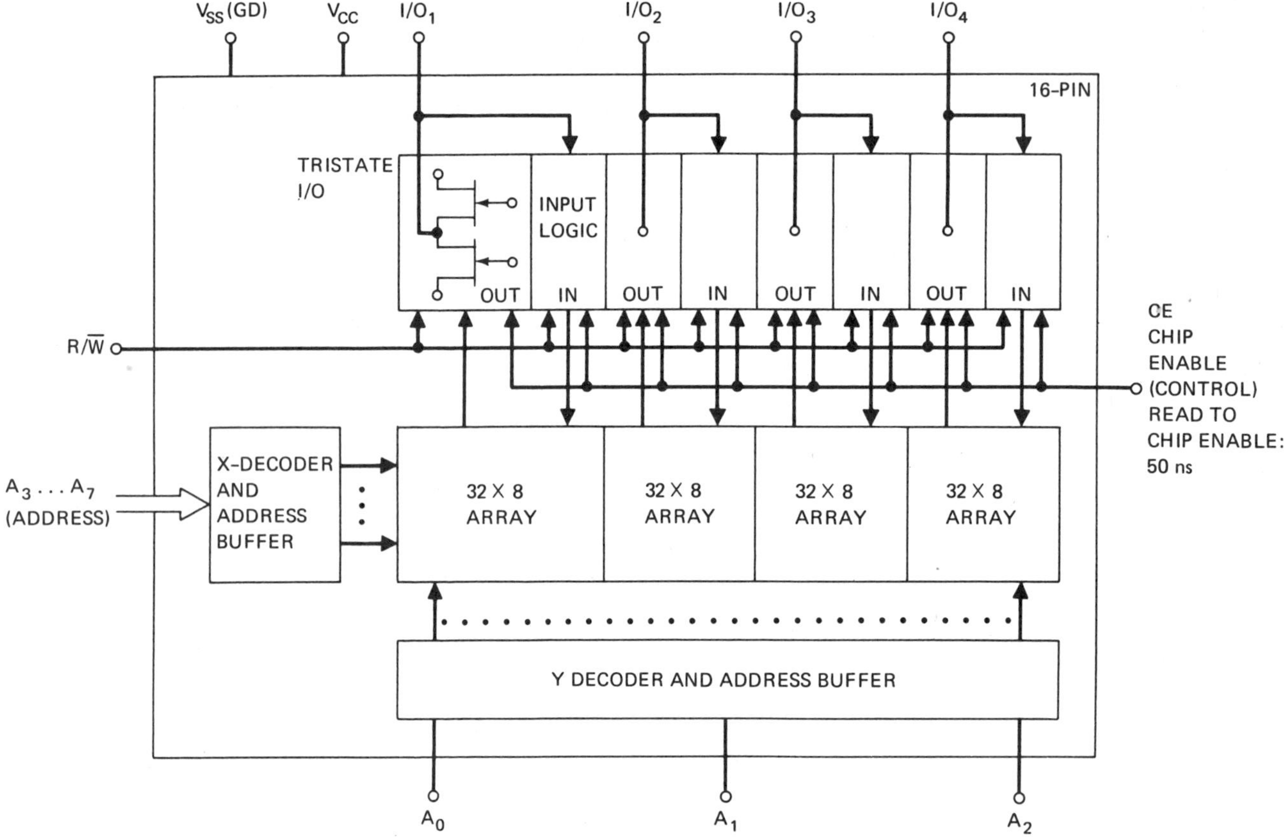

1. TYPE 2606 (SIGNETICS): NMOS, SI-GATE MAIN MEMORY.
2. ACCESS TIME < 750 ns. NO CLOCKS REQUIRED (STATIC): READ-CYCLE TIME: 500 ns.
3. INTERFACE SIGNALS TTL-COMPATIBLE. ADDRESS TO WRITE, TIME: 150 ns; WRITE CYCLE-TIME: 500 μs.
4. TRISTATE OUTPUTS ALLOW EASY EXPANSION OF MEMORY. (OPEN-COLLECTOR TECHNIQUE WITH EXTERNAL PULL-UP RESISTOR OF DIAGRAM 1(2).

Fig. 3-2. Static NMOS RAM, tristate output buffers (256 X 4 bit). (*Courtesy of Signetics*)

tions. Table 3-1 indicates the various types of RAM memory and possible density of each type on a chip, as deduced from the area of a memory cell.

The RAM is both read-and-write. It could be partly low-power static and partly low-power dynamic; however, it is "volatile," unlike the power-consuming nonvolatile core main-memory that presently has an access time varying from 300 ns to 10 μs. Besides the present NMOS/CMOS and bipolar I^2L, high-speed static semiconductor memory using multicell, power-consuming, bipolar TTL and ECL-10K are available; however, they are applicable to large- and medium-scale computers only. The latest ion-implanted bipolar semiconductor memories have access times of about 10 to 100 ns, with gate-switching times of 1 to 2 ns. A memory-instruction cycle-time is usually two to four times the access time. (Gate: logic gate; in the case of MOS, it is the "gate" electrode.)

The access time of the present high-density PMOS/NMOS and CMOS-on-sapphire is comparable to that of the high-speed CORE memory (300 to 1,000 ns), and hence their overwhelming popularity in the place of the CORE in practically all the microcomputer systems. As pointed out earlier, the high-density single-cell NMOS memories (4K, 8K, 16K, 32K) are dynamic and volatile, and their storage function must be constantly replenished during the operation of the microcomputer by single or multiphase clock "refresh" circuitry. The auxiliary bulk or external mass-storage disk, drum, and floppy-disk memories can be also classified under "on-line" random-access memory, but their

TABLE 3-1. Types of RAM memory and possible density on chip.
(Courtesy of McGraw-Hill. From Carr, W. N., and Micze, J. P., 1972, **MOS/LSI Design and Applications.)**

Types of RAM Memory	Single or Multiphase Clocking Pulses	Need for "Refresh"	Area per Cell, mil^2
CMOS (6 transistor)	1	none	9
Static RAM (6 transistor) NMOS	1	none	13
Dynamic RAM (4 transistor) NMOS	2	parallel	11
Dynamic RAM (3 transistor) NMOS	2, 3, 4	serial	9
Dynamic RAM (1 transistor + capacitance) NMOS	2, 3	serial	3.5
CCD (LARAM)	1	none	1
I^2L (bipolar)	1	none	less than 3

access time is very slow indeed, mostly in tens or hundreds of milliseconds. They are best suited to program libraries for software in high-level languages in the case of microcomputer systems. A high-density RAM is illustrated in Fig. 3-3.

16-K Bit EEPROM (1980/81). 16-K bit EPROM (*erasable* programmable read-only-memory), type 2716, is currently one of the most popular solid-state memories in demand for microcomputer systems. It is exposed to ultraviolet light radiation through its *quartz-window* to clear the previous memory contents in a *bulk-erasure* fashion, and reuse the chip afresh for "writing" a new program (or the same program with very minor changes). In the case of the *electrically erasable* programmable ROM (EEPROM) under discussion, *single-byte erasure* is a remarkable advantage in programming or modifying programs on EEPROMs for practically permanent memory—without the need of expensive quartz-window ultraviolet light bulk-erasures for minor changes. Intel has developed a "flotox" process to achieve this result for a 16-K (2-K X 8-bit) EEPROM which functions as a chip-or-byte erasable *nonvolatile* memory. The same power supply that is used for programming enables the erasure of a part of the program *right on the board.* This achievement enables a remote-controlled erasure or modification of an EEPROM program in a microcomputer system (or even a single-chip microcomputer, *if* the ROM portion is originally processed as EEPROM). Automatic program changes can be accomplished as well for reprogramming of future *self-programming* computers.

In 1979, Hitachi Ltd. of Japan achieved this result satisfactorily by using the *MNOS* (*metal-nitride-oxide* semiconductor) storage-element amidst a 6-NMOS-transistor *static* RAM memory-cell to make it practically *nonvolatile. Floating-gate avalanche-injection* used in the *FAMOS* technique in the case of the reliable EPROMs 2716 and 2732 is an alternative successful technique to MNOS processing. A *polysilicon gate* is fully enclosed in a silicon-dioxide film-envelope as the storage-element in the case of the FAMOS nonvolatile memory. But the implementation of the 16-K bit EEPROM with its several advantages is really a fine achievement at the present juncture, because, when these EEPROMs (and possibly 32-K bit and 64-K bit ones in the near future) are available in quantities, one of the greatest needs in the present microcomputer technology will be fulfilled. In this context, the present availability of *static* 64-K bit RAMs from Matsushita Electric Ltd. is another timely achievement, because the necessity of multiphase clocks for the refreshing requirement in the case of the popular 64-K bit *dynamic* RAMs is eliminated; multiphase clock timings sometimes produce *clock-skew* problems unless special precautions are observed in design.

Intel's reliable and consistent processing technique is based on the concept of flotox (*floating-gate-tunnel oxide*), since the electron carriers tunnel to-and-from a special floating-gate of a FET transistor. Intel calls this processing technology by the registered name *HMOS-E* (H for high performance as in HMOS-I etc.). The concept of *bilateral* tunneling goes by the name *Fowler-Nordhelm tunneling* through an insulating oxide of less than 200 Å (angstrom) thickness. Apparently, this concept will therefore consistently work in the case of the *scaled-down* VLSI high-density NMOS techniques that coincidentally require such minimal dimensions. (It is the same remarkable tunnel-diode concept at *superconductivity* temperatures in *liquid-helium* packaging, that makes the Josephson-Junction Interferometer mechanism feasible in the case of the *futuristic subminiature computers* of IBM.)

Both "writing" and "erasing" need a 10-msec program voltage-pulse of 20-volt amplitude (V_{pp}) in EEPROM; but the "read" function at the usual 5-volt supply is identical to that of the type 2716 EPROM. The chip is powered up by $\overline{CE}$ (chip-enable) *low*, and address and data are applied to initiate the "write" with a single 20-volt, 10-msec-wide pulse on V_{pp} pin. Another exclusive pulse $\overline{OE}$ remains *high.* A byte is erased by writing 1's (*high*) for all the 8 bits of the byte; another "write" pulse of 10-msec width will insert the new byte, requiring a total interval of 20 msec for replacing a byte on the EEPROM with a modified byte, as desired. For the chip's total program-erasure operation, the other exclusive pulse $\overline{OE}$ (output enable) is raised to 20-volt level without the involvement of address and data application; that is, 16-K bits are erased with a single 10-msec pulse. The "clear" (erase) and "write" programming is simple enough even for remote control of programs in EEPROMs used in micro- or minicomputer systems.

As a contrast, in the case of other nonvolatile EPROMs such as type 2716, the entire contents of the program are "read" out and loaded into an auxiliary RAM memory, the chip is "erased" with ultraviolet light, and the entire memory is "rewritten" with the altered program in the auxiliary RAM memory or a fresh new program.

In the near future, low-cost mass memory programs for various applications will be readily available off-the-shelf in the silent *all-electronic form* of *plug-in* ROM, EEPROM, and magnetic bubble memories. This is a certainty in the case of most low-cost consumer microcomputer systems to eliminate high-cost time-consuming software programming for private users and small business applications. Under these circumstances, EEPROMs will enable minor programming changes (fine-tuning of programs) as an exceptionally fine attraction. (This is an optimistic forecast of the author.)

64-K Static RAM. During 1980–81, several dynamic 64-K bit dynamic RAMs are available in the market from several manufacturers; but the first static 64-K bit RAM in the market is announced by Matsushita Electric Industrial Company of Japan. Since CMOS memories are rising in popularity due to low power-dissipation, the 64-K static RAM exclusively uses CMOS for the normally power-consuming internal peripheral circuits such as the decoders and selector logic, while the static memory-array employs NMOS on an optimized P-type substrate and a second level of polysilicon for the cell load resistance. The size of the memory-cell in the array is minimized by four NMOS first-layer polysilicon transistors with 2-micron gates and folded resistors over the cell. These double-polysilicon memory-cells are presently used in the static 16-K bit RAMs. The static 64-K bit array structure should provide a model for the future feasible 256-K bit, and 1-M bit static RAMs in potentially the same chip area, when the design rules are scaled down eventually to 1 and 0.5 micron, respectively. So, the future of lower cost microcomputer systems is assured with lower cost main memory on a single microprocessor board (with minicomputer-like computational power).

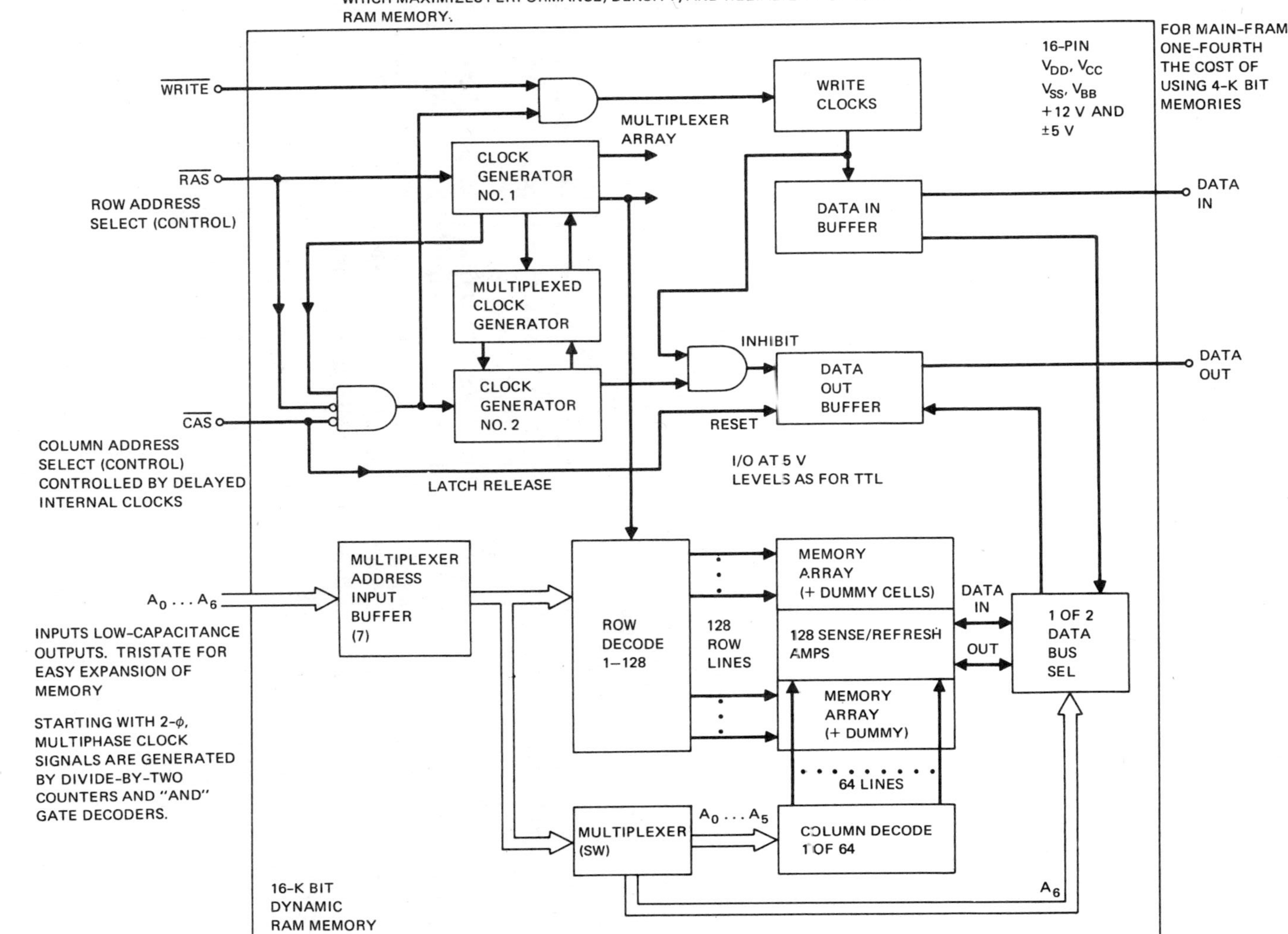

OTHER FEATURES:
1. READ-WHILE-WRITE, (AT SAME MEMORY ADDRESS ALMOST SIMULTANEOUSLY).
2. READ-MODIFY WRITE CYCLE: DATA READ FROM SELECTED CELL, MODIFIED, AND WRITTEN IN MODIFIED FORM IN THE SELECTED LOCATION.
3. PAGE-MODE: PAGE BOUNDARY EXTENDED BEYOND 128-COLUMNS IN A SINGLE RAM.
4. INTERNALLY ORGANIZED AS 2 X 8,192-BIT SUBARRAYS SEPARATED BY 128 SENSE AMPLIFIERS. TO THE USER, IT IS A 128 X 128 MEMORY (SINGLE TRANSISTOR CELL/BIT).
5. INTERNAL CLOCK GENERATORS ARE ACTIVATED BY CAS AND RAS CONTROL SIGNALS. (TESTING THE CHIP IS EASIER.)
6. SENSE AMPLIFIERS DO THE REFRESHING OF THE DYNAMIC MEMORY. (REFRESH EVERY 2 mS.)

Fig. 3-3. Latest high-density RAM main-memory, MOSTEK-MK4116, 16-K bit (volume production). Eight 16-pin chips to provide 16-K byte main-memory. (*Courtesy of Mostek Corporation*)

As far as the processing of the 28-pin static 64-K bit RAM is concerned, it is achieved with the same switching speed as other processes provide, but with fewer total processing steps. Using boron-doped gates, six ion-implants are involved in the process. The chip has an approximate area of 50,000 sq. mil (2.2 times that of static 16-K bit RAM), accommodating 271,400 transistors and 131,000 load resistors. The data are organized as 8 blocks of 8-K bits each for the 256 X 256 row-column cell array. The access-time is a mere 80 nsec at a power dissipation of 300 mW, on a single 5-volt power supply. The standby current intake is 15 mA when the power-down mode is controlled by the chip-enable and chip-select signals.

3-3. REGISTER AND ARITHMETIC LOGIC UNIT (RALU)

To obtain and utilize the high access times, such as 10 to 100 ns in the case of the static semiconductor RAMs, Motorola uses as a building block, a new 4-bit ECL-10K MSI chip or a new I^2L slice. The Motorola system component RALU is illustrated in Fig. 3-4 as a part of a microcontroller.

The microinstruction information is entered simultaneously via two input ports and processed simultaneously by using the twin RAM ports. Complex microinstructions can be executed faster with multiphase clock operation, but this dictates added decoding logic and more control input lines than those required for single-phase clock.

The register and arithmetic logic unit (RALU), consisting of a parallel-loop of RAM and arithmetic logic unit (ALU), is another popular technique at present to replace buffer-registers, counters, and shift-registers used in the hard-wired random-logic designs. The CROM (control ROM memory) of the control section of a microprocessor provides, via the bidirectional-bus, the RALU control function by means of the instructions in the ROM control memory. For example, the software instructions from an external bulk or mass memory can be written in the RAM for this control function. The feedback from the RALU indicates results of a current or previous RALU operation; it is also capable of modifying its sequence of instructions on this basis by "jumps." The control ROM memory thus replaces the gates, flip-flops, decoders, and multiplexers used in hard-wired, random-logic design. The control memory also steers the data into and out of the RALU through the interface logic. Use of the above bidirectional bussing technique thus reduces the number of internal interfacing functions needed.

When a microinstruction is received from the control RAM memory, the RALU operations typically require one or more steps, such as transferring a RAM word to a latch and a shift register and thence to the ALU. The popular dynamic NMOS-RAM cell has a very low steady-state power dissipation (μW's/bit) compared to the conventional static latch (see Table 3-1 for the number of transistors per memory cell.)

3-4. CONTENT-ADDRESSABLE MEMORY (CAM)

Content-addressable memory (CAM) combines the logic at each bit position with a storage facility. It has three modes of operation: Read and Write, such as those of the dynamic RAM, and Match, as a third mode, to compare the data inputs with the selected bits in the memory in several words simultaneously, if so desired. CAM is ideal for (1) search through data files, (2) comparison of numbers, and (3) **associative data processing** that interrelates specific data against sets-of-data in files. As an example, a CAM with a six-word X 12-bit capacity will have an additional complement of two 12-bit registers for "search" and "mask" and two 6-bit "word-select" and "search-result" registers. Through iteration of the simple "match" process, more complex operations, such as

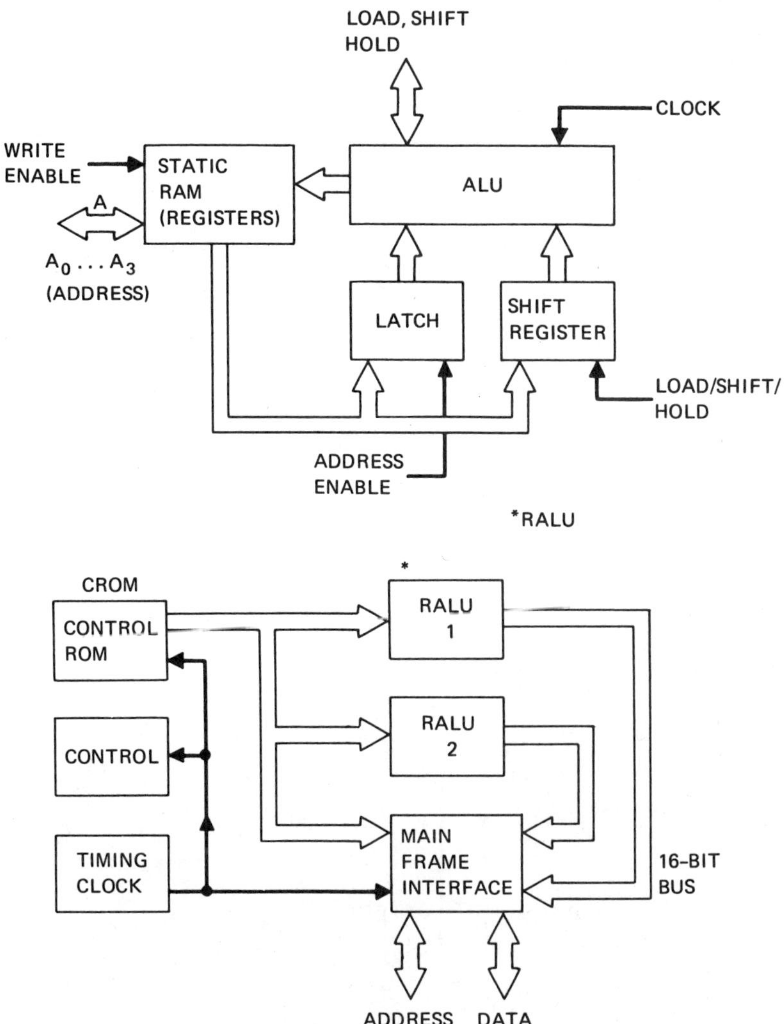

Fig. 3-4. RALU (register arithmetic logic unit). (*Courtesy of Motorola*)

"greater," "less than," "next greater," can be accomplished. The system organization of a content-addressable memory and a 4-word by 4-bit CAM memory are illustrated with notes in Fig. 3-5.

3-5. LSI CCD MEMORIES

Cost-effective 16-K bit, LSI-CCD chips, considered as high-density low-cost mass-storage memory, fill the gap between high-performance, higher-cost NMOS and bipolar memories and lower-performance lower-cost disk and drum memories (0.1 cents/bit). In block-oriented memory applications, CCDs have a cost advantage over RAMs. However, CCDs are neither really "random-access" nor "read only" in operation, since this memory is presently accessible serially by either line or block. Blocks of 4-K bit each, for a total of 16-K bits, will make Fairchild type-460 a line-addressable RAM as a fast-access LARAM (25 μs). In addition, they require, as memory, more interface circuitry than RAMs. The details of the LARAM, consuming medium power, are shown in Fig. 3-6.

Arrays of CCDs consist of an N-silicon substrate covered by a layer of silicon dioxide insulator, which in turn is capped with a row of aluminum-metal "field" plates spaced less than 0.1 mil apart. If all plates are held at a small negative potential, "holes" can be

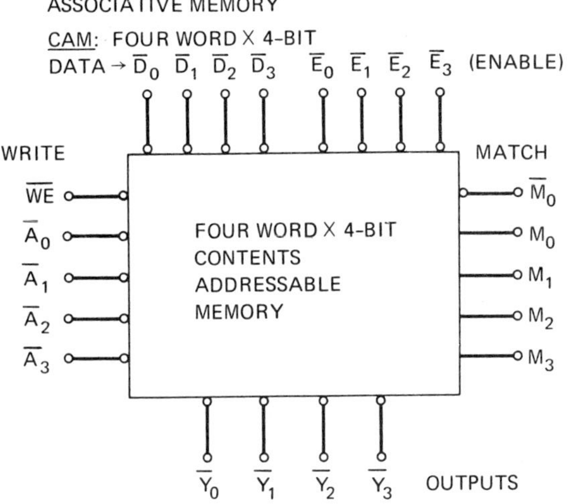

REGISTERS: 1. SEARCH 2. MASK
3. WORD SELECT 4. SEARCH RESULT
WRITE: "O": $\overline{WE}$, $\overline{A}$, $\overline{E}$ (BIT ENABLE) DATA WORD APPLIED AT $\overline{D}$.
MATCH: DATA AT INPUTS COMPARED TO DATA STORED IN MEMORY.
READ MATCH: EACH INPUT BIT D_i ENABLED BY $\overline{E}_i$. COMPARED WITH BIT i OF FOUR STORED WORDS. ANY STORED WORD MATCHING DATA INDICATED BY "I" AT M_i TERMINAL

- UNLIKE COORDINATE-SPECIFIED ROM AND RAM, CAM IS AN ASSOCIATIVE MEMORY FOR MATCHING TO A CONTENT-SPECIFICATION INSTEAD OF AN ADDRESS. ASSOCIATES "KEYS" WITH STORED DATA: IT HAS ABILITY TO MASK DATA COLUMNS.
- INFORMATION RETRIEVAL REQUIRES A MINIMUM OF TWO 8220 CHIPS.
- SIGNETICS 8220 MSI CHIP: ARRAY OF EIGHT MEMORY CELLS, AND LOGIC FOR DATA ASSOCIATION. R/W FUNCTIONS ALSO PERFORMED. CAM IS ORGANIZED FOR PARALLEL SEARCHES ON ENTIRE DATA WORD OR ON SPECIFIC FIELDS, USING MASKING ABILITY. 64-BIT CAM ARRAY: 8 X 8220.

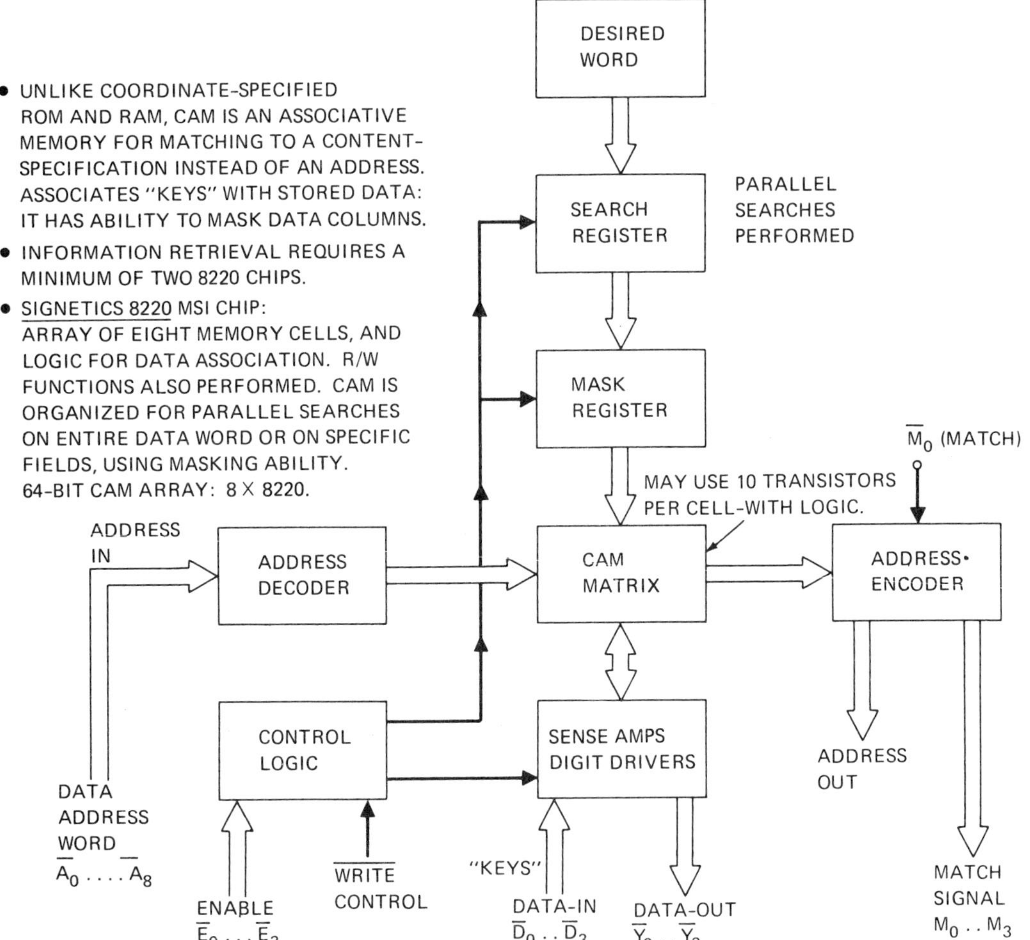

Fig. 3-5. Content-addressable memory (CAM) system organization. (*Courtesy of Signetics*)

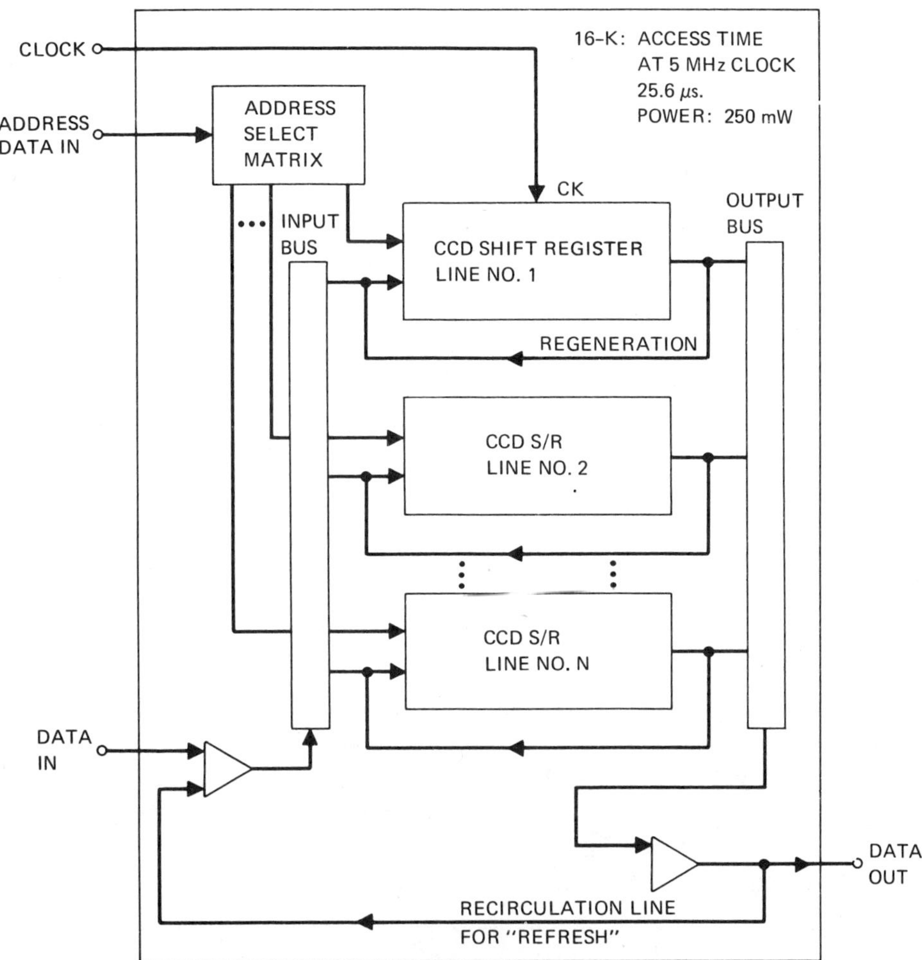

- ORGANIZATION OF THE FASTEST LINE-ADDRESSABLE 16-K BIT RAM (MEDIUM POWER). EACH LINE IS ACCESSED AT RANDOM.
- INTERNAL PARALLEL REGISTERS ARE CLOCKED AT LOW FREQUENCY. CCD MEMORY YIELD IS GREATER THAN MOS-RAM.

Fig. 3-6. CCD line-addressable RAM (LARAM: Fairchild).

stored in the resulting surface-depletion regions or in potential wells below the metal caps. If a more negative pulse is applied to a field-plate adjacent to the one under which the charge is stored, the charge will spill over into the deeper potential well due to higher negative potential, thereby shifting the charge along the MOS-chain; the charge is eventually read out as detection of capacitance-change in the terminal element.

CCDs are presently used to provide memory, shift-register, delay time, and solid-state black-and-white and color television-camera imaging functions at low cost, since the fabrication is much simpler than PMOS or NMOS. (In the case of imaging function, charge or absence of charge are introduced selectively as 1s and 0s, respectively, at the surface of the metal-oxide semiconductor chain of CCDs by, for example, radiation-generated electron-hole pairs.)

The alternative, the previous **bucket-brigade devices (BBD)**, which work on a charge-deficit transfer principle, can be either bipolar junction or unipolar MOS transistors, using regular storage capacitances instead of the "geometrically defined, potential well" of the CCD. And, BBDs do not have the high-density or high-resolution capability of the CCDs.

The charge-coupling technique, as explained earlier, combines storage and transfer mechanics into a single gate region, an N-channel area as minute as that of V-MOS, and four times smaller than that of double-poly silicon-gate used in the 16-K bit NMOS-RAMs. Presently, a 64-K bit RAM is an accomplished feat from several manufacturers as a low-power alternative special memory to the conventional N-channel silicon-gate fabrication.

64-K Bit CCD RAM-Memory: Fairchild's memory component CCD Type-465 has a serial-parallel-serial (SPS) format operation, unlike the line-addressable format of its Laram, which was referred to earlier. With this new SPS technique, it is designed to replace some mass-storage drum and disk memory systems at comparatively less access-time/bit, under 1 msec (at a clock-rate of 4 MHz). The memory is of course volatile; it is inherently dynamic, since it stores data or instruction words as charge. That is, the software from the tape cartridge or floppy-disk will be first loaded into the 64-K bit CCD memory at start. In the said SPS format, data fill a horizontal X-register and then shift in parallel through vertical Y-registers at a slower rate. The CCDs in this technique are used not only as shift-register serial read-out memories, but also as monolithic, read/write, high-speed two-electrode cells with X/Y select-busses and buried-write P-channels. A 64-K chip has an area of 120 X 120 mil^2. In the read/write or read/modify-write modes, it consumes 400 mW at 4 MHz and 300 mW in search mode. The 64-K bit SPS-CCD chip's organization is detailed in Fig. 3-7.

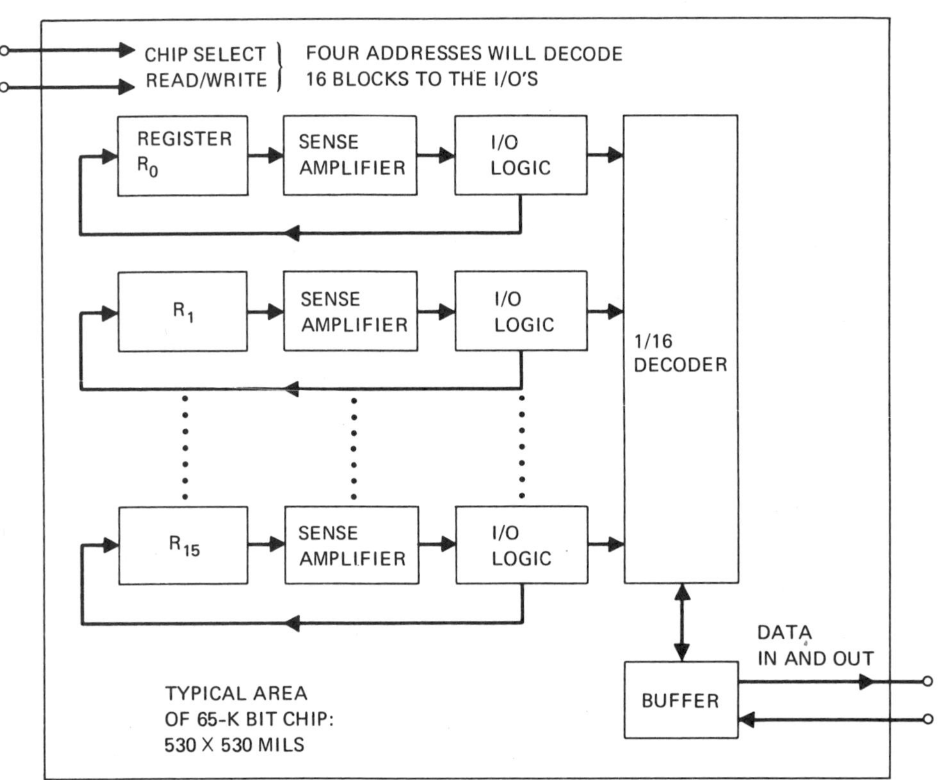

- ORGANIZED AS 16 REGISTERS OF 4,096 BITS EACH.
- COST EFFECTIVE 20-M BIT; TO REPLACE TAPE AND DRUM WHEN THE REQUIREMENT OF MEMORY IS LIMITED.
- WHEN ONE BLOCK IS ACCESSED, THE REMAINING 15 WILL RECIRCUTATE AND SYNCHRONOUSLY REFRESH THEMSELVES WITH THE ACCESSED REGISTER.
- CCD CELL REQUIRES 0.16 MIL^2 COMPARED TO 1 MIL^2 OF MOS CELL.

Fig. 3-7. Organization of 65,384-bit CCD RAM (Fairchild, Texas Instruments, Intel, IBM).

3-6. MAGNETIC BUBBLE-MEMORY AS A MASS-STORAGE OF THE NEAR FUTURE

Magnetic-domain-bubbles (IBM, Rockwell, TI, Nippon, Bell) make a potential low-cost, high-density memory, possibly competitive with magnetic disks. 64-K bit chips with 4-μ bubble-diameter are at the development stage; and, IBM apparently has a new higher-capacity bubble-lattice storage technique, which uses the direction of magnetization on the boundary region of the cylindrical bubble-domain to represent 1s and 0s. Possible density is estimated at 10^9 bits/sq inch. In some bubble-lattices, the direction around the circumference could be reversed to produce two types. Memory is nonvolatile, with speed halfway between semiconductor and disk. A TI chip holds 100-K bits; mass-memory capability can reach up to 300 megabits. Hitachi has a 2-megabit bubble-memory available for prototype mass memory. Bubble-memory has approximately the same access-time as the electromechanical disk, approximately 10 ms. Mass-memory disk-storage access-times may extend up to 100 ms in *on-line* computer Operating Systems. (See Section 4-6 for information on a magnetic bubble mass-memory system.)

3-7. ELECTRON-BEAM-ADDRESSABLE MOS MEMORY (EBAM) OR BEAM-ADDRESSABLE MOS MEMORY (BEAMOS)

EBAM and BEAMOS employ electron beams for accessing memory by scanning targets of silicon in small CRTs. The technique cuts the time of milliseconds access-time of such rotating mass memories as disks and drums to microseconds, while presenting the potential for storing millions of bits of mass memory on silicon targets of about 1 cm^2. The cost/bit is projected at 0.02 cents, and a module that is 12″ X 4″ in diameter provides 32-M bit BEAMOS memory system with a 30-μs access-time and a 10-M bit transfer rate (General Electric Company). IBM also has an electron-beam lithographic technique with ion-implantation for a 8-K bit FET-memory LSI chip (5-M bit/cm^2 makes it a bulk-storage device with a comparable access-time).

3-8. V-MOS

The vertical configuration of the transistor elements on the substrate allows very compact logic and memory. A V-notch allows access to a substrate-level MOS source-cell, while the drain and gate structures are formed on the bias of the notch. The gate area is 100 μ^2. American Microsystems has applied this process to produce a 16-K bit ROM with 200-ns access-time. 16-K bit and 32-K bit ROMs, 8- and 16-bit enhanced microprocessors, and 4-K bit static RAMs, following this technique, are under way from other manufacturers.

3-9. D-MOS

The depletion-mode D-MOS technology employs double-diffused doping profile in the gate region to reduce the effective channel region to 1 μ (micron), and enables LSI-gates to operate at 1 to 5 ns and D-MOS discrete transistors to operate at 1 GHz. Signetics (of Philips) and Nippon Electric have adopted this technique to produce an 8 X 8 cross-point switch at 100-dB isolation (for telecommunications) and a 4-bit ALU at 3-ns/gate propagation-delay (of ECL), respectively.

The V-MOS and D-MOS techniques are also applied by Siliconex to manufacture power FETs (operating at 2 amps and above, and at near-zero input-current without preamps) to compete with present current-controlled, minority-carrier, bipolar Darlington power transistor pairs. V-MOS power FETs are voltage-controlled majority-carrier devices.

3-10. NONVOLATILE MNOS AND FLOATING-GATE MEMORIES

In the field of scientific and programmable calculators, there is an immediate need for low-power nonvolatile semiconductor memory. Clocked static CMOS-RAMs (RCA-1M7507, 4-K bit RAM, Intersil 1M6508/18 series 1-K bit RAMs), drawing a few microamps of trickle-current at 2%/week discharge-rate from an internal backup Ni-Cd (nickel-cadmium) battery-cell is one solution. But Bell Laboratories P-channel, slow-access, metal-nitride-oxide semiconductor "nitride memory" (MNOS), as a charge-trapping device, makes an inherently nonvolatile RAM main-memory that retains information for years at a slightly higher cost. In the case of a ROM, it is electrically alterable. So, in the area of microcomputer systems, the MNOS memory may eventually replace the nonvolatile, power-consuming CORE memory. Plug-in MNOS file cartridges, which are user-alterable and nonvolatile for all practical purposes, are presently available to store up to 240 steps of a program subroutine (as used in National Semiconductors NS-7100 calcula-

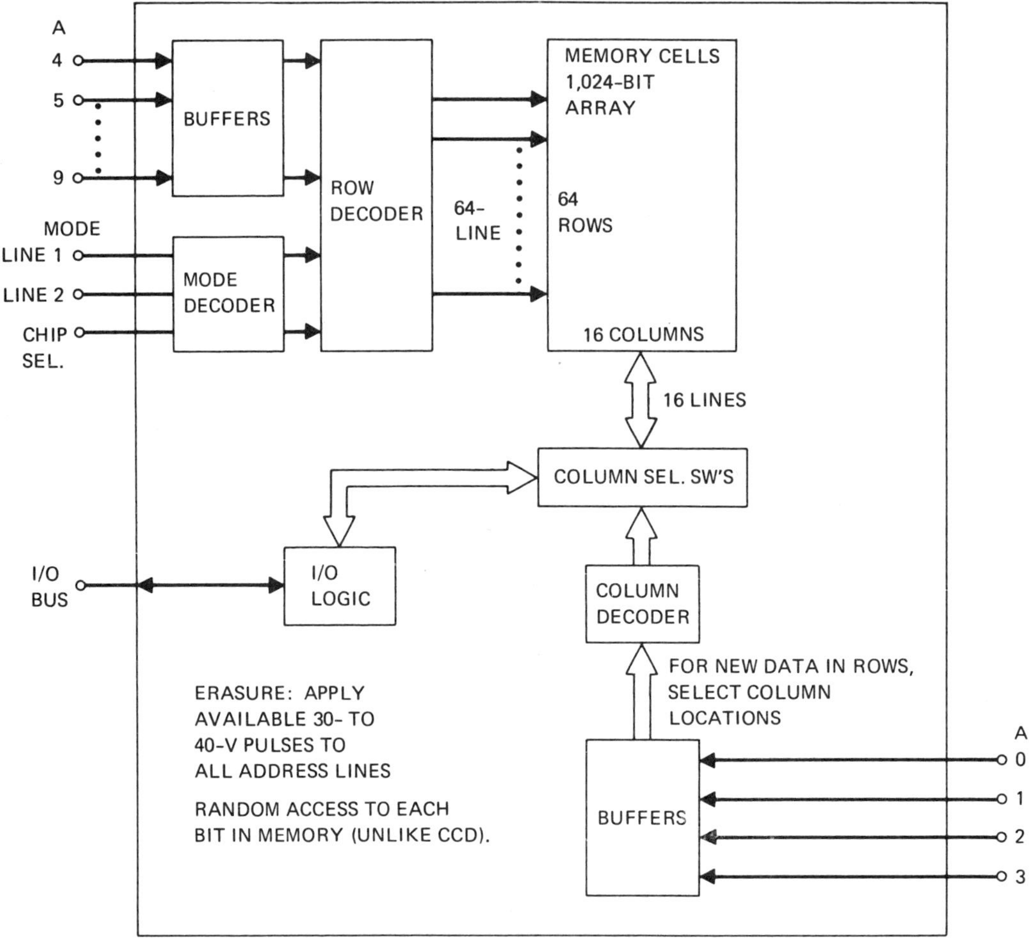

- "NITRIDE" MEMORY, NITRON-7051 (McDONNEL DOUGLAS).
- ELECTRICALLY REPROGRAMMABLE NONVOLATILE MEMORY; ENTIRE OR SELECTIVE.
- READ-TIME 2 TO 5 μs (TOO SLOW FOR REAL-TIME APPLICATIONS; APPLICABLE TO DIGITAL ODOMETERS IN VEHICLES, PROGRAMMABLE CALCULATORS, DIGITAL TELEVISION, FM RADIO TUNERS, CB RADIO TUNING, POINT OF SALE FOR PERIODIC INVENTORY UPDATE, MACHINE-TOOL CONTROLS TO REPLACE PAPER-TAPE PROGRAMMING.

Fig. 3-8. Organization of MNOS nonvolatile memory.

tor). Example: 1,024-bit NCM-7051 MNOS, with internal decoder (Nitron of Cupertino, Calif.) is nonvolatile; 600 mW, 500 ns access, read cycle-time 4 μs, write 2 ms, 64 × 16; $20. The memory organization is shown in Fig. 3-8.

Toshiba's nonvolatile 1,024-bit static RAM, which is usable as an EARAM, can replace CORE memory on a comparable price/bit basis, consuming 500 mW only. Read-access and write cycle-times are approximately 1 μs. For each bit, it employs a P-channel Si-gate MOS cell and an MNOS transistor for storage (256 × 4-bit: $13, with a storage life of over one year).

The N-channel double-gate Nippon Electric nonvolatile μPD-458, 8-K bit EPROM can be electrically erased in 1 minute, and programmed in 80 seconds, by using read and programming voltages. Access time is 500 ns. Each cell employs two N-channel MOS transistors; one responds to external addressing, and the other does the actual memory storage. The internal organization of the memory and the basic memory cell are shown in Fig. 3-9 (see p. 54). The second transistor is said to contain an extra "floating-gate of polysilicon," and the more specialized nitride processing is avoided for nonvolatility of a more permanent nature. The ulrtraviolet erasable EPROM is available in 16-K bit chip capacity. These EPROMs are called **Famos memories.** The **floating-gate injection MOS transistor** is a Si-gate MOSFET in which no connection is made to the floating silicon-gate. Charge is injected by avalanche of high-energy electrons from the source or drain; -28 V applied to the PN junction releases electrons. (In the case of MNOS, carriers tunnel through the thin nonconducting oxide layer into traps at the oxide-nitride interface.)

3-11. I^2L MEMORY AND MICROPROCESSORS

The 5-V, 18-pin, high-density, 4-K bit bipolar I^2L static RAM, S-400 is available from TI with a power dissipation of 0.5 W and a maximum access time of 75 ns—more than twice as fast as the Si-gate NMOS 4-K bit RAMs. IBM, Fairchild, Signetics, and possibly RCA are the other contenders at present. In view of their low power-dissipation, these memories will slowly replace the former bipolar semiconductor main-memories in large- and medium-scale computers. In defense applications, the I^2L appears to be an ideal technique, consuming little power, and operating over the entire temperature range of -55° to 125°C. Other applications at this moment include microprocessors, programmable watch chips, countdown and deflection circuits, frequency synthesizers, organ tone-generators, CB radios, PLL and tone-encoder circuits in telecommunications, and television circuits, all requiring both digital and linear signal processing functions.

In the case of the 16-bit microprocessors, the integrated-injection-logic I^2L, built with isoplanor circuit technology, is considered competitive with popular MOS processors, at 5- to 10-ns/gate price-performance level. And, in the case of television receivers, remote control, digital tuner kits, op-amps, sample-and-hold circuits, and horizontal- and vertical-line processing are some of the tasks that single-chip I^2L processors will eventually take over. In the field of data communications, Philips has developed a digital data transmitter that implements a filter and a vestigial sideband transmitter for 2,400 and 4,500 bauds/sec, respectively, on a single I^2L chip.

The 4-K bit I^2L bipolar main-memory chip (both static and dynamic) is presently available with an access time under 100 ns. In the dynamic version, a single transistor pair, NPN and PNP are merged on the Si-substrate without a capacitor (unlike NMOS). The 1s and 0s are stored in the easily accessible junction-capacitance in the shared collector-base of the merged transistor pair. The efficiency of the charge-storage mechanism in I^2L is high; the junction-capacitance is charged for "0" and discharged for "1."

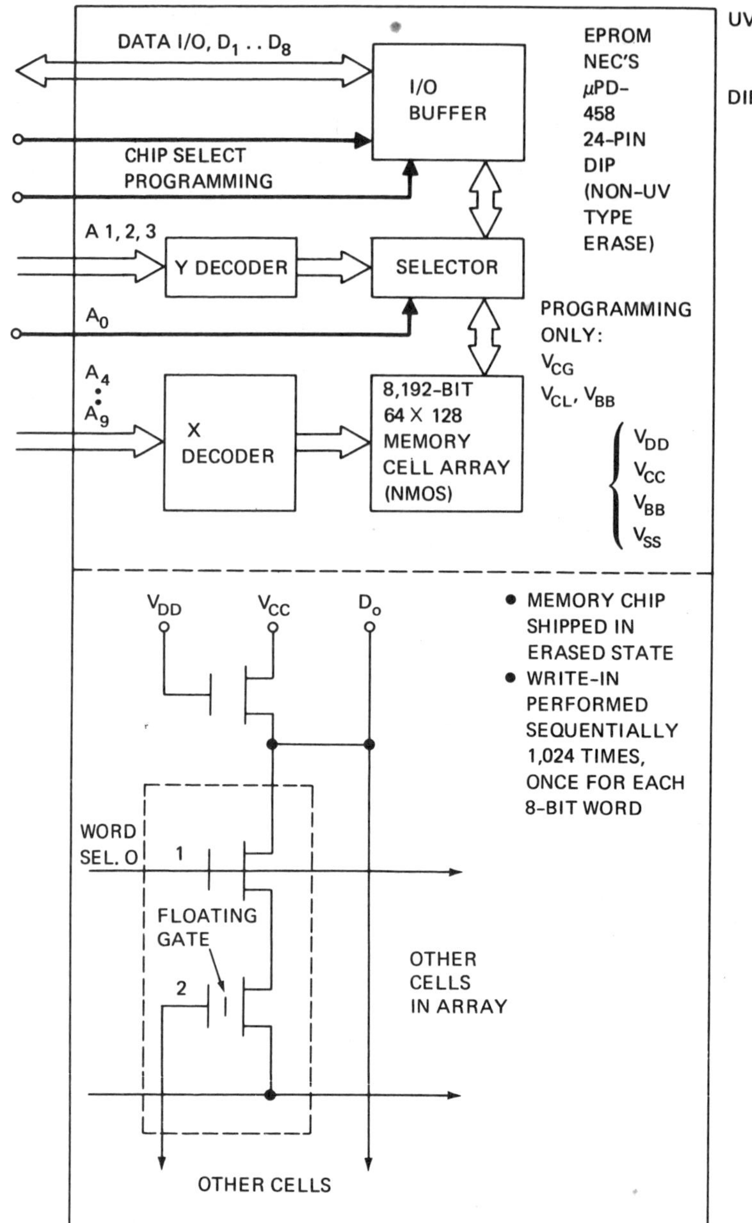

- FAMOS: "FLOATING-GATE AVALANCHE-MOS."
- TECHNIQUE: "FLOATING GATE," USING TWO NMOS TRANSISTORS, ONE ENHANCEMENT MODE, RESPONDING TO ADDRESSING, AND THE OTHER "FLOATING GATE" FOR STORAGE FUNCTION IN MODE 2.

Fig. 3-9. Nippon nonvolatile 8-K bit electrically erased EPROM. ("FAMOS" memory).

3-12. AMORPHOUS SEMICONDUCTOR MEMORY

The amorphous semiconductor memory is another prospective candidate for the choice of the nonvolatile main memory. The technology is called *Ovanics*, as coined by its originator Ovshinsky of Energy Conversion Devices. Burroughs is presently developing a 1,024-bit amorphous semiconductor EAROM for use in main-frame CPUs. An operating speed of 15 ns is feasible; this speed is compatible with that of the high-speed bipolar current-mode logic (CML) used in Burroughs computers. As a nonvolatile alternative to CORE and MNOS memories, it is attractive.

The noncrystalline amorphous semiconductor consists of chalcogenide glasses; it changes in phase- and voltage-current characteristics when energy is applied (Figure 3-10). The method of testing this device is now understood, and it may take its place as one of the new semiconductor memories. The material is generally a conglomerate of the semiconductor elements: silicon, germanium, arsenic, sulfur, selenium, and predominantly tellurium ($_{52}Te^{130}$). The latter occurs as an amorphous compound of the other semiconductors.

The operation of the device depends on the composition of the amorphous material; transfer of a disorderly amorphous state to an orderly crystalline state and vice versa take place when energy (in the form of voltage, light, and heat) is applied and removed to produce a *memory switch*. However, if on applying the energy, the amorphous material still retains its amorphous state at a different level, it produces the effect of a *threshold switch*.

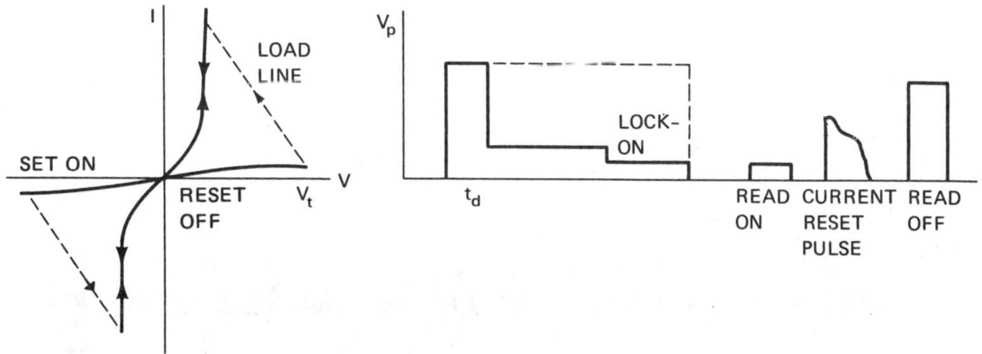

Fig. 3-10. The amorphous semiconductor memory. (*Courtesy of IEEE Spectrum*)

3-13. STATUS OF SOLID-STATE MEMORY CHIPS IN 1981: EXAMPLES

VLSI INMOS IMS1400 16-K static RAM (16-K × 1), using a 5-V supply, sets a new standard with address access and cycle times of 45 nsec at 660 mW of active power and 120 mW of standby. It is TTL-compatible and packaged in a 20-pin 300-mil ceramic DIP with industry standard pinout.

VLSI Motorola MCM6665 64-K bit dynamic RAMs, with a maximum active dissipation of 275 mW at 5 V (30 mW standby) and an access time of 200 nsec, are priced at $150 for 10 chips to provide 64-K bytes of main memory in a microcomputer application. Inputs/outputs are TTL-compatible and upward 16-pin compatible with industry standard 16-K bit RAM memory chips.

Sharp Corp. of Japan has developed a low-power 44-pin flat-package 256-K bit (n-well) CMOS ROM, LH53256 with a typical access time of 500 nsec and chip dimensions of 6 × 5.98 mm. Toshiba Corp. of Japan, using an NMOS 2-micron design-rule, is successfully developing a 256-K bit ROM with a maximum access time of 150 nsec for applications such as compilers and CRT-display of *kanji* (Chinese) characters.

4
Mass-Memory Libraries for Microcomputer Systems

4-1 THE PRESENT HIGH-SPEED AUXILIARY ON-LINE MEMORY CORE

Successful ferrite nonvolatile CORE memory systems are available, which have diameters as small as can be handled, tested, and wired into arrays readily (0.08″ OD, 0.05″ ID, 0.025″ thick). Cores with higher coercive force have shorter switching time (1 to 5 μs) in coincident-current storage units with an optimum current of 0.8 to 0.3A. Random-access-time at a particular address is 1 to 5 μs, depending on serial or parallel access. (Present access-times of semiconductor memories range from 20 to 500 ns.) Cost/bit of core is about 2 cents/bit in 1-K banks. A main-memory capacity of 0.25- to 8-M bytes of 8-bit words, with a memory cycle-time of 2 μs, is available for large-scale computers such as the IBM-375/155. Most minicomputers generally employ quad-size (8.5″ X 10″) core-memory with a capacity of 4,096 words in the usual 16-bit configuration. As a typical example, an 8,192-word core-memory module is logically divided into eight "pages" of 1,024 words each (a page is the largest block of memory that can be addressed by a memory reference instruction). The latest cores (0.03″ OD) have a configuration of 3-D (three-dimensional) and 3-wire; they have a routine capacity of 4-K bytes and an access-time of 600 ns.

The individual bits are stored by magnetizing toroidal ferrite cores in the "1" or "0" direction by applying a "Write" current pulse. "Reading" is done by pulsing the core in the "0" direction; "1" produces a current pulse in a "sense" wire. Coincident-current selection is used to select a particular word. Figure 4-1 illustrates the bit-plane of a 3-D, 3-wire-type core memory. By using additional switching logic, three wires allow both "inhibiting" and "sensing" functions. Since core memory is nonvolatile under power-off conditions, and since reading "destructs" or clears the addressed memory location, the word "Read" into a register enables the rewriting of the word into the core at a new address during the second half of the "Read Memory Cycle" to make it "nondestructive."

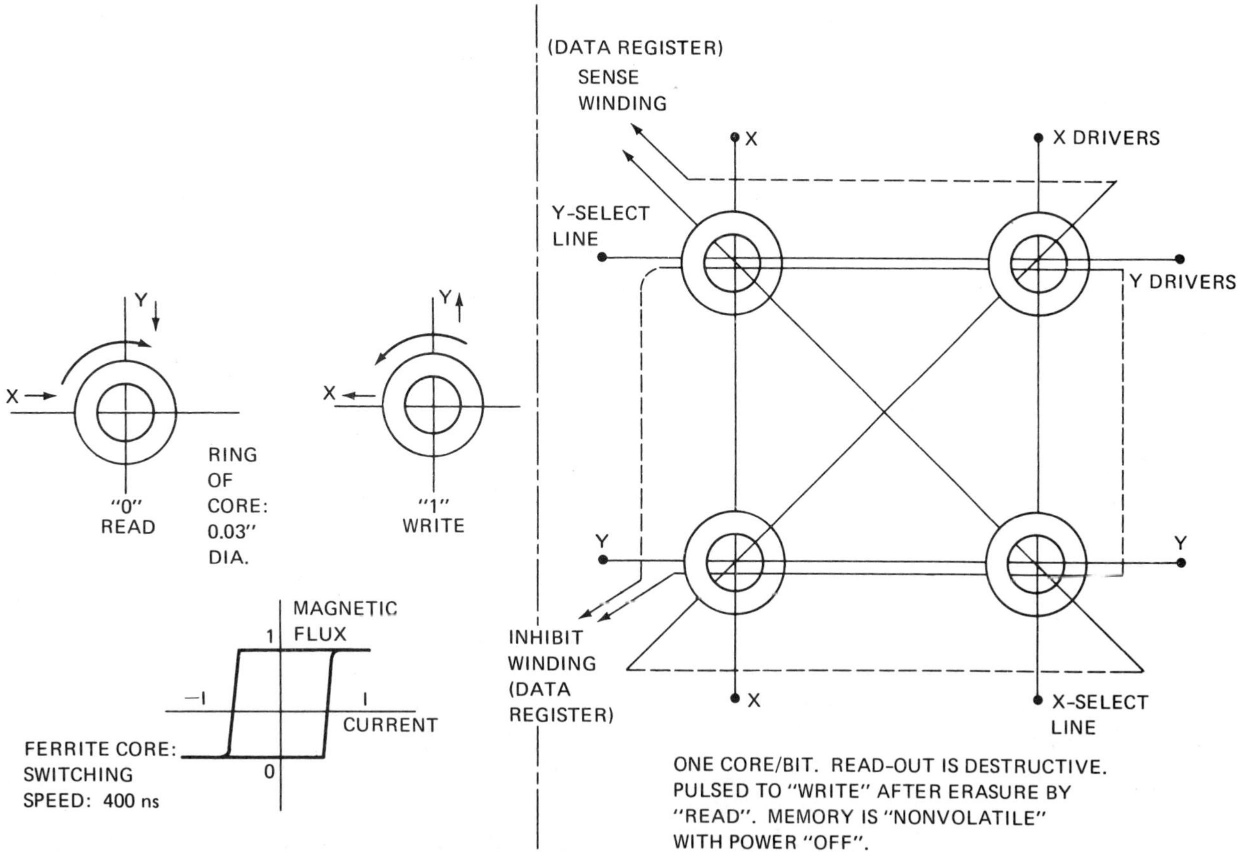

Fig. 4-1. Magnetic CORE: Four cells in the bit-plane of a 3-D, three-wire type, CORE memory.

4-2. MAGNETIC DISK AND FLEXIBLE FLOPPY-DISK

Magnetic disk is the most common on-line bulk-storage medium, in contrast to the off-line slow-access magnetic tape in cassette or cartridge form. The disk operating system (DOS) makes a random-access memory, and it is presently capable of storing 6.4 billion bits in a system consisting of up to eight spindles; each spindle contains 20 recording surfaces (or 10 disks). The typical speed of rotation of a disk is about 1,000 rpm; the disk, in general, is detachable and replaceable in a minute, since the data in one of the files of a disk-pack can be moved to another computer location for data-processing purposes. Each face is divided into a number of concentric tracks or channels, and each track is capable of storing strings of characters serially or in parallel (like the comparatively faster-access magnetic drum). Each track is divided into records separated by interrecord gaps (IRGs). One magnetic head serves to "read" and "write" data or program on the top surface of the disk; another magnetic head simultaneously "reads" and "writes" on the bottom surface if the program is so manipulated in a sophisticated way. A given track is in the same relative position on all disks, so that once the read-write heads are positioned to read data from one track in a "cylinder of disks," all the other tracks on the other disks in the cylinder can be read without repositioning the read-write heads for simultaneous access. Hence, many tracks can be read or written with a single move of the read-write heads to minimize the on-line access-time to reach a comparatively short duration of the order of a few tens of milliseconds.

The floppy-disk random-access memory used with the minicomputer of, for example, the Digital Equipment Corporation comes in either single-disk or dual-disk drive at a comparatively low cost. The disk-storage system is interfaced to DEC, LSI-11 microcomputer system as well, by means of one dual-height interface card that connects either drive to the system backplane. The floppy disk serves:

1. as a mass-storage medium of 256-K (single-density) or 512-K byte-capacity (double-density)
2. for a high-level language programming such as the multiuser BASIC, and FORTRAN-IV.

For this Operating System, 360 rpm, 3,200 bits per inch (bpi), 77 tracks/disk, and a latency of 83 ms make the specification. For personal computer applications, two 8-in. Shugart compatible single-sided, double-density floppy-disk drives are popular for 1-M byte of mass memory. A typical software-controlled IBM format of a track is illustrated in page 79.

4-2.1. Winchester Drives—8-inch Hard Disk. The high-cost Winchester sealed-medium 14-inch high-density mass-memory hard disks used for the main-frame computers' (such as IBM 3350 and 3370) disk-drive systems for expensive data-base computer systems have now stepped down to linear, brushless, dc-motor servo controlled Winchester 8-inch (exact 7.87-in. or 8.27-in. diameter) hard-disk for mini and microcomputers to hold 60-M bytes of memory at 10-M bytes/platter, 8-K bit/in. and 500 tracks/in. in the place of the 1.2-M byte floppy-disks. Access-times are of the order of 25 to 50 ms, and prices range from $900 to $2100. They will be standardized shortly to fit into the 4.6-by-8.5-in. opening of the standard floppy-disk with new LSI-chip control. Sophisticated microprocessor controlled data-base file management can be extended to mini and microcomputer systems for multiprogramming software with this huge mass-memory system, since a floppy-disk will wear out too fast for systems of this kind. As a matter of comparison, magnetic bubble chips must achieve 16-M bits per card at a price of $25. So bubbles and Winchester 8-in. disks will coexist in different software applications for a long time to come.

IBM (62 PC drive, piccollo), Basic-Four Corp., Memorex Corp., Kennedy Co., New World Co., and International Memories Inc. are some of the manufacturers, and there is bound to be some standardization move in this area. The economy 5.25-in. floppy-diskette market with a limited mass-memory demand in the case of personal computing will not be affected by this high-density mass-memory Winchester 8-in. hard disk. On the other hand, with the newly developing high-capacity 5.12-in. hard-disk technology, personal computer users also can add millions of bytes of mass storage to their systems at a reasonably low-cost.

High-density mass-memory hard disk systems will advance still further in density of tracks/in. and bit/in. when the present 1-micron surface-gap ferrite read/write heads are replaced by miniature inductive spiral thin-film heads (or possibly thin-film magneto-resistive heads) in the near future. IBM 3370 disk drive with 700 tracks/in. and 12000 bit/in. does use this inductive thin-film, read/write flying-head assembly system. The thin-film heads "fly" 0.2 micron from the surface of the disk!

4-2.2. Winchester 14-in. Disk Operating System (DOS) for Microcomputers (Hewlett-Packard). The storage is 12-M bytes on a 14-in. single-disk, desk-top 7910-H controller in a portable cabinet adjacent to the microcomputer-keyboard CRT terminal at a price of $8375. The Hewlett-Packard 64000 Logic Development System (LDS) provides a disk operating system with several hundred kilobytes of storage to replace lower mass-storage floppy-disk systems along with their former operating systems. The system provides several relocatable macroassemblers to support 8080, 8085, Z80, 6800, 6805, 6809,

PREAMBLE (46 BYTES)	INDEX ADDRESS MARK (1 BYTE)	POST INDEX GAP (32 BYTES)	SECTOR 1 (188 BYTES)	SECTOR 2 (188 BYTES)	---	SECTOR 25 (188 BYTES)	SECTOR 26 (188 BYTES)	POSTAMBLE

REFERENCE POINT (INDEX HOLE)

ID = { SECTOR IDENTIFICATION

ID ADDRESS MARK (1 BYTE)	TRACK/SECTOR ID (6 BYTES)						ID GAP (17 BYTES)	DATA ADDRESS MARK (1 BYTE)	DATA		DATA GAP (33 BYTES)	NEXT ID ADDRESS MARK
	TRACK NUMBER	0	SECTOR NUMBER	0	CHECK SUM				(128 BYTES)	CHECK SUM (2 BYTES)		

(FOR ERROR-DETECTION IN READ/WRITE DATA TRANSFER)

1. SECTORS IN EACH TRACK AND FIELDS WITHIN EACH SECTOR ARE CLASSIFIED AS DATA, ADDRESS, AND CONTROL FIELDS.
2. THE FIELD IS DIVIDED INTO CODED BYTES SO THAT THEY CAN BE IDENTIFIED BY THE DISK CONTROLLER.
3. THE FORMAT USES THE SYNCHRONIZATION PULSE GENERATED BY THE REFERENCE INDEX HOLE.
4. CLOCK SIGNAL BITS ARE RECORDED PRIOR TO EACH INFORMATION BIT.

NOTE: AS AN ALTERNATIVE TO SOFTWARE-CONTROLLED FORMAT, A FLOPPY DISK CAN BE HARDWARE CONTROLLED. EACH SECTOR IS THEN TRACKED BY MEANS OF HOLE PERFORATIONS THROUGH THE DISK, AWAY FROM THE TRACK, FOR GENERATION OF SYNCHRONIZATION PULSE. SINCE THE NEED FOR STORING ADDRESSES OF THE TRACKS IS THUS AVOIDED, MORE SPACE WILL BE AVAILABLE FOR DATA.

Typical software-controlled format of the track of a floppy disk.

8048, 8021, 8022, 9900, 1802, F8, and 3870 microcomputer systems. Irrespective of the source file size, these macroassemblers (priced at $550 each) can operate at 4000 line/min. This disk operating system with an abundance of user mass-storage is also used in Hewlett-Packard 300-series computers. The DOS has a seek-time of 60 msec, with track-to-track access of 10 msec. The data transfer rate is 100-K byte/sec, and latency is practically zero after first access, since sector placement is optimized. The file structure for this drive is interleaved in such a way that as the data read from one sector are transferred, the disk would revolve to the next consecutive sector for read.

4-3. TAPE CARTRIDGE

As a substitute to the floppy-disk mass-storage, the IBM-5100 portable microcomputer has a system-integrated, miniature 3M built-in tape unit that reads up to 2,850 characters/sec, and simultaneously writes and checks at 950 characters/sec. The tape unit uses a capstan-driven, 0.25″ magnetic-tape, IBM data-cartridge that stores up to 204-K bytes. It searches and rewinds tape at 40 ips. As data and programs are developed, they can be stored off-line on these data cartridges for subsequent usage or for use in other software applications. Data stored on the cartridge is protected from accidental erasure by means of a file-protect feature. Also, data can be secured by removing the cartridge from the microcomputer unit. An optionally available auxiliary tape unit can be connected to the microcomputer system to speed up and simplify the preparation of file-updates of the cartridge plugged in the built-in tape unit. IBM, for example, supplies for its portable computer a library of ready-to-use cartridges for engineering, statistical, and business applications; the interface system is built in. (See Sections 12.1 and 12.2 for tape cassettes.)

A typical specification of a magnetic-tape drive system for the mini- and micro-computers: minireel, single-capstan, 12.5–75 ips, 200–800 bpi (bits; 7-track non-return-to zero interface—a phase-encoder tape-controller is required. **Heads**: single-gap read/write and dual-gap write/read. (Nine-track tape-drive is also used on 0.5″-wide tape.)

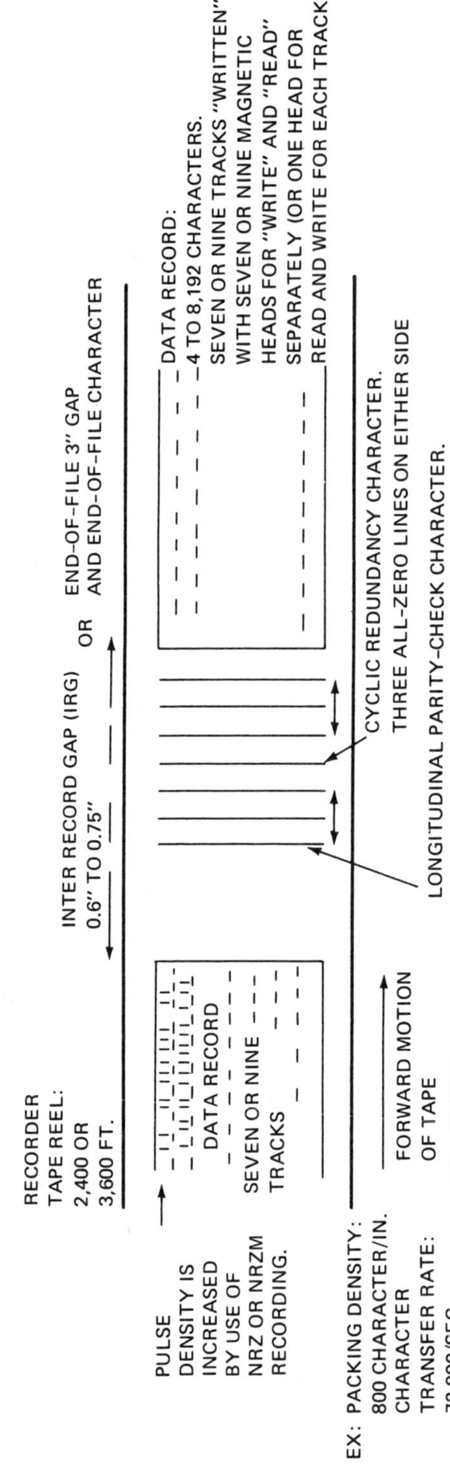

Fig. 4-2. Magnetic tape—Data record on 7/9-track tape.

7 tracks: Numeric **1, 2, 4, 8.** Alphabet-Zone **A, B.** Even parity-bit **C.** Start-stop: 8 ms at 45 ips. Small reels with limited storage are called either tape-cassette or tape-cartridge systems. Limited storage on the reel necessitates multiple cassette drives. Incidentally, flexible disks can easily replace cassettes to provide faster access to data or instruction words. Figure 4-2 illustrates the inter-record gap and data record on a 7- or 9-track magnetic tape.

RZ and NRZ Magnetic Tape Recording. The coding method used for pulse-signal recording is called *return-to-zero* (*RZ*); and DC-level recording is called *non-return-to-zero* (*NRZ*). RZ recording requires one pulse to turn on from zero-to-saturation and another pulse to turn off from saturation-to-zero. As the tape can be positively or negatively saturated about zero, pulse-type RZ recording may have three signal levels. A pulse tape-cell is the significant requirement. The direction of magnetization of the tape-cell determines an area bit-content as a "1" or "0." NRZ recording is a dc-level change to signify plus-saturation level and minus-saturation level. There is no zero-level as such; hence, it is termed *NRZ*. If alternate "1s" and "0s" are to be written, level changes take place between cells, and the waveform resembles RZ recording. The corresponding IBM technique is called "NRZ-MARK" or "NRZ Modulo-2"; however, it is more sophisticated. Figure 4-3 differentiates the RZ, NRZ, and NRZM types of recording.

4-4. TYPES OF MEMORY VERSUS ACCESS TIME

As regards the memory technology applicable to the microcomputer systems, the plot of the access time versus capacity and the cost/bit gives an indication of the latest trends. In the case of the microcomputers, the fast-access, high-density NMOS and the newly introduced I^2L-RAM, and the CMOS-on-sapphire main-memories have practically replaced the nonvolatile CORE memory so indispensable hitherto for high-speed in mini- and general-purpose digital computers. High-density CCDs or the bubble memory will perhaps replace the electromechanical disk and tape mass-memory systems during the next decade, although they serve as the mass-memory software systems for the microcomputers at this time. The various types of internal and external memories used in computers are plotted for capacity versus access-time in Fig. 4-4.

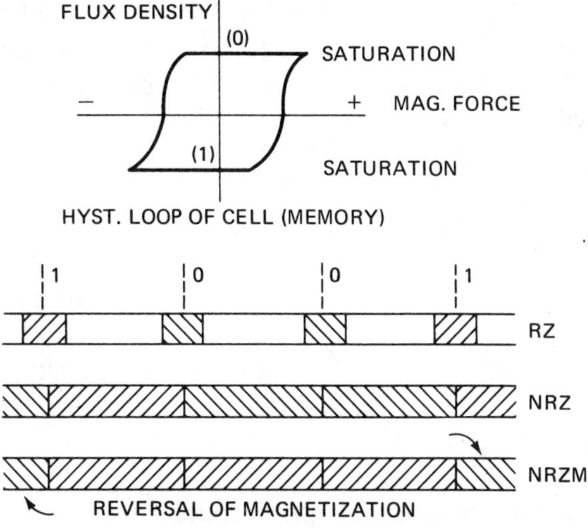

Fig. 4-3. RZ, NRZM tape recording.

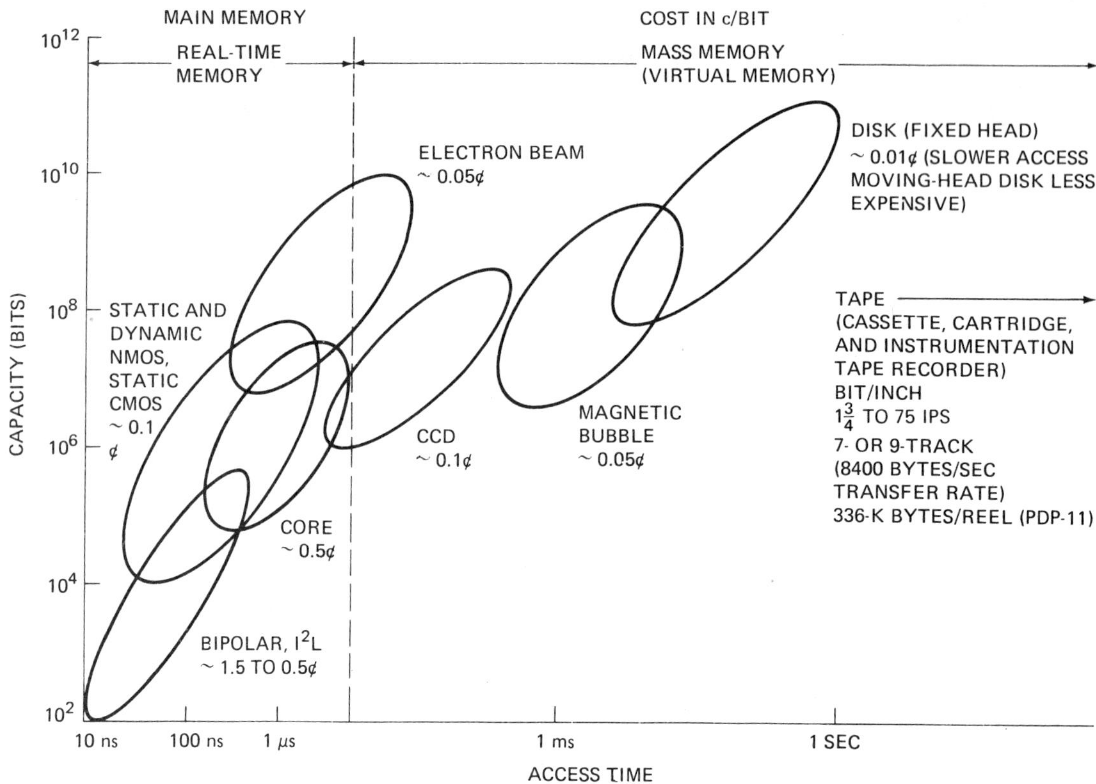

Fig. 4-4. Types of memory and access-time (cost/bit).

4-5. PERIPHERAL INTERFACE AND CONTROLLER CHIPS FOR TAPE CASSETTE OR FLOPPY DISK

A typical peripheral-interface adapter (PIA) interfaces the microprocessor to an external peripheral by means of an 8-bit bidirectional data-request bus, a specified number of chip-select lines, register-select lines, and interrupt-request lines, a read-write line, an enable line, and a reset line. The eight bidirectional data lines allow the transfer of data between the microprocessor and the PIA. The enable-pulse is the only timing signal required for the PIA; timing of the other signals is referenced to the leading- and trailing-edges of a specific E-pulse derived from phase-2 clock. A typical Interface of a Microcomputer to a peripheral Controller is detailed in Fig. 4-5.

NEC LSI Controller Chips: An LSI chip (μPD372) is presently available as a popular single-chip Controller for mini-floppy and floppy-disk mass-memory systems from NEC Microcomputer Systems Inc. It is compatible with the IBM 5.25-in. mini-floppy diskette, 8-in. floppy disk, and other formats. Each chip can control up to four floppy-disk drives in a personal computer system.

Another useful LSI chip for personal computing is the tape cassette controller, μPD371, for up to two tape cassette drives. These chips will replace 50 to 60 TTL chips used in present drive systems to save power, space, and budget in personal computing applications. At the same time, the reliability of mass-memory microcomputer systems is escalating at a phenomenal rate to enable their trouble-free use in consumer quantities of millions during the 1980's. This way, the floppy-disk mass-memory systems can successfully compete with the oncoming rush of magnetic bubble technology for prewritten software.

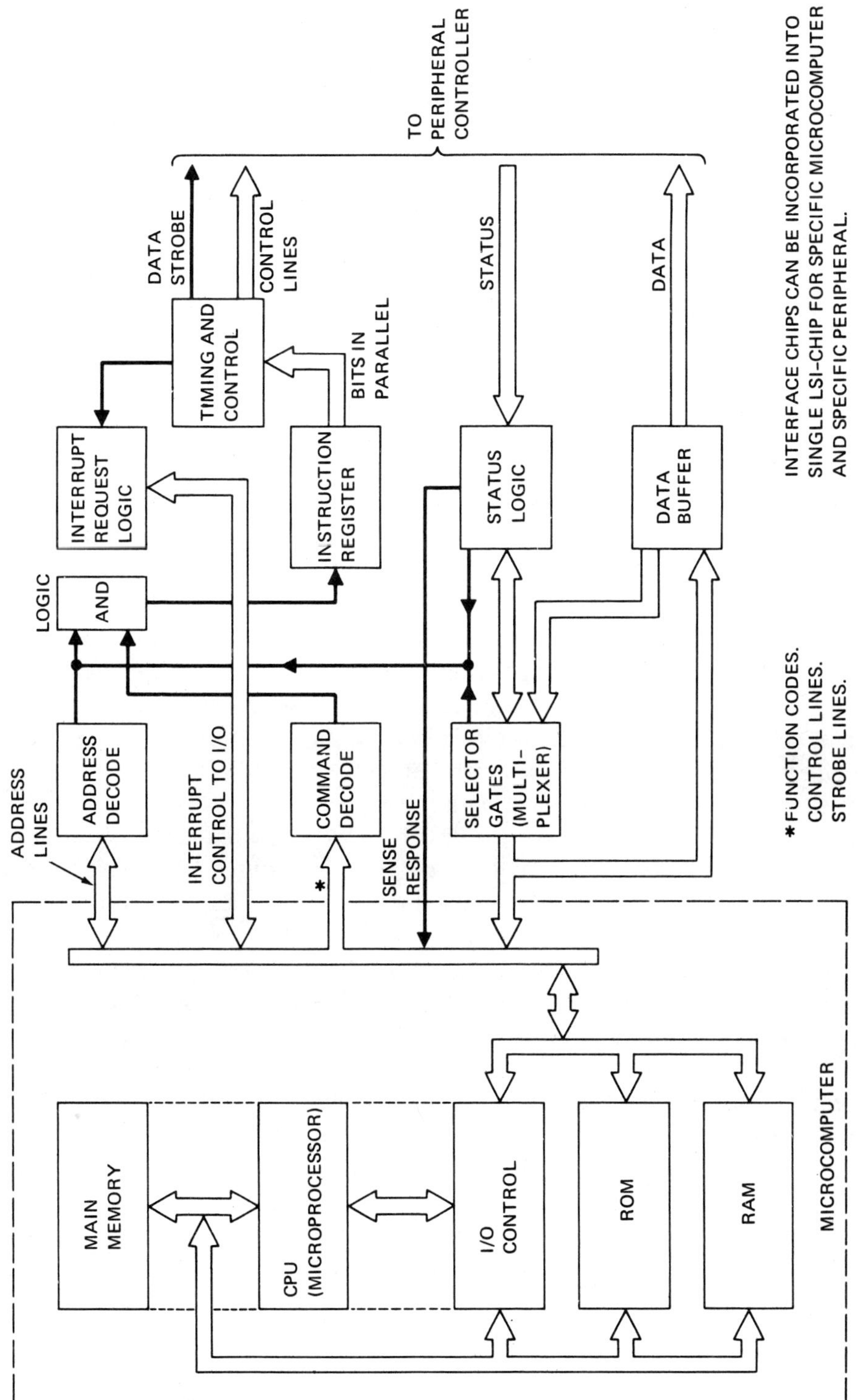

Fig. 4-5. Typical interface of microcomputer to peripheral controller. (*Courtesy of IEEE Spectrum*)

4-6 MAGNETIC "BUBBLE" MASS-MEMORY (MBM)

The Microcomputer Operating System on-a-card along with an **on-line nonvolatile magnetic storage mass-memory** is a timely new development in microcomputer system organization. A 92-K bit, nonvolatile major-minor-loop Bubble-Memory chip, as miniature as 1.1″ X 1″ X 0.4″ (H), is commercially available from Texas Instruments as the first candidate of choice for the low-budget microcomputer systems. Thus, in the case of at least the microcomputer system, with a minor precaution of handling we may have presently eliminated the practical and essential need for a basic, rotating, rack-mounted, floppy-disk, mass-memory system costing approximately $3,000. (In comparison, the main-frame on-line Disk System, IBM-2311, will cost $25,000, and the off-line slow-speed 3-M cartridge tape will cost a minimum of $3,000.) The new bubble memory, as a starter 92-K bit TBM-0103 DIP (dual-in-line package) chip, will currently cost about $75. With popular usage and demand, the price of the bubble memory will go down, and a normal full complement of 1.1-M bit mass-memory, requiring a space of approximately 8″ X 2″ X 0.4″ (H) on the microcomputer card itself, will serve most on-line software requirements in the case of a microcomputer. Associated auxiliary chips require some extra space.

The most attractive feature of the stationary nonvolatile bubble memory is that, with its average 4-ms access time and 100-K bit/sec memory-transfer rate, it is even *faster than the floppy disk.* The practical introduction of the "Bubble" and "CCD" mass-memories to meet the limited on-line software requirements of the microcomputer Real-time Operating Systems will permit, in low-budget applications, the replacement of the hitherto unavoidable, costly and less reliable, rotating, slower mass-memory devices such as floppy disk and cartridge tape. An **LSI Microcontroller chip** is immediately available from Texas Instruments, type TMS-9916, to serve as an Interface, for example, to the CPU, Intel-8080 LSI Microprocessor. (Texas Instruments is a second-source manufacturer of 8080.) The originator of the bubble technology, Bell Labs, Rockwell, IBM, Nippon TTC, and Hewlett-Packard are the other contenders in this field. As a case of precedence and field experience of this sophisticated hardware, a 2-M bit bubble memory has been in continuous use in Japan as a file memory in a telephone switching system for over a year.

In contrast to the medium-scale bubble mass-memory in minicomputer and microcomputer applications, where unlimited software requirements are involved, as in the case of large-scale host-network computer systems, a billion megabit IBM-3300 type moving-head Disk System and its Interface Controller can economically provide mass-memory at 0.005 cent/bit. Since bubble memory is not transferable as disk and tape libraries, it is presently not economically applicable to large-scale computer systems.

"Bubble" Technology. For the bubble memory, the substrate is gadolinium-gallium garnet (3-G); a **magnetic epitaxial film is grown on the substrate to form high-resolution permalloy bubble-domain patterns** when a magnetic field is generated by means of a pair of coils around the chip. The resultant twin-magnet, constant-flux, bias field enables the **nonvolatility of the bubbles in the primary epitaxial magnetic layer.** In the presence of the **rotating magnetic field,** the bubbles induced by a pulsating current in a secondary layer (which functions as a **single-turn "major" loop**) are transferred out, as in a shift register. An **array of resistance elements in a bridge circuit detects the passage of a bubble** in the secondary single-register major-loop, and the then-effective **large number of "endless minor-loops" function as shift registers** to make an overall **major-minor-loop** (MML) system comprising of 157 minor loops, 641 bubble positions per loop, and a **100-K bit memory capacity.** Average access time to the first bit of data is 4 ms. It is the major-loop of the system that provides, as a unidirectional shift register, the read/write facility as the presence or absence of a bubble at a 10-μs period for a bit "1" or "0," respectively. Data-blocks as pages are accessed by rotating the minor-loops until the desired page of data is adjacent to the major-loop. In order to allow maximum reliability in yield of chips, only 92-K functioning bits are specified as active in the minor-loops of each chip, and the nonparticipating minor-loops are automatically invalidated by the manufacturer by means of a preprogrammed 2-K bit PROM in an exclusive Microcontroller TMS-9916 developed for Interface. Each 92-K bit TBM-0103 memory chip in conjunction with its three associated circuit chips—**Function Drive, Coil Drivers,** and **Diode Array**—make one overall **memory cell,** and the cell consumes 10 to 11.5 W at ±12V and ±5V, when continuously active. If the module is automatically turned "ON" only when accessed, it consumes 1W on standby and 5W in operation. **A sense amplifier** and its termination network are shared by two memory cells. A 1.1-M bit mass-memory and the associated interface chips on a card weigh less than a pound. Figure 4-6 illustrates the nonvolatile 1.1-M bit magnetic-bubble mass-memory package in a microcomputer on-line Operating System, using an Intel-8080 CPU and a Texas Instruments TMS-9916 Microcontroller Interface.

In order to access the data for "reading," the CPU selects the memory chips, loads the desired "page" in the NMOS microcontroller, and sends the "read" command. The controller accesses the page from the memory cell and stores the data in its 1- to 20-byte buffer temporary registers and interrupts the CPU to enable the reading of the data in a few milliseconds. For "writing," the CPU sends the data to the buffer temporary storage registers in the controller, initiates the transfer, and waits for the acknowledgment of data-storage from the controller before it continues with the next software instructions.

The microcontroller, by means of its control-ROM and the serial/parallel conversion facility for bubble-bit data-transfer, responds to the CPU software in meeting the requirements of:

1. page-size in 1 to 20 bytes
2. minor-loop size of 1 to 1,024 bits
3. page capacity of 1 to 1,024 pages
4. start/stop of the bubble-shifting manipulations and the generation of the magnetic bubble-domains at the bubble field-rotation period.

Compared to the nonvolatile high-speed magnetic CORE memory, the nonvolatile magnetic bubble chip is susceptible to partial data-loss in the primary major-loop *unless* the relevant data are transferred in time (by the microcontroller) to the secondary minor-loops within a minimum of 12.8 ms at the warning of a power failure.

At larger capacities of over 30-M bits, the electron-beam addressable-memory (EBAM), referred to in Section 3.7, is expected to play a competitive role from the viewpoint of economics. The floppy disk does present in some applications the advantage of software transferability or disk-rentability, but in the present context of the unlimited expansion of the Data Communications Networks via satellites and fiber-optics, the permanent fixture of mass-memory software on a card in the case of a microcomputer is not a deterrent to its potential demand.

4-7 STATUS OF MAGNETIC BUBBLE MEMORIES, 1980–1981

The Texas Instruments technology of magnetic bubbles is called a "field-access" version with the requirement of a high-frequency rotating field generated by X and Y coils. The bubbles in the magnetic film are limited in operation up to 200 kHz as a result of power dissipation due to both skin-effect losses in the coil windings, and eddy-current losses in the metal package components. These conventional memories produce asymmetrical-

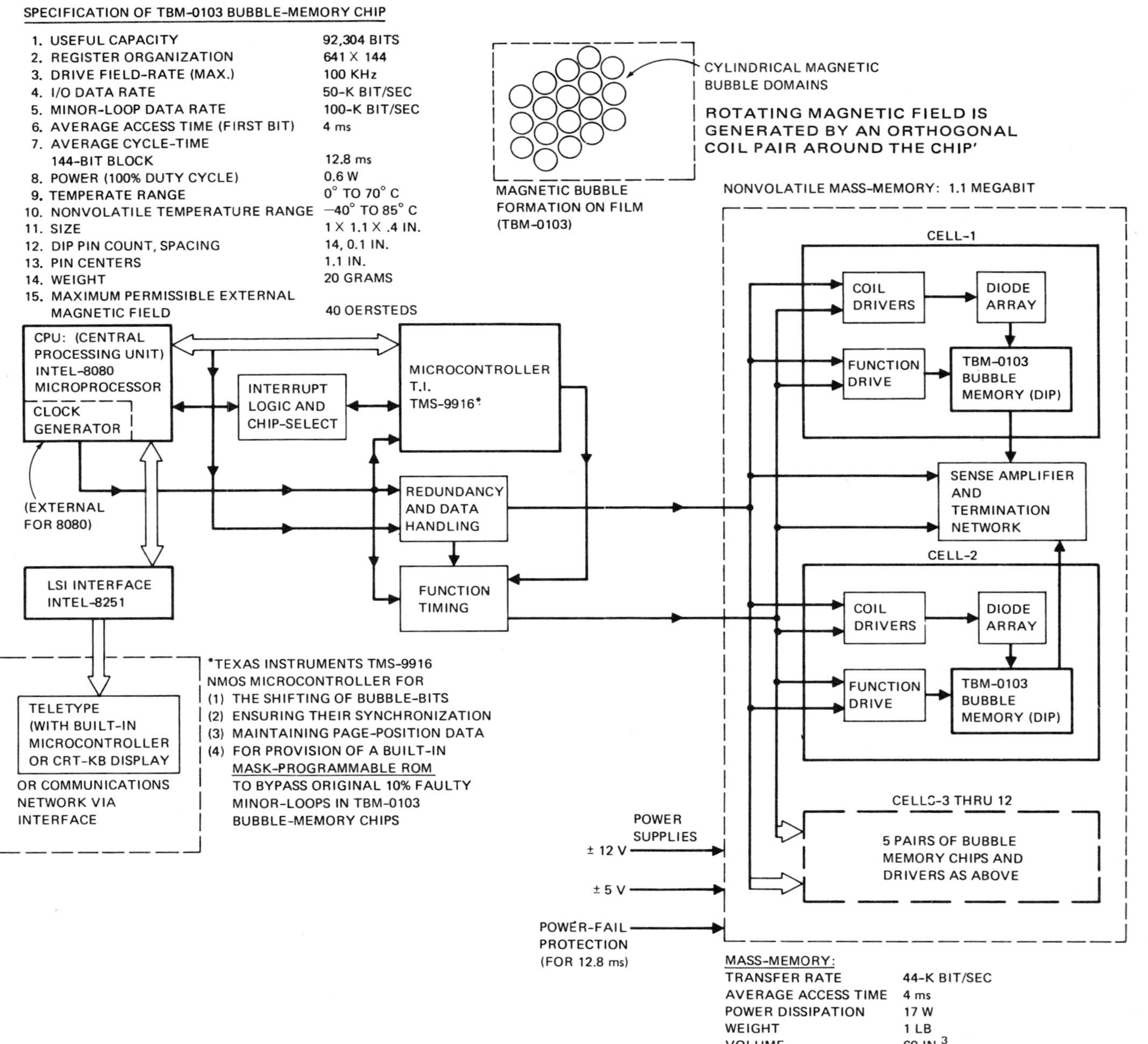

SPECIFICATION OF TBM-0103 BUBBLE-MEMORY CHIP
1. USEFUL CAPACITY 92,304 BITS
2. REGISTER ORGANIZATION 641 X 144
3. DRIVE FIELD-RATE (MAX.) 100 KHz
4. I/O DATA RATE 50-K BIT/SEC
5. MINOR-LOOP DATA RATE 100-K BIT/SEC
6. AVERAGE ACCESS TIME (FIRST BIT) 4 ms
7. AVERAGE CYCLE-TIME 144-BIT BLOCK 12.8 ms
8. POWER (100% DUTY CYCLE) 0.6 W
9. TEMPERATE RANGE 0° TO 70° C
10. NONVOLATILE TEMPERATURE RANGE −40° TO 85° C
11. SIZE 1 X 1.1 X .4 IN.
12. DIP PIN COUNT, SPACING 14, 0.1 IN.
13. PIN CENTERS 1.1 IN.
14. WEIGHT 20 GRAMS
15. MAXIMUM PERMISSIBLE EXTERNAL MAGNETIC FIELD 40 OERSTEDS
CYLINDRICAL MAGNETIC BUBBLE DOMAINS
ROTATING MAGNETIC FIELD IS GENERATED BY AN ORTHOGONAL COIL PAIR AROUND THE CHIP'
MAGNETIC BUBBLE FORMATION ON FILM (TBM-0103)
NONVOLATILE MASS-MEMORY: 1.1 MEGABIT
CELL-1
COIL DRIVERS
DIODE ARRAY
FUNCTION DRIVE
TBM-0103 BUBBLE MEMORY (DIP)
SENSE AMPLIFIER AND TERMINATION NETWORK
CELL-2
COIL DRIVERS
DIODE ARRAY
FUNCTION DRIVE
TBM-0103 BUBBLE MEMORY (DIP)
CELLS-3 THRU 12
5 PAIRS OF BUBBLE MEMORY CHIPS AND DRIVERS AS ABOVE
CPU: (CENTRAL PROCESSING UNIT) INTEL-8080 MICROPROCESSOR
CLOCK GENERATOR
(EXTERNAL FOR 8080)
INTERRUPT LOGIC AND CHIP-SELECT
MICROCONTROLLER T.I. TMS-9916*
REDUNDANCY AND DATA HANDLING
FUNCTION TIMING
LSI INTERFACE INTEL-8251
TELETYPE (WITH BUILT-IN MICROCONTROLLER OR CRT-KB DISPLAY
OR COMMUNICATIONS NETWORK VIA INTERFACE
*TEXAS INSTRUMENTS TMS-9916 NMOS MICROCONTROLLER FOR
(1) THE SHIFTING OF BUBBLE-BITS
(2) ENSURING THEIR SYNCHRONIZATION
(3) MAINTAINING PAGE-POSITION DATA
(4) FOR PROVISION OF A BUILT-IN MASK-PROGRAMMABLE ROM TO BYPASS ORIGINAL 10% FAULTY MINOR-LOOPS IN TBM-0103 BUBBLE-MEMORY CHIPS
POWER SUPPLIES
± 12 V
± 5 V
POWER-FAIL PROTECTION (FOR 12.8 ms)
MASS-MEMORY:
TRANSFER RATE 44-K BIT/SEC
AVERAGE ACCESS TIME 4 ms
POWER DISSIPATION 17 W
WEIGHT 1 LB
VOLUME 60 IN.³

Fig. 4-6. Magnetic bubble-memory, on-the-card mass-storage for a microcomputer-on-a-card.

chevron pattern, cylindrical magnetic domain bubbles in a thin film of magnetic material (synthetic garnet) between two permanent bias magnets formed by X- and Y-coils. The bubbles are organized to travel in major (representing a page of memory) and n/2 minor loops, each representing 2n bits for a total of n^2 bits. Ones and zeros are represented by the presence or absence of reverse domain of magnetization (which causes the bubble) in the thin film (consisting of base epitaxial garnet film), then the storage layer enabling the height of the cylindrical bubble, and a top spacer to represent the hemispherical top of the bubble. The bubble film is deposited on the surface of a substrate terminal chip between the coiled bias plates held in a mu-metal tube. Some manufacturers use permanent magnets to eliminate the coils for the bias plates.

The latest Texas Instruments chips are of three capacities: (1) TIB 0250: 280,850 bits, 20-pin dual-in-line 1.2 X 1.2 in., (2) TIB 0500: 561,426 bits, and (3) TIB 1000: 1,222,852 bits (512-k X 2). This last item is comprised of 300 (X 2) minor loops (each loop consisting of 2-k bits), an access-time of 11.2 ms, average data-rate of 170-k bits/sec, and 1.2-W power dissipation. The magnetic bubble-chip organization with a read-function driver (TIB 0864) for data and redundant replicators, and a write-function driver (TIB 0884) for data generation, data swap logic, and "replicate" swap logic for speeding access are shown in Figure 4-7. There are four accessory chips for each modular bubble-memory chip: (1) bubble memory controller TIB 0904, (2) function timing generator TIB 0954, (3) data corrector and formatter TIB 0934, and (4) sense amplifier TIB 0834 for the two A and B detectors in the memory chip. The common field-rate for the three types of memory chips is 100 kHz.

The manufacturers presently supplying 256-K bit, 18-pin magnetic bubble memory chips with either major-minor/swap or block replicate/transfer organization are: (1) Texas Instruments, (2) Rockwell International, (3) Hitachi, Ltd., (4) Fujitsu, Ltd., and (5) National Semiconductor, and (6) Intel. Intel employs *multiple-block replicate organization* of minor loops to supply type-7110, 1-M bit (256 bits by 4-K) rugged nonvolatile bubble memory chips, with built-in burst-error detection and correction. They are specially suitable for microcomputer systems. The accessory chips for the Intel bubble memory palm-size card are 7242 Formatter/Sense Amplifier, 7230 Current Pulse Generator, 7250 Coil Predriver, two 7254 Quad-Transistor Logic packs, and an Interface 7220 System-Timing Controller for 1 to 8 megabit 13-terminal memory cards. As a replacement of electromechanical rotating floppy-disk memory presently used in personal computer applications, the rugged all-electronic bubble memory cards will be highly attractive to low-cost microcomputer systems. The OEM personal computer manufacturers should start the activity of transferring their high-end slower-access floppy-disk software to plug-in bubble memory cards as this new memory technology gradually establishes itself as a more attractive nonvolatile medium than the volatile and costlier CCDs.

Intel MBM. The interface problem is more complex than that for semiconductor memories and single-chip controllers for mini-floppy diskettes. Besides addressing and control logic, precise current pulse generation, and low-level analog voltage sensing, relatively high current waveforms in a set of coiled drivers are required. Intel has presently come up with a 1-M bit solid-state nonvolatile magnetic bubble memory chip, 7110 with the abovementioned interface chips for a timely mass-storage solution to some new applications in process control and telecommunications, as an addition to mini-floppy diskettes and solid-state ROM memories. The 128-K byte MBM is comprised of a serial-in parallel-loop serial-out shift-register which makes one-half of the 20-pin 7110 BMC (bubble memory chip), and a 7220 controller via an 8257 DMA chip. A minimum performance method by polled I/O requires a status bit in the controller; DMA and interrupt driven I/O make two other means for data transfer. Eight MBM's (9 X 10-in. board) can be

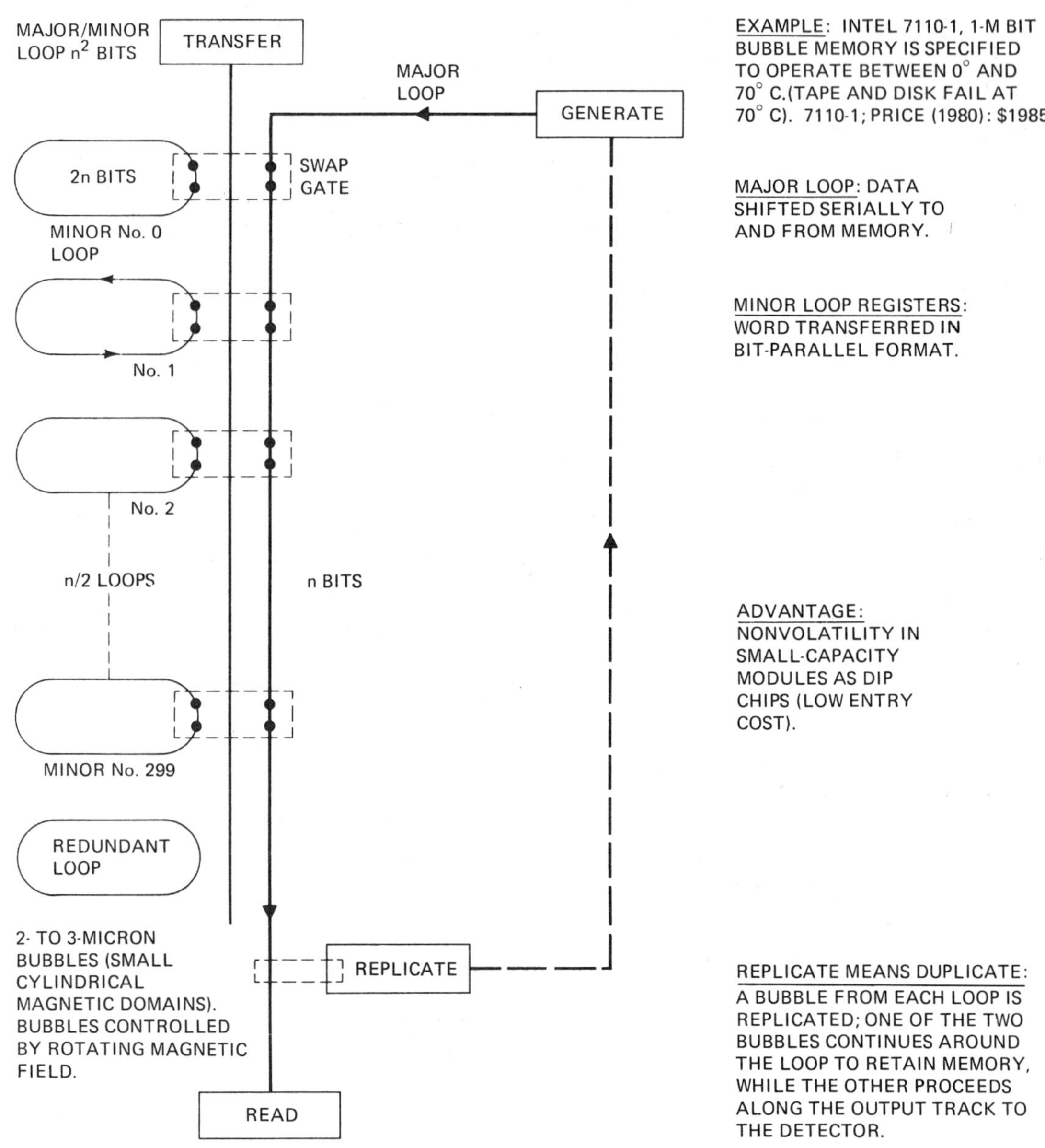

Fig. 4-7. Magnetic-bubble chip organization.

operated in parallel or multiplexed one at a time at 40/11W respectively (at +12V and −5V) for a 1-M byte nonvolatile memory system in microcomputer applications such as word processing systems, at a maximum data transfer rate of 100-K byte/sec or 10 μs/byte.

An MBM can be used as a RAM or a PROM to update data. Unlike disk and tape, the MBM is free from contamination, and hence it can be used with faster access-time in dusty environments, and in the place of a second 1-M byte disk in a single-drive disk controller system. As a start, a one megabyte bubble prototype kit BPK-71 costs $2280 for an 8085-based controller. Reset (initialize), Read for the selected page, and Write for the selected bubble memory page make up the common commands. The defect-tolerant design incorporates 25% redundant storage loops (64), and predicted data-error rates are less than 10^{-10}. The 7110 device has a binary page organization to store 2048 pages of 512 bits each. The pages are divided into two channels of 256 bits each. A total of 128 data storage loops per channel are further divided into two sections of 64 data loops each, with a separate detector for each channel. Bubbles are shifted through each detector in alternate cycles. With all four quads interleaved, the maximum data rate is twice the shift rate. A swap logic operation exchanges a new page for the old at the address location desired. Along with 256 assured storage loops to hold the megabit of useful data, and 16 for an error-correction code, 48 spare, identified, redundant loops can be defective without any fabrication problem in production. A boot-loop identifies the good and spare loops, and thus presents a loop-map, which is read out of the 7110 MBM and stored in the 7242 dual formatter/sense amplifier each time the system is initialized prior to read/write command.

As the popularity of nonvolatile magnetic bubble-memories increases during 1981, the price of a small-card 1-M bit bubble-memory set will be an unprecedented $595 when ordered in large quantities. By August 1982, the unit-price will further go down to $295 on a 25,000-piece order to discourage the use of the formerly indispensable power-consuming CORE memory as the main memory of large computer systems. The bubble-memory set's six special-support peripheral control chips, viz., a controller, a formatter/sense-amplifier, 3 packages for coil-driving, and a current-pulse generator, interface to microcomputer system buses via the above controller. The controller in turn interfaces up to eight 1-M bit bubble-memory packages, and provides powerful protection and error-correction as well. This trend in price of bubble-memories will help the personal computer user immensely, because he will then gradually transfer his allegiance to the lower-cost, low-power consuming, lightweight, all-electronic, silent, reliable bubble-memory software from the present not-so-reliable minifloppy-diskette software. The microcomputer will then have built-in programmability, and portability, at reduced service and maintenance costs, with ensured data integrity. The high-density RAMs will supplement the nonvolatile bubble memory to supersede the CORE Read/Write speed.

IBM has settled for the higher-density **"contiguous-disk" magnetic bubble memory** technology. In the place of the 2-micron bubble permalloy overlay of the above manufacturers, this "field-access" version allows bidirectional propagation of higher lithographic resolution 1-micron bubbles. Patterns of in-plane magnetization are directly ion-implanted into the base garnet film. A 4-M bit asymmetric-chevron bubble memory chip is feasible, since the concept as a 15-K bit wall-encoded structure is already demonstrated without the conventional magnetic coils. Packaging requirements are essentially the same for contiguous-disk memory chips and present bubble technology.

As a contrast to the above field-access technologies requiring rotating magnetic fields, **Bell Laboratories** has eliminated the coils, and come up with an experimental **"current-access" bubble memory technology** that uses two insulator-isolated conductive plates—(1) an insulating layer on the top sheet and (2) a conducting layer at the base of the bottom plate—to move 0.7-micron chevron-shaped bubbles in a storage layer below the conducting layer, by applying high-frequency alternating current across the surface of the conducting layer. A 1-MHz intrinsic data-rate is feasible with 2-micron bubbles at a 5-V single voltage supply and a comparable 1-to-2W power dissipation for a 256-K bit memory chip. In addition to smaller size bubbles and lower costs, high-speed data-rates can go above 10 MHz. The thickness of the storage layer above the substrate determines the height of the bubbles held by the garnet film, and the lower conducting layer's thickness determines the hemispherical portion of the bubble.

The development of the newer second-generation technologies in bubble memory will make sure that the potential advanced bubble memory chips will be directly compatible for integration into the present bubble software systems. Plessey Incorporated of Great Britain and Signetics Corp. (a subsidiary of US-Philips of the Netherlands) will join the bubble-memory race because this new high-density nonvolatile memory technology will *eventually* replace the former indispensable high-speed CORE memory in present computer systems. The compact bubble memory systems at their current data-rate and cost will easily compete with the slightly faster but volatile CCD and slightly slower mass-memory systems. (A 250-K bit, Rockwell RBM 256 bubble-memory chip, with a temperature range of -10 to 70°C, costs $500 at this initial state.)

Watkin-Johnson markets types 1450/1475 automatic magnetic memory testers, using a PDP-11/03 microcomputer, a CRT-terminal, and a dual-drive floppy-disk system to load programs and collect data from the magnetic-bubble memory package. The software approach is based on a Device Independent Software System embodied in a Pascal test program. The procedure and pattern programs work out of a data base to allow testing of other device architectures. The Pascal library consists of macroinstruction subroutines to control loading and execution of patterns for testing any single parameter. The pattern generator uses 32-bit microprogram commands synchronized to X-Y drive field. The memory chip can be tested for maximum and minimum drive fields and temperature range to inspect individual minor loops and the read/write logic gates.

The following preliminary data give the specification and price of a typical magnetic bubble-memory setup:

National Semiconductor Magnetic Bubble Memory

NBM 2256: 256-K bit, 16-pin DIP, Nonvolatile Magnetic Domain Memory

Even/Odd loops of 1024 bits each. Loaded through Swap gates, and Read via Replicate gates at opposite ends of the Storage loops.
Operating frequency: 100 kHz
Data-rate: 100-K bit/sec
Average access-time to first bit of random data-block: 7 msec
No. storage loops, including defect tolerance: 282
Usable data storage: 262,144 bits (32-K bytes)
Power, total: 750 mW
Storage, size: 12 X 12.5 mm (1.5-micron cells)

Associated chips:

1NS 82851: Bubble memory controller
DS 3615: Function driver
DS 3616: Coil driver
DS 3617: Sense amplifier

Price:

Bubble memory chip: $500
Evaluation board: $1300
Memory expansion board: $2500

Bubble Cassette, Fujitsu, America, Inc. Fujitsu's FBM 31CA, FBM 43CA bubble cassettes are portable and detachable nonvolatile magnetic memories. FBM 31CA has a memory capacity equivalent to 20 meters of paper tape, and 65-K bits can be transferred in 0.74 sec. FBM 43 CA has 4 times the above capacity, and an average access-time of 6 msec. The cassette is plugged in a holder, mounted by the side of the screen of a keyboard-CRT microcomputer system. A control card FBC 308 CIA, a holder FBM-U001, a plug-in bubble-memory cassette system, and a small power supply unit FBC 308 CIA make the complete system. Write prevention is automatic with an LED indication. (Ferromagnetics must be avoided near the unit.)

NOTE: In future, two 1-M byte, programmed bubble boards (MBMs) such as those of Intel (with 7110 memory chips) will be plugged in on the CRT keyboard terminal as they do 1 or 2 floppy disks along with a separate unit of the drive.

Fujitsu bubble-memory cassettes may be connected to an 8-bit microprocessor-bus by means of a holder. A card incorporating a monitor program is part of the system. A write prevention key is provided at the holder.

APPLICATIONS: Low-speed files and program memories, testing equipment, and numerical control systems.

Specification	FBM 31CA	FBM 43CA
Organization	Serial loop	Major-minor loop Block replicator transfer
Capacity	70,032 bits 65,536 bits effective	277,745 bits 1,033 bits X 265 loops
Transfer rate	100-K bits/sec	100-K bits/sec
Drive frequency	100 kHz	100 kHz
Access-time	740 msec max.	6 msec average
Power consumption	500 mW	700 mW
Temperature range	0 to 55°C	0 to 55°C
External magnetic field	50 Oe max.	50 Oe max.
Physical structure	24-pin cassette	24-pin cassette
Dimensions	60 X 45 X 20 mm	60 X 45 X 20 mm
Weight	50 grams	50 grams

4-8. DATA BASE MANAGEMENT

Data Base Management is one of the latest software development areas in full activity. Data base machines specialize in mostly disk-memory oriented computer hardware, supporting basic data base management at host and central computing centers in data communications networks. For expansion and reliability, software grows in complexity and in size. How to accelerate access, storage, retrieval, and management of the desired programs in a large mass-memory system is the problem, because off-line, batch, single-user environments are changing over to on-line, concurrent, multiuser environments. Practical verification methods under the circumstance are difficult to visualize. By using new programming techniques in data base management, we might also improve the reliability of software, as the reliability situation in hardware has improved enormously with the advent of LSI solid-state technology.

Moving large amounts of data from the secondary disk or magnetic bubble storage to the main memory nonvolatile CORE or the latest RAM memory, and executing many software modules for finding the answers among the data involve a complex procedure. The data-base management might fall short of memory cycles to extract the desired data, when the I/O traffic to-and-from the secondary storage via the direct memory access is heavy. The response time is naturally degraded under these circumstances. The response time can be improved by incorporating *associative array* modules of the category of microprocessor-based CAM (content addressable memories) and *catche* memory modules. See Figure 4-8 for a block diagram of a "data-base" computer. Large on-line storage and rapid real-time search are complex problems unless new programming techniques are successfully devised with the aid of the latest LSI/VLSI hardware technology.

Data base researchers have realized that the hardware approach might provide a solution to data base management. Monolithic associative memories have been considered too expensive and limited in capacity, but not if the latest 16/32-bit VLSI microprocessor-based higher-capacity monolithic CAM memories are used along some newly devised system techniques. Some researchers are presently working in this direction using multi-microprocessor-based search facilities.

Cellular logic design to provide content addressability in fixed-head disk systems is one

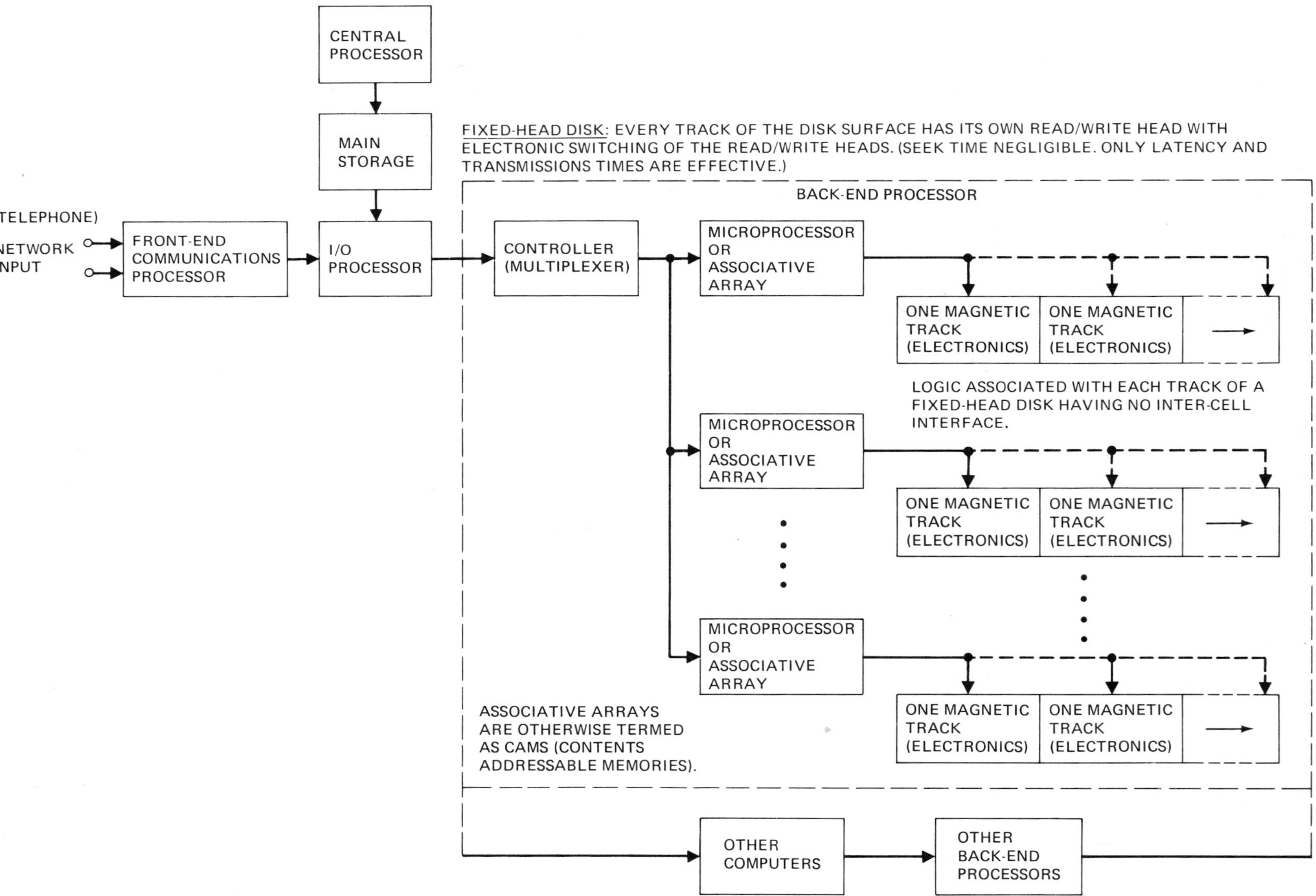

Fig. 4-8. General block diagram of a data-base computer.

of the modern research trends. Processing capabilities may be incorporated in the read/write mechanisms of a fixed-head disk, to furnish intertrack communication, and hence slower-speed associativity in a fairly large-capacity medium up to 10^8 bytes. Each individual track is defined as a cell in this approach. Parallel processing of the data in the cells by content and context addressability is the concept. Before explaining the concept of the cellular logic design, a brief introduction to the present status of the secondary disk memory systems is helpful.

Moving-head and fixed-head disks make the basis for modern large- and medium-scale data-base machines. The metal disk is coated with ferromagnetic particles on one or both sides for storing software/data, and several disks are stacked up as a "cylinder." Each surface is divided into concentric bands or tracks, which in turn are divided into sectors; sectors carry the same capacity of memory bits. Each sector is written into or read through a read/write head that floats above or below the surface of the rotating disk. In a *moving-head* disk, the heads are mounted on a comblike movable arm assembly. When data recorded in a specific sector on a certain track are to be accessed, the appropriate moving head will be selected and moved to seek the track containing the desired data within the *seek time*. The rotation delay during which the proper sector comes under the selected read/write head is called the *latency time*. During I/O operation, the data of several sectors may be written or read, and the total *transmission time* is the time required to read/write a series of sectors, starting at the instant of the first read/write operation. (The IBM 3300 disk pack has an average seek time of 30 msecs and a transmission rate of 806 characters/msec.) In the *fixed-head* disk systems, each track has its own read/write head, and electronic switching from head-to-head enables data to be read/written from different tracks (without any need of seek time) to speed up I/O operations, with minimum latency and transmission delays only.

The architecture of a cellular-logic system is shown in Figure 4-9. Memory cells may or may not have intercommunication facilities; this is more general than that conceived by D. L. Slotnick, which belongs to the second classification. The cellular-logic (CL) device is controlled by a computer that translates the high-level data manipulation requests into commands for the CL device, transfers commands to the device for execution, receives data transferred out of the device, processes and outputs data to the user. M is a set of circular memory elements consisting of storage registers and random access memory handling the useful software words. Electron-beam addressable memories (EBAM), CCD shift registers, magnetic bubble memories, or any delay-line technology elements may take the place of the circular memory elements. P is a set of processing elements containing the logic, and C is the controller to control the execution of an identical instruction by all the processors simultaneously. I/O is the mechanism for moving data to and from the circular memory elements. The input is similar to the input operation of a computer. Output data are based on the priorities preassigned to P's or based on the order in which data are scanned by P's. A more comprehensive bus structure or multiple channels can allow data to be transferred out of memory cells in parallel. It is the parallel processing and the content and context search capabilities of the processors (including microprocessors) of the system that distinguish the cellar-logic devices from the conventional rotating mass memory devices.

For special-purpose data-base tasks, bubble memories are presently used for voice recording, CCDs for buffering, and EBAMs for paging. Some special-purpose data-base systems use relational data-base management for certain unique operations that require frequent and effective use. Some specialize in text-processing that involve rapid search and repetitive scanning without any need of updating. But on-line moving-head technology is expected to remain popular by using the aid of microprocessors for intelligent

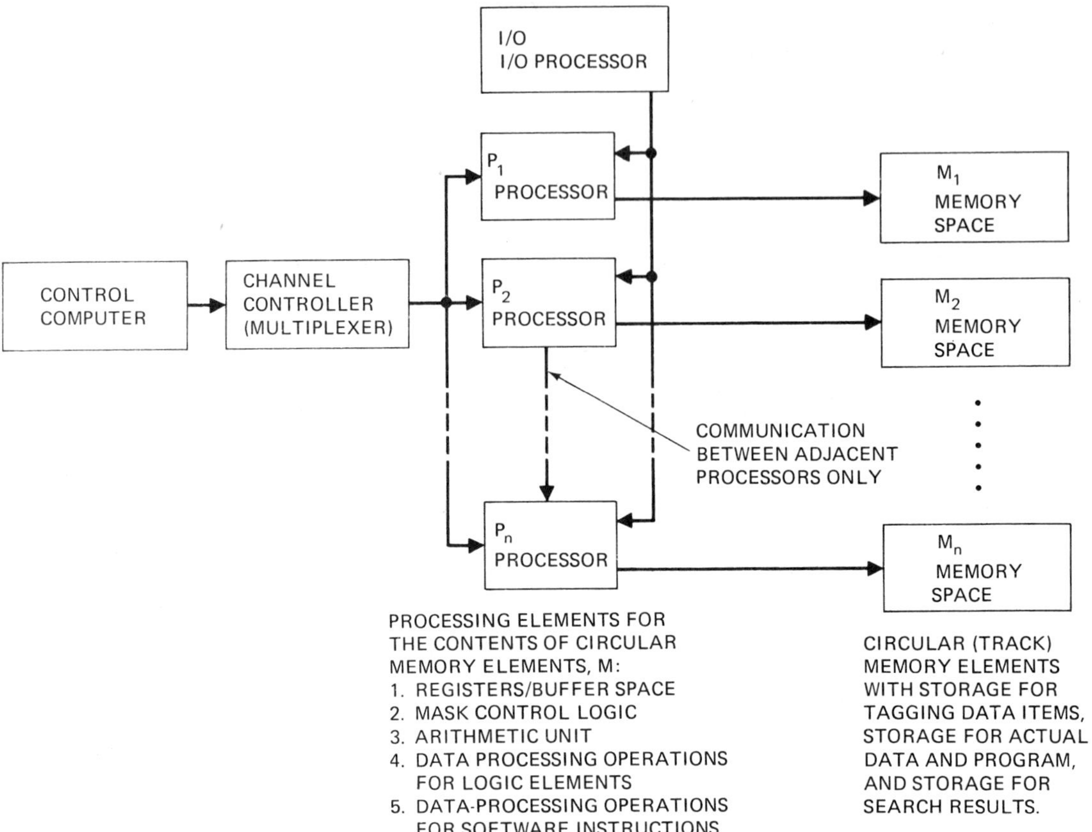

Fig. 4-9. Architecture of a cellular-logic System. ©1979 *IEEE, COMPUTER March.*

search and processing capability required in content-addressability of disk packs. In the near future, by delegating the structural information of a data-base computer system to faster memory devices such as EBAMs, CCDs, and magnetic bubble memories, the number of accesses to the disk-pack data-base may be minimized. At the same time, with the latest distributed processing systems with low-cost 8-M byte range microprocessor-based floppy-disk mass-memory at the individual keyboard CRT terminals, the need for larger central data-base memory systems will be gradually diminished and will reduce the complexity of information storage and retrieval from billions and billions of bytes of mass-memory systems.

Modern Data-Base Management: In general, *from the systems point of view*, data-base management may be classified into data administration, data-base, data communication, and data delivery. The data administration depicts adequate security by encryption, and right usage of data for right purposes. The central or distributed data-base stands for economic storage of information as a virtual mass-storage of random-access in on-line disk-packs, magnetic bubbles, and EEPROM, and off-line tape, cartridges, cassettes and optical film. Duplication must be carefully avoided and economic productivity of computer software must be enhanced by using portable, block-structured, modular high-level languages such as PASCAL and its derivatives. Data communication represents the observance of the right protocols at host computer-concentrators, and keyboard-CRT/printer terminals and the latest economic formats of data communications by facilities such as wideband-multiplexed TDMA satellite communications, packet-switched networks, and fiber-optic links. The data delivery stands for rapid, computer-assisted, systematic retrieval of the requisite error-free data from the data-base for the immediate information of the end user.

LSI/VLSI hardware and firmware from 1980 onward will demonstrate excellent cost/performance ratings. On the final analysis, the integration of the right-mix of decision-making in the above areas should result in a highly efficient portfolio of the task of data base management.

4-9. LOW-COST DIGITAL OPTICAL DISK MEMORY (10-Billion Bits on a Disk by Photoresist Recording with High-Power Laser—Philips Research Laboratories)

The optical prerecording and reading disk presents the *feasibility* of a mass-memory of 10^{10} bits at a bit correction efficiency of 81% on a 128-sector, 46-track, 30-cm-diameter air-sandwich pregrooved recording disk. The servo system involved controls the radial tracking of the optical recording head used for recording and reading the reliable mass-memory archival storage of video or binary data in applications such as geological surveying, banking, historical archives, television broadcasting, and medical archives. An optical disk can replace 25 high-density cartridge tapes with a much lower random access-time on the order of 250 ms at 2.5 rps and 25 ms at 25 rps. The 0.6-micron, 0.07-micron-deep pregroove concept allows for storing synchronization information on the recording disk; and data are written in the groove by melting holes in the recording layer by a high-power infrared 820-nm laser beam. A 5-micron-wide stripe is defined by proton bombardment. Raw bit-error rates of 10^{-5} are measured, and since a bit-error rate of better than 10^{-10}

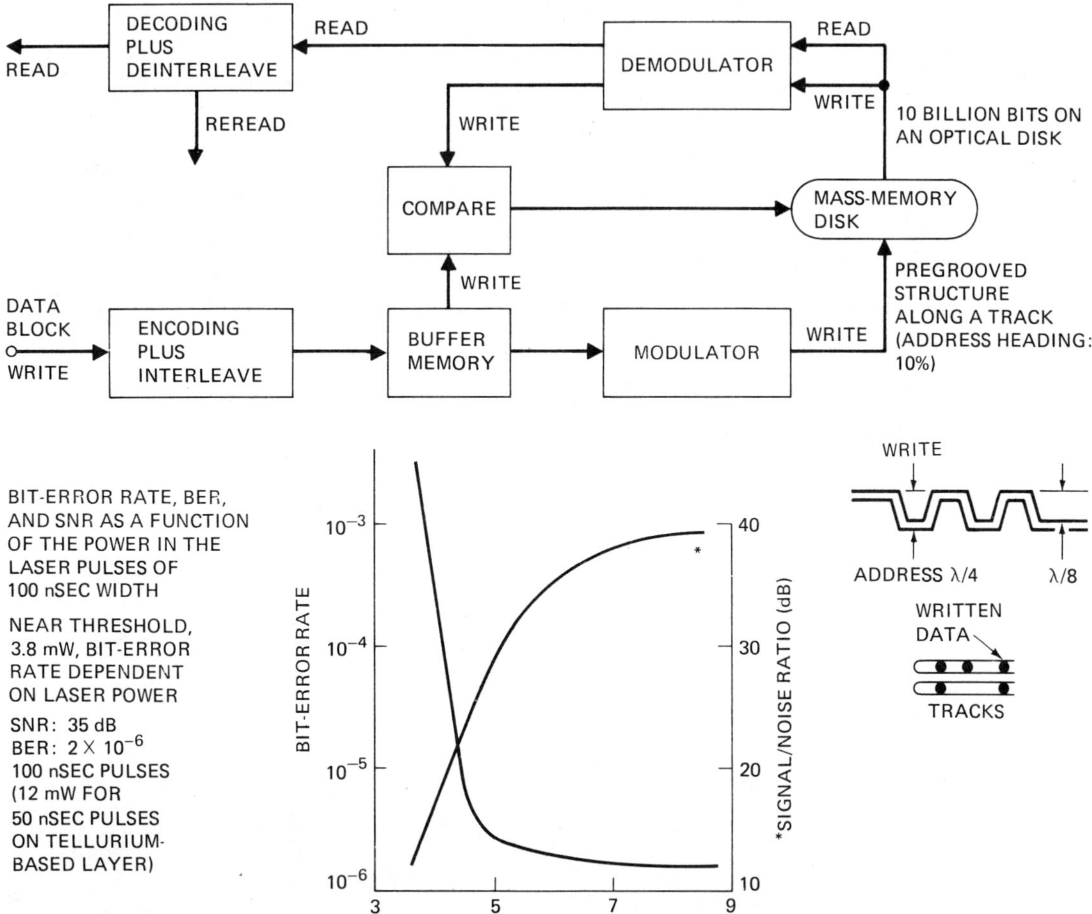

Fig. 4.10. Bit-error corrections, optical disk memory. ©1979 IEEE, *Spectrum, August,* Kees Bulthuis *et. al.*

in data retrieval is essential in many applications, the data are encoded with redundant bits before recording. Short bit-error bursts are corrected by recording the encoded data interleaved on the disk; long error bursts are spread over a whole sector, so that the error-correction code can correct the interleaved error bursts. The bit-error correction scheme is shown in Figure 4-10. The data bits are buffered, modulated, and recorded on the disk, and the data spectrum is matched by modulation against the record/read process. Drop-outs are detected by immediate reading and comparison of the detected and demodulated data with the source data; if the recording is faulty, the sector is invalidated and rewritten in another sector to enable final error-free recording of data during the recording process itself. Exhaustive tests indicate permanent storage is achievable with tellurium-based plastic sandwiches. But practical bit rates are limited from 1-to-10 MBPS at this stage of laser-diode development for recording on tellurium-based materials.

Optics for the recording/reading head are illustrated in Fig. 4-11. The placement of the diode laser with an antireflective-coated front face and the photodetector enables the requisite acquisition range for the servo system. At power levels between 10 and 20 mW with a pulse-duration of 50 ns, the high-bit level is represented by the absence of holes; 0.9 micron holes are effective for the low bits.

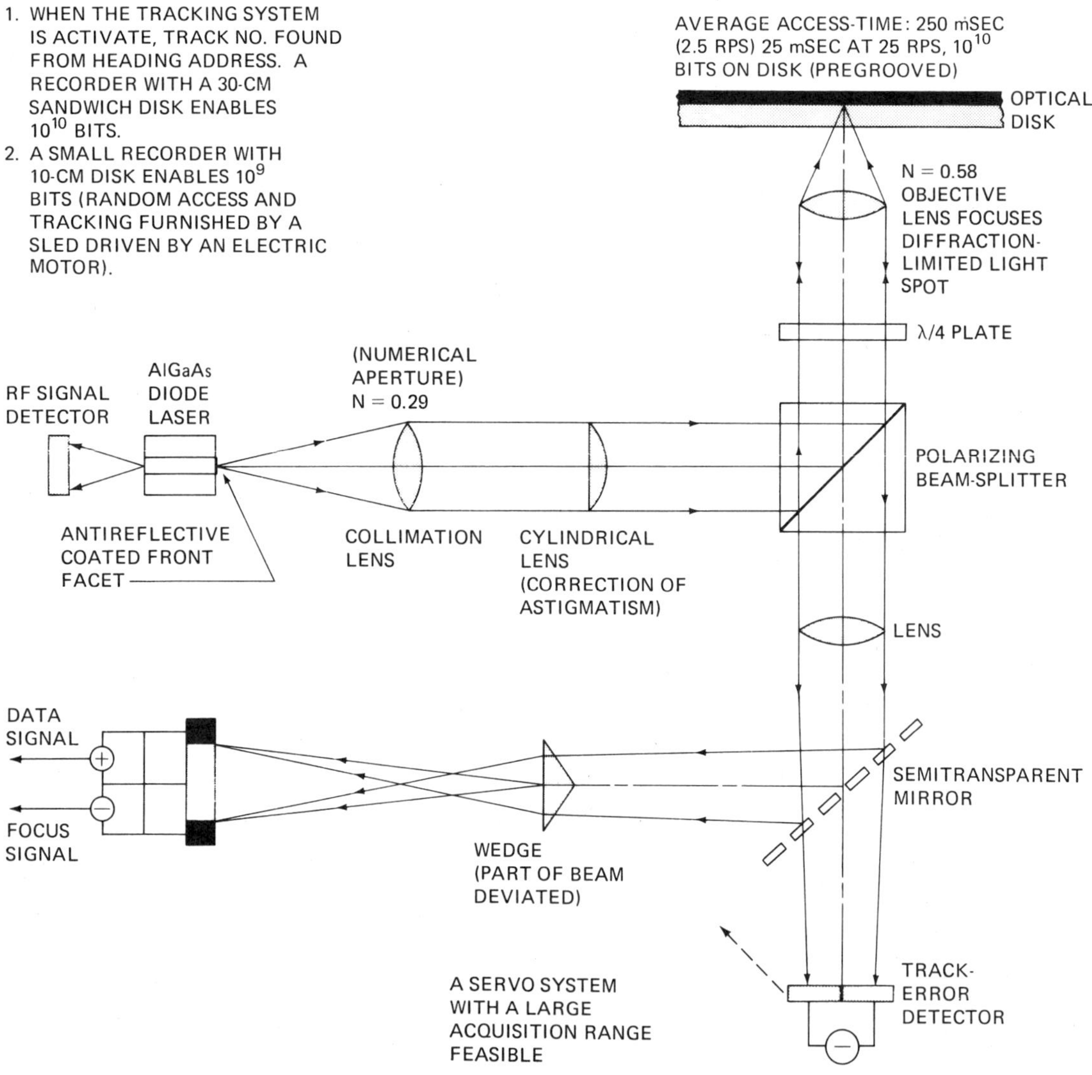

Fig. 4-11. Optics for the recording/read head. ©1979 IEEE, SPECTRUM, August, Kees Bulthuis *et al.*

The optical video disk storage is not a read/write device (data cannot be updated in a computer system); but it is attractive because at much higher recording density than magnetic recording, the stored information lends itself to replication for archival storage applications. The modulated laser beam is focused onto the spinning disk (either to produce a *master* from which copies are later printed or for directly prerecording upon an on-line storage medium) are explained in the above system. The retrieval takes place with a less-intense laser beam, and the modulated data are read or detected by light that is either reflected back or transmitted by the disk. In 15-MHz bandwidth video disks, about 5000 tracks/cm are used. In the high-density portable optical disk recording system, which effectively records 1's for a read-only storage, the photoresist or ablative thin-film make the high-power laser recording medium for the master.

4-10. MASS STORAGE (Vendors' information)

1. **Disk Cartridges**: Oxide-coated aluminum substrate is analyzed for contour and finish after sonic cleaning and rinsing. They are cure monitored and laser-tested for coating voids, and piezo-tested for smoothness. The molded plastic housing on disk cartridges protects data from harmful contamination. They are manufactured in two versions, for front-loading and top-loading. They are usually guaranteed to read/write error-free for 3 years.
   Examples: DEC RK05 (PDP-11, 15), Front loading, price, $85 ea.
   DEC RK06, 13.8-M bytes, Top loading, price $295 ea.
   IBM 1130, 2310, 2315, Front loading, price $85 ea.
   IBM 5022, 5440, 5444, Top loading, price $90 ea.
   Tracking density: 200 TPI (tracks/in.) maximum. Memory capacity varies from 5.2-M to 28-M bytes.

2. **Disk Packs**: To guard against contamination, an acid bath chemically treats the substrate for the proper adhesion of oxide coating. Durable and long-lasting surface is assured by the appropriate incline plane, and optical high-resolution laser-beam tested for coating voids and dispersion of coating. The disk-pack is finally dynamically balanced before format check and final packaging. The pack should not hit the spindle; top and bottom covers should not touch the platters. A chart is supplied by the vendor for the appropriate disk-pack for the available disk drive system. They are usually guaranteed to read/write error-free for a period of 3 years.
   Disk memories presently have the highest bit and track densities and are very cost-effective. The tiniest flaw in the coating can result in a "flag" (error), and it can affect the computer results. "Soft errors" are corrected by error-correction code (ECC) incorporated in the drive circuits; but these circuits cannot detect or correct in the case of "hard errors" (flags). Some drives, however, have special identifying circuitry for flags, so that the drive can assign an alternative track, resulting in an increased memory access-time. Diameter is 14 in.
   Examples: DEC, RP04, RP05, 88-M bytes, $497. (14-in. dia.)
   DEC, RP06, 176-M bytes, $710 each
   IBM, 3330, 3336, 100-M bytes, $497.
   IBM, 3330-11, 3336-11, 200-M bytes, $630.
   These high-density Gigabit mass-memory disk packs are used as *virtual memory* (VM) in central-node mini or large-scale computers in large networks.

3. **Flexible (Floppy) Disks**: The jacket container provides an antistatic, clean environment for handling and storage. The jacket interior is surfaced with a self-cleaning

and smooth material, so that it continuously wipes the floppy-disk from dust and debris from the disk surface. They are tested for uniform thickness, yield strength, flatness, and thermal sensitivity, and finally inspected for proper magnetic coating, amplitude, and resolution. The size and position of the center hole and the index hole are critical to reliable read/write performance and interchangeability; they are especially important in the case of double-density drives. Diameter is 8 in. Types of floppy disks:

Single-Sided: Data are written/read from only one side of the flexible disk.

Double-Sided: Data are written/read on both sides by a drive with dual heads. One pivotal head records or reads data automatically.

Reversible: Data are written/read from both sides. After one side is complete, one must manually turn the disk over (the disk jacket will have 2 identifying black dots against one dot for the above disks).

Single-density: Data are written on each of the 77 tracks at 3408 bits/in. (bpi).

Double-density: Data are written on each of the 77 tracks at 6816 bpi.

Sector: One of several fixed-length subdivisions that identify the data storage position. For a *soft sector*, one hole is used to synchronize the beginning of a track's data. Twenty-six sectors are allotted per track.

Hard sector: For a hard sector, the data content is higher than that for the soft sector. Each one of 32 sectors is assigned its own unique hole.

Shugart approved (one of the floppy-disk drive manufacturers): The flexible disk is tested at a higher clipping-level to permit a greater residual signal. This ensures better quality and reliability in the case of flexible disks. (see Section 12.7)

Examples: IBM 2305830 (Inmac Corp. 7870-KL), single-side, single-density, price $5.40 ea. (file of 10 minimum—blank disks without programs)
IBM 1669045 (Inmac 7859-KL), dual-side, double-density, price $8.00 ea. (file of 10 minimum)
Shugart approved (Inmac 7888-KL), single-side, single-density, hard sector, price $7.30 ea. (file of 10 minimum)
Shugart approved (Inmac 7886-KL), single-side, single-density, soft sector, price $7 ea. (file of 10 minimum)

Sturdy file-folders are used to prevent warping and oxide dropout problems.

4. **Minifloppy Disketts**: Diameter 5.25 in. (see Section 12-7)
   Examples: Inmac Corp., 7897-1-KL, hard sector, 16 sectors, price $4.15 ea. (File of 20 diskettes, 1 year guarantee for error-free operation)
   Vinyl minifloppy envelopes for insertion into binders is a common practice. Each envelope holds two diskettes. The diskettes are highly popular in personal computer applications.

5. **Mag-Tape**: A textured substrate backing on Mylar below the oxide-coating gives one confidence for a 10-year guaranteed error-free use. Uniform sliding action helps stop the damaging effects of cinched tape. Higher static-friction coefficient helps to prevent damaged tape edges. Conductive substrate helps resist scratches and reduce static which attract airborne debris.
   Examples: Inmac Corinthian tape-in-seals with 10-year guarantee:
   600 ft. reel, 7.5 in., $16 ea. (No. 7015-KL)
   1200 ft. reel, 8.5 in., $20 ea. (No. 7065-KL)
   2400 ft. reel, 10.5 in., $25 ea. (No. 7115-KL)
   These tape reels are also available in thin-line canisters.

6. **Mag-Tape Data Cartridges**: They should meet ANSI standards. For use with personal computers such as IBM-5100/5110, etc., 300-ft., 0.25 in.-wide tape cartridges are commonly used to give high-density and simultaneous recording applications for 1, 2, and 4-track applications.
   Example: Inmac 7257-KL, price $23 ea., guarantee 1 year

7. **Minidata Cartridges**: With a specially-formulated gamma ferric-oxide tape, low head-abrasion, and better head-to-tape contact, one-year error-free operation is guaranteed.
   Example: 140 ft./reel, Inmac No. 7255-KL, price $18 ea.

8. **Digital Cassettes**: Cassettes are guaranteed error-free for one year. They are rigorously tested for (1) high reliability, (2) decreased electrical surface resistance and light emittance, (3) greater resistance to humidity and heat, (4) enhanced recording density, (5) improved torsional strength, (6) prevention of skew errors, and (7) maintenance of exact pressure. The cassettes meet ANSI/ECMA/ISO standards.
   Example: DEC TU60, TA-8, TA-11, price $8.50 ea.
   IBM System/7, type 3651, price $6.50 ea.
   (Available from more than 30 manufacturers in the U.S.A. as a highly popular consumer product for personal computers.)

5 Memory Transfer Via Internal Registers

5-1. INTRODUCTION TO REGISTERS

A register stores a bit/byte/word temporarily; basically, one flip-flop per bit is required for this function. A number ranging from 0 to $2^n - 1$ can be stored by using n number of storage "latches" in parallel; a clock signal times the instant of "Set" and "Reset" or "Clear." In general, digital logic necessarily requires this latching and register function to process data according to the instructions in the program (software or firmware). As an example, when data-bits are shifted left, the last most significant bit (MSB) at left may be "rotated" to the least-significant-bit (LSB) position in a register or simply get lost according to the intent of the program. In general, microprocessors use several variations in this respect. Some registers merely provide an intermediate storage facility for later use of the word stored. The control section of the I/O buffers or registers, which have access to the external peripherals, determine according to software the transfer of information stored in these registers in a specific order. Thus, the "control" section of the microprocessor governs the procedural pattern or the architecture of the device. So, an individual programmer's capability is determined by the way one manipulates the sequencing of instructions and data in the various registers available in a minimum number of steps to perform a certain task or an algorithm, which one derives from a preliminary system flowchart. The I/O is an acronym for the input/output section.

The computer machine-language in binary-digit code can manipulate numbers as well as alphabetic letters in the format of numbers; this is data. The combined alphanumeric representation is termed information; this will then associate a specific meaning to the data. The short-form mnemonics, which abbreviate the instructions of the program, can be categorized as information, and the code it is put in then becomes data. Each instruction in a program is also allotted a sequential number for the use of the program counter, and each cell in the main memory is allotted an "address" number for keeping track of the information under transfer during computation.

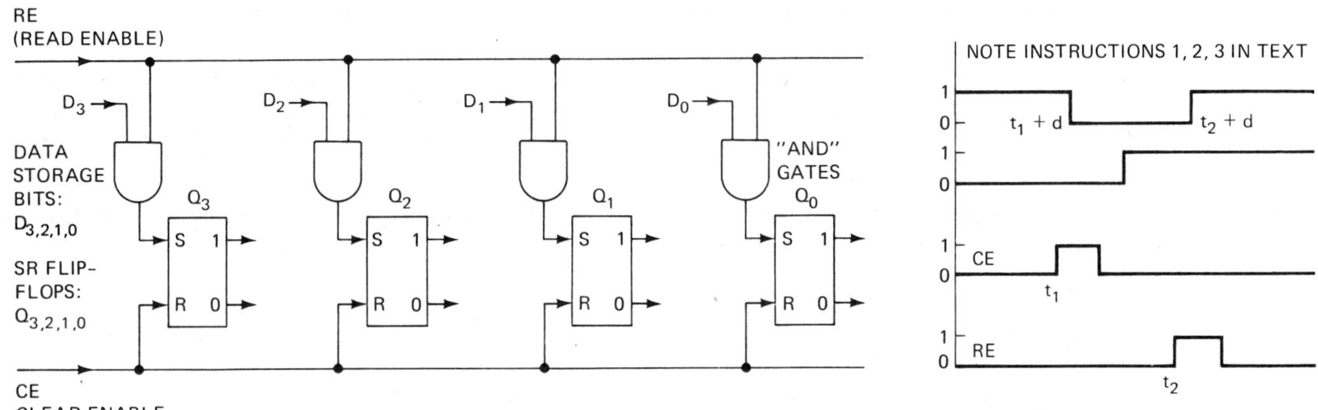

Fig. 5-1. Two-Step read data-storage and pulse timing diagram.

5-2. DATA-STORAGE REGISTER AND SHIFT REGISTER

A register is an assembly of flip-flop storage cells sharing common timing signals (pulses) and a common purpose. A *data-storage register* or *latch* will have the simple function of holding the data from the RAM or ROM memory temporarily as a buffer; and a shift-register will have the flip-flops connected in such a manner that at the end of each clocking pulse-sequence, the data in the flip-flop assembly is shifted one bit to the left or right.

The data-storage register is usually configured in one of two forms:

- *Two-Step Read* data-storage (Fig. 5-1)
  1. RE and CE should not be a logical "1" simultaneously.
  2. Data lines change only when RE is a logical "0" (Read Enable).
  3. After loading, data remain in the storage memory until CE is a logical "1" (clear Enable to Reset R).
- *One-Step Read* data-storage (Fig. 5-2)

A one-step read approach using a single timing signal is thus feasible by gating true and complement data inputs into the flip-flops.

The storage register may be designated, for example, as (8 X 2), (8 X 3). The 8 rep-

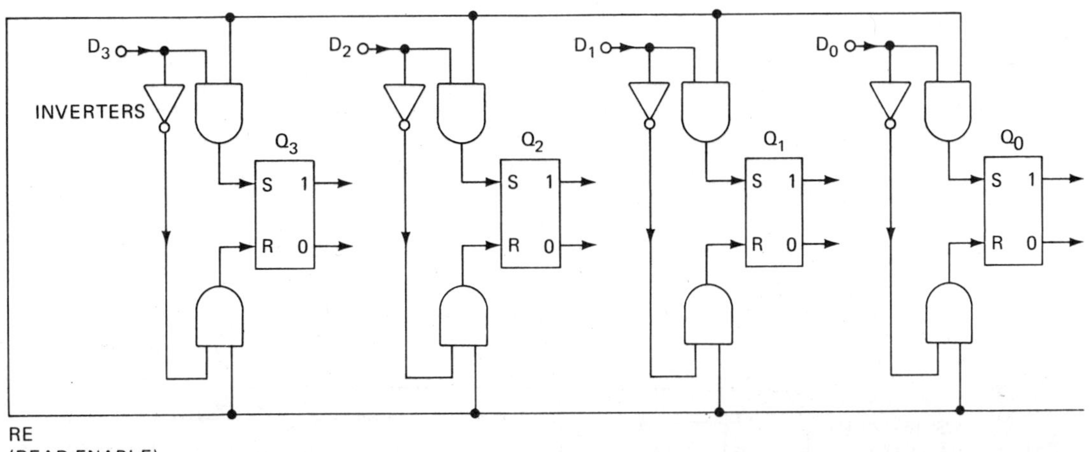

Fig. 5-2. One-Step read 4-bit data-storage.

resents the number of bits per character; the 2 or 3 represents the number of characters in the word.

By using one stored pulse, parallel data (all pulses occurring simultaneously, can be stored in a storage register; then by successively enabling the register for each character of 8 bits, parallel to serial conversion, can be accomplished. Corresponding bits of each register are OR-gated together.

The *shift-register* can be interpreted as a data storage register, which has, as its inputs, the output of a previous stage to its right or left, as shown in Fig. 5-3 in the right-shift register, using clocked J-K flip-flops (see Section 10-12).

1. Flip-flops in shift registers are conventionally numbered in sequence from right to left.
2. Shift-right input will be shifted into the left-most flip-flop.
3. Transitions take place on the leading-edge of the shift timing input signal.
4. Master-slave J-K flip-flop pairs are used to assure the shift of one-bit per clock-pulse (see Section 10-2). As a result, Set-Reset SR flip-flops are not used.
5. The pulse timing chart shows the shift-right pulse-train with respect to the flip-flop pulse timings.

Data are shifted along the chain simultaneously at each flip-flop in a synchronous mode, and all transitions take place at approximately within a time-ınterval that is short

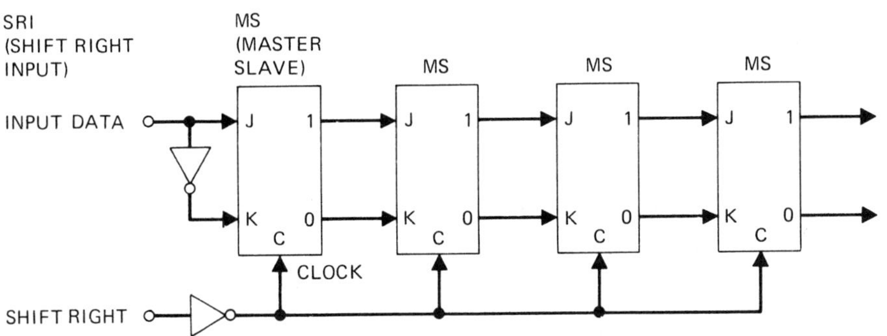

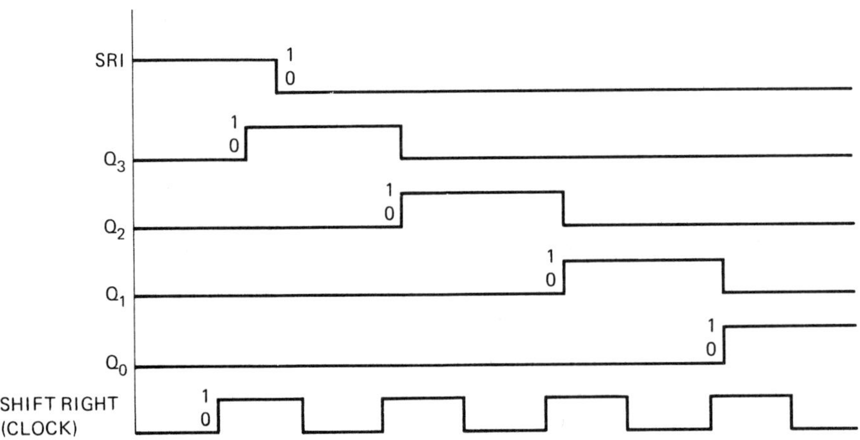

Fig. 5-3. Shift register (shift right) and pulse timing chart.

compared to the propagation-delay of each flip-flop. In high-speed systems, most medium-scale integrated circuit (MSI) shift-register chips commonly use master-slave (MS) flip-flops in order to satisfy the above condition of tolerance concerning propagation-delay of flip-flops. Note that for synchronous operation of circuits, a clock pulse-train input signal is required.

One of the important functions of a shift register is its function in arithmetic for multiplication and division. When a number is multiplied by 10, it is shifted to the left, and a zero is added as the least significant digit. Division, on the other hand, requires a right shift.

A shift register is also used for serial to parallel conversion of binary pulses. When the flip-flops in a shift register are individually set for such a conversion, the flip-flop function is denoted as *preset* or *direct set*. If a clock-pulse is present simultaneously, the flip-flops are set synchronously. Simultaneous use of *synchronous clock* and *direct set* enables a register to be used in either parallel or serial operation or a combination of both. (See Section 10-12.)

5-3. GENERAL-PURPOSE REGISTERS (GPR)

A general-purpose register (GPR) is a short-term storage and data-transfer device for data, such as a word consisting of 4, 8, 12, 16, 18, 24, 32, or 64 bits. The computer handles one word at a time. The microprocessors, presently handle word sizes up to 24 or 32 by bit-slicing techniques. Operations upon the word are at times, performed by bit-picking, editing, and masking—or by considering the word as a natural binary integer (counting number). A 16-bit register can address, for example, $2^{16} = 65{,}536$ memory addresses or locations.

Specific registers are used for such special purposes as program counter (PC), accumulator (for arithmetic operations), instruction register for instruction decoding unit, operand register for processing data, 1-bit carry register, memory-address register (MAR), and memory-data register (MDR) for transferring instruction or data between the CPU and the memory decoding circuits. SAR/SDR are alternative terms using S for storage.

In particular, GPRs in the form of CORE memory cells, instead of flip-flops, are not generally available for the use of the programmer. They can be used for general computing purposes in the control circuitry of the microprocessor system (for example, as RAMs for the registers of the arithmetic logic unit, RALU). Example: The main-frame IBM System-360 has ninety-six 32-bit fixed-point GPRs and four, 8-byte or 64-bit floating-point GPRs, along with 44 GPRs for miscellaneous control functions—all implemented as a local memory in the control unit.

In the case of microcomputers, eight or sixteen 8-bit (or two 8-bit bytes in parallel) general-purpose buffer registers are commonly used internal to the microprocessors, they are available to the programmer (generally). If required, they may be used by the programmer to control the instructions in a control ROM for processing the data in packets between the various sections of the microprocessor via the bidirectional bus system commonly provided. In larger computers, they may be allotted for fixed-point or floating-point arithmetic if a sufficient number of bits are available in each word. These are mainly bipolar, high-speed, parallel or serial-parallel, shift registers for moving data back and forth. Temporary transfer of data to a register effectively increases execution speed.

Registers and Microprocessors. The architecture of microprocessors is generally extended from one to three LSI chips, depending on their computational power. The functional distribution of the registers in these three cases is shown in Fig. 5-4. In the

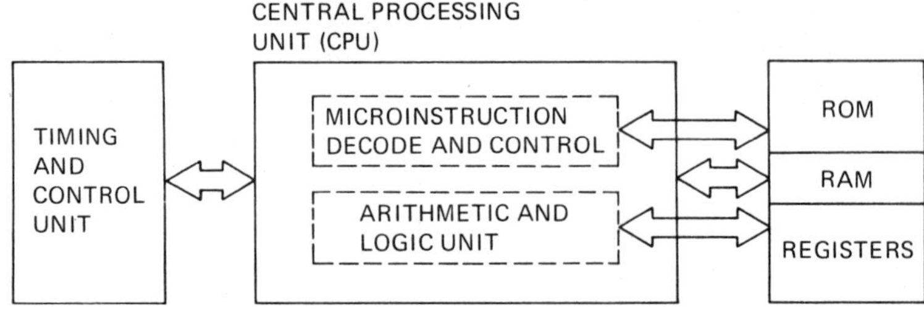

1. 3-LSI-CHIP VERSION OF MICROPROCESSOR ARCHITECTURE AND REGISTERS

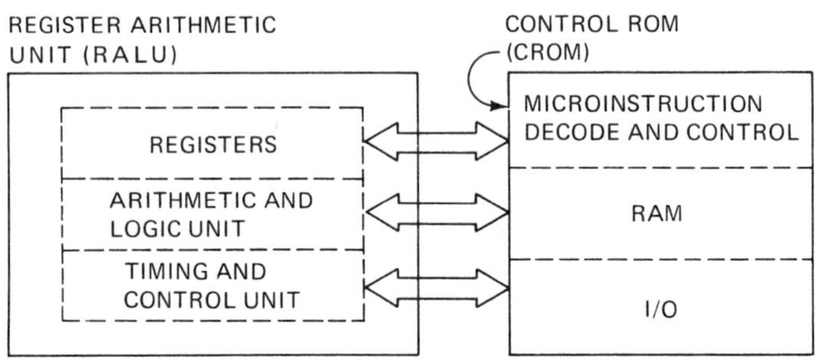

2. 2-LSI-CHIP VERSION OF MICROPROCESSOR ARCHITECTURE AND REGISTERS

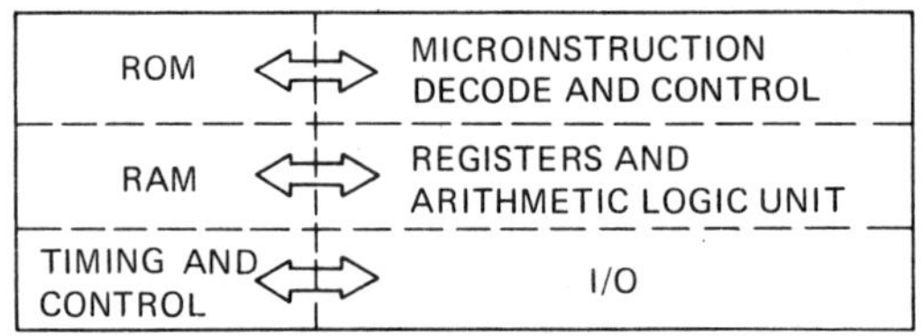

3. SINGLE-LSI-CHIP VERSION OF MICROPROCESSOR ARCHITECTURE AND REGISTERS

Fig. 5-4. The place of registers in three versions of microprocessor architecture.

case of a single-chip microprocessor, all decoding, timing and control circuits, registers, arithmetic logic unit, and a restricted amount of RAM and ROM memory are included. An external input/output chip is required in some cases to interface with the peripherals. In the case of a two-chip architecture, a control read-only memory (CROM) is exclusively used for decoding and control of microinstructions in the ROM area, while the registers, arithmetic logic unit, and timing and control are accommodated in a separate register and arithmetic unit (RALU). Lastly, in the case of a more powerful 3-chip architecture, CPU, registers, and timing and control circuits may be located in individual LSI chips with external ROM and RAM memory to approach the performance of one of the present minicomputers. As the LSI processing extends to the latest VLSI status, 16-bit single-chip microprocessors are capable of reaching equivalent computational power and throughput, to directly compete with present minicomputers in most applications.

5-4. COUNTERS

A counter counts pulses through a sequence of numbers, then resets itself to an initial timing value, and then repeats the counting process. In digital counting circuits, the basic binary counting cell (dividing by 2) can be asynchronous without the use of a clock pulse. Such asynchronous counting cells using flip-flops may be interconnected to form limited "ripple counters." Propagation delays of flip-flops add up to produce "spikes" in ripple counters. The binary counting unit requires additional logic gates in order to discriminate the leading and trailing edges of an input pulse-count. This condition allows the output to change value only after the input signal changes from a logical 1 to 0, that is, at the trailing transition of the input pulse waveform. A master-slave flip-flop unit, using two J-K flip-flops and additional logic gates, can meet this operational property. Hence, asynchronous MSI ring-counters commonly use master-slave flip-flops. As an alternative, edge-triggered flip-flops can be used by adding an inverter to the toggle input line.

Binary up-counters (or modulo-2^n counters) that count in an ascending order are directly derived from n toggle T flip-flops (see Section 10-12). *Modulo-n* is a *modern algebra* term. They start at logical 0-count, count to 2^n-1, and then reset to logical 0. If n = 3, the counter counts through successive binary numbers 0 through 7 as shown in the following *transition diagram* and *state table* for the three T flip-flops. J-K flip-flops can be used by connecting J and K inputs together as a T control-input.

Module-8 synchronous counter (divide by 8):

Present States (outputs)	Next States (outputs)	Control Inputs	Carry Output
Q_2 Q_1 Q_0			
0 0 0	0 0 1	0 0 1	0
0 0 1	0 1 0	0 1 1	0
0 1 0	0 1 1	0 0 1	0
0 1 1	1 0 0	1 1 1	0
1 0 0	1 0 1	0 0 1	0
1 0 1	1 1 0	0 1 1	0
1 1 0	1 1 1	0 0 1	0
1 1 1	0 0 0	1 1 1	1

State Table

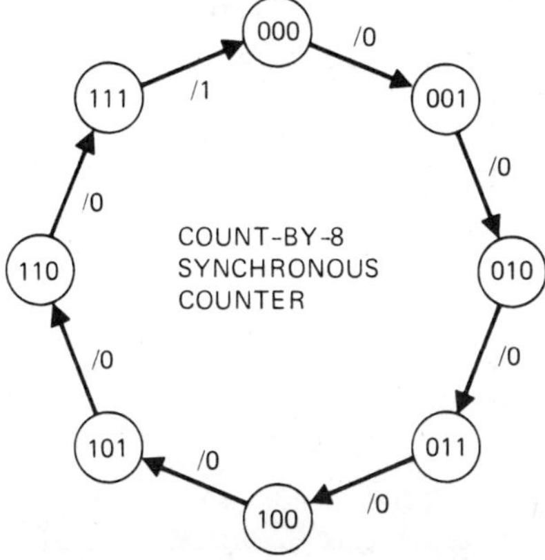

TRANSITION DIAGRAM

In some applications, *binary down counters* are used to operate on a descending order, to count backwards or down. The truth-table for the up-counter is merely sequenced top-down.

Where dual-mode operation is required, a synchronous modulo-2^n *up-down counter* can be designed, using an exclusive mode control line M; then count-down implies M is logical 0 and count-up implies M is logical 1. The circuit involves three additional NAND gates (AND-gate with inverter) for each master-slave flip-flop stage following the input master-slave stage. Up-down binary counters are commonly used in the design of analog-to-digital counters as shown in the following block-diagram. A digital-to-analog converter is required to provide a difference signal from a digital comparator, so that when the difference signal is positive (M = 0), the counter is counted down; it is counted up when M = 1. (See Fig. 5-5.)

5-5. ACCUMULATOR REGISTER (A OR B)

The one or two registers used between the arithmetic logic unit (ALU) and the main RAM memory (or the control RAM buffer in the I/O unit) are, in most microprocessors, designated as accumulators. The A register accumulates the results of (1) arithmetic operations; (2) Boolean logic decisions, such as AND, OR, and EXCLUSIVE OR; (3) comparison for equality with a memory word; (4) shifting or rotating bits to left or right; (5) testing the status of individual flags or bits; (6) test operations such as LOAD, STORE, SHIFT, and ROTATE; (7) complementing bits by INVERTERS; and (8) receiving or holding data for transfer to and from external devices via the I/O. These functions are of course performed by way of logic instructions in the mnemonic assembly language of the microprocessor.

The B register can be considered as the second part of the accumulator in some microprocessors to permit flexible and high-speed arithmetic. This register holds the results of arithmetic and logic operations, independently of the A register. The B register may be addressed by any memory reference instruction for inter-register operation in conjunction with the A register. However, the B register is not involved with the

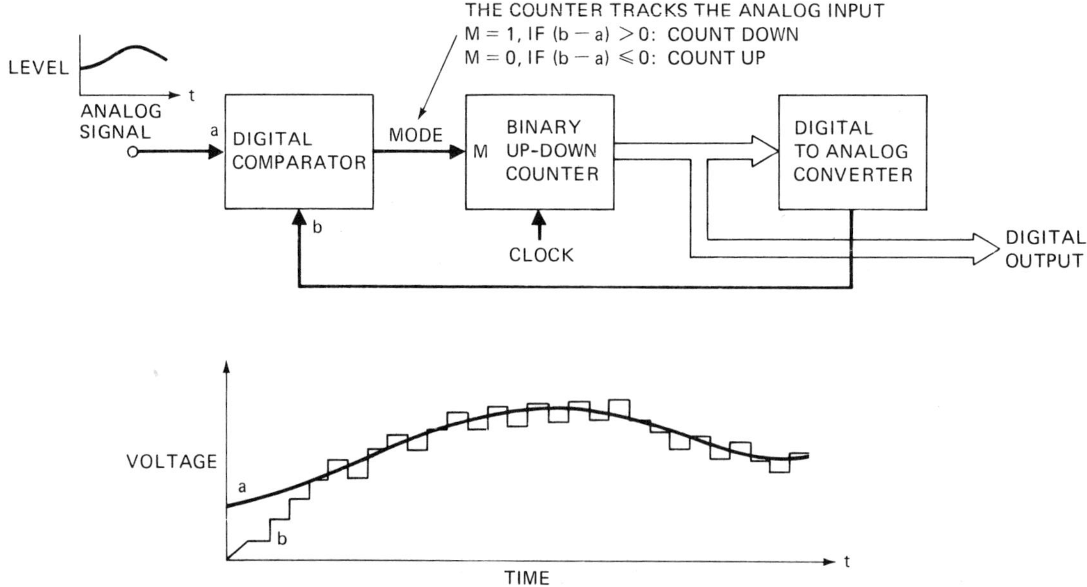

Fig. 5-5. Up-down binary counters.

Boolean logic functions. (Complex operations such as multiplication and division are usually programmed into the system either by software or by *microprogramming*. This software is being replaced by high-speed LSI hardware-multiplier chips, since software is a more expensive, slower operation. TRW Inc. manufactures a 16 X 16-bit multiplier TDC 1010J and 35-bit output accumulation in 115 nsec; 8 X 8: TDC 1000J, 70 nsec. 3.5 to 1–2 W, 5 V. $205–$95, respectively.)

As far as the instruction is concerned, it will involve two operands, the first usually coming from the memory location specified by the instruction, and the second coming from the accumulator. The result of the operation usually remains in the accumulator. In the case of a binary addition, the carry-out of the most significant can be lost from the accumulator unless it is recorded in a 1-bit *link* register.

5-6. SCRATCH-PAD MEMORY

A scratch-pad memory is generally an auxiliary group of registers (for example, 7 words X 8 bits) associated with the accumulator for the address-pointer manipulation of data in scratch-pad addresses. A scratch-pad address multiplexer and decoder are activated by the I/O control for this purpose. 16 X 4 RAM scratch-pad MSI memory chips are exclusively available. (Signetics Inc. 82S25 64-bit).

5-7. STACK-POINTER (SP)

This register performs the same function as the address-pointer in the ROM-microprogramming techniques—as if a secondary microprocessor with a dedicated memory (for example, in the form of a stack of registers) is performing a sequence of instructions under the I/O command of a simple macro-code word. A stack address multiplexer and decoder will be involved in sequencing the microinstructions stored in the I/O-ROM memory to address stack and program-counter (for example, 8 words X 16 bits) on a first-in, first-out (FIFO) basis or last-in, first-out (LIFO) basis. So, at present, the microprocessors have attained a powerful and elegant status by directly using microprogramming as a readily available tool in preprogrammed ROM—control-instruction memory. This fine-tune elegant technique was formerly available to large-scale computers that used the stack principle in hardware design, such as the Burroughs B5500. This facility is presently called *firmware*, since it is a means of converting software into hardware.

The functions of the stack pointer are:

1. The addressing mode of the external stack in the external memory is controlled.
2. Multiple-level interrupts can be conveniently handled, since the system status is saved and restored for an interrupt.
3. Unlimited *subroutine nesting* is rendered feasible, with one subroutine calling another subroutine.

In the Intel 8080 microprocessor, memory locations may be addressed via the 16-bit stack-pointer by way of just two stack operations: *push* for inserting data into the stack, and *pop* for receiving data from the stack (see Figure 5-6). The stacks are located in a static RAM memory for carrying out the read/write instructions. Since the stack-pointer is 16-bit, for push operation, the most significant 8 bits of data are stored at the memory address one less than the contents of the stack-pointer, and the least significant 8-bits of data are stored at the memory address two less than the contents of the stack-pointer. Then the stack-pointer is automatically reduced by two. For pop operation, the 16 bits of data are transferred from the *stack* memory area to a register pair or to the 16-bit

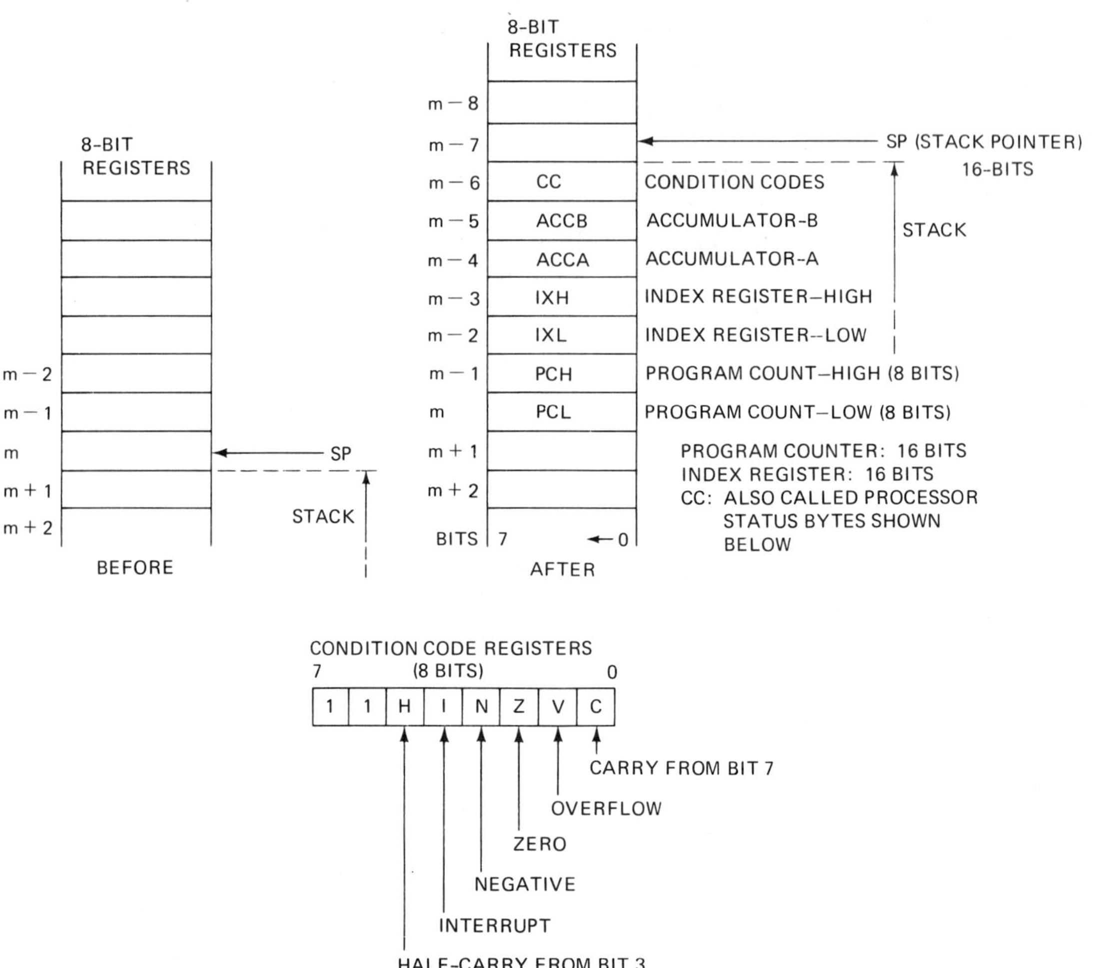

Fig. 5-6. Condition code register; status of results in ALU.

program counter. The addresses of the memory area to be accessed during the stack pop operation are determined by using the stack-pointer as follows: (1) the second register of the pair, or the least significant 8 bits of the program counter, are loaded from the memory address held in the stack-pointer; (2) the first register of the pair, or the most significant 8 bits of the program counter, are loaded from the memory address one greater than the address held in the stack-pointer; and (3) the stack-pointer is automatically decremented by 2. The programmer must initialize the stack-pointer before performing a stack operation to avoid erroneous results. (This is the procedure in expensive assembly programming; in high-level languages, these steps are replaced by a single command to the compiler-translator.)

The preceding example illustrates how the latest 16-bit microprocessors of the rank of Intel type 8086, and Zilog type Z-8000 considerably lessen the task of the assembly programmer and improve the computational power and throughput of microprocessors in order to reach the performance specifications of the present 16-bit minicomputers.

5-8. CONDITION CODE REGISTER

The condition code register indicates the *status* of results in an arithmetic logic operation of the microprocessor. Figure 5-6 describes how the order of saving the microprocessor status is manipulated within a stack in the RAM memory, when the programming instructions involve an interrupt for servicing a peripheral device.

5-9. DIRECT MEMORY ADDRESS

For direct addressing purposes, generally only two memory-pages (0 and 1) of a CORE memory or a static or dynamic RAM memory are allocated. Direct addressing combines the instruction code and the effective address into one word, thus permitting a memory reference instruction to be executed in two machine phases, "fetch" and "execute." (Indirect addressing uses the address part of the instruction word to access another word in the memory, which is considered as a new memory reference for the same instruction.) Direct memory addressing is the simplest addressing scheme for the address bits. The location of the instruction's operand, which specifies the operation to be performed, indicates the source or destination register. The address is of course fetched into the central processing unit of the microprocessor as a part of the instruction and loaded into the memory address register (MAR). If the fetched address needs modification, it is altered in the CPU and the modified address is reloaded in the MAR.

5-10. PROGRAM COUNTER (PC REGISTER)

After the completion of each instruction, the PC register indicates the address of the next instruction to be *fetched* out of the memory. The PC automatically increments by 1 (or more when executing a jump instruction) when the *execution* of the current instruction is completed. It is designated as a P register in some minicomputers. It can be tested through its full range by means of a mnemonic no-operation instruction in the program.

Program Counter and Timer. When it is necessary to monitor external events in real-time, a programmable counter/timer device is used in microcomputer applications. The timer of course needs control logic. The device can be addressed and accessed as a memory location, or in some cases as an I/O port, if the initial value of the 16-bit counter can be set under program control. As mentioned in the case of the PC register, with each clock-pulse input, the contents of the counter are decremented by one. In the case of a periodic clock pulse, the timer is programmable; if the external input signal is aperiodic, the device is called an *external-event counter*. The start signal for initiating the program counter/timer can be generated by hardware or program instructions. Whenever the count reaches zero, the device outputs an end-of-count (EOC) signal or flag.

For example, Intel's 8080 family of LSI chips furnishes a programmable counter/timer, 8253, with three independent programmable timing circuits. Each circuit is operated as an interval timer, an event counter, or a periodic clock-pulse generator and a single-shot. The following description of the various terminal pins (24) gives an idea of the actual usage of this chip in microcomputer applications.

1 through 8: Data bus, tristate bidirectional, D_0–D_7.
9, 10, 11: Timer 0 clock input C_0, output O_0, Gate input G_0, respectively.
13, 14, 15: Timer 1 output O_1, Gate input G_1, clock input C_1 respectively.

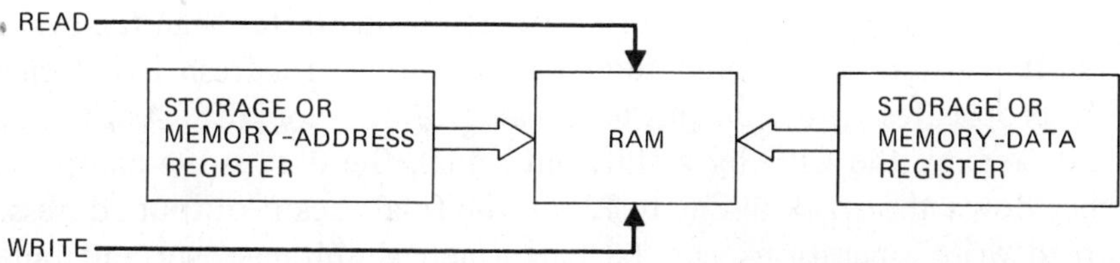

16, 17, 18: Timer 2 Gate input G_2, output O_2, clock input C_2, respectively.
19, 20: Register select input A_0, A_1.
21: Chip select input, CS.
22: Read control input, $\overline{IOR}$ (data bus control signal).
23: Write control input, $\overline{IOW}$ (data bus control signal).
24: V_{cc}, power input.
12: Ground input.

The Timer control logic in the chip controls the mode of operation, the method of counting, and the byte transfers involving the 16-bit counter, as the information from the data bus is read into the *8-bit control register*. The 8 bits of this register B7 through B0 select the modes of operation, the nature of the data transfer operations (when the timers are monitored by the microprocessor type 8080A), and the selection of the timer used for the mode of operation being set.

Mode 0: (B3, B2, B1) . . .	0, 0, 0.	
Mode 1:	0, 0, 1.	
Mode 2:	X, 1, 0 (X = don't care . . . either 1 or 0)	
Mode 3:	X, 1, 1.	
Mode 4:	1, 0, 0.	
Mode 5:	1, 0, 1.	
Latch counter value into register: (B5, B4) . . .		0, 0
Select low-order byte:		0, 1
Select high-order byte:		1, 0
Access low-order byte followed by high-order byte:		1, 1
Select timer 0:	(B7, B6)	0, 0
Select timer 1:		0, 1
Select timer 2:		1, 0

5-11. CACHE-MEMORY (DATA GENERAL)

This is a fast, relatively small semiconductor memory used as a supplement to the main memory. It is accessed by the CPU in minimum possible access time. Whenever the CPU calls for a word from, for instance, a 64-K byte main memory, a firmware algorithm transfers not only that word but also a block of adjacent words into the buffer cache-memory, since a well-written program usually requests words in proximity to each other. In practice, the cache may possibly contain several blocks of words from widely separated areas of the main memory, since in a well-devised software system with this facility, a large majority of the words requested by the processor may be quickly accessed in the relatively small cache-memory supplement. An optimized size can, however, benefit easy programming. (See Section 4-8 for *associative memory array* under data base management.)

5-12. FIRST-IN, FIRST-OUT MEMORY

The first-in, first-out (FIFO) serial-memory, using Schottky-bipolar MSI (or advanced I^2 L-LSI technique) promises to be an order of magnitude faster than the available single-chip FIFO shift register. Data preentered at the input of a fresh FIFO memory-stack automatically propagates to the output terminals without clocking. As the data from the output is collected by the CPU by a shift-out signal, the data subsequently inputted to the FIFO cues down the stack in-line to fill up the final vacant output address. With this technique, read/write operations can be performed simultaneously and independently without any synchronization. (If one uses a regular RAM for this purpose, only one operation can be performed during a given cycle, since only one address can be selected at a time.) The FIFO-memory makes a fine cache-memory.

The typical specifications of a FIFO stack-in memory are presented in Fig. 5-7a for the 28-pin MSI chip AM2813 of Advanced Micro Devices, Inc. Its major function is its buffering capability to accept and output data at two different rates. Whenever a device is ready to receive data up to 32 words of 9-bits each, the FIFO 3-state outputs are readily available at the rate the peripheral device can accept. Once loaded into the FIFO, which is organized as an array-type stack, the data words *ripple through* the FIFO ladder and line up at the output in sequence. The ripple-through time is fast enough for microcomputer applications. As a pointer-type organization in an empty stack, the FIFO allows the transmittal of an input data-word at the output instantaneously. If the device requires more than 32 words, two or three chips can be cross-connected in parallel with a common RESET connection to provide an overall stack handshake depth of 64 or 96 words. Where the word is 8-bit (without a redundant bit for a special use), the 9th bit will, of course, be grounded.

Last-in First-out Register Stack and Status Flags. As an example, the National Semiconductor Corporation's IMP-16C slice-oriented 16-bit microprocessor uses four 4-bit Register and Arithmetic Logic Units (RALUs). Each RALU constitutes an arithmetic section which includes a last-in first-out 16-word stack, along with an I/O multiplexer and 16 status flags. These flags can be stored and retrieved as a 16-bit register. The block-diagram of the complete 16-bit arithmetic section signifies the operation of the LIFO stack and the status flag register (Fig. 5-7b). Since each RALU, as a slice, provides for 4-bits, the 16-bit LIFO stack and the 16-bit flag register require four RALU units in this 16-bit CPU. One or two control ROMs (CROMs) are used on the control bus for *microprogramming* this arithmetic section. (See Section 8-31.) The CROM unit serves

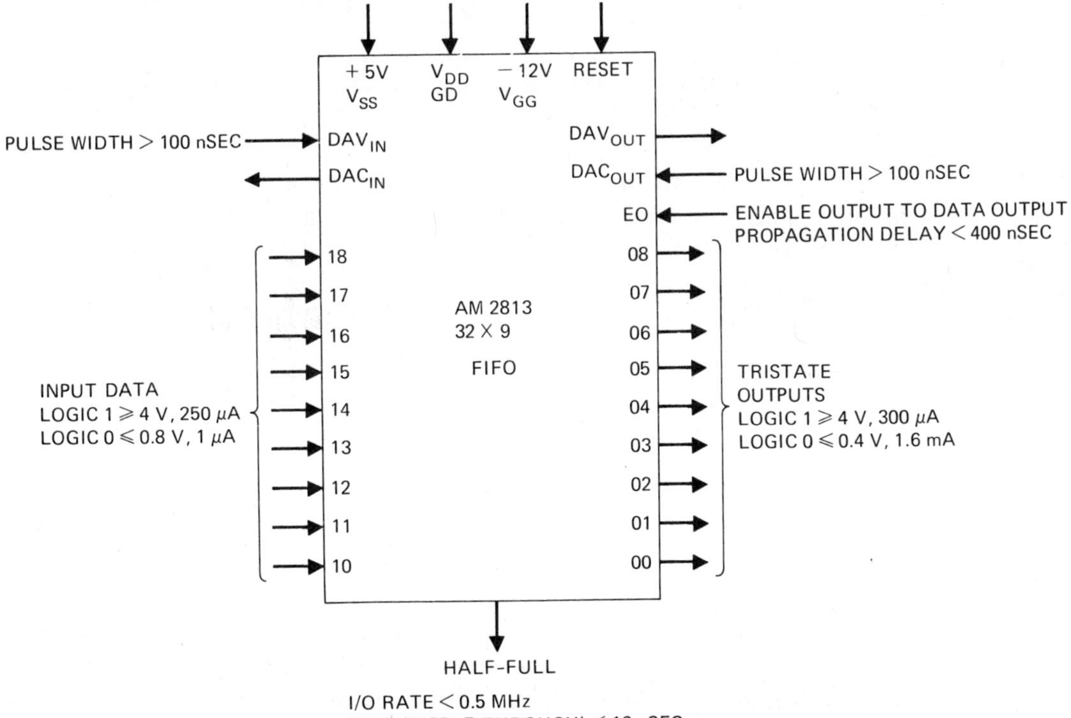

Fig. 5-7a. First-in first-out (FIFO), Advanced Micro Devices, Inc; type Am 2813: 32 X 9.

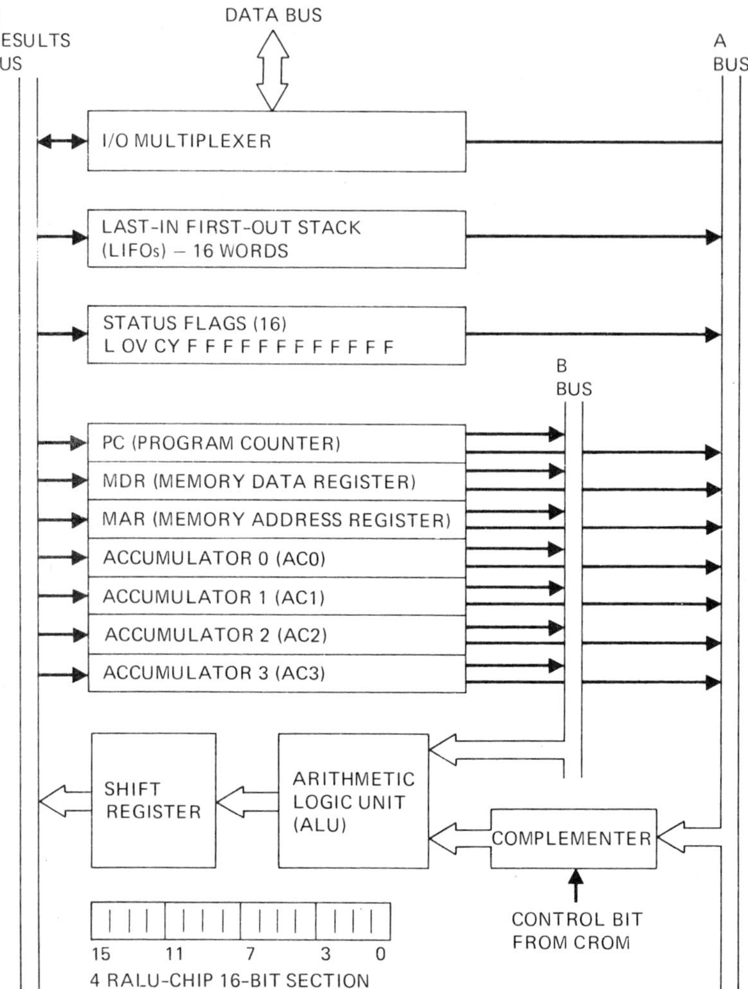

Fig. 5-7b. Last-in, first-out (LIFO) stack and status flag registers in IMP-16C arithmetic section. (Courtesy of National Semiconductor Corporation)

the function of ROM address control, control logic, and 100 words of microprogrammed address and contents. The contents of the four RALU 16-bit registers may be loaded onto the A-bus. The 16-bit data from the top of the LIFO stack and from the status flags, are combined as 16-bit words; these data may be loaded as operands, while the CROM microprogramming control logic complements the data. The data from the RALU via the ALU and shift register is transmitted to the CPU data bus by means of the I/O multiplexer. The contents of the RALU registers, loaded onto the B-bus, may be loaded into the ALU to transfer the results of the ALU operations to the LIFO stacks, and the RALU flags.

LIFO stack. The 16-word high LIFO stack is accessible via the top shelf (location). Note that this word-stack is actually the combination of the four 4-bit RALU slices that make the arithmetic section.

The 16-bit data word is entered via the results R-bus and retrieved via the A-bus; as a new word is inserted into the top shelf, its current 16 bits are pushed down one level. Then the contents of each succeeding lower level are in turn replaced by the contents of the next higher location, so that the contents of the bottom location get lost. On the other hand, if a word is retrieved from the stack, the process reverses to necessitate the insertion of "0"s in the vacant bottom shelf, because the last-in at the top shelf is the first-out. The LIFO stack is in principle used (1) for saving the status during interrupts, (2) for temporary storage of subroutine return addresses and (3) for temporary storage of data with a special instruction.

RALU System Status Flags. RALU system status flags are single-bit status flags (pulses) that are stored and retrieved from a 16-bit register. The flags used in the arithmetic section are Link flag (L), Carry flag (CY), Overflow flag (OV), and 13 general-purpose flags. Link, Carry, and Overflow flags make the first, second, and third most significant bits. Whenever these status flags are activated, the entire 16-bit status word in complemented. They are manipulated by pushing them onto the stack for temporary storage during interrupt processing; after the completion of interrupt service, they are transferred back to their respective flag flip-flops.

5-13. DIRECT-MEMORY-ACCESS (DMA)

The I/O interface generally transfers data directly to the memory unit by means of a special register. The processor indicates this specific type of transfer by supplying the interface with a starting memory-address and a word-count and then proceeds to attend to other tasks. When a transfer is to be made, the interface requests a memory cycle-time and, when acknowledged, causes data to be transferred directly to memory as the processor halts for the cycle-time. The logic that performs this transfer is termed a *channel*; it contains a memory-address-register to control the location in the memory to/from which the data is transferred. It may also contain a word-counter to keep track

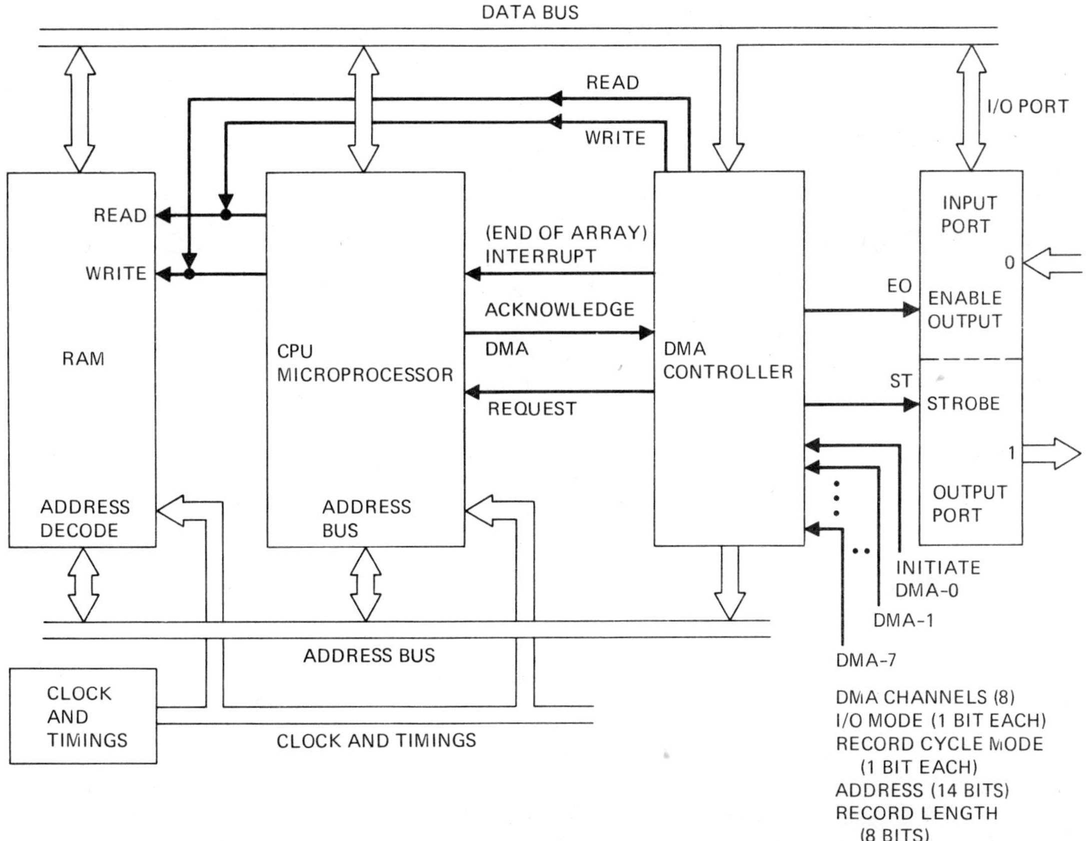

Fig. 5-8. The interconnections of a DMA controller to the CPU.

of the number of direct memory-transfers made. Circuitry must be provided for all related operations, such as timing and control signals. By this means, a processor is allowed to spend minimum time for I/O processing. DMA is mandatory in bulk-data batch-processing applications, such as the CRT terminal.

The major components required in a DMA input transfer are a request flip-flop, address register, and data register for the use of the peripheral device. The transfer of a block of data actually involves initializing the DMA logic to start the DMA during repeated cycle-stealing steps, and terminating the DMA through a program interrupt routine to switch back to the main program. The data output transfer from the computer memory registers is accomplished by buffering into the DMA output lines. Figure 5-8 illustrates the inter-connections of the CPU, the RAM main memory, I/O, and the DMA controller. As an interesting example, RCA Cosmos (CMOS) microprocessor (type 1802) has a built-in DMA facility. The CPU of the chip uses its 16-bit, 16-register array as data pointers to indicate the address locations in the RAM memory. A specific scratch-pad register R(0) in this stack assumes the role of the data pointer during the DMA operation. When a DMA-In or DMA-Out request is received, one machine cycle is "stolen" at the end of the *execute* machine cycle in the current instruction. The data are read from (DMA-Out) or written in (DMA-In), the memory location pointed to the R(0) register. At the end of the transfer, R(0) is incremented by one so that the CPU is ready to act upon the next DMA byte-transfer request. When fast exchanges of data are mandatory in the case of magnetic disk memory or during CRT display-refresh cycles, this built-in DMA facility saves a substantial amount of logic normally required in DMA controllers. Also, a program-load facility with the DMA-In channel is available as a one-step procedure to

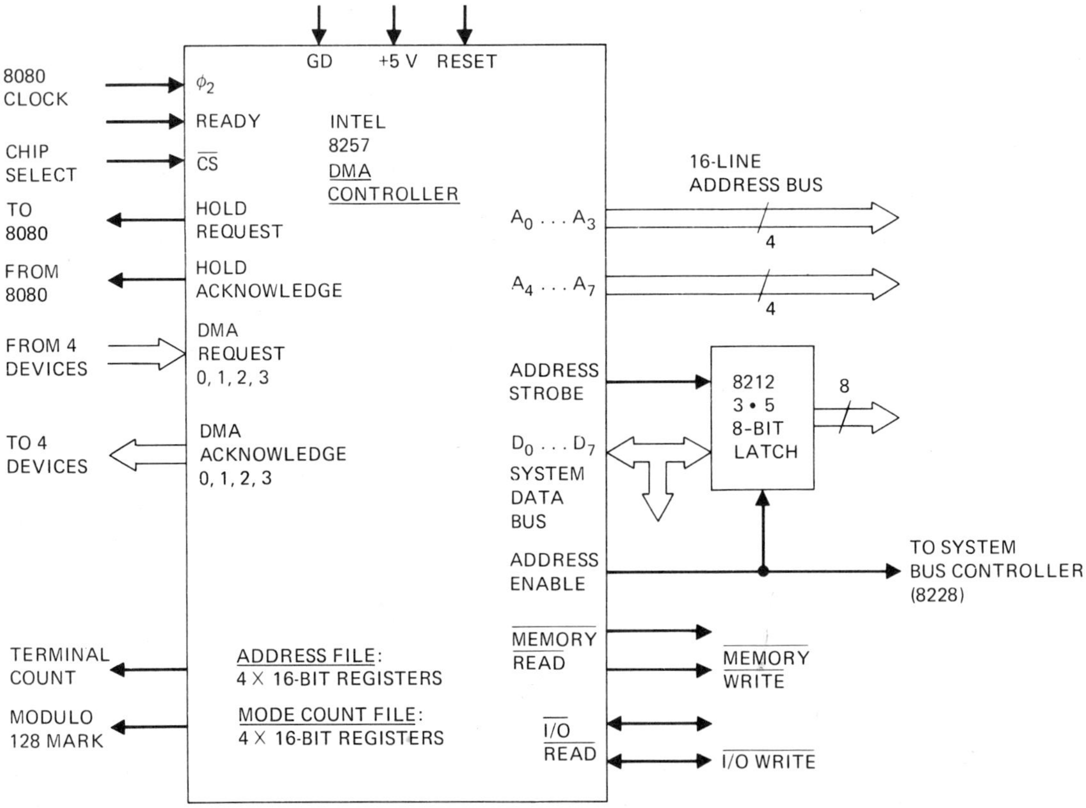

Fig. 5-9. Interconnections of Intel 8257 DMA controller in a microcomputer system.

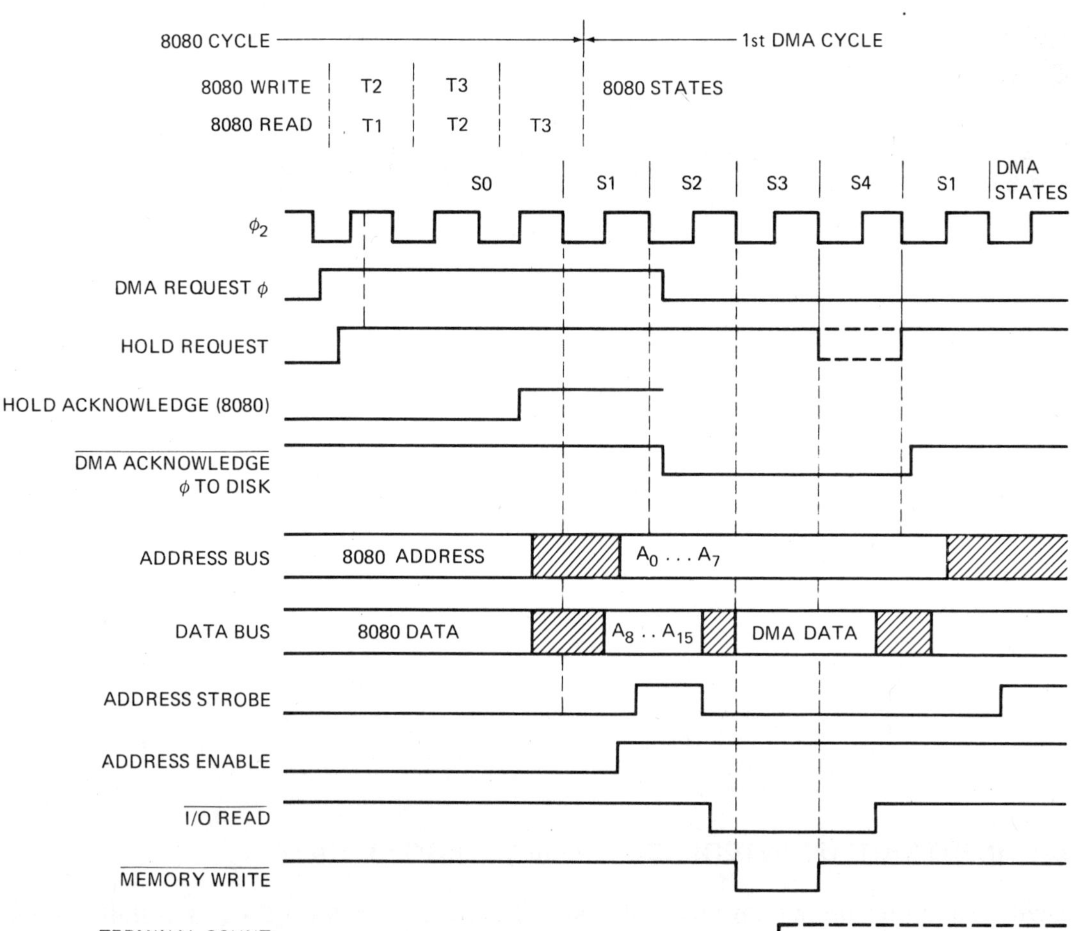

Fig. 5-10. Timing waveforms of DMA cycle.

enable user's load programs into the memory. Thus, specialized program-initializing "bootstrap" ROMs are eliminated by this fine on-chip DMA facility.

INTEL DMA Controller, Type 8257. LSI chips of the category of former 8008 8-bit microprocessors require a considerable effort of programming to provide the DMA function, using external hard-wired MSI logic. Intel 5-V NMOS 8257 DMA controller eliminates the software effort and considerable MSI hard-wired logic design. It contains eight 16-bit registers and control logic.

Intel 8257 can provide for four DMA devices on a priority basis; 8257s can be cascaded to provide for larger number of DMA channels. The details of the interconnection of this chip to the popular 8080 microprocessor are illustrated in Fig. 5-9; the timing waveforms of a DMA cycle are shown in Fig. 5-10. System address and data-buses are conventionally switched between the CPU and the DMA controller by a tristate switching facility (See Section 2-8.7.) The availability of LSI chips of this category makes it clear that the replacement of expensive software by *low-cost* hardware is an obvious time-saving trade-off in high-speed data processing. The increasing popularity of LSI microprocessors in former high-cost main-frame large-scale and minicomputer applications is hence a natural trend at present.

6
Input/Output Interface

6-1. INPUT/OUTPUT INTERFACE: TYPICAL DIGITAL DATA

Digital computer users conventionally establish requirements for the physical, functional and electrical characteristics of the desired I/O Interface for transfer of digital data from the peripherals to the digital computer. It is the task of the Interface designer to provide the necessary hardware to implement this function in terms of the following bidirectional signals.

1. **Parallel data transfer** on twisted pairs up to 4-K 16-bit or 18-bit words on one cable. Binary voltage levels of 0-V(logical-1) and minus 3-V(logical-0) is one standard as an example.
2. **Serial data transfer of words** up to 64-K bits/sec on one twisted pair. (Bipolar ±3.25-V levels.)
3. External Interrupt Enable line
   External Interrupt Request line
   Input Data Acknowledge line
   Input Data lines
   External Function Request line
   External Function Acknowledge line
   Output Data Request line
   Output Data Acknowledge line
   Output Data line
   Input Enable, Output Enable, Control Frame, etc.
4. Drivers and receivers used for sending and receiving the signals on the twisted pairs are in practice differential amplifiers for the signal and its return. Conventionally, both the signal and its complement are sent on two adjacent twisted pairs.

5. Besides the preceding signals, in the case of synchronous digital processing, a digital clock and a strobe pulse-timing for the word accompany the above signals on separate twisted pairs. If provision is not made for a parity-bit in the regular words along with a sign-bit, as in the case of the 18-bit word computers, a separate twisted pair may be specified for the parity check-bit.

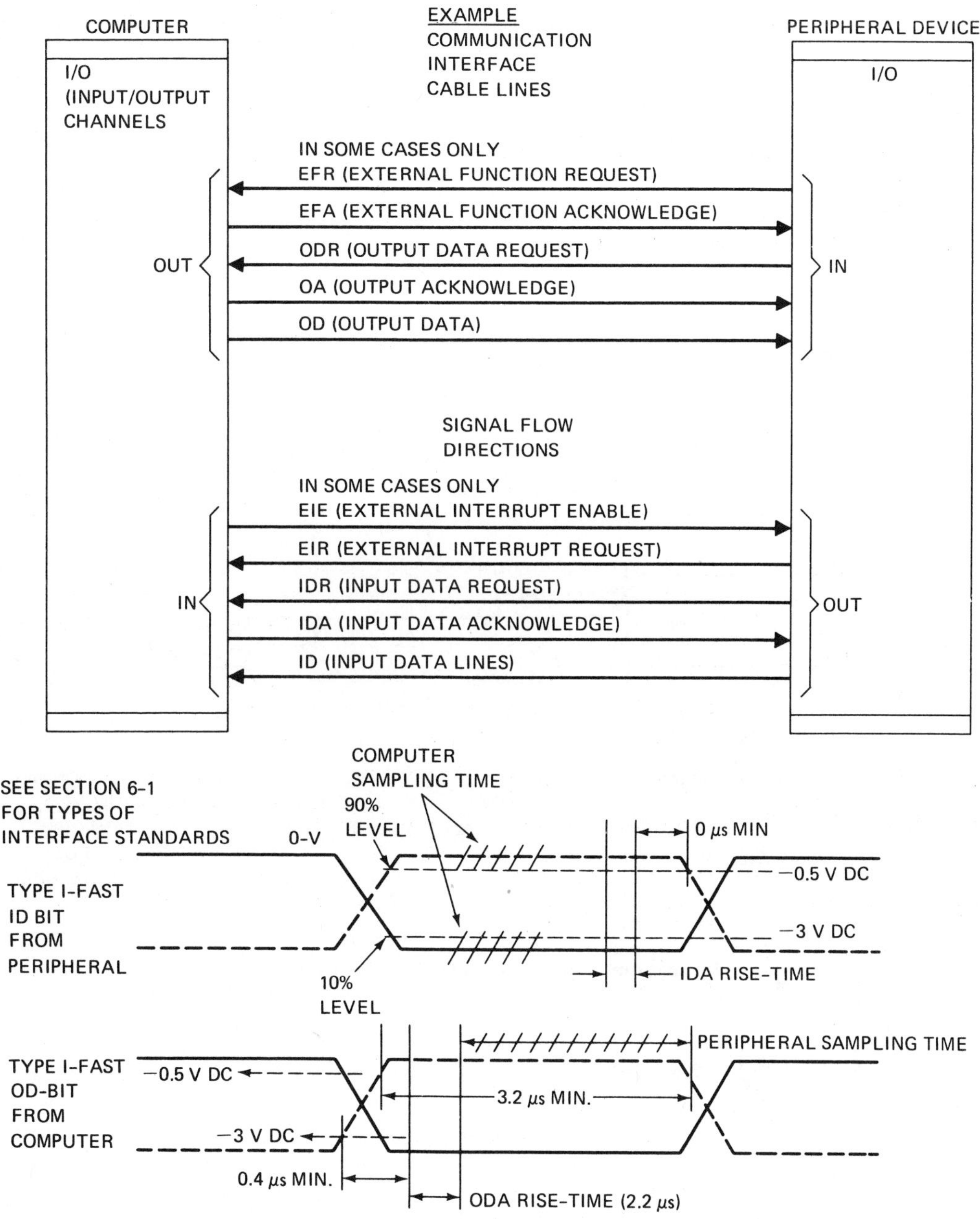

Fig. 6-1a. Typical interface "handshake" signals of a computer and a peripheral device. Pulse waveform timings.

Typical I/O Interface "Handshake" signals of a computer and a peripheral device are shown in Fig. 6-1a, along with typical pulse waveform timings. Figure 6-1b indicates bipolar high-speed real-time Microcontroller timings as a comparison (Signetics Microprogram control unit type N3001).

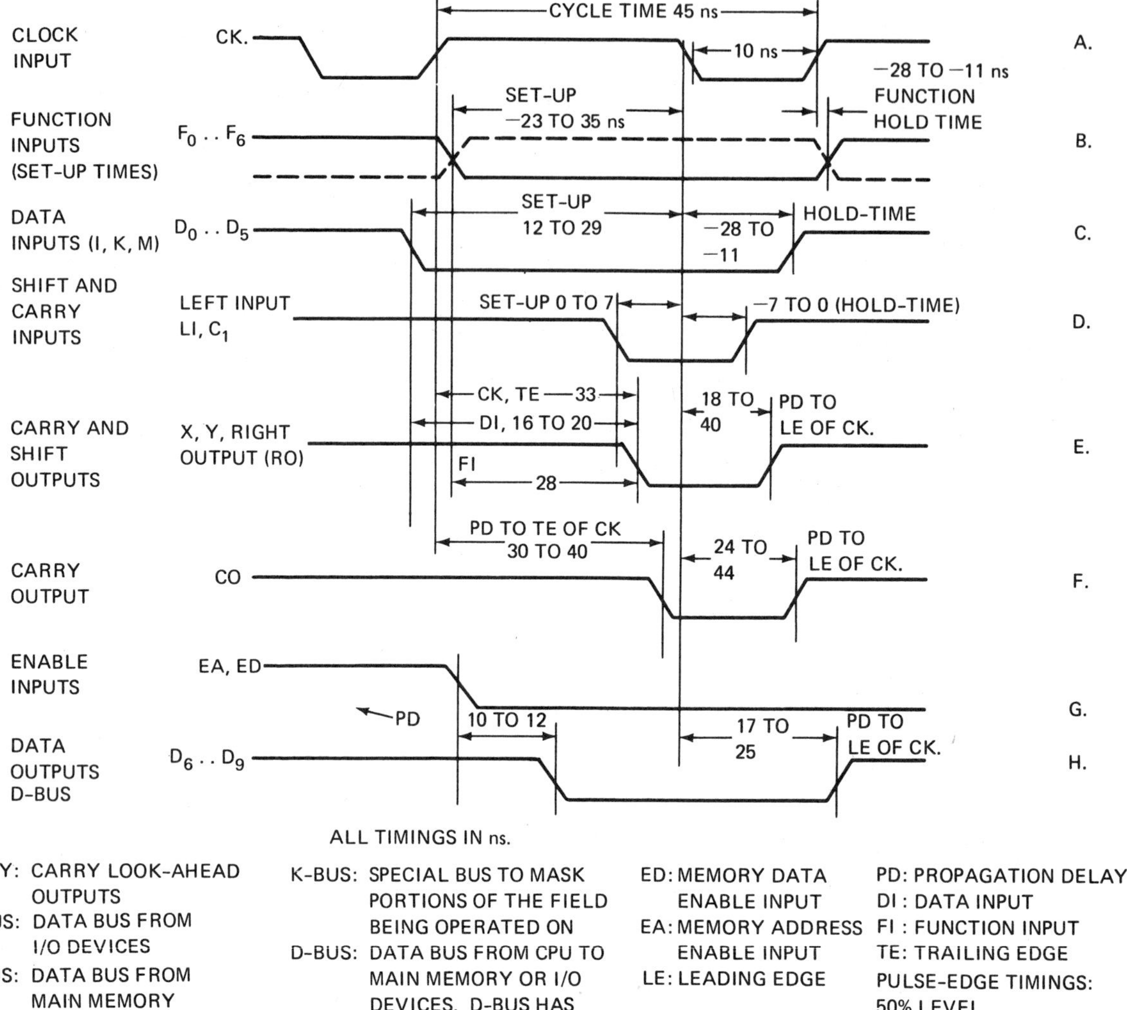

Fig. 6-1b. Bipolar "high-speed" real-time microcontroller (MPU) timings (compatible to latest high-speed minicomputer CPU timings). (*Courtesy of Signetics*)

6. Some of the preferred standards of data transfer to a computer are specified in the following table.

***Interface* (I/O) parallel transfer/cable**

Data Transfer Words/sec; TYPE	Bit 1	0	Logic
I: SLOW 41,667	dc	-15 V	positive
I: FAST 250-K	0	-3 V	positive
II: FAST 250-K	0	+3.5 V	negative

SERIAL: 10-M bits/sec/cable. Bipolar ±3.5 V.

6-2. BUILT-IN INPUT/OUTPUT SECTION OF A MICROPROCESSOR

1. The I/O busses of the Microprocessor apply 4/8/16 bits in parallel, per port, to the bus leading to the peripherals via the Interface MSI chips (or LSI) as shown in Fig. 6-2.
2. There will be a number of I/O ports for each microprocessor.
3. Where the number of I/O ports are excessive, a multiplexer and a serial format are used between the I/O bus and the interface units. The I//O will generally use a serial to parallel data converter to communicate with the device in circuit at any instant.
4. Although all the peripheral Interfaces are connected in parallel, only one of them will be able to decode the device-address issued in the I/O instruction. The other Interfaces will not be able to decode that address, and hence they remain inactive.
5. The general form of the I/O instruction word-format follows:

		OPERAND FIELD	
GROUP CODE	OPERATION CODE (OPCODE)	DEVICE ADDRESS CODE	FUNCTION CODE

The opcode specifies the instruction from one of the general groups of I/O instructions noted below:

INPUT: A word of data is read from the selected peripheral and placed in a working register.

OUTPUT: A word of data is transferred from the relevant working register to the selected peripheral.

CONTROL: A signal is issued by the microcomputer I/O to command a specific control function of the peripheral.

SENSE: The status of the peripheral Interfaces is tested. Conditional branches, which occur in the program, depend on this testing.

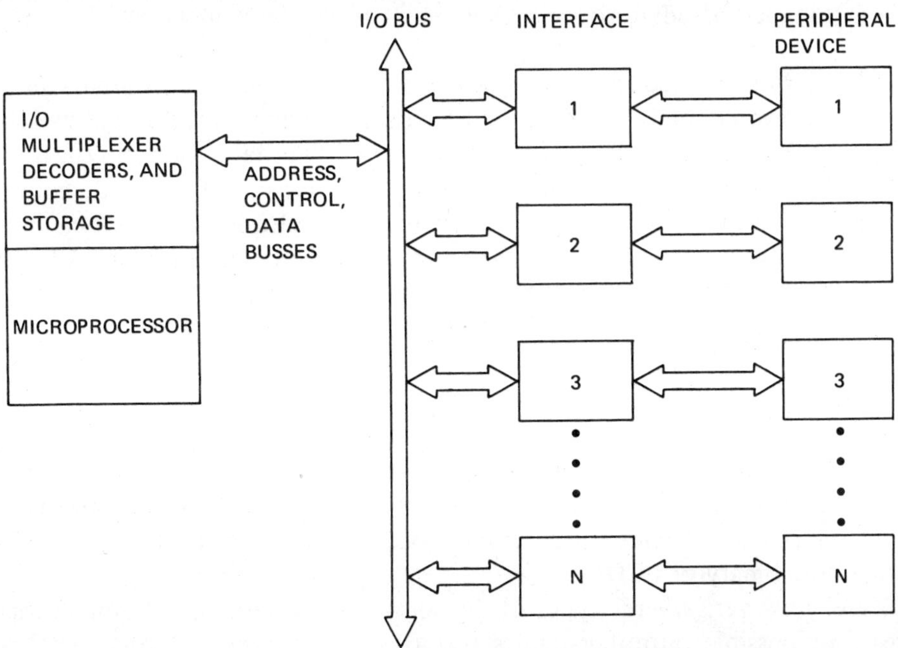

Fig. 6-2. I/O-bus and peripheral devices.

6-3. MULTIPLEXER OR MULTIPLEXER CHANNEL

It is the "channel controller" of a digital computer, connecting several peripherals, either directly or via a common or individual "device controller." Each one of these may in turn take the form of a microprocessor, if they are connected to a central large-scale, medium-scale, or mini-computer. The multiplexer enables the computer to interface with not only the fast devices or peripherals but also slow devices such as TTYs and telephone line-conditioners or data-access units.

The multiplexer thus takes the form of a computer-within-a-computer. Actual data exchange between the main computer and the peripheral device or network terminal takes place at such a slow rate that it is possible to simultaneously service tens or even hundreds of such devices with a single channel-controller. A special microprocessor could be employed as a built-in CPU for the multiplexer and its control, while the multiplexer itself functions as an integral Interface for the main computer.

A peripheral may provide information in bytes or characters that differ in size (number of bits) from those of the words stored in the main memory of the computer. The multiplexer channel must do the necessary reformatting of the data or the instruction words from the peripheral device or the terminal.

Direct communication between the main memory and the multichannel controller can be also achieved by **cycle-stealing** without the awareness of the computer "control" system. The channel sneaks into the main memory and steals a memory cycle for the I/O; most often, the computer may not be held up at all when this transfer takes place.

"Polled" is synonymous with "multiplexed." A digital multiplexer or encoder is in principle equivalent to a single-pole multiposition switch. It is a **combinational logic** network with 4, 8, 16, or more, input or data lines, one synchronized output line (and a complement of output-line), and i-control or data-select lines, where 2^i is the number of input lines. Combinational logic is realized by appropriate application of the input variables or binary constants to the data and data-select inputs. Conversely, a Decoder/Demultiplexer is a combinational network that handles serial input-data, i control inputs, and 2^i outputs, where each decoded output is unique. A combinational logic network is the part of digital logic that does not include memory elements such as flip-flops.

A multiplexer or an encoder may in principle have any number of inputs and outputs; at any instant, several combinations may be true depending on the actual switching logic used. The corresponding "polling" configuration will then take the form of, for instance, a 4-pole, 4-throw switch. A decimal to binary-coded-decimal (BCD) code converter may be called a decimal to BCD/8-4-2-1 weight **encoder** or **multiplexer** since it can multiplex a 10-line input to a 4-bit binary equivalent on 10 X 4 outputs, if required. A typical open-collector 3-input, 4-bit digital multiplexer is illustrated in Fig. 6-3; it is analogous to a 4-pole, three-position switch. (See Fig. 10-15.)

6-4. DECODER/DEMULTIPLEXERS

Corresponding to the multiplexing polling function just described, the multiple-line decoders do the reverse code-conversion process such as obtaining the 10-digit decimal equivalent on 10 output lines for a binary input bit-set of say four weighted lines (8-4-2-1), either pure binary or BCD, etc.

There are, however, several types of decoders. For example, a 2-input variable code produces four possible output variables (00, 01, 10, 11); and a 3-input octal code produces eight possible outputs. The device implementing the necessary logic in these cases

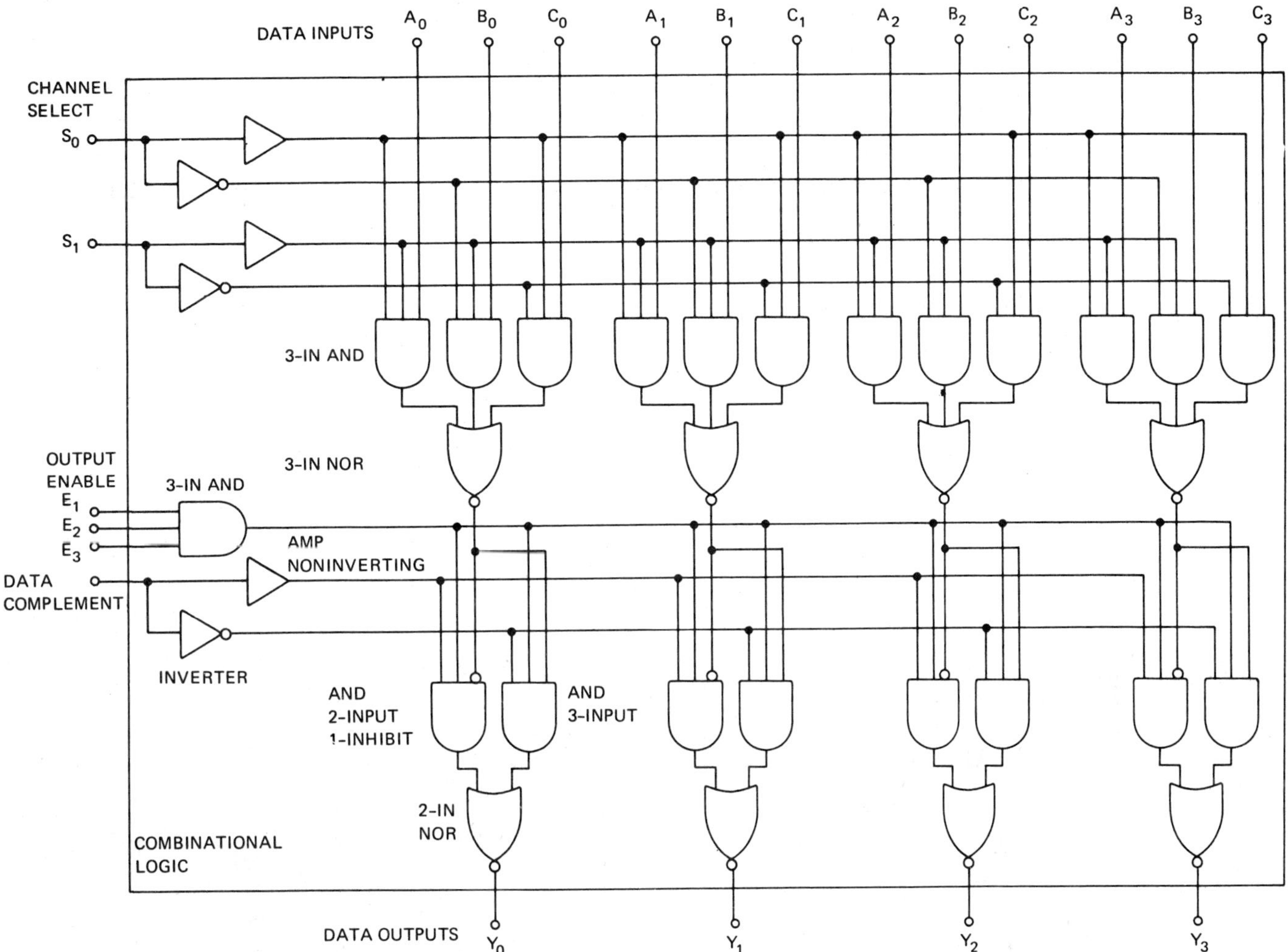

- FOR STORAGE, FOUR INVERTERS AND FOUR R-S FLIP-FLOPS ARE INCLUDED IN THE CHIP WITH A CLOCK INPUT.
- TWO-INPUT CHANNEL-SELECTION CODE DETERMINES WHICH INPUT SHOULD REMAIN ACTIVE.
- DATA COMPLEMENT INPUT CONTROLS CONDITIONAL COMPLEMENT CIRCUIT AT THE OUTPUT TO EFFECT EITHER INVERTING OR NONINVERTING DATA FLOW.
- OPEN-COLLECTOR OUTPUTS ALLOW EXPANSION OF INPUT TERMS.

- EXPANSION: OF ABOVE MSI CHIP TO FOUR-POLE 24-POSITION SETUP
  1. CONNECT ABOVE OUTPUTS TO THE OUTPUTS OF ANOTHER SIMILAR MULTIPLEXER.
  2. PROVISION IS MADE FOR USE OF A 3-BIT CODE (OUTPUT ENABLE E_1, E_2, $E_2 \equiv 2^0, 2^1, 2^2$ AND COMPLEMENTS) TO DETERMINE WHICH MULTIPLEXER IS SELECTED. THUS, EIGHT MULTIPLEXERS ARE USED TO EFFECT A FOUR-POLE 24-POSITION SWITCH.
  3. OPEN-COLLECTORS: USE COMMON COLLECTORS WITH EXTERNAL PULL-UP RESISTORS (ONE/4 OUTPUTS) AND USE OUTPUT ENABLE CODE.

Fig. 6-3. A typical open-collector, three-input, 4-bit digital multiplexer. (TTL MSI-chip; analogous to four-pole, three-position switch). Type 8263, Signetics. (*Courtesy of Signetics*)

to produce an output that indicates the state of the input variables is also a decoder. In this classification, a "majority decoder" using three input variables produces one true output only when two or three inputs are true; the corresponding "minority decoder" produces one true output when only one input is true; if an odd or even number of true inputs produce a true output, the decoders are odd or even, respectively. Similarly, special-purpose counter readouts, adders, subtractors, parity comparators, etc. can be classi-

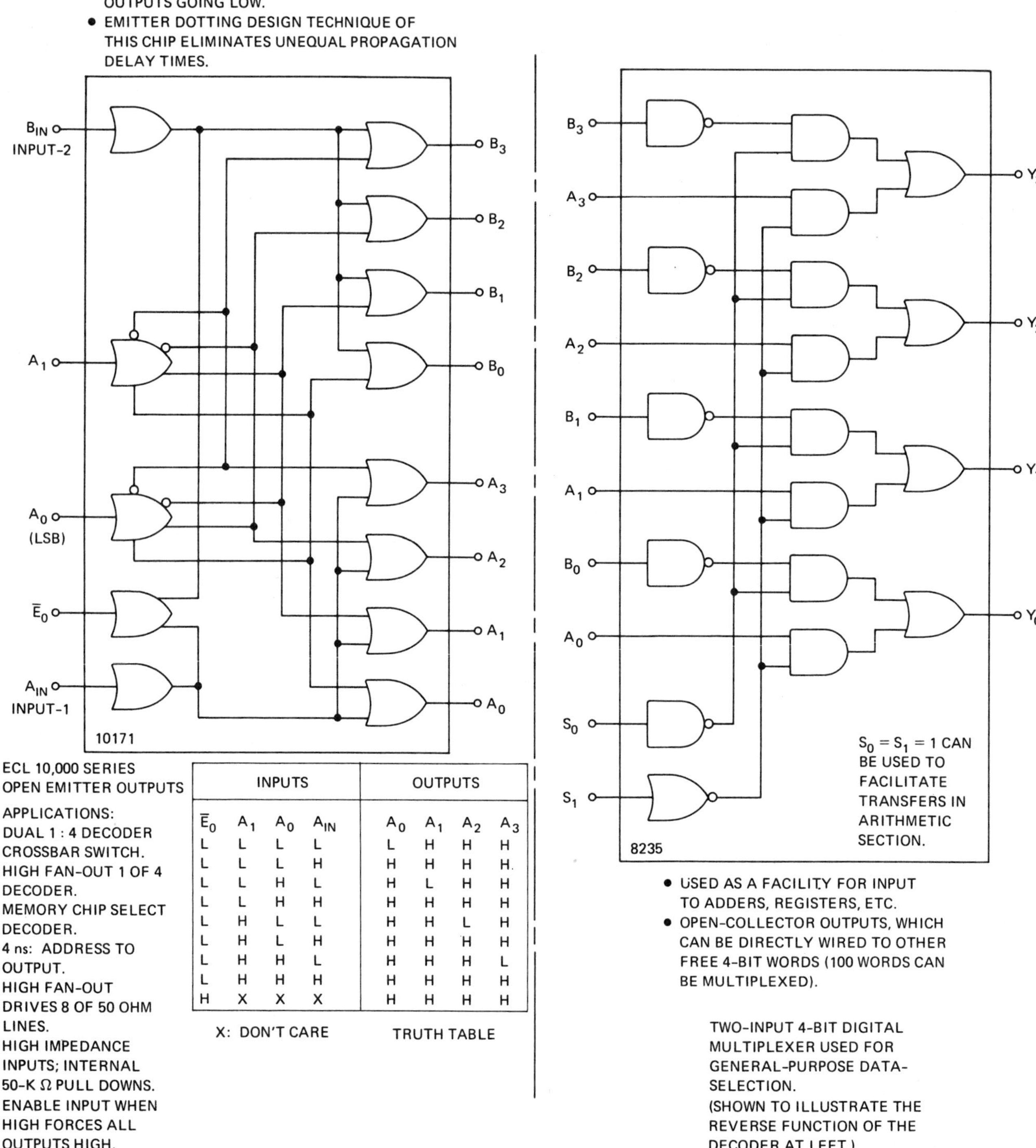
• OUTPUTS NORMALLY HIGH, WITH SELECTED OUTPUTS GOING LOW.
• EMITTER DOTTING DESIGN TECHNIQUE OF THIS CHIP ELIMINATES UNEQUAL PROPAGATION DELAY TIMES.
B_{IN}
INPUT-2
A_1
A_0
(LSB)
$\bar{E}_0$
A_{IN}
INPUT-1
B_3
B_2
B_1
B_0
A_3
A_2
A_1
A_0
10171
ECL 10,000 SERIES
OPEN EMITTER OUTPUTS
• APPLICATIONS: DUAL 1 : 4 DECODER CROSSBAR SWITCH. HIGH FAN-OUT 1 OF 4 DECODER. MEMORY CHIP SELECT DECODER.
• 4 ns: ADDRESS TO OUTPUT.
• HIGH FAN-OUT DRIVES 8 OF 50 OHM LINES.
• HIGH IMPEDANCE INPUTS; INTERNAL 50-K Ω PULL DOWNS.
• ENABLE INPUT WHEN HIGH FORCES ALL OUTPUTS HIGH.
B_3
A_3
B_2
A_2
B_1
A_1
B_0
A_0
S_0
S_1
Y_3
Y_2
Y_1
Y_0
8235
$S_0 = S_1 = 1$ CAN BE USED TO FACILITATE TRANSFERS IN ARITHMETIC SECTION.
• USED AS A FACILITY FOR INPUT TO ADDERS, REGISTERS, ETC.
• OPEN-COLLECTOR OUTPUTS, WHICH CAN BE DIRECTLY WIRED TO OTHER FREE 4-BIT WORDS (100 WORDS CAN BE MULTIPLEXED).
TWO-INPUT 4-BIT DIGITAL MULTIPLEXER USED FOR GENERAL-PURPOSE DATA-SELECTION. (SHOWN TO ILLUSTRATE THE REVERSE FUNCTION OF THE DECODER AT LEFT.)

INPUTS				OUTPUTS			
$\bar{E}_0$	A_1	A_0	A_{IN}	A_0	A_1	A_2	A_3
L	L	L	L	L	H	H	H
L	L	L	H	H	H	H	H.
L	L	H	L	H	L	H	H
L	L	H	H	H	H	H	H
L	H	L	L	H	H	L	H
L	H	L	H	H	H	H	H
L	H	H	L	H	H	H	L
L	H	H	H	H	H	H	H
H	X	X	X	H	H	H	H

X: DON'T CARE

TRUTH TABLE

Fig. 6-4. A typical two-input, dual four-output decoder/demultiplexer. Types 10171 and 8235, Signetics. (*Courtesy of Signetics*)

fied as general decoding functions. (See Fig. 10-11h for "majority voter" and Fig. 10-16 for design of a display decoder.)

A binary coded 2-line to dual 4-output line low-power, high-speed ECL decoder/demultiplexer is shown in Fig. 6-4 as an example, along with its truth table of positive logic. This parallel decoder uses a special technique of internal emitter dotting technique to eliminate unequal delay times, and can be used for demultiplexer, telephone cross-bar switching, **fan-out** for distribution of signals, and memory chip-select decoder applications. For direct comparison, an MSI/TTL 2-input 4-bit multiplexer, used in data applications, is shown adjacent to the decoder.

There are other possible variations of decoders. A simple diode matrix decoder can be represented by two flip-flops with two vertical output lines and matrixed-diodes for detection (or decoding) on horizontal lines. This matrixing feature can be extended to a large number of variables.

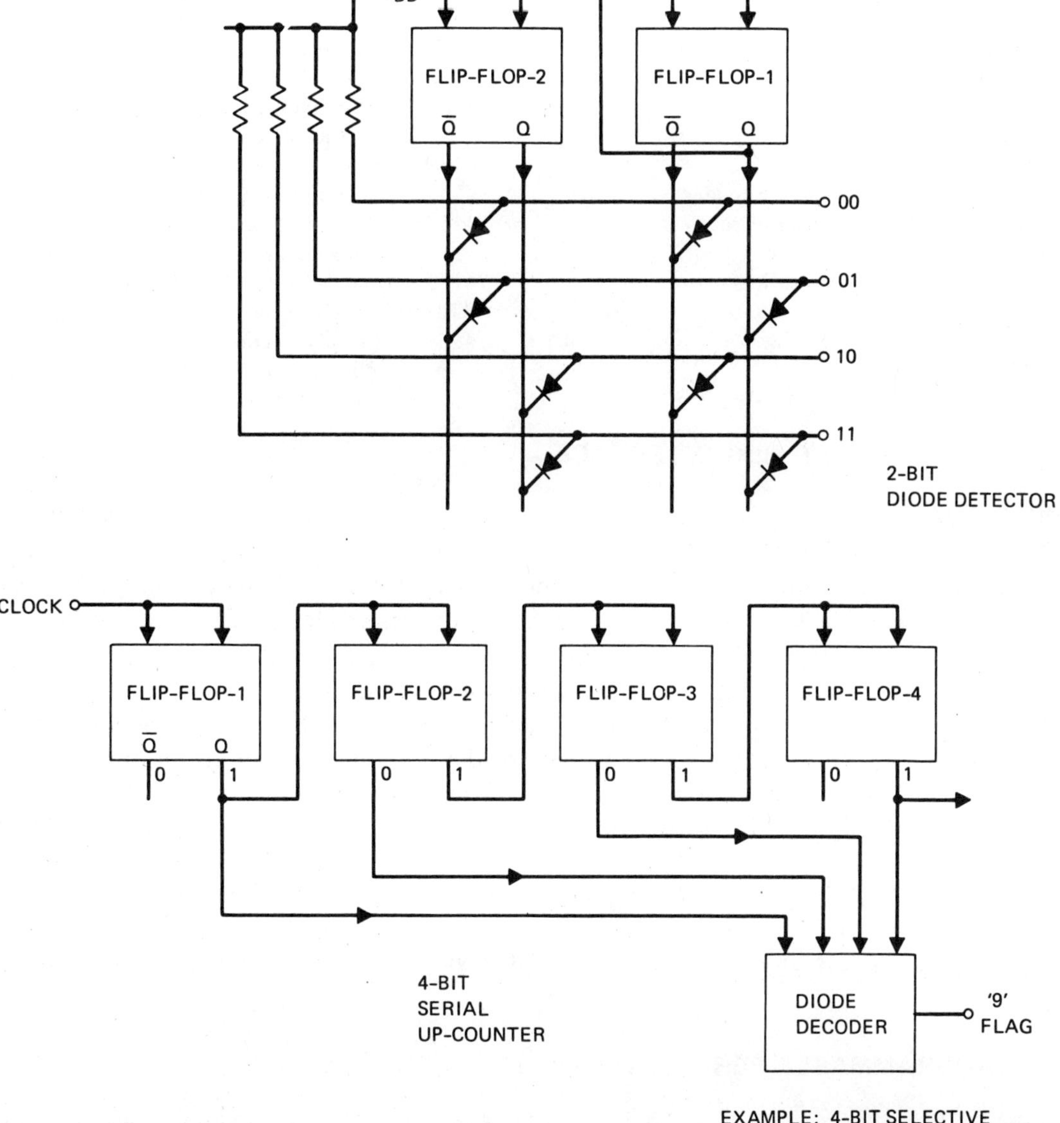

Fig. 6-5. A simple 2-bit diode decoder.

A simple diode decoder, for instance, for decimal 9, from a 4-bit serial up-counter can provide a "flag" for a subsequent ALU function such as "compare." Figure 6-5 illustrates the configurations of a simple 2-bit diode decoder along with its two flip-flops.

MSI/TTL Multiplexers and Demultiplexers (Decoders). Some of the TTL integrated circuits most commonly used in computer switching logic design for data communications networks are listed below.

SIGNETICS/or Texas Instruments (TI)

Note: FIRST two digits of Types 54150, etc. with ceramic packaging in the place of plastic types, starting with 74 . . . , meet military specifications.

	Multiplexer (MUX) Channel Controller		*Decoder*
74150:	16-to-1 line	7442:	BCD-to-Decimal (1 of 10) (4 bits IN)
74151:	8-to-1 (with inhibit strobe)	7443:	XS-3 (Binary)-to-Decimal (1 of 10)
74152:	8-to-1 (without inhibit strobe)	7444:	XS-3 (GRAY)-to-Decimal (1 of 10)
74153:	Dual 4-to-1	7445:	BCD-to-Decimal Decoder/driver
74157:	Quad 2-to-1 (Noninvert)	74145:	BCD-to-Decimal Decoder/driver
74158:	Quad 2-to-1 (Inverting)	7446:	BCD-to-7 Segment Decoder/driver
74251:	8-to-1 with 3-state outputs to connect several MUX-outputs in parallel.	7447A:	BCD-to-7 Segment Decoder/driver
74298:	Quad 2-to-1 with storage	7448:	BCD-to-7 Segment Decoder/driver
9309:	Dual 4-to-1	74138:	3-to-8 line Decoder (1 of 8, with 3-select and 3-enable)
3912:	8-to-1 with strobe	74139:	Dual 2-to-4 line (1 of 8, with 3-select and 3-enable)
74147:	10-to-4 line priority Encoder	74154:	4-line to 16-line Decoder with 2 inhibit strobes
74188:	8-to-3 line priority Encoder	74155:	Dual 2-line to 4-line Decoder
8263:	Open-collector, 3-input 4-bit TTL MUX (4-pole-3 position switching), Fig. 6-3.	9301:	1-to-10 Decoder
		74261:	Multiply/decoder (used in parallel multiplication in 2's complement form, 2-bits at a time)

6-5. USER'S LINE I/O BUS INTERFACE

When a few peripheral devices are used in a microcomputer system, a bidirectional bus of 8 to 18 data-bit lines is adequate by including multiplexers for device selection via data lines. However, a common interface technique used for connecting a large number of peripheral devices, such as displays, A-D/D-A converters, printers, TTYs, etc., to a mini- or micro-computer of a wider scope is the so-called party-line I/O bus system. The peripherals send and receive data to the accumulator or memory by means of a parallel I/O data bus connected via appropriate logic to an I/O register in the microprocessor. Other device-select lines carry control-logic signals for device selection and synchronization of the data-transfers to the memory cycle-time. Figure 6-6 illustrates the simple interface system, and how a 16-bit I/O instruction word is allotted for device selection and control logic. Bits 0 to 4 request an I/O instruction word from the processor; bits 5 to 10 are device-address bits in a device-select code; bits 11 and 12 indicate special functions, if any; and bits 13 to 15 produce sequentially timed commands. A 16-bit I/O instruction word can then select any one of $2^{11} = 2{,}048$ devices or device functions in 4 memory cycles.

6-6. PROGRAMMABLE PERIPHERAL INTERFACE OF INTEL

Intel LSI chip type 8251 is a typical example of the future course of direction in respect to the Interface of a microprocessor and a peripheral device-controller or a transmission

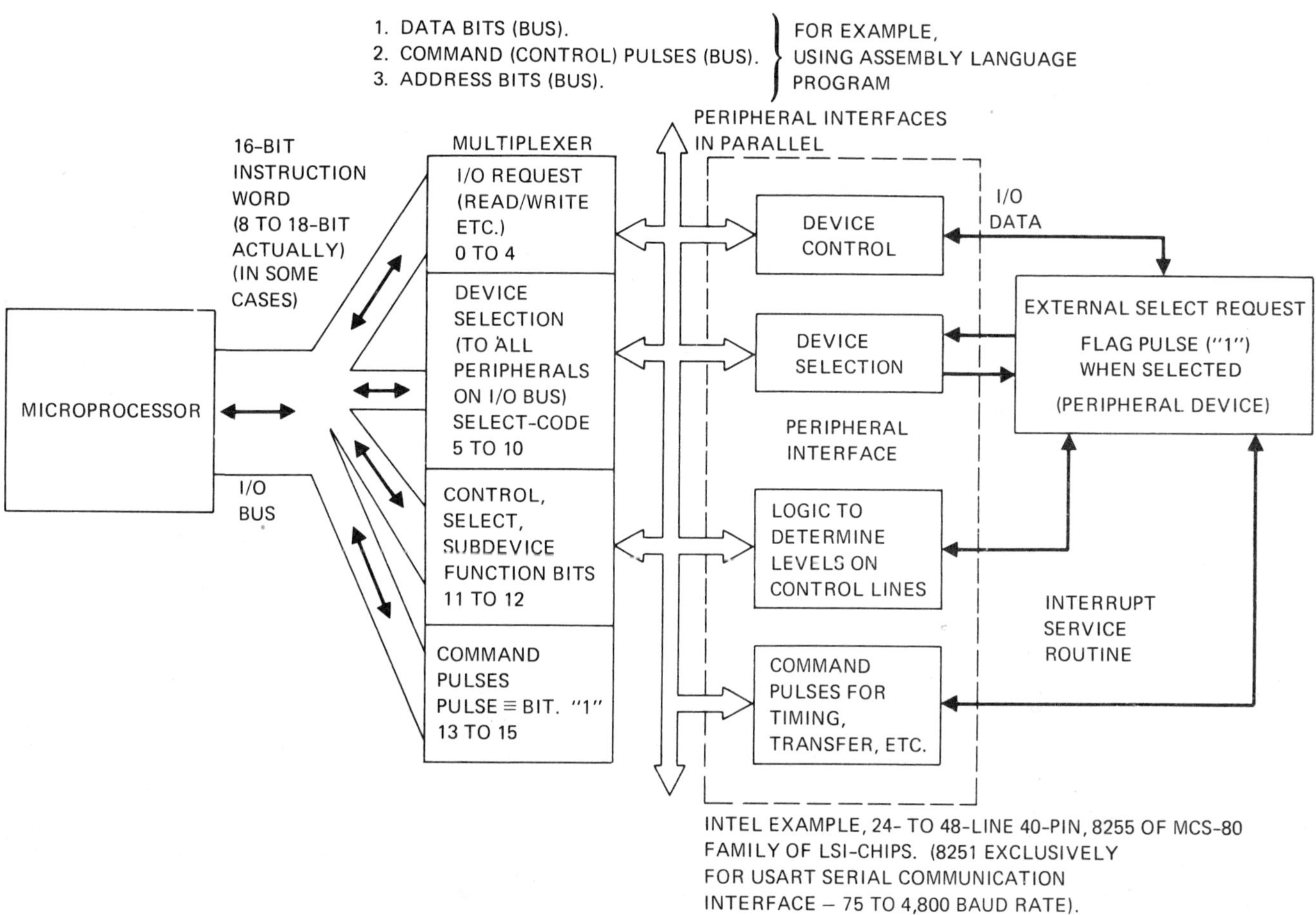

Fig. 6-6. I/O-bus interface data for several peripherals.

link. (An Interface design that includes the necessary decoding and buffering logic usually requires about 20 to 30 TTL or CMOS IC's.)

The Intel type 8251 LSI configuration is shown in Fig. 6-7, along with Intel MCS-80/85 system features. The type of transmission (whether serial synchronous or asynchronous), the length of the instruction word, and so forth have to be defined before starting the program. Each time, at start, the program loads the four control registers shown. A divide-by-four counter, along with a reset control-bit, selects (multiplexes) these registers in sequence to eliminate the need of four exclusive address words. For a dedicated application, the chip is preprogrammed, but the facility of control-ROM programmability makes the LSI chip highly flexible for any other application.

6-7. GENERAL I/O FEATURES

The transfer of data in and out of the microprocessor as *programmed data transfer* is manipulated in terms of the mnemonic I/O instructions. They are part of the assembly program. Interrupt- or event-initiated transfers—that allow microprocessors to be shared by several processes or events simultaneously—require that the concurrent events be embedded in a priority scheme.

The transfer of data from a source to destination basically involves the control and data buses. The control signal provides the start and end timings. Conventional I/O interface

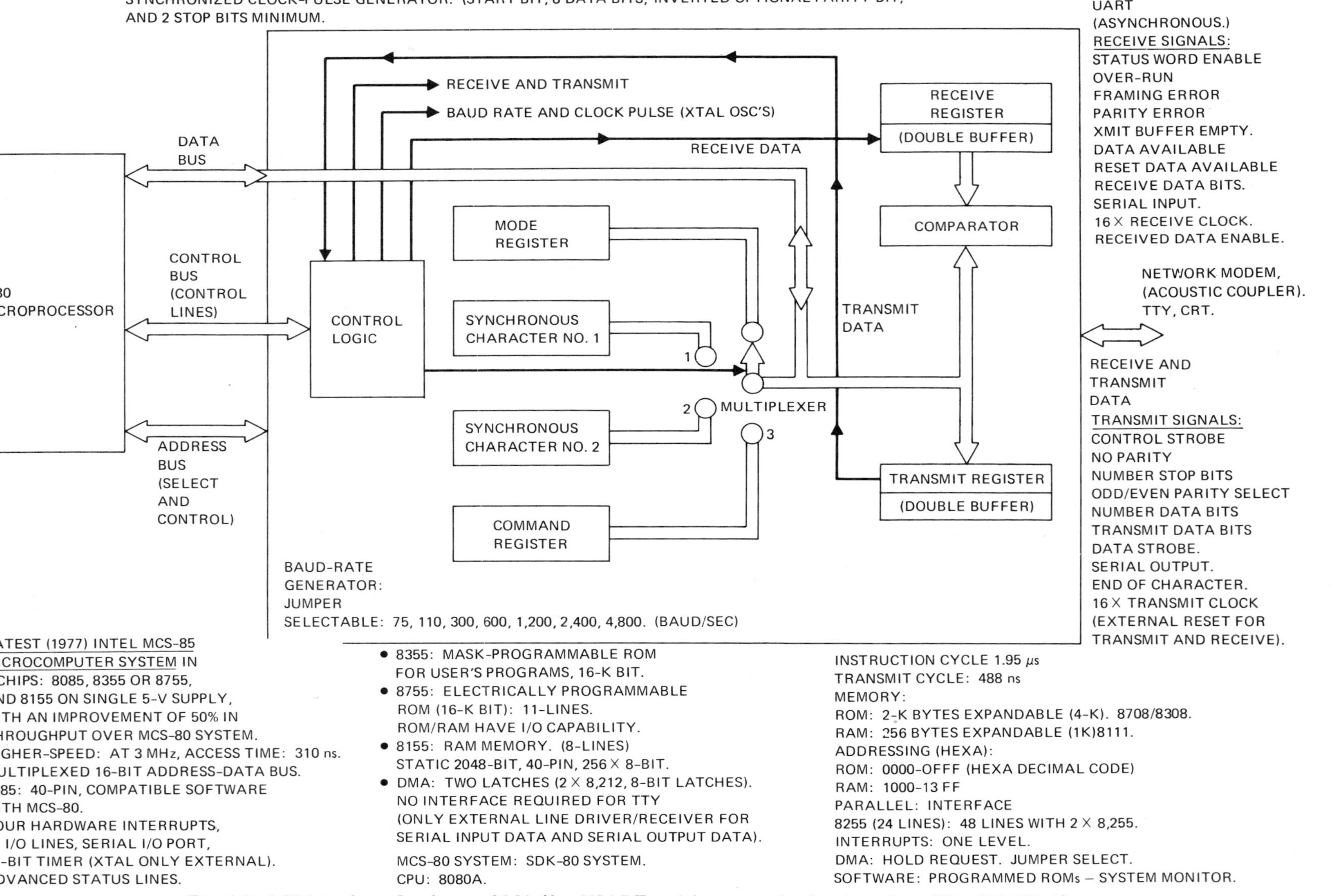

Fig. 6-7. LSI interface, Intel type 8251 (for USART serial communication interface, EIA, RS-232-C). LSI chips used in Intel systems types MCS-80 and MCS-85.

handshaking protocols signify the destination device request and acknowledge the receipt of the data on the control bus by individual control signals in a specific format.

Programmed data transfers are actually asynchronous with synchronization provided by a clock pulse-train on the control bus. When the data arrive in a serial bit stream, control time-slots are used for the clock; parallel data transfers of course dedicate separate lines for control. The peripheral device must wait until the CPU is ready to service the device after its execution of the current instruction in progress. The CPU will *poll* (or test) the device status via the status line. Several peripheral status lines can be tested at a single input port. *Bit-testing* and logical AND instructions for *masking off* undesired bits are generally used for this purpose.

The use of I/O latches or buffers in the data channel is the usual procedure for data transfers. However, *double-buffered* data transfers facilitate transfer of input serial data bit-streams in parallel pipeline fashion for higher throughput of the microprocessor. Since most peripheral devices send data at a slow rate, as compared to the high-speed data processing in the microprocessor, the synchronization of the CPU during the transfers is achieved by a *countdown* loop scheme in conjunction with the clocks to provide for the involved time-delays. In some cases, the use of interval timers tested via status bits is an alternative procedure. Since the I/O interface plays a significant role in increasing the throughput of a high-speed microprocessor, the use of a flexible, intelligent, multifunction

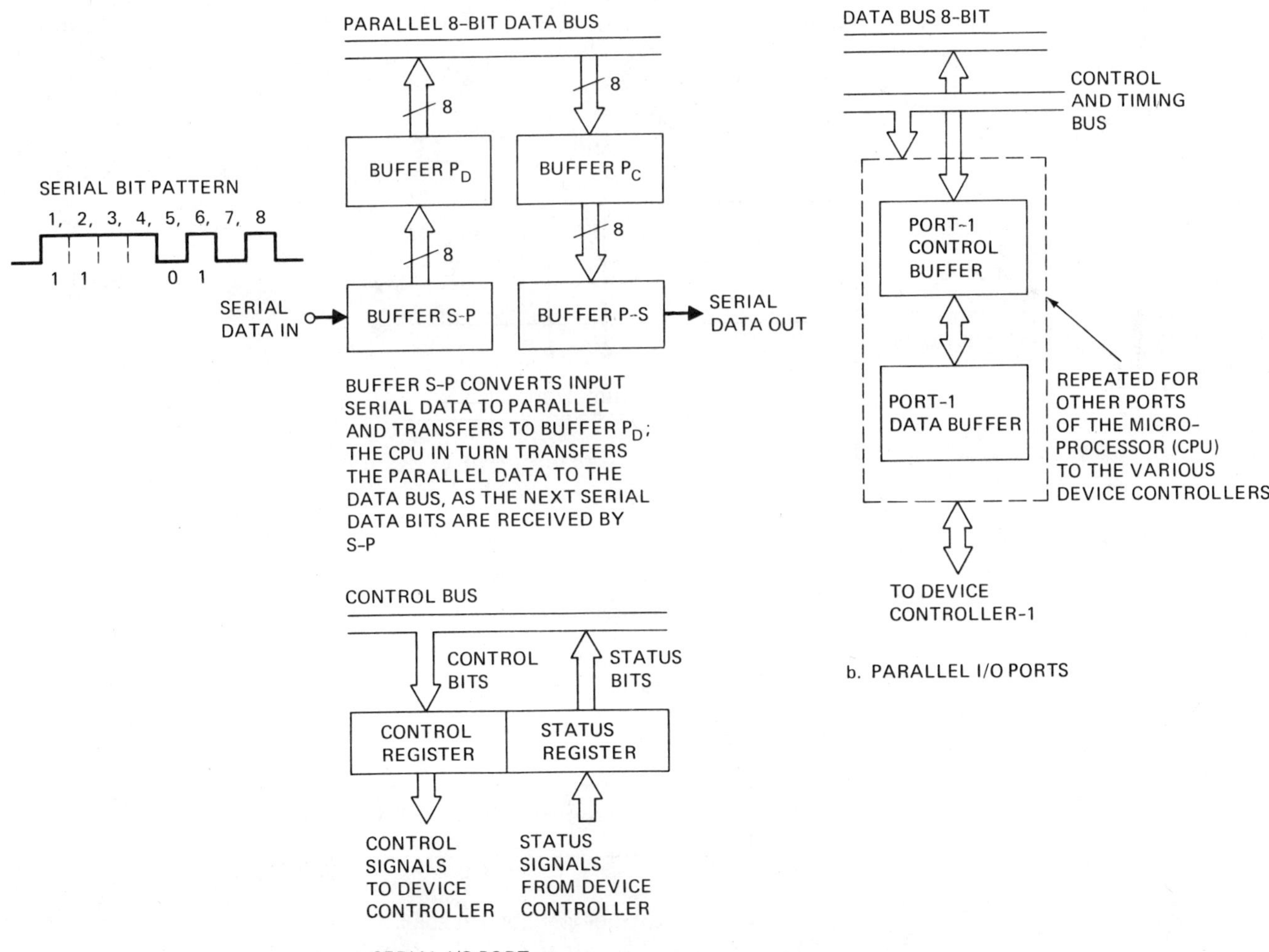

Fig. 6-8. Serial and parallel input/output ports.

input/output facility in the form of an exclusive I/O processor chip such as Intel 8089 processor is an obvious conclusion (see Section 7-33.) Figure 6-8 illustrates the configuration of serial and parallel input/output ports commonly used in microprocessors.

6-7.1. Extended and Nonextended I/O. *Extended I/O.* Signetics type 2650 microprocessor (described in Section 7-7) has several 2-byte I/O instructions that provide a high-order byte for device address. During execution of these instructions, the second byte is fetched from the memory and placed on the low-order address lines. As the $\overline{\text{MEM-I/O}}$ signal line enables the I/O, bit A_{14} specifies the Extended or $\overline{\text{Nonextended}}$ (E/$\overline{\text{NE}}$) mode. If this bit A_{14} is set, the I/O can use the device-address data arriving on the LOW address bus, as shown in the I/O control-signal decoder of Fig. 6-9a. (The over-line indicates an inverted signal.)

Nonextended I/O. The type 2650 microprocessor also has several 1-byte I/O instructions; they facilitate data transfer between an external peripheral device and a specified internal register without any need of device address information. The control information is used at the designer's option, and the Data/$\overline{\text{Control}}$ (D/$\overline{\text{C}}$) bit serves as a one-bit address to select the I/O device. The address bus is used during the nonextended I/O operations. The generalized control channel provides for the two modes Write Control (WRTC) and Read Control (REDC) for sending commands to the I/O devices, and for testing status or receive device commands, respectively. As per address line A_{13}, the I/O instructions operate in either mode. An alternative version with a mode decoder is shown

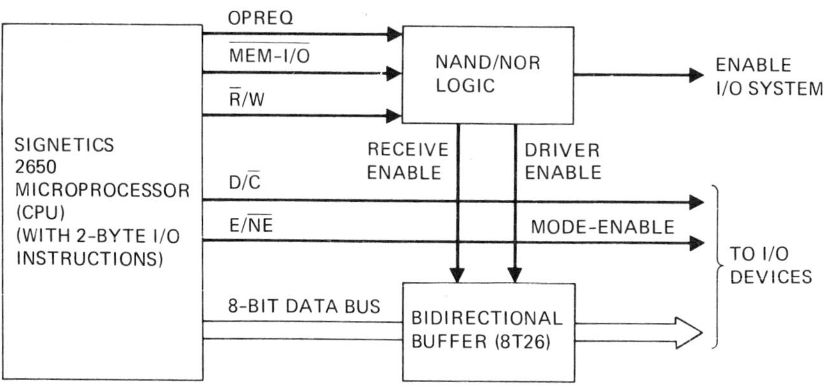

a. EXTENDED OR NONEXTENDED I/O MODES

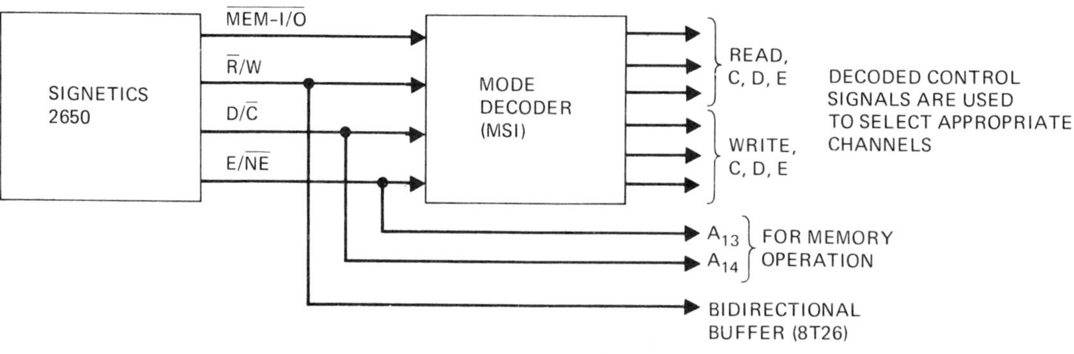

b. MODE-DECODER VERSION

Fig. 6-9a,b. Extended and nonextended I/O modes.

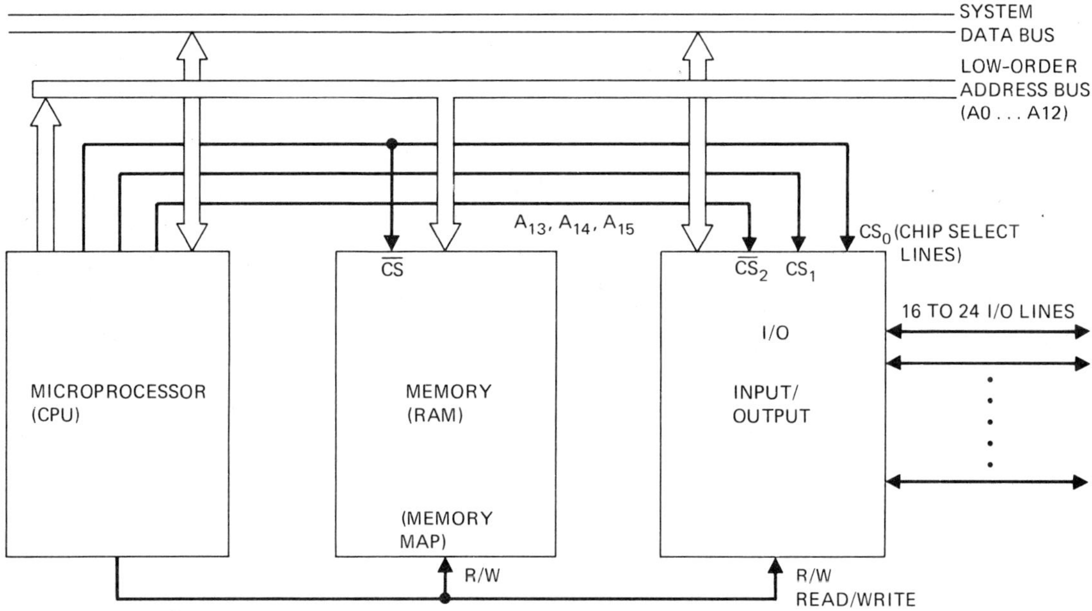

MICROPROCESSOR ARCHITECTURES OF THE POPULAR 6800 AND 6502 CHIPS DO NOT USE I/O INSTRUCTIONS; THEY THEREFORE DEPEND UPON MEMORY-MAPPED I/O. THEY ALLOT SPECIFIC MEMORY LOCATIONS TO I/O DEVICES, AND ADDRESS THESE I/O REGISTERS AS THEY DO MEMORY REGISTERS. IN MICROCOMPUTER SYSTEMS, THE HIGH-ORDER ADDRESS LINES (A_{13}, A_{14}, A_{15} AS ABOVE) CAN BE USED TO SELECT BETWEEN I/O AND MEMORY. I/O SUPPORT CHIPS ARE AVAILABLE, AND THEY ARE OPERATED BY THESE HIGH-ORDER ADDRESS LINES. SPECIAL CONTROL LINES FOR THIS FUNCTION ARE PROVIDED BY THE CPU.

Fig. 6-9c. Memory-mapped I/O address lines (microprocessors Motorola 6800, and MOS technology 6502).

in Fig. 6-9b; the source or destination for a write or read instruction is specified by a 2-bit register field.

6-7.2. Memory-Mapped I/O. The popular Motorola 6800 and Microcomputer Associates 6502 microprocessors use memory-mapped I/O in the place of conventional I/O instructions. Specific word locations in the RAM memory are allotted to I/O devices, and the corresponding I/O registers are addressed in the same manner as regular memory registers. Where large microcomputer systems are concerned, external decoding of the address lines would be necessary. In smaller systems that use only lower-order address lines, the high-order address lines are used to distinguish between memory and I/O address instructions; these I/O address lines are then used in conjunction with special I/O support chips. A simple block diagram in Fig. 6-9c illustrates this feature of memory-mapped I/O technique.

6-8. UNIVERSAL ASYNCHRONOUS RECEIVER TRANSMITTER, UART

Asynchronous serial data transmission is used in data communications systems using former low-speed electromechanical and popular teletype devices (TTYs) operating at dc to 500 character/sec. A TTY transmission speed of 110 characters/sec is common. The UART chip developed by some of the manufacturers for I/O interface to microprocessors implements the real-time asynchronous parallel-to-serial and serial-to-parallel bit conversions. This facility thus enables the incoming characters at low speeds to be converted to the high-speed data-processing words used in microcomputers. The TTY serial characters are comprised of a start bit, 5 to 8 data bits, an optional even or odd parity bit for error-detection, and 1/1.5/2 stop bits. At the end of each character, the line goes high for the stop bit(s), and the beginning of the next character is denoted by the negative-going pulse transition between the high idling bits and low start bit. Synchronization of receive data from a TTY is accomplished by using an external clock in the UART as shown in Fig. 6-10. In this connection, it may be noted that the bit-rate is the reciprocal of the baud-rate of TTY or teleprinter ($\frac{1}{110}$ baud = bit-period of 9.1 msec).

Motorola designates the LSI UART as asynchronous communications interface adapter (ACIA) in order to interface this chip directly to type 6800 microprocessor. The ACIA (or the UART) can receive data from one source and simultaneously transmit data to another source; in this connection, exclusive external clocks can be used for the receiver and transmitter, as long as the data format is the same in both the operations. Double buffering may be used for both receive and transmit data. The ACIA can additionally control a modem to transmit and receive data over telephone lines. Address and data bus structures are used as in exclusive I/O port LSI chips. The internal 8-bit receive data and status registers in the ACIA are read-only, whereas the 8-bit transmit data and control registers are write-only.

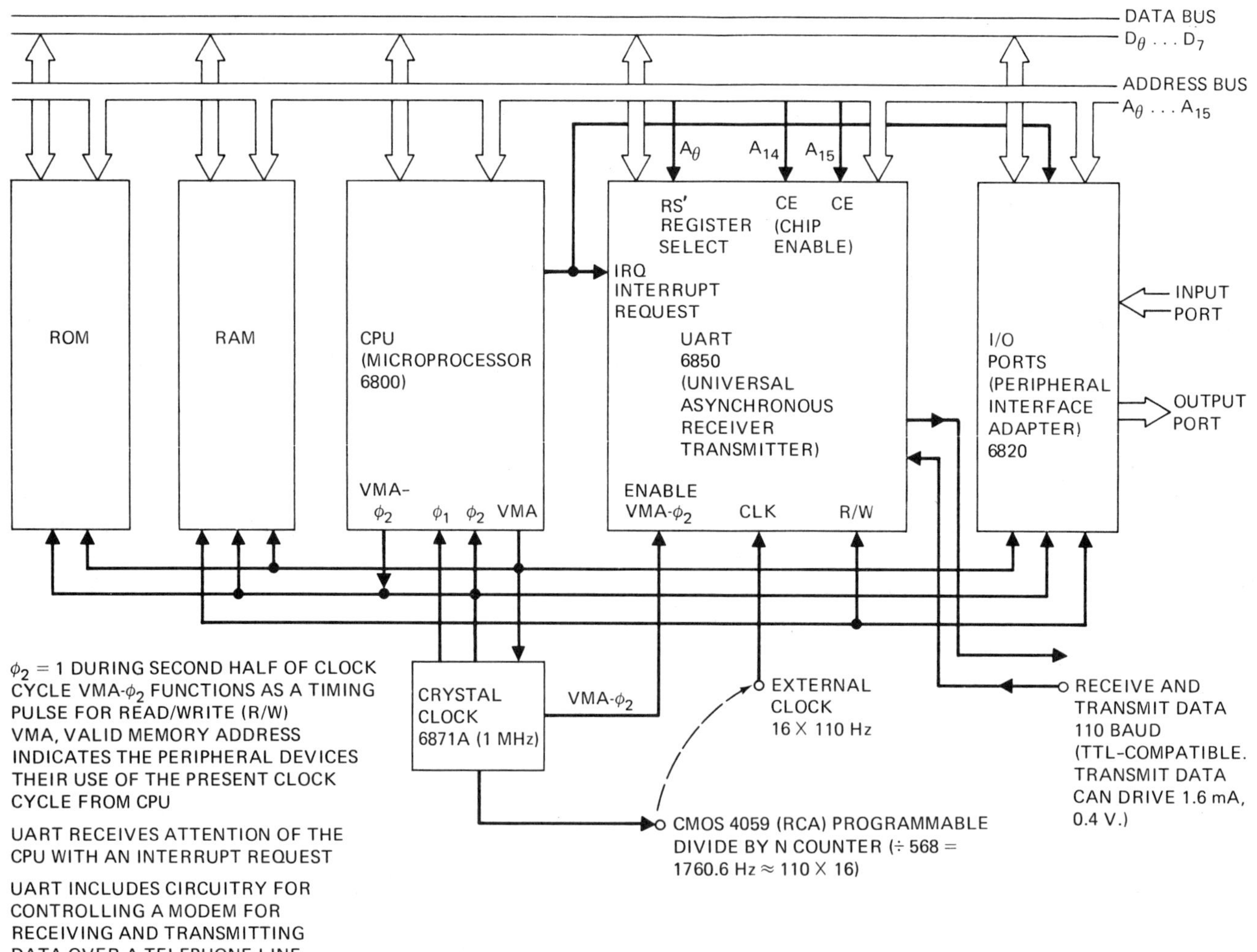

Fig. 6-10. Interface of Motorola type 6850 UART to Motorola type 6800 microprocessor as an asynchronous communications interface adapter (ACIA). (*Courtesy of Motorola Semiconductor Products Inc.*)

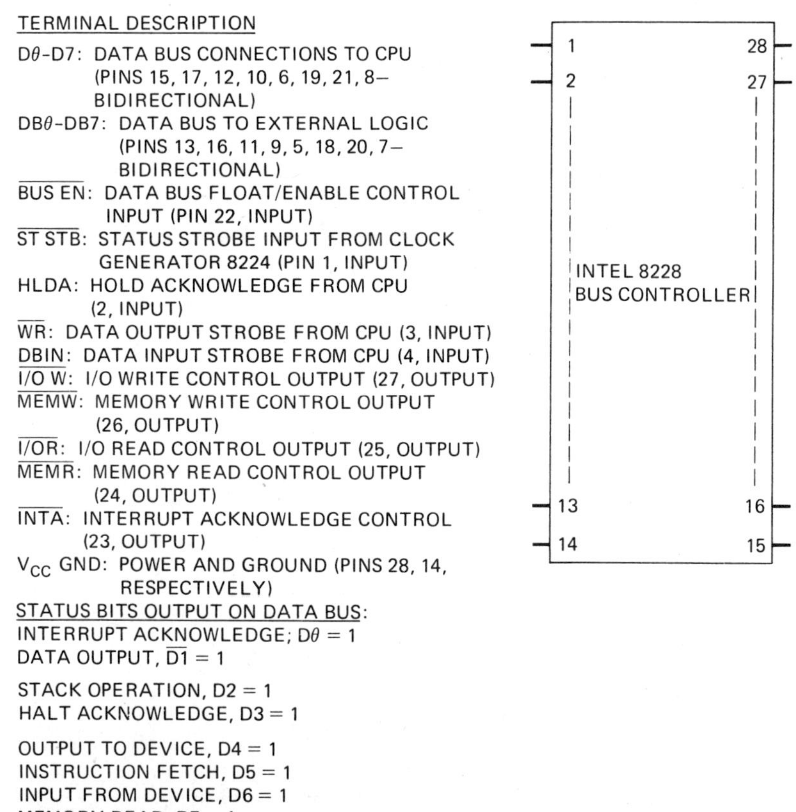

TERMINAL DESCRIPTION
D0-D7: DATA BUS CONNECTIONS TO CPU (PINS 15, 17, 12, 10, 6, 19, 21, 8– BIDIRECTIONAL)
DB0-DB7: DATA BUS TO EXTERNAL LOGIC (PINS 13, 16, 11, 9, 5, 18, 20, 7– BIDIRECTIONAL)
BUS EN: DATA BUS FLOAT/ENABLE CONTROL INPUT (PIN 22, INPUT)
ST STB: STATUS STROBE INPUT FROM CLOCK GENERATOR 8224 (PIN 1, INPUT)
HLDA: HOLD ACKNOWLEDGE FROM CPU (2, INPUT)
WR: DATA OUTPUT STROBE FROM CPU (3, INPUT)
DBIN: DATA INPUT STROBE FROM CPU (4, INPUT)
I/O W: I/O WRITE CONTROL OUTPUT (27, OUTPUT)
MEMW: MEMORY WRITE CONTROL OUTPUT (26, OUTPUT)
I/OR: I/O READ CONTROL OUTPUT (25, OUTPUT)
MEMR: MEMORY READ CONTROL OUTPUT (24, OUTPUT)
INTA: INTERRUPT ACKNOWLEDGE CONTROL (23, OUTPUT)
V_{CC} GND: POWER AND GROUND (PINS 28, 14, RESPECTIVELY)
STATUS BITS OUTPUT ON DATA BUS:
INTERRUPT ACKNOWLEDGE; D0 = 1
DATA OUTPUT, D1 = 1
STACK OPERATION, D2 = 1
HALT ACKNOWLEDGE, D3 = 1
OUTPUT TO DEVICE, D4 = 1
INSTRUCTION FETCH, D5 = 1
INPUT FROM DEVICE, D6 = 1
MEMORY READ, D7 = 1
1
2
28
27
INTEL 8228
BUS CONTROLLER
13
14
16
15

Fig. 6-11. Intel 8228 bus-controller, I/O terminal description. (*Courtesy of Intel Corp.*)

6-9. INTEL TYPE 8228 BUS CONTROLLER AND TYPE 8212 PARALLEL INPUT/OUTPUT PORT

The popular Intel 8080A microprocessor requires type 8228 bus controller and type 8212 parallel input/output port chips in most single-board microcomputer applications. These two chips shown in Figs. 6-11 and 6-12 clarify the I/O interface functions of these two chips, along with the terminal descriptions.

The peripheral devices are not directly connected to the data and control buses of a microcomputer chip; input/output *ports* that provide for data buffering and transfer of control signals are essential as shown in Fig. 6-11. A control register, a data buffer register, and control logic circuits are required in each port. A synchronization scheme of *handshaking* is simultaneously involved to provide for the transfer of asynchronous input data from slow-speed peripheral data. Each port is designated by an identification number, and transmitted over the address bus and decoded by each port, which acknowledges and receives. (If the registers in a port can be directly addressed, they become an extension of the RAM memory as a memory-mapped I/O, without the need of an arbitrary port identification number.)

Interrupt operation. The Intel 8080A microprocessor receives external interrupts by means of the INT and INTE signals. Interrupt facility is enabled and disabled under program control by EI (enable) and DI (disable) instructions. Figure 6-13 shows the timing diagram of the interrupt initiation sequence. The Intel 8228 bus controller plays an important role in the interrupt initiation sequence shown. The start of postinterrupt instruction fetch is indicated when 8080A (1) acknowledges an interrupt by setting INTE to 0 during the leading edge of ϕ_2 in the next clock period and (2) simultaneously trans-

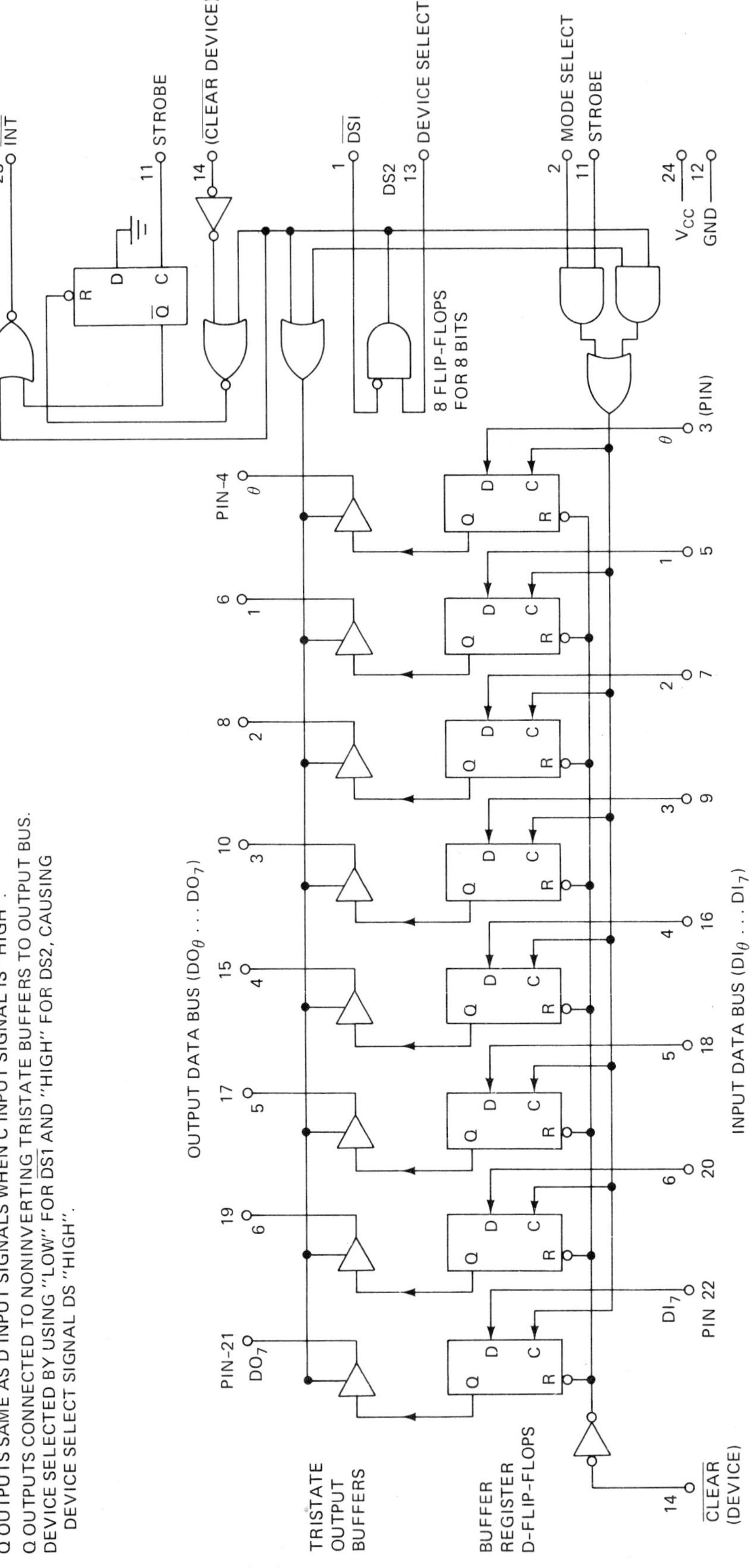

Fig. 6-12. Intel 8212 parallel input/output port: internal logic of a port and nomenclature of terminal pins (24). *(Courtesy of Intel Corp.)*

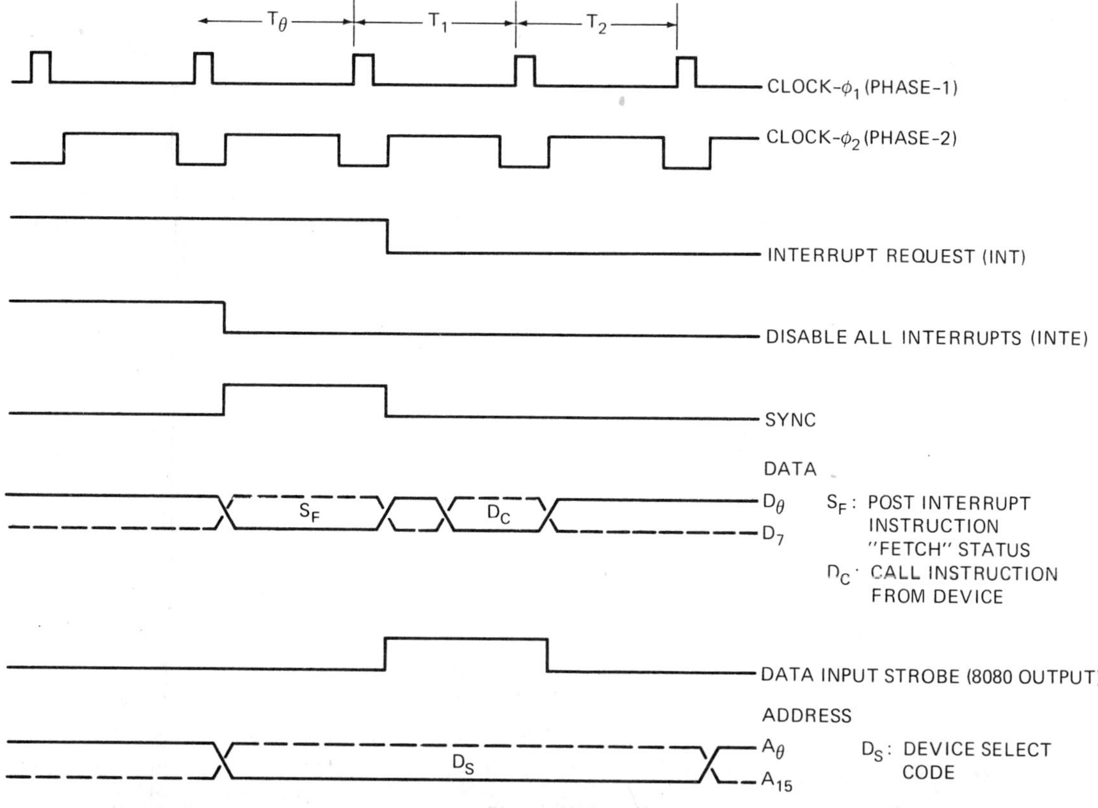

INTEL 8080A ACKNOWLEDGES AN INTERRUPT BY SETTING INTE "LOW" DURING LEADING EDGE OF ϕ_2 IN THE NEXT T_θ CLOCK PERIOD; SIMULTANEOUSLY 8080 SENDS STATUS BITS TO BUS CONTROLLER 8228 FOR POST-INTERRUPT INSTRUCTION FETCH. THIS INTERRUPT START IS SHOWN IN THE TIMING DIAGRAM. 8228 SUPPLIES INTA (ACKNOWLEDGE).

8080A FETCHES INSTRUCTION MACHINE CODE FURNISHED BY INTERRUPTING PERIPHERAL DEVICE. (THE PROGRAM COUNTER MEANWHILE INDICATES THE NEXT INSTRUCTION OF THE INTERRUPTED PROGRAM. THE ADDRESS OF THIS INSTRUCTION IS OF COURSE SAVED, SO THAT THE INTERRUPT SERVICE ROUTINE MAY BE TERMINATED WITH A "RETURN" INSTRUCTION.)

Fig. 6-13. Timing diagram: interrupt acknowledgment and postinterrupt instruction fetching. (*Courtesy of Intel Corp.*)

mits status bits to the 8228 bus controller. For further information on the operation of the bus controller, note the description of the status bits output on the data bus in Fig. 6-11 of the bus controller. Parallel I/O port, Intel 8212 LSI chip can be used as a simple gated buffer for data input if *mode select* is set low and *data strobe* is permanently set high. It can also be used to transfer data according to a handshaking protocol by using the interrupt request signal.

Since the speed of operation of the microprocessor is very high compared to the bit transmission rate of the peripheral device, synchronization in the form of handshaking must precede the data transfer to insure that no data are lost. When the parallel I/O port is ready for data transfer, it signals the microprocessor by means of an *interrupt signal.* The moment the CPU completes the execution of the instruction in progress, it acknowledges the interrupt request, temporarily suspends execution of the program in progress, stores contents of all registers in memory, and starts execution of a routine program (in the software) to service the interrupt request. On the completion of this service request, the CPU resumes its execution of the program in progress at the instant of interrupt.

The peripheral device, outputting its parallel data to the I/O port via the data bus, lowers its *strobe* signal to transfer data into the data buffer-register of the port. The data transfer is delayed only as long as the strobe raises a *buffer-full* "high" signal for the information of the device. The trailing edge of the strobe also activates the interrupt signal in order to request an interrupt service from the CPU. After *acknowledge*, the CPU executes a routine program instruction to transfer the buffer contents over the data bus. After transfer, the interrupt signal is deactivated, and the buffer-full signal returns to its normal "low."

During the parallel output mode of a port, the bus interface logic, upon a CPU request, strobes data from the data bus into the buffer register of the port. The output transfer is accomplished with the signals *data write*, *port busy*, *acknowledge*, and *interrupt*.

6-10. SERIAL INPUT/OUTPUT PORTS

Peripheral devices such as magnetic tape cassettes, teletypes, etc., can transfer data in a serial bit stream only. Since the data bus transfers in the microcomputer system occur in a parallel format, serial I/O ports are essential for conversion to and from parallel format of data in a double-buffered register setup.

The transmission rate of the incoming bit-stream must be specified so that the receiving serial I/O port, with the timing of its clock, can subdivide the incoming bit-period into a number of subintervals, provided the clock is faster than the transmission rate. These incoming high-speed synchronized bits are then shifted into the receiver's buffer register at approximately the center of the bit-period. However, if the period of the receiver clock is much shorter than the bit-period (as in the case of a TTY), the incoming serial bit-stream is not synchronized accurately with respect to the clock, as an asynchronous mode of operation. In the asynchronous mode, the transmitter maintains the data line "High" during silence, and when transmission is resumed, it starts with a "High-to-Low" (Mark) transition signal, a start bit, and ends the transmission of every frame of data byte with a parity-check bit for the purpose of error detection, and one or two stop bits.

When the incoming bit-stream is high-speed, the synchronous mode is effective, as the transmission takes place on a continuous basis; it transmits a preassigned synchronization character in the absence of data. Start of a data byte is signaled by the resumption of two such synchronization characters, followed by "Mark" transition, so that the receiver can (1) start shifting the data bits into its buffer register, and (2) assemble the data byte for transfer to the data bus. The simple block-diagram of a serial I/O port was shown in Fig. 6-8.

Serial I/O interface in common protocols. Serial bit-stream transmission requires a one- or two-wire system to carry all necessary signals between modules or modems. Address, data, and control information are sent bit-by-bit, asynchronous or synchronous.

EIA standard RS-232C specifications require a 25-pin connector with nominal plus and minus 12-V pulses for effective transfer. TTYs use *asynchronous* data at 110, 150, or 300 baud/sec; and CRT terminals use synchronous bit rates above 1200. When serial data are transmitted over dial-up telephone voice-grade lines, in conjunction with acoustic couplers, the data below 300 baud or bit/sec is modulated FSK (frequency-shift keying) with tones corresponding to marking ("1") and spacing ("0"). Bit rates above 300 use PSK (phase-shift keying) over expensive low noise data-grade lines for minimum bit-error-rates (BER). The signals between the communications modem and the computer terminal RS-232C interface use the handshake at the start and end of the serial data, as a contrast to the procedure in IEEE-488 bus protocol, which is used exclusively for systems. *Current-loop* is a similar standard in the former mechanical teletype writers; loop-to-EIA RS-232C data converters are available for maximum line-lengths under 100 ft, and data rates under 20 kb/sec with a receiver input of 1.5 V (single-ended). For longer lengths of lines under 5000 ft and higher data-rates under 1-M bit/sec, with a receiver input of 100 mV (differential), EIA RS422/423 standards are specified, but they are not commonly used in practice.

For high-speed *synchronous* data communications, 8 extra bits are adequate for every 800 bits. IBM's protocol synchronous data link control scheme (SDLC) transmits data-burst as a frame, in blocks of many characters at a time; each frame has seven fields. Each field consists of one or more bytes of data. As all transmitter and receivers share the same wire, only one unit transmits with a start character while the others receive. Each SDLC serial I/O interface waits to identify its own address; when it is matched and recognized, the frame will be received and checked for error bits. A return frame is sent back to the transmitting modem to acknowledge that the data (in ASCII or EBCDIC) were received; if errors were present, the receiver addressed requests retransmission. Two or more types of frames are also transmitted with control byte data or supervisory information. The data frames transmit cyclic redundancy check bits (CRC) of a so-called cyclic or polynomial code for parity check and double-bit error detecting bits at the end of data before the stop-bit in the frequently used 32-bit word. A synchronous serial interface will handle various types of protocols by some combination of software and hardware in the form of a controller chip. The latter identifies the start character, insert and delete sync (synchro-

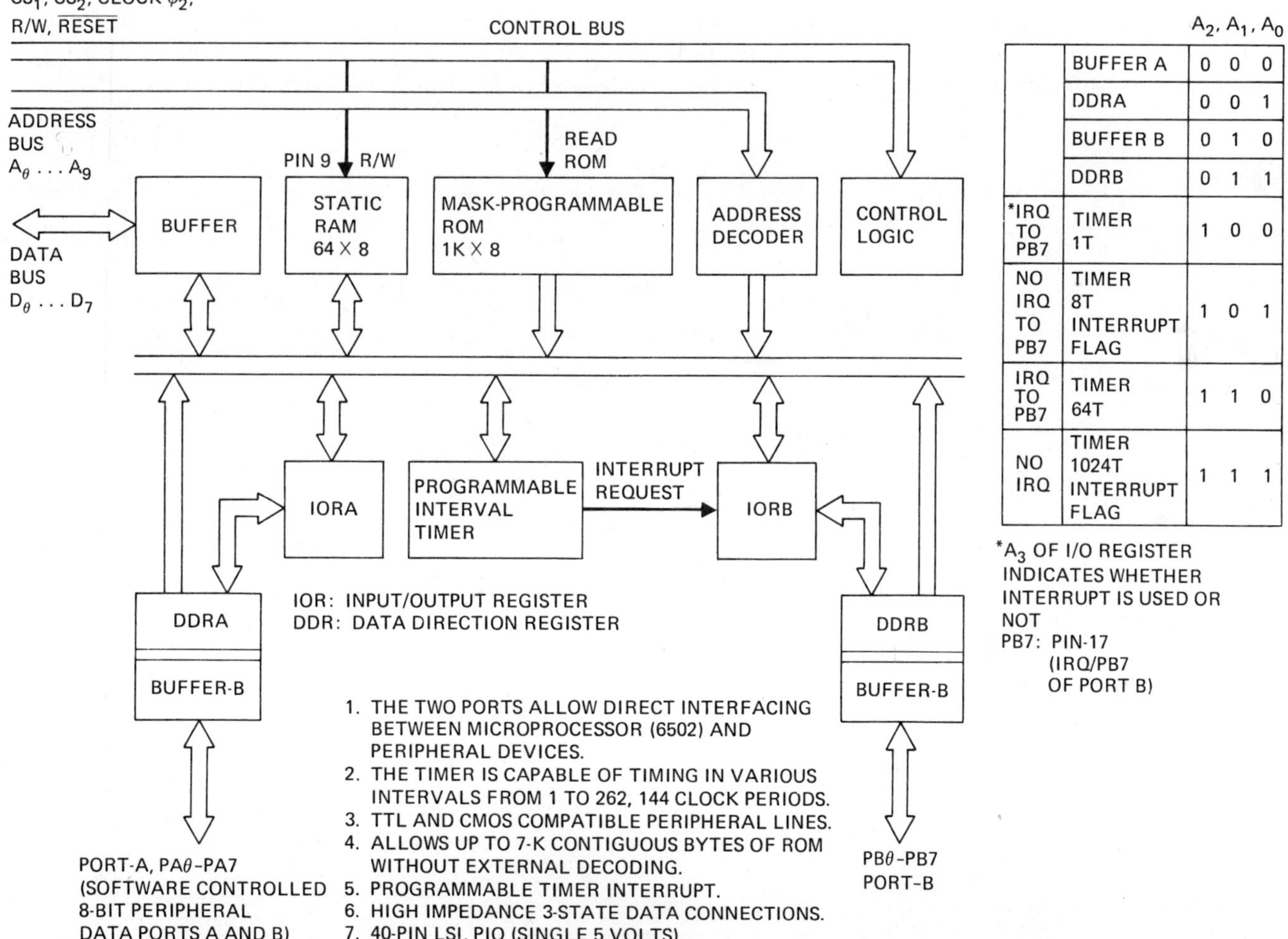

		A_2, A_1, A_0
	BUFFER A	0 0 0
	DDRA	0 0 1
	BUFFER B	0 1 0
	DDRB	0 1 1
*IRQ TO PB7	TIMER 1T	1 0 0
NO IRQ TO PB7	TIMER 8T INTERRUPT FLAG	1 0 1
IRQ TO PB7	TIMER 64T	1 1 0
NO IRQ	TIMER 1024T INTERRUPT FLAG	1 1 1

*A_3 OF I/O REGISTER INDICATES WHETHER INTERRUPT IS USED OR NOT
PB7: PIN-17 (IRQ/PB7 OF PORT B)

Fig. 6-14a. MOS technology 6530 programmable I/O with built-in facilities of ROM, RAM, and I/O timer array. (*Courtesy of MOS Technology Inc.*). b. Memory map.

nizing) bits automatically, and does the needed block checking. The software looks after the assembly and decoding of the frames from the fields.

6-11. PARALLEL I/O CHIPS

Microcomputer Associates type 6502 is one of the most popular microprocessors used in personal computer applications. For examples, the most popular Apple personal computer and Ohio Scientific personal computers (described in Chapter 12) use 6502 as the CPU. Most microcomputer applications need at least two or more I/O ports on one or more LSI parallel I/O chips that belong to the family of 6502 microprocessor. The use of a programmable timer, control logic, and automated shift registers are some of the features these parallel I/O chips (PIOs) provide. Series 6520, 6522, 6530, and 6532 chips furnish two PIO ports with slight variations in their built-in facilities. Figure 6-14a illustrates the internal architecture of 6530, which is one of the most popular chips used in I/O interface. Parallel I/O chip 6530 furnishes two parallel 8-bit ports, a 1-K byte ROM, 64 bytes of RAM, and a timer along with one 10-bit address decoder, seven buffer registers, and control logic.

The timer shown in the memory map of this chip (Fig. 6-14b) appears as a set of 4 memory locations in conjunction with the buffer registers, and the I/O interrupt facility for the peripheral devices.

The timer will generally use the system clock to generate specific *delays*. And delays can be measured by software loops when interrupts are not involved. When interrupts are involved fixed delays are generated by delay flip-flops and logic. The timer measures

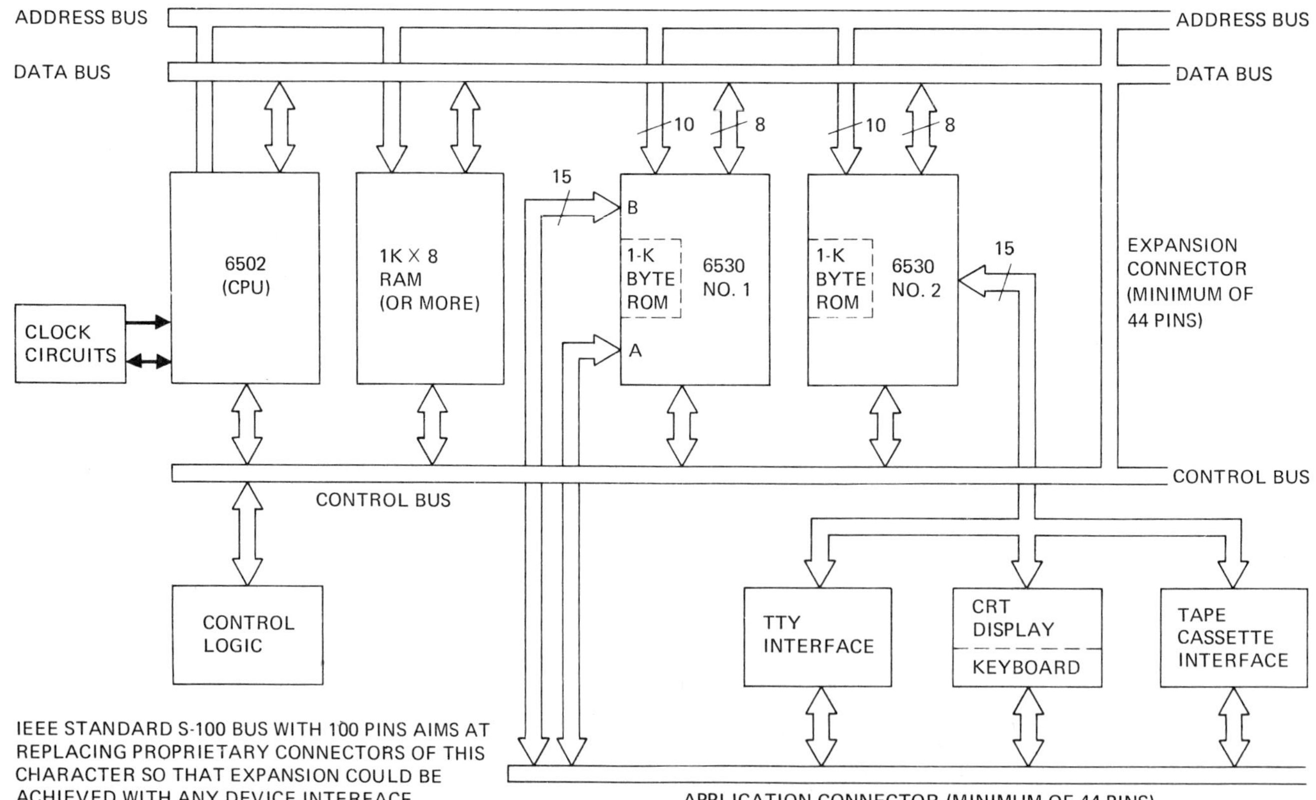

Fig. 6-15. KIM-1 personal computer system with two parallel I/O interface chips. (*Courtesy of MOS Technology Inc.*)

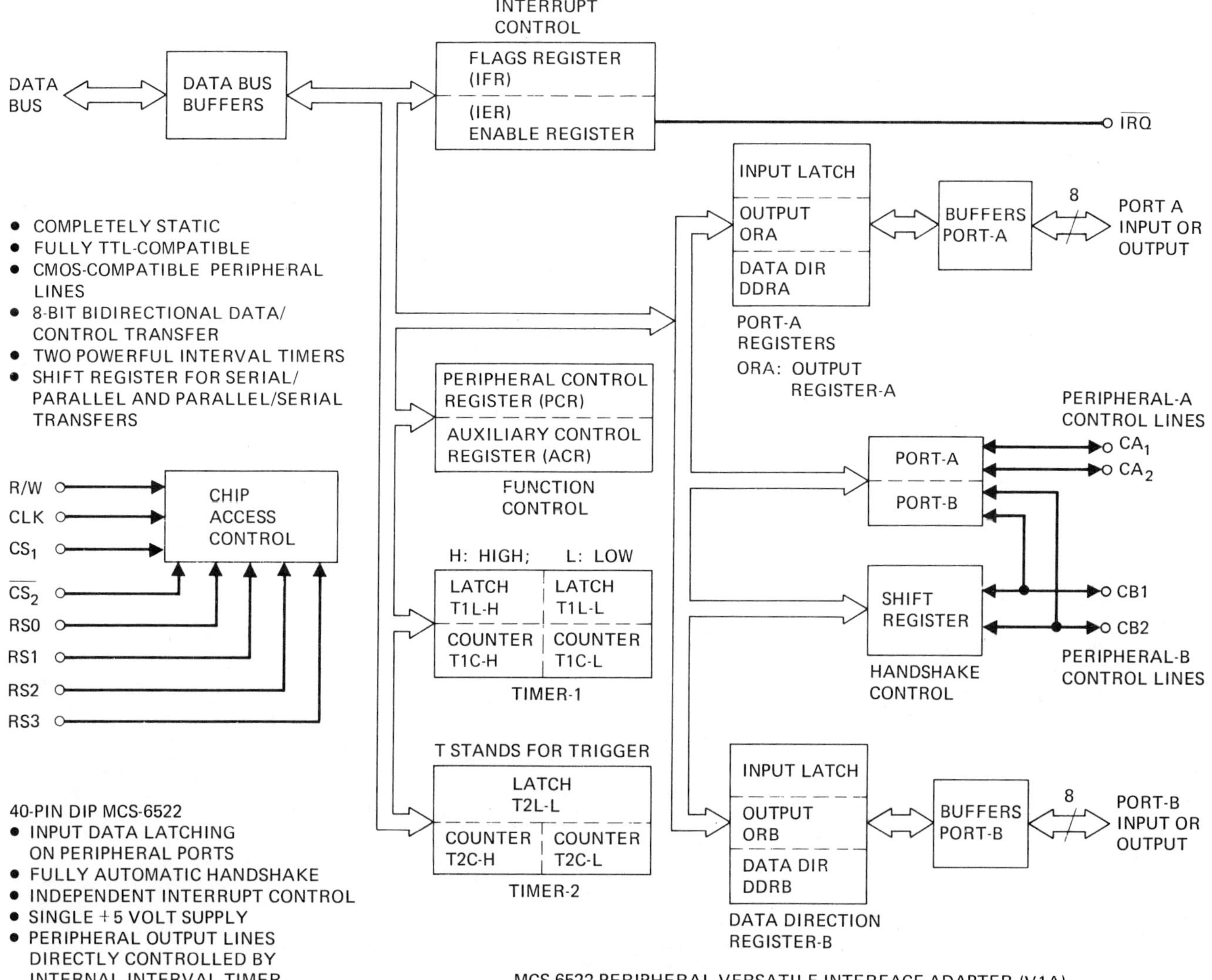

Fig. 6-16. Block-diagram and terminal nomenclature of Versatile Interface Adapter MCS-6522. (*Courtesy of Microcomputer Associates Inc.*)

the duration of an external pulse or time elapsed between 2 flags or pulses. The timer can count from one-to-256 with an 8-bit register or one-to-64K with a 16-bit register. Other popular personal computers that use 6502 and its PIO series are KIM, SYM, and AIM65. For example, KIM-1 personal computer uses two PIO chips in its system for the peripheral devices shown in Fig. 6-15.

MCS6522 Versatile Interface Adapter. The versatile interface adapter (VIA) provides a broad range of peripheral control facilities for the implementation of interface in microcomputer systems. The 6522 is a 5-V, 40-pin DIP (dual-in-line plastic) NMOS, completely static, and fully TTL-compatible chip, allowing the interconnection of CMOS-compatible peripheral control lines. The chip provides for independent interrupt control. It offers a pair of powerful interval timers, a serial-to-parallel/parallel-to-serial shift register, and a facility for input data-latching on the peripheral ports. In multiple microprocessor systems, MCS6522 facilitates handshaking capabilities and control of bidirectional data transfers between the VIAs of the several microprocessors in the system. Figure 6-16 illustrates the block-diagram and terminal nomenclature of the 40-pin DIP MCS6522 chip.

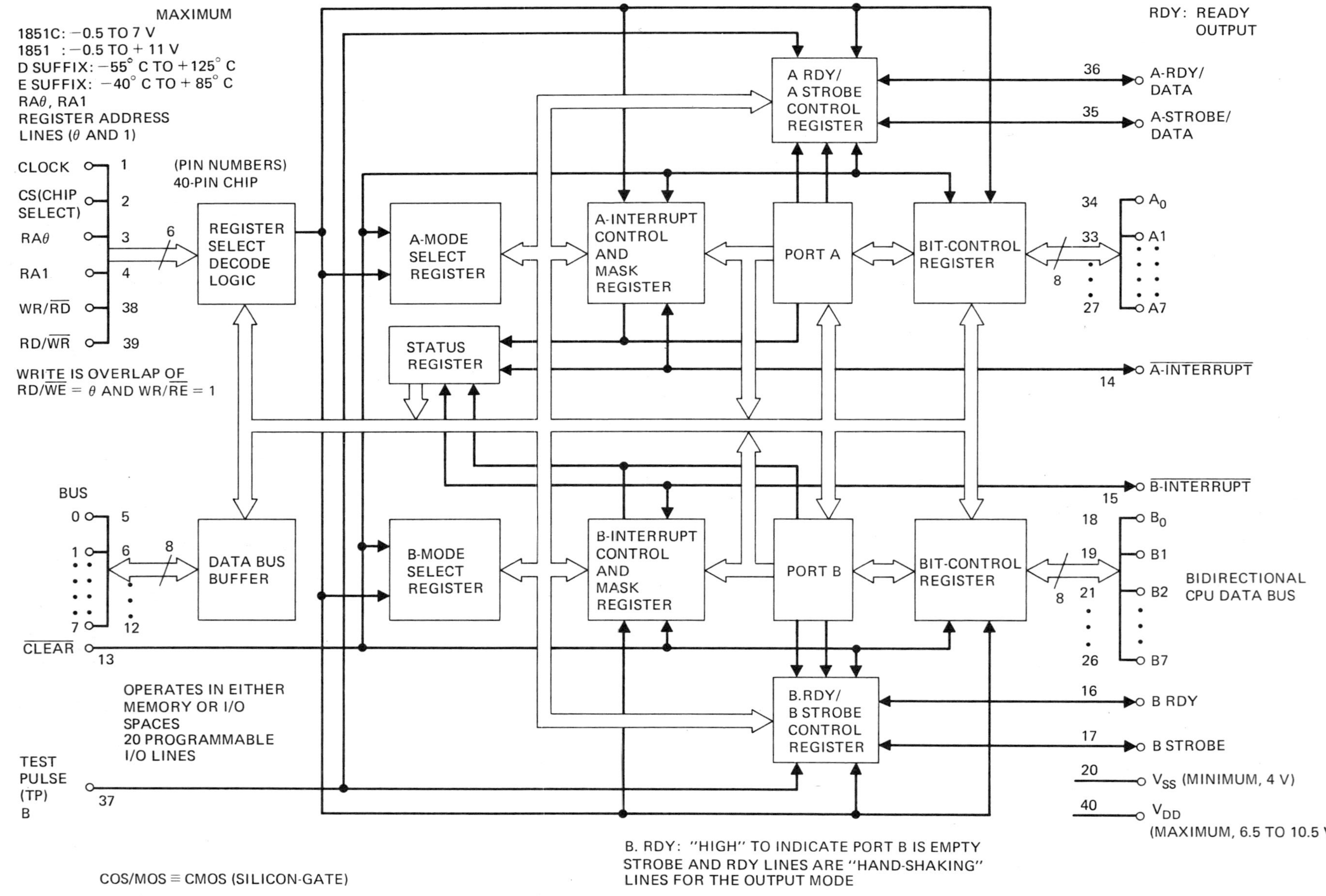

Fig. 6-17a. Internal architecture of RCA Programmable I/O Interface, CDP-1851. *(Courtesy of RCA Solid State Division).*

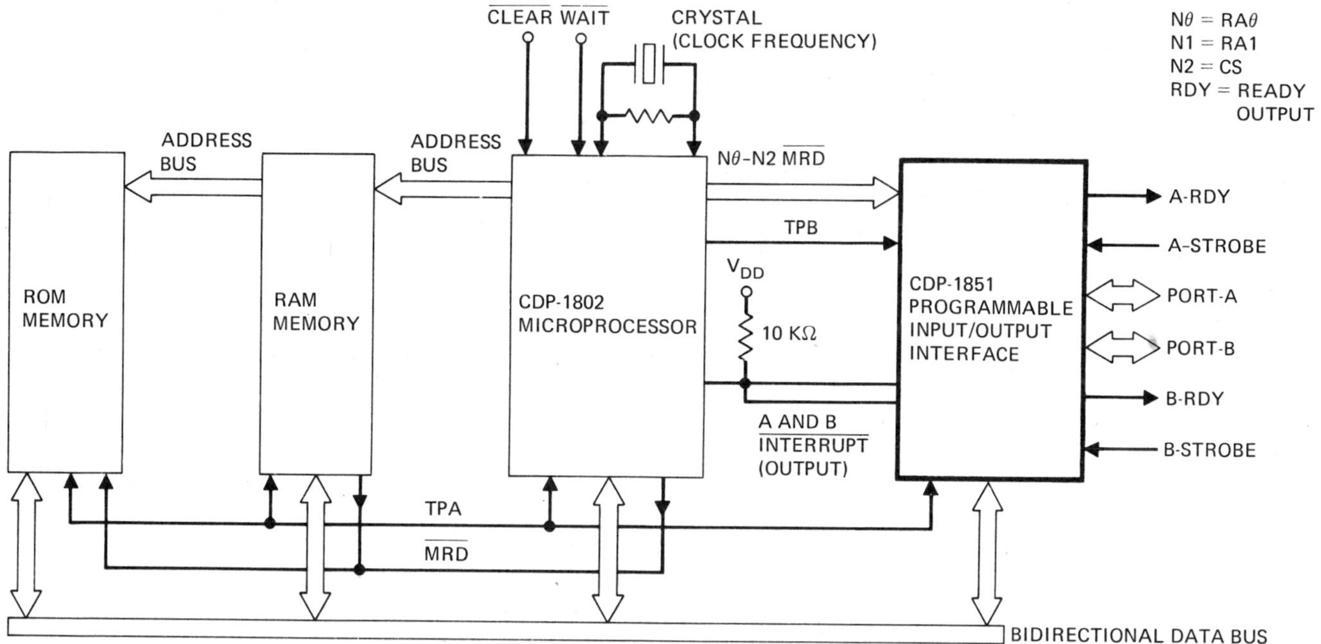

TPB: POSITIVE INPUT PULSE USED AS A DATA-LOAD SET OR RESET STROBE
A-STROBE (INPUT): AN INPUT HAND-SHAKING LINE FOR PORT-A IN INPUT/OUTPUT/ AND BIDIRECTIONAL MODES. USED ALSO AS A DATA-BIT I/O LINE WHEN PORT-A IS IN BIT-PROGRAMMABLE MODE.

TPA: TIMING PULSE A (CLOCK TO 1851).
CS: CHIP SELECT.
$\overline{\text{MRD}}$: MEMORY READ (READ/$\overline{\text{WE}}$ OF 1851). WE: WRITE ENABLE.
TPB: (WRITE/$\overline{\text{RE}}$ OF 1851). RE: READ ENABLE.
ANOTHER CDP-1851 CAN BE CONNECTED IN PARALLEL TO 1802 OUTPUT LEADS IN I/O SPACE TO PROVIDE TWO MORE PORTS. (UP TO 4 OF 1851 IN MEMORY SPACE).

Fig. 6-17b. Interface of 1851 in a CDP-1800 series microcomputer system. (*Courtesy of RCA Solid State Division*)

6-12. PROGRAMMABLE I/O

A CMOS programmable I/O LSI chip is available from RCA's Solid State Division. Type CDP-1851 is a general-purpose two-port, 5-V, I/O device, directly compatible with CDP-1800 series 8-bit CMOS microprocessors CDP-1802, CDP-1802C, and CDP-1804.

CDP-1802, without suffix "C," is the high performance device, with high-noise immunity and an operating temperature range of $-55°$ to $+125°$ C. It has a typical fetch instruction time of 2.5 or 3.75 μsec at V_{DD} = 10V, and 5 or 7.5 μsec at V_{DD} = 5V. With 96 instructions, it is TTL-compatible with an on-chip DMA. Organization is 8-bit parallel, with bidirectional data bus. Any combination of RAM and ROM is acceptable with a memory addressing range of 65,536 bytes in a flexible programmed I/O mode, and program-interrupt mode. Four I/O flag inputs are directly tested by branch instructions. A 16×16 matrix of registers functions as multiple program counters, data pointers, or registers. CDP-1804 contains on-chip ROM, RAM, timer/control, and single-phase clock oscillator; it uses 113 instructions.

CDP-1851 is programmable with 20 I/O lines. It can be operated in four modes: (1) input, (2) output, (3) bidirectional, and (4) bit-programmable. Each one of its two ports can be programmed in either byte-I/O or bit-programmable modes for interfacing with peripheral devices such as keyboards and printers. The chip is available in 40-lead dual-in-line plastic (DIP with suffix E) and hermetic ceramic (suffix D) packages. A block-diagram of its internal architecture is shown in Fig. 6-17a. The simplified system block-diagram of the microcomputer is given in Fig. 6-17b to clarify the interface of the programmable I/O chip with its two ports. Port A is programmable in all four modes, but Port B must be programmed in bit-programmable mode. The STROBE and READY lines provide handshaking in the input and output modes. A High-to-Low transition on the STROBE line will generate an interrupt to indicate that data have been loaded into the port. When the CPU reads the data, the interrupt is reset, and the READY line goes high to indicate that the port is vacant. In all modes, interrupts can be detected on the $\overline{\text{INT}}$ output terminals or by reading status register. The chip can be used in either memory spaces or I/O.

6-13. I/O INTERFACE TO KEYBOARDS AND PRINTERS

User programs and data are entered into a microcomputer by means of a *keyboard* input device like that used by a teletype. It is operated in conjunction with a CRT display system. The keyboard is comprised of pressure-operated or capacitive touch-tactile switches arranged in a matrix array. A combination of hardware and/or software is used for key-recognition, and the two basic types used are either encoded (with LSI interface circuitry) or nonencoded. The encoded keyboard has the necessary complement for key-recognition and for holding the data until a new key-stroke; the nonencoded versions use either hardware or a special software routine for analysis. The decoded version is simple to interface with a parallel I/O port directly. The software routine versions are becoming unpopular since the simpler LSI ASCII decoding hardware is less expensive.

Small low-cost hex keyboards with built-in interface circuitry can be attached to the front panel of a microcomputer system to enter short machine-language programs in hexadecimal code. Figure 6-18a illustrates the simple hex-keyboard with a simple block diagram of the logic involved for interface. A diode matrix is used to convert the key strokes into unique binary patterns.

As the microprocessor accepts (at a typing speed of 10 characters/sec) one character at a time (or several characters in some instances, depending on the memory and logic circuitry involved for some special keys), the microprocessor has plenty of time to execute other programs at approximately 50,000 instructions or more between successive key strokes of a commercially available keyboard/CRT microcomputer. Most personal computers belong to this category.

Key-bounce of a duration of approximately 10 to 20 msec is a problem in pressure-operated switches; it is usually solved by means of an RC-filter or a simple dual-NAND logic circuit across the switch contacts. The nature of the on-off bounce, and the NAND implemented bounce-free switch are shown in Fig. 6-18b. Multiple-key closure or *roll-over* is another problem associated with keyboards. Several types of LSI keyboard encoders, such as static/scanning/converting encoders, are available to successfully solve the problem of bounce and rollover. Some keyboards are equipped with a ROM memory, which automatically supplies an output code such as the ASCII or the EBCDIC corresponding to the key pressed. Separate shift and control inputs are also provided. The block-diagram of a typical sophisticated keyboard system (NEC μPD 364D-022) for microprocessor input-port use is shown in Fig. 6-19. Equipped with an internal mask-programmable 3600-bit ROM, it provides for multikey lockout, multikey roll-over and debounce, frequency control oscillator, and a 4-mode selection of shift, control, and shift plus control. It is a 9 X 10 matrix version with 10 bit/key-stroke in 4 modes, using two ring-counters and an output data-buffer, which is TTL/DTL/MOS compatible.

Another outstanding example is the keyboard used for RCA CMOS VP-3301. This ASCII encoded, interactive data terminal features flexible-membrane key switches with

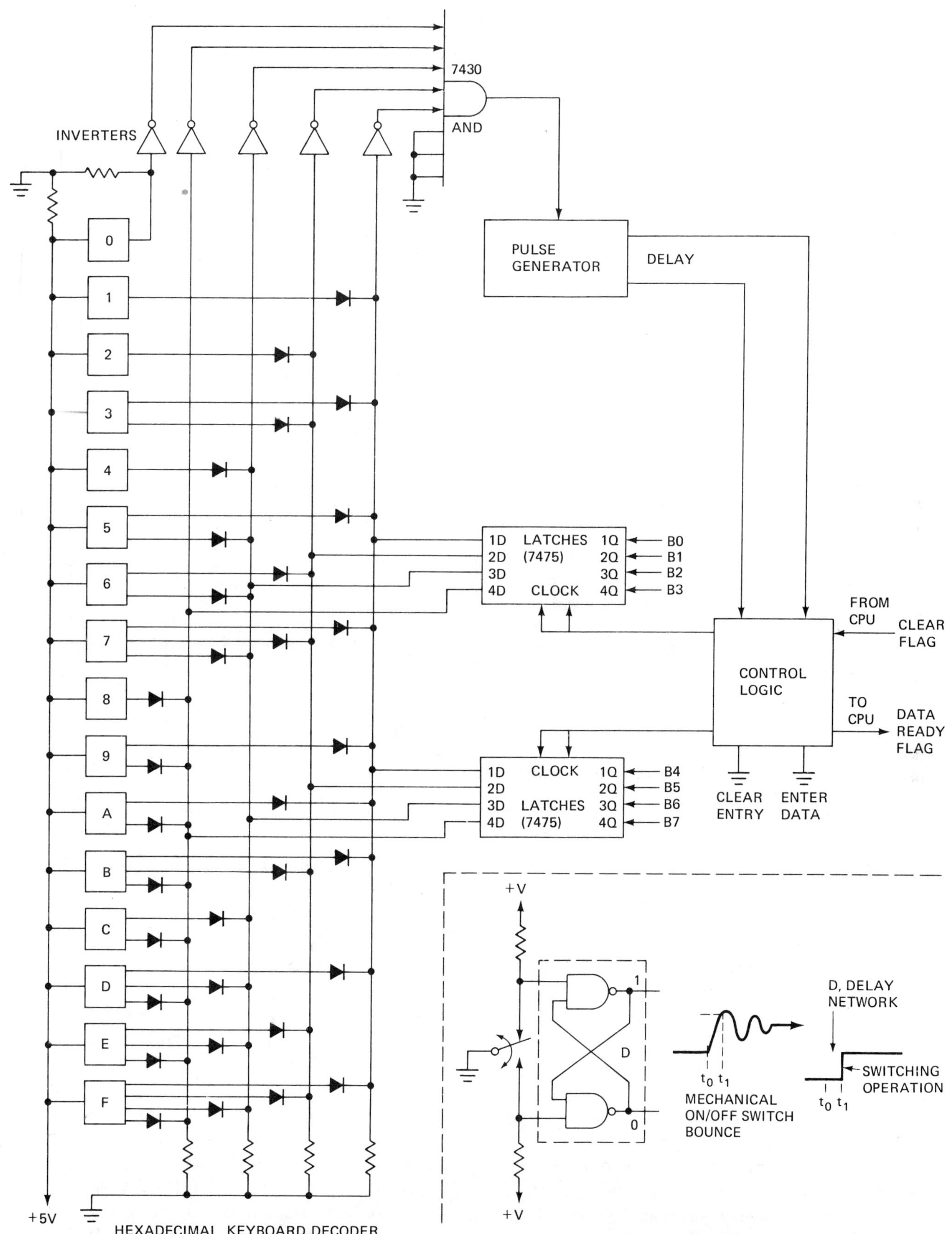

Fig. 6-18a. A simple hexadecimal keyboard interface. b. NAND implemented bounce-free switch and on/off bounce waveform.

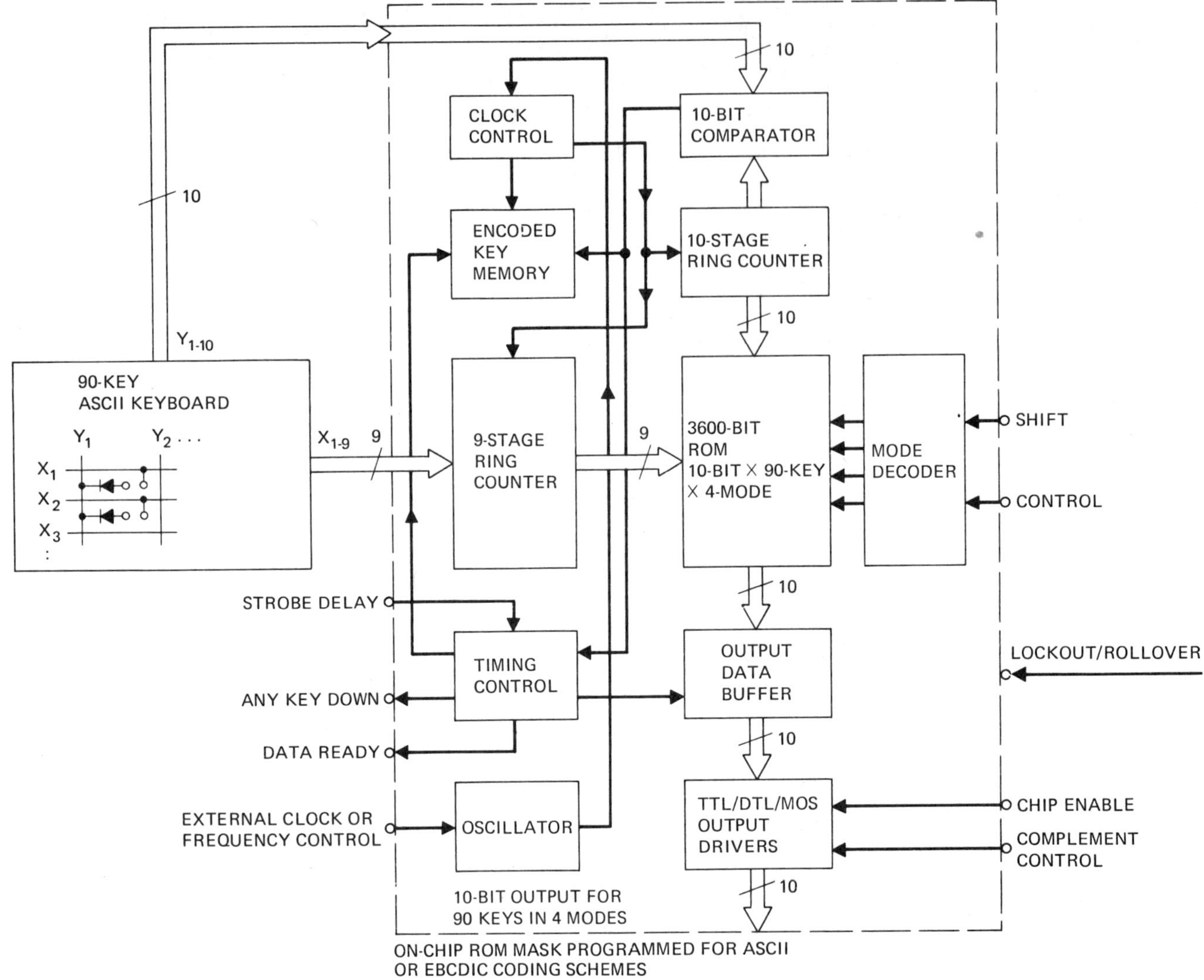

Fig. 6-19. NEC μPD 364D-022 keyboard encoder using a ROM. (*Courtesy of Nippon Electric Company*)

contact-life rated above 5 million operations. A finger positioning overlay and positive keypress action give a fine effortless "feel" for the operator. An on-board sound generator and speaker provides aural feedback for key presses; they can be also activated with escape sequences to provide an audio output. The sealed keyboard is bounceproof and dustproof, and the noise-immunity CMOS circuitry makes the VP-3301 ideal for noisy environments. Operating from a single 5-V built-in power supply, the keyboard connects directly to a computer or to a standard modem for over-the-phone access to time-sharing networks or data-base host computers. Microprocessor intelligence and LSI video control integrated circuits bring performance, features, and flexibility as an interactive data terminal (with color graphics) at a low price ($255). The CMOS-decoded keyboard alone costs less than $50. The VP-3301 interactive data terminal is shown in Fig. 6-20.

The resident character set is comprised of 52 upper- and lower-case alphabetics, 10 numerals, 32 punctuation/math symbols, and 31 control characters, including Greek letters, graphic symbols, etc. The all-inclusive VP-3301 provides for software selectable display formats of 40 characters by 24 lines or 20 characters by 12 lines for color graphics. This interactive color graphics terminal can be directly connected to a (525-line stan-

Fig. 6-20. RCA VP-3301 interactive data terminal. (*Courtesy of RCA Solid State Division*)

dard) color or monochrome monitor, or to a standard television receiver by using an RF modulator for one of the free television channels—to make a personal computer.

Output Printers. Standard electric typewriters used for teletype or teleprinters produce direct *hard* copy; they are known as console, message, or supervisory printers. Long rolls of paper are put into the typewriter carriage for entry and readout of processed data. For high-speed printout of decoded bulk data, two basic types of printers are used: line-at-a-time printers and high-speed character-at-a-time printers. Line printers (*bar* or *gong* printers) enable line-at-a-time by means of solenoid-operated hammers and typebars for 80 characters. Proper positioning of the bars is controlled by the decoder output, to provide a rated speed of about 150 line/min. for numerical printing and about 100 line/min. for alphanumeric printing.

Other large electromechanical printers, such as *wheel* printers, *drum* printers, *chain* printers, and *comb* printers, are used in the case of large-scale and medium-scale computers. A chain printer, for example, can print more than 1000 line/min.; and a comb printer is used where a relatively simple, inexpensive printout is desired at a medium speed of 150 lines/min. The fastest printers presently available belong to the *electrostatic* category on a special paper, that holds the electrostatic charge of ink-dots assembled as characters. They reach very high speeds on the order of 5000 line/min.

In character-at-a-time printers, the type is placed on a square block; it moves from left to right as the desired character is positioned and "hammered" at each print position against an inked ribbon; the teleprinter speed is about 8 line/min. However, character-at-a-time *matrix* printer using a 5 X 7 dot-matrix, have a high-speed capability up to 800 line/min., as good as a line-printer. The character format is accomplished when the appropriate pins strike against the paper. These matrix printers are generally called *impact* printers; they are suitable for multiple carbon copies. In less-noisy *nonimpact* printers, the print mechanism does not touch the paper. *Thermal* printers use pulses of heat shot into heat-sensitive paper in dot-matrix format, and *ink-jet* printers shoot ink droplets onto the appropriate dots of the desired characters. Number of characters can vary from 20 to 132 character/line, with 80 as the medium capacity of columns. Some inexpensive printers give only upper-case printout, using friction feed mechanism for advancing paper.

For use of microcomputer systems and low-cost personal computers, *dot* printers with 20 to 80 character/line are the least expensive; they cost from $500 to $1000. As a typical example, PR-40 dot printer, manufactured by Southwest Technical Products Corporation, is an impact type using the standard 5 X 7 dot matrix. ASCII encoded characters, 40/line, are printed at the rate of 75 line/min. The printer interface uses a FIFO buffer memory for a stack of 40 characters. A line printout occurs when a carriage-return control character is received or when the FIFO is full. The line printer uses the following components for the motor print mechanism: (1) 40-character FIFO, (2) ROM character generator and a dot counter for column-select, (3) control character and carriage-return decoders, and (4) printer solenoid and motor drivers. The dot printer receives ASCII data and data strobe on 8 lines, and returns data-accept signal on 1 line to the output-port of the microcomputer. The ROM outputs the signals for the print hammer-solenoid drivers. No software instructions are needed from the microcomputer. The popular Radio Shack TRS-80 microcomputer uses 5 types of 5 X 7 dot-matrix *impact* printers in the price range of $219 to $1960. The top-end TRS-80 Line Printer III (26-1156) provides full 13-in.-wide, 132 character-lines, 9 X 7 dot-matrix printout at a rate of 120 character/sec. The head prints upper- and lower-case letters and numbers in both directions as it moves across the paper.

6-14. I/O PORTS AND DISPLAY

A display of numerical digit information, using 7-segment light-emitting diodes (LEDs) or liquid crystal display (LCDs in the case of battery-cell operated wristwatches), can be reliably handled in several ways.

6-14.1. LED Display. Former techniques using binary-coded decimal to 7-segment MSI decoder drivers, such as Texas Instruments 74LS47s, require the usage of either several available I/O ports of a microprocessor or as an alternative LSI parallel I/O-port interface chips of the category of 6520, 6530, etc., and prohibitively large number of segment leads to provide a multidigit display. Segment leads can be multiplexed to minimize the number of leads to the lamps in an assembly. For example, LED Litronix 707 requires 7 leads to the 7-segment display at 1.7 V and 20 mA by using a common-anode supply of 5 V and series resistors.

As an alternative, the number of I/O ports required from a microprocessor can be minimized to just one port by using Texas Instruments 74LS259 active-high decoder chip for 3-digit address and strobe; and the remaining 4 lines of the I/O port, out of the total of its 8 lines, are connected in parallel to the 7-segment display package via Signetics latch-and-decode drivers 8T74, one per LED.

In the near future, compact microprocessor-controlled LSI/VLSI decoder chips will be available to interface LED/LCD alphanumerical display assemblies of several digits from a single I/O port of a microprocessor.

6-14.2. LCD Display. Low-power-consuming, liquid crystal displays sensitive to voltage rather than current, have been commonly used in wristwatches and pocket calculators. Now they are also used in other applications. In cases requiring more than 3 or 4 display digits, multiplexing schemes drastically reduce the number of output control leads to the 7-segment LCD displays. An 8-digit numerical display with each segment individually driven would require an IC driver with 67 leads; 3-line (V/3) multiplexing will reduce the package size and cost by using only 28 leads. V depicts voltage.

LCD segments are selectively tested by way of amplitude selection on a time-synchronized basis. If the peak operating voltage is 3 V, the rms voltage across a segment is 1.91 V when it is on, and 1 V when it is off. V_{ON}-to-V_{OFF} ratio of 1.91 is achieved with V/3 multiplexing also. Temperature compensation is essential for wide-temperature applications by using (1) a supply voltage that tracks the LCD temperature or (2) a silicon diode since it compensates the correct negative temperature coefficient (10 mV/°C) for common liquid-crystal materials. Incidentally, the V/3 multiplexing scheme is effective for analog LCD displays; a single CMOS IC can drive a large number of segments, since the drive currents and voltages are very low.

6-14.3. Video Display. The most popular CRT video display is interfaced to the address, data, and control buses of a microcomputer by using a system interface controller, primarily consisting of a RAM memory and video generator circuitry. The basic system concept is shown in Fig. 6-21a. Most video displays use a 16-line-by-32-character/line format on the CRT screen, and this procedure requires 512 bytes of data stored in a RAM. The video generator functions in a loop (1) to access each character in sequence and (2) to continuously display and refresh the display on the screen. If fresh characters or lines are desired, the microprocessor stores them in new address areas in the RAM, or an expanded RAM memory.

One of the low-cost available color graphics CRT display systems, using RCA CMOS video display controller CDP-1861C and RCA CMOS color generator controller CDP-1862C, is illustrated in Fig. 6-21b. Figure 6-21c shows their functional block-diagrams. These two LSI controller chips are directly interfaced to RCA CMOS 1802 microprocessor and the necessary ROM and RAM memory chips. If graphics on black-and-white CRT are desired, CDP-1861C will do.

CDP-1861C CMOS LSI video display controller uses static silicon-gate CMOS architecture to support bit-mapped video display for graphic flexibility. The last digit C in type number indicates 24-pin dual-in-line ceramic package to meet the specifications of defense equipment. While generating composite horizontal and vertical syncs for the digital frame on the screen, it inherently provides a programmable vertical resolution for matrix display of up to 64 × 128 segments. The features include real-time interrupt generator, clear input, external display control, and low quiescent and operating power on a single 4-to-6-V power supply. The operating temperature ranges from −55° to +125° C. The internal DMA feature of the CDP-1802 microprocessor may be conveniently used for direct data transfers from memory to the CDP 1861C. The interrupt input and the I/O command lines are used to perform the necessary handshaking between the microprocessor and the video controller. Timing is simplified by operating the CPU at a clock-frequency of 1.76064 MHz (half that of standard color subcarrier frequency). The clock-frequency equals field/sec (60), times line/field (262), times machine-cycle/line (14), times bit/byte (8). Each machine-cycle requires a memory-access time in DMA operation.

CDP-1862C CMOS LSI color generator controller interfaces conveniently with CDP-1802 microprocessor, and CDP-1861C video display controller to provide CRT graphics in a color television monitor (CRT). The screen background color and video dot color are programmable. There is an on-chip crystal-controlled oscillator (with external crystal connections). The color generator controller is NTSC-color compatible; green, red, and blue luminance signals are available for directly controlling the green, red, and blue amplifiers in the color video monitor. A 7.15909-MHz on-chip crystal-controlled oscillator or an external clock of the same frequency can be used to generate multiple phases of the 3.579545 MHz color burst (subcarrier) frequency for NTSC-compatible color of television programs. An internal counter provides the clock (1.789773 MHz) for the microprocessor and video display controller chips. Two inputs, synchronous timing pulse (STP) and $\overline{\text{SYNC}}$, are used to maintain color system synchronization. The $\overline{\text{RESET}}$ input to CDP-

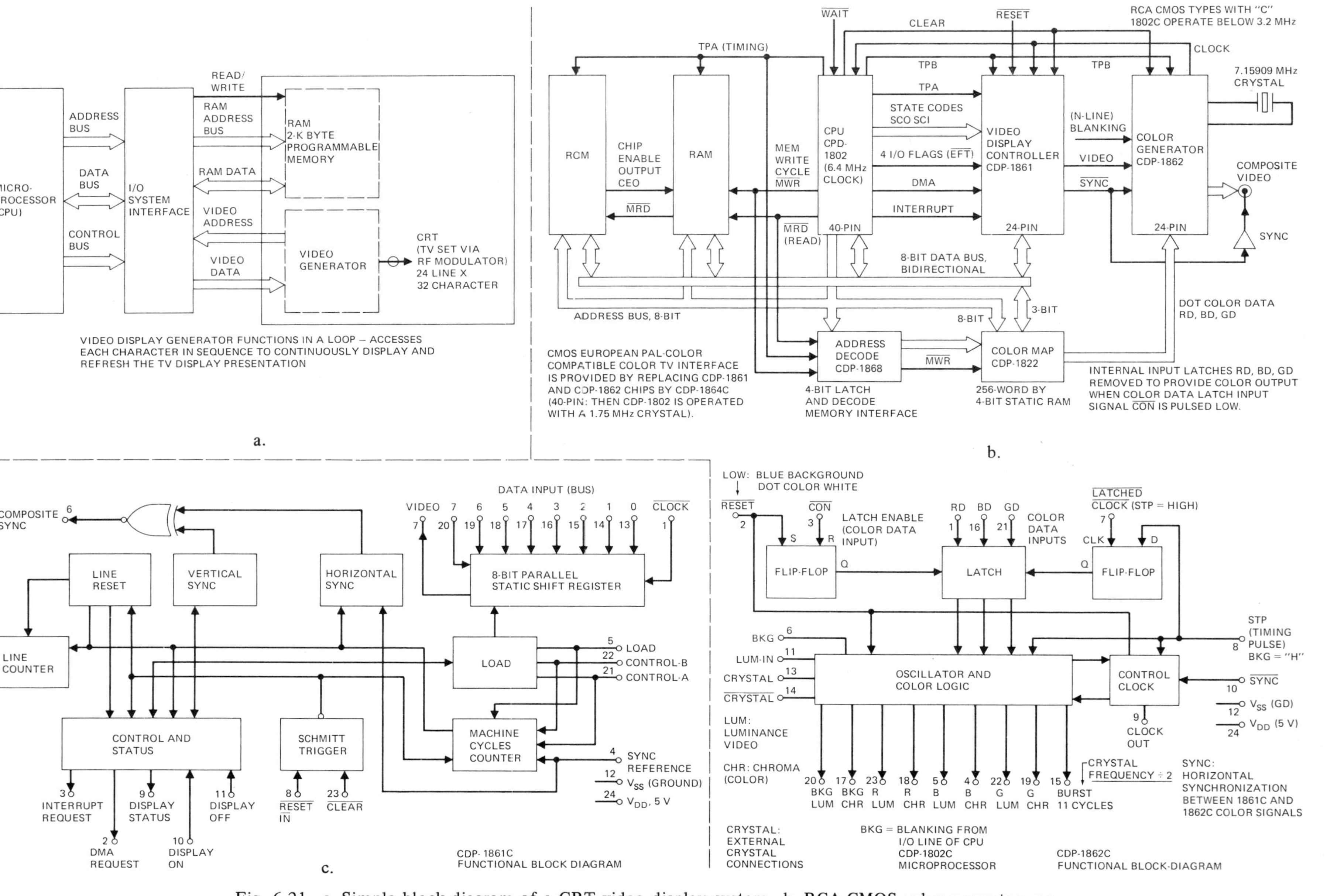

Fig. 6-21. a. Simple block-diagram of a CRT video display system. b. RCA CMOS color generator controller for color graphics. c. Functional block-diagrams of RCA CMOS 1861C video display system and RCA CMOS 1862C color generator controller. (*Courtesy of RCA Solid State Division*)

1862C turns the background color to blue with video display in white dots. CDP-1862C is supplied in 24-lead hermetic dual-in-line side-brazed ceramic packages (D suffix) or plastic package (E suffix). The supply voltage should be maintained within 4 to 6.5 V. The corresponding NMOS video interface chip (VIC) for color graphics is the MOS Technology Inc. MCS6560/6561. It provides for mask-programmable sync generation (NTSC-6560, or PAL Europe-6561), and 600 independently programmable and movable background locations. It has a light-gun/pen facility for interactive graphics.

6-15. I/O INTERFACE-ORIENTED MICROCOMPUTER CHIPS

Motorola MC6801 of the 6800 family can function as a flexible stand-alone 8-bit microcomputer with eight operating modes to serve as a microcontroller in control processing applications. With an on-chip serial communications interface, on-chip ROM, and polled registers, it can be conveniently serviced by interrupts to replace expensive software in serial data communications. The communication format may be half or full duplex with baud-rate selection. MC6801 has 2-K bytes of mask-programmed ROM, 128 bytes of RAM, 29 I/O lines, and 4 I/O ports. Ports 2 and 3 provide I/O in the single-chip mode to transfer data and address information; but these ports can transfer data in the expanded mode by using off-board additional ROM, RAM, and I/O ports.

Modes available (program control with 3 bits on pins 8, 9, 10) are:

Mode 0: Multiplexed test
Mode 1: Multiplexed RAM and ROM
Mode 2: Multiplexed RAM
Mode 3: Multiplexed without RAM and ROM
Mode 4: Single-chip test
Mode 5: Nonmultiplexed/partial decode
Mode 6: Multiplexed/partial decode
Mode 7: Single-chip, stand-alone microcomputer

MC6801 has an electrically programmable EPROM version in MC68701. This chip, when operated in expanded mode with external ROM control program, and external RAM object-code program, is capable of programming itself automatically. There is also a monitor ROM program version MC6801L1, with built-in monitor mask-programmed ROM, to let the user transmit monitor commands to a standard RS-232 C terminal via the serial-port in one of the above 8 modes. The built-in timer serves under software control many timing functions, such as pulse, frequency, and period-synthesis, as well as measurement of these parameters. The timer comprises of a 16-bit counter to increment the system clock-rate, an input buffer-register, and an output compare-register.

Port No. 1, which is byte-oriented, is always available for parallel I/O. Port No. 4 handles I/O in single-chip mode, and addresses in expanded multiplexed/nonmultiplexed modes. All 29 I/O lines are compatible with TTL; 5 of these lines can be shared with the serial interface. The standard multiplexed mode provides for the full addressing of 4-K bytes of RAM memory. A crystal of 4.91520 or 2.4576 MHz must be used for standard-speed serial communication.

Emulation of the 6801 can be implemented with a 6801 in the expanded mode. MC6801 PC, a *peripheral controller* with dual-ported ROM for enabling external access to the on-chip RAM, and a preprogrammed MC6801 controller-version for the IEEE-488 bus, are also available from Motorola Inc.

6-16. I/O SERIAL CONTROLLERS FROM LOW-SPEED TELETYPES TO NETWORK HOST MINICOMPUTER

Setting up a protocol-interfaced serial data communications network from a host computer involves an expensive extent of random logic in the front-end controllers at the TTY terminals. This procedure is simplified for a network of up to 255 terminals in common applications such as a processing plant or gas stations, etc., by using a single LSI chip—Mostek Corporation's serial control unit (SCU-1)—at each network terminal. It is housed in a 40-pin 5-V, 275 mW, DIP, and implemented by an LSI ion-implanted silicon-gate NMOS chip, with a serial-data port and bidirectional port-Ø and port-1 I/O lines (8 each). Asynchronous operation in a half-duplex mode at a rate under 1200 bit/sec is specified. The terminal can change its mode of operation by interpreting 19 preprogrammed commands. The chip contains the processing power of a communications link interface and a CPU consisting of ALU, ROM, 64 × 8-bit scratch-pad registers, indirect address, memory address, instruction, status and accumulator registers, main and interrupt control logic, external crystal-clock, and serial-data port. Bit and word synchronization are provided by the asynchronous format. Eight lines for address selection, two lines for speed selection, and one line for $\overline{\text{RESET}}$ and POWER-ON-CLEAR are also required.

SCU-1 is ideally suitable for controlling analog-to-digital or digital-to-analog converters sending information over a noise-immune RS-422 transmission line. This versatile LSI chip can be also used as a peripheral microcomputer to send data and control the operation of a LED display driver.

6-17. I/O ENCRYPTION INTERFACE IN MULTI-KEY SYSTEMS

Data communications security is an important requirement in modern data terminals such as credit-card validation and verification systems, point-of-sale (POS) terminals, defense data communications, and banking computer hardware that incorporates microprocessors and their peripherals. American Microsystems Inc. has announced a 2-chip S6894 data-encryption and data-decryption set, adaptable to multiple-encryption-key systems, by using minimum of hardware and software. The set, implementing the security task, consists of an S6802 microprocessor with an external crystal and an S6846 ROM with built-in I/O and a timer. Since the set can operate at data rates up to 11.5 Kb/sec, it is suitable for most data terminals in use. The ROM chip interfaces directly with the host minicomputer of the network. Data I/O, key and command input, and interface signals require a total of 8 lines. Eight data lines and 10 address lines interconnect the two chips along with read/write, chip-select, and enable signals. A partial reset interrupt-command from the host computer is optional.

The American Microsystems set briefly described above implements the National Bureau of Standards data encryption standard. There is no end to the applications of the ROM memory usage, on both hardware and software basis, in computer systems.

6-18. PERIPHERAL CONTROLLERS (CUSTOM LSI CHIPS)

Low-speed peripheral devices such as floppy-disk drives, CRT terminals, line printers, and high-speed hard-disk drives can be controlled with minor modifications in the ROM programmability of a Z-80 microprocessor-based LSI peripheral controller as an interface to a host high-speed minicomputer. Control Data Corporation has developed a custom LSI logic chip, for incorporation in a CDC Series/1 controller which uses four of these chips for address, data, status, and poll. The chip uses bipolar integrated-injection logic (I^2L) approach for high-density, high-speed, and low-voltage low-power dissipation. The I/O circuits in the chips are buffered to make them noise-immune and TTL-compatible to the Z-80 microprocessor in the controller. The TTL peripheral control logic and the I/O port of the controller are subject to minor modification depending on the actual peripheral used. The 2600-gate, single-board (7 X 9 in.) peripheral controller is compatible to IBM's Series-1 minicomputers as a plug-in accessory. This kind of interface facility would previously have required a highly expensive hard-wired controller-interface and software for a powerful main-frame computer.

The Series-1 controller has a requirement of 81 lines of communication with the minicomputer channel, 33 lines for interconnect to the Z-80 microprocessor, and 27 lines for interface to the peripheral. In view of the number of lines involved, the organization of the controller is divided into 4 chips for the functions of address, data, status, and poll. A counter on the *address chip* (1) tracks addresses, (2) enables the DMA in the cycle-stealing mode of the Z-80 microprocessor, and (3) decodes instructions for the peripheral program control. The *data chip* provides buffer registers for data transmission and interrupt information between the Z-80 and main-frame CPU. The *status chip* provides the logic circuitry for the status of the CPU and the peripheral subsystem concerning interrupt and monitoring. The *polling* chip keeps track of the CPU's intercommunication with the Z-80 microprocessor in servicing the peripheral device. Some manufacturers would handle the required large number of I/O lines by using either additional LSI multiplexing circuitry or by conserving space to 2 chips only by the expediency of a 2-to-1 piggyback mounting facility in view of the low power dissipation.

7
LSI/VLSI Microprocessors And Single-Chip Microcomputers

7-1. DESCRIPTION OF SOME CHIPS AVAILABLE OFF-THE-SHELF

The types of single-chip LSI/VLSI microprocessors such as CPU, and single-chip stand-alone microcomputers (that include a clock generator with external crystal, ROM and RAM, and I/O) number about 40 at present. For flexibility of system design in various applications, the microprocessor as a CPU is, naturally, the preferred technique. That is, many of the logic and circuit designers will progressively turn into system designers using LSI/VLSI microprocessors, LSI/VLSI memories, LSI/VLSI field-programmable logic arrays FPLAs, and single-chip dedicated microcomputers. Of course, the manufacturer's applications engineers will necessarily play an important role in this function during the learning stage. Several chip- and system-design houses having logic-design capability have already commenced putting together custom LSI/VLSI chips for I/O interface, etc. in NMOS, or in CMOS or I^2L at competitive prices; this implementation is practical within a reasonable period of 3 to 6 months. The latest trend points to 16-bit microprocessors.

The single-chip microcomputers, 4-bit and 8-bit, from about a half dozen manufacturers are mostly based on NMOS technology; however, Fairchild Semiconductors is expected to exploit a 16-bit bipolar isoplanar I^2L microcomputer chip (9440) as a prelude to its successful feasibility and demand in the 1980s. Incidentally, some of the more popular microprocessor types do have second-source suppliers.

7-2. INTEL-8080/LSI MICROPROCESSOR

7-2.1. Intel N-Channel Microprocessor: 8080 with Intellec-8 Program Development Facility. As the most popular "workhorse" among the microprocessors, the 40-pin silicon-gate N-channel microprocessor is TTL-compatible. Processing speeds are up, 10 to 100 times, compared to those of former Intel P-channel microprocessors. It is operationally a parallel CPU with an instruction cycle-time of 2 μs at the nominal clock-rate of 2 MHz, and 78 microinstructions, and clocked with 2-phase, nonoverlapping clock. It has 14 control lines, and 8-line bidirectional data-bus; a 16-line bus is used for addressing the memory along with a 24-I/O line-section. All system controls are decoded on the chip. The CPU accesses up to 64-K bytes of memory, and operates up to 256 input and 256 output 8-bit channels; it has a provision for 8 interrupt levels.

High-speed I/O structure, memory, and control lines permit its use as a controller and a data-processing subsystem. Stack architecture enables the programmer to effectively process both subroutines and interrupts. Instructions are capable of handling strings of data along with decimal and double-byte arithmetic. Both decimal and binary data are handled with equal speed. Source programs can be written in either PL/M high-level system-oriented language or in a macroassembler language; programs written for the previous P-channel Intel-8008 may be compiled or assembled for the use of type-8080, which needs 20% fewer instructions.

The Intel-8080 microprocessor employs the programmable peripheral interface (PPI) 8255 for easy interface to printers, keyboards, displays, and motor drives. It has 13 options for memory circuits, such as 16-K bit ROMs, 8-K bit EPROMs, and 4-K bit RAMs (at high density and low cost) plus CMOS-RAMs for minimum power requirements. Type-M8080A is ruggedized for operation at Military Standards -55 to 125°C; type-8080A-1 is designed for a 1.3-μs instruction cycle-time in higher-speed real-time applications. Intel has a microcomputer hardware/software development system, Intellec-MDS, which employs an ICE-80 in-circuit emulator to simultaneously debug both software and hardware from the initial prototyping stage through production; it is supported by six comprehensive software packages, which include a macroassembler ICE-80, and a diskette operating system. This facility enables the direct availability of a versatile Intel

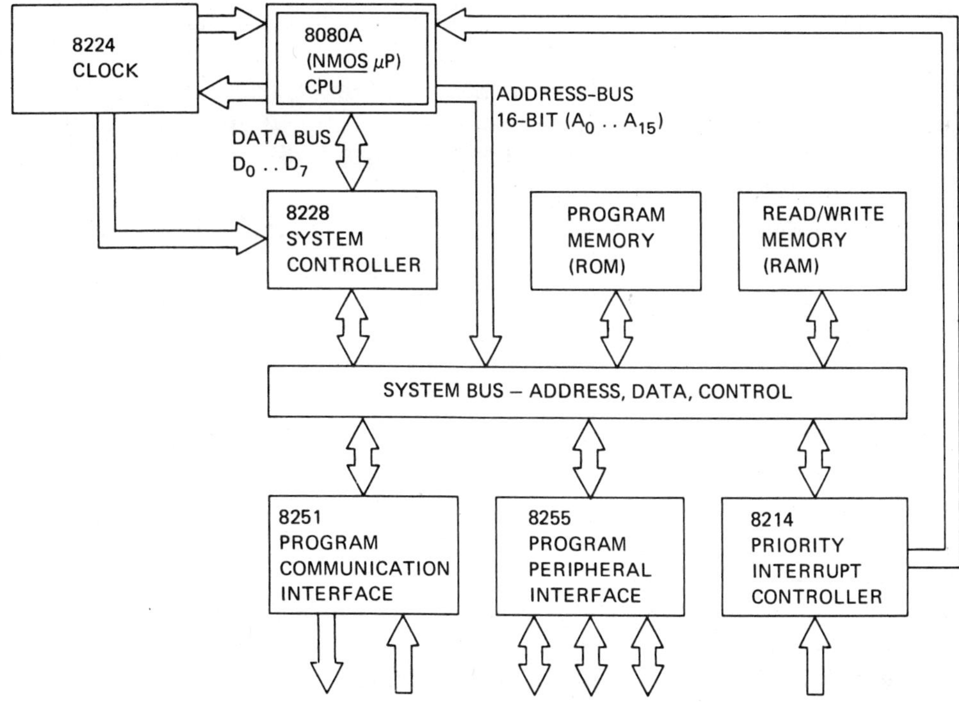

(COURTESY OF INTEL CORPORATION).

Fig. 7-1. Intel MCS-80 microcomputer system.

microcomputer system such as the IBM-5100 or DEC-LS-11 microcomputer systems. With the latest VLSI 64-K bit RAMs, ROMs, and EPROMs, cost-effective microcomputer systems are readily feasible.

Intel's MCS-80 system design-kit is comprised of a type 8080-A CPU, a crystal clock-generator, a system controller, a programmable communications interface (PCI), and a programmable peripheral interface (PPI). The system includes two 1-of-8 binary decoders, 256 bytes of static RAM as main memory, 2-K bytes of EPROM, and a PC board, at a total cost of $350. Figure 7-1 illustrates Intel's MCS-80 system design kit.

Gordon Moore and Robert Noyce of Intel were the initiating pioneers of the microprocessor concept in 1968 with their first PMOS, Intel-4004 microprocessor; Intel's technological track record in the advance of P/NMOS state-of-the-art in both the microprocessor and memory fields has been outstanding since.

Texas Instruments type-TMS-9900, a full-parallel 16-bit NMOS microprocessor, second-sources the above Intel-8080, and operates at 3-MHz clock, 4-phase, and does 16-bit register additions in less than 5 μs just as the present-day minicomputers do.

MICRO-PAC-80 (PCS, Inc.) employs Intel-8080, 1-K bytes of ROM and 4-K bytes of RAM. Pro-log Corp. type SS-1 uses Intel-4004 to provide eight 4-bit I/O lines, and Intel-8008 to provide 32 I/O lines and model ASR-33 TTY interface. Pro-log type-MP4216 and -MP4102 A-D and D-A converter cards serve as plug-in I/O interface.

7-2.2. Intel SBC 80/10 Microcomputer-on-a-Card. The single-card microcomputer SBC 80/10 is an example of a kind of subsystem (or OEM—original equipment manufacturer—supercomponent), employing type-8080A microprocessor and one 8,192-bit EPROM; it includes programmable LSI I/O interface, components to provide customized software for parallel I/O ports, and communications interface. This facility eliminates the need for inefficient specialized hardwired designs for custom applications, and results in the availability of a microcomputer-on-a-card, 6.75" × 12" at a price of $295, in the place of a superfluous minicomputer at a price of thousands of dollars, for most common general-purpose applications. The type-8080A CPU contains over 5,000 transistors on a silicon-substrate chip, 0.164" × 0.19". The organization of this system version is shown in Fig. 7-2a along with the pertinent interface components for most applications. The central processor, using the interrupt-control (LSI-8228 status latches) and the bus-control logic, the crystal-controlled clock (LSI-8224), the high-current drivers for memory and I/O bus expansion, and other CPU-related control functions, is implemented with the NMOS 8080A CPU and two Schottky-bipolar LSI devices. The cycle-time is 1.95 μs. The read/write main memory on the card consists of 1-K bytes of static RAM (two LSI-8101). The card has provision for four sockets to plug in 4-K bytes of EPROMs (LSI-8708) or ROMs (LSI-8303) to facilitate control memory in 1-K byte increments.

The programmable peripheral interface (PPI-LSI, 8255) provides 48 software-configurable parallel I/O lines; sockets are provided for interchangeable quad-line drivers and terminators to enable the user's choice of sink currents, polarities, and so forth. The programmable synchronous and asynchrous communications interface (PCI-LSI, 8251) includes a variable baud-rate generator and a jumper-selectable RS-232C interface with TTY drivers and receivers.

Since active programs are normally stored in a nonvolatile memory to eliminate the need for reloading RAMs every time the system is turned on, formerly external CORE memories were used for this purpose. This requirement is now eliminated by packaging such dedicated active memory on the card itself by using plug-in 1-K byte EPROMs or ROMs. The programmable interface devices mentioned previously accommodate various operating modes and protocols for control of data transfer to a variety of external devices like switches, motor drivers, bistable sensors, analog-to-digital and digital-to-analog converters, displays like CRT/LED, keyboards, line printers, communications modems for the TTYs in centralized or distributed communications networks, cassettes, and other micro- and mini-computers.

7-2.3. Intel 8748/8048 Microcomputer-on-a-Chip. The latest LSI technology introduces a dedicated microcomputer on a single-chip as an all-in-all digital controller by itself. As anticipated, the Intel track record continues unabated as the leading contender in the state-of-the-art microcomputer technology. Not unlike the present low-cost stand-alone 4-bit calculator chips, the Intel type-8748 and type-8048 microcomputer twins have a built-in 8-K bit (1,024 X 8-bit) EPROM, to facilitate a periodic updating of the program in one case and to facilitate a mask-programmable ROM in the other case, respectively. The requisite software-development function is reserved for the electronically programmable prototype 8748, and the finalized application program is established for the regular large-scale mask-programmable production chip 8048. This single-chip microcomputer thus accomplishes a stand-alone computer function in the built-in CPU, programmed ROM memory, 64 bytes of 9-bit scratch-pad data RAM memory, pulse-clocks and timers, and I/O interface for the dedicated application. In the case of the programmable version 8748, the program is altered or debugged by the technique of ultraviolet light-erasure. (Pro-log UV-Erase light system costs $150.)

The 8-bit CPU will provide the function of the ALU and the accumulator for all the binary and decimal arithmetic functions. The I/O function allows three 8-bit I/O ports and three test/interrupt ports—all directly controlled by the program instructions in the masked ROM area. The system details of the microcomputer-on-a-chip are shown in Fig. 7-2b.

One could add flexibility of expansion to this stand-alone microcomputer by directly interfacing an "Expander" chip type-8243, to handle 16 additional I/O lines. At the same time, the program and data bus-oriented architecture of the chip facilitates further expansion of the data-processing capability by means of an external ROM/RAM complement using an external latch (8212)—as in the case of any micro- or mini-computer system.

Present multichip microcomputer designs have an inherent delay in the transfer of the data between the memory and the CPU, and the single-chip microcomputer scores an advantage in eliminating that delay. Direct access to the 64 bytes of the 8-bit dynamic RAM allows the execution of indirect internal instructions, fetching the address of memory location and its contents, and the storage of the resulting information, all in one cycle-time of 2.5 μs. The RAM consumes a mere 75 mW for decoding the sense circuits involved in this operation.

Advantages of the single-chip microcomputer include:

1. In multiple-chip design, some time-delay is involved in transferring data between the memory and the CPU; with single-chip design, the specified instruction cycle-time is all that matters.

2. The inclusion of respective data and program RAMs and ROMs simplifies the user's interface needs.

3. Since the 8-level stack scratch-pad RAM operation is included in the CPU function, no "refresh" is required in this respect, although the internal clock is used for refreshing the low-power access to the dynamic RAM main memory in a fraction of an instruction cycle. Indirect internal instructions, requiring multiple addresses for (1) fetching the memory location to be operated on, (2) fetching the contents of the addressed location, and (3) storing the results of the operation, can be executed in one instruction cycle-time.

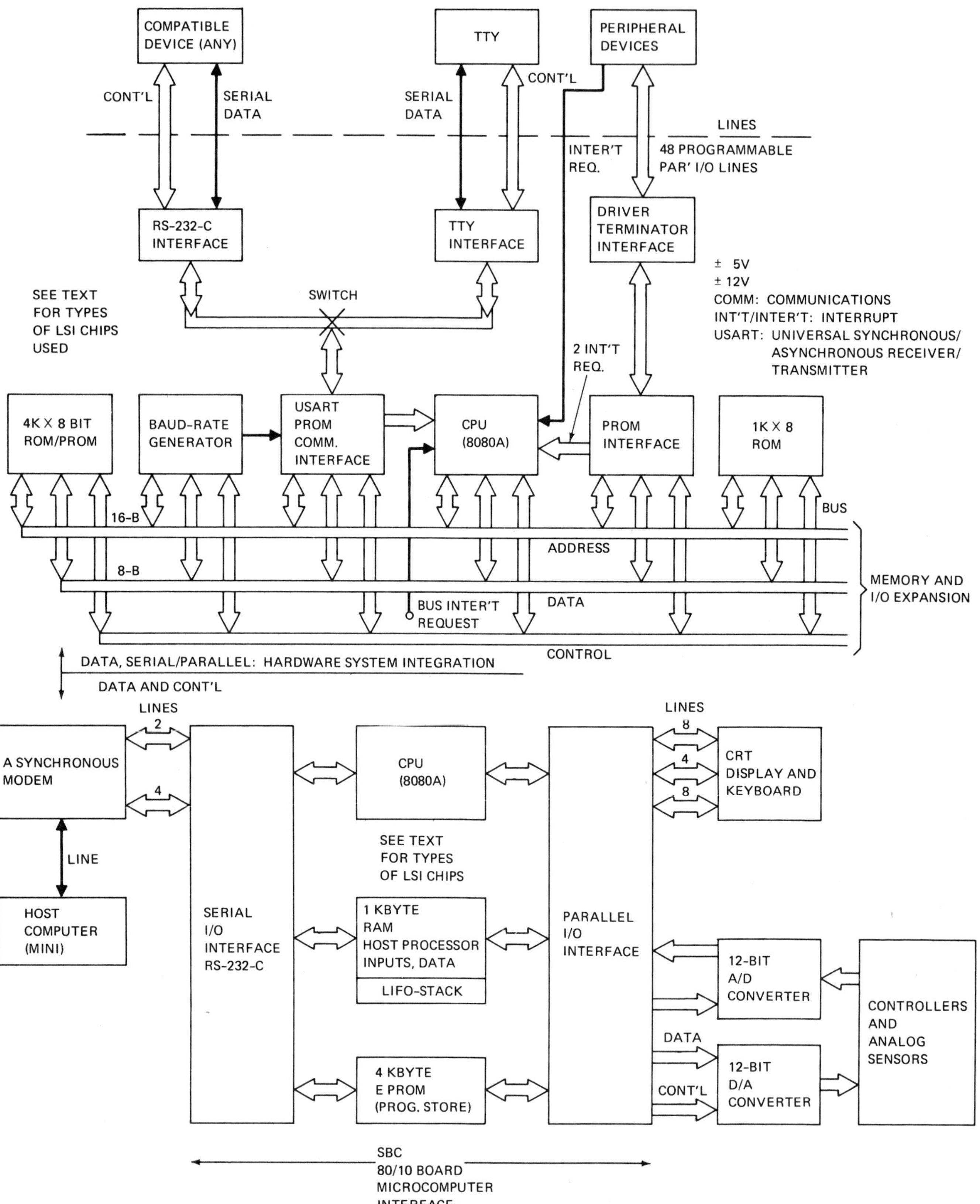

Fig. 7-2a. Organization of Intel SBC 80/10 microcomputer on a card. (*Reprinted by permission of Intel Corporation*)

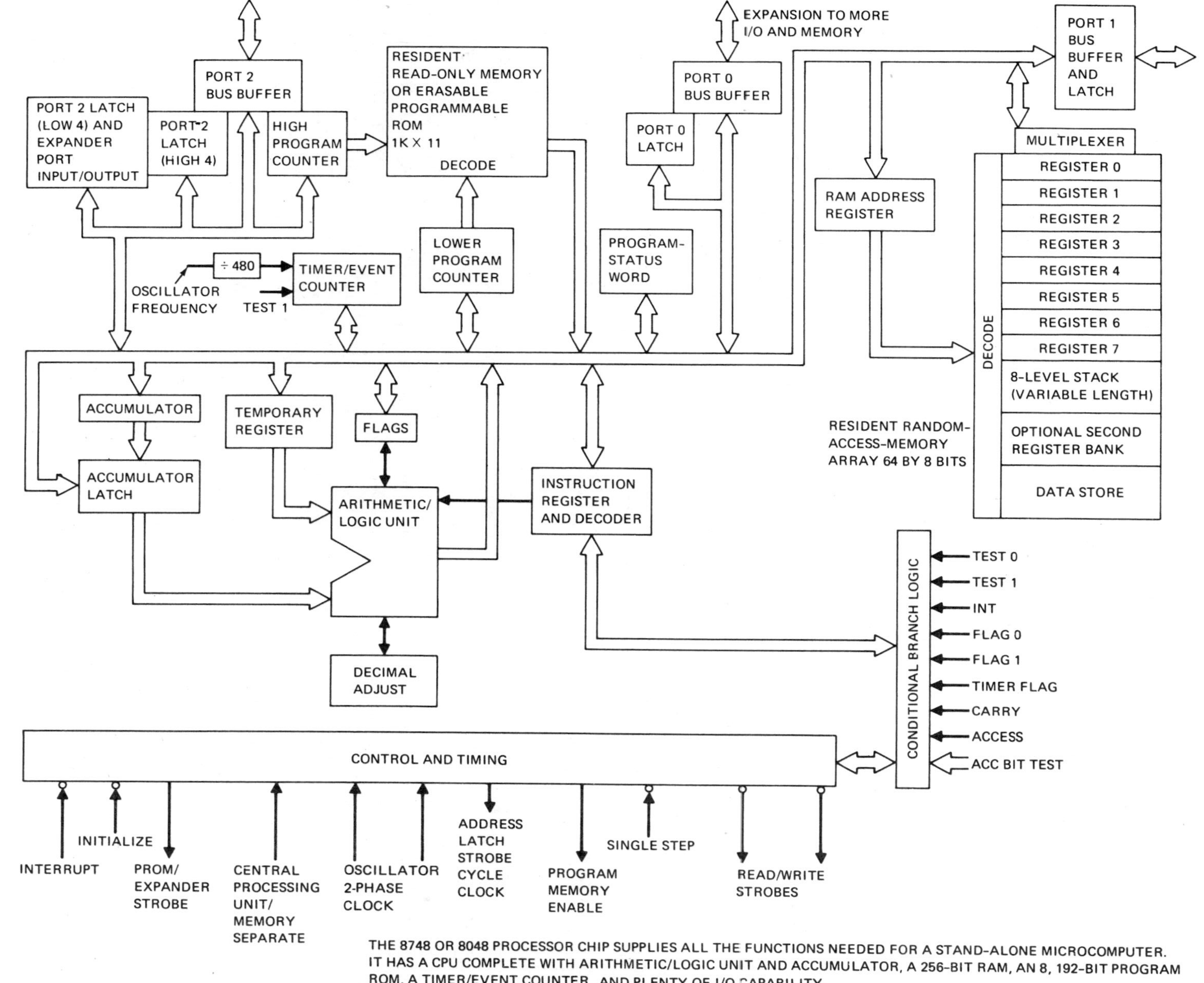

THE 8748 OR 8048 PROCESSOR CHIP SUPPLIES ALL THE FUNCTIONS NEEDED FOR A STAND-ALONE MICROCOMPUTER. IT HAS A CPU COMPLETE WITH ARITHMETIC/LOGIC UNIT AND ACCUMULATOR, A 256-BIT RAM, AN 8, 192-BIT PROGRAM ROM, A TIMER/EVENT COUNTER, AND PLENTY OF I/O CAPABILITY.

Fig 7-2b. Intel 8048 microcomputer on a chip. (*Courtesy Intel Corporation*)

4. The type-8748 with the EPROM can be operated on a special double-cycle instruction-cycle mode (called the third-state mode) for programming and convenient verification of the EPROM.

5. The instruction cycle of the 8748/8048 microcomputer takes place in five states: (1) instruction input, (2) decoding and program counter incrementing, (3) start of the program execution, (4) and (5) program execution while the next cycle's program address is simultaneously rendered effective, as a parallel pipeline operation.

7-2.4. Intel 8085. Intel 8085, a popular NMOS version of Intel 8080A, has the same word and data size 8/8, direct addressing range 64-K words, 80 instruction-set, but a maximum clock frequency-range of 3 MHz at single-phase, and four levels of on-chip interrupt with on-chip clock and serial-I/O data control, as compared to one level of interrupt, and external clock in the case of 8080A. In addition, 8085 operates with a single 5V power supply in the place of ±5 and −12V. Therefore, in most applications, 8085 chip is presently replacing the former 8080A microprocessor. Figure 7-3 illustrates the application of 8085 in the case of a small Private Automatic Branch Control (PABX), in conjunction with 4-K bytes of programmable-ROM (8355), 2-K bit main-memory static-RAM (8155), Programmable Peripheral Interface (8255 A5), I/O Driver/Terminator TTL Interface, Programmable Communications Interface (USART, 8521A) to RS-232C data line or terminal interfaces, Multi-Master-BUS Arbitration Logic (8218), and five Programmable Interval Timers (8253). A 10-ms interrupt-rate would produce an average dial-tone delay upon line seizure (off-hook condition) of 0.5 sec in a 100-port PABX or Concentrator.

7-3. PDP-11/03, DIGITAL EQUIPMENT CORPORATION

Digital Equipment Corporation (DEC) has recently announced its first end-user, microcomputer system PDP-11/03, priced at $9,950, as a packaged version of its microcomputer operating system LSI-11. It has a capacity of 8,192 words of RAM memory, a dual floppy-disk drive holding more than 500-K bytes, a VT-52 CRT terminal (or alternatively, an LA-36 keyboard serial-matrix printer for I/O, and DEC's RT-11 Operating System). The stand-alone floor-model printer operates at 30 characters/sec, while the CRT terminal as a separate tabletop configuration, displays 24 lines.

The basic microcomputer system of the PDP-11/03 and the dual-floppy disks are in one package, measuring 15″ X 17″ X 19″. The CPU is a treble-chip high-speed 16-bit microprocessor.

The LSI-11 microcomputer has been microprogrammed to

1. Emulate the basic instruction set of the previous PDP-11/35/40 minicomputers, along with fixed- and floating-point instructions
2. Perform on ASCII code for interactive communication dialogue with the operator
3. "Refresh" all dynamic MOS memories and provide for microcode expansion.

DEC, as the world leader in minicomputer products, claims that the PDP-11/03 opens a new dimension in microcomputer cost/performance product. (Rockwell International has recently announced a floppy-disk controller, using 8 LSI chips and costing $200, in place of the previous $1,000 hard-wired version.) DEC performs its internal software with the 8-bit octal code (as against the 16-bit hexadecimal code of IBM).

The 16-bit DEC LSI-11 microcomputer is compatible with the PDP-11/40 minicomputer and is exclusively designed to interface with the existing software of DEC's worldwide

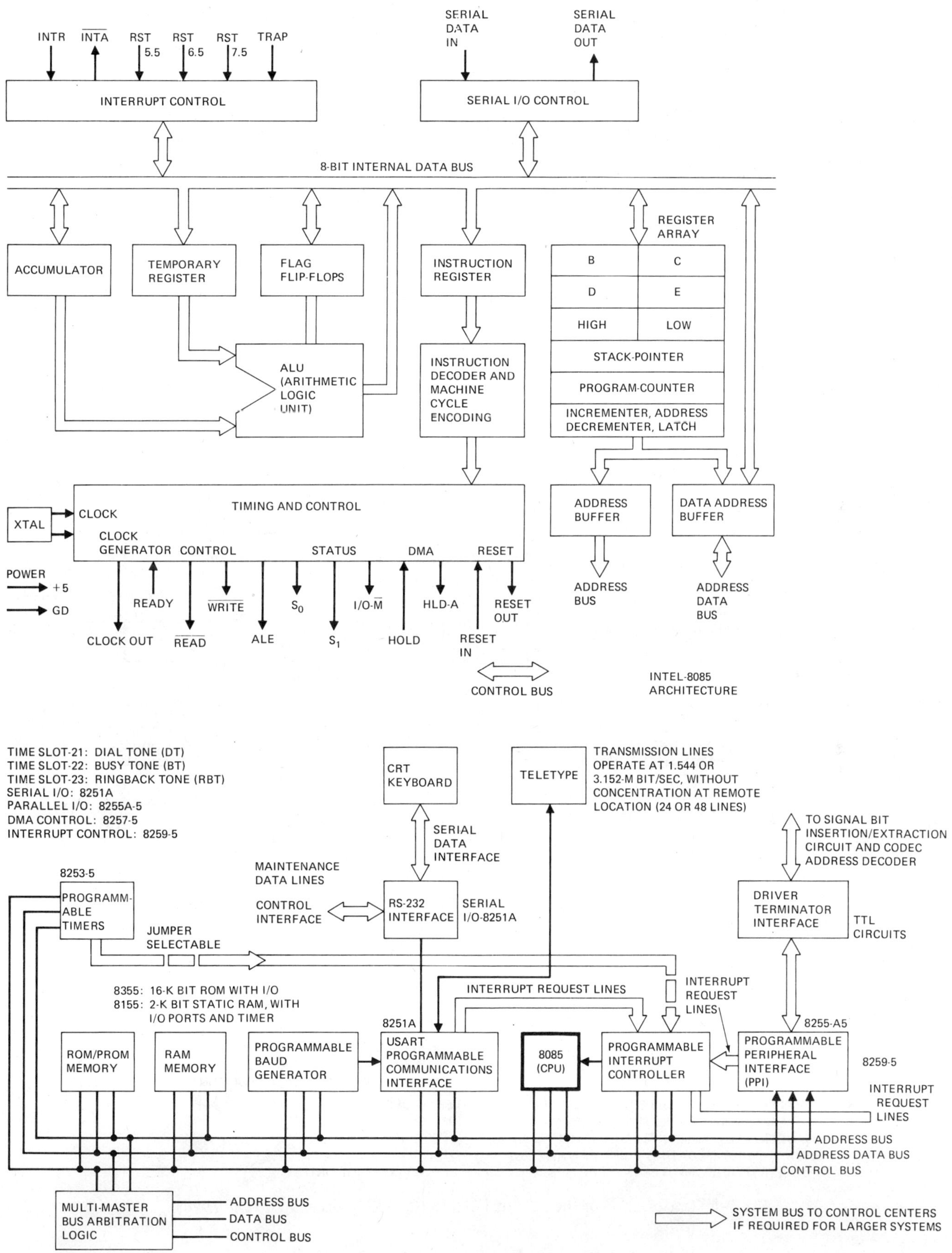

Fig. 7-3. Application of Intel-8085 in a PABX. (*Courtesy of Intel Corp.*)

PDP-series minicomputer operating systems. That is, the basic instruction set of the single-card (8.5" X 10.5") microprogrammed LSI-11 (with 4-K words of 16-bit memory and cycle-time of 350 ns, an ASCII keyboard console, a real-time clock, automatic dynamic-memory refresh, and interface-bus transceivers, and control logic) is identical to that of the PDP-11 series of minicomputers (PDP-11/05, 40, 70). Using the conventional distinction of horizontal (unencoded) and vertical (highly encoded) microorder codes, the LSI-11 can be classified as a vertical GPDC. Only addressing modes are exclusive, as shown in the microinstruction formats in Fig. 7-4 along with the organization of the LSI-11 CPU. The actual implementation of this computer is comprised of several NMOS microprocessor chips and extraneous TTL-MSI/SSI chips.

In the CPU module, provision is made for plug-in of an additional chip for extended arithmetic and floating-point instructions. Accessibility to the bus transceivers allows DMA transfers to and from primary basic 4-K word dynamic NMOS-RAM main memory on the card. As an alternative, either a nonvolatile CORE memory or a combination of 1,024-word static RAM and 4,096-word PROM could be used as main memory.

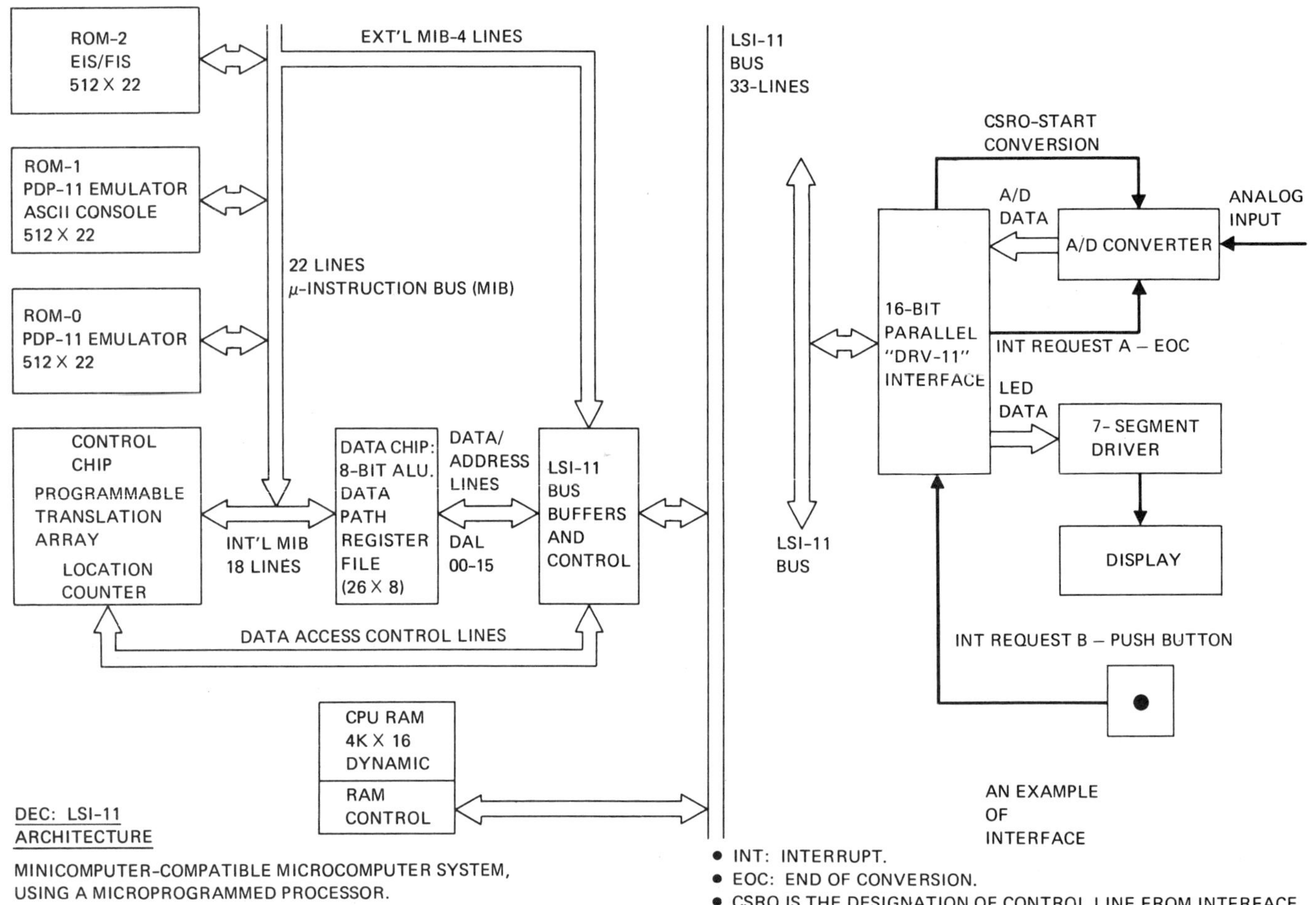

Fig. 7-4. Organization of the CPU of LSI-11. (© *IEEE Proceedings, June 1976*)

In view of the mixed LSI/MSI configuration of the basic high-speed CPU microprocessor card, the DEC microcomputer system is not aimed at the low-end market of the other single-chip microprocessors. The single-chip MPUs are used as CPUs in dedicated and common low/medium-cost/medium-speed applications under a \$500-to-\$1,000 bracket. (This situation is identical in the case of the recently introduced IBM-5600 portable computer.)

DEC subsequently introduced LSI-11/2, a smaller double height version of the original LSI-11. The new version is suitable for incorporation into instrumentation devices; the original 8-K bytes of memory of LSI-11 is relocated.

The newest member of this family, LSI-11/23, has been in use since 1979. It is hardware- and software-compatible with the original versions, but LSI-11/23 is improved functionally to step up the computing power to that of a regular 16-bit minicomputer; LSI-11/23 permits increased memory addressing capability.

LSI-11 and LSI-11/2, assembled with backplane, memory, and power supply are designated as PDP-11/03; and LSI-11/23 with backplane, memory, and power supply is distributed as PDP-11/23 microcomputer system.

7-4. TYPE 3850, FAIRCHILD MICROCOMPUTER SYSTEMS

A 2-chip NMOS microprocessor, as (1) 3850-CPU and (2) 3851-PSU (program storage unit with a 1,024 × 8-bit memory), I/O, Interrupt, Timer, and a Clock generator, make the basic Fairchild Microcomputer System.

Fairchild microcomputer kit (F-8). The architectural design of this microprocessor, according to the manufacturer, is aimed at directly addressing the user application, as an effective minicomputer does. It is a single-chip CPU with internal program storage. A six-chip array on a card allows memory interface and I/O structure, providing 32 latched I/O control lines, 64 bytes of RAM memory, on-chip clock, power-on reset, timer, and interrupt contols. See Fig. 7-4.

The regular microcomputer system consists of 3850/F8/CPU, 3851/F8/PSU, 3852/F8/DMI (dynamic-memory interface), 3853/F8/SMI (static-memory interface), 3854/F8/DMA (direct-memory access), and 3861/F8/PIO (peripheral I/O) device as an expansion unit for I/O ports, interrupts, and timers. An evaluation kit consists of an assembled microcomputer card (CPU, preprogrammed PSU), 1-K bytes of static RAM and SMI, a prewired cable terminating in an edge connector, a TTY connector, and power supply plugs. The PSU has a "bootstrap loader" that loads data from the terminal and stores it in a RAM with a full capacity of 1,000 bytes. The remaining functions of this chip allow:

1. Communication with a TTY at speeds from 10 to 300 bauds/sec
2. Dump memory from RAM for future loading
3. Create a PROM
4. Read from a high-speed paper-tape-reader, and
5. Alter any register or memory location in the F8 system from a terminal.

One could alter any instruction (as part of a subroutine format) by using the PSU and the terminal in this fully assembled microcomputer. The kit costs \$185.00.

F8 Microcomputer. Mostek is the second-source supplier of the F8 microcomputer.

CPU (MK3850). The 8-bit CPU has provision for 16-bit bidirectional I/O lines, which are internally latched either for storing output data or for driving a TTL load in the peripheral. The 64-byte scratch-pad memory eliminates the need for external RAM circuits in many applications. Clock and power-on reset circuitry are included on the chip.

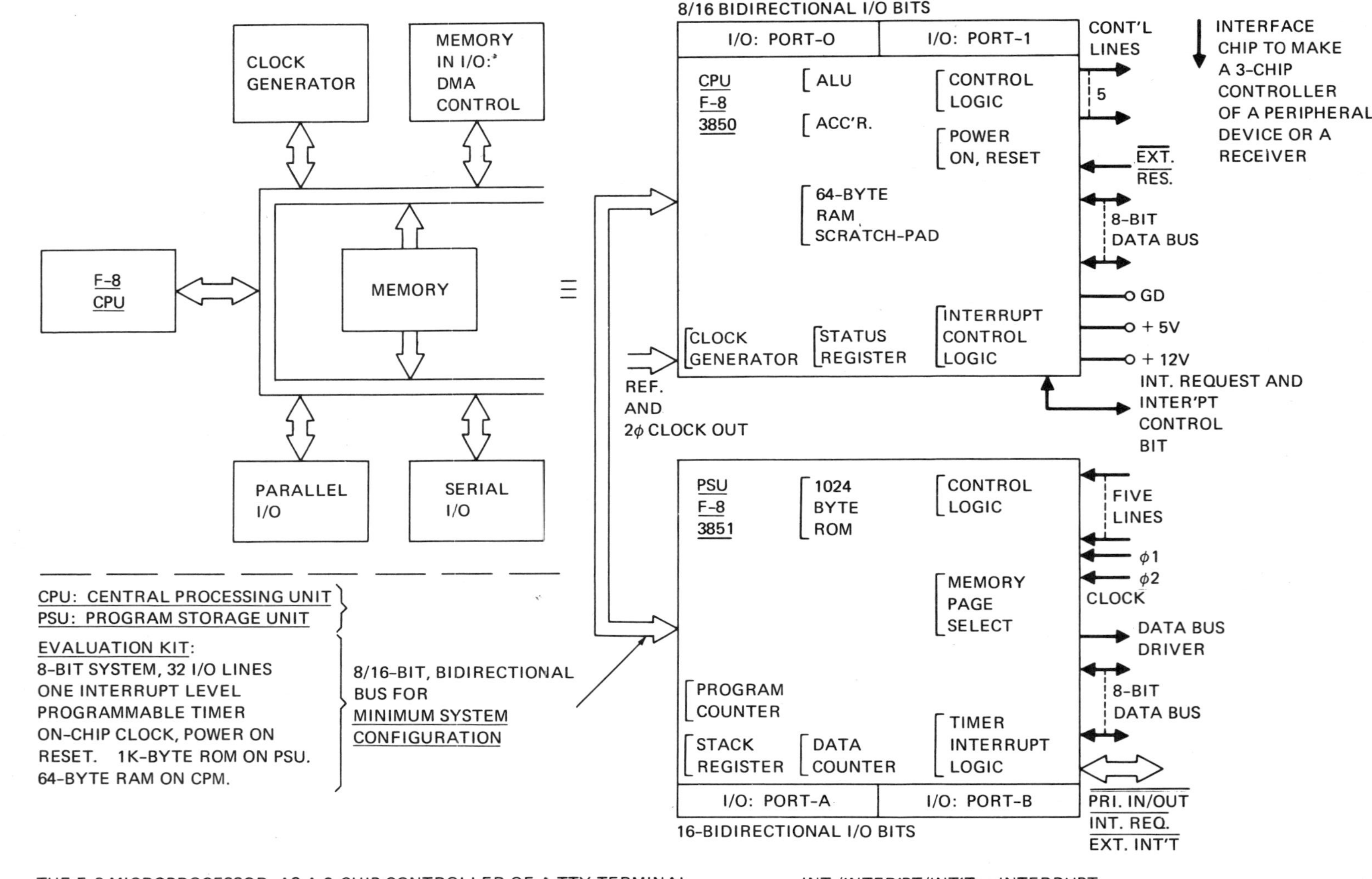

Fig. 7-5. The F-8 microcomputer. (*Courtesy of Fairchild Micro Systems*)

PSU (MK3851). The program storage unit contains:

1. A mask-programmable ROM for programmed permanent storage.
2. Addressing logic for memory referencing, a program counter, an indirect address register, and a stack register.
3. Restored interrupt level with an external interrupt line to alert the CPU.
4. An 8-bit programmable timer for generating real-time delays.
5. An additional 16 bits of TTL compatible, bidirectional latched I/O.

The system design of assignments between the two chips allows some flexibility. One CPU and three PSU chips will furnish a microcomputer system containing 64 bytes of RAM, 3,072 bytes of ROM, and 64 bits of I/O, three interrupt levels, and three programmable timers.

Memory interface circuits MK3852/3853. Each memory interface circuits chip has 16 address lines and the signals necessary to interface with 65-K bytes of RAM, PROM, or ROM.

The Static Memory Interface (MK3853) contains a full level of interrupt capability with a programmable interrupt-vector and a programmable timer. The Dynamic Memory Interface (MK3852) contains the logic necessary to "refresh" MOS dynamic memories.

Direct-memory access (MK3854) enables a high-speed data-link between F8-memory and peripherals. The data transfer is initiated by CPU under program control, and transfer will then continue without CPU intervention to enable its high throughput. The DMA contains an address register and a byte count for 16 address lines, DMA control and control registers, 8-bit data-bus, and miscellaneous control logic.

The **peripheral I/O (MK3861)** provides 16 bidirectional ports and an extra vectored-interrupt.

The **peripheral interface adaptor (MK6820P)** provides for TTL-compatible 8-bit bidirectional data-bus for communication with CPU or memory-interface chip. The peripheral lines are CMOS-compatible. Two programmable peripheral data direction registers, two programmable control registers, and two interrupt I/O control lines, make the other complement of this unit.

Software available for the microcomputer includes Resident Assembler, Text Editor, FORTRAN IV Cross-Assembler, two designer's debugging tools (DDT-1/2).

A typical application of an F-8 microcomputer in a surveillance receiver is shown in Fig. 7-6. The F-8 microprocessor, as a 3-chip controller of a TTY terminal or receiver, reduces the IC count from 91 to 12 or less, the system power by 50%, and the system cost by 20%.

7-5. EXORCISER (MOTOROLA MC-6800)

The architecture of the Motorola MC-6800 microprocessor is shown in Fig. 7-7. It is comprised of 256 bytes of ROM; 3K bytes of RAM (RAM expandable to 64K); teletype interface; 110–9,600 baud/sec, baud-rate switch-selectable; 10 optional modules with 8-bit I/O (expandable to 12 modules). Price $2,640. See Section 8-35 for further details of the MC-6800.

7-6. MICROCOMPUTER (AMERICAN MICROSYSTEMS INC., AMI-6800)

The AMI-6800 microcomputer, as a microcomputer development system, consists of 80 characters by 25-line CRT keyboard display, 1-M byte mass-memory dual floppy-disk on-line operating system, S6834 EPROM programmer, RS-232 interface, 16-K words of

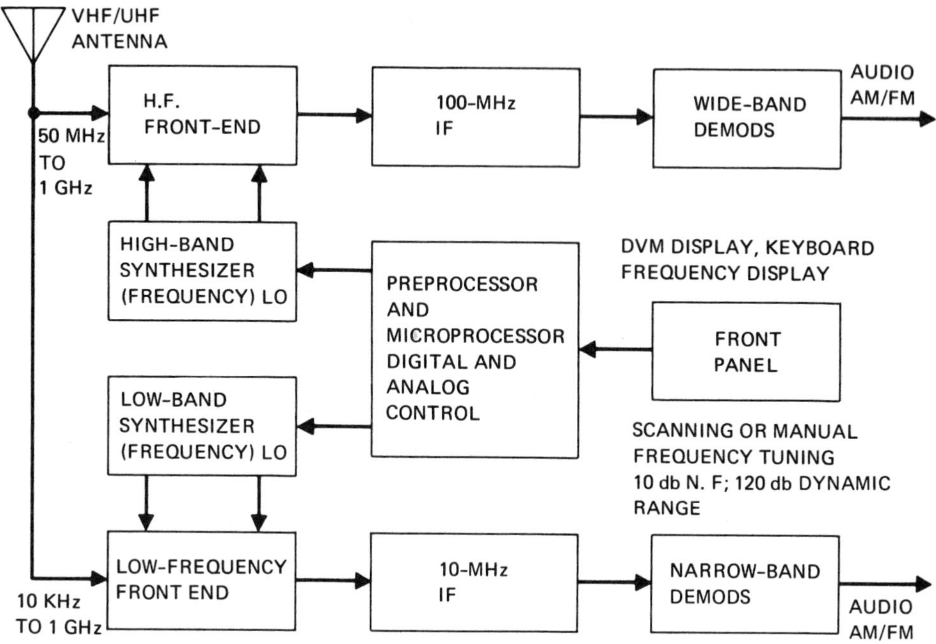

Fig. 7-6. Application of F-8 in a surveillance receiver.

RAM memory, a software debug package, editor, and assembler. The CRT system eliminates the conventional paper tape, the front panel, and the TTY or the cassettes, to cut the programming time from hours to minutes, according to American MicroSystems. With hands on the keyboard, one can modify the program, interrupt after instruction, and examine the data in all of the registers, without translating the addresses into binary to get the required information. Since this is an "intelligent" CRT terminal, and only one instruction set is involved, one could complete a typical edit-assembly sequence in a few minutes as a program-development exercise. A prototyping board with two 36-pin edge connectors is available to

1. Debug programs
2. Develop AMI-6800 toward a microcomputer application.
3. Evaluate parts
4. Program S6834 EPROM in about 1 minute.

One edge-connector is meant for the microprocessor bus extension; the other is for the I/O. The microcomputer board provides 2-K bytes ROM, 2-K bytes EPROM, EPROM programming, 1-K byte RAM, totally buffered microprocessor unit, restart address selection, TTY operating system software, ROM subroutine program library, and serial and parallel I/O ports.

The CPU of AMI-6800 is similar to that of 8080A, with one exception, namely, an index register is available on the chip. It provides DMA capability and two accumulators. The interface adapter provides a bidirectional 8-bit data-transfer device between the processor and up to 16 other peripherals or microprocessors. This feature is attractive for communications networks, since the TTY microcomputer can be directly connected to the telephone lines via one Modem. The comparative architecture of the AMI-6800 and the Intel 8080 is illustrated in Fig. 7-7. The Motorola MC-6800 is used as the AMI-6800.

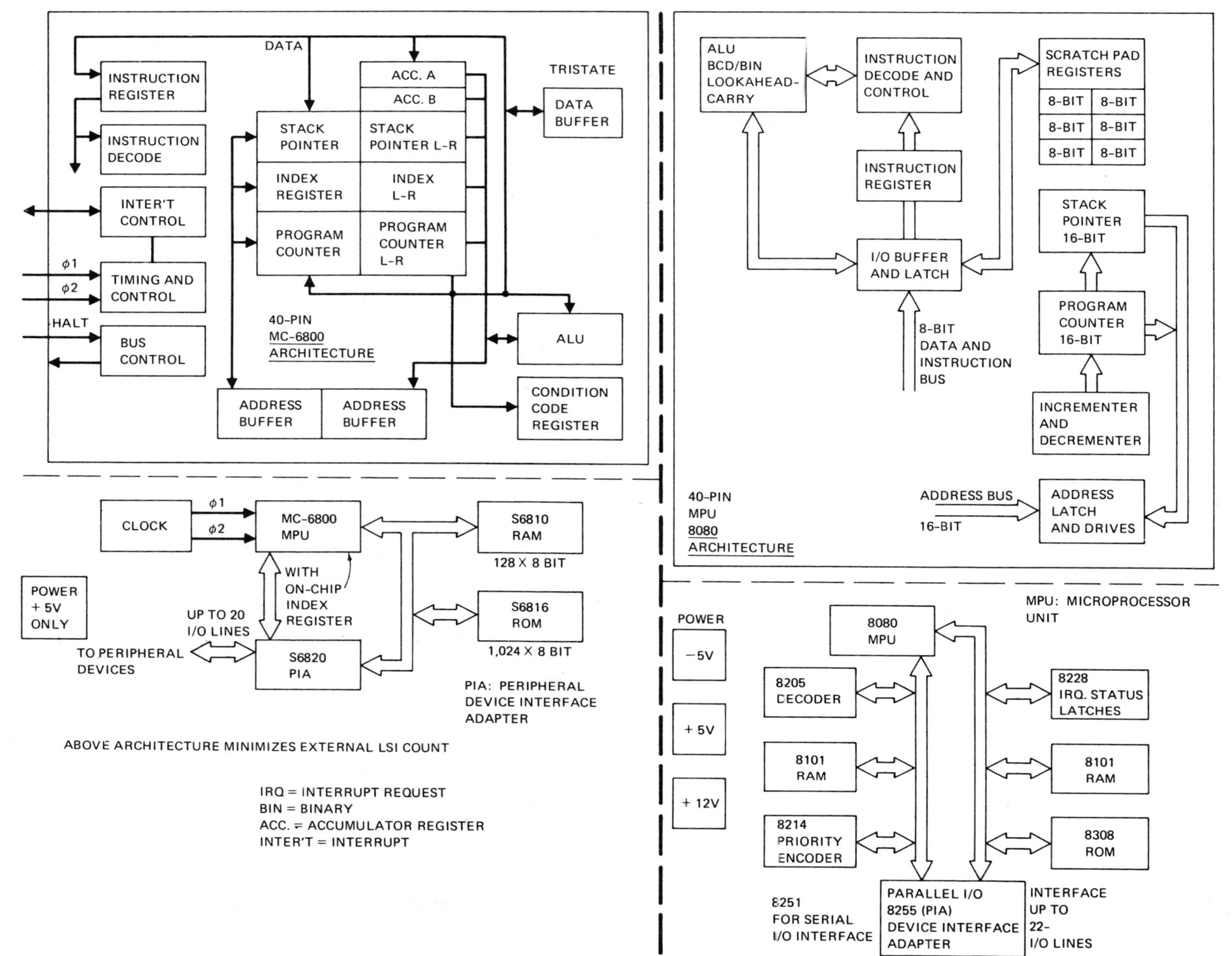

Fig. 7-7. Comparative architecture of MC-6800 and Intel 8080.

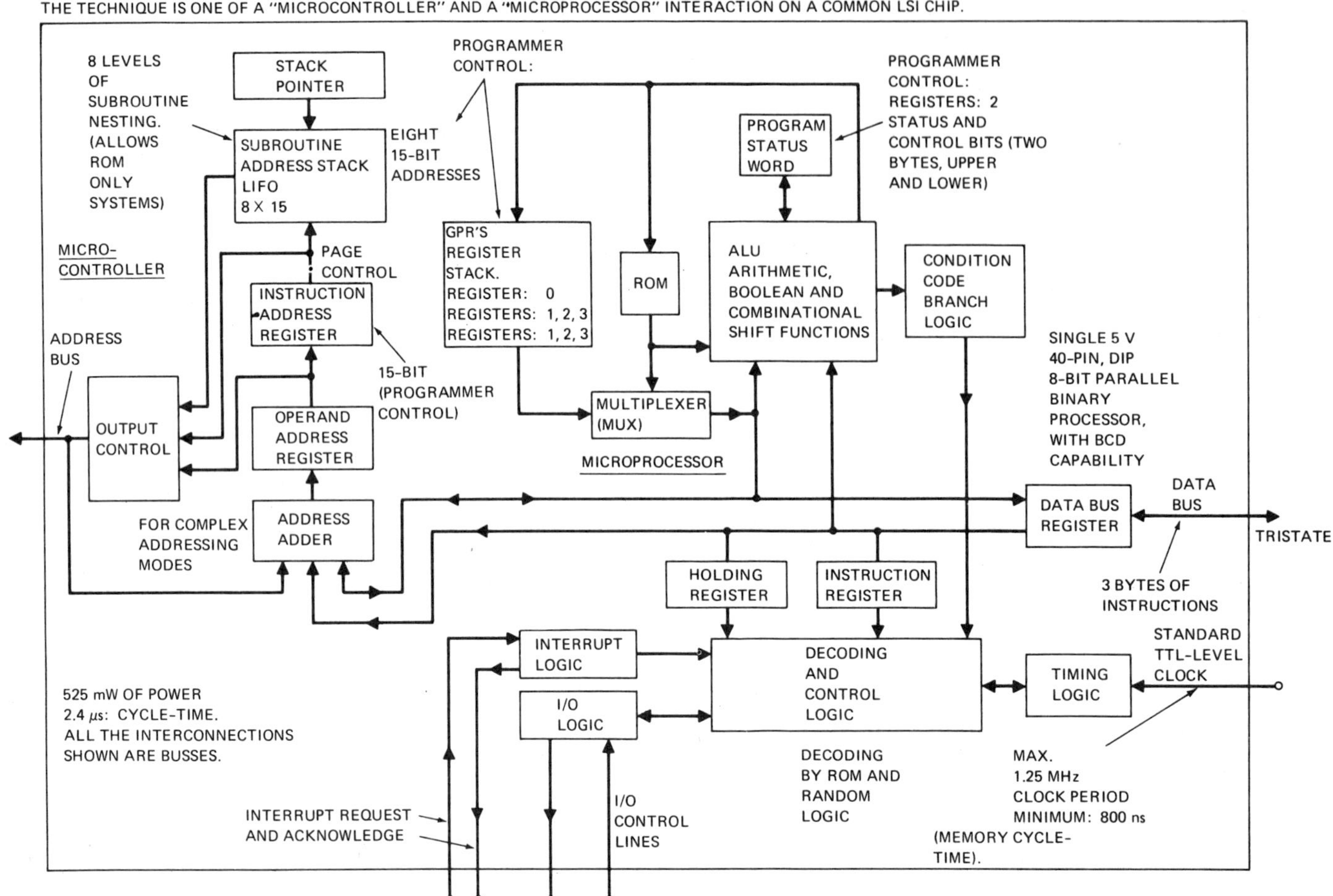

- DIRECT INSTRUCTIONS REQUIRE 2, 3 OR 4 PROCESSOR CYCLES. 4.8 TO 9.6 µs.
- OP. REQ. (OPERATION REQUEST) IS THE MASTER CONTROL SIGNAL TO COORDINATE EXTERNAL OPERATIONS.
- VECTORED INTERRUPT (8 LEVELS) (INTERRUPT SERVICE ROUTINE CAN BEGIN AT ANY ADDRESSABLE MEMORY LOCATION).
- INSTRUCTION SET. (75).
  THREE-LETTER MNEMONIC AND 6-BIT OPCODE).
  LOAD AND STORE (2)
  ARITHMETIC (3)
  LOGICAL (3: AND, OR, EXCL. OR)
  ROTATE COMPARE (3)
  BRANCH (7)
  SUBROUTINE BRANCH/RETURN (6)
  MISCELLANEOUS I/O (9)
  PROGRAM STATUS (5)
- REGISTER-TO-REGISTER INSTRUCTION: 1 BYTE. REGISTER TO STORAGE: 2 OR 3 BYTES LONG (2 BYTES: IMMEDIATE OR RELATIVE ADDRESSING TYPES).
- AUTOMATIC INCREMENTING OR DECREMENTING AN INDEX REGISTER.
- ALL BRANCH INSTRUCTIONS CAN BE CONDITIONAL.
- 1-, 2-, OR 3 - BYTE INSTRUCTIONS FOR THE VARIOUS ADDRESSING MODES.
- <u>A MICROCOMPUTER SYSTEM</u> (TTY)
  REQUIRES SEVEN MINIMAL NO. OF CHIPS:
  2,650 (A_0 . . A_9 ADDRESS BUS; D_0 . . D_7 DATA BUS, SENSE, FLAG, R/W, OPREQ, CLOCK, A_{10})
  2606 (256 X 4 RAM): QUANTITY 3;
  RANGE: 32-K BYTE.
  74123 CLOCK GENERATOR.
  7439 MISCELLANEOUS LOGIC (NAND).
  4049 (INVERTER).

NOTE: SIGNETICS HAS A SCHOTTKY BIPOLAR 2-CHIP MICROPROCESSOR (N-3002 CENTRAL PROCESSING UNIT AND N-3001 MICROCONTROL UNIT, USING STANDARD EXTERNAL TTL/ECL MSI SUPPORT CIRCUITS, FOR A MICROINSTRUCTION CYCLE-TIME OF 100 ns. USING 6 PROMS, INSTRUCTIONS MAY USE 48-BIT WORDS. 512-MICROINSTRUCTION CAPABILITY, WITH 9-BIT MICROPROGRAM ADDRESS REGISTER, ALLOWS 18-BIT PROCESSING.

Fig. 7-8. Signetics type 2650 microprocessor (Si-gate NMOS, ion-implanted). (*Courtesy of Signetics*)

7-7 MICROPROCESSOR (SIGNETICS TYPE 2650, NORTH-AMERICAN PHILIPS)

Five-volt microcomputer system. Interface on the chip; powerful instruction set; fixed instruction set of 75 (40% arithmetic); TTL-compatible; 576-bit ROM; 250-bits of register and 900 logic-gates on processor; 8-bit bidirectional tristate data-bus and separate address-bus; 32,768-byte addressing range; internal 8-bit parallel structure; seven 8-bit GP registers; 8-level on-chip subroutine, return-address stack; program-status-word for flexibility and processing power; separate adder for fast address calculation; low power.

The Signetics 2650 is a multisource microprocessor chip, priced at $21.50. It is available with external MOS/bipolar memories, programmable peripheral interface, communications interface, A-D converters, synchronous data-link converters, 16-K byte NMOS and bipolar RAMs, 4-K byte and 8-K byte NMOS EROMs, and 8-K byte bipolar PROMs. Development software in PL/μs high-level language compiler reduces programming effort and time. Type-2650/AS 1000/1100 assembler and type-2650/SM 1000/1100 simulator are also available in both 32- and 16-bit on GE and NCSS time-sharing BASIC. ANSI-standard FORTRAN IV is applicable. For development, prototyping facilities are provided by means of a twin floppy-disk mass-memory, a resident assembler, and a text editor.

The 2650A microprocessor, using a 77-instruction set, is much smaller in size as a 40-pin DIP; the cycle-time is therefore reduced from 2.4 to 1.5 μs. The NMOS depletion-mode chip, costing less than $20, consumes 625 mW at 5 V. Two prototyping cards and kits, and a 4-K byte card are available along with 16/32-bit assemblers and compilers as software support. For further details, see Fig. 7-8.

Type 2650 is a comparatively faster depletion-mode NMOS unit; it has the capability of 8/16/24-bit instruction words. Internal address capacity is 8-K bytes with 75 instructions. However, it has an addressing capacity of 32-K words. The basic card uses type-2650 microprocessor, two 2606B ICs, one 2608 chip, one N74123, and one N7438A. The instruction formats used for the 2650A microprocessor are presented in detail in Table 7-1.

7-8. Mostek 3872 Single-Chip Microcomputer

Mostek depletion-load 64-register NMOS 3872 is architecturally compatible with 3870 and the multiple-chip Fairchild Camera and Instrument Corporation's F8 family of LSI chips. The 3872, however, differs in size, and mix of 4-K bytes of ROM, 128 bytes of scratch-pad and executable RAM in the main-memory on-chip storage, and an extra address-bit for the extra memory capacity. The overall one-chip microcomputer block diagram is illustrated in Figure 7-9. The system organization conveniently allows addition of external memory. It has the flexibility to operate at 2.8 volts in the place of the normal 5-volt power supply to reduce the current requirement from about 25 mA to 4 mA. Its maximum power-dissipation capability is 435 mW. Like Mostek 3870, Mostek 3872 has 32 I/O lines organized in four ports, of which half the number of lines can be individually mask-programmed for either TTL, open-drive or high-drive. One vector-interrupt out of two is assigned to external interrupts, while the other is assigned to timer interrupts. Out of its 70 basic instructions operable up to a clock of 2 MHz, those that involve the 64 scratch-pad memory instructions are comparatively high-speed. The large-capacity ROM is ideal for the storage of mnemonic instructions, lookup tables for slower recursive-algorithms and mass data-storage. Mostek 3872 is presently used in applications such as gas pumps, point-of-sale terminals, consumer appliances, and push-button radios. Its standby power option allows the protection of a few essential bytes of data in the event of power failure, if other precautions such as power-fail interrupt are not taken.

Table 7-1. Instructions formats—Signetics, type-2650 microprocessor (*Courtesy of Signetics*)

Addressing Modes	R = Register No. V = Value or condition X = Index register No. I = Indirect bit	* Index control 00 : Nonindexed 01 : Indexed with auto-increment 10 : Indexed with auto-decrement 11 : Indexed only		
(Z) Register Addressing (word: 1 byte)	7 6 5 4 3 2 | 1 0 Opcode | R/V	←8-Bit instruction		
(I) Immediate Addressing (word: 2 bytes)	15 14 13 12 11 10 | 9 8 Opcode | R	7 6 5 4 3 2 1 0 Data mask or binary value	←16-Bit instruction	
(R) Relative Addressing (word: 2 bytes)	15 14 13 12 11 10 | 9 8 Opcode | R/V	7 | 6 5 4 3 2 1 0 I | Relative displacement −64 < Displacement < +63	←16-Bit instruction	
(B) Absolute Addressing: Nonbranch Instructions (word: 3 bytes)	23 22 21 20 19 18 | 17 16 Opcode | R/X	15 | 14 13 | 12 11 10 9 8 I | *Index control | Higher-order address	7 6 5 4 3 2 1 0 Lower-order address	←24-Bit instruction
(A) Absolute Addressing: Branch Instructions (word: 3 bytes)	23 22 21 20 19 18 | 17 16 Opcode | R/V	15 | 14 13 12 11 10 9 8 I | Page / Higher-order page address	7 6 5 4 3 2 1 0 Lower-order address	←24-Bit instruction
Indirect Addressing (word: 2 bytes)	15 | 14 13 12 11 10 9 8 | Page / Higher-order address	7 6 5 4 3 2 1 0 Lower-order address	←16-Bit instruction	
(E) Miscellaneous Instructions (word: 1 byte)	7 6 5 4 3 2 1 0 Opcode	←8-Bit instruction		

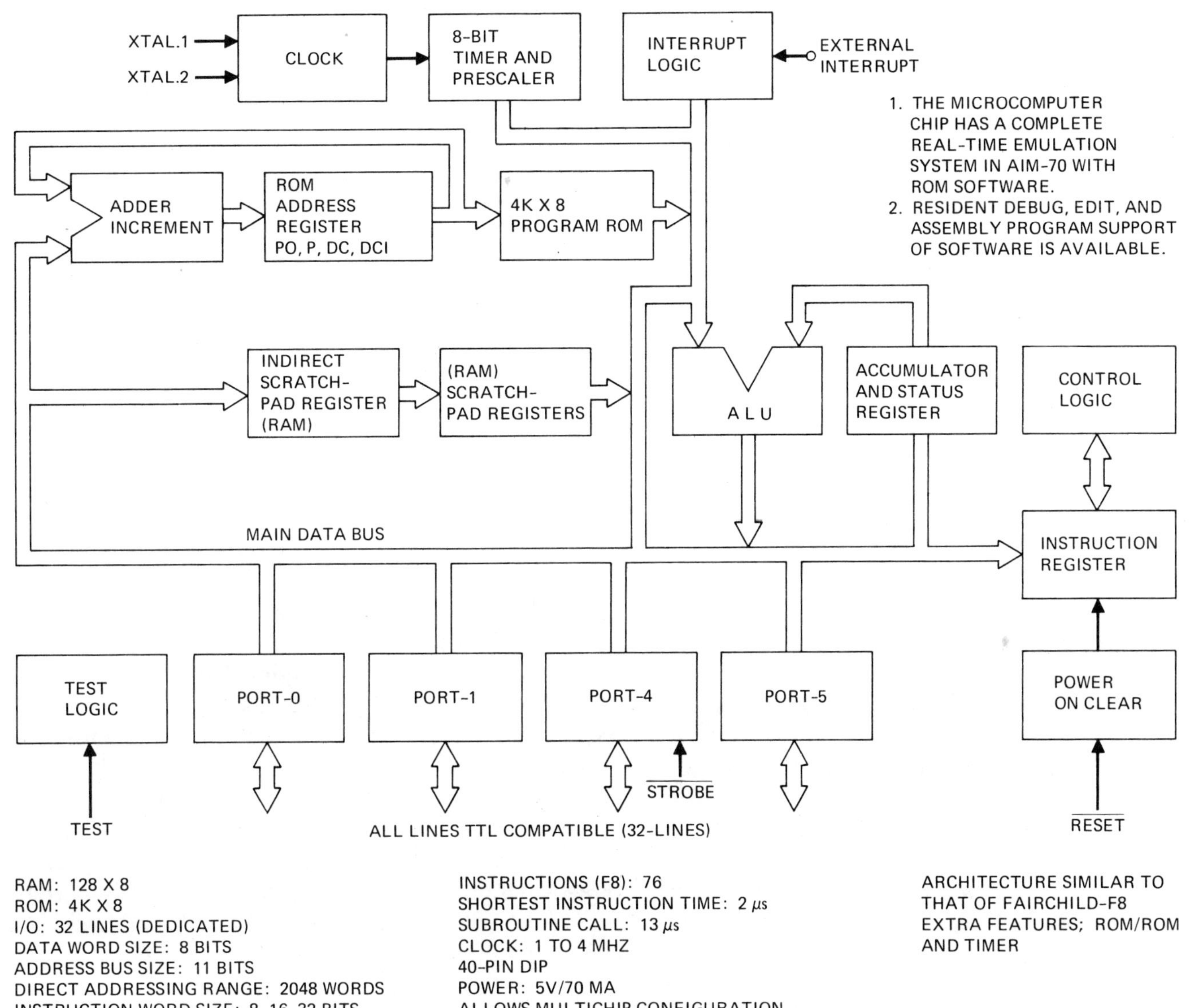

Fig. 7-9. Mostek-3872 single-chip microcomputer. (*Courtesy of Mostek Corp.*)

7-9. PPS-4/1 AND PPS-8 (ROCKWELL INTERNATIONAL)

The 4-bit, PMOS microprocessor series has a wide range of I/O, and ROM/RAM memory sizes for low-speed high-volume applications at low cost under \$5. The power dissipation of the 42-pin package is typically 100 mW at -15 V or alternatively at -10 or 5 V. The three I/O ports are TTL-compatible. ROM: 640 to 2,048 by 8-bits. RAM: 48 to 128 by 4-bits. Incidentally, this was the second source PNP, 4-bit microprocessor for the very first microprocessor that started the microcomputer revolution at Intel under the pioneering direction of Moore and Noyce.

A total of 50 unique instructions have an average execution time of 12.5 μs. It is a BCD arithmetic design with decimal-correction instruction and complement. There are two conditional-interrupt test instructions. Bit setting and testing facility are available in a RAM memory. Cross-assembler on time-sharing network, text editor, two-level subroutine nesting, lookup-table function, assembler, and debug utility on universal assimulator provide software support.

PPS-8 (Rockwell International). The single-chip 8-bit PPS-8 microprocessor is designed for controller and processor applications at a price under $24. Over 90 instructions are used with an average instruction time of 4 μs. PPS-8/2 incorporates on-chip clock, I/O, and ROM/RAM in a 52-pin package. Three levels of priority and 16-level subroutine nesting are available. LSI, DMA-chip has 8 priority levels and allows 250-K byte/sec data transfers. Software support includes time-sharing network, resident text-editor, assembler, and debug utility on universal PPS assimulator.

7-10. COSMAC (CMOS, 2-CHIP MICROKIT; RCA CDP-1801)

RCA introduced CMOS as COSMOS.* (High-speed low-power CMOS-on-sapphire will be highly competitive.) 1-K byte RAM, 512-byte PROM, expandable to 24-K bytes of mixed RAM and PROM; teletype interface; serial communications interface; 8-bit input; 8-bit output-latch; one general interrupt line; four jump-condition I/O Flags, 16 output command lines for use with optional I/O controller cards (12 card-slots); monitor includes hex-loader and terminal I/O; assembler, editor, file system, and full debug-capability. CDP-1801C (5 V) version with 16 registers: $40. CDP-1801 (15 V): $56.

CMOS of the latest RCA CDP-1801 is adaptable to thousands of low-power appliance applications and to high-noise industrial applications with high-temperature range −55° C to +125° C (for arctic equipment and under-hood battery-operated auto controls). Power consumption is just 32 mW at single-phase 3-MHz clock; it has the provision for an addressing capability of 65-K bytes, 4 external flags, on-chip DMA, interrupt, four dedicated programmable device-select lines, direct program-load capability, and reset. The support system consists of one prototyping system-microkit, time-share assembler, stand-alone assembler, stand-alone editor, and time-share simulator/debugger. With the built-in I/O, CDP-1801 interfaces with unlimited choice of I/O devices, driven polled, or interrupt-driven, or DMA. The I/O commands operate at 4-bit; ALU and data-bus operate at 8-bit; and memory- and input-control and decoder operate at 16-bit into a 16 X 16 general-purpose register array. A simple unregulated power supply (with built-in constant-current regulation of nano and microamp currents) will provide high supply-tolerance from 3 to 12 V (absolute maximum rating is 15 V), as a tradeoff against speed.

CDP-1802. This static CMOS chip, operating in the preceding temperature and voltage ranges, dissipates only 40 mW at 10 V and 6.4 MHz clock, as a 40-pin package. Noise immunity is 30% of the drain-voltage applied. It has a 91-command instruction set, requiring 2.5 μs for fetch and execute of each instruction. Addressing is stack-pointer, based in a 16 X 16 register array. 4-bit registers select these 16 X 16 pointers and define their function, I/O or interrupt or DMA, all built into the CPU. All support mentioned is available. A COSMAC development system at $3,200 provides ROM, RAM, power supply, debug card, and TTY interface. Software support of cross-assemblers, editors, and simulators is available for interfacing with 16-bit minicomputer and 32-bit-and-above GPDCs. (See Section 7-11 for further information.)

7-11. CDP-1802, RCA

This is the only 8-bit 40-pin DIP CMOS microprocessor available at $16-to-$20 for commercial and industrial applications. It is distributed as a register-oriented 8-bit data VIP microcomputer system, offering static operation and especially high-noise immunity. With on-chip DMA and clock, it lowers the cost of memory and systems at a low power

*RCA uses the name *COSMOS* for its *complementary symmetry MOS*; other manufacturers use the acronym *CMOS*.

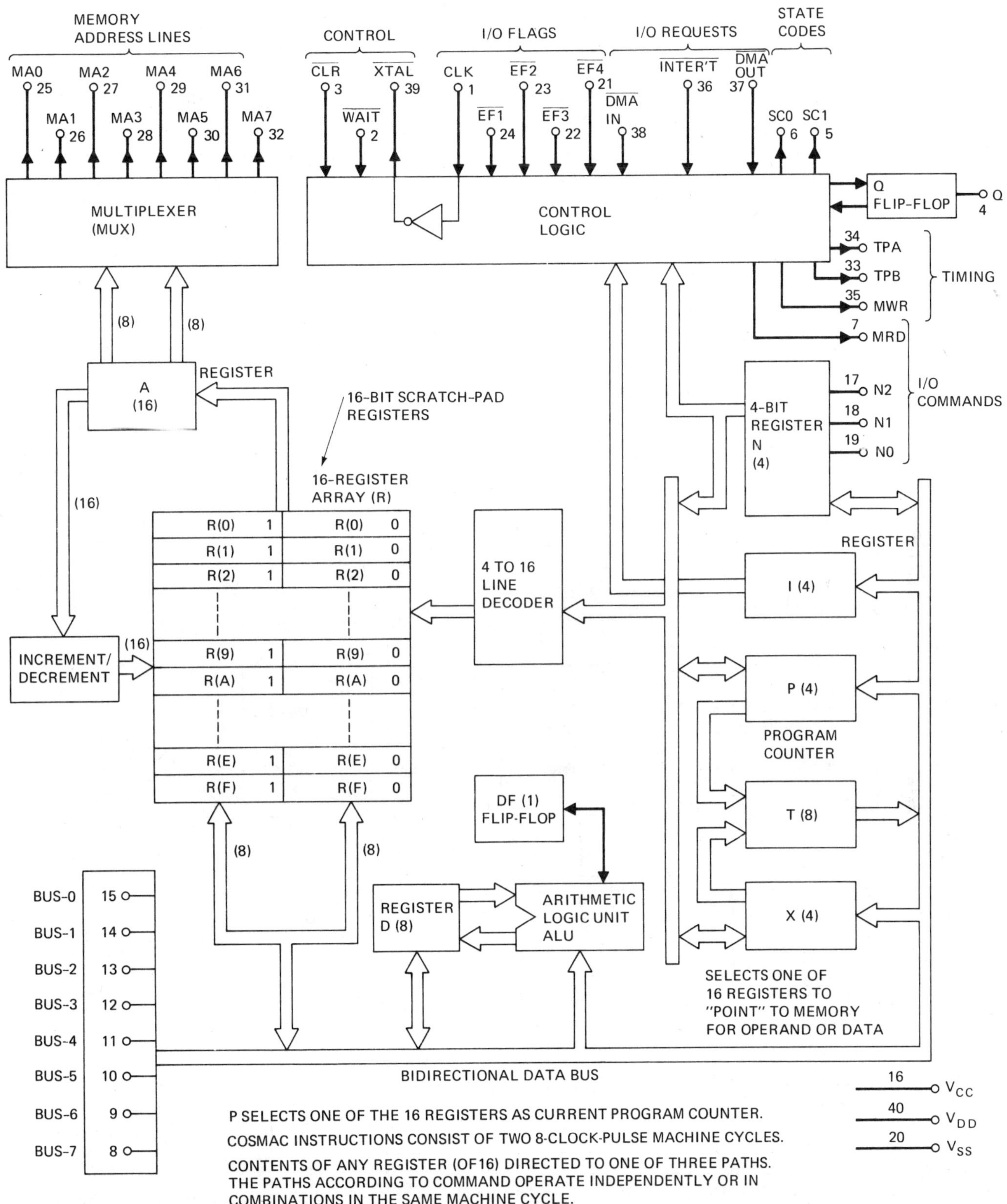

RCA COSMAC CDP-1802/C Types Architecture (CMOS Microprocessor) *Courtesy of RCA Solid State Division*).

dissipation from 4 to 12V/1.6 mA at 5V. Hughes Semiconductor Products Inc. is the alternate second-source manufacturer of the low power-consuming CMOS processor and memory chips for commercial and defense applications. (See Section 6-12.)

The architecture is oriented around the 16 X 16 bit register-file, which simplifies 16-bit addressing and memory reference instructions. A minimal low-cost VIP microcomputer system can be organized with just one 64-K bit CMOS ROM memory for the mnemonic instructions in hexadecimal code. The commands are allotted 12 for logic, 12 for arithmetic, 20 for short-branch, 8 for long-branch, 9 skip, and 14 I/O. On-chip program memory-storage includes a 16 X 16-bit scratchpad CMOS static-RAM.

Software support, based on 1-, 2-, and 3-byte instructions, includes arithmetic resident editor, cross-assembler/simulator, and firmware debug package, as well as a full floppy-disk-based program development system. A high-level interpretive language (such as BASIC) is also available. Branch and skip commands permit rapid selection of a subroutine or program jump. Programmable on-chip serial-port allows direct serial-I/O. Hardware support includes Microtutor-II Learning System, and COSMAC development system for software, and an Evaluation Kit for prototyping and breadboarding. The direct addressing capacity is 64-K words, with instruction-time in the range 2.5-to-3.75 μs. Clock frequency can be varied from dc to 6.4 MHz with one supply voltage and nine dedicated I/O lines.

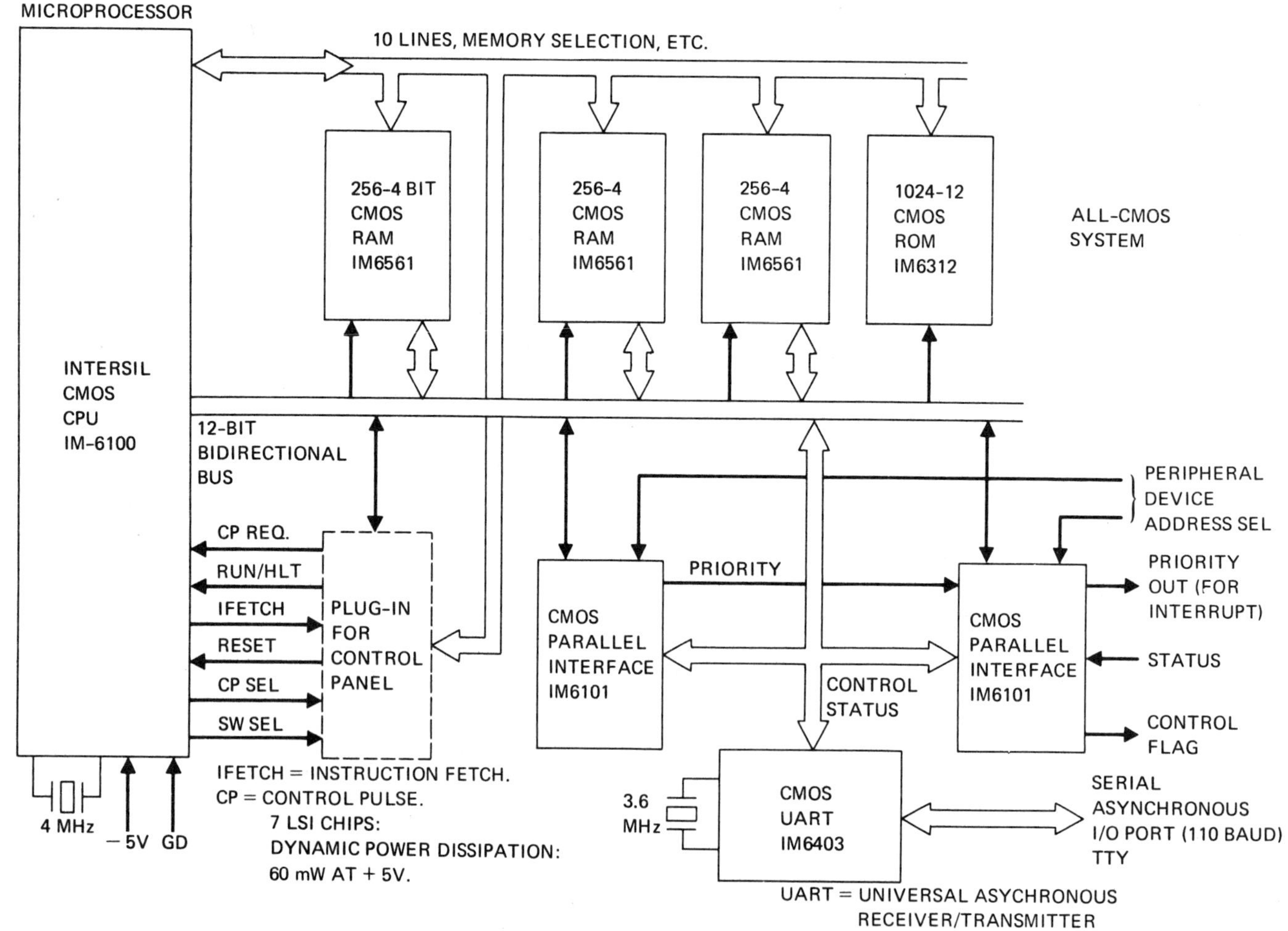

Fig. 7-10a. Intersil CMOS IM-6100 system organization. (©*IEEE Proceedings, June 1976*)

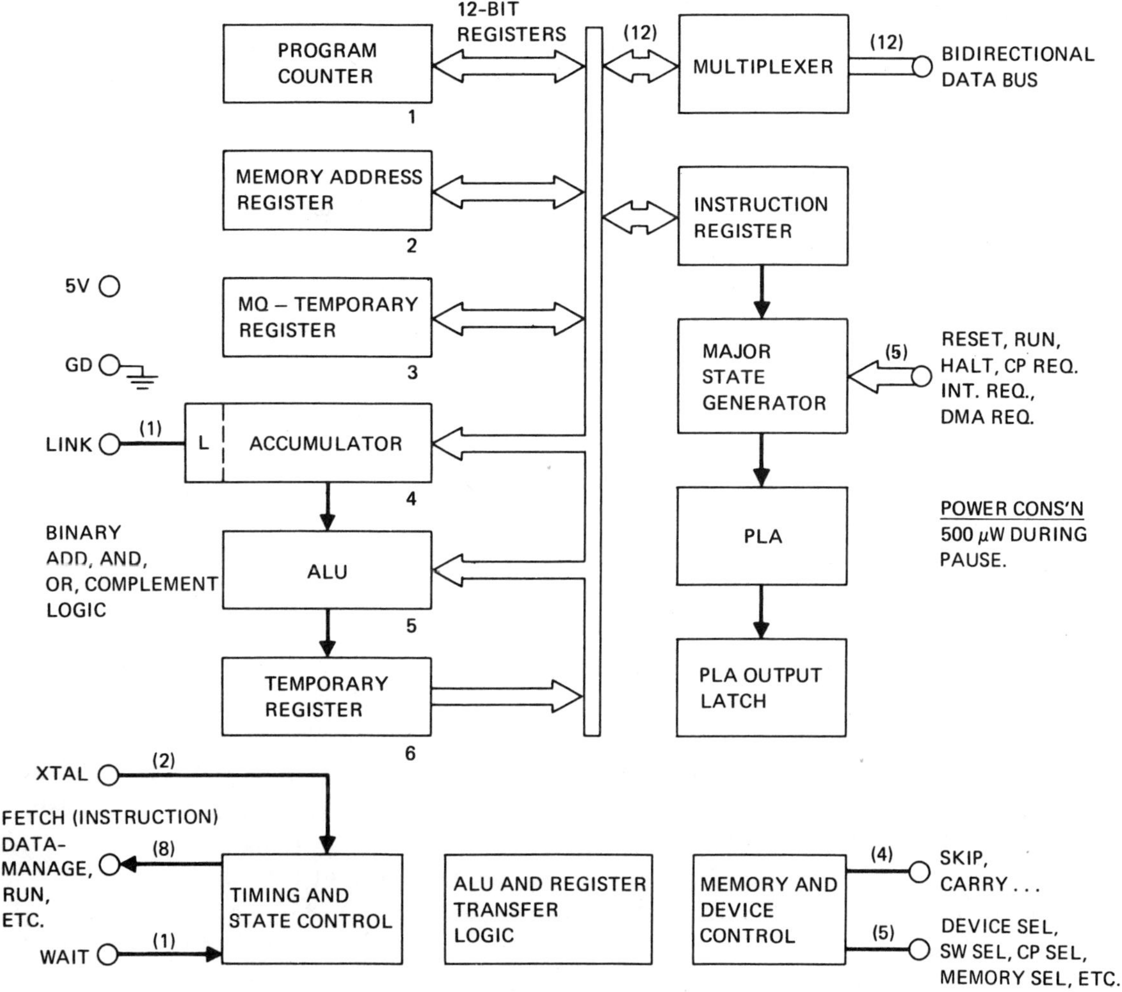

Fig. 7-10b. Architecture of Intersil IM-6100. (*Courtesy of IEEE Proceedings*)

7-12. INTERSIL IM-6100

The 5-volt, 12-bit, Intersil IM-6100 microprocessor is implemented, by low-power silicon-gate CMOS process, for high-noise high-temperature environments. The internal logic levels are insensitive to temperature and process parameters, such as device-ratios, geometrics, or thresholds, and circuits would operate over wide Defense temperature ranges (-55° C to +125° C) and power-supply variations (3 to 15 V). High noise-immunity results from the transfer characteristics. Extremely low operating power (60 mW at 5 V) allows portable operation with RAM main memory and standby nicad battery (at 2% per week of discharge) for nonvolatility. Its instruction set, using octal code and I/O interface, is compatible with that of DEC's popular minicomputer PDP-8/E. The overall microcomputer system requires just seven LSI CMOS chips; they include a programmable asynchronous serial interface port, 256-by-12-bit static RAM main memory, and 1,024-by-12-bit ROM control memory. The 12-bit processor (in the place of the conventional 8-bit chips) provides straightforward memory referencing, and sufficient numerical accuracy for most applications (as a substitute to 2-word double-precision arithmetic).

The seven LSI-chip CMOS Intersil microcomputer system block-diagram is shown in Fig. 7-10a for serial UART-interface (universal asynchronous receiver/transmitter) with a TTY.

The functional block diagram shown in Fig. 7-10b is that of the IM-6100 microprocessor chip, using six 12-bit registers, a programmable logic array (PLA), an ALU, and the associated gating and timing circuitry.

The ALU operations on the data from the memory and I/O are performed with the accumulator register. The accumulator operates in conjunction with a "temporary" register; they may be cleared, complemented, tested, incremented, or rotated under program control. The "link" is a flip-flop, which serves as a "carry" for "2s" complement arithmetic and other manipulations in an accumulator. The memory-address-register contains the address of the memory location that is currently selected for read/write. The program counter contains the address of the memory location from which the next instruction is fetched. If there is a branch to another address in the memory, the branch address is set in the program counter. During an I/O operation, a peripheral device may specify the branch address. A SKIP instruction causes the program counter to skip the next instruction. The ALU performs binary ADD, AND, OR, COMPLEMENT, SHIFT LEFT/RIGHT, and DOUBLE ROTATE in two single-bit shifts. The ALU result is conducted to the destination register, while the "temporary" register latches to avoid possible race conditions whenever a register acts as both the source and destination for an operation. The Instruction Register contains the instruction to be executed during "fetch."

The memory and device control unit provide external control signals to communicate with the peripheral devices, external switch-register, external memory, and control-panel memory. The basic cycle-time is 2.5 μs with a 4 MHz crystal. (With a 10-V power supply, the crystal frequency is 8 MHz and the ADD instruction's execution-time halves to 2.5 μs.)

The internal address-space is limited to 4,096 words for a majority of applications. The memory can be however extended externally. The internal clock generator can be stopped by removing the crystal for indefinite periods without any loss of information; when the processor is "paused," the power dissipation is 0.5 mW for the internal clock generator and the P-N leakage current, which maintain the processor-state indefinitely (for nonvolatility such as that of the CORE memory).

The internal PLA in the chip, organized as 19 words X 110 bits, sequences the processor through a number of optimized control-microinstructions for "fetch" operation. Internal to the PLA there is a bit for every transfer and control instruction, and an 8-bit address-register for priority scan. The PLA outputs are latched to permit pipelining; it fetches the next control microinstruction while the CPU executes the current microinstruction.

The seven LSI-chip CMOS microcomputer system requires one IM6403 programmable Universal Asynchronous Receiver/Transmitter (UART) to interface with an asynchronous serial-data channel from a TTY controller.

The IM6100 microprocessor contains a parallel interface element (PIE) to provide a universal means of interfacing with the industry's standard LSI devices, such as UARTs, FIFOs, keyboard chips, and controllers for external peripheral devices.

7-13. PORTABLE COMPUTER (IBM-5100)

The IBM-5100 basic portable desktop microcomputer system can be used as a dedicated computer system for financial analysis and statistical and engineering applications with appropriate interface. It will serve the function of a general-purpose digital computer, for example, as a process controller. The keyboard of its desktop model is coded for commands in the widely used general-purpose BASIC (Tymshare), or as an alternative or both, APL (the advanced programming language of IBM). The 50-lb microcomputer has a built-in 4″ CRT-display, 16 lines of 64 characters each, plus a new 3M/IBM tape cartridge. The computer provides for control memory, 2-K bit high-speed NMOS-ROM chip (with provision for a total of 24 chips) for translating as an assembler/compiler high-level software from the keyboard or the tape cartridges. As read/write storage memory, the computer uses 16-K byte MOS chips; it can be expanded to 65,536 words or bytes. For mass storage, the tape cartridge holds up to 204,000 characters on 300 ft of 0.25″ tape, operating at 40 ips; it can read at 2,850 character/sec and write at 950 character/sec. An auxiliary tape-cartridge unit of double the storage capacity will cost $2,300. The 18-bit CPU uses TTL bipolar LSI, with a microinstruction time of 1.75 μs. A new matrix printer, type 5103, measuring 12.25″ X 13.25″ X 23″, weighing 60 lb, and priced at $3,675, operates at 80 character/sec, with 132 print-positions/line, 10 character/in., and 6 lines/in. Three problem-solving software libraries on prerecorded tape cartridges are readily available for interactive routines in:

1. Advanced engineering
2. Statistical applications
3. Business applications.

A two-cartridge library set leases at $500. The portable computer is list-priced at $8,975.

The system philosophy is based on the following criteria:

1. The execution time of a microinstruction should be well below 2 μs.
2. The microinstruction set should be rich, particularly in I/O-related statements.
3. The microprocessor should present a large enough number of control and data lines to the interface to limit time, space, power, and decoders.

Unlike the single-chip microprocessors of other manufacturers, this "portable computer" employs a CPU microprocessor-card of 15 chips to perform the computations and play a significant role in controlling the I/O devices; the 18-bit microinstruction is performed in a cycle-time of 1.75 μs. All data are transferred and stored in blocks of 8 data-

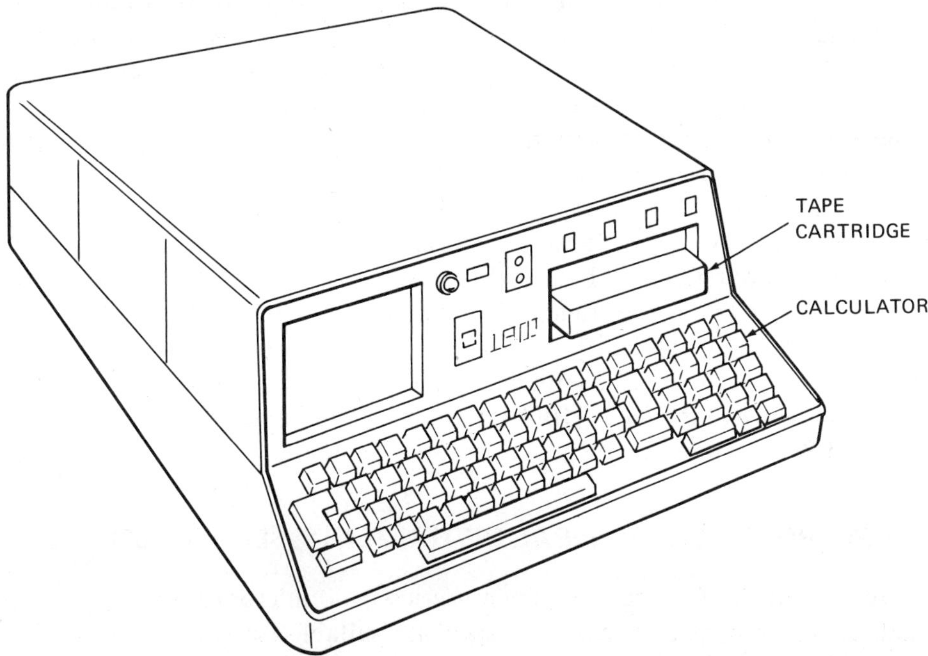

Fig. 7-11. IBM-5100 portable computer. (*Courtesy of IBM*)

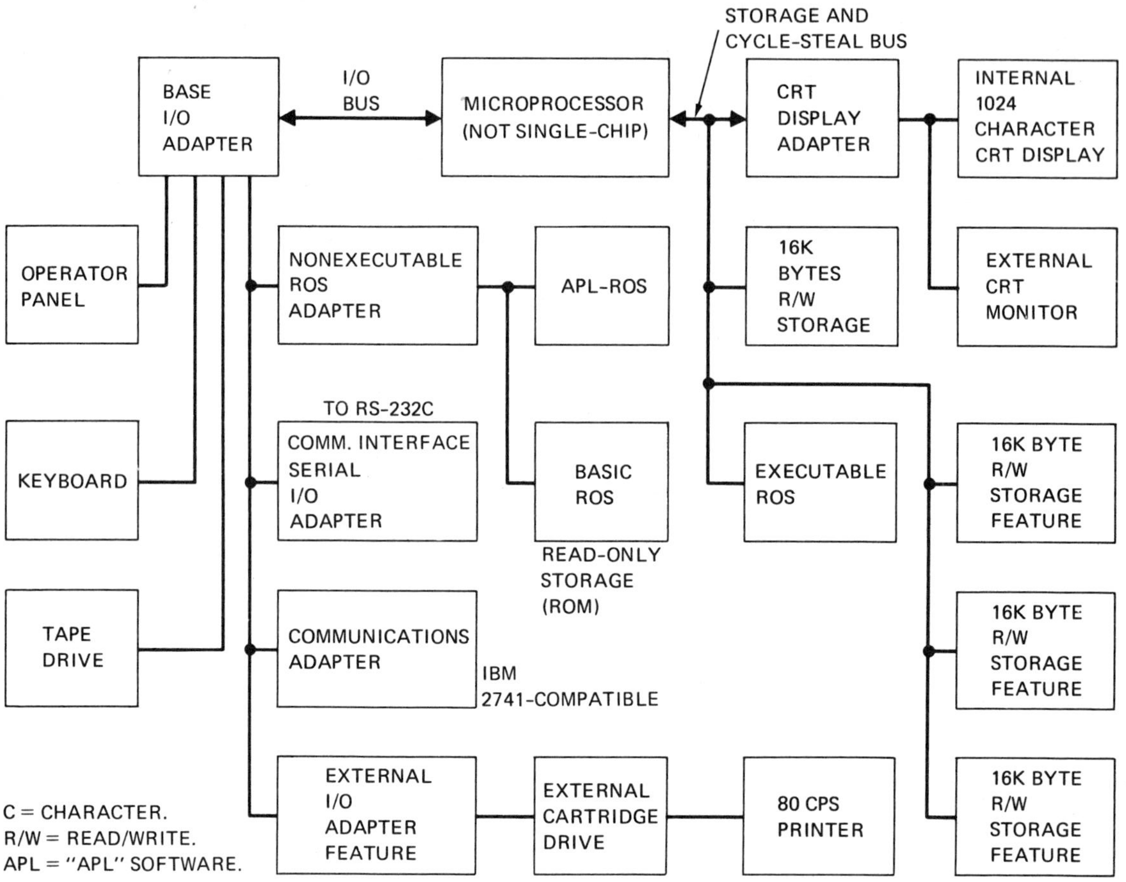

Fig. 7-12. System organization of IBM-5100 portable computer. (©*IEEE Proccedings, June 1976*)

bits and one parity check-bit. The instruction set includes control, device I/O, fetch and store, register-move, arithmetic, and logical/immediate/jump microinstructions that support processing at the high-level APL and BASIC software. As a side facility, a four-function calculator pad is provided on the 1,024-character CRT and keyboard facility so that the computer can be used as a calculator; it enables the rapid inputting of numerical data. The keyboard is used for entering the BASIC programs and character data. The BASIC (Beginners All-Purpose Symbolic Instruction Code) statements are interactive and interpretive, and they are processed immediately on a line-by-line basis. The APL is widely used because it is highly functional and interpretive. Figure 7-11 shows the console of the portable computer, IBM-5100, with its CRT-keyboard display and tape cartridge. This portable computer has two financially improved versions with compatible hardware and software, types 5110 and 5120.

The architecture of the microcomputer system is organized with respect to the microprocessor as shown in Fig. 7-12. (IBM interprets ROMs as executable ROS of user and nonexecutable ROS adapter, and RAMs as read/write storage.)

7-14. MICROPROCESSOR (GENERAL INSTRUMENTS, SERIES-1600)

The architecture of the General Instrument Series-1600 microprocessor presents a 16-bit configuration to the user, and makes it especially suitable for real-time control automation. Unlike other microprocessors, it is not intended for microprogramming, since it employs a fixed instruction set of 68 words for controller applications. Average execution time of a word like ADD is 3.2 μs.

The chip is 40-pin DIP, NMOS metal-gate, with depletion-mode loads requiring +12-, +5-, and -3-V multivoltage sources. The clock frequency extends from 3.3 to 5 MHz.

The 16-bit memory instructions follow the format of those of the popular PDP-11 DEC minicomputer. Although the chip costs as low as $38, a complete minicomputer-like configuration with an 8-K word memory and a peripheral controller costs approximately $3,500. The software includes double-precision arithmetic, cross-assembler, debugs, reloadable linking-loader, text editor and a "super-assembly" high-level language.

The CP-1600 microprocessor (see Fig. 1-2) can directly address the first 1,024 external memory locations by manipulating the I/O as a memory. For data movement, it employs 2-address instructions to utilize its eight general-purpose registers as accumulators. CP-1610 is a low-cost version working at a clock frequency of 2 MHz. (A Japanese 5-volt version is designated as type MN-1610.)

7-15. MCP-1600 MICROPROCESSOR (WESTERN DIGITAL CORP.)

The 16-bit microprocessor (Western Digital Corp., MCP-1600), unlike the single-chip 8-bit microprocessors, is of an entirely different class of architecture; it employs a 3-chip NMOS configuration to make it more compatible with the earlier minicomputer systems. It is microprogrammable and more powerful than the General Instruments CP-1600 chip, and is suitable for both 8- and 16-bit customized instructions. The microinstructions take an average of 500 ns; this includes binary and decimal arithmetic. Sequences of microinstructions can be conveniently encoded in 4-K or 16-K bit ROMs. The DEC LSI-11 microcomputer, described earlier, employs this 3-chip CPU configuration to provide software support at both microcode and macrocode levels. Macroinstructions are fetched by the program counter and interpreted by the exclusive control chip as addresses to the ROM memory; and this ROM provides the actual control instructions to the arithmetic logic unit. The chip requires a multivoltage power source similar to that of the General Instruments microprocessor CP-1600. Western Digital Corp. can provide a macrosoftware version for lower cost microcomputer applications too. (See Fig. 1-2 for the system organization of a microcomputer using MCP-1600.)

7-16. TMS-1000 SERIES (TEXAS INSTRUMENTS)

The Texas Instruments (TI) TMS-1000 microcomputers are reliable, integrated single-chip, 4-bit parallel ALU/memory/I-O, with a self-contained 10-bit, 1,024-word instruction ROM. **TMS 1000/1200** are suitable for low- and medium-complexity applications. Data flow occurs at 4-bit input and 8/11/13-bit output. **TMS 1070/1270,** in addition, allow direct interface to high-voltage indicators such as the neon displays. **TMS 1100/1300** have twice the memory capacity for more complex applications. The software support for this series of microcomputer chips includes:

1. **HE-2 hardware emulator,** to verify the program in real-time for quick design.
2. **SE-1/2 system emulators** for checking the user's single-chip internal ROM instruction programming against externally available instruction memory. Time-share software is available for simulator and assembler programs for user's time-share access at any time. (Texas Instruments data manual CB 177-1). Some typical cost-effective applications of the TI microcomputers include:

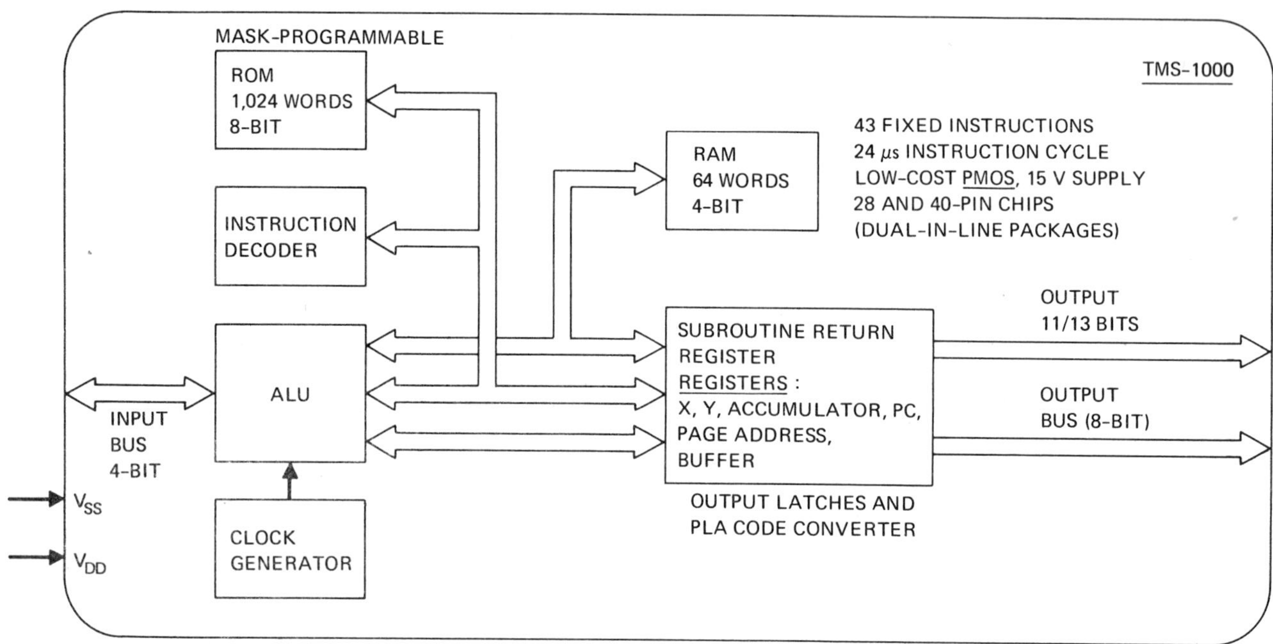

Fig. 7-13. Architecture of the basic TMS-1000 microprocessor. (*Courtesy of Texas Instruments, Inc.*)

printer controllers	smart or intelligent terminals
remote sensing systems	peripheral equipment
cash registers	test instruments
appliance controls	gas pumps
automobiles	credit-card verifiers
vending machines	telephone controls
electronic games	multiple timers
industrial automation	data terminals
communication systems	traffic-light systems

The single-chip architecture of the basic TMS-1000 microprocessor is shown in Fig. 7-13.

TI, TMS 9900 Microprocessor. This microprocessor is a 64-pin silicon-gate NMOS single-chip 16-bit, 16-register CPU from the same manufacturer. The mnemonic and opcode instruction repertoire of 105 includes the capabilities offered by full minicomputers, and uses a 4-phase, 3-MHz-rate clock for "refresh" of dynamic RAMs. The instruction set allows both 16-bit words (including a sign-bit) and 8-bit even/odd byte operands (including a sign-bit each). The 990/4 microcomputer system-on-a-card using this chip provides 32,768 words or 65,536 bytes of memory space. The CPU employs an advanced memory-to-memory architecture as shown in Fig. 7-14.

Blocks of memory designated as workspaces (or scratch pad) replace internal hardware registers with program-data registers. For example, the first 32 words may be allocated for interrupt trap-vectors for the 16 priority interrupt levels, the next contiguous 32 for the extended operation instruction for the same, and so on. The programmed I/O capability includes DMA; the bus configuration separates memory and I/O and interrupts to simplify the system design effort. The system, of course, is fully supported by software and prototyping facilities.

The I/O interface on the card—namely, the communications-register unit (CRU)—provides up to 4,096 directly addressable input and output bits each, and these are addressed individually or in fields from 1 to 16 bits. The TMS 9900 instructions in eight addressing modes perform these functions:

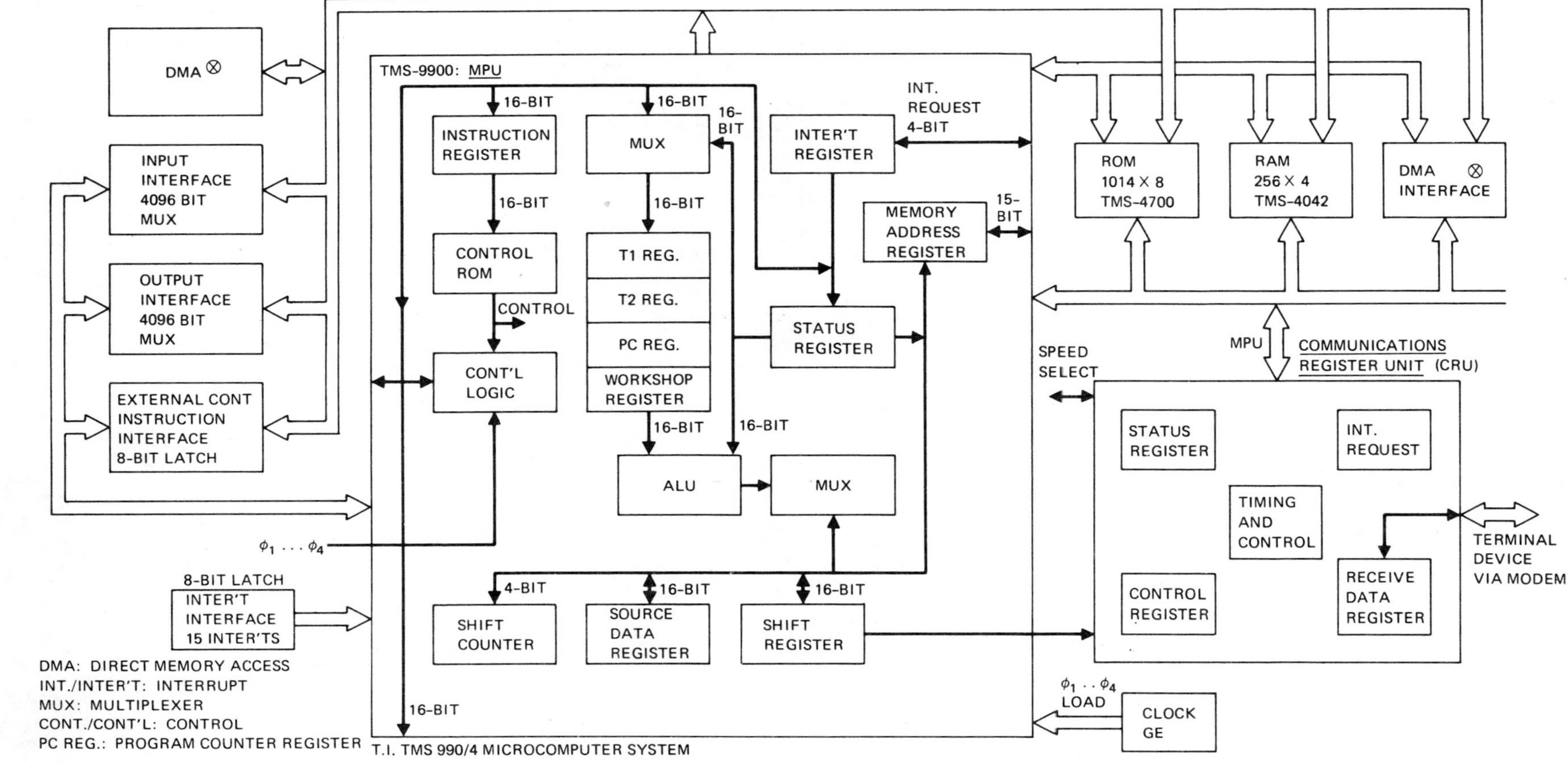

Fig. 7-14. TMS-990/4 16-bit, 3-MHz, 4-phase microcomputer system, using the Texas Instruments NMOS TMS-9900 microprocessor or 2-MHz, single-phase clock, RMS-SBP/9900, 16-bit, I^2L microprocessor. (*Courtesy of Texas Instruments, Inc.*)

1. Arithmetic/logical/comparison/shifting operations on data
2. Loading or storage of internal registers (program counter, workspace pointer, or status)
3. Data transfer between memory and external devices via the CRU
4. Control functions.

Bipolar Microprocessor (TI, SBP-0400 A). The architecture of this high-speed bipolar I^2L, 4-bit microprocessor is fashioned for cascade-connection to 8/12/16/24-bit words, as a **bit-slice technique,** in order to approach the high-speed performance of the minicomputers. The chip has an instruction repertoire similar to that of the popular ALU, SN 74181. The instruction decode is done by means of an instruction-coded PLA at a rate of 512 clock-operations/sec. One of the eight internal working registers performs the clock operations on the result stored in any one of the registers, and the address is outputted on a 4-bit bus. Look-ahead carry is used with the provision of carry-in and carry-out to cascade and expand the processor word length. There is a parallel input and output data-bus and an address-bus, along with an operation-select input. The reg-

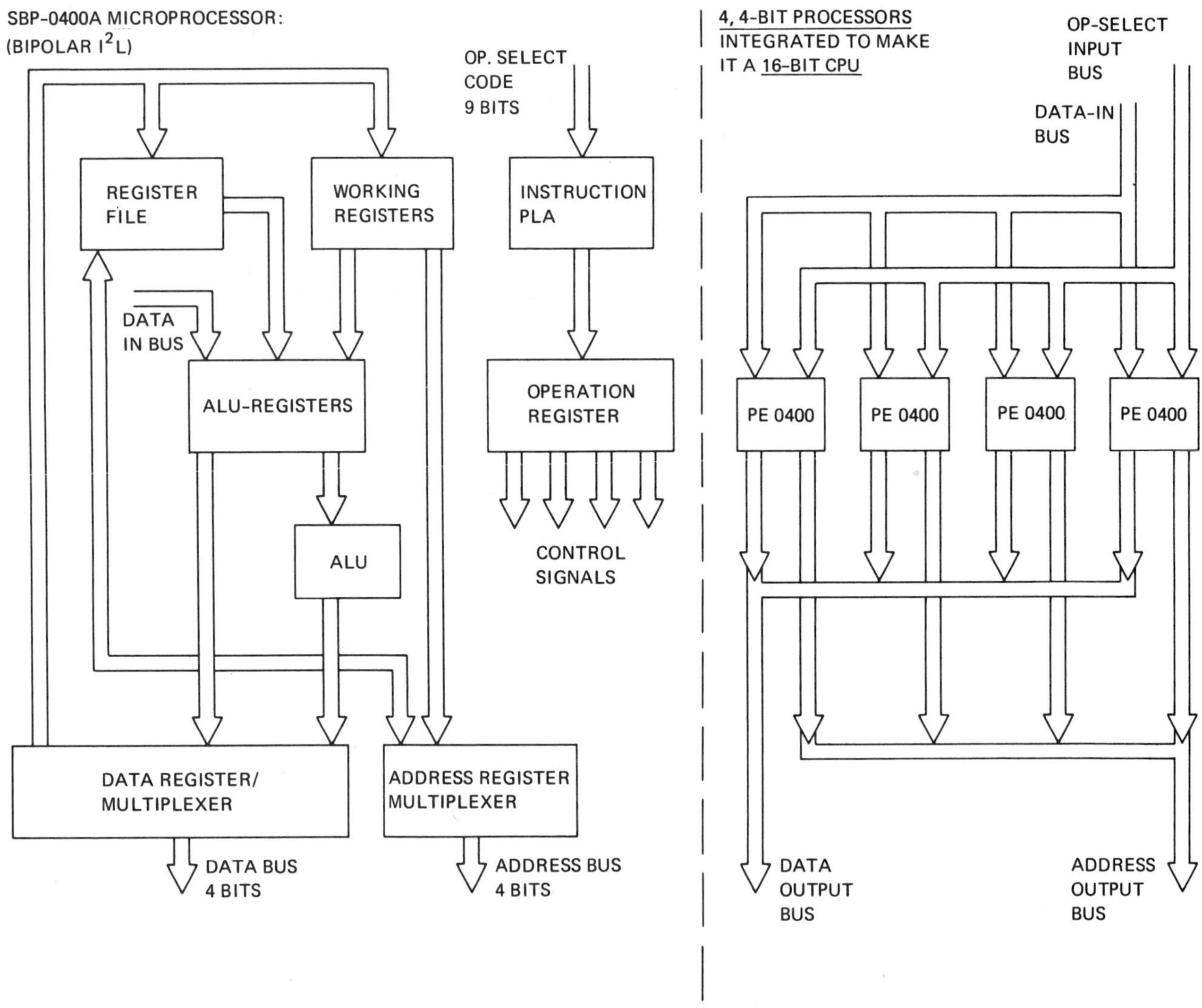

Fig. 7-15. SBP-0400A microprocessor (Texas Instruments); bit-slice technique. (*Courtesy of Texas Instruments, Inc.*)

isters could be manipulated like a combination of a 7-register stack and a stack pointer. When cascaded, the shift-lines for the working registers are connected together.

How the input/output data and address busses are connected, along with the operation-select input, for a cascaded operation of the SBP-0400A bipolar chips is shown in Fig. 7-15 ("cascaded" from the viewpoint of the bits in an instruction).

16-Bit Bipolar I²L Microprocessor (TMS-SBP9900). As compared to its silicon-gate NMOS counterpart TMS-9900, the latest 16-bit isoplanar I²L microprocessor from TI gives a powerful and competitive performance. In addition, it operates at low power to severe Defense temperature-specifications (−55° to +125°C), when ruggedized. At the same time, its software is compatible with that of the powerful minicomputers of the present generation. The device operates at 3-MHz single-phase clock, 500-mA injection-current, and 500-mW power dissipation; it has the flexibility to require only 10 mA at a lower clock-rate of the order of 125 kHz, dissipating a total of 6.4 mW! Thus, a single C- or D-size battery-cell will run the microprocessor. Unlike an NMOS chip, the I²L static RAM main memory will remain nonvolatile by using a penlight backup nicad cell, as in the CMOS case, to allow debug or checkup of a program halfway through a regular program.

The 16-bit device is 64-pin ceramic dual-in-line package (DIP). A commercial plastic 2-MHz version for 0° to 50°C is available at a competitive price. See Fig. 7-14.

Fairchild 9440 "Microflame" is a corresponding Isoplanar I²L, 16-bit, bipolar, 40-pin DIP microprocessor with a direct addressing range of 32-K words, NOVA minicomputer 42-instruction set, 8.33/2-MHz clock, TTL-compatibility, on-chip interrupt, four internal general-purpose registers, RAM stack-register, and on-chip clock. Its DMA-capability along with 9441 Memory and DMA-controller, 9442 I/O Bus-Controller, and performance

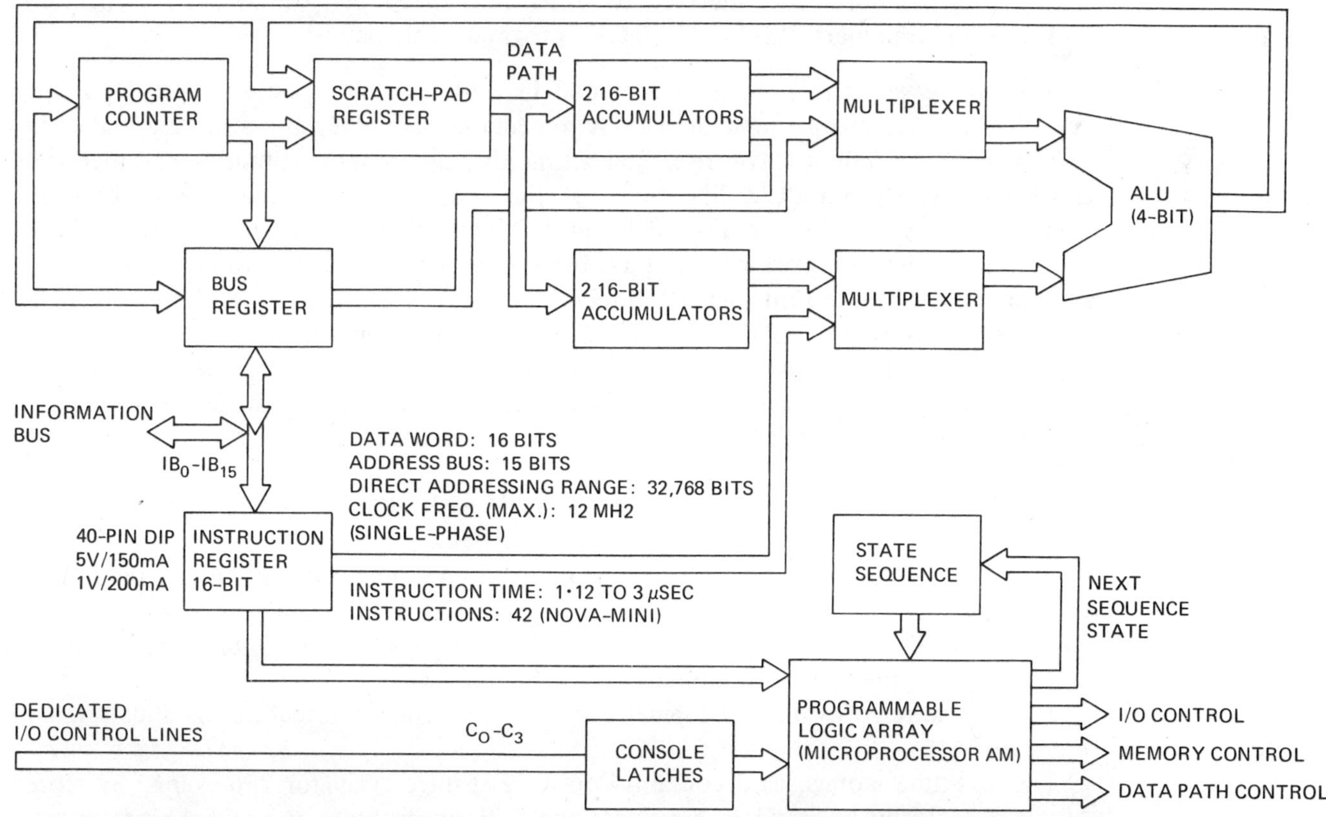

Fairchild 16-bit isoplanar I²L microprocessor. (*Courtesy of Fairchild Camera and Instrument Corp.*)

matched dynamic bipolar RAM makes it equivalent to a 3-chip "minicomputer" with minimum of power-dissipation for intelligence, distributed multiprocessing, and front-end terminal processing computer applications. A hardware multiply/divide processor type 9443 is also available.

7-17. ZILOG Z80-CPU (EXXON)

The Zilog Z80-CPU (Exxon) is a competitive, 5-V, single-chip, enhanced-NMOS, with a throughput claimed several times higher than that of the popular 8080A microprocessor. The chip, available as part of a complete microcomputer system with 1.6-μs cycle time, provides a set of 158 instructions in 1/4/16-bit words (including 78 instructions of the 8080A for compatibility). The new set of powerful instructions allows commands, memory-to-memory, memory-to-I/O block-transfers and searches. 16-bit arithmetic, and nine versions of rotates and shifts. With a single-phase 400-ns clock-speed, direct interface is provided to a wide range of both parallel- and serial-interface peripherals, and dynamic memories, without additional external logic. The chip is high-density Si-gate depletion-load, enhanced-NMOS; it costs $49.

The overall system consists of:

1. Z80-CPU card
2. 16-K bytes of RAM expandable to 64-K
3. 4-K bytes of ROM and 4-K bytes of dynamic RAM monitor-software
4. Real-time event-storage debug module for simultaneous hardware and software debug capability, and in-circuit emulation module for TTL-compatibility to user's equipment
5. Dual mass-memory floppy-disk system
6. Optional I/O-ports for interface to other high-speed peripherals such as printers, PROM programmers, RS-232, Z-80-CTC programmable baud-rate generator.

A complete software package is included in Z80: assembler, editor, Disk Operating System, file maintenance, and debug. A relocatable assembler and a linking loader are also available. Resident software includes time-sharing programs, libraries, and high-level languages BASIC, and PL/Z like those of the other major manufacturers. Z80-CPU microcomputer, which includes CPU and I/O controllers, provides 696 opcodes, 11 addressing modes, 17 working registers, three interrupt modes (up to six times faster), and nonmaskable interrupt—against Intel's 244, 7, 8, 1, and 0, respectively—to enable the claimed five-times-over throughput. The system efficiency is obviously more in line with that of a typical average minicomputer, rather than that of a second-generation NMOS microcomputer. The enhanced NMOS Z80 microprocessor is claimed to be 2 to 12 times faster than Intel's 8080A, and therefore is aimed at the high-end microprocessor market.

Specifications. Standard CPU: 3-K bytes ROM and 1-K bytes static RAM for system monitor, and 16-K bytes general-purpose RAM; clock 2 or 2.5 MHz; optional 8-port parallel I/O modules with interrupt; 16-K byte RAM memory; module extender; extenders for rack-mounting; 115/230 V, 60/50 Hz, 200 W; 0° to 50°C operation; dimensions, 19" X 9" X 15"; weight, 35 lb each for two units, one containing disk drives and power, and the other containing all the other hardware.

The hardware/software development system and chip-architecture are illustrated in Fig. 7-16.

The real-time storage card contains 256 X 32 storage array for 256 events; 32 stored bits include 16-bit address bus, 8-bit data bus, 7-bit control bus, and a final bit to serve as a marker to identify the user's first transaction. The debug software stored can be of any combination of memory: read/writes, I/O-port read/writes.

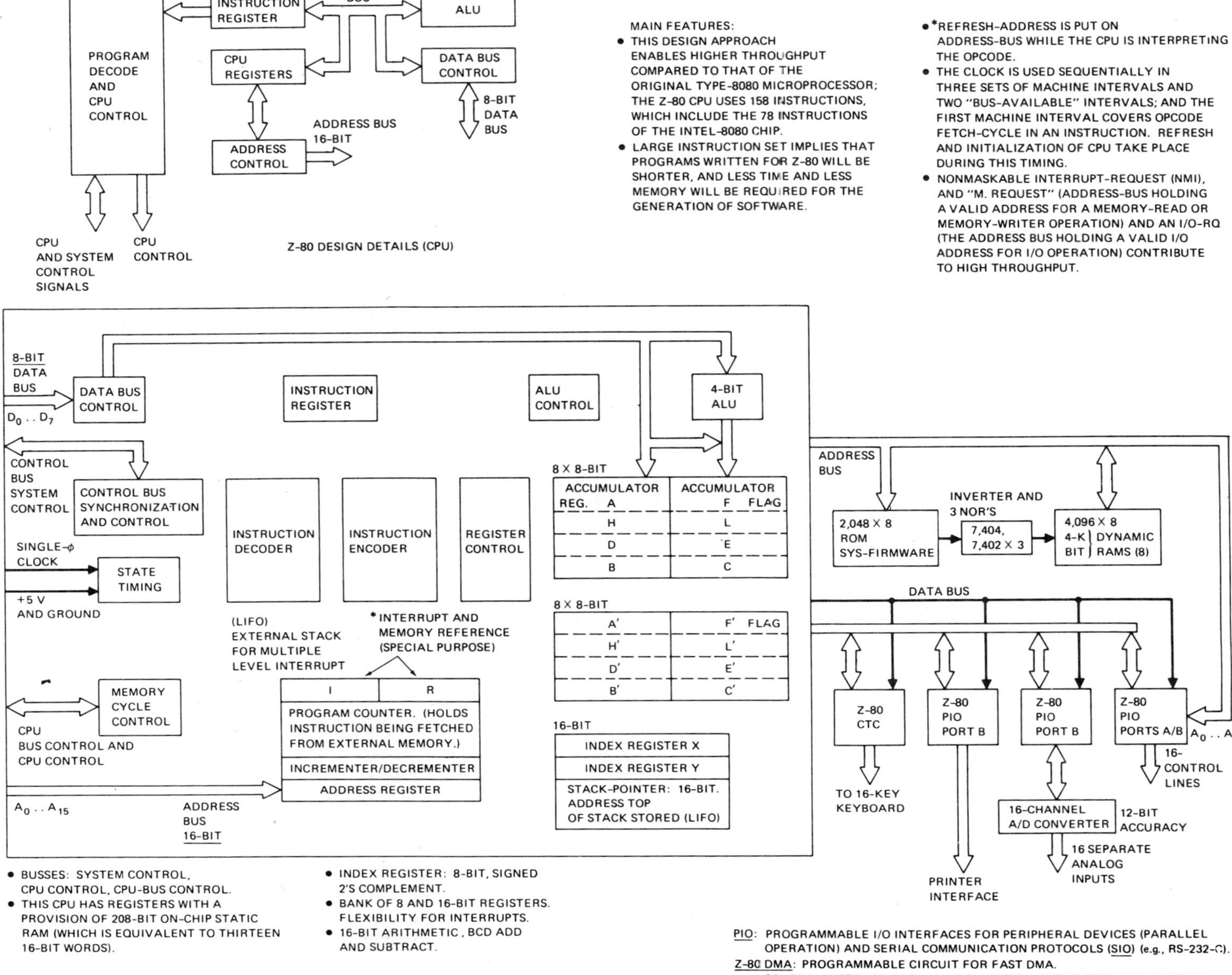

Fig. 7-16. Z-Log, Z-80 microprocessor. (*Courtesy of Zilog Inc., Exxon*)

Any external combination of ROM/RAM/PROM can be used in the place of the standard RAM by way of the in-circuit emulation-bus and a serial-data terminal. For extension to 64-K bytes of memory in 4-K byte increment, the system memory is shared between the monitor mode and the user mode. The monitor-mode programs are entered, edited, assembled, and loaded directly into RAM for immediate execution without the need of any time-consuming programming of PROMs. In the user mode, the RAM memory stores the user's software for complete control of the CPU and peripherals. The ROM-based monitor-software includes the floppy-disk software-driver and bootstrap loader. The in-circuit emulation interface card allows the system to be shared beteeen the monitor and user modes. The standard hardware interconnection cable-port includes 16-bit address bus, 8-bit data bus, all CPU control signals, system clock, and external memory-enable with full buffering.

Zilog-Z8 Microcomputer. As a corresponding chip to Intel's 8048/8748 single-chip microcomputer for dedicated applications, Zilog's Z-8 microcomputer chip is designed for both I/O-intensive microcontroller applications and memory-intensive microprocessor applications (for number-crunching and data-manipulating functions) at a clock-frequency of 4 MHz. Most instructions are executed in 1.5/2.5 μsec. The 16 I/O lines, out of its 32, can be programmed as multiplexed address/data lines for adding external memory in its microprocessor applications. Comprehensive architectural provision is therefore made for 2048 bytes of program memory plus 128-K bytes of external memory, and I/O buffer storage, 144 bytes of RAM register file, a universal asynchronous receiver/transmitter, a pair of 8-bit timer-controllers, and six vectored interrupts. The merged 144-byte file is allocated for four I/O-port registers, 16 status and control registers, and 124 general-

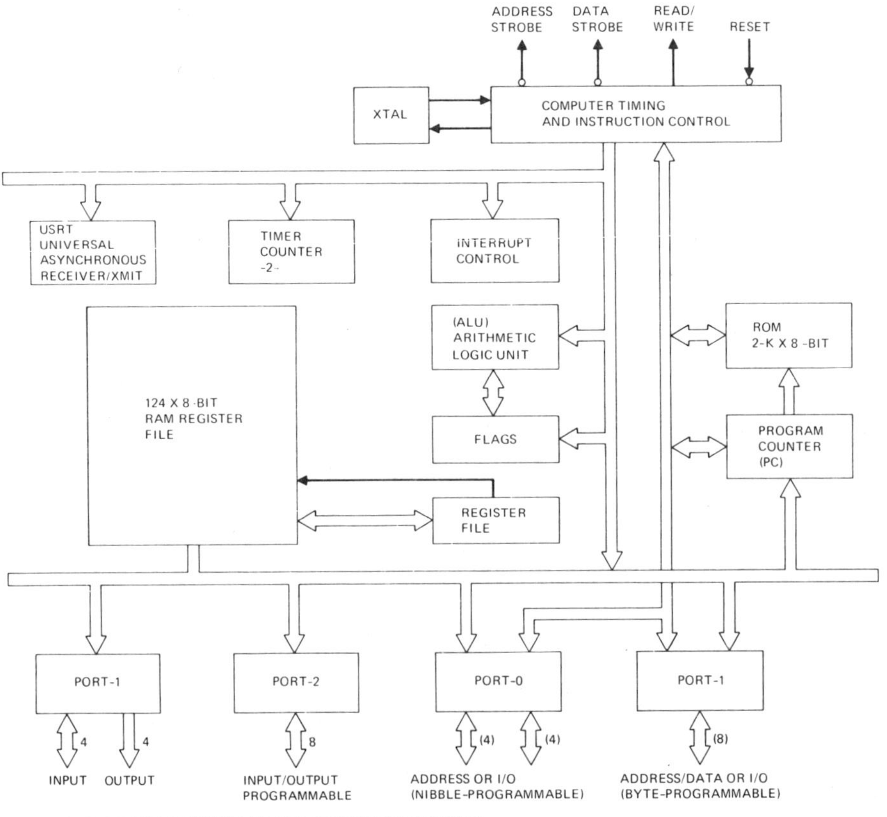

Fig. 7-17. Architecture of the Z-8 microcomputer chip. (*Courtesy of Zilog Inc., Exxon*)

purpose registers. Since the register file is divided into nine sections of 16 locations each, with the aid of a register pointer, 4-bit nibbles can address the registers. The architecture of the chip is shown in Figure 7-17. A 64-pin version is available for Zilog's MCZ or ZDS program development systems.

Z-8's 4-port capability facilitates complex communications and handshake between Z-8 microcomputers or Z-8 microcomputer and several peripheral devices. The six vectored interrupts are individually or combinationally maskable and hence assigned priorities in programming. Since serial communication is a requisite in the latest distributed processing systems, the Z-8's UART facility allows a readily-accessible and efficient means of serial communication.

7-18. DATA GENERAL mN601

The Data General mN601 is the first microprocessor designed by a manufacturer of another popular minicomputer in the international market. The single-chip microprocessor in a 16-bit high-speed silicon-gate NMOS unit, has a 960-ns cycle-time and the fastest instruction-time going, with an ADD time of 2.4 μs and a load-time of 2.9 μs, like a minicomputer. The internal RAM has an access time of 160 ns. The microprocessor uses the 16-bit NOVA instruction-set and the 16-bit data-format. The popular stack-memory is used for easy programming. In addition, it has special hardware for multiply/divide to enable fast program execution, and integral data-channel logic for simplified interface to high-performance peripherals. Control and timing are available for high-density RAM memories. Integral, hidden, refresh logic is used to overlap instruction execution timing. Unique I/O encoding (multiplexing) scheme affords efficient simplified interface design.

Since the single-chip microprocessor is a NOVA product, its software is mostly compatible with the NOVA minicomputer application library; software like the diskette-based Disk Operating System (DOS), FORTRAN IV compiler, assembler, symbolic debugger, relocatable loader, and real-time Operating System are applicable. A more elaborate memory system is available as a single-card microcomputer. This is apparently the first microprocessor that is a step ahead in directly competing with most minicomputers of the last generation—perhaps with some of Data General's own MINIs.

The microcomputer set consists of mN601 CPU, mN606 4-K byte RAM, mN603 I/O controller, and buffer elements. The CPU chip costs $114, and requires ±5- and +15-V supplies. On-chip two-phase real-time clock uses external 8.33-MHz crystal to provide "refresh" control for dynamic RAMs. The CPU chip has multiply/divide hardware stack and pointer registers with stack-overflow protection, DMA, and 16-level priority-interrupt.

7-19. MIPROC-16 (PLESSEY MICROSYSTEMS)

With 350-ns cycle-time, 16-bit word-length, and 82 instructions, the Miproc-16 (Plessey Microsystems) is a real-time high-speed microcomputer-on-a-card. It is available with full hardware and software support on OEM or end-user applications (such as process-control, data acquisition, machine-tools, intelligent terminals, peripheral controller) and data communications, real-time telemetry, FFT processing, and digital filtering. A ruggedized version is available for avionics and navigational systems in Defense and industrial applications. Cross-assembler for use on Tym-share is available. Typical conditional-branch in 700 ns and multiply/divide in 5.6/11.2 μs prove its real-time capability.

The Miproc-16 has an optional 10-M word/sec DMA channel. The instruction-set used eliminates time-consuming microprogramming (like CP-1600), and special hardware design and debugging. The high-speed of this chip allows the use of the less expensive NMOS memories.

At a cost of $500, the chip is claimed to replace high-speed systems with hard-wired logic. With 4-K bytes of RAM, 2-K bytes of ROM, and hardware/software support, the basic Miproc microcomputer system costs $8,000.

Plessey uses PM-1132 CORE main memory with 32-K words on an exclusive memory card for an access-time of 350 ns or, alternatively, a PMS-1132 NMOS RAM memory with 32-K, 18-bit words on a PC board for an access-time of 400 ns and a cycle-time of 500 ns only.

Input/Output ports: 32/256. I/O addressing: separate. The asynchronous maximum baud-rate is 2,400. Board size: 6″ X 9″; dc power: 5 V only at 17-W power-dissipation.

7-20. IMP-16 (NATIONAL SEMICONDUCTOR CORP.)

The architecture of the PMOS microprocessor IMP-16P(L), 4-K byte, 16-bit device, is based around the "register arithmetic logic unit" (RALU) on a bit-slice approach, along with a control ROM (CROM) like that of the popular Data General, NOVA 1200, 16-bit, 43-instruction minicomputer. The bit-slice approach allows the hardware and software configurations for 4, 8, 12, 16, and 18-bit microcomputer-on-a-card design. A 5-chip set costs about $200. Type-L has DMA facility. Direct addressing is accomplished in three modes:

1. Base page
2. Program counter, relative and indexed
3. Indirect addressing is feasible to full 64-K bytes of memory.

Extended CROM will allow block-transfer I/O and memory search. A push-and-pull 16-level stack and multilevel interrupt are provided. Status flag-bits and four Jump-condition inputs allow the movement of all the 16-bit blocks as a whole. Basic CROM provides ADD, SUBSTRACT, and LOGICALs. Cross-assemblers, high-level language (SM/PL), self-assembler, loaders, and debug on paper-tape or cards, time-share, diagnostics, and so on make the software support. The architecture of the IMP-16 is shown in Fig. 7-18. TTY and card-reader interfaces are included in prices under $4,000. The corresponding high-speed NMOS chip will follow.

7-21. CUSTOM MICROPROCESSOR (ADVANCED MICRO-DEVICES, MULTI-CHIP AM-2900)

The AM-2900 follows the architecture-to-custom-design style. The microcomputer is partitioned in bipolar MSI and LSI RALU slices as building blocks, using high-speed Schottky low-power TTL. It is intended for microprogrammable digital computation at a 65-ns cycle-time—as achieved by the latest minicomputers.

The macroinstruction set is defined by the user for microprogramming the ROMs. Actually, one clock-cycle may extend from 50 to 125 ns. A total of 16 working registers in a RALU-RAM can be addressed, two at a time, for simultaneously providing two operands to the ALU, while the latter performs three arithmetic operations on two operands and five logical functions. The following LSI chips are available off-the-shelf for custom designs of microcomputer systems:

1. Interrupt Expander, 2913
2. 1 X 2 Port Register, 2919

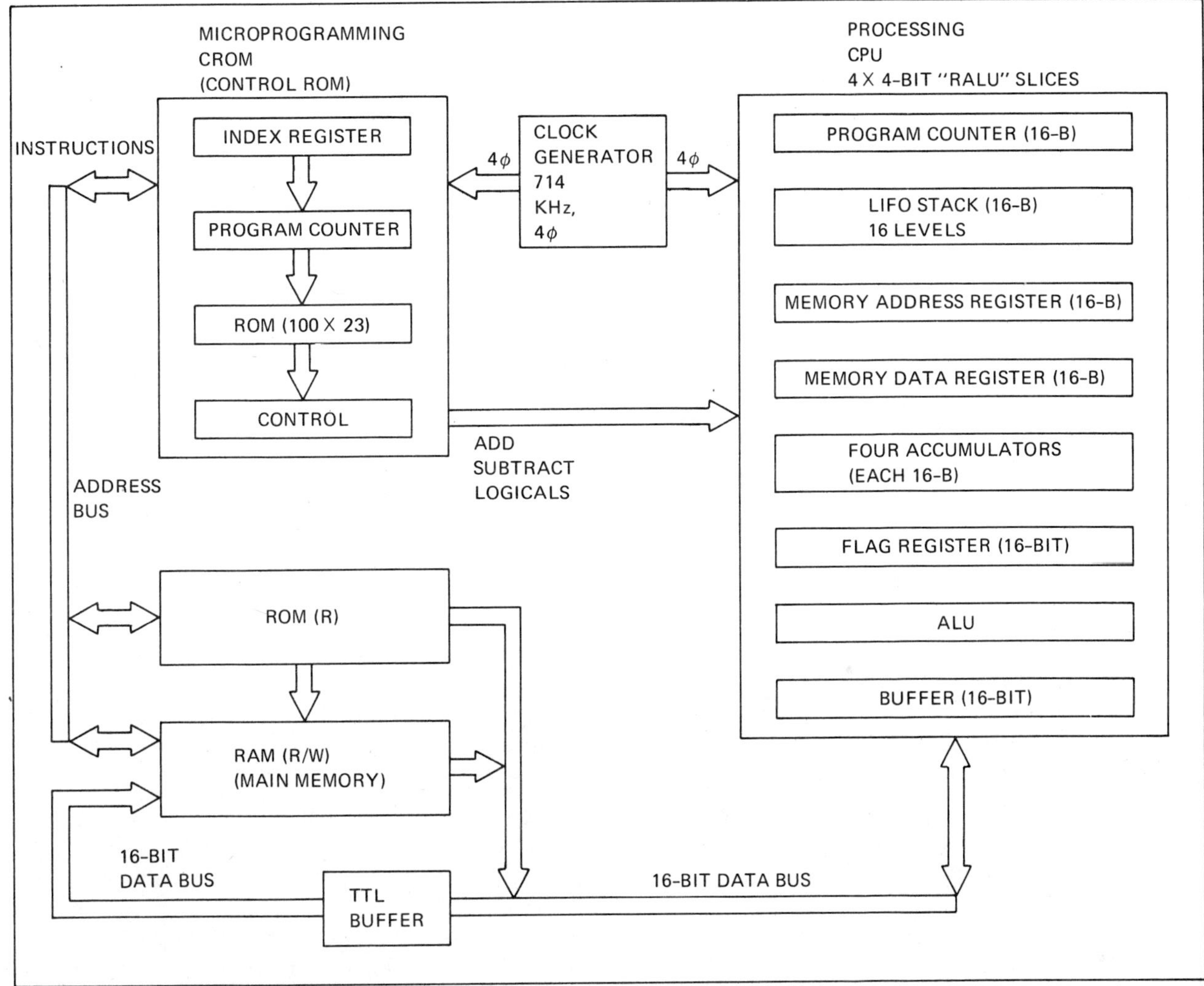

FEATURES:

- 43 INSTRUCTIONS IN 16-BIT WORDS PERFORMED IN 5 TO 10 μs (SLOWER PMOS: CORRESPONDS TO PREVIOUS NOVA 1200 MINICOMPUTER).
- ARCHITECTURE SIMILAR TO PRESENT HIGH-SPEED MICROPROCESSORS WITH CYCLE-TIMES FASTER BY AT LEAST A DECADE. SLOW DUE TO PMOS.
- ADDITIONAL CROM PROVIDES MULTIPLY, DIVIDE, DOUBLE-PRECISION ARITHMETIC, ETC.
- INDIRECT ADDRESSING TO FULL 65-K BYTES OF MEMORY; DIRECT ADDRESSING: BASE PAGE, RELATIVE, AND INDEXED.
- 16-LEVEL STACK; MULTILEVEL INTERRUPT.
- A CORRESPONDING NMOS DESIGN MAY BE AVAILABLE FOR HIGH-SPEED PROCESSING. THIS WAS ONE OF THE FIRST-GENERATION ORIGINAL PMOS VERSIONS.

Fig. 7-18. Architecture of IMP-16, National Semiconductor. PMOS slices are used for CPU and CROM, along with TTL circuits. (*Courtesy of EDN, Cahners publication*)

3. 64-bit 2-Port RAMs, 29704/05
4. 256-bit RAMs, 29720/21
5. 256-bit PROMs, 29750/51
6. RALU Slice: 2901 ($21)
7. Look-ahead Carry, 2902
8. Bus Transceivers, 2905/6/7
9. Interrupt Control, 2914
10. Register Slice, 2918
11. 16-way Branch Controller for Sequencers 2909, 29803

12. Instruction Controller and Controlled Store Sequencer
13. Microprogram Learning and Evaluation Kit: $289
14. Main-memory RAMS: 2950/51/52.

The philosophy behind this system is one of a "transition" between the minicomputer and the microcomputer technologies in the current costlier minicomputer applications.

7-22. MICROCONTROLLER SYSTEM 20 (SCIENTIFIC MICROSYSTEMS)

A microcomputer is generally used as a typical microcontroller to interface several peripheral devices to a medium-scale general-purpose digital computer or a minicomputer operating system. This is the most common application of a microprocessor in large systems. This makes it a computer-within-a-computer.

SMS-300 is a monolithic, high-speed Schottky-bipolar microcontroller, with a 16-bit instruction word and a cycle-time of 300 ns. The unit is specifically capable of working as a controller/interpreter or a multiplexer to interface a medium-scale digital computer or a minicomputer to several peripheral devices, using an "interpreter" octal-repertoire of eight instructions:

1. MOVE
2. ADD
3. AND
4. XOR, exclusive OR for source-data that require eight 8-bit GPRs at a time
5. EXECute
6. NZT (nonzero contents and transfer)
7. XMIT, which requires four 8-bit registers at a time, for "Register-Immediate" and then "Bus-Immediate"
8. JMP-7 (jump to program-address), which requires two 8-bit GPRs.

See Fig. 7-19, which presents the following in somc detail: SMS-300 programmable peripheral microcontroller, SMS-330 processor, SMS-360/361 Interface Vector-bytes, SMS-331 program storage, and SMS-322-02W working storage.

System-20 actually consists of:

1. SMS-330, with SMS-300 interpreter/CPU chip, incremented by 0/512/1024/2048 16-bit words of ten 512 X 8 ROM-chips, in a 64-pin unit

2. SMS-322 Schottky-bipolar RAM working-storage (256 X 8 bits) with 85-ns maximum access-time, as high-speed bit-addressable memory for data-and-status information storage, in another 64-pin chip

3. SMS-331, supplementary 2,048, 16-bit word, program-storage unit with eight 512 X 8 ROM/PROM chips and 1-of-4 ROM decoders

4. Eight, 24-pin SMS 360/361 Interface-Vector (IV) byte chips, each containing an 8-bit bidirectional data-register that works as an I/O tristate or open-collector, TTL-compatible, interface element to the peripheral device. Each IV chip contains, control logic, data-latches, address comparator, and status-latch for transfer of data, and, of course, line receivers/drivers. Thus, the interface element provides byte I/O control, select and write commands, and master-enable and master-clock. A field-programmable address allows one of 512 bytes on a bus to be selected without decoders. I/O-ports are independent, the user-port having priority for data entry. A selected vector byte (IV) deselects itself when another vector byte (IV) is selected.

The storage concept of this microcontroller is that of separating the ROM program storage from the data storage. With the supplementary program-storage unit, the address

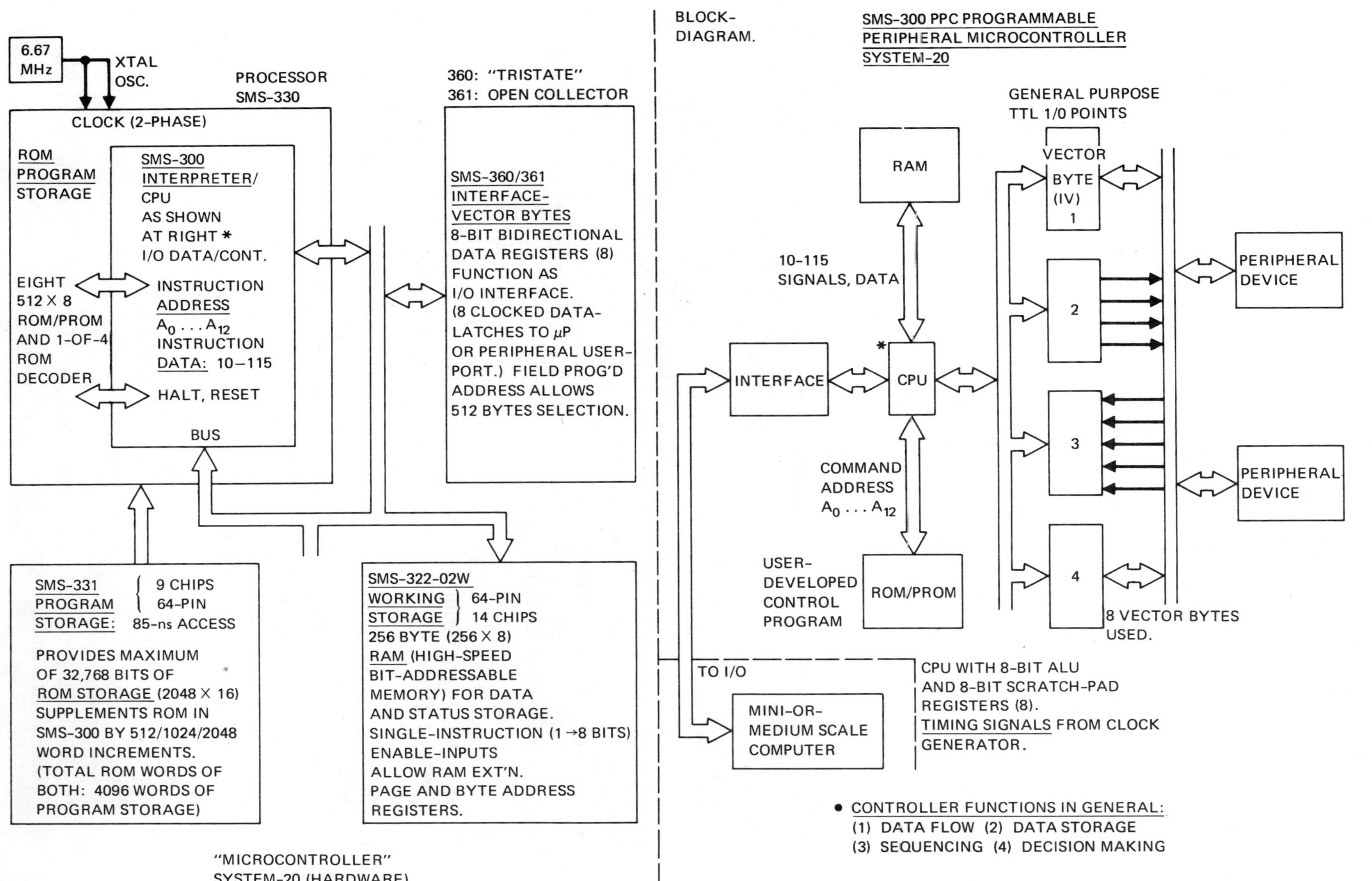

Fig. 7-19. System-20 microcomputer with SMS-300 microcontroller. (*Courtesy of Scientific Microsystems*)

capability of this microcontroller is 8,192, 16-bit words. Simultaneous data-transfer and data-edit take place in a single 16-bit instruction cycle-time of 300 ns. The control-oriented instructions operate with equal speed on 1- to 8-bit data formats, and it is ideal for switching, controlling, and editing applications. And the peripheral-device data can be processed (tested, shifted, added, etc.) without moving them to internal RAM storage, whereas the address of the external device is determined by the program stored in the microcontroller ROMs.

7-23. MICROCOMPUTER SYSTEMS MEETING DEFENSE STANDARDS, 1978

A typical ruggedized microcomputer. The microcomputer system that meets the Defense standards is presently a 16-bit CPU microprocessor-on-a-card introducing advanced, low-cost, high-density LSI with high-reliability logic gates, monolithic semiconductor memories, hybrid power supplies, and innovative packaging concepts. Several options, such as floating-point arithmetic, high-speed extended-precision, "cordic" algorithms, microprogrammed instruction sets, and communications interface make it adaptable to a wide variety of applications. A half-ATR (avionics transport rack) case will hold any avionic configuration with up to 32-K words of CORE, or the less expensive ROM/RAM storage, to meet MIL-E-5400 class-2 aerospace standards and MIL-E-16400 class-4 shipboard standards. Its architecture will go under the classfication of a medium-performance (average high-speed), state-of-the-art, general-purpose microprogrammed multiprocessor. A corresponding advanced space-version may use a 32-bit data-flow along the bit-slice technique.

The 40/48-pin LSI chips, 0.125 in sq, mounted on metallized ceramic substrates of 0.125 in sq, will average about 110 gates/chip by using high-speed Schottky low-power TTL. At this density, 1,700 gates take a card area of 7″ X 3″. Each modular core-memory unit will provide 8-K words of storage, 18-bits/word, with a parity-bit and a store protect-bit. It may use an 8-chip NMOS ROM/I^2L memory on each substrate to provide 12-K bits in each SEM (standard electronic module).

The packaging technique used will contribute to efficient heat-dissipation and accessibility to meet ATR Defense standards.

Cordic algorithms—X, Y, W coordinate-transformation algorithms for vector-rotation of functions in trigonometric and hyperbolic modes—are specially used in navigational software. A cordic algorithm relies on the ability of the ROM microprogram to manipulate the internal registers of the microprocessor. While the interrelation between the registers is maintained by a simple stored algorithm, another register is automatically inserted toward the trigonometric function to minimize execution time to 2 or 3 divide-timings.

The typical features of this microcomputer will be as follows:

1. Fixed-point, binary, fractional 16-bit data flow.
2. Repertoire of at least 108 instructions (16 bits; 32 for double-precision).
3. Program-controlled direct I/O; buffered I/O (multiplexer, block data-transfer, and at least four I/O interrupts); 16-bit parallel direct-memory access; at least four external program interrupts; memory loading.
4. Asynchronous memory-interface for communications.
5. Built-in test; microprogrammed self-test; GO/NO-GO counter and timing step-detector; subassembly test-points.
6. Parallel-shift matrix to support cordic algorithms for exponential and trigonometric functions and coordinate-translation.

7. 32-bit floating-point, hexadecimal, fractional (8/24 format).
8. Interval-counter (16-bits, 3.2-sec duration).
9. Real-time clock (extended interval-timer, 32 bits, 2.48 days).
10. Six discrete inputs, four discrete outputs.
11. Expanded read-only microprogram control storage.
12. Additional instructions for options, 7 for floating-point, 8 for algorithms, 15 for byte handling.
13. 400,000 operations with core; 450-K bytes with RAM; I/O rates: 100K to 400K half-words/sec.
14. Speed: CPU-cycle 250 ns; add: 1.7 to 2.8 μs; floating-point add: 4 to 6 μs; multiply: 4.2 to 5.6 μs; branch: 1.6 to 2.3 μs, depending on small or large instruction.
15. Size: 7.62″ X 4.88″ X 19.56″ (CORE); 7.62″ X 4.88″ X 12.56″–0.27 cubic ft (RAMs).
16. Weight: 28 to 20 lbs (depending on memory expansion).
17. Power: 290 to 285 W, 400 Hz, 3-phase (MIL-STD-704A).
18. Software: Support software contains assembler, linkage editor, interpretive functional simulator, and readily accessed self-test program, which coresides with operational program.
19. Optional software: Program verification package, self-hosted support package, microdiagnostic programs, subroutine library, high-level language compiler.
20. Optional Test Set: For factory checkout and debugging, as a software development tool, it performs:
    a. Memory load-and-verify
    b. Computer test and maintenance
    c. Software test-and-verify
    d. System functional-test, and
    e. Self-hosted software verification.

7-24. SCP-234 MICROCOMPUTER SYSTEM (RCA AVIONICS CMOS)

Availability of small payload, low-power, flight computers enable overall spacecraft performance or capabilities such as enhancing

1. Command and control
2. Precision attitude control
3. EW system applications
4. Communications subsystems.

The **SCP-234 MICROCOMPUTER** was specifically developed by Astro-Electronics Division of RCA for Aerospace applications. The unit, eight cards in all, weighs 8 lbs at 300-cubic-in space requirement and consumes 5 W of power. The computer uses CMOS-LSI, both for the CPU and the memory (RAMs). In one application, its read/write memory, with a write-protect feature, has a capacity of 16-K words of 16 bits each, plus 256 words of PMOS ROM control. The RAM is assigned areas by the jumper wiring, in blocks of 1,024 words, to separate the data areas from the area of instructions and constants.

Arithmetic is binary 2's complement, fixed-point. (2's complement: subtract by inverting all bits and adding 1.) Since 15-bit precision is inadequate in precision control, software uses double-precision with two words without a speed penalty. Cued priority-interrupt system uses 16 levels, of which 14 are external. Single-word, 16-bit instruction execution is controlled by a ROM-microprogram. A total of 52 instructions are imple-

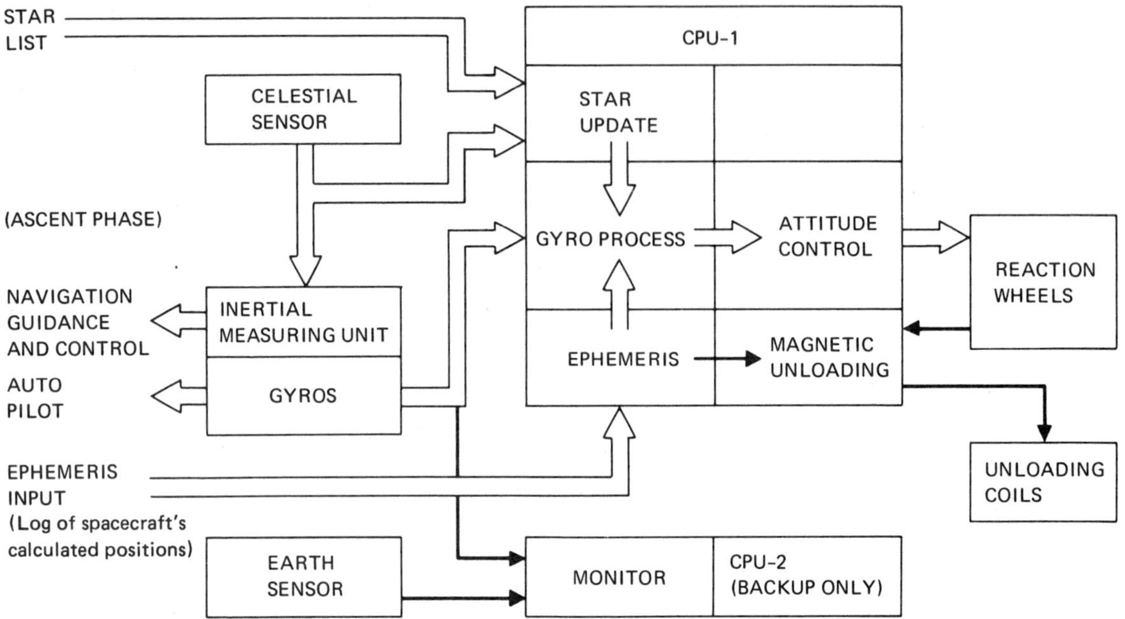

Fig. 7-20. Application of the RCA Avionics, SCP-234 microcomputer system for attitude-control. (*Courtesy of IEEE Aerospace and Electronics Systems Society Newsletter*)

mented: 12 arithmetic, 8 logical, 16 branch/skip, 13 load/store/transfer, 2 I/O, 1 control. ADD, in either the single- or double-precision format, takes 4.68 μs.

I/O interface of the CPU is 16-bit parallel bidirectional-bus. The ROM contains the bootstrap loader; software can be written in a high-level language (SPL). A simpler assembler is also available for coding functions such as the command-control.

A block diagram of the attitude-control system in aerospace applications, given in Fig. 7-20, indicates the computer's functions:

7-25. INTEL-M8080A MICROPROCESSOR (A RUGGEDIZED VERSION)

M8080A is an NMOS, silicon-gate, 8-bit microprocessor intended for processing and control applications. The block diagram of the CPU is shown in Fig. 7-21. The six GPRs can be addressed individually or in pairs to provide single- or double-precision arithmetic. An accumulator and five testable flags are the additional features. An external 16-bit stack feature allows multiple-level priority-interrupts by rapidly storing and restoring processor-status, by use of a part of the memory as "LIFO" for the contents of the accumulator, flags, and program counter, and the GPRs. Simple interface to the memory and I/O is made possible by the 16-line address and 8-line bidirectional data-busses, which are controlled by a HOLD signal to suspend the data processing and permit "OR-tying" with other control devices for the DMA or multiprocessor operation. The unit is specifically suitable for Defense and space applications, with:

1. 2 μs instruction cycle
2. 16-bit program counter for addressing up to 64-K bytes of memory
3. Decimal, binary, and double-precision arithmetic
4. 512 directly addressed I/O ports, and capability of priority vectored-interrupts
5. TTL-compatibility.

Data is stored in 8-bit binary integers, but instructions may be 1 to 3 bytes in length.

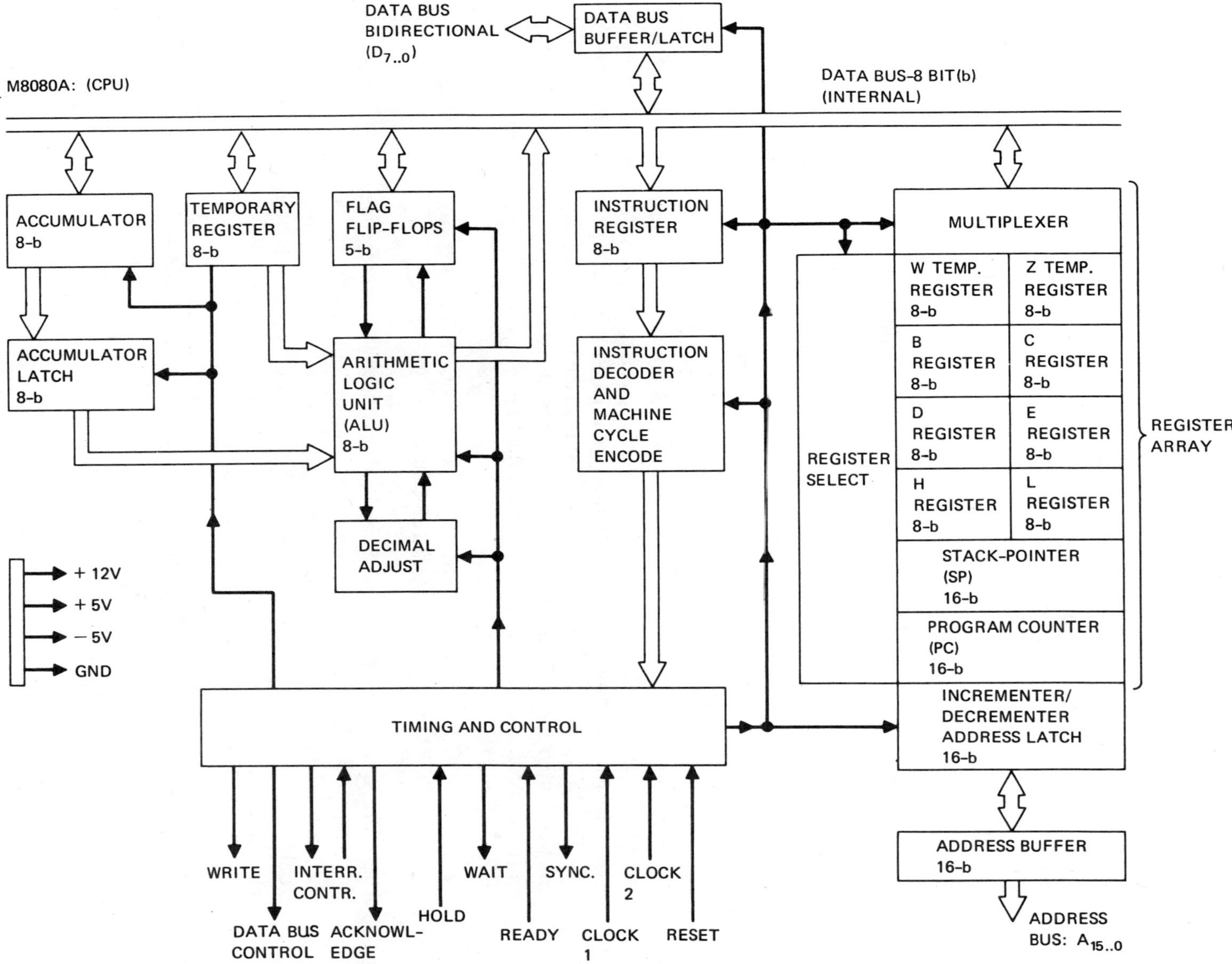

Fig. 7-21. Intel 8080A (ruggedized to meet Defense standards). (*Courtesy of Intel Corporation*)

7-26. ROLM AN/AYK-28 (16/64)

Three microprocessors in one, the rugged ROLM AN/AYK-28 (16/64) microcomputer package meets Defense standards. That is,

1. It is a microprogrammed general-purpose processor for data manipulation applications
2. Variable-precision, floating-point arithmetic is handled by a second processor, which allows the choice of 32-, 48-, or 64-bit precision to get the accuracy and speed normally obtained in medium and mini general-purpose digital computers
3. A direct-memory-access (DMA) processor handles I/O traffic as a multiplexer (or as a computer within a computer).

System and program protection is rendered feasible by a new executer/user hardware-mode, and 200 instructions handle data, irrespective of whether the format is bit, byte, field, block, or list. A total of 64-K bytes of main-memory are allowed, with possible extension to 512-K bytes of dual-port memory. Upward-compatible, standard software package is part of the system at no extra cost.

With the advent of high-speed 16-bit microprocessors, the latest trend in aerospace applications in general is a gradual substitution of dedicated ruggedized microcomputer systems in place of the previous minicomputer systems—due to the obvious weight and power considerations. For example, the first Avionics microcomputer to go into an aircraft digital autopilot system is the one designed by Hughes Aircraft Company for an average instruction cycle-time of 100 ns (in a 16-bit microcomputer operating through the -55° to +125°C Defense standards). Similar dedicated microcomputer systems are being evaluated for such applications as missile guidance, synthetic array radars, airborne gunfire control, and point-to-point communications.

7-27. MICROCOMPUTER ASSOCIATES, MOS TECHNOLOGY, AND ROCKWELL MICROELECTRONIC DEVICES 6502

The 6502 is a popular, 40-pin, $10.90, 8-bit pipelined microprocessor with on-board single-phase clock. It is also available in several 28-pin variants. The two-phase clock version 6512 works with external clock-pulses for high-precision timing control at 2 MHz clock. The 6502 is normally used for TTL-compatible operation from 20 kHz to 1 MHz; and 6502A also extends the clock to 2 MHz for high-speed processing applications. KIM single-board computers have several versions with different amounts of RAM. A synertec SYM-board has a provision for high-current/high-voltage devices. An MDT 650 program development terminal, a TIM 6530 with monitor software, and a BASIC interpreter are available for interfacing serial terminals. The 6502 allows add/subtract and automatic correction in decimal mode, with powerful addressing modes that include *indexed-indirect/indirect-indexed* modes. Both 6502 and 6512 models can address up to 65-K bytes of RAM.

The architecture of the microprocessor, illustrated in Figure 7-22, facilitates all registers to accept data from/to the data bus, since they are all internally routed to the same bus. The 56-instruction set is memory-oriented, and emphasis is placed on convenient addressing of data in memory tables.

The following addressing modes are provided for programming: immediate and absolute addressing, indexed zero page, indexed absolute addressing, implied and relative addressing, indexed indirect, indirect indexed, and absolute indirect addressing. Software support includes a cross-assembler for the DEC minicomputers PDP-8, -10, and -11, a text

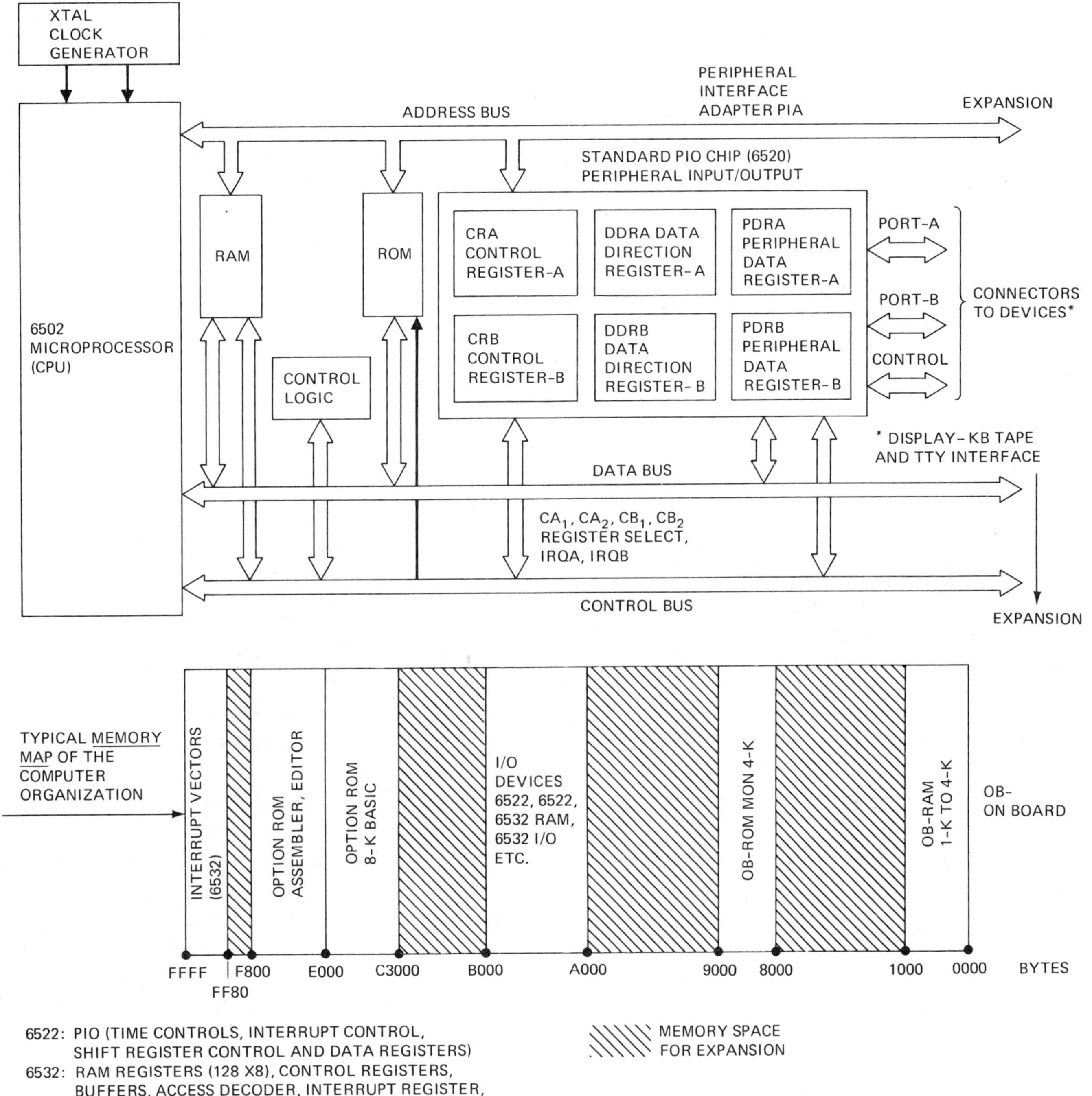

Fig. 7-22. Architecture of the 6502 microprocessor chip. (*Courtesy of Microcomputer Associates*)

editor, a debugger, a resident assembler, a math package, a Fortran compiler, a cross-emulator and BASIC/Extended BASIC.

Other specifications: 16-bit-addressing bus, 65-K byte direct addressing range, 8- to 24-bit instruction words (like those of MC-6800), 1-to-3-μs instruction words, three dedicated I/O control lines, and 5V/140 mA power requirement.

Other LSI interface chips include 6520 peripheral interface adaptor, 6522 peripheral interface adaptor and two timers, 6530 integrated chip containing 16 I/O, 8-K bit ROM, 65 X 8 RAM and timer, and 6532 with 128 X 8 static RAM in the place of 65 X 8 RAM.

Mnemonic Instruction Set

ADC	Add with carry	JSR	Jump to subroutine
AND	Logical AND	LDA	Load accumulator
ASL	Arithmetic shift left	LDX	Load X
BCC	Branch if carry clear	LDY	Load Y
BCS	Branch if carry set	LSR	Logical shift right
BEQ	Branch if result = ∅	NOP	No operation
BIT	Test bit	ORA	Logical OR
BMI	Branch if minus	PHA	Push A
BNE	Branch if not equal to ∅	PHP	Push P status
BPL	Branch if plus	PLA	Pull A
BRK	Break	PLP	Pull P status
BVC	Branch if overflow clear	ROL	Rotate left
BVS	Branch if overflow set	ROR	Rotate right
CLC	Clear carry	RTI	Return from interrupt
CLD	Clear decimal flag	RTS	Return from subroutine
CLI	Clear interrupt disable	SBC	Subtract with carry
CLV	Clear overflow	SEC	Set carry
CMP	Compare to accumulator	SED	Set decimal
CPX	Compare to X	SEI	Set interrupt disable
CPY	Compare to Y	STA	Store accumulator
DEC	Decrement memory	STX	Store X
DEX	Decrement X	STY	Store Y
DEY	Decrement Y	TAX	Transfer A to X
EOR	Exclusive OR	TAY	Transfer A to Y
INC	Increment memory	TSX	Transfer SP to X
INX	Increment X	TXA	Transfer X to A
INY	Increment Y	TXS	Transfer X to SP
JMP	Jump	TYA	Transfer Y to A

6500/1, one-chip microcomputer. Assembly-line programming gains speed if the processor, memory, timing and control are all incorporated on a single 40 pin-chip, 6500/1. Since debugging becomes difficult in this production version, 6500/1 is available in a 64-pin emulator model as well with the same instruction set and 13 modes of addressing as those of 6502. The emulator chip has the address, data, and control buses accessible through 24 extra pins, to enable the user to link them to the external memory being used for software development. After the program is debugged, it can be masked into the 2048 bytes ROM of the 40-pin 6500/1 production chip. The additional facilities of 6500/1 are shown dotted in the blockdiagram of 6502 microprocessor. As an additional facility, a third-generation development system is available in System-65 to allow the interface of mini-floppy drives, high-speed terminals, and *high-speed* printers. As in 6502, the instructions are pipelined so that the fetching of one instruction overlaps the execution of the immediately preceding instruction. Since 6500/1 has the facility to directly address all memory space, unlike other similar single-chip systems, it can store constant tables in its ROM. For peripheral I/O, the chip has the provision of four bidirectional ports (A, B, C, D), and each of these pins may be assigned an input or TTL output function. Two leads of port A enable edge-deleting logic capability for requesting interrupts.

Two interrupt-request lines $\overline{\text{NMI}}$ and $\overline{\text{IRQ}}$, as in 6502, are vector interrupts, so that when they are serviced, program-return processor-status information is automatically saved on the stack. Minimum interrupt response time is eight memory cycles for access to the first instruction of service routine. That is, when the maskable interrupt request ($\overline{IRQ}$) and the nonmaskable interrupt ($\overline{NMI}$) are received from the monitor program, the microcomputer 6500/1 handles the interrupt by first completing the execution of its current instruction and then saving the results on the stack; the appropriate vector address for the computer is then available in the program handshaking procedure. At that specific address, it expects to find the beginning address of the selected interrupt service routine from the peripheral involved, as prearranged in original program development. This entire procedure involves a delay of at least eight memory cycles to commence the required service routine. After handling the service routine, the computer returns to the next instruction after collecting the stored results from the stack.

System 65 supports hardware/software development for the entire 6500 family of microprocessors. The system may be connected to other terminals via current loop or RS-232C interface, and to a dot-matrix printer for hard copy via standard parallel interface.

For debugging, nine break-points are provided, eight for software and one for real-time hardware. Writing into protected memory is always done by the monitor program. A personality card matches the 6500/1 to the System 65 program development system. When the emulator is executing in real-time, a TTL sync pulse output provides the oscilloscope trigger for real-time debugging. Provision is made in the hardware used for Program Development System-65, the requisite operational 5-V dc power supply, reset pulse timing, and the crystal for the clock frequency.

7-28. MAC-4 MICROCOMPUTER, BELL LABORATORIES

MAC-4 is a low-end, low power-consumming CMOS, 40-pin microcomputer chip specially designed as an I/O-intensive controller for telecommunications applications. With a bus-structured architecture and a powerful instruction set oriented toward efficient bit manipulation, it has a flexible I/O structure, event counter, nonmaskable DMA, interrupt facility, and a PLA encoder that can work as a code converter. Although the internal data bus is 4 bits wide, the operand width can extend from 4 to 16 bits in a programmable extension register. The program memory efficiency and the contents of memory addressable locations are emphasized. The halt instruction puts the chip in standby microwatt power consumption as an asset in a telephone loop. The 1024-nibble (4-bit) ROM program memory as well as the 64-nibble RAM user memory can be easily expanded to 3840 and 192 nibbles, respectively.

The five basic sections of the architecture, controller, arithmetic logic unit (ALU), special registers, address arithmetic unit (AAU), user memory, and I/O are shown in Figure 7-23. The AAU, under the direct supervision of the controller, performs the following tasks: (1) formatting of the proper addresses for each of the four destination and four source addressing modes, (2) incrementing of the data in the 12-bit address latches, (3) formatting of the special addresses dedicated to interrupt and trap, and (4) formatting of the special register addresses. The AAU also comprises of a block of RAM dedicated to the special registers: (1) program counter, (2) stack-pointer, (3) DMA pointer DP, (4) two memory pointers, (5) group pointer, (6) extension register as part of opcode, (7) I/O control register, and (8) two temporary storage registers. The rich and homogeneous repertoire of 43 instructions, with the memory-mapped I/O and special registers as the source and destination for all instructions, can be arranged under four categories: 9 monadic, 9 diadic, 10 program transfer, and 6 miscellaneous. Unlike most microprocessors, the RAM space provides for the following source and destination addressing modes, as well as the memory pointer registers and the group memory registers. A register in this group acts as the accumulator thus enabling true memory-to-memory data transfer without the conventional accumulator.

Mode	*Destination*	*Source*
0	Indirect via group pointer	Indirect via group pointer
1	Direct addressing	Direct addressing
2	Indirect via memory pointer 1	Indirect via memory pointer 1
3	Indirect via memory pointer 2	Immediate data

The 8-bit stack-pointer enables the user to address the stack for storing and restoring current addresses for calls, traps, and interrupts in the RAM. However, the stack-pointer must be initialized through software, since there is no reserved stack in the RAM memory. The condition register has four user-accessible flag-bits carry, overflow, zero, and parity, and they signify the results of certain arithmetic and logic operations. Program transfer instructions such as branch, jump, call, return, and halt have no effect on the condition register. All other instructions affect two or four conditions for logic and arithmetic operations, respectively.

The I/O related functions of MAC-4 are: (1) nonmaskable DMA (serial I/O, parallel I/O, or interrupt), (2) maskable interrupt, (3) maskable event counter, (4) bus-structured functions (8-bit I/O port as levels or strobed, 16 I/O latches, and 4-bit input port), and (5) 4-bit PLA encoder (external or internal). The I/O mode of operation is selected by an 8-bit I/O control register; the lower 4 bits control the flow of data among the input port,

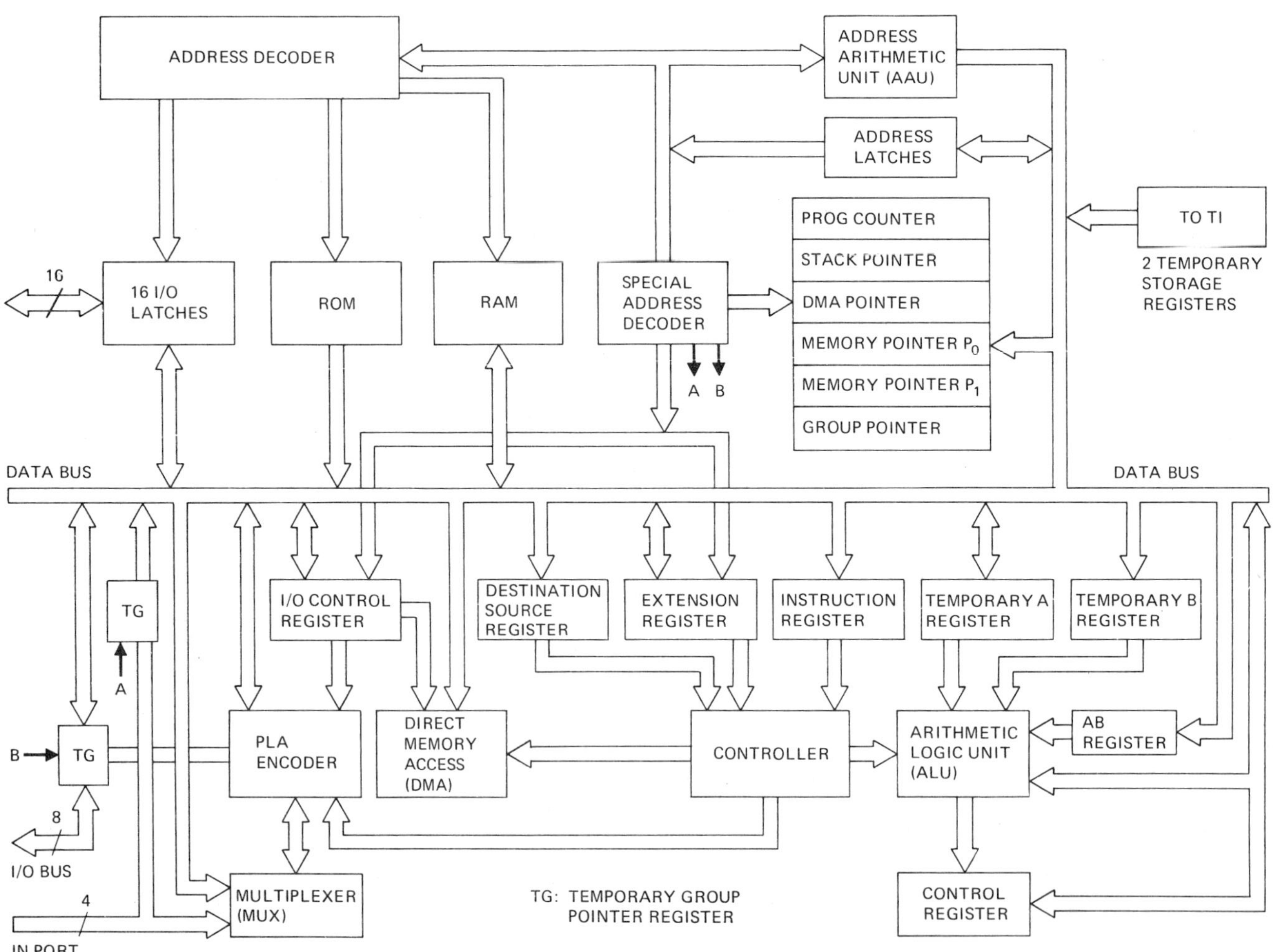

Fig. 7-23. Bell Laboratories MAC-4 microcomputer chip. (© *IEEE, COMPCON, 1979*)

the I/O bus, and the internal data bus; and the upper 4 bits control the data for DMA in/out, DMA serial/parallel, event counter enable, and interrupt enable. The DMA pointer serves also as a 12-bit event counter, if the DMA request is maintained high, and the asynchronous clock is pulsed low, when the event counter bit of the I/O control register is enabled. Each asynchronous clock pulse increments the pointer, and a transition from Hex FFF to ØØØ results in an overflow that generates an interrupt.

The MAC-4 designed for optimum cost effectiveness in high-volume telecommunications applications illustrates the design methodology of a typical very-low-cost microcomputer chip in modern mass-production applications.

7-29. TRADE-OFFS BETWEEN HARDWARE IMPLEMENTATION BY LSI AND RESTRUCTURED SOFTWARE—INTEL 8253

The following example describes the latest design trend in systems and control engineering applications. **Intel 8253 LSI programmable counter/timer chip** is architecturally organized to control three active intervals of time with three independent 16-bit counters (binary or BCD) at dc to 2 MHz. It operates in several modes to generate different waveforms and timing requirements. As a typical systems-method of its application as a feedback controller for dc motor speed, R. D. Grappel of the Massachusetts Institute of Technology's Lincoln Laboratory improvised this chip to enable a microcomputer (1) to control the power supplied to the motor-load on a proportional basis and (2) to generate a motor-parameter such as revolutions per minute to be digitally fed back to the microcomputer.

It is obvious from the technique illustrated that the simple form of control algorithm, depicted by the direct implementation of hardware in Fig. 7-24, naturally results in a minimization of time and effort on computer software. Most of the tasks involved were formally assigned to the expensive software implementation for this specific digital control system. The flowchart for the CPU interrupt-handler and the main program are included in Fig. 7-24.

Timer 1 of 8253 provides overall system control and generates periodic interrupts to command the computer that a new power pulse is required. It is programmed to provide a 1-sec interval between interrupts by using a 10-kHz clock. Timer 2 is triggered to generate the power pulse. Timer 0 is gated to count feedback pulses from the motor load: it acts as a gated counter to feed back the state of the load to the computer; the computer interrupt-software modifies this count to a new count for timer 2.

A disk-encoder with 10 perforations and a lamp/photocell arrangement are used as a transducer to indicate motor speed. A single-shot integrated circuit 74121 shapes the photocell signals for timer 0. The motor speed-range from 600 to 6000 rpm translates to 100 to 1000 pulse/sec. The pulse generator of timer 2 drives a buffer (7407) and an opto-isolator. The motor is driven by a Darlington (2N6037) capable of handling loads up to 100 W.

At start, the first task of the microcomputer is to initialize the three timers. One interrupt/sec is received to read timer 0, and the corresponding count is compared to that in the program to increment/decrement the preset count of timer 2 within the set limits. Then, the microcomputer reloads timers 2, 1, and 0 for returning control to interrupt.

With the technique illustrated, one microcomputer (having cycle-times of the order of 1 to 2 μsec) can attend to several control tasks in parallel by using different control algorithms. The LSI hardware technology is thus instrumental at this time in economizing fairly complex digital control systems by minimizing space and comparatively more expensive and time-consuming software demands.

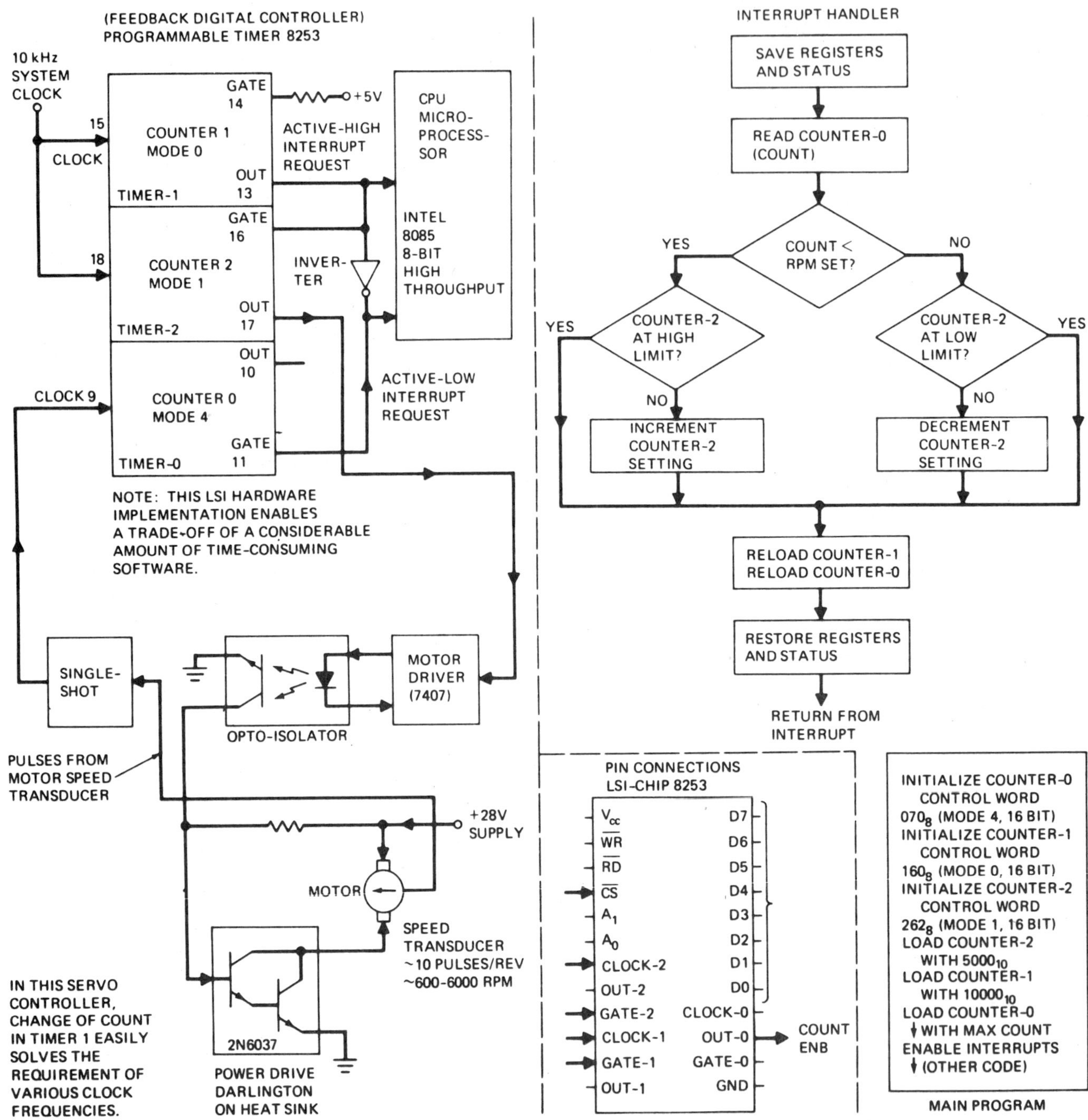

Fig. 7-24. Feedback controller. Intel-8253 as a programmable interval-timer in motor-speed application. (*Courtesy of EDN, Cahners Publishing Company*)

7-30. VLSI SCALED-DOWN MICROPROCESSORS

Zilog-8000, 32/16-bit scaled-NMOS Microprocessor (Zilog, Inc., Cupertino, California). The Zilog-8000 is the first VLSI (*very large-scale integrated*) microprocessor that is architecturally *register-oriented* instead of byte to rival the former average minicomputers in trends of application. Multiple registers reduce the instructions necessary for execution in order to simplify programming. At the same time, Z-8000 fits into the applications of the present 8/16-bit microprocessors. The VLSI feature means 17,500 transistors in

5833 gates at a power dissipation of 1.5 W, compared to 4800 transistors in 1600 gates of the LSI Intel 8080 (1974) at 1.2-W dissipation. (Intel's VLSI, 16-bit 8086 microprocessor is comprised of 20,000 transistors.) The Assembly language notation, the 81 distinct operation-code instructions, data types, and addressing modes all amount to a powerful set of 414 instructions, compared to a corresponding 65 of 8080. Therefore, the throughput of Z-8000 is as much as 10 times that of the present microprocessors. The VLSI Motorola scaled-NMOS 68000 microprocessor, expected during 1979, boasts 68,000 transistors; it can handle 32-bit arithmetic operations like any minicomputer and interface with 1 megabyte of random access memory.

With 24 registers of 16 bits each and a minimum need of memory reference, the Z-8000 may be considered as a *fourth-generation microprocessor* in the lineage 8080, Z-80, Z-80A/Intel 8085, and Z-8000.

A large majority of the instructions can use any of five main addressing modes with 8-bit byte and 16- or 32-bit data words.

With a direct-memory-addressing capability of 8 megabytes, the Z-8000 organizes memory into a set of 128 segments of up to 64-K bytes each, in order to simplify programming. As in large-scale and minicomputers, the Z-8000 accomplishes *dynamic relocation* and memory protection by using an auxiliary *memory-management chip* in a *data-base setup*. The NMOS chip is processed in VLSI scaled-down depletion-load silicon-gate technology, requiring a 5-V supply and a single-phase 4-MHz clock for timing.

To meet the requirement of compatibility with both the present series of microprocessors and new minicomputer applications, Z-8000 is available in (1) a 40-pin version that uses 16 lines to address a single segment of 64-K bytes and (2) a 48-pin version that uses

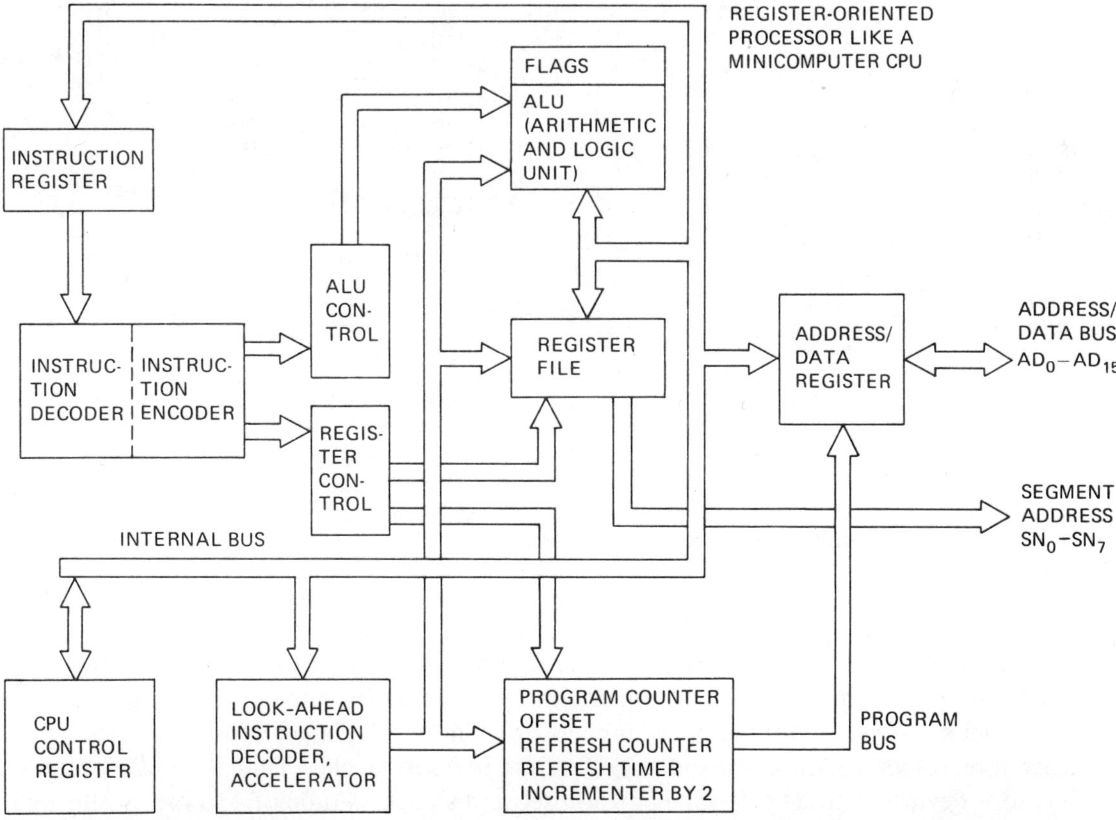

Fig. 7-25. Zilog-8000 Architecture. (Reprinted from *Electronics*, December 21, 1978: Copyright © McGraw-Hill, Inc., 1978.)

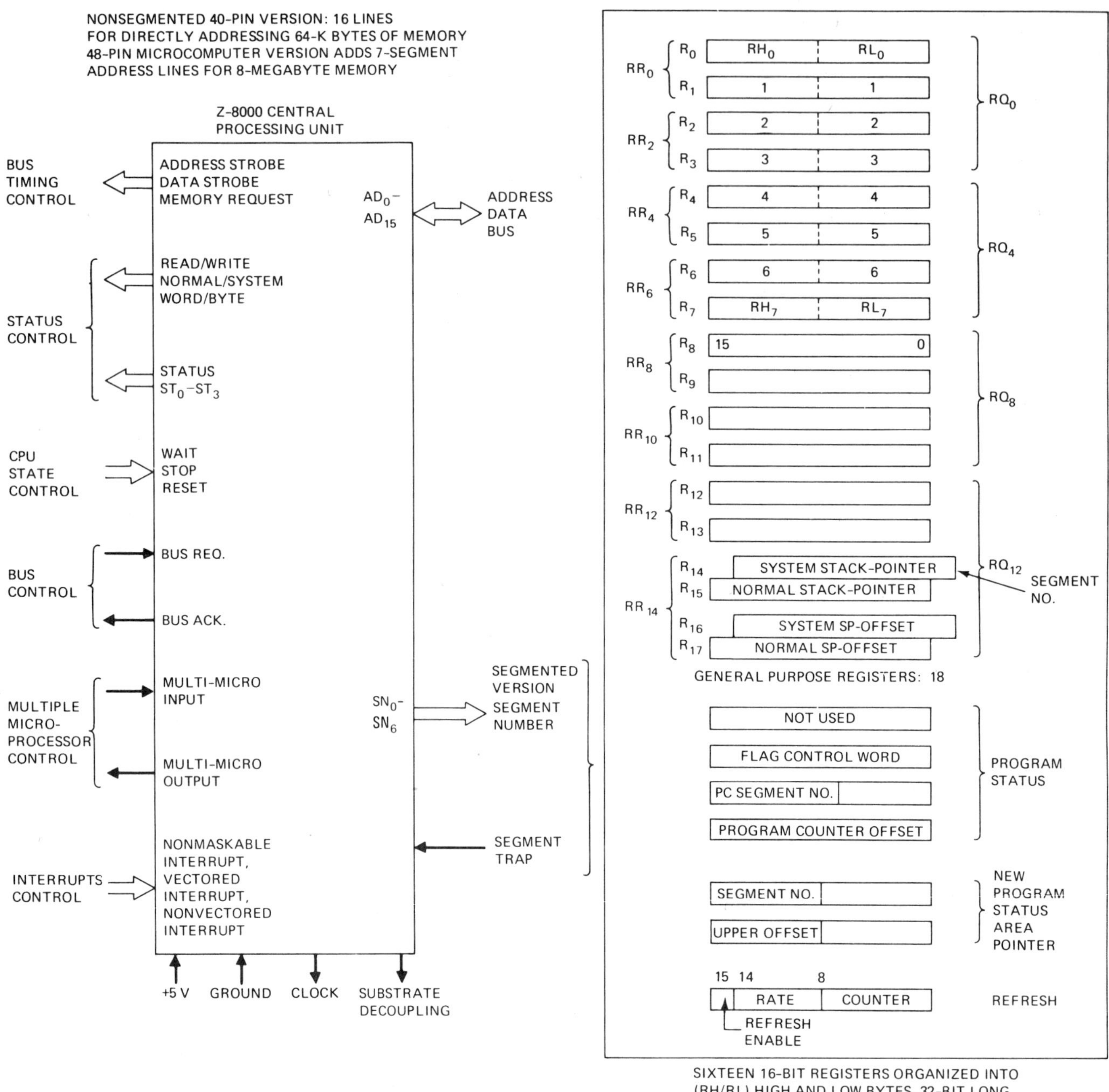

Fig. 7-26. Zilog-8000 Microprocessor: Nonsegmented version (40-pin); minicomputer-like 48-pin version, and register organization. (Reprinted from *Electronics*, December 21, 1978: Copyright © McGraw-Hill, Inc., 1978.)

23 lines to address memory-segmented random-access memory of 8 megabytes. Real-time operating system and application programming features are isolated for maximum throughput under system- and normal-operating modes as in modern larger computer systems. At least three clock-cycles are mandatory for one memory-cycle. That is, Z-8000 requires memory devices with a cycle-time of 750 nsec and an access-time of 430 nsec. The architecture of Z-8000 is illustrated in Fig. 7-25. The organization of the registers and the chip-interface signal requirements are shown in Fig. 7-26. The throughput of this micro-

processor is boosted by means of a look-ahead instruction decoder and accelerator on its internal bus. The systematic instruction-set allows an instruction to begin actuation as it enters the instruction register.

How an up-to-date intricate VLSI microprocessor is actually designed to specifications in the semiconductor industry can be obtained by the detailed example of the **Zilog-8000 microprocessor.** The following brief summary of the design methodology and procedure is a fine complement to the subject of VLSI in this context. (This Zilog VLSI development project was managed by Masatoshi Shima with C. N. Patel as the associate designer.)

The design is formulated on the basis of the governing concepts: (1) top-down modular design, (2) accurate product cost predictions, (3) product definition, (4) second-source availability for large-scale production of consumer products, (5) well-organized methods of intercommunication between the members of the design team, (6) experience of designing the original LSI chips such as Z-80, etc., in order to speed up the design effort according to the research and development schedules, and (7) interactive communication between the hardware, firmware, and software skills available for optimization of chip layout. At the outset, it must be noted that the design time of a VLSI logic chip does not necessarily follow a linear relationship to the number of several hundred thousand "scaled-down" NMOS silicon-gate transistors involved.

The objectives of the design were aimed at: (1) a large memory address with optional segmentation and memory management, (2) abundant resources, including sixteen 16-bit general-purpose registers, (3) software regularity with most-used instructions in various addressing modes and data lengths to extend to 32 bits so as to gain high execution-speed with minimum set of instructions, (4) compact instruction format to insure that frequently used instructions have fewest bits with minimum number of bits in op-code, and (5) maximum effective use of the memory bus up to 85% for high-speed execution of frequently

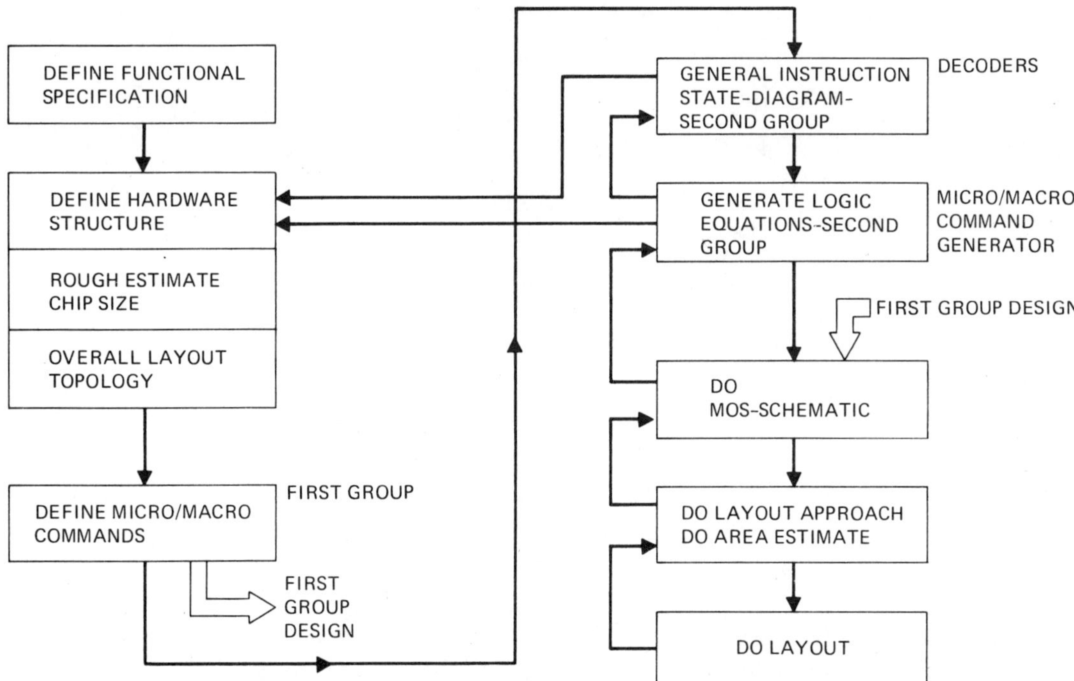

THE DESIGN PROCEDURE INDICATES THAT A CONSIDERABLE EXTENT OF HEURISTIC MEASURE-AND-OPTIMIZATION DEVELOPMENT IS INVOLVED IN LSI/VLSI DESIGNS, BESIDES SUBSEQUENT CAD (COMPUTER-AIDED-DESIGN) TESTING FOR ANALYSIS AND SYNTHESIS OF BASIC CIRCUITS.

Fig. 7-27. Top-down design methodology of Zilog-8000. © *IEEE Spectrum, July 1979.*

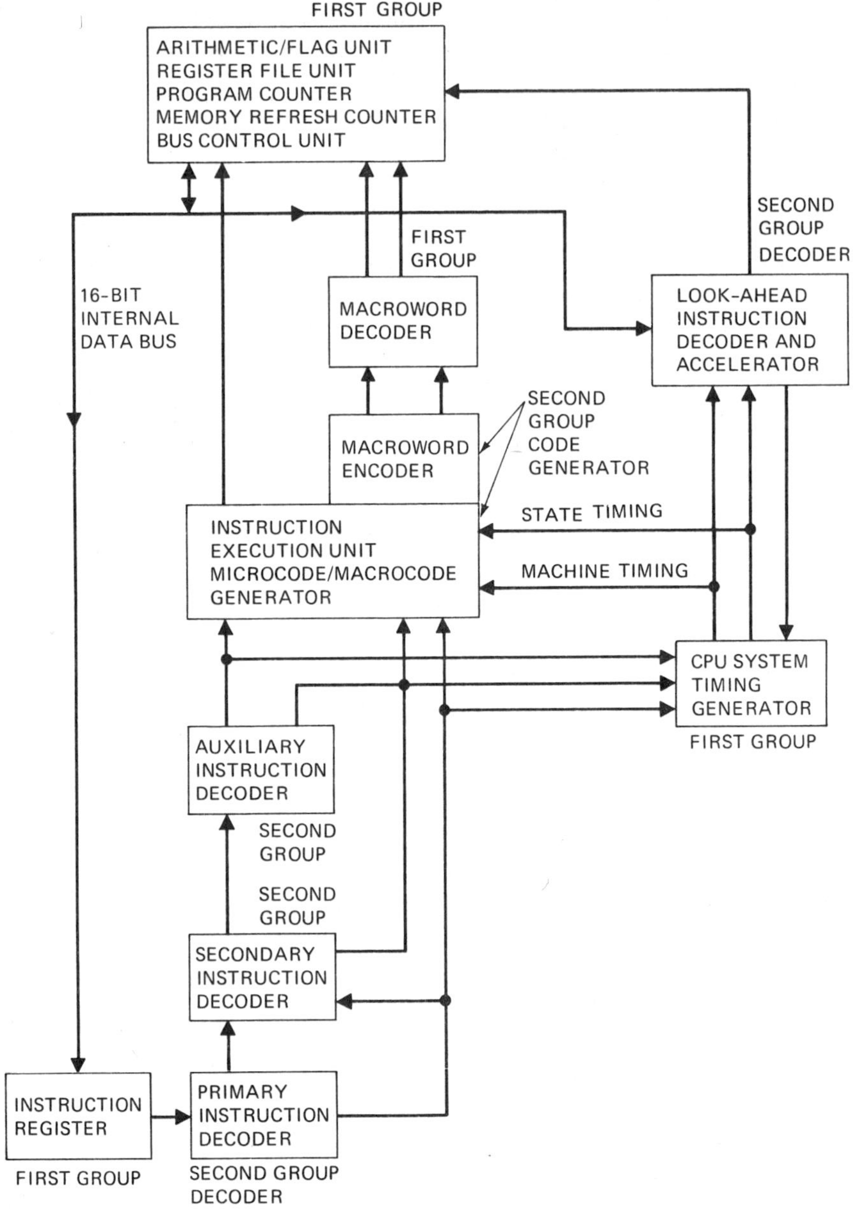

Fig. 7-28. Zilog-8000, the subsystem block-diagram. ©*IEEE Spectrum,* July 1979.

used instructions. The heuristic top-down design methodology of the microprocessor with repeated feedback check against design/layout errors is shown in Figure 7-27. The subsystem organization of the microprocessor was divided into two groups, one for execution and the other for instruction-implementation. The subsystem block diagram is shown in Figure 7-28.

Execution Group	*Instruction-implementation Group*
Arithmetic and flag section	Instruction register
Register file	Look-ahead instruction decoder
Program counter	Primary decoder
Dynamic RAM memory refresh counter	Secondary decoder

Execution Group (cont.)	*Instruction-implementation Group (cont.)*
External address data and control busses and their controllers	Auxiliary decoder
Interrupt-handling controllers	Instruction-execution unit
CPU mode-selection unit, for selecting segmented or non-segmented memory operation and system or normal modes	CPU timing generator

By using this directive, the first group design and layout will remain unchanged if the second group design is changed drastically from random logic to microprogram control.

The instruction implementation unit uses random logic with an extension of the minimal-node designs used for 8080 and Z-80 in order to minimize chip area and layout time. (The alternative extensive multilevel programmable logic arrays—PLAs—with ROM-like organization introduce large capacitive loading of the nodes to increase internal delay times.)

In a look-ahead decoder for DIRECT/INDEX addressing modes, for the micro/macro level ADD command, the three-input NAND-gate's state-timing and machine-timing circuitry for output of primary or secondary decoders, as an example of the data-manipulation time overlapping the fetch-time of the next instruction word, the timing waveforms and design layout are shown in Fig. 7-29. All together, 700 such NAND gates are used in the execution unit. The microcommand is generated when the clock goes low. One NAND input selects one of eight clock-cycles per machine cycle, the second input one of eight machine states per instruction, and the third input an output of the instruction decoder. Each state and machine timing signal is generated at the trailing edge of the clock pulse.

The major subsystems of the chip layout are enumerated as follows:

1. Flags and condition code
2. 16-bit ALU (arithmetic logic unit)
3. Register file
4. Program counter and refresh
5. Instruction execution section
6. Secondary instruction decoder
7. Primary instruction decoder
8. Instruction register
9. CPU system timing
10. Main bus control and CPU mode control
11. Auxiliary bus control

Converting instruction state diagrams to logic equations, and then interpreting these equations to the NMOS schematic was one of the most cumbersome aspects of design. The checking process was reversed to eliminate possible errors in design.

Computer-aided circuit simulation was used to determine delay times for a matrix of preassigned capacities at each important node. Approximately similar results were predicted by the designers by extrapolation of results. The logical operations are checked for throughput versus clock speed and temperature by means of production dies obtained from masks of layout, which were in turn prepared by computer digitization. Masatoshi Shima finally used a microprocessor-controlled die checkout system to determine the state of all registers, flags, and the address/data control bus at each machine cycle. As a

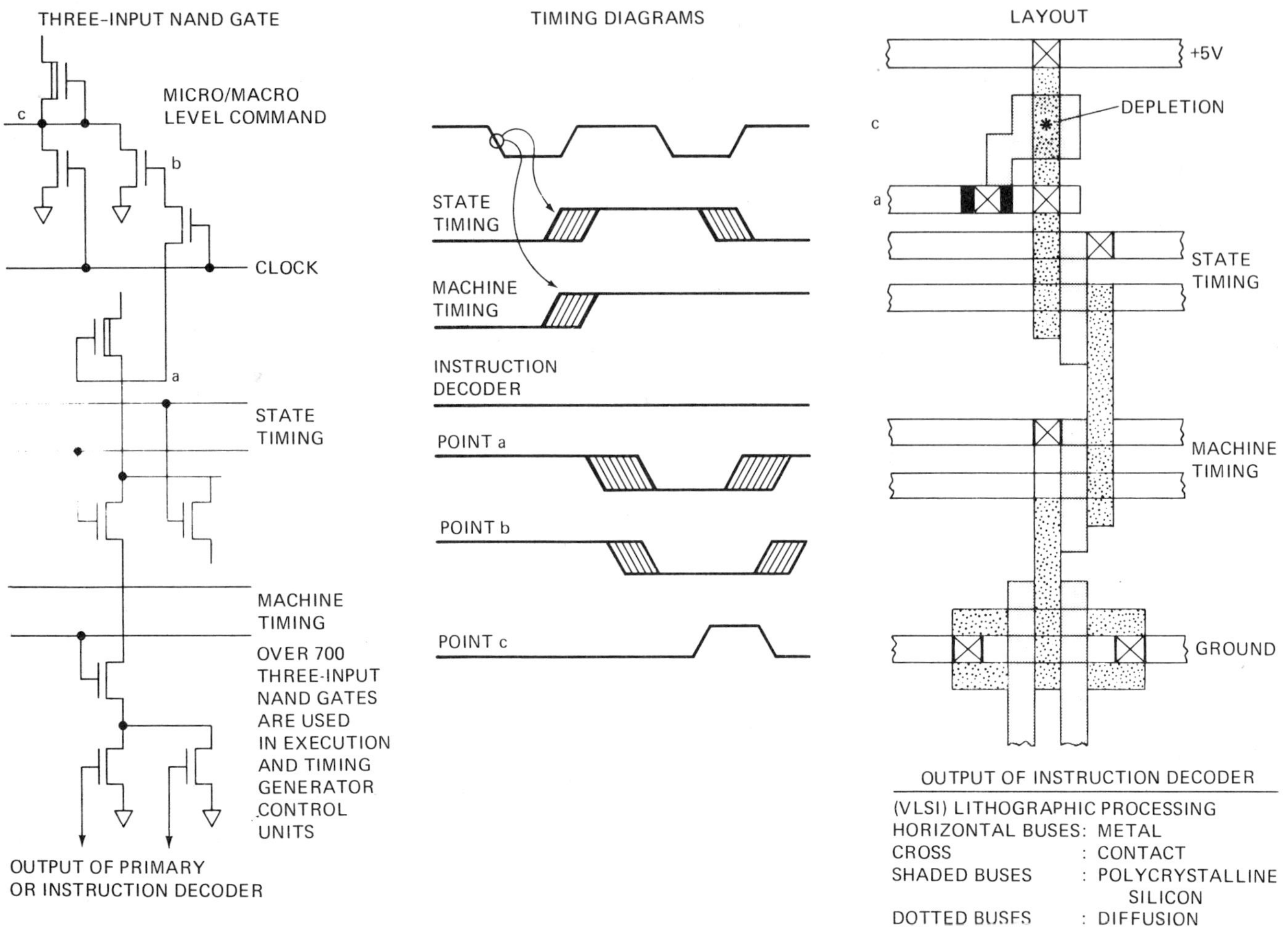

Fig. 7-29. *a*, overlap of data manipulation-time, and fetch-time of next instruction word; *b*, timing waveforms; *c*, design layout. ©*IEEE Spectrum,* July 1979.

debugging procedure, they could be modified and stored on a floppy disk and displayed on CRT or printed to obtain functional test patterns.

Z-8081, Z-8002, Z-8010

These three VLSI chips of the Z-8000 series are fabricated in the high-density, high-performance scaled-down NMOS, silicon-gate, depletion-load processing technique. The three powerful chips are housed in dual-in-line packages. Z-8001 is a 48-pin segmented CPU, and Z-8002 is a 40-pin nonsegmented CPU. The difference is addressing range: Z-8001 can directly address 8-M bytes of memory, Z-8002 can address only 64-K bytes of memory. The Z-8001 has a two-operating-mode facility to extend its memory to 48-M bytes, besides its normal mode of operation. The Z-8002 can extend its memory to 384-K bytes in a single mode only. (Z-8000 Microprocessor unit is a high-performance *microcomputer board* using 16-bit segmented Z-8001 microprocessor. *NOTE*: This is a modification of **Zilog's original definition of Z-8000 in 1979**).

The Z-8001 has a versatile 414 instruction-set that handles seven data types ranging from bits to word-strings. The functions included on the Z-8001 microcomputer board include real-time clock, parity-checking and generation, on-board 32-K bytes of protected dynamic RAM, and two serial I/O ports that can support all standard protocols. The addressing space of Z-8001 is divided into 128 relocatable segments up to 64-K bytes each. A 23-bit segmented address uses 7-segment address to point to the segment, and a 16-bit off-set to address any location relative to the start of the segment. Segmented Z-8001 can run any code written for nonsegmented Z-8002 in any one of its 128 segments, when it is set to the nonsegmented mode (of Z-8002).

Z-8010 is the *memory management unit*; it manages the large address space of Zilog microprocessor systems by facilitating features such as segment relocation and memory protection. However, Z-8001 can be used without the need of Z-8010 for both 8-M byte and 48-M byte address spaces.

ZCM-1: This is Zilog's floppy-disk controller for Z-8, Z-80, Z-8000, Z-8001, and Z-8002 systems. Four single- or double-sided, single- and double-density minifloppy disks can be driven by one controller. The controller includes an LSI controller chip to support programmable record lengths, 15 control commands, and built-in format function. Another controller chip ZCM-2 provides DMA transfer capability and parity generation besides.

ZRTS: Board-level real-time software offers a versatile base, around which the operating system of a specific application can be built. It consists of a small real-time, multi-tasking kernel, tool-kit of operating system, including primitives, real-time priority-scheduling of tasks, inter-task communication, real-time clock control, and interrupt handling. As an option, file management primitives and memory management units are supported. The kernel and primitives are ROMable, and hence ZRTS software is best for ROM-based applications.

Z-bus backplane interconnects ZCM-1 single-board (1 X 96-pin, 6.3 X 3.9 in.) and ZCM-2 double-boards (2 X 96-pin, 6.3 X 92. in.). The former is designed for Z-8 systems, and the latter is designed for Z-80 and Z-8000 series microcomputer systems.

7-31. Intel VLSI 16-bit 8086 Microcomputer (Gordon Moore). The processing capability of the Intel 16-bit 8086 microcomputer, with its clock-rate of 5 MHz or alternatively 8 MHz, enables execution speeds about 10 times faster than those of 8080A-based computation, using roughly 10% to 25% of shorter programming effort. Its architecture aims at bridging the gap between 8- and 16-bit microcomputers, because the 8-bit 8080 software package and program development scheme could be easily adapted.

The advantages include signed 8- and 16-bit arithmetic, multiply and divide, interruptible bit-string operations, and improved bit manipulation. Minicomputer features such as reentrant code, position-independent code, dynamically relocatable programs, direct-address capability up to 1 megabyte of RAM or disk/bubble-memory, and flexibility for multiple-processor operation are available.

The VLSI high-performance NMOS, using 29,000-transistor, scaled-down, depletion-load, silicon-gate fabrication (H-MOS), enables propagation delays of 2 nsec per gate. Memory with cycle-times of 500 to 800 nsec is suitable, and access-time of data is from 300 to 460 nsec. Powerful 8- or 16-bit register structure, unlimited levels of interrupts, efficient input/output interface, and a new segment register-file contribute to a high computational throughput.

For control and timing, a bus-interface unit (BIU) maintains an optimized 6-byte fetch-ahead instruction queue for overlapping the execution and fetching of instructions. The instruction set supports stack management in block-structured high-level language of PL/M-86, which is an extension of the former PL/M language developed for 8080/8085 microprocessors.

The register-structure, the BIU, and execution unit (EU) of 8086 are illustrated in Fig. 7-30a and b. In the minimum-mode system (Fig. 7-30c), the access-times required of

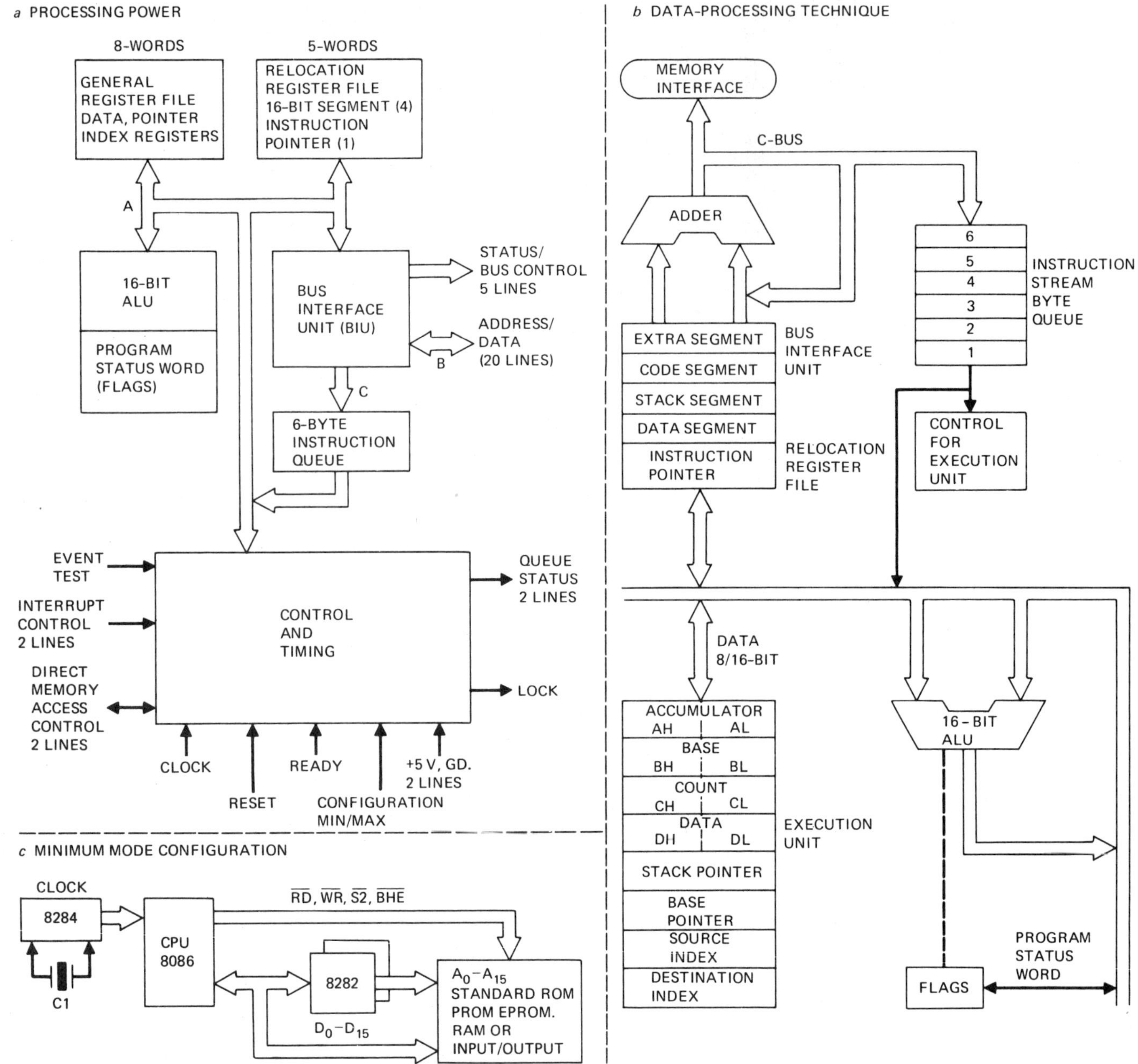

Fig. 7-30. *a*, INTEL 8086 CPU processing power. *b*, Processing data. *c*, Minimum mode microcomputer configuration needs 11 components to form a complete system. Large systems feasible with more components. (Reprinted from *Electronics*, February 16, 1978. Copyright © McGraw-Hill, Inc., 1978.)

memory and I/O devices for the high-speed 8-MHz CPU operation are 265 nsec from receipt of address and 130 ns from receipt of read- or write-enable, respectively.

Intel 8087, Numeric Data Processor (NDP). Intel iAPX 86, 88 product line provides: (1) distributed multitasking system functions with specialized VLSI components, (2) multiprocessing capabilities, and (3) hierarchical bus organization capable of complex data flows of high-performance systems or simpler stand-alone microcomputer systems.

Intel 8087, 80-bit numeric data processor (NDP), in conjunction with Intel 8089, Input/Output processor (IOP), makes the Intel 8086, 16-bit third-generation microprocessor (or its alternative chip 8088), using a segment-oriented register file architecture, approximately as powerful as modern high-speed minicomputers such as DEC VAX-11/780. These minicomputeis provide powerful features of the category of floating point accelerators (FPA), high-speed associative RAM memory stacks, and writable diagnostic control storage (WDCS), and virtual mass memory and bus adaptors/ channel multiplexers etc.; the microcomputers presently furnish similar features with the added advantage of compatibility with up-to-date structured programming of high-level languages.

In turn, the Intel 8087 Math-Extension chip is architecturally divided into two processing elements: (1) control unit (CU) for decoding and READ/WRITE memory operand instructions in synchronism with the CPU, 8086, and (2) numeric executive unit (NEU) that uses a data path 84 bits wide (68 fraction bits, 15 exponent bits, and a sign bit). The NDP extends the overall instruction set to trigonometric, logarithmic, exponential, and arithmetical instructions for all data types. Special instructions that complement the 8086 instruction set belong to the classifications of data transfer, arithmetic comparison, transcendental tangent and arc tangent, constants $\log_{10}$ and $\log_e$, and NDP coprocessor control. Data types furnished are word integer (16 bits), short integer (32 bits), long integer (64 bits), packed decimal (80 bits), short REAL single-precision (32 bits), long REAL (64 bits), and temporary REAL (80 bits).

A floating-point accelerator like that of the powerful high-speed minicomputers is available to minimize timings of double precision floating-point arithmetic. As a 40-pin ceramic package (to meet Defense specification requirements), it is capable of meeting the proposed IEEE-standard for double-precision.

To the programmer, the 8086/8087 combination appears like a powerful single mainframe CPU, operating at 5 or 8 MHz clock (with cycle-times of 200 nsec and under). The processor effectively operates on 8-, 16-, 32-, 64-, and 8-bit character and string data, with the internal data paths at least 16 bits wide. Up to 1-M byte of high-speed solid-state RAM memory (or electronically erasable programmable read-only memory, EEPROM) can be addressed along with a separate 64-K byte I/O buffer memory space. The address/ data and status interfaces of the processors are compatible since the address and data buses are time-multiplexed at the processor to allow compatibility with common bipolar bus support components.

The advanced architectural features of 8087 lower software development costs; the interprocessor coordination is automatic. Internal operand paths are used for 64-bit transfer at high-speed. While 80-bit registers operate as a stack, the instructions operate on the top one or two stack elements. A status field (ST) identifies the correct top-of-stack register. The 8087 register file grows down toward lower addressed registers. The 8087 takes advantage of the addressing modes of the CPU, 8086 to relocate code and data during execution, and 8087 can access data in any location of the 1-M byte of the main memory.

The 8087 enables convenient programming of numerical arrays, structure-based variables, and routines in high-level languages. LOAD and STORE instructions convert operands and REAL numbers in temporary registers. The 32-bit and 64-bit REAL numbers are multiplied in 19 μs and 27 μs, respectively. More constants and REAL numbers are held in registers during computation, reducing access time and increasing throughput at high-speed execution. Fetching and decoding of instruction bit streams are accomplished in parallel.

In numerical control applications, the NDP can move and position machine-tool heads with extreme accuracy. In X- and Y-axis control application positioning, the hardware trigonometric support is effective. In data acquisition systems, the scan-and-scale feature reduces large quantities of data as they are collected and analyzed.

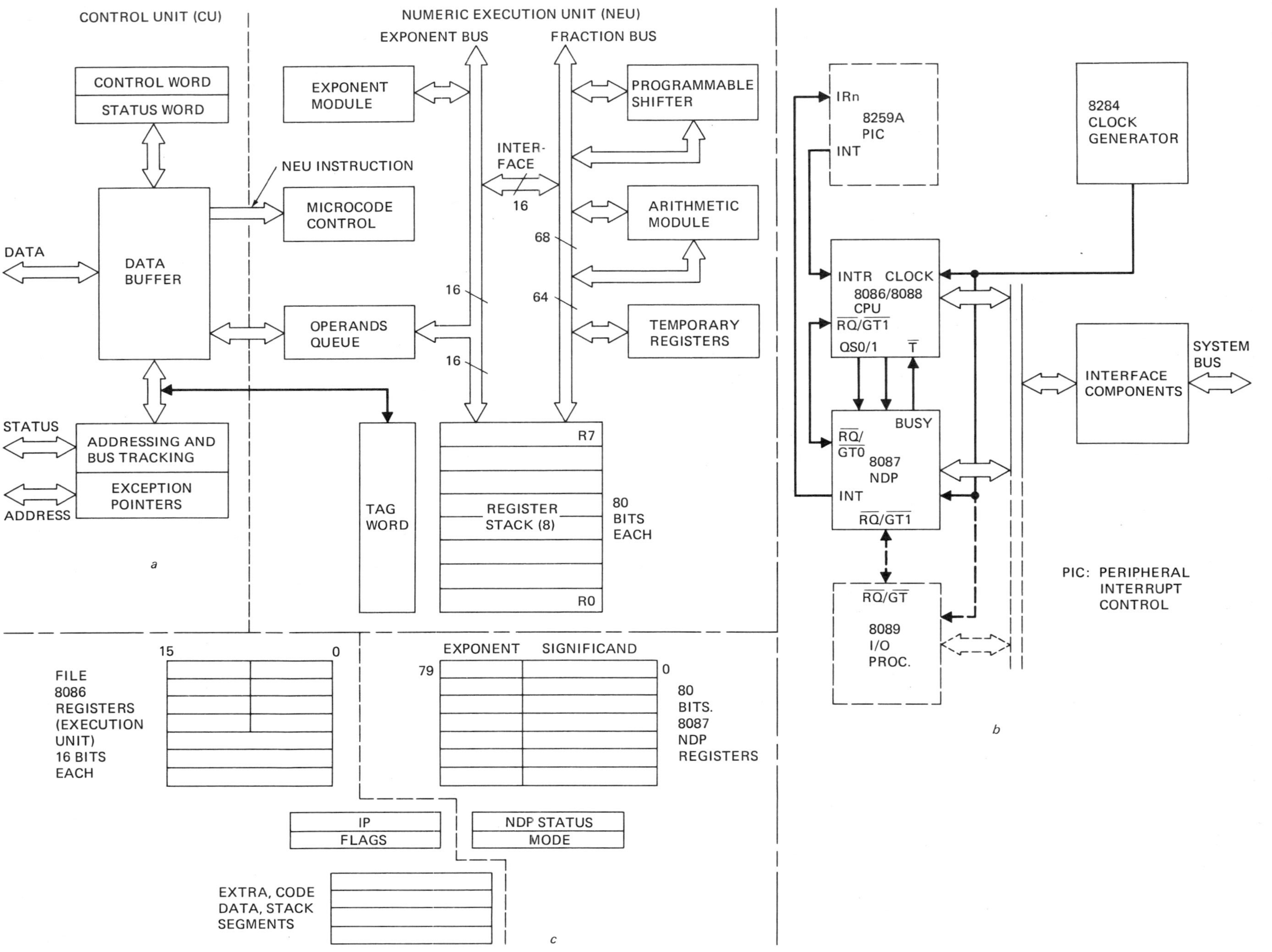

a, Architecture, 8087 numeric data processor; *b*, 8086/8087 system integration; *c*, 8086/8087 register formats. (*Courtesy of Intel Corporation*)

8086/8087: Execution Time for Selected Instructions (Less at 8-MHz Clock)

Floating Point Instructions	Clock—5 MHz
Add/subtract magnitude	14/18 μs
Multiply (single-precision) 32-bit	19 μs
Multiply (double-precision) 64-bit	27
Divide	39
Compare	9
Load (double-precision)	10
Store (double-precision)	21
Square-root	36
Tangent	90
Exponentiation	100

The INTEL 8089 I/O processor, along with system and local buses, gives the capability of parallel distributed processing in multitask environments by allowing independent direct memory access (DMA) transfers.

The architecture and system integration of the onboard 8086/8087 are shown in the accompanying diagram (see *a* and *b*); the combined register stacks for the overall 8086/8087 high-throughput microcomputer system are shown in *c*.

7-32. INTEL-2920, REAL-TIME VLSI MICROCOMPUTER FOR LINEAR SIGNAL PROCESSING IN CONTROL SYSTEMS

A programmable general-purpose microcomputer, Intel-2920, with built-in EPROM program control, 40-word RAM working memory, control and arithmetic logic units, and A/D and D/A converters, is a timely arrival for popularizing the direct application of VLSI microcomputers in automatic control and data communications.

It can be programmed with 192 instructions in 24-bit words. The RAM working memory uses 25-bit words. The digital section enables parallel instructions to boost throughput and interface with the analog section by way of a data-register, which actually takes the role of a memory location.

With the availability of this VLSI chip, complex programmable devices such as modems, equalizers, tone generators and receivers, process controllers and motor or servo-motor drives can be readily designed without a large number of passive components and linear-amp integrated circuits.

The system organization of this NMOS VLSI microcomputer is shown in Fig. 7-31. The technique of architecture in this chip maintains total program control, and execution time remains constant. The program execution time is determined by the fixed sampling-rate that is mandatory with this digital-control chip. The high-speed, number-crunching, pipelined architecture of the CPU using a much simpler algorithm (in place of the usual shift-and-add multiplier) facilitates, in particular, the needed high-capacity computation between real-time sampling in processor control applications. External LSI digital filters and additional 2920 microcomputer chips can be provided for more complex digital control systems. The simulation of the microcomputer chip as a digital filter is interpreted in Fig. 7-31.

From the hardware point of view, the design of fairly complex digital control systems, requiring dynamic memory relocation, memory protection, and multitasking programmability, is economically feasible at the present stage. A new breed of combined hardware and software professionals are needed in order to minimize the current high cost of software. Companion VLSI chips are available for "memory management;" they enable

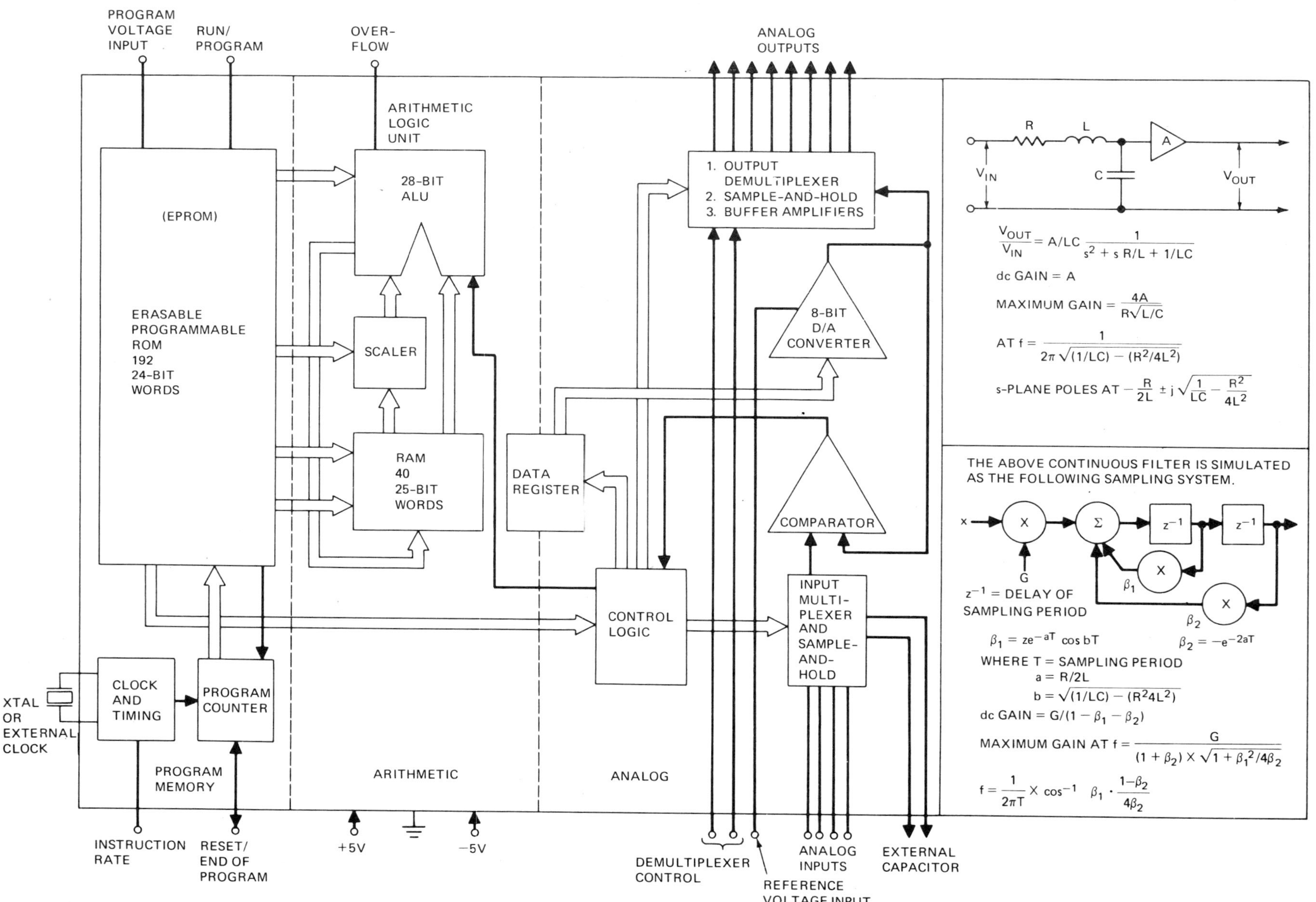

Fig. 7-31. Intel-2920. NMOS microcomputer for real-time signal processing in control systems. (Reprinted from *Electronics*, March 1, 1979: Copyright © McGraw-Hill, Inc., 1979.)

VLSI 16/32-bit microcomputers of the category of Intel 8086, Zilog 8000, Motorola 68000, etc., to make full use of 8-megabit external addressing capability for such complex digital control systems. High-capacity 64-kilobit and 131.072-kilobit (28-pin) ROMs, having an initial access-time under 450 nsec are presently available to speed up most processors. External real-time high-capacity working memory is also readily available with 5-V dynamic 64-kbit RAMs, which use a single pin to control self-refreshing for both active and idle states. All this economy hardware naturally facilitates the scope of long-term development of software for plant digital automation in the near future.

Power tools, toys, food-processing appliances, floppy-disk drives, radio-controlled automobiles, etc., use millions of new universal motors. Single-chip digital microcomputer chips costing $2.00 can replace bulky analog feedback control circuitry hitherto used for speed-control. The mirocomputer, besides adjusting speed, checks motor current against a list of maximum current values, stored in a high-capacity ROM lookup table right on the chip, to limit instantaneous long-duration surge and peak currents. This makes it feasible to use a smaller economy motor for most applications.

7-33. INTEL-8089 I/O PROCESSOR AND MCS^R-86 SYSTEM

Intel 8089 HMOS 40-pin I/O processor serves as an intelligent I/O subsystem. This is the conventional technique in mainframe and minicomputer systems for significantly improving system throughput. A typical low-cost VLSI single-bus microcomputer system, as shown in Figure 7-32, whether it is using an 8-bit or 16-bit microprocessor, has the following inherent disadvantage as compared to high throughput mainframe and minicomputer systems. The CPU (microprocessor) itself is responsible for system and application program execution as well as I/O task execution; since the I/O peripherals reside on the same system bus, the CPU is restricted to the use of the bus for system and application program execution at its full capability, resulting in limited throughput. As an alternative, Figure 7-32 illustrates a system with two independent CPU microprocessors, the CPU and a separate I/O processor, that execute their respective tasks over two independent buses. Intel 8089 I/O processor, as a parallel to mainframe I/O subsystem processors, supports such a configuration in "remote mode" and enhances total system performance as presently accomplished in high-speed minicomputer systems.

The architecture of 8089 I/O processor is dedicated to control all I/O operations to enhance I/O throughput. The 8089 relieves the main processor 8086 in the MCS-86 system, shown in Figure 7-32c, from the additional burdensome tasks of I/O operations. Main processing and data manipulation tasks are performed by operating in parallel with the CPU of 8089; and the exclusive I/O tasks are executed at a high throughput rate over its separate remote I/O bus, as clearly shown in Figure 7-32b and c. This dual-bus technique naturally achieves a significant improvement in system efficiency and throughput. When system memory references operations are desired, the main system bus alone is effective. But arbitration in this configuration is performed by a bus arbiter chip 8289 and a bus controller 8288, which interface the use of the system MULTIBUS™ between the two CPUs. The I/O remote bus is used for all I/O transfers. Two 8089s may share the same local I/O bus with arbiter and bus controller.

The internal architectural details of 8089 I/O processor are separately illustrated in Figure 7-33a. All internal resources of 8089, except registers, channel controller (multiplexer) logic, and flip-flops controlling the state of the channel are shared. Figure 7-33b explains the communications routes internal to the 8089 I/O processor between the CPU and I/O processing. The 8089 I/O processor consists of two separate I/O channels alternating with an internal cycle of 4–8 clock pulses, a CPU, bus interface unit, an assembly/

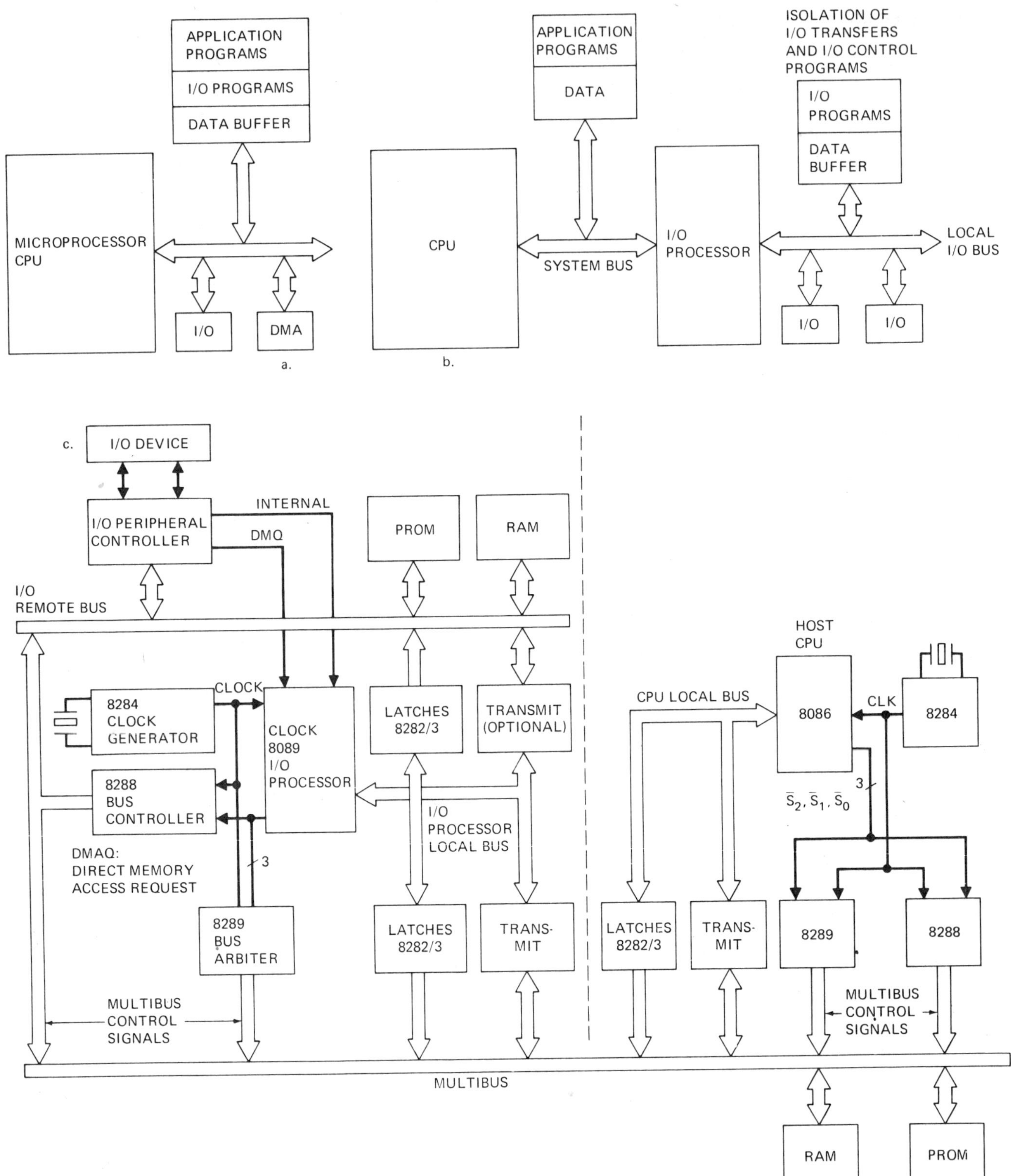

Fig. 7-32. Intel VLSI single/dual bus MCS[R]-86 Microcomputer System. (*Courtesy of Intel Corp.*)

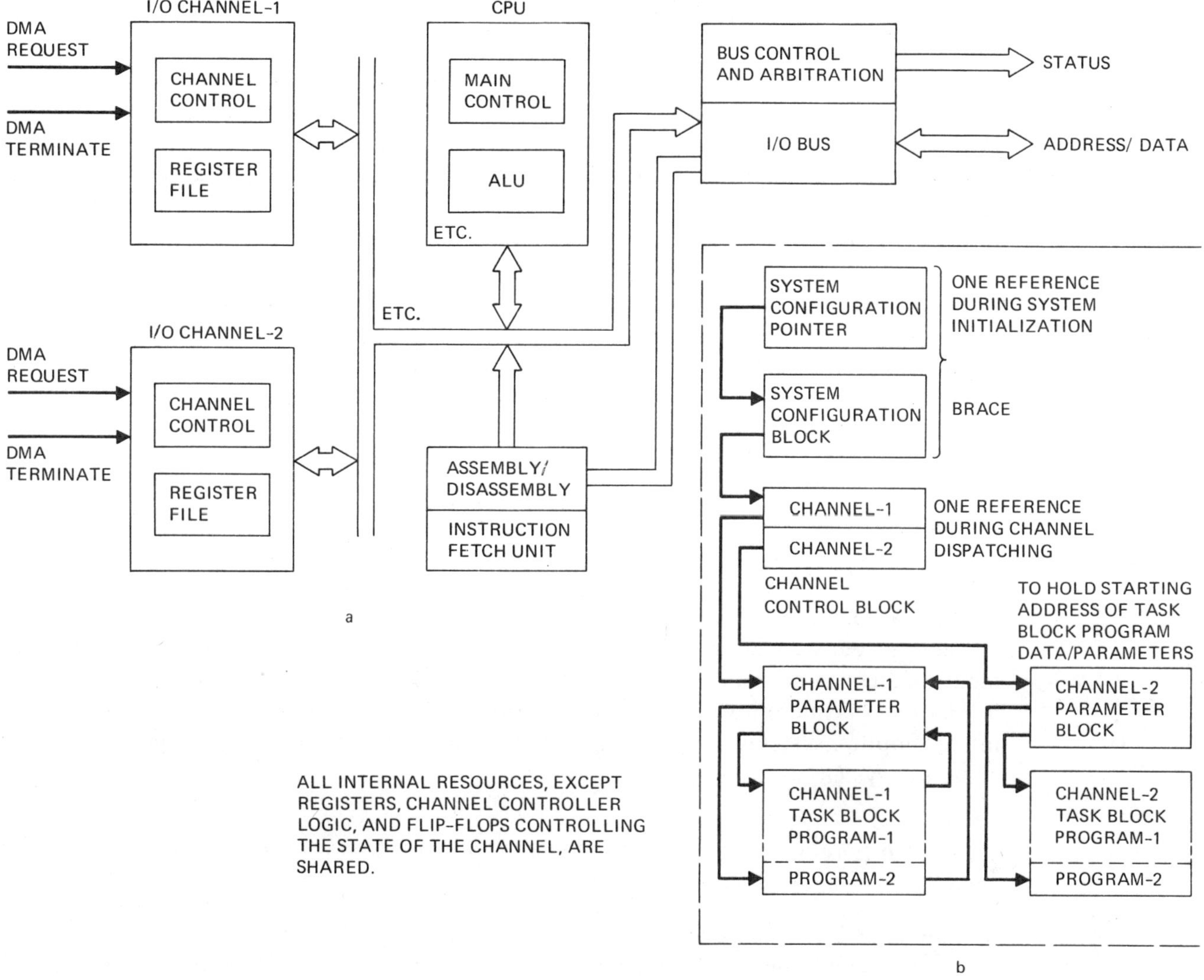

Fig. 7-33. *a*, Intel-8089 I/O processor, Architecture. *b*, Communication routes between the CPU and I/O processing–8089. (*Courtesy of Intel Corp.*)

disassembly register file, and an instruction FETCH unit. Each channel maintains its own register set, control and status words, and a flexible channel controller. Both channels may operate concurrently, executing channel programs or performing high-speed DMA transfers by time multiplexing the fast access and the use of the external bus intake. The I/O processor maintains an optimized special I/O-intensive instruction set. As to the communications routing, the system configuration pointer and system configuration block are referenced once, upon system initialization (reset). The channel control block is referenced during channel selection. The channel parameter block holds the starting address of the task block, as well as data and parameters.

Communications between 8089 I/O processor and the main microprocessor 8086 CPU occur in a flexible hierarchical way only when necessary, enhancing the overall system performance like that of a main-frame computer. Under the control of task programs in two channels, the I/O processor can expedite DMA transfers at up to 1.25-M byte/sec at a standard clock of 5 MHz.

An example of this trend in microcomputer technology is the Zilog-8 single-chip microcomputer, which excels in I/O and memory-intensive applications.

7-34. 3-CHIP 32-BIT MICROPROCESSOR (INTEL), 1980

Intel has announced the design of a 32-bit, software-intensive microcomputer system, using a VLSI, 3-chip microprocessor, main-frame CPU. The iAPX 432 *Data processor*, iAPX 432 *storage chip*, and iAPX 432 *interface processor* make the CPU. It is organized toward a **high-level language operating system using the new architecture**. The performance is aimed at that of minicomputers such as IBM System/38. The hardware architecture relieves programmers of considerable effort since it automatically takes off operations embodying differing data structures. Each chip, consisting of as many as 120,000 transistors (approximately twice the density of Motorola 68000), is housed in a 64-pin quad in-line package, with geometrics approaching 0.5-micron processing levels. Two high-level language instruction sets are oriented to PASCAL and PASCAL-based Ada high-level language of the Defense and other administrations. This feature provides a framework for an unrestricted software engineering methodology, according to Intel.

A high-speed 16-bit iAPX-86 based series-III microcomputer is available to support PASCAL-86 and FORTRAN-86 in a similar fashion. A network system is simultaneously planned for development of a *disk and file-sharing system* (D/FSS), so that up to 8 terminal computers will have access to a large mass-storage facility at the central node, such as an iAPX-432 based host computer. Another iAPX-286 system (to be announced shortly) will have a performance capability of up to 5 times that of the iAPX-86 system.

These systems are expected to support 10 to 200 tasks in a multiprogramming environment, addressing a 16-megabyte physical memory or a 1-Gigabit virtual-memory on disk by means of microprocessor-based memory-management and protection logic. The microcomputer systems have commenced to compete directly with former powerful minicomputer systems.

Intel Corporation's LSI/VSLI Products, 1980/81. Prefixes used in Intel's microcomputer series using VLSI configurations follow:

- iAPX 86/10 denotes 16-bit 8086-based microcomputer systems
- iAPX 86/11 denotes a system using 8086 as CPU, and 8089 (I/O processor, IOP)
- iAPX 88/11 denotes highly integrated high-performance systems using the popular 8-bit 8085-series of components such as 8155 RAM and I/O Timer, 8755A EPROM and I/O, and 8155 (8-K bit) RAM with the 8/16-bit 8088 as the CPU. The 8/16-bit 8088 can replace 8086 as a CPU.
- iAPX 88/20 denotes a system using 8086 *or* 8088 as CPU and 8087 as Math extension.
- iAPX 88/21 denotes a system using 8086 *or* 8088 as CPU, and 8087 as Math extension, and 8089 as IOP.
- iAPX-432 denotes a system using an Intel 3-chip 32-bit CPU.
- iAPX-286 denotes a 3-chip 16-bit processor (see 7-34) featuring a pipelined architecture and virtual-memory management and memory protection right on the 16-bit processor chip. The *Address chip* consists of an adder and a high-speed cache memory with facilities of base address and protection fields. The *Execution chip* consists of an ALU, control ROM, registers, and multiply/divide hardware. The third *Instruction-Decode* unit and a data-channel bus to 8087 Math unit, and external bubble or floppy-disk memory make the overall system, such as a powerful minicomputer-like microcomputer.

Prefixes used for Intel Microcomputer **System-80 product line are**:

- iAPX: processing series
- iRMX: operating system

- iSBC: single-board computers
- iSBX: multi-module boards
- iAPX-86 etc. identify various series of Intel processor families. (Examples are cited under LSI/VLSI Products, 1980/81.)

Intel 8087, 80-Bit Numeric Data Processor. This 40-pin Math-chip is an NMOS, depletion-load, silicon-gate high-performance (HMOS) VLSI integrated circuit for powerful computational applications with minimal software requirements, as far as the mathematical computations go. The architecture of the chip is based on the following built-in hardware:

1. Eight individually addressable numeric 80-bit register stacks and a tag-word for their individual access from a control data-buffer.
2. The control unit consists of 6 addressing and bus-tracking status registers and addressing of exception pointers. The data buffer has the provision of control and status words, and queueing of operands.
3. The numeric execution unit has the provision of (1) a 16-bit interface between a numeric execution-instruction based microcode control unit and an exponent module with an exponent bus, and (2) a fraction bus with a programmable shifter, a 68-bit oriented arithmetic module and 64-bit oriented temporary registers. (See 7-31 for its use).

This sophisticated architecture enables the following facilities:

- full high-performance internal 80-bit Math capability
- implementation of proposed IEEE floating-point standard
- total numeric support for Intel's iAPX-86/20 and iAPX-88/20 microcomputer systems
- capability for expanding the data types of the iAPX-86/10 system to 32- and 64-bit integers, 32-, 64-, and 80-bit floating-point, and 18-digit BCD operands
- availability of the addressing modes of all iAPX-86/10 and iAPX-88/10 microcomputer systems
- extension of the instruction sets of the above systems to data types involving trigonometric, logarithmic, exponential, and arithmetical instructions
- built-in handling functions for exceptions

Architectural Features of iAPX-86 and iAPX-88 Product Lines

1. Distribution of system functions among specialized VLSI components.
2. Multiprocessing hardware capabilities are inherent.
3. Hierarchical bus organization enables complex data flows required by high-performance systems, while allowing simpler systems without superfluous facilities.
4. Availability of 5-MNz clock (for 200-nsec cycle-time) and 8-MHz clock rate as well for higher speed.
5. Provision of both 8-bit and 16-bit data paths.
6. Processors can operate on 8-, 16-, 32-, 64-, and 80-bit character and string data types. (Internal data is at least 16-bit oriented.)
7. Up to 1-M byte of external memory can be addressed along a separate 64-K byte I/O memory space.
8. Address/data and status interfaces of processors are compatible with time-multiplexing of address and data buses.
9. Multiple processor systems are feasible for medium-to-large-scale systems with several advantages over a centralized approach that uses a single CPU and high-speed memory. Special tasks are assigned to individual processors (as a distributed processing system) for increased flexibility and parallel/distributed processing of the overall system.

10. Increased reliability of the overall cost-effective flexible and powerful microcomputer system for a large spectrum of applications.

The Intel 8086-family of system configuration devices are quoted below. The bus structure of the **Intel MCS-86 system** for the 40-pin 16-bit 8086 VLSI microprocessor is compatible with the former **MCS-80** (of 8080A) and **MCS-85** (of 8085A) peripherals.

1. 8284, 18-pin clock generator and driver
2. 8282/8283, 20-pin 8-bit I/O ports (8-line latch and inverting 8-line latch)
3. 8286/8287, 20-pin 8-bit parallel bidirectional bus drivers (or 8-line three-state transceiver and inverting 8-line three-state transceiver)
4. 8288, 20-pin bus controller for bipolar drive capability and three-state command output drivers
5. 8259A, 28-pin programmable interrupt controller with 8-level priority controller
6. 8041/8741, 40-pin universal peripheral interface
7. 8212, 24-pin 8-bit I/O port (for fully parallel 8-bit data register and buffer)
8. 8253/8253-5, 24-pin programmable interval timer for 3 independent 16-bit counters (binary or BCD)
9. 8257/8257-5, 40-pin programmable DMA controller for 4 channel DMA
10. 8273, 40-pin programmable HDLC/SDLC protocol controller for full/half duplex or loop SDLC operation, and programmable NRZI encode/decode with digital phase-lock loop clock recovery, up to 64-K baud transfers
11. 8278, 40-pin programmable keyboard interface for simultaneous keyboard and display operations, 16- or 18-character 7-segment display interface, right or left entry display RAM, 8-character keyboard FIFO (first-in first-out stack) and 128-key scanning logic at 6-MHz clock
12. 8291, 40-pin GPIB talker/listener for complete source and acceptor handshake to IEEE standard-488 (General-Purpose) Interface-Bus
13. 8275, 40-pin programmer CRT controller with 11-character graphic capability, light-pen detection and registers, dual-row buffers, programmable DMA burst mode, and programmable screen and character format
14. 8294, 40-pin microprocessor-controlled data encryption unit for 80-byte/sec data conversion rate, 64-bit data encryption using 56-bit key, DMA interface, encrypt/decrypt modes, and certified by National Bureau of Standards
15. 8295, 40-pin dot-matrix printer controller for dot-matrix impact printers, with on-chip 40-character buffer, DMA transfer and serial/parallel communication
16. 8292, 40-pin microprocessor-controlled general-purpose interface-bus controller for complete IEEE standard-488 controller function
17. 8279, 40-pin programmable keyboard/display interface for simultaneous keyboard display operations, dual 8- or 16-numerical display, 16-byte display RAM, 8-character keyboard FIFO and programmable scan timing
18. 8271, 40-pin programmable floppy-disk controller: IBM-3740 soft sectored format-compatible; programmable record length, automatic Read/Write headpositioning and verification; dual/drive (expandable to 4 drives); multi-sector capability; programmable step-rate, settle-time, head-load time, head-unload index count; and internal CRC (cyclic redundancy check) generation and checking (single +5V supply)
19. 8255A, 40-pin programmable peripheral interface with 24 programmable I/O circuits used in 3 major modes of operation
20. 8251A, 20-pin programmable communication interface for synchronous/asynchronous operation; baud rate DC to 64-K; error-detection—parity overrun and framing; and full-duplex, double-buffered, transmitter/receiver

21. 8205, 16-pin high-speed Schottky bipolar 1-out-of-8 binary decoder with 18-nsec maximum delay

Intel, 8051 Single-Chip Microcomputer (1980). As a further development on the former 8048 single-chip microcomputer, 8051 provides a functional/speed improvement up to ten times with access to additional program and data memory. External peripheral capabilities such as 32 programmable I/O lines, a full-duplex UART facility, two 16-bit timer/event counters, and a unique built-in Boolean (logic) processor make high-performance 8051 very attractive in stand-alone sophisticated single-chip microcomputer applications. Multiply-and-divide executes in 4 μsec, and most instructions require 1 or 2 μsec.

In many applications, 4-K bytes of ROM/EPROM, 128 bytes of RAM for internal scratchpad, and 20 registers for controlling peripheral functions provide ample facilities. The external memory space is expandable to 64-K bytes of RAM and 64-K bytes of ROM.

Extended built-in CPU processing capabilities are available by the provision of multiple addressing modes, four 8-register banks, and duplex serial I/O port for terminals and UARTs at baud rates from 122,000 to 31,250/sec. The port can link multiple 8051s to enable transmission rates up to 187.5-K baud, using standard asynchronous protocols, and an address-driven automatic initiation.

The advanced interrupt system provides for five sources, two priority levels, and a nested structure that allows efficient monitoring of internal/external alarms. The Boolean bit manipulation allows for 8-bit binary/BCD arithmetic and 8-bit logic operations in especially microcontroller applications in the industry. As an integral part of the CPU, the Boolean processor uses 12 exclusive instructions, independent accumulator, bit-addressable RAM and I/O to enable bit manipulation with minimal data movement, byte masking/shifting, or test-and-branch tree procedures.

Intel provides software support with an ASM-51 macroassembler and a CONV-51 conversion program to upgrade prior 8048 source code to operate on 8051. An Intel ICE-51 In-circuit Emulator allows the testing of a new system with all its I/O functions at full processor speed. This specific provision enables debugging of a system before committing code to EPROMs or ROM. The type 8051 chip has the corresponding 8751 EPROM version in the place of the final ROM for prototyping and initial production. External program memory can be provided by type 8031 off-chip program memory.

Intel 8741A Peripheral Controller. It is a well-supported, flexible, and intelligent universal peripheral interface (UPI) controller with built-in EPROM memory, for minimum design and debug time of keyboard control and complex process tasks. Macrocommands are executed from the host computer by using on-chip program memory and operating in parallel with the host. The controller is comprised of an 8-bit CPU (microprocessor), 1-K byte program memory, 64-byte data memory, clock, timer/counter, and I/O ports. After the user's program is developed, 8741A can be switched over to Intel's pin-compatible ROM version of the controller, viz., 8041A for volume production applications.

The majority of 8741A's instructions are control-oriented for a wide range of I/O tasks. With Intel's ICE-41A in-circuit emulator, Multi-ICE software packages, and Intellec development system, debugging becomes simple in complex multiprocessor designs. ICE-41A allows easy modification of registers, memory locations, and I/O ports.

7-35. MOTOROLA MC-68000 VLSI MICROPROCESSOR

Former LSI microprocessor and microcomputer chips using less than 10,000 gates (or transistors/chip) are strictly limited in number of registers and data-path width. Hence, the power of the instruction-set; this resulted in higher assembler software costs by increasing the number of program instructions. The obvious VLSI solutions are: (1) higher density with improved processing techniques such as high-density HMOS in the place of the former NMOS, and (2) direct support of high-level languages such as PASCAL and structured PL-series of languages via the interpretive channel of high-density ROM solid-state memories. Computer design aided HMOS architecture results in twice the circuit-densities and four-times the speed-power product in order to approach the performance standards of most minicomputers. The 32-bit architecture of the new Motorola-68000 microprocessor is implemented on the above basis to enable a versatile addressing facility for various types and word-sizes of data. Complex operations, multilevel interrupt structure, and fast, asynchronous, nonmultiplexed bus architecture are feasible with an effective instruction set for meeting the requirement of a broad spectrum of general-purpose applications. Provision is made as "unused" areas for future implementation of advanced versions of MC 68000 for floating-point arithmetic and string operations, since the chip is oriented in design for high-level language support. The flexibility of architecture allows different versions of implementation. The throughput of 68000 is 10 to 25 times that of the original Motorola-6800 microprocessor chip.

7-35.1. System Architecture

1. The computer architecture is expected to specify flexible interface between the processor and its environment for facilities such as interrupt, memory-segmentation, bus interface, and I/O structure.

2. I/O device registers are addressed as memory-mapped I/O locations as in previous Motorola microprocessors to give the programmer the flexibility and power of the entire instruction set for organizing data-registers and peripheral control. I/O space and critical areas of memory are thus protected by memory management logic.

3. Address and data lines are separated on an asynchronous bus to avoid multiplexing and demultiplexing and ensure speed. Transfers on the bus are controlled by handshake signals that allow large variation in response-time of devices and memories.

4. The system bus is cooperatively shared by processors and direct-memory-access devices by using a request/grant protocol. For memory protection, a bus-fault input pin causes instruction execution to terminate in a "trap" if an improper memory access is made.

5. Vector-interrupt is similar to that in most minicomputers. Trap and interrupt vector allocation are shown in Figure 7-34a. Vector-interrupt allows software control over placement and execution of interrupt-handling routines. Current priority level of the processor is stored in its status word, and interrupt handling is nested with 256 vectors in an interrupt-handler, which serves eight priority levels without device-polling. The vector-table is assigned by the processor and stored in the main memory for program access.

6. For routine applications, the processor manipulates the memory directly as the program generates the addresses. For multiple tasks and multiple users (as in minicomputer applications), a separate Motorola LSI-chip is now available to provide memory segmentation, address translation, and memory protection.

7. Present VLSI Si-gate NMOS packaging technology, with one transistor/square-mil and speed-power product of one picojoule, allows 24 bits for addresses in a 64-pin package. (See Fig. 7-34b.) Therefore, a 32-bit word requires two accesses to memory as the data-path is limited to only 16 bits. Circuit density currently limits the operable instruction set; therefore, space is allocated for the future implementation of floating-point and string operations, which constitute one-eighth of the operation-code map. (Increased circuit density in the near future is expected to allow on-chip memory and sophisticated high-speed techniques.)

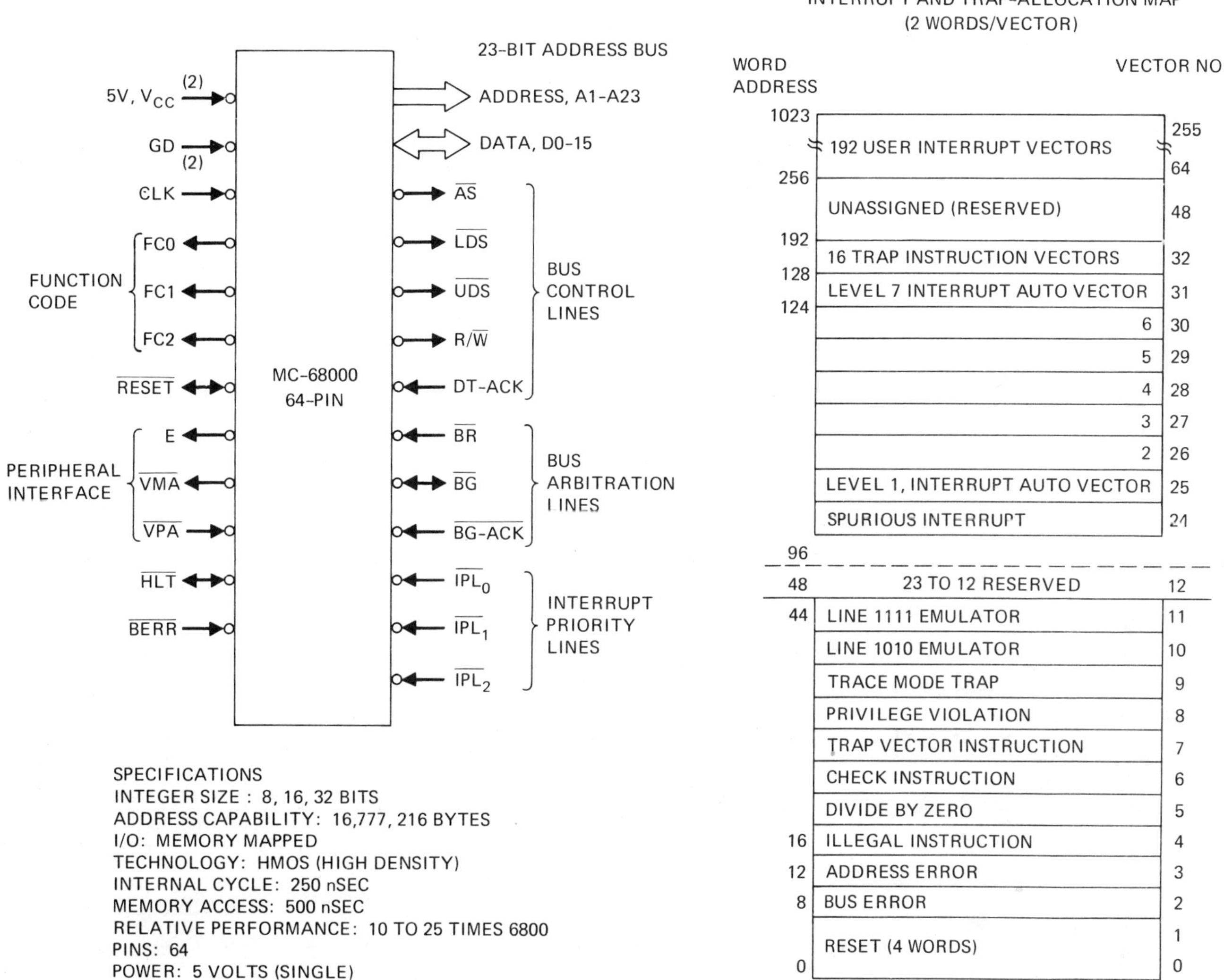

Fig. 7-34. *a*, Trap and Interrupt vector allocation. *b*, MC68000: 64-pin package allows the use of separate Address-bus and Data-bus. (©*IEEE, COMPCON 1979*)

8. The execution unit, consisting of three arithmetic logic units for use of control microcode, has a dual 16-bit bus structure to receive both input operands from registers simultaneously, as shown in Figure 7-35. The unit is independent of the external timings of the bus, but interfaces directly to external bus logic and buffers. The microcode is a two-level microprogrammed control structure, with level-1 microinstructions in short "vertical" format having complex branching capabilities. Level-2 nanoinstructions are in wide "horizontal" control address words; these nanoinstructions control the execution unit.

7-35.2. Major Features

1. *Memory* may be accessed in unit sizes of 1, 8, 16, and 32 bits, and integer size varies in 8, 16, and 32 bits. Bits are individually addressable in the bit-manipulation instructions. Variable-length segmentation of the address space as well as memory mangement schemes are allowed. Address calculations are specified by 6-bit fields of the instruction. The addresses in 8-bit bytes or 16/24/32 bit words are individually specified for each instruction in order to intermix either efficient small addresses or larger addresses in a program. A variety of addressing modes are available with eight address registers, requiring fewer

memory accesses for loading and storing temporary address values. This feature minimizes the program time spent in manipulation of addresses in most microprocessors. The addressing capability extends to 16-M bytes, with a memory-mapped input/output facility. The main-memory access-time is 500 nsec and the internal cycle-time is limited to 250 nsec.

2. *Registers* are divided into two classifications, eight 32-bit data registers and eight 32-bit address registers (one of which is used as a user or supervisory stackpointer). An extendable 24-bit program counter and 16-bit status register are available in addition. The address registers specifically use 16 bits for addressing modes such as "add register differed," "add indexed," "move," and "conditional branch," "jump to subroutine," etc. See Fig. 7-35.

3. *Data types and supporting operations* include integers in 1/2/4 bytes (for add, subtract, multiply, divide, negate, compare, and arithmetic shift), multiprecision integers, logical operations (AND, OR, XOR, complement, shift, and rotate), one-byte Booleans, flags (for set, clear, change, and test), decimal BCD operations, character instructions (for move and compare), address operations (that include increment, decrement, add/subtract

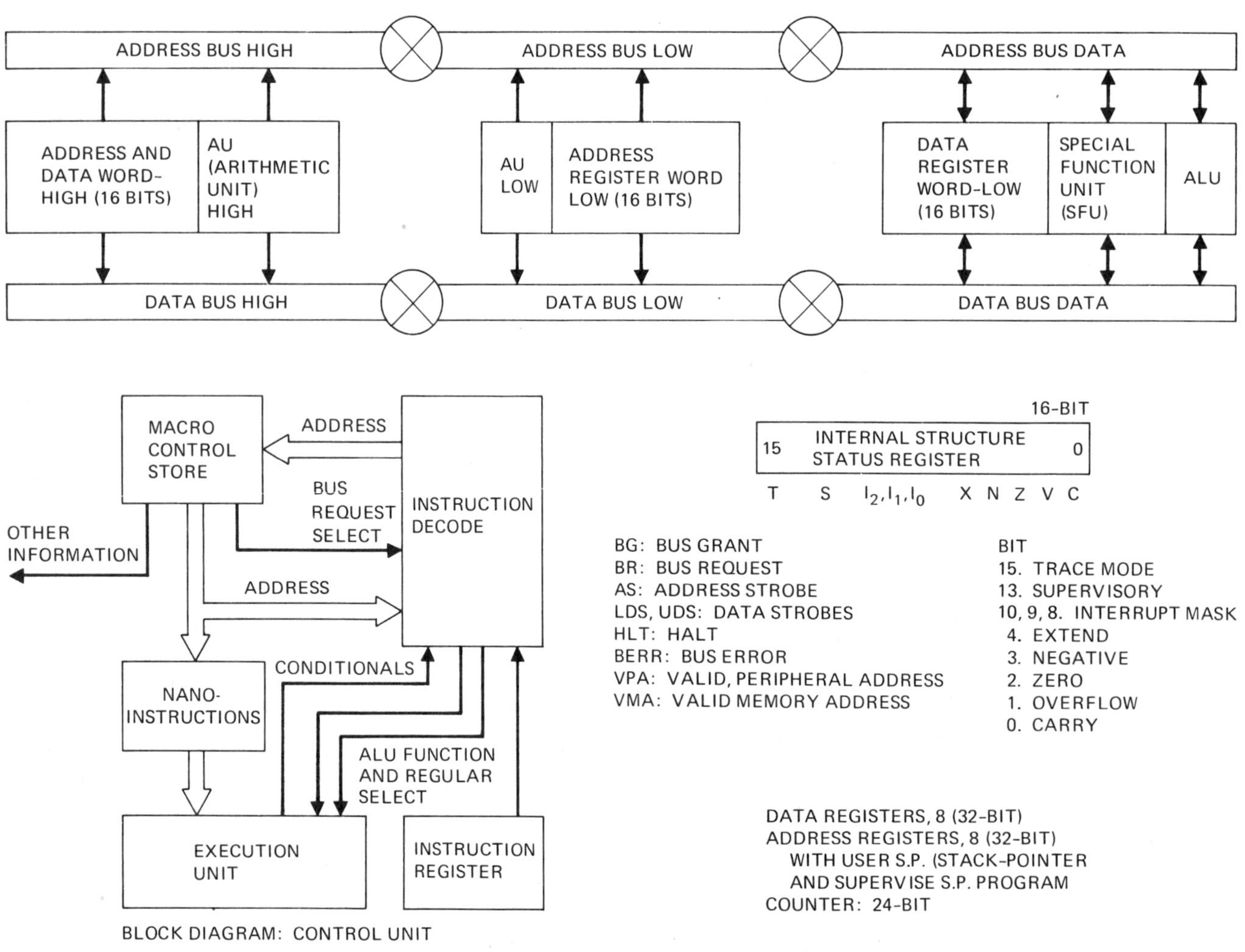

Fig. 7-35. MC-68000, Execution Unit's Architecture.
Registers,
Status Register Format, and
Block-diagram of Control Unit.
(© *IEEE, COMPCON 1979*)

integer, compare and load effective-address) and future provision for floating-point and bit-strings (for move, search, and translate). The size of the operand may be specified as independent of the operation, and operand sources may be either registers or addressed memory locations in order to minimize the number of registers required to save the results. Most operations specify memory-to-register, register-to-register, register-to-memory, immediate-to-register, or immediate-to-memory.

4. *Programming.* "Interrupts," "conditional branch," and "jump and return from subroutine" are conventional. "Trap" instruction specifies 16 different operating-system calls. "Stop" halts the processor, "Reset" reinitializes the system environment, and "move" manipulates the processor status word. The CPU operates in user or supervisor state. Address translation is inhibited in the supervisor state, and stop/reset/change status word are not allowed in user state. Improper instructions cause CPU to "trap" and switch to supervisor state. Two stack-pointer registers facilitate this precaution. The instruction set extends to the total of 59 instructions in the supervisor state only.

7-35.3. High-Level Language Support. The architecture of the Motorola VLSI 68000 microprocessor is implemented to support a high-level language such as PASCAL. The method "provides adequate instructions to support the required run-time representation" and transformations on that representation "without extensive in-line computation." The support is effective at both compilation time and execution time with a clean, consistent instruction set. Hardware implementation (circuit design) of commonly used functions such as multiply, divide, and address calculation occurs in parallel with firmware implementation (or microprogramming) or "a set of special-purpose instructions that manipulate the run-time environment of a high-level language program." The language constructs aided by these special-purpose instructions include: (1) array accessing (bounds check), (2) limited-precision arithmetic (trap on overflow), (3) looping (for-loop construct), (4) Boolean-expression evaluation (with the same "conditional set" and "conditional branch" instructions), and (5) procedure calls that use a stack-pointer to build the nested environments of called procedures. (A sample PASCAL program, the equivalent 68000-code, and the stack-activity on procedure call are presented in the COMPCON paper.)

The MC68000 thus integrates the state-of-the-art technology, advanced circuit design techniques, and latest computer science findings to present an architecturally advanced VLSI 16/32-bit microprocessor for most of the former minicomputer applications. This advanced microprocessor uses a two-level microprogrammed control unit that is tightly coupled to the execution unit and the bus interface. Tight coupling is an expediency for permitting full overlap of fetch, decode, and execute cycles across every macroinstruction boundary for high-speed. The block-diagram of the control unit in Figure 7-35 illustrates the two-level control of MC68000. The microcontrol storage has a set of routines, and each routine is a sequence of microcommands. They implement a macroinstruction or a position thereof, such as an addressing mode. The macroinstruction decode (instruction decode in the block diagram) in turn provides a starting address to the microcontrol storage to continue the microcommands. The nano control storage has a set of unique control words to support the entire instruction set. These words are field encoded so that, with two or three levels of decoding, they will directly drive control points in the execution unit. The microroutines will make as many accesses to the instruction stream as there are words in the associated macroinstruction.

The system features of MC68000 facilitate easier program and memory management. The processor operates in one of two privilege states—the lower user state and the higher supervisory state. Each privilege state determines the legality of operations by using its stack-pointer in instruction references. The supervisory state is defined by an S-bit of the status register. Some instructions which have major system effects are considered illegal. In addition, the processor is always in one of three processing states, normal, exception, or stop. The stop is a special case of the normal instructions to prevent further bus cycles. The exception processing is associated with seven levels of auto-vectored priority interrupts, trap, trace, and other exceptional conditions such as catastrophic and noncatastrophic (bus/address-error, etc.) from the viewpoints of processor hardware. Exception processing is limited to the supervisory state, regardless of the S-bit in status register. The processing halts if bus or address errors occur during exception processing. A hierarchy exception priority network is used to provide hardware arbitration among possible multiple exception conditions. Such features as these enable the minimization of the usual conflicts between architecture and implementation of intelligent software implementation, once the programmer masters the implications of the various features of this advanced VLSI microprocessor.

EXORmac Development System for MC68000 16-bit Microprocessor

EXORmac incorporates a 5-MHz bus structure called VERSAbus having the following features for industrial control, communications, multiple-processor applications, and business applications.

- A very fast bus cycle-time
- Asynchronous bidirectional operation
- 8-, 16- or 32-bit data transfers and single-byte feasibility of designation in 16- and 32-bit data transfers
- 32 address lines for direct access to 4 billion words of memory
- DMA and multiple processor support
- 7-level priority interrupt control
- 5-level daisy-chained bus arbitration
- Up to 50 I/O lines with mating ground returns
- Standard 5-volt 12-volt power to logic as well as 15-volt process control and standby power support
- Serial communication
- Distinct I/O mapping
- Bus error and reentry signals
- Integration of a separate analog board

The standard board, 6.5 in. X 9.26 in., uses two connectors, one 120-pin and one 140-pin. This ample provision will take care of future incorporation of new VLSI/LSI chips in the system. The dedicated memory management system has the following features:

- Address relocation memory protection
- Multiple-segment definitions and memory management, such as logical address segment location, offset to physical address, and address space parameters for memory protection
- Variable-length segment (256 bytes to 16-M bytes in 256-byte increments)
- Cascadability of multiple MMUs enables more segment definitions
- Bus error is generated on unauthorized attempted access (Encryption)
- Fast efficient context switching

The dedicated DMA controller (DMAC) has the following features

- 4 independent channels
- 16-M byte addressing range with 32/16-bit data transfer counter
- Byte, word, long-word transfer modes

- Programmable fixed and rotating priority control
- Memory-to-memory block transfer
- 3 data chaining modes with facility of independent chaining of each channel
- Interrupt vector register for each channel
- The DMAC is fully compatible with other MC 68000 LSI peripherals such as:
    - MC 6821, PIA (Peripheral interface adapter)
    - MC 6840, PTM (Peripheral timing module)
    - MC 6843, FDC (Floppy-disk controller)
    - MC 6845, CRTC (CRT controller)
    - MC 6847, VDG (Video display generator)
    - MC 6849, DDFDC (Dual-density floppy-disk controller)
    - MC 6850, ACIA (Asynchronous communications interface adapter)
    - MC 6852, SSDA (Serial synchronous data adapter)
    - MC 6854, ADLC (Advanced data link controller)
    - MC 68488, GPIA (IEEE-488 bus interface adapter)

The address and data buses terminate in a Bus Arbitration Adapter module (BAM) with the following facilities:

- Provision for interfacing microprocessors in larger systems.
- Arbitration of bus conflicts between local and global buses.
- Generation and response to all global bus handshake signals.
- Provision of address mapping relocation to eliminate interprocessor address conflicts.
- The BAM appears to the local microprocessor unit as an I/O device.
- Compatibility with other peripheral controllers of MC 68000.

The MC 68000 has a consistent set of just 60 instructions to facilitate assembly programmers a minimum number of mnemonics and maximum flexibility. For example, MOVE EA can be *any* of the sixteen 32-bit registers or *any* memory location. Most instructions operate on bits, bytes, words (16 bits) and long words (32 bits). It provides for 5 addressing modes with 15 variations. Privileged instructions MOVE the EOR, AND, and OR to the system byte of the status register; and RESET, RTE, and STOP can be executed in the supervisory mode only. The MC 68000 has the following software features:

- Real-time multi-tasking operating system
- Resident PASCAL compiler, providing a superset of these present PASCAL standard Calls to executive routines, I/O routines, and assembly language routines, makes the MPU MC 68000 flexible to other Motorola systems. Absolute address and interrupt handling are well supported.
- A secondary memory map provides unrestricted use of supervisory and user modes of MC 68000
- A complete self-test is executed at power up. The operating system incorporates diagnostic routines. Device level fault isolation is provided by means of the serial and parallel I/O ports of a one-chip 6801 microcomputer. Programs can be monitored, executed, and break-points set via the serial port. The parallel port enables factory testing and *signature analysis routines.* *
- Intelligent communications controller and hard-disk software can be added to support multiple users.
- Macroassembler allows conditional assembly, complex expressions, and position-

*A device can be designed so that the probability of two bit streams having the same value or "signature" is extremely small. A recirculating shift-register is used for this purpose in a Signature Analyzer.

independent code generation. The set of cross-software includes macro and cross PASCAL compiler and an MC 68000 simulator for IBM 370, PDP-11, and EXORcisor development system.

- As far as the software testability is concerned, system programmers have the facilities to detect the occurrence of programming errors and allow run time checks. Hardware traps indicate abnormal internal problems such as illegal instructions, unimplemented instructions, address error, divide by zero, and overflow condition code (TRAPV). Software traps include 16 software instructions, checking register-content against bounds (CHK), and TRACE mode (which provides a capability to trace a program instruction by instruction).
- Software instructions are specially structured for high-level languages.

7-36. MOTOROLA MC68000-SERIES VLSI INTEGRATED CIRCUITS (1980/81)

The MC68000-series VLSI chips are developed to provide a set of building-blocks for cost-effective highly reliable performance in complex third-generation 16/32-bit microcomputer applications; internally microcoded 32-bit architecture is the preferred approach. Efficient block-structured, portable high-level language support provided by PASCAL is the norm in microcomputer systems of the 1980s to allow upward compatibility of software from 8-to-16-to 32-bit microprocessors. The former Motorola 8-bit MC6800-family processors can be directly accessed via one physical 24-bit address bus from a memory-management unit and one direct data bus from the 64-pin MC-68000 processor.

The following information gives an overview of the entire Motorola series in this classification; it is offered in 1980/81 as a full-scale general-purpose microcomputer organization. Use of 32-bit data and address registers, 56 powerful instructions with five main data types, memory-mapped I/O, and 14 addressing modes are the major features of these sophisticated microcomputer systems.

A microcomputer system comprised of the following VLSI and LSI multiprocessor organization can successfully compete with most of the former minicomputer systems; and that with extra merits such as higher reliability, comparable speed, low power consumption, low cost, and compact size, etc. In satellite applications, we are approaching the stage of satellite on-board automatic attitude control (by telemetry commands from the ground computer facilities), and automatic time-division multiple-access data communication facilities to interconnect terrestrial or shipboard subscribers (as a telecommunications exchange in the sky!). The secret is that former large PC boards are gradually replaced by individual VLSI chips.

MC68000 uses seventeen 32-bit registers (as alternate index registers), a 32-bit program counter, and a 16-bit status register. The first eight registers are used as data registers for byte, word, and 32-bit long words; the second set of seven registers and system stack-pointer may be used as software stack-pointers and base address registers. A 23-bit logical address bus from MC68000 goes to the memory management unit (MMU), MC68451; and the MMU output 16-bit physical address bus and the 16-bit data bus from MC68000 are connected directly to all the following VLSI peripherals of the MC68000 in the system organization.

MC68451 Memory Management Unit (MMU). Multiple MMUs are allowed in a system. The MMU provides address translation and write protection of the 16-M byte addressing space of the MC68000. The 64-pin MMU can be accessed by any potential bus master, such as instruction set processors or DMA controllers. Virtual memory, paging, and segmentation are supported. A total of 32 segments with variable segment sizes, simplification of the programming model of address space, minimization of the overhead of operating system with quick-context switches, interprocess communication through shared resources, provision of efficient *memory relocation*, high *multiprocess system* reliability, and separate address spaces of system and user resources are the other features of the MMU. The function code provided by MC68000 specifies an address space, while the address specifies a location within that address space. The function codes distinguish supervisor and user spaces as well.

MC68120 Intelligent Peripheral Controller (IPC). The IPC, a 48-pin programmable counter, has a built-in 8-bit CPU, system interface, serial communication interface, 21 parallel I/O lines and 2 handshake lines, a 16-bit timer, 2048 bytes of ROM, 128 bytes of dual-ported RAM, and 8 operating modes. Six internal registers can be accessed by both the system and IPC CPUs, as well as an external CPU or a device via the system interface. Control signals for an asynchronous bus of MC68000 are also available. It is bus compatible with the 8-bit MC6800. External clock input, interrupt and DMA capability, 8 X 8 built-in multiplier are the other major features. The registers, 16-bit timer, serial communications interface, parallel I/O ports, and interrupt can be controlled by software. With its additional exclusive 8-bit address and data buses, external memory and I/O chips can be accessed.

Memory (Off-the-Shelf VLSI Memory Chips of Motorola)

MCM68764 (8-K X 8 EPROM); MCM68732 (4-K X 8 EPROM);
MCM68364 (8-K X 8 ROM); MCM68332 (4-K X 8 ROM);
MCM68316 (2-K X 8 ROM); MCM 6664 (64-K X 1 Dynamic ROM)

MC68540 Error Detector/Correction Unit (EDCC). The 48-pin unit is interconnected to the ROM/RAM memory aggregate. Single devices check 8-bit and 16-bit operation, and two devices check for 32-bit operation. Other features are bidirectional data and check bits; single-error correction and double-error detection; detects catastrophic error of all 1's and all 0's; independent byte control; supports parity (Read and Write); error flags; flexible diagnostic operating modes; internal diagnostic register; and facilities for latching to hardware and I/O data. MC68000 is connected via control, address and data buses.

MC68453 Bubble Memory Controller to Bubble Memory. High-density (HMOS), 40-pin N-channel, silicon-gate, depletion-load device; control logic available for up to 64 separate bubble memory devices; access for 1, 2, 4, or 8 memory devices in parallel; complete bubble memory timing generator; 128-byte FIFO buffer; error detection and correction logic; logic to ignore defective loops in bubble memory; single or multiple data transfer; multiple options such as software polling, interrupt, external DMA controller for data transfer from associated bubble memory chips; and extensive command structure for control and verification of bubble memories.

MC68341 Floating-Point ROM. Two separate IEEE-standard 24-pin chips provided for lower and upper bytes for direct interconnection to address and data buses of MC68000; position-independent/reentrant floating-point ROM; uses unimplemented instruction trap to simulate hardware floating-point; single, double, and extended precision formats; includes add, subtract, multiply, divide, remainder, square-root, compare, absolute value, negate, integer part, and inter-integer-floating point and inter-binary-decimal conversion.

MC68122 Direct Memory Access (DMA) Controller. The 64-pin device enables high-performance speed and flexibility in data transfer rates to 4 Mb/sec. Features include sophisticated array or link-array chained/unchained operations and memory-to-memory block data transfers. Variable bus-bandwidth utilization results in optimum data transfers. Internal 32-bit address registers provide upward software compatibility with future Motorola peripheral processors. Other features include four fully independent channels, single/dual address transfers, support of vectored interrupts and programmable interrupt priorities.

MC68230 Parallel Interface/Timer (PI/T). The 48-pin unit is a parallel interface device for parallel I/O and timing requirements to interface a wide variety of peripheral devices. Features include 24 programmable I/O lines, selectable handshaking modes, 24-bit programmable timer, several timer modes, interrupt prioritization logic, and unique interrupt vectors for each source. The device supports interrupt and DMA service requests, and includes port and timer status-registers. Registers are Read/Write, and directly addressable. Port modes include bit-mode, bidirectional, and unidirectional 8-bit and 16-bit modes. The PI/T can be directly interfaced to the DMA controller on the physical address and data bus.

MC68122 Cluster Terminal Controller (CTC). The 48-pin controller device relieves the host CPU in a network of the task of coordinating communications between one or more keyboard CRT terminals. Messages containing either text or control commands between the host and the controller follow the application program. Standard I/O protocols are supported with CRT terminals and printers. The controller's local bus is used for message buffering and interface to devices. Broadcast feature provides for automatic generation of text to all the terminals with status reporting capability, echo control, carriage-return option, and automatic error recovery.

MC68560 Serial DMA Processor (SDMA). The 64-pin serial DMA processor provides a serial high-speed (4-M bit/sec transfer rate) link between microprocessors and "intelligent" controllers in distributed processing (DP) network environment. With IBM's SDLC link-control protocol or HDLC protocol, multidrop, point-to-point, and loop network operation is rendered feasible under simplex or duplex requirements. Data-chaining capability of one primary SDMA for data link-control (polling) and one or more secondary SDMAs, for responding to link-level commands over serial bus, is implemented with some error-recovery facility. Data integrity and validation are assured. Internal byte synchronization, external clocks, 24-bit address bus, and 16-bit data bus operation are the other features.

MC68561 Multiprotocol Communications Controller (MPCC). The 48-pin controller is an I/O serial data communications interface for MC68000 in this series (via control, address, and data buses) for asynchronous, and bit-oriented (such as X.25, SDLC, and HDLC handshaking protocols), and byte-oriented synchronous communication protocols (such as BYSYNC and DDCMP). Internal crystal oscillator and baud rate generator are available. Microprocessor interface is compatible with the DMA controller of the series in self-test loop mode. Multiple character generation and error detection and complete status reporting capability are provided for by the inclusion of transmit/receive buffer registers and vectored interrupts.

MC68340 Dual-Port RAM. The 48-pin dual-port RAM is meant for primary data and control communications path between two processing elements in a multiprocessing system. It can be also used as a CRT refresh or disk-interface buffer. Compatibility with both 6800/68000 and HOLD/ACKNOWLEDGE line applications, support of vectored interrupts, and internal refresh-cycling are the main features. It can be expandable to any width and depth (2-K X 8 to 4-K X 8 RAM).

7-37. STATUS OF COMPUTER TECHNOLOGY, 1981

Some of the new microelectronics arrivals from Japan in 1981 offer competitive and attractive features. An 8-bit microprocessor from Hitachi Ltd. provides on-chip nonvolatile memory for the first time. A single-chip graphics display controller is available from

Nippon Electric Company; it means a regular consumer television receiver using a few additional chips and a keyboard with a built-in decoder can shape up as a personal computer at consumer product prices. NEC, by the way, eliminates alpha-particle radiation in high-density microelectronics chips for negligible bit-error-rates by using the acceptor impurity of boron under each cell node as a buried junction to sweep away alpha-particle-generated carriers. Also, NEC's ACOS 1000 large-scale computer successfully competes with the IBM mainframe 4341 and 3081 large-scale computers. Hitachi Ltd. and Fujitsu Ltd. are two other Japanese Manufacturers of large-scale computers; they compete in the international market by profuse use of LSI/VLSI microelectronics.

The 32-bit microprocessors are coming! Bell Laboratories Mac-32, a 100,000-transistor CMOS microprocessor, is archtiecturally register-based and CAD-designed using a 17-by-32-bit file. As in the case of Intel 8086 and Texas Instruments' new 99000 microprocessors, fetching and execution are accomplished in parallel by using an instruction-queue cache memory and a secondary arithmetic unit for address computation. The regular ALU performs a 32-bit addition in 60 nsec. The execution section employs a *barrel* shift register to shift 1 to 32 bits in a single machine cycle-time. A 32-MHz clock is derived from two phase-shifted 8-MHz external clock sources. By using on-chip 4-K bit CMOS static RAM memory with access time of 20 nsec, Mac-32's application in multiplexed high-speed telecommunications networks will boost AT&T's leadership in data communications.

Hewlett-Packard's 450,000-transistor, 8-mask, silicon-gate, 32-bit NMOS microprocessor employs a high-resistance substrate. This microprocessor achieves its enormous density by using 1-micron channel-widths by way of electron-beam lithography. A special on-chip multiplier section computes a 64-bit multiplication from two operands in 1.8 μsec; 64-bit floating-point multiplication is performed in 10.4 μsec! A machine cycle-time of 55 nsec is achieved by using as 18-MHz clock.

National Semiconductor's register-oriented, 60,000-transistor, 48-pin DIP, NS16032 microprocessor, using 32-bit internal data bus and a 16-bit memory interface works in conjunction with a type NS16082 VLSI memory management chip to provide a true virtual memory facility. Fetching and execution are done in parallel as in the case of Intel 8086; and NS16032 is primarily microcoded with an extensive memory-space of 1300 by 18 bits at a cycle-time of 100 nsec. The chip also includes a self-testing routine.

High-speed National Semiconductor double-polysilicon dry plasma processing, using selective field-oxidation, allows low-power CMOS linear circuits at NMOS high speeds. A P^2CMOS type TP3040 telecom 8-kHz PCM codec filter is a successful product for digital electronic switching systems. The fabrication technique uses ion-implantation for opamp configurations with lower noise and improved power rejection ratio.

8
Software and Firmware

8-1. THE SOFTWARE PROCEDURE IN MICROCOMPUTER SYSTEMS

The programming techniques applicable to minicomputer systems do apply, although the actual number of instructions add up to need external ROM and RAM memories, in view of the limitation of instruction lengths to one-to-three 8-bit bytes. Programming experience with such high-level languages as BASIC, minicomputer FORTRAN, or APL cannot be directly utilized to apply to the low-level language required by most microprocessors. Sofware talent in program planning and in testing or debugging of minicomputers should be augmented with some familiarity of the details of the microcomputer hardware system and a specific programming technique for a specific microcomputer system.

Latest developments in hardware/firmware. With a drastic cut in engineering turnaround time, the hardware/firmware field is experiencing a kind of explosion in both developments and applications that reach most minicomputer levels of complexity. The latest microprocessors, mass-produced at low cost and custom-designed along economically feasible techniques, make the previous task of logic design much easier in microcomputer applications. The system and logic designers presently work with firmware of compilers, assemblers, editors, and debugging software related to special and custom hardware from microprocessor manufacturers; engineering changes are mostly made by altering a pattern here and there on a programmable electronically-erasable ROM or by plugging in an alternative ROM or PLA. Complexity of testing new microcomputer systems depends on the degree of assurance required and hence cost, whereas mass-produced dedicated systems enjoy an advantage in this respect.

Firmware allowing hardware/software trade-off. The hardware cost of computer systems is presently declining at a rapid rate, and LSI memories can economically provide computer functions that were normally performed by software. LSI chips (meeting Defense standards) with custom-designed gates (as field programmable logic arrays, or

FPLAs) operate at speeds about twice as fast as those of LSI-ROMs, presently used for microprograms. Computational speed is basically the main reason for replacing such hardware for software, especially for such complex computations as sorting, Fast Fourier Transforms in digital signal process, and floating-point arithmetic. For example, an algorithm for recognizing hand-printed characters, programmed in IBM PL-I high-level language, required 7 sec to run on an IBM-360/65; a hardwired processor or FPLA would take 7 ms to run the same algorithm. Memory management is best performed by hardware in the new micro- and mini-computing systems. A list is given below to indicate software features that can be presently implemented by hardware:

1. Memory allocation, memory reclamation, virtual memory management, paging, segmentation (absent segment interrupt), memory and data protection, stack operations, address generation, indexing, indirect addressing, storage protection.
2. Multiple-precision arithmetic, decimal multiply-and-divide, floating-point arithmetic, sorting, algorithms for data manipulation.
3. Program linking and binding, program relocation, data relocation, data structure, formal checking, character-string manipulation, data-type conversion.
4. Symbolic addressing, variable-field lengths (16, 32, 64 bits), variable data structures, alphameric field manipulation, context switching, emulation, queues, links, compilation, task-dispatching, next software-instruction fetch.
5. Interrupts, interrupt checking, trap catchers, peripheral data transfer, time-sharing supervision, text-editing, control command instructions, format checking.
6. Parity checks, error-control coding (detecting and correcting), automatic retry, automatic diagnosis.

8-2. TIME-SHARE COMPUTER SERVICES

Time-share computer services offer proprietary programs, supplied by the microprocessor vendors, which allow the assembly of "source" high-level programs into "object" code suitable for execution in a microprocessor. The source program written in the **assembly language** of the microprocessor in mnemonics comprises the symbolic operation-code and the symbolic label that corresponds to the actual binary address at which the instruction Opcode will reside during program execution. This assembly language also keeps track of the start addresses of subroutines utilized by the main program. The object-code generated by the assembler loads the processor's instruction-PROM memory in the desired sequence. An **"interpretive" language** like BASIC can thus be stored on a semipermanent basis.

In actual practice, the logical sequence of events in the program are established by a flowchart, and each step in the flowchart is converted to one or more instructions in the Assembly language. The instructions are keyed into a data-file in a time-shared computer, and the program or source-file is processed by the assembler program in the time-shared system. The error-free output-record renders the object-file in a suitable format for storage; the object-file of bit-patterns is "burned" by a vendor into usable ROM memory chips as permanent "stored program" of the microcomputer system.

Central time-sharing computer. Real-time interaction between humans and machines in **high-level language** provides a continuous dialogue for quick results, instead of the one-program-at-a-time batch-processing. The time-sharing computer, therefore, serves as a powerful library for an entire community. The system organization of a time-sharing computer is illustrated in Fig. 8-1. As a contrast to the time-sharing network, a **distributed network** and a **hierarchical network** are illustrated in Fig. 8-2.

Software

Source Code	Translation	Object Code in Bits
High-level BASIC, FORTRAN, or APL	Compiler	Machine instructions and data addresses
High-level BASIC, FORTRAN, or APL	Interpreter (hardware or firmware)	Machine instructions and data addresses
Assembly Language (phrased in Mnemonic–alphanumeric commands)	Assembler	Machine instructions and data addresses

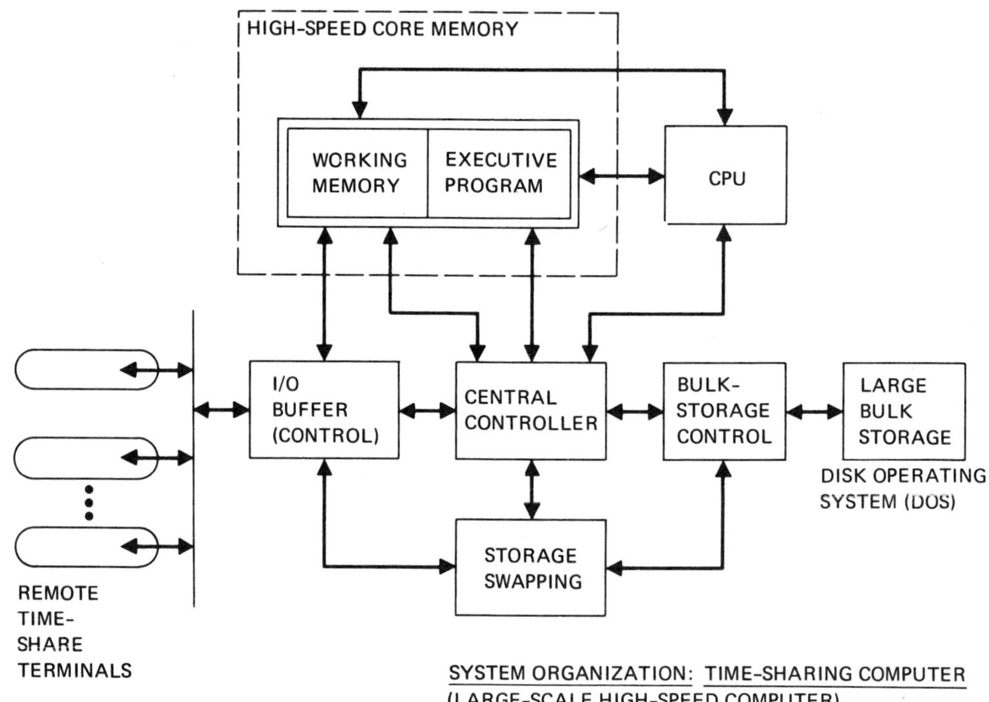

Fig. 8-1. Organization of a time-share system.

8-3. PROTOTYPING SYSTEMS

As an alternative, for a distributed network or a microcomputer, manufacturers provide, at costs ranging from $3 to $10 thousand depending on its complexity and features, a prototype system that can provide an operating setup to enter and edit source programs in the assembly language, and execute the effective machine code with actual microprocessor hardware. The prototype system allows direct hardware interface to the controller under development via plug-in "kluge" cards. These cards contain the actual hardware required for the interface system. This technique allows the design of the Interface between a specific microprocessor and a specific controller of a peripheral or an industrial digital control-device. A *program development system* is an alternative term for the prototyping system.

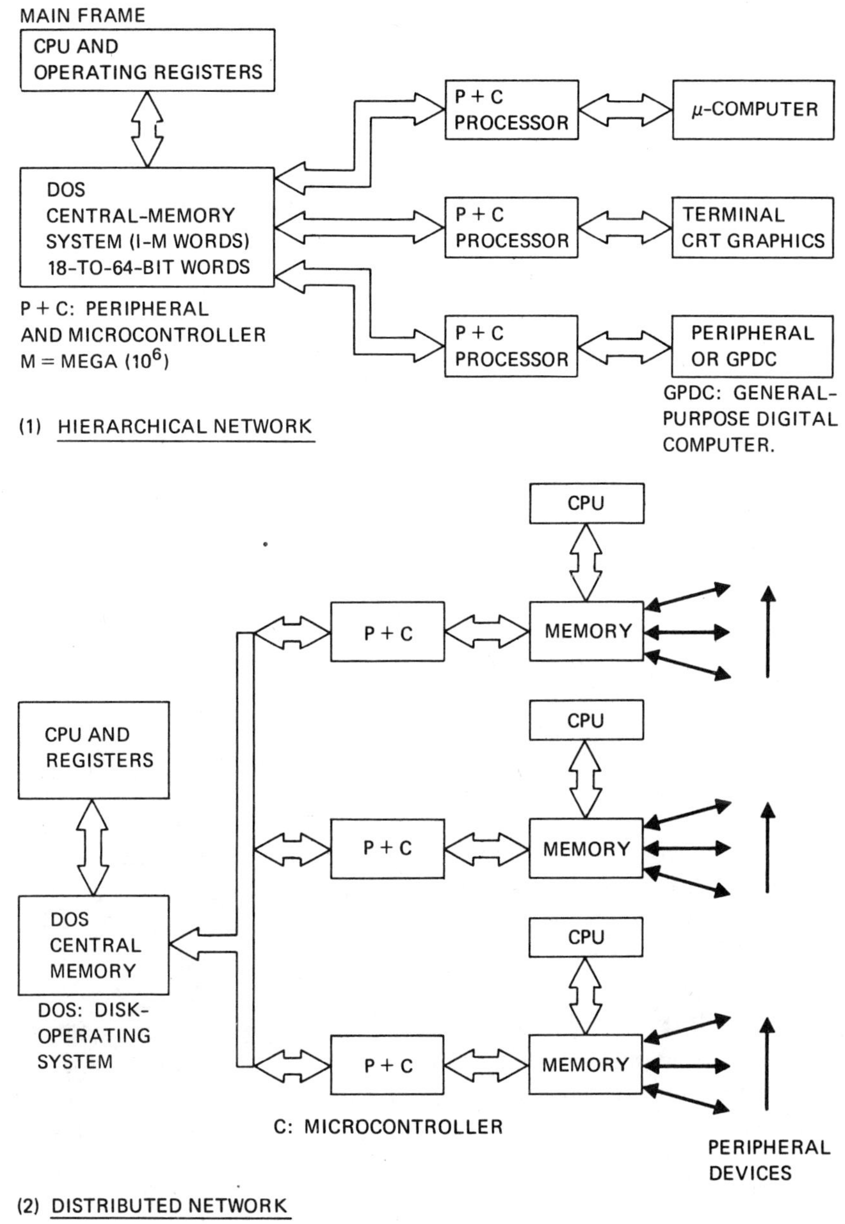

Fig. 8-2. Hierarchical and distributed networks.

8-4. MEMORY ORGANIZATION, VIRTUAL MEMORY, AND BOOTSTRAP LOADER

The microcomputer's memory is composed of several thousand words, each consisting of a number of binary digits or bits (e.g., 16 for a 16-bit word), and *the word at any address may represent either an operating instruction* (for instance, of the stored program at address 55) *or a block of binary-coded-decimal data* such as the number 2,730 in 3-bit octal (base 8) or 4-bit hexadecimal (base 16) code. The most significant bit 15 (MSB) of a word is often used to indicate sign (0 = +; 1 = -). The least significant bit of the word is numbered bit 0, as shown in the following diagram.

Conventional numbering of bits in a 16-bit computer

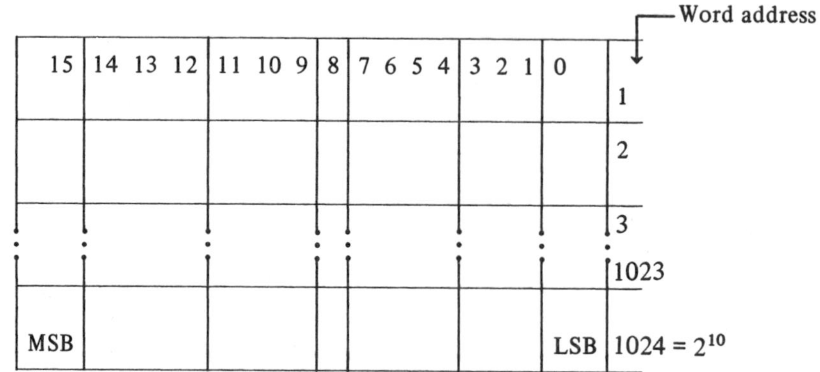

(1-K word of memory stored in a ROM is equivalent to 16-K bits or 2-K bytes of a short program of commands and data.)

The computer handles one word at a time in a clock cycle-time, a word size may vary from 4 to 8, 12, 16, 18, 24, 32, or 64 bits. The microprocessor normally uses the memory under the jurisdiction of the control logic. But an I/O control or multiplexer can "sneak" into memory and steal a memory cycle without the awareness of the control, by way of a special "direct memory access" facility and "steal" a memory-cycle by not necessarily holding up the regular control circuitry by a memory-cycle.

Usually the program is stored in consecutive memory locations and is executed sequentially unless a "jump" or "branching" instruction comes along. It is actually the sophisticated software, the logic of the program, that determines whether the contents of a memory word is data or an instruction. Firmware, via the medium of the latest LSI hardware in the form of the programmable logic array (PLA) and ROM's, is the fastest system of software presently available.

Virtual memory. Software programs, such as loaders, assemblers, and compilers, are generally provided by the microcomputer manufacturer. An **Executive program**, for instance, collects a sequence of software programs, such as write/edit/assemble or compile/ and execute, into an operating system. The Executive program is also responsible for:

1. **Job scheduling**, such as sequencing the loading and execution of a user's program, for example, by way of teletype or the start punch-cards of a job-deck.
2. **Monitoring programs and I/O controls** for such utilities as debug. Larger Operating Systems using this Executive software have bulk-memory peripherals such as disk or drum or external RAM/ROM memory-stacks. The Executive software will transfer programs from its internal memory to the said external bulk-memory when out of use, loading each one back again when required. This kind of handling memory is termed *virtual memory*, since this configuration of the transferable software memory appears almost unlimited to the programmer.

Managing virtual-memory in modern host minicomputers such as IBM System/38 is accomplished by considering the main memory and auxiliary storage on disk-drives as a homogeneous unit. The virtual-memory addresses may extend to capacities like 281 trillion bytes. For processing a program from any time-sharing terminal, the information must be moved from the disk-drives to the main memory such as CORE or RAM and back. The transfer of information with an unvarying (virtual) address is transparent to the time-sharing user; the user need not know the location of the memory, although the location actually changes while the computer keeps track of its address. This task is accomplished by the effective data-base management scheme used.

The System/38 implements the algorithm that uniformly distributes the virtual addresses on the basis of a 2-tier translation scheme. The virtual address-memory space is divided into segments, that are in turn subdivided into 512-byte blocks or pages. When this page is transferred to the main RAM (CORE) memory, it is called a frame, and the interrelationship between the page- and frame-addresses is the task of the translator.

The virtual address will have page-address (with a segment and page parts) and a byte-identifier for the page, while the main-memory address will have frame-address and its own byte identifier for identification by the page-address. A page-directory, and an index-value of the entry in a separate table are used for this function.

The above scheme for virtual-memory translation gives an idea of the software complexity involved when such large disk-drive systems are incorporated in modern minicomputer concentrators, which in turn serve tens or hundreds of microprocessor-based CRT terminals or workstations in the network. For data-base management, there are schemes that use multi-microprocessor setups to minimize virtual-memory access-time.

Bootstrap loader. The bootstrap loader is a small program that enables at start in an empty memory the loading of a few instructions or data (for instance, for commanding a peripheral device to input the program instruction codes.) It may typically consist of 5 to 10 instructions, which may be either read from an internal ROM or keyed in via:

1. The control panel switches.
2. The keyboard, if the microcomputer console has a built-in keyboard facility.

8-5. ASSEMBLER

The assembler programs are powerful but simple at the lowest level of program-development software. (The IBM BAL–Basic Assembly Language–is an example.) They allow the programmer to design programs up to several thousand words and to specify the instructions, addresses, and data by name in decimal, octal, or hexadecimal formats by using **mnemonics** (abbreviated symbolic words) for the instruction words, address names, and data numerical constants. The mnemonics are usually three to five characters long. Special user programs are usually developed by computer manufacturers for the specific hardware and peripherals involved.

The source-language assembler allows the inputting of a user program via the keyboard or TTY in the form of coded symbolic instructions. In addition, the assembler program will:

1. Translate these codes into the object binary machine-language
2. Calculate all the necessary memory reference addresses from the start address given
3. Convert all formats of data to the binary machine language.

Label is the equivalent of a memory address–where referenced only. Instruction mnemonic specifies type of operation. **Operand** is the operand part of the instruction word (a constant or a memory address).

The remarks under a separate column in the program-format are added for only understanding the program during "debugging."

In the event an instruction word needs a modification, it can be typed in; the assembler recalculates the memory addresses. If the assembler is commanded to assemble the input program, it will list the user program on a line printer, if one is available.

Macroassembler. A **Macroassembler** allows the programmer to develop and specify blocks of instructions. As an example, if the programmer specifies a four-instruction sequence for interfacing an I/O device, the Macroassembler allows the programmer to define the sequence by a simple four-character mnemonic. When this mnemonic is encountered by the Macroassembler during the processing of a source program, it will automatically go through the four-instruction sequence. These user-defined multiple-words are called *macroinstructions.* So, this is a mix of the assembler and the high-level language programs.

8-6. COMPILERS FOR HIGH-LEVEL LANGUAGES SUCH AS FORTRAN AND BASIC

The Macroassembler is a start in the direction of a high-level language. The compiler translates the high-level language and provides the following simplifying software facilities to the programmer.

1. A mathematical operation can be specified in algebraic form, and the compiler converts it into a series of instructions in the form of binary words; it is the machine-language for actually operating the computer.
2. Real numbers can be conveniently handled in shifting floating-point notation. Since most computers are binary fixed-point machines, the compiler provides a floating-point feature.
3. Data can be specified in matrix (table) or subscript format to handle large amounts of data.
4. Macroassemblers can be indexed for a loop sequence, which requires several instructions at the start and end of each loop. Example: Program to evaluate $y = \frac{AX + B}{5.6}$, requires only 4 commands in FORTRAN.
   a. READ A, B, X
   b. Y = (A*X + B)/5.6
   c. PRINT Y
   d. END

In the machine code or Assembly language, a large number of program instructions are involved for this computation.

The compiler assigns the CPU-registers, calculates addresses, and assigns memory areas to programs and subroutines without the programmer ever knowing the working registers and actual instruction set. The demerit is that a much faster method of computing a function is not feasible by using a lesser number of internal machine instructions (as could be optimized by using Assembly language and mnemonics). At the same time, obviously the compiler needs high overhead of memory. Presently, the compilers are rendered "intelligent" by automatically rearranging the sequence of operations for the optimum throughput.

8-7. INTERPRETER

The interpreter differs from the compiler in that it translates the high-level instructions one by one, and executes each immediately to slow up the execution of the program. However, the program can be more conveniently modified on a one-by-one basis. This software technique is especially convenient in a programmable calculator. **Interpretive BASIC** commands are also stored in a ROM for a preprogrammed microcomputer in **personal computing** systems.

8-8. DEBUGGING A PROGRAM

Debugging is an essential **utility routine** during the generation of software for a specific application. A simple TTY debugger-program will include the ability to load memory from a paper-tape, and dump a section of the memory to a TTY printer in a readable format. It will have the ability to examine and modify a memory address or the contents of a memory address, and execute a program starting at a specific address. A **break-point facility** allows the programmer to stop the program at a specific step, by inserting a breakpoint at an address in the program. The **debugging program** then goes to that address, removes and stores the instruction, and then inserts a command that causes the computer to jump back to the debugging program; then, the stored original instruction is replaced to execute a program up to the point and then stop. This allows the programmer to examine the memory to see if any failures have occurred in the user's program. The debugging program also duplicates many front-panel hardware functions to check the relevant software aspects.

Generally, if a program is less than 200 words, **support software** may not be required. The program can then be generated directly in binary, octal, or hexadecimal format by entering it through the front panel and debugging it manually via the front-panel controls. For programs of 200 to 4,000 words, a **paper-tape assembler** or a 16-K bit PROM and a debug-package are sufficient. For multiprocessing of several programs, more sophisticated software packages are required. It is only during the debugging procedure that a system programmer, using the BASIC or FORTRAN, may have to deal with the machine-language instructions.

The use of available program-development software supplied by the manufacturer results in fewer program errors, because such automatic tools provide many design-checking features. **Software diagnostics** are called the debugging programs, and these diagnostic programs determine whether a system failure is due to hardware or software. The **CPU hardware diagnostics** are generally supplied by the manufacturer. When one designs an I/O interface, one must write corresponding diagnostics to debug the hardware design.

8-9. TEXT EDITOR

Text editor has the function of inserting or deleting information from words. If the memory-word outputted is 002350000, the editing procedure may involve reformatting this word by:

1. "Extracting" the meaningful part of the word, and
2. "Writing or masking" new characters over part of the word according to a "mask."

After editing, the word may take the format "$23.50." The editing procedure may thus involve shifting bits or characters in a register with respect to the word, so that a decimal point, if any, can be inserted at the appropriate place. In general, delete, insert, copy, or mask-and-shift make the requisite manipulations.

8-10. LINKAGE EDITOR

In programs, "Load" instruction may have several functions, such as

1. Loading and relocating the machine-language program in the main memory, which may be CORE or RAM
2. Communicating with the various segments of the main program

3. Bringing in names, masks (or overlays), and addresses, and link to the subroutines from a subroutine library of look-in tables like ROMs
4. Monitor the contents of the memory to see that its capacity bounds are not exceeded.

More flexible software systems distribute these functions on different passes by using a Linkage Editor, which may take a basic assembly-language program from a tape or disk and convert it into the corresponding "absolute" machine-language on a one-to-one instruction basis, and append or "link" subroutines from a relocatable library like an array of external static RAMs; at this stage, if the program exceeds the limits of the CORE/RAM main-memory, it is rejected.

8-11. BATCH PROCESSING OF PROGRAMS

It is a programming technique where all information to be processed is coded and collected into separate "decks" or batches of cards off-line before actually processing through the computer in a sequence. This is the free-standing configuration, when a bulk-storage medium such as an on-line random-access disk operating system (DOS) is not the case. Microcomputer Systems, with "RAM" memories and floppy-disk mass-memories, make on-line random-access systems. When slow-access tape cartridges are used, software loading into the popular static RAM main-memory is off-line.

8-12. STACK INTERRUPT PROCESSING

The stack is a reserved area of the main-memory where the CPU automatically sets aside the contents of the program-counter and the working registers when a program interrupt occurs via the I/O control system. The stack normally forces the CPU to return to resumption of processing from the interrupts in the same order that the sequence of the interrupts from the external devices occurred in the first instance.

8-13. SOFTWARE TRENDS

As noticed in the case of the more sophisticated IBM-5600 and DEC-LSI-11 microcomputer systems, the software previously developed for minicomputers will be adapted for the direct use of microcomputer systems in the form of external miniature tape or floppy-disk facilities and internal RAM and ROM memory. Loading of the internal or extended external RAM memory from the tape or disk mass-memory software may be considered an off-line operation.

The distinction between the large-scale general-purpose digital computers and minicomputer systems with LSI hardware is presently determined by mostly software differences. A modern minicomputer operating system is as powerful as some of the original medium-scale general-purpose digital computer Operating Systems of IBM-360. The minicomputers are highly competitive in throughput, speed, access time, and so on, with latest medium-scale machines in the IBM-370 series too. (Large-scale IBM, CDC, and Burroughs Computers would be mainly reserved for the central multiprogrammed function of pipelined time-share and distributed network centers. There are several other large-scale main-frame manufacturers.)

The previous situation will be repeated for the eventual distinction between the latest microcomputers and the present medium-speed real-time minicomputer operating systems. For example, the word sizes in minicomputers have been increasing to 32 and 64 bits for handling larger word lengths during each memory cycle, to allow less programming effort and faster run-times for the same computational accuracy of the double-precision floating-point arithmetic. To keep in step, the latest 16-bit, bit-slicing microcomputers can now handle 4, 8, 16, and 24-bit word sizes in a memory cycle in medium-speed real-time applications, and they show signs of replacing some of the original minicomputer systems by exhibiting a more powerful architecture and performance. During the next few years, when the high-density, high-speed, low-power bipolar, Schottky I^2 L-LSI processing reaches maturity, microcomputer Operating Systems are expected to reach the standards of the latest minicomputer systems in both performance and scope, and gain an advantage with the claimed higher MTBF of 12,000 hours (for Intel 8080) as compared to the average 500-hour figure for most minicomputers.

8-14. HIGH-LEVEL LANGUAGE–BASIC

BASIC programming language is presently used on the teletype time-sharing computer systems (e.g., GE-265, GE-645). It is ideal for solution of scientific or business problems of moderate size and complexity. The BASIC consists of 31 commands, using:

1. Variable name
2. Expression
3. Message, line number
4. Counter
5. Beginning value
6. Ending value
7. Step size
8. Numeric value
9. Alpha value
10. Dimension value
11. Operand
12. Relation
13. Function name
14. Function argument
15. Function definition.

One uses a teletype machine with a built-in digital microcontroller and dials the computer's telephone number to hear a high-pitched tone for connection. The computer is told the problem in the proper form of "line statements" and asked to print the answer via the keyboard-printer. The computer prints back the answer in line statements. IBM-5100 microcomputer system uses BASIC in conjunction with its own keyboard and CRT output display, as do several other microcomputer systems at this moment. BASIC, originally designed as a simple interactive programming language for beginners in time-sharing computers, is available as a subset of any of the languages in the machine-oriented class, plus the essential I/O instructions and the math packages that rely on the operating system. The syntax (or phrasing of statements) of BASIC is so direct that source statements can be conveniently executed by an *interpreter* (rather than a compiler) to facilitate easy debugging and on-line modification. However, BASIC does require a fairly large run-time system. In view of its poor data-structuring facilities for modularization and its single-character variable names, it is not quite satisfactory for large professional programming applications. The extended LLL-BASIC, however, facilitates interfacing with assembly routines; therefore, it is successful in real-time environment.

Specialized system software for language processing purposes is essential to make a high-level language executable in any computer. This software includes translators such as compilers, macroassemblers, assemblers, interpreters, linkaging, and bootstrap loaders. Utility programs such as debuggers, editors, and text for machine code are also important. A *translator* essentially converts a source text written in a high-level language to a program in machine code, assembly language, or an intermediate "abstract-machine" language (which is usually referred to as the machine code of a virtual machine). On the other hand, the simpler *interpreter* software used as the high-level BASIC, prewritten on ROMs,

TABLE 8-1. General Evaluation of Software in terms of Program Execution, Preparation, and Portability.[a] AMC. Abstract Machine Code as Used in UCSD-PASCAL (© *1980, IEEE, COMPUTER, January*)

Type of software	Complete Translation	Translation to Assembler	Translation to AMC and AMC Interpretation	Source Language Interpretation
Program Execution				
Size of object program	3	3	2	1 (Best)
Execution speed	1	1	2	3
Size of run-time system	1	1	2	3
Run-time diagnostic and debugging	3	3	2	1
Program Preparation				
Total size of program package	3	4 Includes Assembler	2	1
Preparation time	3	4	2	1
Diagnostics and interactivity	2	3	3	1
Memory size to compile	3	2	1	OK with ROMs
Portability				
Portability to other machines by bootstrapping	3 OK with retargetting	2	1	2

[a]Evaluation dependent on actual source language and target machine.

in microcomputers, executes a source program (such as BASIC), and in conjunction with its input data, directly produces output results. This prewritten programming trend is called BASIC-in-ROM in personal computing applications for nonprofessional microcomputer users. Table 8-1 explicitly explains the distinctions in trade-offs, programming parameters, and portability between compilers, assemblers, and BASIC Interpreters. Portability of a program/software is the characteristic that makes a high-level language run on different computer systems.

The Abstract Machine Code enables translation to the intermediate Interpreter Language for the high-level PASCAL software. It was first proposed by University of California, San Diego—UCSD-PASCAL.

BASIC Versus other high-level languages. All the high-level languages (Fortran, COBOL, PASCAL, etc.) use a regular compiler for written software program to translate the high-level language into *compiled* assembly language of several steps in terms of the mnemonic instructions pertaining to the CPU or minicomputer or microprocessor. The high-level language is portable from computer to computer, because each computer has its own specifically designed, built-in translator to convert the high-level language statements into individual Assembly programming statements up to 10 or more directly (or in some cases via a macro/interpreter-style intermediate translator, to do the translation in two stages).

The BASIC high-level language used in microcomputers combines the features of a *compiler and interpreter* to generate an intermediate form of code in a permanent memory of the form of ROM. This expendiency reduces the number of assembly steps by at least three times. This code is more compact and will execute faster than the source code statements one types into the computer. (However, in the case of PASCAL, if it is to be portable or suitable for all microcomputers, each microcomputer must have a built-in, respective, interpretive Intermediate Code available so that the high-level language PASCAL could be first interpreted and then translated as two steps.) Each BASIC key command or Verb (for example, PRINT or INPUT) in a program is first replaced or compacted (or compiled) by a single character (or byte), and it may be termed a *token*. Arithmetic commands will have tokens, such as +, -, *, /, and some other commands may have special symbols such as (,), ", ', and #. These symbols stored in ROM in ASCII Code may sometimes vary from microcomputer to microcomputer. Therefore, BASIC software programs available for one microcomputer may not be identically suitable for use in another microcomputer. This of course involves the manufacturer's business interest. Thus, the user of a particular personal computer must rely on the particular manufacturer's own software programs in BASIC. After all, the microcomputer hardware is presently so inexpensive; a variety of software programs in quantity are the basis for the manufacturer's business in the microcomputer field. When a program is in ROM in this reduced Interpreter-style form, the BASIC commands must do the compaction (or compiling) procedure everytime the command LIST is typed in order to allow the program to be printed on the CRT terminal (or printer). Alternately, the command SAVE preserves the source code for the program on the chosen permanent, mass-memory tape or diskette. So, it must be remembered that the BASIC-in-ROM used in the case of the microcomputers is fundamentally an "Interpretive Compiler."

To minimize this problem of BASIC program interchange, a nominally standard ANSI BASIC has been adapted, but it is doubtful whether manufacturers of low-cost microcomputer systems will follow this standard. However, it may be noted that BASIC-11, introduced by the Heath Company's H-11 and DEC (Digital Equipment Corporation), is a small family of languages that run on several minicomputers or microcomputers with many types of peripheral devices. Hobbyists who adopt this multiuser MU-BASIC refer to programs of this standard as "DECUS library."

An "Interpreter" does not immediately generate the object machine (hexadecimal binary) program for each source statement to be saved for later execution; an Interpreter actually executes a part of the code each time the source statement is encountered. In a way, the Interpreter is an advantage over the conventional compiler because the executing program can be easily interrupted, changed, and then resumed. Thus, each source statement is translated anew each time it is to be executed, with only one drawback, namely, the slower speed of execution as compared to a conventional compiler.

The compilers produce two to three times more code than an Assembler to define source code thoroughly and execute programs relatively fast as compared to an Interpreter. In most applications, however, the combined size of an Interpreter and its source code (BASIC-in-ROM) will still be much smaller than the code produced by a compiler from the same language. The Interpreter's comparatively slower execution speed is not important in microcomputer applications, where the CPU is actually computing for only a small percentage of the time. There is plenty of time at the disposal of the Interpreter, while the program in general spends a large percentage of time in an idle loop waiting for effective action in slow steps. Hence, BASIC-in-ROM is an ideal solution for the programming of microcomputers—instead of the former approach of the time-consuming and difficult mnemonic Assembly language for each microprocessor encountered. Therefore, the training of microcomputer programmers in Assembly language is not really essential in light of the availability of fairly inexpensive 64-K bit ROM memory chips with relatively fast-access time for on-board plug-in ROMs or programmable EPROMs in high-level languages such as BASIC and PASCAL.

VLSI 256-K bit ROM and dynamic RAM memories will be available in the near future. As a result, more expensive and less reliable floppy-disk memory programs will be accessible in plug-in ROMs at comparatively lower cost. In addition, small, all-electronic, 256-K

1. FULL TRANSLATION (MISTRAL M, PLM, PLS, PLZ-SYS)

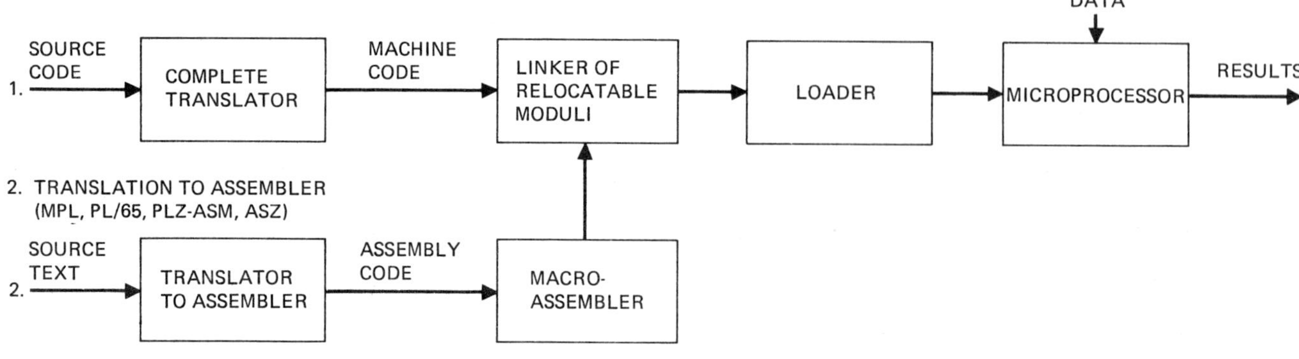

3. TRANSLATION TO ABSTRACT MACHINE CODE AND PARTIAL INTERPRETATION (PLZ-SYS, UCSD PASCAL, RTL/2)

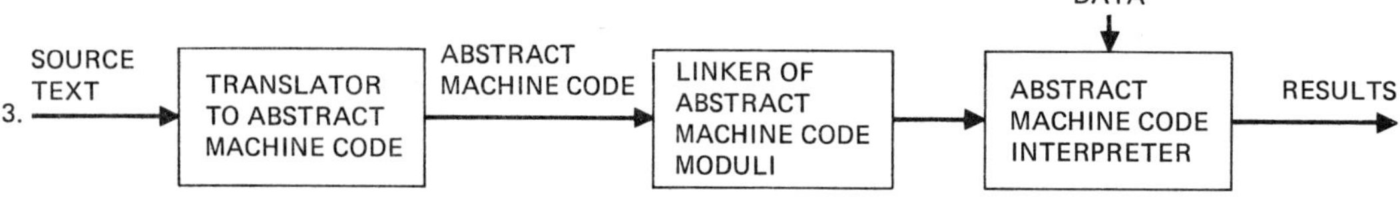

4. FULL INTERPRETATION (BASIC, APL)

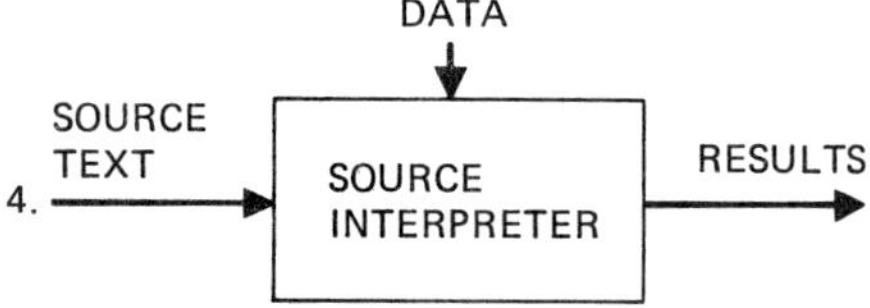

Fig. 8-3. BASIC-in-ROM Interpreter-Compiler versus Compilers and Assemblers. (© *1980 IEEE, COMPUTER, January*)

byte, prewritten program cards could easily displace diskettes for low-cost microcomputer systems (as an alternative to high-density slow-access nonvolatile bubble memory cards). Routines and subroutines could be readily packaged for plug-in in firmware systems to replace the present software on cassettes, cartridges, and floppy diskettes. As an example, 4-K byte ROM chips are presently used for such purposes as the storage of a complete font of 5 X 7 dot-matrix characters, code-conversion tables, and bit-patterns of video games on the screen. That is, prewritten ROM BASIC programs for video games desired can be directly plugged-in on easily accessible cards in the slots of the microcomputer, preferably following a standard S-100 BUS. Or, individual manufacturers will provide the games for use on their exclusive special BUS in the microcomputer unit.

Since optimized high-speed Assembly programs are not mandatory for 90% of applications, ROM-resident production firmware may be the norm in microcomputer system's software during the 1980s. Host minicomputers using the present 14-in. hard-disk systems for billion-byte mass-memory software libraries eventually might be partially replaced by resident high-density low-cost, compact, all-electronic magnetic bubble memory systems.

The evaluation of the BASIC-in-ROM Interpreter-Compiler used in the Ohio Scientific and other Personal Computing systems versus conventional Compilers is shown in a simplified block-diagram in Figure 8-3. A memory-map for the BASIC Interpreter and associated bootstrap and other I/O routines are presented in Table 8-2 for the 8-K bytes of BASIC-in-ROM. A hexadecimal-to-decimal and decimal-to-hexadecimal conversion table is shown in Table 8-3 for ready reference, since memory maps for microcomputer

TABLE 8-2. BASIC-in-ROM—Memory Map for BASIC Interpreter 8-K bytes in 64-K bit ROM (Example).

ROM-Address		No. bits	Routines and Interpreter
Hex	*Decimal*		
1000–1090	4096–4240	144	BASIC—Bootstrap Initialization
1091–1498	4241–5288	1,176	BASIC I/O Routines
1499–14C9	5289–5325	36	PACK Routine
14CA–D04E	5326–53326	48,000	BASIC Interpreter
D04F–EAOE	53327–56918	3,592	Debugging Routine and Loaders

systems are usually represented in hexadecimal code. BASIC Interpreters are commonly accommodated in 8-K bytes of ROM memory that could be easily mass-produced in a single 64-K bit VLSI chip. One version, the 3-L BASIC, developed at the Lawrence Livermore Laboratory, Livermore, California, and tailored for instrumentation, data-acquisition and process-control applications, requires 6-K bytes of ROM; this is obviously a fine way to go in microcomputer systems. Actually, compilers can also be accommodated in modular VLSI ROMs of the future in order to minimize application program effort. The ROM software also allows language conversion, since ROMs are ideal for code conversion and translation. The debugging and utility portion in the BASIC memory-map

TABLE 8-3. Hexadecimal-to-Decimal and Decimal-to-Hexadecimal Conversion.

Hexadecimal Columns											
Byte				Byte				Byte			
6		5		4		3		2		1	
HEX	DEC	HEX	DEC	HEX	DEC	HEX	DEC	HEX	DEC	HEX	DEC
0	0	0	0	0	0	0	0	0	0	0	0
1	1048576	1	65536	1	4096	1	256	1	16	1	1
2	2097152	2	131072	2	8192	2	512	2	32	2	2
3	3145728	3	196608	3	12288	3	768	3	48	3	3
4	4194304	4	262144	4	16384	4	1024	4	64	4	4
5	5242880	5	327680	5	20480	5	1280	5	80	5	5
6	6291456	6	393216	6	24576	6	1536	6	96	6	6
7	7340032	7	458752	7	28672	7	1792	7	112	7	7
8	8388608	8	524288	8	32768	8	2048	8	128	8	8
9	9437184	9	589824	9	36864	9	2304	9	144	9	9
A	10485760	A	655360	A	40960	A	2560	A	160	A	10
B	11534336	B	720896	B	45056	B	2816	B	176	B	11
C	12582912	C	786432	C	49152	C	3072	C	192	C	12
D	13631488	D	851968	D	53248	D	3328	D	208	D	13
E	14680064	E	917504	E	54344	E	3584	E	224	E	14
F	15728640	F	983040	F	61440	F	3840	F	240	F	15
0123		4567		0123		4567		0123		4567	

HEX:DEC—Locate each HEX digit in its corresponding column position, and note the decimal equivalents. Add these to get DEC value.

DEC:HEX—Locate the largest DEC value above that will fit into the DEC number to be converted.
Note its HEX equivalent and HEX column position.
Find the DEC remainder. Repeat the process on this and subsequent remainders.

(Courtesy of Motorola Semiconductor products Inc.)

shown in Table 8-2 allows the programmer/engineer to examine internal registers and memory locations and modify their contents if necessary.

Tiny BASIC is a limited version of the standard BASIC high-level language, specially tuned for video games and simple educational programs. As a nominal extension of this BASIC, NIBL (National Industrial BASIC Language) is another interesting version of BASIC oriented to industrial control applications. NIBL can be now easily implemented by a single-chip 32-K bit ROM, which furnishes approximately 120 average BASIC steps of program for a microcomputer used in industrial process applications.

8-15. HIGH-LEVEL LANGUAGE—APL

As an alternative to BASIC, or as an advanced computational facility, the IBM-5100 "portable" computer system provides predeveloped APL software via its ROS/RAM internal memory system and external tape cartridges. The APL has a close similarity to the notation of vector algebra, but it is more simple and is further extended in applicability. APL contains a rich set of conveniently usable well-defined "primitives"—built-in functions that make it applicable over a wide area of arithmetic, trigonometric, and hyperbolic functions (and their inverses); matrix products and inverses, look-up lists or tables; set of relations; and logic.

APL (a programming language, IBM). The APL, an interactive high-level language used for problem-solving, enables a concise expression of complex mathematical statements. It was developed by R. V. Iverson of IBM especially for DC/AC circuit analysis and computer-aided design (CAD).

1. It contains mathematical operators that allow the systems analyst to perform array processing functions, trigonometric and hyperbolic functions, and common arithmetic, logical, and relational operations.
2. It treats scalars, vectors, and matrix arrays with equal facility and lets one store data (or the results of computation) using a variable name, so that the current value is automatically subsituted.
3. It permits previously defined programs to be used as a function and to perform operations on arrays of up to 63 dimensions.

The APL software is available on tape cartridges for various applications in statistics and mathematics—approximations to functions, advanced mathematical functions including calculus and linear equations, and matrix analysis. The main-memory storage in the form of fast-access 2-K bit NMOS RAMs is available in increments of 16-K bytes up to 64-K bytes (16,384 to 65,536 memory cells of words). Fourteen program command-keys for the BASIC and APL software permit direct inputting of the system-commands via the CRT keyboard in the case of the IBM-5100.

The set of primitive scalar functions in monadic and dyadic forms includes plus, negative, signum [xB ⟶ (B > O) - $\overline{\text{B} < \text{O}}$], reciprocal, ceiling Γ, floor L, exponential, natural logarithm ⊕, magnitude (|), factorial (!), roll (?), pi-times (o), not (~), dyadic functions (all trigonometric functions), and ∧, or ∨, nand ⍲, Nor ⍱, less <, not greater ⩽, equal =, not less ⩾, greater >, and not equal ≠. The set of primitive mixed functions includes size (ρ A), reshape (V ρ A), ravel (, A ⟷ ⍳, or first A integers), catenate (V, V ⟷ VV), index (V [A]), index generator (⍳ S), index of (V ⍳ A), take (V ↑ A), drop (V ↓ A), grade-up (⍋A), grade-down (⍒A), compress (V/A), expand (V\A), reverse (⌽A), rotate (A ⌽ A), transpose (V ⍉A, ⍉A), membership (A ∈ A), decode (V ⊥ V), encode (V ⊤ S), and deal (S?A, random deal of S elements from first A integers). Restrictions on argument ranks are indicated by S for scalar, V for vector, M for matrix and A for Any.

8-16. COBOL (COMMON BUSINESS-ORIENTED LANGUAGE)

Since typical business-oriented computation requires more data manipulation as input and output than extensive computation (as required in scientific applications), the high-level language COBOL is the preferred programming approach in business applications. The format of the I/O data on files, either on cards or tape, is comprehensively edited in COBOL:

1. For exchange of programs on different computers
2. For facilitating minor alterations in programs
3. For minimizing person-hours to write and debug new programs.

The COBOL program is composed of four "decisions":

1. "Identification," the name of the programmer, title, date.
2. "Environment," basic data on the machine to assign "special names" to various units of equipment and switches.
3. "Data," "data-names," and "condition-names" to define I/O files used in the program as "working storage" and "constant" sections
4. "Procedure," to describe the operation as "procedure-names," and the preceding data-names and condition-names.

The 25-line, 80-column format or coding sheet is written in sequences of tens (010, 020 . . .) to make the punching of the card deck as simple as possible. For example, 007230 means page 7, line 23. The following flow chart symbols are used: >, <, ≠, I/O card, tape I/O, printed output, processing block, decision block, → ① connectors, O start, and halt.

8-17. PL/1 (PROGRAMMING LANGUAGE/ONE), "ALGOL," AND "PolyFORTH"

PL/1, a user's high-level source program originated by IBM for large-scale computer users, aims at minimizing clerical work involved in writing an assembler program. The rigidly "coded" program with appropriate "syntax" of 60 (or 48) characters, divided into three goups, is keypunched and entered into the computer as data input for a standard "library program" preloaded in the computer as "PL/1 compiler." (In IBM system 360 operating system 0/5-F level, and in tape/disk operating system T/DOS, PL/1 compilers are used.) The cards use columns 2–72 only; 73–80 are reserved for identifying the program. The computer outputs a listing of the program input and an equivalent program in machine language for subsequent debug or computation.

ALGOL 60. ALGOL 60 is a high-level language that was originated at Princeton University on a Control Data Corp. 1604 computer for translation to the Assembly-language of this machine; it is used more commonly in Europe. The language aims at separating the functions of "defining the language" and "translating to another." The sytem operates in three phases. The first enables the translator's "diagraming program" to output syntax definitions pertinent to the particular ALGOL program, e.g., "defining identifiers." The second phase enables DIAGRAM to output Assembly language program. The third phase is the actual assembly of the code. This compiler of CDC-1604 outputs about 300 assembly-language instructions per sec.

PolyFORTH is one of the newest software languages that could be programmed at both the assembler and the high-level language levels. It has been developed by FORTH INC., Hermosa Beach, California, for use on both mini- and microcomputers. The software is available in a minimum of 8-K bytes on a disk-based operating system, assembler, compiler, interpreters, editor, virtual memory, and device drivers. In personal computers, a PROM could be used for program development, with a floppy-disk as a peripheral.

The software available is suitable for on-line multiprogramming capability like the other popular software languages. The sponsor claims reduced program development time, less number of program steps, and transportability for transferring application programs between different types of computer systems.

The language is oriented toward stack architecture, postfix notation, dictionary-wise high-level, low-level, and data structures, and interactive programming. Constants, variables, arrays, separate text interpreter, and address interpreters are included. Design of logical control structures is based on DO . . . LOOPs, BEGIN . . . END, IF . . . ELSE . . . THEN.

8-18. PASCAL

First implemented in 1970 by Niklaus Wirth of Zurich, PASCAL is a modern, established high-level language that relieves the tedius recordkeeping requirements of time-consuming (and hence expensive) assembly languages. It is organized on a systematic basis as a structured programming technique with top-down modular design and recursive routines. A structured programming technique for data eliminates the former problems due to indiscriminate use of transfers of control in terms of arrays or files, and provides systematic guidelines to enable easier programming and efficient use of high-speed memory. (This language, preferred presently for microcomputers, is named after Blaise Pascal, the famous French mathematician.)

PASCAL has the following advantages:

1. A complex powerful problem can be treated in simpler manageable sections with less-expensive hardware.
2. It has a built-in error-checking process for syntax testing and type- and range-checking to lower debugging time and costs.

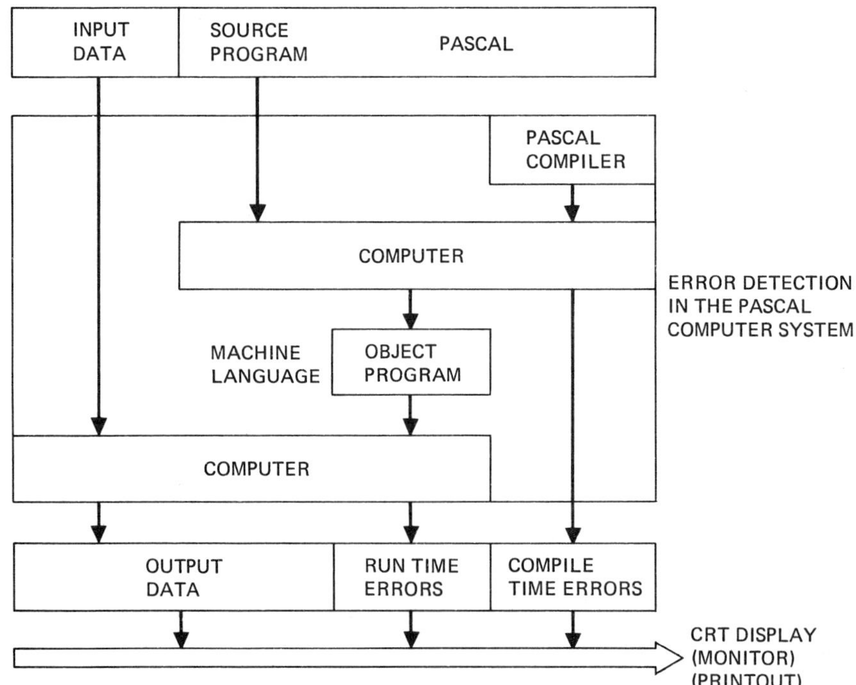

ERROR DETECTION IN THE PASCAL COMPUTER SYSTEM

3. It minimizes maintenance costs by enabling a second programmer to modify the program to new specifications.
4. The compiled PASCAL programs take less storage space than BASIC.
5. Commands and data types can be extended to meet individual needs (unlike FORTRAN/BASIC/COBOL).

Thus, a sophisticated language is readily available for low-cost microcomputer systems. (BASIC programmers can learn PASCAL programming with some practice.) Professional UCSD (University of California, San Diego) PASCAL is standardized and complete for operating systems, utilities, and extensions for system development. The language is easily "portable"; that is, programs written in UCSD PASCAL can run directly on most real-time microcomputer systems using one floppy-disk, 48-K bytes of RAM, and 16-K bytes of "Interpreter" (auto-start) ROM that is used for BASIC. Where the facility of horizontal scrolling is available, the above system package is suitable for either 80- or 40-character CRT microcomputer systems.

The correct output data are displayed provided there are no errors during compiling and execution.

PASCAL programs are written by using letters, digits, and characters used in typewriters and computer peripherals. Synonyms are defined if such characters are not available. In some cases, PASCAL may use only available upper-case letters.

Reserved words are used as indivisible specifically defined symbols in PASCAL.

AND	ARRAY	BEGIN	CASE	CONST
DIV	DO	DOWNTO	ELSE	END
FILE	FOR	FUNCTION	GOTO	IF
IN	LABEL	MOD	NIL	NOT
OF	OR	PACKED	PROCEDURE	PROGRAM
RECORD	REPEAT	SET	THEN	TO
TYPE	UNTIL	VAR	WHILE	WITH

Identifiers are names chosen by the programmer to denote constants, types, variables, procedures, and functions. An Identifier consists of a letter followed by any combination of letters and digits. The compiler will regard two identifiers as distinct if they differ in their first eight characters. There are some *standard identifiers* the compiler can recognize without a definition:

Constants			
false	time	maxit	
Types			
integer	boolean	real	char
text			
Files			
input	output		
Functions			
abs	arctan	chr	cos
eof	eoln	exp	ln
odd	ord	pred	round
sin	sqr	sqrt	succ
trunc			

Procedures

get	new	pack	page
put	read	readin	reset
rewrite	unpack	write	writeln

Special or Metalanguage Symbols

:=	becomes	,	separates items in a list
;	separates statements	'	delimits character and string literals
..	subrange specifier	↑	file and pointer variable indicator
.	end of definition	¦	alternatively
=	shall be defined to be	{x}	0 or more repetitions of x
{ }	start and end of comment	[x]	0 or 1 instance of x

(x¦y¦ . . . ¦z) grouping: any one of x,y, . . .z or nested expression
"xyz" the terminal symbol xyz
lower-case-name a non-terminal symbol

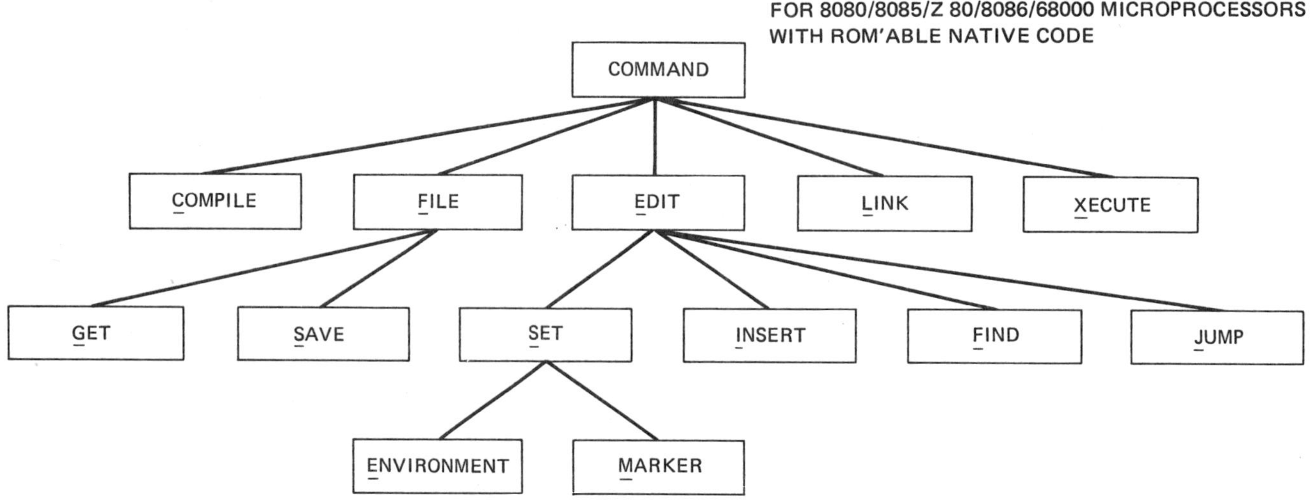

Example of an interactive program in PASCAL (*Courtesy of Addison-Wesley Publishing Co., "Programming in PASCAL"*)

```
PROGRAM interact (ttyin, ttyout, output);
  TYPE
    ttyfile = SEGMENTED FILE OF Char
  VAR
    ttyin, ttyout:ttyfile;
  PROCEDURE getchar (VAR ch:char);
    BEGIN
      IF NOT eof (ttyin)
        THEN
          IF eos (ttyin)
            THEN
              BEGIN
                putseg (ttyout);
                getseg (ttyin);
```

```
                ch:= ' ';
              END
            ELSE read (ch)
    END;
  BEGIN
    . . .
  END.
```

Methods used for describing the syntax of PASCAL. In English, for given words and symbols, the syntax allows the clarification of the proper definition of a sentence or phrase. In PASCAL, syntax is defined as follows:
Syntax: The pattern of formation of sentences and phrases from *words*, such as VAR, BEGIN, END, etc. The rules for constructing identifiers are summarized in syntax charts.
Syntax Chart: A graphical chart for quick reference. Follow the lines to see how to make up any given entity. For named entities, use square boxes; for terminal symbols, use rounded boxes. (Examples: unsigned integer and unsigned number.)

Example of a BLOCK structure is shown in Fig. 8-4.

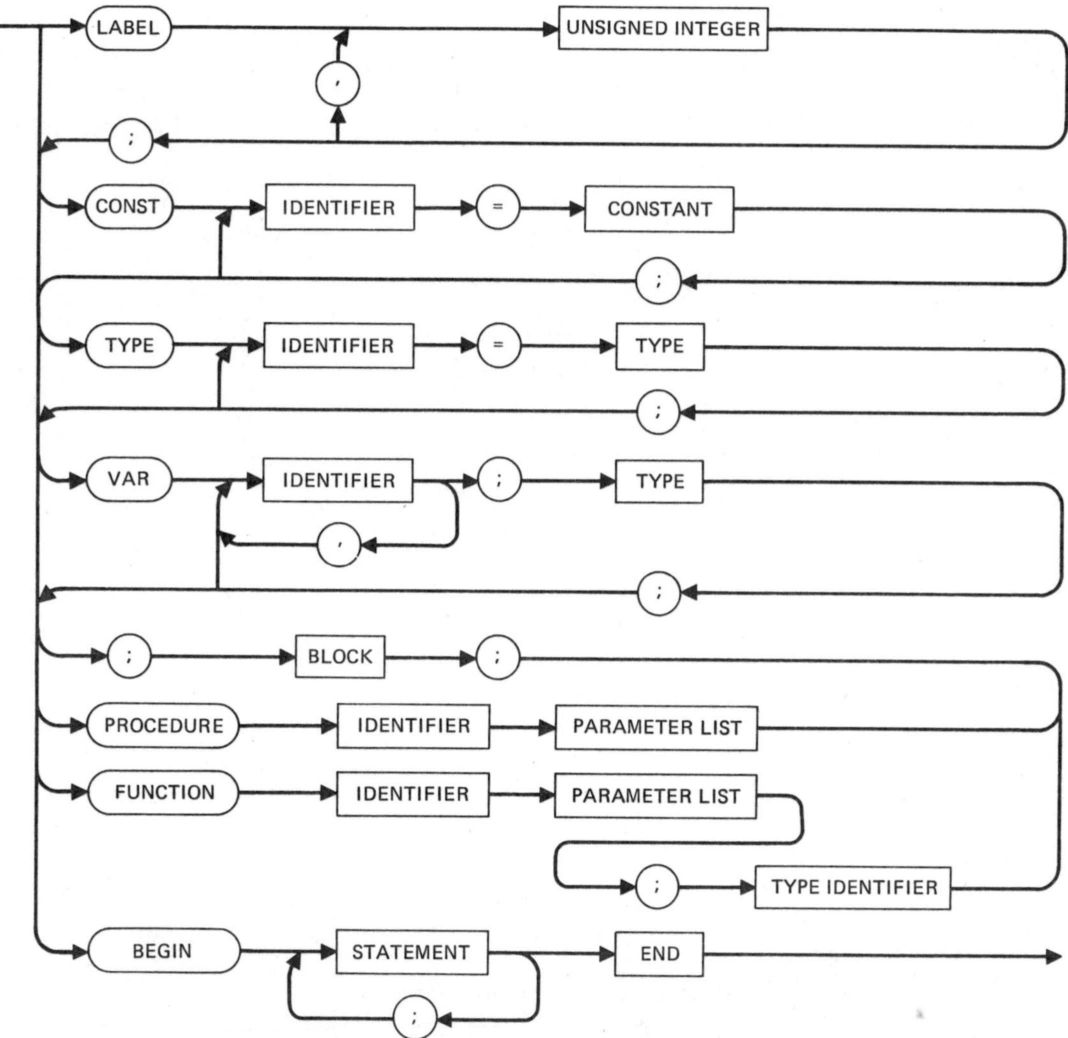

Fig. 8-4. Block structure–syntax chart.

Data Types in PASCAL:

1. *Scalar:*		2. *Structured:*	3. *Pointer:*
1.1. Standard	1.2. Extensions	2.1. Array	3.1. Lists
Integer	Subrange	2.2. Record	3.2. Trees
Real	User-defined	2.3. Set	3.3. Graphs
Boolean		2.4. File	
Character			

In brief, a PASCAL program has the form of a *procedure* declaration, except for the heading, which follows the order: (1) the symbol program, (2) a program name-identifier, and (3) program parameter identifiers. The parameters signify external *file variables* with a statement of associated system I/O resources, and they must be declared in the main program. The monolithic programs are *block-structured* as shown in the procedure diagram. The procedure declarations may be *nested to any depth*, and unnamed blocks are not admissible. Structured data types defined may include indexed *arrays*, *records* with variable and field *identifiers*, sets of integers (or *bit strings*) or a list of identifiers, and dynamic files of I/O. As a special requirement, declaration of a *pointer* yields a data type that is associated with some other variable, such as a record. Data structures such as *lists*, *trees*, and *graphs* can be defined by linking their elements together with pointers.

Microprocessor-PASCAL from Texas Instruments. The Texas Instruments FS990 floppy-diskette–based development system with 56-K bytes of RAM and KB-CRT display is the minimum hardware necessary to develop software programs in PASCAL. These

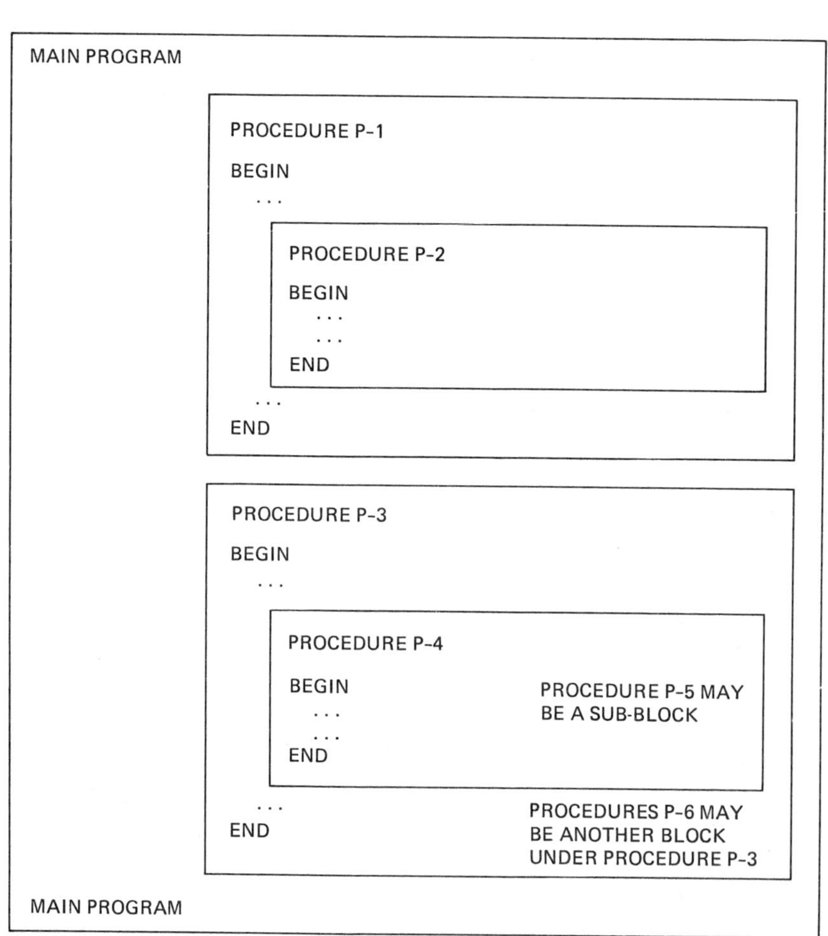

programs execute on Texas Instruments 9900 microprocessor-based products and 990 minicomputer-based systems. Texas Instruments PASCAL is a virtual superset of the proposed international PASCAL standard. Concurrent multitask execution, expanded I/O capability, and specific library utilities are all provided for in a cost-effective way on ROM-resident target system operation for real-time production environment. For multiuser requirements, Diablo disk DS 990 multiuser hard-disk–based minicomputer with 64-K bytes of RAM will suffice. The PASCAL consists of six sections:

1. Source Editor to generate/edit programs and check program syntax
2. Compiler to compile source programs into intermediate code which can be executed directly or converted into 9900 machine code via mnemonic instructions in Hex-Code
3. Host debugger via AMPL™ with 15 options for tracing variables and modifying data
4. Configurator to enable target system to retain only the parts of the run-time support necessary for program execution
5. Native code generator to convert PASCAL *intermediate code* into the machine code for the 9900-family of microcomputer hardware
6. Interpretive or Native code run-time support for two methods of execution to provide speed/memory trade-off

Disk-based or 1600 bpi magnetic-tape–based microprocessor PASCAL costs under $2.8 K. The software does have built-in features of program modification, error-checking, position-independent code, multitask concurrency and reentry, interpretive execution for minimal memory requirements, direct bit and byte access, Read/Write I/O statements, and assembly language interface for time-critical subroutines.

The concept of the Texas Instruments approach to PASCAL is shown in the following diagram:

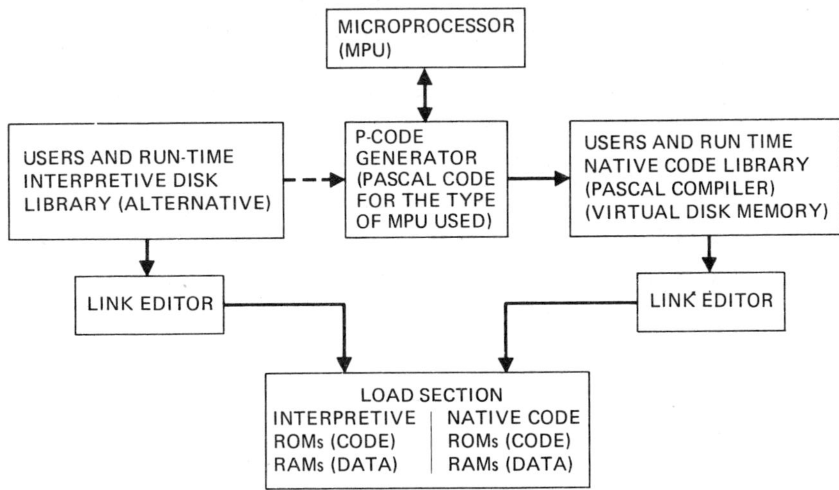

Concept of portable PASCAL code (Texas Instruments approach)

ADA is a standardized version of PASCAL, developed as a portable high-level language for the various types of general-purpose digital computers used by the United States government. ADA honors Charles Babbage and the historical mechanical computing machine he developed in the nineteenth century; Babbage engaged Lord Byron's daughter Ada Byron as a pioneering programmer of his machine.

PASCAL Software Programs. The following example illustrates how software firms use their ingenuity in making high-level language programs such as PASCAL portable (common usage) for several types of popular microprocessors.*

A sophisticated **compiler** is developed for Intel's 8-bit 8080/8085 and 16-bit 8086/8088/8087 Math-chip/8089 I/O processor by using portable PASCAL high-level language and Intel's assembly language. The PASCAL software can also be run on a number of host computing systems such as Computer Data Control's very high-speed Cyber computer, Digital Equipment's PDP-11/Unix, Intel's MDS/ISIS-II, and personal computer systems using the popular CP/M-8080 programs. The compiler can switch the host machines, since it follows machine-independent coding standards and top-down modular program design.

The typical compiler described is organized into six adaptable phases for operation in a single-pass, multiple-pass, or parallel pipeline approach. The ability to switch the Intel's microprocessors is accomplished by selecting algorithms that are independent of target microprocessors for several tasks of the compiler's nucleus. These tasks are selected for a particular microprocessor by providing minimal information needed for identifying each processor. This approach of a fixed compiler algorithm produces minimum number of errors at higher compiling speed. The complete $2500 PASCAL package includes the compiler and protected diskettes; it consists of a binder that allows iterative linking, a loader program that supports symbolic debugging, an assembler, and run-time library modules. The specific portable package described is written in a subset of the standard PASCAL. Binder linking is feasible because the module's I/O is identically encoded.

8-19. FORTRAN

FORTRAN (Formula Translation) is developed for numerical methods, statistics, engineering applications, matrix and Boolean algebra, Monte Carlo techniques, and so forth. FORTRAN programming has several versions such as Data General, DEC 4-K, DEC 8-K, H.P. 4-K, H.P. 8-K, and General Automation FORTRAN for synchronous transmission of binary coded decimal (BCD) data in telecommunications. The form of FORTRAN that is used for minicomputers will be directly adapted for microcomputer system software by each manufacturer. The software facilities involved in two of the aforementioned versions are described below.

Data General (NOVA). The larger versions of the FORTRAN are as powerful as the FORTRAN IV used on IBM-360 machines. The simpler versions have:

1. Double-precision complex variables
2. Array-index lower-bounds other than one
3. Formatted I/O
4. Unformatted I/O
5. 128 array-dimensions
6. Text-variables. If 12-K byte CORE or RAM main memory is used, features like data initialization, external statements, mixed-mode arithmetic, and equivalence statements appear in the program.

A two-pass compilation procedure is used to produce a binary tape from FORTRAN source statements; the tape contents are relocatable in different memory locations. The user's manual describes language syntax, operating and compilation procedures, and diagnostic messages.

*Courtesy of Language Resources Inc., Sunnyvale, California.

DEC 8-K Word FORTRAN. The language is similar to the standard ASA FORTRAN II, providing single-precision arithmetic only (and no mixed-mode arithmetic) and two array-dimensions. A two-pass compilation procedure is used to produce a relocatable binary-coded tape from the FORTRAN source statements. Maximum program size is from 200 to 300 lines of coding (excluding comments), depending on the size of the storage arrays and the number of the library-routines used. The software used for the compilation, loading, and running of the FORTRAN programs include an 8-K word compiler, plus assembler, linking loader, and a two-part FORTRAN library. This software runs on a DEC PDP-8/81 minicomputer with 8-K words of storage, using the floppy-disk facilities for the compilation, loading, and handling of the programs. DEC has adapted this software for use with its PDP-11/03 microcomputer system. Binary-coded tape copies (DEC minireels), available at $30 per set for the minicomputers, will be adapted for the new DEC microcomputer systems.

FORTRAN IV and Structured FORTRAN 77* The widely used unstructured FORTRAN IV program written by the programmer, and dispatched to the computer as a punched deck of IBM 80-column Hollerith cards, consists of the following sequence:

1. Identification (ID) card
2. FORTRAN deck (FORTRAN program)
3. Data deck (data that are read as input to the computer)
4. End-of-file (EOF) card (end of package)

These four sets of cards may be separated by one or more control cards. Each statement in a program must be punched on a separate card. The computer follows a *procedure* to solve a problem in a sequence of steps called an *algorithm* (usually in the configuration of a flowchart). The algorithm is written as statements, each statement extending to just one line.

The first few lines in a FORTRAN program begin with C, which stands for *comment*. These lines identify and explain program to others. C's are part of the program but not statements as commands to the computer.

A FORTRAN *real variable* is indicated by an initial letter followed by any desired letter or digit up to 6 characters together. A *variable* signifies a memory element. If a memory location is used to store *integer constants*, it is called an integer variable. *Constants* are quantities appearing as numbers without names, but representing themselves as *real constants* and integer constants. The real or integer variables may be different in different systems. *Integers* are numbers used for counting, and *reals* are numbers used for measurement. An integer constant is also called a *fixed-point* constant; it is a signed or unsigned whole number without a decimal point or any punctuation mark. Unsigned numbers are taken for granted as positive. The maximum length of any integer usually does not exceed 9 digits (of course, it depends on the computer). A *real constant* is called a *floating-point* constant in FORTRAN, and it is written in decimal form or exponential form. The decimal point distinguishes the real constant from the integer constant; the real constant may be a signed or unsigned finite sequence of digits, but a decimal point must appear. The number of digits retained by the computer after computation depends on the word-length of the computer. (REAL INT denotes a real variable.) Here is a short program as an example of FORTRAN (blanks within a FORTRAN statement are ignored):

*For further information, refer to *Programming with Fortran* by Seymour Lipscutz and Arthur Poe (New York: McGraw-Hill Book Company, 1978).

```
     READ (5, 50) HOURS, RATE
 50  FORMAT (F4.1)
     PAY = HOURS * RATE
     WRITE (6, 100) HOURS, RATE, PAY
100  FORMAT (IX, F5.1)
     STOP
     END
```

The first statement begins with the word READ for reading data. The first digit in parentheses specifies an integer such as 5, which signifies a card reader in the computer system used; 50 stands for the program count of next statement to enable the program counter in the CPU move to the next statement. Next, the FORMAT statement describes how the data values are arranged on the card in terms of the columns. Field descripters enclosed in parentheses, such as (F4.1), signify a four-column field having one digit after the assumed decimal point so that, if the datum punched is 0312, it actually stands for 031.2 dollars per hour (since the READ data in the first statement states RATE. Any value that is given a name like HOURS or RATE is a variable.

An *assignment* statement is a command to assign a value to a variable. Formulas can be written on the right-hand side of an assignment statement as an implication of FORTRAN for formula statement.

Next, in the WRITE statement, 6 stands for a printer and 100 points to the statement in sequence for the program counter for following the steps of the algorithm. In the next statement, 100 for FORMAT, IX signifies the carriage control specification of the printer, and F5.1 indicates the result printed after the computation involved. The number 5 signifies the number of printing positions on the printer, and 1 represents the number of digits after the decimal point for the data punched on the card. STOP is a command to the CPU to stop processing, and END implies that there are no further statements in the program.

Arithmetic expressions. Parentheses-free expressions are sequenced as follows. Exponentiation (**), multiplication (*), division (/), addition (+), and subtraction (-). FORTRAN does not allow two arithmetic expressions to follow one another; as an example, 4* -3 must be written as 4*(-3). Parentheses have precedence over all arithmetic operations.

Library of mathematical functions (subroutines). SQRT(X), ABS(X), EXP(X), SIN(X), COS(X), ALOGIO(X), and ALOG(X) for natural logarithm.
Convert integer I into real: FLOAT(I).
Truncate real X into integer: IFIX(X).

Unconditional transfer.

```
20 GO TO 50
```

50 is the statement number, and the computer is commanded to proceed to statement 50 if the sequential statement numbers are 20, 30, 40, 50.

Conditional transfer. The flowchart indicates a decision block.

```
50 IF AMT ⩽ 1000 THEN RATE = 0.06
                 ELSE RATE = 0.05
```

The figure 1000 is the amount of loan; repeat the process, if yes. STOP is the next statement; terminate the process otherwise. An example of a short program involving a logical expression (logexp) is:

```
    REAL INT . . . . . . (INT = Interest)
    READ (5, 20) AMT
20  FORMAT (F15.2)
```

Relational expressions:
.LT. for less than
.LE. for less than or equalto

```
      IF(AMT.LE.1000) GO TO 100        .EQ. for equalto
      RATE = 0.05                      .NE. for not equalto
      GO TO 200                        .GT. for greater than
100   RATE = 0.06                      .GE. for greater than or equalto
. . . . . . .
200   STOP
```

Unstructured FORTRAN with DO loop. DO statement is a powerful construct of FORTRAN. Here is a macrocommand:

```
DO . . . WHILE I ≤ I ≤ N      C (I = counter)
DO (the steps of the process are repeated)
WHILE I ≤ I ≤ N     C (I is set to 1; with increments of 1, the cycling is stopped when
                       I exceeds N.)
```

A DO statement may refer to a CONTINUE statement at some step in the program. But CONTINUE merely acts as the end of the range of DO.

Other characteristic features of FORTRAN include arrays, subscribed variables, functions and subroutines, searching, sorting, merging, numerical calculations, vectors/matrices, and logical expressions such as:

```
lexp 1. AND. lexp2
lexp.OR. lexp2
    .NOT. lex1
```

Special INPUT/OUTPUT features include: G-FIELD for integer, real, logical or complex data. Data statement and Scale factor sP, and miscellaneous features such as IMPLICIT statement, DOUBLE PRECISION, COMPLEX variables, COMMON and EQUIVALENCE statements, and BLOCK DATA.

Structured FORTRAN. *FORTRAN IV constructs*, especially the GO TO statement, is at times a source of confusion and error; structured IF, WHILE, FOR, and DO loop structure with iteration count designated by KOUNT, etc., in a new version of structured FORTRAN 77, makes this hitherto popular high-level language more easily understood for modification of programs.

Some of these new program steps take the following form:

```
1. IF(logexp) THEN
   . . . (IF- Block)
   ENDIF
2. IF(.NOT.logexp) GO TO 10 (Program step number 10)
   . . . . (Group T statement)
   10 . . .
3. WHILE (logexp) DO
   . . . (Body of the loop)
   ENDWHILE
4. DO n VAR = INV, ENDV, INCR     (loop initial and end or test value parameters)
   . . . (Body of DO loop)     (n = program step; VAR = loop control variable, name
   CONTINUE (Step n)                               of an integer or a real value)
```

8-20. ROUTINE SOFTWARE NEEDS

The system manufacturer delivers an initial hardware with a free-standing Operating System, so named because it does not use slower bulk-storage devices such as tape and disk during real-time operation. The routine software consists of an Executive program, which controls:

1. Loaders, including a link-editor (linkage editor)
2. Text editor
3. Assembler
4. Debug monitor
5. I/O subsystem control software, for driving the peripheral devices via the appropriate interfaces
6. Utilities library of mathematical subroutines
7. High-level language translator such as a FORTRAN/APL/BASIC-compiler.

Assembly language programs use the I/O subsystem for all peripheral device communication and the utilities library for all arithmetic operations.

Once the Executive program is loaded into the memory via the memory data and address registers, a peripheral such as the TTY sends commands to the Executive Editor, and the Debug program initiates the execution of all subsequent system operations. See section 8-8, Debugging a Program.

Additional software in the mass-storage system is transferred to the compiler for source-to-object language translation, for occasional secondary applications that run when the microprocessor is otherwise idle during the data-processing intervals.

8-21. EXECUTIVE PROGRAM

The Executive program brings together the various items of the software mentioned previously to make an **operating system** (O/S), which may include (1) a Disk-Operating System and (2) a Real-Time Operating System. **With a disk assembler/compiler O/S,** at the command of, for example, a TTY, the Executive will load all the other program modules of the O/S onto the bulk-storage unit and recall them when necessary, leaving the rest of the RAM main-memory free for user program. The user programs can be automatically transferred to the disk if they exceed the capacity of the main internal microcomputer memory. Also, too many infrequent user programs and data clutter up the disk storage.

8-22. REAL-TIME OPERATING SYSTEM

As an addition to the above Disk O/S, the Real-time O/S:

1. Allows the execution of the programs to be scheduled by time of day.
2. Allows the programs to "queue up" for execution, waiting for the CPU to finish the more important jobs such as monitoring experiments and so on.
3. Every program is assigned a priority in an O/S; for example, emergency control programs (0), monitor experimental run (1), reduction of the data in between the runs and calculation of the settings for the next run (2), and compilation of some of the FORTRAN source programs and running these programs (3).

The CPU keeps track of time by way of a built-in crystal-controlled **"real-time" clock (RTC), which generates interrupts at specified times.** The RTC-interrupts, one by one, return control to the Executive, and the Executive checks if a higher-priority program needs immediate attention. Thus, a Real-time O/S provides maximum utilization of a computer system. With a memory cycle-time of 2 μs, a microcomputer can execute half-a-million instructions/sec; however, it waits most of the time for the I/O devices transmit or receive data at rates of 1,000 characters/sec. A TTY, for example, outputs 10 char. per sec, and an IBM Communications Interface Adapter operates at 800-bits (bauds)/sec line-rate using an EIA RS-232C standard modem Interface.

As a typical example, in an Operating System, a computer, running intermittently, may take:

1. About 1 min at the start to monitor the instruments, during the early phase of an experiment at 1% of the busy-time.
2. Collect data during the next minute at 40% of the busy-time.
3. Process collected data during the next 2 min at 25% of the busy-time.
4. Set the starting conditions for the next run during the fifth minute at 10% of the busy-time.

8-23. INTERFACE ADAPTOR

A terminal digital controller (e.g., a microprocessor with its I/O Interface) using a TTY will be interconnected to a central large-scale computer system via a data-communication line or a telephone line by means of an Interface Adapter, which is otherwise called a **front-end processor, data set, or modem**; it is a terminal for conditioning the outgoing data and for accepting and recording the incoming data. The **modem** accomplishes its mod/demod functions by converting an input dc signal into an ac format and vice versa, mostly using **PSK modulation** (phase shift keying). The modem performs, in addition, automatic equalization for the line-losses in preferably a two-way full-duplex operation and provides the automatic level-limiting facility. The PSK Encoder/Decoder may have a data-rate capability from 75 to 9,600 baud/sec, and several channels may be multiplexed on high-speed transmission lines at 40-K bits/sec. The low-speed data sets are generally asynchronous and compatible with one another. However, the high-speed modems above 32-K bits per second are intended for synchronous operation, phase-locked to the multiple of a crystal-controlled reference frequency.

The **high-speed synchronous units will phase-lock** transmitting and receiving modems in a matter of hundreds or tens of milliseconds. The cost of a modem in general is about $1/baud. The baud represents a basic rate of transmission in pulses/sec, and the baud-rate is theoretically limited to twice the bandwidth in Hz. In low-speed systems, baud and bit rates are equivalent. Low baud-rate asynchronous modems can operate with about 20% distortion, while the high-speed synchronous modem is restricted to 7% distortion to enable minimal error-rate at the desired SNR. **Tymshare,** which effectively enables many users to use a central large-scale computer via terminal controllers such as TTY or CRT keyboard, requires the use of the Interface Adapter at each terminal. The computer Operating System actually services each user in sequence at its high data-speed, but the users operate as if they are served individually in one of the commonly used high-level languages such as FORTRAN or BASIC in serial 8-bit ASCII or IBM/EBCDIC code of characters.

8-24. PERIPHERAL INTERFACE OF A MICROCOMPUTER SYSTEM

Peripheral selection starts with the decoding of the I/O instruction in the digital computer.

Function selection (Example: writing and reading data, rewinding tape, back-spacing in a tape cassette or floppy disk.) Sensing the status of the conditions and service routines in the peripheral devices and their Interfaces is indicated by the error-checking schemes used in the peripheral with mostly an even or odd parity-bit (and occasionally additional correcting bits). The microcomputer addresses a peripheral device to interrogate via the control lines and takes the appropriate action on the sensed condition. A two-way data-transfer path between the high-speed computer and the peripheral must be established without any loss of data due to the inevitable slow data-handling rate of the peripheral.

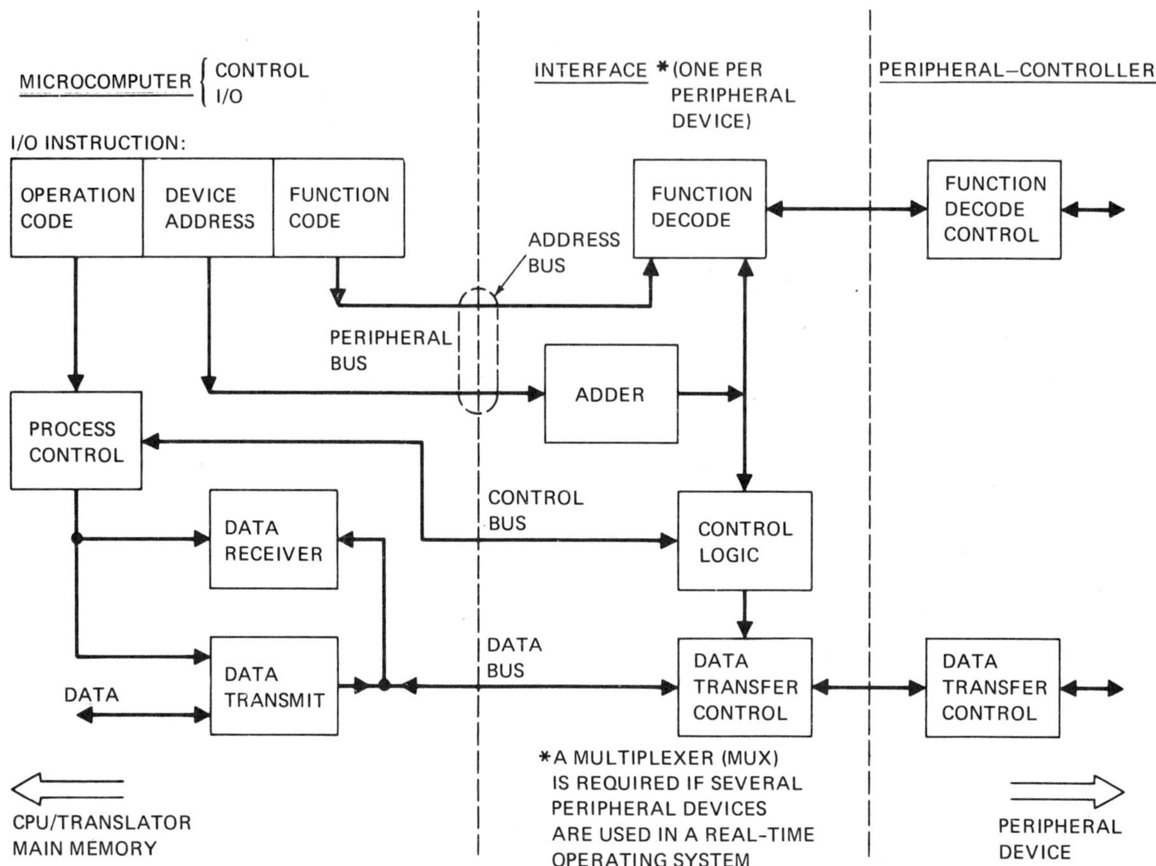

8-25. ADDRESSING MODES

The microprocessor has the inherent ability to access a large amount of memory due to its high-speed cycle-time of the order of 1 or 2 μs. A 16-bit program counter can address 64-K memory locations ($2^{16} = 65,536$). However, a regular 16-bit instruction word may actually specify the instruction in 8-bits and the memory-address in 8-bits to practically enable the addressing of only 256 locations ($2^8 = 256$). A few bits in the instruction are required for the opcode. To overcome this restriction, several addressing modes are used. Thus, the programming versatility increases with the number of modes available.

8-25.1. Direct Addressing. The memory reference address is obtained directly from the address bits of the **memory reference instruction.**

Simple memory addressing can use the limited addressing range of the 8 bits (256 locations) for only groups of subroutines or limited program sections. For an extended addressing range, the processor can use two instruction words of 16-bits each, one 64-K word memory for instruction, and another 64-K word memory for the large main-memory, to give the memory-address of data.

Paging. Memory is divided into blocks or pages of 256 words (2^8), and program modules or subroutines must fit within these page boundaries. Then a program of instructions overlapping a specific page-boundary is ineffective; extra instructions are therefore necessary to transfer the memory reference from page to page, thus imposing inefficient usage of the available memory.

Relative addressing (or addressing relative to the program-counter). An 8-bit memory address as a reference allows forward or backward references of 255 cells each. The address bits are interpreted as a signed integer, which is added to the current program-counter reading to obtain the effective address.

8-25.2. Indirect Addressing.

In contrast to direct addressing, indirect addressing defines the effective memory-address of the instruction (called the *Address Pointer*) from a second word specified by the usual memory-reference instruction. It takes longer to complete as two instruction cycle-times are involved. On a paged-memory computer, an address-pointer on the current page contains the address of a word on any other page. Indirect addressing has, however, the advantage of allowing a single instruction to access the starting number of a sequence of memory locations from the contents of the address pointer. For example, a subroutine or a lookup table in the memory can be relocated by changing the starting address in the address pointer.

Indexed addressing, if used, requires one or more extra working registers called *Index Registers (X)*. The memory address indicated by the address bits of the instruction has, in addition, the contents of the index register to determine the effective address of the memory reference. This mode is useful in particular for the access of data in a table with reference to a starting address. In conjunction with the indirect addressing mode, post-indexing and preindexing are possible from the contents of the address pointer.

Scratch-pad addressing typically uses 256 words (2^8), starting from location 0 of the main memory (as the **base-page** of memory); it allows the storage of common facilities such as interrupt addresses, and indirect address-pointers for the linkage of different sections of a program. (The scratch-pad memory cells are addressed directly by the typical 8 address bits of the memory-reference instructions of a 16-bit microcomputer.)

Register addressing by way of additional working registers allows the storage of a memory-address for the memory-reference instructions such as LOAD, STORE, and ADD. The latter contain only a code to indicate the register involved. This type of addressing is more common in LSI microprocessors.

With the use of the various addressing modes described, it is obvious that a program of instructions can only be as efficient as the time required for reaching a specific memory-address and moving the data.

8-26. NUMBER OF INSTRUCTIONS IN A MICROCOMPUTER SYSTEM

The set of instructions varying anywhere from 40 to 400 according to the direction of the programmer are stored in the computer memory along with the data. The actual instruction set is based on the computational technique (or the algorithm) used and on the flowchart devised for the logical sequence of the computer manipulation to solve a certain problem or to process a large quantity of statistical data. The flowchart serves as a valuable aid in debugging when the programmer checks the written program for possible errors.

In the case of a microcomputer, the instruction set is, to some extent, determined mostly by the internal hardware design of the microprocessor and the specific stand-alone dedicated application. They are usually "microprogrammable" with "microinstructions" on a semipermanent basis. From the software point of view, sophisticated microprogramming may make different microcomputer systems appear identical in spite of possible design differences.

The type of instructions used in a general-purpose digital computer (a GPDC of this 16-bit scale) may be divided into seven groups as follows shortly. First, a typical instruction format for a 16-bit microcomputer is presented.

15 14 13 12	11 10 9 8	7 6 5 4 3 2 1 0
INSTRUCTION GROUP CODE	OPERATION CODE (OPCODE)	OPERAND FIELD

The Group Code places the instruction in one of the following seven categories. The Opcode defines the specific instruction; for example, what type of conditional jump or what register to operate on are indicated. The Operand-field designates the memory-address, data-code, or shift count, etc.

1. The **memory reference instructions** perform the arithmetic or logic operations involving the data stored in the indicated memory-cell addresses or registers. These instructions dedicate some bits to define the addressing mode of the control instructions, indirect or indexed addressing, etc. For example, an instruction such as LOAD 200 would signify that the contents of the memory-address location 200 should be transferred to a specific register or the accumulator.

2. The **immediate addressing instructions** are similar to the above memory reference instructions in format only; however, the memory data, like the constants or the number of counts, is stored within the immediate instruction itself as the operand, rather than in a separate location, to gain not only one extra memory-cell but also speed by requiring only one memory cycle-time for the execution of the instruction. This naturally involves the restricted definition of the operand with half the number of bits. The gain in speed, however, points out the advantage of using a larger bit-capacity such as 24 or 32 in an instruction word. As an example, an "immediate" operand section of the command may be required to be added to the contents of a specific register.

3. The **Conditional-Jump** will command the program counter to depart from the normal sequence of instructions to the JUMP instruction and to transfer the control to a different part of the program to satisfy the specific condition stated. As an example, the commands take the form:

JUMP if accumulator contents >0, or
JUMP if carry register = 1

4. The **Shift Instructions** move the bit-patterns in the shift register to the right or to the left by one or more bits. This may require one or more registers to UNPACK the data for the I/O operations. Or, the data-bits may be shifted to the carry-register for the purpose of testing. Code conversion and arithmetic may be involved too. (UNPACK may mean the translation of a code to the corresponding bit pattern.)

5. The **Register Change Instructions** perform arithmetic and logic operations involving the general-purpose working registers only (and not the main memory). For example, "COMPLEMENT 200" would perform the 1's complement operation (of the contents of the address 200) in the accumulator.

6. The **Control Instructions** command the general status-manipulations within the

computer, such as Interrupts, HALT, NO OPERATION, and SET CARRY. The command "NO OPERATION," for example, would imply that the program-counter register is merely incremented by one step without any other action.

7. The **I/O instructions** transfer data IN/OUT usually via the working registers or the buffers in the Control Memory to the external peripheral devices, or the twisted-pair transmission lines, in multiplexed serial-words, along with a strobe-pulse signal/clock. The I/O instructions, in turn, may involve all of the preceding six groups of instructions. The CPU of the microprocessor executes an I/O instruction in about 1 or 2 μs memory cycle-time, and the TTY, for example, requires 10-ms to move an 8-bit byte of character or word of data. The CPU actually transfers a bit/line, in parallel mode as "0"/"1" voltage levels. The TTY transmits in a bit-serial mode on one data-line in the presence of some current flow. Obviously, a special hardware Interface is required for the appropriate control and data transfer from a specific microcomputer to a specific peripheral device. The control busses which connect the computer to the Interface must perform device selection, function selection, sense status, and data-transfer by way of the commands issued as I/O instructions. The two-way data-transfer also requires line drivers and line receivers.

8-27. CROSS SOFTWARE

Microcomputer software can be divided into three categories as shown in the following diagram. All computers–micro, mini, medium-scale, and large-scale main-frames–require the following software programming facilities:

Program-Development Software	Diagnostic Software	Operating Software
Assemblers	CPU diagnostics	User-application programs
Relocatable assemblers	Memory diagnostics	Binary loaders
Paper-tape editors	I/O device diagnostics	Relocatable binary loaders
Macroassemblers	Software diagnostics	Real-time and Disk Operating Systems
Microassemblers	(Debuggers and Simulators)	Utility programs
		Math subroutines
Compilers for high-level languages		I/O control subroutines
		Paper-tape copy and list programs

During the last few years, the leading computer manufacturers have generated software for several systems and stand-alone applications along the tabulated lines on disk, floppy-disk, tape-cassette, tape-cartridge, core memory, and semiconductor memory. With the latest advances in microcomputer systems, mass-memories, and semiconductor RAMs and ROMs, the designated software can be conveniently cross-correlated with necessary modifications to interface minicomputer systems and microcomputer systems, which use common peripheral devices such as floppy disk, cassette and cartridge, CRT-keyboard terminals, and printers. The cross-software is mostly available in the form of external disk and tape-cartridges and LSI high-capacity dynamic RAMs and ROMs to the extent required. Some of the manufacturers have ruggedized the mass-memory systems to meet Defense standards. As an example, DEC provides readily available cross-software for its LSI-11, PDP-11/03 microcomputer system, along the lines previously generated for the PDP-11/40 minicomputer system.

8-28. ROM/PROM EMULATION

The most common applications of the read-only memory are:

1. Code conversion
2. Microprogamming
3. Character generation
4. Process control
5. Mathematical function lookup tables.

During the development of software (firmware as specially designated), it is often desirable that the user be able to program a ROM in his facility. Such ROMs are referred to as programmable ROMs (PROMs). In one method of field programming, each cell in an array incorporates a metallic link at one of its electrodes. During programming, the link is fused by the application of a high-current pulse of a specific duration. A broken link in a cell defines one binary state, and the unbroken link defines the other state. The programming implementation is defined in detail so that an accidental application of a pulse to the cell does not change its binary state.

ROM and PROM programs, when first operated in the System, need debugging for possible failures in hardware or software. For this and other purposes, 2 kilobytes of RAM or CORE may be reserved in the main memory for loading and emulating the machine-language program written on a PROM or a vendor-supplied ROM for that program. This is actually a debugging procedure.

Data words written into a PROM cell are irreversible. Although users may have a facility to program a programmable ROM, they have no recourse to change a bit other than programming an entirely new ROM. When a new System is being developed, this is a handicap in an experimental situation. Therefore, use of an EPROM (erasable PROM) in place of a PROM is a more convenient procedure in this aspect. Erasure is accomplished by sealing the EPROM with a quartz window that transmits ultraviolet light. The photocurrent discharges all the memory cells to the "0-state." Then reprogramming is done by applying a large voltage or pulse of a specific duration to the selected output data terminals, while addressing the requisite word through its x-y coincidence. In READ operation, a word is selected using the same address circuits to output the corresponding ROM bit-pattern. The EPROM may be reprogrammed many times for the final bit-pattern. Then a conventional ROM may be fabricated against the final version. (Presently, the more convenient electronically alterable EAROMs go a step further by altering only the faulty bits.)

8-29. VECTORED INTERRUPT

The general program-interrupt facility allows the microprocessor to continue processing the regular program and yet be able to service I/O requests from the peripheral devices on demand, by branching to a special routine, which will deal with the requirements of the interrupting device. After it is dealt with, the control returns to the program in process, to exactly where it got diverted. If the request comes from a second peripheral device when the computer is already servicing the first interrupt, a **priority-interrupt** scheme becomes effective. That is, if the second interrupt has a higher priority, the control instantly turns the microprocessor to the second interrupt; otherwise the second device must wait for service until the first interrupt is completed. Some microprocessors provide up to eight or more such **levels of priority or vectored interrupt service**, and the priority is determined mainly by the external circuit connections to the peripheral interface.

If the internal crystal-controlled clock (e.g., 10 MHz) generates a timing-sequence for the read/write memory-cycles every 1.6 μs, the microprocessor may operate on the instructions as a four-phase system in four modes (fetch, indirect-address, execute, and interrupt), of which the first three take a memory-cycle each, but not in sequence. The computer can go directly from one of the first three modes to any of the two remaining modes according to choice, or to the fourth interrupt mode upon the completion of a current mode. The corresponding logic of **vectored priority interrupt lines** allow faster identification and service, at lower memory cost.

In general, the implementation of an interrupt system consists of replacing a waiting-loop in the program with an equivalent logic (hardware) in the I/O control; the logic configuration used tests for the presence of any interrupt at regular intervals, e.g., just before every "fetch" instruction. A stack-memory, which enables the CPU to store its current state at an "interrupt" in a few instructions in the stack, makes an excellent real-time process control. Normally, the arrival of the interrupt-acknowledge signal makes the I/O control send the address of the interrupt to the CPU, and the CPU finds the location of the routine to service the interrupt of the peripheral device (or the device-controller). In some microprocessors, the I/O control can shorten this procedure by sending the actual location of the service-routine, and the CPU can then reach the routine by an "indirect" jump instruction. This is generally called the *vectored-interrupt*, the fastest selective servicing procedure. For example, an anticipated power-failure would enable the transfer of the critical contents of the registers in use to the nonvolatile storage memory by means of an automatic "jump" command.

8-30. GRAPHICS

The **computer graphics** is characterized by real-time graphic interactive human-machine communication. The designer is assisted in conceptualizing and analyzing a design by an iterative feedback process at a number of hierarchical levels. A graphics system consists of a digital computer of the scale of a mini or microcomputer, a CRT and an associated-function keyboard, a display processor, and a light-pen.

The light-pen is actually a photocell and fiber-optic combination that includes a photomultiplier at the other end. Whenever the light-pen "sees" an illuminated spot, the point is determinated because of the correlation between the time the flash is received and the position of the electron beam. Using x- and y-coordinate data, writing is accomplished by calling onto the screen *a tracking-cross under the pen's field of view*; the cross generates a line as it moves. The display processor, as a stored program-counter, implements coordinate-incrementing instructions, display subroutine jumps and returns, ROM character generation (called by appropriate control words), and output to multiple CRT consoles, since the distribution to several CRT terminals, by way of coax cables, is simple enough.

The display processor's operations involve:

1. Arithmetic for scaling of the picture or a portion thereof
2. Rotation by high-speed digital-to-analog converters.

With a working memory of 8-K words, and a 300-K byte cartridge tape-drive, a Tektronix type 4051, CRT Graphics Terminal (with upper and lower alphanumerics and BASIC firmware) may cost just under $7,000. The display file for a simple graphics picture is simply a block of words containing the display point-coordinates and the display control information. (See Section 13-4 for further information.)

8-31. MULTITASKING AND MULTIPROGRAMMING

Multitasking is a technique of achieving concurrency by separating a single program or several programs into two or more interrelated tasks that share code, buffers, and files while the computer is running. This requires considerable ingenuity on the part of the programmer.

Multi-programming. The concept of multiprogramming involves:

1. Dynamic or temporary allocation of information to a hierarchy of memory devices, such as RAMs and ROMs.
2. Providing means for programs to interrelate reference procedures and data manipulation, independent of their actual location in physical memory.
3. Providing common procedure and data-formatting by several programs.
4. Preventing unauthorized access of system resources.
5. Expedited switching of actual computation hardware from one program to the other.

Both hardware and software must be organized so that the computation hardware—namely, main memory, processing units, auxiliary storage, and I/O channels—are shared by many concurrent computations. This is a common task in central large-scale computers used for time-sharing.

Pipelining. Parallel-processing and pipelining are usually oriented to the aspect of architecture in the case of the mini- and micro-computers, so that several distinct tasks are compacted in time-domain for simultaneous processing.

In the structure of a CPU, the preceding requirement is usually reflected in the techniques of the instruction "fetch" process and the design of the arithmetic section ALU. For example, while the processor is engaged in decoding and executing one instruction, a few additional registers on the data-bus could be involved in a prefetch or lookahead manipulation for another instruction simultaneously. The registers particularly suitable for this technique of parallel handling of instructions are FIFO or LIFO, and tandem or toggle-mode registers for alternate routing of the other instruction.

Pipelining techniques are frequently used in microcomputer systems to increase the throughput of low- or medium-speed microprocessors. By using several chips as CPUs functioning in parallel on several macroinstructions simultaneously, the speed of computation can be upgraded to reach the performance standards of the high-speed mini- and medium-scale computers.

The symbol of a pipelined ALU used in microprocessors is shown in the case of the Intel 8048 microprocessor of Fig. 7-2b.

The **interrupt call program** will *poll* or determine if any other programs are waiting to execute; in the event a new program is on-line waiting for attention, the program saves all registers and flags in the stack, while simultaneously saving the address of the stack-pointer in the memory table. The new program's stack-pointer is then loaded from the same table, while the registers and flags connected with the new program are popped out of the stack for returning to the new program. If the computer gets trapped in an "infinite loop" of a faulty program, an external interrupt becomes effective after every 10 msec. If there are several users (or tasks), a task number and a priority on an arbitrary scale are allotted to the interrupts. The programmers usually find it convenient for *vectoring* all the I/O functions through one subroutine, because the I/O controllers are very complex without processor intervention. In the case of small microcomputer systems, software techniques are used if any special timing or flag is desired; in large systems, the solution is sought by extra hardware. With the latest I/O chips in use, extra hardware is no problem.

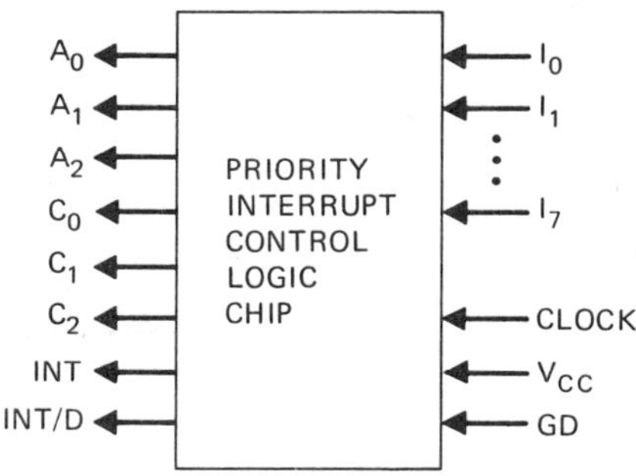

Provision is made for *priority arbitration* by assigning a fixed priority of service to each interrupt signal. A priority control logic chip will have the configuration shown here. With the incoming interrupt signals I_0 through I_7, the "INT" interrupt signal is polled for execution in the microprocessor. A_0, A_1, and A_2 indicate, by their binary identification, pending priority for the other incoming interrupt signals. Input control lines C_0, C_1, and C_2 transfer respective priority control words in a buffer control register to selectively disable groups of interrupts according to the program. The microprocessor can disable the whole interrupt procedure by means of the "INT/D" control signal.

A **multiprogramming system** can be controlled at several levels of activity. A lower level operating system such as a BASIC interpreter allows the users to generate assembler level code. The popular microprocessors used in operating systems have built-in features to safeguard the operating system and its users from accidental loss of programs or data. In practice, the use of vectored interrupts assures an even distribution of the throughput, processing power, and cycle-times of the popular microprocessors to approximately eight tasks in a multiprogramming environment.

A multiprogramming or multiuser system is entirely permissible in the case of the present microcomputer systems. The concept does not mean simultaneous execution of several programs; simultaneous execution stands for a **multiprocessor system** involving several microprocessors on a common bus of the nature of the S-100 bus, which IEEE is presently sponsoring for using several processors with a shared local virtual memory-base management, to increase the throughput of microcomputer systems to a limit of six times that of a single microprocessor system. A multiprocessor system is described in Section 11-2 as an adjunct to S-100 IEEE bus.

Multiprogramming allows more than one user to use a microcomputer system as well—according to the common practice of time-sharing in data communication networks. The concept increases the productivity of a microcomputer system by handling a million instructions per second to effectively allow other programs to run while the main user program awaits input, access to a disk, etc. And the common methodology involves the connection of several keyboard CRT terminals operating on the I/O lines with real-time interrupts for a more efficient use of the computing power of the microcomputer system. Upon receiving the interrupt request from a second keyboard out of a *limited* number of terminals, the computer saves the status of the current program in a stack, and enters or transfers control to the second keyboard read routine. As soon as the second user has made the desired change of program, the computer returns to the original program. The process of passing control from one program to the next is commonly handled by an *operating system* module (O/S), and it is usually designated as the **interrupt call routine**. The routine is imbedded as part of I/O driver routines or other standard utility subroutines in the operating system, along with bootstrap loader, and time-sharing support program.

8-32. MICROPROGRAMMING APPROACH

In contrast to the "fixed-control" computers that use a hard-wired set of logic circuits in machine language for the control function, the modern microprogrammable computer is primarily a multipurpose machine with a "flexible" control section (whether it is large-scale using a 90-bit instruction, or a miniscale using a 16-to-64-bit instruction, or a micro-scale microcomputer that presently uses 4-to 32-bits by bit-slice techniques). Stored microinstructions from replaceable or alterable high-speed ROM via RAM control-memory sections make it feasible to make even a microcomputer highly powerful at the present stage of computer technology.

1. A microprocessor with special interface decodes each instruction word into a sequence of control-bit slices for various microoperations (e.g., the microinstruction word may be a combination of four slices of bits: opcode, register 1, register 2, and a flag).
2. The successive microinstruction words can be "fetched" from a ROM or a loaded-RAM lookup table.
3. A complete set of computer instructions may be produced as a microprogram in machine language in several cycle-times of the main memory. Thus, the control unit functions as an "internal" stored-program auxiliary computer within the regular computer to address, fetch, and execute a sequence of microinstructions from the control memory in a fixed set of cycle-times. The large-scale machines that use large instruction words in a multifield format require fewer cycle-times and hence are more powerful than the microcomputers, which necessarily use smaller instruction words and thus longer microprograms and more control-memory references. This is the major distinction between the large-scale and mini- and micro-computers at the present state-of-the-art. Latest high-speed CORE and RAM and ROM semiconductor memories have made this feasible.

Microprogramming is an effective tool in implementing a sophisticated instruction set with a relatively simple processor and reduced random logic. It permits the user to change the instruction sets and evaluate different interfaces for external controllers, thus allowing a flexible transition for various applications or software. Microprogramming is thus increasingly efficient for complex operations that otherwise would require subroutines in the previous "fixed" control third-generation machines. In short, microprograms replace the core-memory references with the faster control-memory references.

The following software programming features are rendered practical with the microprogramming technique:

1. Floating-point arithmetic, complete routines for trigonometric functions, FFT, integration, etc.
2. I/O routines, which can automate complex interrupt service routines, buffer management, or formatting.
3. Automatic stacking of nested routines are implemented by microprogramming instructions such as JUMP TO SUBROUTINE, RETURN FROM SUBROUTINE, and RETURN FROM INTERRUPT.
4. Manufacturers presently supply a **microassembly language** using a mnemonic-version of microinstructions and possibly two translation programs, one for substituting the CORE as RAM main-memory in the place of the control-memory for debugging a simulated program and the second for allowing a paper-tape to load the internal RAM memory. The best way to implement and change new microprograms is afforded by the latest electronically alterable EPROM memories in the control section.
5. Microprogram execution times depend on ROM access-time, which ought to be shorter than one-fifth to one-third of main-memory cycle-time. Semiconductor ROMs,

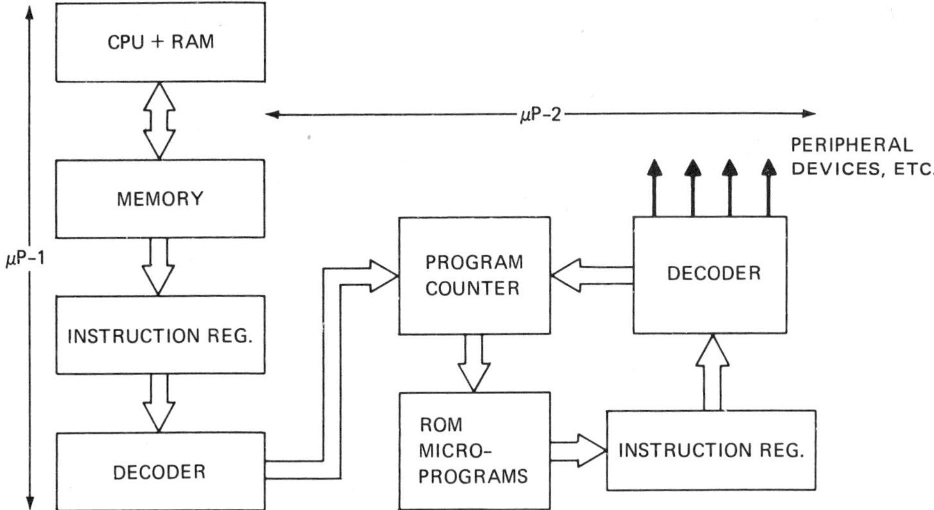

Fig. 8-5a. Microprogram-controlled processor.

rugged and reliable, have access times from 50 to 500 ns depending on the kilo-bits available on the LSI chips. (This is slow compared to the speed of the hard-wired logic; hence, it does not pay to microprogram a mini- or micro-computer that requires a simple fixed instruction set for a dedicated application—from the speed point-of-view only.)

6. The instruction-code bits of the "outer or virtual" memory of the microcomputer system set the program-counter to a starting address in the control memory, and the microprogram counter is incremented after each microinstruction is executed. This does not of course interfere with the conditional or unconditional branching or decisions in the program.

A typical microprogram-controlled microcomputer system that employs two microprocessors is shown along with a typical microprogramming subsystem in Fig. 8-5a,b.

The latest 12/16-bit microcomputers implement instruction sets (including double-precision floating-point arithmetic) through microprogramming with 12-, 16-, 18-, 24-, and 32-bit microinstructions. This is fast enough to work, even with 300-ns solid-state main memories. A further trend is to incorporate such microprogrammed microprocessors into the asynchronous-bus architectures of the larger minicomputer systems that can readily accommodate different memories, peripherals, and multiple processors. And, the

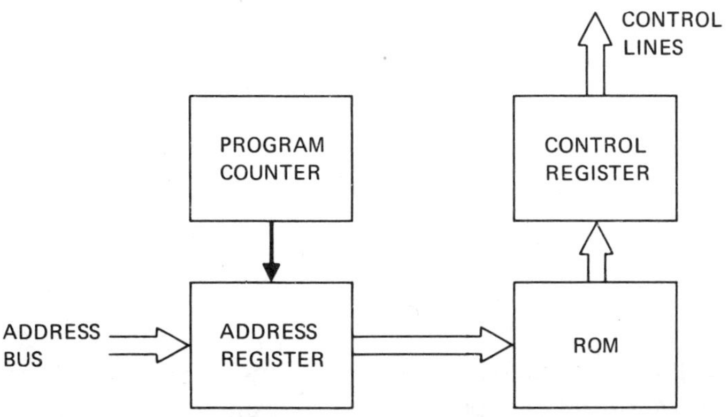

Fig. 8-5b. Typical microprogramming subsystem for addressing microinstructions. MICROPROGRAM CONTROL ROM (CROM).

latest high-speed NMOS, CMOS-on-sapphire, and I^2L semiconductor memories close the gap between the memory-speed and the logic-speed of the processor. Formerly, incompatibility in this aspect was a serious problem in the design of hardware and software systems. The ROMs presently permit one to use microprogramming with a 100- to 600-ns cycle-time of the main-memory without any sacrifice in computing speed and throughput.

8-33. FAST FOURIER TRANSFORM, FFT

A series of oscillations, the frequencies of which are integral multiples of the fundamental frequency, can be represented by the Fourier series when the function X(t) is single-valued and finite and has a finite number of maxima and minima in the interval of one oscillation.

Frequency and Time Domains

1. Analog continuous Fourier transform pair, **CFT**

$$X(f) = \int_{-\infty}^{\infty} x(t)\, e^{-i2\pi ft}\, dt. \qquad x(t) = \int_{-\infty}^{\infty} X(f)\, e^{i2\pi ft}\, df. \qquad \begin{cases} -\infty < f < \infty \\ -\infty < t < \infty \\ i = \sqrt{-1} \end{cases}$$

2. Digital form for a complex series, **DFT**

$$X(j) = \frac{1}{N} \sum_{k=0}^{N-1} x(k)\, e^{-i2\pi jk}$$

$$x(k) = \sum_{j=0}^{N-1} X(j)\, e^{i2\pi jk} \qquad \begin{cases} j = 0, 1 \ldots N-1 \\ k = 0, 1 \ldots N-1 \end{cases}$$

Substitute $e^{2\pi i/N} \equiv W_N$ to obtain the following

3. Cooley-Tukey Fast Fourier Transform (FFT) algorithm:

$$X(j) = \frac{1}{N} \left[\sum_{k=0}^{N-1} x(k)^* \, W_N{}^{jk} \right]^*$$

*Complex conjugate operation.

$$X^*(j) = \hat{X}(j) = \sum_{k=0}^{N-1} A(k)\, W^{jk}$$

$$j = 0, 1 \ldots N-1;\ W = e^{2\pi i/N};\ A = X^*/N.$$

When N = 8: j and k are 0, 1, . . 7

$$W^8 = [e^{2\pi i/8}]^8 = e^{2\pi i} = 1.$$

For N = 8, a direct evaluation of the DFT algorithm requires 64 operations of complex multiply-and-add operations. But for FFT, the number of multiply-and-add operations are reduced to 24 only. Computation of N^2 operations in DFT are actually reduced to $\frac{N}{2} \log_2 N$ complex multiplications in FFT. When N = 1,024, the simplification in computation is as much as 200 to 1. (G. D. Bergland, Bell Telephone Labs.)

The FFT technique has practically become conventional, not only in computing spectograms for short-term power spectrums as function of time, but also for correlation of two time series and for digital filtering in convolution of two series of data samples. Using a mini- or micro-computer system and 8-K words of memory, a 1,024-point transformation can be presently achieved in less than 1 sec without using the floating-point format. At this time, an accessory CCD processor appears ideal in a microcomputer system for high-speed FFT computation—since the basic operations needed to perform this computation are arithmetic and delay elements.

The **Fast Fourier Transform is ideal for digital processing of waveforms** in a literal sense, since the frequency components of a continuous waveform can be rapidly identified by first sampling it at finite intervals to enable the **discrete DFT form** of analysis in principle. The **FFT algorithm is merely a rapid computational technique to translate the time-domain to the frequency-domain components.** The closer the samples are taken, the more accurately the resulting digital series represents the original waveform. The sum of the finite series, considered as coefficients of successive harmonic frequencies, is an approximation in DFT. The coefficient of the first term is the average value of all the samples (i.e., their sum divided by N). Without FFT, each coefficient would require the summation of N real and N imaginary terms, each of which is a sample value and a trigonometric weight. For the real and complex conjugates, N^2 products would be required to compute the coefficients. **The simplifying FFT algorithm requires the combining of the Fourier coefficients for two interleaved sets to obtain the coefficients of the composite set.** A single set of coefficients for all the sets of the even- and odd-numbered samples is the actual computational simplification. Hence, in the final analysis, the FFT digital signal processing, as stated previously, requires a total of N/2 real multiplications in regular DFT signal process. The **Cooley-Tukey FFT approach** is, in short, based on a set of nested multiplications using **full-adders** and **delay elements**—hence the popularity of the CCDs for simplifying the processing of waveforms by means of the FFT algorithm.

Special-purpose digital hardware, interfaced to a minicomputer or microcomputer, is currently available to compute 1,024 real-point FFT in 139 ms. Complete real-time control software is provided along with the FFT processor. Some 1,024 real-points correspond to 512 complex points, and actual FFT processor time is only 18 ms out of the overall computer time of 139 ms. With full 16-bit accuracy, **Elsytec Company's FFT Array Processor 306/MFFT** transforms from 16 to 16,384 real points. The processor is also capable of high-speed correlation and digital filtering, forward and inverse FFT, spectral magnitude and complex multiplication, and arithmetic processing of arrays or blocks of numbers. The control software needs only 1,100 RAM cells. FFT calculations utilize block floating-point scaling. Complex array multiplications require 17 μs per complete point.

LSI MULTIPLIERS. For designing digital filters and Fast Fourier Transform processors, using a 16-bit microprocessor, a high computational-speed multiplier is mandatory. The software involved in such a requirement is prohibitive. Bipolar monolithic 16 X 16-bit multipliers are available in 1980 to do the multiplication in just 100 nsec. The chip has the processing power of 24 MSI chips and it costs $157 in 100's.

Type MY-16HJ of TRW Inc. has the following important features:

- On-chip I/O registers with 3-state outputs
- 2's complement or unsigned magnitude
- Controllable transparent output registers
- Double-precision product
- TTL compatibility
- Single 5-volt power supply with power consumption of 3 watts
- Temperature range −55°C to +125°C (at extra cost)

Because of the high speed attainable, the power consumed by this bipolar chip is not ordinary for an LSI chip. (As a comparison, one of the latest LSI 16-K bit static CMOS

ROMs, type 5316 from Solid-state Scientific Inc., as a replacement to an NMOS 2316, or an EPROM 2716, each consuming about half-a-watt, requires approximately 10% to 20% of this power in microcomputer applications. Since the CMOS LSI chips are energy efficient they run cool with extremely high reliability.)

8-34. FLOWCHART AND PROGRAMMING

The flowchart is a logical representation of the path of the processing or computation control to arrive at a set of instructions (a program) for obtaining the solution of a problem. A recursion or iteration procedure in the algorithm of the problem is indicated by a closed loop in the diagram. A simple linear path indicates that no control decisions are required. Each block in the flowchart presents the status of the variables and constants in a logical sequence. An example of the said iterative procedure is shown in the following diagram when a control decision with an iterative loop is involved.

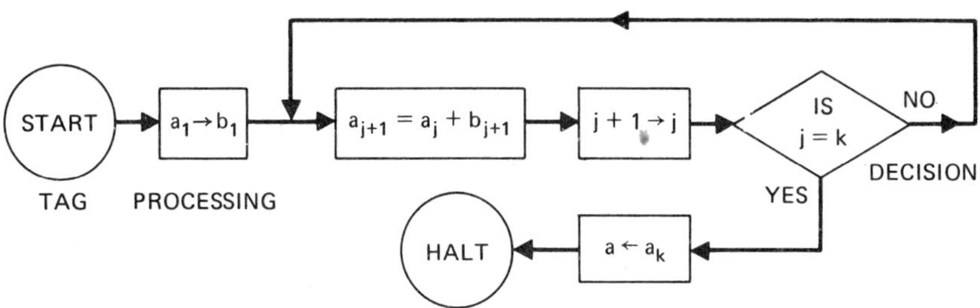

The standard form of the symbolic blocks used in the flowcharts are shown in Fig. 8-6.

Example. **Addition and subtraction in 10's complement notation.** Start with two numbers, x and y, each of n decimal digits. The 10's complement decimal notation method is similar to the 9's complement method except for a slight modification. The 10^n complement of y is added to x instead of the $(10^n - 1)$ complement. This is accomplished by adding a "carry" to the 10^0 stage during the ADD procedure.

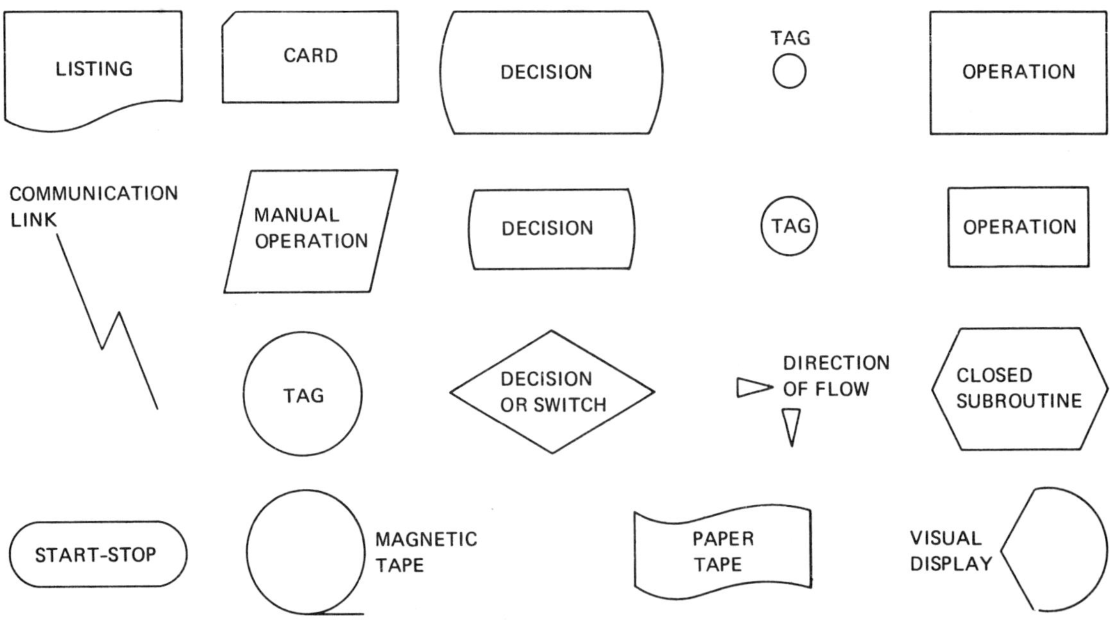

Fig. 8-6. Symbolic blocks used in flowcharts.

If a carry results from the most significant 10^{n-1} stage, it is discarded, but serves as an indication that $x \geqslant y$ and that the result is correct as it stands. If no carry results from the most significant stage, it indicates that $y > x$ and that it is necessary to take the 10^n complement of the sum in order to obtain the absolute value of the correct difference.

Case (i) $x \geqslant y$: Sum $= x + (10^n - 1 \pm y) + 1$
$= (x \pm y) \ldots$ by ignoring carry from the most significant 10^{n-1} stage.

In the case of subtraction, x is the minuend and y is the subtrahend. The absolute value of the correct difference $= x - y$.

Case (ii) $x < y$: Sum $= x + (10^n - 1 - y) + 1$
$= 10^n - (y - x) \ldots$ no carry from the msd

Recomplement the result to obtain the absolute value of the correct difference.

$$\text{Sum} = 10^n - 1 - [10^n - (y - x)] + 1 = y - x.$$

The flowchart clarifies the combined procedure for the preceding addition and subtraction in 10's complement notation.

S = Absolute value of sum or difference. Start with the instruction:
$(x \pm y) \rightarrow \alpha$

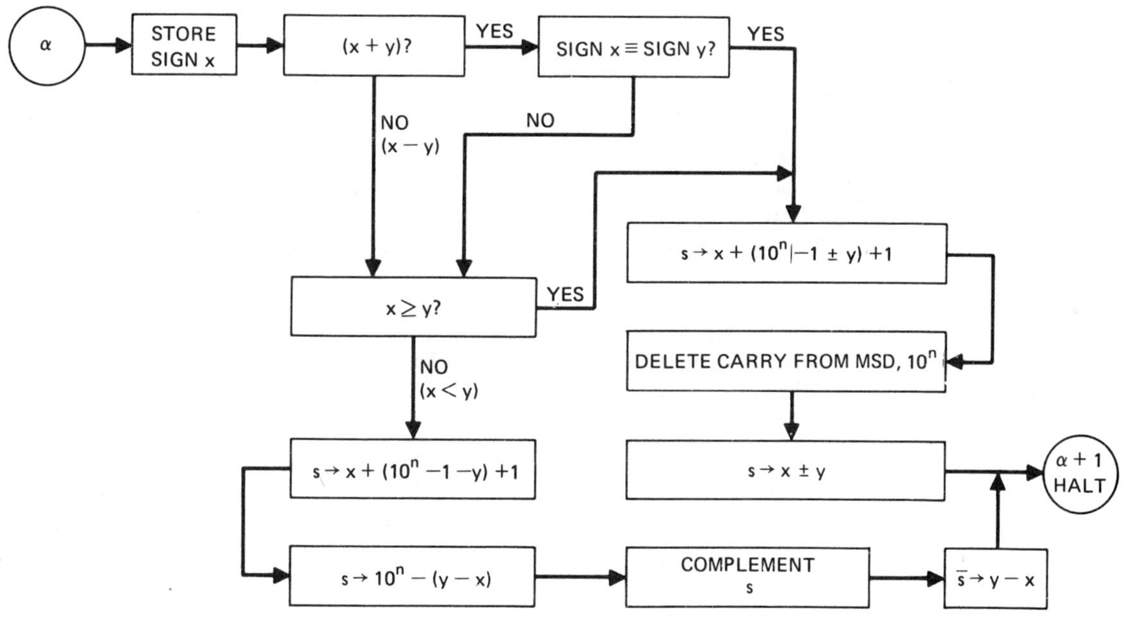

As a contrast to such conventional programming techniques, the present Network **computer-aided services for design (CAD)**, using a TTY or a CRT terminal, readily provide a simple programming approach as a problem-solving facility. One needs to understand only the basic principles of communicating with the distant large-scale computer by using the routine BASIC Network language. An example follows to illustrate this technique.

A simple example of a program in BASIC to make 73 arithmetic computations:

```
100 LET J = 1
200 LET A = 1
300 LET S = J + A
400 PRINT S
```

```
 500. IF S = 73 THEN 9999
 600  LET J = J + 1
 700  LET S = S + 1
 800  GØ TØ 300.
9999  END.
```

8-35. VENDOR'S INFORMATION ON MICROPROCESSORS

The following example of the LSI chip MC-6800, the microprocessor unit/MPU of Motorola Semiconductor Products, illustrates the comprehensive information typically available from the various manufacturers.

The **features of MC-6800** are:

8-bit parallel processing
Bidirectional data-bus
16-bit address-bus–65-K bytes of addressing
72 instructions–variable length
Seven addressing modes–direct, relative, immediate, indexed, extended, implied, and accumulator
Variable-length stack
Vectored restart

TABLE 8-4. Microprocessor instruction set—Alphabetic sequence *(Courtesy of Motorola Semiconductor Products, Inc.)*

ABA	Add Accumulators
ADC	Add with Carry
ADD	Add
AND	Logical AND
ASL	Arithmetic Shift Left
ASR	Arithmetic Shift Right
BCC	Branch if Carry Clear
BCS	Branch if Carry Set
BEQ	Branch if Equal to Zero
BGE	Branch if Greater than or Equal to Zero
BGT	Branch if Greater than Zero
BHI	Branch if Higher
BIT	Bit Test
BLE	Branch if Less or Equal
BLS	Branch if Lower or Same
BLT	Branch if Less than Zero
BMI	Branch if Minus
BNE	Branch if Not Equal to Zero
BPL	Branch if Plus
BRA	Branch Always
BSR	Branch to Subroutine
BVC	Branch if Overflow Clear
BVS	Branch if Overflow Set
CBA	Compare Accumulators
CLC	Clear Carry
CLI	Clear Interrupt Mask
CLR	Clear
CLV	Clear Overflow
CMP	Compare
COM	Complement
CPX	Compare Index Register
DAA	Decimal Adjust
DEC	Decrement
DES	Decrement Stack Pointer
DEX	Decrement Index Register
EOR	Exclusive OR
INC	Increment
INS	Increment Stack Pointer
INX	Increment Index Register
JMP	Jump
JSR	Jump to Subroutine
LDA	Load Accumulator
LDS	Load Stack Pointer
LDX	Load Index Register
LSR	Logical Shift Right
NEG	Negate
NOP	No Operation
ORA	Inclusive OR Accumulator
PSH	Push Data
PUL	Pull Data
ROL	Rotate Left
ROR	Rotate Right
RTI	Return from Interrupt
RTS	Return from Subroutine
SBA	Subtrace Accumulators
SBC	Subtrace with Carry
SEC	Set Carry
SEI	Set Interrupt Mask
SEV	Set Overflow
STA	Store Accumulator
STS	Store Stack Register
STX	Store Index Register
SUB	Subtract
SWI	Software Interrupt
TAB	Transfer Accumulators
TAP	Transfer Accumulators to Condition Code Register
TBA	Transfer Accumulators
TPA	Transfer Condition Code Register to Accumulator
TST	Test
TSX	Transfer Stack Pointer to Index Register
TXS	Transfer Index Register to Stack Pointer
WAI	Wait for Interrupt

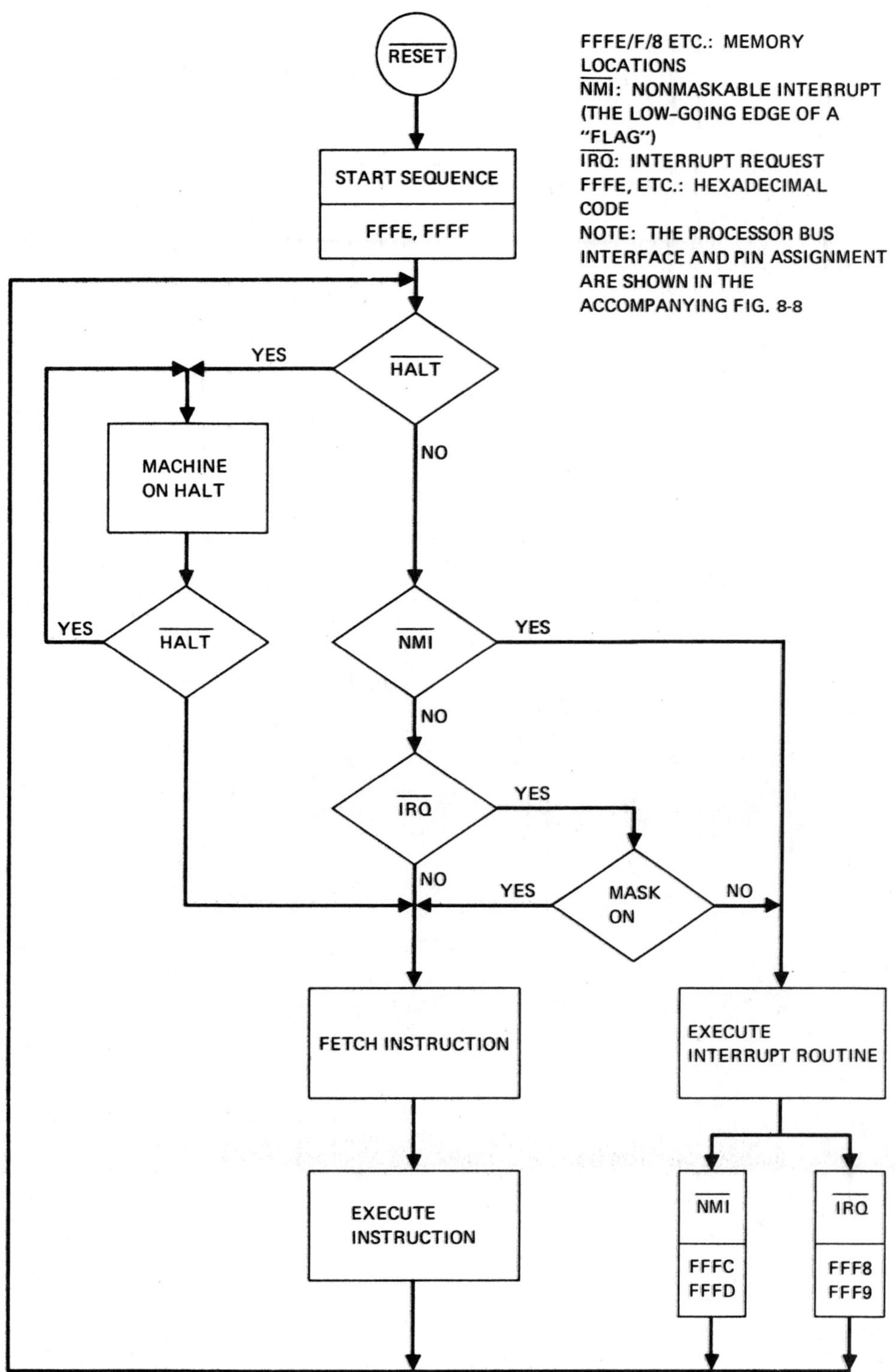

Fig. 8-7. MPU flowchart, MC-6800. (*Courtesy of Motorola Semiconductor Products, Inc.*)

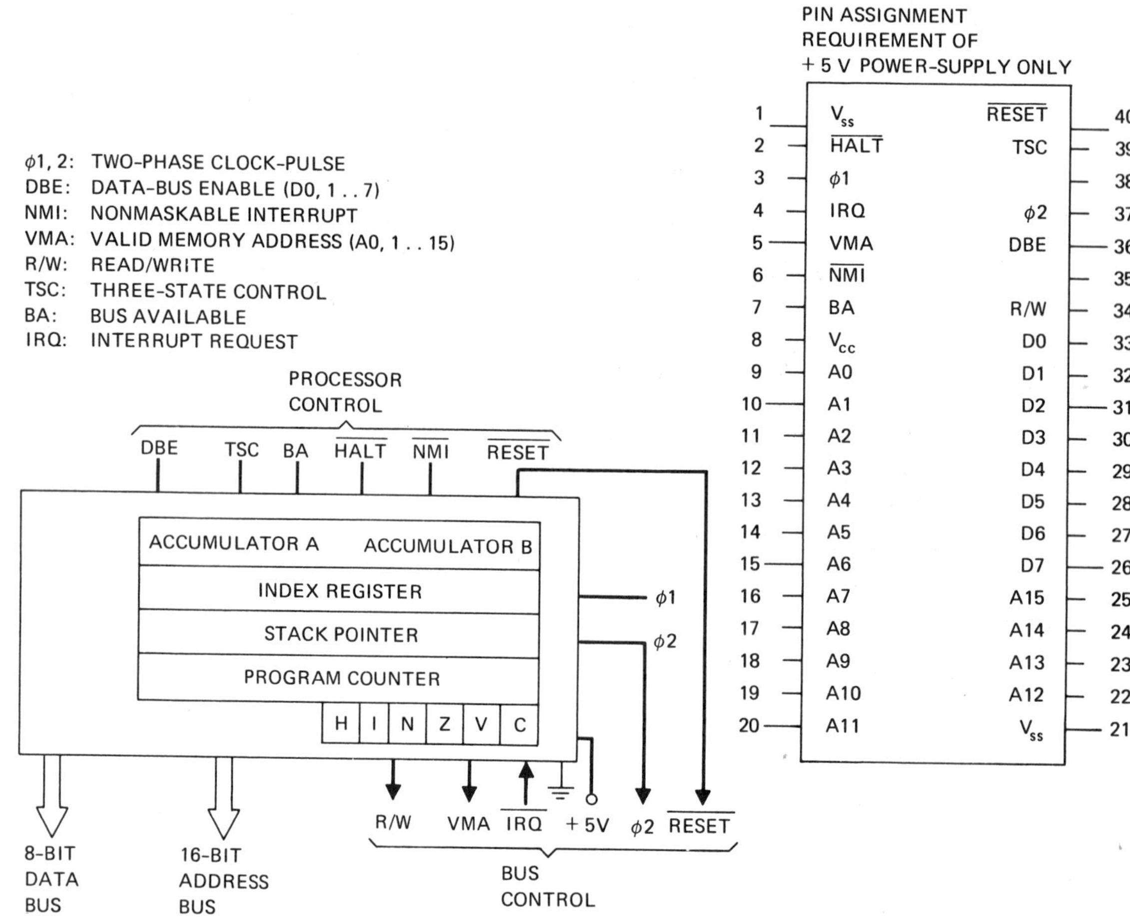

Fig. 8-8. Processor bus-interface, MC-6800. (*Courtesy of Motorola Semiconductor Products, Inc.*)

Maskable interrupt vector
Separate nonmaskable interrupt–internal registers saved in stack
Six internal registers–two accumulators, index register, program counter, stack-pointer, and condition code register
Direct memory addressing (DMA) and multiple processor capability
Clock-rates as high as 1 MHz
Simple bus-interface without TTL
HALT and single-instruction execution capability

A set of 72 instructions used for programming the Motorola type MC6800 microprocessing unit (MPU) are given in Table 8-4. The Flowchart and Bus-interface for this particular 8-bit parallel-processing MPU are shown in Figs. 8-7 and 8-8.

When inserting CMOS devices, it is recommended that a low wattage soldering iron with a grounded tip be used. This will prevent damaging the part. Another alternative is to use sockets for the parts.

The cable assembly consists of five items:

1. Edge connector
2. Edge connector cover
3. 50 pin PC board connector
4. PC board connector cover
5. Approximately 3 feet of 50 conductor flat cable

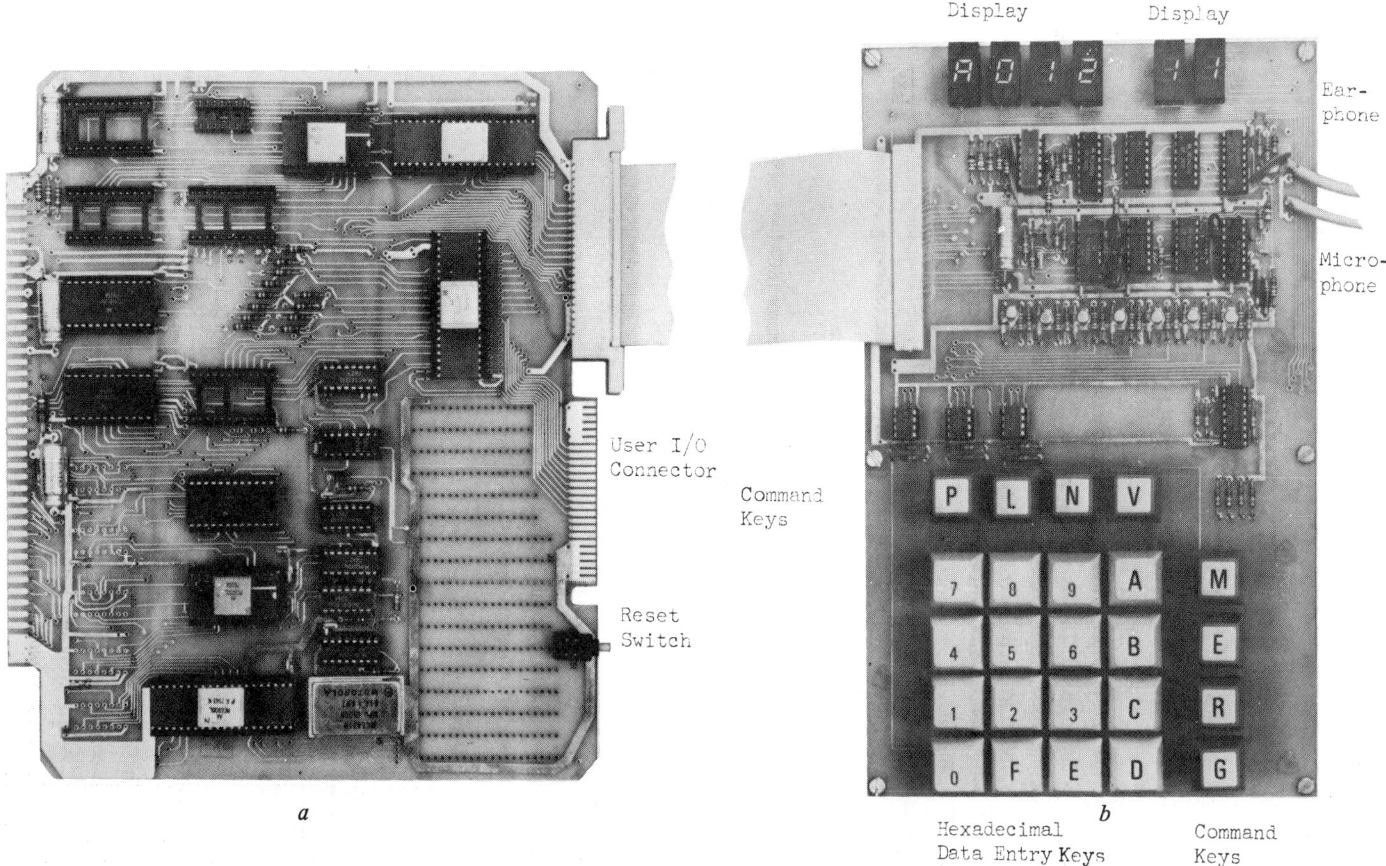

Fig. 8-9. *a*, Microcomputer module. *b*, Keyboard display module. (*Courtesy of Motorola*).

Motorola MEK6800 D2 Evaluation Kit-II. For introductory training of programmers in Assembly language, Motorola provides this kit of two printed circuit boards as a fully functional microcomputing system. The main board consists of:

- microprocessor MC 6800 (MPU)
- MCM6830 (ROM) monitor program (1024 bytes)
- Three MCM6810 (RAM) main memory chips (128 X 8)
- Two MC6820 peripheral interface adaptors (PIA)
- MC6850 asynchronous communications interface adaptor (ACIA)
- MC6871B clock generator

And has a provision for:

- Additional RAM memory (two)
- MCM68708 electrically programmable EPROMs (two)
- MC8T97 buffer (three)
- MC8T26 bidirectional buffer (two)

This expansion capability allows the programmer to use several operating modes.

The associated keyboard/display module allows the programmer to enter and debug programs as an adjunct to the prewritten program on the MCM6830 ROM in the main board. This auxiliary KB/Display board is furnished with audio cassette circuitry to allow the programmer access to RS-232 interface to a modem or a Teletype terminal. The two

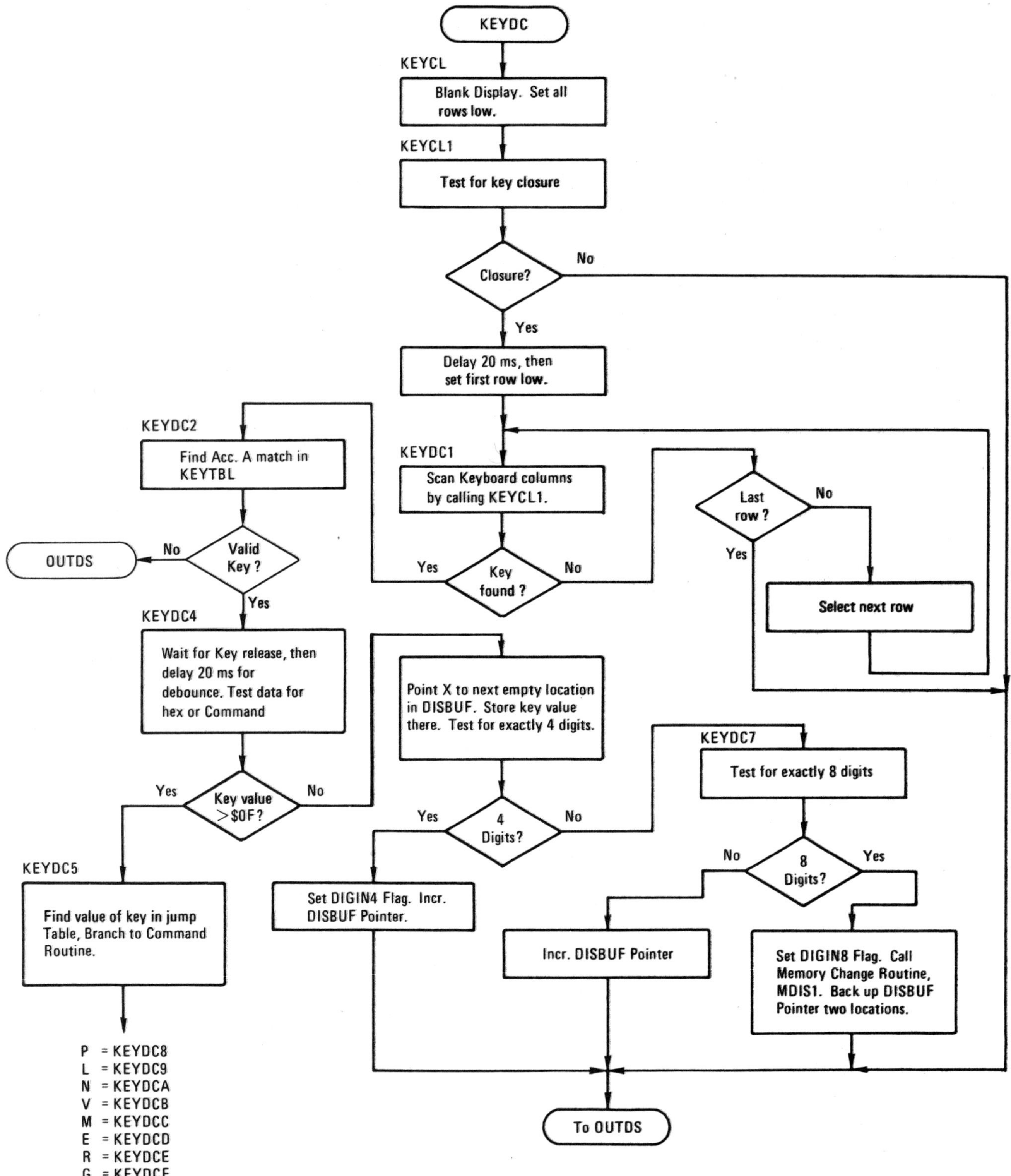

Fig. 8-10. Program flow for keyboard scan and decode routine. (*Courtesy of Motorola*)

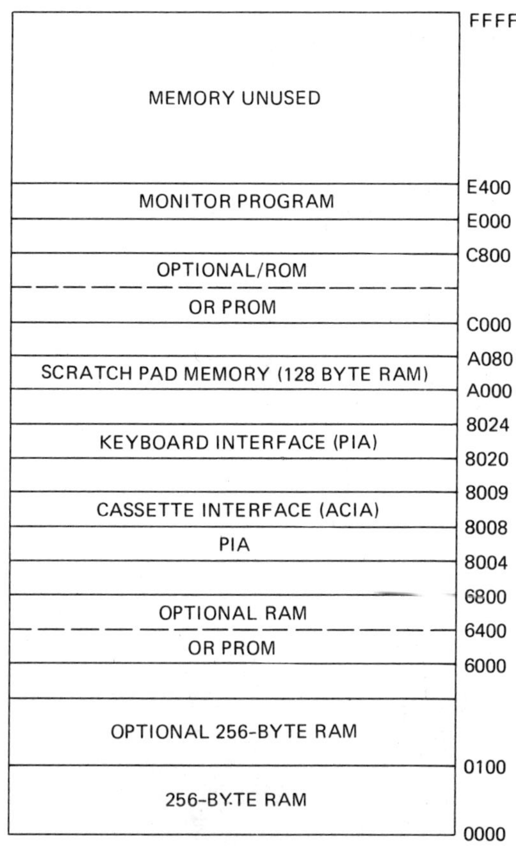

Fig. 8-11. Memory map for MEK 6800 D2 microcomputer. (*Courtesy of Motorola*)

PC boards are interconnected with a cable assembly consisting of edge connectors, 50-pin board connectors, covers, and 50-connector flat cable. Figure 8-9a,b illustrates the layout of the LSI chips on the two Motorola PC boards. Figure 8-10 shows the program flowchart for keyboard scan and decode routine.

The keypad of the auxiliary board has provision for 16 keys, labeled 0,1,2, through F for entry of hexadecimal data and eight blue control keys for commanding the various functions in program evaluation. Table 8-5 presents an Instruction Map for the facility of writing the mnemonics of the assembly program in hexadecimal code in various operating modes. Figure 8-11 presents a Memory Map for the MEK6800 D2 Microcomputer System. The control commands used in this Evaluation Kit are described in the following list:

M: Examine and Change Memory

E: Escape (abort) from operation in progress

R: Examine contents of MPU Registers P (Program Counter), X (Index Register), A (Accumulator A), B (Accumulator B), CC (Condition Code Register), and S (Stack Pointer)

G: Go to specified program, and begin execution of designated program

P: Punch data from Memory to Magnetic Tape. Before invoking Punch, the Memory Change function must be used to establish which part of the memory is to be recorded. (A 30-sec. string of ones is recorded as "prompt," ahead of data.)

MSB \ LSB	0	1	2	3	4	5	6	7	8	9	A	B	C	D	E	F
0	•	NOP (INH)	•	•	•	•	TAP (INH)	TPA (INH)	INX (INH)	DEX (INH)	CLV (INH)	SEV (INH)	CLC (INH)	SEC (INH)	CLI (INH)	SEI (INH)
1	SBA	CBA	•	•	•	•	TAB (INH)	TBA (INH)	•	DAA (INH)	•	ABA (INH)	•	•	•	•
2	BRA (REL)	•	BHI (REL)	BLS (REL)	BCC (REL)	BCS (REL)	BNE (REL)	BEQ (REL)	BVC (REL)	BVS (REL)	BPL (REL)	BMI (REL)	BGE (REL)	BLT (REL)	BGT (REL)	BLE (REL)
3	TSX (INH)	INS (INH)	PUL (A)	PUL (B)	DES (INH)	TXS (INH)	PSH (A)	PSH (B)	•	RTS (INH)	•	RTI (INH)	•	•	WAI (INH)	SWI (INH)
4	NEG (A)	•	•	COM (A)	LSR (A)	•	ROR (A)	ASR (A)	ASL (A)	ROL (A)	DEC (A)	•	INC (A)	TST (A)	•	CLR (A)
5	NEG (B)	•	•	COM (B)	LSR (B)	•	ROR (B)	ASR (B)	ASL (B)	ROL (B)	DEC (B)	•	INC (B)	TST (B)	•	CLR (B)
6	NEG (IND)	•	•	COM (IND)	LSR (IND)	•	ROR (IND)	ASR (IND)	ASL (IND)	ROL (IND)	DEC (IND)	•	INC (IND)	TST (IND)	JMP (IND)	CLR (IND)
7	NEG (EXT)	•	•	COM (EXT)	LSR (EXT)	•	ROR (EXT)	ASR (EXT)	ASL (EXT)	ROL (EXT)	DEC (EXT)	•	INC (EXT)	TST (EXT)	JMP (EXT)	CLR (EXT)
8	SUB (A) (IMM)	CMP (A) (IMM)	SBC (A) (IMM)	•	AND (A) (IMM)	BIT (A) (IMM)	LDA (A) (IMM)	•	EOR (A) (IMM)	ADC (A) (IMM)	ORA (A) (IMM)	ADD (A) (IMM)	CPX (A) (IMM)	BSR (REL)	LDS (IMM)	•
9	SUB (A) (DIR)	CMP (A) (DIR)	SBC (A) (DIR)	•	AND (A) (DIR)	BIT (A) (DIR)	LDA (A) (DIR)	STA (A) (DIR)	EOR (A) (DIR)	ADC (A) (DIR)	ORA (A) (DIR)	ADD (A) (DIR)	CPX (A) (DIR)	•	LDS (DIR)	STS (DIR)
A	SUB (A) (IND)	CMP (A) (IND)	SBC (A) (IND)	•	AND (A) (IND)	BIT (A) (IND)	LDA (A) (IND)	STA (A) (IND)	EOR (A) (IND)	ADC (A) (IND)	ORA (A) (IND)	ADD (A) (IND)	CPX (A) (IND)	JSR (IND)	LDS (IND)	STS (IND)
B	SUB (A) (EXT)	CMP (A) (EXT)	SBC (A) (EXT)	•	AND (A) (EXT)	BIT (A) (EXT)	LDA (A) (EXT)	STA (A) (EXT)	EOR (A) (EXT)	ADC (A) (EXT)	ORA (A) (EXT)	ADD (A) (EXT)	CPX (A) (EXT)	JSR (EXT)	LDS (EXT)	STS (EXT)
C	SUB (B) (IMM)	CMP (B) (IMM)	SBC (B) (IMM)	•	AND (B) (IMM)	BIT (B) (IMM)	LDA (B) (IMM)	•	EOR (B) (IMM)	ADC (B) (IMM)	ORA (B) (IMM)	ADD (B) (IMM)	•	•	LDX (IMM)	•
D	SUB (B) (DIR)	CMP (B) (DIR)	SBC (B) (DIR)	•	AND (B) (DIR)	BIT (B) (DIR)	LDA (B) (DIR)	STA (B) (DIR)	EOR (B) (DIR)	ADC (B) (DIR)	ORA (B) (DIR)	ADD (B) (DIR)	•	•	LDX (B) (DIR)	STX (B) (DIR)
E	SUB (B) (IND)	CMP (B) (IND)	SBC (B) (IND)	•	AND (B) (IND)	BIT (B) (IND)	LDA (B) (IND)	STA (B) (IND)	EOR (B) (IND)	ADC (B) (IND)	ORA (B) (IND)	ADD (B) (IND)	•	•	LDX (IND)	STX (IND)
F	SUB (B) (EXT)	CMP (B) (EXT)	SBC (B) (EXT)	•	AND (B) (EXT)	BIT (B) (EXT)	LDA (B) (EXT)	STA (B) (EXT)	EOR (B) (EXT)	ADC (B) (EXT)	ORA (B) (EXT)	ADD (B) (EXT)	•	•	LDX (EXT)	STX (EXT)

DIR = Direct Addressing Mode
EXT = Extended Addressing Mode
IMM = Immediate Addressing Mode
IND = Index Addressing Mode
INH = Inherent Addressing Mode
REL = Relative Addressing Mode
A = Accumulator A
B = Accumulator B

*Unimplemented Op Code

Table 8-5. M6800 instruction map. (*Courtesy of Motorola*)

L: Load Memory from Magnetic Tape. The load function is used to retrieve from audio magnetic-tape data that was recorded using the Punch function described against P.

N: Trace one instruction. This function permits stepping through an assembly program one instruction at a time for checking the program from a "break-point" (as designated by the following V function). The user IRQ interrupts are an exception for this function.

V: Set (and Remove) Breakpoints. To facilitate debugging, Breakpoints are set at preselected program steps. The breakpoint is set by entering the hex address of the desired breakpoint, followed by a V key closure (hhhhV)—repeated up to five times. The breakpoint entry function can be excited after any entry by using the escape function E. The monitor program on EPROMs will retain all the breakpoints until they are cleared.

LED display on the auxiliary board: The left-hand side 4 alphanumeric characters indicate the address display, and the right-hand side 2 alphanumeric characters provide the display of data.

As an example of Assembly Programming, the following program adds the five values in location numbers $10 through $14 using Accumulator A and stores the final result in location $15. The intermediate total is kept in Accumulator A; Accumulator B is used as a counter to count down the loop. The Index Register X contains a "pointer" (address) of the next location to be added.

The leftmost column of the following example in Assembly Programming contains the "Memory Address" where one byte of the program is stored. The next column contains the machine language OP-code and data for a particular instruction of MC6800 (as obtained by reference to Table 8-5). The next four columns contain the mnemonic representation of the program in assembly format. (The last column is merely reserved for remarks, as an aid to the programmer or follow-up.)

M6800 Coding Form: Title . . . , Problem . . .*, By . . . (*Courtesy of Motorola*)

Location	Hex		Instruction	Accumulator	Operand		Comment
							*Add five numbers at locations 10 through 14. *Put answer in location 15.
0020	8E	STRT	LDS		00	$FF	DEFINE STACK IN USER AREA
0021	00						
0022	FF						
0023	4F		CLR	A			TOTAL #0
0024	C6		LDA	B	#05		INITIALIZE COUNTER
0025	05						
0026	CE		LDX		00	#$10	POINT X TO LOCATION 10
0027	00						
0028	10						
0029	AB	LOOP	ADD	A	00	,X	ADD 1 LOCATION TO TOTAL
002A	00						
002B	08		INX				POINT X TO NEXT LOCATION
002C	5A		DEC	B			DONE ALL 5 LOCATIONS?
002D	26		BNE		LOOP		BRANCH IF NOT
002E	FA						
002F	97		STA	A	$15		SAVE ANSWER
0030	15						
0031	3F		SWI				GO TO MONITOR (SOFTWARE INTERRUPT)

If any error is made while writing the preceding program, it is corrected during the step-by-step "debugging," using up to five breakpoints, Register Display, and Trace through. When a single instruction is executed and traced through, associated timing waveforms at the binary counters and flip-flops aid in debugging if the error is connected with hardware circuitry (and not one of software).

8-36. STATUS OF MICROCOMPUTER SOFTWARE WITH HIGH-LEVEL LANGUAGES (HLL-SOFTWARE)

8-36.1. Intel PL/M Software Engineering.* PL/M is a high-level language exclusively developed to simplify the programming of Intel 8008/8080/8085/8086 microcomputer systems using *either 8-bit or 16-bit words.* (A corresponding PL/Z software is available for the higher throughput chips Z-80/Z-80A/Z-8000 of Zilog.)

Along the lines of the Fortran-IV/V and PL/1 high-level languages, by using *structured design techniques* for writing *correct* programs, the PL/M *compiler* facilitates the automatic control of the internal registers, main memory, and stacks, and the external memory and peripherals in disk and tape operating systems via the input/output interface. With the use of high-capacity 64-K bit RAMs, PROMs, and PLAs, reliable PL/M software development, checkout, portability, and documentation for program maintenance and modification are presently feasible in microcomputer systems as well—and at comparatively low cost.

The characteristics and modular-software development methodology are explained with simple explanatory definitions in Section 8-36.3. The PL/M compilers look after the details of machine and assembly language programming, while the programmer concentrates on the effective software and logic design. A PL/M compiler may be directly outputted into the Intel series of 8- and 16-bit *simulator programs* for interactive, symbolic debugging, or may be punched to paper tape in hexadecimal (hex) format for loading into an Intellec microcomputer development system. The PL/M compilers are written in ANSI standard Fortran IV, and are designed to *run on timeshare* on any minicomputer or large-scale computer system using minimum 32-bit integer format (word size).

8-36.2. PL/M Features.* Salient features of the PL/M include:

1. A sequence of *declarations* and *executable statements* make the program.

2. The declarations allow the control of *memory allocation* and define simple *textual macros* and *procedures.* As a *block-structured language,* the procedures may involve secondary declarations and their subsidiary functions, which in turn might include further procedures.

3. The procedural facility reflects *modular programming* as a sectional *division into subprocedures* such as keyboard input, binary-to-decimal conversion, and output printing. The subprocedures facilitate easy formulation and debugging, and make a convenient *library* for direct incorporation into *other programs.*

4. The *data* are made up of (1) BYTE, variable or constant, as an 8-bit identity and (2) ADDRESS, variable or constant, as a 16-bit (2-byte) word. The programmer can declare variable *names* or *vectors* (*arrays*) to represent BYTE or ADDRESS.

5. The executable statements specify computation such as arithmetic, boolean algebra, and operators BYTE and ADDRESS for comparison. Combined, these *relational operators* and *operands* make the *algebraic* EXPRESSIONS such as A/(B - 1)*C—which are actually the PL/M ASSIGNMENT *statements.* They compute the result and store it in a *memory location* defined by a *variable name* such as Q in the statement,

*All mnemonics copyright Intel Corporation 1975.

$$Q = A/(B - 1)*C$$

The computation to the right of equal sign is done first and saved in a memory location labeled by Q.

6. Conditional tests, branching, loop control, and procedure invocation with parameter passing make similar statements. Powerful *control block-structures* specify the *flow of program execution*. Basic *I/O statements* to read and write BYTES to and from the microprocessors may be defined by other procedures for more complex I/O operations.

7. A *compile-time macro* facility in the compiler provides a method of *automatic text-substitution* of a *character string* for a *symbolic name*. (A *string* is an arbitrary sequence of characters or alphanumerics.)

8. Programs are written *free-form*, with column-independent freely inserted *spaces*. The *character set* is a subset of both ASCII and EBCDIC codes. The following represent the valid PL/M alphanumeric and special characters:

ABCD . . . WXYZ 012 . . 789 $ = ./( ) +-'*, <> : ;

Any other characters are merely invalid, and they are substituted by respective spaces. Special characters and combinations of special characters have special meanings in a PL/M program.

9. An *identifier* (up to 31 characters in length) names variables, procedures, macros, and statement labels. The identifier must be part alphabetic first and then alphabetic or numeric. Dollar signs are for readability only and are ignored by compiler. There are, however, 34 RESERVED WORDS, as part of PL/M language, but *not* used by programmer as identifiers. (An example of an identifier: X GAMMA LONGIDENTIFIERWITH-NUMBER3.) Blanks may or may not be used in PL/M statements of identifiers and reserved and special characters. For readability, explanation, and documentation, a comment in the form shown is permissible; the delimiters enable the compiler to ignore the comment.

/*THIS IS A COMMENT*/

8-36.3. Structured Programming and Top-Down Design in PL/M.† Former programming techniques of general-purpose digital computers were without any standardized discipline, and hence most of those operating systems had too many errors. The situation has changed for the better with the latest techniques, just in time for the high-level language (HLL) programming of the new generation of a multitude of low-cost microcomputer systems. The PL-series of HLLs, and PASCAL in its modified forms are gradually taking a predominant role in fairly efficient and economic software engineering applications in these new systems, which apparently have an explosive character in demand and high-quality software. The latest programming techniques under consideration relate to two powerful software techniques: *structured programming* and *top-down design*. They enable error-free programming with a minimum of experience.

Structured programming is designed in terms of four *control structures–sequencing, selection, repetition,* and *subroutine* or *function invocation*—without the need of any elaborate flowcharts and the confusing, excessive GO TO statements common in most languages previously. Next, the *top-down design* relates to a hierarchical procedure or collection of statements in the form of *modules*, shown in the following multilevel hier-

†All mnemonics copyright Intel Corporation 1975.

archical *tree*. Ready *documentation* is provided by mixing comments right inside the actual programs written in the high-level languages under consideration.

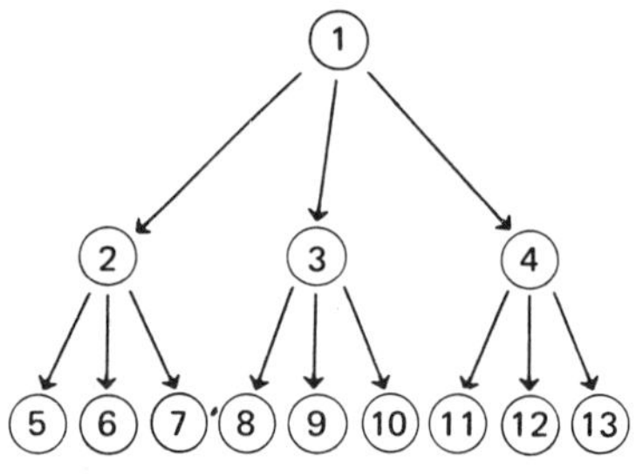

Entire program calls on *modules* 2, 3, and 4 to perform its *function* as *functional blocks* on level 2.

Independent modules in level 3 implement software with operations available in the HLL used (5 . . . 13) . . . (last statement section).

Niklaus Wirth, who initiated the PASCAL high-level language, defines *structured programming* as the formulation of programs in hierarchical, nested structures of statements and objects of computation. The decomposition of the modular hierarchical problem structure is described as a *stepwise refinement* or fine-tuning procedure. The four basic constructs and the corresponding formatting of well-formed structured programming of stepwise refinement are illustrated in the diagram on page 281. These constructs are presently introduced in many of the popular high-level languages including FORTRAN. The constructs, which help logical thinking processes, are the constituent submodules of Programmable Logic Trees shown in the structured hierarchical tree. This is the modular way the hardware is designed.

8-36.3.1. Definitions

1. *Data structure* can be organized into structures, arrays, stacks, strings, trees, plexes, graphs, queues, deques, etc.

2. *Structure* is a PL/ high-level-language term that refers to a *block of memory*. It can be organized into several *levels*. For example, if a 4-BYTE location is named PIECE, it can be DECLARED with four contiguous addresses into (level 1) PIECE TYPE; (level 2) PIECE COLOR; (level 3) PIECE POSITION ROW; (level 3) PIECE POSITION COLUMN. The three levels are actually termed *offsets* 0, 1, 2 in this example. A structure is designated by a POINTER, which in turn is the name of a WORD; COUNTER is the corresponding name of a BYTE. An address calculation is carried out at the *translation time* into the machine code at the *run-time* of the computer.

3. *Linear array* is similar to the structure; however, with the structure, the offset is known at the translation time, whereas the *array*, as a group of bytes or words, must be calculated at the run-time with extra access-time. An array will consist of several PIECES (or blocks of BYTES).

4. A two-dimensional array stored by *rows* or *columns* is declared a TABLE.

5. A *queue* is a linear list whose ends are labeled *front* and *rear*; it is implemented by a circular list (or *circular array*).

6. A *deque* (pronounced "deck") is a double-ended queue. A *bottomless stack* implements the deque with an *overflow* into tape or disk storage.

7. A *string* is a sequence of *characters*; it is stored in the computer as a linear array of character codes. One large array is preferred for all the strings in a program. The computer itself allocates space from this array for newly formed strings. A string is denoted by its *length* and the *address* of its leftmost byte, which together make a *descriptor*—it is declared as LIKE STRING. The length of the strings, called SIZE, is limited to the range,

1. Sequence: concatenation

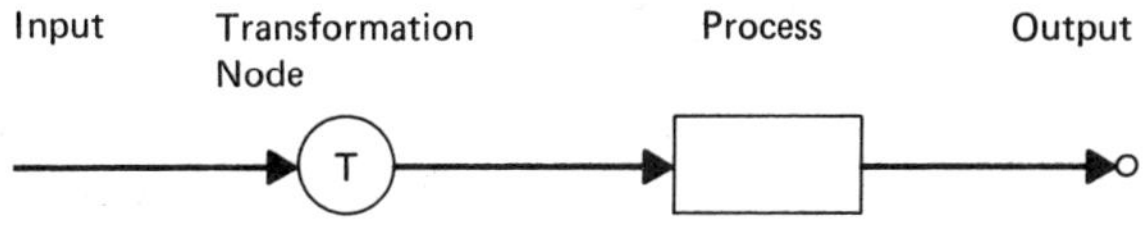

A process may be an algorithmic procedure or a submodule of one of these constructs with input and output T-nodes.

2. Selection:

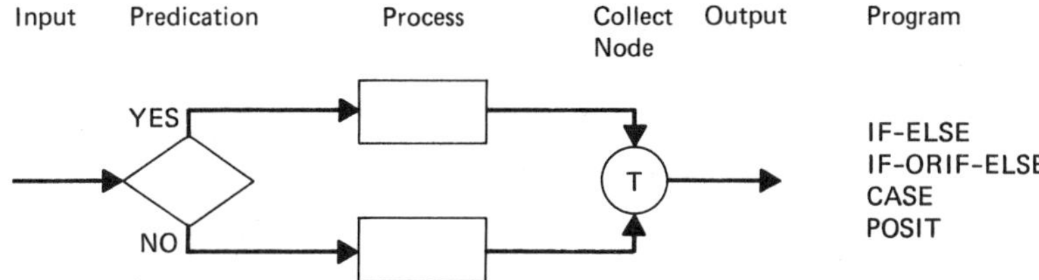

Program

IF-ELSE
IF-ORIF-ELSE
CASE
POSIT

POSIT stands for abnormal exit involving a False codition after an initial True condition.

3. Iteration:

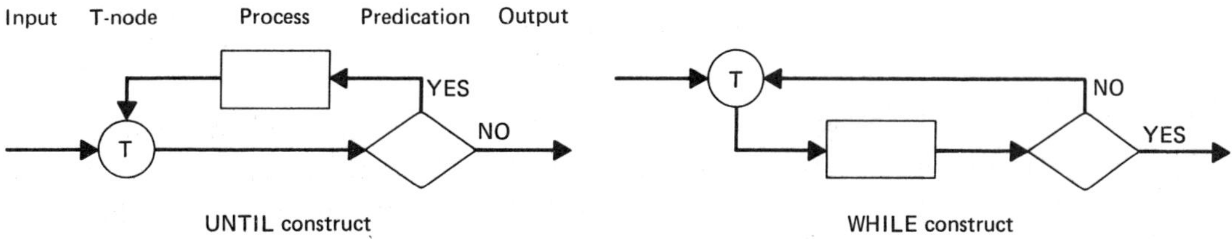

4. EXIT: escape

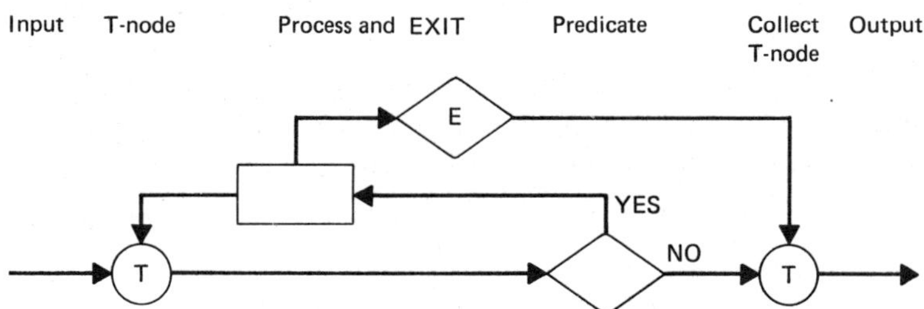

null-string 0 to a maximum length of 255. This limit facilitates the sensing of when a *garbage collection* (or recovery of unused space) is required.

8. A *plex* is a *set of memory-blocks* interrelated with *pointers*. These memory-blocks are called *nodes*, and, since a memory-block is also a *structure*, a node is defined by a structure declaration. In general, one such *structure declaration* will do if all the nodes of a plex have the same structure.

9. A *chain* is a *linked list* implemented as a plex. If the last element of the list is linked back to the first, it is a *ring*. A chain may be searched by a *sequential search*.

10. A *computer tree* branches downward with the "root" of the tree at the top, and "leaves" at the bottom; the tree represents (1) hierarchical, (2) nested, (3) branching, and (4) converging structures. A collection of trees is called a *forest*. A tree in which each node has exactly two branches is called a *binary tree*. If every node that is not a "leaf" has two branches, left and right, it is called a *complete binary tree*. A *preorder traversal* represents node to branches left to right, and the inverse traversal from branches to the node is *postorder*. Compact bit tables require a single bit for each entry. Complicated

programming, involving *shifting and masking operations*, is required to extract the desired bits from the bytes or words in which they are stored. Algorithms are *recursive* when the data structure being manipulated is itself recursively defined. *Recursive* indicates bounded nonoscillatory stable parameters.

11. Maps, networks, mazes, signal flowcharts, schematic diagrams, state transition diagrams, syntax diagrams, and so forth are all known as *graphs*; they consist of *points* or *nodes* connected by lines or *arcs*. If the arcs have arrowheads, they are *directed graphs* with initial and terminal nodes.

12. A *record* is a block of data referring to a single entity. The record is usually a structure, and the components of the structure define the components or *fields*. Each entity will have certain properties or *attributes*. The information stored refers to an entity. When a program has *constructed an internal entity* as an aid to its manipulation, compilers make frequent use of such *internal constructs*.

13. A *binary search* requires an average of $\log_2 N - 1$ probes, and a maximum of $\log_2 N + 1$ probes, where N is the length of the list and $\log_2 N = \log N/\log 2$.

14. *Hashing* is a special technique used to store the records of a list in *random order*. The hashing function converts a key into an address or more commonly a *subscript*. The technique is ineffective after the list is about 80% filled. To avoid collisions as much as possible, the hashing function should distribute the stored records throughout the table and should *avoid clustering* them all in one or two areas. A hash table consists of a *prime area* and an *overflow area*.

15. *Bubble sort* is the simplest of the *exchange-sorting routines* to program for lists stored in *internal main memory* of a computer. It is the least efficient because the time required is proportional to N^2, if it is the number of records to be sorted. The *shell sort* is more efficient since the time required is proportional to $N^{1.2}$. The more complex *Quicksort* is the most efficient sorting technique with the corresponding figure $N*\log_2 N$.

The *external sorting* techniques for tape and disk memory are comparatively slow. *Merging* is the technique used for sequential access to files. Given two or more *ordered sequences* of records, we can merge them into a single sequence that is also ordered.*

The following tables present (1) a sample PL/M program, (2) PL/M vocabulary, (3) special characters, (4) reserved words, (5) predeclared identifiers, (6) list of instructions for the original Intel 8-bit 8080 microprocessor, and (7) a typical set of macro-assembly programs with mnemonics.

*For further information, see Neil Graham, *Microprocessor Programming for Computer Hobbyists* (Blue Ridge Summit, Pennsylvania: Tab Books, 1977).

8-36.3.2. Typical HLL software associated with microcomputer systems.

PL/M PROGRAMMING
PL/M Reserved Words

RESERVED WORD	USE
IF THEN ELSE	conditional tests and alternative execution
DO PROCEDURE INTERRUPT END	statement grouping and procedure definition
DECLARE BYTE ADDRESS LABEL INITIAL DATA LITERALLY BASED	data declarations
GO TO BY GOTO CASE WHILE	unconditional branching and loop control
CALL	procedure call
RETURN	procedure return
HALT	machine stop
ENABLE	interrupt enable
DISABLE	interrupt disable
OR AND XOR NOT	boolean operators
MOD	remainder after division
PLUS	add with carry
MINUS	subtract with borrow
EOF	end of input file (compiler control)

PL/M PROGRAMMING
PL/M Special Characters

SYMBOL	NAME	USE
$	dollar sign	compiler toggles, number and identifier spacer
=	equal sign	relational test operator, assignment operator
:=	assign	imbedded assignment operator
.	dot	address operator
/	slash	division operator
/*		left comment delimiter
*/		right comment delimiter
(	left paren	left delimiter of lists, subscripts, and expressions
)	right paren	right delimiter of lists, subscripts, and expressions
+	plus	addition operator
-	minus	subtraction operator
'	apostrophe	string delimiter
*	asterisk	multiplication operator
<	less than	relational test operator
>	greater than	relational test operator
<=	less or equal	relational test operator
>=	greater or equal	relational test operator
<>	not equal	relational test operator
:	colon	label delimiter
;	semicolon	statement delimiter
,	comma	list element delimiter

PL/M PROGRAMMING
PL/M Pre-declared Identifiers

CARRY
DEC
DOUBLE
HIGH
INPUT
LAST
LENGTH
LOW
MEMORY
OUTPUT
PARITY
ROL
ROR
SCL
SCR
SHL
SHR
SIGN
STACKPTR
TIME
ZERO

PL/M PROGRAMMING
ASCII codes

The ASCII (American Standard Code for Information Interchange) was adopted by the American National Standards Institute, Inc. (ANSI) in 1968. The standard itself, as distinct from the summary here presented, is available from ANSI, 1430 Broadway, New York, NY 10018, as USAS X3.4-1968. A previous version of this standard was adopted by the National Bureau of Standards as a Federal Information Processing Standard (FIPS 1). ASCII is a seven-bit code, which we are representing here by a pair of hexadecimal digits.

00	NUL	20	SP	40	@	60	
01	SOH	21	!	41	A	61	a
02	STX	22	"	42	B	62	b
03	ETX	23	#	43	C	63	c
04	EOT	24	$	44	D	64	d
05	ENQ	25	%	45	E	65	e
06	ACK	26	&	46	F	66	f
07	BEL	27	´	47	G	67	g
08	BS	28	(	48	H	68	h
09	HT	29	)	49	I	69	i
0A	LF	2A	*	4A	J	6A	j
0B	VT	2B	+	4B	K	6B	k
0C	FF	2C	,	4C	L	6C	l
0D	CR	2D	-	4D	M	6D	m
0E	SO	2E	.	4E	N	6E	n
0F	SI	2F	/	4F	O	6F	o
10	DLE	30	0	50	P	70	p
11	DC1	31	1	51	Q	71	q
12	DC2	32	2	52	R	72	r
13	DC3	33	3	53	S	73	s
14	DC4	34	4	54	T	74	t
15	NAK	35	5	55	U	75	u
16	SYN	36	6	56	V	76	v
17	ETB	37	7	57	W	77	w
18	CAN	38	8	58	X	78	x
19	EM	39	9	59	Y	79	y
1A	SUB	3A	:	5A	Z	7A	z
1B	ESC	3B	;	5B	[	7B	[(braces)
1C	FS	3C	<	5C	\	7C	! (bar)
1D	GS	3D	=	5D	]	7D	] (braces)
1E	RS	3E	>	5E	^	7E	(tilde)
1F	US	3F	_	5F	_	7F	DEL

PL/M PROGRAMMING
Grammar of the PL/M Language

VOCABULARY

	terminal symbols	nonterminals
1	!	<program>
2	;	<statement list>
3	HALT	<statement>
4	ENABLE	<basic statement>
5	DISABLE	<if statement>
6	IF	<assignment>
7	THEN	<group>
8	ELSE	<procedure definition>
9	DO	<return statement>
10	CASE	<call statement>
11	INTERRUPT	<go to statement>
12	<number>	<declaration statement>
13	PROCEDURE	<label definition>
14	<identifier>	<if clause>
15	)	<true part>
16	(	<expression>
17	,	<group head>
18	END	<ending>
19	:	<step definition>
20	RETURN	<while clause>
21	CALL	<case selector>
22	GO	<variable>
23	TO	<replace>
24	GOTO	<iteration control>
25	DECLARE	<to>
26	LITERALLY	<by>
27	<string>	<while>
28	DATA	<procedure head>
29	BYTE	<procedure name>
30	ADDRESS	<type>
31	LABEL	<parameter list>
32	BASED	<parameter head>
33	INITIAL	<go to>
34	=	<declaration element>
35	:=	<type declaration>
36	OR	<data list>
37	XOR	<data head>
38	AND	<constant>
39	NOT	<identifier specification>
40	<	<bound head>
41	>	<initial list>
42	+	<variable name>
43	-	<identifier list>
44	PLUS	<based variable>
45	MINUS	<initial head>
46	*	<left part>
47	/	<logical expression>
48	MOD	<logical factor>
49	.	<logical secondary>
50	BY	<logical primary>
51	WHILE	<arithmetic expression>
52		<relation>
53		<comp>
54		<term>
55		<primary>
56		<constant head>
57		<subscript head>

PL/M PROGRAMMING
Sort Program

A SORTING PROGRAM

Now we construct an example program using expressions, do-groups, and subscripted variables. Suppose a vector A contains a set of numbers in an arbitrary order, and we wish to sort them into ascending order.

```
/* INITIAL ORDERING OF 'A' IS ARBITRARY */

DECLARE A(10) ADDRESS INITIAL
  (33, 10, 2000, 400, 410, 3, 3, 33, 500, 1999);

                /* BUBBLE SORT */

/* SWITCHED = (BOOLEAN) HAVE WE DONE ANY
              SWITCHING YET THIS SCAN? */
DECLARE (I, SWITCHED) BYTE, TEMP ADDRESS;

SWITCHED = 1;         /* SWITCHED=TRUE MEANS NOT DONE YET */
DO WHILE SWITCHED;

  SWITCHED = 0;           /* BEGIN NEXT SCAN OF A */
  DO I = 0 TO 8;
    IF A(I) > A(I+1) THEN
      DO;                 /* FOUND A PAIR OUT OF ORDER */
      SWITCHED = 1;       /* SET SWITCHED = TRUE */
      TEMP = A(I);        /* SWITCH THEM INTO ORDER */
      A(I) = A(I+1);
      A(I+1) = TEMP;
      END;
  END;
  /* HAVE NOW COMPLETED A SCAN */

END /*WHILE*/;
/* HAVE NOW COMPLETED A SCAN WITH NO SWITCHING */

EOF
```

This program scans the vector A, comparing each adjacent pair of elements. When it finds a pair out of order, it swaps them. It does this repeatedly, until it completes an entire scan of A without having swapped any pair. Then it is done.

The variable SWITCHED keeps track of whether we have done a swap yet, this time through the array. So we zero it each time we start a new scan, and set it each time we do a swap.

PL/M PROGRAMMING
Interrupt Processing

```
DECLARE KEYMAX LITERALLY '72';
DECLARE KEYBUFF (KEYMAX) BYTE, KEYPTR BYTE;
DECLARE OVERFLOW LABEL;

KEYBOARD$PROCESS: PROCEDURE INTERRUPT 3;
   DECLARE CHAR BYTE;
   KEYPTR = KEYPTR+1;
   IF KEYPTR > KEYMAX THEN GO TO OVERFLOW;
   IF (CHAR := INPUT(5)) = '$' THEN RETURN;
   KEYBUFF(KEYPTR) = CHAR;
END KEYBOARD$PROCESS;

KEYPTR = .(KEYBUFF);
ENABLE;
/* MAIN PROGRAM */
...

OVERFLOW:
/* KEYBOARD BUFFER OVERFLOW */
...

EOF
```

In this example, KEYBOARDPROCESS operates on the global variables KEYPTR and KEYBUFF each time RST 3 is executed. If KEYPTR exceeds KEYMAX then control is transferred to the outer block label OVERFLOW and the saved machine state is discarded -- control never returns to the interrupted process. If KEYPTR does not exceed KEYMAX then the value of input port 5 is read and stored into CHAR. If the value of CHAR is ASCII dollar sign, then the interrupt procedure returns immediately to the interrupted process. Otherwise the value of CHAR is placed in the vector KEYBUFF and control returns to the interrupted process.

The 8080 interrupt mechanism is disabled by the occurence of an interrupt, and may be explicitly enabled with an ENABLE statement inside the interrupt procedure. Interrupts are enabled by a return from an interrupt procedure. Caution should be exercised when enabling interrupts inside an interrupt procedure: two activations of the same interrupt procedure must never be in process simultaneously, since there is only one data area for both activations. This exclusion can be accomplished by specifically disabling the interrupt source, or by establishing a priority of interrupts with external circuitry. The safest method is to leave interrupts disabled during all interrupt processing.

Interrupt procedures may contain nested non-interrupt procedures. On completion of a call, these nested procedures return to their point of call inside the interrupt procedure in which they are defined; it is only the RETURN's at the outermost interrupt procedure level which cause the machine state of the interrupted process to be restored.

Instruction set, Intel 8080 microprocessor.

Summary of Processor Instructions
By Alphabetical Order

Mnemonic	Description	Instruction Code[1] D_7	D_6	D_5	D_4	D_3	D_2	D_1	D_0	Clock[2] Cycles
ACI	Add immediate to A with carry	1	1	0	0	1	1	1	0	7
ADC M	Add memory to A with carry	1	0	0	0	1	1	1	0	7
ADC r	Add register to A with carry	1	0	0	0	1	S	S	S	4
ADD M	Add memory to A	1	0	0	0	0	1	0	1	7
ADD r	Add register to A	1	0	0	0	0	S	S	S	4
ADI	Add immediate to A	1	1	0	0	0	1	1	0	7
ANA M	And memory with A	1	0	1	0	0	1	1	0	7
ANA r	And register with A	1	0	1	0	0	S	S	S	4
ANI	And immediate with A	1	1	1	0	0	1	1	0	7
CALL	Call unconditional	1	1	0	0	1	1	0	1	17
CC	Call on carry	1	1	0	1	1	1	0	0	11/17
CM	Call on minus	1	1	1	1	1	1	0	0	11/17
CMA	Compliment A	0	0	1	0	1	1	1	1	4
CMC	Compliment carry	0	0	1	1	1	1	1	1	4
CMP M	Compare memory with A	1	0	1	1	1	1	1	0	7
CMP r	Compare register with A	1	0	1	1	1	S	S	S	4
CNC	Call on no carry	1	1	0	1	0	1	0	0	11/17
CNZ	Call on no zero	1	1	0	0	0	1	0	0	11/17
CP	Call on positive	1	1	1	1	0	1	0	0	11/17
CPE	Call on parity even	1	1	1	0	1	1	0	0	11/17
CPI	Compare immediate with A	1	1	1	1	1	1	1	0	7
CPO	Call on parity odd	1	1	1	0	0	1	0	0	11/17
CZ	Call on zero	1	1	0	0	1	1	0	0	11/17
DAA	Decimal adjust A	0	0	1	0	0	1	1	1	4
DAD B	Add B & C to H & L	0	0	0	0	1	0	0	1	10
DAD D	Add D & E to H & L	0	0	0	1	1	0	0	1	10
DAD H	Add H & L to H & L	0	0	1	0	1	0	0	1	10
DAD SP	Add stack pointer to H & L	0	0	1	1	1	0	0	1	10
DCR M	Decrement memory	0	0	1	1	0	1	0	1	10
DCR r	Decrement register	0	0	D	D	D	1	0	1	5
DCX B	Decrement B & C	0	0	0	0	1	0	1	1	5
DCX D	Decrement D & E	0	0	0	1	1	0	1	1	5
DCX H	Decrement H & L	0	0	1	0	1	0	1	1	5
DCX SP	Decrement stack pointer	0	0	1	1	1	0	1	1	5
DI	Disable Interrupt	1	1	1	1	0	0	1	1	4
EI	Enable Interrupts	1	1	1	1	1	0	1	1	4
HLT	Halt	0	1	1	1	0	1	1	0	7
IN	Input	1	1	0	1	1	0	1	1	10
INR M	Increment memory	0	0	1	1	0	1	0	0	10
INR r	Increment register	0	0	D	D	D	1	0	0	5
INX B	Increment B & C registers	0	0	0	0	0	0	1	1	5
INX D	Increment D & E registers	0	0	0	1	0	0	1	1	5
INX H	Increment H & L registers	0	0	1	0	0	0	1	1	5
INX SP	Increment stack pointer	0	0	1	1	0	0	1	1	5
JC	Jump on carry	1	1	0	1	1	0	1	0	10
JM	Jump on minus	1	1	1	1	1	0	1	0	10
JMP	Jump unconditional	1	1	0	0	0	0	1	1	10
JNC	Jump on no carry	1	1	0	1	0	0	1	0	10
JNZ	Jump on no zero	1	1	0	0	0	0	1	0	10
JP	Jump on positive	1	1	1	1	0	0	1	0	10
JPE	Jump on parity even	1	1	1	0	1	0	1	0	10
JPO	Jump on parity odd	1	1	1	0	0	0	1	0	10
JZ	Jump on zero	1	1	0	0	1	0	1	0	10
LDA	Load A direct	0	0	1	1	1	0	1	0	13
LDAX B	Load A indirect	0	0	0	0	1	0	1	0	7
LDAX D	Load A indirect	0	0	0	1	1	0	1	0	7
LHLD	Load H & L direct	0	0	1	0	1	0	1	0	16
LXI B	Load immediate register Pair B & C	0	0	0	0	0	0	0	1	10
LXI D	Load immediate register Pair D & E	0	0	0	1	0	0	0	1	10
LXI H	Load immediate register Pair H & L	0	0	1	0	0	0	0	1	10
LXI SP	Load immediate stack pointer	0	0	1	1	0	0	0	1	10

Mnemonic	Description	Instruction Code[1] D_7	D_6	D_5	D_4	D_3	D_2	D_1	D_0	Clock[2] Cycles
MVI M	Move immediate memory	0	0	1	1	0	1	1	0	10
MVI r	Move immediate register	0	0	D	D	D	1	1	0	7
MOV M, r	Move register to memory	0	1	1	1	0	S	S	S	7
MOV r, M	Move memory to register	0	1	D	D	D	1	1	0	7
MOV r1, r2	Move register to register	0	1	D	D	D	S	S	S	5
NOP	No operation	0	0	0	0	0	0	0	0	4
ORA M	Or memory with A	1	0	1	1	0	1	1	0	7
ORA r	Or register with A	1	0	1	1	0	S	S	S	4
ORI	Or immediate with A	1	1	1	1	0	1	1	0	7
OUT	Output	1	1	0	1	0	0	1	1	10
PCHL	H & L to program counter	1	1	1	0	1	0	0	1	5
POP B	Pop register pair B & C off stack	1	1	0	0	0	0	0	1	10
POP D	Pop register pair D & E off stack	1	1	0	1	0	0	0	1	10
POP H	Pop register pair H & L off stack	1	1	1	0	0	0	0	1	10
POP PSW	Pop A and Flags off stack	1	1	1	1	0	0	0	1	10
PUSH B	Push register Pair B & C on stack	1	1	0	0	0	1	0	1	11
PUSH D	Push register Pair D & E on stack	1	1	0	1	0	1	0	1	11
PUSH H	Push register Pair H & L on stack	1	1	1	0	0	1	0	1	11
PUSH PSW	Push A and Flags on stack	1	1	1	1	0	1	0	1	11
RAL	Rotate A left through carry	0	0	0	1	0	1	1	1	4
RAR	Rotate A right through carry	0	0	0	1	1	1	1	1	4
RC	Return on carry	1	1	0	1	1	0	0	0	5/11
RET	Return	1	1	0	0	1	0	0	1	10
RLC	Rotate A left	0	0	0	0	0	1	1	1	4
RM	Return on minus	1	1	1	1	1	0	0	0	5/11
RNC	Return on no carry	1	1	0	1	0	0	0	0	5/11
RNZ	Return on no zero	1	1	0	0	0	0	0	0	5/11
RP	Return on positive	1	1	1	1	0	0	0	0	5/11
RPE	Return on parity even	1	1	1	0	1	0	0	0	5/11
RPO	Return on parity odd	1	1	1	0	0	0	0	0	5/11
RRC	Rotate A right	0	0	0	0	1	1	1	1	4
RST	Restart	1	1	A	A	A	1	1	1	11
RZ	Return on zero	1	1	0	0	1	0	0	0	5/11
SBB M	Subtract memory from A with borrow	1	0	0	1	1	1	1	0	7
SBB r	Subtract register from A with borrow	1	0	0	1	1	S	S	S	4
SBI	Subtract immediate from A with borrow	1	1	0	1	1	1	1	0	7
SHLD	Store H & L direct	0	0	1	0	0	0	1	0	16
SPHL	H & L to stack pointer	1	1	1	1	1	0	0	1	5
STA	Store A direct	0	0	1	1	0	0	1	0	13
STAX B	Store A indirect	0	0	0	0	0	0	1	0	7
STAX D	Store A indirect	0	0	0	1	0	0	1	0	7
STC	Set carry	0	0	1	1	0	1	1	1	4
SUB M	Subtract memory from A	1	0	0	1	0	1	1	0	7
SUB r	Subtract register from A	1	0	0	1	0	S	S	S	4
SUI	Subtract immediate from A	1	1	0	1	0	1	1	0	7
XCHG	Exchange D & E, H & L Registers	1	1	1	0	1	0	1	1	4
XRA M	Exclusive Or memory with A	1	0	1	0	1	1	1	0	7
XRA r	Exclusive Or register with A	1	0	1	0	1	S	S	S	4
XRI	Exclusive Or immediate with A	1	1	1	0	1	1	1	0	7
XTHL	Exchange top of stack, H & L	1	1	1	0	0	0	1	1	18

NOTES: 1. DDD or SSS – 000 B – 001 C – 010 D – 011E – 100H – 101L – 110 Memory – 111 A.
2. Two possible cycle times, (5/11) indicate instruction cycles dependent on condition flags.

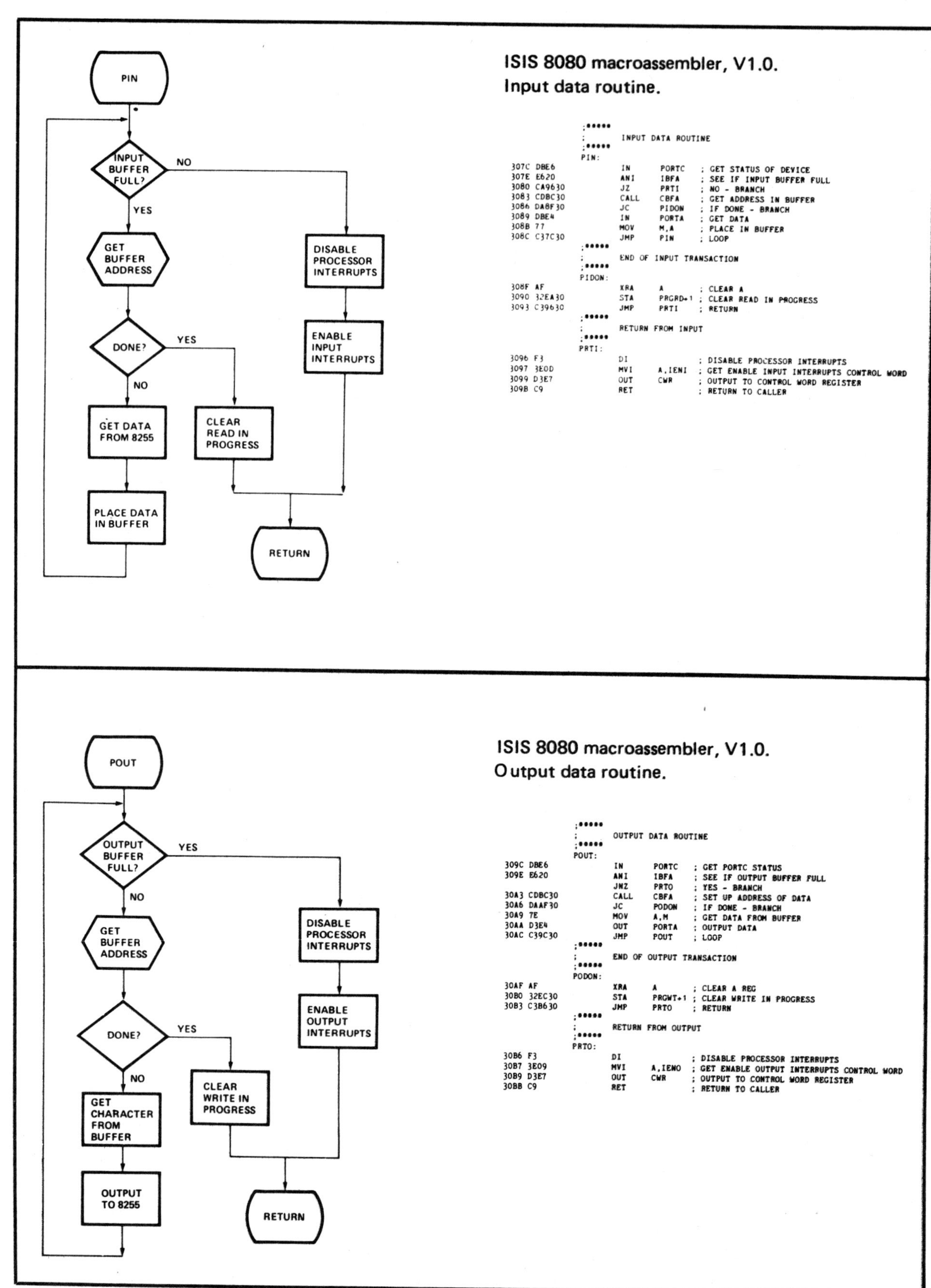

ISIS 8080 macroassembler, V1.0.
Input data routine.

```
                ;*****
                ;       INPUT DATA ROUTINE
                ;*****
                PIN:
307C DBE6               IN      PORTC   ; GET STATUS OF DEVICE
307E E620               ANI     IBFA    ; SEE IF INPUT BUFFER FULL
3080 CA9630             JZ      PRTI    ; NO - BRANCH
3083 CDBC30             CALL    CBFA    ; GET ADDRESS IN BUFFER
3086 DA8F30             JC      PIDON   ; IF DONE - BRANCH
3089 DBE4               IN      PORTA   ; GET DATA
308B 77                 MOV     M,A     ; PLACE IN BUFFER
308C C37C30             JMP     PIN     ; LOOP
                ;*****
                ;       END OF INPUT TRANSACTION
                ;*****
                PIDON:
308F AF                 XRA     A       ; CLEAR A
3090 32EA30             STA     PRGRD+1 ; CLEAR READ IN PROGRESS
3093 C39630             JMP     PRTI    ; RETURN
                ;*****
                ;       RETURN FROM INPUT
                ;*****
                PRTI:
3096 F3                 DI              ; DISABLE PROCESSOR INTERRUPTS
3097 3E0D               MVI     A,IENI  ; GET ENABLE INPUT INTERRUPTS CONTROL WORD
3099 D3E7               OUT     CWR     ; OUTPUT TO CONTROL WORD REGISTER
309B C9                 RET             ; RETURN TO CALLER
```


ISIS 8080 macroassembler, V1.0.
Output data routine.

```
                ;*****
                ;       OUTPUT DATA ROUTINE
                ;*****
                POUT:
309C DBE6               IN      PORTC   ; GET PORTC STATUS
309E E620               ANI     IBFA    ; SEE IF OUTPUT BUFFER FULL
                        JNZ     PRTO    ; YES - BRANCH
30A3 CDBC30             CALL    CBFA    ; SET UP ADDRESS OF DATA
30A6 DAAF30             JC      PODON   ; IF DONE - BRANCH
30A9 7E                 MOV     A,M     ; GET DATA FROM BUFFER
30AA D3E4               OUT     PORTA   ; OUTPUT DATA
30AC C39C30             JMP     POUT    ; LOOP
                ;*****
                ;       END OF OUTPUT TRANSACTION
                ;*****
                PODON:
30AF AF                 XRA     A       ; CLEAR A REG
30B0 32EC30             STA     PRGWT+1 ; CLEAR WRITE IN PROGRESS
30B3 C3B630             JMP     PRTO    ; RETURN
                ;*****
                ;       RETURN FROM OUTPUT
                ;*****
                PRTO:
30B6 F3                 DI              ; DISABLE PROCESSOR INTERRUPTS
30B7 3E09               MVI     A,IENO  ; GET ENABLE OUTPUT INTERRUPTS CONTROL WORD
30B9 D3E7               OUT     CWR     ; OUTPUT TO CONTROL WORD REGISTER
30BB C9                 RET             ; RETURN TO CALLER
```

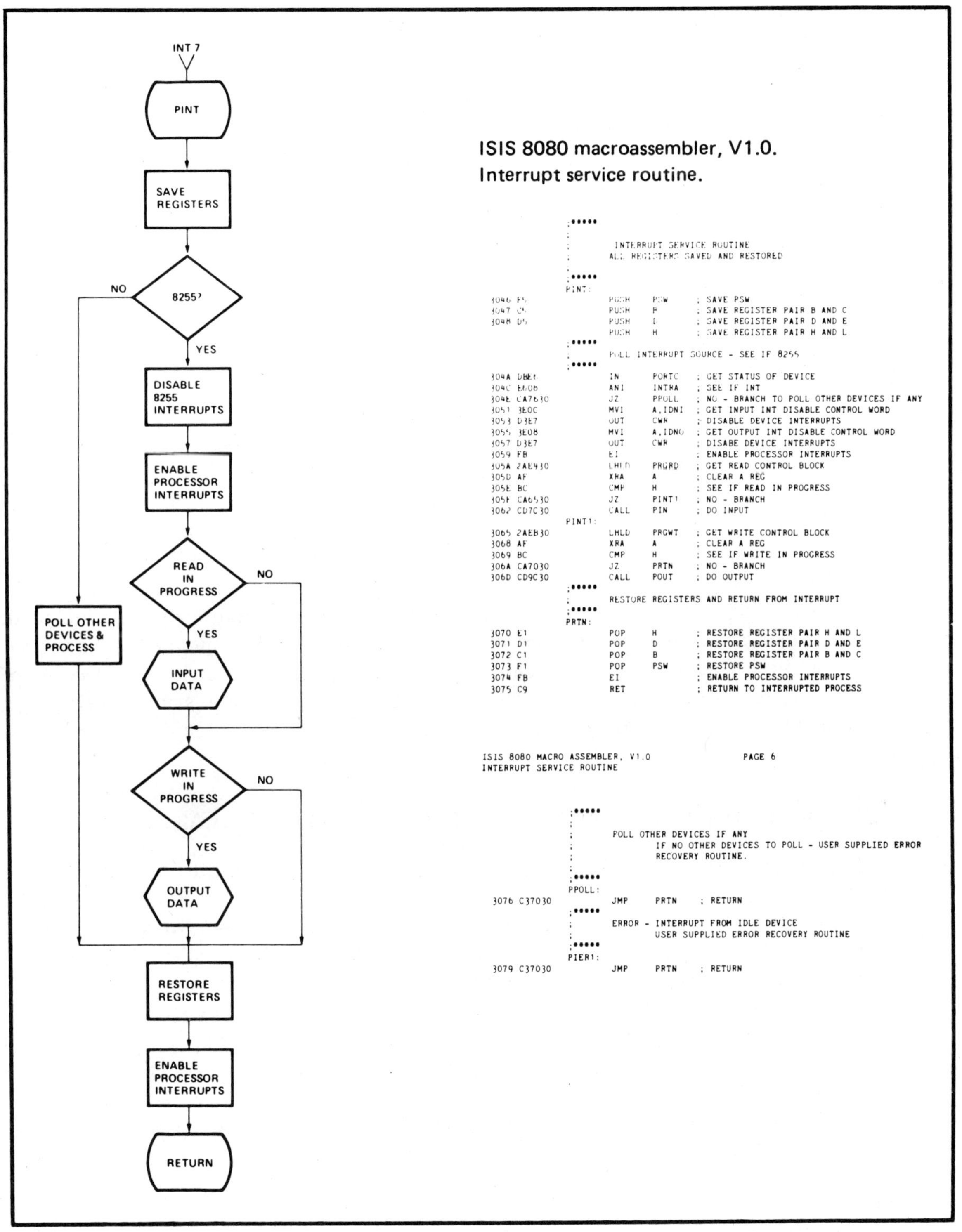

ISIS 8080 macroassembler, V1.0.
Interrupt service routine.

```
                ;*****
                ;
                ;       INTERRUPT SERVICE ROUTINE
                ;       ALL REGISTERS SAVED AND RESTORED
                ;
                ;*****
                PINT:
3046 F5                 PUSH    PSW     ; SAVE PSW
3047 C5                 PUSH    B       ; SAVE REGISTER PAIR B AND C
3048 D5                 PUSH    D       ; SAVE REGISTER PAIR D AND E
                        PUSH    H       ; SAVE REGISTER PAIR H AND L
                ;*****
                ;       POLL INTERRUPT SOURCE - SEE IF 8255
                ;*****
304A DBE6               IN      PORTC   ; GET STATUS OF DEVICE
304C E608               ANI     INTRA   ; SEE IF INT
304E CA7630             JZ      PPOLL   ; NO - BRANCH TO POLL OTHER DEVICES IF ANY
3051 3E0C               MVI     A,IDNI  ; GET INPUT INT DISABLE CONTROL WORD
3053 D3E7               OUT     CWR     ; DISABLE DEVICE INTERRUPTS
3055 3E08               MVI     A,IDNO  ; GET OUTPUT INT DISABLE CONTROL WORD
3057 D3E7               OUT     CWR     ; DISABE DEVICE INTERRUPTS
3059 FB                 EI              ; ENABLE PROCESSOR INTERRUPTS
305A 2AE930             LHLD    PRGRD   ; GET READ CONTROL BLOCK
305D AF                 XRA     A       ; CLEAR A REG
305E BC                 CMP     H       ; SEE IF READ IN PROGRESS
305F CA6530             JZ      PINT1   ; NO - BRANCH
3062 CD7C30             CALL    PIN     ; DO INPUT
                PINT1:
3065 2AEB30             LHLD    PRGWT   ; GET WRITE CONTROL BLOCK
3068 AF                 XRA     A       ; CLEAR A REG
3069 BC                 CMP     H       ; SEE IF WRITE IN PROGRESS
306A CA7030             JZ      PRTN    ; NO - BRANCH
306D CD9C30             CALL    POUT    ; DO OUTPUT
                ;*****
                ;       RESTORE REGISTERS AND RETURN FROM INTERRUPT
                ;*****
                PRTN:
3070 E1                 POP     H       ; RESTORE REGISTER PAIR H AND L
3071 D1                 POP     D       ; RESTORE REGISTER PAIR D AND E
3072 C1                 POP     B       ; RESTORE REGISTER PAIR B AND C
3073 F1                 POP     PSW     ; RESTORE PSW
3074 FB                 EI              ; ENABLE PROCESSOR INTERRUPTS
3075 C9                 RET             ; RETURN TO INTERRUPTED PROCESS


ISIS 8080 MACRO ASSEMBLER, V1.0                 PAGE 6
INTERRUPT SERVICE ROUTINE


                ;*****
                ;
                ;       POLL OTHER DEVICES IF ANY
                ;               IF NO OTHER DEVICES TO POLL - USER SUPPLIED ERROR
                ;               RECOVERY ROUTINE.
                ;
                ;*****
                PPOLL:
3076 C37030             JMP     PRTN    ; RETURN
                ;*****
                ;       ERROR - INTERRUPT FROM IDLE DEVICE
                ;               USER SUPPLIED ERROR RECOVERY ROUTINE
                ;*****
                PIER1:
3079 C37030             JMP     PRTN    ; RETURN
```

Intel RMX/86 Operating System (O/S) Software on ROM or Disk for the 16-Bit 8086 Microprocessor. The following is an example of how the user is generally trained in application software. The RMX/86 software is engineered for megabyte-addressing capability. The software, as a nucleus, is applicable for basic as well as extended I/O system and programmer interface. The modular O/S software runs on Intel's multibus-compatible iSBC systems, providing an environment for the execution of multiple programs via a priority-structured, event-initiated scheduling algorithm. RMS/86 is actually a library of functions to which the users extensions are complementary.

RMS/86, as a real-time O/S, can monitor and control concurrent asynchronous events with features such as priority-based system resource allocation, interprogram and inter-task communication and control, real-time clock-control, and interrupt handling. A total of 255 priority execution levels, as designated by the user, respond to the interrupts. The nucleus of the software supports multiple tasks and programs, while maintaining synchronization and mutual exclusion. Software diagnostics are handled by several recovery methods. The I/O system is device-independent to simplify interchange of peripheral devices. Drivers for iSBC-204 single-density diskette and iSBC-206 hard disk controllers are included in the system. A random-access driver is available for custom applications. The human interface feature allows extensive console services for applications and utilities by decoding a command-line interpreter. Commands from a terminal or a disk file can be originated, added, or deleted. Start, stop, and line-editing are handled by key-stroke control.

Error-handling and debugging by memory examination and modification are included. Errors in new programs and tasks are detected and trapped. Breakpoints can be set for task execution, and stack overflow examined. RMX/86 software carries a license fee of $7500 plus royalties of $300/application. The base price includes eight diskettes, six manuals, registration, one week of programmer training, an iSBC execution vehicle, and free updates for 12 months.

8-37. MICROCOMPUTER PROGRAMMING WITH HIGH-LEVEL LANGUAGES

High-level languages such as PL/1, BASIC, FORTRAN, APL, PL/M, PL/Z, ALGOL, and PASCAL require less coding time, and new complex systems can be built expeditiously in neat, available system modules. However, they all require a comparatively large amount of memory. With low-cost 64-K bit LSI RAM/ROM memory chips and external magnetic bubble/CCD memories around, the possible waste of hardware memory space is not a problem anymore. The number of assembly instructions generated by a single HLL-statement may be as high as 12, and that is the potential range of software costs saved in the case of complex programming tasks. Logical system procedures and thinking are facilitated when one does not have to keep track of what every accumulator and register hold at any instant in any particular computer. English language statements such as DECLARE, IF, THEN, ELSE, DO, BEGIN, REPEAT, CALL, PLUS, BYTE, etc., ease the programmer's task of translating thinking processes the computer can understand via the *compiler* and any subsidiary *interpreter.*

The costly *flow-charting phase* of Assembly language programming in low-cost firmware is mostly eliminated. The costly *debugging* of assembly language instructions in mnemonics is also avoided. The block-structured PASCAL, with its data-handling versatility, is presently becoming popular with *ROM-able* mass-storage. For example, in most microcomputer applications, (HLL) PASCAL or BASIC coding would use one ROM for holding the interpreter (intermediate P-code) and another ROM for the mnemonic instructions in hexadecimal code; in most applications, the comparatively slower access-times are not a problem at all. The standardization of a powerful, universal high-level language such as one of the present PASCAL modified versions would be ideal from the viewpoint of inexpensive software for the multiplicity of microcomputer applications presently under consideration. The high-technology of microelectronics has cut the cost of LSI microcomputer system hardware enormously; given a chance, it will likewise do so during the 1980s for the present time-consuming and expensive software/firmware that make the real-time operating systems "go," especially in the case of personal and small business computers.

As far as the latest status of high-level languages for microcomputers is concerned, PASCAL (and its modified versions, especially the "C" language of Bell labs), as a block-structured programming language in the style of Algol, enjoys a leading position as a more powerful HLL than BASIC, FORTRAN, and PL/I. PASCAL programs are first *compiled* into the *intermediate P-code*, which in turn gets interpreted on the various types of *target microprocessors*. The native assembly languages of each target unit will be coded on a single ROM interpreter. Then the PASCAL compiler system-package developed at the University of California at San Diego (UCSD) will take over the task for the simple PASCAL program written for any application. Kenneth Bowles of UCSD claims that his PASCAL programs run on the Intel 8080, Zilog Z-80, Motorola 6800, Western Digital MCP-1600, Texas Instruments 9900, Rockwell 6502, and American Microsystems custom-unit microprocessors. The compiler has extensions for strings, disk files, interactive graphics and system programming, text-editor, file-manager, debugger, and utilities. The PASCAL programs are comprised of three levels of "modules": the "root" names the program and specifies the variables. The "functional block" follows as the body of the program. The block is divided into six "leaves." The first four declare the labels, constants, data types, and variables. The fifth names and precedes an actual "procedure" (or function). The sixth "statement" section will consist of the executable code for the named "procedure," *Labels* identify statements for reference. *Constants* equate numbers with names for use throughout the program (example, $\pi = 3.14$). *Data types* can be numerous. *Structured types* can be defined to include arrays, records, sets, and files (see *Definitions*, p. 409). Each variable named will be followed by its type; procedures can be written within procedures; and statements for each must be preceded with "BEGIN" and terminated with "END." *Operators* are defined for multiply, divide, add, subtract, logical, and relational. *Numerous control statements* are allowed. PASCAL is similar to other *block-structured programming languages*, but it is more powerful and elegant; it is potentially international for standardization, since the originator of this language, Nicklaus Wirth of Switzerland, named it PASCAL to honor the seventeenth-century French mathematician. For further information on PASCAL, see Section 8-18. We can see on the horizon the eventual demise of the Babel of languages—that is, if the international body politic is willing. Where secrecy is mandatory, *cryptography* is easily accomplished with the aid of protective ROM-software that could be translated to the standard HLL.

The *major advantages of a standardized HLL* include:

1. Assembly language coding produces a significant number of errors, since it is difficult to keep track of what is in each index register. The problem of debugging is minimized by the use of a high-level language.

2. The modular software engineering in a block-structured HLL improves program reliability and reduces costs.

3. The programmer feels that the compiler design itself executes the flowcharts.

4. After some experience with it, the HLL firmware enables the checkup of a product design much sooner than does other firmware.

5. Code written in a HLL is *portable*, since it is not machine-dependent like the assem-

bly language. This portability is cost-effective since utility routines such as stack and queue processing, floating-point arithmetic, and number-conversion packaging are common in most applications.

6. Maintenance in firmware is simplified since programming in HLL is simpler to write. In practice, about 25% development time is saved.

7. The programmer becomes familiar with the efficient code-constructs when the HLL compiler furnishes, with its sophisticated macroinstruction capability of benchmark routines and subroutines, a listing of the assembly-language object code along with the source HLL-code. This kind of learning on the part of the HLL programmer (by way of CRT-presentation in particular) substantiates the efficiency realized to an extent of at least 30% in a short time.

8. The HLLs presently require expensive disk-based operating systems for their use. The latest and the next generation of extra high-capacity bubble-memory and ROMs will hold complex interpreter and compiler HLL software packages at the economy price levels of mass-produced VLSI chips—and that at error rates, orders of magnitude better than disk.

8-38. GLOSSARY OF COMMON SOFTWARE TERMS

8-38.1. Bit/Byte/Character/Word/BCD/Baud/Flag/Statistical data/Word Length/I/O Bus

1. **Bit:** Binary digit of data (High/Low: "1"-"0"). *Bit density* refers to the number of bits recorded per unit length or area (e.g., 1,000 bits/in^2 of tape).

2. **Byte:** A group of contiguous bits; in most computer systems, there are 8. (IBM uses one additional parity-bit to make a 9-bit byte.) Bytes are successive and nonoverlapping in the computer memory and are addressable. The byte may, but not necessarily, make up a complete character or word.

3. **(IBM) character:** The general term includes all alphanumeric punctuation marks, mathematical operators, and the coded representation of such symbols.

4. **Word:** A set of bits (e.g., cores or memory cells of a RAM) stored in the main memory and handled by the computer as a unit of information. The word length is thus determined by the hardware design, number of cores per address, and number of storage units (e.g., flip-flops in a register).

5. **BCD:** Binary coded decimal notation. Each successive decimal digit is represented by four binary digits of weights 8, 4, 2, and 1, respectively, from the most significant bit (MSB) to the least significant bit (LSB).

6. **Baud:** A unit of signaling speed equal to the number of signal events/sec. In Morse code, 1 baud/sec is one-half dot cycle/sec. For binary systems, a baud is the same as a bit. Practically, baud rate is limited to the width in hertz.

7. **Flag:** *Flag* can be defined as a 1-bit register, a simple flip-flop, triggered by a strobe of the appropriate timing. For example, a peripheral device may request the computer for a specific service by sending a "flag" on its interrupt input line, to enable the "interrupt request."

8. **Statistical data:** Masses of data can be best interpreted in terms of their characteristic patterns, namely, *sample mean*, *variance*, *standard deviation*, and *mean deviation*.

1. Sample mean (the average value of data), $\overline{X} = \Sigma X_i/n$
2. Variance (the amount of variation or dispersion of an item form the central average),

$$s^2 = \frac{\Sigma X^2 - (\Sigma X)^2}{n(n-1)}$$

3. Standard deviation, $s = \sqrt{s^2}$

4. Mean deviation is a simpler alternative to variance and is not commonly used, i.e.,

$$M = \frac{\Sigma |X - \overline{X}|}{n} .$$

8-38.2. Table of Common Codes and Parity Bit.

TABLE 8-2. Table of common codes and parity-bit

Decimal	Binary	Binary-Coded Decimal (Decimal Computer)	Octal[a]	Hexadecimal[b]	ASCII: 8-bit[c]
0	0000	0000	0	0	00110000
1	0001	0001	1	1	10110001
2	0010	0010	2	2	10110010
3	0011	0011	3	3	00110011
4	0100	0100	4	4	10110100
5	0101	0101	5	5	00110101
6	0110	0110	6	6	00110110
7	0111	0111	7	7	10110111
8	1000	1000	10	8	10111000
9	1001	1001	11	9	00111001
10	1010	00010000	12	A	01000001
11	1011	00010001	13	B	01000010
12	1100	00010010	14	C	11000011
13	1101	00010011	15	D	01000100
14	1110	00010100	16	E	11000101
15	1111	00010101	17	F	11000110
16	10000	00010110	20	10	Etc.

a. Octal (DEC mini- and micro-computer). Radix = 8.
b. Hexadecimal code (IBM). Radix or base = 16.
c. ASCII: American Standards Code for Information Interchange.

9. **Word length**: The hexadecimal digits given in Table 8-2 each require 4 bits in the place of the 3 bits of octal. This is a convenient facility for two 8-bit bytes in a 16-bit word; hence, most microprocessors use software in hexa-notation. Two 8-bit ASCII (American Standards Code for Information Interchange) can be packed into a single 16-bit word, and separate byte addressing is feasible in 16-bit format.

Some minicomputers, such as PDP-7/9/15, use 18-bit words. The extra word length is convenient for addressing 8-K words of memory, especially for a fair resolution of the CRT display (512 X 512) with 9-bit x and y coordinate values; this halves both refresh memory and refresh time. Three octal digits allow 9 bits conveniently.

For microprogramming, 8-bit words and 16/24/32-bit multiword operations are quite proper. The ASCII parity-bit is allowed in 8 bits, and it can represent two BCD digits.

The 12-bit words accommodate 1-in-4,000 resolution of medium-accuracy instruments.

10. **I/O BUS LINES**: The video coax lines used generally have a characteristic impedance of 93 ohms. Twisted pairs (No. 26 or 28) with about 30 turns/ft have a characteristic impedance of 100 ohms with a ground return. Shielding of the twisted pairs is recommended for lengths greater than 3 feet. A diode or Schottky-diode in a reverse termination at the output-end limits negative overshoots in I/O bus lines.

Parity-Bit: In order to verify correct data, a redundancy check-bit is used (most significant bit). The 8th bit even-parity is used in ASCII as modulo-2 sum = 0. Odd-parity, as modulo-2 sum = 1, is also used.

Alphanumeric: Alphabetic, numeric, and special characters. (Abbreviated **alphameric.**)

EBCDIC: Extended Binary Coded Decimal Interchange Code of IBM (8-bit).

8-38.3. Error-Correcting Codes. A parity-bit check with a "distance-2 code" will enable only the detection of the erroneous bits in a code word. "Distance-d" is the number of elements in which the code symbols (words) differ. Correction of errors is not feasible with the distance-2 codes.

A distance of at least 3 ($d \geqslant 3$) is required to allow the correction of one error-bit in a code symbol. For correction of two errors, $d = 5$. The **Hamming code is a distance-3 code** capable of detecting and correcting one error-bit in a word, by incorporating three additional check-bits along with the information bits. (See p. 356.)

8-38.4. Unit-Distance Codes. Unit-distance codes derive their name from their property that only one-bit changes between representation of two consecutive numbers. They are unweighted; that is, the numerical value can be found only from a specific table showing the state assignments. The **unweighted Gray-code** used for the output comparator signals in a digital quantizer, immediately after conversion to the digital format, is an example of a unit-distance code.

Original Gray-code. The Gray-code is one of a series of codes known as *reflected binary codes*. The Gray-code in particular has the same bit-length and MSB as the binary; two adjacent numbers in the code differ in one bit as in the previously mentioned unit-distance codes. It is commonly used as a special facility in position transducers of digital feedback control systems to minimize transient errors.

Decimal:	0,	1,	2,	3,	4,	5,	6,	7,	8,	9,	10
Binary:	0000,	0001,	0010,	0011,	0100,	0101,	0110,	0111,	1000,	1001,	1010
Gray:	0,	01,	11,	10,	110,	111,	101,	100,	1100,	1101,	1111

"Exclusive-OR" gate logic is generally used to convert the unit-distance codes to the regular binary format of the computers.

8-38.5. Fetch: A predetermined phase of the state of the internal computer logic that enables the computer to interpret the word read out of the memory during a memory cycle as an instruction word.

Execute: The execute phase of the computer operation is similar to "fetch," except that it will interpret the word as a data word.

Interrupt: As in "fetch," but the interrupt phase will interrupt a program in progress and branch to a specific service routine, conditionally or unconditionally.

8-38.6. IRG: Interrecord gap or the space deliberately left between the recording portions of data or records to prevent errors, through loss of data or overwriting, and to allow tape start-stop operations.

8-38.7. Macroinstruction: An instruction (similar in binary coding to the computer's basic machine instructions) that is capable of generating a sequence of machine-language instructions.

Microinstruction: An instruction that forms part of a larger, composite set of instructions.

8-38.8. Base Page. The lowest numbered page of a computer's memory. It can be directly addressed from any other page. The direct-addressing range of the memory-reference instructions dictates the artificial division of a memory into several pages, each containing a fixed number of locations.

8.38.9. Program Status Word (PSW). In many computers, a special register, called the *program-address, PSW,* or *P register*, is used to keep track of the address of the next instruction to be executed. It is typically two words of 32 bits each in a 64-bit control-area of the computers.

8-38.10. Relocatable Loader. The programmer is enabled to load several programs at the same time and to stack them in the main memory automatically; the loader simultaneously provides communication of "linkage" if the program calls for several branch programs of mathematical subroutines. The relocatable loader must be capable of modifying all the relevant addresses used in a given program, since these addresses depend on where a particular program finally ends up in the main memory.

Relocatable memory pertains to the programs whose instruction words can be loaded into any stated area of the memory.

8-38.11. Linking Loader/Editor. The linkage-editor takes a program from the library of the source high-level languages of the assembly programs on the disk or the cassette/cartridge or from some other external bulk memory and converts it into "absolute," as opposed to "relocatable" machine language. To meet this requirement, all subroutines located in the relocatable mass-memory library are appended to the program and appropriately linked thereto.

Incidentally, if a program exceeds the CORE or RAM main-memory limits, it is rejected. After such editing, the absolute machine-language program is transferred to either the absolute machine-language library or the program loader used for the absolute machine-language program. The loader transfers the program directly into the main memory in a serial placement of locations. Then, it turns control over to the program.

8-38.12. Jump Conditions. A conditional "jump" instruction causes a transfer of control from one part of the program to another; the program-counter indicates this as a "jump" from the normal sequencing of instructions. The conditional jump occurs only if a specified test condition, such as "Jump, if accumulator contents $>$ 0," or "Jump, if carry register = 1," is logically satisfied.

However, an unconditional jump instruction can take place in the case of the memory reference instructions, which perform arithmetic or logical operations involving data stored not only in the memory, but also in the operating registers of the microcomputer.

8-38.13. Cycle-Time and Cycle-Stealing. A memory is said to be a random-access memory when it requires a fixed time interval—the cycle-time—in either the read or the write mode, regardless of the address of the datum in question. For some memories, data can be ready before the end of the cycle. "Read" is nondestructive in static or dynamic memories, whereas "write" involves erasure of any previous information. The memory-control unit controls the memory cycle.

Cycle-stealing. A channel-controller or multiplexer of the interface system may steal a memory cycle-time to transmit a word from the external data-storage medium into the main memory or from the main memory into the external data storage via the **direct-memory access (DMA) register.** Since the fastest peripheral may require at least 10 μs before another access is required, and since latest micro- and mini-computers have cycle times of the order of 0.2 to 1.5 μs, the computer can attend to its computing function while attending to the peripherals via DMA from time to time. The method speeds up data processing.

8-38.14. Single and Multiaddress Machines. The command or instruction may contain one or more operand addresses. In a single-operand specification of the computer, there will be room for only one location or address-field. Some high-speed large-scale three-address machines provide a command with addresses for three operand addresses, and an instruction word with as many as 64-bits or more.

8-38.15. Fixed and Variable Field-Length. Most microcomputers using 8- to 16-bit instruction words are fixed word-length computers. Some large-scale machines use variable field-length words, because they can handle sets of words whose size is specified in the command.

8-38.16. Fixed-Point and Floating-Point. The *fixed-point* is the numeric notation in which the fractional point (in the decimal, octal, hexadecimal, or binary format) is predetermined at a constant position.

The *floating-point* is the numeric notation in which the integer and the exponent of a number are separately represented (frequently by two computer words stored at adjacent locations in the memory), so that the implied position of the fractional-point can be freely varied with respect to the integer digits. Double-precision arithmetic or logic thus involves two computer words to represent the number.

8-38.17. File/Record. The *file* is a complete set of data on tape/disk, etc., usually consisting of more than one record and containing all information relating to a single test or computing run. The *record* is a block of data, read as a single group into the computer. Record length is limited by the storage capacity within the computer.

8-38.18. Real-Time. Real-time is the time elapsed between events occurring externally to the computer. A computer in a real-time environment accepts and processes information from one such event and is ready for new information before the next event occurs. A clock incorporated in the computer reflects the real passage of time and hence is called a *real-time clock*. The clock reading is accessible to, and sometimes is resettable by, system software to time intervals, rather than a continuous run.

8-38.19. Subroutine. A subroutine is a sequence of instructions that perform a single task, with the inclusion of a provision to allow some other program to cause the execution of the task sequence, as though it were part of the said "other" program.

8-38.20. Diagnostic Programs. Diagnostic programs determine whether a system failure is caused by the hardware or the software. The **hardware diagnostics** are supplied by the manufacturer for the CPU, memory, and each I/O device.

The **software-diagnostics are called the *debugger programs***; they constitute part of the **program development software. Simulators** are the diagnostic tools for the debugging of software. A simulator makes a software model of a hardware computer, as each single step of the internal operation of the simulated CPU is envisioned by the programmer. Problems of interaction between the software and the hardware can be slowly solved, only if they are not time-related problems. That is, timing is an important criterion in hardware design.

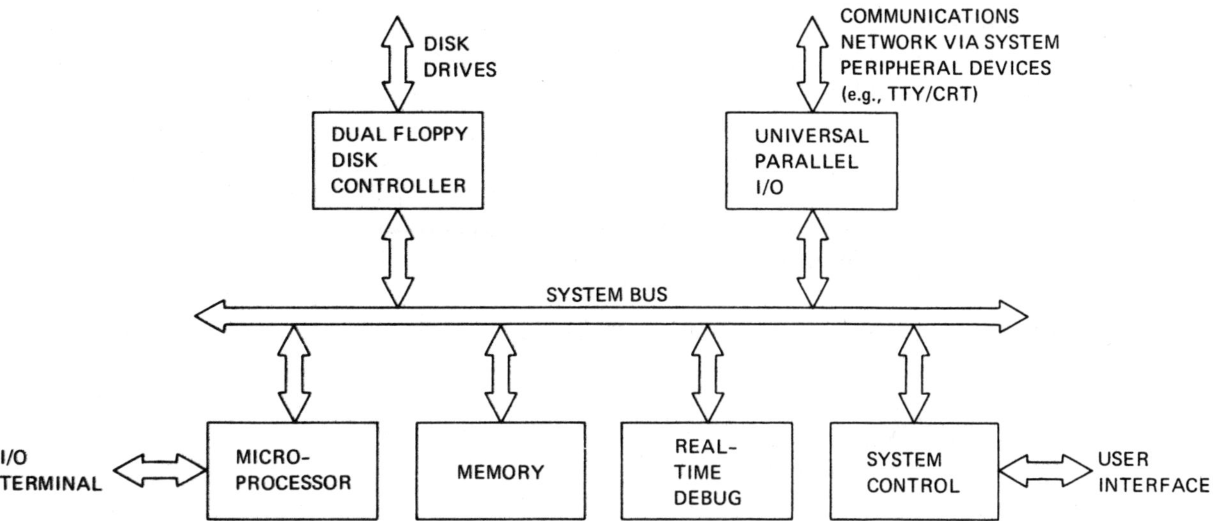

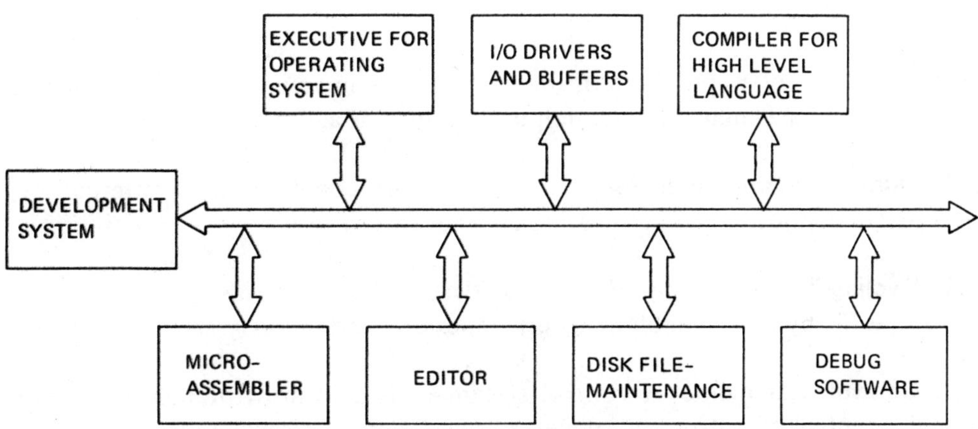

Fig. 8-12. Typical microprocessor system development, hardware/software.

8-38.21. Microassembler. A general-purpose assembler, the microassembler allows the programmer to define the word-size of the machine, the instruction mnemonics, and their corresponding binary bit-patterns. Thus, a microassembler can be used to generate an optimized assembler for a specific computer as an advantage over a higher-level compiler.

8-38.22. Typical Microprocessor System Development, Hardware and Software. This is illustrated in Figure

8-38.23. Initialization. Initialization is a programming step that sets certain counters and clears certain registers in preparation for entering s subroutine. Then the subroutine can be tested within a single loop to see that it is satisfactorily performed several times before the exit is made to the main program in progress. (The initialization procedure sets the relevant sections of the stored program to starting values, so that the program will remain unchanged when repeated. The procedure is then included as part of the software.)

8-38.24. Utility routine. A utility routine is a standard routine such as peripheral driver, sorting routine, merging, etc., which assures the operation of a digital computer, as distinguished from a library mathematical routine in software.

8-38.25. Waiting Loop. In a waiting loop, a sequence of one or two instructions are repeated indefinitely to enable the effect of a delay until a desired external event occurs, such as the receipt of a flag (timing pulse) from usually an external device to indicate that it is ready to transfer or receive information.

8-38.26. Relocatable. Programs whose instructions can be loaded into any specific area of memory are *relocatable.*

8-38.27. Packed Word. A packed word is a computer word containing 2 or more independent bits of information. This is an expediency to conserve storage when actual information involved requires relatively fewer number of bits compared to the number of bits in a computer word.

8-38.28. Documentation. Documentation is conventionally printed *software* material such as user instruction manual for providing an overview and description. Tables, listings, and baseline drawing are included.

8-38.29. Field. In software, the term *field* represents an area on a data card or magnetic tape assigned to a particular classification of data such as address in a word.

8-38.30. Dump. *Dump* stands for recording memory contents on an external medium, such as a magnetic tape, while monitoring on a CRT.

8-38.31. Cycling Tape. Cycling tape is a software reference to the preparation of a new magnetic tape file by updating old magnetic tapes of a certain program.

8-38.32. Control Statement. A control statement is a form of branch instruction that transfers the control of instruction sequence to a statement elsewhere in the program.

8-38.33. Compile. *Compile* means to translate a program (mnemonic assembly language) to the desired high-level language with considerably fewer program steps.

8-38.34. Coding. Coding is the translation of a flow diagram (flowchart of an algorithm) into a computer program.

8-38.35. Clear/reset. With *clear/reset*, all relevant data are reset to binary "O" state.

8-38.36. Buffer. A buffer usually holds information by means of temporary storage, such as a static or dynamic RAM memory or a register, to compensate for the delay of different rates of data flow between a peripheral device and a computer. The buffer is usually part of the I/O section of the computer. In some cases, double buffering is preferred.

8-38.37. Absolute address. Absolute address is fully defined by a memory address number in mostly hexadecimal code. A program may refer to absolute address as distinguished from *symbolic* address in bits.

8-38.38. Overflow. Overflow is a one- or two-bit register indicating that the result of an addition has exceeded the maximum permitted value; the result indicates that one or more significant bits are missing. A signal or alarm indicates that the capacity of generally a register has been exceeded.

8-38.39. Nonreturn to zero (NRZ). In magnetic tape recording, NRZ is a technique by which the recording medium does not turn off the magnetic flux between the recording of individual characters; the flux remains at *saturation* level during recording, and bits are indicated by reversals of flux polarity.

8-38.40. Information. A unit or contents of memory represented in the form of discrete words can be interpreted as information; it consists of a pattern of symbols or, in the case of the digital computer, bits (binary digits).

8-38.41. Indirect phase. Indirect phase is a state of the internal computer logic that causes the computer to interpret as an address the information readout of the memory during a memory cycle.

8-38.42. Software. Essentially, *software* indicates the use of control words or instructions in a program to steer data along prescribed paths by using computer hardware such as latches, storage and shift registers, and an arithmetic logic unit.

8-38.43. Reentrant code. The reentrant code allows the program to be interrupted during execution. (A program with an intermediate state of execution is totally restorable when it is reentered after an interrupt.)

8-38.44. Breakpoint insertion. When *debugging* a program, it is a provision to implant a "trap," so that when the trap is executed, the control automatically activates the monitor. The trap is inserted by a command at a specific address. Whenever this trap or breakpoint is set, any prior breakpoint is deleted to enable its replacement by the original code. The breakpoint functions by removing a small portion of the code from the specified address and by inserting a reference to the monitor in place of the code removed. The code removed is saved in a specific register so that it can be replaced in its proper place when the program moves away from the breakpoint area after the checkup.

8-38.45. Benchmark program. An application-dependent benchmark program assures the programmer that the architecture and computational power of the CPU is known to justify the decisions that the programmer makes while writing programs for a particular microprocessor. The benchmark program may consist of approximately 150 commands preferably involving I/O. One should select at least two processors of differing cycle-times. The benchmark program is then used to check the speed of performance in relation to the set of instructions for both the processors. While writing the program, one must step through each instruction with test data, so that the accuracy can be verified. Minimum execution time through the benchmark program naturally provides a means for choosing the processor for the application under consideration. If the benchmark program involves the processing of an event four times a second and the processor requires above 250 msec for each turn, the processor is not fast enough. If the other processor needs less time, it will be used to perform the programs in less time.

8-38.46. Modem. A modem is a combined unit or chip of modulator and demodulator for sending and receiving coded data in PSK (phase-shift-keying) or any other type of modulation on a high-frequency carrier meant for radio or line/coax/fiber-optic transmission in modern data communications and communications satellites.

8-38.47. Message switching. In data communications, message switching is the method of receiving a message, storing it until an appropriate line is available, and then transmitting the message. In **line switching**, a direct connection is available between the sender and receiver.

8-38.48. Bias distortion. In teletype (TTY) applications, the bias distortion causes a uniform shifting (due to line capacitance effects) of all marking pulses from their exact timing in relation to the beginning of the start pulse in asynchronous transmission at low speed. Hence, phase-lock loop (PLL) controlled synchronous transmission at high speeds of data is essential in time-division multiplex (TDM) and other data communications.

8-38.49. TWX. TWX is a teletypewriter exchange serivce (AT&T) using Baudot and ASCII coded machines from a central-office switched network. **TELEX or TEX** is a direct-dial telegraph service for intercommunication among subscribers by start-stop equipment on the public telegraph network. **WATS** is a wide-area dial-up telephone service within a specific zone provided by telephone companies in the United States for a monthly charge.

8-38.50. Teleprocessing. In modern data communications, teleprocessing is the conventional form of computer-controlled data-processing systems for intercommunication among subscribers on public telephone networks. The transreceiving equipment at the subscriber's premises is usually called a *concentrator*.

9

Reference Data on the Microprocessors and Microcomputer Systems (Tabular Format)

A single 8-to-16-bit mass-produced microprocessor chip will, in general, replace five average-size cards consisting of hard-wired MSI logic and MSI semiconductor memory in any digital system—e.g., a minicomputer that was designed and produced around the year 1970. This outstanding characteristic of the architecture of microprocessors is illustrated by the exclusive design features of several types presently available off the shelf from the various manufacturers.

An overview of their specifications and special features is presented in Tables 9-1 through 9-7. The abbreviations used in the reference tables are explained in the following list.

A-t:	Access time	No.:	Number
Asy:	Asynchronous	ns:	Nanoseconds
b:	Bit or baud/s	OEM:	Original equipment manufacturers
C-t:	Cycle-time	O/S:	Operating system
Cartr:	Cartridge	Par':	Parallel bus
Comp'l:	Compatible	P.C.:	Printed-circuit board
CPU:	Central processing unit	ph:	Phase
CROM:	Control ROM	R-t:	Real-time
DMA:	Direct-memory access	RALU:	Register arithmetic logic unit
GPDC:	General-purpose digital computer	Reqd:	Required
GPR:	General-purpose registers	s:	Second(s)
Instr:	Instructions	Size″:	Size in inches
K:	Kilo (10^3)	Sy:	Synchronous
K-B:	Keyboard	Sys:	System
M:	Mega (10^6)	Temp:	Temperature
MDS:	Microcomputer development system	T/S:	Time-share
M-M:	Main memory	TTL:	Transistor-transistor logic
Mem:	Memory	TTY:	Teletype, EIA RS-232-C interface
Min:	Minimum	Unlim:	Unlimited
ms:	Milliseconds	Wd:	Word
MUX:	Multiplexer	μC:	Microcomputer chip or system

Peripheral options: paper tape, keyboard, line-printer, mag-tape cassette/cartridge, floppy-disk, CRT, VRAM-TV, calculator K-B/display.

TABLE 9-1. Comparative reference data—Microprocessors and microcomputer systems

No.	Manufacturer	Type	Word: Data, Instr.	Address Capacity	M-M RAM: Byte/A-t	ROM Byte/A-t	PROM Byte/A-t	Input Ports	Output Ports	Interface
1	IBM	5100, portable computer (NMOS)	18-b, 2-byte, parity, sign	16-K to 64-K byte	16-K, 500 ns	48-K b/ROS 190-K: 500 ns	–	14-key K-B tape cartridge	CRT, tape, VRAM-TV printer	Asy: 134.5/300-b. TTY and RS232C; CRT; tape cartridge; printer.
2	DEC (Western DIG WD-16 MCP-1600 NMOS)	LSI-11/ PDP-11-03	16/16	32-K 400 custom instr.	16-K: 450 512-K: 1,200	4-K: 100 512-K: 1,200	4-K 512-K	I/O: 33 lines, Par'. DMA, 16:1 MUX	I/O: DMA 833-K, BUS Wd/S	Asy: 50 thru 9.6-K baud/s TTY, floppy disk, tape, CRT, TTL comp'l.
3	RCA	CDP-1801 (CMOS)-1802	8/8, 16 I/O: 4	64-K 59 instr.	4-K: 300 512-K: 500	512-K: 1,000	4-K 512-K: 1,000	8 ports 256 lines	8/256 8-b/port	Asy: 1,200 b/s. TTY, TTL Comp'l. I/O address separate.
4	INTEL Intellec 4-AMD	4004 (PMOS)	4/8	4-K 46 instr.	32-K 42-K	–	8-K 32-K	16 4-b/port	32 4-b/port	TTY, I/O address separate from mem.
5	INTEL Model MDS	8080 (NMOS)	8, 16/8, 16/24 Bit-slice	64-K 78 instr.	128-K: 450 512-K:	16-K: 450 112-K:	2-K 96-K: 1,300	44 4-b/port	44 4-b/port	Asy:/Sy. 9.6-K baud/s. All options external.

No.	Clock and Cycle-Time	Interrupts	Temp. (°C)	Voltage Power	Price ($)	Size (in)	Peripherals	Software	Features and Remarks
1	R-t, 1.75 μs	4	0–70 (–55 to +125)	115-V, AC ~500 W	8,975 to 19,975	8 × 17.5 × 24 (46–50 lbs)	CRT, TV, K-B, tape, printer	BASIC O/S, APL (Resident) APL and BASIC	Auxiliary tape cartridge. Microprogrammable 5-chip set.
2	R-t, 11 MHz, 4-ph	16-b/port levels unlim.	0–50	±5, +12 9 W	990 P.C.: 630	8.5 × 5/10 CPU-P.C.	CRT (VT-50) Paper-tape	BASIC, FORTRAN IV, Diagnostics, O/S. T/S; Macro II, etc.	O/S: RT/11; CORE, edit, linkage. Minicompatible.
3	2 MHz, 1-ph	unlim. MUX. I/O and interrupts	0–70 (–55 to +125)	10 V, 32 mW (3–10 V)	2,250 (CDP-1801: 40)	P.C.: 3 × 4 Min.: 10 P.C.	CRT, TTY, Paper-tape cassette	Assembler (nonresident) s-package CDP, 18S900: $2,000	Sys. support: CDP 18S002: $3,000 Hardware (assembler and edit)
4	0.74 MHz, 2-ph, 10.8 μs	–	0–55	–5, +10 V	2,545 Chip: 5–15	24-pin 6.2 × 8 3 P.C.	Paper tape, K-B, printer	No high-level language	Used by several OEM applications.
5	2 MHz, 2-ph, 2 μs	eight levels priority and vectored	0–55	Chip: 0.8 W ±5, 12 Max: 150 W	2,545 Chip: 20	42-pin. 12 × 6.75 P.C. 4 P.C.	All options except tape	All options external Mem. nonrelocatable. PL/M.	Most popular original NMOS chip for OEM applications.

Note: Second sources and OEMs for Intel 8080A microprocessor: American Microdevices, Texas Instruments, Nippon Microcomputer Company (Japan), Hitachi (Japan), National Semiconductors Inc., Sieman's, Cramer, Pro-Log, MuPro, Control Logic, Monolithic Systems, Technitrol, Martin Research, DEC, IMS Associates.

TABLE 9-2. Comparative reference data—Microprocessors and microcomputer systems

No.	Manufacturer	Type	Word: Data, Instr.	Address Capacity	M-M RAM: Byte/A-t	ROM Byte/A-t	PROM Byte/A-t	Input Ports	Output Ports	Interface
6	Intersil (6900/ TAWGFN)	IM-6100 (CMOS)	12-b, 12-b	32-K byte 60 instr.	48-K: 500 ns 384-K	0/384-K	0/384-K	64/256 12-b/port	64/256 12-b/port	Asy: 200-K baud Sy: 1-M baud All options.
7	MC Associates (JOLT)	6502 (NMOS)	8/8, 16, 24	64-K 139 instr.	4-K: 1,000 ns 512-K: 2,500	2-K: 1,000 ns 256-K	2-K: 1,000 ns 256-K	2/MUX unlim. 8-b/port	2 8-b/port	Asy: 600 baud.
8	MOSTEK	5065 (NMOS)	8/8, 16, 24	32-K 51 instr.	8-K: 500 96-K	4-K: 500 8-K	0/8-K	—[a]	—[a]	Asy: 40-K baud Auto-start, bootstrap load.
9	Fairchild Micro Systems (F-8)	3850 (NMOS)	8/8	64-K 70 instr.	512-K: 81 512-K	0/512-K	0/512-K	2/252 8-b/port	2/252 8-b/port	Not TTL-compatible. Asy: 9.6-K baud Sy: 9.6-K baud
10	General Instruments Corp.	CP-1600A (NMOS)	16/10	64-K 87 instr.	128-K: 400 1-M	30-K: 500 1-M	0/1-M: 1,000	2/unlim. 16-b/port	2/unlim. 16-b/port	Asy: 9.6-K baud TTY, TTL interface. Not microprogrammable.

No.	Clock and Cycle-Time	Interrupts	Temp. (°C)	Voltage Power	Price ($)	Size (in)	Peripherals	Software	Features and Remarks
6	8 MHz, 1-ph, 5 μs	1 level vectored	0–70	+5 (2 W) 10 mW at 4 MHz	25 to 100 (specification dependent)	6.5 × 8 3 P.C.	All options	All options are available externally	Architecture similar to Mini PDP-8E, except DMA.
7	0.75 MHz, 2-ph, 2.6 μs	3 levels priority and vectored	0–50	+5 or −10 4 W	20 3 MHz: 32	4.25 × 7 1 P.C.	All options except tape and disk	All options except high-level language	MOS Tech. Inc. NMOS: Si-gate. Similar to 6800.
8	2 MHz, 3-ph, 7 μs	3 levels priority	0–70	−5, 5, 12 24 W	995	9.6 × 6.75 1 P.C.	Interface required	Interface controller	Custom high-speed data communications.
9	2 MHz, 1-ph, 2 μs	64 levels priority vectored	0–70	−5, +12 300 mW	9.95 kit: 300	6 × 9 1 P.C.	All options	Debug, text edit, application programs.	MOSTEK too. 4/8-bit controllers, 4-chip μC. DMA.
10	5 MHz, 2-ph, 2.4 μs	5 levels priority vectored	0–50	−5, ±12 54 W	134 2 K to 3.3 K	40-pin 9.25 × 9.75 4 P.C.	All options except disk, cassette	O/S, applications prog's, no macro and high-level.	Metal-gate tech. console, DMA, MUX, real-time.

a. Figure unavailable.

TABLE 9-3. Comparative reference data—Microprocessors and microcomputer systems

No.	Manufacturer	Type	Word: Data, Instr.	Address Capacity	M-M RAM: Byte/A-t	ROM Byte/A-t	PROM Byte/A-t	Input Ports	Output Ports	Interface
11	Motorola (Exorciser)	MC-6800 (NMOS) Si-gate	8-b/ 8, 16, 24	64-K byte 72 instr.	0/512-K byte 550 ns	24-K/512-K byte, 550 ns	0/512-K byte 550 ns	0/104 8-b/port	0/104 8-b/port	Asy: 9.6-K baud TTY-, TTL-compatible
12	National Semiconductor (PACE)	IMP-8/16 (NMOS)	8/16/16	64-K 387 instr.	64-K/512-K 500 ns	12-K/512-K 200 ns	0/512-K 1,000 ns	0/unlim. MUX 8/16-b port	0/unlim. 8/16-b port	Asy: 1.2-K baud TTY
13	National Semiconductor	SC/MP (PMOS)	8/16, 14	1,024-byte	1.2-K	16-K	0/512-K	0/unlim.	0/unlim.	Economy calculator K-B and Hexadecimal alphanumeric display.
14	Plessey	Miproc-16 (bipolar)	16/16	64-K 82-instr.	16-K/32-K 80 ns/	4-K/1-M 80/	32/256 16-b/port	32/256 16-b/port	Unlim. with ext'l MUX	Asy: 2.4-K baud TTY etc. (not TTL compatible)
15	Intel, on-chip µC (MCS-48)	8048/8748 Si-gate NMOS	2 working banks 8-b registers	8-K 90 instr.	64-byte (External Expansion)	8-K (Masked 8048)	8-K EAROM (8748)	I/O resident 17 lines	I/O resident 17 lines	Intellec MDS development system 8071 Sy: Data-link.

No.	Clock and Cycle-Time	Interrupts	Temp. (°C)	Voltage Power	Price ($)	Size (in)	Peripherals	Software	Features and Remarks
11	1 MHz, 2-ph, 2 µs 4 MHz, (6801 is used in new computers)	4-level priority vectored	0–70	±5 V, 100 W	29.95, 5 LSI Set: 210	42-pin. 6 × 9.75 2 P.C.	All options (no K-B).	Debug, macro. All options, PL/M.	AMI, Hitachi, T-CSF Mini capability with LSI-MC chips.
12	2 MHz, 2-ph, 8 µs	4-level priority	0–50	115/230 V AC, 50 W	210 (5-chip set)	8 × 11 4 P.C.	All options and tape cartridge	Self-assembler, debug, time-share etc. High-level SM/PL	4-bit 'RALU' slices CPU, CROM (TTL extras).
13	2 MHz, 10–50 µs	4-level	0–50	14 V	<10	40-pin	Special K-B/ display or custom.	Pointer addressing. Auto-index. Hex software for economy calculator K-B/display.	Communications and low-control applications. Hobbyists (NMOS to come).
14	2.87 MHz, 1-ph, 350 ns	8-level option priority	0–70	+5 V 17 W	2,655 4-K ROM 2-K ROM	6 × 9 1 P.C.	All options. No cassette tape.	All options except macro assembler. No O/S.	(British/USA) CORE to meet mini performance.
15	On-chip Clock: RC[a]: 2.5 µs	8-level stack or option	0–70	+5 V	10 (8048)	Single-chip (dedicated use), 40-pin	Floppy disk, CRT/K-B chips.	MDS based assembler, editor, monitor. (Hexa.)	Single-chip microcomputer. Emulation

a. Resistor-capacitance.

TABLE 9-4. Comparative reference data—Microprocessors and microcomputer systems

No.	Manufacturer	Type	Word: Data, Instr.	Address Capacity	M-M RAM: Byte/A-t	ROM Byte/A-t	PROM Byte/A-t	Input Ports	Output Ports	Interface
16	Rockwell International Type-I System	PPS-8 (PMOS)	8/8	32-K byte 109 Instr.	4-K/128-K byte 1,800 ns	0/128-K byte 1,800 ns	0/128-K byte 1,800 ns	4/30 8-b/port	4/30 8-b/port	Asy: 18-K baud Sy: 32-K baud TTY (options)
17	Scientific Microsystems (MC-SIM)	SMS-300 (bipolar)	8/8, 16 8 instr. types	8-K as required	16-K/64-K 65 ns	–	1.5-K words	1/512 8-b/port	1/512 8-b/port	TTY, I/O has reserved address area in memory. Data 1 to 8 bits.
18	Texas Instruments (990/4)	TMS-9900 (NMOS Si-gate)	8, 16/16, 32, 48 Data flow 16-b	32-K 69 instr.	4-K/512-K 333 ns	0/16-K 700 ns	0/256-K	1/256 16-b/port	1/256 16-b/port	Asy: 9.6-K baud Sy: 48-K, TTY, CRT.
19	Fairchild Micro Systems "Microflame"	F-9440 (I^2L-16 bit) bipolar	8, 16/16, 32, 48 16-bit data	32-K 69 instr.	4-K/512-K 333 ns	0/16-K 700 ns	0/256-K	1/256 16-b/port	1/256 16-b/port	Asy: 9.6-K baud Sy: 48-K: TTY, CRT. Multiply requires 17.3 μs.
20	Texas Instruments	SBP-9900 (I^2L-16 bit) bipolar	9-b control word 12-b: 3 × 4	I^2L-MM as required 512 instr.	I^2L-RAMs as required	I^2L-ROMs	I^2L-PROMs	Data-in 12-b	Data-out 12-b	Custom-design to requirements.

No.	Clock and Cycle-Time	Interrupts	Temp. (°C)	Voltage Power	Price ($)	Size (in)	Peripherals	Software	Features and Remarks
16	256 KHz, 4-ph, 4 μs	3-level priority vectored	0–70	+5, –12 2.8 W	CPU: 24 μC: 350	42-pin 5 × 7 1 P.C.	All options except cartridge.	No resident memory. All other options. PPS assemulator and system analysis module.	PDS-8/2 has on-chip clock, I/O, RAM/ROM. (52-pin)
17	6.6 MHz, 4-ph, 250 ns	priority vectored	0–70	+5, 10 W	CPU: 90–233 μC: 4,890	CPU: 50-pin 6 × 7, 1 P.C.	K-B paper-tape	Assembler resident or nonresident. Relocatable macro applications programs.	Proprietary TTL-360, 1, 2, 3 LSI chips. Fast bit/byte oriented microcontroller.
18	3 MHz, 4-ph, 770 ns	8-level priority vectored	0–65	±5, 12 14 W	CPU: 50–100 μC: 575	64-pin 11 × 14, 1 P.C.	All options except cartridge.	I/O memory merged or separate. Portable ANSI FORTRAN assembler. All options.	Memory-to-memory architecture. (No accumulator or working registers in CPU to allow multiprocess.)
19	3 MHz, 4-ph to 125 KHz	8-level priority vectored	–55 to +125	5 V, 500 mW 6.4 mW at 125 KHz clock.	~350	64-pin	Same	Same software. Airborne navigational processor, guidance system.	"Workspace" in RAM selected for the 16 GPRs.
20	1–5 MHz variable	As required.	0–70	1.5 low-power (battery)	28/4-b chip	As required. 1 P.C.	User's peripherals	Assembler on PROMs according to user's needs.	The chip is used as a building block for custom-design of μC to high-speed R-t applications.

TABLE 9-5. Comparative reference data—Microprocessors and microcomputer systems

No.	Manufacturer	Type	Word: Data, Instr.	Address Capacity	M-M RAM: Byte/A-t	ROM Byte/A-t	PROM Byte/A-t	Input Ports	Output Ports	Interface
21	Signetics (2650-PC 1000)	2650 (NMOS-depletion mode)	8/8, 16, 24	32-K 77 Instr.	8-K Static 625 ns	8-K 625 ns	–	2 8-b/port	2 8-b/port	Asy: 300 baud. TTY: "TWIN" program-development system.
22	NEC (Japan) (PDA-80)	μ PD-8080D (NMOS)	8, 16/8, 16, 24 8-b CPU	64-K 78 Instr.	8-K/32-K 350 ns	16-K/64-K 450 ns	16-K/64-K 450 ns	1/1,280 8-b/port	1/1280 8-b/port	Asy: 1.2-K baud. TTY: Not TTL-compatible.
23	Electronic Arrays	EA 9002 (NMOS)	12/5, 8, 12	As required. 46 Instrs.	As required.	–	–	Standard I/O	Standard I/O	64 scratch-pad and 8 GP registers.
24	Advanced Micro Devices (RALU architecture)	AM 2900 (Schottky-TTL-LSI)	16/16	As required. User defined.	Type 2950, 2952 RAMs	Type 2960, 2962 ROMs	User defined. Instr. set	2,905/6/7 Type bus transceiver	2905/6/7	16 working registers "RALU" slices Type 2901.
25	Zilog	Z-80 (NMOS)	8, 16/8, 16, 24 Bit-slicing	64-K 128 Instr.	128-K/512-K 450 ns	16-K/112-K 450	2-K/96-K	Option: 44 8-b/port	Option: 44 8-b/port	I/O pins TTL-compatible. Asy, Sy: 9.6-K baud. 16-bit stack pointer with LIFO stack.

No.	Clock and Cycle-Time	Interrupts	Temp. (°C)	Voltage Power	Price ($)	Size (in)	Peripherals	Software	Features and Remarks
21	1.25 MHz, 3-ph, 10/4.8 μs	1-level vectored	0–70	CPU: 5, 625 mW	21.50	40-pin, 6 × 9 As required.	All options.	Resident FORTRAN assembler absolute memory–debug. O/S (16/32-b)	Communications and control mini applications–2650 A-1 is a faster version.
22	2 MHz, 2-ph, 2 μs	Unlim (MUX) priority vectored	0–50	AC-in 50 W	μC: 4,500	40-pin, 6 × 9 1 P.C.	All options. No K-B.	All options. Memory not relocatable. No linking loader.	Evaluation kit and PDA-8 proto-development kit.
23	4 MHz, 1-ph, 2 μs	7-level subroutine nesting with LIFO stack	0–70	5 20 W	20 995	28-pin 1 P.C.	Controller applications	All options. FORTRAN emulator editor.	Control bus interfaces directly with standard memories and I/O system. Prototyping board (295S)
24	8-20 MHz, 65 ns	2914 Type control	0–70	5 20 W	RALU: 29 reprog. kit 289	1 P.C.	All options.	AMD ASM microprogram Assembler: user's own software.	Second source: Motorola, Raytheon. MSI/LSI building blocks.
25	2 MHz, 2-ph, 1.5 μs	Two banks of GPRs allow fast interrupts 8 levels priority, vectored.	–55 to +125 0–70	5 CPU: 0.8 W	49	42-pin 1 P.C.	All options.	Software compatible to 8080A. R-t disk O/S, files of any size Macroassembler. BASIC, PL/Z; 16-bit BCD add, subtract.	Second source: Mostek. Second generation 8080A, but not pin–compatible with auto refresh dynamic RAMs (32-K)–2 index registers.

TABLE 9-6. Comparative reference data—Microprocessors and microcomputer systems

No.	Manufacturer	Type	Word: Data, Instr.	Address Capacity	M-M RAM: Byte/A-t	ROM Byte/A-t	PROM Byte/A-t	Input Ports	Output Ports	Interface
26	MOS Tech. Inc.	MCS-6602/ 6612 (NMOS-Si-gate)	8/8, 16, 24 More instr. per byte	2-K 57 Instr.	32/192 bytes 50 ns	512/2-K bytes 50 ns	512/2-K bytes 50 ns	I/O port and address bus or I/O port.	Simplified I/O bus, serial port.	Low-cost microcontroller applications. Full program development system. Two-indexed addressing.
27	MicroNova Data General	μ Nova mN601 (NMOS-Si-gate)	16/16 2.4 μs	1-K word	16-K words	As required. External	As required. External	47-line I/O controller	47-line I/O controller	Special communications interface system available.
28	Essex International	Sx-200 (PMOS)	4/8	1-K byte 41 Instr.	64 × 4-b	1-K byte	External emulator	2-lines	1-line	On-chip interface for capacitive touchplate switches.
29	General Instruments AEG, Germany; SGS, Italy	8000 (PMOS) 3-chip	Data: 8 Address: 6 Control: 4	48 Reg's 8-b 48 Instr.	48 × 8 GPRs	1-K byte	–	3-lines 8-b	3-lines 8-b	Dedicated application. Interface to user's needs. Interface support for time-share networks.
30	Mostek	3870 NMOS-Si-gate	8/8, 16, 24	64-K 70 Instr.	64 byte 4-K/512-K External	2-K byte 512-K External	512-K External	4-lines 8-b/port	4-lines 8-b/port	Not TTL-compatible. Sy, Asy: 9.6-K baud.

No.	Clock and Cycle-Time	Interrupts	Temp. (°C)	Voltage Power	Price ($)	Size (in) Weight	Peripherals	Software	Features and Remarks
26	2 and 3 MHz, 2-ph, 1 to 2 μs	Any (MUX) priority and vectored	0–70	±5 650 mW	CPU: 50	40-pin 1 P.C.	Appliance controller	Not compatible to 6800 software. More instructions with single-byte of code. Decimal mode.	Similar to MOS 6502 and MC-6800. Single-chip μC. More powerful than 6502.
27	8–33 MHz, 2-ph, 700 ns	16 levels priority	0–70	±5, 15	CPU: 114 printer DOS: 511-K 630-K byte	1 P.C. cabinet rack	All options.	R-t O/S. BASIC. Extensive library; multiply/divide stack; diskette DOS system.	Mini-architecture mN 601 CPU; mN 606, 4-K RAM; mN 603 I/O controller; DMA (NOVA-3D Mini: $37.6 K with CRT)
28	400 kHz, 3-ph, 20 μs	Bit test (add and subtract)	0–50	+50 to 20	μC: 7 emulator $5K	28-pin	Dedicated applications.	Assembler FORTRAN: decimal adjust arithmetic.	Economy appliance use. Single-chip μC. Prototyping system (emulator with PROMs).
29	800 kHz, 2-ph, 10 μs	1-level	0–70	+5, −12	CPU: 22	40-pin 1 P.C.	All options.	BCD arithmetic. 48 × 1 scratch-pad. Assembler and simulator in FORTRAN.	Predecessor of Fairchild's F-8 GIMINI program-development system.
30	2 MHz, 1-ph, 2 μs	64-level priority vectored	0–70	5 500 mW	μC: 15	40-pin	All options.	Binary timer with programmable prescaler. Emulation and prototyping are PROM-based.	μC on single-chip. Fairchild F-8 hardware compatibility. Software development board with assembler debug: $1,300.

TABLE 9-7. Comparative reference data—Latest microprocessors with the computing power of minicomputers.

No.	Manufacturer	Type	Word: Data, Instruction	Address Capacity	RAM	ROM	PROM	Input Ports	Output Ports	Interface
31	Bell Telephone Labs (For use of Bell Telephone Systems and AT&T)	MAC-4 CMOS μC (Latest: 32-bit MAC-32)$_a$	Operand width set to 4/8/ 12/16 by software; 43 Instructions, 4 addressing modes: Source/ destination.	Flexible via DMA and asynchronous clock	64-to-192 4-bit nibbles. Standard version: 80 × 4	1024 to 3840 nibbles. Standard version: 1280 × 4-bit	–	Flexible 16 I/O latches. 8-bit bidirectional I/O bus, 1 Serial IN, 1 Serial OUT		Memory-mapped I/O Interface. Programmable Logic Array Encoder for Code Conversion.
32	Intel Corp. 3065 Bover Ave., Santa Clara, CA 95051	8086 VLSI, Scaled-down, Si-gate NMOS (HMOS) 29000 transistors	8/16/32-bit words. 8080 Instructions, subset of the Instructions of 8086.	1-M byte of RAM or Disk/ Bubble memory	For minimum mode configuration, Control bus ($\overline{RD}$, $\overline{WR}$, $\overline{S2}$, $\overline{BHE}$) and Data bus D_0–D_{15} go directly to RAM/ROM/PROM/and I/O; address bus A_0–A_{15} needs 8282 chip. For large systems: Control via 8288 and Random logic, address A_0–A_{19} via 8283 and 8287, and data via 8287's.					Main-frame-like programmability, on-line, to allow maintenance and upgrade. Multi-user applications with virtual memory security. Bus-Interface Unit (BIU) optimizes overhead Execute/ Fetch instructions. Programs relocatable.

33	Zilog (Exxon) 10460 Bubb Rd. Cupertino, CA 95014	Z-8000 VLSI like 8086. 17500 transistors Z-8000 Microprocessor unit is a microcomputer board built around Zilog's 16-bit segmented microprocessor Z-8001.	Data: 1 bit to 32 bits. 414 Instructions compatible to Z-80A.	Direct addressing: 8-M bytes. 8 User selectable addressing modes. (Z-8001: 48-M byte)	External RAM/ROM/PROM/and I/O as in the case of 8086. 1-M byte range Programmable Counter refreshes dynamic RAM automatically (refresh period 1-to-64 μS) with 4-MHz clock. Common I/O 16-bit address/data bus used.	Segmented CPU with 8 lines SN_0–SN_7 and segment trap. Bus control status 4 lines ST_0–ST_3. Multi-microprocessor control: microcode I/O'. Bus Timing: $\overline{AS}$, $\overline{DS}$, $\overline{MReg}$. Nonsegmented CPU: Z-8002 8-to-48-M bytes, Segmented CPU. Z-8001, 64-to-384-K bytes.
34	Motorola 3501 Ed Bluestein Blvd. Austin, TX 78721	MC68000 VLSI–NMOS like 8086.	8/16/32-bit words. 70 Instructions	32-K bytes to 128-K External RAM	Address A_1–A_{23} and Data D_0–D_{15} to Bus Arbitration Module, BAM for multi-processor interface. RAM/ROM/and I/O. DMA and Memory Management Unit MMU are external.	Interface organization includes Peripheral Processor Unit, PIA, ACIA, PTM, GPIA, CRTC, VDG, ADLC, SSDA, and DDFDC (See Text, MC68000)
35	National Semiconductor Santa Clara, CA	NS16032 NMOS, as 8086, VLSI	16/24/32 bit words. 100 Instructions	16-M bytes. 3200 Pages, 512 bytes	RAM main-memory, ROM, PROM, and I/O external to CPU as for main-frame Minicomputers with virtual memory, and MMU, NS16082.	Peripheral Memory Management Unit plays an important role for address relocation/memory protection.

a. Hewlett-Packard, NMOS 32-bit, VLSI 450,000-transistor microprocessor (for Desk-top Computers) will be available during 1982; it will operate at 18-MHz clock-rate.

TABLE 9-7. Continued.

No.	Clock and Cycle-Time	Interrupts	Temperature (°C)	Voltage Power	Price	Size	Peripherals	Software/Firmware	Features and Remarks
31	Asynchronous clock or external clock generator	One level of flexible interrupt and trap	0–70°	1.5 to 10V Low power dissipation	–	40-pin DIP; I/O requires 34 pins	Mostly telephone and communications equipment	Nonmaskable DMA uninhibited. Auto width, auto load, auto increment. Interrupt is produced by overflow as well.	Powerful instructions for efficient bit manipulation. Bus structured architecture. HALT minimizes phone loop-power until reset. PLA Encoder in I/O for Code Conversion. Phone usage likely.
32	5 or 8 MHz, 500/800 ns Access: 300 to 400 ns	256 Types including division/overflow errors. Program transfer on interrupt.	0–70° Defense temperature range OK	5V	–	40-pin DIP	All minicomputer options acceptable in multiprogram/multiprocessor applications	First multiuser/multijob modern real-time Operating Systems with memory protection. 8085 PL/M OK. 4 levels available. Synchro auto signal processing	Architecture aimed at open-ended visible addressability by internal segmentation at 64-K to 1-M bytes. Portability of 8086-based software. 16-bit architecture ideal for usual minicomputer applications.
33	4 MHz, external clk, generator. 250 ns to 2 μsec	Nonmaskable vectored/nonvectored interrupts. Structure includes trap also.	0–70° Defense Temperature range OK	5V 300 mA	–	48-pin (Z-8001); 40-pin (Z-8002)	All minicomputer options acceptable by using Zilog interface chips.	Time sharing easy-to-use. Compiler support by Z-8010 memory management unit. 32-bit instructions include × and ÷. Throughput enhanced by nondedicated registers	High-end advanced 16-bit μP (CPU) with an instruction set of a minicomputer. More powerful than many minis. Z-Bus compatible for multiprocessing systems. MMU facilitates segment relocation and memory protection.

34	8-MHz Master clock, 1-Ø TTL input	Seven levels of encoded interrupt priority. Seven auto vectors. A 256 vector allocation. Trap and interrupt	0–70°	5V single supply "TRAPs" are interrupts explicitly caused by instructions or abnormal processing conditions.	–	64-pin	Compatible MC 6800 peripherals (10 chips) RS-232/IEEE-488 interface OK with "Host" computers IBM-370 PDP-11.	5/15 addressing modes. User/Supervisor modes. Support of all high-level languages. Easy program debugging. Position-independent reentry/recursion. Modular.	Synchronous/Asynchronous peripheral interface. 32-bit words for data/address registers. Nonsegmented 16-M-byte address space via 23-bit address bus. Architecture versatile to bits, BCD, 16/32-bit words. 192 fully-vectored interrupts.
35	–	–	–	–	–	–	24/25-bit MUX (multiplexer) for address/data bus. O/S software enables disk storage.	32-bit addressing will eventually access 4-billion byte disk memory by 32-entry associative memory page table-pointers.	16000-family of VLSI chips starting with NS16032 16/32-bit CPU chip. Its 32-bit pipeline organization supports virtual-memory software along with MMU NS16082. Modular software design.

10 Microprocessor-Associated Hardware

10-1. HARDWARE IN GENERAL

In the digital-computer field, hardware and software are essentially interchangeable. Thus, since hardware is less expensive to implement with latest high-capacity PROMs, RAMs, shift registers and character generators, and exclusive programmable logic arrays for custom circuitry, there is a special need for the hardware designers and the programmers to coordinate their effort in each application to economize the costs of the final debugged microcomputer system. In fact, the custom microprogrammed interface circuits used for the desired peripherals of a microcomputer system make the system in general a "dedicated processor" with a flexible and preset program. In the case of the communications network interface, the additional requirement is by routine much simpler in the form of a parallel-to-serial conversion of the interface of the I/O data in either direction. Powerful hardware, such as the first in first-out stack-registers and the DMA, commonly associated with the microcomputer, considerably reduce the software effort needed in stand-alone applications. Even if the microprogrammed throughput of the microprocessor is medium-speed, these stand-alone applications will still meet the real-time requirement.

Compared to the popular power-consuming bipolar TTL/MSI circuits, NMOS/LSI appears to dominate the recent scene with its high-density low-cost logic per chip; however, the bipolar technology, in the new format of the low-power high density I^2 L/LSI, appears to compete with the NMOS/LSI on an equal footing–if not at an advantage of speed and power consumption–in both processing and memory devices. For example, compared to the popular 4-K bit NMOS static-RAM with an access-time of 150 to 300 ns at 0.5W dissipation, the latest 4-K bit I^2 L static-RAM is leading with an access-time of 90 ns at an equivalent power dissipation. One has the choice of trading speed for power consumption in the Schottky I^2 L case.

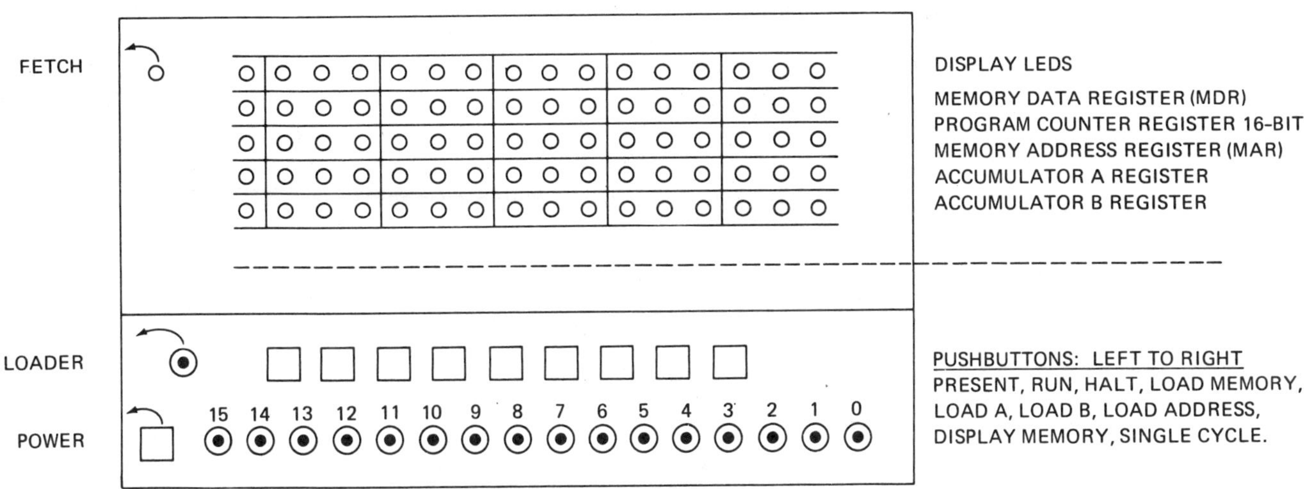

Fig. 10-1. Typical operating console of a mini- or micro-computer.

10-2. OPERATING CONSOLE OF A TYPICAL MINI- OR MICRO-COMPUTER

The general-purpose digital computer operates on the basis of the instructions inserted into its memory by the programmer. However, front-panel controls are generally available for entering the instructions and data into the memory, and for initiating the operation by way of loading with a starting instruction. For example, binary numbers can be loaded via 16 switches into the computer memory. The switches actually represent a 16-bit register for an instruction word. "Load address" and "load memory" push-buttons are used for this task.

After the RAM main memory is loaded with the program of instructions, the user can enter the address of the starting instruction, as just described, and then press the "run" push-button, which enables the computer to automatically follow the sequence of program instructions, until the "halt" instruction is reached. Activation of the load-address and the display-memory push-buttons displays the answer on the front panel. A typical operating console is shown with the various switching and display facilities in Fig. 10-1.

10-3. BUS-ORIENTED ARCHITECTURE

Most microcomputer systems use the bus-oriented architecture illustrated in Fig. 1-2 for the General Instruments CP-1600 microcomputer system. The architecture of the 8-bit microprocessor is organized for intertransfer of parallel-bit information via

1. An address and control-bus (8 lines in parallel actually)
2. A 16-bit bidirectional bus to the RAM/ROM memories and input-output control.

The use of this **bussing technique in general reduces the number of interfacing functions** needed. By using the bus-oriented architecture, the I/O data can be handled just like the memory by the limited number of instructions stored in the internal control ROM memory. A 16-bit (parallel) data-bus can also transmit data in "bit-slices" of 4, 8, or 16 bits. The number of bits in the address-bus limits memory capacity unless multiple-cycle addressing techniques are used to expand the memory. As an example, two 8-bit input busses from the accumulator and the memory-address registers can be inputted in parallel to the arithmetic unit to combine their contents. During the execution of an instruction, the combined output can be read into a **16-bit memory-data register** to indicate what is written or read out of a memory-cell during the preceding memory cycle. The memory-data register output is then accessible for arithmetic or transfer to other registers via the bus system. The **bit-slice** microprocessor architecture for a 16-bit microcomputer system is shown in Fig. 10-2; the system employs four 4-bit microprocessors as individual CPUs.

The I/O busses of the microprocessor apply the data in parallel to the peripherals used, but only one of the device interfaces will be able to address the device in question, and the other device-interfaces will not be able to decode and respond to the data on the busses at the same time.

As another example, the DEC, LSI-11 microcomputer has a two-way bidirectional bus from the I/O for the control and data lines; it is actually composed of 16 multiplexed data/address lines, and 18 control/synchronization signal lines including the basic essential power and maintenance lines. The highest-priority peripheral device (from the "interrupt" point of view) is the one closest to the microcomputer module.

The data/address bus could be synchronous, open-collector, or low-impedance tristate lines, with "don't care" conditions, besides the 0-(Low) and 1-(High), for the facility of increasing the external memory size by adding RAMs to the main memory and ROMs to the instruction set, e.g., for additional floating-point arithmetic functions.

10-4. BUFFERS

Buffers in hardware generally do not translate the data from one form to another like an encoder/decoder/multiplexer, etc., but act to hold information as a device register. In some computers, a buffer may also be a storage device used to compensate for a difference in time of occurrence of events or a different rate of flow. Then it could be termed a *buffer register.*

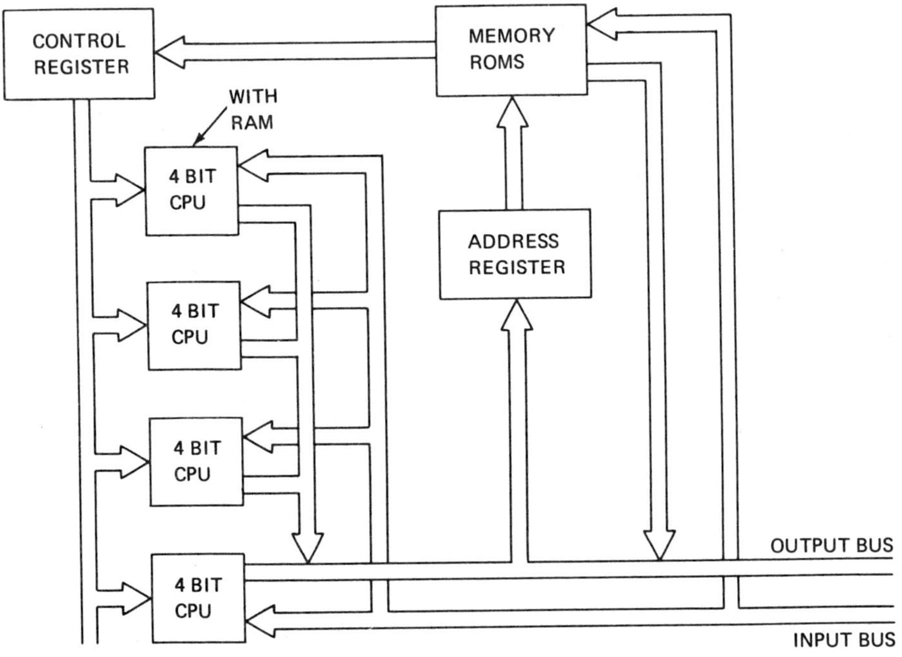

Fig. 10-2. Bus-oriented architecture.

If a digital-to-analog or analog-to-digital converter is involved in the interface, the data transfer may require a double-buffered register. Data is first inputted or outputted into the buffer register and then into the device register proper; this hardware facility will then enable the simultaneous operation of all the device registers by means of a simple clock-pulse.

In the I/O interface structure, some practical program applications involve multiple data-transfers from the main memory that include ADCs and cell-arrays of the order of hundreds. Temporary storage areas used in I/O for cell-array requirements of this magnitude are also conventionally called *buffers*. This is an essential function because external peripherals such as TTY or CRT process data at much slower rates compared to the normal high-speed cycle-times of the main-memory and CPU. Interference between data processing and I/O operations is avoided by careful assignment of the buffers during the preparation of the program—especially how they are managed during services interrupts. *Error routines* involving **parity errors** and **improper I/O requests** and **code-formatting routines** (general character "packing" and "unpacking") also need the careful assignment of the I/O buffers during this programming effort.

In some sophisticated minicomputer systems, a *microprocessor* is deputed to organize the buffers and the multiplexer/channel-controllers in handling the above assignments.

10-5. ARITHMETIC AND LOGIC UNIT (ALU)

Some terms pertinent to arithmetic and logic unit (ALU). Binary point, sign and magnitude, 1's complement and 2's complement notation, half and full-adders, race conditions. The ALU operates with binary arithmetic irrespective of the code (hexadecimal, octal, BCD, Gray, etc.) used for writing the assembly-language program. The specific computation procedure used for obtaining a solution is called an **algorithm.**

Binary integer 2^3 2^2 2^1 2^0 (Bits "0" or "1" with "weights" 8 + 4 + 2 + 1)
Fractional numbers after binary point 2^{-1} 2^{-2} 2^{-3} 2^{-4}

The preceding binary point notation is the same as decimal-point notation.

2^0 and 2^{-4} are the least significant bits (**LSB**) for the integer and the fraction, respectively.

2^3 and 2^{-1} are the most significant bits (**MSB**) for the integer and the fraction, respectively.

Sign and magnitude notation. Example: 5-bit magnitude part with a 6th sign-bit:

S (sign-bit)
↓
010111 = +23
↓
110111 = −23

In floating-point notation, the binary fractional point can be chosen between any two adjacent bits of the magnitude part. An arithmetic shift should not affect the "sign" position.

1's and 2's complement notation. In sign-and-magnitude notation, a positive number is identical to that in the 1's complement notation. For a negative number, however, it is subtracted from "1" to provide the complements of the bits, 1 for 0 and 0 for 1, in the 1's complement notation. In the 2's complement notation, "1" must be added to the above 1's complement notation for a negative number. As above, a positive number is not affected.

The **binary adder** that performs such arithmetic tasks is essentially a simple form of

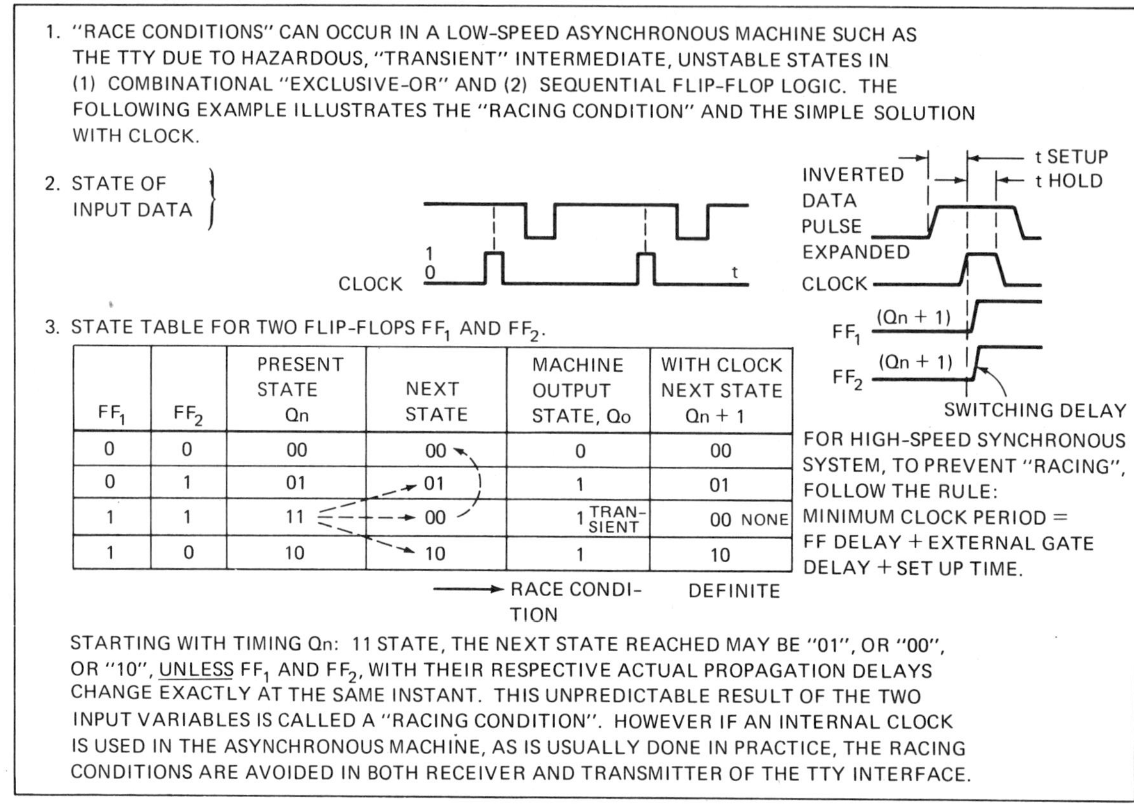

1. "RACE CONDITIONS" CAN OCCUR IN A LOW-SPEED ASYNCHRONOUS MACHINE SUCH AS THE TTY DUE TO HAZARDOUS, "TRANSIENT" INTERMEDIATE, UNSTABLE STATES IN (1) COMBINATIONAL "EXCLUSIVE-OR" AND (2) SEQUENTIAL FLIP-FLOP LOGIC. THE FOLLOWING EXAMPLE ILLUSTRATES THE "RACING CONDITION" AND THE SIMPLE SOLUTION WITH CLOCK.
2. STATE OF INPUT DATA
CLOCK
1
0
t
INVERTED DATA PULSE
EXPANDED CLOCK
t SETUP
t HOLD
FF1 (Qn + 1)
FF2 (Qn + 1)
SWITCHING DELAY
3. STATE TABLE FOR TWO FLIP-FLOPS FF1 AND FF2.
FF1 | FF2 | PRESENT STATE Qn | NEXT STATE | MACHINE OUTPUT STATE, Qo | WITH CLOCK NEXT STATE Qn + 1
0 | 0 | 00 | 00 | 0 | 00
0 | 1 | 01 | 01 | 1 | 01
1 | 1 | 11 | 00 | 1 TRAN-SIENT | 00 NONE
1 | 0 | 10 | 10 | 1 | 10
RACE CONDI-TION
DEFINITE
FOR HIGH-SPEED SYNCHRONOUS SYSTEM, TO PREVENT "RACING", FOLLOW THE RULE: MINIMUM CLOCK PERIOD = FF DELAY + EXTERNAL GATE DELAY + SET UP TIME.
STARTING WITH TIMING Qn: 11 STATE, THE NEXT STATE REACHED MAY BE "01", OR "00", OR "10", UNLESS FF1 AND FF2, WITH THEIR RESPECTIVE ACTUAL PROPAGATION DELAYS CHANGE EXACTLY AT THE SAME INSTANT. THIS UNPREDICTABLE RESULT OF THE TWO INPUT VARIABLES IS CALLED A "RACING CONDITION". HOWEVER IF AN INTERNAL CLOCK IS USED IN THE ASYNCHRONOUS MACHINE, AS IS USUALLY DONE IN PRACTICE, THE RACING CONDITIONS ARE AVOIDED IN BOTH RECEIVER AND TRANSMITTER OF THE TTY INTERFACE.

Fig. 10-3. "Race conditions," waveform timings. (*Courtesy of Texas Instruments, Inc.*)

ALU. Binary subtraction is commonly performed by complement addition and by **end-around carry**. Whenever a **carry-bit** is generated during summing, it is added to the LSB of the sum.

The **half-adder** is a simple adder with no provision for carry-in from the preceding addition of two binary numbers; however, the **full adder** makes provision for the "carry" from the preceding addition. However, both adders produce two outputs, "sum" and "carry." These adders are usually called **asynchronous adders** since each stage is delayed until the preceding stage has produced its "carry" output. In another technique termed **"carry" look-ahead**, the "carry" for each of the stages is simultaneously predicted in parallel to shorten the delay and the final add-time.

Race conditions. *Race condition* is a timing situation related to asynchronous operation, when two variables are asked to change state simultaneously. The device state is then "critical." Figure 10-3 illustrates the involved waveform timings. (See Section 10-12, System Logic Design.)

10-6. PROGRAMMABLE LOGIC ARRAY (PLA)

There are presently two basic hardware methods for implementing the usual software functions:

1. The hard-wired or custom-wired logic-gates, using the MSI integrated circuits or the field-programmed PLAs
2. The Read-only-Memories.

When the gates are designed in the large-scale-integrated form, the result is a custom-wired PLA-chip capable of performing the desired software functions. The Field Programmable Logic Array is illustrated in Figs. 10-4a and b.

A
B
L
INPUT
PRODUCT, "AND" LOGIC ROM
SUMMING "OR" ROM
Q_0
Q_1
Q_n
OUTPUT
FEED-BACK LOOP CLOCKED
FLIP-FLOPS (CLOCKED TO PREVENT "RACING")
CLOCK
RESET
SEQUENTIAL AND COMBINATIONAL "LOGIC" FUNCTIONS PERFORMED BY DESIGNING A SINGLE "GATE MASK" DURING CIRCUIT FABRICATION.

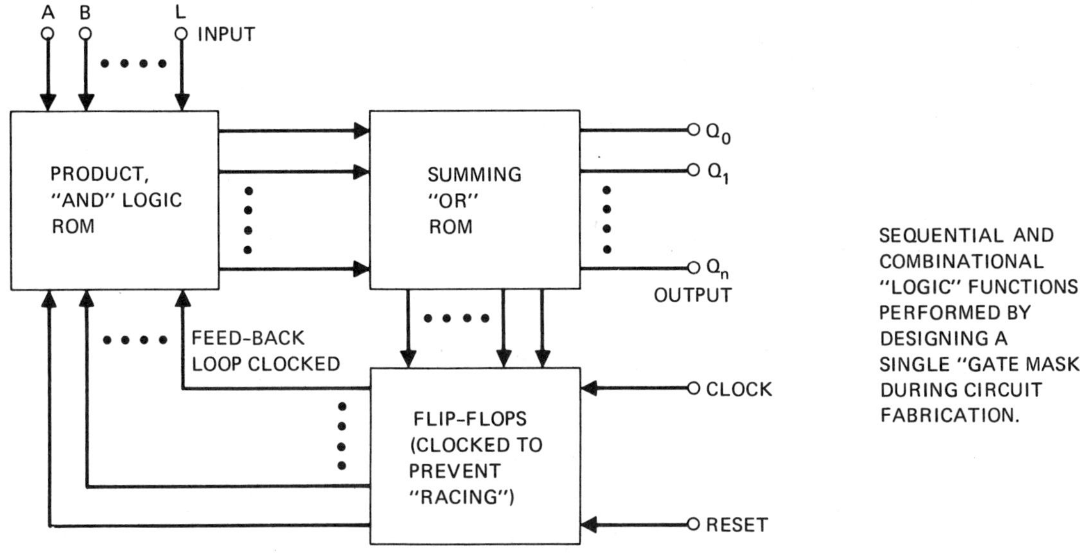

Fig. 10-4a. Field programmable logic array (FPLA).

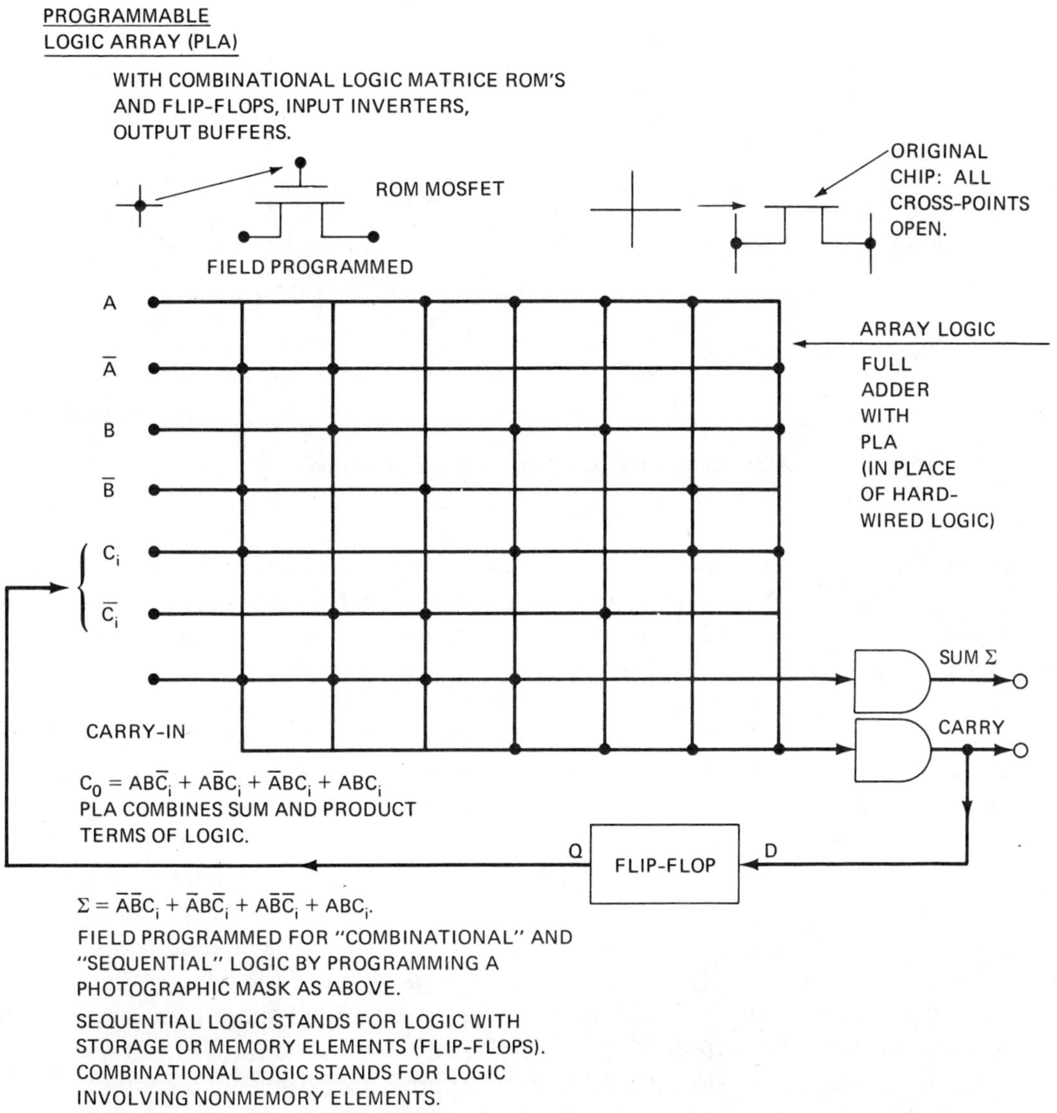

PROGRAMMABLE LOGIC ARRAY (PLA)
WITH COMBINATIONAL LOGIC MATRICE ROM'S AND FLIP-FLOPS, INPUT INVERTERS, OUTPUT BUFFERS.
ROM MOSFET
FIELD PROGRAMMED
ORIGINAL CHIP: ALL CROSS-POINTS OPEN.
A
$\bar{A}$
B
$\bar{B}$
C_i
$\bar{C}_i$
ARRAY LOGIC
FULL ADDER WITH PLA (IN PLACE OF HARD-WIRED LOGIC)
SUM Σ
CARRY
CARRY-IN
$C_0 = AB\bar{C}_i + A\bar{B}C_i + \bar{A}BC_i + ABC_i$
PLA COMBINES SUM AND PRODUCT TERMS OF LOGIC.
Q
FLIP-FLOP
D
$\Sigma = \bar{A}\bar{B}C_i + \bar{A}B\bar{C}_i + A\bar{B}\bar{C}_i + ABC_i$.
FIELD PROGRAMMED FOR "COMBINATIONAL" AND "SEQUENTIAL" LOGIC BY PROGRAMMING A PHOTOGRAPHIC MASK AS ABOVE.
SEQUENTIAL LOGIC STANDS FOR LOGIC WITH STORAGE OR MEMORY ELEMENTS (FLIP-FLOPS).
COMBINATIONAL LOGIC STANDS FOR LOGIC INVOLVING NONMEMORY ELEMENTS.

Fig. 10-4b. Programmable logic array (PLA).

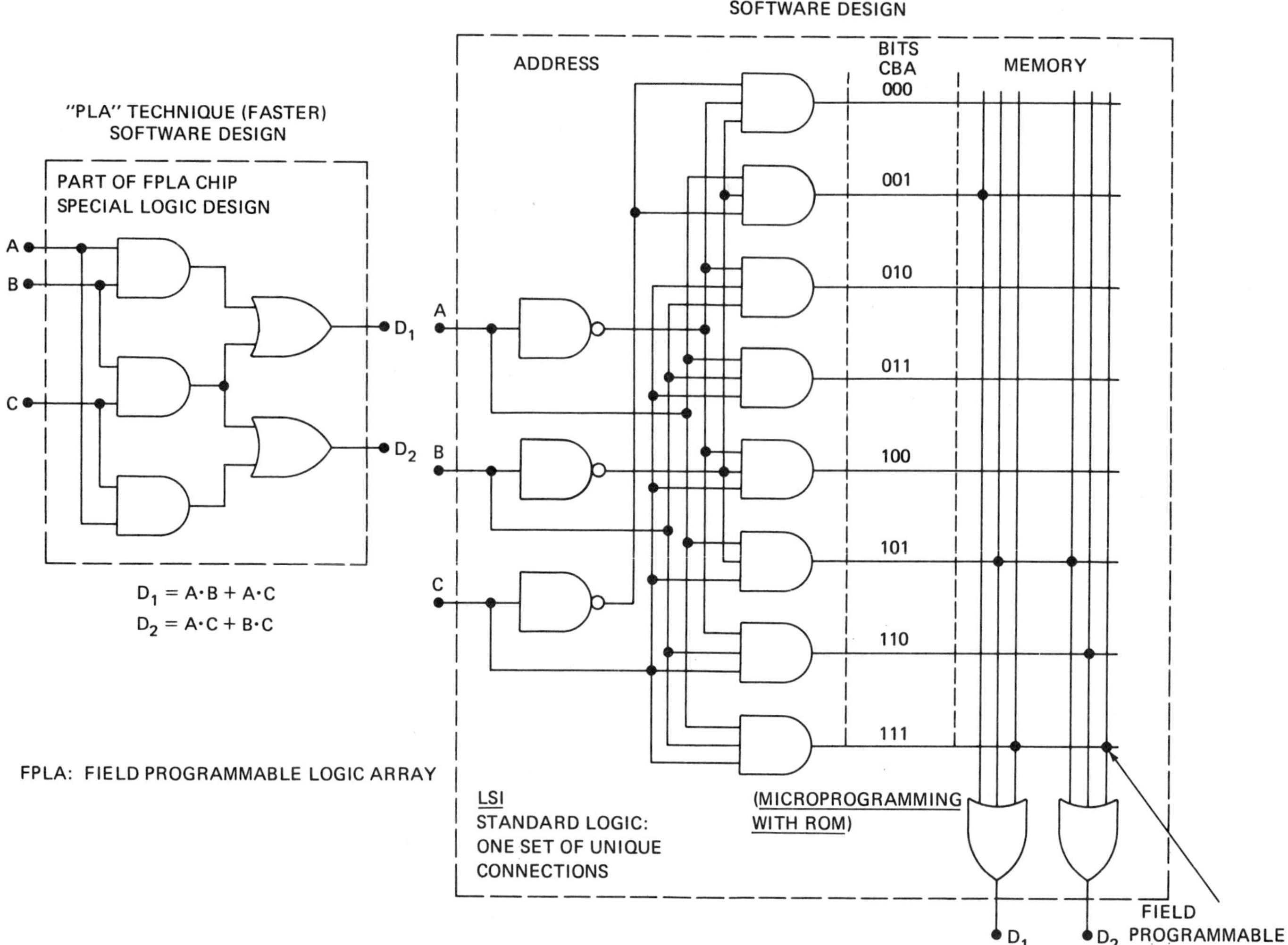

Fig. 10-5. PLA and ROM techniques. (*Courtesy of IEEE Spectrum*)

Integrated-circuit chips can also be produced as standard arrays of ROM elements and processed for the desired logic connections as a stored pattern of 0's and 1's, such as the stored-program in the computer memory. A sequence of a few logical events of this pattern makes a microprogram. The ROM technique is illustrated in Fig. 10-5.

But the custom-wired logic chip, such as the Signetics 82S100 (FPLA, Fig. 10-6), can perform the computation function much faster than the ROM's version of logic shown in Fig. 10-5. However, both of these techniques are considerably faster than the MSI hard-wired method of software design. Design time of course is involved in laying out the logic connections for the custom-wired FPLA chip. The ROM version of design is easier, but the microprogram coding requires more person-hours. To effect a simple instruction such as adding two numbers, the operand "fetch" and the data "transfer" must be specified in the microprogram in 3 to 10 microinstructions. So, this is a large-scale investment, which must be considered only for the dedicated application of the microcomputer for a specific controller or business application. Design turnaround times of several months can be tolerated for this method of "firmware" (software in the form of LSI hardware). In short, the comparatively slower PROM/ROM approach of firmware is simple and convenient for most dedicated applications of microcomputer systems.

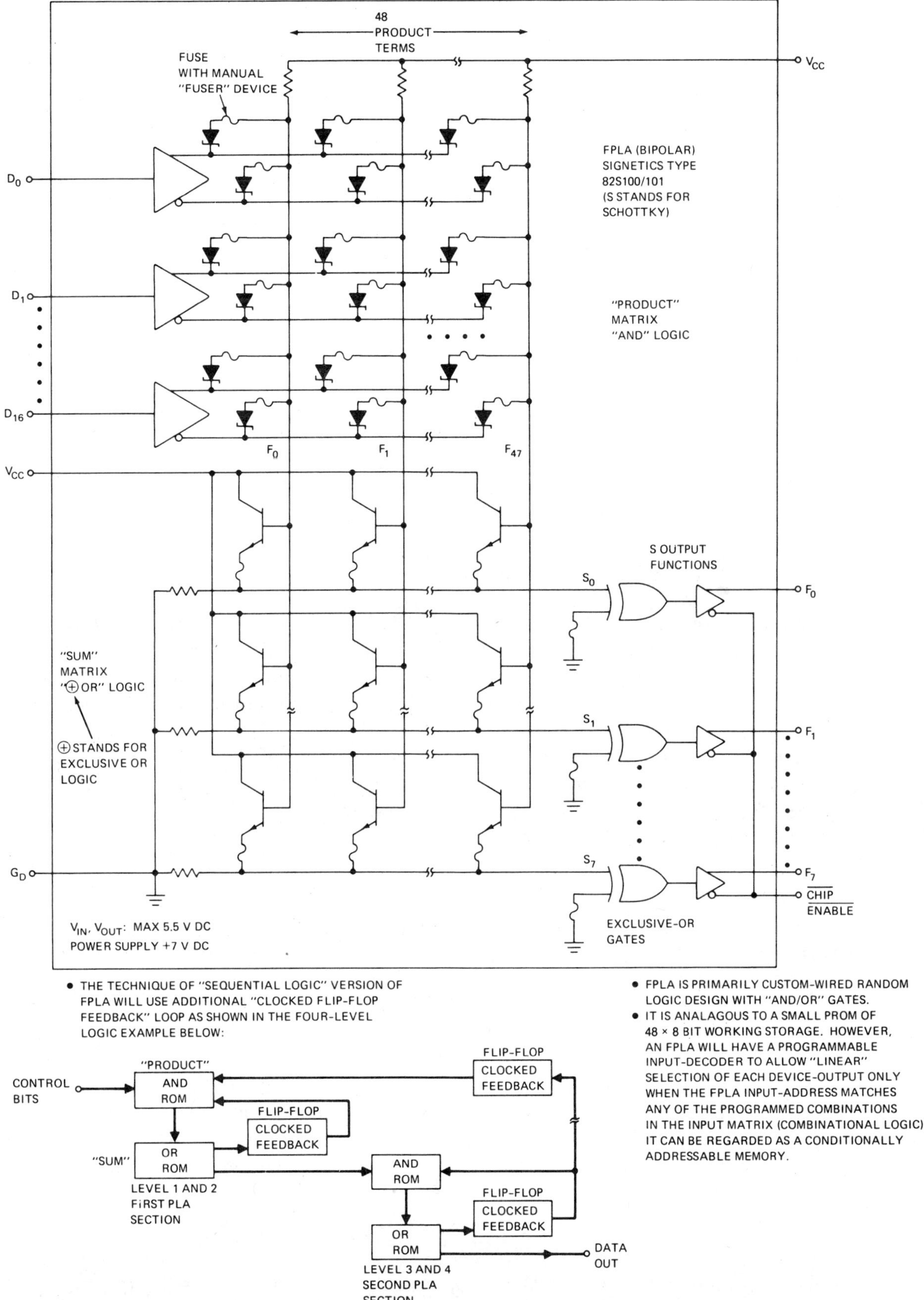

Fig. 10-6. Custom-wired field programmable logic array, bipolar version (FPLA). (*Courtesy of Signetics*)

For complex computations, high speed is achieved by using a programmable logic array (PLA); it is definitely advantageous for specialized sorting, Fast Fourier Transforms (FFT), and floating-point arithmetic. Figure 10-4b illustrates the programmable logic array (PLA).

FPLA (LSI, field-programmable logic array). An FPLA—for example, Intersil IM5200—is used for implementing random logic functions to interface the external LSI or bulk-storage memory (from disk or tape) to the microprocessors.

The FPLA chip is functionally equivalent to a collection of AND/NAND gates, which may be OR/NOR-ed at any of its outputs. For example, with 14 inputs, the designer has a choice of 48 product (AND) terms, and a complexity of over 480, 4-input logic gates. Field programming is done by electrical pulses. **Nonprogrammable PLAs** are also available for a wide variety of logic; they provide greater flexibility than the ROMs, and conveniently replace the present hard-wired logic that requires a large number of printed-circuit boards for a combination of MSI and SSI integrated cirucits.

Programmable logic array (PLA) or **uncommitted logic array (ULA).** Some manufacturers (e.g., Plessey) are producing the versatile PLAs for low-volume custom circuits that cost less for combined high-speed and low-power logic as compared to CMOS or TTL. One Plessey 14 X 14 matrix of unconnected cells on a diffused silicon-chip, 147 X 154 mils, with a voltage-rail coming up through the substrate, is presently available. A 1,000 cell PLA, using the high-speed bipolar I^2L technique, will be commercially available off the shelf in the near future.

10-7 TWO-PHASE NONOVERLAPPING CLOCK

Operation of dynamic (ratio-less) PMOS and NMOS logic used for dynamic RAMs, etc., requires two or more clock pulses and is independent of the ratio of transistor geometrics. A minimum clock-frequency is therefore specified for dynamic logic circuits to "refresh" circuit-capacitances through periodic recharging and to prevent loss of data due to discharge leakage currents.

To meet this requirement, the low-frequency operation of the PMOS and NMOS dynamic shift-registers is assured by using master-slave J-K flip-flops at a 4-phase clock frequency for minimum power-dissipation, cell-area, and highest operating frequencies. If 2-$\emptyset$, the lowest operating frequency, is determined by

$$f_{min} = 1/(t_m + t_s)$$

where t_m and t_s are the refresh times for the master and slave J-K flip-flops, respectively. This frequency is minimum when $t_m = t_s$. The minimum clock frequency allowed decreases at lower temperatures.

In the more common 2-phase shift-register, the high frequency is limited by the time-constants of the node-capacitances (transistor-geometrics); these impose a minimum of duration for $\emptyset_1$ and $\emptyset_2$.

To prevent the clock signals from overlapping each other, a "clock-skew" becomes necessary. A clock-skew is defined as the "time-interval between the trailing edge of one clock phase and the leading edge of the subsequent clock phase." In the absence of the clock-skew, the data could propagate through several shift-register bits during the clock-overlap and cause errors in logic.

$$f_{max} = \tfrac{1}{2}\,(t_\phi + t_t + t_s)$$

where t_ϕ = minimum duration of the $\emptyset_1$ and $\emptyset_2$ clocks, when $\emptyset_1 = \emptyset_2$; t_t = transition duration; and t_s = minimum skew-time between the 2-phase clock-pulses. A 2-$\emptyset$ ratio-less dynamic shift-register with 2-$\emptyset$ nonoverlapping clock pulses is shown in Fig. 10-7.

The nonoverlap clock in this figure is required mostly for the slower MOS logic only. By combining the dynamic storage of MOS with a simple dc flip-flop, the need for a nonoverlapping clock is avoided (STL Ltd). In general, the method of positive edge-trigger is effective in preventing clock overlaps.

Multiphase clock signals (2-, 3-, 4-phase). These clock signals are generated from a single master-clock crystal-controlled oscillator, generally temperature-controlled in an oven by means of a thermostat to obtain a frequency stability of the order of ±10 Hz at 10 MHz or so. The clock-frequency of course depends upon the memory instruction cycle-time feasible due to the technique of processing and the circuit logic used. Multiphase

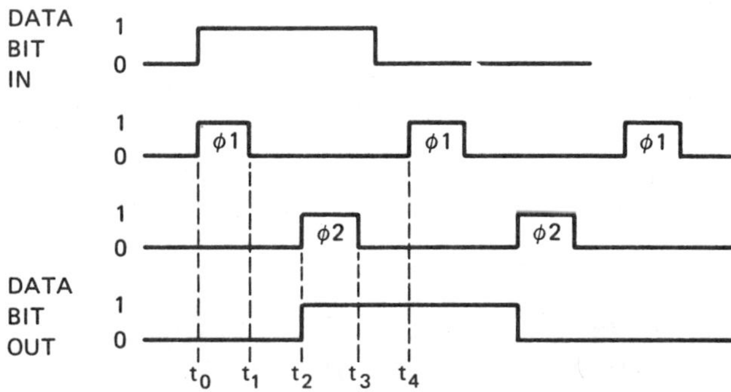

- ONE BIT OF INFORMATION UNDERGOES TWO INVERSIONS IN TWO SUCCESSIVE CLOCK PULSES FOR THE DATA SHIFT SHOWN ABOVE.
- ONE BIT OF A TWO-PHASE RATIOLESS DYNAMIC MOS SHIFT REGISTER REQUIRING THE NONOVERLAPPING TWO-PHASE CLOCK IS SHOWN BELOW. (THE SHIFT REGISTER DOES NOT USE DRAIN VOLTAGE SUPPLY.)

(THE SHIFT REGISTER

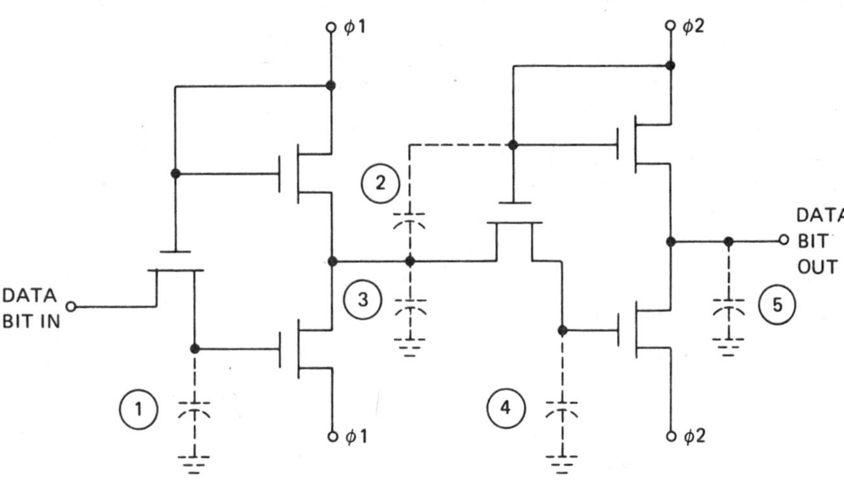

THE CHARGES ON FIVE GEOMETRIC CAPACITANCES REQUIRE A TWO-PHASE NONOVERLAPPING CLOCK FOR SHIFTING A DATA-BIT FROM THE INPUT-TERMINAL TO THE OUTPUT.

Fig. 10-7. Two-phase dynamic MOS shift register with two-phase nonoverlapping clock pulses. (*Courtesy of Motorola Semiconductor Products*)

clocks for dynamic memories, etc., are usually generated by using a master clock followed by a ring-counter or some form of counter decoding logic.

10-8. MICROCOMPUTER PERIPHERALS

1. Peripheral device such as a powerful source-program editing CRT-display (in place of a TTY)
2. Line-printer hard-copy device for hard-copying the listings of the source-programs connected with debugging and documentation
3. Mass-storage device, such as a cassette and/or floppy-disk, for rapid access to the assemblers of microprogramming and the compilers of high-level languages
4. High-speed paper-tape system to handle paper-taped programs.

All four are effective for the successful development of compatible software of minicomputer systems. Using available minicomputer hardware-interface, they are all applicable to the microprogrammable microcomputer systems. If efficient software development were attempted afresh for the microcomputer systems, such a development system would cost 75% of the whole microcomputer operating system. However, the latest high-speed miniperipherals would reduce such software development cost by at least 50%. As a long-range perspective, exclusive efficient software development is in order for the future microcomputer systems by using a few LSI programmable-logic-array (PLA) chips in the place of the present bulky hard-wired logic designs.

For example, by using microprocessor-controlled CRT intelligent terminals, Raytheon, has evolved a PTS-1200 **distributed data processing system** that performs the following six functions:

1. Source data-entry and preprocessing
2. File and record maintenance
3. Unattended two-way point-to-point or multipoint communications
4. Stand-alone batch-processing
5. Local report-printing
6. On-line IBM-3270 emulation.

Some of the more common **peripheral devices** presently available for the use of the microcomputer systems are described in the following paragraphs.

1. **Punched-card** is widely used unique form of computer input with the following advantages:

   a. Each card is discrete as a unit-record.
   b. It provides the convenience of manipulation for addition, deletion, and rearrangement in records.
   c. It provides the facility of direct manual reference to individual records.

The **keypunch** machine is a typewriterlike machine for punching the character code of a word as holes in a 12-bit X 80-column card. The IBM punched-card dimensions are specified as 3.25" X 7.375" X 0.0067".

2. TI model-84 **Card-Reader** is a column-oriented device that reads punched-hole data in 80-column cards at approximately 400 cards/min. The data is transferred through fiber-optics to an array of photosensors. The Card Reader is complete with input hopper, feed mechanism, read station, stacker mechanism, output stacker, and timing mechanism with supporting drive-belt and motor, control-and-error electronics, and power supply.

3. TI model-306 **line-printer** is a medium-speed, impact printer that uses a standard 10-

point type 5 X 7 dot-matrix for character generation and prints 80 characters/line/sec. Standard sprocketed paper is sprocket-fed, and paper widths from 4" to 9.5" can be used. One master copy and up to four copies are available. Standard print-format is 10 characters/inch and six lines vertical/inch. The other specifications are:

Transmission rate: 100 to 9,600 baud/sec
Code: ASCII, 64 characters printed
Character buffer: 80 characters (one line)
Paper feed: Adjustable to 9.5 inches.
Dimensions: 12.75" X 18.75" X 23.5"; weight: 66 pounds

4. **Punched paper-tape** has remained the most popular program-loading device for minicomputers. In view of the electronically alterable semiconductor programmable ROMs, program-loading by paper tape may not prove to be as popular for the microcomputer. Sophisticated microcomputer systems would prefer tape-cartridges or floppy-disk mass-memories; stand-alone special-purpose microcomputers would use PROMs and ROMs. However, where TTYs are involved as peripherals, the paper tape as a program-loader will continue in usage, especially in the extensive communications field. **Teletypewriter types ASR-33 and ASR-35** have built-in 10 characters/sec **paper-tape-punches and readers** to feed the program tapes in the binary machine-language for occasional program preparation. Digital Equipment Corporation markets a 50-character/sec punch and a 300 characters/sec reader, using a fanfold paper tape that does not require rewinding (price, $300 to $3,000, depending on the tape handling speed).

In the case of the TTYs ASR 33/35, an 8-character paper tape in ASCII code appears with binary 1-2-4 weighted 3-bit groups, one group of holes on either side of the sprocket holes, and a third 2-bit group at the bottom for characters 7/8. The 212 line-feed and 215 carriage-return codes function as controls in the abovementioned TTYs.

5. **Tape and CRT-keyboard interface (IBM-5100)**

a. The large-capacity magnetic tape-storage employs plug-in capstan-driven data cartridges with file-protect features. Each cartridge holds up to 204,000 characters on a 300-foot, 0.25" magnetic tape. Searching or rewinding are both performed at 40 ips.

b. The visual display-screen presents up to 1,024 alphanumeric characters in 16 lines on a 5" diagonal CRT.

c. A full-function keyboard and a 10-function calculator pad are provided.

d. An optional **type-5103 desktop printer** (12.25" X 13.25" X 23", 60 lbs, at a price of $3,675) can be easily integrated into the portable computer system.

e. An optional **auxiliary tape unit** is also available as an added software facility. Each of these peripheral devices has a built-in controller and the necessary interface-electronics on a plug-in MSI printed-circuit board.

A **back-plane card guide-assembly** provides the facility for plug-in of the controllers and additional memory adjacent to the CPU. This system organization appears to be universal in all the existing and upcoming microcomputer systems.

Tape cartridges, reading and writing speed (IBM). The magnetic tape-cartridge unit driven at 40 ips has an effective reading-rate of up to 2,850 alphanumeric characters/sec; however, in the record mode, the machine can write up to 950 character/sec only, because, during the write-mode, a self-checking read-head is involved with its own time allotment for output information.

6. **Video-RAM (V-RAM).** As used in the IBM-5100 portable computer system, the video random access memory is a modular device that provides an interface between the microcomputer system and an ordinary TV-monitor of any picture size. The V-RAM functions like any other static-RAM; it is organized in 128 words of 8 bits each, and its output is presented as a conventional analog composite video signal that can be directly

connected to any standard TV monitor. A single V-RAM has the provision to drive 25 television monitors. The device has a large repertoire of characters (ASCII large- and small-case alphanumerics, various symbols, and Greek letters) and operates at 5 V, 1 W. Price: $94.

10-9. A CUSTOM SINGLE-CARD MICROCOMPUTER SUBSYSTEM

A custom single-card microcomputer subsystem will typically use an Intel 8080A NMOS microprocessor, 1 kilobyte of RAMs, and 4 kilobytes of ROMs, and I/O drivers for the address, data, and control busses. The dimensions of the card will be nominally 6.75" × 12". Programmable serial interface for a compatible data-communications terminal or, as an alternative, a serial TTY interface and, for instance, 48 parallel I/O lines to a peripheral device will complete the single-card microcomputer system with external ±5-V and ±12-V regulated dc. Provision will be included for at least one interrupt line. The said communications interface will include a programmable synchronous and asynchronous communications interface device, a variable baud-rate generator, and jumper-selectable RS-232-C and TTY drivers and receivers. This kind of microcomputer is readily available as an original-equipment manufacturer's (OEM) item from Intel as SBC 80/10. (Most computer manufacturers supply similar single-card microcomputers.) The programs can be written in a natural algorithmic language such as the PL/M of Intel; the compiler available will eliminate the need to manage register usage or allocation of memory. One could develop, debug, and execute software directly on this unit by means of an Intellec MDS, resident macroassembler, a text editor, and an external optional diskette-operating system. MDS has an **in-circuit emulator** ICE-80 for debugging purposes. (A 16-K bit RAM/ROM is available in one LSI chip.)

10-10. "SC/MP," NATIONAL SEMICONDUCTOR "KITBUG" KEYBOARD-SCAN

In a microcomputer system, the low-cost CPU microprocessor and possibly a low-cost LSI interface-chip—to the real-word peripheral such as an expensive TTY or a CRT terminal—are a gross mismatch for applications by amateurs and schools. National Semiconductor has a timely solution to this problem of an expensive peripheral in a low-cost hand-held calculator-type keyboard-display, which uses only 20 keys and an 8-digit 7-segment output-display. It goes by the name "Kitbug" and is shown in Fig. 10-8. Timing is accomplished by way of a programmable delay-instruction (13 to 131,593 microcycles), and the 20 keys used have the following command functions: 16 keys for the more popular 16-versus 8-bit hexadecimal code, 0 through 9 and A through F, Abort, Memory, GO, Terminate, and Power ON/OFF for start. The Abort-key disables the current-command for return to "wait-loop"; the operation of the memory-key then displays the last referenced address and its data. If pressed in memory mode, it will increment memory address and display data at that address. The GO-key displays the last referenced address. The terminate-key will begin execution at the last referenced address. A 21-pin cord connects the keyboard-display to the microcomputer on a card. The details of the hardware of eight interface parts for this peripheral Calculator Keyboard and Display are given in Fig. 10-9. The Read/Write RAM memory allocation and the calling sequence for the Keyboard-Scan routine are reproduced in Table 10-1. The calling sequence indicates how, for example, an **"XPPC P3"** instruction is completed **(Return to the Monitor Program).**

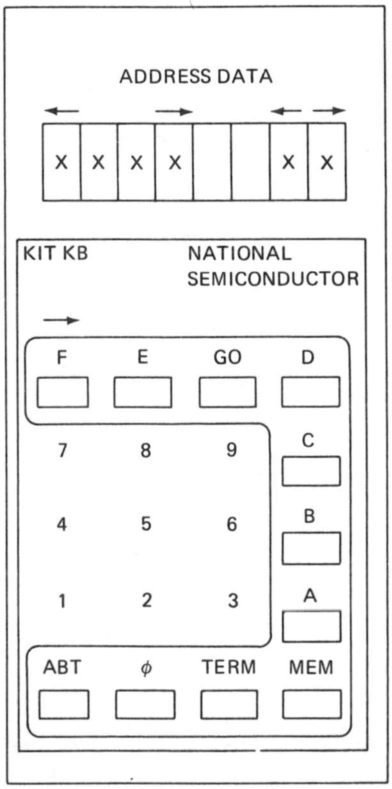

ADDRESS DATA

X X X X X X

KIT KB NATIONAL SEMICONDUCTOR

F E GO D

7 8 9 C

4 5 6 B

1 2 3 A

ABT ϕ TERM MEM

- THE CALCULATOR-TYPE KEYBOARD FACILITATES MANUAL INPUT COMMANDS TO THE MICROCOMPUTER SC/MP.
- SIX-DIGIT HEX DISPLAY FACILITATES VISUAL OUTPUT.
- THE KEYBOARD HAS AN 8 X 4 MATRIX-ARRAY (20 OF POSSIBLE 32 KEYS ONLY ARE USED; SEE TEXT.
- COST: $95.00 (WITH INTERFACE AND SPECIAL ROM WITH DEBUG KEYBOARD/DISPLAY SCANNING PROGRAM).
- ABT-ABORT KEY; TERM-TERMINATE PRESENT MODE OF OPERATION; MEM-MEMORY MODE (THE FIRST PUSH OF TERM WILL END THE INPUT OF ADDRESS AND ALLOW INPUT OF DATA).

Fig. 10-8. SC/MP "Kitbug" (economy keyboard-display peripheral device used to interface with SC/MP microcomputer system). (*Courtesy of National Semiconductor Corp.*)

TABLE 10-1. Basis of software for the Keyboard-Scan (*Courtesy of National Semiconductor Corp.*)

R/W RAM Memory Allocation			Calling Sequence		
1	FØØ	SEGMENT FOR DIGIT 1	KYB	=	Ø185
2	FØ1	SEGMENT FOR DIGIT 2	RAM	=	ØFØØ
3	FØ2	SEGMENT FOR DIGIT 3			
4	FØ3	SEGMENT FOR DIGIT 4		LD I	H(RAM)
5	FØ4	SEGMENT FOR DIGIT 5		XPAH	2
6	FØ5	SEGMENT FOR DIGIT 6		LD I	L(RAM)
7	FØ6	SEGMENT FOR DIGIT 7		XPAL	2
8	FØ7	SEGMENT FOR DIGIT 8			
9	FØ8	EXTRA LOCATION		LD I	H(KYB)
10	FØ9	COUNTER		XPAH	3
11	FØA	KEY PUSHED		LD I	L(KYB)-1
12	FØB	CHAR READ		XPAL	3
13	FØC	MEMORY ADDRESS LOW			
14	FØD	MEMORY WORD		XPPC	3
15	FØE	MEMORY ADDRESS HI			
16	FØF	FIRST FLAG		JMP	CMND
17	F1Ø	ROW COUNTER			
18	F11	FLAG FOR NEW DATA			
19			CMND		
20					

18 Words of RAM

CHAR: Character
CMND: Command
LD: LOAD
KYB: Keyboard

1, 2, 3: P1, P2, P3 instruction words.
P1, P2, P3, A, E, S: Registers
XPPC: Return to the monitor program.
Next instruction: Jump command to the command-key return.

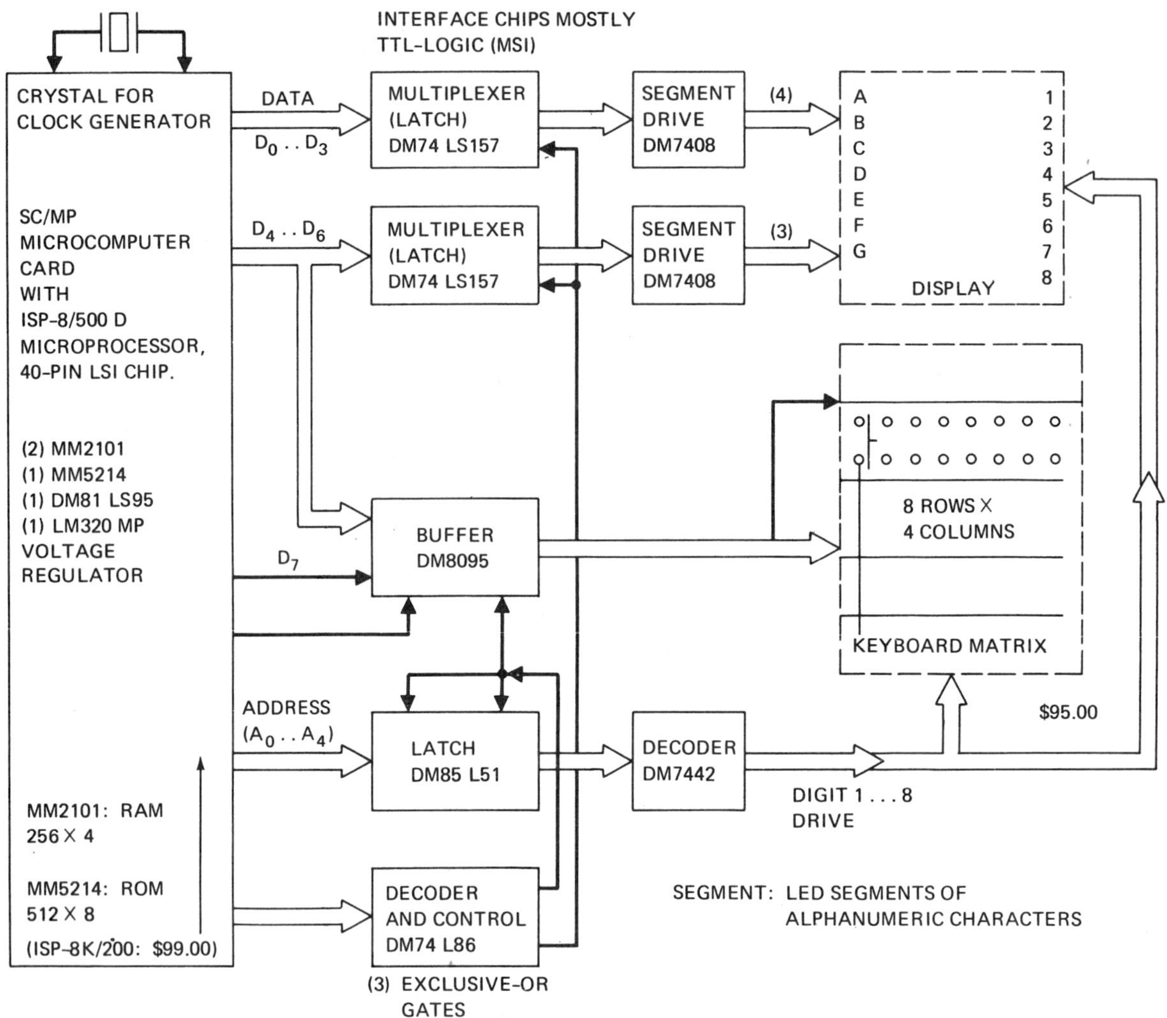

Fig. 10-9. "Calculator" keyboard-display system–Interface for SC/MP microcomputer. (*Courtesy of National Semiconductor Corp.*)

10-11. PROGRAMMING ACCESSORIES

1. **Programming an erasable PROM.** Intel 4-K bit type-2704 and 8-K bit type-2708 PROMs can be readily programmed by using the model PR-2708 programmer from Curtiss Electro Devices, Mountainview, California. Price: $998. Size: 16″ X 10″ X 4″. Verification is automatic by using an internal RAM memory; the RAM is loaded from the PROM by means of eight data switches and an octal address switch. Automatic verification can also be accomplished from a master ROM or a microcomputer. With the microcomputer, the programmer serves as a 1-K X 8-bit RAM for debugging the prospective erasable PROM contents with the aid of eight status lamp-indicators.

2. **The "Sponge."** For a single-card microcomputer system using a microprocessor and external RAMs and I/O PROMs, **a universal wire-wrap panel** called "Sponge" is available with 270 I/O pins at $245 from Mupack Corp., Brackton, Massachusetts. Pin-spacing is a multiple of 0.1″.

3. **Microcomputer cross-assembler.** A Micro-Tek microcomputer cross-assembler is available for $300 (Micro-Tek Inc., Wichita, Kansas) to give the programmer the

advantages of large-scale computer processing, editing, and high-speed I/O capabilities. The program written in ANSI FORTRAN IV will execute on any 16-bit, 8-K word mini- or micro-computer, furnished with a compiler supporting this high-level language.

4. **Microprocessor tester,** type MPU-1 (Micro Control's Co.). This device compares the microprocessor chip under test with a standard microprocessor chip, using worst-case voltages and timing, at both fast and slow pulse-repetition rates. The test program is stored in a 4-K bit RAM that can be loaded from a TTY. For high-speed loading, a mag-tape drive is available as an option. The panel controls provide for entering and displaying data, and for manually stepping through the program instructions in STEP mode. The program breakpoint and other facilities are included for debugging new programs and developing software. Test program and TTY software-loader are also included at a total price of $8,500 (Micro Control's Co., Minneapolis, Minnesota).

5. **Portable Microcomputer Analyzers** (Pro-Log Corp). A series of individual lightweight analyzers for 8-bit Intel-8008 and -8080 and Motorola MC-6800 microprocessors are used in conjunction with a standard oscilloscope to test hardware and software separately or together. With a strobe, they display the data related to a selected instruction cycle. An accessory DIP connector, with 3 feet of cable, clips onto the microprocessor. Prices range from $550 to $750. (Prolog Corp., Monterey, California).

6. **EPROM eraser** (Parametrics, Inc.). An adjustable timer is included to shut off the interlocked and **well-shielded ultraviolet radiation source** when the set-in time has elapsed. This facility assures against damage to EPROMs. Complete erasure of devices rated at 6 W/sec/cm^2 **integrated-erasure-dose** (for such types as 1702A and 4702A) requires less than 5 min at 30 W AC power requirement. (Parametrics, Inc., Chicago, Illinois).

7. **Clock oscillator for microprocessors** (Vectron Labs). Vectron CO-636-2, DIP compatible clock oscillator operates from 5 to 15 V DC thru 6 MHz and 10 to 15 V DC at 10 MHz; it is factory-set to within ±0.005% of specified clock frequency, -55°C to +125°C. Pricing of thermostat-controlled crystal oscillators depends on specifications concerning accuracy and temperature range. The oscillator provides high-stability CMOS-compatible output.

8. **8080 real-time in-circuit Emulator** (muPro Inc.). **muPro-80E:**

Real-time program execution is achieved at a cycle-time of 350 to 650 ns.

User programs may reside anywhere in the 64-K byte address space.

256 I/O device codes are available to the user's system.

Breakpoint is allowed on program/data/stack in PROM or RAM.

Comprehensive, fully transparent Control/Display Console is built-in.

Convenient memory and I/O Device allocation are feasible between the user's system and the Emulator, via four hexadecimal switches (multiplexers) on the Emulator.

Either the the user's or the internal clock can be automatically selected.

Program-trace provides 64-instruction history, preceding a Halt or breakpoint.

Terminal is required for only software development.

The unit fits in a suitcase with its dimensions of 4.6" H × 6.6" W × 15" D and weight of 18 lbs. Price: $3,250.

9. **muPro-80 Microcomputer Development System.** The complete system consists of the CPU, using Intel-8080, memory as required, and a transparent control/display console

that provides total debug capabilities. Automatic bootstrap is available from paper-tape or floppy-disk. The 64-K word memory-address system avoids the need for any monitor program. A total of 256 I/O device codes are available. Breakpoint can occur when the program is in ROM or RAM. There is a provision of eight card-slots on a mother-board for the CPU, hardware of multiply/divide option, memory refresh, 24-K word memory, floppy-disk interface, real-time clock, CRT/line printer/reader/punch interfaces. The chassis is extendable for full 64-K word memory, and additional I/O (serial, parallel, analog, and DMA). Total software support is available for a multiuser, multitask Disk Operating System (80-D), Resident BSAL-80 Block-structured assembly language, relocating/linking loader, text-editor, and BASIC high-level language. Dimensions: 4.6″ H × 6.6″ W × 15″ D; weight: 15 lbs; price: $3,950. A heavy-duty power supply system with regulated +5V at 15A and ±17V at 2A is included.

mu-Pro-80D Multiuser/Multitask Disk Operating System. The **dual-drive system** includes additional memory as required. The system will allow more than one program to run at the same time and will therefore support multiple terminals or users. System development time is minimized by eliminating the need for paper tape. The controller supports two dual-drives (four diskettes). The disk operating system is high-speed and single-density with **250-K bytes/diskette and 100 ms maximum search-time** from track 0 to track 76.

The RAM requirements are as follows:

muPro-80: 24-K bytes
Operating System: 8-K bytes
BSAL-80 Assembler: 8-K bytes (8-K Symbol Tables)
Text editor: 4-K bytes (12-K text buffer)
Linking-loader: 2-K bytes (14-K symbol table)

The muPro-80D, at a price of $3,765 provides comprehensive file management. Dimensions are identical to those of muPro-80. That is, the microcomputer system and the Disk Operating System together require 5.25″ rack-mount side-by-side, with a total weight of 50 lbs. Total price: $7,715 (1977). Both the Development and Disk Operating Systems could be directly integrated without any need of redesign in CPU, memory, and I/O cards.

Comments. It will be noted, incidentally, that the latest low-cost microcomputer systems are gradually assuming the powerful real-time tasks and increased throughput of the original medium-scale and subsequent minicomputer systems. And, the solid-state RAM memory is slowly replacing the former power-consuming nonvolatile CORE memory. The starting time required for loading the RAM memory from the permanent or semipermanent software on disk and tape is, after all, not that significant.

The sectored software on Diskettes of this system is compatible with IBM-3740, with the powerful DMA data-transfer facility.

The source BSAL-80 software used in this system has a high-level language syntax with ALGOL-like commands (e.g., IF, THEN BEGIN, END ELSE BEGIN, END CONSTRUCTS); the object machine-language output is "relocatable" like that in larger computers, with automatic variable memory allocation for program and data. BSAL-80 includes latest software features such as intuitive statement formats, extensive Error Diagnostics (36 descriptive error messages), extensive Macro instructions, Symbol cross-reference table for the assembler, and the Linking-loader (which combines the relocatable modules into the absolute program with a Load map).

The Text Editor uses commands that are meaningful, such as ADD, DELETE, COPY, GATHER, FIND, MODIFY, LIST, REPLACE, KEEP, TEXT, and SET. This is all, of course, the result of the latest capability of turning software logic into low-cost subminiature LSI hardware. It conveniently enables sophisticated features of the nature of line and string modification, block-copying and moving, multiple commands per instruction word, single-character command option, local-edit during command or text-entry, and automatic instruction numbering by ADD, COPY, GATHER, and TEXT.

10. **PROM programmer (muPro-80P-**2708). The PROM programmer enables **on-card programming** and thus avoids unnecessary chip-handling. Erasure and data verification each take less than 1 sec. Error conditions and program data from RAM, ROM, and emulator memories are displayed directly on the system control-display. It is transparent to CPU-timing, and no memory or I/O device codes are required. The accessory for programming up to eight type-2708 PROMs in about 5 minutes costs $775; and 8-K byte ROM card is included. (An independent programmer for the insertion and programming of eight chips in about 40 minutes is priced at $1,115.)

11. **VRAM-TV Monitor Display**. The latest low-cost CRT digital computer display system is the VRAM-TV monitor display. One merely adds a card of hardware to a regular low-cost (under $100) television video monitor, operating at 15.75-kHz line-scan rate and 60-Hz interfaced-field (30-frame) vertical-scan rate. The VRAM-TV display is the compatible economy CRT-Terminal for the present economy microcomputer systems. Within a year or two, a few LSI chips will be available to enable **home monochrome or color-television sets** to interface with data-communications systems.

The system block-diagram of the VRAM (video random-access memory) technique that converts the computer digital format to the regular composite black-and-white or color television signal is shown in Fig. 10-10. Incidentally, the television signal is a composite of synchronizing pulses at the horizontal 15.75 kHz/sec rate and the vertical 60 Hz/sec rate and analog black-and-white or color video (picture) information. The color signal is compatible to the black-and-white information in that merely additional chroma (in green, red, and blue) and color-synchronizing information, amplitude-and-phase modulated on a color subcarrier of 3.58 MHz, is added to the black-and-white monochrome information. The recent IBM portable-computer type-5100 provides the VRAM-TV monitor facility.

Video random-access memory. VRAM operates like a regular RAM; data and address bits are similarly processed, and the location of an element of the picture on the television screen corresponds to the cell location of the VRAM address. As explained in Chapter 12, the digital part of the VRAM system processes the microprocessor instruction words and formats alphanumeric data; a ROM character-generator in conjunction with a shift register feeds the data to a video generator to obtain the analog ("linear") video information for the television monitor. (I^2L) LSI chips would be ideal for processing in VRAM terminals. Special high-resolution television monitors with extended bandwidth could handle **graphics** that demand the configuration of line-segments along with alphanumerics in a 256 × 256 dot-matrix arrangement. The ROM character generator in the VRAM-TV will actually receive ASCII codes and output digital pulses that form letters in, for instance, a 7 × 9 format. The alphanumeric digital format may include all the present special features such as blinking, variable intensity, brightness reversal, and scrolling. The television sets may be conveniently switchable to the European line, field and color frequency standards, if they are easily portable.

10-12. BASIC CIRCUIT CONCEPTS OF DIGITAL LOGIC

The common logic circuits used in microcomputer systems are briefly covered in Figures 10-11A-Z, 10-12 through 10-20, and Table 10-2 through 10-6. Basically, they are the same as in any digital computer.

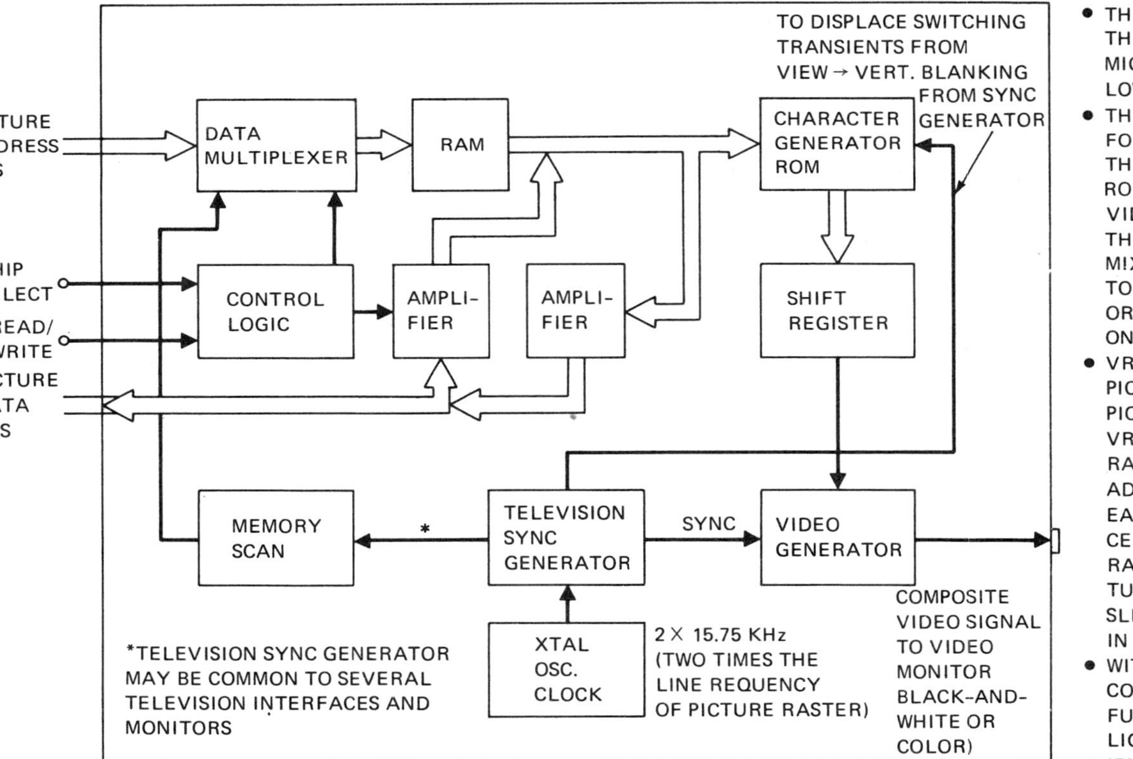

- THE ABOVE INTERFACE SYSTEM FOR A REGULAR TELEVISION RECEIVER (OR TELEVISION MONITOR) CAN BE REDUCED TO TWO LSI CHIPS (A MICROPROCESSOR AND AN INTERFACE CHIP).

- THE (ANALOG) TELEVISION RECEIVER WILL THEN SERVE AS A CRT-DISPLAY FOR THE MICROCOMPUTER SYSTEM TO PROVIDE A LOW-COST CRT-DEVICE.
- THE DIGITAL PROCESSING SECTION FORMATS THE ALPHANUMERIC DATA. THE VIDEO GENERATOR CONVERTS THE ROM VIDEO CHARACTERS TO NONCOMPOSITE VIDEO. WITH TELEVISION SYNC LOCKED TO THE CLOCK OF THE MICROCOMPUTER, IT IS MIXED WITH THE ABOVE NONCOMPOSITE VIDEO TO RUN THE ORDINARY TELEVISION MONITOR OR RECEIVER (WITH THE VIDEO MODULATED ON A VHF OSC. CHANNEL).
- VRAM INPUTS (IN ASCII CODE)
  PICTURE ADDRESS BITS: $A_0 \ldots A_8$.
  PICTURE DATA BITS : $D_0 \ldots D_7$.
  VRAM FUNCTIONS LIKE AN ORDINARY RAM IN MANIPULATION OF PICTURE ADDRESS AND DATA INFORMATION. EACH ADDRESS CORRESPONDS TO A CELL LOCATION ON THE TELEVISION-RASTER DISPLAY. AS THE TELEVISION TUBE SWEEPS A LINE, IT WRITES OUT A SLICE THROUGH A SERIES OF CHARACTERS IN THE ASCII CODE, 5 X 7 OR 7 X 9 FORMAT.
- WITH ANOTHER LSI CHIP, THE FACILITY COULD BE EVENTUALLY EXTENDED TO FULL "GRAPHICS" ADAPTATION WITH LIGHT-PEN.
- IBM PORTABLE-5100 PROVIDES THIS VRAM-TELEVISION MONITOR FACILITY AS AN EXTENSION TO ITS SMALL-SCREEN CRT-DISPLAY PERIPHERAL.

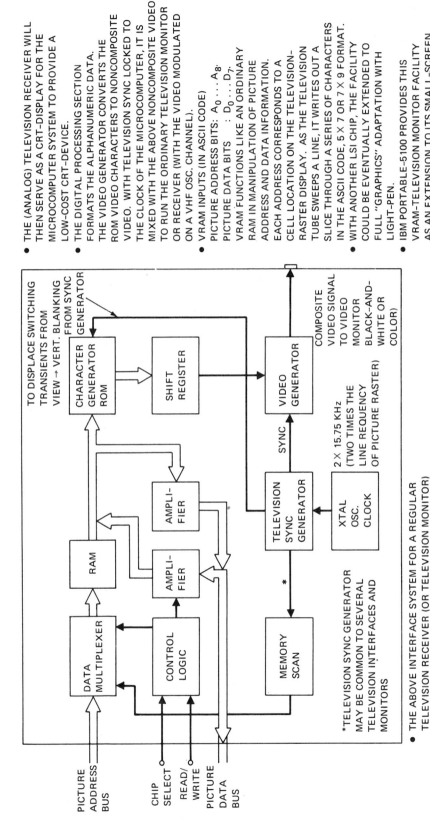

Fig. 10-10. "VRAM-converter" for black-and-white or color television monitor or receiver. (*Courtesy of EDN, March 5, 1977*)

COMBINATIONAL LOGIC

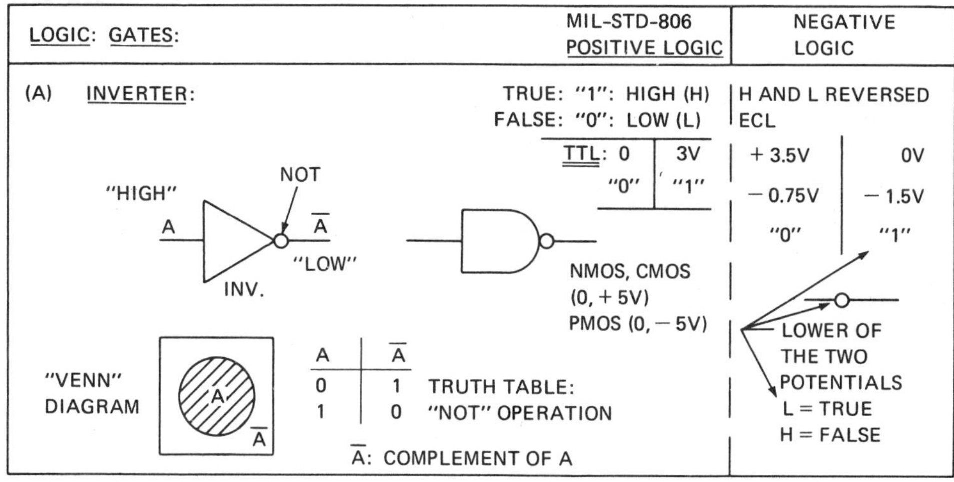

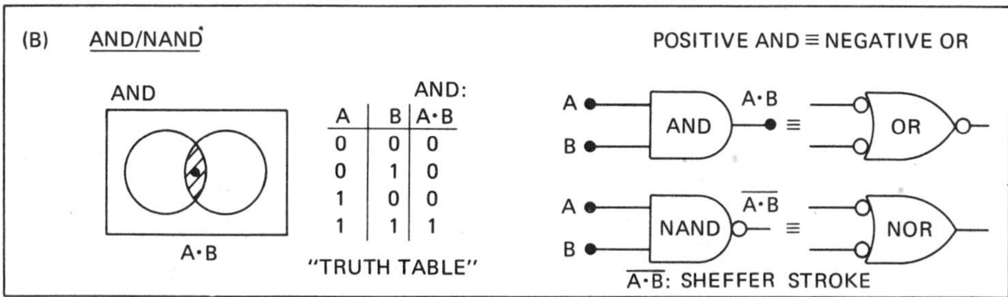

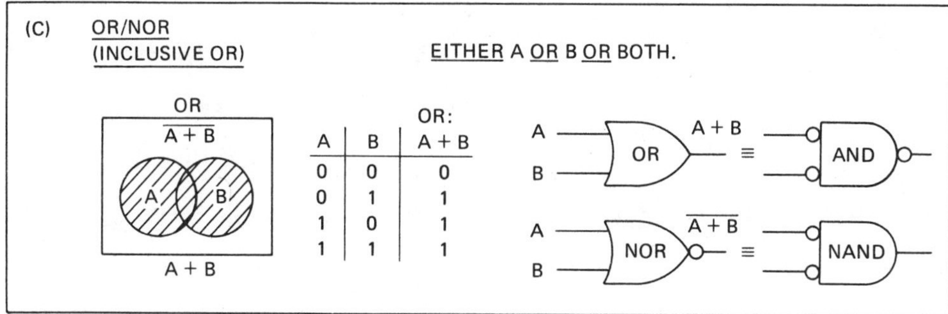

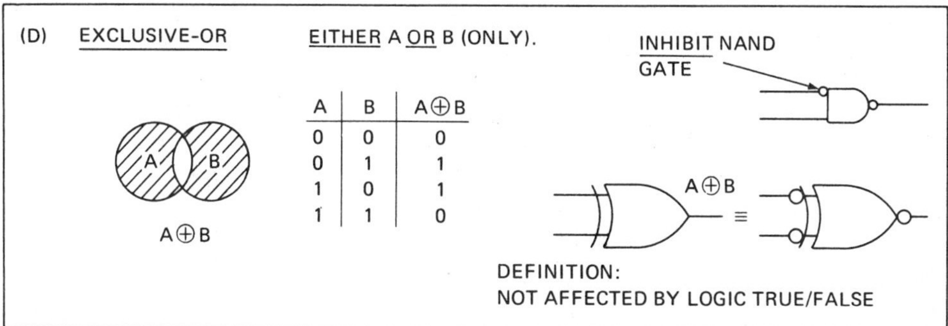

Fig. 10-11A-Z. Basic circuit concepts of digital logic.

The microelectronics hardware is developed by computer aided design (CAD) and interactive graphics.

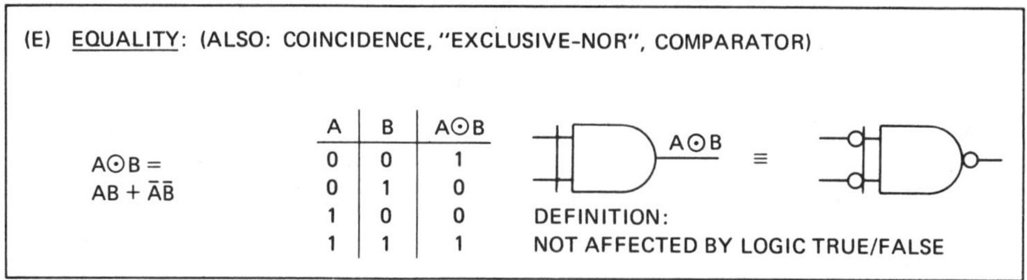

(E) EQUALITY: (ALSO: COINCIDENCE, "EXCLUSIVE-NOR", COMPARATOR)
A⊙B =
AB + $\bar{A}\bar{B}$
A B A⊙B
0 0 1
0 1 0
1 0 0
1 1 1
A⊙B
≡
DEFINITION:
NOT AFFECTED BY LOGIC TRUE/FALSE

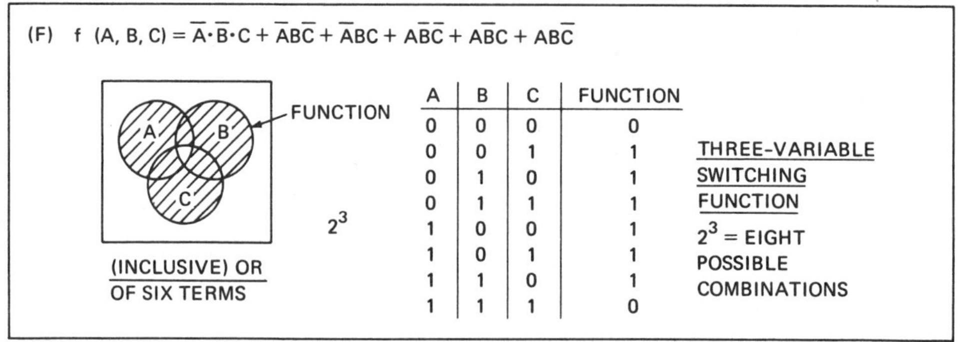

(F) f (A, B, C) = $\bar{A}\cdot\bar{B}\cdot C + \bar{A}B\bar{C} + \bar{A}BC + A\bar{B}\bar{C} + A\bar{B}C + AB\bar{C}$
FUNCTION
A
B
C
(INCLUSIVE) OR
OF SIX TERMS
2^3
A B C FUNCTION
0 0 0 0
0 0 1 1
0 1 0 1
0 1 1 1
1 0 0 1
1 0 1 1
1 1 0 1
1 1 1 0
THREE-VARIABLE
SWITCHING
FUNCTION
2^3 = EIGHT
POSSIBLE
COMBINATIONS

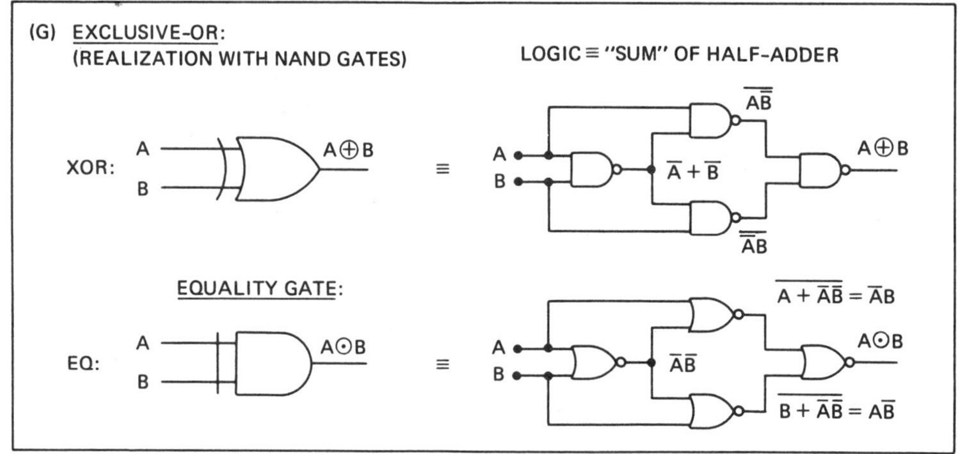

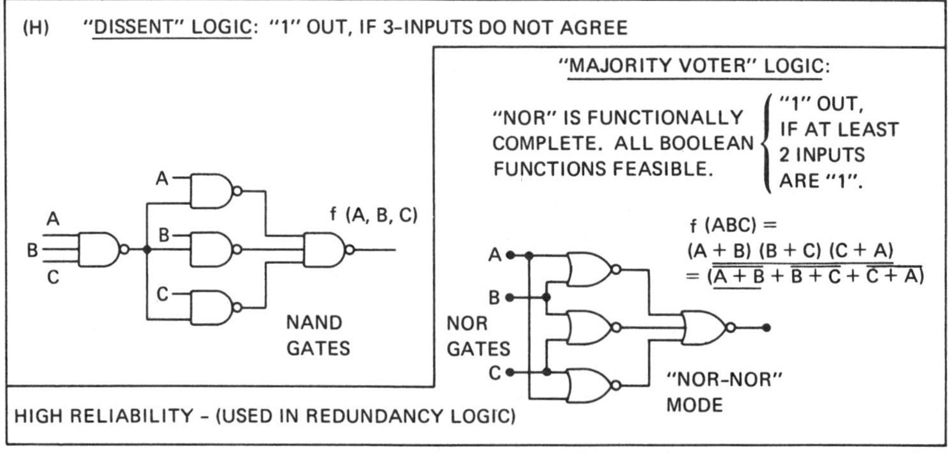

Fig. 10-11A-Z. (*Continued*)

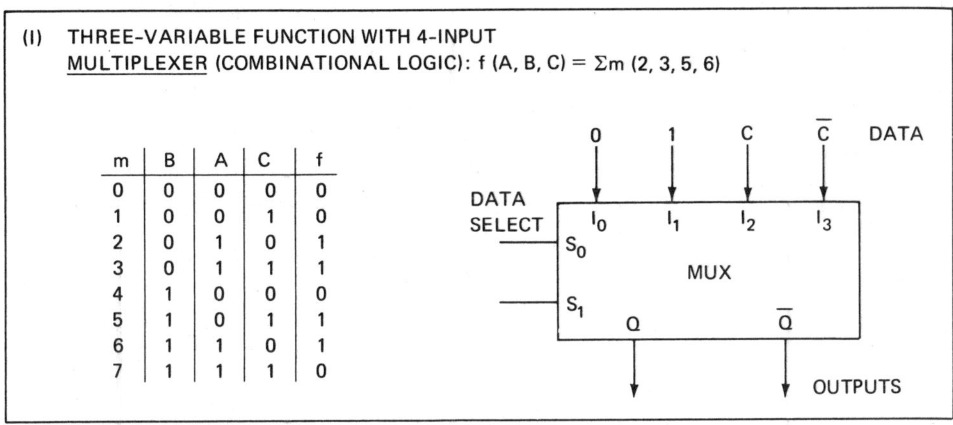

(I) THREE-VARIABLE FUNCTION WITH 4-INPUT MULTIPLEXER (COMBINATIONAL LOGIC): f (A, B, C) = Σm (2, 3, 5, 6)
0
1
C
C̄
DATA
DATA SELECT
I0
I1
I2
I3
S0
S1
MUX
Q
Q̄
OUTPUTS

m	B	A	C	f
0	0	0	0	0
1	0	0	1	0
2	0	1	0	1
3	0	1	1	1
4	1	0	0	0
5	1	0	1	1
6	1	1	0	1
7	1	1	1	0

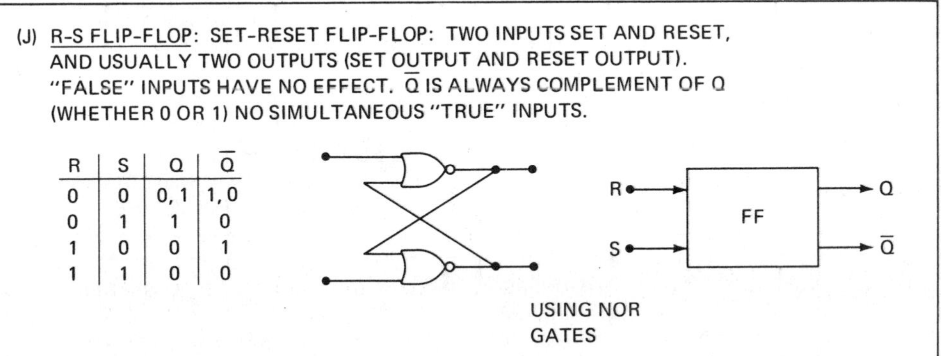

(J) R-S FLIP-FLOP: SET-RESET FLIP-FLOP: TWO INPUTS SET AND RESET, AND USUALLY TWO OUTPUTS (SET OUTPUT AND RESET OUTPUT). "FALSE" INPUTS HAVE NO EFFECT. Q̄ IS ALWAYS COMPLEMENT OF Q (WHETHER 0 OR 1) NO SIMULTANEOUS "TRUE" INPUTS.
R
S
FF
Q
Q̄
USING NOR GATES

R	S	Q	Q̄
0	0	0, 1	1, 0
0	1	1	0
1	0	0	1
1	1	0	0

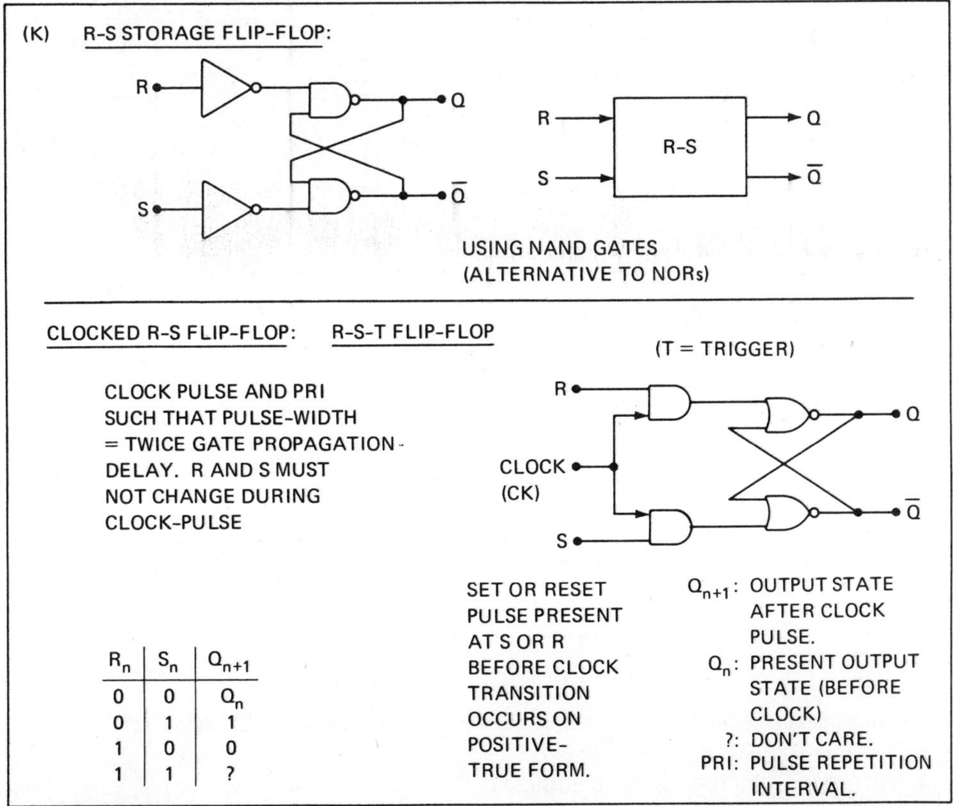

(K) R-S STORAGE FLIP-FLOP:
R
S
Q
Q̄
R-S
USING NAND GATES (ALTERNATIVE TO NORs)
CLOCKED R-S FLIP-FLOP: R-S-T FLIP-FLOP
(T = TRIGGER)
CLOCK PULSE AND PRI SUCH THAT PULSE-WIDTH = TWICE GATE PROPAGATION DELAY. R AND S MUST NOT CHANGE DURING CLOCK-PULSE
CLOCK (CK)
SET OR RESET PULSE PRESENT AT S OR R BEFORE CLOCK TRANSITION OCCURS ON POSITIVE-TRUE FORM.
Qn+1: OUTPUT STATE AFTER CLOCK PULSE.
Qn: PRESENT OUTPUT STATE (BEFORE CLOCK)
?: DON'T CARE.
PRI: PULSE REPETITION INTERVAL.

R_n	S_n	Q_{n+1}
0	0	Q_n
0	1	1
1	0	0
1	1	?

Fig. 10-11A-Z. (*Continued*)

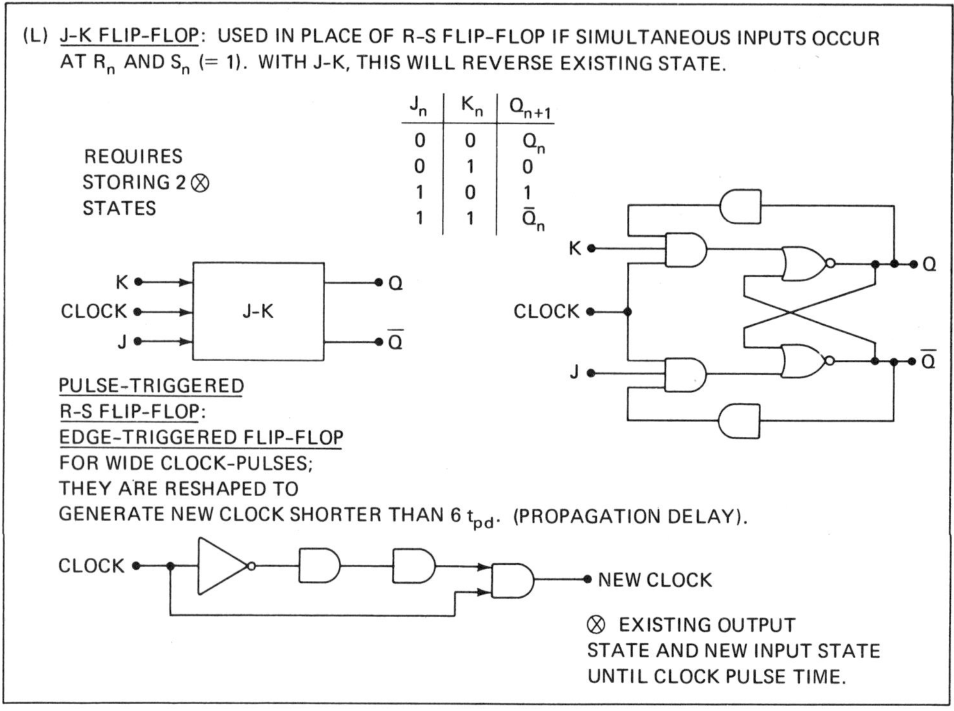

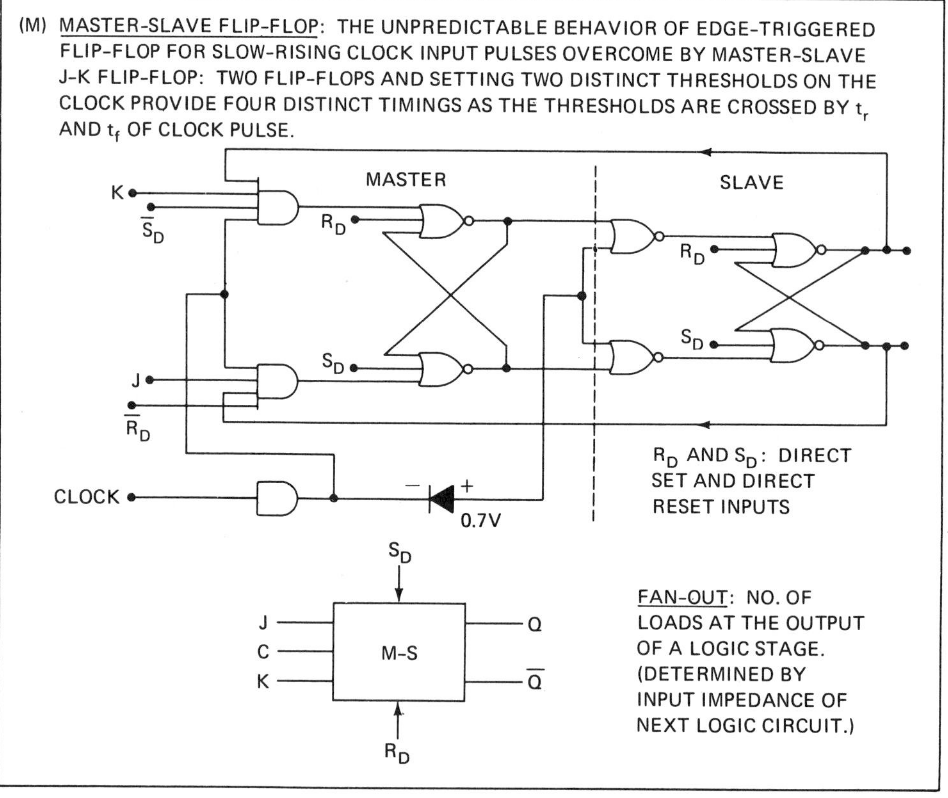

(M) MASTER-SLAVE FLIP-FLOP: THE UNPREDICTABLE BEHAVIOR OF EDGE-TRIGGERED FLIP-FLOP FOR SLOW-RISING CLOCK INPUT PULSES OVERCOME BY MASTER-SLAVE J-K FLIP-FLOP: TWO FLIP-FLOPS AND SETTING TWO DISTINCT THRESHOLDS ON THE CLOCK PROVIDE FOUR DISTINCT TIMINGS AS THE THRESHOLDS ARE CROSSED BY t_r AND t_f OF CLOCK PULSE.
MASTER
SLAVE
K
$\bar{S}_D$
R_D
R_D
S_D
S_D
J
$\bar{R}_D$
CLOCK
− +
0.7V
R_D AND S_D: DIRECT SET AND DIRECT RESET INPUTS
S_D
J
C
K
M-S
Q
$\bar{Q}$
R_D
FAN-OUT: NO. OF LOADS AT THE OUTPUT OF A LOGIC STAGE. (DETERMINED BY INPUT IMPEDANCE OF NEXT LOGIC CIRCUIT.)

t_r = RISE-TIME
t_f = FALL-TIME

CLOCK (HIGH-SPEED "SCHOTTKY" SWITCHING EFFECTIVE UP TO 45 MHz. 5 ns/GATE IS COMMON. MECL-10,000 SERIES: 2 ns/GATE.)

MECL: MOTOROLA EMITTER-COUPLED LOGIC.

Fig. 10-11A-Z. (*Continued*)

(N) TOGGLE FLIP-FLOP: ONE INPUT ONLY. AS INPUT A GOES TRUE, Q AND $\overline{Q}$ SWITCH STATES. 2 INPUT PULSES REQUIRED TO GET ONE OUTPUT CYCLE: TOGGLE FLIP-FLOP USED AS ÷2 IN COUNTERS.

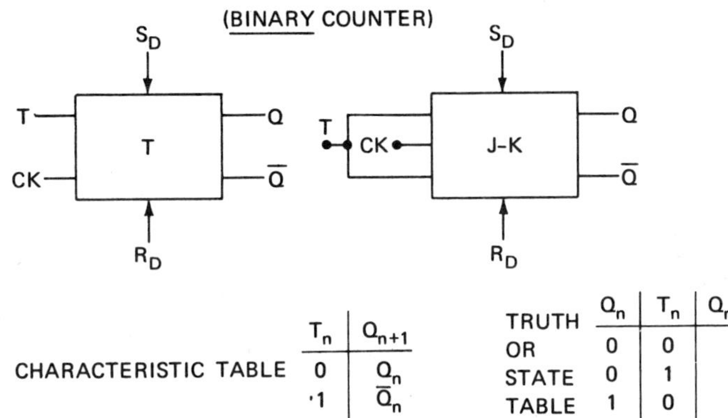

CHARACTERISTIC TABLE

T_n	Q_{n+1}
0	Q_n
1	$\overline{Q}_n$

TRUTH OR STATE TABLE

Q_n	T_n	Q_{n+1}
0	0	0
0	1	1
1	0	1
1	1	0

LATCHING FLIP-FLOP: WHEN A CLOCK IS NECESSARILY APPLIED TO THE SINGLE (TOGGLE) INPUT FLIP-FLOP AS ABOVE, IT IS CALLED LATCHING FLIP-FLOP. THE FLIP-FLOP WILL GO INTO T-IN STATE WHEN THE CLOCK PULSE GOES FROM TRUE TO FALSE (TRAILING EDGE USUALLY). DURING CLOCK PULSE, FLIP-FLOP "UNLATCHED" AND Q SWITCHING TAKES PLACE IF T-IN CHANGES.

(P) DELAY FLIP-FLOP: THE DELAY FLIP-FLOP DOES NOT HAVE AN "UNLATCHED" STATE AS IN CASE (N). IT IS SIMILAR TO "LATCH", SINCE IT LATCHES INTO STATE AT T-IN WHEN CLOCK GOES FROM TRUE TO FALSE; BUT Q DELAYED FROM SWITCHING UNTIL TRAILING EDGE OF CLOCK PULSE OCCURS.

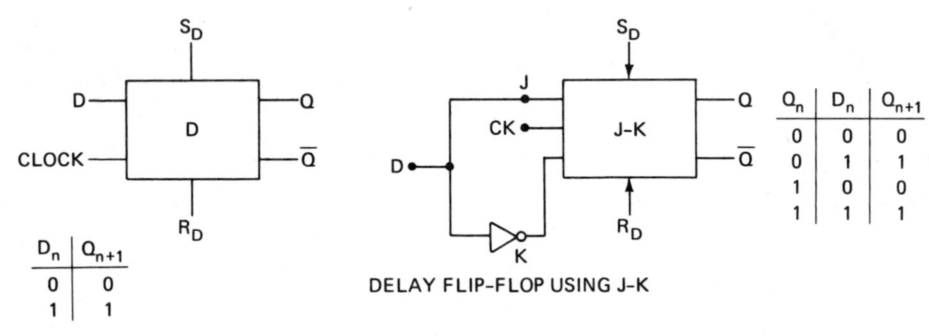

D_n	Q_{n+1}
0	0
1	1

Q_n	D_n	Q_{n+1}
0	0	0
0	1	1
1	0	0
1	1	1

Fig. 10-11A-Z. (*Continued*)

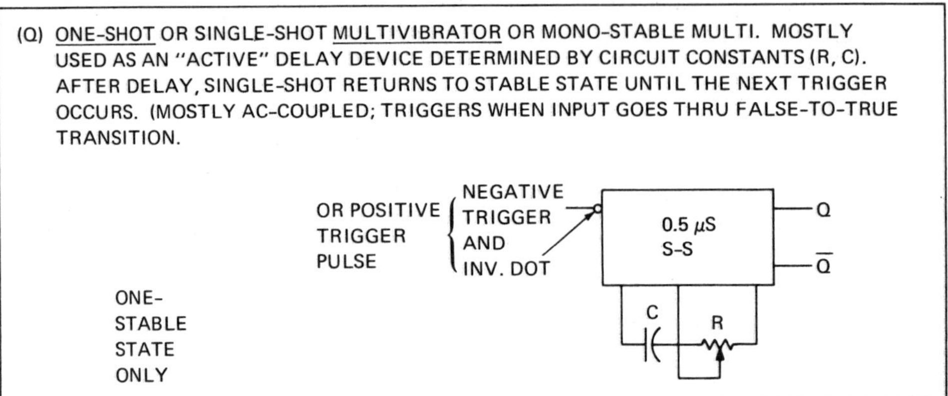

(Q) ONE-SHOT OR SINGLE-SHOT MULTIVIBRATOR OR MONO-STABLE MULTI. MOSTLY USED AS AN "ACTIVE" DELAY DEVICE DETERMINED BY CIRCUIT CONSTANTS (R, C). AFTER DELAY, SINGLE-SHOT RETURNS TO STABLE STATE UNTIL THE NEXT TRIGGER OCCURS. (MOSTLY AC-COUPLED; TRIGGERS WHEN INPUT GOES THRU FALSE-TO-TRUE TRANSITION.
OR POSITIVE TRIGGER PULSE
NEGATIVE TRIGGER AND INV. DOT
0.5 μS
S-S
Q
Q̄
C
R
ONE-STABLE STATE ONLY

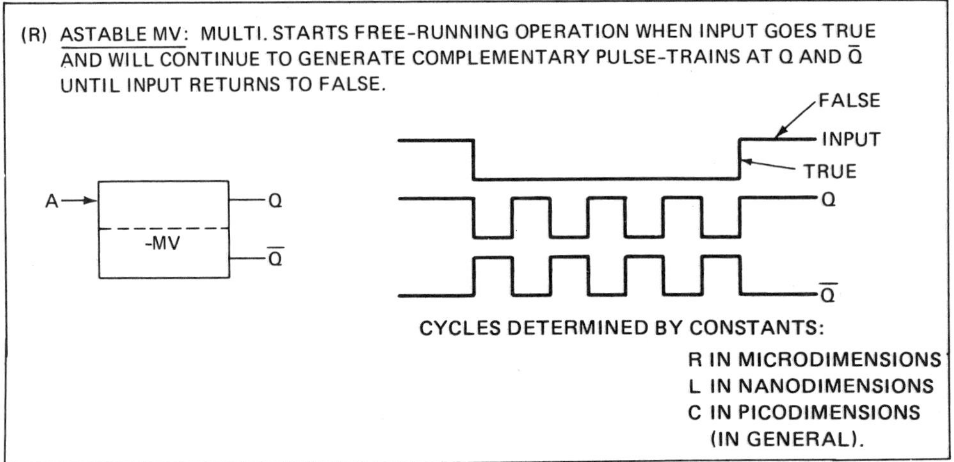

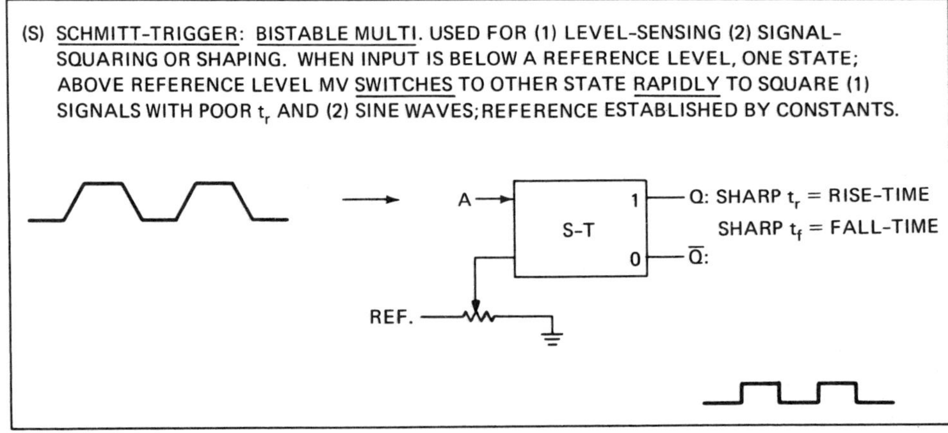

(R) ASTABLE MV: MULTI. STARTS FREE-RUNNING OPERATION WHEN INPUT GOES TRUE AND WILL CONTINUE TO GENERATE COMPLEMENTARY PULSE-TRAINS AT Q AND Q̄ UNTIL INPUT RETURNS TO FALSE.

R IN MICRODIMENSIONS
L IN NANODIMENSIONS
C IN PICODIMENSIONS

(S) SCHMITT-TRIGGER: BISTABLE MULTI. USED FOR (1) LEVEL-SENSING (2) SIGNAL-SQUARING OR SHAPING. WHEN INPUT IS BELOW A REFERENCE LEVEL, ONE STATE; ABOVE REFERENCE LEVEL MV SWITCHES TO OTHER STATE RAPIDLY TO SQUARE (1) SIGNALS WITH POOR t_r AND (2) SINE WAVES; REFERENCE ESTABLISHED BY CONSTANTS.
A
S-T
1
0
Q: SHARP t_r = RISE-TIME
SHARP t_f = FALL-TIME
Q̄:
REF.

Fig. 10-11A-Z. (*Continued*)

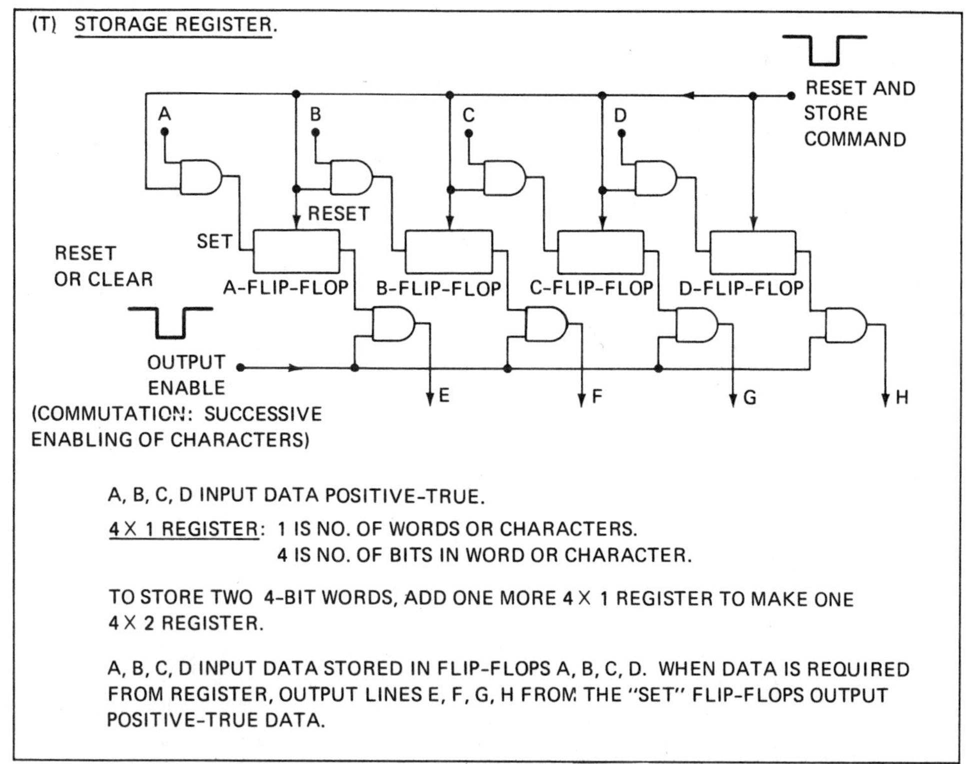

A, B, C, D INPUT DATA POSITIVE-TRUE.

4 X 1 REGISTER: 1 IS NO. OF WORDS OR CHARACTERS.
4 IS NO. OF BITS IN WORD OR CHARACTER.

TO STORE TWO 4-BIT WORDS, ADD ONE MORE 4 X 1 REGISTER TO MAKE ONE 4 X 2 REGISTER.

A, B, C, D INPUT DATA STORED IN FLIP-FLOPS A, B, C, D. WHEN DATA IS REQUIRED FROM REGISTER, OUTPUT LINES E, F, G, H FROM THE "SET" FLIP-FLOPS OUTPUT POSITIVE-TRUE DATA.

Fig. 10-11A-Z. *(Continued)*

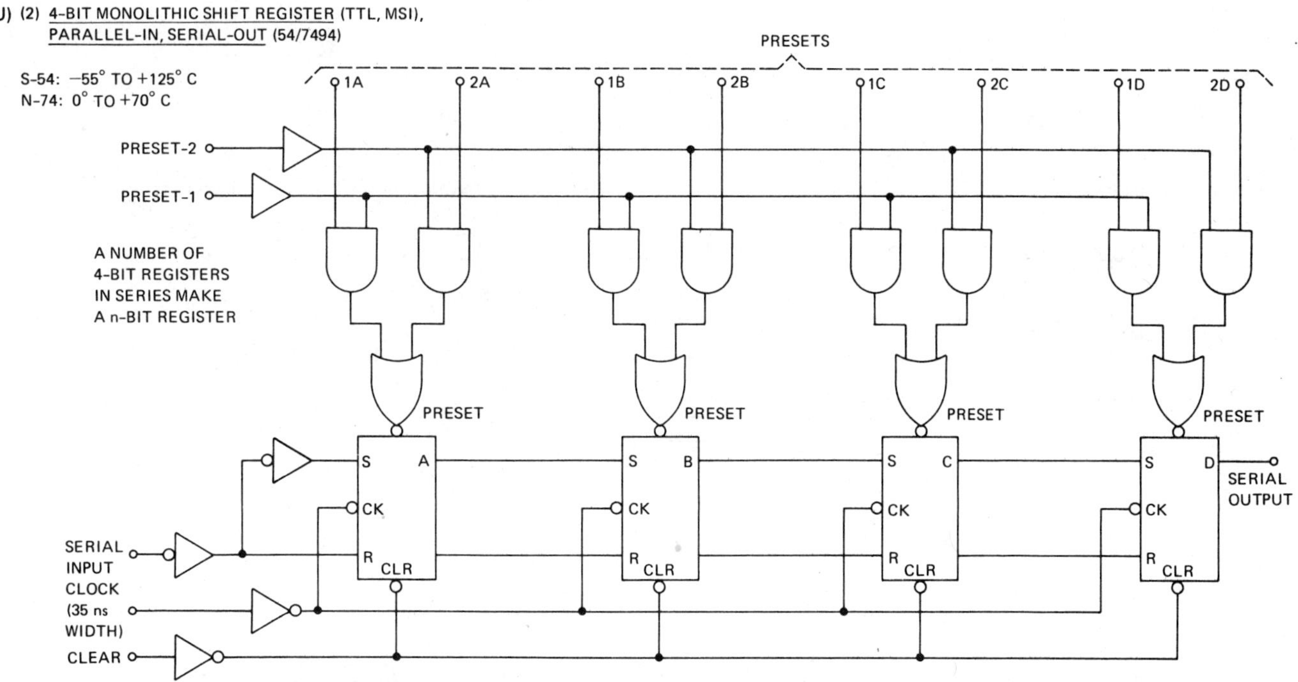

1. THIS S/R IS COMPOSED OF 4 R-S MASTER-SLAVE FLIP-FLOPS, 4 AND-OR-INVERT GATES, AND 4 INVERTER-DRIVERS.
2. IT MAKES A VERSATILE REGISTER TO PERFORM RIGHT-SHIFT OPERATION AS A SERIAL-IN, SERIAL-OUT REGISTER OR AS A DUAL-SOURCE PARALLEL TO SERIAL CONVERTER.
3. PROPAGATION DELAY FROM CLOCK TO OUTPUT ≈ 25 ns. (AVERAGE POWER: 175 mW at V_{CC} = 5 V.
4. WHEN CLOCKING OCCURS, CLEAR INPUT, PRESET 1, AND PRESET 2 MUST BE AT LOGICAL "0".

(Courtesy of Signetics)

Fig. 10-11A-Z. *(Continued)*

(U) (1) 4-BIT PARALLEL ACCESS SHIFT REGISTER

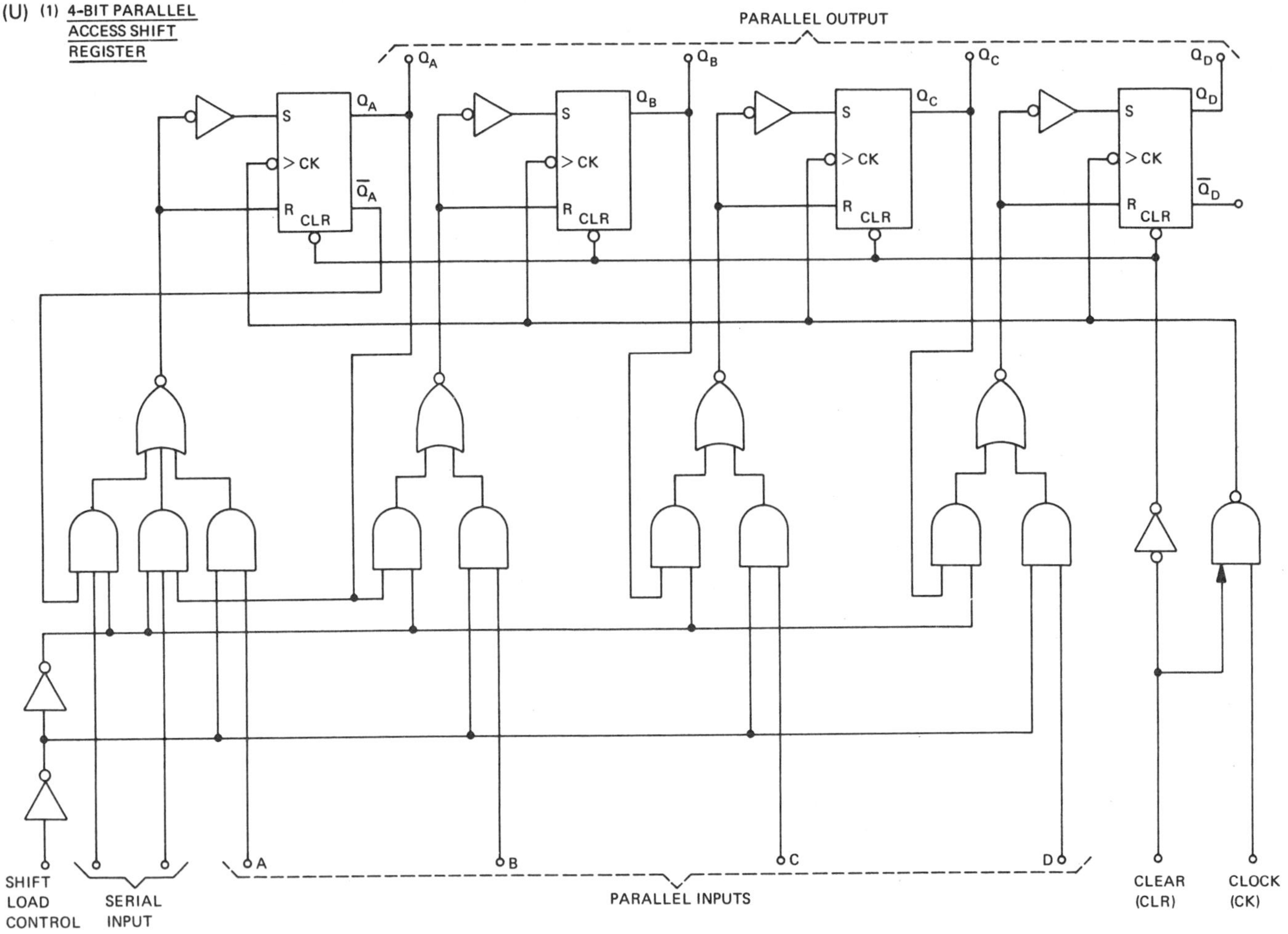

PARALLEL OUTPUT

Q_A Q_B Q_C Q_D

S, > CK, R, CLR, Q_A, $\overline{Q}_A$, Q_B, Q_C, Q_D, $\overline{Q}_D$

SHIFT LOAD CONTROL

SERIAL INPUT

A B C D

PARALLEL INPUTS

CLEAR (CLR)

CLOCK (CK)

TTL, MSI:
TYPICAL CLEAR, SHIFT AND LOAD SEQUENCES

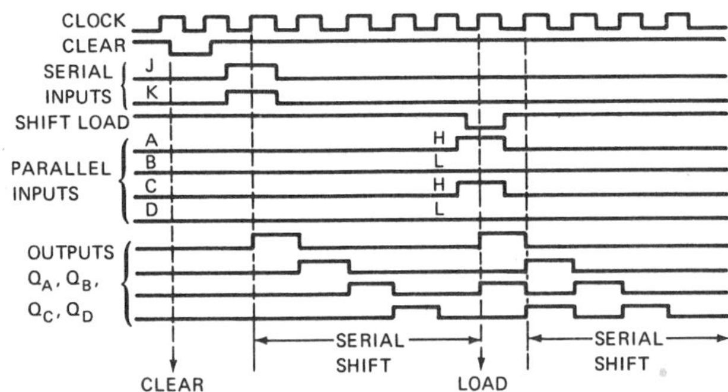

TYPICAL (MSI) 4-BIT MONOLITHIC SHIFT REGISTER.
CLOCK PULSE GENERATOR: 50 Ω, PULSE RATE ≤ 1 MHz.
THE 4-BIT REGISTER (54/74195) ALLOWS PARALLEL INPUTS, PARALLEL OUTPUTS, J-$\overline{K}$ SERIAL INPUTS, SHIFT/LOAD CONTROL INPUT, AND A DIRECT OVER-RIDING CLEAR. ALL INPUTS ARE BUFFERED TO ALLOW LOWER INPUT DRIVES.

REGISTERS HAVE 2 MODES OF OPERATION:

1. PARALLEL LOAD: BY APPLYING 4 BITS OF DATA AND MAKING SHIFT/LOAD CONTROL INPUT LOW. THE DATA IS LOADED INTO THE ASSOCIATED FLIP-FLOP. IT APPEARS AT THE OUTPUT AFTER THE POSITIVE TRANSITION OF THE CLOCK-INPUT. DURING LOADING, SERIAL DATA FLOW IS INHIBITED.
2. SHIFTING: DONE SYNCHRONOUSLY WHEN SHIFT/LOAD CONTROL IS HIGH: SERIAL DATA FOR THIS MODE IS ENTERED AT THE J-$\overline{K}$ INPUTS. THESE INPUTS ALLOW THE FIRST STAGE OPERATION AS J-$\overline{K}$, D OR T-TYPE FLIP-FLOP (SHIFTING REQUIRED IN MULTIPLY/DIVIDE ARITHMETIC).

(Courtesy of Signetics)

Fig. 10-11A-Z. *(Continued)*

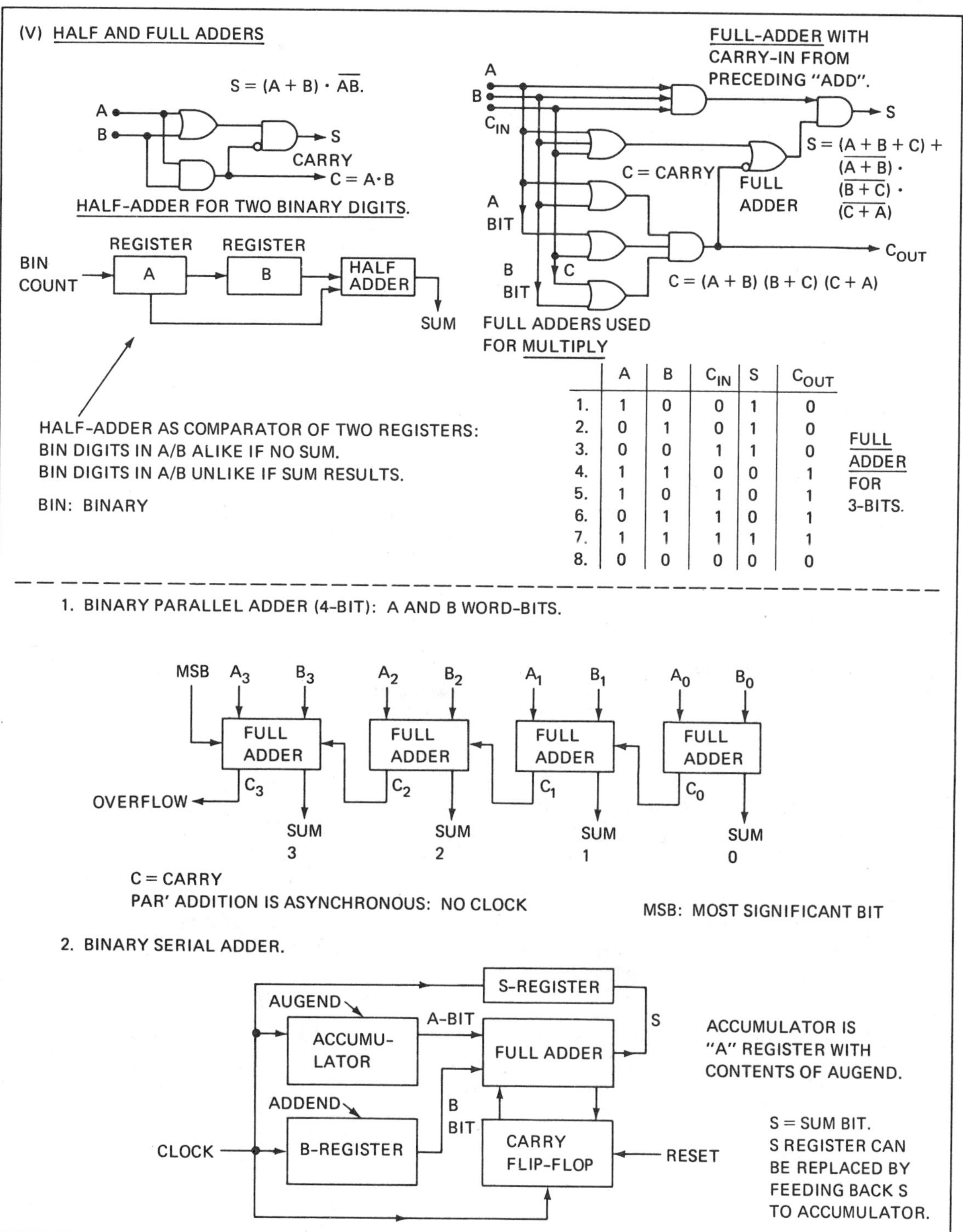

	A	B	C_{IN}	S	C_{OUT}
1.	1	0	0	1	0
2.	0	1	0	1	0
3.	0	0	1	1	0
4.	1	1	0	0	1
5.	1	0	1	0	1
6.	0	1	1	0	1
7.	1	1	1	1	1
8.	0	0	0	0	0

(*Courtesy of Motorola*)

Fig. 10-11A-Z. (*Continued*)

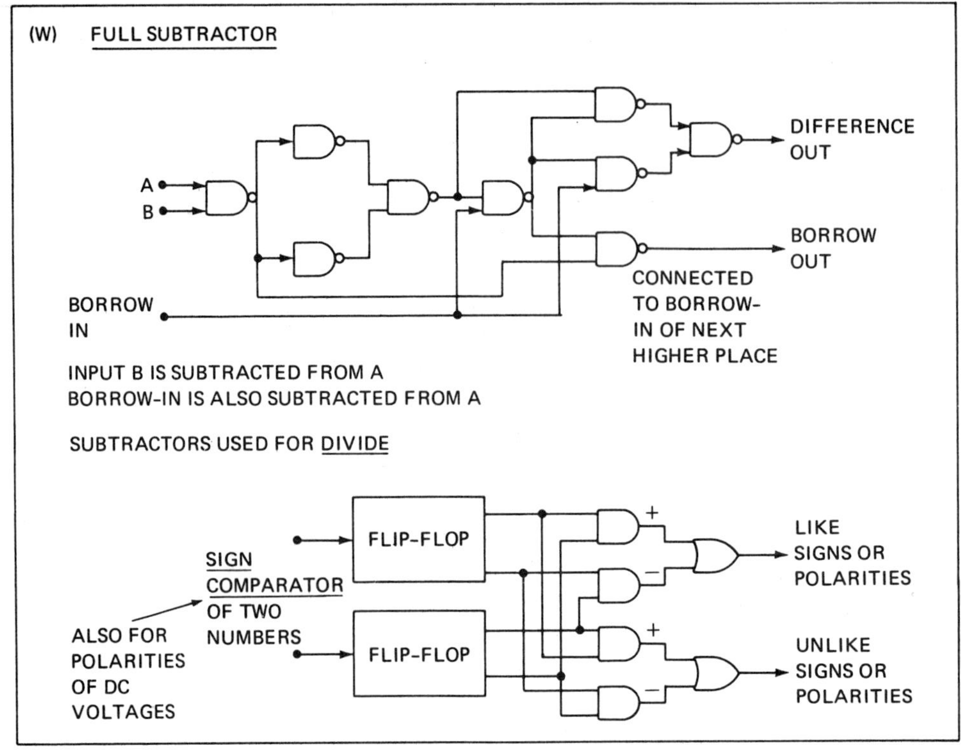

(*Courtesy of Motorola*)

Fig. 10-11A-Z. (*Continued*)

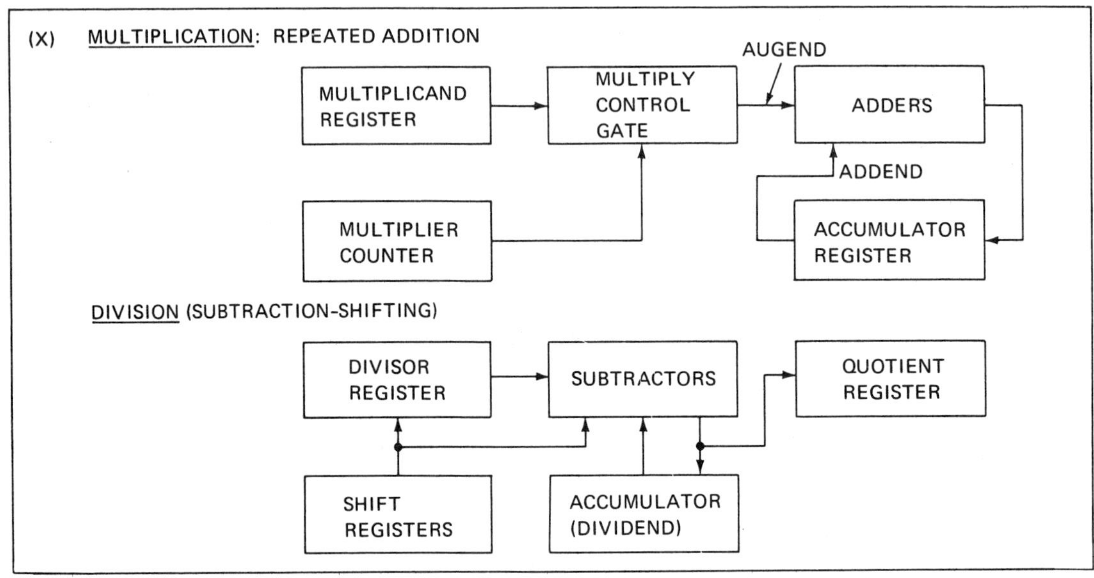

(*Courtesy of Motorola*)

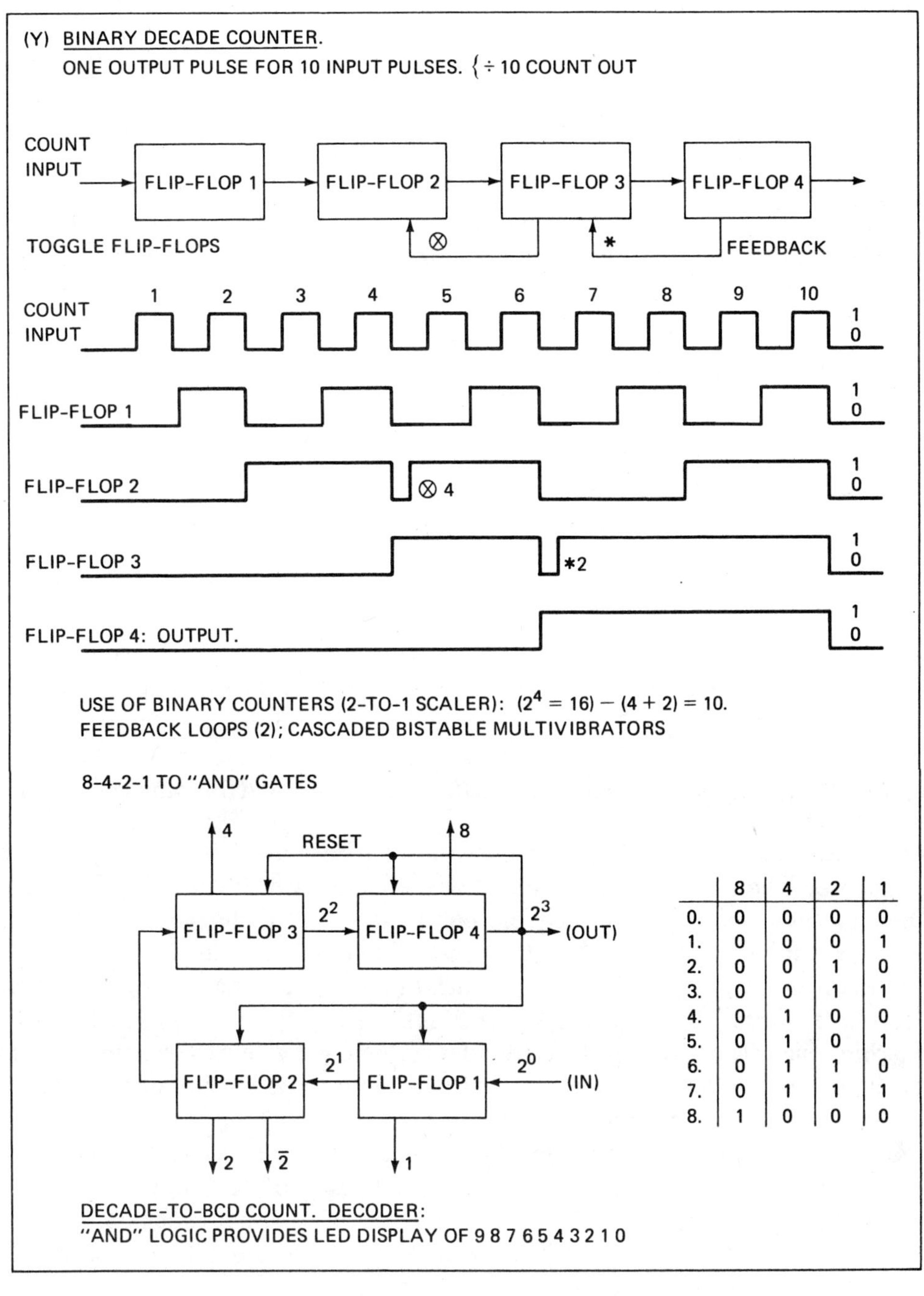

	8	4	2	1
0.	0	0	0	0
1.	0	0	0	1
2.	0	0	1	0
3.	0	0	1	1
4.	0	1	0	0
5.	0	1	0	1
6.	0	1	1	0
7.	0	1	1	1
8.	1	0	0	0

(Z) SWITCHING ALGEBRA: **CUMULATIVE:** A · B = B · A; A + B = B + A.
ASSOCIATIVE: A · (B · C) = (A · B) · C; A + (B + C) = (A + B) + C.
COMPLEMENTS: A · A = 0; A + A = 1.
DISTRIBUTIVE: A · (B + C) = A · B + A · C; A + B · C = (A + B) · (A + C).
IDEM POTENT: A · A = A; A + A = A.
IDENTITY: A · 1 = A; A + 0 = A.
NULL: A · 0 = 0; A + 1 = 1.
ABSORPTION: A + A · B = A; A · (A + B) = A.
INVOLUTION: (A) = A;
DEMORGAN'S THEOREM: (A · B · C . .) = A + B + C . . . ;(A + B + C + . .) = A · B · C . . . .

Fig. 10-11A-Z. (*Continued*)

System Logic Design. *K-Map* (Kavanaugh map) method is the most popular classical two-level Boolean minimization procedure in digital logic. There are *no* known procedures for assuring minimum multi-input and multi-output Boolean functions. Time, effort, and common sense play the deciding role in arriving at the best possible logic for minimum signal propagation-delay time in multilevel logical gates; however, the two-level logic provides some assurance. Elegant logical design procedure is workable by using the common NAND or NOR structure of logic on a system basis. The latest LSI/VLSI signal processing techniques, such as low-power I^2L, CMOS, and Si-gate NMOS, and higher-power MSI Schottky TTL and ECL techniques do enable high-speed system architecture in circuit design by using computer-aided design. Programmable logic-arrays (PLAs) implying sum-and-product logic components is one of the preferred techniques that enable instruction word times of the order of 50 ns to 1/2 μs memory *cycle-times* in present VLSI/LSI designs. The *access-time* from the instant of command may be on the order of approximately 50% of that of the instruction memory cycle-time, where memory and control logic are both involved.

Usually restricted to a particular logic design are: (1) Trade-offs between high-speed and low-power dissipation and (2) circuit configurations of the two-level AND-OR, OR-AND, NAND-NAND, and NOR-NOR combinations. Gate input-loading and *fan-in* (number of inputs allowed for each gate) are not a problem for functions up to four variables. For a larger number of variables, the levels of logic in hardware design are increased by using a tree-circuit realization, as is done in modern block-structured implementation of modular software. True and complement inputs provide a flexible aid in this procedure. If the sum of input and output variables is greater than 8 in the case of a multiple output function or a *fan-out* situation, the use of CAD (computer-aided design) becomes mandatory.

In some cases, a minimum logic circuit is not the absolute criterion. Low power, low cost, and prevention of "race conditions" or *dynamic hazards* (unwanted output spikes that might cause digital errors when the input variables are changing from one state to the other) are the conventional objectives in hardware design. In the VLSI state-of-the-art, the engineering effort in rigorous minimization of logic is more costly than the saving of a few gates when about 100,000 gate functions are available on a single monolithic silicon chip—there is even room for redundancy logic gates (e.g., the neural logic of the human brain) at minimum power and cost. In the case of the mass-produced 100-gate high-speed MSI chips (reaching the sub-nanosecond switching rates), the engineering effort for minimization of logic gates is of course worthwhile. However, it is best to always remember the following five performance trade-off objectives: (1) low-power dissipation (for occasional use of battery cells in portable applications), (2) short propagation-delay, (3) adequate output driving capability, (4) operational range of temperature, and (5) good noise-immunity for minimal bit-error rates.

In combinational logic using NAND/NOR gates, some input switching combinations may never occur, and certain switching results may have no effect on the overall logic. Such "*don't-care* one/zero" switching conditions (represented by d's in a K-Map logic simplification procedure) can be useful in practical simplification of logic. In general, "d"s provide greater flexibility in the design of a combinational logic network that controls a set of flip-flops, such as one or more registers.

In the *analysis* of network logic, a *state-table* provides the following information for each state listed: (1) identification of the present-state x(t) in binary, (2) the next-states of x(t + Δ or τ) for various combinations of input to the system, as predicted from present-states of gate outputs, and (3) outputs resulting from each of these combinations. As a contrast, for *synthesis* of network logic, the characteristics of the digital system are defined in the following steps: (1) the specified characteristics are translated to a state-table, and (2) the types(s) of flip-flops are chosen and logic circuits for control inputs are designed by using the excitation tables. The *excitation table* relates the known state-transition of the flip-flops to the control signals necessary to produce the said state-transitions.

Static and Dynamic Hazards (SH/DH). Spurious output signals that cause bit errors in sequential circuits using storage flip-flops are called *hazards.* In the VLSI high-speed logic, bit-errors are caused by alpha-particles in X-ray/ion-beam/electron-beam lithographic processing techniques. If the initial and final output of a logic device are the same, then the erroneous output signals, which result from input signals and change an *even* number of times during propagation, are called *static hazards.* They do not affect combinational logic. On the other hand, if the initial and final output waveform-timings differ, and output signal waveforms change an *odd* number of times during propagation, the spurious error signals produced are called *dynamic hazards;* they result in "race conditions." (See p. 318.) A Boolean logic circuit function is free from SH/DH, if a single input to a logic circuit alone is allowed to change at a given instant, and the effect of this change is allowed to propagate through the circuit before an additional input change. Use of "min" terms (sum of products) is thus preferable in high-speed sequential logic.

The spurs (spurious output signals) will not disturb the purely combinational circuits, which in principle do not include flip-flop memory cells, because the outputs concerned are a function of the steady-state input signals only. Circuit transients, however, may result and disturb operation, if the output signals under reference are used as inputs to sequential flip-flop circuits. (The logical design of digital computer systems is continued through pages 346 to 360.)

TABLE 10-2. Boolean Switching Logic in a Chart.

H(High) = TRUE = 1: (Positive) L(Low) = FALSE = 0: (Logic, TTL) (Negative Logic, ECL: L = H; H = L) Machine language: BINARY LOGIC		BOOLEAN ALGEBRA (BOOLE'S SYMBOLIC LOGIC) (Enables the system designer to realize a set of given specifications with minimum number of components in logic equations	*TTL: Transistor-Transistor Logic H = 3V; L = 0V. ECL = Emitter coupled logic (High-speed): H = -.75V(0), L = -1.5V(1)
Postulates	**Shannon's Analysis of Relay Switching**	**Theorem No. (These theorems enable manipulation of logic equations to simplified logic)**	**Miscellaneous Information**
P.1a: 0 · 0 = 0 Series P.1b: 1 + 1 = 1 Parallel	a: b: 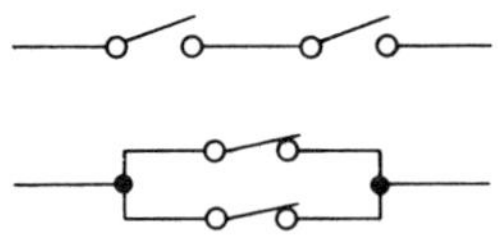	1a: x · y = y · x COMMUTATIVE LAW 1b: x + y = y + x 2a: (x · y) · z = x · (y · z), ASSOCIATE LAW 2b: (x + y) + z = x + (y + z): (For all x,y,z in ϵK)	1. The theorems can be proved, using postulates 2. Checked by use of switching diagrams by perfect induction method.
P.2a: 0 · 1 = 0 1 · 0 = 0 ($x \cdot \overline{x} = 0$)	c: d: 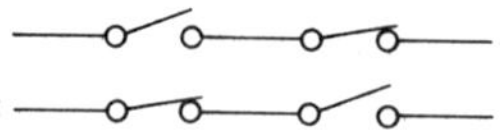	3a: x · (y + z) = (x · y) + (x · z), DISTRIBUTIVE LAW 3b: x + (y · z) = (x + y) · (x + z): (For all x,y,z in ϵK)	
P.2b: 1 + 0 = 1 0 + 1 = 1 $x + \overline{x} = 1$ x + 0 = x	e: f: 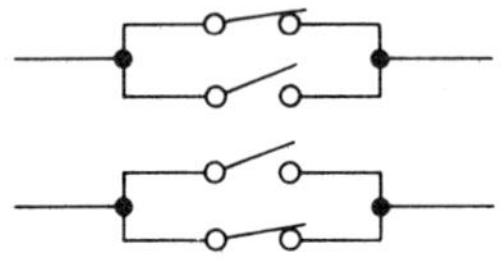	4a: x · 1 = x LAW of IDENTITIES 4b: x + 0 = x If x + y = y, and x · y = y, then x = y 5a: x · 0 = 0 NULL ELEMENTS 5b: x + 1 = 1 (Special law of 0 and 1)	AND: a x · y b OR: + a x y b NOT: x (NOT) $\overline{x}$
P.3a: 1 · 1 = 1 x · 1 = x x · x = x P.3b: 0 + 0 = 0	g: h: 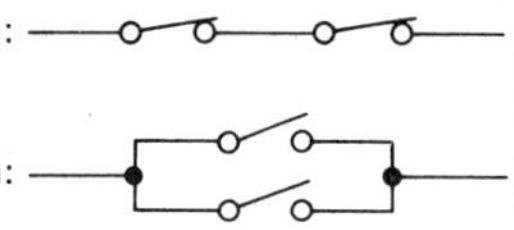	LAW: If x + y = 1,x · y = 0 6a: $x \cdot \overline{x} = 0$ COMPLEMENTS: then y = x 6b: $x + \overline{x} = 1$ Each element has unique complement)	Logical operations
P.4a $\overline{0} = 1$ P.4b $\overline{1} = 0$	NOT OF 'OPEN' IS 'CLOSED' $\overline{x}$ NOT OF 'CLOSED' IS 'OPEN' 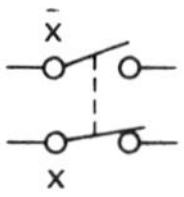 x	7a: x · x = x 7b: x + x = x IDEMPOTENT 8a: x + (x · y) = x ABSORPTION*; 2nd: $x + \overline{x} \cdot y = x + y$ 8b: x · (x + y) = x Ist. law; $x \cdot \overline{x} + y = x \cdot y$	BINARY OPERATIONS ON K: [K, +, ·] 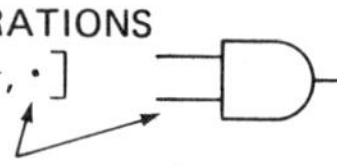 Boolean functions $0, 1, x, \overline{x}$
P.5a: x = 1 if x ≠ 0 P.5b: x = 0 if x ≠ 1 P.6: Elements 0 and 1 unique.	A circuit cannot assume both states simultaneously. There exist at least 2 elements x and y in ϵK, such that x ≠ y	9: $\overline{(\overline{x})} = x$ INVOLUTION (Double negation) 10a: $\overline{(x \cdot y \cdot z \ldots)} = \overline{x} + \overline{y} + \overline{z} + \ldots$ DEMORGAN'S 10b: $\overline{(x + y + z + \ldots)} = \overline{x} \cdot \overline{y} \cdot \overline{z} \ldots$ THEOREM NAND: AND , NOT (LOGIC) NOR: OR , NOT (LOGIC) 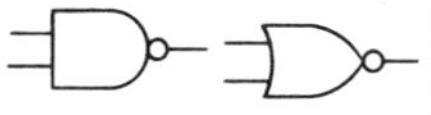	If x and y are Boolean functions so are $\overline{x}, \overline{y}$, x + y, and x · y

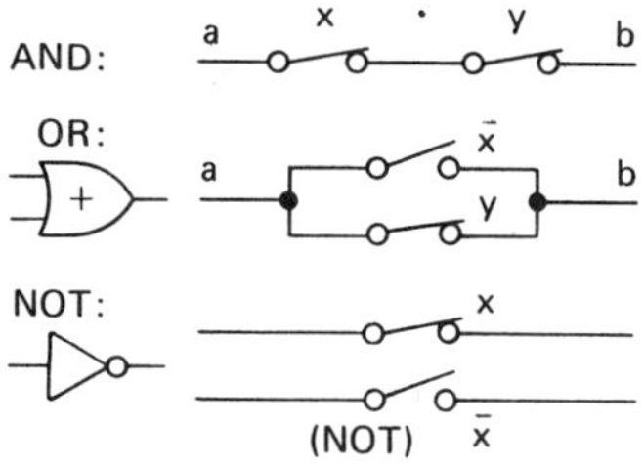

Note: Fig. 10-11z is expanded and explained with x, y, z for A,B,C
*Special Law of Absorption:
x((x + y) + z) = x   x + (x · y) · z = x
((x + y) + z) x = x   ((x · y) · z) + x = x

(*Schottky TTL is popular fairly high-speed; ECL is relatively high-power dissipating: see Chapter 2.)

TABLE 10-3. "Min" and "Max" Terms, Digital Logic (Canonical Forms)

The duality of *min* (function of *sum of products*, FSP) terms and *Max* (function of *product of sum* terms, FPS) for a 3-variable function, f(ABC): 2^3 : 8 terms.

	Example	A B C	FPS terms: min (V)	FPS terms: Max (Λ)
0	0	0 0 0	$\bar{A}\,\bar{B}\,\bar{C} = m_0$	$(A + B + C) = M_0$
1	0	0 0 1	$\bar{A}\,\bar{B}\,C = m_1$	$(A + B + \bar{C}) = M_1$
2	1	0 1 0	$\bar{A}\,B\,\bar{C} = m_2$	$(A + \bar{B} + C) = M_2$
3	1	0 1 1	$\bar{A}\,B\,C = m_3$	$(A + \bar{B} + \bar{C}) = M_3$
4	0	1 0 0	$A\,\bar{B}\,\bar{C} = m_4$	$(\bar{A} + B + C) = M_4$
5	1	1 0 1	$A\,\bar{B}\,C = m_5$	$(\bar{A} + B + \bar{C}) = M_5$
6	1	1 1 0	$A\,B\,\bar{C} = m_6$	$(\bar{A} + \bar{B} + C) = M_6$
7	0	1 1 1	$A\,B\,C = m_7$	$(\bar{A} + \bar{B} + \bar{C}) = M_7$
			Σ m in 1's	ΠM in 0's

Example: Characteristic function in 1's = $\Sigma m\,(6,5,3,2)$

$0.m = 0$ ⎤ $= 0.m_7 + 1.m_6 + 1.m_5 + 0.m_4 + 1.m_3 + 1.m_2 + 0.m_1 + 0.m_0$
$1.m = 1$ ⎦ $(108)_{10}$ = D108 = 0 1 1 0 1 1 0 0
Binary weight: 128 64 32 16 8 4 2 1

Characteristic function in 0's = $\Pi M\,(7, 4, 1, 0)$

$0 + M = M$ ⎤ $= (0 + M_7)(1 + M_6)(1 + M_5)(0 + M_4)(1 + M_3)(1 + M_2)(0 + M_1)(0 + M_0)$
$1 + M = 1$ ⎦ $=$ 0/M 1 1 0/M 1 1 0/M 0/M = $(108)_{10}$

Logic Simplification by Karnaugh K-Maps ("min" logic technique)

The K-Map is the most extensively used tool for simplification of logic functions up to six variables; it is easy to apply because a pattern-recognition procedure is generally very simple. The assignment locations of min-terms are such that two adjacent terms (adjacencies) differ in one literal only.

One form of a *3-variable K-Map*, with 0-to-7 min-terms: Map $F(A, B, C) = \bar{A} + \bar{B}C + B\bar{C}$

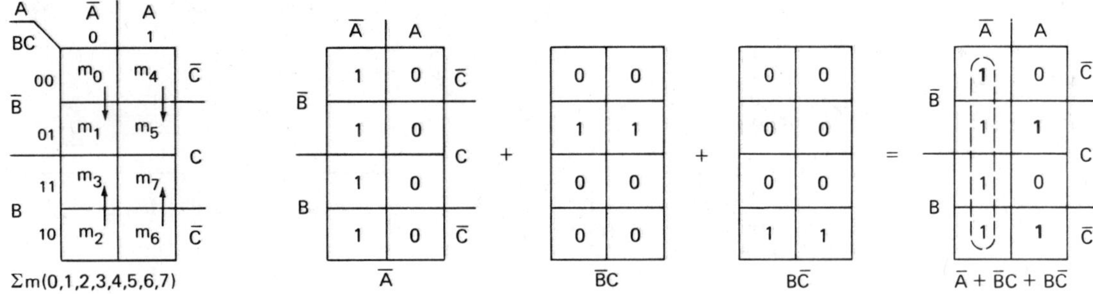

4-Variable K-Map Simplification

$F(A, B, C, D) = \Sigma m(4, 6, 12, 13, 14)$; with four input variables, 0-to-15 min-term Truth table is effective.

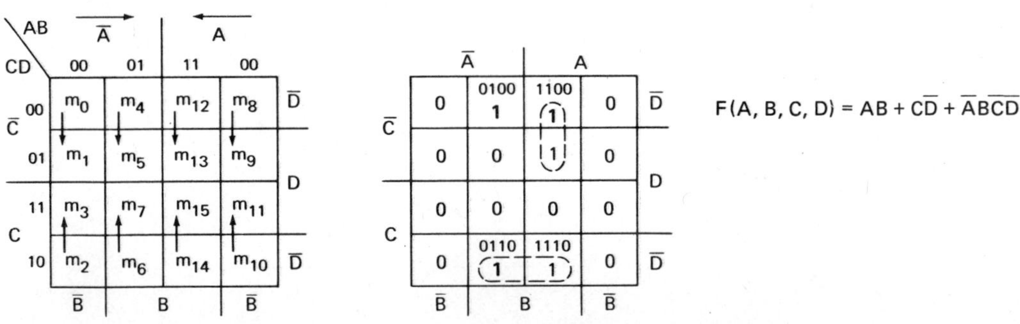

In general 2^i adjacent cells represent a product term of (n − 1) variables in an n-variable function.

Fig. 10-12. Logic simplification by K-maps ("min" technique).

Essential Prime Implicant or the Core of a Function in a K-Map

If at least one square in a *prime implicant* grouping is not shared by another prime implicant, then the prime implicant is defined as *essential*.

Simplification of K-Map logic using s-of-p K-Map with 1's min-term logic, and p-of-s K-Map with 0's Max-terms: s − p = sum or products
p − s = product of sums

F(A, B, C, D)—Six terms of 1's min logic (simplified to 3 s − p terms), and cost of number of inputs, and logic gates are compared to 10 terms of 0's Max logic (simplified to 3 p − s terms), and cost of required number of inputs and logic gates. In logic designs, both functions and complimentary input variables are generally made available.

K-Map of 1's:

$F(A, B, C, D) = \bar{B}\bar{D} + \bar{A}\bar{C}\bar{D} + AC\bar{D}$

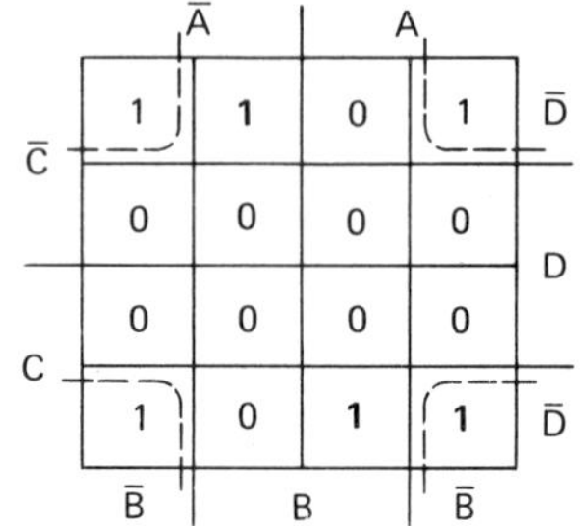

COST = 11 inputs and 4 Logic Gates for output

K-Map of 0's:

$F(A, B, C, D) = \bar{D}(\bar{A} + \bar{B} + \bar{C})(\bar{A} + \bar{B} + C)$

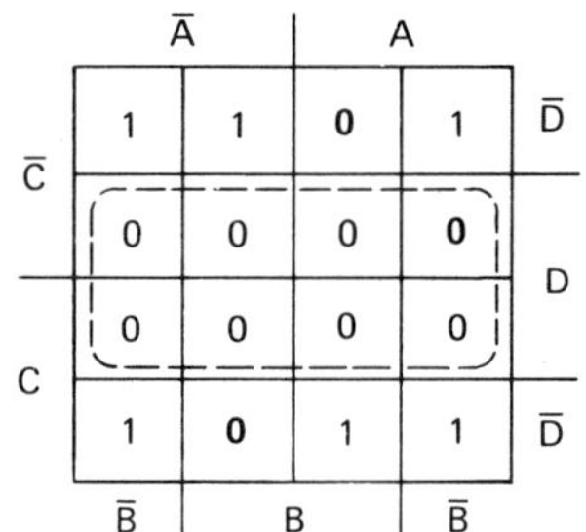

COST = 9 inputs and 3 Logic Gates. This Logic is therefore preferred in this particular case with 0's Max-terms. The Logic Circuit derived is of the following configuration:

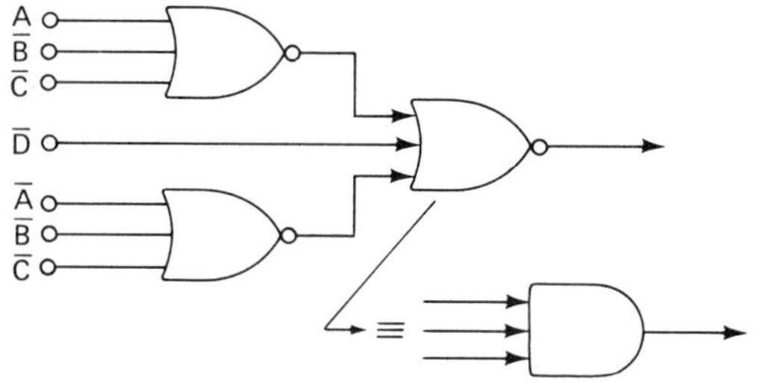

Fig. 10-13. Comparison of Logic Simplification with K-Maps using 1's min logic terms and 0's Max Logic terms in a specific case. (In most cases, 1's min-logic is more effective.)

Design of Multiplexer as a Combinational Logic Device. The Multiplexer is a Logic Equivalent to a rotary multipole switch—with 2^n input lines for each section, and n control lines (bit-operated, 0/1) to determine the line to be transferred to output of each section.

Ex. 1: 4-in-MUX.

$$
\begin{aligned}
F(A, B, C) &= A\overline{B} + BC + \overline{A\,C} \\
&= A\overline{B} + BC(A + \overline{A}) + \overline{A}(B + \overline{B})\overline{C} \\
&= A\overline{B} + ABC + (\overline{A}BC + \overline{A}B\overline{C}) + \overline{A}\overline{B}\overline{C} \\
&= ABC + A\overline{B} + \overline{A}B + \overline{A}\,\overline{B}\,\overline{C} \ldots (1)
\end{aligned}
$$

$(A + \overline{A})$ etc. = 1

$a_0 = F(0, 0, C)$
$a_1 = F(0, 1, C)$
$a_2 = F(1, 0, C)$
$a_3 = F(1, 1, C)$

If a_0, a_1, a_2, a_3 are the input data lines (input variables of the Boolean function) and A, B are the 2 control lines:

$F(A, B, C) = ABa_3 + A\overline{B}a_2 + \overline{A}Ba_1 + \overline{A}\,\overline{B}a_0 \ldots (2)$

Compare (1) and (2) to determine the input data lines to the multiplexer.

Hence the following design of the 4-in-MUX:

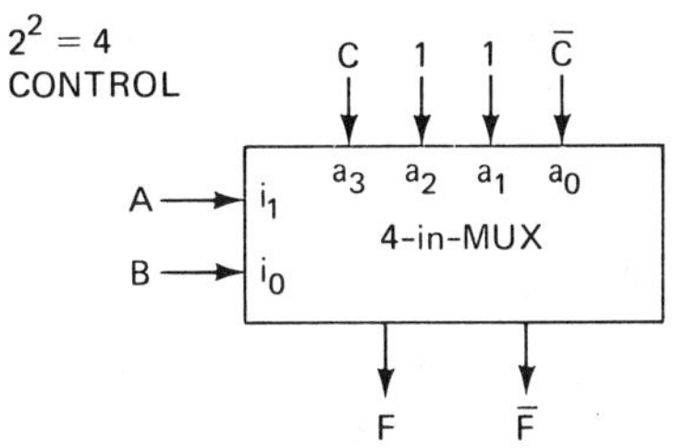

Ex. 2: Implement an 8-to-1 Multiplexer for $F(A, B, C, D) = \Sigma m(1, 4, 5, 10, 11, 14)$ by expanding the function about the variables A, B, C.

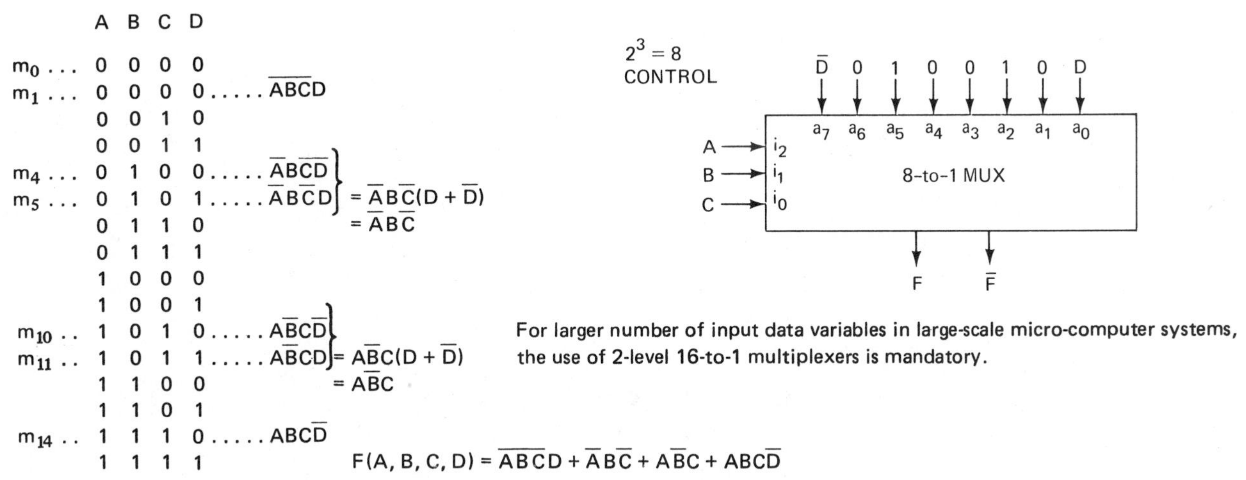

	A	B	C	D	
m_0 ...	0	0	0	0	
m_1 ...	0	0	0	0	..... $\overline{ABC}D$
	0	0	1	0	
	0	0	1	1	
m_4 ...	0	1	0	0	..... $\overline{A}B\overline{CD}$
m_5 ...	0	1	0	1	..... $\overline{A}B\overline{C}D$
	0	1	1	0	
	0	1	1	1	
	1	0	0	0	
	1	0	0	1	
m_{10} ..	1	0	1	0	..... $A\overline{B}C\overline{D}$
m_{11} ..	1	0	1	1	..... $A\overline{B}CD$
	1	1	0	0	
	1	1	0	1	
m_{14} ..	1	1	1	0	..... $ABC\overline{D}$
	1	1	1	1	

m_4, m_5: $= \overline{A}B\overline{C}(D + \overline{D}) = \overline{A}B\overline{C}$

m_{10}, m_{11}: $= A\overline{B}C(D + \overline{D}) = A\overline{B}C$

For larger number of input data variables in large-scale micro-computer systems, the use of 2-level 16-to-1 multiplexers is mandatory.

$F(A, B, C, D) = \overline{A\,B\,C}D + \overline{A}B\overline{C} + A\overline{B}C + ABC\overline{D}$

Expanding about A, B, C means that specific combination of the input variables A, B, C will control the switching of certain inputs off the a_i inputs to pass through.

$\overline{A\,B\,C}$ selects a_0: D is therefore inputted to a_0
$\overline{A}\,B\,\overline{C}$ selects a_2: 1 is therefore inputted to a_2
$A\overline{B}C$ selects a_5: 1 is therefore inputted to a_5
ABC selects a_7: D is therefore inputted to a_7

0's are therefore connected to the rest of the input data terminals a_1, a_3, a_4, a_6 to complete the design of this MUX.

Fig. 10-14. Design of multiplexers.

Design of BCD-to-7 Segment LED/LCD Display Decoders

By selectively actuating several of 7 independent segments, a binary-coded decimal to 7-segment decoder (MSI-IC chip, viz., 7447A) can be used for one LED or LCD display of decimal numeral. (With other appropriate decoder IC chips, the display can be extended to Hexadecimal code and Mnemonic alphabetical characters of Assembly language instructions (or commands).

7447A BCD-to-7 segment Decoder

Numeral	D	C	B	A
0	0	0	0	0
1	0	0	0	1
2	0	0	1	0
3	0	0	1	1
4	0	1	0	0
5	0	1	0	1
6	0	1	1	0
7	0	1	1	1
8	1	0	0	0
9	1	0	0	1
10	1	0	1	0
11	1	0	1	1
12	1	1	0	0
13	1	1	0	1
14	1	1	1	0
15	1	1	1	1

$DEMUX_8$

Rows 8 through 15 invalid for decimal output; they can be d's (don't cares)

Decimal Output

0	1	2	3	4	5	6	7	(8	9)	
0	1	1	1	1	1	1	1	1	1	0
1	0	1	1	1	1	1	1	1	1	1
1	1	0	1	1	1	1	1	1	1	2
1	1	1	0	1	1	1	1	1	1	3
1	1	1	1	0	1	1	1	1	1	4
1	1	1	1	1	0	1	1	1	1	5
1	1	1	1	1	1	0	1	1	1	6
1	1	1	1	1	1	1	0	1	1	7
1	1	1	1	1	1	1	1	0	1	8
1	1	1	1	1	1	1	1	1	0	9

Besides the DECODER 7447A, 2/inverter chips, 1/2-in NAND, 3/3-in NAND's and 2/4-in NAND's are required for segment logic.

If D is considered a LOW-TRUE enable, the decoder becomes an output decimal decoder with a common enable for 7-segment display, ($DEMUX_8$).

A combination min-terms input is applied for each 0 in the truth-table at right. The min-terms effective for each segment are indicated for the 7-segment display shown in the following logic diagram.

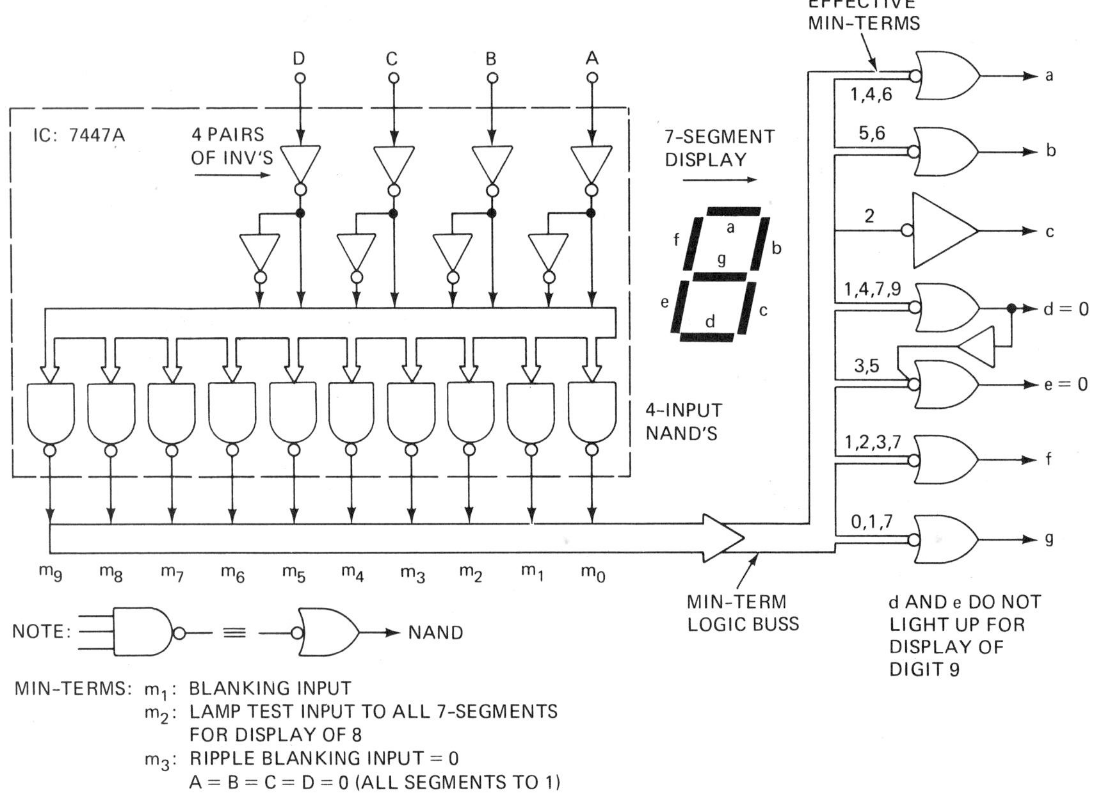

Fig. 10-15. Design of a 7-segment display decoder.

Combinational and Sequential Logic. In *combinational logic*, steady-state outputs depend on *present* inputs only (for AND, OR, INV logic). In sequential logic, steady-state outputs depend on both *present* state and *next-state* outputs as a result of feedback from output to input (as required when storage or memory elements such as flip-flops are involved in logic).

Transition Table of a network presents the properties of the Next-state (NS) and output functions. Columns give possible input signals, and rows correspond to possible states of network. *State Table* of network interprets Transition Table in terms of the symbolic representation of states.

A *State Transition Diagram* shows the resulting state transitions in terms of the *Nodes* (one circle for each Node), and a set labeled *Transition Arrows* leaving each state, and terminating on outputs.

States in a Transition Diagram:

ENTER EXIT — BRANCH : REGULAR STATES

EXIT ONLY : TRANSIENT STATE (CANNOT BE ENTERED)

ENTER ONLY NO EXIT — 0 OR 1 : PERSISTENT STATE

0,0 : ISOLATED STATE (REFLECTING BRANCH)

The *next-state* results from the present values of the inputs and gate feedback outputs, as in the example of a *gated oscillator*:

1.

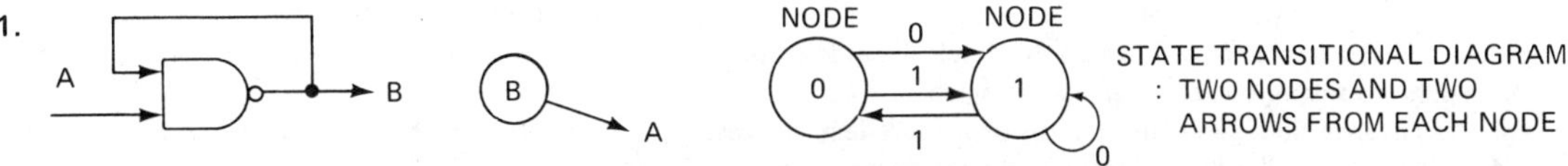

A = 0, State 1 stable, State 0 transitional.
A = 1, States 0/1 . . . pair of oscillatory states.

2. *Binary Case:* n gates, k inputs. 2^n nodes and 2^k state transition arrows per Node, with 1 delay unit per gate (τ). In some cases, inverters are added just to increase propagation delay and maintain positive feedback for oscillation of a gated pulse generator.
3. *Lumped Logic Model:*

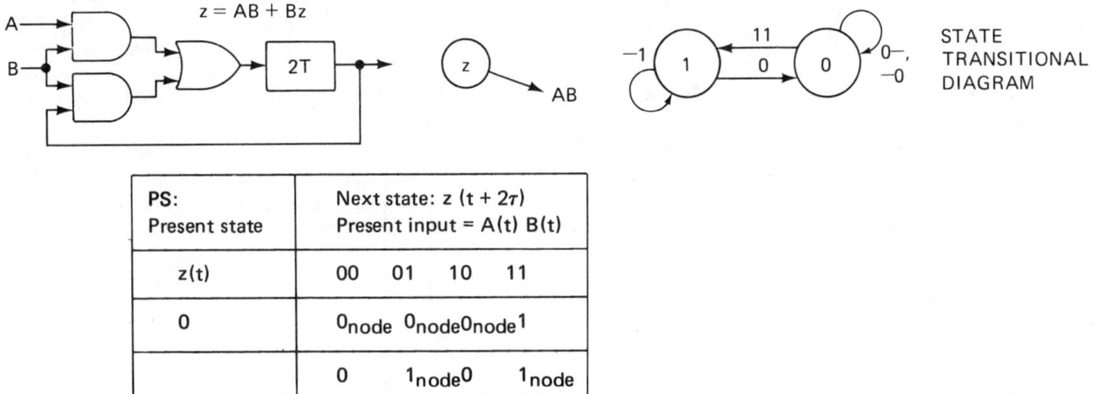

PS: Present state	Next state: z (t + 2τ) Present input = A(t) B(t)
z(t)	00 01 10 11
0	0node 0node 0node 1
	0 1node 0 1node

Analysis of a Sequential Network: The procedure involves the determination of the combinational logic equations for the common J and K inputs of the J-K flip-flop memory cells. Then the next-state logic equations are realized, assuming a lumped-delay model as above from the equation:

$$X(t+\tau) = J(t)\,\overline{X}(t) + \overline{K}(t)\,X(t)$$

Fig. 10-16. Combinational and sequential logic, analysis and synthesis.

Synthesis of a Sequential Logic Network. Starting with J-K flip-flops as before, a set of next-state logic equations are specified. The model then assumes the following system configuration.

The example illustrated shows how combinational and sequential logic are interrelated in logic design:

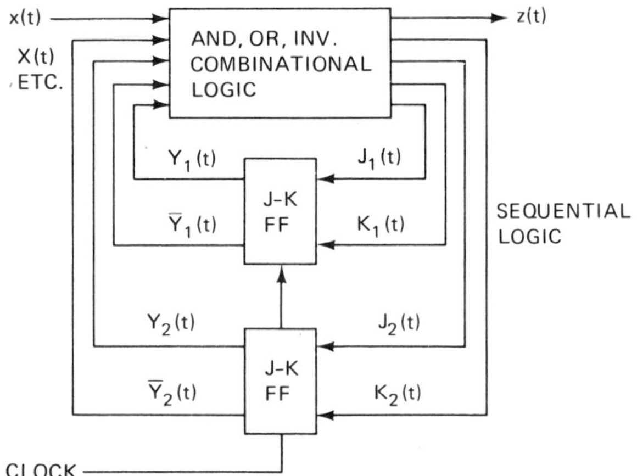

The properties of a flip-flop are described by a characteristic state table or *excitational table* as shown: Using J-K FF's,

PS	NS	Input J(t)	Input K(t)
0	0	0	d
0	1	1	d
1	0	d	1
1	1	d	0

d = 1 or 0. Note: **A state table** is also called a **state transition table.** (d is designated as *"don't care"* as a facility toward K-Map logic simplification.)

External binary input signals and internal state variables X(t), etc., corresponding to the outputs of the J-K flip-flops are required for the synthesis. Combinational logic circuits are used to provide the necessary excitation signals for the J-K inputs of each flip-flop. These excitation equations are functions of both present inputs and present state variables. To avoid timing problems and "race" conditions, external input signals are allowed to change only when the clock signal is at logical '0'. We also assume that the J-K excitation inputs reach steady-state value prior to setting the clock signal to logical '1'.

The next state equation as specified under the analysis procedure is in the case of synthesis realized by using the state transition table and the generation of K-Maps for the excitation inputs and next state equation.

	Present Input		PS Output	NS Output	Excitation Inputs	
	J(t)	K(t)	X(t)	X(t + τ)	S_X(t)	R_X(t)
m_0	0	0	0	0	0	d
m_1	0	0	1	1	d	0
m_2	0	1	0	0	0	d
m_3	0	1	1	0	0	1
m_4	1	0	0	1	1	0
m_5	1	0	1	1	d	0
m_6	1	1	0	1	1	0
m_7	1	1	1	0	0	1

State Transition diagrams give a graphical representation of the operation of a sequential logic network. Verticals or Nodes correspond to the states of the network. *Note: Combinational and sequential logic system design of this character is gradually becoming out-of-date as microprocessors replace many of these functions. This task is taken over by CAD.*

3-INPUT K-MAPS

	$\overline{J}$	$\overline{J}$	J	J
$\overline{X}$	0	0	1	1
X	d	0	0	d
	$\overline{K}$	K	K	$\overline{K}$

$S_X(t) = J(t)\overline{X}(t)$

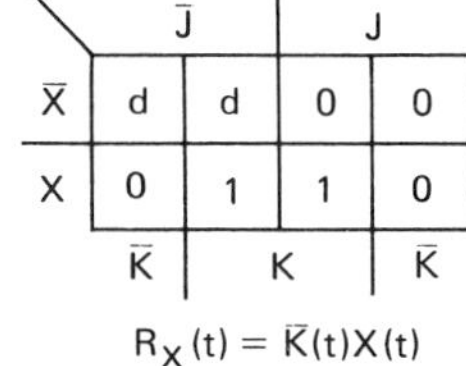

$R_X(t) = \overline{K}(t)X(t)$

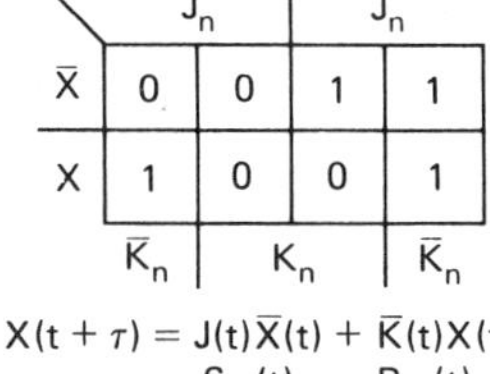

$$X(t + \tau) = \underset{S_X(t)}{J(t)\overline{X}(t)} + \underset{R_X(t)}{\overline{K}(t)X(t)}$$

It is not practical to judge the behavior of a network from the tables under different input conditions. Hence, state transition diagrams present a graphic practical solution to this problem.

With a J-K, simultaneous Set and Reset will reverse the present state of FF instead of resulting in an unpredictable next state (like SRT FF).

Figure 10-16 (continued)

1. A *Binary Counter* counts through a sequence of numbers, and then resets itself to an initial value to recycle the counting process. *Asynchronous* binary counting cells (Flip-flops) form ripple counters when interconnected. After initiation, they may go out of phase in timing. *Synchronous* counters using a clock pulse are designed with master-slave and edge-triggered flip-flops to assure counting without static and dynamic hazards or errors. Autonomous binary counters require that the next-state counting be dependent on the present state counting.

K-modulo-N counter counts a series of events that occur at most N – 1 times. The actual count in this case is K/N, where N is a positive integer.

2. *The division by binary counters,* using feedback from counter to counter is formulated by the expression, $2^n - 2^p$. The flip-flops $2^0, 2^1, 2^2$, etc., are sequential.

Decimal count 10: $2^4 - (2^1 + 2^2) = 16 - 6 = 10$ (n = 4; p = 1, 2.)

Count 43: $2^6 - (2^0 + 2^2 + 2^4) = 64 - 21 = 43$

The expression inside the parentheses represents the feedback of output timing to sequential counters $(2^0, 2^2, 2^4)$ via inverting buffers. A binary counter does not respond to an input pulse timing instantaneously; there is some inherent delay before the binary output reaches full amplitude '1.' The negative going pulses from the feedback buffers trigger back the state '0' binaries to state '1.' Then the count proceeds to repeat the cycle.

Television sync-pulse count from a clock pulse generator of 31.5 KHz/sec. 525 lines interlaced and 60 fields/sec. Interlaced 2 fields = 1 picture frame.

$$2^5 - (2^0 + 2^1 + 2^2) \times 5^2 - (2^0 + 2^1 + 2^3) = 25 \times 21 = 525.$$

31.5 KHz/525 = 60 fields/sec

To maintain *synchronization,* a digital feedback control loop is required from the final counter output of 60 to the clock pulse generator 31.5 KHz/sec. An appropriate digital filter is also required.

3. *Programmable (presettable) counters:* Motorola MC9316, 4-bit modulo-16 direct reset decoder type binary counter. MC9310L: Decimal decoder for fixed count 10

Clock up to 20 MHz.
Clock generally used:
1MHz/sec.
Count of 7:
16 – (P_3, P_0, C_{EP}) = 16 – 9 = 7
5v
P_2, P_1 to Gd.
Count of 14: P_1 and C_{EP} to +5v (Vcc)
P_3, P_2, P_0 to Gd.

	Q_3	Q_2	Q_1	Q_0
m_0	0	0	0	0
m_1	0	0	0	1
m_2	0	0	1	0
m_7	0	1	1	1
m_{15}	1	1	1	1
	8	4	2	1
	P_3	P_2	P_1	P_0

The counter is programmed with P's.

MC9316

Pin	Left	Right	Pin
1	MR	Q_0	14
2	Ck	Q_1	13
3	P_0	Q_2	12
4	P_1	Q_3	11
5	P_2	C_{ET}	10
6	P_3	PE	9
7	C_{EP}	TC	15
8	Gd. (L)	(H) + 5V V_{CC}	16

C_{EP} – Count enable program.
MR: Master Reset.
C_{ET}: Count enable trickle.
PE: Program enable.
TC: Terminal count

L: LOW; H: HIGH
300 mW, loading: 6
Propagation Delay of 15 to 30 nsec.

4. *Bite Pattern Generator* for built-in test equipment of systems.
Start with a clock of 1MHz (1μs)
Ex.: Count of 16380 μs (Period). Five chips of MC9316 are required. The counter is explained with a block diagram (5 X 14 X 13 X 9 X 2 = 16380.)

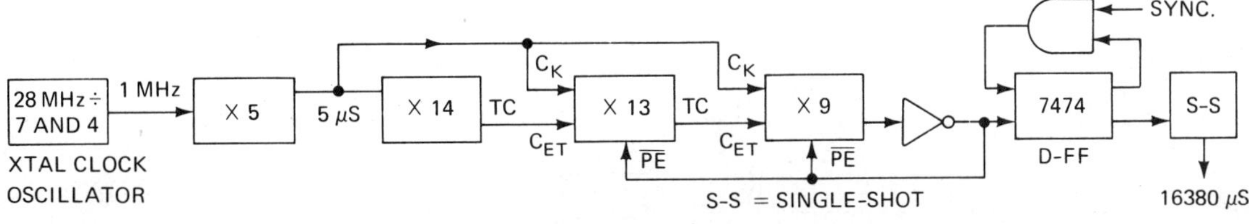

Fig. 10-17. Design of binary counters.

1. Most common full adder logic circuit and the corresponding logic equations:

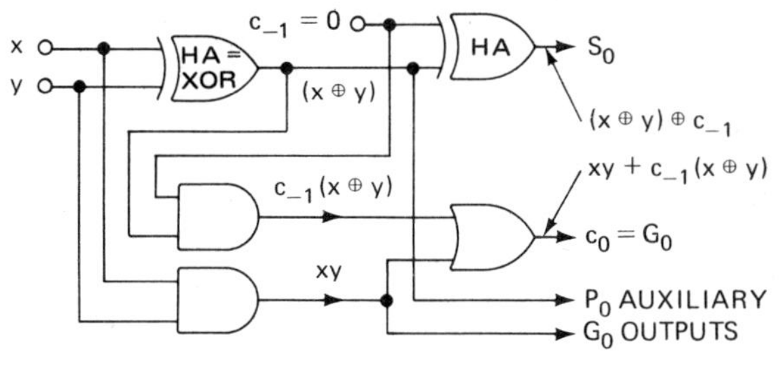

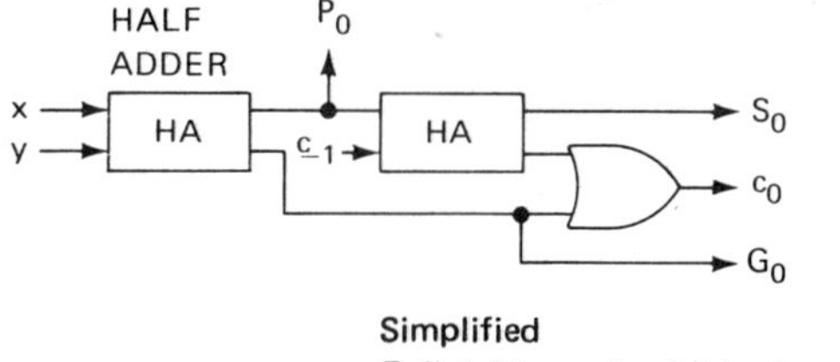

Simplified Full Adder FA

S_0 = Sum

c_0 = carry

An Adder for two n-bit numbers can be realized by cascading n FA's in a Ripple-Carry Adder configuration.

Half Adder can be realized by an Exclusive-OR circuit, (XOR).

Ripple-Carry Full Adder Circuit (for low-speed ALU):

M: Complement Enable. c from HA or FA.

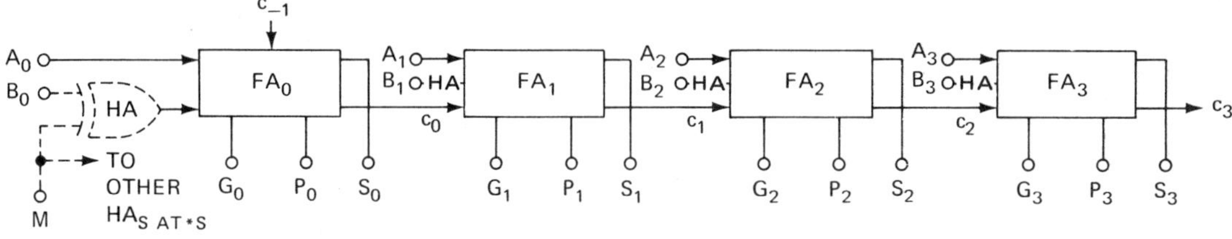

M HA's at x

M = 1 for subtraction, and 0 for addition of 4 bits. c_3 is Ripple Carry. Auxiliary outputs (G_0, P_0, etc.,) are not used in Ripple Carry Full Adders used in slow-speed logic.

Because of the long propagation delay of the asynchronous ripple carry adders and the increasing complexity of 2-level adders for large n (number of bits) a *look-ahead carry adder with a simultaneous carry restorer circuit* is used.

2. 4-bit Full Adder with Carry Look Ahead:

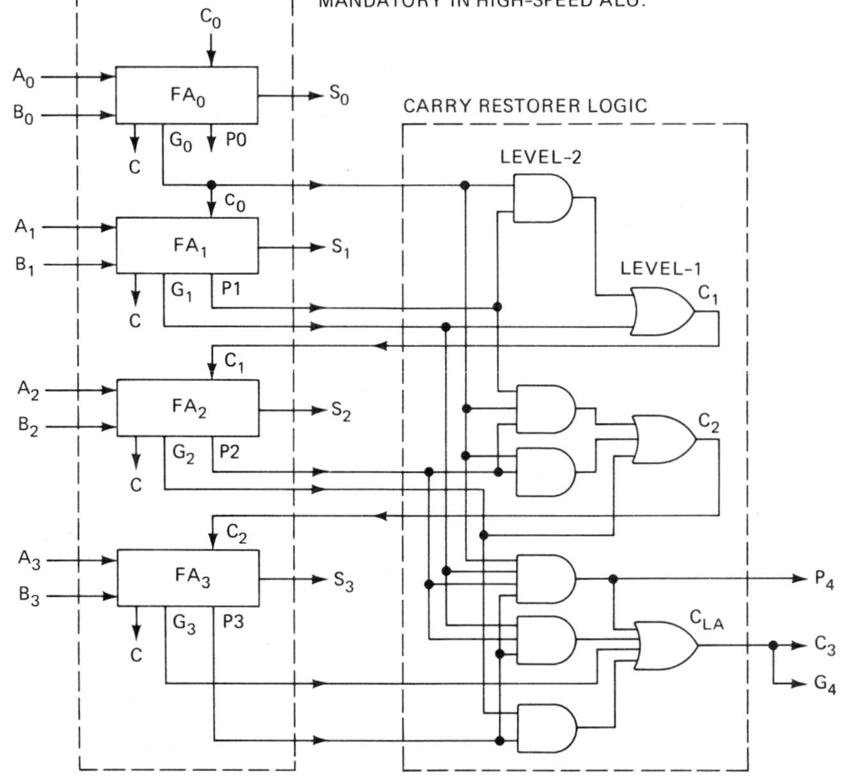

Carry restorer logic equations:

$C_0 = G_0$

$C_1 = G_1 + G_0P_1$

$C_2 = G_2 + G_1P_2 + G_0P_1P_2$

$C_3 = G_3 + G_2P_3 + G_1P_2P_3 + G_0P_1P_2P_3$

This is all the logic that is required for 8/16/32/ . . . bit full adders by using Motorola 74182 MSI Carry Look Ahead Generator, one chip per 16-bit adder, which comprises of four 4-bit adders 7483.

Fig. 10-18. Design of adders with carry look ahead.

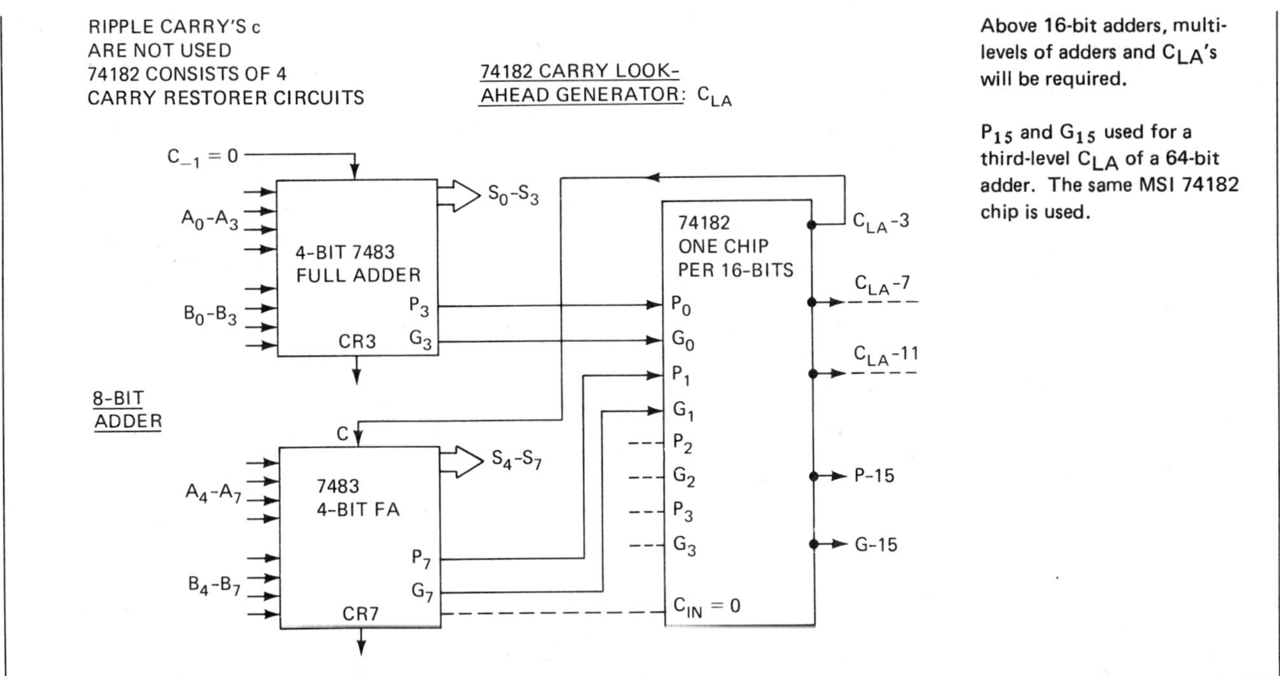

Fig. 10-18 (*cont.*)

1. *Error Detection:* 8-bit *even parity* checking and *odd parity* checking. ASCII (American Standard Code for Information Interchange) For even parity, output B is in 'O' state for no error (Most significant bit, MSB). For odd parity, output A is in 'O' state for no error (least significant bit, LSB).

Logic Tree for Error Detection:

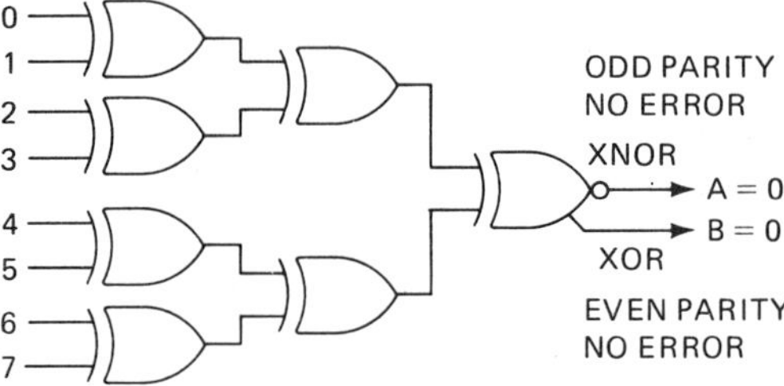

Dec.	*Binary*	*Even parity*	*Odd parity*
0	0 0 0 0	00110000	00000
1	0 0 0 1	10110001	00010
2	0 0 1 0	10110010	00100
3	0 0 1 1	00110011	00111
. . . .		MSB	LSB

EX
16-BIT WORD
PARITY
8
4
4
1
TREES AS SHOWN AT LEFT
4-BIT TREE
L = 0
B = 1
A = 1
ODD PARITY
OK
EVEN PARITY CHECK

2. *Hamming Code One-Bit Error Correction*
For one-bit correction, distance-3 code requires three Hamming correction bits be added to a 4-bit binary word.

Example: Binary Word: 1001 (Decimal/Hex: 9)

The Hamming correction-bits' positions are indicated by H's in the following Hamming Word of 7 bits.

A *Hamming Code Transmitter* is used to insert the correction bits in the binary words as even parity check bits. The technique is illustrated for the binary word 1001, using a 7-bit combined Hamming-Binary Word for a 'soft' error.

	B_7	B_6	B_5	H_4	B_3	H_2	H_1
Binary word =	1	0	0		1		
(1) $H_4 = B_5 \oplus B_6 \oplus B_7 = 1$	1	0	0	1	1		
(2) $H_2 = B_3 \oplus B_6 \oplus B_7 = 0$	1	0	0	1	1	0	
(3) $H_1 = B_3 \oplus B_5 \oplus B_7 = 0$	1	0	0	1	1	0	0

For 2-bit error correction, 5 H-bits are needed.

Fig. 10-19. Error detection and Hamming single-bit error correction.

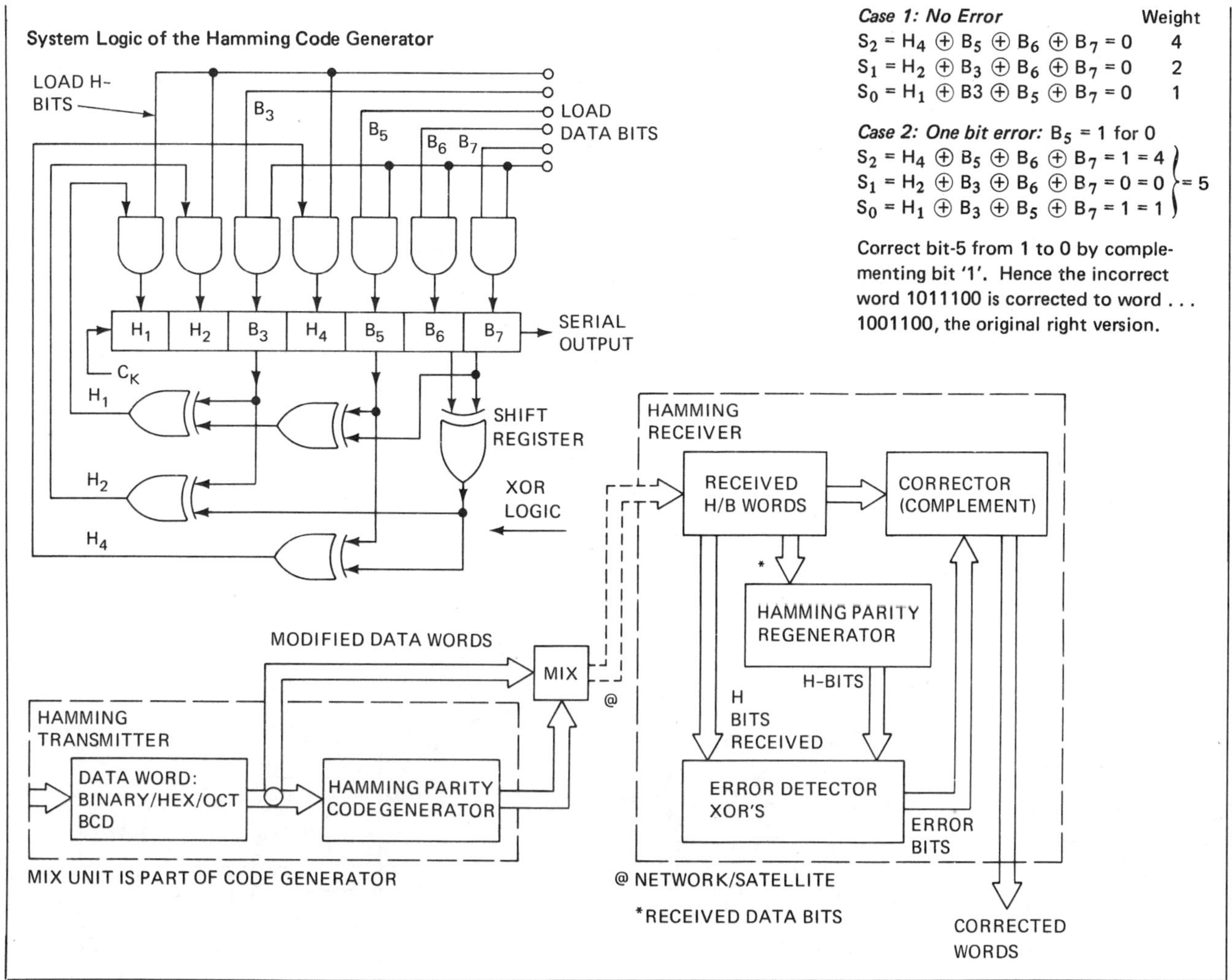

Fig. 10-19 (*cont.*)

Use of PROM in Microprocessor or Microcontroller Applications (Prior to Burning in Program Instructions on ROM). A Signetics type 2650 microprocessor with 3-K bytes of ROM and 3-K bytes of RAM is illustrated in the digital microcomputer system shown in Fig. 10-20. Two input/output ports can be conveniently designed by means of a 32 X 8 bit programmable read-only memory as the decoding logic element and eliminate expensive hard-wired logic. The technique shown here is one of the most common

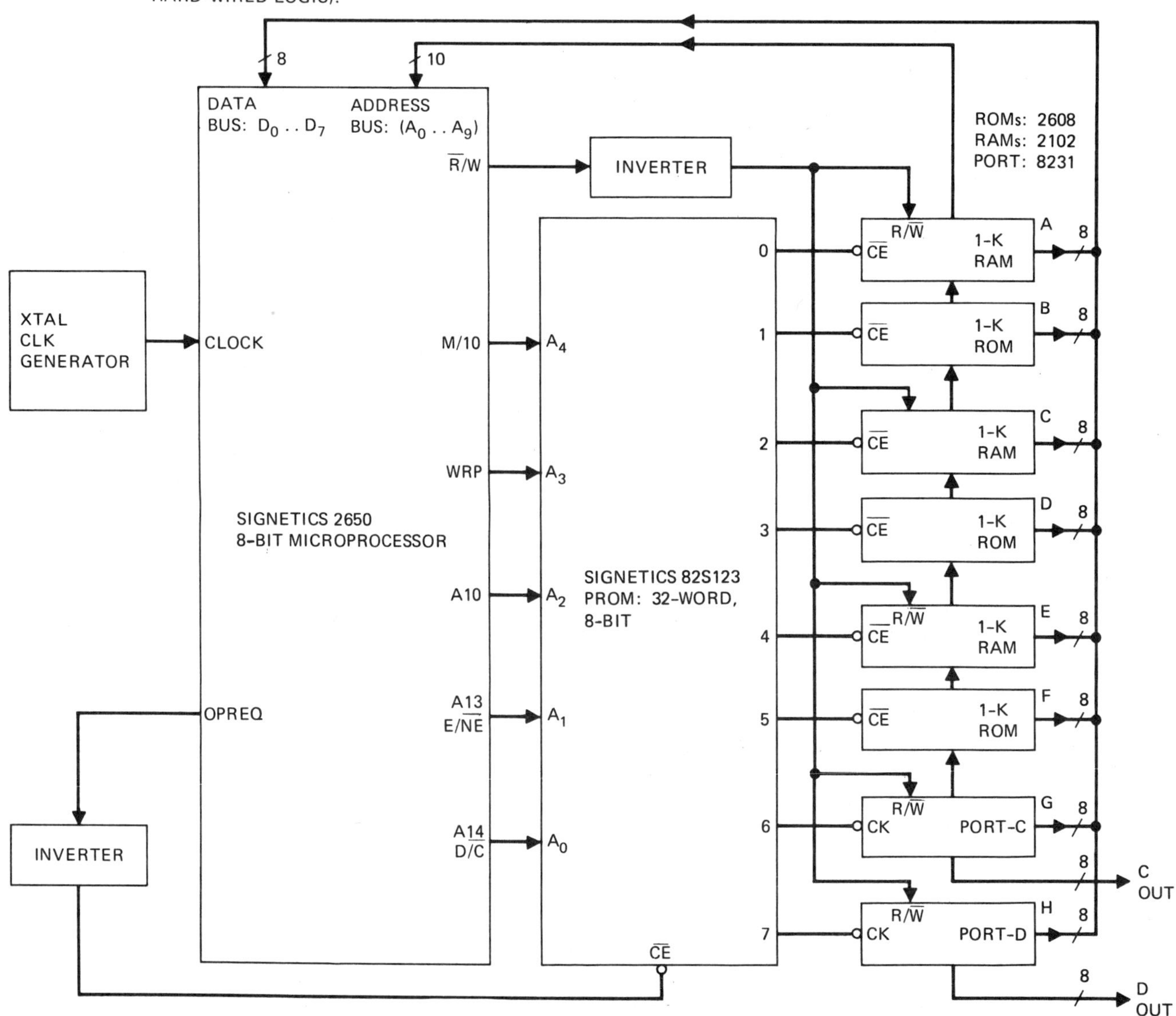

Fig. 10-20. PROM implementation in computer-controlled system. (Reprinted from *Electronics*, September 2, 1976: Copyright © McGraw-Hill, Inc., 1976.)

implementation procedures one should get acquainted with in the application of microcomputer systems in digital control applications.

In the application shown in Fig. 10-20, the PROM is programmed to generate the chip-enable signals for the 6-K byte memory and provides the clock pulses to the I/O ports. The PROM actually decodes the control and address lines from the microprocessor to enable any one of the memory banks or I/O ports and functions as a kind of programmable logic array.

Signetics 2650 allows 18-bit processing by means of its 9-bit microprogram address-register and microinstruction capability. With its 77-instruction set and 8-level vectored interrupt, the operation request is the master control signal to coordinate external operations. The NMOS depletion-mode 40-pin DIP (dual-in-line package) has a cycle-time of 1.5 μsec, and consumes 625 mW at 5 V. It has the capability of 8/16/24-bit instruction words, 8-level on-chip subroutine, internal 8-bit parallel structure, and seven 8-bit general-purpose registers. A separate adder enables fast address calculation. The architecture reflects interfacing of a microcontroller and a microprocessor on a common LSI chip. Each RAM bank consists of eight 2108 1 K × 1-bit static RAMs, and each ROM bank consists of a single 2608 1-K byte ROM. Each of the I/O ports is an 8T31 8-bit bi-directional I/O interface structure. The PROM enables just one of the ROM/RAMs to read or write at a memory location command by the 10-address line memory-bus between the 2650 and the six memory banks. This bus can have 2^{10}(=1024) addresses, and the enable signals from the PROM under consideration can select these to any one of the six memory banks for 6-K bytes of memory locations for data via the 8-bit data-bus.

The two highest-order address lines that determine the 8-K byte page of memory and I/O operations are multiplexed on lines A14 (E/$\overline{\text{NE}}$) and A13 (D/$\overline{\text{C}}$) by the microprocessor. If E/$\overline{\text{NE}}$ (A1) is low, port D or C is enabled depending on whether D/$\overline{\text{C}}$ (A0) is high or low, when M/$\overline{\text{I,O}}$ line of the microprocessor selects the memory and I,O operation. That is, A4 must be high in any PROM input that enables one of the six memory banks, and A4 must be low to enable or clock either I/O port. The exclusive write-pulse (WRP) line at A3 must be high to enable any ROM for R/W. A2 must be high to enable a ROM and low to enable a RAM. The OPREQ, going to $\overline{\text{CE}}$ (chip-enable) of PROM must be high to enable any ROM/RAM/PORT D/$\overline{\text{C}}$. ROMs and RAMs are enabled at low (and hence $\overline{\text{ROM-A}}$ or $\overline{\text{ROM-B}}$) but I/O ports are enabled at high. For example, Port "C" is enabled at high. (R/W = read or write.)

Table 10-5 indicates the program that charts the operating conditions for ROMs, RAMs, or I/O ports. The coding of this program on the PROM is indicated in Table 10-4. As an example of clarification, words 0 through 15 all have A4 low for I/O operation, and words 16 through 31 have A4 high for memory operation. The first 10 address lines of the address bus A0 through A9 of the microprocessor and two page-address/I/O port lines are all thus decoded by this program. Undecoded A11/A12 are "don't care" lines, so that the same 1-K byte of information can appear at four places on one page, but the first three pages only are significant. (The ROM and RAM position on each page can be revised by merely recoding the PROM.) The coding in the blank rows is all redundancy and hence "don't care." If the PROM enables one of the I/O ports instead of a memory bank, the $\overline{\text{R}}$/W signal determines whether the port reads data on to the data-bus for write or reads the data off the bus.

PROMs can be used to drive 7-segment display to show the decimal value of a 4-bit input signal. A 32 × 8-bit programmed PROM can directly provide the drive signals from a machine-generated 4-bit binary code to a $1\frac{1}{2}$ digit display of the numbers 0 to 15, and also include lamp test and inhibit commands. (Otherwise, a binary-to-BCD converter, and BCD-to-7 segment decoder/drive ICs are required.)

Table 10-4. ASCII coding of 82S123 PROM. (*Courtesy of McGraw-Hill*)

	INPUTS					OUTPUTS H	G	F	E	D	C	B	A	COMPONENT ENABLED		
WORD	A_4	A_3	A_2	A_1	A_0	7	6	5	4	3	2	1	0		H	G
0	0	0	0	0	0	0	1	1	1	1	1	1	1	PORT C	0	1
1	0	0	0	0	1	1	0	1	1	1	1	1	1	PORT D	1	0
2	0	0	0	1	0	0	0	1	1	1	1	1	1	–		
3	0	0	0	1	1	0	0	1	1	1	1	1	1	–		
4	0	0	1	0	0	0	1	1	1	1	1	1	1	PORT C	0	1
5	0	0	1	0	1	1	0	1	1	1	1	1	1	PORT D	1	0
6	0	0	1	1	0	0	0	1	1	1	1	1	1	–		
7	0	0	1	1	1	0	0	1	1	1	1	1	1	–		
8	0	1	0	0	0	0	1	1	1	1	1	1	1	PORT C	0	1
9	0	1	0	0	1	1	0	1	1	1	1	1	1	PORT D	1	0
10	0	1	0	1	0	0	0	1	1	1	1	1	1	–		
11	0	1	0	1	1	0	0	1	1	1	1	1	1	–		
12	0	1	1	0	0	0	1	1	1	1	1	1	1	PORT C	0	1
13	0	1	1	0	1	1	0	1	1	1	1	1	1	PORT D	1	0
14	0	1	1	1	0	0	0	1	1	1	1	1	1	–		
15	0	1	1	1	1	0	0	1	1	1	1	1	1	–		
16	1	0	0	0	0	0	0	1	1	1	1	1	1	–		
17	1	0	0	0	1	0	0	1	1	1	1	1	1	–		
18	1	0	0	1	0	0	0	1	1	1	1	1	1	–		
19	1	0	0	1	1	0	0	1	1	1	1	1	1	–		
20	1	0	1	0	0	0	0	1	1	1	1	0	1	ROM BANK B (PAGE 0)		
21	1	0	1	0	1	0	0	0	1	1	1	1	1	ROM BANK F (PAGE 2)		
22	1	0	1	1	0	0	0	1	1	0	1	1	1	ROM BANK D (PAGE 1)		
23	1	0	1	1	1	0	0	1	1	1	1	1	1	–		
24	1	1	0	0	0	0	0	1	1	1	1	1	0	RAM BANK A (PAGE 0)		
25	1	1	0	0	1	0	0	1	0	1	1	1	1	RAM BANK E (PAGE 2)		
26	1	1	0	1	0	0	0	1	1	1	0	1	1	RAM BANK C (PAGE 1)		
27	1	1	0	1	1	0	0	1	1	1	1	1	1	–		
28	1	1	1	0	0	0	0	1	1	1	1	0	1	ROM BANK B (PAGE 0)		
29	1	1	1	0	1	0	0	0	1	1	1	1	1	ROM BANK F (PAGE 2)		
30	1	1	1	1	0	0	0	1	1	0	1	1	1	ROM BANK D (PAGE 1)		
31	1	1	1	1	1	0	0	1	1	1	1	1	1	–		

Table 10-5. ASCII enabling conditions for ROMs, RAMs, or I/O ports. *(Courtesy of McGraw-Hill)*

$(\overline{\mathrm{RAM\ A}}) = (\mathrm{OPREQ})\,(\mathrm{M}/\overline{\mathrm{IO}})\,(\mathrm{WRP})\,(\overline{\mathrm{A13} \cdot \mathrm{E}/\overline{\mathrm{NE}}})\,(\overline{\mathrm{A14} \cdot \mathrm{D}/\overline{\mathrm{C}}})\,(\overline{\mathrm{A10}})$
$(\overline{\mathrm{ROM\ B}}) = (\mathrm{OPREQ})\,(\mathrm{M}/\overline{\mathrm{IO}})\,(\overline{\mathrm{A13} \cdot \mathrm{E}/\overline{\mathrm{NE}}})\,(\overline{\mathrm{A14} \cdot \mathrm{D}/\overline{\mathrm{C}}})\,(\mathrm{A10})$
$(\overline{\mathrm{RAM\ C}}) = (\mathrm{OPREQ})\,(\mathrm{M}/\overline{\mathrm{IO}})\,(\mathrm{WRP})\,(\mathrm{A13} \cdot \mathrm{E}/\overline{\mathrm{NE}})\,(\overline{\mathrm{A14} \cdot \mathrm{D}/\overline{\mathrm{C}}})\,(\overline{\mathrm{A10}})$
$(\overline{\mathrm{ROM\ D}}) = (\mathrm{OPREQ})\,(\mathrm{M}/\overline{\mathrm{IO}})\,(\mathrm{A13} \cdot \mathrm{E}/\overline{\mathrm{NE}})\,(\overline{\mathrm{A14} \cdot \mathrm{D}/\overline{\mathrm{C}}})\,(\mathrm{A10})$
$(\overline{\mathrm{RAM\ E}}) = (\mathrm{OPREQ})\,(\mathrm{M}/\overline{\mathrm{IO}})\,(\mathrm{WRP})\,(\overline{\mathrm{A13} \cdot \mathrm{E}/\overline{\mathrm{NE}}})\,(\mathrm{A14} \cdot \mathrm{D}/\mathrm{C})\,(\overline{\mathrm{A10}})$
$(\overline{\mathrm{ROM\ F}}) = (\mathrm{OPREQ})\,(\mathrm{M}/\overline{\mathrm{IO}})\,(\overline{\mathrm{A13} \cdot \mathrm{E}/\overline{\mathrm{NE}}})\,(\mathrm{A14} \cdot \mathrm{D}/\overline{\mathrm{C}})\,(\mathrm{A10})$
$(\mathrm{PORT\ C}) = (\mathrm{OPREQ})\,(\overline{\mathrm{M}/\overline{\mathrm{IO}}})\,(\overline{\mathrm{A13} \cdot \mathrm{E}/\overline{\mathrm{NE}}})\,(\overline{\mathrm{A14} \cdot \mathrm{D}/\overline{\mathrm{C}}})$
$(\mathrm{PORT\ D}) = (\mathrm{OPREQ})\,(\overline{\mathrm{M}/\overline{\mathrm{IO}}})\,(\overline{\mathrm{A13} \cdot \mathrm{E}/\overline{\mathrm{NE}}})\,(\mathrm{A14} \cdot \mathrm{D}/\overline{\mathrm{C}})$

10-13. GLOSSARY OF HARDWARE TERMS

1. **Timings** encountered in the microcomputer and microwave areas:

$T = \frac{1}{f} = 1$, if f = 1 MHz; then T = 10 for 100 kHz T = period; f = frequency.

Millisecond, ms = 10^{-3}: kilohertz, kHz: 10^3 Hz/sec
Microsecond, μs = 10^{-6}: megahertz, MHz = 10^6 Hz/sec (million)
Nanosecond, ns = 10^{-9}: gigahertz, GHz = 10^9 Hz/sec (billion)
Picosecond, ps: 10^{-12}: terahertz, THz = 10^{12} Hz/sec (trillion)
Mil: (1/1000) inch; micron, μ = 10^{-6} meter; millimicron: 10^{-9} meter
Angstrom, Å: 10^{-10} meter. Wavelength of 1 eV photon = 1.24 μ
t_r = **pulse rise-time** = 1 μs: **bandwidth** of 1 MHz; 1 ns: 1 GHz **(BW)**; 1 ps: 1,000 GHz (BW)
Noise temperature in degrees Kelvin (290° K = Ambient); 67° K = 1 dB of insertion-loss in a graphic plot depicting a linear-scale from 5 to 200° K approximately. This linear relationship gives the db-equivalent to noise-temperature.

2. **Batch-processing of microprocessors.** Both MOS and Bipolar (I^2L) LSI fabrication are done by starting with a 2-inch-diameter intrinsic seed-grown Silicon ingot. The crystal is sliced into thin (approximately 20-mils thick), 2-inch-diamter Silicon wafers, parallel to the preferred crystallographic plane. For example, 138 cells of 2,560-bit dynamic ROMs are simultaneously formed on the surface of the wafer by means of photolithographic process, oxidation, diffusion, metallization, etc. The wafer is then scribed and cut into 138 chips, each containing a possible ROM, since the actual yield is perhaps around 50%, depending on the learning period of production. After processing, a 200-micron-thick, 1 inch-diameter, P-type substrate wafer yields 625 differential amplifiers in a linear IC chip. (Presently, MOS technology allows slice diameters from 3 to 5 inches.)

3. **Flag (pulse-timing).** A pulse, or the stored indication of a signal (from a flip-flop) that indicates the readiness of especially a peripheral device to transfer information. (The control-bit then enables the transfer of information to and from a peripheral device.)

4. **Logic-clip** is a test-device used to detect and indicate logic levels (high/low) present at the terminals of dual-in line IC logic packages (DIP).

5. **Bit-plane** indicates one of the planes of a CORE memory-stack, in which the ferrite cores, which represent the bits, form a single matrix for sensing and control wires. Eight bit-planes or four pairs, back-to-back, make a frame; each frame may contain 32 pages.

6. **Propagation-delay (t_p), rise-time (t_r), fall-time (t_f), slewing rate.**

TABLE 10-6. Some available LSI/VLSI memory chips.

The Latest Status of the Availability of LSI/VLSI ROM and RAM Memory Chips, Multipliers (for FFT/Digital Filters) Single 5V supply is common.

Intel Corporation; 3065 Bowers Ave, Santa Clara, CA 95051
Static RAMs: 4096 × 1-bit (2141/2147/2147H), H: High Speed (45 to 70 nsec)
NMOS 1-K × 4 (2148H/2149H, 180mA/30mA, 45 to 70 nsec address access)
1-K × 1 (2115H/2147/2147H, 20 to 35 nsec)
8-K × 1 (8185 HMOS, compatible with 8085A: 1-K × 8-bit)
1-K × 4 (2114A, HMOS, 40 to 70mA, 120/250 nsec)
16,384 × 1-bit (2117/2118, 16-pin, 150/120 nsec, $28) –Also Fujitsu
Dynamic RAM: 64-K (2164, Refresh cycles/period: 128/2, access: 100 to 200 nsec, 5V)
EPROM, UV-Erasable: 1-K × 8 (2708)
2-K × 8 (2716, 450 nsec)
4-K × 8 (2732, 450 nsec); (2732A, 250 nsec), 24-pin.
EPROM with I/O ports: 16, 384-bit (8755)
ROM 1-K × 8 (2308/8308, 350/350 nsec), 3-State output, On-Chip address-latch.

NEC (Japan): μPD7801 μComputer chip: *32-K bit ROM, 1-K RAM, 48 I/O,* External Memory: 64-Kbyte, (NMOS), 5v

Texas Instruments: P. O. Box 5012, M/S 308, Dallas, TX 75222
Series EPROM: 64-K bit: 8-K × 8-bit (TMS2564, 840mW/131mW, access 450 nsec, 28-pin DIP, 5V, single TTL-level pulse for loading)
32-K bit: 4-K × 8-bit (TMS 25L32, 500 mW/131mW, access 450 nsec, 5V)
16-K bit: 2-K × 8-bit (TMS 2516-35, 525mW/131mW, access 350 nsec, 5V)
8-K bit: 1-K × 8-bit (TMS 2508-25, 446mW/131mW, access 250 nsec, 5V)
Static Ram: 4-K × 1-bit or 1-K × 4-bit (TMS 40L47, 200 nsec, 18/20-pin, 5V)
4-K × 1-bit (TMS 21L47-7, 18-pin, R/W cycle-time 320 nsec, 5V)
Error Detection and Correction: (SN 54 LS30, 31, 74, 28-pin)
Magnetic Bubble Memory: (TIB-1000, External, 512-K × 2, access 11 ms, Binary Megabit)
(Nonvolatile) (TIB-0500, 512 × 1-bit, 11 ms)

Fairchild Semiconductor Operations Division, 464 Ellis St., Mountain View, CA 94042
Static RAM: 128 × 8-bit (F3876, 64 × 8-bits available–low current power-down)
ROM: 4-K × 8-bit (F3878)
S-Isoplanar RAM: 4-K × 1-bit (ECL/TTl, access 35 nsec to 10 nsec at 1 micron for main-frame computers: in production.)
" PLAs: 2000-Gate Array at 0.5 nsec gate-delay

RCA: Solid State Division, Box 3200, Somerville, NJ 08876
Static Ram, *CMOS:* 1-K × 1-bit(CDP 1821) ROM: 1-K × 8-bit (1833/1834)
(8-K × 8: 18S622), 128 × 8-bit(CDP 1823) PROM: 1-K × 8-bit (1833/1834)
CMOS: Second source: EAROM: 512 × 8-bit (1831/1832)
Hughes Semiconductor Products. Also Harris Semiconductor, 64-K bit Dyn. RAM.

TRW LSI Products: P.O. Box 1125, Redondo Beach, CA 90278
Multipliers: 16-bit × 16-bit (MPY-16HJ, 100 nsec, 3W, $157)
12-bit × 12-bit (MPY-12HJ, 80 nsec, 2W, $103)
8-bit × 8-bit (MPY-8HJ-1, 45 nsec, 1W, $57)

Solid State Scientific: Montgomeryville, PA 18936
Static CMOS: *16-K bit ROM* in 2048 × 8-bit format replaces 2716 EPROMs, (2)1833 CMOS ROMs, 2316/2616 NMOS ROMs–SSS, *SCM 5316E*

National Semiconductor: 2900 Semiconductor Drive, Santa Clara, CA 95051
EPROM: 2-K × 8-bit (MM2716M, 450 nsec, $123)

Fujitsu Bubble Memory Chip: 293-K bit, 16-pin, DIP (FBM 0301); NMOS RAM, 4-K Static, 55 nsec.

Hitachi CMOS, 6116, 16-K Static RAM, 120 nsec, 200 mW (Plastic)

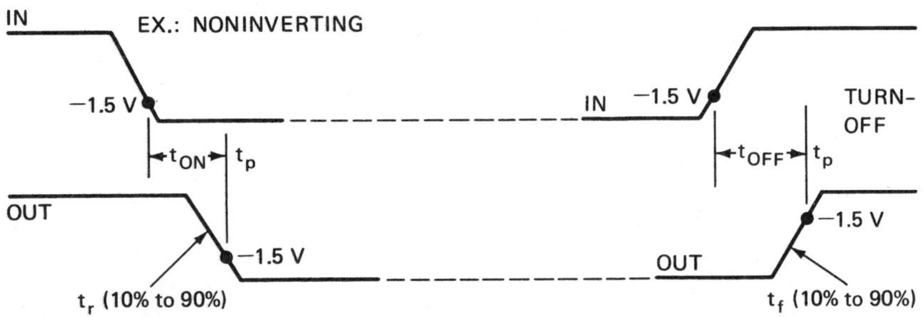

SLEW-RATE INDICATES THE RATE OF VOLTAGE CHANGE IN ANALOG/LINEAR AMPLIFIERS. IT IS DEFINED AS THE INTERNALLY LIMITED RATE OF CHANGE IN OUTPUT VOLTAGE WITH A LARGE AMPLITUDE STEP FUNCTION APPLIED TO THE INPUT. THESE RATES VARY FROM 1 TO 1,500 V/μs.

7. **Schottky.** In a Schottky diode or hot-carrier barrier-diode, current flows by electron majority-carriers across a metal-semiconductor contact, unlike the minority-carrier drift of holes in a P-N junction. When the diode junction-field is reverse-biased with the metal (gold or aluminum) positive, the hole-conduction ceases and electron-flow enables a high-speed switching phenomenon, shorter than 10 ns, in the reverse recovery-time of the Schottky diode. All high-speed MSI and bipolar I^2L microprocessors make common use of the Schottky junctions.

8. **Boolean algebra.** George Boole (1854) originally developed the logic concepts of "true" as binary "1" and "false" as binary "0." During the 1930s, Shannon founded the practical application of this concept to switching-theory using relays.

9. **Sample-and-hold.** Analog quantities, as distinguished from discrete "digital" information, are measured in a brief time-interval by "sampling" with a periodic pulse-train, and "held" constant by a capacitance within a tolerance, and instantly applied via an analog switch or a multiplexer to an analog-to-digital converter (ADC) for processing the "continuous" analog information in a digital format. Where a high degree of accuracy is desired, a digital format is the ideal solution, since the digital word can be extended to the desired number of digits conveniently. The resolution or "quantization error" of the ADC is then obtained by the number of bits chosen to represent the analog quantity. The resolution is specified to have a maximum value of "±½ Least Significant Bit" of the chosen number of bits. If the sampling period is T, and each sample is converted to N bits, the *bandwidth* required is given by N/2T.

10. **Analog voltage comparator.** The comparator is a DC-coupled high-gain amplifier with a differential input and a binary "1" or "0" output. The practical output threshold-of-crossing determines the sensitivity and stability of the logical decision made. The

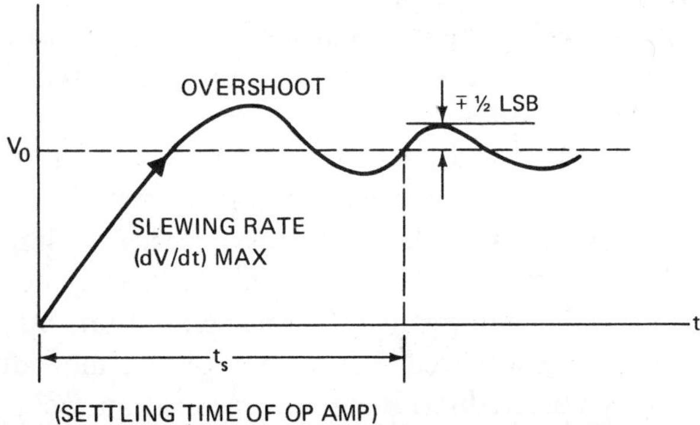

Step-response of an operational amplifier.

THE SCHOTTKY-CLAMPED TRANSISTORS ARE FORMED BY USING SCHOTTKY-BARRIER DIODES IN PARALLEL WITH THE BASE-COLLECTOR JUNCTION TO ENABLE THE EFFECT DISCUSSED IN THE TEXT IN (7).

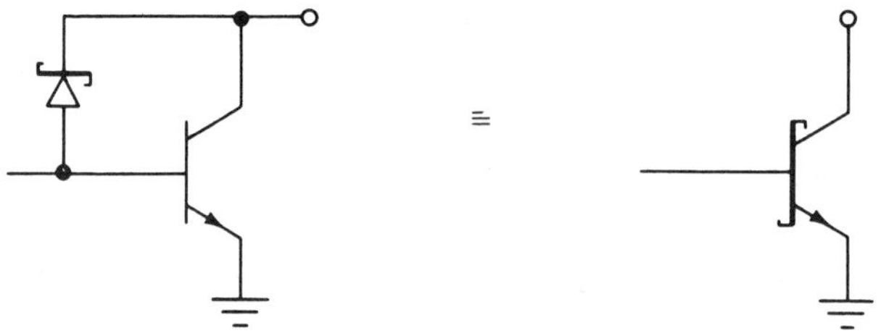

SCHOTTKY DIODE: EQUIVALENT REPRESENTATION WITH TRANSISTOR

SYMBOL FOR SCHOTTKY TRANSISTOR

offset voltage is then determined by the change in input voltage that actually brings the output to the logic threshold voltage. The difference in the *turn-on* and *turn-off* input voltages is termed the *hysteresis* of the comparator. An input overdrive results in *cutoff* or *saturation* to slow down the operation due to the actual nonlinear regions involved. So, a fast "recovery time" is a desirable property of all voltage comparators.

11. **"Don't Care" condition.** In combinational logic involving NAND and NOR gates, some input switching combinations may never occur, and certain switching results may have no effect on the overall logic. Such "don't care" switching conditions can be useful in practical simplification of digital logic.

12. **MIN and MAX terms.** A function of n variables has 2^n standard product terms called the *minterms*, and 2^n standard sum terms called the *maxterms*. Example: 7 = Binary, 111: ABC (Min); $\overline{A} + \overline{B} + \overline{C}$ (Max).

13. **Latch.** A latch is a storage element implemented by a (Set/Reset) R-S flip-flop. A flip-flop can in turn be implemented by interconnecting two NAND gates, with or without inversion, for the Set/Reset inputs, respectively. Using a NOR-gate as a building-block is slightly more involved than a NAND.

14. **Modulo-2^n.** An "ADD" operation of Modulo-2^n (or mod-2^n) ignores the bit of weight 2^n, which is called the *modulus* of the arithmetic. The *residue*, consisting of all the lower weight bits, makes the output of the ADDER. In other words, a *modulo-sum* is a sum with respect to the modulus, when the *carry* is ignored.

15. **Redundancy** is the general method of improving circuit reliability by including elements intended to provide a *parallel-function* capability, when the work load is heavy. The human brain adopts the neural principle of *passive redundancy*, and the microprocessors will do so during the learning-cycle of production. The theory was originated by Von Neumann, Moore, and Shannon (1956).

Some failure-sensing and switching mechanisms are usually involved in bringing the alternative *active redundant* elements into operation, when *standby active redundant elements* are used in a complex system.

16. **Reliability**. The soldered and mechanically associated interconnections of the former technology, often a common source of failure, are wholly or partially replaced by the chemically bonded interfaces in the microelectronics to improve the reliability. Reduction of size in microelectronics makes it easier to isolate the chip from such environmental stresses as excessive temperature, shock, vibration, nuclear irradiation, and corrosion. Also, the microminaturized dimensions of the individual circuits, and the facility of automation and cost reduction in the fabrication technology allow the economic feasibility of the principle of passive redundancy in circuit elements. In view of

these aspects, the *reliability*, defined as *the probability that a system will not fail during a specified period of time while operating under a given set of conditions*, is comparatively much greater in the case of the microprocessor.

The sum of the reliability and Q, the probability of failure, must be unity. That is, if λ is the *failure-rate* then

$$Q = 1 - e^{-\lambda t}$$

For several components, the parallel system *reliability*,

$$R_S = \exp\left[-(\lambda_1 + \lambda_2 + ..)\,t\right] = \exp\left(-\lambda t \times 10^{-5}\right)$$

Where failure-rate λ is expressed in percentage/1,000 hrs.

17. **Hall-effect (solid-state relay).** Semiconductor materials such as indium-antimony and indium-arsenic have high electron-mobility, and they exhibit a special property of "Hall-effect."

When a current I is flowing through a bar of the aforementioned materials at an applied voltage of V, if a magnetic field B is applied perpendicular to the current, the electric field E produced is perpendicular to both B and I (in a three-dimensional field), then E is proportional to BI, and an open-circuit voltage V_H is produced, and V_H is proportional to μ_H BI, where μ_H is the Hall mobility.

Sprague type-ULN-3006T is an example of such a magnetically operated solid-state switch with a digital current-sinking output. The "T" pack will interface directly with most transistors, integrated circuits, and silicon-controlled rectifier with no problem of noise or bounce caused by electrical contacts. The solid-state switch is integrated with a Hall-sensor, voltage regulator, Schmitt-trigger, and amplifier. The sensor is not rate-sensitive like magnetic and variable-reluctance signal pick-ups. The switch operates at 100 kHz.

18. **Gunn-effect (Gunn-diode).** The transferred-electron or Gunn-effect is associated with the radio-frequency generation at GHz and amplification at a *high power-rating in "bulk" semiconductor materials such as gallium-arsenide or indium-phosphide*; they exhibit high electron-mobility on a "two-valley basis." Electrons gain energy from an applied electric field and at fields of several KV/cm enough energy is gained by the electrons for transfer to a conduction-band valley of lower mobility. This "bulk negative-resistance" effect in these materials enables the implementation of Gunn-diode oscillators at 2 GHz and above, 100 W pulsed, and 100 mW, CW. The frequency is determined by the electron transit-time in the bulk-semiconductor used.

19. **PNPN switching device and silicon-controlled rectifier (SCR).**

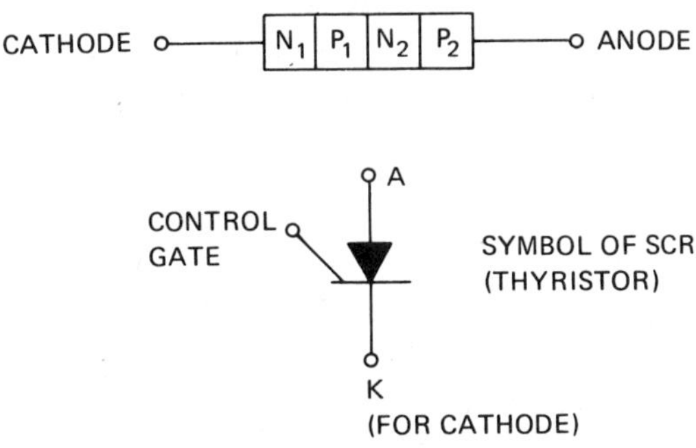

The PNPN device is a three-junction bistable device such as a gas thyratron; it is also called a four-layer diode. With the gate terminal shown in the diagram, it is called a

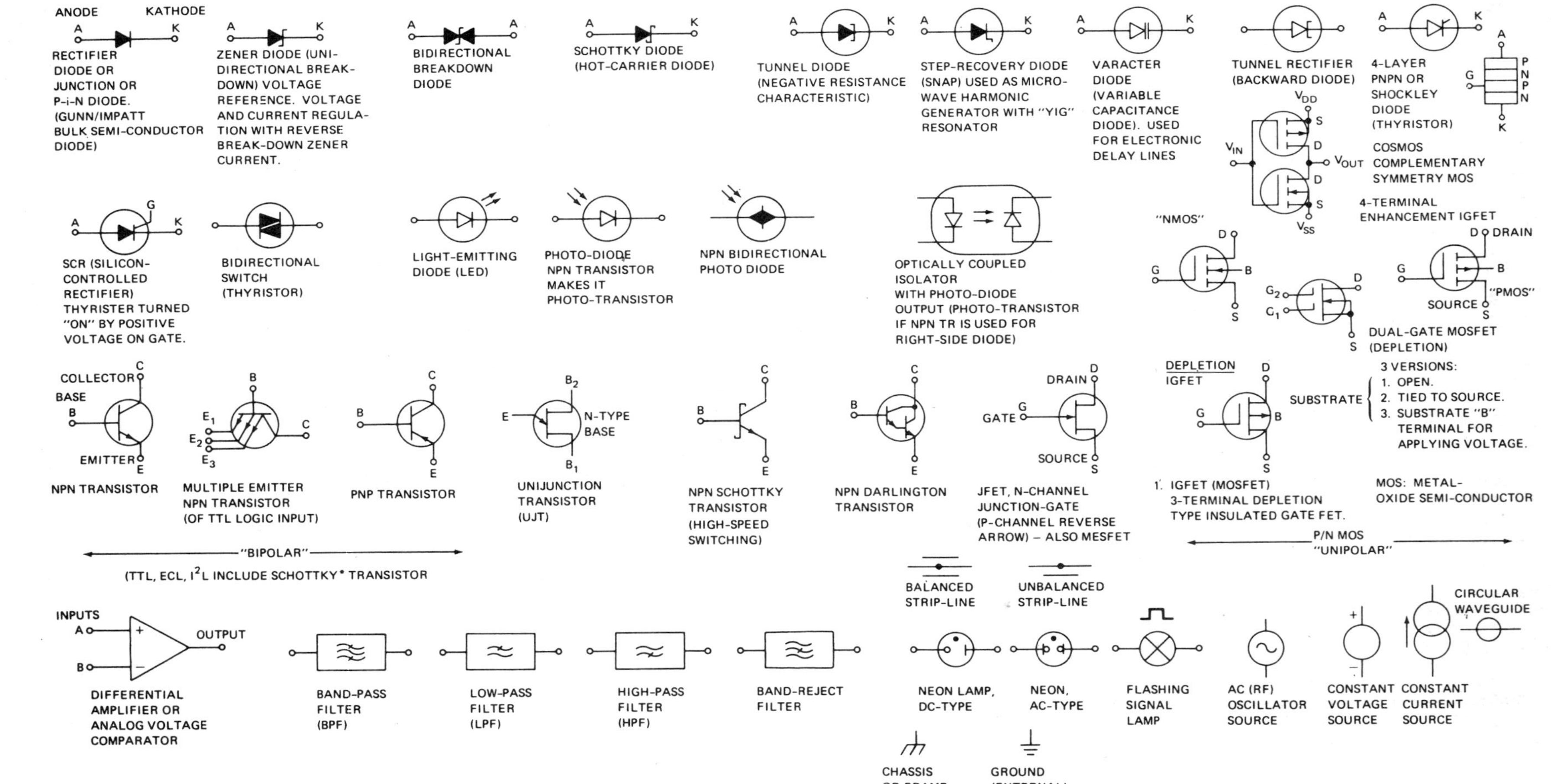

Fig. 10-21. Symbolic representation of diodes, transistors, etc.

silicon-controlled rectifier when the switching results in a state of very low impedance at the appropriate voltages. Total turn-on times range from about 0.1 μs for small-area devices (1 A, 400 V) to about 10 μs for large-area devices (400 A, 1,200 V). Gate-controlled switches turn off the load-current by reverse gate-current in 2 to 50 μs. For AC-power control applications, five-layer diode configurations are available to enable switching action in either polarity of applied voltage.

20. **Thin- and thick-film resistors and capacitors.** Thin-film resistors are processed by vacuum-evaporation, vapor-plating, and sputtering of materials like nichrome, tin oxide, tantalum-tantalum nitride, and cermet chromium-silicon monoxide. *Thick-film* resistors use palladium-silver and palladium-oxide-silver and glass, and processing is done by *silk-screen* techniques.

Thin-film dielectrics for capacitors are processed by vacuum-evaporation, vapor-plating, anodization of aluminum films, steam oxidation, and anodization of such materials as silicon monoxide, silicon dioxide, aluminum oxide, and tantalum oxide. For thick-films, titanium dioxide and glass mixtures, or simply barium-titanium-dioxide, are processed by *silk-screen*.

For conducting terminals and plates, the materials used generally are chromium-gold or copper, aluminum, nickel or ceramic, gold-glass and silver-glass. Processing techniques are vacuum-evaporation, electroless-plating, and silk-screen.

21. **Voltage-variable capacitors and varactors.** *Voltage-variable capacitors* are small-signal PN junctions of silicon or *gallium-arsenide* with special impurity profiles; their junction-capacitance is rendered variable by controlling the reverse bias. *Varactors* are high-power devices designed as *charge-storage* or *step-recovery* diodes, in which minority-carrier charge, injected during a short forward-bias pulse, can be largely recovered on current reversal, both to enhance capacitance-voltage nonlinearity and allow frequency multiplication. Varactors give output powers of 20 W at 1 GHz, 1 W at 5 GHz, and 50 MW at 20 GHz. (Step-recovery diodes or SRDs, are used for harmonic generation in frequency synthesizers–along with YIG tuner filters.)

22. **P-i-N diode.** The *pin diode* consists of heavily doped end-layers separated by a lightly doped, thick (10 to 100 μ) **central-layer**, which is practically **intrinsic** or pure silicon. The device makes a high-voltage rectifier with a low forward-drop at high currents due to conductivity-modulation of the intrinsic central-layer by the carriers injected from the thin end-layers. The *pin diode* makes a variable attenuator at microwave frequencies, because the frequency is too high for any rectification to take place, as a result of the large recovery-time of the central thick i-layer. At zero or reverse-bias, the i-layer introduces high resistance; the resistance reduces to as low as 1 ohm, when a forward-bias such as 50 mA is applied, to make it a microwave switch or a microwave amplitude-modulator. The TV-Plumbicon camera tube uses the P-i-N concept for charge-imaging purpose.

23. The symbolic representation of the semiconductior diodes and transistors is shown in the chart of Fig. 10-22.

24. ANALOG MULTIPLEXER.

The analog multiplexer enables the time-sharing of an A/D converter by several analog signal channels. The analog multiplexer operates with the aid of a sample-and-hold circuit to hold the analog voltage long enough for A/D conversion.

For an 8-channel multiplexer, a 1-to-8 decoder is required to switch the analog channels to the time-shared A/D converter.

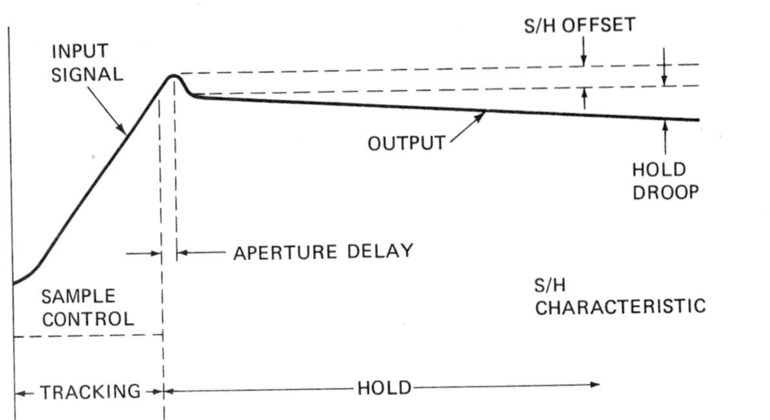

SAMPLE-AND-HOLD (S/H)

The S/H stores analog information and reduces the aperture time of an A/D converter. It is simply a voltage memory device using a high-quality storage capacitor. It is sometimes used as a *deglitcher* at the output of a D/A converter. It is also used in a data acquisition system as a *zero-order hold* or data recovery or *signal reconstruction filter*, when a train of analog samples are reconstructed into the original signal. It is then a low-pass filter actually, with a cut-off frequency slightly less than half the sampling frequency.

QUANTIZATION ERROR (OR NOISE)

When an analog signal is divided into a number of digital bits, a quantization error is inherent as a result of the division process. One part in 2^{10} is an output uncertainty in a 10-bit converter, and it is equivalent to $\pm\frac{1}{2}$ least-significant bit, the same as that for linearity. It is reduced by increasing the resolution of the converter.

USE OF A/D CONVERTERS IN DATA ACQUISITION

1. A central high-speed A/D converter with a regular microcomputer system is the obvious choice as part of a *multiplexed data acquisition system* using several transducer input measurement or process-monitoring analog signals and a sample-and-hold output to a high-speed successive approximation type A/D converter.
2. Alternatively, several remote A/D converters can be used in conjunction with a CMOS-multiplexed data acquisition system. At each remote site, one UART (universal asynchronous receiver/transmitter) will be used to control the A/D converter and the multiplexer. Two-wire UART serial-data outputs of several remote acquisition stations can be transmitted to a central computer-processing system.

ULTRA-FAST SAMPLE-AND-HOLD

The ultra-fast sample-and-hold operates open-loop with a 4-coil pulse transformer and a diode-bridge switch. The diodes are blocked by a bias voltage until a control command arrives and connects the bridge to an output buffer amplifier with a small input capacitor in the circuit. An input signal connected to the diode-bridge enables a connection to the buffer within an interval less than 30-nsec.

CHOPPER-STABILIZED AMPLIFIER

The chopper-stabilized amplifier is an operational amplifier with a special mod-demod circuit that reduced input offset voltage drift to an extremely low value.

HYSTERESIS AND OFF-SET ERRORS IN A/D CONVERTERS

When small variations in analog transition points of an A/D converter depend on the direction of approach, the error is called *hysteresis.* It is caused by the analog comparator used in the circuit of the A/D converter.

Off-set error is the error at analog zero for a data-converter operating in the bipolar mode.

A/D AND D/A CONVERTERS

The common successive approximation principle of analog-to-digital and digital-to-analog converters is illustrated in the following simplified diagram.

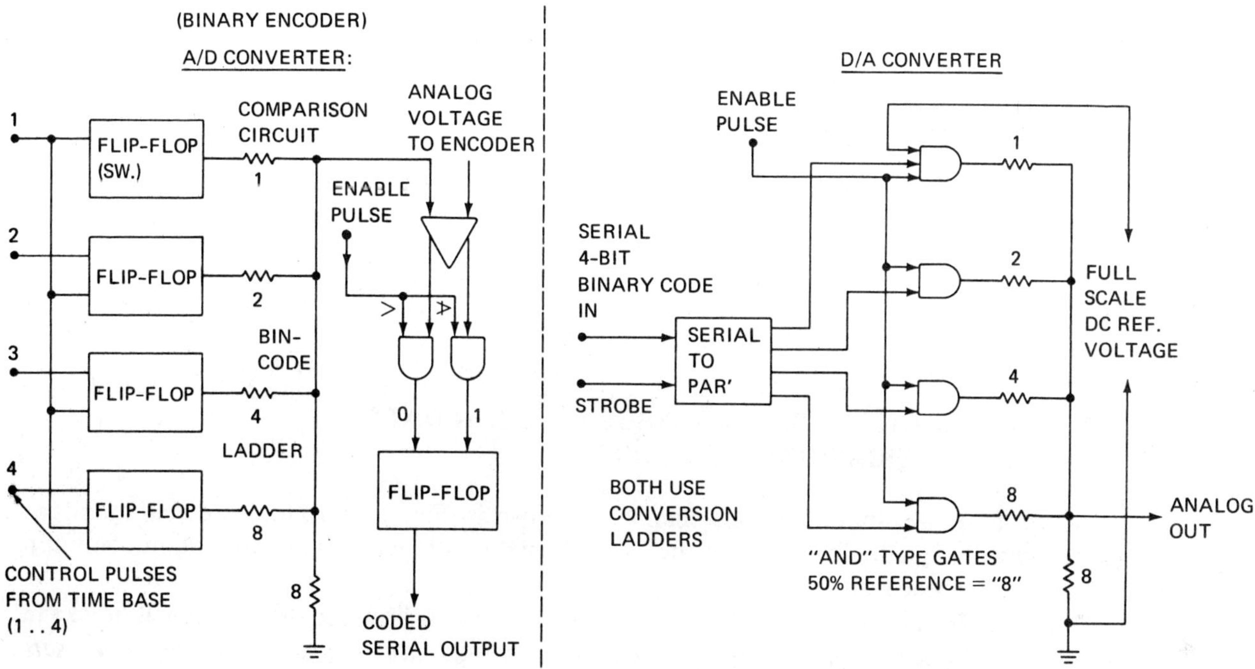

11
Applications of Microprocessors

11-1. APPLICATIONS OF MICROPROCESSORS IN DATA COMMUNICATIONS NETWORKS

A typical data communications channel is shown in Fig. 11-1 to indicate how microprocessors would gradually take over the several functions generally encountered in communications **Teleprocessing networks.**

To clarify the various functions, brief descriptions follow for the functional blocks involved in the data communications network; namely, *data terminals*, *modems* or *data sets*, *radio frequency/satellite/line communications channels*, *multiplexers* and *remote data concentrators*, *software* and *error-control devices*, *transmission control units* and *front-end processors*, and *fault isolation* and *backup functions*.

Data terminals. Data is typically entered from a remote data communications terminal, such as a teletype send-receive set (TTY), or an alphanumeric CRT keyboard/display, or a remote batch processing terminal, or a remote group center that consists of a real-time high-speed minicomputer system using disk and card reader/puncher and line printers. Most terminal message characters are encoded into bits (asynchronous low-speed, below 200 bauds/sec, base-band ON–OFF waveforms) and transmitted serially bit-by-bit into the transmitting modem, a device that signifies its modulation/demodulation functions. The modem takes a dc signal and converts into an AC-format using mostly PSK (phase-shift-keying) or sometimes FSK (frequency) and ASK (amplitude) or combinations thereof. The analog continuous signals thus modulated can be transmitted by voice-grade telephone lines or–after further frequency-division multiplex or time-division multiplex processing– by repeater furnished, high-speed, 500-meter cable-lengths of EMI-proof* fiber-optic cables or the present HF/Microwave/Satellite Links. The modem at the re-

*EMI: electromagnetic induction.

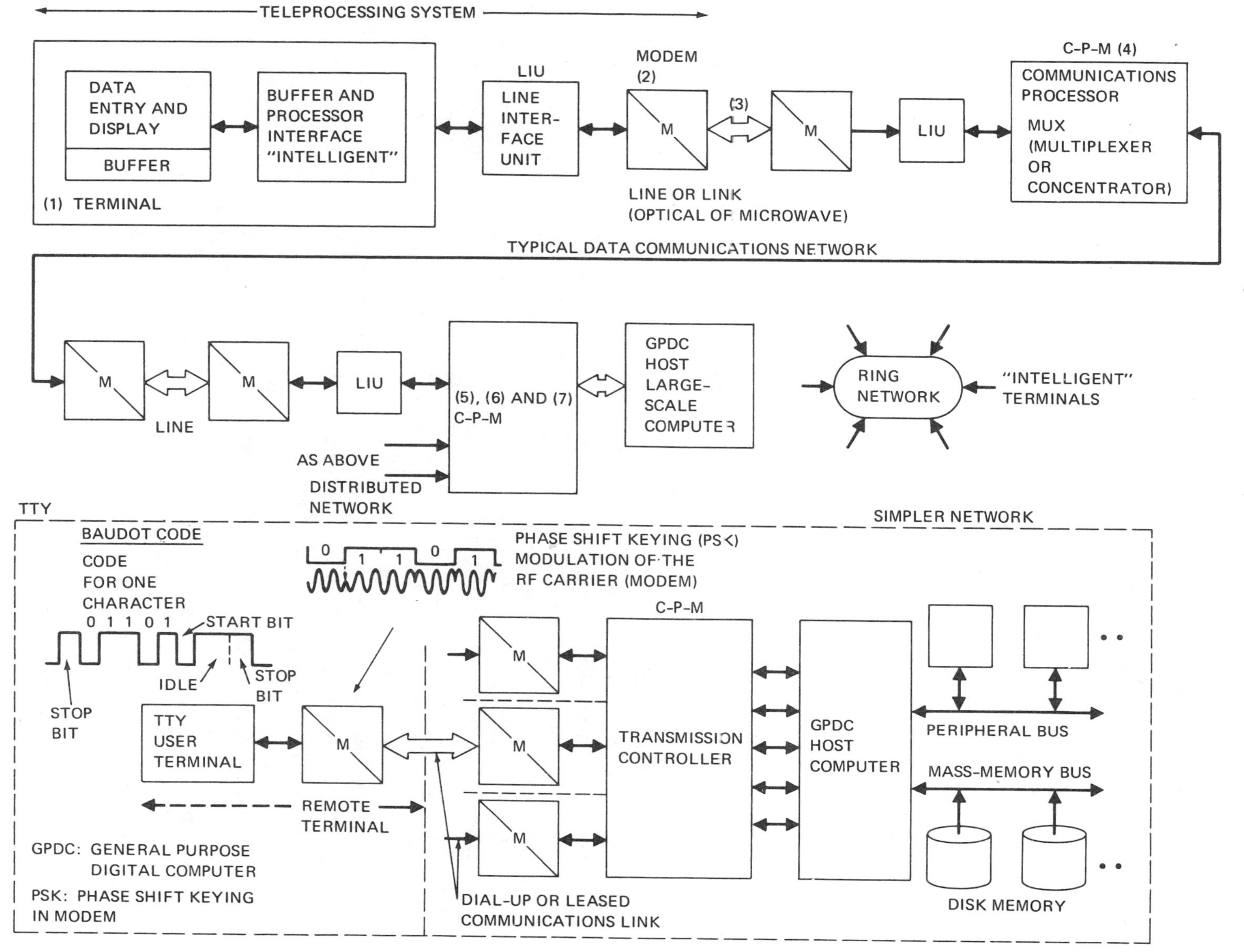

Fig. 11-1. Typical data communications channel. *(Courtesy of McGraw-Hill Publications, partial)*

ceiving terminal demodulates the analog signal back into the bit-stream for the computer interface. This could be a large-scale general-purpose digital computer.

The **source base-band signal modems** may have other features such as automatic equalization, provision for on-line "half-duplex" transmission (two-wire lines operating in either direction sequentially) or "full-duplex" transmission (four-wire lines operating in either direction simultaneously) and the requisite channel encoders/decoders in the case of the high-speed multiplexed transmissions.† In low-speed TTY terminal modems, the transmission includes some type of manual/automatic error detection and retransmission scheme. But in medium-speed (above 1,200 bauds/sec) synchronous data applications, the terminal includes a "buffer" to temporarily store a character or word, along with redundant bits, for parity or parity-and-correction check, in order to permit an automatic approach for the control of possible transmission errors in data bits. The receiving terminal uses the redundant bits for automatic error detection (or correction as well, if no feedback channel is available to give a positive acknowledgement ACK). If an error is detected, a negative acknowledgement (NACK) is returned to the sender to repeat the block-of-bits containing the error. This is, for example, mandatory in the IBM's binary synchronous communications (BSC) protocol or line-control discipline. Digital Equipment Corporation's digital data communications message protocol (DDCMP), and IBM's synchronous data link control (SDLC) of Systems Network Architecture (SNA) are furnished for full-duplex carrier facilities when either higher error rates or larger propagation delay of the COMSAT satellite links are involved. In fact, COMSAT is proposing CODEX "selective repeat method" for sending several blocks of data at a time via a special storage-and-shift-register device so that only one block-with-error out of several correct blocks could be repeated automatically to minimize overall delay; the system should include echo-suppressing devices too for satellite communications.

The microprocessor and its interface can function as a Line Interface Unit (LIU) to implement the above protocol; the procedure includes a cyclic redundancy-check for control of error, and to perform code conversion (5-bit Baudot Code plus parity bit to 8-bit ASCII) and subsequent data-formatting. The microprocessor can also perform modulation and demodulation by digital (LSI) CCD Fast-Fourier-Transform techniques, as a substitute to the present analog mod/demod methods, which necessarily use phase-locked oscillators and filters. So, along with a modem on a chip, the terminal is no longer a simple I/O device, but a complete remote "intelligent" terminal. The miniature hardware required for these devices could be merely a part of the TTY and CRT terminals. In addition, the microprocessor can perform such functions as line equalization, programmable speed-selector (9,600. . . 1,200. . . 150. . . 110 baud/sec from a bit-rate generator) and diagnostics, all at comparatively low cost in the range of hundreds of dollars only, instead of thousands as at present. The Line Interface Unit may have processing time left over, in which case, with added firmware, it could handle up to 16 voice-grade data lines, each 1,200 bauds/sec.

11-2. EIA STANDARD RS-232C, IEEE-488–1978 AND IEEE S-100 BUS INTERFACES

The EIA standard RS-232C Interface between computers and modems consists of the following signals and circuits "from" and "to" data communications equipment (DCE) at the terminals:

†A hybrid transformer device is required at either end to operate full-duplex on a two-wire system to allow the transmission of analog PSK signals from Modems.

Ground (as a basic reference)
Common Return
Transmitted Data (to)
Received Data (from)
Request to Send (to)
Clear to Send (from)
Data-Set Ready (from)
Data Terminal Ready (to)
Ring Indicator (from)
Received Line Signal Detector (from)
Signal Quality Detector (from)
Two Data-Rate Selectors (to data terminal equipment or DTE source, and from data communications equipment or DCE source)
Two transmitter signal element timings (to DTE source and from DCE source)
Receiver signal element timing (from)
Secondary Transmitted Data (to)
Secondary Received Data (from)
Secondary Request to Send (to)
Secondary Clear to Send (from)
Secondary Received Line Signal Detector (from).

The various circuits determine the "handshaking" needed to establish Interface connections. These *interface* or *line adapter* or *line termination units* are presently hardwired transmission control units of the class of IBM-270X controllers. In general, a *TTY* or a *CRT-display* makes the basic *terminal*. Line-sharing equipment such as *multiplexers* and *remote data concentrators* connect clusters of remote terminals to *data processing centers* by employing voice-grade or synchronous wide-band lines rather than a large number of asynchronous low-speed circuits. A voice-grade line (Series 3000) can carry the equivalent of 20 to 50 low-speed lines (Series 1000) in terms of bauds or bits/sec at low speed. So multiplexing is actually a cost-reduction technique.

Both *frequency division multiplex (FDM)* and *time division multiplex (TDM)* are generally used to raise bit rates to 9,600. Wideband FM/FDMA (*frequency division multiple access*) or TDMA microwave-link data rates go up to 55-K, 1.544-M, and 33-M/48-M bits/sec respectively. The last rate applies to digital color-television transmission via satellites.

PROTOCOLS AND OTHER STANDARDS IN DATA COMMUNICATIONS

RS-232-C: Interface standard for data terminal equipment (DTE) to data-circuit terminating equipment (DCE). RS stands for *recommended standard* of Electronic Industries Association (EIA)

RS-422: Electrical standard for interfacing balanced circuits

RS-423: Electrical standard for interfacing unbalanced circuits (such as coax cables)

RS-449 Mechanical standard for connector pin assignments

X3.28: Character-code control standards, American National Standards Institute (ANSI)

1748: Basic-mode control standard, International Standards Organization (ISO)

V.35: 48-K bit/sec data transmission standard (International Consultative Committee for Telegraphy and Telephony, CCITT)

X.21: General-purpose DTE-to-DTC standard for public networks (CCITT)

X.25: Interface standard for packet-switched service on public networks (CCITT)

SDLC: Synchronous data-link control (IBM Protocol)
SNA: Systems network architecture (IBM)
UART: Universal asynchronous receiver/transmitter
USRT: Universal synchronous receiver/transmitter
USART: Universal synchronous/asynchronous receiver/transmitter
NCP: Network control program (IBM)
NRZI: Non-return to zero inverted (mag tape)
NSP: Network services protocol (Digital Equipment Corporation, DEC)
HDLC: High-level data-link control
DLC: Data-link control
ASCII: American Standard Code for Information Interchange
BISYNC: Binary synchronous communication (International Business Machines, IBM)
EBCDIC: Extended binary-coded decimal interchange code (IBM)
DDCMP: Digital data-communications message protocol (DEC)
DDD: Direct distance dialing (AT&T service–American Telegraph & Telephone Company)
ADCCP: Advanced data-communications control procedure
BOP: Bit-oriented protocol
CCP: Character-controlled protocol (also character count protocol)
CRC: Cyclic redundancy check
ATDM: Asynchronous time-division multiplexing
FDMA: Frequency-division multiple access
TDMA: Time-division multiple access
LAP: Link-access procedure (X.25)
PAD: Packet assembly/disassembly facility (X.29 etc.)
ITU: International Telecommunications Union

IEEE-488-1978 Standard Digital Interface. The standard applies to interface systems used to interconnect programmable and nonprogrammable electronic measuring instrumentation and accessories in which (1) the data communication exchanged unambiguously is digital, (2) the number of devices interconnected by one continguous bus does not exceed 15, (3) the limited total transmission length of cables does not exceed 20 meters, and (4) the data rate across the interface on any signal line does not exceed 1 Mb/sec.

The standard enables the interconnection of equipment from various manufacturers into a single functional system without requiring any intermediate adapters. The data communications system may be asynchronous over a wide range of data rates, allowing remote control for programmability. The *handshake* digital-signals' interconnect-process effects the transfer of each data-byte across the interface by means of an interlocked (nonsimultaneous) sequence of status and control signals. A bidirectional bus used by any individual device such as a transmitter/receiver/controller at the interface allows two-way transmission of digital input/output data.

A *serial poll* sequence may be initiated when a transmit device requires some action by the controller, by transmitting the service request message. The controller in response obtains the status byte of all possible devices in sequence to ascertain which required service. A *parallel poll* function, on the other hand, enables the device to transmit, on the controller's demand, one bit of status information simultaneously with several other devices. The assignment of data line to a particular device, in response to a parallel poll, may be accomplished through interface messages. The Interface capabilities and bus structure are shown in Fig. 11-2. The Interface Functional Repertoire and Relevant Message paths:

Source handshake (SH)–1, 2, 4, 5
Acceptor handshake (AH)–1, 2, 4, 5
Talker or extender talker-transmit (T/TE)–1, 2, 3, 4, 5
Listener or extender listener-receive (L/LE)–1, 2, 3, 4, 5
Device trigger (DT)–1, 2, 4, 5
Service request (SR)–1, 2, 4, 5
Remote local (RL)–1, 2, 4, 5
Parallel poll (PP)–1, 2, 4, 5
Device clear (DC)–1, 2, 4, 5
Controller (C)–1, 2, 4, 5, 6

Messages sent between a device function and an interface function are called local messages. Messages sent via the interface between the interface functions of different devices

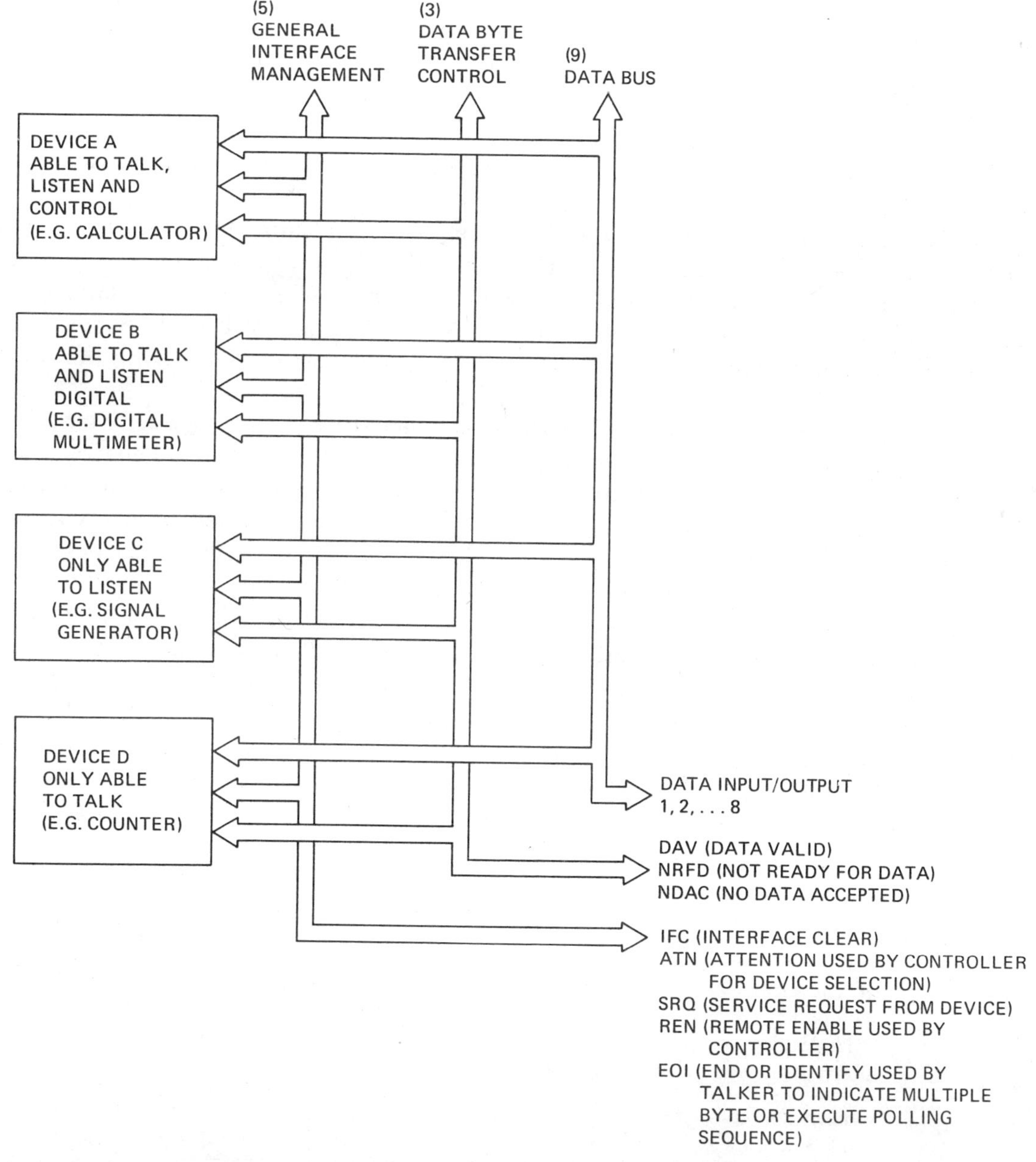

Fig. 11-2. IEEE-488–1978. Interface capabilities and bus structure. (*Courtesy of IEEE*)

are called remote messages. Message coding is the process of translating remote messages to or from interface signal values of highs (true) and lows (false) of digital signals.

Source handshake function provides a device with the capability to guarantee the proper transfer of multiline messages. An interlocked handshake sequence between the source handshake function and one or more *acceptor handshake* functions guarantees *asynchronous* transfer of each multiline message. The source handshake function controls the initiation and termination of a multiline byte. This function uses DAV (data valid), RFD (ready for data), and DAC (data accepted) messages to effect each message byte transfer.

The handshake functions are generally implemented according to *State Diagrams* to specify the set of messages and states required to effect transition from one active state to another. Each state that an interface function can assume is represented graphically by a circle, and a four-letter upper-case mnemonic, always ending in S, is used within the circle to identify the state. All permissible transitions between states of an interface function are represented graphically by arrows between the various states or circles. Each transition (from one state to the other) is qualified by an expression whose value is either true or false. The interface function remains in its current state if all expressions which qualify transitions to other states are false. The interface function becomes effective if, and only if, one of these permissible transitions between states becomes true at any time or after any specified time interval. State linkages are used in conjunction with the logical operators AND/OR/NOT.

Mechanical specifications for the interface giving the connector type, number of contacts, dimensions, etc., are included. Basic environmental performance relative to temperature and humidity criteria should follow in accordance with the tests of MIL-STD-202E. (For the exact details of Interface, refer to IEEE Standard Digital Interface for Programmable Instrumentation, IEEE Std 488-1978, Revision of ANSI/IEEE Std 488-1975.)

Multiprocessing Systems and IEEE S-100 Bus. The IEEE Microprocessor Standards Committee has developed and published a standard specification for S-100 bus interface devices, specially oriented toward not only single processor systems but also large multiprocessor systems. A majority of single processor systems are not oriented to a standard bus, since manufacturers are inclined to a vertically-integrated product line to a proprietary bus standard of their own, without "mix and match" products from a plethora of manufacturers. A total of 16 DMA devices are rendered feasible with a 4-bus line, dynamically allocated encoded-arbitration-priorities technique that provides a fast priority resolution less than 100 nsec—by using devices of any level of intelligence, including programmable or parallel general-purpose processors/controllers. The compatibility of 8/16-bit multimicroprocessor environment during the 1980s is a highly attractive implementation. The interconnection of parallel/concurrent microprocessor systems sharing a common memory, as shown in Fig. 11-3, is a highly commendable proposition for the 1980s.

Bus Capabilities	Small Systems	Large Systems
Memory addressing	16-bit	24-bit
I/O addressing	8-bit	16-bit
Data paths	8/16-bit	8/16-bit
DMA devices	1 device	16 devices
Interrupts	to 10 levels	to 10 levels
Memory address space		16-M bytes
No. I/O devices		64-K devices

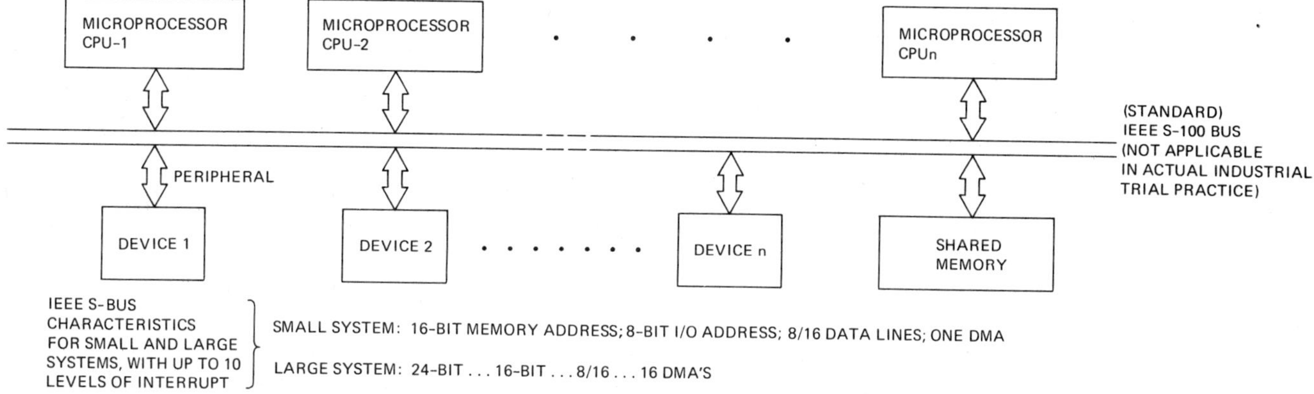

MULTIPROCESSING ON THE S-100 BUS: TOTAL SYSTEM THROUGHPUT WITH SHARED MEMORY HAS BEEN DETERMINED AS A FUNCTION OF THE NUMBER OF PROCESSORS, THE THROUGHPUT OF EACH PROCESSOR, AND THE AMOUNT OF BUS INTERFERENCE WITH RESPECT TO CONTENTION FOR THE COMMON S-BUS IN THE WORST CASE OF BUS SATURATION, ON AN AVERAGE THROUGHPUT IS LIMITED AT ABOUT 6 CPU CHIPS AT 10 TIMES THE THROUGHPUT OF A SINGLE MICROPROSSOR. (LATEST SCALED-DOWN VLSI MICROPROCESSORS IN GENERAL, FURNISH 10 TIMES THE FORMER THROUGHPUT OF FORMER MICROPROCESSORS; THUS, MULTIPROCESSORS OF THE ABOVE FORMAT ARE ALREADY OBSOLETE FOR THE ABOVE PERFORMANCE. HOWEVER LATEST GENERATION OF INTEL-8086/ZILOG-8000/MC-6800 IN SUCH MULTIPROCESSOR CONFIGURATIONS WILL APPROACH THE PERFORMANCE OBJECTIVES OF MODERN ADVANCED MINI-AND MEDIUM-SCALE COMPUTERS WITHOUT ANY PROBLEM IN SPECIAL DATA COMMUNICATION NETWORKS.

A MULTIPROCESSOR DISTRIBUTED PROCESSING SYSTEM

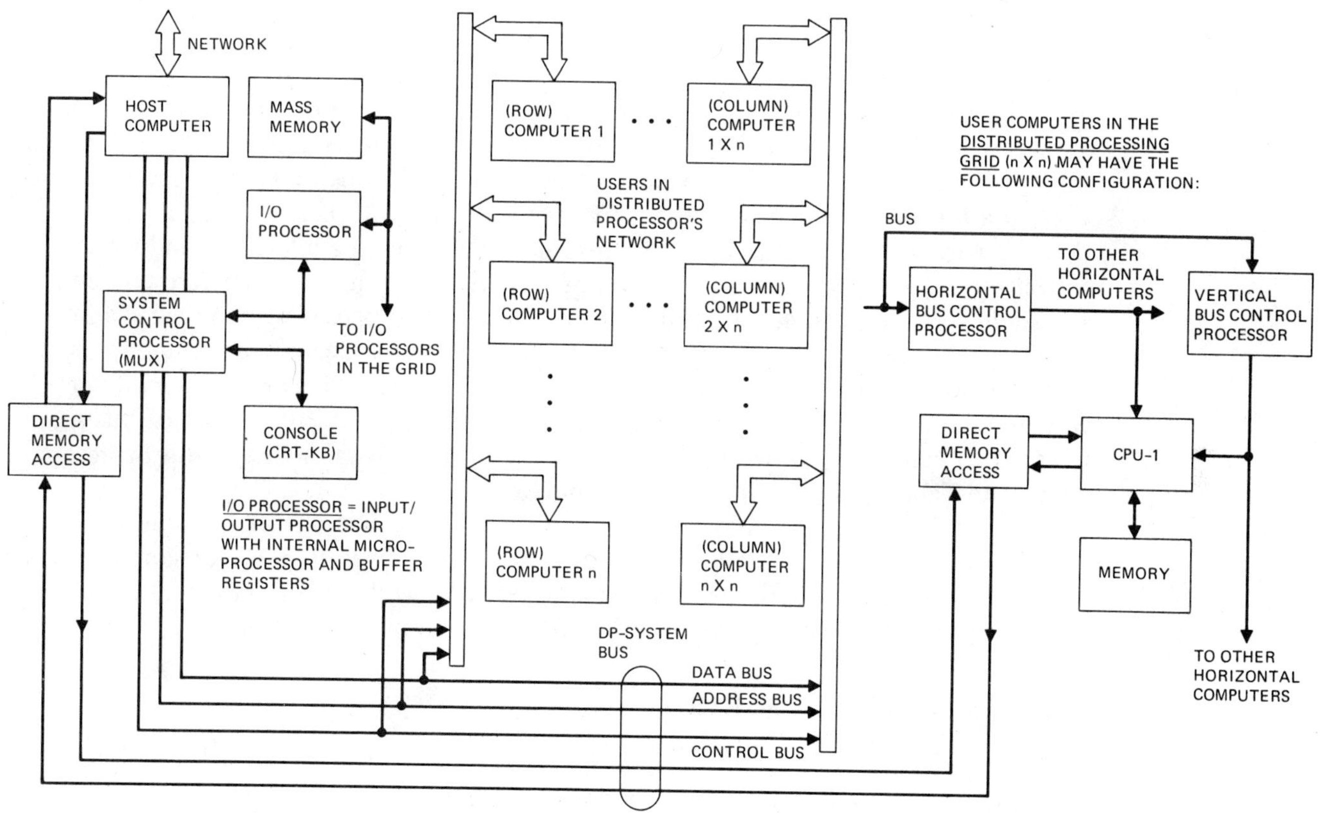

Fig. 11-3. Interconnection of parallel/concurrent microprocessor systems sharing a common memory.

The flexibility of modularity facilitates the systems engineer to add devices with dedicated and general-purpose functions. The bandwidth of the common bus S-100 limits the total system-throughput. In the worst case, for bus saturation it can be shown that the throughput is limited at about six processors, whereas, on an average, the system throughput for several processors is approximately 10 times that of a single processor.

With one option, access to the local memory of a processor may be controlled by the local processor to load the memory with programs and data, and then *dump* the results back to a common system memory such as magnetic tape. This approach degrades system throughput.

With a second option, the local memory may be configured as a write-through high-speed *cache* memory. All memory would be homogeneously common to all the processors, and any program could be located anywhere in the memory. This approach requires a dedicated local processor for the management of high-speed access to the cache memory—thus increasing the complexity of the system. (See Section 5-11.)

With a third expedient approach, the local memory is configured as a dual-port unit. It may accept memory requests from its local processor without requiring a system bus access. From the system bus, it appears as a single-port memory to allow a system bus access for the local processor. Then all memory is accessible to all processors, and the operating system is rendered complex. Heuristics may be mandatory for trade-offs between hardware and software.

The proposed S-100 Bus Standard was published in July 1979. A modified standard specification was subsequently issued to upgrade the specification for the use of the new 16-bit microprocessors. (These standards are **subject to revision** by IEEE).

The proposed standards for exchange of digital data among the devices in the microprocessor interface systems, using 100-line parallel backplane (S-100 Bus), are herein covered in brief. The number of devices in a system is finalized to 22 or less. The total transmission path length is 25 in. or less in order to minimize the total transmission-line propagation delays at a maximum data rate of 6 MHz or less. Flow of the information among the devices is managed by specifying one device, which generates interface messages in a bus cycle, as a *bus master*; any second device will then act as an addressed *bus slave*, as part of the bus cycle. Slave intercapability is permissible either individually or collectively. Device signals acting as bus masters initiate bus cycle; they are termed *type M signals* with address, status, and control buses. Bus masters are subdivided into one permanent bus master and 16 temporary bus masters in a single system. A temporary bus master is not subject to a DMA (direct memory access) cycle; this bus master will have no vested DMA operation. A bus slave will examine and generate the subset of bus signals required to communicate with bus masters. Table 11-1 shows the S-100 Bus Structure in detail, and Table 11-2 gives the S-100 bus pin list.

Universal interface connects general-purpose interface bus (GPIB) with all microprocessor systems using IEEE-696(S-100) Bus. That is, universal interface complies with IEEE-488 and IEEE-S-100 Bus Standards. Presently, Dylan Corporation of San Diego, CA, is providing this universal interface for its microcomputer systems.

11-3. POLLING PROCEDURES

Polling procedures control Terminal access to the computer Network in most private line systems. The line-control program queries the terminals to solicit messages in a prescribed cyclic sequence according to an internal subroutine of the Terminal addresses. Access by polling is not controlled by the user but by the communications control software. In dial-up applications, selective polling to various terminals is controlled from the control center. Dial-up time-sharing systems and facsimile terminals gain access on a first-come, first-served basis, as a *contention* procedure. In centralized applications involving dial-network, the Bell Telephone Systems **Wide Area Telecommunications Service (WATS)** is a means for reducing cost of inward and outward traffic. Computer programs evaluate and optimize services to the Terminals and the Data Processing Centers; **Multiplexers** and **Concentrators** are used only if lower net costs result as compared to an optimally configured message-switched network based on multidrop lines.

TABLE 11-1. Proposed S-100 Bus Structure for Data Bus and Address Bus, and mnemonic software information for Status Bus, Control Output Bus, Control Input Bus, DMA Control Bus, and Utility Bus. (© *IEEE Computer, July 1979*)

1. Data Bus	2. Address Bus	3. Status Bus	4. Control Output Bus
16 signal output lines: DO_7-DO_0 (MSB-LSB)[a] Input: DI_{17}-DI_{10} For 16-bit data transfers DI bus and DO bus are ganged together. Two signal control lines: sXTRQ: sixteen request SIXTN: sixteen acknowledge Both true Low. 16-bit data: DI_{17}-DO_0. a: MSB (Most significant bit; LSB (Least ")	16- or 24-bit parallel signal lines to select address or 256 I/O devices A_7–A_0 during current bus cycle. 24 address bits A_{23}–A_0 for extended address capability. Bus masters assert at least 16 bits A_{15}–A_0 for 1–64K memory locations. Extended I/O device address bus A_{15}–A_0 for 1–64K devices.	8 status bus lines to identify bus cycle in progress. Signals generated by current bus master (s: status). 1. sMEMR: memory read 2. sMI: opcode fetch 3. sINP: input 4. sOUT: output 5. sWO*: write cycle 6. sINTA: interrupt acknowledge 7. sHLTA: halt acknowledge 8. sXTRQ: 16-bit data transfer request sMemory Write: (-sOUT) . sWO*	5 control output bus lines: 1. pSYNC: start of new bus cycle 2. pSTVAL* stable address and status sampled from bus in current cycle 3. pDBIN: read strobe gates data from addressed slave to data bus 4. pWR*: write strobe writes data from data bus to addressed slave 5. pHLDA: hold acknowledge to priority temporary master that bus is free of permanent master
5. Control Input Bus	**6. DMA Control Bus**	**7. Vectored Interrupt Bus**	**8. Utility Bus**
6 control input bus lines: 1. RDY: synchronize bus masters to slave speed (open collector line) 2. XRDY: stop and single-step bus master (used by front panel devices) 3. INT*: interrupt line to request service from permanent bus master. Group interrupt with vectored interrupt request bus. INT* masked off by bus master via software. 4. NMI*: nonmaskable INT. 5. HOLD*: Hold request line (open collector line) 6. SIXTN*: 16-bit acknowledge line as response to status signal request sXTRQ*	8 lines of DMA control bus along with HOLD* and pHLDA. 4 lines arbitrate among simultaneous requests for bus control by temporary masters; (encoded priority is asserted) 1. DMA0* 2. DMAl* 3. DMA2* 4. DMA3* 4. signals on bus to disable line drivers of permanent bus master. 5. ADSB: address disable 6. DODSB*: data out disable. 7. SDSB*: status disable 8. CDSB*: control output disable.	8 lines of vectored interrupt bus along with INT* to arbitrate among 8 levels of INT V_{17}–V_{10}* (request priorities). V_{10}*: highest priority INT. Vectored interrupt lines implemented as levels: held active until service is received. Interrupt request priorities are implemented as inputs to a bus slave that masks and gives priorities to the requests, asserts interrupt request to the permanent bus master, and responds to interrupt acknowledge bus cycle with appropriate vectoring data. (INT: interrupt)	20 signal lines. 9 lines: two 8-volt lines, one 16-volts, one -16 volts, five Ground lines. 1 line: system clock ϕ, master clock generator signal for the use of bus cycles only. 1 line: clock, 2 MHz. Timing for counters, timers, and baud rate generator. 12. RESET* to reset all bus masters (open collector line). 13. SLAVE CLR*: to reset all bus slaves (open collector line). 14. POC*: power on clear power on; asserts 12 and 13. Minimum active period 10 msec. 15. PHANTOM* for overlaying bus slaves at a common address location. 16. ERROR*: for parity, write to protected memory. 17. PWRFAIL*: power failure; restored when POC* is true. MWRT: memory write strobe: pWR. (-sOUT) 18,19,20: optional. NDEF (not to be defined).

[a] Refer to S-100 Bus, List of Pins, Table 11-2. (These standards are subject to revision by IEEE.)

TABLE 11-2 Proposed S-100 Bus Pin List (1 to 54). (Subject to revision).

Pin No.	Signal and Type	Active Level		Description
1	+8 VOLTS (B)			Instantaneous minimum greater than 7 volts, instantaneous maximum less than 25 volts, average maximum less than 11 volts.
2	+16 VOLTS (B)			Instantaneous minimum greater than 14.5 volts, instantaneous maximum less than 35 volts, average maximum less than 21.5 volts.
3	XRDY (S)	H		One of two ready inputs to the current bus master. The bus is ready when both these ready inputs are true. See pin 72.
4	VI0*(S)	L	O.C.	Vectored interrupt line 0.
5	VI1*(S)	L	O.C.	Vectored interrupt line 1.
6	VI2*(S)	L	O.C.	Vectored interrupt line 2.
7	VI3*(S)	L	O.C.	Vectored interrupt line 3.
8	VI4*(S)	L	O.C.	Vectored interrupt line 4.
9	VI5*(S)	L	O.C.	Vectored interrupt line 5.
10	VI6*(S)	L	O.C.	Vectored interrupt line 6.
11	VI7*(S)	L	O.C.	Vectored interrupt line 7.
12	NMI*(S)	L	O.C.	Nonmaskable interrupt.
13	PWRFAIL*(B)	L		Power fail bus signal.
14	DMA3* (M)	L	O.C.	Temporary master priority bit 3.
15	A18 (M)	H		Extended address bit 18.
16	A16 (M)	H		Extended address bit 16.
17	A17 (M)	H		Extended address bit 17.
18	SDSB* (M)	L	O.C.	The control signal to disable the 8 status signals.
19	CDSB* (M)	L	O.C.	The control signal to disable the 5 control output signals.
20	GND (B)			Common with pin 100.
21	NDEF			Not to be defined. Manufacturer must specify any use in detail.
22	ADSB* (M)	L	O.C.	The control signal to disable the 16 address signals.
23	DODSB* (M)	L	O.C.	The control signal to disable the 8 data output signals.
24	ϕ (B)	H		The master timing signal for the bus.
25	pSTVAL*(M)	L		Status valid strobe.
26	pHLDA (M)	H		A control signal used in conjunction with HOLD* to coordinate bus master transfer operations.
27	RFU			Reserved for future use.
28	RFU			Reserved for future use.
29	A5 (M)	H		Address bit 5.
30	A4 (M)	H		Address bit 4.
31	A3 (M)	H		Address bit 3.
32	A15 (M)	H		Address bit 15 (most significant for non-extended addressing.)
33	A12 (M)	H		Address bit 12.
34	A9 (M)	H		Address bit 9.
35	DO1 (M)/DATA1 (M/S)	H		Data out bit 1, bidirectional data bit 1.
36	DO0 (M)/DATA0 (M/S)	H		Data out bit 0, bidirectional data bit 0.
37	A10 (M)	H		Address bit 10.
38	DO4 (M)/DATA4 (M/S)	H		Data out bit 4, bidirectional data bit 4.
39	DO5 (M)/DATA5 (M/S)	H		Data out bit 5, bidirectional data bit 5.
40	DO6 (M)/DATA6 (M/S)	H		Data out bit 6, bidirectional data bit 6.
41	DI2 (S)/DATA10 (M/S)	H		Data in bit 2, bidirectional data bit 10.
42	DI3 (S)/DATA11 (M/S)	H		Data in bit 3, bidirectional data bit 11.
43	DI7 (S)/DATA15 (M/S)	H		Data in bit 7, bidirectional data bit 15.
44	sM1 (M)	H		The status signal which indicates that the current cycle is an op-code fetch.
45	sOUT (M)	H		The status signal identifying the data transfer bus cycle to an output device.
46	sINP (M)	H		The status signal identifying the data transfer bus cycle from an input device.
47	sMEMR (M)	H		The status signal identifying bus cycles which transfer data from memory to a bus master, which are not interrupt acknowledge instruction fetch cycle(s).
48	sHLTA (M)	H		The status signal which acknowledges that a HLT instruction has been executed.
49	CLOCK(B)			2 MHz (0.5%) 40-60% duty cycle. Not required to be synchronous with any other bus signal.
50	GND (B)			Common with pin 100.
51	+8 VOLTS (B)			Common with pin 1.
52	−16 VOLTS (B)			Instantaneous maximum less than −14.5 volts, instantaneous minimum greater than −35 volts, average minimum greater than −21.5 volts.
53	GND (B)			Common with pin 100.
54	SLAVE CLR* (B)	L	O.C.	A reset signal to reset bus slaves. Must be active with POC* and may also be generated by external means.

TABLE 11-3 (cont.)

Pin No.	Signal and Type	Active Level		Description
55	DMAO* (M)	L	O.C.	Temporary master priority bit 0.
56	DMA1* (M)	L	O.C.	Temporary master priority bit 1.
57	DMA2* (M)	L	O.C.	Temporary master priority bit 2.
58	sXTRQ* (M)	L		The status signal which requests 16-bit slaves to assert SIXTN*.
59	A19 (M)	H		Extended address bit 19.
60	SIXTN* (S)	L	O.C.	The signal generated by 16-bit slaves in response to the 16-bit request signal sXTRQ*.
61	A20 (M)	H		Extended address bit 20.
62	A21 (M)	H		Extended address bit 21.
63	A22 (M)	H		Extended address bit 22.
64	A23 (M)	H		Extended address bit 23.
65	NDEF	•		Not to be defined signal.
66	NDEF			Not to be defined signal.
67	PHANTOM* (M/S)	L	O.C.	A bus signal which disables normal slave devices and enables phantom slaves—primarily used for bootstrapping systems without hardware front panels.
68	MWRT (B)	H		pWR·—sOUT (logic equation). This signal must follow pWR* by not more than 30 ns.
69	RFU			Reserved for future use.
70	GND (B)			Common with pin 100.
71	RFU			Reserved for future use.
72	RDY (S)	H	O.C.	See comments for pin 3.
73	INT* (S)	L	O.C.	The primary interrupt request bus signal.
74	HOLD* (M)	L	O.C.	The control signal used in conjunction with pHLDA to coordinate bus master transfer operations.
75	RESET*(B)	L	O.C.	The reset signal to reset bus master devices. This signal must be active with POC* and may also be generated by external means.
76	pSYNC (M)	H		The control signal identifying BS_1.
77	pWR* (M)	L		The control signal signifying the presence of valid data on DO bus or data bus.
78	pDBIN (M)	H		The control signal that requests data on the DI bus or data bus from the currently addressed slave.
79	A0 (M)	H		Address bit 0 (least significant).
80	A1 (M)	H		Address bit 1.
81	A2 (M)	H		Address bit 2.
82	A6 (M)	H		Address bit 6.
83	A7 (M)	H		Address bit 7.
84	A8 (M)	H		Address bit 8.
85	A13 (M)	H		Address bit 13.
86	A14 (M)	H		Address bit 14.
87	A11 (M)	H		Address bit 11.
88	DO2 (M)/DATA2 (M/S)	H		Data out bit 2, bidirectional data bit 2.
89	DO3 (M)/DATA3 (M/S)	H		Data out bit 3, bidirectional data bit 3.
90	DO7 (M)/DATA7 (M/S)	H		Data out bit 7, bidirectional data bit 7.
91	DI4 (S)/DATA12 (M/S)	H		Data in bit 4 and bidirectional data bit 12.
92	DI5 (S)/DATA13 (M/S)	H		Data in bit 5 and bidirectional data bit 13.
93	DI6 (S)/DATA14 (M/S)	H		Data in bit 6 and bidirectional data bit 14.
94	DI1 (S)/DATA9 (M/S)	H		Data in bit 1 and bidirectional data bit 9.
95	DI0 (S)/DATA8 (M/S)	H		Data in bit 0 (least significant for 8-bit data) and bidirectional data bit 8.
96	sINTA (M)	H		The status signal identifying the bus input cycle(s) that may follow an accepted interrupt request presented on INT*.
97	sWO* (M)	L		The status signal identifying a bus cycle which transfers data from a bus master to a slave.
98	ERROR* (S)	L	O.C.	The bus status signal signifying an error condition during present bus cycle.
99	POC* (B)	L		The power-on clear signal for all bus devices; when this signal goes low, it must stay low for at least 10 ms.
100	GND (B)			System ground.

In the communications network system shown in Figure 11-1, the present high-end minicomputer is cost-effective to improvise all the functions of a communications processor. Sould it reach saturation, however, the low-speed functions can be transferred to a microprocessor serving as a preprocessor. It is not too optimistic to visualize that with regard to system-architecture, a few microprocessor chips will, in the near future, take over the functions of a "communications processor" of this status to further reduce the cost at the throughput and efficiency of the high-speed minicomputer. This is the so-called **pipeline architecture**, which refers to the principle of parallel compacting of CPU operations in time-domain, so that several distinct tasks–for example, the "instruction fetch" and "arithmetic computation"–proceed simultaneously. It is for this reason that, in the case of the new microprocessor technology, knowledge of both system architecture and programming concepts are equally important. Incidentally, high-speed pipeline CPU arrangement of logic elements, which compute algebraic, trigonometric, and exponential functions by way of an array, accomplishes real-time processing of sensor-data if an adequate programming facility is furnished.

CONTENTION QUEUING AND POLLING IN DATA COMMUNICATIONS. In designing data communication networks, the primary planning steps should first involve the determination of the constants of the application environment, such as: (1) number and location of CRT time-sharing terminals, local and remote, (2) patterns of information flow, (3) types and volume of transaction, (4) priority of processing information, (5) acceptable bit or block error-rate, (6) reliability consideration, and (7) potential ultimate capacity of data flow. Then the specific characteristics of the network variables should be considered for the desired options and cost-effectiveness. The network variables come under the category of: (1) centralized or distributed processing, (2) dial-up/leased-line and combinations thereof, (3) routing of data lines from several types of terminals and their transmission speed, (4) locations of the terminals and their control procedures, and (5) types of software and error-control procedure. Due consideration must be given for trade-offs between various conflicting factors in constants and variables.

In leased-line networks using frequency division multiplexing (FDM), and in high-speed synchronous time-division multiplexing (STDM) and point-to-point links, the nature of line control is predetermined since a dedicated line is available to the CPU. But, in cases involving multipoint lines, switched lines, *concentrators*, and multiprocessor environment, exclusive line control is provided to dial-up line ports on the basis of emitter *contention-queuing* or *polling*. In the simple contention-queuing model of a serial-sequence of network terminals to a central or host CPU, congestion and response times become excessive with a large number of network terminals. Contention procedure is commonly used in switched networks when user requests for access are random and unpredictable, but it is unacceptable on a line if the throughput requirements exceed one-third of the maximum transmission capacity. Different classes of user terminals and strict priorities are not desirable in contention-queuing.

Contention. The high-capacity channel may be shared in a free-for-all procedure, if network terminals are permitted to send short bursts of data at a time on a random basis. The contention line control signals lead the burst of data as (1) a synchronization pattern for recovering clock timing, (2) start data-bit, and (3) error-detecting code. With unlimited number of network terminals, congestion of data may result in interference of inter-terminal TDM data. Excessive delay is the other alternative if retransmission is used as a solution to interference.

Polling with extra hardware/software is more desirable than contention-queuing if a tight control of line usage and different levels of message priority are essential for transmission efficiency. Then the polling procedure may be designed to query the message-priority terminal more often by program control. In general, a combination of polling (for heavily loaded lines) and contention (for lightly loaded lines) is a preferred procedure, since mathematical models of polling strategies are available for the design of software involved.

11-4. LINE MONITOR

In a communications network, a Line Monitor plays an important role by trapping and displaying data and control signals, as an aid to isolating faults on, for example, RS-232C contol leads. The readouts are converted to appropriate code and displayed by LED's and alphanumeric CRT displays. The line monitor is usually built around serial buffer memories that store the data selected for inspection. Data Line Monitors from Digi-Log Systems and Spectron Corp. are examples. Figure 11-4, a block diagram of a typical Line Monitor, clarifies the functions of this unit; a microcomputer could be used for its design to minimize hardware. Special Line Monitors measure signal phase-jitter, noise, harmonic-distortion, delay-distortion, amplitude and threshold-level, drop-out of pulses, and so on.

11-5. SOME COMMUNICATIONS NETWORKS IN OPERATION

1. ARPA (Advanced Research Projects Agency): 35 to 40 computers.
2. MERIT: three large-scale university computers of IBM and CDC.
3. TUCC: several IBM host university computing centers.
4. DCS: Distributed Computing System, connecting mini- and medium-size computers.
5. IBM Network/440: IBM locations, universities.
6. CYBERNET: CDC's network of about 40 computers or nodes with voice-grade lines and private lines operating at 40.8-K bit/sec.
7. OCTOPUS: CDC, using a 12-M bits/sec digital loop.
8. IBM TSS: interconnected to switched dial-up voice-grade lines.
9. INFONET: Computer Sciences Corporation's commercial network handling remote batch and job-entry applications.
10. MARK III: General Electric Company's information services commercial network.
11. TYMNET: TymShare's commercial Xerox host computer network, using packet-switched, store-and-forward concept.

With the advent of microcomputer intelligent terminals, the preceding networks are ex-

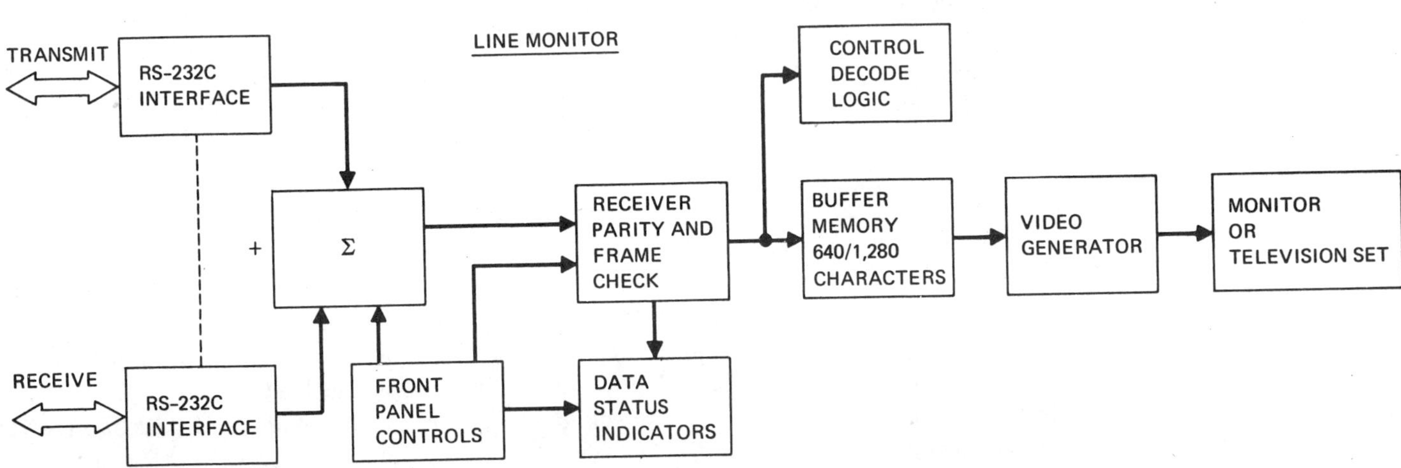

Fig. 11-4. Line monitor for an interface. (*Courtesy of McGraw-Hill, Basics of Data Communication*)

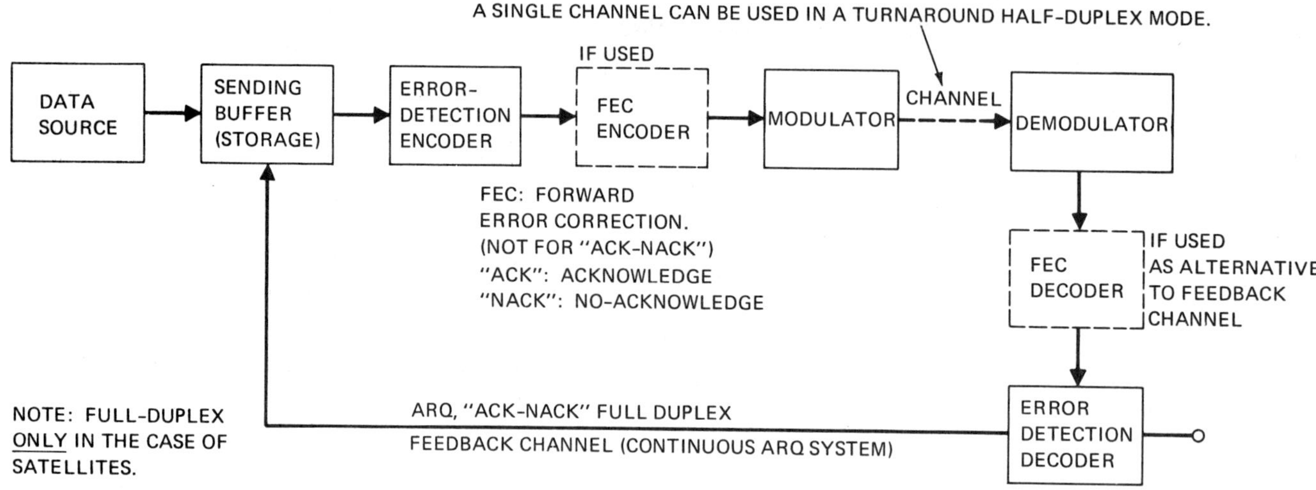

Fig. 11-5. Ack-nack "store-and-forward" transmission. (© *IEEE Proceedings, June 1973*)

pected to grow at an enormous rate. During the next 10 years, the communications market is expected to grow a hundredfold in dollar volume in order to minimize the pressure on the postal delivery of communications.

11-6. ACK-NACK STORE-AND-FORWARD TRANSMISSION OF DATA

"Store-and-forward" is the most common data communications technique. The alternative Forward Error Correction, which includes error correction at the receiving end in place of the feedback channel, is less common. In the first case, the feedback channel allows Ack-Nack procedure. Figure 11-5 illustrates this type of data-transmission. *Store-and-forward technique* is generally accomplished in *packet-switching network architecture*. In SNA (system network architecture of IBM) and DECNET (of Digital Equipment Corporation), the actual management and control of the communications links and nodes in the networks are transparent to the network user by appropriate network control software.

Most networks around the world are presently implementing intelligent networks based on packet-switching to accomplish the store-and-forward feature. In the United States *value added carriers* must develop standardized software-dependent interfaces to the existing networks. X-25 protocol is designed to specify all interface standards for interfacing terminals and computers to public data networks operating in packet-switching mode. The high-speed, multiplexed (TDM) communications network employs "concentrators" as host minicomputers for customer microcomputers and local data microcontroller terminal ports working at several speeds. The *concentrators* are also called "city collection centers" (CCC) communicating with other concentrators mostly in megabit-rate time-division multiplex. They are presently suitable for domestic TDMA satellites.

The high-speed minicomputer concentrators accept the messages of the user terminals and mini or microcomputer in real-time, and break them down into fixed-length segments called *packets*. These packets are transmitted through the network on a *store-and-forward* basis. As the packets are individually transmitted along the best available path to their destination (sink), they are error-checked each time another wideband path is involved. The concentrators (used in the Advanced Research Projects Agency, ARPA) dynamically reroute packets (as bursts of data) over alternative paths. The concentrator (host computer) at the destination site reassembles the complete message from their constituent packets for transmission to the local user-terminal or computer. Thus the relatively expensive wideband lines are shared by way of the *interleaving* action that the packet switching technique enables. The carrier-provided lines between the concentrators may be lines of any speed from 2400 b/sec through 230,400 b/sec. The ack-nack and Request for Next Message (RNM) individual feedback lines between the various concentrator host minicomputers run parallel to the packet-switching wideband lines. Source messages can extend up to 8095 bits in transparent binary, while the packets consist of bursts up to 1008 bits, control-bit header, check bits, and framing bits. The basic rules governing the concentrators working in real-time are minimization of end-to-end delay and number of queuing stages.

High-speed response-time is achieved for various speeds of user messages because the packets are held momentarily and transmitted on the wideband lines at wideband speeds. As an example, the ARPA network takes less than half-a-second to send 8000 bits between any two sites; this includes time for acknowledgment-return signaling to the originating concentrator. Individual pairs of concentrators (or nodes) may use lines with different speeds without any noticeable impact on the speed of network transmission. Compared to conventional leased lines, automatic rerouting feature prevents congestion or outages at intermediate nodes. However, during heavy traffic, some delays are unpredictable if alternative routing is not available for use immediately.

11-7 COMPUTER AIDED SERVICES (CAD AND MONTE CARLO SIMULATION)

Computer Aided Design (CAD) for design of linear and digital integrated circuits—e.g., ECAP/360, Electronic Circuit Analysis Program (ECAP) of IBM—and the Interactive Financial Modeling system (CYBERNET of Control Data Corp.) for development of decision-oriented models as an aid to management planning in the industrial and public sectors are presently common computer-aided features in engineering and business organizations.

Computer Aided Design. The example just mentioned, ECAP, is basically an electronic circuit simulator that enables the designer to check the performance of the circuit under design against the requirements of specifications from the design viewpoints of Steady-state dc, ac, and Transient analysis. In ECAP, only six different simple input statements of a high-level language are required:

1. the topology of the circuit
2. circuit element values

3, 4. type of analysis desired (dc and ac/transient)

5. the circuit excitation
6. a list of the desired outputs.

Of course, the design engineer need not know the actual software involved in the program; by means of the input English-language statements, communication with the computer is maintained with a little practice.

ECAP can, in general, handle complex electrical networks with as many as 50 nodes and 200 branches in circuit topology. For instance, if a **dc analysis** is required, the user can predict the steady-state solution in voltages, currents, and power dissipation of linear electrical networks (and also the partial derivatives and sensitivity-coefficients of the network voltages with respect to the input parameters, if desired.)

Worst-case and **standard-deviation analyses** of the network voltages, and automatic parameter modification capability, may also be included in the program. The source input statements are entered into the central computer with its disk memory of the various programs by way of the usual channels, such as a punched deck of cards (if the computer is onsite), or a remote TTY, or a CRT-keyboard terminal in conjunction with a telephone "acoustic coupler" to the line. The solutions desired are printed out in the appropriate format at the user's terminal in the time-sharing network.

Monte Carlo Simulation. A list of some common business applications is enumerated at the end of this section. The programs are usually based on **probability and statistics** and, more specifically, on the so-called Monte-Carlo simulation. The mathematical simulation models involve *stochastic* or probabilistic variables. Distribution theory and random numbers evolve **realistic or lifelike** data by means of the Monte Carlo process; the uncertainty and risk factors involved in the input variables are described by **statistical distributions** of the order of Normal, Triangular, or Uniform types. The estimates of uncertainty may be oriented on historical data or subjective judgments based on actual experience. In principle, a simulation process is an iterative process that outputs several solutions to a mathematical model. In each iteration, a value is selected at random for each of the problem variables according to their probability of occurrence, and the iteration output data is systematically organized and reported as typical simulation output of the computer. An output statement for a particular profit-margin problem may take the format, namely the return for a certain investment will be from 12 and 16 percent with a *confidence factor* of 80%. That is, the decision technique allows the manager to "quantify" uncertainty in the possible results of a venture.

Examples of management applications are:

1. Budget planning
2. Investment planning
3. Planning market and profit strategies
4. Engineering cost-estimation
5. Cash-flow projection
6. Research-and-development project selection
7. Real-estate evaluation
8. Plant expansion
9. Manufacture-or-buy decisions
10. Bidding-and-risk analysis, etc.

On the other hand, the **simplex linear programming technique** in some business applications is highly reliable for a specific solution, since a large amount of substantial input (statistical) data is accumulated and put in the mathematical format of simultaneous algebraic equations of several variables and entered into the computer for a solution by means of a special "simplex" iterative computational technique–for maximum profit or best performance.

11-8. DATA COMMUNICATIONS

BASE BAND SIGNALS. If there are 100 bit/sec, the pulse repetition interval PRI is 1/100 = 0.01 sec, and the frequency is 1/0.01 = 100 Hz. And, as a square pulse (at 50% duty-cycle), the pulse-duration is 0.01/2 = 0.005 sec or 5 ms.

A *baud* is the unit used for signaling speed in data communications; it is the reciprocal of the shortest signal element: 1/0.005 = 200 bauds in the preceding example.

If T is the period of a return-to-zero train of pulses, the baud-rate, as shown, is twice the bit-rate. Incidentally, the baud is related to the bandwidth as bit/sec of transmission-speed, signal-power, and noise; that is, the baud-rate determines the type of the transmission channel required.

The teletype-unit code of 7 bit/character uses 25-msec *start*, 30-msec *stop*, and five 20-msec information pulse/channel for a total of 155 msec for one character. Therefore, the corresponding bit-rate = 1/0.155 X 5 = 32.3 information bit/sec.

If the space between the stop of one character and the start of the next is 40 msec, the baud-rate is identical but the *rate of information flow* is reduced:

$$\frac{1}{(0.155 + 0.40)} \times 5 = 25.6 \text{ information bit/sec}$$

The information bits include the *parity-bits* generally used for *error-detection*. Channel-capacity in bit/sec: $C = B \log_2 (1 + SNR)$

$$\text{(i.e.) } SNR_{dB} = 10 \log (2^{C/B} - 1) \ldots \text{ Shannon's relationship}$$

where

B is the bandwidth in hertz

$$SNR = \frac{\text{Average signal power}}{\text{Average noise power}}$$

Owing to limitations in transmission channels, bandwidth-limited processing becomes necessary in a binary system, as shown in the following diagram:

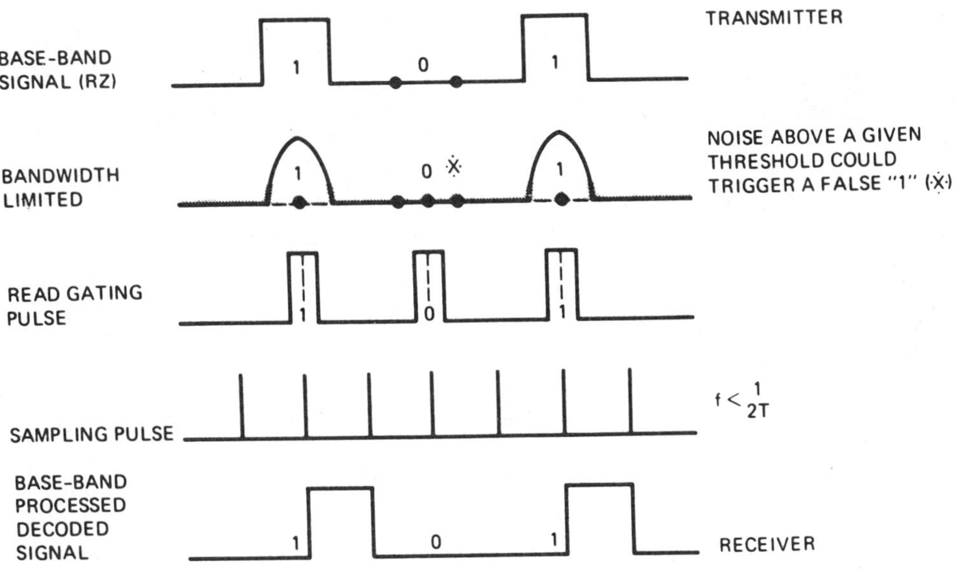

The noise-power increases as the square-root of bandwidth. This fact is taken into consideration when message enhancement is achieved by redundant-bit transmission in, for example, *error-correcting codes* with both information and redundant bits.

A parity-bit check with a *distance-2 code* will enable only the detection of one erroneous bit in a code word. "Distance-d" is the number of elements in which the code symbols (words) differ.

A distance of at least 3 ($d \geqslant 3$) is essential for the correction of one error-bit in a code

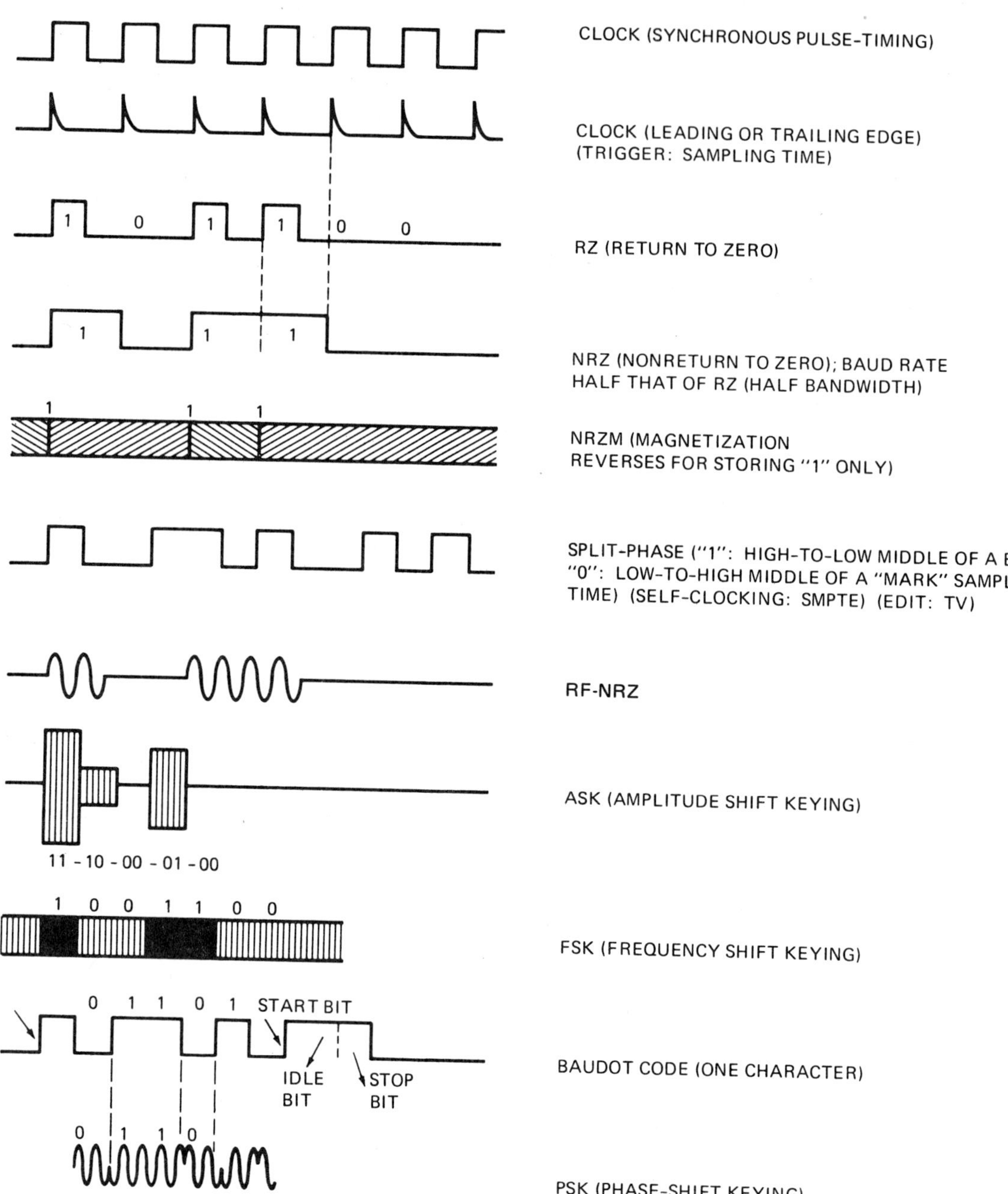

Fig. 11-6a. RZ, NRZ, NRZM, split-phase, RF-NRZ, ASK, FSK, and PSK, digital/analog signals.

symbol. For correction of two error-bits, d is 5. The popular Hamming code is a distance - 3 code capable of detecting and correcting one error-bit in a word.

Complement parity is another technique for reliability in data transmission. A command word of 8 or 16 bits is transmitted in practice in conjunction with its complement (of inverted 1's and 0's) on twisted pairs, via line-drivers and line-receivers for random or impulse noise-immunity.

11-9. PULSE-FORMATTING (QUANTIZERS AND ANALOG-TO-DIGITAL CONVERTERS)

The synchronizing clock-pulse at rates of up to 20 MHz for high-speed digital computers makes the basis for pulse-timing in synchronous digital processing systems. (Asynchronous digital computer systems operate without this basic synchronization by using alternative methods of logic.) The clock-frequency is divided by down-counters to provide other timings at lower rates. Figure 11-6a illustrates the various pulse formats normally encountered in practice. The sampling-time may be either the leading- or trailing-edge of the clock-pulse at several rates. Unlike the continuously varying analog, video, audio, and carrier signals, the digital data signal change in only discrete levels with rise- and fall-times, as governed by bandwidth in Hz/sec. The binary machine language used in digital computers naturally operates at two discrete levels, 1's and 0's (High and Low or True and False). A fast rise-time of course corresponds to higher bandwidth. Digital systems are comprised of either the directly coded *base-band* data signals on a network transmission line or a frequency- or time-division-multiplexed pulse-modulated signals; teletype (Baudot) and high-speed data communications systems are typical examples, respectively. Analog information is converted by a sample-and-hold circuit to a digital format by sampling the continuous signals at discrete timings, and converting each instantaneously

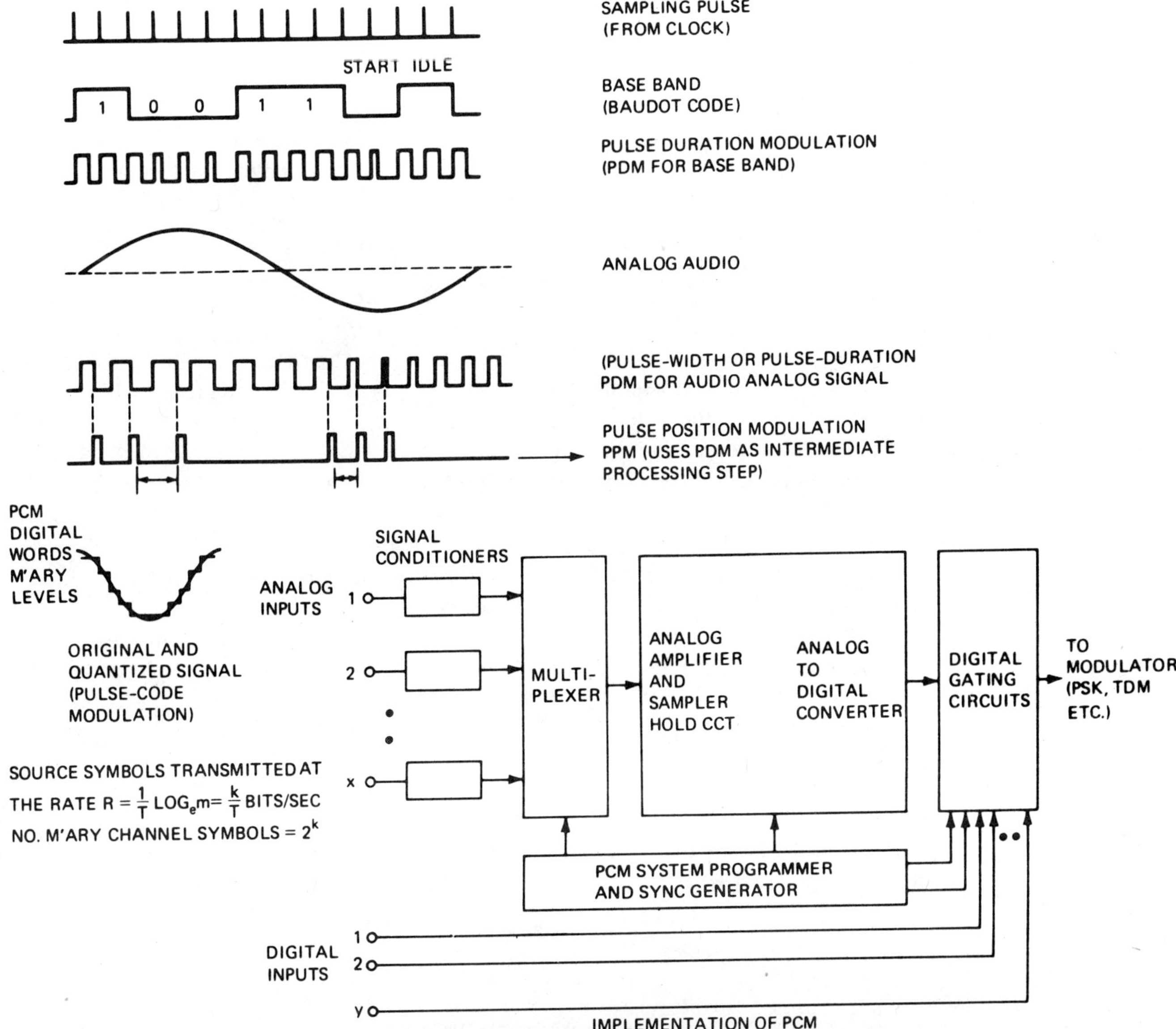

Fig. 11-6b. Base band and analog signals. PDM, PPM, and PCM.

sampled-level to a corresponding binary number to formulate a pulse-code modulation (PCM) system. The common PAM (pulse-amplitude modulation), PCM, PDM (pulse-width modulation), and PPM (pulse-period modulation) waveforms for the base-band and analog signals are illustrated in Fig. 11-6b.

11-9.1. Quantizers. The latest digital filter technique in digital control systems naturally require the use of finite number of bits to express the filter state-variables as coefficient values. The continuous analog signal is therefore digitized in amplitude and timing by the sampling process. The process introduces samples of amplitude at several levels and involves quantization-noise and quantizing-errors.

An analog *ramp* (or sawtooth) signal is converted to a PCM format by momentarily holding each instantaneously sampled voltage level in a sample-and-hold circuit. The quantized step, quantum E_q is actually a pulse-amplitude modulated signal. A 7-bit code PCM signal represents (2^7 =)128 possible amplitude levels or M channel-symbols or words. The code is a set of characters that, taken in order, correspond to the set of levels.

In data communications networks, the source-symbols transmitted at a rate,

$$R = \frac{1}{T} \log_e M = k/T \text{ bit/sec}$$

with k source-bits or $\log_e$ M binary signals (or 2^k "M-ary" channel-symbols = 2^7 in the above example), are processed in a *block encoder* to provide the channel signals.

The maximum quantizing error or noise for 128 levels in PCM is given by

$$E_q/2 = \frac{1}{2} \text{ quantum} = \frac{1}{2 \times 128} = 0.4\%$$

The quantized signal is thus 99.6% accurate, as far as the original analog information is concerned. The basic sample-and-hold circuit and a typical 4-bit quantizer with its binary formatting circuit are illustrated in Fig. 11-7.

The subjects of quantizing and coding in PCM are extensively treated by K. W. Cattermole in his book on pulse code modulation.* Although it is more complex than other pulse modulation methods, it is the most appropriate technique for digitizing audio and video signals for modern computer-controlled time-division multiplex transmission. Each instantaneously sampled voltage level (*quantum*) of the ramp-function is held momentarily by the *sample-and-hold circuit*, as the conversion to PCM takes place with pulse-amplitude modulation as an intermediate step. The midpoint of each amplitude-step is the corresponding sampling time. Figure 11-8 illustrates the basic principle of the TDM (time-division multiplex) used for data transmission. The clock-rate must be at least equal to the sampling-rate times the number of channels being sampled, including the sync channel.

11-9.2. Analog-to-Digital Converter. The analog-to-digital (A/D) converter (ADC) is an encoder that accepts an analog signal A_i and reference voltage A_r, and provides an approximated digital output with a resolution of

$$\chi \equiv (A_i/A_r)$$

**Principles of Pulse Code Modulation*, Iliffe Books, London, 1969.

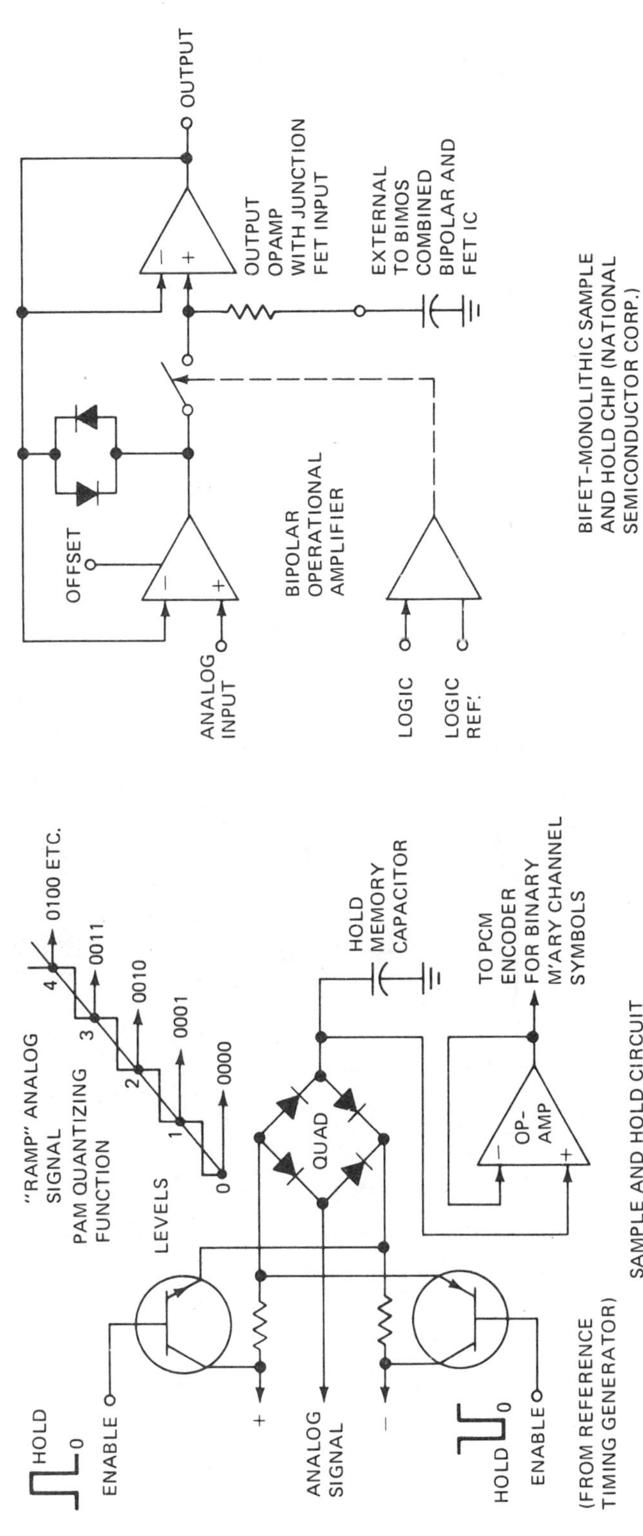

Fig. 11-7. Sample-and-hold circuit and 4-bit PCM encoder.

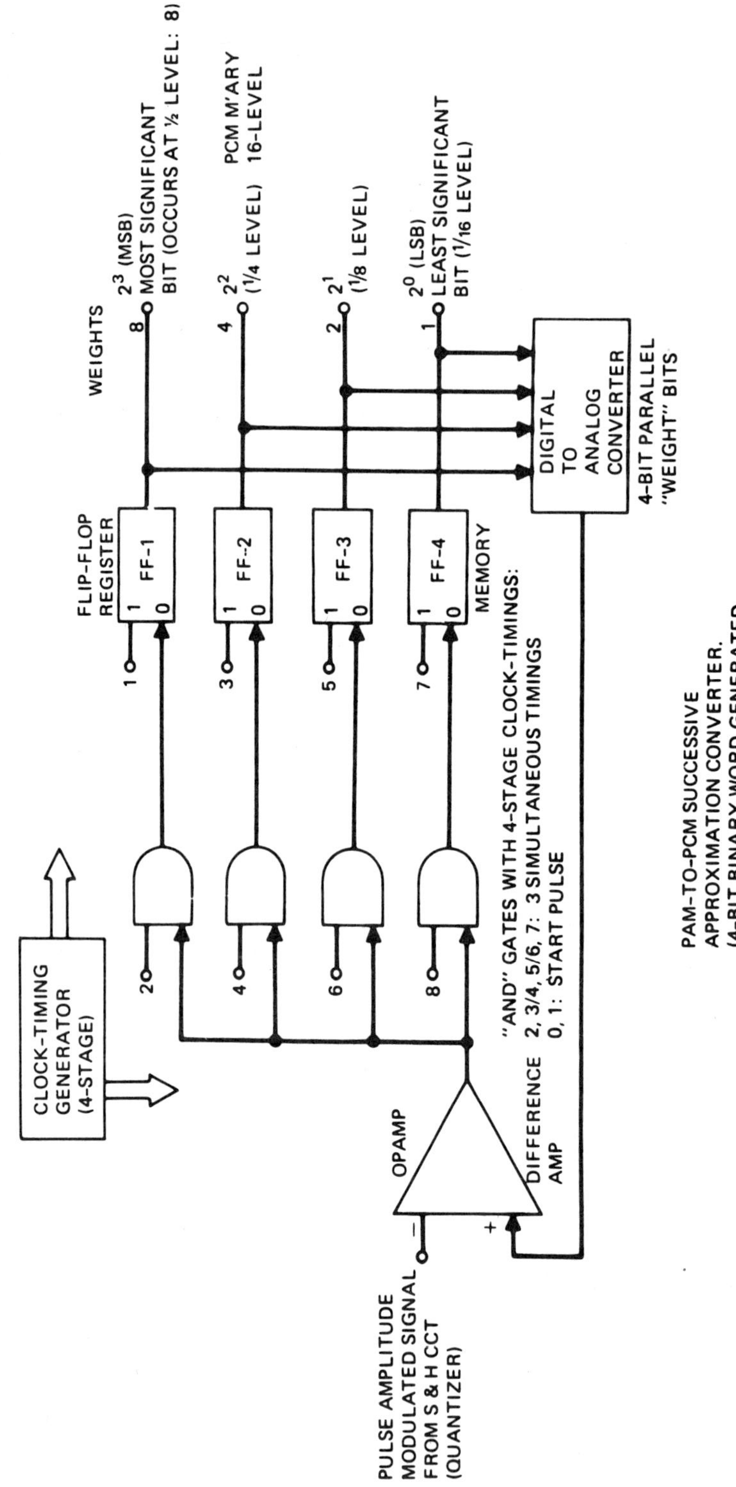

PAM-TO-PCM SUCCESSIVE APPROXIMATION CONVERTER. (4-BIT BINARY WORD GENERATED FROM THE INSTANTANEOUS VOLTAGE LEVEL OF THE ANALOG SIGNAL SAMPLED).

Fig. 11-7 (*cont.*)

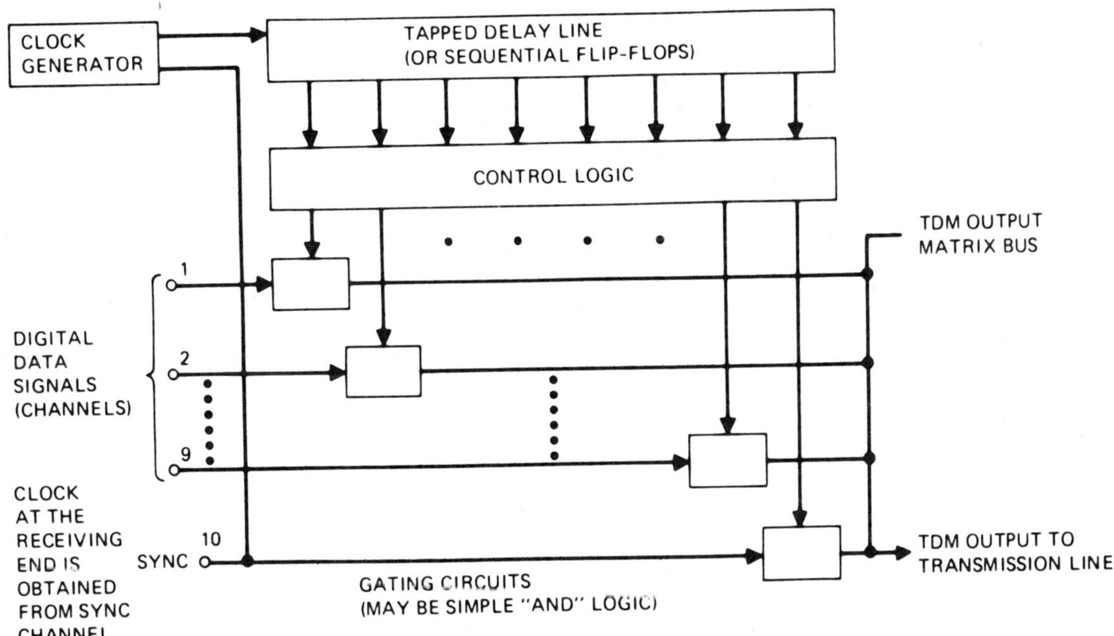
CLOCK GENERATOR
TAPPED DELAY LINE (OR SEQUENTIAL FLIP-FLOPS)
CONTROL LOGIC
TDM OUTPUT MATRIX BUS
DIGITAL DATA SIGNALS (CHANNELS)
1
2
9
CLOCK AT THE RECEIVING END IS OBTAINED FROM SYNC CHANNEL
10
SYNC
TDM OUTPUT TO TRANSMISSION LINE
GATING CIRCUITS (MAY BE SIMPLE "AND" LOGIC)
(See Fig. 11-17 for a typical data packet)
A TDM MODEM WILL CONSIST OF A SWITCHER (COMMUTATOR) OF THE ABOVE CONFIGURATION AT BOTH THE CODING TRANSMITTING AND THE DECODING RECEIVING ENDS.
THE CLOCK RATE MUST BE AT LEAST EQUAL TO SAMPLING-RATE TIMES THE NUMBER OF CHANNELS SAMPLED (10 AS ABOVE).

Fig. 11-8. Concept of time-division multiplex (TDM).

The binary approximate form

$$\frac{A_i}{A_r} \approx (a_1 2^{-1} + a_2 2^{-2} + \cdots a_n 2^{-n})$$

The quantization error $\Delta A_i = A_i/r^n$ where r is the radix and n is the number of digits in χ. A sampling error is also present if the input-frequency is high relative to the conversion-rate of the A/D converter.

There are several types of A/D converters, including:

1. *parallel-feedback* with a comparator consisting of a summing circuit (for input and feedback analog signal from a D/A converter) and a threshold voltage to output an error of either polarity, which drives a bank of counters that register and store the updated count,
2. *successive approximation*, which makes n successive comparisons at each conversion between the input analog signal value and a time-dependent feedback voltage
3. *servo* with the digital output changing in such a direction as to reduce the error from a detector
4. *indirect converter*, which derives the digital format from an intermediate (partly or overall) analog-step
5. *simple-ramp comparison* with a precise ramp generator and comparator. (see 11-13.)

The successive approximation A/D converter is the most popular type; at a clock frequency of 500 kHz and 12-bit words, the device using MSI requires 1 to 24 μsec for the conversion of small or large values of the input signal. A 12-bit successive approxima-

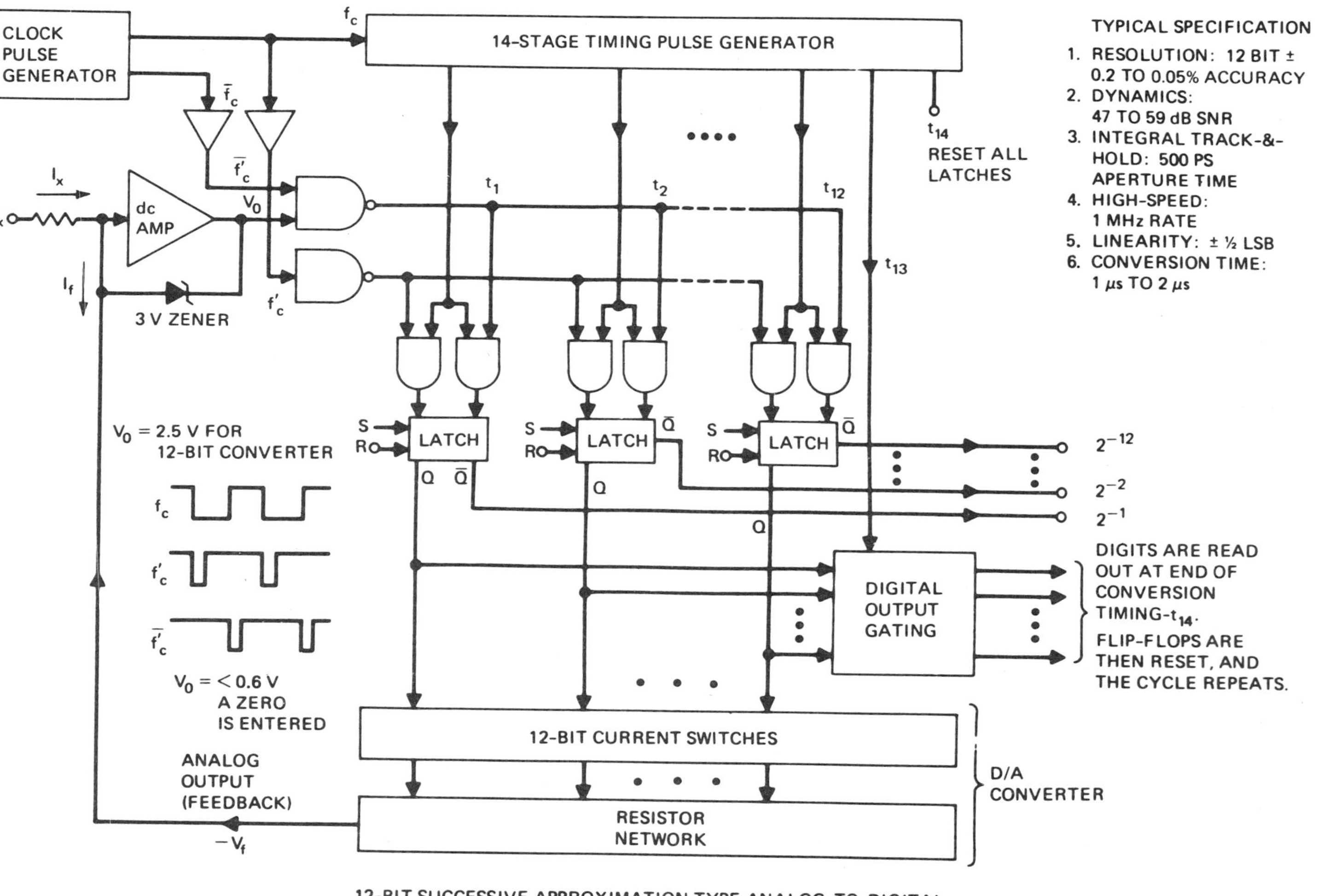

Fig. 11-9. Twelve-bit analog-to-digital converter (successive approximation technique).

tion A/D converter is shown in Fig. 11-9. The timing generator output is properly sequenced to trigger bistable-latches and inhibit readout until conversion is complete.

Transducers. A transducer is a device that converts a change in some form of energy (such as heat, radiation, sound, pressure, motion, or angular velocity), or a natural phenomenon or event, into a change of a variable appearing as a measurable electrical parameter. And, transducers are in general affected by more than one of the preceding forms of energy.

An *active transducer* produces a variable output voltage or current that can be measured with or without external power, while a *passive transducer* produces a change in a passive parameter such as resistance/inductance/capacitance. All feedback analog/continuous or digital control systems derive their basic control information from some form of transducer, governing displacement, flow, force, humidity, level, light, mass, pressure, angular velocity, acceleration, strain, temperature, thickness, velocity, viscosity, etc. After sufficient amplification, this basic analog control information is converted to the digital format in digital systems.

Piezoelectric crystals, photoelectric (phototransistor), thermoelectric, magnetoelectric, electronic, and electrochemical and radioactive voltages/current generating devices are active transducers, while a variable R/L/C device, or a magnetostrictive element or a differential transformer make a passive type. All of these devices are mostly nonlinear beyond a linear range, and the operation of the control systems is generally approximated to the linear range or compensated appropriately.

11-9.3. SMPTE Control Time-Card. The Society of Motion Pictures and Television Engineers (SMPTE) has standardized videotape and audio time-control codes for the editing of the videotape and the synchronization of the audiotape. The code includes a biphase mark, with BCD time of day, BCD frame-count, and optional binary-word information. The code, consisting of 80 bit/television frame or 40 bit/field at 2400 (=60 X 40) bit/sec, is recorded on the audio-cue track of the videotape recorder; the bandwidth is consistent with normal forward tape speeds. In editing, the code is used to search for the required edit timings during fast-forward and reverse shuttling of the tape, requiring a bandwidth approaching 100 kHz. The sync word (bits 4 through 79), with twelve 1 bits followed by 0 and 1 indicate *end of frame* and forward direction of tape. The reverse direction is indicated if twelve 1's are followed by two 0's.

Starting with bit-number 0, the 80 bits are sequenced thus: frame units (4), first binary group (4), frame tens including "drop-frame" (4), second binary group (4), seconds units (4), third binary group (4), seconds tens (3), unassigned address bit-number 27, fourth binary group (4), minutes units (4), fifth binary group (4), minutes tens (3), unassigned address bit-number 43, sixth binary group (4), hours units (4), seventh binary group (4), hours tens (2), unassigned address bit-number 58, fixed bit-0 (1), eighth binary group, and sync word from bit-number 64 to bit-number 0 of next frame. NTSC color video requires a drop-frame because the NTSC color frame-rate is 29.97002/sec in the place of the monochrome 30/sec. To allow for this difference, two frames are dropped every minute except every tenth minute.

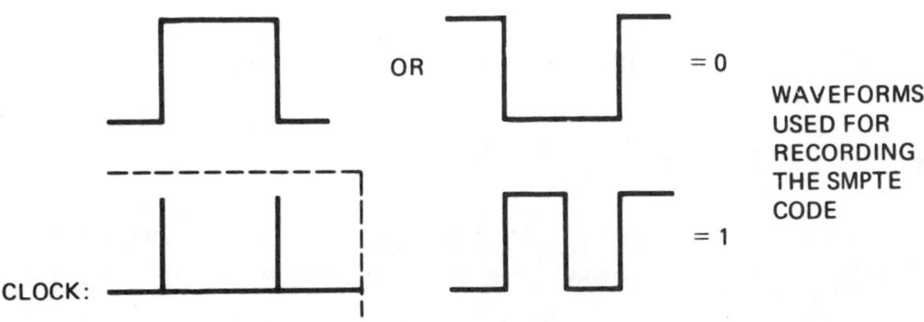

WAVEFORMS USED FOR RECORDING THE SMPTE CODE

Table 11-3. ASCII Encoding Chart (7-bit code)

				$b_7 \rightarrow$	0	0	0	0	1	1	1	1
				$b_6 \rightarrow$	0	0	1	1	0	0	1	1
Bits				$b_5 \rightarrow$	0	1	0	1	0	1	0	1
b_4 ↓	b_3 ↓	b_2 ↓	b_1 ↓	COL / ROW	0	1	2	3	4	5	6	7
0	0	0	0	0	NUL	DLE	SP	0	@	P		p
0	0	0	1	1	SOH	DC1	!	1	A	Q	a	q
0	0	1	0	2	STX	DC2	"	2	B	R	b	r
0	0	1	1	3	ETX	DC3	#	3	C	S	c	s
0	1	0	0	4	EOT	DC4	$	4	D	T	d	t
0	1	0	1	5	ENQ	NAK	%	5	E	U	e	u
0	1	1	0	6	ACK	SYN	&	6	F	V	f	v
0	1	1	1	7	BEL	ETB		7	G	W	g	w
1	0	0	0	8	BS	CAN	(	8	H	X	h	x
1	0	0	1	9	HT	EM	)	9	I	Y	i	y
1	0	1	0	10	LF	SUB	*	:	J	Z	j	z
1	0	1	1	11	VT	ESC	+	;	K	[	k	{
1	1	0	0	12	FF	FS	,	<	L	\	l	¦
1	1	0	1	13	CR	GS	-	=	M	]	m	}
1	1	1	0	14	SO	RS	.	>	N	^	n	~
1	1	1	1	15	SI	US	/	?	O	_	o	DEL

ANSI (American National Standards Institute), ASCII encoding chart is modified for television broadcast use in video character generators. Alphanumeric characters may be made to "crawl," usually from right to left across the bottom one-fourth of the picture to present statistics, or the display may be made to "roll" usually from bottom to top for information of "credits." Only capital letters are used for the ASCII decoding chart, and columns 6 and 7 are deleted. In column 1, row 3, CRSR abbreviates the word *cursor*—which when turned ON indicates the position of the next character to be typed on the keyboard; it appears as a white square on the monitor. The cursor control actually replaces BS (back space), HT (horizontal tabulation), VT (vertical tabulation), FF (form feed), and GS (group separator) in the standard ASCII code. *Home* position is the upper left of the *page*. The function of the crawl and roll are selected on a separate group of control buttons on the keyboard unit. FLASH, OPEN, CLOSE, ETX (end of transmission), SND MSG, SND LINE, ERASE, RM (stop code enters memory), HOME, LOAD REQ, and CRSR are the major functions included in this chart. The ASCII Encoding Chart and the ASCII Decoding Chart for television are presented in Tables 11-3 and 11-4.

11-10. DIGITIZING AUDIO SIGNALS

Digitized audio (and video) signals can be conveniently "stored" in LSI (large-scale integrated) PROMs (programmable read-only-memories) and RAMs (random-access

Table 11-4. ASCII Decoding Chart for Special Television Use

			Bits	$b_7 \rightarrow$	0	0	0	0	1	1	1	1
				$b_6 \rightarrow$	0	0	1	1	0	0	1	1
				$b_5 \rightarrow$	0	1	0	1	0	1	0	1
b_4 ↓	b_3 ↓	b_2 ↓	b_1 ↓	ROW \ COL	0	1	2	3	4	5	6	7
0	0	0	0	0	NUL		SP	0		P		
0	0	0	1	1	SOH	FLASH	!	1	A	Q		
0	0	1	0	2		OPEN	"	2	B	R		
0	0	1	1	3	ETX	CRSR	#	3	C	S		
0	1	0	0	4	EOT	CLOSE	$	4	D	T		
0	1	0	1	5			%	5	E	U		
0	1	1	0	6			&	6	F	V		
0	1	1	1	7	BEL			7	G	W		
1	0	0	0	8	CRSR LEFT		(	8	H	X		
1	0	0	1	9	CRSR RIGHT	EM	)	9	I	Y		
1	0	1	0	10	LF	ERASE	*	:	J	Z		
1	0	1	1	11	CRSR DOWN		+	;	K	[		
1	1	0	0	12	CRSR UP	CRSR HOME	,	<	L	~		
1	1	0	1	13	CR	CRSR NEW LINE	-	=	M	]		
1	1	1	0	14		SND		>	N	^		
1	1	1	1	15		SEND MSG	/	?	O	.		

memories), so that the information can be read-out or manipulated on any convenient time-base desired. With LSI microprocessors and microcontrollers becoming extremely popular at economy prices, it is natural such information will gradually become a part of the worldwide PCM (pulse-code modulation) data control and communications systems.

A digitized voice channel of the telephone network with a frequency response up to 3000 Hz is shown in Fig. 11-10. Sampling at 8-kHz rate is converted to a 7-bit binary word from "0" on (2^7 =)128 levels at 10-V peak audio level and 0.078-V quantum. The quantizing error is 0.39% of 10-V peak. *Signal-to-*(quantizing) *distortion ratio* (sdr) at maximum input level or full load is given by

$$\text{sdr} = 6n + 1.8 \text{ dB} = 43.8 \text{ dB (if } n = 7)$$

An sdr of 43.8 dB is approximately equivalent to 1.2% of *total harmonic distortion* (*thd*)—a

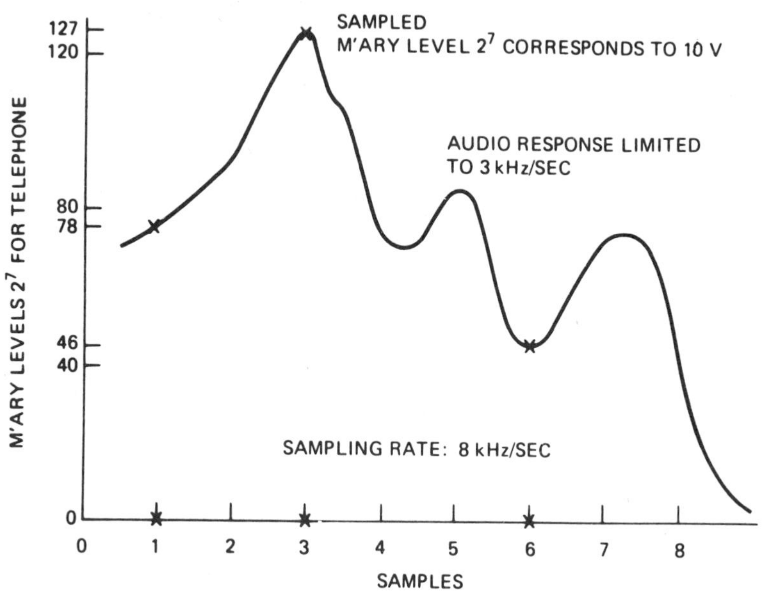

PCM: AUDIO M'ARY LEVELS IN BINARY WORDS REPRESENTING BINARY WORD HIGH'S POSITIVE-GOING AND LOW'S NEGATIVE-GOING:

EX.: SAMPLE 1:

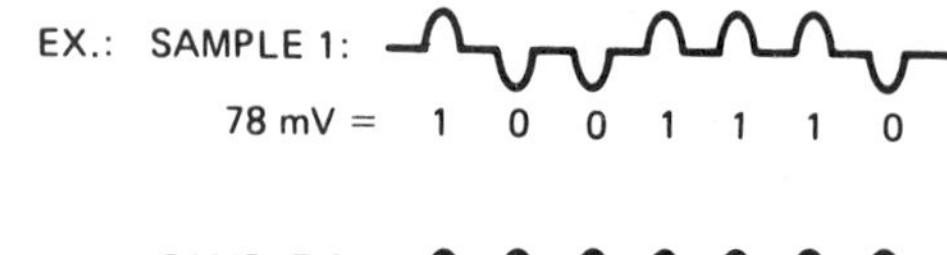

78 mV = 1 0 0 1 1 1 0

SAMPLE 3:

2^7 = 127 mV = 1 1 1 1 1 1 1

SAMPLE 6:

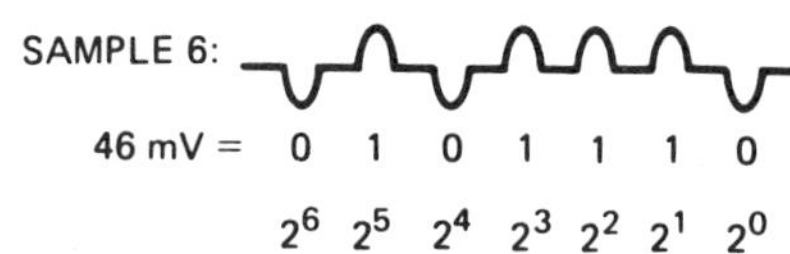

46 mV = 0 1 0 1 1 1 0

2^6 2^5 2^4 2^3 2^2 2^1 2^0

LEVEL	VOLTAGE
127	10 V
78	6.14 V
46	3.62 V
*1	0.078 V
0	0 V

*EACH QUANTUM LEAST SIGNIFICANT BIT (LSB) = 78 mV ∴ MAXIMUM QUANTIZING ERROR = 39 mV. (½ Q)

SIGNAL/DISTORTION = 6 X BITS/WORD + 1.8 dB; TOTAL HARMONIC DISTORTION = 1.2% (THD)
TELEPHONE: AN SDR OF (6 X 7) + 1.8 = 43.8 dB CORRESPONDS APPROXIMATELY TO 1.2% THD
TELEVISION: AN SDR OF (6 X 14) + 1.8 = 85.8 dB CORRESPONDS APPROXIMATELY TO 0.01% THD
(M'ARY LEVELS = 2^{14} FOR HIGH-FREQUENCY RESPONSE TO 15 kHz AND A CORRESPONDING HIGH SAMPLING RATE OF 33 kHz/SEC)

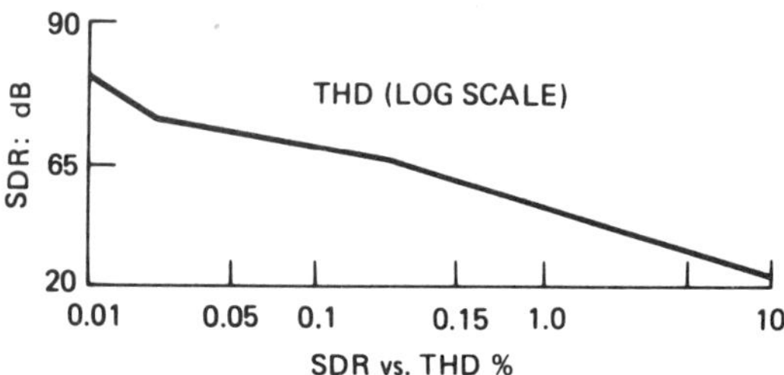

Fig. 11-10. Digitized voice channel in a telephone network. (*Courtesy of Sam's Publications*)

fine tolerance from the distortion point of view. Where high-quality broadcast music is involved, 12-to 14-bit binary word is in order with an sdr of 85.8 dB (n = 14). When the signal is 40 dB below full level, the thd at 1% is still fine.

For broadcast music at 15-kHz bandwidth and a sampling rate of 33 kHz and 14-bit binary words, the transmission rate is 462 kb/sec (33000 X 14); the bandwidth achieved at an SNR of 40 dB is given by:

$$BW = \frac{\text{channel capacity}}{\log_2 \text{SNR}} = \frac{462 \text{ kb}}{\log_2 10000} = 35 \text{ kHz}$$

In practice, 10- to 12-bit M-ary levels are used for a channel bandwidth of 20 kHz. Bandwidth is further reduced by using such concepts as *companding* to truncate the three MSBs during soft passages and the three LSBs during loud passages, and automatically reinstating them during decoding. Program-modulated noise due to quantizing, etc., is eliminated by the usual technique of preemphasis and deemphasis prior to quantization. Another technique, *digital audio delay*, which is adjustable, is a common *special effects* feature in sound systems to minimize the effects of distracting echoes and loss intelligibility.

11-11. DIGITAL AUDIO FOR TELEVISION

The accompanying diagram indicates how the binary audio data are carried by a 5.5-MHz digital subcarrier when audio accompanies the digitized video in a television transmission system. The color subcarrier 3.579545 MHz is divided by 104 to provide a 34.42 kHz sampling rate at a 13-bit word level for four audio input signals.

$$33.42 \text{ kHz} \times 13 \times 4 = 1.79 \text{ Mbit/sec}$$

The 5.5-MHz digital subcarrier furnishes four-phase phase-shift-keying modulation for the four audio channels. The encoder receives this signal along with a filtered video signal (of 4.5 MHz bandwidth), so that the base-band output is a 5.5 MHz subcarrier. The audio and video signals are separated at the decoder, and the four audio channels are separated by filtering.

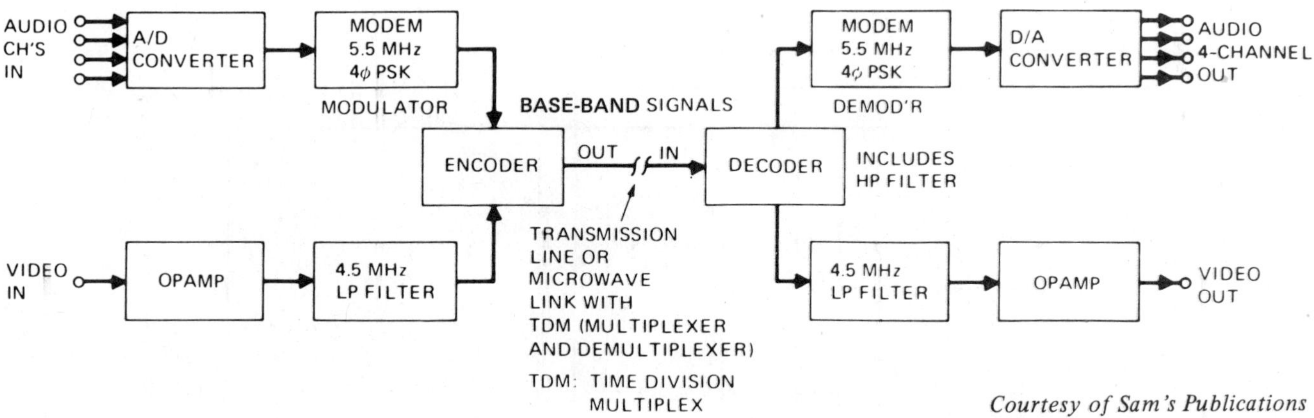

Courtesy of Sam's Publications

There is a possibility that the audio information may be inserted in future as digital data within the horizontal blanking intervals of the composite television signals with the sync content.

11-12. LSI VIDEO A/D CONVERTERS (TRW LSI PRODUCTS)

Digital television is presently an accomplished fact in the highly reliable, medium-cost LSI format. No doubt the processing will eventually become a popular low-cost technique when digital television becomes a mass medium around the world via synchronous domestic satellites. The following analog-to-digital converter is a timely new LSI component for the low-cost implementation of digital television:

1. TRW TDC 1007J is an 8-bit monolithic bipolar (TTL) fully parallel A/D converter, using 255 sampling comparators, combinatorial Exclusive-OR logic, and an output buffer for digitizing 7-MHz analog black-and-white or NTSC/PAL color-television signals or radar signals at rates from dc to 30 megasamples/sec (MSPS). The combinational logic is involved in the conversion of unit-distance code to binary. The sample-and-hold circuit is built in; recovery from a step-input occurs within 20 nsec with the sampling comparators

of 40-MHz bandwidth. The aperture jitter is hardly 30 psec at a differential phase of 0.5° and a differential gain of 1.5%.

Peak-signal to rms noise at 2.438-MHz input is 54 dB, and noise power ratio (at dc to 7 MHz white noise-bandwidth) is 38 dB. The 64-pin LSI chip operates through a temperature range of −55° to +130°C, and requires a drive of 1-V peak-to-peak composite video signal (or −0.5-to-5.5-V radar pulse) and provides an 8-bit binary or two's complement output, using ± 15- and +5-V power supplies. The system organization of the converter is shown in the accompanying block diagram. The cost of the plug-in PC-board is $550, complete with the chip, selectable input impedance and amplitude, and adjustable offset for unipolar or bipolar input.

2. For lower-cost closed-circuit television and other applications, a 6-bit resolution TRW TDC 1014J is available in a 24-pin ceramic dual in-line package at a lower cost of $186 and power dissipation of $\frac{3}{4}$ W. Compared to the 8-bit converter, the 6-bit chip uses 63 strobed sampling comparators; the other details are identical to those in the 8-bit chip; linearity in this case is specified as ± $\frac{1}{4}$ least-significant-bit (LSB). The device requires a single command to digitize an analog waveform of amplitude between 0 and −1 V. The peak-signal to rms noise with 2.438-MHz pass-band input is 42 dB, and the noise power ratio for dc to 7-MHz white-noise bandwidth is 27 dB.

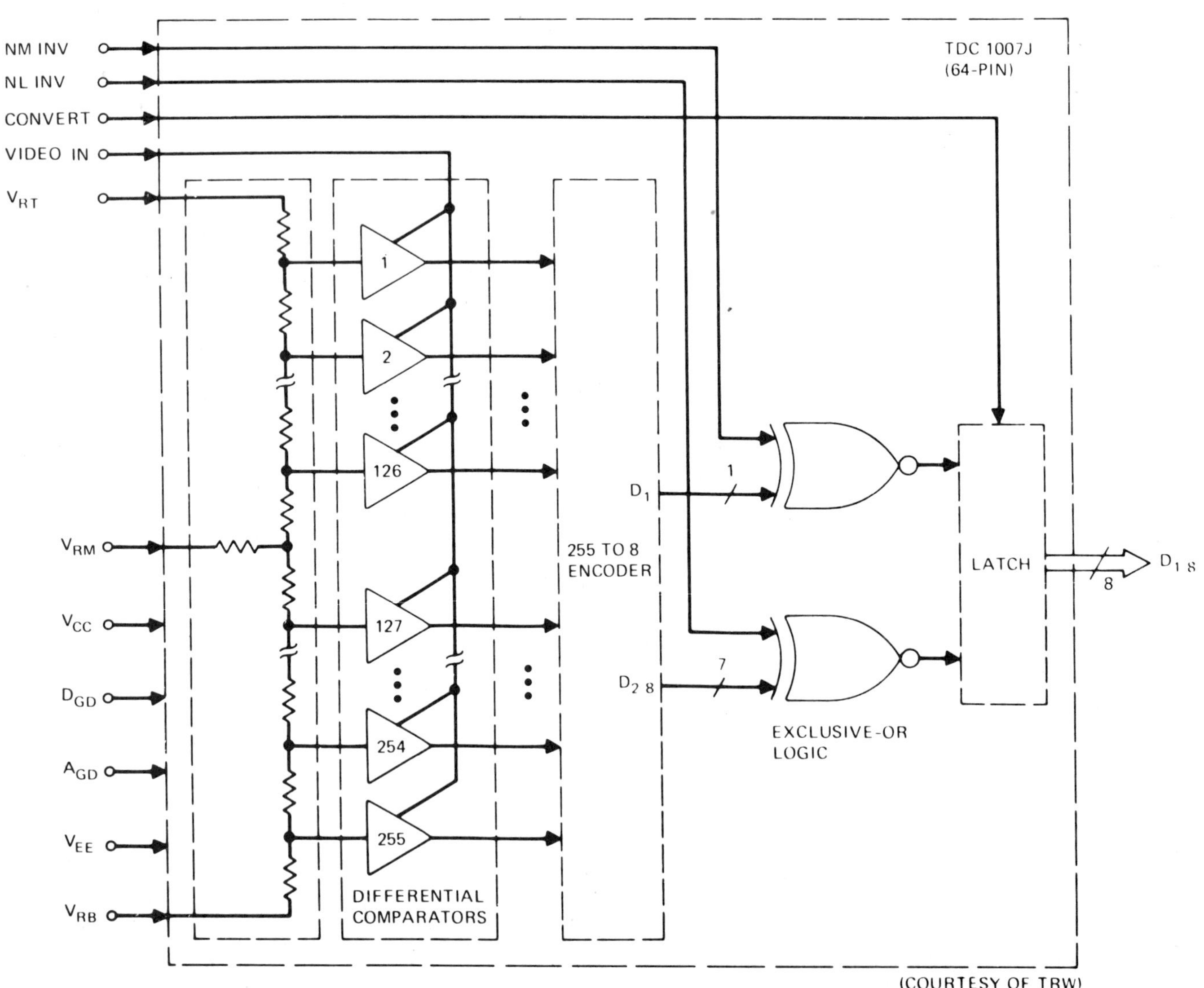

(COURTESY OF TRW)

11-13. DIGITIZED VIDEO SIGNALS

With the recent introduction of worldwide color television broadcasts via satellites, digitized video is an accomplished fact. Other digitized video applications include (1) automatic raster-and-color synchronizers and timers, (2) time-base correctors for video recorders, (3) image enhancers, (4) automatic international standards conversion, and (5) video bandwidth compressors and expanders. At this time, temporary storage via LSI RAMs at a clocked rate is an inherent processing technique in all of these applications. Sample-and-hold circuits to convert the low-pass filtered analog signal to a PAM signal, and the subsequent ADC to generate the format corresponding to the instantaneously sampled PCM signal, are the other two stages in this signal processing technique.

In the case of video, the whole synchronous picture information occurs at even-multiples of the horizontal line-scanning frequency, and color information is "interleaved" at odd multiples of one-half the line frequency by starting with a color subcarrier at 3.579545 MHz. Unlike the audio, a smaller 8-bit binary word can be used at three times the color subcarrier in the case of video ($2^8 = 256$ levels) for very high-quality color picture of a bandwidth of 4.5 MHz. For closed-circuit television and VTRs, 6- and 7-bit (64 to 128 levels) binary words will do for peak-to-peak signal-to-RMS noise ratios from 43 to 49 dB.

Transmission rate at the above high-quality sampling rate of 3 times the color subcarrier rate:

$$10.7 \text{ MHz} \times 8 = 86 \text{ Mb/sec}$$

Quantizing aperture effect is generally frequency compensated by preemphasis and deemphasis before quantizing and decoding, respectively. COMSAT has experimentally demonstrated satisfactory international satellite telecasts with its DITEC-PCM and comb-filters at a transmission-rate of 33.6 Mb/sec in the place of 86 Mb/sec. The *teeth* of a luminance comb-filter have maximum response at the harmonics of the line-frequency (15.75 kHz) and nulls at the odd harmonics at half the line-frequency for color. And the *teeth* of the color comb-filter occur at the odd harmonics of half the line frequency for color, and nulls at the even harmonics of the line frequency for luminance. When four times the color subcarrier frequency is used for sampling the I and Q components of color, the samples on all the time-sequential picture lines are well-aligned for the comb-filters. However, by employing a Phase-Alternation Line Encoding (PALE) technique, the digital comb-filters perform equally well at three times the subcarrier (10.7 MHz) sampling-rate, using one-third fewer digits for the binary words. A simplified block-diagram of the PALE technique is illustrated in Fig. 11-11a. The phase of the sampling frequency is shifted by 180° on alternate horizontal scan lines during the breezeway at the leading-edge of the color-sync burst. When a signal is stored in a shift-register, the stored data are read out as a reconstructed PALE-clock, which is phase-synchronized with the samples on each scan-line. Switching transients and ringing at the output of the digital-to-analog converter are minimized by the *resampling* process using a filter, as shown in Fig. 11-11b. The high-frequency performance is redeemed by aperture compensation.

Digital-comb-filtering and a matrix network recover the in-phase I and quadrature Q color information as shown in Fig. 11-11c. They are superimposed on the dc luminance component M. The sampling is shown at the 10.7-MHz rate. The I and Q signals are digitally extracted with the following matrix:

$$I = A - C; Q = B - D; \text{and } M = \tfrac{1}{2}(A + C) \text{ or } \tfrac{1}{2}(B + D)$$

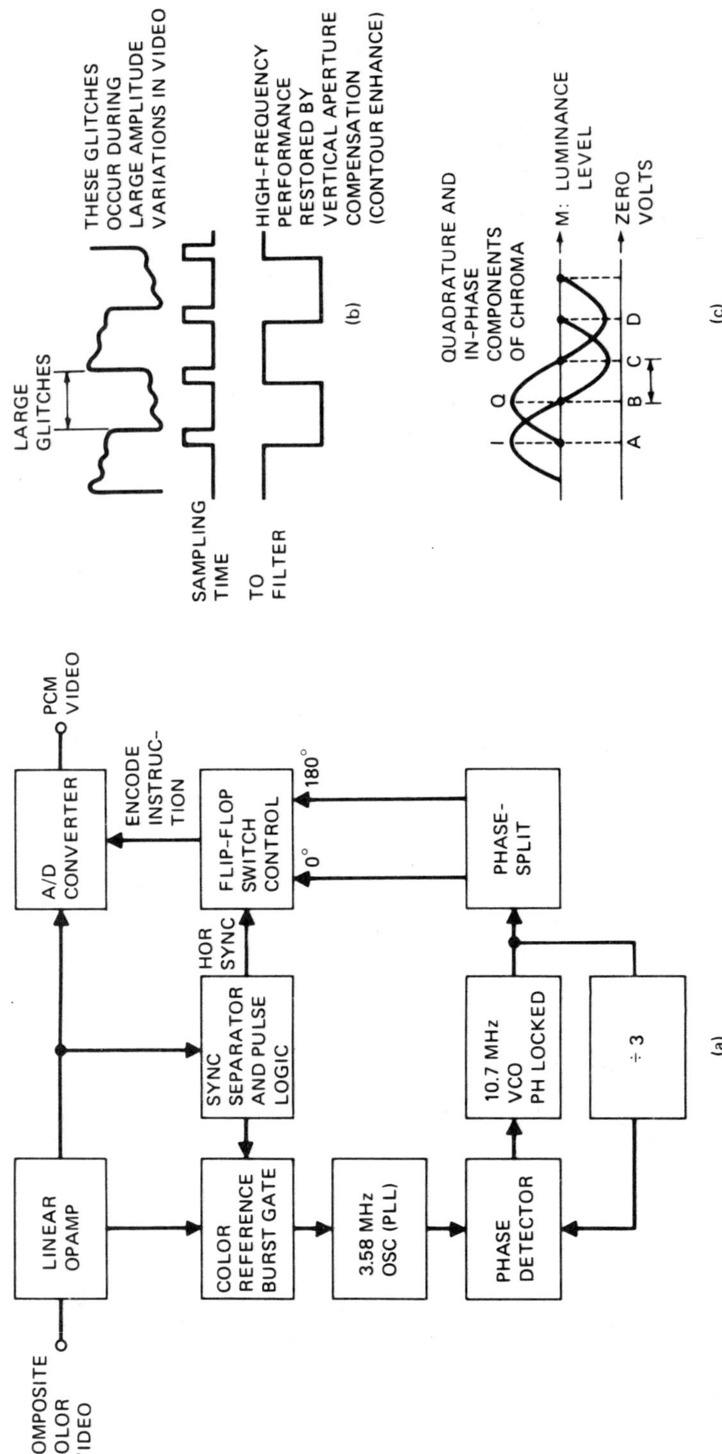

Fig. 11-11. "Pale" technique of digitizing composite color-television signal. (*Courtesy of Sam's Publications*)

Analog-to-Digital (A/D) Converters

There are six feasible versions of A/D converters. The type actually used in an application depends on the resolution and speed required.

1. *Counter type*: Also called a *servo type* it uses a digital counter and a clock to control the input of a digital to analog (D/A) counter with a *ramp* output. Since it is too simple and slow, a *tracking type* A/D converter replaces this version; this is controlled by an up-down counter that is in turn controlled by a comparator and a clock.
2. *Successive-approximation (s-a) type*: This version is the most *popular* version in moderate or high-speed applications. The s-a A/D uses a D/A converter in the feedback loop of a digital control circuit, which adjusts its output in n-steps to equal the analog input, n being the *resolution* in bits. In both the successive approximation and counter types, a clock and comparator are involved.
3. *Parallel A/D converter* (*Flash* or simultaneous version): It is popularly used in video and radar applications below a resolution of 8-bits at rates of 20 MHz. A reference voltage divider and (2^8-1) *analog comparators* (using operational amplifier integrated-circuits) are used for an 8-bit decoder to implement this A/D converter. Since all comparators change state simultaneously, the quantization process takes place in one step, and hence high-speed. An 8-bit converter needs 255 comparators, and with modern LSI processing, this is no problem. For higher rates such as 50 to 100 MHz, two 4-bit stages of parallel A/D converters can be used in conjunction with a 4-bit D/A and an 8-bit output register. (TRW LSI 6-bit and 8-bit A/D converters are based on the flash parallel A/D conversion technique.)
4. *Integrating type*: It is an indirect, slow, but highly linear signal processing circuit, using the conversion of the input analog signal into a time period, which is in turn measured by a clock and counter. Single-slope, dual-slope, charge-balancing, or quantized methods are alternative versions of the integrating principle. National Semiconductor Corp. announced in 1980 a *single-slope* A/D converter that operates with the aid of a microcomputer INS-8070 and control logic to deliver a *linearity of 20 bits* and a feasible *absolute accuracy of 20 bits* (depending on the accuracy of the voltage reference used.
5. *Dual-slope type*: This version of A/D converter uses an integrator with a reference, comparator, clock, and counter. Since this version is slow in A/D conversion, it is exclusively used in instrumentation such as digital multimeters and panel meters.
6. *Charge-balancing type*: This A/D conversion technique is also called *quantized feedback* processing. The principle of operation is based on generating a pulse-train with a frequency repetition-rate that varies in proportion to the input analog voltage. The output pulses are counted for a fixed time-interval. It consists of an integrator, comparator, precision pulse generator, timer, and counter. It is, in principle, a voltage-to-frequency converter.

11-14. HIGH-SPEED DATA ACQUISITION AND PROCESSING WITH A/D AND D/A CONVERTERS

The simple block diagram shown in Fig. 11-12 illustrates the use of analog-to-digital (A/D) and digital-to-analog (D/A) converters in a microcomputer system.

The A/D Converter (ADC) involves the use of an encoder that produces in a serial form (all the bits on one line sequentially); in addition, a conversion ladder is used to implement a 4-bit (or higher resolution) binary-coding system. The ladder provides a comparison voltage to a comparison circuit, which compares the voltage to be encoded against the

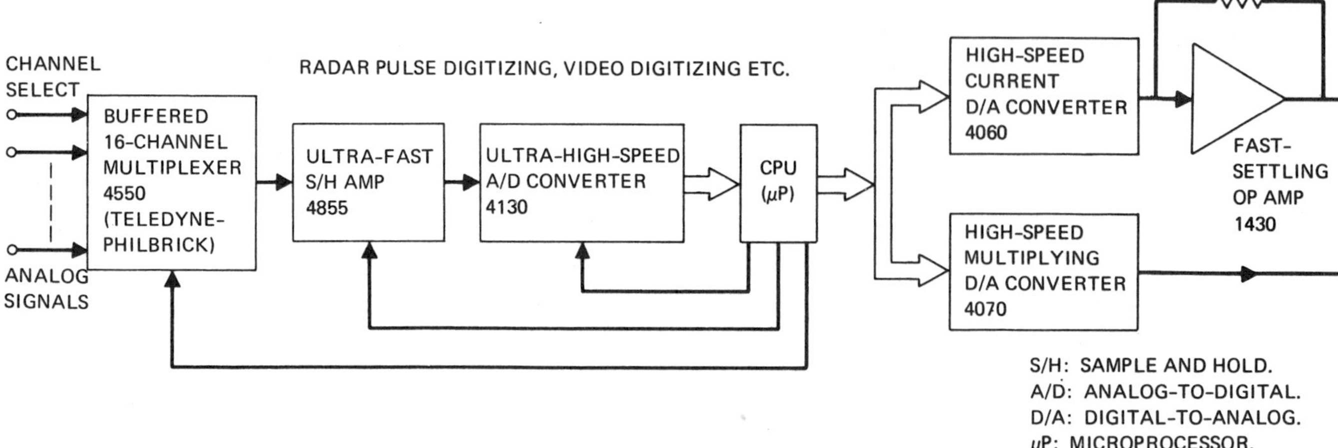

Fig. 11-12. Radar video/pulse digitizing system. (*Courtesy of Teledyne Philbrick*)

binary-coded voltage from the ladder. The output of the comparison circuit is the desired digital binary code in serial format. These devices are presently available in hybrid packaging with 8-, 10-, and 12-bit resolution, and conversion times from 0.75 μs to 2.5 μs.* In conjunction with a buffered multiplexer such as Teledyne 4550, and an ultrafast Sample/Hold amplifier type 4855, the 8-bit 4130 ADC has a gated throughput-rate of 909 KHz at 1.1 μs. The ADC system block-diagram of the chips on a 5″ X 5″ card is shown in Fig. 11-13. Typical specifications of an A/D converter (ADH-10/1 of Data Devices Corporation) are:

Resolution: 10 bit ± 0.2 to 0.05% accuracy
Dynamics: 47 to 59 dB, signal-to-noise ratio
Integral track-and-hold: 500-ps aperture-time
High-speed: 1-MHz word-rate.

*The Latest TRW *monolithic ADC*, with linearity ± $\frac{1}{2}$ LSB, has a conversion time from 400 ns (type IDC = 1001J) to 1 μs (type 1002J); price: \$75 to \$175.

ECL- and TTL-compatible, and processed to MIL-STD-883, Level B, the D/A converter (DAC) performs the reverse function by producing a normal dc output voltage that corresponds to the binary code in a serial or parallel format. A conversion ladder outputs a dc that represents a percentage of the full-scale reference voltage; an AND-gate using an

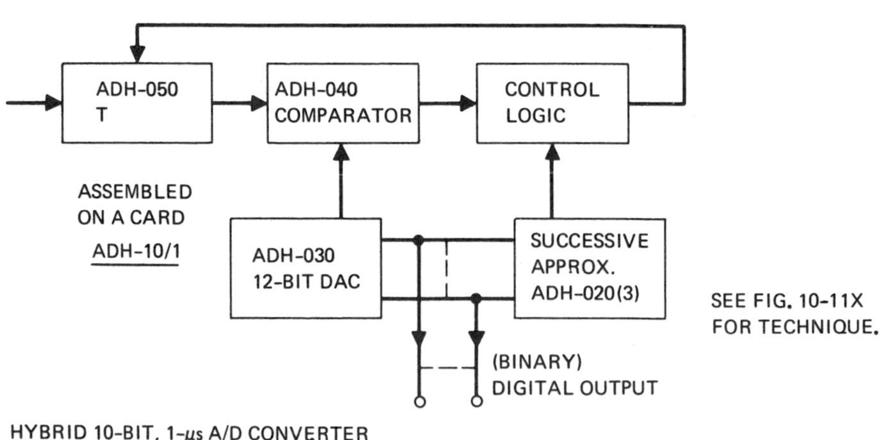

Fig. 11-13. Hybrid 10-bit, 1 μs A/D converter. (*Courtesy of ILC Data Devices Corp.*)

enable-pulse and the binary-pulse produces the output-dc. Shift and storage registers are involved when a parallel-format input is involved. A simple system block-diagram of a high-speed current-output, 12-bit/3-decade, DAC-3 of Data Devices Corporation, is shown in Figure 11-14. Specifications of the DAC-3 are:

(2″ X 1″ X 0.375″ plug-in module)
High Resolution: 12-bit or 3-decade BCD
Output current: up to 2 mA (full scale)
Unipolar or bipolar output: (pin-programmable)
Choice of BCD, binary, off-set, or 2's complement binary input format
Temperature-coefficient: 15 ppm/°C
Linearity: ±0.0125%; settling-time 500 ns to 0.1%
Reference: built-in, temperature-compensated

TTL- and DIP-pin compatible, and meeting MIL-STD-883 level B, the Teledyne's fastest DAC, type 4060, has a settling-time of 85 ns. It is suitable for radar-pulse digitizing, video digitizing, simultaneous sample-hold systems, CRT displays, and waveform analysis.

LSI, I^2L 8-Bit D/A Converter

Analog Devices, Inc., Wilmington, Pa., announced in 1980 a monolithic I^2L 8-bit AD558 D/A Converter (DacPort) operating with 5-to-15-volt dc power supply. Higher speeds are feasible at voltages of up to 15. The device includes 8 integrated-injection logic data-latches, 8 lateral PNP current sources, an R/2R ladder-resistive-network, reference and control amplifier, and an on-chip output amplifier with an analog output of 0 to 2.55 volts at 10 mA, or alternatively 0 to ±10 volts at 10 mA. Fifty-to-150 mW is a surpris-

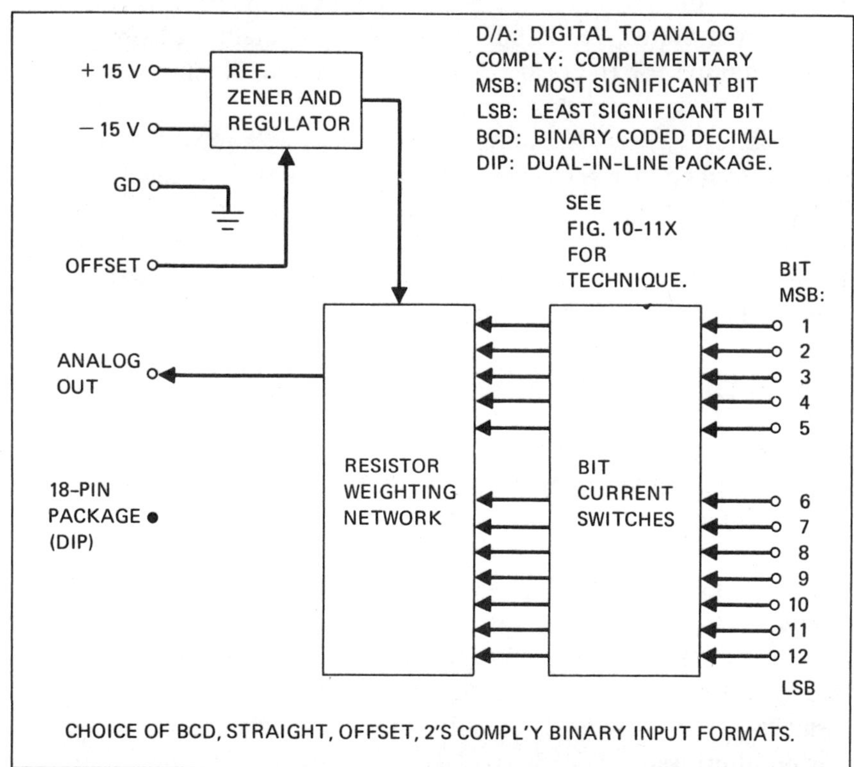

DAC-3 D/A CONVERTER (ILC DATA DEVICES CORP.)

Fig. 11-14. Data Devices DAC-3 D/A converter. (*Courtesy of ILC Data Devices Corp.*)

ingly low-power consumption for a D/A converter. It, however, needs an external decoupling electrolytic capacitor. I^2L processing employs the same diffusion processing steps as a standard bipolar process; hence analog and digital functions are feasible on the same chip.

The PNP current-sources eliminate errors due to *alpha particles*, and allows TTL-compatible input levels on the data-bus for the 8 I^2L data-latches. The input control signals are (1) Read/$\overline{\text{write}}$ for chip-enable input $\overline{\text{CE}}$, and (2) Address bit A_{15}, Enable clock-ϕ_2, and (3) Valid Memory Address, all three signals Nand-gated to on-chip control logic via chip-select $\overline{\text{CS}}$ control input. It can be easily interfaced to a type 6800 microcomputer system with a 3-transistor SSI chip. A single one-shot delay is required for deglitching in the case of a CRT display system. (In a write-cycle, the data delay-time to the rising-edge of R/$\overline{\text{W}}$ pulse is 225 nsec and hence the possibility of glitches.)

AD558 can be used as an A/D converter also by controlling the appropriate processing with a microprocessor.

11-15. "TELETEXT" OR CAPTIONING ON A DEDICATED TELEVISION-CABLE

Digitized data can be sent during two line-intervals of the vertical-blanking-interval of the regular monochrome or color composite-video signal of television transmission. The average data-rate used in the United Kingdom with this technique is 36-K bits/sec; the access-time for a full-page or caption is 0.24 sec. The page or caption capacity is 24 lines and 40 characters/line. With the present microcomputer systems, the cost of the television-studio processing system along with the pertinent peripherals can be reduced to a few thousand dollars. In addition, the special digital "decoding" unit required in the normal television receiver or monitor should not at this time cost more than \$75 on a large-scale production basis. The British Reuters Business News Service is available for this particular TV application. In the United States, the Public Broadcasting System is planning to use this caption-broadcast technique for the deaf. A simplified system block-diagram of the teletext is shown for the Encoder/Decoder system in Fig. 11-15.

In the United States, Reuters Manhattan Cable-TV project provides a dedicated pay-TV channel to its subscribers for receiving transactions on the Chicago Board of Trade or Financial News as "packets" of data (12 lines × 64 characters). A full-page of information appears in a few seconds by automatically deleting the regular picture video.

Hazeltine in the United States has developed a scheme to insert two bits of data on each odd-even line-pairs of the 525-line television picture at 30 frames/sec.

11-16. FDM AND TDM IN DATA COMMUNICATIONS

The data user may choose to transmit the data either in a serial or a parallel mode. The choice usually depends on the original format of data to be transmitted or it may depend upon the optimization of the channel in use. For parallel transmission, the channel is band-split into narrow-band subchannels for **Frequency Division Multiplex (FDM)**. Each bit of a character (e.g., ASCII 8-bit word) is transmitted over a separate narrow-band channel as shown in Fig. 11-16. The bit-rate of each narrow-band channel is reduced by a factor equal to the number of channel segments. By multiplexing, the incoming channels are contiguously put side-by-side in frequency. In serial transmission, each bit of an individual character is transmitted sequentially over a single channel.

Time Division Multiplex (TDM) is the latest preferred technique, since the concept is more **appropriate to digital data communications**, although FDM is easier to implement and less costly. A typical FDM multiplexer may put together twelve 110-baud channels,

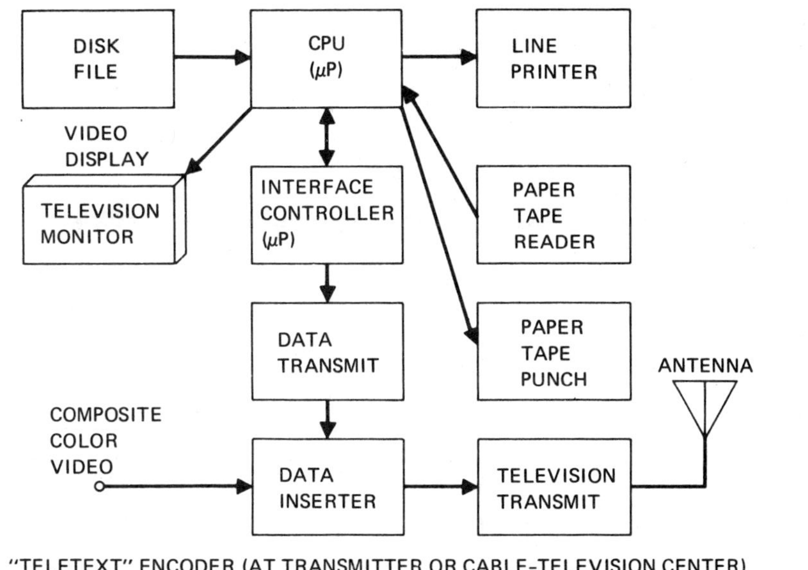

"TELETEXT" ENCODER (AT TRANSMITTER OR CABLE-TELEVISION CENTER)

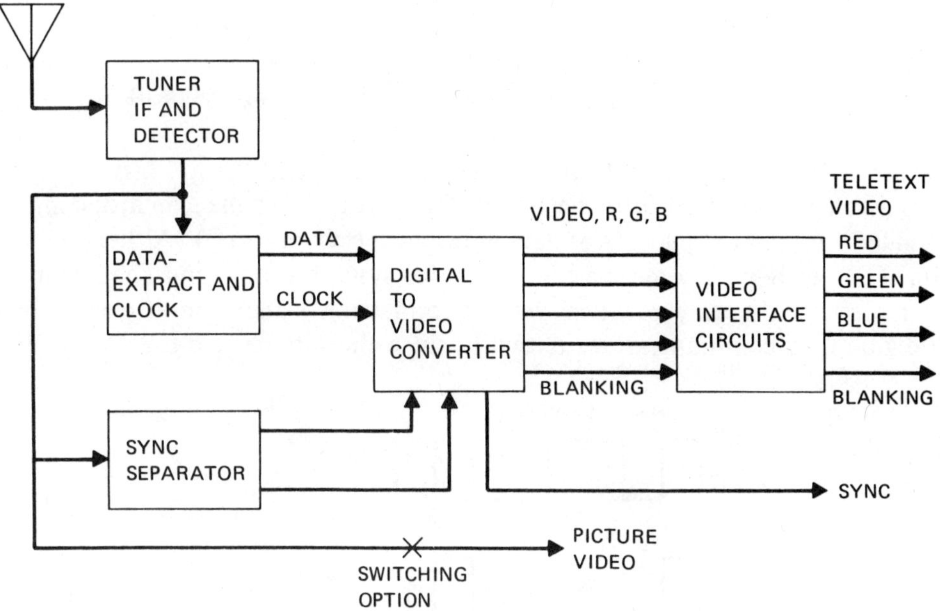

"TELETEXT" DECODER IN COLOR-TELEVISION RECEIVER

Fig. 11-15. "Teletext" captioning, system block-diagram.

or alternatively two 600-baud channels over one voice-grade 1,200-baud line. A small part of the usable bandwidth must, however, be reserved as an allowance for channel "guarding."

TDM is also termed *nonmessage switching*, and the relatively short time-intervals are repeatedly assigned to the same user; this is called *Time Division Multiple Access* (TDMA). The present FDMA satellite links are due for conversion to the TDMA at the next opportunity.

A typical character-interleaved TDM system is illustrated for the coded message. (A),

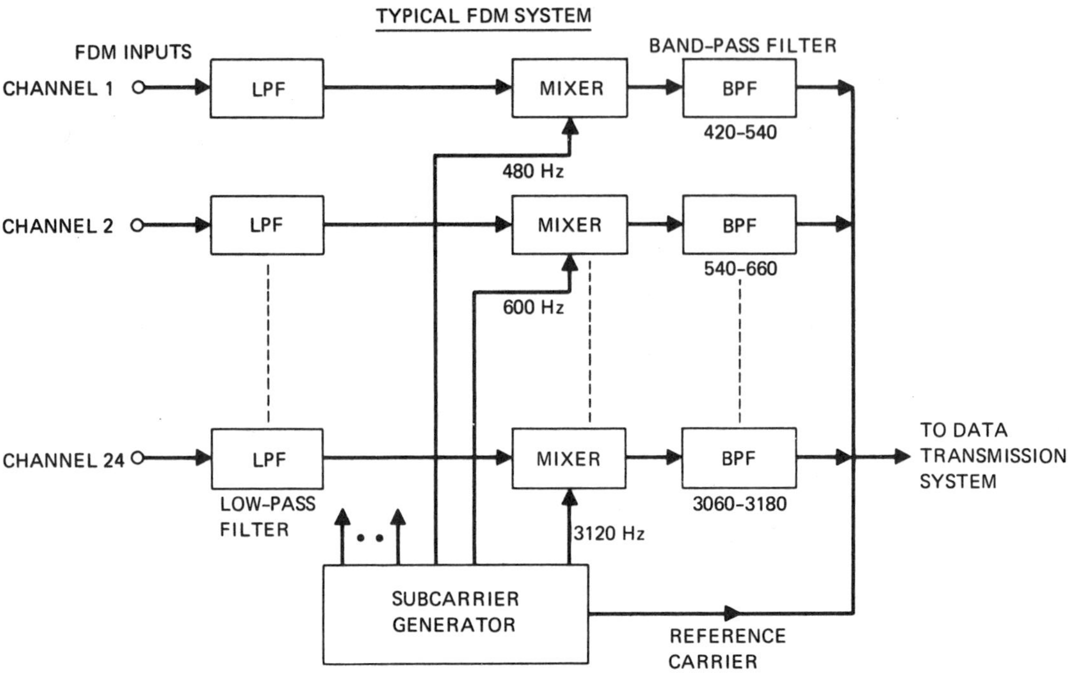

Fig. 11-16. Typical FDM system. (*Courtesy of IEEE Spectrum, February 1971*)

shown in Fig. 11-17. It is first stripped of its "start" and "stop" bits (B). The character of channel-1 is moved into the frame (C). Then, the frame synchronizing information is added for the next packets of data in respective channels (D). Although it is mandatory for TDM to reserve some message space for sync, framing, and channel-identifying bits, it represents the only practical way of formatting a digital multiplexing technique over a digital data communications network, since the bits packed-together need not be

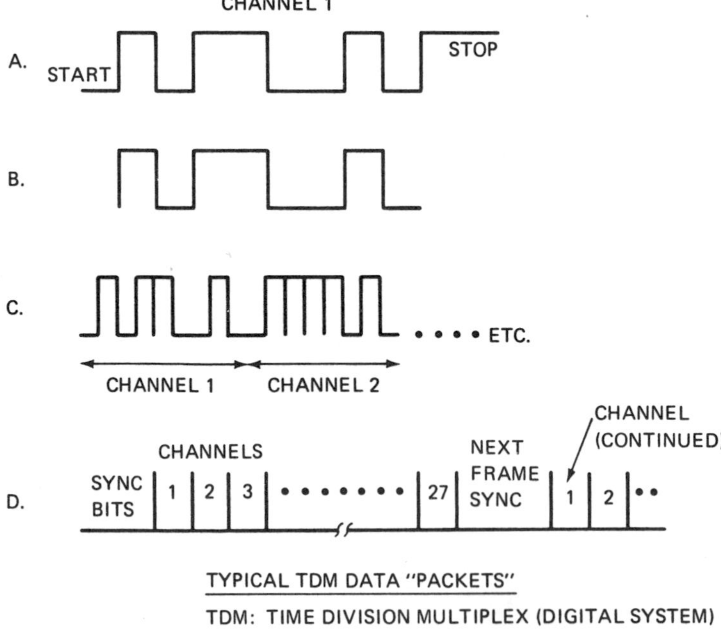

Fig. 11-17. Typical TDM data packets. (*Courtesy of IEEE Spectrum*)

put through D/A and A/D converters at either end. With TDM, low-cost microprocessor hardware will lower the costs too. (See Time-Division Multiple-Access, Appendix C.)

TDMA (Westar Satellite of Western Union)

The traffic capacity of a satellite transponder decreases when more than one carrier frequency is used for transmission in FDM/FDMA (frequency-division multiple access), whereas the traffic capacity is not affected in a TDM/TDMA system. Also, TDMA facilitates the use of low-cost microcomputers in small roof-top earth stations. So, all the latest domestic satellites going up in various countries should be using TDM/TDMA hereon. American Satellite Corporation and Digital Communications Corporation are the manufacturers of Westar equipment.

The transmitting central office uses a *channel processor* with up to 28 nonredundant terrestrial interface modules (TIMs) for up to 39 asynchronous Bell Telephone's T1 lines of 1.544 Mb/s (multiplexed with data, voice and wideband analog signals). The following *multiplexer/demultiplexer* equipment combines and compands the terrestrial input digital information into 2 high-speed multiplexed data-buses of 32 Mb/s each in *burst* format to make an overall TDMA bit-rate of 64 Mb/s. The *common control equipment* (CCE) is designed for redundancy; it involves scrambling (for security), preamble generation, and quadri-phase-shift keying (QPSK) of the uplink microwave channel. The receive downlink equipment of the satellite similarly consists of QPSK demodulation, preamble detection, and high-speed descrambling. An auto-entry and steady-state burst synchronization are the other functions involved.

A microprocessor-based *performance monitoring unit* (PMU) is essential, for continuous monitoring of the on-line equipment with a hard-copy printout of status and alarm, routine checkout, fail-safe use of redundant equipment, and diagnostics of faulty equipment. Typical uncoded BER (bit-error-rate) performance ranges between 10^{-7} and 10^{-8}, and energy/bit to noise-power-density required to achieve a BER of 10^{-6} is determined to be 16.5 dB.

The TDMA burst-frame of a duration of 750 μsec uses 2 reference sync bursts, each burst consisting of 60 bits of carrier recovery/clock recovery, 20 bits of unique word, and 8 bits of station identification. A guard-time of 12 bits separates the two adjacent bursts. A data-burst *preamble* is provided to accommodate overhead channels for voice and teletype orderwires and a BER monitoring procedure operating at 10.67 Kb/sec. A 5.33 Kb/sec alarm channel is included to transmit the alarms from the earth stations, microwave repeaters, etc., to the operational control center. (See Appendix C.)

The Westar TDMA burst-frame format is shown in the following diagram.

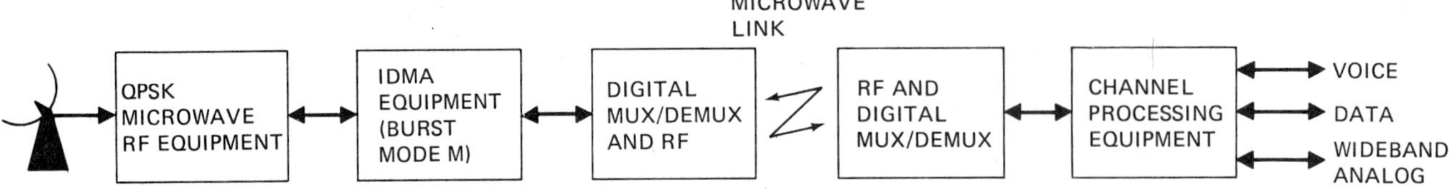

ORGANIZATION OF A TYPICAL WESTAR EARTH STATION FOR TIME-DIVISION MULTIPLE-ACCESS SATELLITE

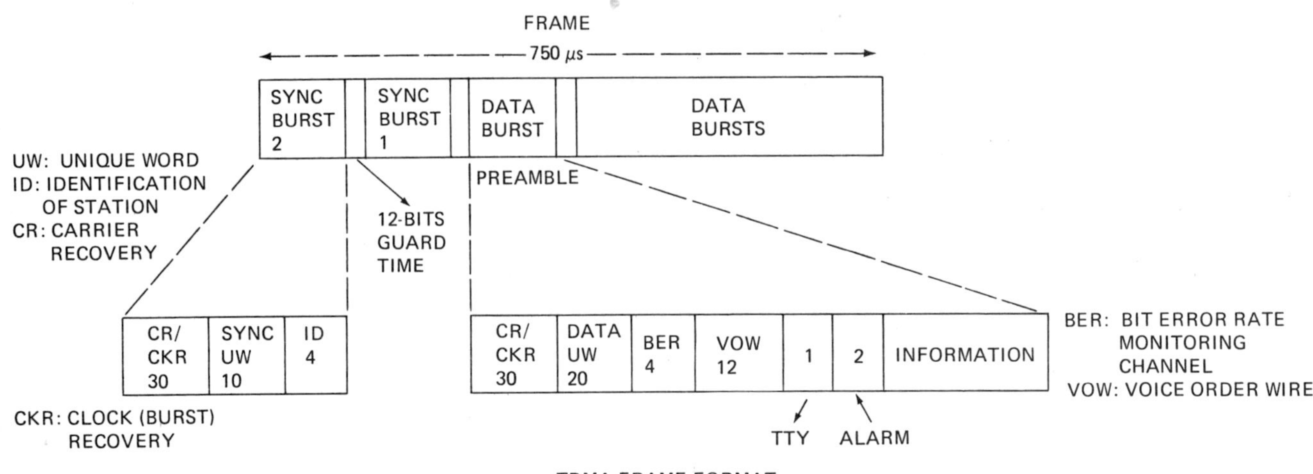

TDMA FRAME FORMAT

11-17. DATA COMMUNICATIONS BY FORWARD TRANSMISSION

The components in a forward transmission "ARQ" network are shown in Fig. 11-18. ARQ stands for **Acknowledge Request** on a supplementary **feedback channel.**

The source-symbols are transmitted at the rate R with an acceptable probability of information-bit error (P_B) in the presence of noise.

$$R = \frac{1}{T} \log_e m = k/T \text{ bits/sec}$$

where k = source-bits
= $\log_e m$ binary-signals.

Coding involves relating k source information-bits, on a "Block" or "Convolution" basis, to bandwidth and power for efficient use of these communication channel resources.

The **Block Encoder** output produces one of M channel symbols (words), and the modulator converts the binary-M or "M-ary" channel symbols given by 2^k into channel signals. If the channel is *bandwidth-limited* with adequate power (as on telephone lines), the encoder groups k information-bits to form M channel-symbols. If the channel is *power-limited* (as in satellites), the encoder adds redundancy to the k bits to effect a lower P_B at the expense of increased bandwidth and complexity. In the case of the ACK-NACK ARQ network with a feedback channel, the encoding consists of an error-detection code, and it is used in both these cases in forward transmission.

Data transmission involves digital modulation of an analog carrier. With ASK, amplitude-shift-keying, one of M amplitudes is sent in the signaling interval; with MPSK, one of M phases of a sine-wave segment is sent; PSK alone implies binary M = 2. The conventional technique of PSK requires phase coherence at the receiver, and hence, the common use of phase-lock-loops in modems. Message formatting, for example, allows

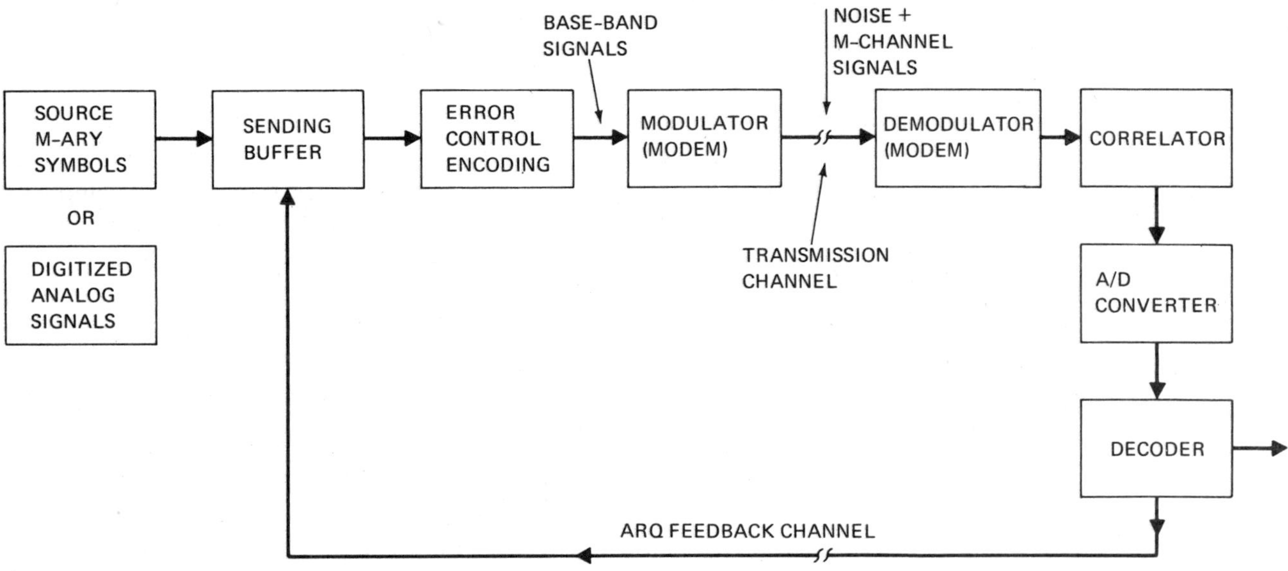

Fig. 11-18. Forward-transmission, ARQ network transmission. (© *IEEE Proceedings, June 1973*)

128 messages if a sequence of k(=7) source-bits are used ($m = 2^7 = 128$ messages or levels).

Convolution Encoding. As an alternative to block-encoding, channel symbols may be assembled by convolving information-bits k and the impulse response of a shift-register encoder with its modulo-2 adders. Convolution coding with a so-called Viterbi-decoding algorithm is termed maximum-likelihood decoding in the most cost-effective forward error-control technique devised for medium accuracy (P_B) requirements. This obviously involves **forward error correction (FEC)** in the absence of a feedback channel (as in satellite data communications).

11-18. PULSE CODE MODULATION AND SPREAD SPECTRUM SYSTEMS

In pulse code modulation (PCM), the analog signal is first sampled at a rate exceeding twice the highest significant frequency in the signal (according to Shannon's theorem), and each sample is quantized to one of a finite number of M levels, as noted previously. Each of these levels is a digital symbol or word. The quantized sample is reconstructed at the receiver by filtering and recovering the analog signal. PCM, with its high bit-rate, is mainly practical for multiplexing several source signals in a common channel.

The PCM format of grouping binary-symbols to represent M levels is exactly the format needed for digital characters from microcomputers; hence, the common-carrier digital multiplex facilities, such as the Bell T_1 and T_2 digital carriers, use the PCM format at 64-K bits/sec and above for grouping binary-symbols into characters in ASCII code.

Differential pulse code modulation (DPCM) allows a 20-K bit/sec speech transmission-rate for the PCM-encoded error between the current sample and a predicted value. The prediction computation is time-variant. DPCM turns to a CORE RAM technique in video recordings; for example, picture-phone video is transmitted DPCM at a 1.544-M bits/sec rate for the 1-MHz analog video signal. (Bandwidth-consuming PCM actually requires 14-M bits/sec for phone-video.)

Delta Modulation (DM) is the simplest type of DPCM, as a binary error coding signal. The predictor simply integrates the past history of the information at a variable gain and remains mostly close to the actual waveform. With this technique, the 20-K bits/sec can be lowered to 10-K bits/sec.

Spread Spectrum Systems. The technique spreads the transmitted voice or television signal or any other analog signal over a wide frequency band, much wider than the bandwidth of the analog signal. For example, the narrow-band voice signal from a telephone is distributed over a wide megahertz bandwidth by encoding the voice signal with a wideband encoding signal. As another example, a 4-MHz bandwidth color television signal is transmitted over a bandwidth of 43 MHz by quadriphase-shift keying modulation of a microwave signal (for one transponder) in satellite data communications systems. The technique is adopted for the following *advantages*: selective addressing facility; code-division multiplexing in satellite multiple-access data communications; encryption in data transmission; high-resolution range; low-density power-spectra hiding the signal (even in noise); and above all, interference rejection. Three types of modulation are used to achieve these results by spread spectrum concept:

1. '*Direct sequence*' modulated system by modulation of the carrier by a digital code-sequence, whose bit-rate is much higher than the information signal bandwidth. The following simple diagram shows how it is accomplished.

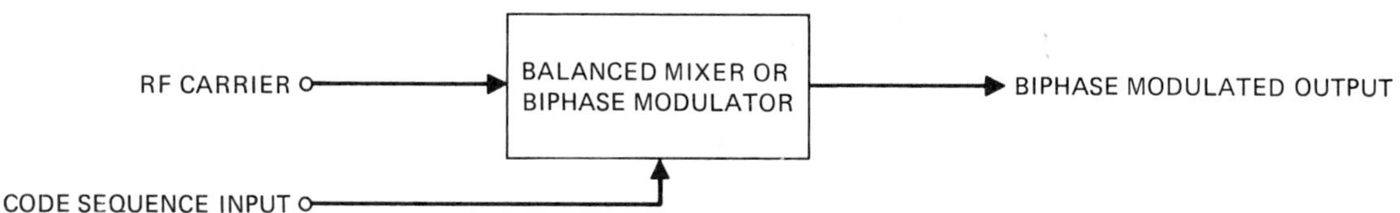

2. '*Frequency Hop*'. The carrier frequency is shifted in discrete increments in a pattern that follows a code-sequence. The transmitter involved hops from frequency to frequency within a set range of frequencies. The following diagram illustrates the concept.

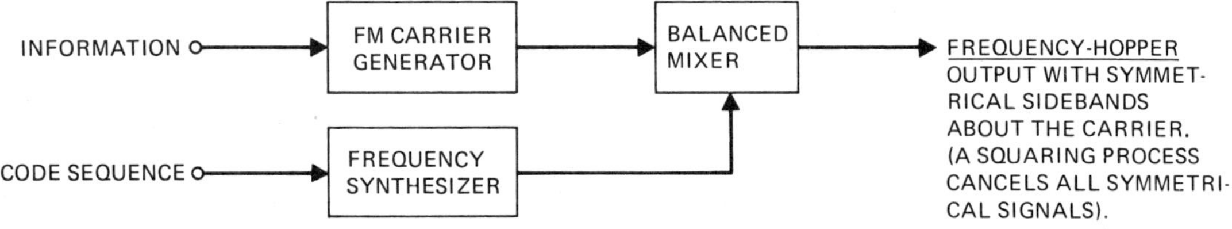

3. *Pulsed-FM* or '*chirp*' modulation is accomplished by *sweeping* the carrier over a wideband during a given pulse-interval. (The 'sweeping' is similar to that commonly performed in 'signal frequency generators' used for tracing the bandwidth envelope of an audio or video amplifier.)

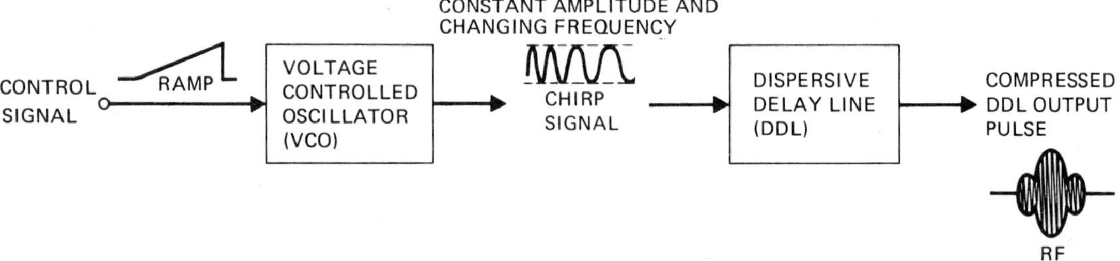

3-Bit PCM (Pulse Code Modulation) Digitizer

In telephone transmission for voice, 3-bit PCM that generates 8 levels in digital information ($2^3 = 8$) is quite satisfactory (for a decoded, clear, audio signal). The analog audio signal is *quantized* into 8 levels (called *M-ary levels.*)

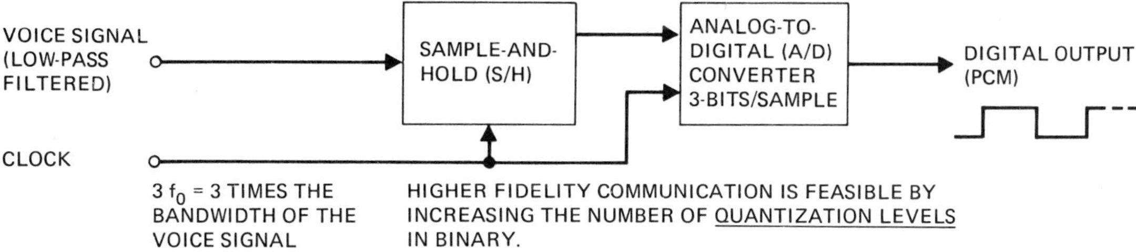

Quadriphase Modulation

Satellite microwave transmissions use Quadri (or quaternary) phase-shift keying modulation (QPSK) for the *multiplexed wideband* digital information used for thousands of telephone channels and broadcast color television signals.

Advantages: The QPSK data communications information is not degraded in BER (bit-error-rate) when passed through a nonlinear amplifier with low signal/noise ratio as a biphase signal. Also, for the same data-rate, the RF (radio frequency) bandwidth for a quadriphase signal is half that required for a biphase signal. Alternatively, twice as much data can be transmitted in the same bandwidth with a quadriphase compared to a biphase signal.

The quadriphase modulator shifts one of 4 carrier-phases spaced at 90° intervals (in-quadrature). Two bits of binary data are required to select the phase to be transmitted. If the binary bits are A and B, the following data/phase relationships result.

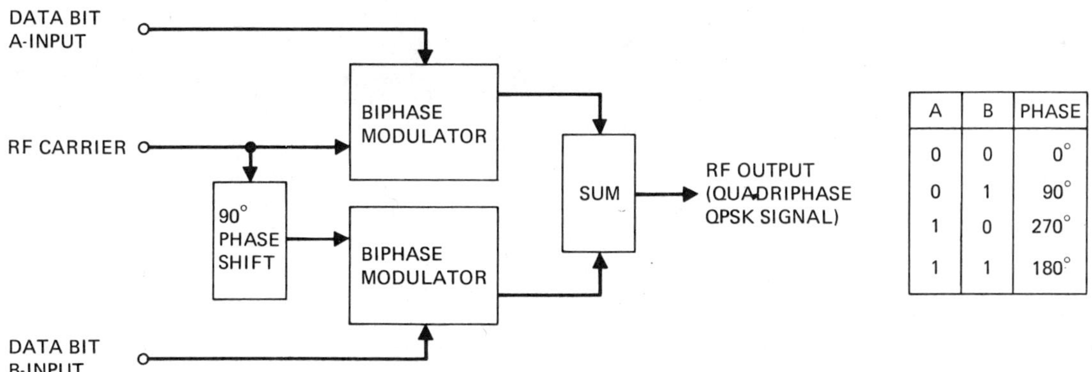

A	B	PHASE
0	0	0°
0	1	90°
1	0	270°
1	1	180°

PCM CODEC (Pulse Code Modulation, Coder/Decoder). The high-density NMOS silicon-gate technology has produced one of the most popular devices for data communications applications (see p. 372). Intel 2910A 8-bit companded A/D and D/A converter provides combined analog and digital circuits on a common chip to replace one of the important units in telecommunications systems with a low-power consumption, 230 mW (standby 33 mW). The chip comprises of the sample-and-hold circuits, built-in digital-to-analog converter, the comparator, the successive approximation register, the logic required to interface a 4-wire full-duplex voice telephone circuit in a PCM link, and in-band signaling for time-division multiplex (TDM) systems.

The wide 78-dB dynamic range, and the minimal conversion time of 80 μsec, with

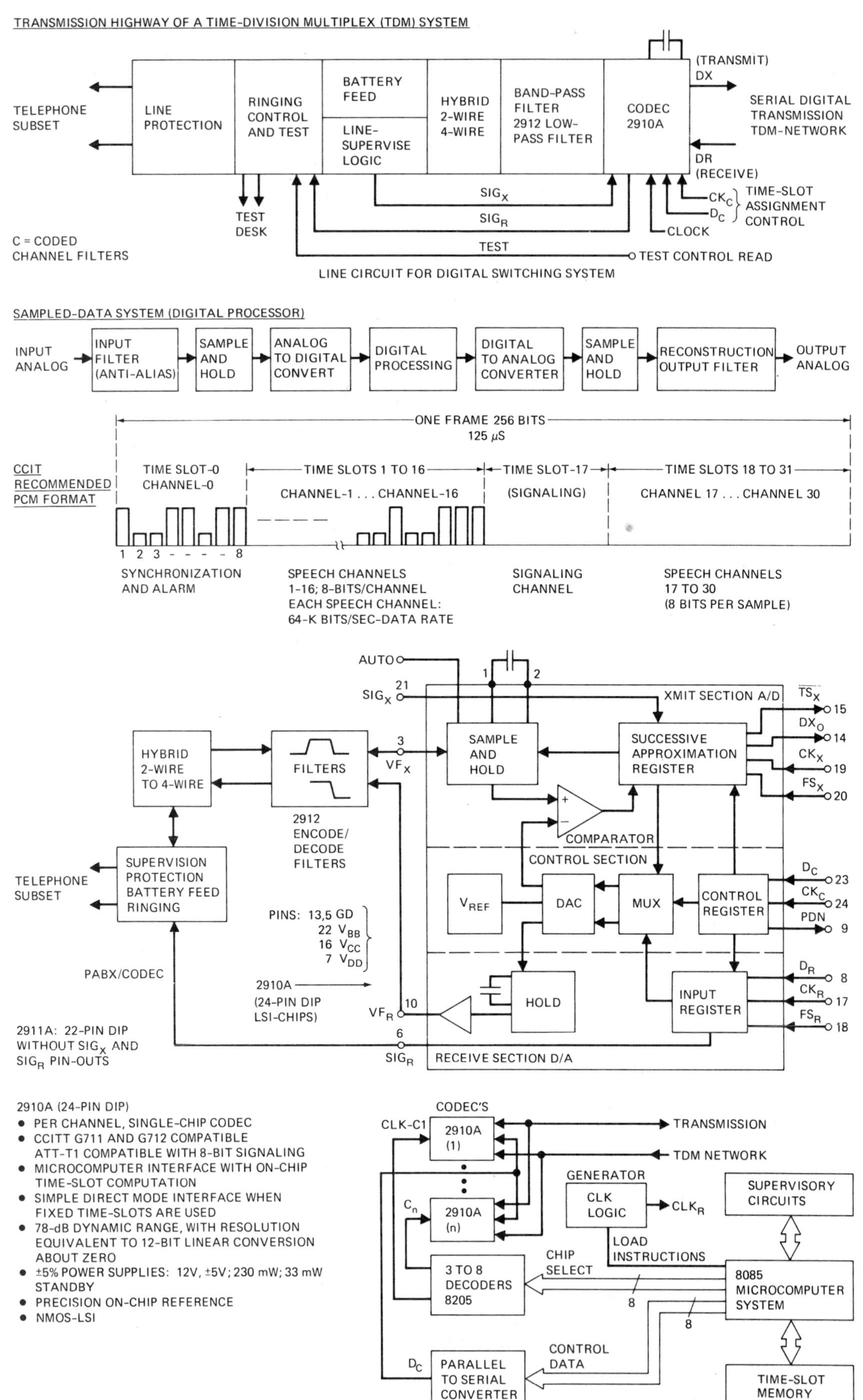

Fig. 11-19. Intel 2910A, PCM CODEC, LSI chip. (*Courtesy of Intel Corp.*)

resolution equivalent to 12-bit linear conversion about zero, makes it an ideal LSI chip for applications such as data acquisition, telemetry, signal processing systems, and secure data communications. In the telecommunications area, it can be used for: (1) T1 carrier transmission, (2) digital PBXs and central switching systems, and (3) subscriber carrier/concentrators. The functional block-diagram of its usage in transmission line circuits (in conjunction with two PCM line filters–supplied by Intel as a common monolithic integrated chip 2912), and the block-diagram of the chip 2910A and its pin configuration are shown in Fig. 11-19. The chip is CCITT/G711 and G712 compatible and ATT/T1 compatible with 8-bit signaling. Microcomputer interface with on-chip time-slot computation is applicable in modern TDM systems for tele- and satellite data communications.

Functional Description. The two foremost functions of the unit are: (1) encoding and decoding of analog signals for both voice and call-progress tones and (2) encoding and decoding of the signaling and supervision information.

The Codec encodes the incoming analog voice signal at the frame rate into an 8-bit PCM word on a nonsignaling frame. The word is sent out on pin D_X at the proper interval. The Codec fetches an 8-bit PCM word from the receive path D_R and decodes an analog value, which will remain constant on VF_R until the next receive frame. Transmit/Receive frames are independent, asynchronous (transmission), or synchronous (switching) with each other.

For signaling associated with the channel, the transmit path encodes the incoming signal as above and substitutes the signal present on Sig_X for the least significant bit of the encoded PCM word. In the same way, the Codec decodes the 7 most significant bits according to CCITT/G733 recommendation on the receive signaling frame, and outputs the least significant bit value on Sig_R until the next signaling frame. Signaling frames on the send/receive sides are independent of each other and are selected by a double-width frame sync pulse on the appropriate channel.

2910A can be used on line and trunk (long-distance) terminals. The call progress tones (dial tone, busy tone, ring-back tone, recorder tone), and the pre-tape-recorded announcements can be sent on the voice path; the signaling path takes care of off-hook and disconnect supervision, rotary dial pulses, and ring control.

The transmit and receive time-slots are defined in the circuitry to eliminate external time-slot exchange in small systems. In large systems, the Codec provides one level of concentration, but it can be bypassed, and discrete time-slots can be allotted to each Codec within a system. In the standby mode, most functions are disabled to minimize power consumption.

Companding and Coding. The PCM bit-rate required to maintain a 72-dB voice dynamic range with minimum 40-dB below-signal distortion level is of utmost importance. The dynamic range is determined from speech characteristics and power losses over long lines compared to short lines. This dynamic range would require at least 12 bits for linear A/D conversion. Since minimum number of bits/time-slot are desirable for more time-slots at a given bit rate, T1 carrier uses 8 bits/time-slot. Compression and expansion of the signal during A/D conversion allows 8 bits to represent the full 72-dB dynamic range and maintain a constant signal/distortion ratio (SDR). Companding is a nonlinear signal process wherein low-level signals are amplified and high-level signals are attenuated to reduce output dynamic range while maintaining signal characteristics independent of input signal amplitude. An expander does the reverse process.

Companding during quantizing or A/D conversion is also called "coding for telephony," and it is achieved by using nonlinear spacing of quantizing levels. The threshold levels are more closely spaced for small amplitude levels than for large amplitude levels thus causing quantizing distortion to be favorable to small signals. The signal-to-quantizing distortion ratios are far better quantitatively when companding is used. The compression curves are piecewise linear approximations to the following equations.

μ-law: (USA/Japan) $F(X) = \text{Sgn}(X).\ \ln(1 + \mu\,|X|)/\ln(1 + \mu)\ ..\qquad 0 \leqslant |X| \leqslant 1$

A-law: (Europe) $F(X) = \text{Sgn}(X).\ 1 + \log_{10}(A|X|)/1 + \log_{10} A\ ..\qquad \frac{1}{A} \leqslant |X| \leqslant 1$

$= \text{Sgn}(X).\ A|X|/1 + \log_{10} A\ ..\qquad 0 \leqslant |X| \leqslant \frac{1}{A}$

X = Input signal; Sgn (X) = Sign of input; μ = 255 (AT&T); A = 87.6 (CCITT)

Codecs use 8-bits/time-slot to specify amplitude as a piecewise linear approximation to the log curves. (μ-law uses 15-segment approximation, and A-law uses 13.) The 8-bit digital code has a sign-bit, 3 bits for chord selection, and 4 bits for step selection within the chosen chord. Figure 11-20 illustrates the compression effect through use of non-uniform quantizing levels and the transfer characteristics of the coder and the decoder for μ-law. The μ-law Codec has a dead-zone around zero, requiring two code words for plus and minus zero. The A-law Codec has a threshold at zero; that is, for a zero input, the output must have an offset of plus or minus half a step.

11-19. AUTOMOTIVE MICROPROCESSOR APPLICATIONS

The Intersil 12-bit IM-6100 or the RCA 8/16-bit CDP-1801 CMOS microprocessors are ideal for cost-conscious automotive applications in view of their immunity to noise and temperature. Systems with two microprocessors, one as the CPU and the other as a multiplexer-controller for the various functions in the following list, are feasible in the immediate future.

Motor and chassis:

1. Electronic fuel injection
2. Ignition control and electronic advance
3. Alternator diodes and voltage regulators
4. Cruise control
5. Tire pressure monitor
6. Electric fuel pump
7. Antiskid, 2/4 wheel
8. Seat-belt ignition interlock.

Steering-wheel mechanism:

1. Tachometer with speed-threshold indicator
2. True velocity sensing by radar
3. Windshield wiper control
4. Heater/air-conditioning temperature control
5. Speed indicator and mileage totalizer
6. Automatic transmission
7. Airbag-trip for automobile-crash
8. Cockpit instrumentation.

Figure 11-21 illustrates an automotive application that uses two microprocessor chips.

Detroit's 1981 Cars. With the introduction of the microprocessor chips in the automobile, Detroit's new cars will get better gas mileage, emit far less pollution, and provide

- COMPANDING CODING IN TELEPHONY FOR PCM CODEC DIGITAL PROCESSING IN TIME-DIVISION MULTIPLEX TRANSMISSION SYSTEMS: μ-LAW FOR U.S. AND JAPAN, AND A-LAW FOR EUROPE, ETC. BOTH INVOLVE PIECEWISE APPROXIMATIONS TO LOGARITHMIC COMPRESSION CURVES.

- μ-LAW: $F(x) = \text{SGN}(x)\,\dfrac{\ln(1 + \mu|x|)}{\ln(1 + \mu)}$ . . $0 \leqslant |x| \leqslant 1$, WHERE x IS INPUT SIGNAL.

- A-LAW: $F(x) = \text{SGN}(x)\left[\dfrac{1 + \log_{10}(A|x|)}{1 + \log_{10}A}\right], \dfrac{1}{A} \leqslant |x| \leqslant 1$

  SGN (x) = SIGN OF INPUT
  $\mu = 255$ (AT&T)
  $A = 87.6$ (CCITT)

- μ-LAW USES 15-SEGMENT APPROXIMATION; A-LAW USES 13-SEGMENT CURVE.

- CODEC'S USE 8-BIT/TIME-SLOT TO SPECIFY AMPLITUDE AS PIECEWISE APPROXIMATION TO THE ABOVE LOGARITHMIC CURVES (8-BITS: 1 SIGN BIT, 3 BITS FOR CHORD SELECTION, AND 4 BITS FOR STEP-SELECTION).

- CODER/DECODER CHARACTERISTICS COMBINED PROVIDE THE QUANTIZATION STEPS AS A FUNCTION OF SIGNAL AMPLITUDE.

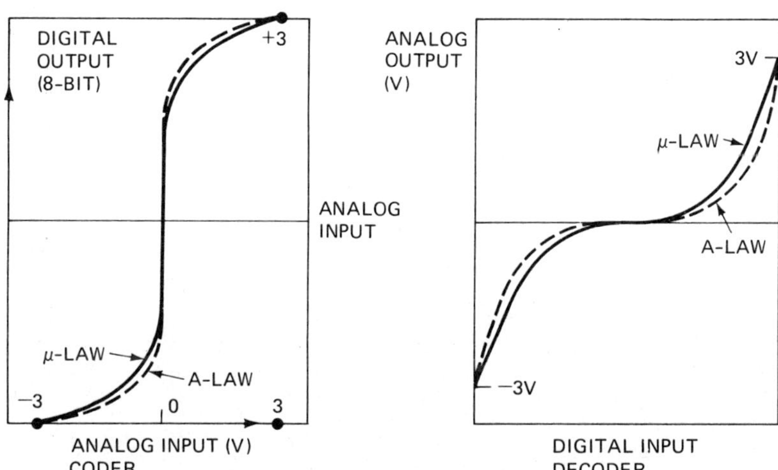

- DECODER OUTPUT CHARACTERISTICS AROUND ZERO AMPLITUDE DIFFER IN μ AND A-LAWS

- COMPRESSION ENABLES THE REDUCTION OF SIGNAL'S DYNAMIC RANGE IN SUCH A WAY THAT SMALL SIGNAL CHARACTERISTICS ARE MAINTAINED. (THE CONVERSION IS LOGARITHMIC TYPE).

- 2910A CODEC: $\mu = 255$ LAW USES A 15-SEGMENT APPROXIMATION TO THE LOGARITHMIC LAW. EACH SEGMENT CONSISTS OF 16 STEPS. IN ADJACENT SEGMENTS, THE STEP SIZES ARE IN A RATIO OF 2 TO 1. (FOR FURTHER INFORMATION ON μ/A-LAWS, 8-BIT COMPANDED A/D AND D/A CONVERTERS, REFER TO INTEL APPLICATION NOTES ON 2910A CODEC.)

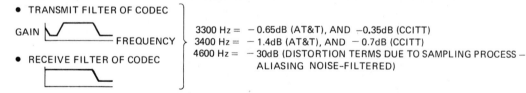

- TRANSMIT FILTER OF CODEC

  GAIN — FREQUENCY

- RECEIVE FILTER OF CODEC

  3300 Hz = − 0.65dB (AT&T), AND −0.35dB (CCITT)
  3400 Hz = − 1.4dB (AT&T), AND − 0.7dB (CCITT)
  4600 Hz = − 30dB (DISTORTION TERMS DUE TO SAMPLING PROCESS – ALIASING NOISE-FILTERED)

- FILTER 2912 IS DESIGNED TO WORK WITH THREE CLOCK FREQUENCIES: 1.536, 1.544, 2.084 MHz THE ABOVE FREQUENCY CUTOFF IS MAINTAINED AT THE THREE CLOCK FREQUENCIES. CORRECTION FILTER (SIN x/x) OUTPUT RESPONSE FOR 2910A PROVIDES THE ABOVE ROLL-OFF $x = \pi f/8000$, WHERE 8000 Hz IS THE SAMPLING FREQUENCY

Fig. 11-20. Transfer characteristics of the coder/decoder for μ-law—compression effect. (*Courtesy of Intel Corp.*)

the driver with useful electronic devices to make driving safer, less expensive, and more interesting. Some of the computer-controlled facilities available in 1981 cars are:

- Engine control unit
- Diagnostic unit
- Brake unit
- Transmission control
- Electronic ignition unit
- Throttle body
- Throttle position sensor
- Vacuum sensor
- Barometric pressure sensor
- Exhaust gas recirculation valve
- Air temperature sensor
- Radar unit

- Fuel injector
- Distributor
- Timing control
- Crankshaft position sensor
- Oxygen sensor
- Coolant temperature sensor
- Knock sensor
- Brake sensor
- Keyless lock
- Dashboard displays: Fuel gauge, diagnostics, speed, time, temperature and temperature control, trip computer, radio/cassette, navigation unit, and map display.

11-20. TELECOMMUNICATIONS, ELECTRONIC SWITCHING SYSTEMS

There is presently a vigorous activity in Europe and elsewhere, where the existing direct-control step-by-step and crossbar electromechanical telephone-switching systems are comparatively small-scale, to replace the electromechanical telecommunications systems, which include private branch exchanges (PBEX), by electronic switching systems (ESS) before the end of the century. The ESS take two forms, the Time Division Multiplex (TDM) digital switching system and the Stored Program Space-Division (SPSD) digital computer switching system. In the approaching twenty-first century, it is quite likely that at least 50% of the Bell Telephone System will, by either one or both of the approaches mentioned, go toward a super large-scale Digital Telecommunications Computer Network (DTCN) using a microcomputer-chip in each terminal telephone set. These subscriber-line (SL) sets will handle local, long-distance, and international calls, including Facsimile News and Picture-Phone. The present large-scale computer Networks and Cable-Television may be interconnected to this Telecommunications Network at option.

1. The TDM system operates as a common transmission path, on which all of the subscriber's digitized conversations take place simultaneously on a PCM time-sharing basis. The Bell Telephone System No. 101 ESS and the Automatic Electric Company EAX (Electronic Automatic Exchanges), both of which are in the development stage, follow the TDM approach. The principle of the TDM telephone system is illustrated in Fig. 11-22. A speech or picture signal is sampled on a repetitive basis and transmitted in a specific time-sequence with respect to the other subscriber signals, as a pulse-code-

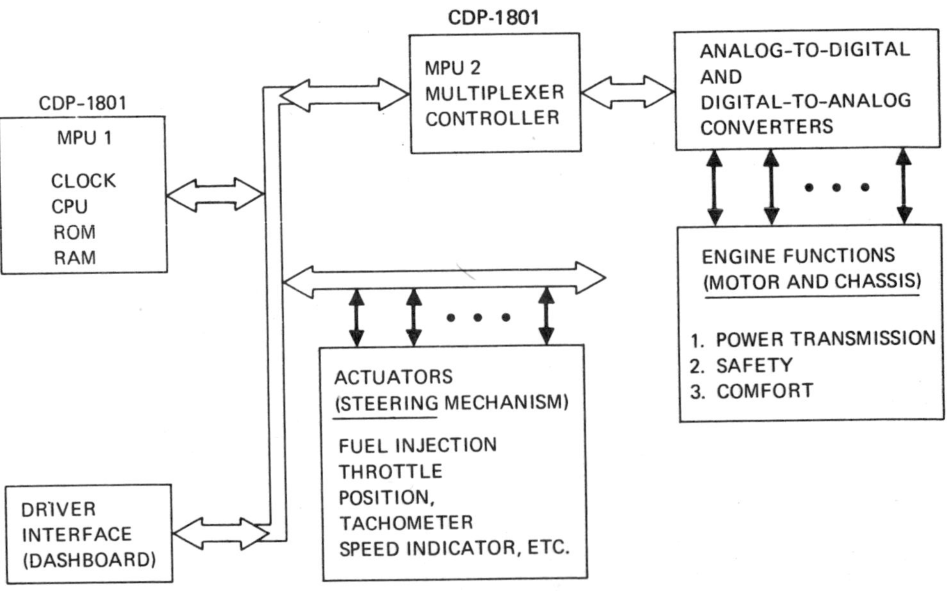

Fig. 11-21. Automobile application with two microprocessor chips.

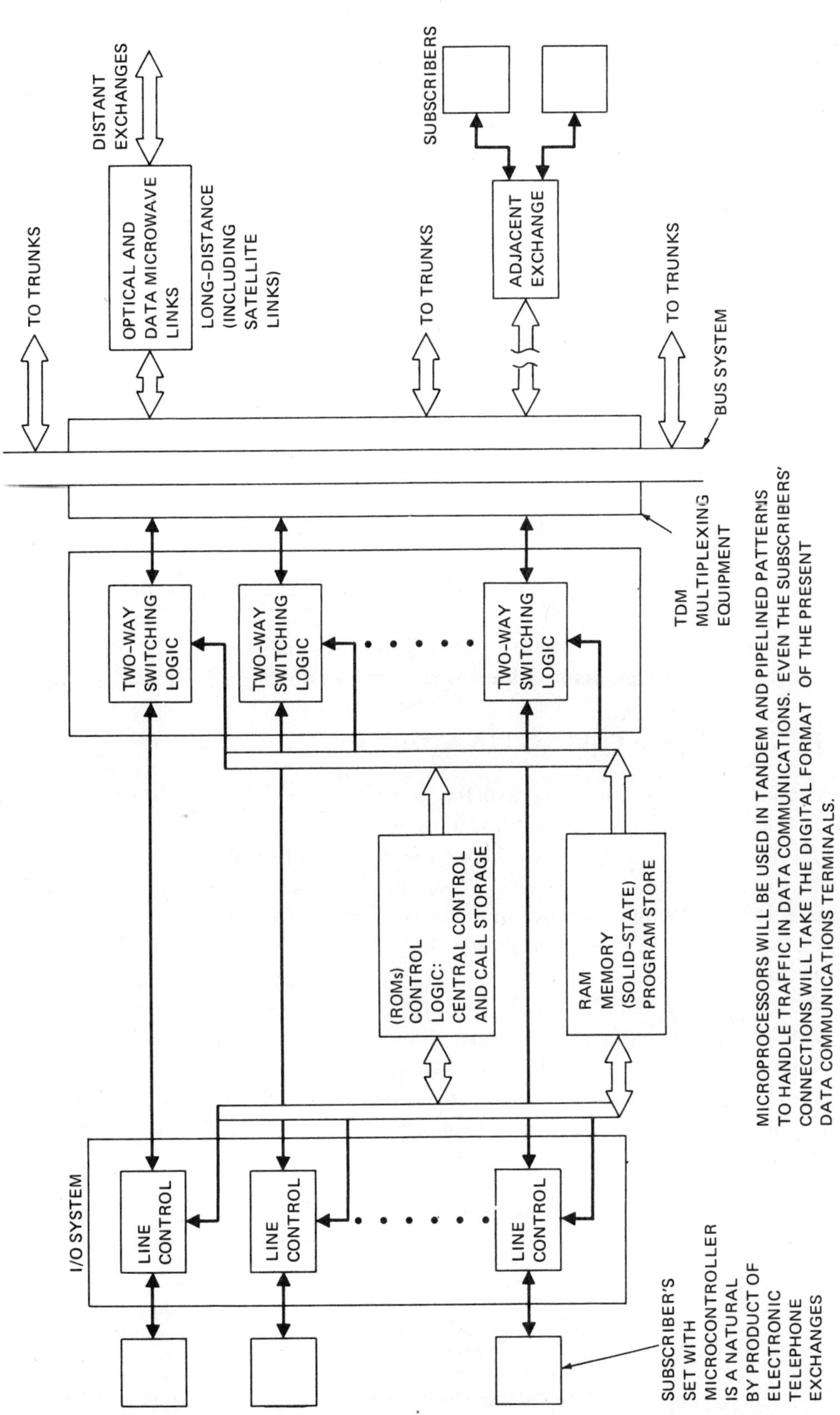

Fig. 11-22. Telephone network, using TDM electronic switching system. (*Courtesy of Hayden Book Company, Inc.*)

modulated, high-speed digital pulse-train. Present heavy telephone cables will be replaced by light fiber-optic cables and optical links.

2. The alternative, **stored program No. 1 ESS** (Bell Telephone System), will have greater flexibility, as a **space-division concept** in two separate sections, central control and switching network. The central control is interfaced with:

1. Subscriber line-scanner
2. Program storage-memory
3. Call storage-memory
4. Switching network in conjunction with line-scanning
5. Administration and maintenance center with teleprinters.

The switching network leads to outgoing trunks for long-distance calls. The stored-program concept allows a continuously changing memory and logic in terms of RAMs and PLA control logic. Microprocessors, in "pipeline" system organization, make elegant switching centers with automatic testing facilities.

Figure 11-23 explains the systems concept in five steps:

1. The input programs collect status-data on subscriber lines.
2. Real-time operational program conducts output action as required.
3. Subroutines on ROMs translate dialed digits, trunks, and network paths for the control of output action.
4. Output programs do the necessary system hardware switching.
5. **Executive control programs** provide the **supervisory software** for the whole operation.

11-21. MOS LSI SINGLE-CHIP CALCULATOR

The first consumer application to reap the benefit of the high-density LSI-PMOS mass-production at high-yields in the early 1970s was the low-priced calculator chip. The implementation technique has been based mostly on the PLA approach using master-slave J-K flip-flops and static RAMs. Sequential and combinational logic is achieved on a single LSI-chip (minimizing requirements of space for intraconnections) by means of the PLA approach. Texas Instruments first achieved this objective in a 13-bit fixed-point calculator, by using four chips during 1969. Within 4 or 5 years, the single-chip calculators flooded the markets around the world at unbelievably low prices.

The external clock requirements were minimized to one, and both functions and numbers are inserted directly to the function and sequence-control section with the aid of PLAs and J-K flip-flops; the ROM is implemented as a look-up table for the stored-program. Parallel arithmetic-unit operation is performed at the digit-level, and a RAM is

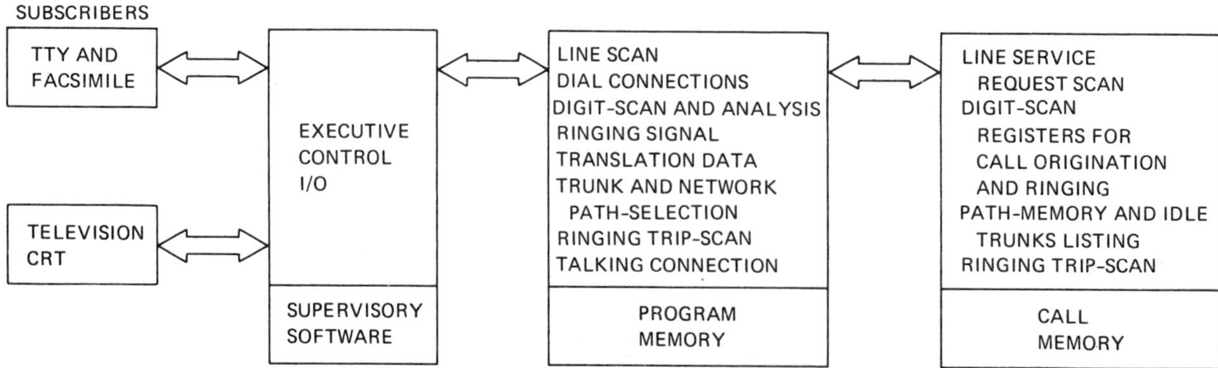

Fig. 11-23. Telephone microcomputer switching center. (*Courtesy of Hayden Book Company, Inc.*)

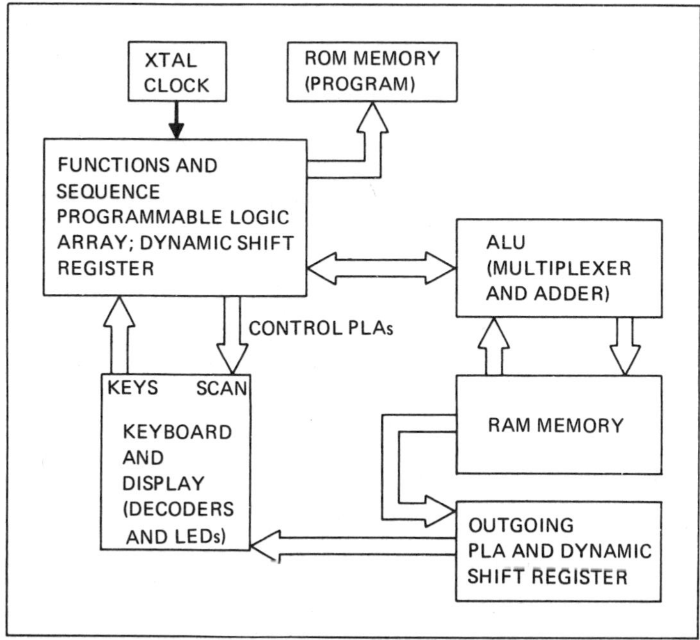

SLOW-SPEED PMOS-LSI (EASIER TO FABRICATE, COMPARED TO NMOS).

Fig. 11-24. Architecture of a typical "calculator" chip.

employed for handling the data transfers, as an improvement to the usual dynamic shift-registers. The keyboard interface is simplified by taking the scan-signal used for the display and using it for encoding the keyboard entries. A typical chip-architecture of the low-cost low-speed PMOS calculator is shown in Fig. 11-24. Automatic display shutoff after a few seconds is mandatory to minimize battery power consumption due to light-emitting diodes (LED). In future, LCD display would eliminate this need.

Sophisticated low-priced calculators, available at low-cost slide-rule prices, use logic of Reverse Polish Notation (RPN). The RPN uses four to three registers in a stack, with the display-register at the bottom. Numbers and functions are keyed into this register, and simple arithmetic operations involve the use of these three registers and not the memory register and its specific memory function. Only intermediate results are displayed and stored automatically; each function is evaluated immediately after the function key is pressed. As compared to algebraic logic, the RPN logic is faster without the need of any parenthesis keys.

11-22. HEWLETT-PACKARD 9825 PROGRAMMABLE DESKTOP PROFESSIONAL CALCULATOR

The Hewlett-Packard calculator belongs to the class of IBM-5100 portable computer, and employs Tektronix-4051 and Graphics 11" CRT-display. The display system includes the interactive light-pen, and 32-K bytes of memory, 300-K byte cartridge tape-drive, and BASIC firmware, and fills in for a large number of applications, bordering those of a minicomputer and a peripheral controller. It can be used as a dedicated computer, oriented toward solution of engineering problems.

Capabilities are:

1. Number-crunching
2. Two levels of 14 interrupts, and interface for a programmable controller

3. Buffered display and high-speed CPU, using H.P.'s own NMOS, Si-gate microprocessor
4. 16-bit parallel processor with 6-MHz clock
5. 16-K ROMs and 4-K RAMs
6. Direct-memory access (DMA)
7. Auto-memory record and load
8. Extended internal calculation range from $\pm 10^{511}$ to $\pm 10^{-511}$
9. Interface capability is provided for plug-in ROMs and I/O modules: **IEEE standard 488-1975 interface BUS requirements** are met at 55 kilobytes/sec data in the "burst mode"; 16-bit parallel-I/O input-speeds up to 400-K, 16-bit words, output-speeds up to 200-K, 16-bit words
10. 32-channel LED-display
11. Optional, Hewlett-Packard 9866B, 80-characters/line, 240-line/min, thermal Line-Printer.

11-23. DISTRIBUTED DATA PROCESSING

11-23.1. Distributed Processing Networks. As a concept, distributed processing networks involve application and/or *data-base processing activity at two or more network nodes. Distributed data processing* (*DDP*) in generally the term connected with the system integration of *computer networking* and *data-base management* associated with *time-share*, using high-level programming languages BASIC, ALGOL, PL/1, APL, FORTRAN, and the latest block-structured languages such as PL/M or PL/Z (Zilog) or PASCAL/C (all ROM-able in the present microcomputer systems). The concept involves an economically flexible and reliable computer system that distributes the power of a *central* large-scale network computer to "Node" computer terminals where some raw information is generated and processed in *real-time*; the customer's host mini- or micro-computers at the terminals share resources such as software and data stored in libraries of disk and other peripherals. Such systems naturally reach a high degree of sophistication as a (difficult-to-implement) standardization takes place in ultimately deciding on a common high-level language, and they minimize undesired additional hardware at the terminals for necessary translation. The Nodes in turn may serve subscriber terminals such as CRTs and TTYs with built-in microcontrollers.

For example, IBM's latest distributed processing unit 8100 offers more stand-alone programming and processing power in a network without requiring a system/370 mainframe as the host computer. This facilitates on-the-spot computing in order to minimize data communication costs in the system network architecture and upgrade reliability via decentralization, since one unit's failure does not shut down the entire system. Today's 8-in. double-sided double-density floppy disk in a PDP-11 low-cost microcomputer system can store over a megabyte of data (1 megabyte of main memory was unheard of in the high-cost medium-scale computers of the early 1960s). Present real-time economy operating systems have become versatile enough to process concurrent tasks.

Network topologies can vary in DDP. However, network control may be hierarchical under a central or host computer; up to five levels of satellite processors are not uncommon. The goal is a network operating system that can allocate network resources.

Latest network software has an *automatic routing capability* that selects the shortest operable links between two points at data rates as fast as 56 kilobit/sec, using modems that allow synchronous speeds up to 9600 baud/sec over dial-up voice-grade lines. The increasingly powerful mini- and micro-computers at the remote terminals do not have to transmit raw data to the host computer for processing over expensive communication lines. Presently, a remote mini- or micro-computer in a systems network architecture

(SNA) has the capability to develop, compile, and execute programs. That is, the hierarchical aspect from a central system/370 computer is eliminated by a set of remote 8100s (concentrators) that use central disk application programs in real-time in a peer network. IBM's synchronous data link control uses time-division-multiplex packet-switching techniques at data communications rates up to 56 kilobit/sec. In addition to IBM, other decentralized distributed data-processing networks are:

Burroughs	Honeywell
Computer Automation	Modular Computer Systems
Control Data	NCR
Datapoint	Sperry Univac
Digital Equipment	Sycor
General Automation	Tandem Computers
Hewlett-Packard	Infonet (Computer Science Corp.)

Most nations have their own DDP networks. As far as standardization of high-level languages is concerned in the case of the microcomputer systems, it is still not too late to decide upon a common block-structured language such as PASCAL or Bell Telephone's C (modified PASCAL) for full implementation in an exclusive network in the near future. The newly standardized ADA language of United States federal government systems, with a translator and interpreter, is another development along the lines of PASCAL. Zilog's distributed data base processor uses a Z-80 microprocessor to sort out the protocols and talk with other computers in a "virtual network."

As a typical example of DDP, the DECnet architecture of Digital Equipment Corporation shown in the diagram on p. 424 employs three protocols: (1) data access for input/output, (2) network services, and (3) digital data communications message for supporting communications.

11-23.2. Distributed Digital Processing Techniques. The following techniques are encountered in distributed digital processing:

1. *Bit rates of physical channels*
   a. *Asynchronous channels* up to 1200 baud/sec

Telex: single-speed of 50 baud/sec. Digital information is transmitted in a 5-bit Baudot code between compatible subscriber-teletypewriter terminals in a Telex network, which provides international message-transfer service via public telegraph circuits.

TWX: Arbitrary codes or transmission rates under 150 baud/sec. The TWX (teletypewriter exchange) network of Western Union provides dial-up service between compatible teletypewriters. It uses analog transmission over the public telephone network.

Baud: Baud is the unit of signaling speed. It is the number of discrete conditions or signaling events per second on a transmission line. Baud is the same as bit for binary digital transmission. It may be a group of two bits in 4-phase modulation as dibit (00, 01, 10, 11).

   b. *Synchronous channels* at higher bit rates
      2.4, 4.8, 9.6, 19.2, 56, 112, 224, 1544 kilobit/sec

The switching time for the lower-speed channels of the Datran network is a fraction of that on the telephone network; it is therefore called a fast-connect network with full-duplex (FDX) two-way transmission. The channels are digital end-to-end, and the users should not need modems. However, modems must be used on analog telephone lines to convert the data transmitted in PSK analog form.

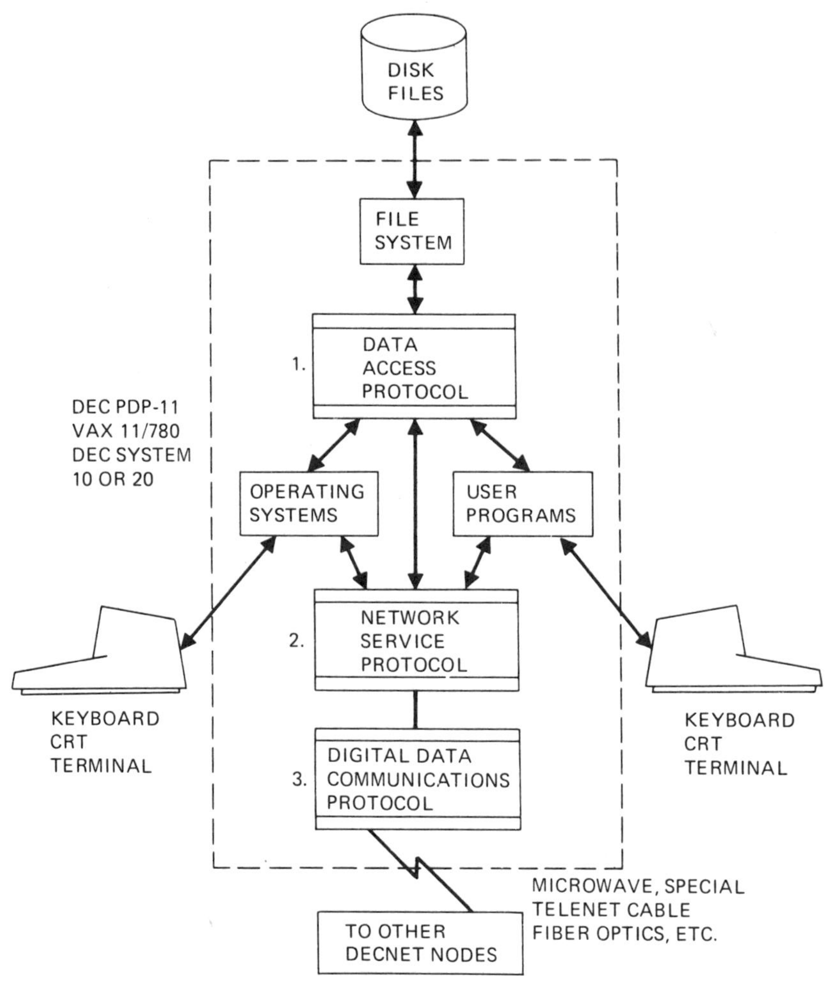

DEC PDP-11, VAX 11/780, DEC SYSTEM 10 OR 20

Other bit rates are:

64 Kb/sec: Digitized telephone channel (CCITT)
1.544 Mb/sec: T1 carrier wire-pair cable
6.312 Mb/sec: T2 carrier wire-pair cable
50-Mb/sec: Satellite transponder
274-Mb/sec: T4 carrier channels in various transmission systems
800-Mb/sec: Satellite throughput, cable television, optical-fiber transmission
16-Gb/sec: WT4 waveguide transmission system

2. *Vocoder:* 4.8 Kb/sec PCM (pulse code modulation) is processed to convey intelligence with enough information to synthesize a voice for human perception only.

3. *Picturephone:* 1-MHz bandwidth video signal is carried by a bit stream of 6.3 Mb/sec, using a 2-MHz sampling rate. For standard PCM, this gives 3 bits/sample, and hence eight discrete amplitude levels can be reconstructed to present a grainy picture. (As a comparison, presently 4.2-MHz bandwidth color television signals are transmitted using 8 to 10 bits per sample.) The coarse picture-phone signals and voice are improved by using differential PCM and delta modulation.

4. *Message-switching:* Non-real-time people-to-people message traffic is stored at the switch nodes and then transmitted onward to its destination on a *store-and-forward*

centralized (star/tree) switching basis in a fraction of an hour. A long message sent in a single transmission is filed for possible retrieval in future.

5. *Packet switching:* The international standards organization for telephony and telegraphy (CCITT) defines a *packet* as a group of binary digits (including data and call control signals), which is switched as a composite whole. The data, call-control signals, and possible error-control information are arranged in a specific format. *Packet switching* is defined by the transmission of data by means of addressed packets, whereby a transmission channel is occupied for the duration of transmission of the packet only. The channel is then available for use by packets being transferred between some other data-terminal equipment. (The data may be formatted into a packet or divided and then formatted into a number of packets for transmission and multiplexing purposes.)

Packet-switching is high-speed, and it is primarily intended for *real-time distributed data processing* in computer networks using several terminals. Long messages are segmented into small slices: 1008 bits per packet on the United States Telenet system; the Datapac system in Canada processes 255 bytes of 8 bits each. The segmented packets in a message can be *queued* in the main memory of the switching nodes and transmitted from node to node. At the destination, the whole message is reassembled. The computers that the network serves are called *host computers.*

A methodology in which the selected rates vary with the conditions of traffic in the network is called *adaptive routing.* The ARPA (Advanced Research Project Agency of the Department of Defense) and Telenet network use adaptive routing, with each node sending a service message every half-second. If, due to some error, the packet is not delivered at the correct destination, it is returned to the origin after a certain count in its field. Traffic congestion is prevented by controlling the *input* node, using control messages such as "ready-for-next-message (RFNM)."

6. *Frequency Division Multiple Access (FDMA):* FDM is *frequency division multiplex* in which the available transmission bandwidth is split by linear-phase filters into narrower bands as separate channels. FDMA implies that separate narrow-frequency bands are allocated to different users (as in broadcasting), and a transmitting or receiving terminal must be tuned to the frequency that is assigned to it.

Multiple-access techniques (used in satellite data communications) can operate as (1) analog fixed-channel assignments to the various users or (2) with channels assigned according to demand, as *demand-assignment.* When the user makes a request, a channel is allocated to the user after a short time-lag depending on the traffic in the channel circuits. It is *demand-assigned multiple access* (DAMA) as used in cable television (CATV). In cases where optical-fiber CATV cables are used, the high-speed digitized bit-rate will allow video (picture) communication between homes and terminal stations.

7. *Time Division Multiple Access (TDMA):* TDM (time-division multiplex) is the procedure in which high-capacity PCM channels are shared between user terminals by time division (time-slots)—as in digital radio and microwave links, CATV cables, waveguides (and fiber-optics), and satellites. If there are many access points for the time-slots by several terminals (in the place of only point-to-point send-receive multiplex terminals), the technique becomes *time-division multiple-access* (TDMA). Unlike synchronous TDM, TDM can have different aggregate bit-rates for incoming and outgoing lines. In general, *multiplexing* refers to static channel-assignment schemes in which given time-slots (or frequency bands) on a shared channel are assigned on a fixed, predetermined (*a priori*) basis with mostly balanced input/output capacities. Dedicated time-slots or subchannels for each port in the sharing group are categorized as synchronous time-division multiplex (STDM). *Asynchronous or statistical TDM* dynamically allocates time-slots on a statistical basis and increases transmission line efficiency by providing time-slots for ports actively transmitting data. The terminals naturally use digital computers

for this purpose. STDMs share a synchronous communication line by cyclically scanning incoming data from I/O ports, gating bits, or characters and interleaving them into *frames* off a single high-speed multiplexed data pulse-train.

A *concentration* technique describes a methodology in which a number of ports dynamically share a limited number of output subchannels on a *demand* basis. As the aggregate I/O bit-rates need not be matched in a concentrator, the digital mini- or micro-computer used in a concentrator at the terminal node will generally use software algorithms based on statistics and queuing. Therefore, a statistical TDM may be referred to as a *multiplexer-concentrator* or simply a *dynamic multiplexer*. Incidentally, a line-switching concentration is sometimes referred to as *space-division multiplex*. The following block-diagram points out the features in a modern satellite TDMA system.

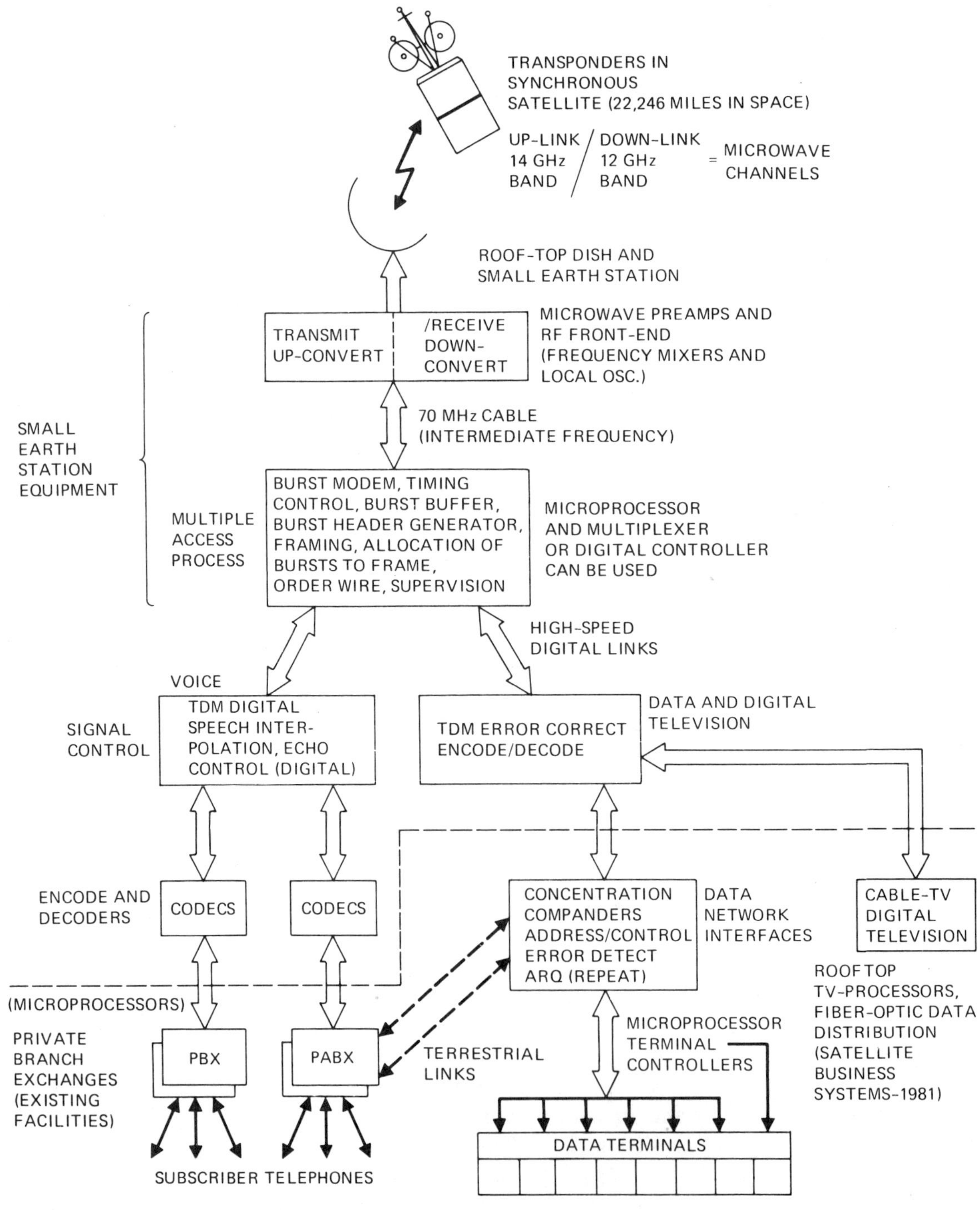

11-24. PRESENT STATUS OF DIRECT DIGITAL CONTROL

Data General's data acquisition and control subsystem (DG/DAC) is a new *complete* I/O modular subsystem that performs both A/D and D/A, and digital I/O multiplexing in any mix, up to 256 lines. *Modularity* allows ready expansion to several units to meet complex requirements, catering up to 1000 lines. As shown in the following block-diagram, two microcomputers, using two VSLI microprocessors of the class of Zilog, register-oriented, 32/16-bit Z-8001 CPU chips, and associated soft-ware, may be incorporated in a system to develop a complex process-control function. For system interface, two LSI micro-controllers would perform the above tasks of DG/DAC as I/O multiplexers, A/D and D/A converters. Should one computer fail, the other would conveniently take over critical operations with no interruption or data loss. While one computer is handling critical process operations, the secondary computer would take over lower priority tasks such as program development.

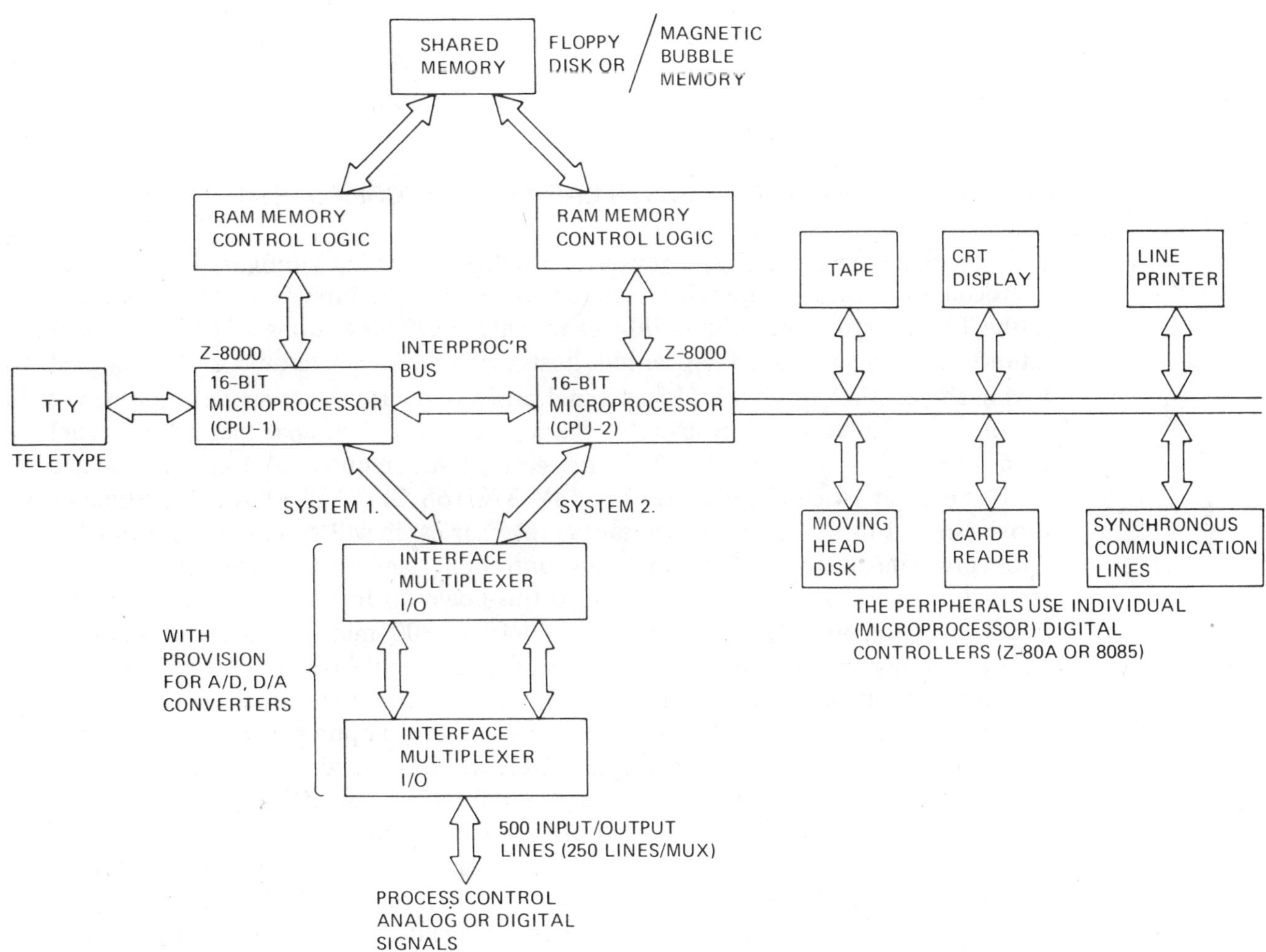

With large-scale mass production, the hardware is comparatively low-cost. However, the initial capital investment in software/firmware is both costly and time-consuming; only affluent nations could afford it. *But*, once the software for a specific process is established in an internationally standardized high-level language code, subsequent mass- and working-memory for software of dedicated process applications will naturally assume the form of low-cost mass-produced hardware as compact magnetic bubbles/CCDs, ROMs/RAMs/ PLAs, and similar, more advanced, high-density, long-term and short-term storage memory. This is going to be the way of automation and mass-production in the twenty-first century.

World-wide automation and satellite communications will be able to distribute basic living comforts (presently restricted to a very small percentage of the world population) to the remote corners of the earth during the twenty-first century (irrespective of the ideological differences):

1. if the affluent nations and the labor unions observe patience, restraint, and a give-and-take philosophy in solving temporary international problems such as unemployment in the face of universal automation and successfully avoid atomic warfare and other forms of self-destruction, and
2. if nations work hard to prevent a population explosion and maintain a demographical zero population growth, and
3. if nations and individuals observe dedication against self-indulgent life-styles, alcohol and drug addiction, and explore ways and means to use the ever-increasing amount of leisure time more constructively.

With unlimited and safe fusion energy on the horizon, the remaining 20 years of the current century can prepare the way for this challenging goal in the evolution of *Homo sapiens*, and it is hence a magnificent opportunity for the present generation.

11-25. MICRO- AND MINI- VERSUS LARGE-SCALE COMPUTERS

In the computing hierarchy, a powerful parallel processing configuration of 10 to 20 microcomputer cards, employing high-speed bit-slice I^2L bipolar microprocessors (such as the Texas Instruments SBP-0400A or the Intel 3000 series using a 16-bit ALU computation), interfaced around a central host-minicomputer real-time operating system, having a cycle-time of about 145 ns, can drastically reduce the computation time needed to solve a highly complex problem of the nature of aerial combat simulation, from hundreds of hours on a system 370/168 large-scale IBM computer, to a manageable average of 10 hours at much lower cost. The IBM 370/168 GPDC also has a cycle-time of approximately 145 ns. The bit-slice microprocessor cards will typically use a fast bipolar 256-word data-memory, a microprogram control unit, and a 512 × 280 bit microprogram instruction-memory. Grumman employed this powerful technique, using the Intel-3000 series microcomputers and Data General NOVA 800 minicomputer to perform this highly complex simulation. Each microprocessor module performs the same program, but on different data, in a pipeline fashion. The central minicomputer programmed in APL would evaluate the results from the various microcomputers and adjust the situation to a new set of variables or commands. Also, from the viewpoint of cost estimate, the hardware and firmware required with the mini-micro GPDC setup would be about $80,000 versus the $4-million-plus cost of system 370/168.

"Hyper-cube" Architecture of Microcomputers. A large **network-array of microcomputers** (each consisting of two Intel 8080A microprocessors, one functioning as the user's task-processor and the other as the controller) is capable of exceeding two or three times the computing power of the large-scale main-frame computers of IBM and CDC at a fraction of power, area, and cost. IMS Associates (San Leandro, California) has developed a prototype system using 16 microcomputers to simulate the computing power of one of the present medium-scale digital computers. A 256-microcomputer network is on the drawing boards. The "Hypercube" architecture is shown in Fig. 11-25.

The individual microprocessor units (MPU) operate independently on separate parts of the problem or different problems or algorithms. IMS's "Hyper-cube" Microcomputer system employs several nodes, each node using a distributed program in a low-level

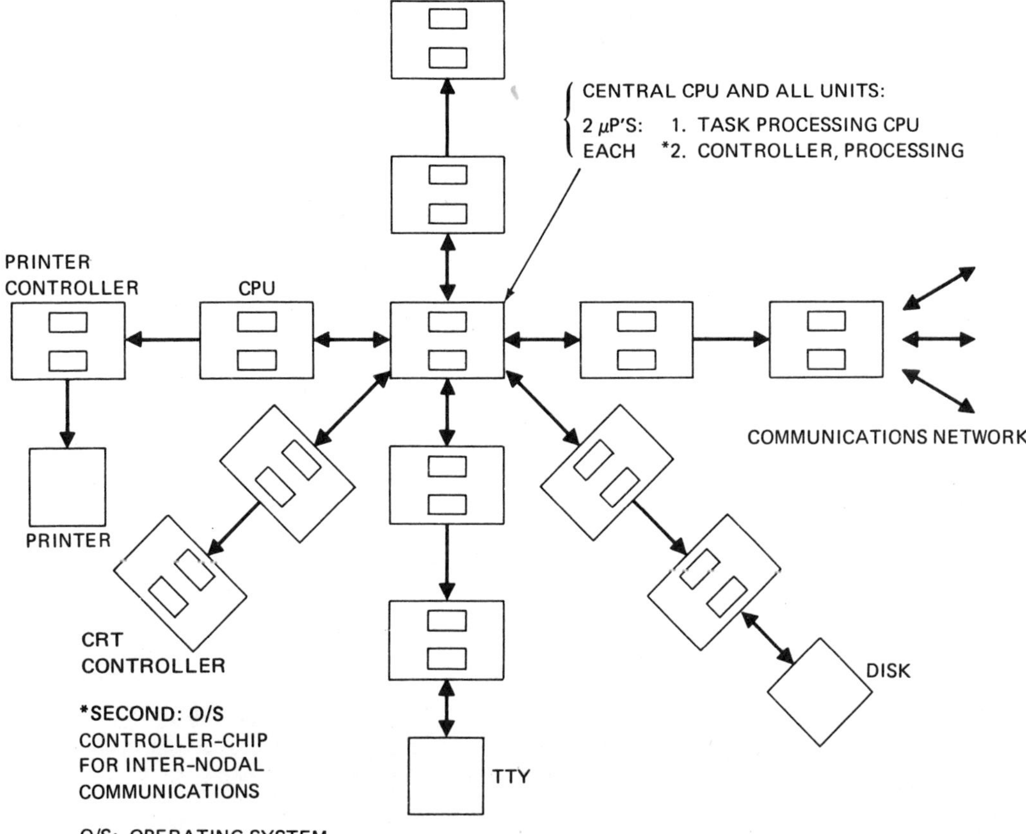

Fig. 11-25. "Hypercube" architecture of microcomputers.

assembly language. Each node is capable of handling 1 million instructions/sec, with a DMA capacity of 2 megabytes/sec, and 16-K bytes of user program, which is extendable to 64-K bytes. Each subsystem located at each node is linked to eight other microcomputers in the adjacent nodes. One MPU of each node handles the user's program, while the second MPU oversees the communications tasks and Operating-System software by using a DMA. Some nodes may operate on I/O data only, or interface with TTY, line printer, or disk mass-memory. This multiprogramming concept is more complex than handling successive programs on the same CPU. Some telemetry and complex simulation systems, large-scale data bases, and data communications networks are being planned with this approach under research contracts.

11-26. LOGIC-STATE ANALYZER (H.P. MODEL 1600A/1607A)

The **Hewlett-Packard CRT Terminal Controller** enables debugging of a microcomputer system, by displaying 16 lines of two sequential 16-bit machine-language words in a parallel mode. The various routines involved in the hardware, software, firmware, and information to and from a peripheral device across an I/O port can all be reviewed in succession. The data is displayed on the left-half, while the right-half is reserved for any auxiliary memory used or for the data acquired from the companion instrument, Model 1607A. Monitoring is done in parallel on several different lines by way of a miniature multiprobe system. Synchronization is achieved by either the clock or the various strobes available from the system under test. A display system of this kind is thus an indispensable medium for analyzing and debugging microcomputer systems. Model-

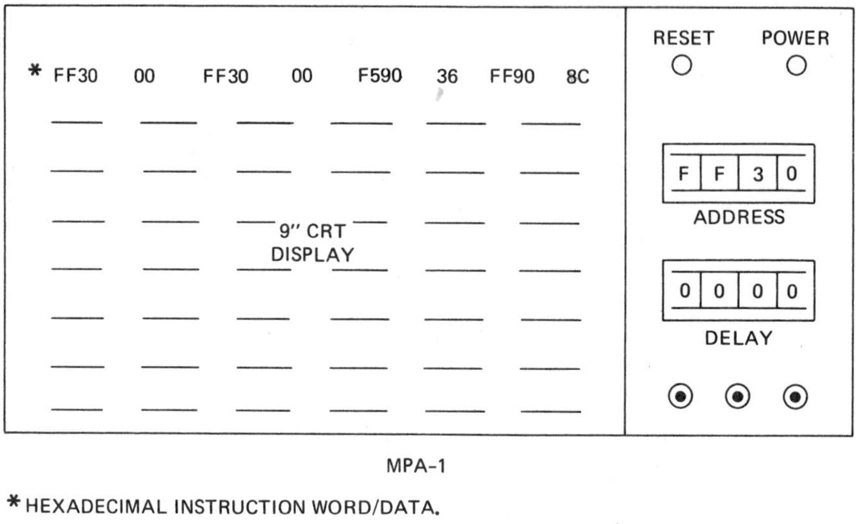

* FF30 00 FF30 00 F590 36 FF90 8C

9" CRT DISPLAY

RESET POWER

F F 3 0

ADDRESS

0 0 0 0

DELAY

MPA-1

* HEXADECIMAL INSTRUCTION WORD/DATA.

Fig. 11-26. Motorola microprocessor analyzer display, MPA-1. (*Courtesy of Motorola*)

1600A display provides for an auxiliary memory for the storage of data. A push-button control enables the transfer of data from the main-memory to the auxiliary-memory, and the contents of each memory may be displayed separately or simultaneously side-by-side. The CRT-display provides also a MAP-mode to display the position of a digital word as a dot on an x-y scale, accompanied by a pattern to show the actual sequence of digital words.

Motorola microprocessor analyzer (MPA-1) belongs to the same class as the Hewlett-Packard diagnostic instrument. The CRT character-display aids in debugging the hardware and firmware of microcomputers. The analyzer, costing under $3,000, eliminates the need for the clumsy hookup of individual leads, buffers, and probes that require special quick-clip connectors. The interface of the analyzer is directly feasible with such microprocessor types as 8080A, AMD 9080, TI-TMS 8080, NEC-8080A, Rockwell PPS-8, AMI-S6800, Mostek 6500 Series, Synertek 6500 Series, and Motorola MC-6800 and EXORcisor. Three probe-connectors and one probe-buffer of choice are provided as plug-in accessories.

A 32-word segment of the program execution can be captured and displayed in the hexadecimal or octal codes to compare against the written program instructions. No manual binary-to-hexa decimal or octal translation is required. The word displayed on the 9" CRT screen consists of four characters for the address and two characters for the associated data-bus information. Status information from the microprocessor can be ignored or captured and alternated with the data from 16 locations. The CRT-display console of the Motorola MPA-1 analyzer is shown in Fig. 11-26.

11-27. AUTOMATIC TEST SYSTEMS

The Automatic test systems (ATS) equipment available from Hewlett-Packard, General Dynamics, and other manufacturers provide a wide range of testing capability for individual subassemblies (e.g., shop replaceable assemblies SRAs) to complex Naval and Avionics Systems (e.g., WRA/LRU, as major assemblies are termed.) The test system usually consists of a minicomputer- or microcomputer-based hardware setup with facilities for stimulus-switching. Measurement subsystems include commercial analog and digital instruments, as shown in two typical test systems in Figs. 11-27 and 11-28.

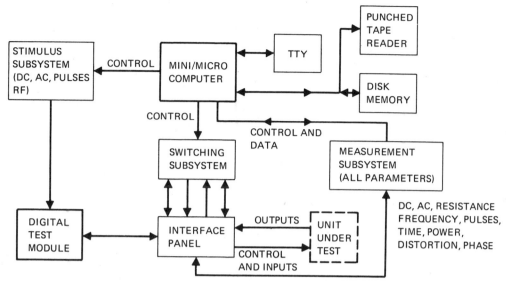

STIMULUS SUBSYSTEM (DC, AC, PULSES RF)
CONTROL
MINI/MICRO COMPUTER
TTY
PUNCHED TAPE READER
DISK MEMORY
CONTROL
CONTROL AND DATA
SWITCHING SUBSYSTEM
MEASUREMENT SUBSYSTEM (ALL PARAMETERS)
DIGITAL TEST MODULE
INTERFACE PANEL
OUTPUTS
UNIT UNDER TEST
CONTROL AND INPUTS
DC, AC, RESISTANCE FREQUENCY, PULSES, TIME, POWER, DISTORTION, PHASE
H. P.'S AUTOMATIC STIMULUS-RESPONSE TESTING CONCEPT

Fig. 11-27. Hewlett-Packard automatic stimulus-response testing concept. *(Courtesy of Hewlett-Packard, Inc.)*

Microcomputers are ideal for low-cost Automatic Test and Measurement Systems geared to instrumentation. Hewlett-Packard is presently marketing several dedicated ATS systems for:

1. Automatic network analysis using Hewlett-Packard Network Analyzer
2. Automatic Spectrum Analysis
3. Automatic Transceiver Test System
4. Instrument Calibration System
5. Distributed Systems capability for multiple test-station applications at Remote Test Sites
6. Digital Logic Simulator.

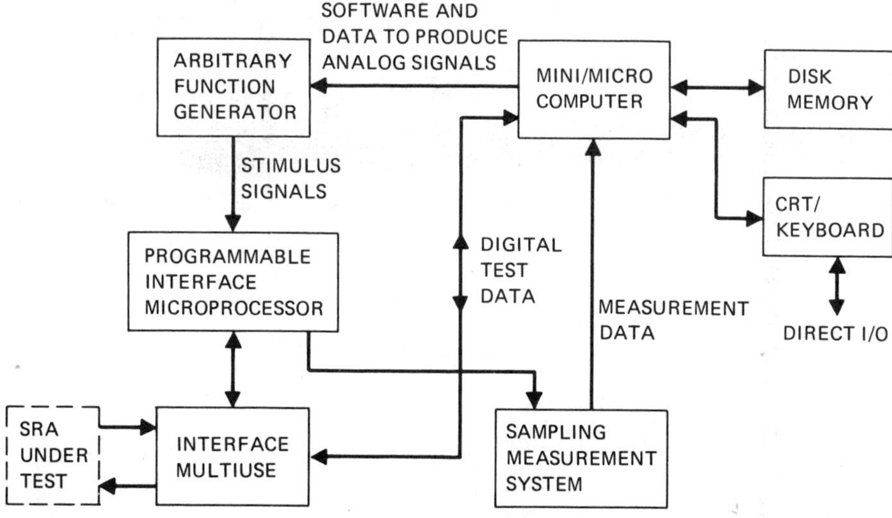

Fig. 11-28. Hybrid automatic testing system (General Dynamics). *(Courtesy of IEEE Aerospace and Electronics Systems Society Newsletter)*

Litton Systems has an ATS real-time Inertial Measurement Unit (IMU with a CRT-display) for a Stabilized-Platform Inertial Navigation System (INS) to check for power-ON sequencing, alignment and navigation performance, attitude accuracy, and auto calibration capability.

A typical ATS concept may include plug-in interface hardware that is applicable to latest programmable instruments, such as "Bite Pattern" generators, and software such as CPOL (Communications Procedure Oriented Language). No full-time programmer or operator is required, and technicians could use the control panel and operate the ATS. For example, a test-oriented paper-tape system merely requires that a test program be loaded into the system to begin a test sequence, which may involve the testing of the RF analog-only (using an off-line "Bite Pattern" and "Fault Dictionaries"), the combined analog-digital, and the digital-only. On-line odd parity-checking is generally used for static functions. For the Series-9500 Hewlett-Packard test system shown in Fig. 11-27, the simple ATS-BASIC is used as the programming language for automatic testing, instrument control, and timing statements. In the case of several SRAs, the programs may be loaded onto a mass-memory such as floppy-disk as a multiprogramming facility, and the segments automatically loaded into the RAM main memory of the mini/microcomputer for execution, as each SRA is plugged into the test system.

In the case of the **General Dynamics test system**, an assembly WRA/LRU is tested on the Versatile Avionics Shop Tester, to isolate the problem to one or more SRAs. A subassembly SRA is usually replaced by a spare one, while the General Dynamics ATS System shown in Fig. 11-28 isolates the faulty component or group of components in the SRA. The mini- or micro-computer system complex of the ATS synthesizes the stimulus signals and analyzes the response signals. The Test Program Set (TPS) development costs can be minimized by a Graphics version of interactive programming capability, using a CRT-display and a light-pen. A microprocessor using a programmable-interface will allow testing of new SRAs with no increase in hardware. Programs for this particular test system were stored on a 2.4-M X 16-bit word disk-memory system. The system software provided performs all the common measurements such as the ac and dc voltages, resistances, timings, frequency, waveform analysis, distortion, spectrum analysis, and statistical analysis.

Software. A standard high-level language ATLAS has been approved by the Institute of Electrical and Electronics Engineers as IEEE Standard 416-1976, because of its direct applicability to the IEEE Interface Standards for automated measuring techniques. ATLAS is a test-oriented language for specifications and procedures—independent of the specific test equipment used. The language was originally developed for manual or automatic or semiautomatic implementation of test procedures. IEEE-Standard "ATLAS Syntax," as a companion document to the ATLAS Test Language, helps to validate or debug the programs of test specifications written in ATLAS manually or automatically by means of metalanguage parsing processors. (Price of documents: $25.)

11-28. LIST OF TYPICAL APPLICATIONS OF MICROPROCESSORS

1. Communications Terminals (including subscriber sets in Telecommunications)
2. CRT-Displays and Graphics-Controller
3. Line-Printer Controller
4. Plotters (X-Y)
5. Keyboard Controller
6. Calculators

7. "Smart" Instruments (self-calibrating), with accuracy improved by two orders of magnitude
8. Vending Machines, Electronic Scales
9. Point-of-Sale (POS) Systems
10. Accounting and Data-Processing Systems
11. Process Control–Chemical, Industrial
12. Numerical Control–Machine Tools
13. Computer-Aided Design (CAD)
14. Medical Diagnostic Instruments
15. Sophisticated Games, Toys, and Robots
16. Video Entertainment Systems (VES)
17. General Peripheral Control
18. Test and Evaluation
19. Digital Signal Processing, Fast Fourier Transforms (FFT)
20. General Mobile Civil and Defense Applications
21. Traffic Lights
22. Parallel "Hyper-Cube" Systems of Economy Microprocessors for More Powerful Low-Cost Medium-Scale and Large-Scale Computers
23. Photo-type Setting and Other Photocomposition Products
24. Optical and Television Color Cameras
25. Automatic Radio/Television Program-Switching Systems
26. Electronic Telephone Exchanges
27. Composition of Music
28. Composition of Modern Art and Cartoons, etc.

These are just a few examples of microprocessor applications. Imagination is the limit regarding custom (MOS/I^2L) LSI computer chips especially designed and mass-produced for dedicated applications.

In the near future, the economy VLSI/LSI microprocessor and high-density solid-state memory chips are definitely going to play a dominating role all over the world in the following disciplines and applications associated with communications.

1. Personal Computers of interest to home and small-business applications
2. Communication and information systems
3. Cellular Radio Systems
4. Image Processing Systems
5. Communications security
6. Communications Software
7. Computer Network Communications
8. Data Communications in General
9. Distributed Communication Systems
10. Integrated Switching
11. Laser (Optical) Communications
12. Millimeter Wave Communications
13. Radio Communications in General
14. Space and Satellite Digital Communications
15. Spread Spectrum Communications
16. Transmission Systems with Remote Automatic Microcomputer Terminals
17. Private Automatic Branch Exchanges, and Home Telephone Terminals
18. Cable Television Networks and Fiber Optic Channel Distribution

19. Automatic International Dialling (Long-Distance)
20. International and Space Telemetering Systems, etc.

11-29. MICROPROCESSOR-BASED APPLICATIONS IN PATIENT CARE

Microprocessor-based applications in patient care include.

1. Testing, therapy, diagnosis, and monitoring on keyboard-CRT microcomputer system and recordkeeping on cassette (or floppy diskette) and line printer.
2. The microcomputer system is centrally interfaced to location digital/analog controllers in the following areas: clinical laboratory, intensive care unit, operating room, outpatient clinic, and general patient and nonpatient areas.
3. The system may be monitored by nurse, patient, physician, lab technician, or nonpatient medical care personnel.
4. The microcomputer operating systems may be bought at low cost or leased by hospital/clinic/health medical officer or physician, or the patient, unlike former exorbitantly expensive minicomputer systems that required time-consuming costly software to boost medical costs.
5. Program adaptability is desired as a standard routine or custom-programmed by vendor in BASIC or PASCAL to be available in low-cost cartridge or floppy disk for common use by hospitals and physicians for KB-CRT display and printers.
6. Algorithmic procedures of a medical character may be nonmedical, or subjective/objective, or deterministic/nondeterministic self-learning.

Microcomputers allow patients to have personal access to their own medical records. Patients can have easy access to data banks provided by microcomputers.

Unlike elaborate medical instrumentation, low-cost microcomputers with input sensors and built-in A/D converters have the general capability to reduce health-care costs, if the tasks involved are adequately controlled to follow a routine. Also, paramedics involved may have better experience with the monitoring techniques, and may serve better in a consulting capacity to retrieve the right information from the storage system of the microcomputer.

Microprocessor-based monitoring devices may allow the development of reliable new health-care systems for the satisfaction and psychological well-being of the patient.

Traditionally medical education has been concerned with memorization of detail. Microcomputers will change this to a concern with broader judgment. Special software and pattern recognition techniques associated with microcomputers, such as electrocardiogram analysis, might be better able to deal with unprecedented situations than *those* medical decisions that are based on intuition, and, in some cases, conjecture and vague recollection of symptoms. In addition, microcomputers decrease the cost and length of medical education by facilitating the use of computer-aided instruction at the individual student's own pace. Computer-aided instruction can also serve as a method of continuing education as medical research produces more reliable methodologies.

Microprocessor-based information systems could present organizational support to physicians by providing detailed diagnostic and therapeutic regimens on an automatic sequential basis. Researchers have discovered that most errors in medical treatment, particularly in chronic diseases, are errors of omission rather than commission. These investigators have pointed out that timely inference from computer-aided documentation via interactive graphics result in better patient care due to improved follow-ups. Microprocessor-based recordkeeping systems enhance the comprehensive and orderly presentation of medical records of an individual patient from disk or tape files to assist the physician in properly evaluating the care the patient should receive. In new applications such as "intelligent" prosthetic links, portable cardiac monitors, or voice-controlled wheelchairs, microprocessors administer proper treatment or take steps to correct the problems by means of devices controlled by artificial intelligence. Biomedical engineers and neural specialists are about to play an increasing role in medicine due to the signal-processing capabilities of microprocessors and the newly developing science of artificial intelligence. Students in medical schools will become acquainted with microprocessor-based miniature medical or biomedical instrumentation, and use of these reliable aids in medical practice should improve the quality of general health care.

In summary, market conditions definitely favor the development of microprocessor-based portable medical devices. Since it is simple enough to mass-produce these miniature low-cost devices (using a strictly limited number of VLSI-signal-processing and ROM/RAM memory chips), medical costs will certainly decline during the 1980s, provided the medical profession, and the FDA make the necessary initial investment to encourage the research and development in this encouraging health-care service on a radically new base.

11-30. FIBER-OPTICS AND OPTICAL DATA COMMUNICATIONS

With the advantages that fiber-optics present in data communications, the projections are excellent for the advance of their usage during the 1980s. The features include:

- low transmission loss (4.4 dB/km and less) between repeaters spaced 4 km apart
- wide transmission range-bandwidth products (640 MHz-km) at 44.7 Mb/sec for high-resolution color television signals
- potential low cost (in the place of highly expensive equalized video repeaters in coaxial cable systems)
- insensitivity to electromagnetic and radio frequency interference, immunity to ground-loop problems and cross-talk among parallel fibers—one to six fibers are common
- improved security compared with former electronic cabling in computer network channels
- relatively small size, lightweight, high strength, and flexibility
- elimination of combustion or sparks caused by former short-circuits
- flexibility in upgrading system capacity without adding new cables
- suitability for relatively high temperatures
- fewer government regulatory difficulties due to elimination of frequency allocation
- suitability for modern broad-band time-division multiplexed (TDM) digital communications and PCM data

Cable losses are independent of transmission frequency, and hence no equalization is required. Route-lengths extending to 50 km, with low-cost repeaters spaced 4 km apart, are used. Bit rates extend to multiplexed 322.2 Mb/sec with 15 television channels, 12 FM channels, and stereo. Nippon Telegraph and Telephone Corp. has developed a two-way digital television conference system using four wavelength-multiplexed channels at 1.544 Mb/sec bit rate. (Satellite Business Systems will be using a digital multiplex system of this kind.)

Some of the manufacturers of the fiber-optics cables are Bell Northern Research Laboratories, Corning-Philips Inc., Siecor Optical Cables Inc., Canstar-Corning Glass Works, Math Associates Inc., ITT Corp., Valtec Corp., Nippon Electric Company, Nippon Telegraph and Telephone Company, General Cable Company, Western Electric Co., and a few European companies, such as Plessey, AEG-Telefunken, Ericksson, and Thomson-CSF.

For transmission, injection laser diodes operating at infrared wavelength of 830 nm are commonly used. Some installations use an LED laser source. For detection (or receiver), avalanche photodiodes are commonly used. A few PiN diodes are also encountered. Fiber cables are spliced by fusion or epoxy techniques. Between 100 and 200 reliable systems are in operation in Canada, the United States, Japan, and Europe. With the spread of domestic satellite systems around the world, especially with the latest SBS and other TDMA data communications systems, high-quality cable television, and small-dish community antenna systems, the use of fiber-optic cable systems will expand at an enormous rate during the 1980s for the education of large masses of people, especially in the developing nations. Low-cost microprocessor and microcomputer systems will naturally play a major role in the distribution of TDM data communications. The schematic block-diagram of a recent subway fiber-optics monitoring system is shown in Fig. 11-29. Six optical fibers in a reinforced 0.527-in.-diameter cable, along with several other advantages, exceed the signal-carrying capacity of 900 pairs of conventional heavyweight copper telephone wires in a 3-in.-diameter telephone cable.

Following are typical specifications of two fiber-optics cables and an optical link (Valtec Fiber data™: Fiber type, MG05, graded refractive-index, glass-on-glass—Valtec Corp. West Boylston, MA):

Type 440

4 dB/km at 900 nm, 400 MHz-km, digital cable-TV application
Price, 10 to 100 km: $0.9/meter
Numerical aperture: 0.20
Pulse broadening: 2 ns/km
Core diameter = 62.5 μm; cladding diameter = 125 μm; buffer diameter = 350 μm

Type, HD

MG05: Temperature, -20°C to +55°C
Humidity, 0 to 100 (storage and operation)
8 dB/km at 800–900 nm, bandwidth 200 MHz-km
Duplex computer cable, 6 X 9 mm diameter, 43 kg/km,
Price: $3.45/m

MU8-1, 8-port Multiplexer/Demultiplexer, TTL BNC Connectors

Multiplexed I/O: 9-pin connector
PS-232C (V-24): Each port can operate full duplex, simultaneously at 20-K bits/sec with full handshaking and monitoring features. The Interface is designed for TTK-D1 fiber-optic duplex transceiver.
EIA (Electronic Industries Association) I/O connector: 25-pin standard
Multiplex asynchronous data output jitter: 12 μs (max)
Operating temperature: 0 to 55°C
Power 2W (115V, 60 Hz)
Bit error rate: 10^{-9}, permitted data rates: DC-20 KBPS
Link distance: 1 km

Model TTK Transceiver

I/O: Standard and differential TTL levels
Data rates: 10 KBPS to 10 MBPS (NRZ)
Transmission loss of fiber-optic cable: 20 dB, 820 nm
Transmission distance: 1 km
Power supply: 6 W (115V, 60 Hz)

APPLICATION IN BROADCASTING AND CABLE TELEVISION – VALTEC VS-100 FIBER-OPTICS SYSTEM

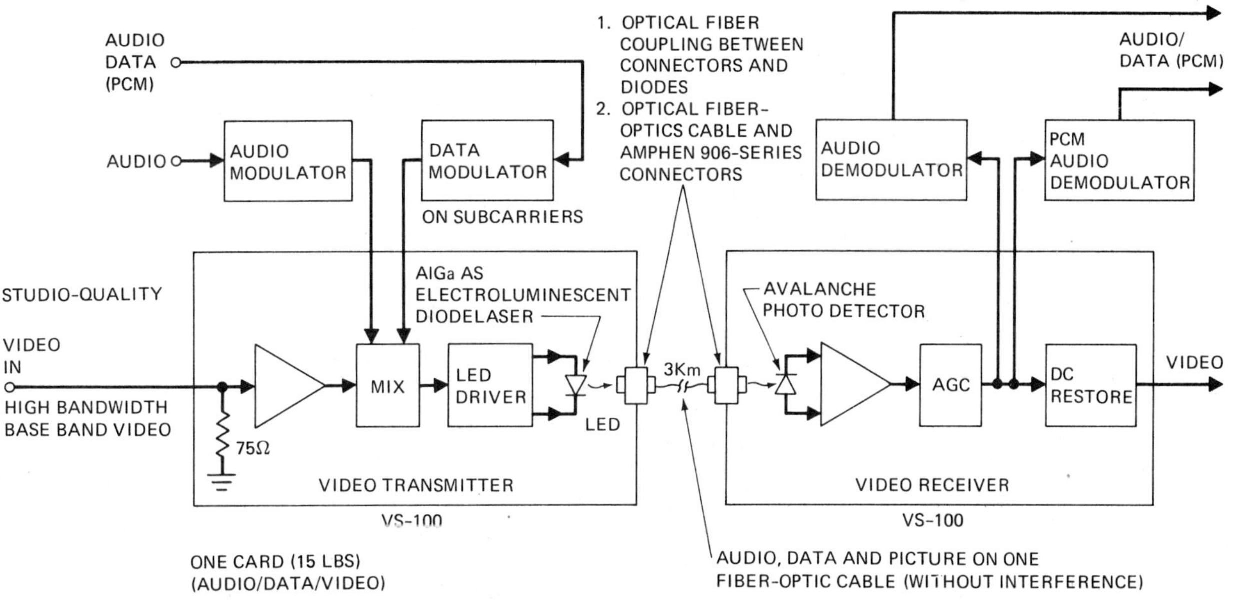

TYPICAL BASIC LASER, DRIVE CIRCUIT:

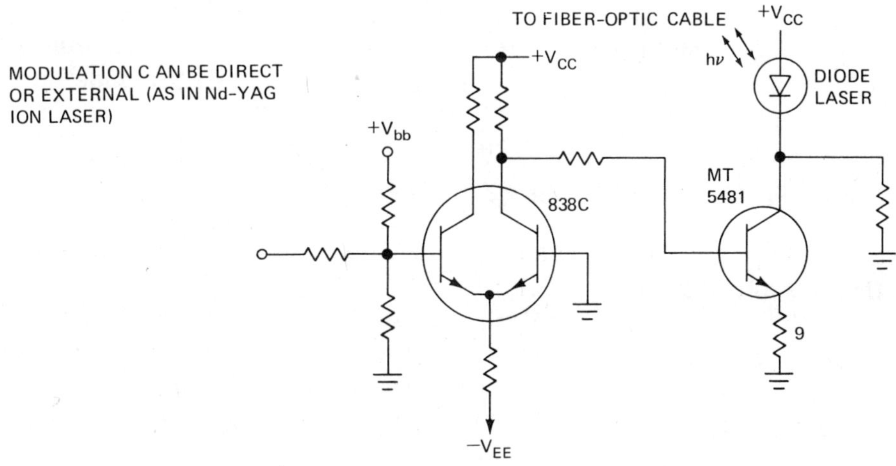

TYPICAL GALLIUM ARSENIDE (ALUMINUM GALLIUM ARSENIDE, AlGa As) INJECTION LASER WITH LATERAL CONFINEMENT

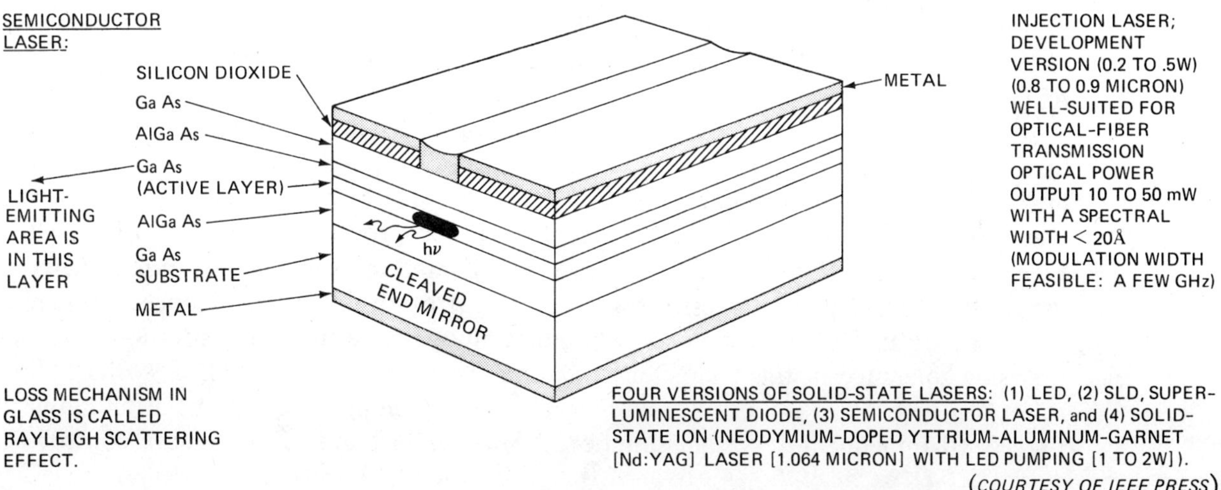

Fig. 11-29. Fiber-optics monitoring system. (*Courtesy of Voltek Inc.*)

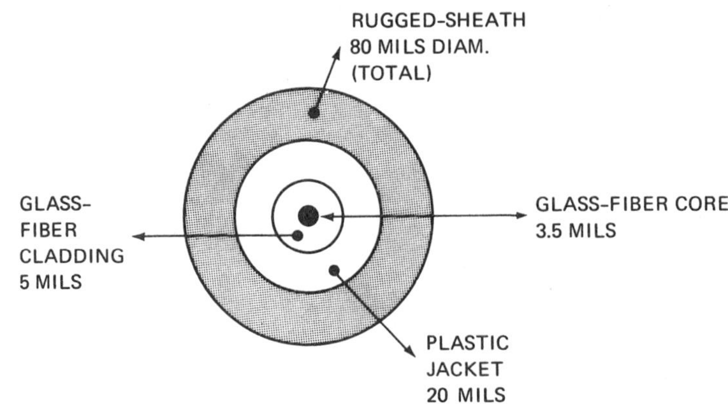

Fig. 11-30. Fiber guide (Fiber-Optics cable).

Low-loss fiber-optic waveguides for multiplexed optical data communications. Bandwidths up to 20 MHz are realized by this glass fiber-optics transmission medium, which is especially applicable to short hops up to 500 meters. Fiberguide (Fiber Communications, Orange, New Jersey) offers high tensile-strength with a ruggedized sheath, and cost-effectiveness at $1.00/ft for lengths varying from 500 to 2,000 ft. The attenuation is 25-to-30 dB/km (0.61 mile) and the 0.1″-diameter fiber-guide's bending-radius is 2.5″ (like coax-cables). Previously, 0.5″-diameter cabled-fibers have been procurable only in fiber bundles or cables with six channels in one sheath. But the new fiber-guide weighs only 1.5lb/1,000 ft, and it can be stripped easily to access the fiber. Humid and underwater environments are acceptable. The cross-section of a "fiber-guide" used in optical communications is illustrated in Fig. 11-30.

11-31. ARTIFICIAL INTELLIGENCE AND ROBOTICS

Artificial Intelligence (AI) is the newest branch of computer science devoted to software tasks that would require intelligence "if carried out by human beings." The areas covered in this branch extend to: (1) problem solving, (2) natural language processing of speech/writing, (3) perception and pattern recognition, (4) information storage and retrieval, (5) automatic programming, (6) computational logic, and (7) control of robots or robotics. The programs are organized to follow a step-by-step strategy or methodology in solving a problem and to systematically carry out those steps as top-down design, block-structured, and iterative, enhanced program modules. The modern high-level language PASCAL is organized along these lines. Playing chess or charting the navigation route of a spaceship or a maze give an idea of the complexity involved. Television cameras, microphones, and radar patterns in an obscure environment furnish some common source signals for these AI programs.

A revolutionary trend is using microprocessor-controlled mechanical assembly to perform both dangerous and *monotonous* tasks that previously required much costlier human handling. General Motors Corp. and Unimation Inc. have recently introduced a PUMA (programmable universal manipulator for assembly) in regular production jobs that require high-precision manipulation within a tolerance of 0.1 mm (the thickness of human hair). It uses a DEC LSI-11 microprocessor that in turn controls five other microprocessors devoted to five robot axes of motion (waist, shoulder, elbow, wrist and hand rotation). A high-precision tolerance of this character is beyond the capability of a skilled worker! So, a robot can be used to aid a skilled worker who merely monitors a high-precision industrial process to implement a certain function. Another instance is the remote control of a normal material-handling manipulation in a dangerous (e.g., nuclear), unpleasant (e.g., spray-painting), or telemetry space environment. Why, the modern ubiquitous microprocessor itself is the result of a score of chemical and industrial mass-production processes of the "robotic" high-technology electronics art of LSI/VLSI in the last quarter of the twentieth century. One must remember that these revolutionary "modern times" started as a movie joke and science fiction only 40 years ago! (Charlie Chaplin produced a wonderful film satire on the early birth pangs of assembly work in production plants in *Modern Times.*) The human evolutionary processes change for the better in spontaneous jumps, and general living standards and international political yardsticks of democracies must advance in step with advances in science and technology without undue resistance if maintenance of peace is the responsibility of every nation. AI is here to stay, and we must make the most intelligent use of this science in conjunction with satellite data communications in every facet of the home and industry.

A robot, by definition, is a machine that functions under its own power and control; a television camera in the robot is the sensor that enables it to perceive, manipulate, or respond to its environment according to the stored-program commands of a microcomputer. (They actually started with complex mechanisms automatically controlled by intricate clockwork a long time ago.) With a television camera, robots can recognize patterns and analyze images of superficially simple detail of established configurations. They may transmit or respond to sonar pulses to locate themselves with reference to obstacles in the immediate environment, or for higher precision, they may use an LED lasar beam by means of effectors or manipulators (hands and arms). The control program must maintain a data base or world model containing a description of the surroundings; and programming is commonly effective in LISP for its movement in the external workspace coordinates, as its built-in microprocessor computes the transformation between its internal and external coordinates. A block diagram of a typical elementary microprocessor-controlled robot is shown in Fig. 11-31 along with its proportional-integral-derivative control system.

The preceding technique can be extended to highly complex problems that could perhaps be solved by systematically solving all of the individual interacting problems involved one by one. This is presently done in complex digital control systems where the stabilized individual interacting phase-lock loops in a complex system are subjected to some form of "adaptive supervisory control." This form of control is successfully accomplished in laboratory practice.* The highly complex conglomerate of sampled-data digital control systems in the system described at length in this reference is used at present; it was successfully solved by heuristic (measure-and-optimize techniques) about 18 years ago when computer hardware and software were in their infancy. *Exponential* algorithmic approaches (factorials, square and cubic laws) are nonlinear and theoretically insoluble. But, when a large number of techniques of the algorithmic character of *polynominal time* (n^0, n^1, n^2 . . .) are encountered, heuristics plays a prominant role. Heuristics, combined with practical guidelines based on the concepts of feedback control systems, provide the only possible route to solve such complex systems in minimum time. Cost-effective research and development schedules in laboratory practice essentially determine the heuristic approach. So it is in the case of heuristic methods in Artificial Intelligence, which use the present software/firmware aspects of multi-microprocessor technology to solve and implement complex digital/data control systems. These heuristic methods in the field of Artificial Intelligence are in their infancy.

The latest theoretical and technological problems encountered in Pattern Recognition

*See *Complex Digital Control Systems* by G. V. Rao, Van Nostrand Reinhold Co., New York, 1979.

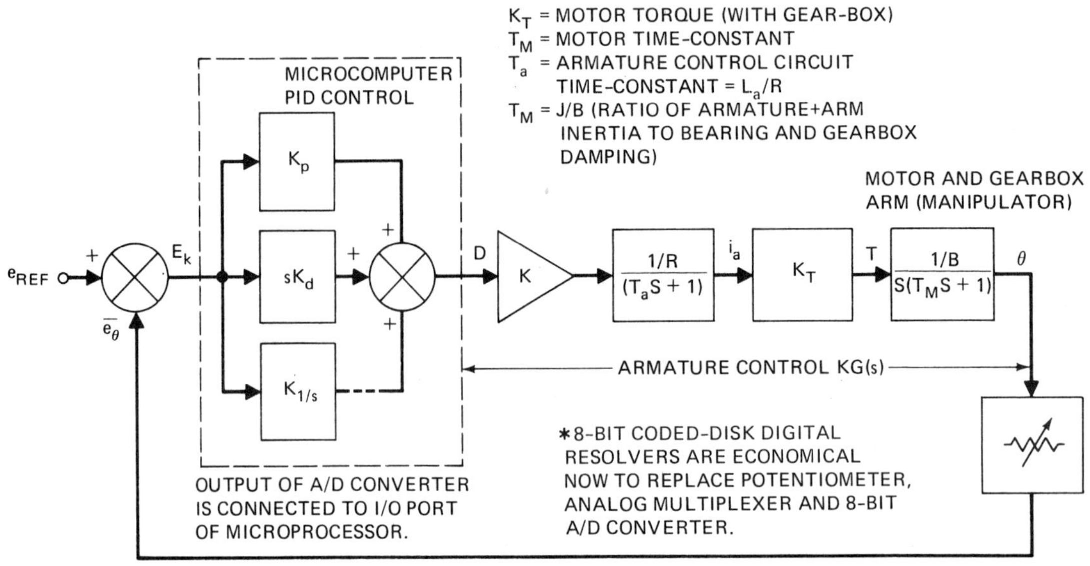

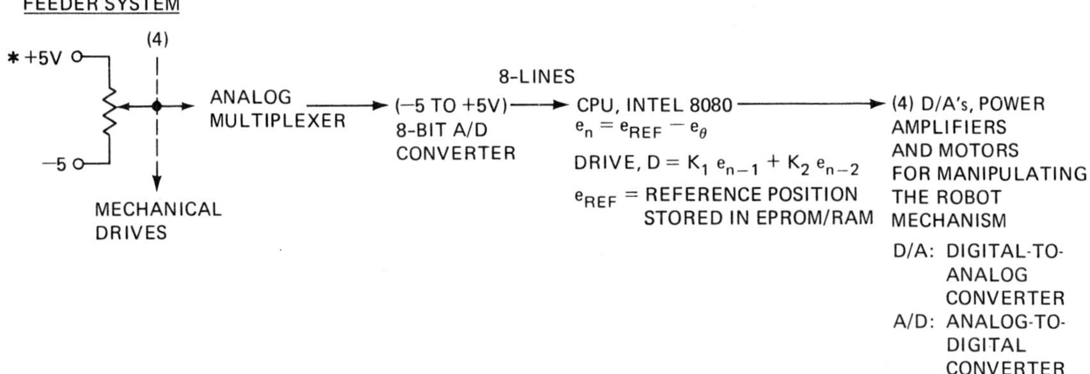

Fig. 11-31. A simple microprocessor-controlled robot and its PID control. (© IEEE, *COMPUTER* January, 1979)

also fall under this category. The "problematic situation" corresponds to the "patterns," and we apply the heuristic aspects of search to find the right solution to recognize the pattern, memorize the same, and then retrieve it from the storage base and interpret the solution in the context of the environment. For example, such AI techniques are presently used in advancing the art of high-resolution space photographs, crispening satellite color television, and image-enhancing. The latter is one of the major branches of microprocessor-based research in AI.

Video games in personal computing represent another aspect of AI. We can use Graphics to display on CRT the board for such games as chess, checkers, dominoes, and backgammon; store the rules of the game in ROM as a reference standard; and write game-software of the computer on a cartridge or floppy disk so that it can manipulate the control and the arithmetic logic unit. The correct interactive move of the computer against the player is determined by reading the pertinent data available in RAM. By actually playing in a tournament or by simulating corresponding benchmark comparisons, the computer software initially devised by an expert programmer can receive a rating as if the microcomputer were a player!

One of the interacting applications of AI is State-Graph Search, which resembles simplex linear programming. For example, one starts with the initial state and explores the state graph of a maze to find the least obstructive path to the goal in minimum time. The exhibit of the 1979 IEEE annual convention, viz., "the best amazing micromice," has given a lot of promotion to the maze concepts of AI. A simple maze and its corresponding state graph are shown in Fig. 11-32 to illustrate software block-structure of the search tree, which could be part of a more complex larger tree. The software involved is mostly identical to the latest top-down modular design of PASCAL and other high-level languages.

AI software can also be used for deduction of theorems, given a set of hypothetic statements to aid mathematicians. As an alternative to automatic programming, computer programs could be devised to debug programs written by beginners. Research in this field is usually conducted so that the computer can either initiate the methodology of a certain programmer or act as an aid to a programmer to achieve a certain result. Automatic programming, as one of the branches of AI, is a definite possibility before the end of the present decade. We are just scratching the surface of AI; its enormous and fascinating potential during the 1980s using multi-microprocessor systems is still a matter of justifiably optimistic expectation. The science-fiction movie *2001:A Space Odyssey* has merely given a glimpse of its possibilities.* What the hardware automation in LSI/VLSI technology has accomplished in minimizing the need for unlimited number of circuit designers, AI will eventually accomplish in minimizing the need for unlimited number of software engineers for writing repetitive programs in countless applications of microcomputer systems.

11-32. TWO-CHIP RADIO CONTROL OF TOY-MODELS

Radio controlled toy-models are popular with children all over the world. LSI chips at a cost of only $10 for both transmit/receive chips will create a huge market for low-cost toy-models. National Semiconductor Corp. has announced a two-chip radio control system with type LM1871 encoder-transmitter and type LM1872 receiver-decoder. The transmit chip allows up to 6 analog channels of pulse-width modulated control informa-

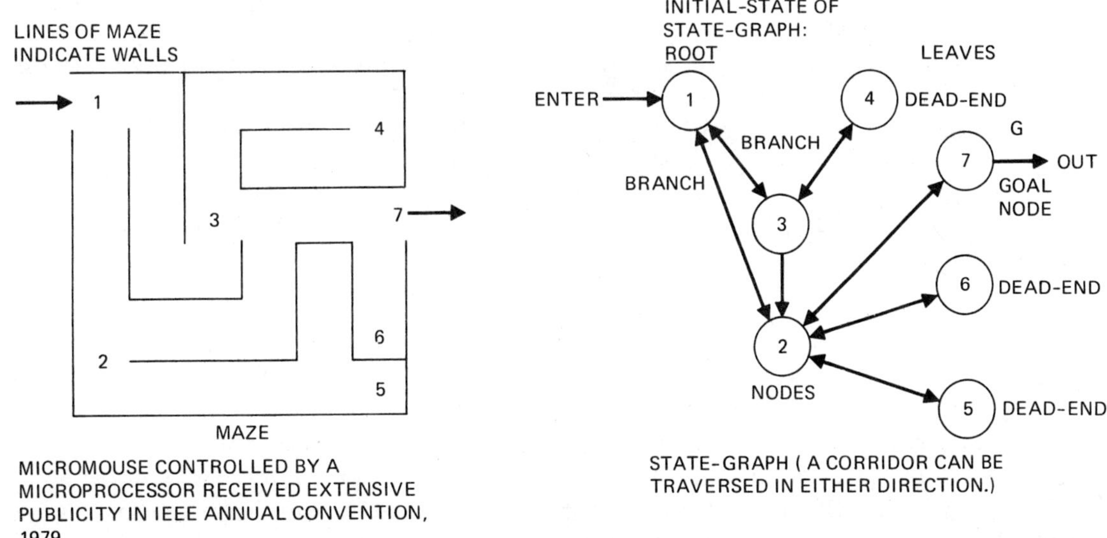

Fig. 11-32. A simple maze and its state-graph.

Artificial Intelligence by Neil Graham, 1979, Tab Books, Blue Ridge Summit, Pa.

tion to modulate an RF (radio frequency) carrier up to 80 MHz. The built-in encoder is a 6-channel combination of digital and proportional type information. The receive chip uses combined pulse-width and pulse-count techniques to handle 4 independent channels of analog or digital formats. Remote television channel control, data links, burglar alarms, etc., are other applications.

No FCC license is required for hobbyists and children using toy-models for operation at 49.83 to 49.89 MHz at 15-kHz spacing. However, maximum field-strength is restricted to 10 mV/meter at a distance of 3 meters. Other citizens band (CB) frequencies require FCC license.

The LM1871 encoder-transmit chip, consisting of a modulator and oscillator, requires a complement of components for the frequencies stated in the above paragraph: a crystal (for the internal oscillator), and 20 low-cost components such as resistors, capacitors, 2 coils, and 2 potentiometers. The LM1872 decoder-receive chip, consisting of local oscillator, mixer, IF-amp with *AGC, detector, sync, and decoding logic, requires external IF (intermediate frequency) transformers (2), RF transformer, one diode, 14 resistors and capacitors, 6-volt battery, and miniature motor of the toy-model. The transmit chip can use ac-supply derived dc or a chargeable battery. The individual transmit/receive chips and the required components can be integrated into a tiny low-cost microcomputer board for various applications and toy models.

11-33. OFFICE INFORMATION SYSTEMS (OIS), WANG LABORATORIES

LSI/VLSI high-speed microprocessor, minicomputer, and solid-state memory-oriented *distributed logic systems*, and intelligent terminals (classified as work-stations that perform local functions with speed and power) make these OIS Wang modular office systems. *Word processing* is the governing concept for the local facilities that include such advanced features as automatic paragraph numbering, indexing, and generation of tables of contents in order to minimize typing effort. Lists are sorted, and mathematical computations are performed with due provision of security. (see 12-24)

Language-compatible word processing systems are initiated for the first time. They are introduced as *ideographic* word processing systems that generate disk-memory based text processors in keyboard-CRT intelligent terminals. They can edit and print documents in Chinese, basic Chinese, Japanese, and English. OIS systems are systematically integrated with such exceptional features. Because of these features, export markets are created for small and large business systems in the Far East including the People's Republic of China. Support intelligent terminals and OIS systems of flexible complexity are provided for numerous other languages. They require minimum of operator training for operation of standard characters, and transaction keys in Japanese Hiragana, Katakana, Japanese-accent English pronunciation, and stylized quotation marks. Provision is also made for 8 phonetically "silent" Japanese characters by special keystrokes, and for special key-pads for Chinese-Japanese Kanji characters by means of special character-generator chips. All these features can be incorporated in each work-station because of the extensive use of low-cost VLSI chips.

The basic Wang system-OIS is a processor with a single diskette drive, a model 5536 IWS keyboard-CRT work-station with internal 64-K bytes of memory, and a model 5531-IP impact printer. Standard disk operating system capacity can range up to 137.5-M bytes. Provision is made for filing, document backup, and libraries or archives of informa-

*AGC: Automatic gain control
Sync: Synchronizing signal generator (clock)
IF amp: Intermediate frequency amplifier at 455-kHz standards.

tion. As a competition for business in the Far East along these lines, IBM has introduced in 1980 a low-priced Displaywriter as a comparable product in this field, which An Wang of Boston initiated about eight years ago to become the second largest supplier of small business computer systems in the world—second to Digital Equipment Corporation.

Some of the OIS business systems produced by Wang in 1980 are as follows:

1. Wang 2200-series MVP starts as a small business computer using a floppy-disk based personal computer. It supports a Wang-enhanced interpretive BASIC language for interactive programming, writing, documenting, and debugging programs. This system can modularly expand to central processor and up to 16 keyboard CRT terminals for concurrent (parallel) and batch-processing word processing business applications such as accounting, business forecasting, order entry, inventory, research, and scientific computation etc. Appropriate application software for manufacturing is readily available for business graphics, accounting, engineering and design, bills of material processing, costing, estimating, and planning material requirements. Files can be interactively updated after entry and validation of incoming data.

   Over 300-M bytes of disk-storage are furnished for the central processor for larger systems. The processor supports full access to asynchronous and bisynchronous international data communications on the basis of industry-standard protocols.
2. Wang 2200 PCS-III personal computer systems: The basic system with internal plug-in double mini-diskette storage file is oriented toward engineering and research, and big-business point-of-sale (POS) (1) to combined finance and insurance revenues, (2) to tailor mortgage and insurance plans, (3) to serve a medical-clinic administrator and a research operation in a medical laboratory, (4) to perform complex calculations on a calculator, (5) to aid an insurance broker in estimating estate planning, insurance, and annuity options, and (6) to enable a small retailer in booking reliable accounts receivable/payables and general ledger reports. Software is readily available for all these individual applications. User memory is 32-K bytes; diskette storage extends to 140-K bytes/drive; provision is made for either 16 lines of 64 characters or 24 lines of 80 characters on a 9-in. screen CRT display. The system can be conveniently integrated into a data communications network.
3. Wang VS for Data Base Management (DBMS): This system provides facilities for (1) flexible data storage techniques without need for renewing programs, (2) structuring data records, (3) fast automated data retrieval, (4) data management language, (5) data encryption, (6) data sharing, and (7) error detection for maintaining accuracy.

   Wang VS-100 is a virtual storage processor for EDP (electronic data processing) function. It has 2-M bytes of internal memory, 32-K bytes of cache memory, CPU with 64-bit fetch and 32-bit word-lengths, and 16 I/O ports for 128 intelligent word processing work-stations. The central storage capacity is 4.6-Gigabytes on disk.
4. Wang OIS Office-BASIC Integrated Information System is a flexible modular design for convenient expansion. This system has the full capability of total word processing, data processing, printing, and data communications. Office operations such as text editing, sorting lists, and merging names and addresses with standardized letters are performed at high speed. Up to 32 peripheral devices such as work-stations, printers, photocomposition units, optical character recognition readers, or Wang's Intelligent Image Printers can be integrated into the system. The image printer is a high-quality multifont printing device producing multiple copies or copy-sets of original documents. The system uses the popular Extended BASIC with an interpreter compiler to facilitate business transactions such as general accounting, insurance, cash-flow analysis, project scheduling, sales transactions for communication with customers, and monthly sales reports.

5. Wang VS/WP: This large-scale or medium-scale system can provide for 1 to 128 work-stations with facilities such as printers and other peripherals with automatic format control for concurrent operation. The printers are connected to keyboard-CRT intelligent terminals or work-stations with 32-K bytes of internal memory. The display is 24 lines of 80 characters per frame. Software in COBOL, BASIC, RPG-II, FORTRAN, and PL/1 is available on an interactive basis. Data, word processing, and communications are all integrated. Information storage and retrieval is effortless since data and text are combined in one integrated system. The overall system is flexible for medium and big business applications, including international data communications. Extensive use of LSI/VLSI chips makes these systems highly reliable.

11-35. CYBER 205

Computer aided design (CAD) simulation techniques have enabled Control Data Corporation to use 29 different types of LSI microprocessor, multiplexer, and memory chips for implementing the highest speed (super) computer CYBER-205 with increased reliability. As a complete system, it can perform 800 million operations in a second—three times faster than any high-speed computer in the world.

The central memory is capable of storing up to 4 million words. The arithmetic operations use both 64-bit and 32-bit words. The virtual-memory capacity may extend up to 2×10^6 million words.

The main-frame CPU can process combined vector and scalar information. A total of 16 I/O ports are used, and each port is capable of handling 200 Mb/sec; this is equivalent to an expanded bandwidth of 3.2 Gb/sec, the maximum in the computer industry.

The components of the computer architecture are as follows: a separate scalar processor links the memory interface to the elaborate vector processor, consisting of (1) I/O combined with setup and recovery, (2) vector stream and string section, and (3) vector floating-point operable in 4 pipelines. The built-in computer memory of 4 million words is organized in 4 pairs of sections via 2 paths, each individual section comprising of 512K memory words.

11.36 MODERN LARGE-SCALE COMPUTERS USING PROPRIETARY LSI/VLSI CHIPS OF PRICE/PERFORMANCE ADVANTAGE

IBM 4341 (64-bit) main-frame Processor, marketed in 1980, is taken as an example of the cost-effective use of LSI technology; its dominant features and its peripheral devices are briefly described. It is a successor to the former system/370, Models 138/148, with excellent cost/performance advantages and efficiency in power and cooling requirements (43% of Model 138). The compact 4341 processor's instruction execution time is 3.14 times faster than that of Model 148 on a complex FORTRAN job in a scientific application. The 64-bit (8-byte) instructions are fetched, decoded, and executed in the main-frame 4341 processor with a cycle-time of 150 to 300 nsec. A double-word (16 byte) of data can be fetched from a high-speed buffer storage (cache/associative memory) of 8-K bytes in the processor in 220 nsec without the need of repetitive references to storage. The buffer uses data-base store-in management. The 4341 is introduced with a wide variety of sophisticated I/O devices for storage and communications.

The main memory is 2-M bytes in Model K1, and 4-M bytes in Model K2 used for distributed processing in data communications environment. Such a large storage capacity is feasible because of the extensive use of VLSI static RAM memory chips. Depending on the configuration, it can be reduced to 108-K bytes according to the needs of the user. When the contents of a buffer location are changed, the updating of the processor storage is automatic and hence transparent to the programmer, thus making his task easier. Exclusive control storage is reloadable to accommodate the microcode (microinstructions) requirements of the processor; the microcode is not addressable by the programmer. The microcode address translation tables are part of this control storage. A processing time reduction up to 84% of Virtual-Memory/system 370 is feasible with 4341 control-program in an operating system.

The 4341 operates in 2 modes, viz., *system/370 mode* (to facilitate the upward compatibility of system/360 and system/370 from the viewpoint of available software), and extended control-program support with virtual-storage extended (*ECPS-VSE*) *mode* for improved processor performance in executing major supervisory functions. Mode-1 above obviously attracts the present IBM systems user to avail the cost/performance benefits of the new high-speed 4341 processor. In the ECPS-VSE mode, an internal mapping function supports virtual-storage units (by address translation tables) and I/O multiplexer channel-programs at execution time. The multiplexer (MUX) channels permit instruction-execution and I/O operations to proceed concurrently. The small portion of the processor-storage not available to the programmer depends on the programmer's choice of the processor's mode of operation, and the number of *unit control words* (*UCWs*) selected. The available 1024 UCWs require 64-K bytes of processor storage, and all these UCWs are effective in the installed multiplexer channels of the 4341 system. Each channel can use up to 8 control units.

In the system 370-mode, dynamic address-translation and channel indirect data-addressing are available to the virtual disk-storage. The 4341 processor makes use of the standard instruction set of system 370 (except READ DIRECT and WRITE DIRECT and 4 multiprocessing instructions), besides its own complement of new instructions that are effective in ECPS-VSE mode only.

In general, I/O control units work in conjunction with either a *byte MUX-channel* or a *block MUX-channel* for selecting the peripheral devices required. A channel can overlap the I/O device operation in an *interleaved mode* or a *burst mode* for a single device, operating at a high speed up to 1-M bytes/sec. Interleaved mode permits several low-speed devices of speeds up to 32-K bytes to operate in parallel (concurrently).

One byte-multiplexer channel is standard for a 4341 processor. *Two block-multiplexer channels*, using multiple subchannels and 2-M byte data-transfer-rate per block-MUX, can increase system throughput by increasing data entering and leaving from the I/O devices in a given interval of time. The block-MUX can support interleaved concurrent execution of multiple high-speed I/O operations (they are equivalent to system 370 processors). The block-MUX operates in 2 modes, viz., *selector channel mode* for compatibility to systems 360/370 selector channels, and *block-MUX mode* for interleaved other I/O data-transfer operations by disconnecting the channel-program in effect during certain non-data transfer operations. Three block-MUX channel units are optional for increasing the total data-rate of transfer in 5 block-MUX channels to 9-M bytes/sec.

For former users of systems 360/370, one *channel-to-channel adapter* is available for interconnection to 4341 processor by way of one control-unit position on the channel.

Two control operation-modes are available, viz., a *display mode* for a 3278 Model-2A (24 lines × 80 characters) display console, and a *printer-keyboard mode* for a 3287 Model-1 or -2 output printer. The combined display and keyboard-printer console operate with one I/O device-address of the processor. A control table is optional.

A *system diskette drive* is provided for *microcode* (microinstructions) and *diagnostic program-loading*. The diskette drive reads and writes on removable diskettes, and allows for storage of system failure-data for the information of the service engineers later. Storage protection is provided for both fetch and store. Failing instruction types are handled automatically by merely *retry*. Channel retry, data and command retry enhance processor availability and serviceability.

Single-bit error correction, and double-bit or many multiple-bit error detection, by error-checking and correction hardware (ECC) are provided. High-precision up to 28 hexadecimal digits (equivalent to 34 decimal digits) is standard with extended-precision floating-point computation. A clock comparator is used to cause an interrupt when the time-of-day (which is updated every microsecond) reaches a preset time. An interval-timer with a resolution of 3.3 μsec is also available.

Standard 4341 processor uses 24 control units, with up to 8 channels/unit. Automatic power-sequencing expansion is optional for 24 additional control units. The following diagram gives a simple concept of the system organization of this computer.

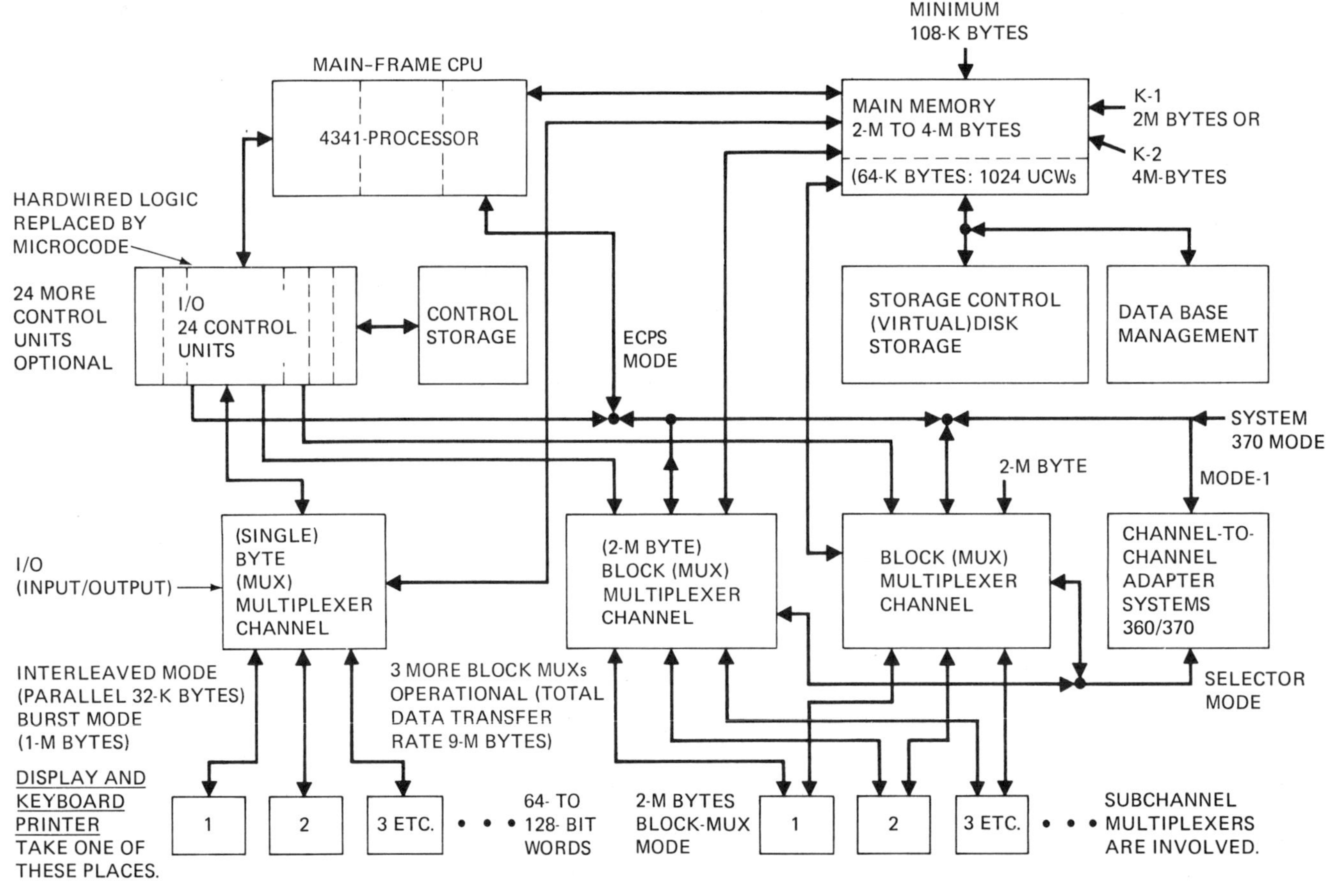

The IBM peripheral devices selected in a typical installation for the use of the *4341 processor* (consisting of a 3-unit console) are shown in italics in the following list:

- Direct access storage: *3880 storage control facility*, *3370 disk storage* (4), *3340 direct access storage facility* (4), 3344 direct access storage, 3340 disk storage, 3333 disk storage and control, 3350 direct access storage, 2314/2319 direct access storage.
- Storage systems: 3850 mass storage system.
  (Virtual memory capacity extends to 10's and 100's of gigabytes; VLSI micro-computer-assisted data-base management and data-retrieval are essential.)
- Magnetic tape equipment: 3803/*3420 mag. tape subsystem* (6), 2400-series mag. tape units.
- Diskette equipment: 3540 diskette I/O device.
- Card readers and punches: *3505 card reader*, *3525 card punch*, 2540 card reader/punch.
- Printers: *3203 printer model-5* line-printer, 3211 printer, 1403 printer, *3800 printing subsystem*.
- Optical readers: 3881 optical mark reader, 3886 optical character reader.
- Magnetic character readers: 3890 document processor.
- Auxiliary processors: 3838 array processor.
- Graphic system: 3250 graphic display system, 2250 display unit.
- Communications terminals and terminal system options: 3270 information display system, 3600 finance communication system, 3650 retail store system, 3660 supermarket system, 3735 programmable buffered terminal, 3767 communications terminal, 3740 data entry system, 3770 data communications system, 3780 data communications terminal, 3790 communication system, 8100 information system.
- Communication control: *3704*/3705 *communications controllers*, 270X transmission control units.
- Display stations: *3278 Model-2* (*display console*) and *3278 display stations* (2).

IBM H-Series 3081, and Amdahl 5880, ETC. Parallel pipeline processing architecture is the way to go for increased throughputs such as 10 million instructions per second, as compared to 1.2 million in the case of the 4341 mainframe. During the 1980s, higher speeds on the order of a cycle-time of 26 nsec, a main memory of up to 16-M bytes, 16 data channels, and a maximum data transfer rate of 72-M bytes/sec will be offered in the case of the $4 million price-performance category of large-scale computers.

Two central processing units of the capability of 4341 are used in parallel to share the execution of operation in IBM 3081 large-scale computer. The main memory in this classification of machines may eventually extend up to an amazing figure of 64-M bytes to cover a huge host-computer network. This is the kind of powerful computation technology that is feasible by using LSI/VLSI integrated circuits as building-blocks in huge but comparatively compact large-scale computers.

As a parallel, the current competition in this category, Amdahl Corporation, offers a 5880 IBM plug-compatible machine with 32-M bytes of main memory and 36 multiplex data channels in an air-cooled 10-tiered mainframe packaging system. Higher speed, LSI emitter-coupled logic (ECL) integrated circuits enable a 0.4 nsec gate-delay, and 7-nsec access-time for a clustered 4-chip 4-K bit RAM, as a memory building-block. The ideal execution of one instruction per machine cycle is feasible in 24 nsec.

Hitachi Ltd. of Japan (type H-200H mainframe), Siemens AG (type 7882), Nippon Electric Co. (type ACOS-1000), and Sperry Univac Corporation (1100/84, 4-processor system) are the other large-scale computers in this classification that make use of the modern trends in LSI/VLSI technology.

Imagine the amazing impact of the microprocessor-based instantaneous access of a single statement or several pages of exhaustive information on the desired subject, residing in the colossal storage capacities of these large-scale computers, via TDMA data communications networks and satellites on a microprocessor-controlled television receiver, or a keyboard CRT, in a remote village or a ship on the high seas around the world! The huge storage capacities may be considered to be large libraries of information.

Note on IBM Personal Computers: IBM Portable computer type 5120, introduced in 1980, is priced at $13,500. A multi-terminal version, type 5130, will be announced during 1981. At a much lower personal-computer-price of $4500, IBM is expected to announce a Model 5105 during 1980/81, meeting the requirements of the IEEE-standardized S-100-bus system, from plug-in point of view, so that IBM peripherals to personal computers can be plugged in other personal computer systems using S-100 bus. As is usual, 5105 will be programmed in BASIC with a main memory capacity of 16-K to 32-K bytes; it will have a cycle-time of 500 nsec. For software, magnetic tape cartridges and a cathode-ray-tube readout device will be used. A 30-character/sec thermal printer will be available as an accessory for the personal computer.

11.37. COMPUTER-BASED LEARNING

As an effective aid to teachers, PLATO, a computer-based instruction system developed by Control Data Corporation, has been uniquely successful in helping schoolchildren learn subjects such as mathematics, basic reading skills, and basic language skills. The basic reading skills course includes fundamentals of word structure, vocabulary development, and basic comprehension skills. In a small pilot operation, 12 microcomputer-controlled keyboard video terminals were used in one Baltimore school. The system consistently increased the achievement level of up to 90% of the schoolchildren. The programs are run on a separate floppy-disk for each course.

The interactive PLATO methodology encourages the child with immediate feedback—unlike that feasible in a coventional class-room environment. The computer instruction technique reinforces and motivates the child to concentrate and work harder. PLATO terminals provide an individualized, self-paced training environment in which the student competes with himself or herself, eliminating unnecessary discouraging peer pressure and embarrassment. What is needed for this application is a very low-cost video terminal for use in developing nations.

11-38. TREND OF NEW MICROPROCESSOR APPLICATIONS

1. The technique of measuring hypertension blood pressure by physically hearing the blood flow (Korotkoff sounds) while watching a pressure meter, as an occluding cuff on the arm is deflated, is a critical procedure. Honeywell's Microswitch Division, Freeport. Ill. uses a microprocessor-based self-calibrating instrument (BPI-420, price $400) to display definite systolic and diastolic blood-pressure readings in 30 seconds.

2. Intel 8748 eight-bit microcomputer displays one of 48 preprogrammed messages to aid victims of cerebral palsy or stroke, when they manipulate a simple control stick. (Georgia Institute of Technology Center, Atlanta, Georgia, price $250.)

3. Z-80 microprocessor-based X-band commercial small-boat radar device developed by Marine Electronics Co. of Seattle, Washington displays the location of targets within 80 miles on a color television set (price $2500).

4. CMOS microcomputer-based watch with a speech-synthesizer provides a liquid-crystal time display, audible time announcement and musical alarm. (Sharp Electronics, Osaka, Japan, price under $100.)

12
Personal Computing

12-1. INTRODUCTION

You need not learn sophisticated professional computing techniques (software) to use your low-cost personal microcomputer system. You can become an expert, after a few days' practice, in interactively communicating with the computer. Using the keyboard and CRT display, you can communicate by means of a few commands of what is generally known as BASIC. It uses a high-level language "compiler" in the form of an Interpreter for the microprocessor type used. The interpreter is built-in as a prewritten ROM facility in the low-cost computer system. The time-consuming intricate mnemonic assembly language need not be learned.

"Canned" specially written programs are available for various applications. You can buy low-cost (approximately \$6) tape cassettes for your home computer (\$500 and up). These programs can be purchased from vendors as well as from the manufacturer of your computer. If you are interested in further extending the capability of your computer to sophisticated programs of "small business application," advanced educational or scientific programs, chess, etc., you can ask the manufacturer to incorporate an additional unit at extra cost (\$600) in your cassette computer system to enable the use of mass-memory mini (5.25-in.) floppy diskette programs which are usually available at an approximate cost under \$30. The diskette facility makes your computer a disk operating system (DOS). (In the case of personal computers, before the year 1985, the expensive diskette electromechanical DOS will be replaced by more reliable, *mass-produced*, all-electronic, plug-in magnetic bubble memory chips of capacities up to **1-M byte**, at a low cost under approximately \$500.) As an example, a mini-floppy diskette contains a permanent memory of 92-K bytes of program. Along with the cassettes and diskettes, you receive instructions for using the programs concerned in BASIC. You give the pertinent commands in BASIC, and you input data of your problem via your keyboard. The computer manipulates the

Note: As a day-to-day developing technology, minor details of Ohio Scientific personal computers are subject to change.

"canned" program and outputs the pertinent information, in answer to your query, in alphanumerics or graphics (such as histograms) by display on the tube. If *you* make an error, the computer tells you so, and *you* give a fresh command or input.

Personal computing, is an explosive nonprofessional branch of Computer Sciences. This is the activity that will develop rapidly during the 1980s with the introduction of the low-cost solid-state LSI/VLSI components of data-processing hardware/filmware, solid-state high-density memory chips, readily available BASIC low-cost programs in tape-cassette (cartridge), mini-floppy diskette, and eventually magnetic-bubble memory format. The personal computing products of one of the popular manufacturers in this field is described in detail in the following pages. The products of several other manufacturers in this field present similar features in competitive price ranges.

Under FCC (Federal Communications Commission) rules, a Personal or Home Computer is classified as a restricted radiation device subject to specifications in Sec. 15.7 (47 CFR Sec. 15.7), FCC Docket No. 20780, 1976. Special power-supply filtering precautions and radiation suppression are required to minimize possible severe radio interference to television reception and other radio services from the high-speed digital logic used in these devices. Both line-conducted and radiated emissions are measured for the Personal Computers before they are distributed as practical consumer products. (Chief, RF Devices & Experimental Branch, FCC, Washington, DC, 20554, 202-632 7095). In practice, this is the responsibility of the manufacturer. Radiated emission causes beat-frequency interference in television receivers if video-RAM data signal from the microcomputer is modulated on a separate oscillator and connected to a free VHF channel of the television receiver for display of digital data. (This procedure requires FCC certification in the case of the user.) In general, this specific procedure is avoided by connecting the Video-RAM digital data from the computer, in the form of a direct video signal, to the CRT of the television receiver.

If your computer system is equipped with the auxiliary facility of a hard-copy miniprinter, you have, for a bookkeeping application, a complete VLSI computer system under approximately $2500. For example, an Ohio Scientific Inc. (Aurora, Ohio) C1P-MF, with 10-K bytes of ultrafast BASIC-in-ROM and 24-K bytes of RAM, can be used as a powerful real-time operating system (OS-65D-V3.1) with random and sequential access capabilities. This system includes a cassette tape recorder, a printer (AC-18P), modem, real-time clock, dual mini-floppy disks, AC remote interface, and full graphics display capability with relatively high resolution on 12-in. color monitor. A more powerful operating system, C8P-DF, has 32-K bytes of RAM, dual 8-in. floppies (OS-65D-3.1 and two demo disks) and costs $2600. It can use a Centronics 779 tractor feed (110 cps) business printer with interface ($1250) and a universal telephone interface CA-15 with touch-tone encoder/decoder (300-baud originate/answer modem, analog signal multiplex/demultiplexer ($500), to make it an equivalent of one of the former minicomputer systems costing above $35,000. This system thus enables the use of your home computer as a professional "time-share" video terminal for access to unlimited programs from a local large-scale host computer in a Network.

The low-cost (micro)computer systems using LSI/VLSI hardware and minimum space and consuming significantly less energy are highly reliable as compared to the former mini and large-scale computers. The simpler microcomputer systems have almost no downtime in practice.

Ohio Scientific mini-floppy diskette (5.25 in. diameter) software is much less expensive than the C1P basic computer cassette software, because of the naturally low cost of mass duplicating diskettes. A typical Ohio Scientific C1P-MF computer mini-floppy diskette will furnish 10 equivalent cassette programs. While the limited cassette programs cost approximately $6 to $8 each, the diskette multiprogram set or a diskette with an equivalent large program costs only $29 retail. Thus, in conjunction with the LOAD and SAVE capabilities of a much faster program and random access file capability, for accumulating a large software library using the mini-floppy diskette prewritten software, a system will actually be much more cost-effective than purchasing a large number of audio cassettes for the starter C1P basic computer system (under $600). With the additional MF hardware unit required for C1P-MF computer system (that allows the use of mini-floppy diskette software), the computer retail cost is approximately $990. Another attractive feature of the mini-floppy diskette system is that Ohio Scientific has previously been involved with the manufacture of regular floppy disk (8 in.) software for small business applications, a word processing system and a data-base management system, etc., for its slightly more costly C8P-DF microcomputer systems. It is therefore gradually transferring its readily available 8-in. floppy- and hard-disk software to mini-floppy diskette format. The transfer will enable low-cost C1P-MF computer systems avail that higher-cost software on cost-effective mini-floppy diskettes. This diskette system is attractively priced at under $1000.

12-2. PROGRAMS (LISTING)

Following is a list of the Ohio Scientific cassette and mini-floppy diskette programs for (1) Educational, (2) Business, (3) Personal, (4) Special Utility cassettes and (5) Video Games. A brief description of the programs is given as a follow-up. Bytes of RAM indicate required RAM capacity in C1P-MF microcomputer with facility of plug-in RAMs, and mini-floppy diskette programs.

Program	C1P Cassette No.	C1P-MF Mini-Floppy Diskette
Educational Programs	(6 unless specified otherwise)	($29 unless specified otherwise)
Add Game	SCE-316	ED-1 (8-program diskette 20-K bytes RAM)
Bar Graph	SCE-327	BD-1 (6-programs, 20-K RAM)
Base Conversions	SCE-321	PD-2 (5-programs, 20-K RAM)
Basic Math	SCE-334	–
BASIC Tutor Series	SCE-336 ($29)	ED-2 (6-BASIC tutor, 20-K RAM)
Clock Tutor	Available	ED-5 (5-programs, 20-K RAM)
Continents Quiz, Geography Quiz	SCE-332	ED-1
Counter (8K)	SCE-317	ED-1
Definite Integral	SCE-326	PD-2
Electronics Equations	SCE-312	PD-2
French Drill & Tutor	Available	ED-8 (3-programs, 20-K)
Function Grapher	Available	ED-6 (5-programs, 20-K)
Genetics, 1 to 7	Available	ED-6
German Tutors and Drill	Available	ED-8
Hangman	SCE-324 ($8)	ED-1
Hangman II	Not available	ED-1
Homonym Quiz (8K)	SCE-328	ED-3 (7-programs, 20-K RAM)
Log Tutor 1 to 3	Available	ED-4 (4-programs, 20-K RAM)
Math Blitz	SCE-329	ED-1
Math Challenge	Available	–
Math Introduction	SCE-319	ED-3

Program	C1P Cassette No.	C1P-MF Mini-Floppy Diskette
Math Library	SCE-335	ED-4
Mathink	SCD-337 ($8)	ED-1
Matrix Tutors 1 to 3	Available	ED-4
Metric Converter	Available	ED-5
Metric Tutor & Quiz	Available	ED-5
Nuclear Chemistry, Tutor & Quiz	Available	ED-6
Organic Chemistry, Tutor& Quiz	Available	ED-6
Physics Equations	Available	ED-6
Powers	SCE-331	PD-2
Presidents Quiz	SCE-320	ED-3
Roman Numeral Tutor	Available	ED-5
Solar System Quiz	SCE-325	ED-3
Spanish Drill and Tutor	Available	ED-8
Spelling Quiz	SCE-333	ED-1
Trend Line	SCE-330	PD-2
Trig Tutor I & II	SCE-318 (8K)	ED-4
Small Business Applications		
Address Book	SCB-523 ($8)	BD-2 (5 programs, 24-K RAM)
Advertisement Demo	SCB-520	BD-2
Bond Evaluation	SCB-514	BD-1 (6 programs, 24-K RAM)
Break/Even Analysis	SCB-515	BD-1
Buzzword Generator	Available	Available
Histogram	–	BD-3 (Full, 24-K RAM)
Inventory Demo	SCB-501	BD-2
Mailing List (8K)	Available	BD-2
Percentile	SCB-513	Available
Programmable Calculator	SCB-522 ($12)	Available
Ratio Analysis I	SCB-517	BD-1
Ratio Analysis II	SCB-516	BD-1
Salary Demo	SCB-511	Available
Statistics, I	SCB-510 (8K)	Available
Straight and Constant Depreciation	SCB-500	Available
Time Calculator	Available	Available
Word Processor (BASIC)	–	BD-2
Personal		
Annuity I	SCP-714	PD-1 (7-programs)
Annuity II	SCP-701	PD-1
Biorhythm	SCP-716 ($8)	PD-1
Calorie Counter	SCP-708	PD-1
Checking Account	SCP-719 ($8)	PD-1
Digital Clock	Available	Available
Kitchen Aid	SCP-713	Available
Loan Finance	SCP-717	BD-1
Personal Calendar	SCP-718	–
Savings Account	SCP-720 ($8)	PD-1
Stock Market Simulation	Available	Available
Uneven Cash Flows	SCP-715	PD-1

Special Utility Cassettes

Assembler/Editor with Manual (C1P) . . . $35.
Extended Monitor with Manual (C1P) . . . $15.

Program	C1P Cassette No.	C1P-MF Mini-Floppy Diskette
Video Games		
Battleship	SCC-947	GD-2 (6-programs, 24-K RAM)
Black Jack	SCG-955	GD-6 (5-programs, 20-K RAM)
Blockade	Available	GD-7 (5-programs, Joystick, 24-K RAM)
Bomber	SCG-948	GD-8 (5-programs, 24-K RAM)
Breakout	SCG-952	GD-1 (6-programs, 20-K RAM)
Civil War	Available	Available
Concentration	Available	GD-9 (5-programs, 24-K RAM)
Cryptography (secrecy)	SCG-931	GD-3 (5-programs, 20-K RAM)
Destroyer	SCG-951	GD-2
Dodge 'Em	Available	Available
Etch-A-Sketch	SCG-934	GD-7
Flip-Flop	Available	GD-9
Frustration	SCG-943	GD-4 (4-programs, 20-K RAM)
Hearts	Available	Available
Hectic	SCG-932 ($8)	GD-1
Hide & Seek	SCG-957	GD-2
High Noon	Available	GD-8
Hockey	Available	Available
Illusion	Available	GD-9
Kaleidoscope	SCG-957	–
Lander	SCG-925	GD-2
Mastermind	SCG-954	GD-4
23 Matches	Available	GD-4
New York Taxi	SCG-956	Available
Othello	Available	GD-9
Poker	Available	GD-6
Racer	SCG-949	GD-2
Slot Machine	Available	Available
Space Attack	Available	Available
Space War	SCG-942	GD-1
Star Trek	SCG-946	GD-3
Star Wars	SCG-926	GD-1
Tic-Tac-Toe	SCG-945	GD-4
Tiger Tank	SCG-950 ($12)	GD-2
Torpedo	SCG-953	GD-1
Zulu 9	Available	GD-8

12-3. SPECIFICATIONS OF A PERSONAL COMPUTER AND ACCESSORIES

A typical low-cost personal or home computer (from $990 up) will have the following specifications and accessories (**Ohio Scientific, C1P-MF**):

Microprocessor (popular type used): 6502, Microcomputer Associates
BASIC-on-ROM: 8-K bytes
BASIC on mini-floppy diskettes (5.25-in.: 92-K bytes each): 1 to 2 drives
Minimal Configuration in RAM (Static): 8- to 32-K bytes
TV/Video Monitor: Accessory
Keyboard (ASCII): Full 53-Key
Video display: 30 ch. X 30 lines.
Upper- and lower-case Graphics + Gaming elements: Available
Effective screen resolution (Horizontal and Vertical): 256 X 256
AC Remote Control Interface: Available
Audio (digital) cassette interface: Available

Real-time clock: Available
Printer Interface: Available
Modem Interface (RS-232 port) 1-300 baud/sec: Available
Built-in +5V (3A) power supply: Available

More sophisticated personal computers such as Ohio Scientific (C8P-DF), Radio-Shack 80-II, Apple-II, Texas Instruments 99/4, Commodore-2000 series PET, etc., use LSI/VLSI microprocessors, LSI/VLSI memories and self-contained peripherals and cost under $3990. With dual 8-in. floppy-disk memory, they serve small business applications, word processing, and Universal Telephone Interface. The above price includes Vortrax voice I/O output or stored message system, AC-Remote Control Interface and Home Security. The user does have the facility to program them in high-level languages such as BASIC, PASCAL, FORTRAN, and COBOL. It is, however, not mandatory since prewritten programs are readily available from under $30 to $300 each for various business applications such as general accounting, information management, word processing, and financial consulting. That is, tasks done by programmers of minicomputers are gradually taken over by personal computer manufacturers employing large groups of software engineers.

According to the Japan Electronic Industries Development association, 790 microcomputer systems were used for 1290 different applications annually in industrial, computer, communications, and instrumentation fields. Consumer, office, transportation, and especially medical applications are expected to grow at the same phenomenal rate during the 1980s. These microcomputer systems include 4-, 8-, 12-, and 16-bit versions of microprocessors. SM-4 was the first microcomputer chip using CMOS; M58840 was the first microcomputer chip with built-in A-D converter; and μCOM-83 was the first multiprocessor-oriented single-chip microcomputer. The notable manufacturers in Japan are Fujitsu, Ltd. Matsushita, Electric Industrial Co., Nippon Electric Co., OKI Semiconductor Inc., Sharp Electronics Corp., and Toshiba Corporation; and the common processing techniques such as NMOS, PMOS, and CMOS are involved. And Japanese manufacturers second-source the American versions Intel 8080A, 8085, AMD-2900, the Motorola 680 family, Z80, and Fairchild F8 for under $5000 "personal computer" applications with BASIC as the standard language. Japan's most advanced chip 64-pin, 5 volt μCOM-1600, developed by NEC, is architecturally suitable for master/slave multiprocessor configuration at a clock-rate of 6.7 MHz. Some of the personal computers include a graphic character set like that of the American versions. It must be realized that Japan is running neck and neck with the explosive personal computer markets as it did with the calculator business. Since there is no professional activity that is not influenced by the economy microcomputers, personal and industrial microcomputer systems will be used in millions during the 1980s.

During 1979, personal computers, consumer electronics, and video games using 65-K bytes of memory on one mini-floppy disk dominated the field of microcomputers. For example, SORD M200 series (with seven models) using one diskette, high-speed serial printer, XY plotter-printer, are quite common in the video-game oriented field. Some I/O modules are supplied, and the standard S-100 bus is adopted as standard with extended BASIC as well as assembler software. A TV controller for a 64-character × 23-line display, a 12-in. black-and-white TV, an audio cassette interface at 1200 baud/sec, an audio-cassette two-channel × 8-bit ADCs with a joystick, a digital clock, built-in 5-V power supply, digital I/Os with relay drivers and photo-couplers, a speaker, a full keyboard with graphics patterns, a printer interface, and S-100 bus interface are common in most of these systems. Hitachi's MB-6800 is oriented in design for hobby and software training applications common in the United States. The BASIC for this machine has a special command, MUSIC, which enables it to play music from cassettes.

The proportion of 16-bit processors and bit-slice I^2L processors is high in the fields of communications, computer, and transportation categories, where high throughput and performance are of primary consideration.

Another dominant feature is the gradual replacement of minicomputers by LSI/VLSI microcomputer chips, with 25% of replacement in office equipment. Replacement of hard-wired logic with LSI programmable logic arrays (PLAs) is another dominant factor in the fields of communications and transportation because of their size, reliability, and minimum power. The manpower expended in hardware system design and in software (firmware) system development is almost *the same*, with longer development time naturally allotted for software.

The overwhelming trend toward microcomputer-controlled consumer products in the following application areas (amounting to more than 10,000 units at approximately $930 each) is a common feature: (1) record changers, (2) tape decks, (3) radios, (4) transceivers, (5) washers, (6) microwave ovens, (7) gas heaters, (8) air conditioners, (9) television sets, (10) copiers, (11) typewriters for word processing, (12) 8-mm movie projectors, (13) home-knitting machines, (14) icemakers, (15) refrigerators, and (16) video cassette recorders. Timers are commonly used in most applications. In industrial applications, sequence control, device control, data processing, data-base management, instrumentation, data transmission, data monitoring, optimal control as well as PID (Proportional Integral and Differentiator) control, logging pattern processing, and arithmetic operation in signal processing are the major application areas. Thus, Japan is going full steam ahead in economy microcomputer systems applications in many parts of the world. This business competition from Japan will hasten the leading, advanced high technology in the computer field from the United States toward international markets at a rapid pace. Unless America takes advantage of its leading position, what happened in the case of color television, CB radio, and other radio markets might repeat in the case of microcomputer systems too; Japan is presently monopolizing the markets mentioned in many countries. Video cassette recording in color television is one field where the United States, Japan, and Europe are competing on an equal footing. The stakes are very high indeed for cassette recording in color television when international broadcasting is a reality via digital satellite communications. Satellite television in broadcasting and video cassette recording will eventually contribute to the education of the people all over the world.

Hardware and software/firmware (or programmability) areas will be closely examined, as an example, with one of the microcomputer systems from a leading manufacturer (Ohio Scientific, Inc., Aurora, Ohio) in the United States. (See section 12-4).

12-3.1. WORD PROCESSING SOFTWARE

For professional word-processing applications in English, a popular software program, AUTOSCRIBE, based on a floppy-disk, is available for the Z-80 and 8080-based microcomputer systems. An associated Hazeltine terminal and a letter-quality printer complete the system.

With AUTOSCRIBE, the typed text will appear on a keyboard CRT screen for the delivery of a hard copy on the associated printer. The text is corrected, and deletions or revisions are made within the desired paragraph structure by the author, so that at the operator can produce the final draft at the keyboard CRT. The finished document is automatically typed at hundreds of lines/minute. The data are stored on a floppy-disk for subsequent reprints.

The AUTOSCRIBE program disk is available from MicroAge Whole Sale, 1425 West 12th Street, Tempe, Arizona 85281. (See p. 494 for a word processing system).

12-4. CHALLENGER 1P PERSONAL COMPUTER SYSTEM

12.4.1. Real-time Clock and Floppy-disk Operating System (FDOS). The 610 board of C1P-MF incorporates a real-time clock circuitry that can be activated by a jumper if required. These circuits enable interrupts at several intervals between 1 sec and 1 ms to control IRQ (interrupt request from external devices) in conjunction with the real-time clock and the supporting software. The board also includes full buffering hardware for additional system expansion by another 40-pin ribbon connector, which mates with model 620 passive connector board to an OSI 48-line BUS backplane.

The total power consumption of the 610 board and the C1P-MF single mini-floppy diskette drive controller at +5V and +12V is approximately 3A, and the requisite regulated power supplies are available in the disk-drive C1P-MF unit. The disk-drive has its own internal data separator and activity light. The format and capacity of each mini-floppy are determined by the actual operating system (OS-65D 3.0) used. The diskette has a storage capacity, usually of an appropriately-formatted 70-K bytes, although the unformatted capacity may extend from 92 K to 100 K bytes. (The maximum dual disk drive system (A/B) requires up to 32-K bytes of RAM.) Drive A directly plugs into a 610 board equipped with a maximum of 24-K bytes of RAM; when the "D" key on the keyboard is pressed after reset (the "break" key), the disk software "boots up" (that is, it is loaded into the static RAM memory within a second or so).

Other options for OS-65D 3.0 CIP-MF floppy-disk operating system (FDOS) with 600/610 board system include any or all of 430B (Super I/O & Manual) A/D, D/A or RS-232 port options–such as CA-6S (Single RS-232 port), CA-6C (cassette interface), CA-7C (two 8-bit D/A, 8-bit A/D and 8-channel multiplexer with 8 I/O lines for cassette interface) or CA-7S (two 8-bit D/A, 8-bit A/D, 8-channel multiplexer with 8 I/O lines for RS-232 interface). CA-9 (parallel Centronics compatible line printer interface), CA-10X (standard 2 ports of RS-232) or 550 (2-to 16-port serial board), CA-12 (96-line remote parallel interface), and CA-14 (Voice I/O using Votrax output modules) may also be implemented as part of the OS-65D 3.0 operating system with C1P-MF 600/610 board system. In addition to these peripheral devices, PROM boards, prototyping boards, and card edge-extender boards may also be used in special applications. Provision is being made at this time for an educational interface board that allows interfaces to external devices, such as detection of switch enclosures, TTL outputs, AC on/off control, and thermostats for home computer applications. An AC remote interface would provide control signals over the AC power BUS.

12-4.2. Software. The software of the C1P-MF system can be divided into the following classifications: (1) BASIC-in-ROM Firmware, (2) optional systems level software, in particular, the software that is available on either the tape cassettes or the mini-floppy diskettes, (3) disk and cassette software for program development, and (4) the applications software on cassettes and mini-floppy diskettes.

12-4.2.1. Firmware. BASIC-in-ROM is the macroinstruction (or Interpretor) code permanently housed into the ROMs of the microcomputer system on the 600 board. It supports 2-K bytes of monitor and support routines and 8-K bytes of BASIC high-level language. The 8-K BASIC is highly sophisticated and debugged in Microsoft™ for the 6502 mnemonic program instruction set in hex for the various addressing modes. The

BASIC is self-sufficient for $6\frac{1}{2}$-digit precision, along with full scientific notation, trigonometric functions, string manipulations, logicals, etc., presently used in refined high-level languages such as PASCAL, PL/1, FORTRAN, etc. Even at the 1 MHz-clock execution speed used in the economy C1P Computer System, it is one of the fastest BASICs available for microcomputer systems; as a benchmark comparison, it needs less ROM capacity than conventional 8080-based computers and other personal computers. A *benchmark* is a program used to test and evaluate the performance characteristics of different microprocessors. OSI claims this trade-off between $6\frac{1}{2}$-digit precision, and execution speed is an excellent trade-off in low-cost personal computers. The high-speed execution makes real-time operation practical for animation, full arithmetic capability for routine "number-crunching" in small business and advanced educational prewritten programming applications. For real-time operating systems using mini-floppy diskettes, $9\frac{1}{2}$-digit extended BASIC does not, however, match the faster BASIC-in-ROM.

The 2-K bytes of BASIC-in-ROM for the support routines, such as I/O support subroutines of tape cassettes, video display, and keyboard scan make the computer system appear like an "intelligent video-keyboard terminal." The video display interface has the capability of scrolls and other common features of stand-alone monitors/video displays. The normal BASIC programming procedure gives programmers the impression that they are using a stand-alone video terminal for the computer system.

The support BASIC-in-ROM includes the complete machine code to allow the programmer to examine memory locations and load and execute machine code programs. Thus, the system has the capability to cater to both professional programmers and non-professionals using prewritten cassette and mini-floppy diskette programs. In the case of the FDOS (floppy disk operating system), the conventional bootstrap routine is loaded from the diskette at start. Since logicals are included in the firmware, the BASIC-in-ROM supports the RAM memory loaded from the mini-floppy diskette, as an alternative to cassette I/O.

12-4.2.2 Standard Cassette Software for C1P Microcomputer. The starter C1P computer system using *600 board* comes with a "Demonstration Library" on cassette to give the user some insight into the special capability of the computer. The Demo Library consists of 10 short programs that introduce the user to BASIC programming—as a kind of self-teaching tutorial. The Educational program and video-game cassettes are designed to inprove familiarity with BASIC programming, if one is programming-oriented. These programs are also available on mini-floppy diskettes.

12-4.2.3. Program Development. An Assembler/Editor for machine code on tape cassette or mini-floppy diskette is available for the programming-oriented user. For the hobbyist, extended monitor for machine code, diagnostics tests, and programs that perform specific I/O functions are also available with optional hardware.

12-4.2.4. The C1P-MF Computer System, Using the 610 Board, and the Diskette Controller can be used in three alternate modes.

a. As a BASIC-in-ROM C1P Computer using cassette programs only.
b. As an FDOS operating system that does not use the BASIC-in-ROM on the 600 board.
c. As a complete operating system using both BASIC-in-ROM and FDOS for diskette I/O operations.

With the C1P-MF computer system, the mini-floppy diskette facility and the 610 board, a small-scale, high-speed real-time OS-65D Level 3 operating system is readily available.

It supports 9-digit precision BASIC with named files and random/sequential access data files under BASIC. The C1P-MF incidentally supports a high-speed, concise interactive assembler, text editor and on-line debugging facility, while featuring an I/O distributor that allows the integration of the cassette, data modem, and line printer output. This is perhaps the first operating system under $1000 that the present microprocessors have made feasible.

For higher execution speed of this low-cost operating system, 6-digit precision BASIC is more desirable than the 9-digit precision when RAM memory space is at a premium, because the 6-digit precision BASIC-in-ROM in conjunction with limited diskette I/O capabilities makes it more efficient in throughput and speed. The 9-digit BASIC with sufficient RAM main memory is more compatible with a larger computer system that allows "open and close files," print to file, print from file or I/O device, and GET and PUT (record number) capabilities. This small-scale operating system can maintain a 6-character file name for diskette files and has complete directory facilities in conjunction with DELETE, RENAME, and file CREATE capabilities. The operating system includes additional utilities such as diskette duplicating and data file dump (monitoring) utilities.

All the software programs available on individual cassettes are grouped on diskettes along with large-scale programs, since the diskette with its 92-K byte capacity has enough room from 70-to-75-K bytes of program and data space. Large-scale programs such as personal calendar, address book, telephone directory, and some small-scale business programs are a common feature of diskette files. Of course, for still larger scale programs and voluminous data, 8-in. floppy or hard disk is ideal, as in minicomputer operating systems. Lower cost high-speed mass-duplicating of disk files makes diskettes less expensive than cassettes in personal computer operating systems, since each diskette may hold an equivalent capacity of to approximately 10 cassettes. A retail price of approximately $29 is common for a diskette, while the individual cassette program may cost as much as $6. Ohio Scientific is presently transferring most of its 8-in. floppy disk software of the former minicomputers to 5.25-in. diskettes for the convenience of the personal computers of its C1P-MF classification.

12-4.3. Instructions for the Operation of the OSI Challenger C1P Microcomputer (using OSI polled keyboard 600-board, 8-K byte RAM, and cassette tape recorder). The C1P personal computer is connected with the short video cable provided to the high-impedance video input of the closed-circuit television monitor (AC-3P). The top connector at the back of the keyboard computer unit is used for this purpose. The Panasonic RQ-2745 cassette tape recorder with its original *starter* cassette, will have two output jacks, one for recorder audio output (labeled "earphone" or "speaker") and the other for microphone input. The audio output of the recorder is connected to the middle connector of the C1P, and the microphone input is connected to the bottom connector of the C1P. See Figure 12-1. The interconnections between the three units is simple enough for anybody to use the personal computer system in BASIC. BASIC, the high-level computer language, is permanently stored in the computer's ROM (read-only memory) to get the computer running when the computer, and Video monitor are turned "ON". Figure 12-2 shows the details of the ASCII, 53-key, "polled" keyboard and the keyboard operating instructions. "Polled" stands for software-scanned. The significant keyboard operating instructions are as follows:

- A latching "shift-lock" key immediately to the right of the "+/;" key must be latched in the "down" position before BASIC hexa-numerals and commands can be entered.
- The machine is then "reset" by hitting "Break." Conventionally, brackets (⟨BREAK⟩)

signify that the corresponding key must be hit for momentary operation. When the monitor is turned on, the screen will be filled up with random characters, but on hitting ⟨break⟩, prompt C/W/M? or D/C/W/M? will appear in the lower left corner of the screen. (D stands for *boot* from disk; boot is an abridged form of *boot-strap*.)

- Press ⟨C⟩. C stands for cold-start. The screen will *scroll* up one line. C *initializes* computer and *clears* system RAM.

  "MEMORY SIZE?" (Computer BASIC asks)

- Press ⟨RETURN⟩. The screen will scroll up another line.

  "TERMINAL WIDTH?" (Computer BASIC asks: 24 characters available on 600-board system)

- Press ⟨RETURN⟩
  The computer will reply:
  XXXX BYTES FREE
  OS1 6502 BASIC VERSION 1 REV. 3.2
  COPYRIGHT 1977 BY MICROSOFT CO.
  OK
  For the C1P computer with 4-K bytes of RAM, XXXX="3327" and with 8-K bytes of RAM, XXXX="7423".

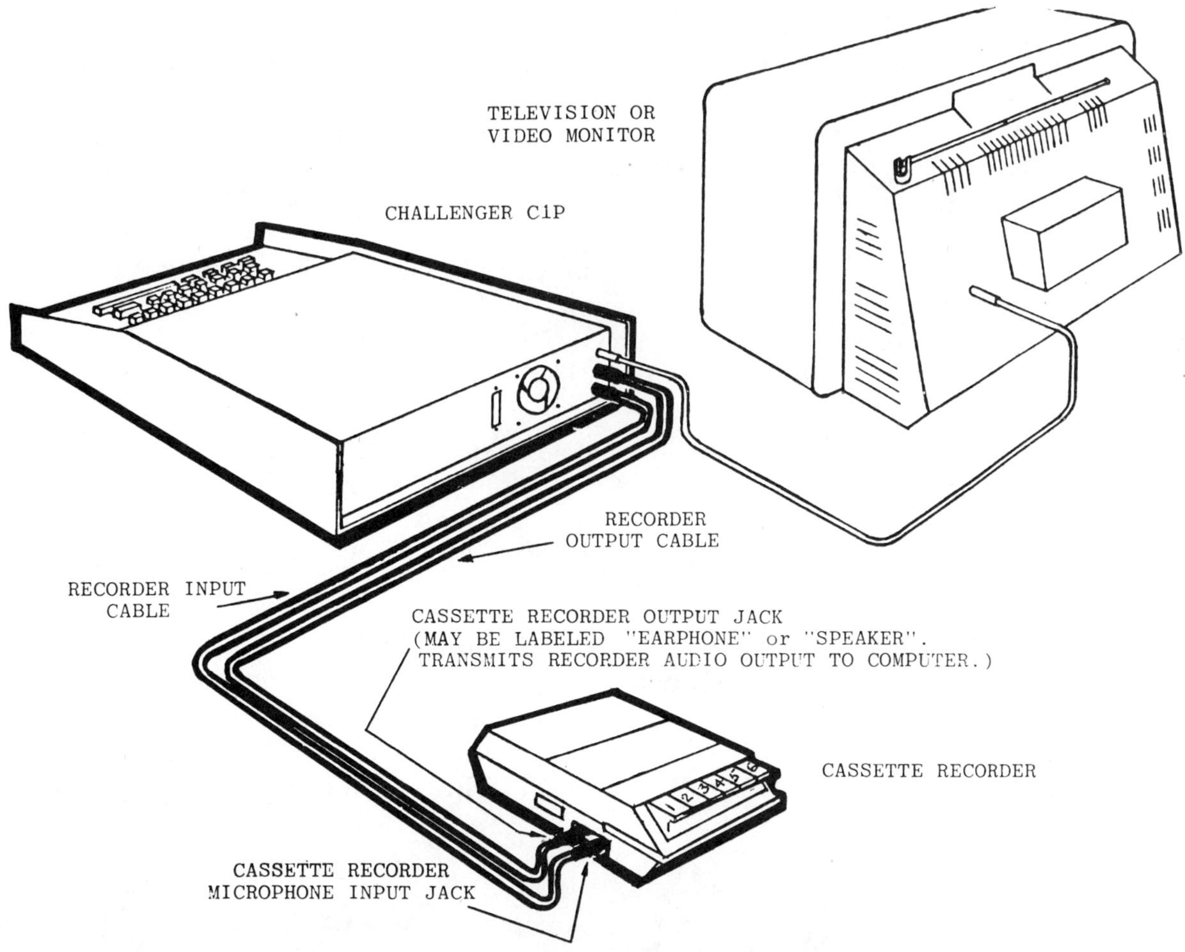

Fig. 12-1. Challenger C1P Cassette recorder connections. (*Courtesy of Ohio Scientific Inc.*)

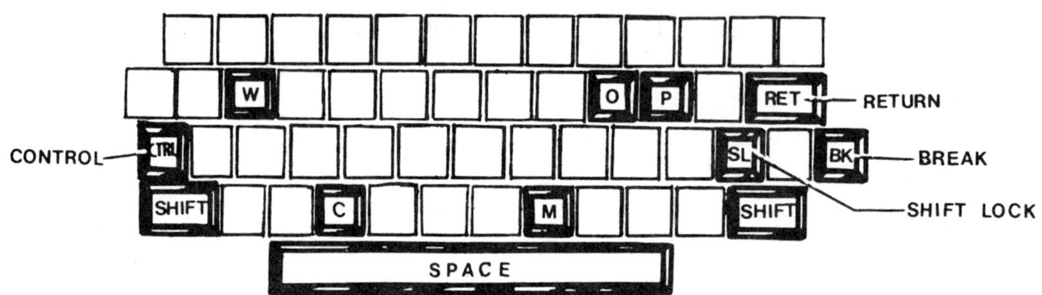

1. <> - Brackets - Instruct user to press key whose label is contained between the brackets. DO NOT type in word between brackets.
2. SHIFT LOCK - (latching key) - must be in the locked (depressed) position before BASIC may be entered; or capital letters, numerals, etc., may be entered.
3. <BREAK> - Places computer in the "RESET" state any time after system is powered up.
4. C - May be pressed after <BREAK> . Initializes computer and clears system RAM.
5. W - May be pressed after <BREAK> except when computer is first powered up (C must be used). Initializes computer, DOES NOT clear system RAM. Any programs in RAM are preserved.
6. M - May be pressed after <BREAK> . Initializes computer, clears system RAM. Computer enters machine language monitor.
7. < SPACE > - provides a space when pressed.
8. < RETURN > - must be entered after a line is typed. Typed material is then stored in program memory space.
9. < SHIFT O > - Press <SHIFT> first, add O - erases last character typed.
10. < SHIFT P > - Press <SHIFT> first, add P - erases current line being typed. Provides a "@" carriage return and line feed.
11. < CONTROL C > - Press <CONTROL> first, add C. Program listing or execution is interrupted, "BREAK IN LINE XXX" is printed.

Fig. 12.2. Operation notes–OSI polled keyboard. (*Courtesy of Ohio Scientific Inc.*)

- W may be pressed after ⟨BREAK⟩, *except* when computer is *first turned on* (*then* only "C" must be used). W initializes computer; it does not clear system RAM. Any programs in RAM are preserved as long as the computer is "ON." W stands for "Warm-start."
- M may be pressed after ⟨BREAK⟩ initializes computer, clears system RAM. Computer enters machine language monitor.
- ⟨SPACE⟩ provides a space when pressed.
- ⟨RETURN⟩ must be pressed after a line is typed. Typed material is then stored in program memory space.
- ⟨Shift⟩ first and then press 0: last character typed is erased.
- ⟨Shift⟩ first and then press P: erases current line being typed. Presents a "@" carriage return, and line feed.
- ⟨Control⟩ first and then press C: program "listing" or "execution" is interrupted. "BREAK IN LINE XXX" is printed.

12-4.4. Program Example. The following program illustrates the fundamental concepts of BASIC. When the computer replies OK under step (5), enter the following program exactly as it appears, including punctuation marks, etc.

```
1Ø PRINT "HELLO! I'M YOUR NEW COMPUTER!" ⟨RETURN⟩
2Ø PRINT ⟨RETURN⟩
3Ø END ⟨RETURN⟩
```

Now, you can check the program you have entered in the RAM (main memory). Type in the word LIST. Press ⟨RETURN⟩. This instructs the computer to print out the program as stored within the computer's memory.

LIST ⟨RETURN⟩

To have the computer execute the program, type in:

RUN ⟨RETURN⟩

The computer should then print:

HELLO! I'M YOUR NEW COMPUTER!

BASIC makes it simple to modify (or EDIT) a program. Errors within a line may be corrected by retyping the line as explained in ⟨shift⟩ instructions. Additional statements may be incorporated into a program by sequencing the new line numbers within the existing program. The following addition demonstrates this EDIT concept:

```
5 FOR X = Ø TO 3Ø ⟨RETURN⟩
25 NEXT X ⟨RETURN⟩
```

Examine the program as amended; type

LIST ⟨RETURN⟩

Then execute the new program; type

RUN ⟨RETURN⟩

The computer then prints the edited program.

12-4.5. Cassette Storage Technique. A "Kansas City" standard cassette tape recorder, such as Panasonic Model RQ-2745 with built-in counter may be used for (1) playback of prewritten OSI BASIC programs for specific applications, (2) for program storage of BASIC programs you initiate, and (3) playback of your own prerecorded programs.

Specification of a typical tape recorder. Panasonic Model RQ-2745 slim-line cassette tape recorder (Price: $42).

Power: AC, 120V, 60 Hz (with AC adaptor RP-65), 4W
Battery: 6V (4, "C"-size dry batteries)
Car battery: with optional Panasonic car adaptor RP-911
Operation: pushbutton one-touch recording with cue, review, and mechanical pause
Jacks: MIC-in (200-600 ohm), DC-in (6V), Monitor (8-ohm) remote
Speaker: 3-in. (8 cm) PM dynamic speaker
Dimensions: $1\frac{1}{4} \times 5\frac{1}{2} \times 9\frac{7}{8}$ in,; weight: 1 lb 12 oz, without batteries.

12-4.5.1. Playing Back a Program

The following steps show how to load computer with a program stored on cassette.

- Check for correct cable connections between the recorder and the C1P computer.
- Rewind the cassette so that the tape "leader" is visible on the takeup spool.
- Turn on the computer, and get into BASIC as indicated by the letters "OK" in the lower left corner of the screen.
- Type in NEW ⟨RETURN⟩. This erases anything that is stored in the computer.
- Type LOAD. Do not press ⟨RETURN⟩.

- Turn on the recorder to PLAY the tape.
- As soon as the tape (dark brown) begins to wind onto the spool, press ⟨RETURN⟩.
- Shortly, the program will begin listing on the screen. When program loading is complete, the following lines appear in the lower left corner of screen.
  OK
  S┘ERROR
  OK
- Press ⟨SPACE⟩.
- Press ⟨RETURN⟩.
- To inspect the program, type in LIST ⟨RETURN⟩.
- To execute the program, type RUN ⟨RETURN⟩.

12-4.5.2. Recording a Program from the Computer's RAM Memory

- Check for correct cable connections between the recorder and the computer.
- Use a new or thoroughly erased cassette. This will minimize noise and other problems of old cassettes.
- Have your program in BASIC ready in the computer.
- Rewind the cassette so that the tape "leader" is visible on the take-up spool.
- Type SAVE ⟨RETURN⟩.
- Type LIST. Do not press ⟨RETURN⟩.
- Turn on the cassette recorder in the RECORD mode. When the tape (dark brown) begins winding onto the take-up spool, wait 5 sec and press ⟨RETURN⟩.
- Observe the program listing on the screen. When the last line of the program is listed, wait a few seconds and turn off the recorder.
- Type in LOAD ⟨RETURN⟩.
- Press ⟨SPACE⟩ ⟨RETURN⟩.
- Label the cassette. If you wish to protect the contents from accidental erasure, break off the appropriate "record protect" tab located on the cassette's rear edge. With these preliminary steps, one can use commercially available OSI program cassettes for various applications. Learning to write programs in BASIC from BASIC manuals is the next stage for those who wish to know how. Here is an example of how one writes a BASIC program to get an answer from the computer.

12-4.6. Problem: Decimal to Binary Conversion. One must be familiar with binary in hexadecimal notation to master machine language or assembly language.

Program in BASIC: (Courtesy of Ohio Scientific)

```
3Ø PRINT
4Ø PRINT
5Ø PRINT "DECIMAL TO BINARY"
6Ø PRINT "CONVERTER"
7Ø PRINT
8Ø PRINT
9Ø INPUT X
1ØØ IF X < Ø THEN GO TO 25Ø
11Ø IF X > 32767 THEN GO TO 25Ø
12Ø PRINT
13Ø PRINT "X=";
14Ø Y = 16384
15Ø A = INT (X/Y)
16Ø IF A = Ø THEN GO TO 2ØØ
```

```
17Ø PRINT "1";
18Ø X = X - Y
19Ø GO TO 22Ø
2ØØ PRINT "Ø";
21Ø Y = Y/Z
22Ø IF INT (Y) = Ø THEN GO TO 24Ø
23Ø GO TO 15Ø
24Ø GO TO 7Ø
25Ø END
```

Table 12-1 presents the machine address numbers against the corresponding static RAM memory chips, and the free bytes available for loading the programs and data in the main memory used on 600 and 610 boards of the C1P-MF microcomputer. Figure 12-3 illustrates the interconnection of the LSI and MSI chips used in the C1P MF microcomputer on 600 and 610 PC boards.

TABLE 12-1. Memory map. *(Courtesy of Ohio Scientific)*

Challenger 1-P Memory Map BASIC-in-ROM Configuration		Memory Map under P-DOS Formatted diskette Pico-DOS	
ØØØØ - ØØFF	Page Zero	ØØØØ - ØØFF	Page Zero
Ø1ØØ - Ø1FF	Stack	Ø1ØØ - Ø1FF	Stack
Ø13Ø	NMI Vector	Ø13Ø	NMI Vector
Ø1CØ	IRQ Vector	Ø1CØ	IRQ Vector
ØØ2Ø - Ø221	BASIC Flags & Vectors	ØØ2Ø - Ø221	BASIC Flags & Vectors
Ø2Ø3	LOAD Flag	Ø2Ø3	LOAD Flag
Ø2Ø5	SAVE Flag	Ø2Ø5	SAVE Flag
Ø218	Input Vector	Ø218	Input Vector
Ø21A	Output Vector	Ø21A	Output Vector
Ø21C	Control C Check Vector	Ø21C	Control C Check Vector
Ø21E	Load Vector	Ø21E	Load Vector
Ø22Ø	Save Vector	Ø22Ø	Save Vector
Ø222 - Ø2FA	Unused	Ø222 - Ø2FA	Unused
		Memory Map P-DOS-1 is included above	
		Ø3ØØ	End of RAM BASIC Workspace
		02FB - 20FF	P-DOS Workspace Pointers
		- 22FA	BASIC Workspace under P-DOS (8-K)
		23ØØ - 317D	P-DOS
		317E - 3FFF	Free
			End of 16-K
		4ØØØ - 7FFF	Free
			End of 32-K
		AØØØ - BFFF	BASIC-in-ROM
		CØØØ - CØØ3	Floppy PIA
		CØ1Ø - CØ11	Floppy ACIA
DØØØ - D3FF	Video RAM	DØØØ - D3FF	Video RAM
DFØØ	Polled Keyboard	DFØØ	Polled Keyboard
FØØØ - FØØ1	ACIA Serial Cassette Port	FØØØ - FØØ1	ACIA Serial Cassette Port
F8ØØ - FBFF	ROM	F8ØØ - FBFF	ROM
FCØØ - FCFF	ROM-Floppy Bootstrap	FCØØ - FCFF	ROM-Floppy Bootstrap
FDØØ - FDFF	ROM-Polled Keyboard Input Routine	FDØØ - FDFF	ROM-Polled Keyboard Input Routine
FEØØ - FEFF	ROM-65V Monitor	FEØØ - FEFF	ROM-65V Monitor
FFØØ - FFFF	ROM-BASIC Support	FFØØ - FFFF	ROM-BASIC Support
FFFA	NMI Vector	FFFA	NMI Vector
FFFC	Reset Vector	FFFC	Reset Vector
FFFE	IRQ Vector	FFFE	IRQ Vector

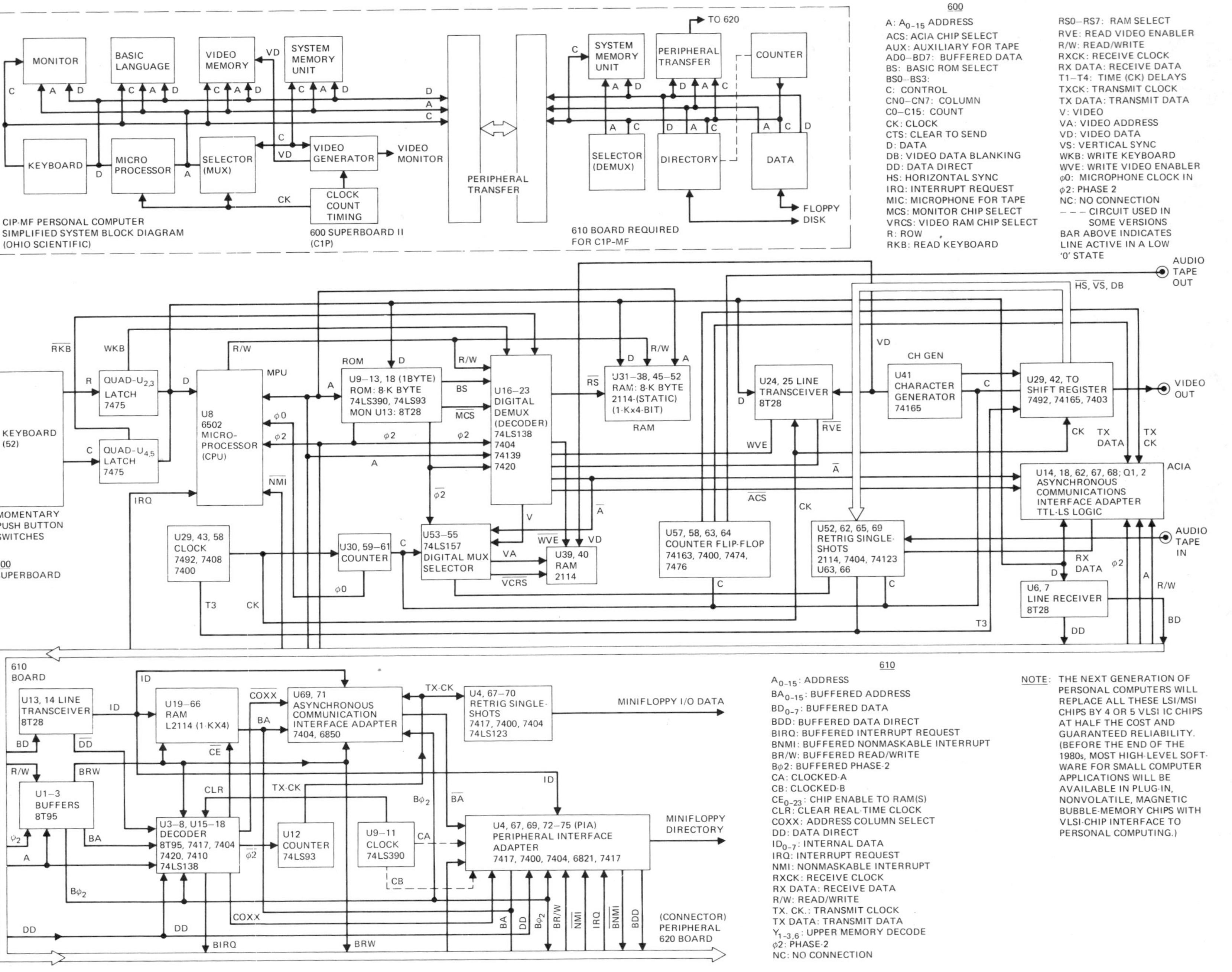

Fig. 12-3. Interconnection of LSI/MSI chips used in the C1P-MF personal computer PC boards 600/610.

Code Conversions. In microcomputer programming, hexadecimal code is almost universal. Four examples will be given to show how code conversions are performed between hexadecimal to decimal, decimal to haxadecimal, hexadecimal to binary, and binary to hexadecimal.

Example 1. Hexa. 3C7 to Decimal?

```
                  3     C     7    → Hexadecimal
Multiply by      16     :     :
                 48     :     :
  Add            12.....:     :
                 60           :
Multiply by      16           :
                960           :
  Add             7...........:
                967 ←──────────── Decimal Equivalent
```

Example 2. Decimal 967

Divide by: 967 ÷ 16 = 60 . . . Reminder 7 is LSD
Divide by: 60 ÷ 16 = 3 . . . Reminder 12 is C (hexa)
Divide by: 3 ÷ 16 = 0 . . . Reminder 3 is MSD . . . 3 C 7

For Decimal 967: Hexadecimal = 3C7

Example 3. Hexadecimal to Binary

Hexa: 3D6 . . . . . . 3 D 6

Binary ⟶ 0011 1101 0110

Binary equivalent: $(001111010110)_2$

Example 4. Binary to Hexadecimal

Binary: 11110101011

Add MSD of 0: LSD

0111 1010 1011
7 A B

Hence $(11110101011)_2$ = 7AB in Hexadecimal

Hexa	Decimal	Pure Binary
0	0	0000
1	1	0001
2	2	0010
3	3	0011
4	4	0100
5	5	0101
6	6	0110
7	7	0111
8	8	1000
9	9	1001
A	10	1010
B	11	1011
C	12	1100
D	13	1101
E	14	1110
F	15	1111

12-4.7. Pico-DOS (Hardware/Software Configuration). The 12-K RAM system with Pico-DOS (P-DOS) uses the internal BASIC-in-ROM with 8-K of program workspace in RAM and 4-K of Disk Operating System. P-DOS allows eight BASIC programs up to 8-K bytes long to be LOADed and SAVEd on disk, using BASIC-in-ROM's LOAD and SAVE commands. This configuration can be upgraded to the disk operating system OS-65D V3.0 by adding memory and software.

C1P-MF Pico DOS Computer Operation. Pico-DOS is a modified version of the operating system OS-65D V3.0. With this, mini-floppies can be used on C1P-MF with only 12-K RAM. This system extends the 6-digit BASIC-in-ROM LOAD and SAVE commands to permit files to be saved on a diskette as well as on the usual tape cassettes on C1P-MF.

In order to use the Pico-DOS, insert a Pico-DOS diskette into the A mini-floppy drive and type a ⟨D⟩ in respect to the start D/C/W/M? message after Reset with ⟨BREAK⟩. The Pico-DOS will boot up with the message:

MINI-65D3 V1.0
MEMORY SIZE? 8955
TERMINAL WIDTH?

Note that the memory size has been specified automatically, because the Pico-DOS occupies memory above this point. Continue with the initialization by entering terminal width as usual, 24 or 20 characters/line.

The new commands available under Pico-DOS are:

LOAD n
SAVE n

where n is a program number 1 through 8 on diskette. To SAVE a program, simply enter it into the machine and type SAVE n where n is 1 through 8. For example, to SAVE a game in the fifth space on the diskette, type SAVE 5. To recall this program at a later date from this diskette, type LOAD 5 and then RUN.

Precautions. Floppy diskettes and disk drives should be treated as mechanical devices, and the observation of the following precautions will maintain them in good condition.

12-4.7.1. Handling Floppy Diskettes

- Do not touch the surface of the diskette or allow any dirt or dust to come in contact with it.
- Be very careful in labeling diskettes without causing any damage.
- Do not bend or fold diskettes.
- Store the diskette at temperatures from 10° to 125°F (-18° to 51°C) only, and only use a diskette in a drive controller if both are at the same temperature.
- Do not allow magnets to come near diskettes.
- Always place the diskette in its jacket, and store it upright in its box when not in use.
- If you must lay a diskette on a table, place it with the label side down, to avoid damaging the recording side.
- When inserting a diskette in a drive, insert it carefully with both hands and an even pressure, until you hear a click. Before you close the drive, make sure that the diskette does not protrude at all.
- Do not try to clean the surface of a diskette.
- Turn on the power to your computer before you insert the diskette, and turn power off *after* you remove the diskette from the drive. *Never* turn the power ON or OFF while the diskette is in the drive.
- Insert the diskette in the disk drive with the label side up.
- Use only 100% certified, single index-hole diskettes, such as the ones offered by OSI.

12-4.7.2. Handling Disk Drives

- The disk drive should only be turned on or off when the computer has been turned ON.
- Diskette should be inserted in the drive after the drive has been turned ON, and removed before it is turned off.
- Do not obstruct the airflow to the disk drive in the rear.

- Disk drives and diskettes will not operate in very high or very low humidity. Air conditioning is generally not required unless the unit is operated in a basement or other area where condensed moisture is likely to occur. Rugs and carpets in the vicinity of the computer should be treated with antistatic spray.
- The disk drive, being a mechanical rotating device, is susceptible to line voltage and line frequency variations. The unit must be operated at 60.0 Hz for SAVE operations to work.
- The floppy disk system is mechanical, and thus subject to wear on pulleys, belts, and bearings, etc. It is a good practice to remove diskettes from disk drives when disk operations are not anticipated during the next hour or so. Also turn off disk drives when not in use for prolonged periods of time. (It is no wonder that the personal computing field has been anxiously looking forward to the highly competitive, stationary, all-electronic, nonvolatile, magnetic bubble memory cards for storage of programs in the place of the present universal usage of 8-in. and 5.25-in. floppy disks. Highly reliable Winchester 14-in. hard-disk systems are too expensive for economy microcomputer operating systems.)

12-5. POPULAR MICROCOMPUTERS USED IN PERSONAL COMPUTING (OHIO SCIENTIFIC INC.)

One of the powerful microcomputers used in the explosive field of personal computing, the Ohio Scientific Challenger 1P Microcomputer System, is described in detail to explain the various features incorporated from the viewpoints of the hardware and software/firmware. The term *firmware* is commonly used for the stored program control by the ROMs, the permanent (nonvolatile) read-only memory in which the ASCII programming of hexadecimal code is burned as mnemonic characters of the macro/microcomputer instructions in various addressing modes. This is commonlly referred to in personal computing as a ROM-Compiler of an "interpreter" version.

The introductory popular Personal C1P Keyboard-CRT microcomputer has built-in 8-K byte ROM for the above function in the BASIC high-level language to furnish a fully-packaged personal computer that is ready to run as delivered. Another 2-K bytes of ROM can be added for monitoring purposes. And the C1P's 8-K bytes of program/data memory can be expanded to 24-K bytes to allow the use of two plug- in mini-floppy diskettes, in addition to a cassette tape-recorder (1-K RAM is required for CRT display; 4-K bytes of static RAM cost $69). The software (programs) for various popular applications is supplied in BASIC on tape cassettes or single-drive mini-floppy diskettes, depending on the complexity of the prewritten programming involved. A floppy-disk-based powerful personal computer, C1P-MF (Mini-Floppy), is available at less than $1000. The system can be easily extended to Ohio Scientific's OS-65D V3.0 disk operating system, with 12-K byte ROM and 32-K byte static RAM, to furnish named program and data files, monitoring, and random and sequential access RS-232 interface capabilities. The C1P-MF can also support a printer, modem, real-time clock, and AC remote interface, as well as the abovementioned OS-65D V3.0 development diskette operating system for instant program and data retrieval.

Ohio Scientific manufactures a full business system as a popular personal computer. It is comprised of a C8P-DF microcomputer unit with slots, which are readily available for plug-in cards of external memory, peripheral interface, etc. The speed is doubled to 2-MHz by using a 6502C microprocessor in place of the 6502 and high-speed static RAMs of the desired memory capacity. This execution speed is reputed to be higher than that of any other personal computer on the market (over 1.2 million instructions per second, average memory time of 600 nsec for accumulator ADD, and 900 nsec for JUMP extended). The C8P-DF allows a 2048-character/frame display (32 rows of 64 columns) with upper and lower case. Long display-width makes it easier to program and read instructions. The effective 16-color graphics resolution of 256 X 512 pixels (picture elements) enables this microcomputer to match the display resolution of expensive color television sets.

Note: The comparatively low-cost Type-C8P uses 6502, BASIC in ROM with a maximum of 32-K bytes of high-speed static RAM, 8-in. floppy or Winchester hard disk, audio cassette Interface, Joystick Interface, AC Remote Control Interface, Printer Interface, Voice I/O, Telephone Interface, and time-sharing and color graphics.

The more advanced Type-C8P-DF system (just under $2600), comparable to average high-end minicomputers, has a provision for full capabilities as a personal computer, a small business and word-processing computer, a home monitoring security system, and an advanced process controller. It offers two versions of Information Management Systems, OS-MDMS and OS-DMS. Some of the disk software available in this category (at $300 each) is listed on p. 485. This Personal and Home Computer incorporates for process control a real-time clock and a unique powerful *dual* operating system that enables a computer to operate with normal BASIC programs while allowing the monitoring of external programs simultaneously. The AC remote control interface used enables, without wiring, the conventional remote control of a range of AC appliances, lights, and a home security monitoring system for fire, intrusion, car theft, water levels, and freezer temperature. The Ohio Scientific universal telephone interface (UTI) connects the computer to any touch-tone or rotary-dial telephone line. Voice, music, or 300-baud modem signals are acceptable. Thus, the main-frame class C8P-DF personal computer can use 48-K bytes of RAM, Dual 8-in. floppy or Winchester hard disk, printer, 16 parallel lines plus accessory bus for 48 additional lines of parallel I/O, and a complete analog signal I/O board with A/D, D/A, and multiplexers. The system allows the use of Joysticks and key-pads, but with its BASIC on disk does not allow BASIC on ROM, cassettes, and mini-floppy diskettes like the C8P personal computing system.

12-6. C1P MICROCOMPUTER

For beginners, a single-board computer system with a built-in ASCII 53-key keyboard system is available as a Superboard-II (at a cost of $279). The regular C1P computer with BASIC-in-ROM (8-K bytes) for full graphics capability and 4-K bytes of RAM (expandable to 8-K) uses a 600-type Superboard II as a consumer product at $349. Technical features are described in the following list of facilities:

1. It is directly connected to the video monitor via conventional NTSC 75-ohm coaxial standard video output, complete with scrolling and character-editing capability.
2. The tape cassette programmer for the C1P low-cost microcomputers are standardized, and one can watch the program step-by-step as the BASIC program from the cassette is loaded into the computer, as a unique feature.
3. The BASIC-in-ROM used is written in Microsoft, compatible with the industry standard nomenclature for BASIC. The 8-K byte RAM memory available is adequate for all the cassette programs available, and 2-K bytes of additional ROM is included for monitor-in-ROM to allow direct accessibility to machine code programming.
4. Full upper/lower-case capability for practical word-processing, and comprehensive graphics facility for standard ASCII characters, text-editing, graphics, lines, geometric, and video-game figures enable extensive video graphics capability with minimum of software.

5. No other low-cost personal computing microcomputer in the field offers high-speed $6\frac{1}{2}$-digit BASIC-in-ROM execution for real-time applications, and full scientific and financial arithmetic capability simultaneously. Noise-free display for animation and real-time graphics achieves the highest "performance-to-cost" ratio in the personal computing field.
6. Data storage in cassette-based files, though limited, is a fine facility in the small-business applications area.
7. The capabilities of the OSI C1P microcomputer system can be conveniently expanded to the economical C1P-MF system by incorporating a second type-610 Accessory Board for a total of 32-K bytes of RAM, a dual mini-floppy diskette controller, and a BUS-expansion facility. A fully expanded C1P-MF personal computer will have BASIC-in-ROM of 10-K bytes (2-K for monitoring), 32-K bytes of RAM main memory, dual 70-K byte mini-floppies, cassette facility, RS-232 interface, modem, printer, real-time clock, AC remote interface, random/sequential access, and OSI 48-line BUS for access to 40 devices (such as A/D, D/A, voice, I/O multiplexer, and memory expansion, etc.). That is, a personal computer is readily available for taking over the tasks of the former high-cost average medium-scale and minicomputers at a reasonable high-speed in actual extent of applications.
8. The on-line mini-floppy diskette drive facility enables instantaneous virtual memory storage for programs and data, instead of requiring several minutes for off-line batch-processing cassette-based software. That is, the effective operating system directly supports sequential and random access files directly in the BASIC high-level language to simulate in small business and scientific applications the operation of the former highly expensive, ultrafast hardware and software in high-cost computers. C1P's BASIC has advanced arithmetic capability with full scientific notation. This feature in both immediate mode and stored program mode makes it an advanced scientific calculator; one can type in an equation on a line and press "return" to get an answer. (The VLSI microprocessors at the introductory and drawing board level are aimed at very high nsec-speed levels, as VHSIC (very high-speed integrated-circuit) components for complex defense international data and signal-processing control and communications systems.)
9. According to OSI, personal computers of comparable price classification from other manufacturers are much less powerful and versatile than C1P. Instead of a calculator-style auxiliary keyboard in some, OSI's full ASCII-type keyboard is more convenient from the viewpoint of interaction with the computer. Most lack decimal arithmetic capability and scientific-math capability. The capabilities of the OSI C1P-class personal computers are considered a "dramatic breakthrough" as seen from the detailed list of significant educational, personal, business, utility, and recreation programs, available in both cassette and diskette form at low-cost (see p. 451). *The performance and application status* of the personal computers available is *clear proof* that the cost of software will follow the trends of hardware gradually—and need not remain highly expensive as in the case of the former high-cost minicomputer era. That is, in the future, computers can be easily handled by professionals and public alike, without any professional knowledge in time-consuming, expensive assembly programming capabilities. For example, personal computers will take a predominant role at both school and adult education levels on a universal basis. For the first time in history, people all over the world will have an opportunity via sattelite facilities to receive education at a potentially more or less uniform level to bring better understanding and peace on a permanent basis. There are approximately 70 satellites in geo-stationary orbit, and several more domestic satel-

lite systems with digital television broadcasting facility are on the drawing board. Meanwhile, LSI/VLSI technology and optical fiber communications systems are rendering small earth stations less and less expensive to enable poorer nations to take full advantage. So, the personal computer (both as a Home Computer and Tutor) has brought about a revolution by taking over most routine tiresome tasks, to enable progress toward a better life in general.

12-7. TECHNICAL DETAILS OF C1P AND C1P-MF PERSONAL COMPUTER SYSTEM

The C1P personal computer system uses *Model-600 single-board* computer, incorporating the CPU (Central Processing Unit), 8-K byte BASIC in ROM, 8-K byte RAM, AC-3P Combination TV/Monitor for video display, cassette storage (on a Panasonic RQ-2745 audio tape recorder), ASCII full 53-key Keyboard, built-in +5V, 3A power supply.

The microcomputer uses MOS Technology, silicon-gate NMOS 6502 microprocessor. It is an 8-bit pipeline-architectured microprocessor available in nine different versions. An internal single-phase clock (at 1 or 2 MHz) generator is used with an external crystal. (The 6512 version requires an external two-phase clock for systems that need high-precision timing control at 4 MHz.) The register and control section of the microprocessor's architecture is illustrated in Fig. 12-4. The 40-pin CPU chip can directly address up to 65-K bytes of data and program. Although the data word size is 8-bit with bidirectional data bus, the address-bus size is defined as 16-bit. Instruction word size can vary from 8 to 24 bits, as in the case of Motorola 6800 microprocessor. The number of basic memory-oriented instructions is 56, the instruction-time varying from 1 to 3 μs. With a clock voltage-swing of 2/5V, it uses three dedicated I/O control lines. It is TTL-compatible and requires +5V at 140mA. It has a powerful set of facilities from the software point of view, such as ADD and SUBTRACT in decimal mode with automatic correction, and 13 instruction addressing modes such as, accumulator immediate and absolute addressing, (true) indexed indirect and indirect indexed, implied and relative addressing, and zero-page indexed. The architecture of the CPU allows all conventionally required registers to accept data from the data bus and transfer data back and forth from the common internal bus. The stack-pointer is programmable with a variable length, and interrupt capability is nonmaskable like that of 6800. There is the direct memory access (DMA) capability and bus-compatibility with 6800. Another advantage is a 1- or 2-MHz clock option, which facilitates operation with a memory of any access-time.

The C1P-600 board operates with a single-speed crystal-controlled clock at approximately 1 MHz, with the computer master-reset by the "break" key of the keyboard. In the C1P configuration, the two available interrupts are not used, but in the C1P-MF, using the 610-Expander board, they are on the 48-line expansion BUS. Ohio Scientific 8-K byte BASIC-in-ROM occupies address range AØØØ to BFFF (hex). Either one 64-K bit masked ROM or four 2316B-type 16-K bit are acceptable with a jumper facility. (If desired, 2716-type EPROMs can be substituted.) Another 2-K byte or 16-K bit ROM is used for system monitor and support functions.

A maximum of 8-K byte of low-power-consuming 2114 Static RAM is used in the base configuration with an access-speed of at least 550 nsec. The 600-board uses an integrated computer-type, intelligent, ASCII, full 53-key standard keyboard with double-shot key caps, unerasable legends, and sealed-contact key switches. Upper- and lower-case characters are validated by using the conventional shift-lock key. The keyboard routine in ROM is effective to scan the keyboard for key closure. Full auto-repeat is effective when any key is held down for more than half-a-second, to produce five characters/sec, in place of the normal single character. Since the microprocessor directly accesses the keyboard, individ-

SECOND SOURCES: MOS TECHNOLOGY, ROCKWELL MICROELECTRONIC DEVICES, SYNERTEC

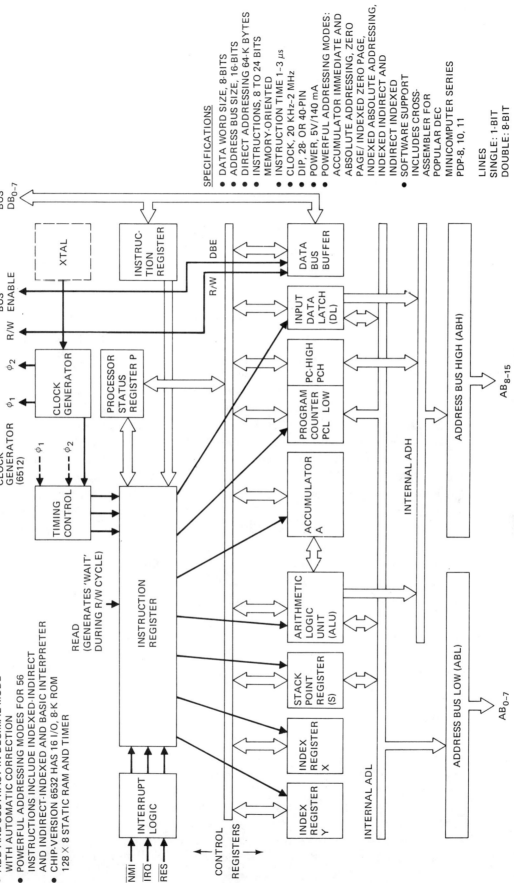

POPULAR 8-BIT PIPELINED MICROPROCESSORS WITH ON-CHIP CLOCK GENERATOR AND EXTERNAL 1-MHz CRYSTAL (2-MHz CRYSTAL WITH HIGHER SPEED 6502A CHIP, AND EXTERNAL TWO-PHASE CLOCK GENERATOR ARE REQUIRED FOR 6512 VARIANT TO ENABLE MAXIMUM TIMING CONTROL.) THE PIPELINED ARCHITECTURE FACILITATES ALL REGISTERS TO ACCEPT DATA FROM THE DATA BUS AND TRANSFER DATA BACK AND FORTH FROM A COMMON INTERNAL BUS.

MAJOR FEATURES (SOFTWARE/HARDWARE)
- ADD AND SUBTRACT IN DECIMAL MODE WITH AUTOMATIC CORRECTION
- POWERFUL ADDRESSING MODES FOR 56 INSTRUCTIONS INCLUDE INDEXED-INDIRECT AND INDIRECT-INDEXED AND BASIC INTERPRETER
- CHIP-VERSION 6532 HAS 16 I/O, 8-K ROM 128 × 8 STATIC RAM AND TIMER

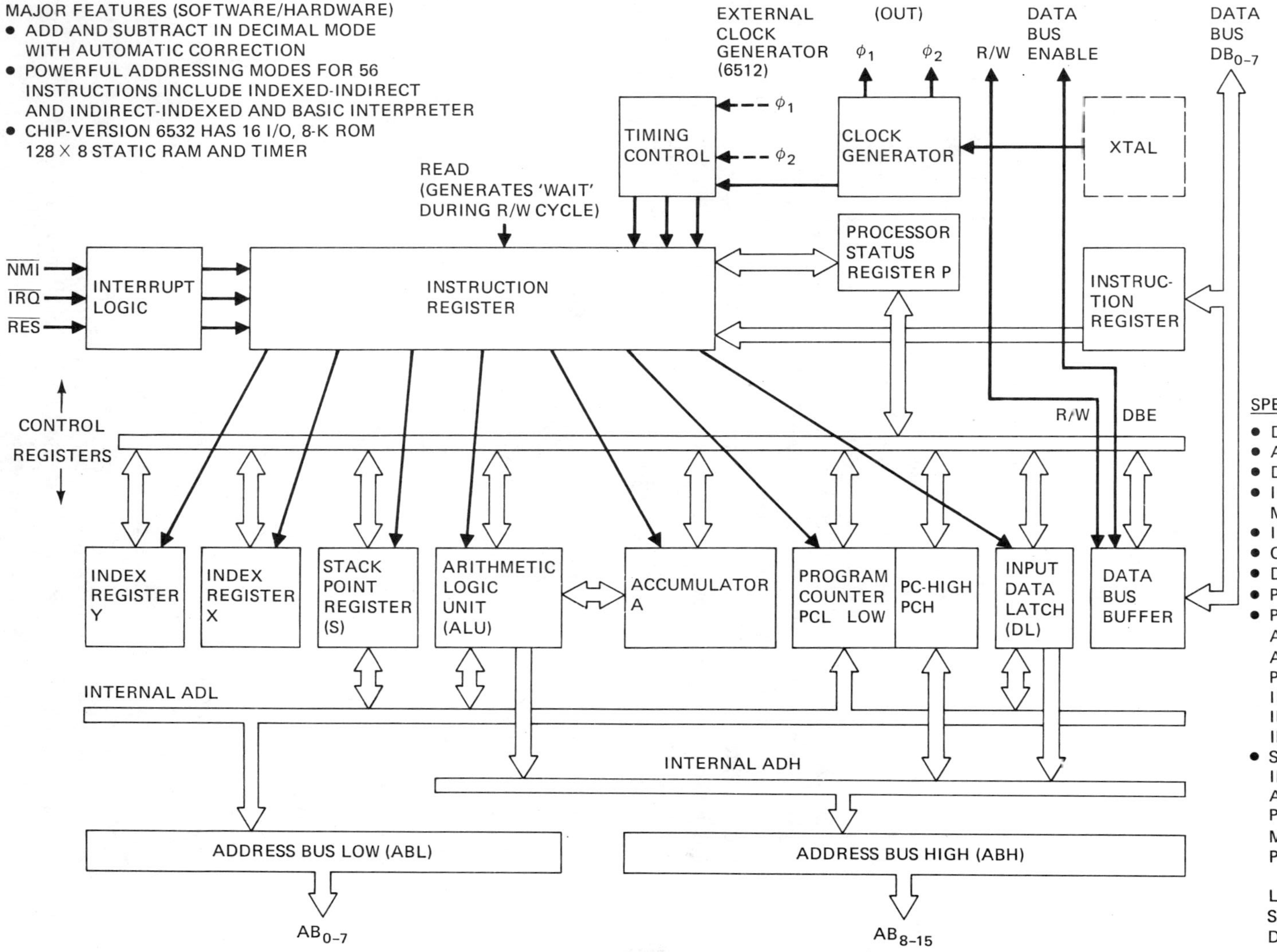

EXTERNAL CLOCK GENERATOR (6512)
ϕ_1
ϕ_2
(OUT)
ϕ_1 ϕ_2
R/W
DATA BUS ENABLE
DATA BUS DB_{0-7}
TIMING CONTROL
CLOCK GENERATOR
XTAL
READ (GENERATES 'WAIT' DURING R/W CYCLE)
PROCESSOR STATUS REGISTER P
$\overline{NMI}$
$\overline{IRQ}$
$\overline{RES}$
INTERRUPT LOGIC
INSTRUCTION REGISTER
INSTRUCTION REGISTER
CONTROL
REGISTERS
R/W
DBE
INDEX REGISTER Y
INDEX REGISTER X
STACK POINT REGISTER (S)
ARITHMETIC LOGIC UNIT (ALU)
ACCUMULATOR A
PROGRAM COUNTER PCL LOW
PC-HIGH PCH
INPUT DATA LATCH (DL)
DATA BUS BUFFER
INTERNAL ADL
INTERNAL ADH
ADDRESS BUS LOW (ABL)
ADDRESS BUS HIGH (ABH)
AB_{0-7}
AB_{8-15}

SPECIFICATIONS
- DATA WORD SIZE, 8-BITS
- ADDRESS BUS SIZE, 16-BITS
- DIRECT ADDRESSING 64-K BYTES
- INSTRUCTIONS, 8 TO 24 BITS MEMORY-ORIENTED
- INSTRUCTION TIME 1–3 μs
- CLOCK, 20 KHz–2 MHz
- DIP, 28- OR 40-PIN
- POWER, 5V/140 mA
- POWERFUL ADDRESSING MODES: ACCUMULATOR IMMEDIATE AND ABSOLUTE ADDRESSING, ZERO PAGE/ INDEXED ZERO PAGE, INDEXED ABSOLUTE ADDRESSING, INDEXED INDIRECT AND INDIRECT INDEXED
- SOFTWARE SUPPORT INCLUDES CROSS-ASSEMBLER FOR POPULAR DEC MINICOMPUTER SERIES PDP-8, 10, 11

LINES
SINGLE: 1-BIT
DOUBLE: 8-BIT

Fig. 12-4. Architecture of the microprocessor (as a central processing unit) MCS-6502. (*Courtesy of Microcomputer Associates*)

ual key strokes can be directly programmed in BASIC for specific functions. Real-time multiple-player video games are feasible since eight key-closures can be detected simultaneously, in conjunction with parallel-switching joystick operation. The dc power-pack with a 5A series-pass regulator-IC on the 600-board incorporates overcurrent protection fuse, reverse polarity diode, and a power-on LED indicator.

Video Display Interface. A direct-access 1-K byte video display memory located at DØØØ hex, is accessed by the CRT video circuitry on the 600-board. The display memory is updated by the noise-immune video control circuitry of the microprocessor. The CRT display format of 32 rows by 32 columns for 8 X 8 pixel characters (picture elements or dots) is generated by an OSI character-generator ROM, which specifies the desired character in 8-bit code ($2^8 = 256$). The 256-character set includes the alphabet (upper and lower case), numerals, special punctuation marks, graphic characters, and video-game characters. The original crystal-controlled synchronizing pulses in the NTSC composite video output are separated. The video display interface circuit transfers the video data at 4-MHz rate (or 8 megabit/sec character dots). Since no vertical or horizontal guardbands are involved, the first character starts after horizontal sync. Normal television equipment has overscan, and the data scan would start and end horizontally and vertically off-screen. The use of guardbands would increase the video data transfer rate of the screen and complicate the use of a conventional television set without modifications. The required character resolution would exceed the resolution capability of the television monitor. Therefore, numeric and graphics information of the C1P computer software is displayed in 24 rows by 24 columns in a conventional overscan television set. (In contrast, broadcast compatible color television signals with a bandwidth of 4.2 MHz are sampled at approximately 43 megabits/sec in digital data communications to obtain the high analog resolution in monochrome/color television receivers for an interlaced 525-line, 30-frame display.)

Audio Cassette. The system needs one LSI 6850 Asynchronous Interface Adapter connected to a crystal-controlled 300-baud audio cassette interface. The interface incorporates reasonable data transfer rate at high reliability and good program exchange capability. The model-600 board incorporates a switching network and connections for a 300-baud RS-232 port specifically for a modem, and an output-only RS-232 board for a printer. Thus, depending on the RS-232 interface, a selector switch and connectors must be provided by the user in the printer and modem used. RS-232 standard requires a negative voltage to the interface; note that there is no provision for negative supply in the 600-board. In addition to these facilities, the serial interface can support higher asynchronous baud rates. At the same time, it allows fully synchronous operation in a OS-65U Level 1 distributed processing system. Thus, in an educational environment, the C1P can function as an intelligent terminal in a network of other personal computers. Audio tape cassettes in personal computer systems use *Kansas City Standard (1975)* for exchange of programs on audio cassettes. The data are recorded serially, using a standard UART (universal asynchronous receive/transmit) format (1 start bit, 8 data bits, and 2 stop bits) at 300 baud/sec. A logic-1 is 2400-Hz sine-wave tone and a logic-0 is 1200-Hz sine-wave tone; the clock pulses are recorded on the tape with the data. Using the KC standard, about 100-K bytes can be recorded on a C-30 tape cassette, and the loading of an 8-K byte program (formatted) would take about 5 min. (This is three times faster than the speed of a Teletype using paper tape; hence, audio cassettes have become very popular in low-cost home-computer systems.) The serial FSK (frequency-shift keying) modulated audio tone is read from the tape and converted into a self-clocking signal that can tolerate 30% recorder speed variations. The Cassette Interface unit using the KC standard consists of an FSK modulator and demodulator.

As an example, the FSK mod-demod of a SWTP model AC-30 tape recorder uses a

4800-Hz clock to the modulator; it is turned on or off by a carrier-enable input to the integrated circuit used. This signal is divided to 2400-Hz and 1200-Hz for reading the FSK data. High-pass filtering and delay-compensation are essential for the correct operation of the audio cassette tape-recorder/player. A controller circuit permits automatic starting and stopping of one or two tape recorders. (Another Tarbell system, interfacing directly to S-100 bus, uses a more sophisticated phase-encoding technique to enable speeds up to 1800 baud/sec.) A cassette tape recorder should have a good high-frequency response to 8-kHz, minimum speed fluctuation, and a good tape-handling system to minimize tape wear. Low-cost Panasonic and Sharp cassette tape recorders are popular. It takes approximately 1 min to load one 8-K byte program from a tape cassette into the computer RAM memory. A counter is used in these recorders to prefix the start and duration of programs.

Model-610 Expansion Board. The C1P-MF Microcomputer system requires this second PC board (mounted below the type-600 Main Board) for the use of a dual mini-floppy (Diskette) Controller, Real-time Clock, 24-K bytes of RAM for loading the programs from diskettes, and an Expansion Interface to a *Model-620 BUS Adapter*, which is merely a passive connector board and a ribbon cable adapter from the 610-board to an OSI 48-line BUS *back-plane.*

RAM Memory. The Main Board-600 must have the maximum 8-K bytes of RAM when the 610-board is used in the C1P-MF system. The 24-K byte RAM array used in 610 starts at 8K-byte up from the base address. A minimum of 16K of RAM is required for mini-floppy operation. Type 2114, 1K by 4-bit (0.5 K-byte), fully static RAM memory chip with an access-time of 550 nsec, is used in this system. Each chip requires 40 mA at +5 V. (Dynamic RAMs at lower cost require additional clock circuitry to refresh memory after loading and are hence not preferred.)

Floppy Disk Interface. The popular and successful OSI Type-470 floppy disk controller is used. This controller, which has been in use for several years, is reputed to be one of the most reliable floppy disk systems.

Floppy disks are recorded with data in concentric circles or tracks. Each track is further divided into "sectors" of 128 bytes each. An 8-in.-diameter floppy disk has 77 usable tracks. Mini-floppy diskettes have from 35 to 40 usable tracks depending on the quality of the floppy disk type. Tracks are numbered from zero (outermost track) up. Ohio Scientific operating system OS-65D, (version 3.0) stores BASIC programs starting on boundary track (zero) and uses an integral number of tracks to store each program. Small programs are stored on a single sector/track. Programs extending to multiple number of tracks in extent are stored on contiguous tracks. (A 3-track-long program, starting at 0, will be stored on 0, 1, and 2.) Eight-inch floppies allow 2800 bytes or characters/track, while 5.25-in. mini floppies allow approximately 2000 bytes or characters/track. Recently double-density floppy disks are introduced.

Typical Floppy Disk Drive System. The disk is inserted into the drive through a horizontal slit opening. When the opening is closed, the disk is automatically clamped. The spindle is driven at a constant speed of 360 rpm by a synchronous motor to rotate the disk inside a felt-lined envelope. The video head on a carriage moves radially in or out from the center of the disk by a stepping motor. In the case of an 8-in. floppy, the video head can be positioned at any one of 77 tracks; the stepping ranges from 100 to 400 step/sec. The recording head protrudes through the slot in the disk envelope. When reading or writing occurs, a pressure pad on the other side of the disk presses the disk against the head. The storage medium on the disk is a large round piece of 0.003-in. Mylar covered with a thin layer of magnetic oxide, and it is housed in an 8-in.-square protective envelope with cutouts for the drive spindle, recording head, and index position

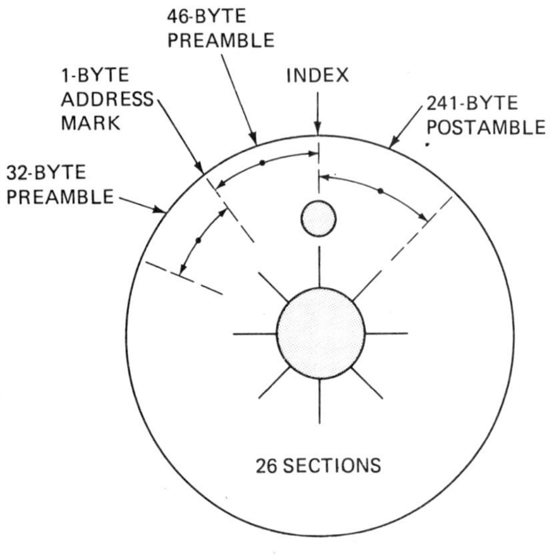

A FLOPPY-DISK IS A ROUND PLATTER OF PLASTIC COATED WITH APPROPRIATE MAGNETIC OXIDE IN CODE-FORMATTED AS SHOWN.

PRINCIPLE OF DATA-BIT RECORDING.

A FLOPPY-DISK DRIVE SYSTEM GENERALLY INCLUDES INDEX AND SECTOR DETECTION, READ/WRITE-HEAD POSITION ACTUATOR HEAD LOAD ACTUATOR DRIVERS, WRITE DRIVERS, READ AMPLIFIER, TRANSITION DETECTORS, WRITE-PROTECT DETECTOR, AND MOTOR CONTROL CIRCUITS.

VERTICAL ARROW
INDICATES FLUX
CURRENT
(R/W COIL)
DIRECTION
OF
MOTION
OF DISK
OXIDE RECORDING FILM
MYLAR BASE

SIGNALS GENERALLY REQUIRED:

1. MOTOR ON
2. DIRECTION SELECT
3. STEP (HEAD MOVEMENT TRACK BY TRACK (IN/OUT))
4. WRITE GATE (INACTIVE MEANS 'READ')
5. TRACK 00 (OUTMOST)
6. INDEX/SECTOR

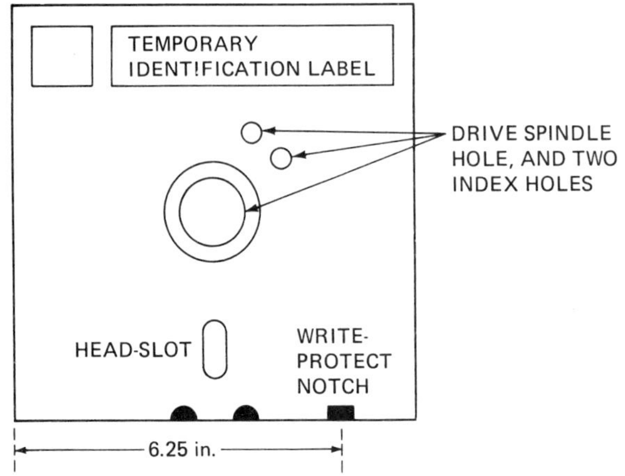

8" FLOPPY-DISK GENERALLY USED IN MINICOMPUTER AND MICROCOMPUTER SYSTEMS FOR NON-VOLATILE PORTABLE RANDOM-ACCESS MEMORY (FOR APPLICATIONS SOFTWARE IN HIGH-LEVEL LANGUAGES, FORTRAN, PASCAL, AND INTERPRETIVE BASIC.)

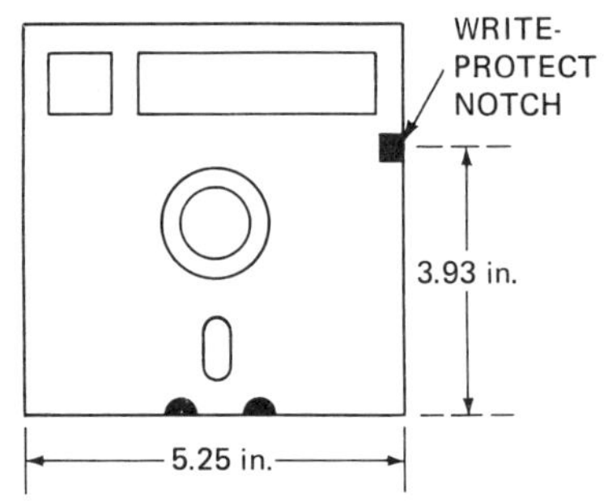

$5\frac{1}{4}$"—MINIFLOPPY DISKETTE PREFERRED FOR LOW-COST MICROCOMPUTER PROGRAMS. TWO DISKS ARE NORMALLY LOADED IN A FLOPPY-DISK DRIVE SYSTEM. (SHUGART SA-800 IS ONE OF THE POPULAR DRIVE CONTROLLERS WITH 2 CONTROL-LOGIC PC-BOARDS)

Fig. 12-5a. Floppy disk and mini-floppy diskette in their standard envelopes. (*Courtesy of EDN, Cahner Publications*)

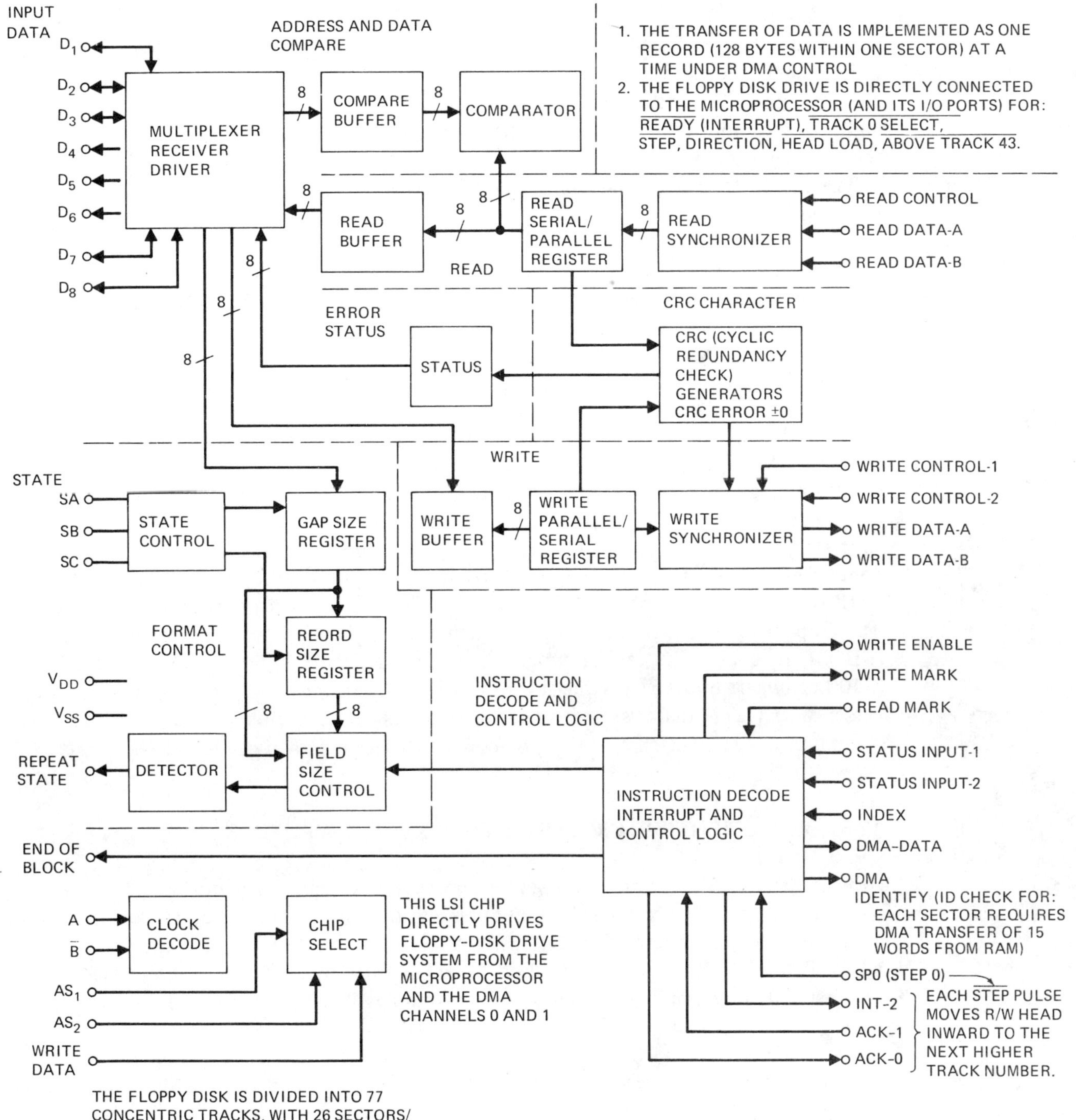

Fig. 12-5b. Rockwell International's single-chip LSI floppy disk controller–architectural details. (*Courtesy of Rockwell International Corp.*)

hole. A typical floppy disk in its envelope is shown in Figure 12-5a. Actually, two versions of disk are used soft- and hard-sectored. The standard *soft-sectored* floppy disk uses a single index hole, and the sectoring format information is prerecorded on the disk (one pulse/rev, every 200 msec, for each track). The *hard-sectoring* disk contains an index-hole and holes to indicate 32 sectors on the hard disk. A photocell and indicator lamp detect the index and sector holes.

The record format on the disk usually consists of a pattern of leading zeros, the data identifying pattern (ID), a data of 128 bytes, cyclic redundancy check (CRC) characters, and a pattern of trailing zeros. If the drive stops in the wrong position, the controller corrects the error by noting the ID pattern.

The drive, controller, and interface electronics circuitry include the read, write, motor control, head-positioning, and loading functions. The controller may use an LSI microprocessor to decode the CPU digital commands and data to provide the correct signals, such as computed step counts, sector and ID information, CRC checking, serialization, etc., of data, and memory data. Control circuitry may be also involved for handling multiple drives, usually a dual floppy-disk system for plugging in a second floppy-disk in a floppy-disk controller. NEC Microcomputers Inc. was the first manufacturer to distribute a single-chip LSI floppy-disk controller μPD372 for turning any microcomputer or minicomputer into a floppy-disk system directly. This chip can actually drive up to four floppy-disk drives. (μPD371 serves a single-chip function as a direct tape cassette controller.) Direct memory access is a common feature to directly read and write in the CPU's memory. The system is usually optimized by a supporting program to manage the whole operation in a high-level language such as BASIC for a floppy-disk operating system (FDOS), to enable the call of programs or data by name. Shugart SA400 mini-floppy ($400), Shugart 850/851 double-side drive ($1050), Shugart standard floppy ($900), and Persci Model 277 dual disk drive ($1575) are the other popular floppy disk controller systems used. A single-chip LSI floppy-disk controller is shown in Fig. 12-5b.

12-8. OHIO SCIENTIFIC C8P SERIES PERSONAL COMPUTERS

Advanced personal computers using microprocessors are already featuring system capabilities in speed and device facilities that approach the operation and computional power of an average minicomputer of the 1970s, at prices under $3000. We are arriving at a stage where Personal Computers can be used for most small-business applications without any professional programming assistance. This trend will naturally expand the use, in the home, of under-$1000 computers for educational and recreation purposes.

The Ohio Scientific C8P series of microcomputer systems based on one of the *microprocessors 6502A (2 MHz clock), 6800, 8080, and Z-80* (and their higher-clock equivalents), belong to this trend in industrial and small-business applications. According to the manufacturer, the organization of the C8P series microcomputers is unique. The large amount of software presently applicable to the OSI's three other popular microcomputers can be directly used for the C8P series of OSI personal computers. For example, the C8P-DF working with 48-K byte RAM and dual 8-in. floppy or 70-M byte Winchester hard-disk drive is a close low-cost competitive parallel to the present higher-cost minicomputer systems. The C8P series of microcomputers use a family of NMOS LSI circuits to derive a common BUS structure such as a special S-40 or *S-100* for a backplane (or mother board) that can directly accept a number of cards containing one or more functions. An accessory such as *RS-232* or *IEEE-488 interface* consists of three or four integrated circuits with one or two peripheral LSI chips, as opposed to scores of integrated circuits for the hard-wired logic in the former minicomputers. This advance in hardware technology with reduced number of external MSI integrated circuits naturally results in favorable hardware/software trade-offs for powerful minimal circuitry configurations with effective advantages of high-speed, throughput, maintainability, and intrinsic reliability, all at the same time. One rarely hears about downtime with microcomputers, as was the case with the former high-cost computers consuming a lot of power. Quality and performance standards of both hardware and software at lower cost enormously benefit microcomputers—thus, their explosive application capabilities. The tens of thousands of microcomputers used for various applications bring down the cost of high-quality, high-performance software available mostly in the form of 8- or 5.25-in. floppy disks. As an example, ANSI standard FORTRAN or COBOL or the latest BASIC or PASCAL for various business, educational, industrial, signal-processing, medical, and scientific applications will be available for a few hundred dollars instead of the thousands formerly required for any standard minicomputer. (As the nonvolatile magnetic-bubble technology gets established to partially replace floppy-disk software, the cost of more reliable all-electronic software will soon take a further downturn.)

Ohio Scientific, with its C8P-DF (48-in. high rack) microcomputer system has a fast-access file system with 74-M byte hard-disk drive. A wide range of standard innovative accessories for advanced scientific applications are available on a full-time ownership basis, as an alternative to a "shared" host main-frame minicomputer. Economically feasible, possible areas of research with this computer include voice processing, image recognition, language processing, and artificial intelligence. According to OSI, its *type-470 floppy-disk controller* has a fine reputation for virtually soft-error-free high reliability. It supports one or two single or dual-headed industry-standard 8-in. floppies with a soft-sectored single-density recording format. Storage ranges of the order of 250-K bytes/surface yields up to 1.15-M bytes on-line with a dual-headed dual-drive configuration. On the other hand, the 14-in. (Winchester) sealed nonremovable OSI CD-74 hard-disk backup system presents a fast-access 74-M byte mass memory. It utilizes the IBM-3340 2940-rpm disk-drive technology, consisting of four 14-in. hard-surface disk platters, operated on by 13 flying heads, that can automatically reposition in 5 ms. The heads deliberately come in contact with the disk in "power-down" and "off" conditions for improved reliability against head misalignment and contamination.

Printer options include: (1) CA-9 Centronics-779, 110-cps Matrix printer for 132 characters on 8.25-in. paper, (2) AC-5 Okidata Model-22, 125-line/min. upper-and lower-case, 14-in.-width, tractor-feed silent printer, and (3) AC-7 Hazeltine-1500 printer with 7-by-9 font upper- and lower-case characters.

For small business applications, the following software support is offered for the C8P-DF computer system:

1. A complete *word-processing system* suitable for both text and letter generation uses a word-processing printer or matrix printer. The features include disk-based text files and editing capabilities in line or cursor oriented modes, line justification, automatic paging, global change and edit commands, and the ability to rearrange blocks of text. (See Section 12-24.)
2. A complete *turnkey small business system* includes a full general ledger, accounts receivable, accounts payable, inventory, invoicing, and payroll.
3. *A data-base management system* for larger business applications and custom applications include general-purpose inquiry, transaction processing, report generation, and specific business programs such as mailing lists, inventory, order entry, and ledger programs for use with the data base.

The OSI operating system based on C8P-DF computer is termed OS-65U, Level 1. If the system is a Zilog Z-80–based floppy disk, it is termed OS-GP/M with disk-extended

BASIC, ANSI standard FORTRAN, and COBOL. In addition, this package, contains an Intel 8080 mnemonic-compatible assembler and text-editor and an on-line debugging system. This single software package is consistent with software used on S-100–based microcomputers. However, OSI software based on 6502 microprocessor (namely, OS-65D, Version 3.0) gives the highest performance due to its "pipelined" architecture—the microprocessor starts to execute the next instruction while completing the instruction it is on. OS-65U (Levels 1, 2, 3) for multiple-user extensions uses Extended-BASIC, oriented toward end-user applications. It incorporates a high-performance *virtual* data-file memory technique in which BASIC programs can address any locations within an open data file without any limitation of block/sector/track structures. With hard disk, the BASIC can access any character in a 74-M byte business data file. This system can support up to 18 of RS-232 interface boards, or 16-terminal distributed processing systems.

OS-65U, Level 3, supports up to 16 independent tables in a multiprocessing, multitasking environment under the supervision of a real-time clock, with a memory capacity of 768-K bytes. OS-DMS is a complete data-base management system operating under OS-65U. Both floppy and hard disk drives are acceptable in this program development operating system, using plug-in "bootstrap" PROM memory and hard disk controller. The OS-DMS data-base management system, meant for *collection of data*, provides a fast and easy method of adding, modifying, deleting, and retrieving information. OS-DMS nucleus and supporting business software packages cost $300 each. When the user needs information, or a decision based on information in the file, a report of a specific format is generated on the CRT terminal or a printer.

12-9. PERSONAL COMPUTING SOFTWARE (*Courtesy of Ohio Scientific*)

12-9.1. Educational Programs

1. *Add Game* combines an additional exercise with a simple game that can be played at two levels of difficulty. The player and the computer take turns selecting numbers from one through nine and adding them up. The first one to reach 50 wins. Addition mistakes may be corrected during the game.

2. *Alphabet Tutor* is a lively and colorful interactive tutor for preschoolers. Each letter is shown in upper and lower case along with some descriptive picture, such as a whale for W. After seeing the entire alphabet, the young users will try to reproduce the alphabet on their own. (Transferred to diskette from 8-in. floppy disk.)

3. *Bar Graph* is a stand-alone program that generates bar graphs on the screen. This program will be particularly useful if used as a subroutine to some other program. It allows you to plot up to 30 distinct points on the screen with reference lines as desired.

4. *Base Ten Converter* allows the user to convert any base ten integer (−99999 to 99999) to its equivalent in base N where N ranges from 2 to 36. Base 2, 8, and 16 are useful for binary, octal, and hexadecimal codes.

5. *Basic Math* is an excellent math-tutoring exercise, which randomly generates addition, subtraction, multiplication, and division problems for the user. It is an excellent example of how the computer system can be used in repetitive routine exercises.

6. *BASIC Tutor Series* cassette contains six separate programs covering the elementary statements and operating in the BASIC computer language. This instruction tape is aimed at the beginning programmer and is only intended to be an introduction to BASIC.

7. *Clock Tutor* can help teach children how to tell time. The face of a clock fills the screen and can illustrate or quiz the user, and correct improper responses.

8. *Continents Quiz* gives the student (elementary level) a list of continents with each question. The answers are corrected during the quiz.

9. *Counter* is a combination educational game and cartoon for youngsters. It is designed to be a youngster's first encounter with the computer. It presents a concept of the numbers 1 through 10 in conjunction with interaction with the computer. It can be successfully used with children from preschool to about first grade. It is also an example of how a computer's cartoon capability can be used effectively.

10. *Definite Integral* calculates definite integrals for a single integral of one variable. It uses an iterative process (Simpson's method) in which the user can specify the number of iterations.

11. *Electronics Equations* contain 10 commonly used equations from electronics: magnetic field at a solenoid, power dissipation (current and voltage), Ohm's law, series and parallel resistance, series and parallel inductance, series and parallel capacitance. The program solves for the variable indicated by the user—very handy.

12. *French Drill and Tutor.* Elementary vocabulary and verb training via computer is easy with these programs (both of these programs are on one tape).

Function Grapher. This handy BASIC program sketches rough pictures of function but does not use high-resolution graphics; thus, it runs on C2-4P's as well as C8P's. (Transferred to diskette from 8-in. floppy disk.)

13. *Genetics Tutors 1–7.* These seven programs form an introduction to the terminology and ideas of modern genetics.

14. *Geography Quiz* is an elementary-level multiple-choice geography quiz.

15. *German Drill and Tutor.* Introductory German vocabulary and verb training can be studied on your personal computer with these programs. (Both of these programs are on one tape.)

16. *Hangman* is a popular educational game in which a person attempts to guess the spelling of a word from clues. As the user makes false guesses, the man in the gallows is constructed. The object of the game is to guess the word before the man is hanged.

17. *Homonyms* is an example of an academic test in which a student attempts to select homonyms. This is one type of testing that is possible on a computer. The data for the program can be easily changed for other specific applications. In this method of testing, the computer runs all the test questions through and, at the end, gives a summary of the right and wrong answers.

18. *Least Squares.* The user inputs the data points in (x, y) format, and Least Squares finds the equation of the straight line of "best fit" via Least Squares approximation.

19. *Log Tutors 1–3* introduce the fundamental concepts and rules for the use and understanding of logarithms. (The programs are on one tape.)

20. *Math Blitz.* Fifty problems (+, −, ×, ÷) are flashed on the screen in random positions. There is a time limit for solving them. This is a good exercise to increase a student's skill and accuracy.

21. *Math Intro* gives addition and subtraction problems in the classic form; for example,

$$\begin{array}{r} 18 \\ \underline{+23} \\ ? \end{array}$$

The user can predetermine the upper and lower limits of the numbers involved; thus, the program can be adapted to young and adult students at different levels.

22. *Math Library.* Evaluate and solve problems with factorials, prime factors, least common multiple, quadratic roots, Pythagorean theorem, distance slope midpoint, and regular and inverse trig functions.

23. *Mathink* is an intellectual mathematical game in which the user attempts to guess an equation in which three numbers will be used to obtain the desired answer. It is an interesting game that cultivates mathematical thinking.

24. *Matrix Tutors 1–3.* Elementary matrix properties are explained in the three tutors in this package.

25. *Metric Converter.* Now it is easy to convert many standard measurements to their equivalent metric values.

26. *Metric Tutor and Quiz.* Study the basics of the metric system and take the quiz to test your understanding.

27. *Nuclear Chemistry Tutors 1-4 and Quiz.* Introductory nuclear physics overview including a quiz to check your grasp of the fundamental principles.

28. *Organic Chemistry Tutors 1-4.* Four programs introduce the fundamental concepts of organic chemistry.

29. *Physics Equations.* Solve equations for uniform acceleration, force, general gas law, electrostatics, light reflection and relativity.

30. *Powers* is a program which will calculate the power of a specified number up to 60 digits in length. If the user enters one, it generates factorials instead. It is an interesting program for showing the trends in large numbers. It is also interesting because it demonstrates multiple precision operation on BASIC up to 60 digit numbers. NOTE: C1P Version - Generates powers up to 22 digits in length.

31. *Presidents* is a questions and answer quiz on the Presidents of the United States. This sample educational program contains a large data base of information on the presidents. However, it doesn't really check the answers, it simply gives you the right answer after your answer is entered. It is a good example of a particular class of exercise or drill that can be performed on a computer.

32. *Roman Numeral Tutor* introduces and explains the Roman numeral counting system.

33. *Solar System Quiz* is aimed at elementary school students. The student is given a list that may be consulted at any time during the quiz. Fifteen basic questions are presented. At the end of the quiz, the student gets a grade and can compare his or her answers to the computer's.

34. *Spanish Drill and Tutor.* Introductory-level Spanish vocabulary and verbs are available with these programs. (Both programs are on one tape.)

35. *Spelling Quiz.* The student is given the phonetic representation of 27 commonly misspelled words and the opportunity to spell the words correctly. At the end of the quiz, the computer gives the student's answer, the correct answer, and a grade.

36. *Trend Line* calculates the slope of the straight line that is the "best fit" to a set of user specified points. This is accomplished by a least-squares analysis. The program will then provide a graph of the points and calculate x or y values that fall on the line of best fit. Trend Line is an excellent demonstration of mathematical analysis by computer.

37. *Trig Tutor I* is an interactive educational program that provides tutoring and testing in conjunction with interesting graphics. An introduction to trigonometry, it includes sine, cosine, and tangent. The program provides an excellent example of a personal computer's capability to convey topics in an interesting fashion when its graphics and conditional response capability are used according to this procedure.

38. *Trig Tutor II.* Similar to Trig Tutor I, it covers the secant, cosecant, and cotangent functions.

39. *Word Search.* This disk-based program randomly selects and places words (from a 300-word data file) on a rectangular block of letters. It is up to the user to find these words. If users give up on any word, they just ask the computer. The word-search puzzles can be output to a printer for hard copies (Transferred to 5.25-in. mini-floppy diskette of your computer from 8-in. floppy disk.)

12-9.2. Business Programs

1. *Address Book* gives the user a versatile method to store and retrieve names, addresses, phone numbers, and related comments. The stored information may be accessed in a variety of methods, i.e., by name, address, or phone number.

2. *Advertisement.* Designed to be used as a display program, the user inputs up to ten lines of advertisement and selects one of three cartoon-type animations. Advertisement will continuously run the selected ad with the eye-catching cartoon. Great for store windows and counter displays.

3. *Bond Evaluation* is intended to be an aid in determining the initial price of a bond in order to achieve a specified rate of return.

4. *Break-Even Analysis* performs the analysis based on either dollar sales or units sold, making the assumption that income and total cost increase linearly. The break-even point is reached when total costs equal total income. After this point, a profit is made.

5. *Histogram.* A disk-based system for entering, storing, and editing annual histogram data. One can simultaneously display any two years for comparison analysis.

6. *Inventory Demo* demonstrates some of the basic principles of computer-based inventories for small businesses. It maintains a file of inventory items as an integral part of the program including part number, description, quantity on hand, wholesale price, retail price, and vendor. It allows the user to quickly access this information. This program is just a demo. It is impractical for any real inventory situation because of its limited memory capacity and lack of random access storage; i.e., one needs a floppy disk drive to perform inventory on a computer.

7. *Mailing List* for storing and printing mailing lists.

8. *Percentile.* Input a set of data and find percentile from rank or vice versa.

9. *Programmable Calculator* is designed to allow programmable calculator users to program the computer without any knowledge of BASIC. Five modes are available: immediate, program, clear, edit, and run. In immediate mode, just key-in the steps as you would with any calculator. In program mode, the operations you key-in are stored in memory. Clear allows you to input a new program. Edit allows corrections and modifications of existing programs. When running the "program," you have a trace option allowing you to follow calculations step-by-step.

Graphics are available through GET and PUT commands. Also, diagnostics are built into Programmable Calculator. There are two types of logical branching: absolute and relative.

There is a 100-step program limit with up to 20 memories. Subroutines may be nested up to 10 deep. A user's manual is provided.

10. *Ratio Analysis I* is an aid to planning and evaluating a company's financial future by considering two classes of ratios: liquidity ratios and leverage ratios.

11. *Ratio Analysis II* calculates activity ratio and profitability ratio. More specifically, inventory turnover, collection period, asset ratio, pure profit, return on assets, and return on net worth are evaluated. This program works well with Trend Line for long-term planning.

12. *Salary Demo* calculates a single biweekly paycheck for a salaried or hourly employee taking into account local, state, and federal taxes. As with Inventory Demo, this program is designed to illustrate a specific computer application.

13. *Statistics I.* The user simply inputs a set of values, and Statistics I outputs the arithmetic mean, geometric mean, median, mode, and standard deviation.

14. *Straight & Constant Depreciation* calculates the depreciation for equipment via the straight and constant depreciation methods.

15. *Time Calculator* is a time card cruncher, with provisions for lunch and overtime.

16. *Word Processor (BASIC)* will edit up to 32 lines of text. Your options include:

insert or delete lines or characters, global replacement of strings, find strings anywhere in the text, remove blank lines, and print out edited material as data (with numbered lines) or text. This program comes with a user's manual. *Note:* Word Processor must be used on computers with a minimum of 12-K bytes of RAM.

12-9.3. Personal Programs

1. *Annuity I* is a program that calculates return on investments, either working from a desired resultant sum or initial sum, taking into account the amount of time money is invested, the interest rate, and the method of interest compounding.
2. *Annuity II* calculates a resultant sum of money accumulated based on the payment in regular intervals of a fixed sum of money. The program takes into account an interest rate, period of time, payment period, and method of compounding interest.
3. *Biorhythm* graphs personal biorhythms (physical, emotional, and intellectual) for any specified 30-day period.
4. *Calorie Counter* considers the user's height, weight, sex, and age, and then estimates the user's metabolism. Next, by considering the user's activity levels, the computer predicts his or her average caloric requirement.
5. *Checking Account* will balance a checkbook when given the initial amount, deposits, and check amounts. There is a limit of 20 checks per run.
6. *Digital Clock.* Using the real time clock capability of the C1P-MF, this program displays a digital clock on the video display.
7. *Kitchen Aid.* Give the computer any recipe, and it will give the proper amount of each ingredient needed to serve the number of people that the user specifies.
8. *Loan Finance* allows the user to specify several variables in conjunction with a possible loan. The program then creates a loan schedule from this input. Loan Finance will either determine the monthly payment or the number of years to pay off the loan from the input information such as amount of loan, interest rate, and payback period.
9. *Personal Calendar* provides the user with a very flexible, easily expanded personal calendar. The program includes instructions for storing appointment information on the tape. Appointments may be added, deleted, reviewed, or stored on the tape at any time.
10. *Savings Account* calculates the balance on a savings account when given the initial amount, interest rate, compounding frequency, deposits, withdrawals, and dates.
11. *Stockmarket (Simulation).* This entertaining simulation of the stock market allows the user to buy and sell stocks in several companies. Very educational but financially safe!
12. *Uneven Cash Flows* program gives the user effective interest rate from uneven cash flows. It is specifically designed to yield the interest rate of a loan on which there are uneven payments, but can also be applied to any uneven cash flow situation to generate the effective annual rate of return. The user specifies a number of uneven periods, the payment for each period, and the number of months in each period.

12-9.4. Utility Programs

1. *Special Utility Cassettes*
2. *Assembler/Editor* with Manual
3. *Extended Monitor* with Manual

12-9.5. Games

1. *Battleship.* The user is pitted against the computer in this nautical warfare game. Five ships are hidden on separate 10 X 10 grids; the player tries to sink the enemy's ships.
2. *Black Jack.* The old gamblers' favorite—for one to five players. Players have the

option of getting an extra card, doubling bets, or holding. The dealer keeps track of winnings and losings. *Note:* In C1P version, one player plays against the computer.

3. *Blockade.* Two players try to avoid running into each other before reaching the opposite side. They can play from the keyboard or use the joysticks of the microcomputer system.

4. *Bomber.* The player is the pilot of a bomber. The object of the game is to get as many points as possible by shooting down planes and bombing ground targets before an enemy plane gets the bomber! Higher speeds can be selected for oncoming aircraft.

5. *Breakout* is a pong-type game in which the user can serve a ball and then steer a paddle to direct the ball to knock down targets. It is a challenging video game that requires manual dexterity.

6. *Civil War.* The user is the general of the Confederate forces in this simulation game. The outcome of the war can be changed if the user makes the right decisions.

7. *Concentration.* The popular television game can be played on the personal computer.

8. *Cryptography* is a two-player game. One player inputs a message of up to 20 letters and a clue. The opponent tries to decipher the computer's coded version of the message.

9. *Destroyer.* The user, in command of a destroyer patrolling enemy waters, tries to sink the enemy submarines by controlling the level at which depth charges explode.

10. *Dodge' Em.* The player must try to maneuver to the right side of the screen through an increasing number of moving barriers. The farther the player gets, the faster the barriers go!

11. *Etch-A-Sketch* is a computer version of a toy with the same name. The user either controls the display or lets the computer create random patterns. Control options are: regular or reversed screen and create or erase lines.

12. *Flip-Flop.* Try to change the row of 10 crosses to zeros by flipping the crosses. The problem is one never knows which pieces will flip.

13. *Frustration* is basically the playing board for a popular puzzle in which the player removes one item from a triangular grid and then jumps over items to remove them from the board. The object of the game is to leave only one. This particular game requires no inherent intelligence on the part of the computer–that is, it is not an interactive game. However, it is a clever implementation of this puzzle.

14. *Hearts.* The computer will shuffle, deal three hands, and play two of the hands against the user. Standard rules for hearts are followed, and scoring is automatic.

15. *Hectic* is an intriguing and challenging video game that is ideally suited for microcomputers. The player has a turret from which he or she attempts to shoot down bombs that can ultimately penetrate the player's shield. It has an outer-space setting.

16. *Hide & Seek.* The computer randomly places 1 to 10 objects in an opaque box. Try to find them by shining rays of light into the box and observing where they exit.

17. *High Noon.* The cowboy and the Indian square off again–the player must hide behind the cactus at the right time.

18. *Hockey* is a keyboard game for two players. They select the score to which they want to play.

19. *Illusion* is tic-tac-toe–type board game for one person. The object is to end up with one zero in the center and crosses in the other boxes.

20. *Kaleidoscope* is a geometric pattern generator that continuously creates geometric images. This program, which is useful for display, is an example of some of the things one can do on a graphics system. There is no user intervention once it is started.

21. *Lunar Lander* is a classical computer game in which a person attempts to land successfully on the moon by varying the amount of fuel burned per unit time. It is an interesting mathematical game. This version of Lander has no graphics. It can be used on virtually any OSI computer.

22. *Mastermind* is a one-player game. The player selects the number of positions or chances allowed.

23. *Matches* is an old strategy game. The player goes first and removes one to three matches; then the computer gets a turn. Whoever picks up the last match loses.

24. *New York Taxi* is a game in which the player is a pedestrian attempting to get a taxi in a hurry in New York City without being run over.

25. *Othello* can be played by two players or by one player against the computer. It can be played in color or on a black-and-white system. The score is available at any time.

26. *Poker.* The OSI dealer plays a good hand of Poker. The player can draw up to three cards and bet against the computer.

27. *Racer.* The player steers a car in and out of many other cars while shifting through five gears. It's a race to see who can go the farthest in a set amount of time.

28. *Slot Machine.* "Pull the lever" and see what turns up! If you can win against this program, you should go to Las Vegas.

29. *Space Attack.* Two players try to destroy as many invading space vehicles as possible.

30. *Space War* is an outstanding two-player arcade-type video game. Two ground weapons fight it out with the Enterprise. The first to break through the other's energy shields is the winner.

31. *Star Trek* is a classical implementation of the most popular computer game in existence including sensors, photon torpedoes, warp drives, phasers, and galactic maps. It is one of the most challenging and interesting character-oriented games available for computers.

32. *Star Wars* is an advanced video game in which a player moves crosshairs around. The object of the game is to get the moving target ship into the crosshairs of a laser. The player can fire at the target ship, and the target ship fires back. This program requires keyboard dexterity.

33. *Tic-Tac-Toe* is a classical implementation of the popular game. The player can go first or second. The computer plays a random or a reasonably tough game, but it can be defeated.

34. *Tiger Tank,* is a highly sophisticated one- or two-player tank game, is similar to arcade tank games. However, it has an option to allow the computer to operate one of the tanks. Tiger Tank requires manual dexterity at the keyboard.

35. *Torpedo* is a typical video arcade game in which the user fires a torpedo at a passing submarine.

36. *Zulu 9.* Real-time animation in a fast-paced space game. The user controls a ship's speed and direction while flying through space.

12-10. UTILITY MINI-FLOPPY DISKETTES (for advanced C4P micro-computer system)

- *Graphics I:* 2 diskette set; provides easy keyboard screen setup and storage, high-resolution (64 X 128) graphing of functions and parametric equations via fast assembler routines (24-K bytes of RAM are required in C4P computer system) . . . $29.
- *DAC-I.* 2 diskette set, State-of-the-art DAC music generator keyboard. Note entry and disk storage for up to 4-part music. (24-K bytes RAM for C4P micro-computer) . . . $39.
- *Utility.* 8-in. floppy disk (presently being transferred to mini-floppy diskette; also 8-in. floppy for C8P-MF microcomputer). Editor for 6502 and 6800 Assembler programs . . . $99.

1. *Graphics I (2-disk set).* Disk I of this set contains a graphics system which allows for

easy keyboard manipulation of graphics color CRT monitor screens, including commands for connecting two screen points with a straight line (optionally specifying character and/or color), print text on the screen anywhere (without using the time-consuming POKE method), change the screen color at any time, store and recall up to 10 full screens with two key strokes.

Disk 2 of the Graphics I package contains two high-resolution (64 X 128) plotting routines. It should be noted that the 64 X 128 resolution becomes possible only with the inverted color capability of OSI's new color video board. These routines plot functions and parametric equations using assembler subroutines for video display generation.

2. *DAC I:* OSI's C4P personal computer is equipped with an 8-bit companding digital-to-analog converter (DAC) as standard equipment. In use, this DAC will approach the tone quality of a 12-bit DAC. Sophisticated assembler level programming is required to use the DAC.

This two-disk set has sample programs which demonstrate DAC output of single notes, four-note chords, single notes from the keyboard, chords from the keyboard, entry editing storage, and retrieval of one-part and four-part music. Five tempos are available (and can be changed at any time). Also, four "voices" for each of the four parts are optional; these parts are square wave, ramp wave, triangle wave, and sine wave.

3. *WP-1B* (available for C8P-MF systems only): Ohio Scientific's WP-1B incorporates complete 6502 and 6800 assemblers in conjunction with a powerful text editor interactively. The tedious job of entering assembler source code is greatly simplified by a comprehensive integral text editor. Creating and editing code is greatly facilitated by this package. Two levels of editing line editing and character editing, are possible.

WP-1B includes a 6500/6800 run package. It allows the user, for example, JSR (jump to subroutine) out of 6500 code, to run a 6800 subroutine, and RTS (return from subroutine) to the 6500 program and vice versa.

The minimum hardware requirements for WP-1B are on OSI C8P-MF micro-computer with a serial port, a serial terminal located on the ACIA at FCØØ, single-or dual-drive floppy disk, and 16K RAM. A terminal with nondestructive backspace capability must be used in order to fully utilize the text editor. The recommended WP-1B system requires a 48K RAM and dual floppy disk controller, a TEC Series 500 terminal, and an Okidata Model 22 line printer. The Hazeltine Model 1500 and Lear-Siegler ADM-3A are also directly supported. Documentation is included to customize WP-1B for use with virtually any conventional terminal or printer.

An elaborate *error-checking routine* is incorporated into WP-1B making it essentially fool-proof. Whenever an error is encountered, the error is indicated by an arrow and explained via a short message.

In 1980, Ohio Scientific Inc. introduced a new model, Challenger 8P-HD. It has integrated Winchester disk-drive with a random access memory of 10.67-M bytes. It has voice recognition capability and provision for home-security facilities.

Application of Microcomputers in Home and Industry. The detailed architecture and organization of a typical personal computer described in this chapter expose the user to the general intricacies of the hardware and software involved in the system. The brief description should give one a background of familiarity and adequacy when a complex device such as a computer is used for his or her particular routine applications(s). As part of this comprehensive introduction to an up-to-date, economy, personal or home computer of the 1980s, some of the popular personal computers are briefly described in the following pages. Since many professional and personal activities will be involved with these microcomputers in the near future, a brief familiarity with the various American-made models is helpful. Millions of economy personal computers will be in use before the end of the decade. Japanese manufacturers will undoubtedly play a major role as far as worldwide distribution is concerned—as it did with calculators and television receivers during the 1970s.

The latest satellite data communications and microcomputers make VLSI in electronics the real revolution of the later twentieth century. The facilities for basic education and good life are gradually being spread throughout the world via advanced audio and visual aids, and other labor-saving gadgetry via automatic mass-production for the first time. No nation need remain isolated from the invigorating capacity of economic modern technology, for every nation could, on a long-term low-interest basis, afford it. With the aid of affluent nations, the underdeveloped countries could organize and take expedited advantage for uplifting the illiterate and superstitious masses by way of universal education on a modern scientific basis. The affluent industrial nations have a stake in preventing a worldwide population explosion; universal education is one of the effective solutions to this problem. In this nuclear age, if maintenance of peace is the expressed policy and primary objective of every nation, the computer and television accentuated media, with their instant access to the living room, must maintain responsible and unfailing restraint by discouraging ideological confrontations around the world—modern research and technology are an idealist's dream of a better life on a global scale come true. Research and technology are the products of the Laws of Nature—and they are scientific truths. Truth is sacred!

12-11. APPLE II (Apple Computer Inc.)

The profile of the popular personal computer and its organization based on microprocessor 6502 is similar to that of Ohio Scientific C1P computer system. The later versions of Apple II with 8-slot motherboard for extensions of memory and I/O facilities etc. follow similar system and operating system concepts. Apple Computer Co. is one of the leading corporations in personal computer business, and it is extending its original BASIC to the high-level language facility of PASCAL as Systems Engineering Enterprises (page 501), Texas Instruments, and other microcomputer manufacturers do at this time. Apple's software-selectable graphics display area is a 40 horizontal by 48 vertical grid; for high-resolution color graphics, the display area is extended to a 280 X 192 grid. In 1980, Apple Computer Inc. introduced a new model Apple-III with integrated floppy-disk drive. It executes a superset of 6502 instructions, and includes relocatable base-page register, relocatable stack memory, and an address range of 128-K bytes.

12-12. PET (Personal Electronic Translator) Computer, 2001—Commodore Corporation

The self-contained cassette-based system unit combines a 9-in. video display, keyboard, cassette recorder, and the microcomputer based on 6502. 14-K bytes of extension ROM provides resident software. The keyboard has a provision of 64 ASCII characters with a separate calculator-style numeric key-pad at the right—like that of the higher-priced IBM portable 5100/5110/5120 computer systems. Software programs are provided for operating system, diagnostic routines, machine language monitor and BASIC. Additional I/O devices can be connected via IEEE-488 Interface. Special keyboard featuring 64 graphics characters on the keyboard itself provides for convenient entry of graphics or video game oriented special characters. (There is a similar facility for the Ohio Scientific personal computer systems, but the graphics characters versus respective keys are presented in the form of a special illustration in the instruction book.)

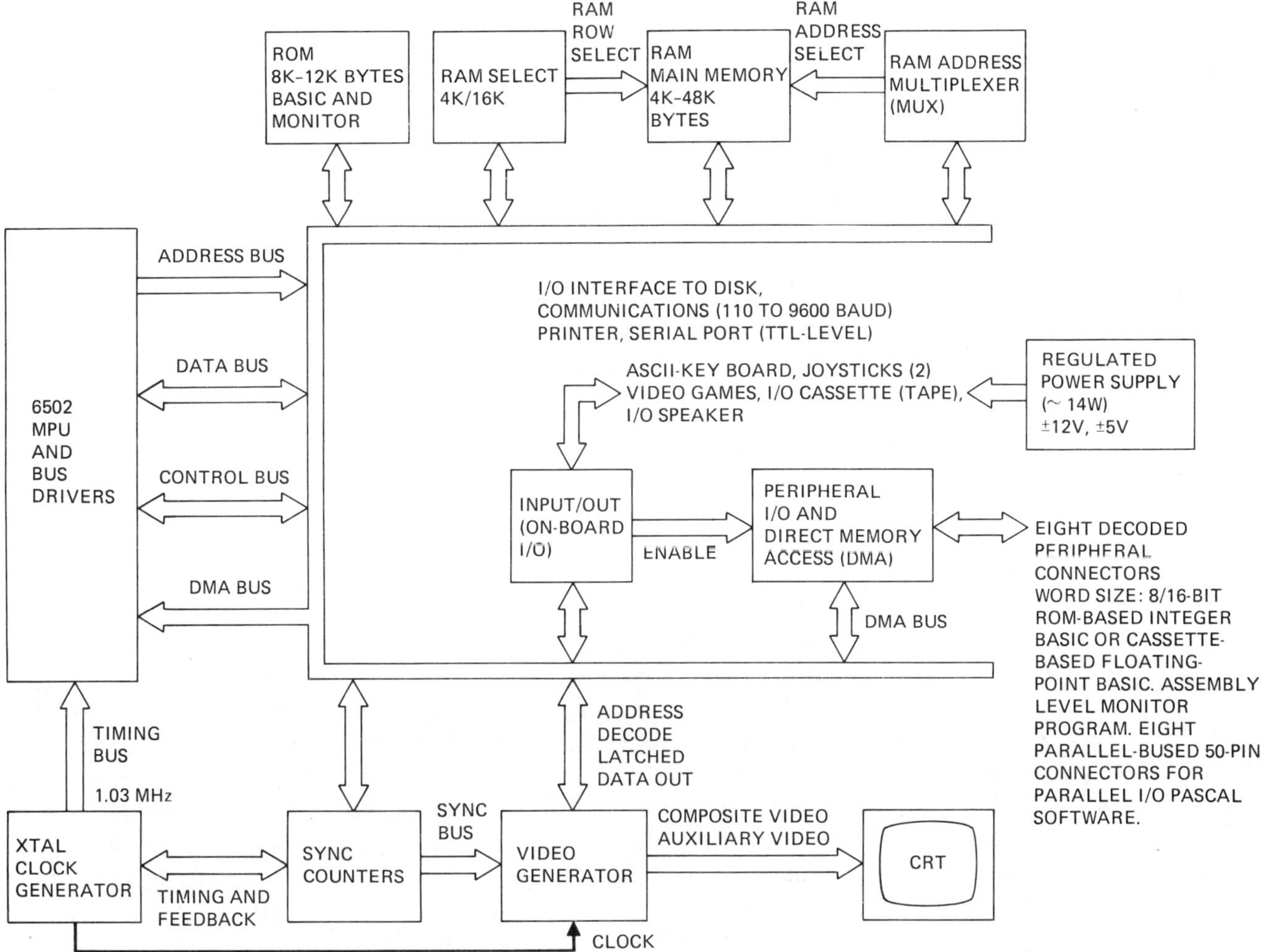

Fig. 12-6. Apple-II keyboard-CRT microcomputer system organization. (*Apple Computer Inc. 10260 Bandly Drive, Cupertino, CA 95014*)

12-13. HEATHKIT H-8 MICROCOMPUTER KIT (Heath Company)

The Microcomputer H-8/9 is based on the Intel 8080A microprocessor, with a cassette tape recorder, video display terminal, and an alphanumeric keyboard, in two small cabinets. The front panel of the H-8 cabinet has a calculator-style numeric key-pad and LED digital display. Since the unit is oriented to Assembly programming using 8080A mnemonic instruction code, the 9-digit display facility provides for display of address and data contents of registers, etc., to indicate the result as the programmer assembles, edits, and debugs a program.

The system monitor program provides for 1-K bytes of ROM. The H-8 cabinet has 10-slots for the extension of RAM main memory, PROM, and other interface option cards. Like the OSI's special 48-line BUS, Heathkit uses a special 50-line BUS, although there is presently a token trend to standardize the BUS to S-100. The cassette tape recorder serves as an off-line storage device for serial I/O interface. The serial I/O port is suitable for either RS-232 interface or current-loop (CL) mode of a serial data communication channel. The same port is internally used for the 12-in. screen, 12-line/80-character, CRT video display terminal, and 67-key alphanumeric keyboard located in the H-9 cabinet. Special function keys facilitate application programs, and such features as erase, page-transmit, and graphics. A BASIC Interpreter-style compiler and cassette-based assembler/editor/debug software facilities are available. The independent H-9 keyboard-display cabinet, as a stand-alone unit, facilitates the availability of an independent lower-cost H-8 kit. The kit-configuration of several optional packages in a system for assembly by the user allows a 5% discount on the list price of the regular Heathkit computer system. An all-in-one H-89-CA CRT keyboard model with 48-K RAM, Serial I/O, and 5.25-in. floppy uses MICROSOFT™ FORTRAN software. It is compatible with the H-8 microcomputer.

12-14. TRS-80 (Tandy Corp./Radio Shack)

TRS-80 BASIC personal computer receives wide publicity due to the large number of Radio Shack sales outlets. CPU/Keyboard TRS-80/I/II/III is a modular Z-80 microprocessor-based system, varying in price from $500 to $5000. Starting with 4-K/16-K byte of RAM, one could complement extensions such as RAM up to 48-K, mini-diskette drives with on-line storage of 307-K bytes and printers. The system includes standard RS-232C Interface (at 300 baud rate), originate/answer acoustic coupler, switches for originate/off/answer and full/half-duplex/test, with a carrier-detect sensitivity of -50 dBm, and a voice synthesizer that responds to 62 phonemes to create any English word ($400). This accessory is meant for computer-aided teaching. An 8-in. 8-character line-printer II ($1000), and wide-carriage 13-in. 132-channel line-printer III ($2000) are available. As in OSI systems, TRS-80/II uses Extended-BASIC for increased computing power at the high-price end, providing formatted printing, program editing, error trapping, named files, multidimension arrays, comprehensive string-variable handling, automatic line numbering, tracing, and keyboard rollover.

OSI's 6502 has a faster instruction at the same clock-speed, while the Z-80 has a more memory-efficient instruction set with a large number of instructions. This results in the feasibility of the same program in less memory. With low-cost static RAM memory at this time, OSI's faster instruction set is an advantage. TRS-80/II has the provision of IEEE-bus Interface, and a fine off-line cassette program library.

Like OSI, Level II BASIC-in-ROM includes 23 specific error codes that can generate an error to test error-trapping routines. Single/double character and integer-precision numeric variables, and string variables, program lines, and logical lines extending to 255 characters long, are allowed, although video screen lines are limited to 64 characters. Access to external devices and ports is provided by commands. The latest TRS-80, Model III, Deluxe 2-M byte business sytems, with 64-K byte RAM, 3 disks, and high-speed printer, cost $8737.

12-15. COMPUCOLOR 8001 (Compucolor, Inc.)

The microcomputer, based on Intel 8080, is located in the 8-color, 19-in. diagonal CRT unit with its display of 80 characters by 48 lines. In the graphics mode, a grid area of 160 horizontals by 192 verticals enables high-resolution color pictures. Color selection for characters and optional blink of selected characters are an attractive feature. Tape drive, which is equivalent to an 8-track, 4800-baud rate, facilitates storage and retrieval of high-speed mass-memory. The basic system costs under $3K with BASIC-in-ROM and a provision for extension of PROM and RAM memories.

12-16. VECTOR-1 COMPUTER (Vector Graphics Inc.)

Based on 8080A, an 8-level vectored interrupt capability and a real-time clock, Vector-1 is an 18-slot S-100 BUS microcomputer system for extensions to original 512-byte PROM memory. A choice of optional software is available with a system monitor facility. The standard 100-pin, S-100, bus allows plug-in of chosen cards from other manufacturers. A cassette tape recorder provides an assembler and program development facility.

12-17. BYTE-80 MICROCOMPUTER (The Byte Shops Inc.)

This 8080A-based microcomputer comes in a cabinet with a 10-slot, S-100 BUS system. The CPU cards include an 8-level priority interrupt system. It is a low-priced beginner's kit with front-panel switches and LED indicators.

For obvious reasons, most specialist vertically-integrated manufacturers do not encourage a *standard S-100 bus* to allow the plug-in of memory or I/O circuits, etc. However, there are at least 50 small companies that allow this facility. As an example, Space Byte, Inc. has an Intel 8085-based S-100 bus system that contains two RS-232 ports, 22 parallel I/O lines, ROM and RAM combinations, a programmable 14-bit timer/counter, and 4 levels of vectored interrupts. It must be noted, however, that some buses are bandwidth-limited to less than 1 MHz, while other buses, such as the Intel SBC-80, can handle data transfer rates up to 5 MHz.

12-18. IMSAI-8080 MICROCOMPUTER (IMSAI Manufacturing Corporation)

This is another popular 8080-based low-priced S-100 BUS microcomputer system in a large cabinet with front-panel switches and LEDs. There is provision for software such as system monitor, Assembler, Loader, Editor, and Debugger.

12-19. KIM-1 MICROCOMPUTER SYSTEM (MOS Technology Inc.)

It is a single-card, calculator-style, keyboard/display unit, based on 6502 microprocessor. It has a built-in provision of 2-K bytes of ROM for a system monitor program, 128 bytes of RAM, 30 I/O lines, and two general-purpose timers. A 23-key keyboard and a 6-digit LED display allow input of numeric data or hex mnemonic commands to the system monitor. The Motorola MEK6800D2 dual-card microcomputer Evaluation Kit II described in detail (on p. 000) features a similar low-priced system set up to enable the training of beginners in Assembly language. Both these systems allow interface of a cassette tape recorder, so that the beginner can record and play back an assembled program or a debugging program. The debugging procedure then allows the checkup of whether or not the instructions are correctly interpreted in machine language.

12-20. COSMAC VIP MICROCOMPUTER (RCA Corp.)

Based on CDP-1802 CMOS microprocessor (which supersedes an earlier 2-chip version), the COSMAC VIP microcomputer card includes a small low-priced, 16-key calculator-style keyboard, and a single-chip graphic video display interface. The video interface can present alphanumeric and graphic display on a video monitor (or on a television set with a facility of a small RF-modulator for a selected-channel). A cassette tape recorder facility is also available. With a limited RAM, COSMAC VIP has a versatile operating system program that provides several utility functions and an interpretive language termed "CHIP-8." It includes test programs to ensure proper operation of the system, and a list of 20 video games on cassettes.

RCA markets (1) an under-$50, ASCII-encoded 58-key, typewriter-format, VP-601 keyboard for alphanumeric entry, and (2) a VP-611 with an additional 16-key calculator keypad. They use the latest flexible membrane key switches, plus 2-key rollover circuitry. A finger positioning overlay, combined with light positive activation key-pressure gives a good operator "feel," and an on-board tone generator gives aural key-press feedback. The high noise-immunity of 5-volt CMOS circuitry makes these keyboards well suited for use in noisy environments. The buffered output is TTL-compatible.

12-21. Z-2 COMPUTER SYSTEM (Cromemco Inc.)

Based on the 4-MHz version of Z-80A microprocessor, the microcomputer is supplied in a rack-mountable metal cabinet furnished with an S-100 bus and a 21-slot motherboard. Clock is switch-selectable 2/4-MHz, and the computer uses automatic power-on jump circuitry to go to a specific memory address when switched 'ON.' For the convenience of former low-cost minicomputer users, it uses paper-tape system monitor; a PROM optional system monitor is also available. Cromemco computer software is available on floppy disk. For software on paper tape, one requires a paper-tape reader to directly load the software into the microcomputer. Z-80 instruction set allows software compatibility to 8080 software.

The Cromemco computer system is expandable to high-priced configurations under $3000 with a "TV-dazzler" color graphics facility. A color kaleidoscope diskette program was originated for distribution to other users on S-100 bus system. Several versions of this computer system are available at lower price levels.

12-22. BASIC CONTROLLER BC1-1 (Dynabyte Inc.)

The Dynabyte Controller is a Z-80 based microcomputer system with a dynamic RAM expandable to 16-K bytes, 2-slot 2-K byte EPROM programmer, 4-slot 8-K byte ROM, 32 TTL-I/O lines, a cassette recorder interface, four 0.75A reed relays, four 5A, 115-V general-purpose relays, a composite video output for a 16-line by 64-character video display, and two extra parallel 8-bit I/O ports.

Data/address word-size is 8/16 bits, and addressable memory is 64-K bytes at a clock frequency of 2.5 MHz. Power supplies required are ±5V, +12V, and +28V. The beginner's system is priced just under $1000. Eight user-definable LED indicators, and 8 LEDs for port data display are included on the board. Of the Z-80's 158 instruction-set, 78 instructions are code-compatible with those of 8080A. The Z-80 commands include 8-bit load directives (21 commands), 16-bit load instructions (20), 14 exchange, block-transfer and search operations, 40 arithmetic and logic operations, 16 shift and rotate instructions, 21 bit and I/O operations, and 11 jump instructions.

Z1BL, the original industrial version of BASIC used by Dynabyte, may be considered as the forerunner of the use of BASIC-in-ROM in most of the present 6502-based microcomputer systems. For the first time, this high-level BASIC approach discouraged the use of time-consuming, expensive and large mnemonic Assembler language programs for the usual *low-cost* microcomputer systems.

12-23. ATARI-800 (Pertec Computer Corporation)

ATARI-800 can normally use high-capacity tape cartridges (217-K bytes) for optional Assembler language. With 8-K bytes of BASIC-in-ROM, cassette programs, 16-color graphics at 8 luminance levels, 8 graphics modes, and 48-K bytes of RAM, a 57-character ASCII keyboard controls the color-CRT microcomputer system. The BASIC versatile system costs just under $1000. Readily available cassette, cartridge, and four individually accessive floppy-disk programs facilitate color graphics, entertainment, home management, and small-business applications. Peripherals such as printers and type-410 audio/digital recorder for talk-and-teach educational system cassettes are an interesting asset of the system. An internal speaker and four separate sound channels are provided for this application. It is a fully programmable computer.

12-24. HP-85 PERSONAL/PROFESSIONAL COMPUTER (Hewlett-Packard Company)

Weighing approximately 20 lb, the self-contained Hewlett-Packard HP-85 provides professional computing power with 16-K bytes of RAM and interactive graphics under keyboard control. Standard typewriter keyboard has a separate numeric keypad and 8 user-definable special function keys. The high-resolution 32 character/16-line CRT display with a 256 X 192-dot plotting area has a powerful editing capability, and a built-in thermal printer can produce a hard copy of the display on command. The microcomputer system has a built-in tape cartridge drive with 217-K bytes of storage capacity. Search speed is 60-in./sec and read/write speed is 10-in/sec. As in most personal computing systems, operating system and BASIC-in-ROM are the major characteristic features. A total of 16 graphic commands have been added to the HP-85's Extended BASIC to enhance its graphics capability for plotting graphs, label axes, and set scales for independent x-and y-axes. For engineering, industrial, and scientific applications, the capacity of RAM can be extended to 32-K bytes while extending ROM-firmware to 80-K bytes. Peripherals such as high-speed full-width line printer, full-size X-Y plotter, or floppy disk drives are acceptable.

Advanced software capabilities include software security, flexible string commands, internal clock for real-time operating system, programmable beeps, and more than 150 commands and statements. Data communications protocols are being added. For a price of $3250, Hewlett-Packard assures warranty, software support, documentation, and service.

The HP-85 personal computer is advanced to a more versatile status by the addition of an HP-IB interface module for implementation of IEEE-488-1978 standard; three I/O ROMs are also included. These accessories can be plugged into the ports of HP-85. The interface allows the computer to intercommunicate with 14 peripherals such as instruments, plotters, and printers. The I/O ROM provides the necessary BASIC commands for configuration of graphics, control, pass data, and check status of devices. The other two ROMs are meant for HP-7225A plotter and HP-2631A printer and one- and two-dimensional matrix array manipulation. Twelve software application packages are available for science, engineering, and finance. These are in addition to the software for text editing, games, BASIC training, and linear programming. The HP-2631A printer is a bidirectional impact version that permits 180 characters/sec on inexpensive computer paper or custom multipart forms.

Interface modules are also available for bit-serial RS-232, general-purpose 16-bit parallel and Binary Coded Decimal formats. The HP-IB interface can operate into an Extender 37203A to operate over a coaxial cable or a fiber optic link 1000 meters long; a second Extender is required at the remote end. The Extenders serialize the data at the transmitting end and convert the serial data to a parallel format at the receiving end.

The following extended (Dartmouth) BASIC program is a typical sample of the printout of the HP-85 for the radio amateur AMSAT OSCAR satellite tracking procedure; the resultant graphics plot accompanies the program.

HP SYSTEM-45 is the top-of-the-line, powerful, single-chassis desktop computer for the scientist or the engineer who has to solve complex, real-time computational, design,

```
  10 REM   RANGE CIRCLES
  20 REM  AND ISO-ELEVATION CURVE
     S
  30 REM  FIRST INITIALIZE
  40 DEG
  50 PEN 1
  60 GCLEAR
  70 SCALE -150,0,0,90
  80 Z=0
  85 X=0
  90 XAXIS 0,10,-150,0
 100 XAXIS 90,10,-150,0
 110 YAXIS -150,10,0,90
 120 YAXIS 0,10,0,90
 400 REM ** ENTER VARIABLES**
 410 DISP "WHAT IS QTH LAT"
 411 INPUT D
 420 DISP " WHAT IS QTH LONG"
 421 INPUT G
 422 DISP "WHAT SAT. (7/8)"
 423 INPUT Q
 424 IF Q=7 THEN H1=740
 425 IF Q=8 THEN H1=565
 426 IF Q<>7 AND Q<>8 THEN DISP "
     SORRY.. DON'T KNOW THAT ONE"
      @ WAIT 800 @ BEEP 500,100 @
      GOTO 422
 427 H=3963/(3963+H1)
 430 FOR B=0 TO 61 STEP 10
 440 FOR E=0 TO 360 STEP 10
 500 REM ** CALC ARC DISTANCE**
 510 REM
 520 REM   A=ARC DISTANCE
 530 REM   B=ELEVATION ANGLE
 540 REM
 550 A=90-B-ASN(H*COS(B))
 600 REM ** CALC SSP LATITUDE**
 610 REM
 620 REM   C=SSP LAT
 630 REM   D=GND STAT LAT
 640 REM   E=AZ ANGLE TO SAT.
 650 REM
 660 C=ASN(COS(A)*SIN(D)+SIN(A)*C
     OS(D)*COS(E))
 670 REM
 672 REM   MOVE PEN TO START PNT
 674 REM   IFF FIRST GO
 676 IF Z=0 THEN MOVE -G,C ELSE 7
     00
 678 Z=1
 700 REM ** CALC SSP LONGITUDE**
 710 REM
 720 REM   F=SSP LONGITUDE
 730 REM   G=GND STAT LONG.
 740 REM
 750 T=COS(A)-SIN(D)*SIN(C)
 760 U=COS(D)*COS(C)
 761 V=T/U
 762 IF V>1 THEN V=1
 790 IF E>=180 THEN GOTO 900
 800 F=G-ACS(V)
 810 GOTO 1000
 900 F=G+ACS(V)
1000 REM ** PLOT RESULTS**
1010 REM   "E=";IP(B);"A=";E;TAB(
     15);"σ=";FNR(C);TAB(23);"∩=
     ";FNR(F)
1015 DRAW -F,C
1020 NEXT E
1030 NEXT B
1040 DEF FNR(D1) = INT(D1*10+.5)
     /10
2000 REM    DRAW AZ LINES
2010 REM
2020 FOR E=0 TO 360 STEP 10
2030 FOR B=70.01 TO 0 STEP -10
2500 REM ** CALC ARC DISTANCE**
2510 REM
2520 REM  A=ARC DISTANCE
2530 REM  B=ELEVATION ANGLE
2540 REM
2550 A=90-B-ASN(H*COS(B))
2560 REM ** CALC SSP LATITUDE**
2570 REM
2580 REM  C=SSP LAT
2590 REM  D=GND STAT LAT
2600 REM  E=AZ ANGLE TO SAT.
2610 REM
2620 C=ASN(COS(A)*SIN(D)+SIN(A)*
     COS(D)*COS(E))
2630 REM
2680 REM ** CALC SSP LONGITUDE**
2690 REM
2700 REM  F=SSP LONGITUDE
2710 REM  G=GND STAT LONG.
2720 REM
2730 T=COS(A)-SIN(D)*SIN(C)
2740 U=COS(D)*COS(C)
2750 V=T/U
2760 IF V>1 THEN V=1
2770 IF E>=180 THEN GOTO 2900
2800 F=G-ACS(V)
2810 GOTO 3000
2900 F=G+ACS(V)
3000 REM ** PLOT RESULTS**
3005 IF X=1 THEN GOTO 3020
3010 MOVE -G,D
3011 X=1
3020 DRAW -F,C
3030 NEXT B
3031 X=0
3040 NEXT E
3050 CHAIN "USA-3"
3060 END
```

(Courtesy of Vern Reportella of AMSAT)

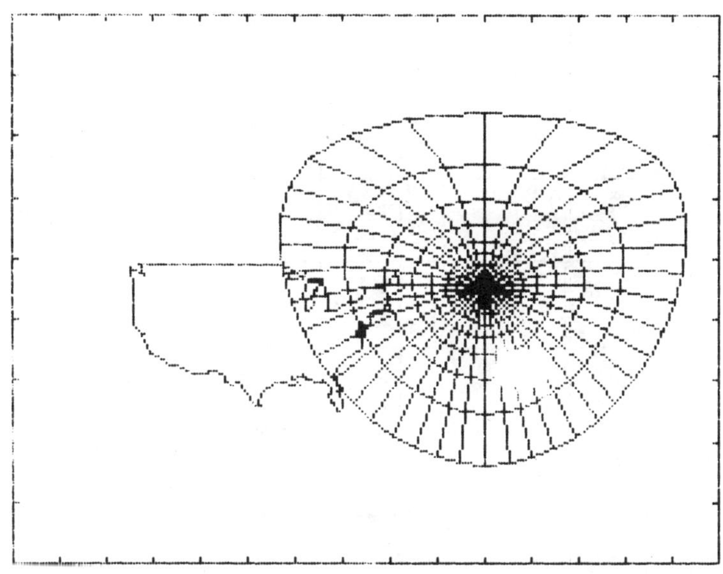

(Courtesy of Vern Reportella of AMSAT)

data-acquisition, and control problems. System-45B provides from 56-K bytes to 449-K bytes of user memory, monochrome graphics CRT display, high-performance I/O, typewriter-like keyboard, mass-storage ROMs, thermal printer, and enhanced BASIC, equivalent in versatility to FORTRAN and APL high-level languages. System-45C extends the system to color graphics capable of 4913 shades of different colors; it includes a light pen that enables the user to rapidly pick, move, and draw diagrams of objects directly on screen for reproduction on a hard-copy. HP-45C is capable of handling problems such as Fast Fourier Transforms on 65000 data points, multiple Linear Regressions on 50 variables, organizational PERT/CPM programs of analysis, all without an external mass-memory accessory.

The model consists of dual microprocessors, high-performance I/O for automatic data acquisition, control, and powerful graphics. The system's 120-K byte operating system resides in a built-in ROM package, and it provides the entire read/write memory for scientific programs and associated data. Unlike System-85, System-45 features a 24-line/80 characters per line 13-in. color graphics CRT—which is a high-resolution tri-color shadow-mask tube. The CRT has a high-speed vector generator to reproduce both alphanumerics and fast area-fills for color shading. CRT displays can be captured in hard-copy printout form on a built-in thermal printer with 80 characters/line and a speed of 480 lines/min. Color displays can be transferred to an HP-9872 color plotter or a 217-K byte tape cartridge storage.

Hewlett-Packard's Popular 2647A Intelligent Graphics Terminal Keyboard is shown in Figure 12-7 and described in Table 12-1. This small computer, as a personal computer of medium higher price under $10K, is used in Word-Processing applications.

12-25. TEKTRONIX COMPUTER DISPLAY TERMINAL, 4006-1.

Interactive high-resolution Graphics on a direct view bi-stable Storage CRT, with a TTY (ANSI-character) 63-character set keyboard, is now feasible with a Tektronix LSI Computer Display Terminal starting at a price under $3K. (Model 4027 scrolling Color Graphics Terminal costs up to $9K, and Model-4632 Video Hard Copy Unit for color copies of graphs and alphanumeric data costs $5K along with a 4-channel multiplexer.)

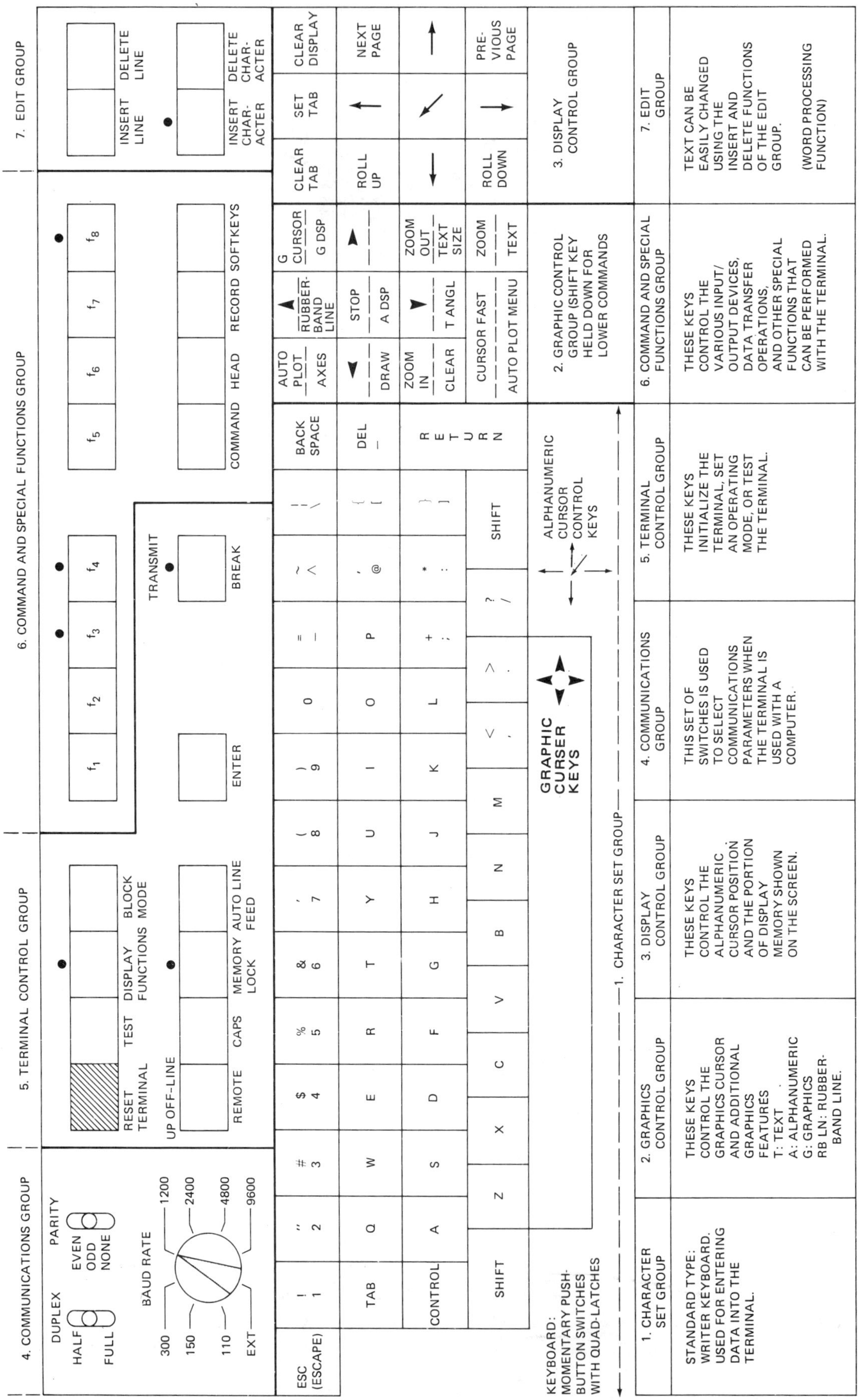

4. COMMUNICATIONS GROUP
DUPLEX: HALF / FULL
PARITY: EVEN / ODD / NONE
BAUD RATE: 300, 150, 110, EXT, 1200, 2400, 4800, 9600

5. TERMINAL CONTROL GROUP
RESET TERMINAL | TEST | DISPLAY FUNCTIONS | BLOCK MODE
UP OFF-LINE
REMOTE | CAPS | MEMORY LOCK | AUTO LINE FEED

6. COMMAND AND SPECIAL FUNCTIONS GROUP
f_1 | f_2 | f_3 | f_4 | f_5 | f_6 | f_7 | f_8
ENTER | TRANSMIT | BREAK
COMMAND | HEAD | RECORD | SOFTKEYS

7. EDIT GROUP
INSERT LINE | DELETE LINE
INSERT CHAR-ACTER | DELETE CHAR-ACTER

ESC (ESCAPE) | ! 1 | " 2 | # 3 | $ 4 | % 5 | & 6 | ' 7 | (8 |) 9 | 0 | = – | ~ ^ | ¦ \ | BACK SPACE | AUTO PLOT / AXES | ▲ RUBBER-BAND LINE | G CURSOR / G DSP | CLEAR TAB | SET TAB | CLEAR DISPLAY
TAB | Q | W | E | R | T | Y | U | I | O | P | ' @ | { [| DEL – | ◄ / DRAW | STOP / A DSP | ► | ROLL UP | ↑ | NEXT PAGE
CONTROL | A | S | D | F | G | H | J | K | L | + ; | * : | }] | RETURN | ZOOM IN / CLEAR | ▼ / T ANGL | ZOOM OUT / TEXT SIZE | ← | ↖ | →
SHIFT | Z | X | C | V | B | N | M | < , | > . | ? / | SHIFT | CURSOR FAST / AUTO PLOT MENU | ZOOM / TEXT | ROLL DOWN | ↓ | PRE-VIOUS PAGE

KEYBOARD: MOMENTARY PUSH-BUTTON SWITCHES WITH QUAD-LATCHES
GRAPHIC CURSER KEYS
ALPHANUMERIC CURSOR CONTROL KEYS
1. CHARACTER SET GROUP
2. GRAPHIC CONTROL GROUP (SHIFT KEY HELD DOWN FOR LOWER COMMANDS)
3. DISPLAY CONTROL GROUP

1. CHARACTER SET GROUP	2. GRAPHICS CONTROL GROUP	3. DISPLAY CONTROL GROUP	4. COMMUNICATIONS GROUP	5. TERMINAL CONTROL GROUP	6. COMMAND AND SPECIAL FUNCTIONS GROUP	7. EDIT GROUP
STANDARD TYPE-WRITER KEYBOARD. USED FOR ENTERING DATA INTO THE TERMINAL.	THESE KEYS CONTROL THE GRAPHICS CURSOR AND ADDITIONAL GRAPHICS FEATURES T: TEXT A: ALPHANUMERIC G: GRAPHICS RB LN: RUBBER-BAND LINE.	THESE KEYS CONTROL THE ALPHANUMERIC CURSOR POSITION AND THE PORTION OF DISPLAY MEMORY SHOWN ON THE SCREEN.	THIS SET OF SWITCHES IS USED TO SELECT COMMUNICATIONS PARAMETERS WHEN THE TERMINAL IS USED WITH A COMPUTER.	THESE KEYS INITIALIZE THE TERMINAL, SET AN OPERATING MODE, OR TEST THE TERMINAL.	THESE KEYS CONTROL THE VARIOUS INPUT/OUTPUT DEVICES, DATA TRANSFER OPERATIONS, AND OTHER SPECIAL FUNCTIONS THAT CAN BE PERFORMED WITH THE TERMINAL.	TEXT CAN BE EASILY CHANGED USING THE INSERT AND DELETE FUNCTIONS OF THE EDIT GROUP. (WORD PROCESSING FUNCTION)

Fig. 12-7. Word-processing keyboard of Hewlett-Packard's 2647A intelligent graphics terminal (*word processing small computer system*). See Table 12-1 for further details.

TABLE 12-1. Hewlett-Packard 2647A Intelligent Graphics: Special Features/Key Operations/Graphics Control.

Special Features	Key Operations	Functions	Graphics Control Group
• BASIC language programmable	Control, tab or backspace	Backtabs to previous tab position	1. *Draw/Move* executed on display
• High-level graphic commands	Control, clear tab	Clears all previously set tabs	2. *Graphics keys* "repeat" if held down for 0.5. sec.
• Shared hard-copy and peripheral devices with other word-processing units	Control, clear display	Clears line from cursor position to end of line	3. *Multiplot:* multiple automatic plotting. Terminated on Stop or character keying
• Simple user interface	Control, next page	Presents special function key assignments on the display	4. *Graphics Cursor:* press 2 keys for diagonal motion
• Independent graphics and alphanumeric memories	Control,	Cursor home down. Places cursor in next available line of display memory	5. *Zoom:* area about cursor magnified as set by zoom-in/out
• Bright display with selective erase	Control,	Sets left margin at current cursor position	6. *Axes:* draws axes, tics, labels
• Vector generation	Control,	Sets right margin at current position	7. *Multiplot menu:* toggles multiplot parameter menu on/off
• Hardware zoom and pan	Control, Ins. character	Character wraparound mode. Characters inserted at cursor position, wraparound to next line after the present line is filled	8. *Rubberband line:* connects current pen position with cursor
• Industry code compatibility	Control display function	Monitor mode: displays all codes on command lines	9. *Clear:* erases graphics image memory
• Multiple automatic plotting	Control, delete character	Delete character having wraparound to next line	10. *Draw:* draws a vector from current pen position to cursor
• Full editing capability and User-definable keys	Control, f_1	Turns on display enhancement	11. *Move:* moves pen to cursor without vector
• Choice of communications capabilities	Control, f_2	Starts an unprotected field	12. *Text:* selects graphics image memory as destination of cell
• Dual mini-cartridege mass storage	Control, f_3	Ends an unprotected field	13. *T sze:* Text Size. Increases character size 8-times. (Character size: 5 X 7 matrix in a 7/10 cell
• Self-test	Control, f_4	Turns on forms mode	14. *T ang:* Sets character orientation, multiples of 90°
• The character set makes 128 (alphabetic, numeric, symbol)	Control, f_5	Turns off forms mode	15. *G DSP:* Toggles display. When off inhibits graphics image without erasing it.
• 4 workspaces, 24 lines, 80 characters	Control, f_6	Starts a transmit only field	
	Control, G Curs	Displays graphics cursor coordinates	
	Control, read	When in block mode, cartridge data	
	Control, soft keys	Executes cursor line in display workspace	
	Control, previous page	Displays next display wordspace	
	Control, command	Enters commands in a display workspace at present cursor position as each function key (f_1–f_8) is pressed	

Model 4006-1 displays a 35-line by 74-character format on a 7.5 X 5.6-in. screen for stock-room/class-room/conference room applications.

A brief specification of the Model 4006-1 follows.

- Character generation: 5 X 7 dot-matrix.
- Cursor: 8 X 8 dot matrix.
- Graphics display mode: Vector only (3.6 ±2 ms).
- Information density 1024 X 1024 addressable points.
- Baud rate: Transmit and Receive, independently selectable; 75 to 4800 baud.
- A standard data communications Interface (EIA, RS-232C).
- Asynchronous full-duplex (Half-duplex option is available).
- Software packages for 10 plots are a regular feature. (More advanced computer Display Terminals 4010, 4012, 4013, 4016 cost up to $20K.)

12-26. TEXAS INSTRUMENTS TMS/9900, TMS/SBP9900

Texas Instruments 16-bit (instruction and data) microcomputer on a board has the exclusive feature of supplying the system either with a NMOS, silicon-gate 9900 microprocessor or an I^2L SBP9900 microprocessor, working at a clock frequency of 3 MHz. Data/address word size is 16/15 bits. 4-K byte RAM and 8-K byte EPROM are mounted on board. Programmable serial and parallel I/O is provided, with all address, data, and control lines on the connector for convenient expansion. The Interface chip handles TTL-compatible, 16 parallel I/O lines, while serial I/O is RS-232C or 20 mA current loop. The instruction set includes 16 arithmetic (multiply and divide), 20 program control, 14 data control, 6 logical, 4 shift, 5-bit I/O, and 6 external, totaling 69 commands. Software support includes a line-by-line assembler, interactive debug monitor, and transportable cross support-software consisting of an assembler and simulator with the utility functions on a ROM. Memory and I/O expansion boards are provided by means of a 4-slot motherboard. Power is required at 5V and ±12V.

A complete prototyping system, AMPL, includes a keyboard video terminal, dual floppy, and a special high-level language and PASCAL. Presently, the latest PASCAL is the chosen in-house high-level language at Texas Instruments. A second serial port is added in the later versions.

The model numbers of the various LSI signal processing and memory chips go under the insignia TM-9901. The software is an emulated version of Texas Instruments 990/ minicomputer family. It requires minimum number of assembler statements and program memory-byte requirements and 2 to 3 times less execution time, as compared to such processors as 8080 and 6800.

Incidentally, Texas Instruments specializes in programmable calculators such as TI-58C and TI-59, with custom plug-in modules containing prewritten programs. Each relatively low-priced module may contain up to 5000 program steps, the equivalent of a multi-card library of magnetic cards. The optional general-purpose software modules are available in a variety of applications in engineering, science, statistics, and business.

12-27. DEC STATION 78 (Digital Equipment Corporation)

In 1978, DEC introduced the high-speed, high-cost, 16-bit microcomputer series DEC-11/03, 11/2, 11/23, consisting of a 3-chip CPU, two NMOS chips for data and control and a third for memory management, MMU. Its original 12-bit PDP-8 minicomputer system was earlier replaced by a CMOS, 12-bit, 6100-based microcomputer operating system in order to utilize the extensive software (about 60,000 programs in all) of the PDP-8. This software is available around the world with a price tag under $8K. The system DEC-station is comprised of a keyboard-CRT microcomputer terminal with a dual floppy disk unit. For a full real-time operating system, the user merely presses the start switch to load the needed program from the floppy disk or ROM memory. The floppy disk has a capacity of 8-bit 256,256 bytes/disk. The alphanumeric display consists of 24 lines of 80 characters each (upper and lower case), and graphics with 32 special graphic characters for graphs, plots, and diagrams. Editing and special function keys are available. The single-card microcomputer system employs 12-bit 16-K words of RAM. ROM memory is available for the system monitor program with features such as automatic self-test software and a bootstrap loader to retrieve the disk operating system from the floppy disk. A parallel I/O 12-bit port and 2-serial RS-232C I/O Interface ports are provided, in addition to the port required for video display. Both RAM and ROM memory are extendable.

The Disk Operating System in BASIC is comprised of the following commands: COMPILE, COPY, DELETE, DIRECT, DATE, EDIT, EXECUTE, HELP, LIST, LOAD, RENAME, RUN, SAVE, TYPE, and SUBMIT. The software includes the operating system, system monitor, command language, BASIC and Fortran compilers, Editor, Assembler, Debugger, Loader, Disk file handler, and time-sharing and data-communications package—all the software formerly available in octal code for the 12-bit PDP-8.

12-28. IBM 5100/5110/5120 PORTABLE COMPUTER

IBM 5100 portable computer system is described on p. 000. In concept, most of the personal computing systems described in this chapter follow the system philosophy of the original IBM-5100, although the present on-line, low-cost, mini-floppy diskette, software mass-memory systems are an improvement over the original IBM off-line tape cartridge software. Of course, IBM does provide on-line disk mass-memory as an optional feature in later costlier versions. IBM-5100/5110/5120/5130 models provide the choice of large-capacity diskette and/or tape cartridge for program and data storage, and RAM to the extent of 64-K bytes. The line printer as an option presents 80/120 characters/sec. BASIC and/or APL-2 interactive languages, designed to speed up program-writing, make the system convenient to use. Software is available to handle business reports related to the generation of journals, trial debit/credit balances, balance sheets for asset/liability/capital status, and income statements. The reports facilitate documentary support designed to ensure accuracy in auditing, and thus they reduce clerical, accounting, and auditing time by eliminating many typing and verification functions. The system is flexible enough to perform other cost-cutting applications such as payroll and accounts receivable. That is, IBM is marketing this high-end ($10- to 20-K) portable computer to the upper-bracket small-business applications, while most of the personal computers (priced under $3K to $4K) take over the hitherto unpromoted low-end, small-business and personal-budget applications. They will gradually complement the present cash-box used in millions of small-business firms.

12-29. OTHER TYPES OF PERSONAL COMPUTERS

As a final reference, the many very low-cost (approximately $100 to $500) **single-card OEM and personal computers** presently available are listed here, along with the types of popular microprocessors they are based on. They usually have a small complement of ROM and RAM memory and marginal I/O capability. They are meant for industrial applications and hobbyists.

8080/8080A/8085:

1. SDK-85 System Design Kit (Intel Corp.)
   SBC-80/05 Single Board Computer (Intel Corp.)
2. MIKE-3 Microcomputer System (Martin Research Inc.)
3. EQUINOX-100 Microcomputer (Parasitic Engineering Inc.)
4. TK-80 Microcomputer (NEC Microcomputers Inc.)
5. 8080A CPU Card (The Byte Shops Inc.)
6. 8080 CPU Card (Electronic Control Technology Inc.)
7. SOL-PC Single Board Terminal Computer (Processor Technology Corporation)
8. ALTAIR 8800 (MITS, Pioneer Micro Instrumentation and Telemetry Systems, Pertec Computer Corporation)
9. CCS-1025-1 General-Purpose Single Board Microcomputer (Control Logic Inc.)
10. ABACUS Micromodules (Information Control Corporation)
11. 8080A CPU Board (Vector Graphics Inc.)
12. IMSAI 8048 Single Board Control Computer (Imsai Manufacturing Corporation)
13. SYNCRON: KB-TV, $3-K Class (Symbiotic Systems Inc.)

Z-80/Z-80A:

1. Z-80-3 Board Microcomputer System (Digital Group Inc.)
2. AZPU Z-80 CPU Card (Affordable Computer Products Inc.)
3. Z-80 Software Development Board, SDB-80 (Mostek Corporation)
4. QUAY-80 AI-Microcomputer (Quay Corporation)
5. ZILOG Z-80 MCB-Microcomputer Board (Zilog Inc.)
6. Microsystem/10 MOD-Z80: KB-CRT: $4-K Class (Futuredata Computer Corporation)

6800:

1. Evaluation Kit II, MEK 6800 D2 (Motorola Inc.)
2. M68C Micro-68 Computer (Electronic Products Associates Inc.)
3. EVK 99 Microprocessor Evaluation Kit (American Microsystems Inc.)
4. WINCE Control Module (Wintek Corporation)
5. 8611 CPU Board (Pro-log Corporation)
6. 6800 SYSI-Microcomputer (Digital Group Inc.)
7. SWTPC 6800/2 Computer System (Southwest Technical Products Corporation)
8. ALTAIR 680b (Mits Inc.–Pertec Computer Corporation)
9. JUPITER-II Microcomputer System: KB-CRT: $4-K Class (Wave Mate Inc.)
10. SYSTEM-310: KB-CRT: $2-K Class (Sphere Corporation)

6502:

1. DATA HANDLER (Western Data Systems Inc.)
2. Model 500-1 Microcomputer (Ohio Scientific Inc.)
3. MCS-6502 (Microcomputer Associates Inc.)
4. ETC-1000 Basic System (Electronic Tool Company)

Popular proprietary personal computers

F8: Fairchild Micropro Microcomputer Card (Fairchild Camera and Instrument Corp.)
2650: Signetics, ABC-1500 Adaptable Board Computer (Signetics Inc.)
SBP0400 (4-bit slice): Microcomputer Learning System (Texas Instruments Inc.)
PPS-4/1: Microcomputer Chip on a Card, XPO-1 System Development Microcomputer (Rockwell International)
SC/MP Evaluation Kit and Keyboard (National Semiconductor)
IM/6100 (12-bit CMOS), Intercept Jr. Tutorial System (Intersil)

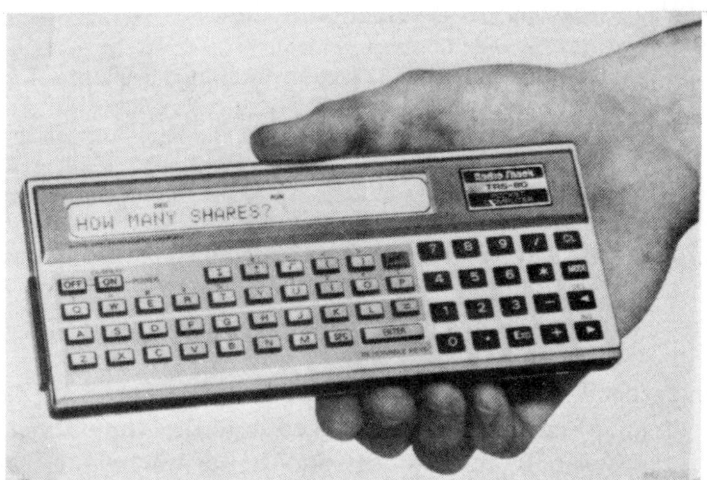

Fig. 12-8a. A typical pocket personal computer (Radio Shack TRS-80 series). It executes instructions in BASIC-on-CMOS-ROM or tape cassette. (*Courtesy of Tandy Corp.*)

GI/CP1600 (General Instrument)
COSMAC (CDP 1802), ELF II (Netronics)
AM2900 (Advanced Microdevices)

Pocket Personal Computers. Figure 12-8a shows a 6502-based Radio Shack TRS-80 series pocket personal computer, using BASIC instructions (price $249). Matsushita Electric Corporation of America (Japan) and Panasonic Electronics Inc. introduced the first hand-held personal computer (HHC). As a stand-alone, the HHC can be used as a language translator, electronic memo pad for 500 characters, and an "electronics secretary" with an alarm and message display, clock, and calendar (price $800).

Computer Chess. Fidelity Electronics Ltd. of Florida introduced microcomputer-based chess and video games such as backgammon, bridge, and checkers. The computer-based chessboard (Chess Challenger "7") facilitates chess players at different levels of capability to learn, improve, and match their skills against the computer's mind (program) (Figure 12-8b). The intelligent machine provides varying levels of responses in every game, and plays against a single player or against itself. A sensory chess challenger that "sees" every move the player makes and a voice chess challenger that speaks to the player are also available.

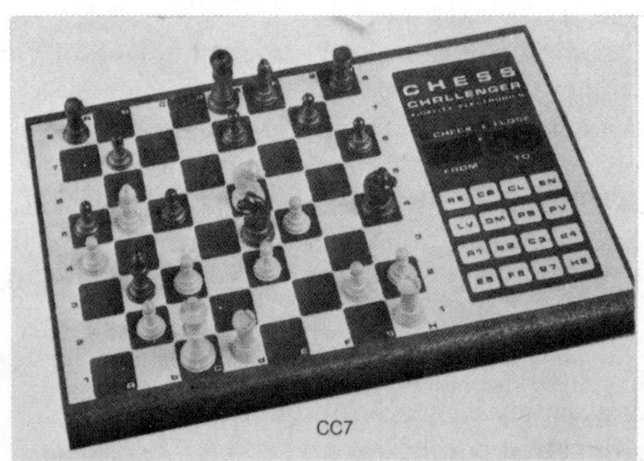

Fig. 12-8b. Chess Challenger "7." (*Courtesy of Fidelity Electronics Ltd., Florida*)

High-Level Language Software for Personal Computers

Microsoft™ Software

XENIX-OS operating system software written in high-level C **programming language** (an alternative to PASCAL of Bell Telephone Laboratories) will provide hardware-independence and portability; switching to a new microprocessor is made simple, since Microsoft XENIX-OS will simultaneously support BASIC, COBOL, and PASCAL.

XENIX-OS is an interactive, multi-user, multi-tasking system with extensive utility packages. The programs will fully utilize the powerful instruction sets and large addressing capability of the new 16-bit microprocessors such as Intel 8086, Zilog 8000, and Motorola 68000. The establishment of a typical 16-bit standard operating system is a timely support with its portability.

For systems and general applications, a **MICROSOFT Z-80 softcard** (Z-80 microprocessor-based BASIC program) can be directly plugged in to the **Apple II** personal computer, which is based on the type 6502 microprocessor. The software was originally writted for a Z-80 based personal computer. The software on the Z-80 softcard allows one to switch between the 6502 of the Apple II computer and a Z-80 personal computer with simple commands. This facility allows one to use software written for one processor for either microprocessor. That is, the softcard provides a facility of limited "portability."

CP/M™ is a versatile, widely used software language for microcomputer operating systems, commonly stored on a diskette in the softcard package, and it readily runs an Apple II keyboard-CRT personal computer, according to the application the software is intended for. With the above Softcard from MICROSOFT one can then run CP/M based business, scientific, and educational programs on Apple II. Actually, the MICROSOFT Z-80 softcard, requiring 48-K btyes on a diskette and its drive is compatible with both Apple II and its 1980 version **Apple III**. Independent peripherals of the Apple personal computer are supported as well. (CP/M is a registered trade mark of Digital Research.) (Courtesy of MICROSOFT Consumer Products, 10800 Northeast Eight, Bellevue, WA 98004.)

Cybernatics, another software firm supplies CP/M operating system with editor, assembler, debugger, utilities at a price of $150 for the Z-80 based popular personal computer of Radio Shack, TRS-80.

DOWNLOAD, TR80 to TR80 of TR5-80 Computers: A data program in CP/M at one location can be communicated to another location by telephone line, provided the other end uses CP/M. An RS-232C interface is required at either end for communication purposes. (Cost: $95.) (Courtesy of Cybernatics, 8041, Newman Avenue, Huntingdon Beach, California.)

BASIC Compiler, Microsoft

MICROSOFT BASIC compiler is an ideal programming tool for developing BASIC applications or microcomputer software. The BASIC compiler is 3 to 10 times faster than MICROSOFT BASIC interpreter. It has the same language features as MICROSOFT 5.0 BASIC and runs on a 32-K byte CP/M system provided by MICROSOFT. For information, "compiled" BASIC programs are considerably faster than "interpreted" BASIC programs, due to extensive optimization procedures during compilation. BASIC language compiler supports all the language features of the MICROSOFT BASIC-80 interpreter, including

- WHILE/WEND conditional for structured programming
- CALL statement for assembly language subroutines
- PRINT USING for formatted output
- Long variable names, up to 40 characters

BASIC compiler supports double-precision transcendental functions SIN, COS, TAN, ATN, LOG, EXP, SQR. The compiler can generate relocatable machine-language module from MICROSOFT BASIC programs. The compiler also includes MICROSOFT macro-assembler and loader. BASIC programs are easily linked to assembly subroutines, and MICROSOFT FORTRAN and COBOL programs. MICROSOFT BASIC compiler costs $395.

A microcomputer programmed at the Northwestern University computer laboratory, in Evanston, Illinois, plays with such skill that it approaches the rank of 80 to 100 compared to the grand masters of *chess in world championships*. The chess experts call the method of programming the "brute force" approach, because the computer apparently does not exhibit the characteristic patience which the grand masters observe during play. With the above program, the computer can consider 3600 logical steps (*hypothetical moves*) in a split second before it makes a move in response to that of the skilled player playing against it. The move is actually implemented by the flicker of an LED (light emitting diode) in the current position of a magnetized chess-piece and the flicker of the LED in the next position it intends to move to after the move of the regular player. In practice, a child can be taught to move the computer's chess-pieces according to the flicker, as the computer and the child play with the champion in championship matches. A typical chess microcomputer requires up to 24-K bytes of ROM for the program, and 4-K bytes of RAM. The computer finally displays the number of moves it made before it won or lost the game.

The Bell Laboratories have a project for devising a program that would analyze 120,000 positions/second along the so-called brute force approach—a program that should enable the computer to beat a grand master!

12-30. MORE ADVANCED MICROCOMPUTERS (Systems Engineering Enterprises)

Among microcomputer systems, sophisticated systems ($3995 and up) provide some basic high standard features on all systems, and flexible optional features of peripherals, etc., in both hardware and software at extra cost to replace former minicomputers used in higher-speed business, industrial, communications, and scientific applications. One such manufacturer is Systems Engineering Enterprises (SEE, Rockville, Md).

1. **SEE System 6684.** The CPU, using the microprocessor 6512A or 6809 (operating at 4-MHz clock), or microprocessor 6502 or 6800 (operating at 2 MHz clock), is integrated into an 8-in. hard-disk or floppy-disk cabinet with peripheral ports in rear of cabinet. It can support four full RS232 data communications ports with 12 lines/port or 20 mA/60 mA closed loop, and bit-speeds 75 to 19,200/sec.

2. **SEE System 6784.** As in System 6684, the CPU is integrated into a 12-in. screen, 80-character by 24-line CRT video terminal cabinet with peripheral ports in rear. 16 programmable function keys control the video. A 128 high-resolution character set, including lower case and 32 graphics, with 8 X 10 dot-matrix block/character, is provided for full-editing and reversible video facility.

3. **Hardware—Standard and Optional Features.** Basic systems with 12 slots for the card cage allow 8 free slots for expansion. The systems operate in pipeline architecture at 4-MHz clock. 16-K bit (2-K X 8-bit), 2716 PROMs can be used. Basic 16-K bit RAM capacity of 442, 368 characters of memory with 200-nsec access-time can be expanded to 12 Megabyte of RAM with 150-nsec access-time. For synchronous, 4-port, 12-line/port communications, RS-232 interface board is crystal-controlled. The systems have provision for 8 vectored interrupts, with interrupt-driven I/O. The systems are expandable from 1.2 Megabyte, double-sided, dual 8-in. floppy-disk (IBM-3740 compatible) to 4 Megabytes

of disk random access memory. Facility of 660-Megabyte hard-disk storage memory is available for a true real-time distributed processing operating system, which can use 64 RS-232 ports and interconnected, intelligent terminals, with no degradation in response-time. Both fixed and removable hard-disk facility is available with a four-driver hard-disk controller. Four 165-MB disk units provide 660-MB storage memory. ANSI standard 10.5-in. 9-track tape-drive controller at 18 ips and 1600 bpi can be incorporated into the system along with a backup IBM-compatible 450-ft, 6400-bpi 3-M controller for cartridge tape. 100-CPS, 132-character (upper-case), 8.5-in. field, tractor-feed unidirectional printers, and 150-CPS, 132-character (upper-case), 14-$\frac{7}{8}$-in. field, RS-232 Interface, 75 to 9600 baud, auto top-of-form, 11-in. format printers are acceptable. Options include: (1) Parallel-interface Centronics printers, (2) 160/300-LPM, 132-character matrix printers, (3) 55-CPS letter quality word-processing printers, (4) 1400-LPM, 132-character electrostatic single-copy matrix printers, (5) multiuser traffic controller with multiuser software for 16 terminals that comes with optional RS-232 port.

4. Software. Very high-speed, full text-editing Magnum BASIC, with sequential and random files, integer and high-precision 16-digit floating-point arithmetic is standard. N-dimensional matrices and superset of Microsoft 16-K extended disk BASIC are also standard. Interactive conversational macroassembler and text-editor for 6800-family microprocessors are available. Interactive, relocatable macroassembler development system and Disk Operating System for 6502 and 6512 microprocessors are options. Source programs up to 2 Megabytes extent can be assembled. Compilers for high-level languages—PASCAL, FORTRAN, BASIC, and COBOL—for comprehensive business software are all available as options for the systems. The Process Control Language for a Disk Operating System is also available as an option. Some of the Application Software Packages are quoted as: (1) comprehensive word processing, (2) mailing-list package, (3) General business package with general ledger, accounts payable, and receivable, (4) inventory and payroll, (5) medical billing packages include statements, aging of accounts, automatic filing of insurance forms, and schedule of appointments, (6) publisher's package with automatic calculation of author's royalties, debiting of inventory, crediting of returned books, etc., (7) comprehensive travel agency package, and (8) manufacturer's inventory with automating debiting of raw materials, finished goods, invoicing, billing, accounts receivable for wholesale/retail, etc.

12-31. INTELLIGENT SYSTEMS CORPORATION—CP/M2

The CP/M2 Operating System, using an Intercolor® 8963 personal computer with 19-in. CRT display, is available with a wide variety of small-business programs in BASIC, COBOL, and FORTRAN IV. It does not require preparation of new software. New high-level languages such as PASCAL can be incorporated, if desired. The built-in operating system is comprised of 32-K bytes of RAM, 591-K bytes of dual 8-in.-floppy disk drive, CP/M2 O/S, and a color version of MICROSOFT® Business BASIC (cost: $6395).

Personal Computing is a rapidly accelerating phenomenon of the 1980s. The number of these low-cost small computers in use is expected to reach as many as 2 million before 1985.

12-32. THINGS TO COME

The author's forecast of a typical Home Color Television Receiver as a consumer product in 1988/1990: the color-TV may be renamed the "Keyboard Color TV" alias "BOEE"

(Box of Education and Entertainment), as an instrument meeting the demands of increased leisure time, since the microcomputer is going to impose production and office automation in a world community. The microcomputer will create millions of jobs while replacing routine manual work that is below norms. The BOEE will have the following characteristic features.

- Satellite digital color-television channels (in time-division multiple access) will be available on a local satellite community antenna system with an economy 7- to 15-foot-diameter parabola dish. The domestic satellites will pick up international satellite programs. The local community antenna system, if sufficiently budgeted, will directly receive programs from an adjacent country. The programs can be automatically distributed in a village community by means of a "fiber optics" cable, somewhat like a telephone connection. As an alternative, a "cable-TV" or "pay-TV" company will provide large-scale distribution of educational and entertainment programs from a local satellite television center. As things stand in countries like the United States and Japan, they would not be allowed to distribute commercial or political or religious programs, because these programs will remain in the domain of the present commercial networks.
- The BOEE will serve the dual function of (1) channel switching and color television controls, and (2) personal computing by means of two additional keys, TV and Computer.
- A remote control unit about as big as a pocket calculator will be available for remote push-button control of the BOEE—for both television and computing.
- In the computer mode, the color television receiver will serve as (1) a personal computer using plug-in color video cassette programs in digital format on magnetic bubble memory cards and (2) a CRT (cathode-ray tube) terminal, with access to educational, scientific, and "small-business" programs on the local computer network by telephone line. Programs will be available in high-level languages such as BASIC or ADA (an American version of PASCAL).
- The distributed processing of programming will remain universal for years to come.
- The BOEE can be accessed by any home-user by means of a pocket-size push-button keyboard for normal 10/20-foot distant-viewing of magnified data as if it were a television program in TV-Mode.
- Since 64-K/256-K and above static RAMs and high-density EEPROMs will be quite common, the BOEE in the computing mode will have the computational power of a present minicomputer plus a capability of digital storage in color of movie/educational documentary/scientific/and small-business program material on magnetic-bubble color video cassettes—"Bubble-cassettes". Two to six cassettes can be plugged in like tape cassettes. Electromechanical disk systems will not be used in this advanced version of personal computing.
- In order to eliminate the problem of cross-talk between the regular color television programs with 3.579545-MHz color crystal frequency and the clock of the microcomputer in the BOEE, the central processing unit (CPU) will use a clock standard of 3.579545 MHz in the place of the 5- to 18-MHz clocks commonly used in the new 16-bit and 32-bit professional microcomputers. Europe will use the color frequency standard of Europe, viz., 4.43361875 MHz.
- The BOEE will be a regular consumer product with price tags in the range of $500 to $1500.
- With special bubble program material, governments in general can educate their common citizens against the corruptions of inflation, narcotics, etc.
- Local neighborhood clubs can be formed to view special educational bubble program

material; government participation in social antidiscrimination measures may be included. After all, special education is meant for developing harmony in communities.

- Strict FCC regulations will be essential in the distribution of bubble educational material.
- During the next decade, plug-in mass-storage optical disks will be available for unlimited educational and scientific program material, since a broad spectrum of knowledge is going to be the main theme of the BOEE era of general enlightenment.
- Above all, the BOEE will be capable of serving as a fundamental United Nations tool to eradicate poverty and ignorance all over the world in the era of the BOEE. (See Table D-3 in Appendix D.)

12-33. LATEST MICROPROCESSORS AND MEMORY CHIPS FOR PERSONAL COMPUTING USE

1. **National Semiconductor NSC-800.** New P^2CMOS NSC-800, 50-mW (!) microprocessor features the speed and throughput of the popular NMOS Z-80 and 8085 microprocessors at a clock of 2.5 MHz. On a single 5-volt power supply, NSC-800 provides the multiplexed address and data bus of the 8085, and the sophisticated 10-addressing mode, 22-register, 158-instruction computational power of the Z-80.

Two complementary P^2CMOS chips (1) NSC-810 RAM-I/O Timer with 42 I/O lines, and (2) NSC-830 with 2-K bytes of ROM and 20 more I/O lines enable fine system interface in high-density, low-cost, low power-consuming, highly reliable personal computing applications. With these attractive features, the Si-gate, oxide-isolated P^2CMOS technology achieves these goals by using two layers of polysilicon, in addition to a metal layer for interconnects. NSC-800 is ruggedized for aerospace applications at 125°C.

2. **National Semiconductor NMOS COP2440**, with *dual* on-chip CPU's, ROM and RAM, simplifies programmability of industrial-process microcontrollers by scanning 35 I/O lines, while simultaneously processing data.

3. **Motorola 6809**, used in Radio Shack "Color Computer" and Fujitsu Micro-8 Personal Computer enables the computing power of a mainframe minicomputer. 16-bit address space for a 64-K byte RAM, 8-bit data bus, relocatable accumulator registers A and B and 2 index registers in two stacks are the new refinements of this chip.

4. **Intel 2816 EEPROM**, highly attractive electrically erasable 16-K bit nonvolatile memory chip is both byte and chip erasable to replace previous CORE memory.

5. **New IBM Personal Computer** for use with home television and audio cassette recorder, starting at $1600, is announced. It employs high-speed Intel 16-bit 8088 microprocessor as the CPU, allows 16-K to 256-K bytes of RAM, and 40-K bytes of ROM. BASIC or PASCAL software is provided by 2 Diskette drives with 160-K bytes/diskette. High-resolution green-phosphor display screen allows 80 characters by 25 lines, and upper/lower case letters. Diagnostic facility of power-on self-testing parity checking, Color Graphics for concurrent graphics and text capability, and RS-232C plus asynchronous start/stop protocols up to 9600 bits are available. An 80-character/sec, 12-character style bidirectional printer with 132 characters/line and 9×9 character-matrix is an attractive option.

13
Displays: Solid-State, Gas-Discharge, and CRT

Alphanumeric and graphic displays are common I/O functions in microcomputer applications, especially in human-machine interactive, graphic CRT displays.

13-1. LIGHT-EMITTING DIODES AND LIGHT DETECTORS

P-i-N Photodiodes are ultrafast silicon planar light detectors for visible and infrared radiation. The "i" represents the intrinsic silicon-layer that produces the electric field. The low dark-current of these noise-immune devices operating on less than 20 volts enables detection of very low light intensity. The capacitance decreases sharply through a large dynamic range of up to about 10 volts of reverse-bias and continues down to 20 volts. Laser pulses shorter than 0.1 ns may be observed, and frequency response extends from DC to 1 GHz. **Example**: Hewlett-Packard 5082-4205, Kovar and ceramic package with a hemispherical lens (4,203 has a flat glass window).

Figure 13-1 illustrates an Optically Coupled Isolator with the complement of a Light-Emitting Diode. The device serves as a Remote Control facility.

The photodiode is used as a high-speed, optically coupled isolator by coupling it with a light-emitting input diode such as a GaAsP diode that emits photons in proportion to the forward-current. An internal high-speed transistor amplifier maximizes gain-bandwidth product for direct-coupling to TTL loads at TTL speeds.

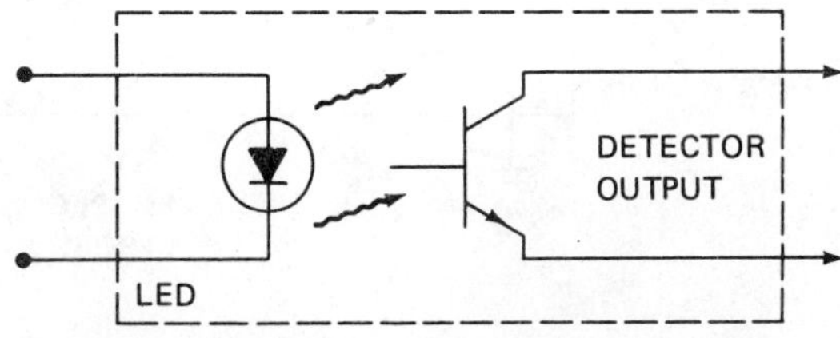

Fig. 13-1. Optically coupled isolator with LED for remote control.

Example: Hewlett-Packard 5082-4350. They are suitable as isolators for high-speed digital and analog line-receivers, and as replacements for pulse transformers and mechanical relays. They can be used to eliminate ground-loop currents between modules of a system. By combining a Nand-logic gate inside the unit, a diode/IC isolator Hewlett-Packard 5082-4360 is available as a special-purpose logic element. These devices can be used as optically coupled ac/dc amplifiers. An example of the application of those devices for eliminating ground-loop currents between peripheral equipment is shown in Fig. 13-2. Solid-state relays (SSR) employ optical coupling for isolation.

As long as the enable-input remains "high," the electrically isolated outputs from the optically coupled isolators will respond to changes of state at the inputs, with a delay of about 45 ns, as a result of the delay in generating and detecting the optical signals. The strobe incidentally eliminates the change-of-state glitches.

Light-emitting diodes. The solid-state GaAsP and GaP discrete light-emitting diodes (LED) provide a complete line of numeric and alphanumeric displays, electrically compatible with LSI microprocessors. The LEDs are practically lifelong (100,000 hours) as far as any electronics hardware is concerned. Available in green, yellow, and red, they are mini-sized for maximum front-panel density and easy panel-mounting with high luminous intensity at low cost. They are vibration- and shock-resistant for alphanumeric-displays presenting wide viewing angles, and ideal for logic-state fault-indicator applications, since they can be directly driven from diode-transistor logic (DTL) and TTL.

The LED displays are available in plastic-encapsulated or hermetic packages, with a typical luminous intensity of 0.7 to 1.8 mcd (milli-candella of light intensity) at a forward voltage of 1.6 V and 20 mA. **Example**: Hewlett-Packard 5082-4860 (red lamp); speed of response 15 ns with an integral resistor for TTL-compatibility at 5-V, 16-mA operation. Hewlett-Packard type 5082-7405: 14-pin epoxy, 0.3" Dual-In-Line Package (DIP), four-digit with decimal point.

Hewlett-Packard 5082-7000 is a **single-digit 5 X 7 LED matrix-display with built in decoder driver** that indicates numeral 0 to 9 when presented with a BCD code. It uses

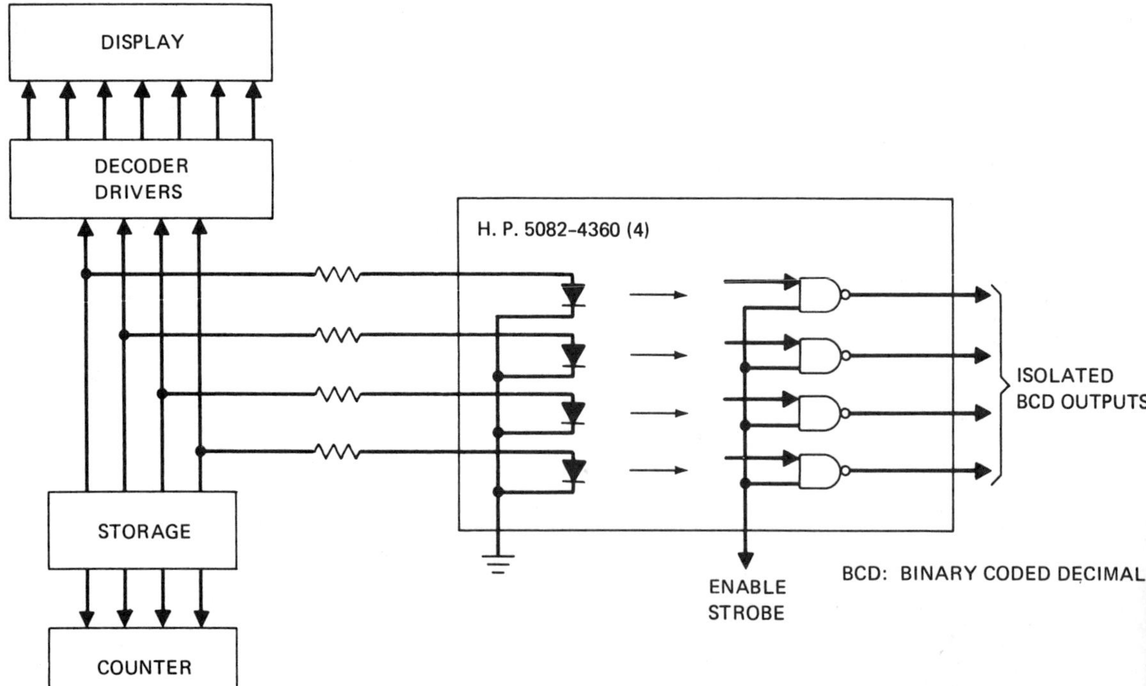

Fig. 13-2. Strobed optically coupled isolators. (*Courtesy of Hewlett-Packard, Inc.*)

negative logic, separate luminous intensity control, and current-limited left-hand decimal point. Each segment of the unit draws about 3 mA at 1.6V. (High-efficiency red LEDs, seven-segment, 0.43″ high (5082-7650) cost $3.95 each.) Displays capable of producing the alphanumeric characters, using the 5 X 7 dot-arrays of GaAsP LEDs, are available. These arrays are X-Y addressable to allow a simple addressing, decoding, and driving scheme between the display module and the external logic. X-Y addressing allows sharing of a ROM character generator for a five-column, seven-row, 35-dot array, using minimum number of pin connections.

Fairchild Semiconductor has the largest size 5 X 7 LED matrix-display, 0.8″ high (common cathode or common anode with either a left-hand decimal or a right-hand decimal). Each segment draws 5 mA at 1.7 V at an average intensity/segment of 0.15 mcd. The 0.25″ LEDs can be used with any BCD-coded thumb-wheel switches to provide luminosity in the place of the more common printed numerals. Litronix seven-segment LEDs have reached 1″ size for two to four digits. LEDs dissipate more power than liquid crystal displays (LCD); a seven-segment LED may require a minimum of 1 mW as compared to 0.2 μW in the case of an LCD display.

Long-distance visibility and wider range of alphanumeric characters are feasible by multiplexing tens of discrete **LED matrix-arrays** in place of the 5 X 7 segment LEDs.

As a result of this feasibility, 0.55″ orange-glow, high-voltage, gas-discharge display panels used in dc and multiplexed applications may not prove as popular for large-size display panels.

LED infrared lasers (light amplification by stimulated emission of radiation) are presently used for optical communications through the medium of fiber-optic cables. An 8,400-Å LED has an output of 30 mW. Receiver uses P-i-N photodiode to demodulate amplitude-modulated data (40-MHz bandwidth) on a coherent, narrow beam of light.

Four-Character Solid-State Alphanumeric Display

HDSP-2000, Hewlett-Packard, is a **5 X 7 LED array** for display of alphanumeric information. The LSI device is available off-the-shelf in 4-character clusters. It is packaged in a 12-pin dual-in-line type package, avoiding a large number of leads from a card of MSI integrated circuits.

An on-chip serial-in parallel-out 7-bit shift register associated with each digit controls constant-current LED row-drivers.

Full character display is achieved by external column strobing.

The constant-current LED drivers are externally programmable; each driver is capable of sinking 13.5 mA peak per diode.

The 5 X 7 LED matrix is capable of displaying the full ASCII code. The LEDs have a wide viewing angle.

The circuitry is suitable for direct interface with TTL circuits. Interactive I/O terminals, point-of-scale mini/microcomputers, portable data communications units, and hand-held microcomputers that require displays are some of the applications.

A basic display system is illustrated in the following block diagram to clarify the display interconnections of HDSP-2000 in a typical display system. The pin connections of the display chip are shown in the diagram. (HDSP-2000 consists of four 7-bit serial-in parallel-out shift registers and four 5 X 7 LED diode matrixes for the 4 characters).

13-2. LIQUID CRYSTAL DISPLAY

The former dynamic-scattered mode did not prove successful from the viewpoints of visibility and reliability, but the **field-effect seven-segment liquid crystal displays (LCD)** with a contrast-ratio of 20:1 use a lower voltage (3 V) to operate and have a faster response and erase-time without producing ghosts. Beckman series-705, 3.5-digit watch-

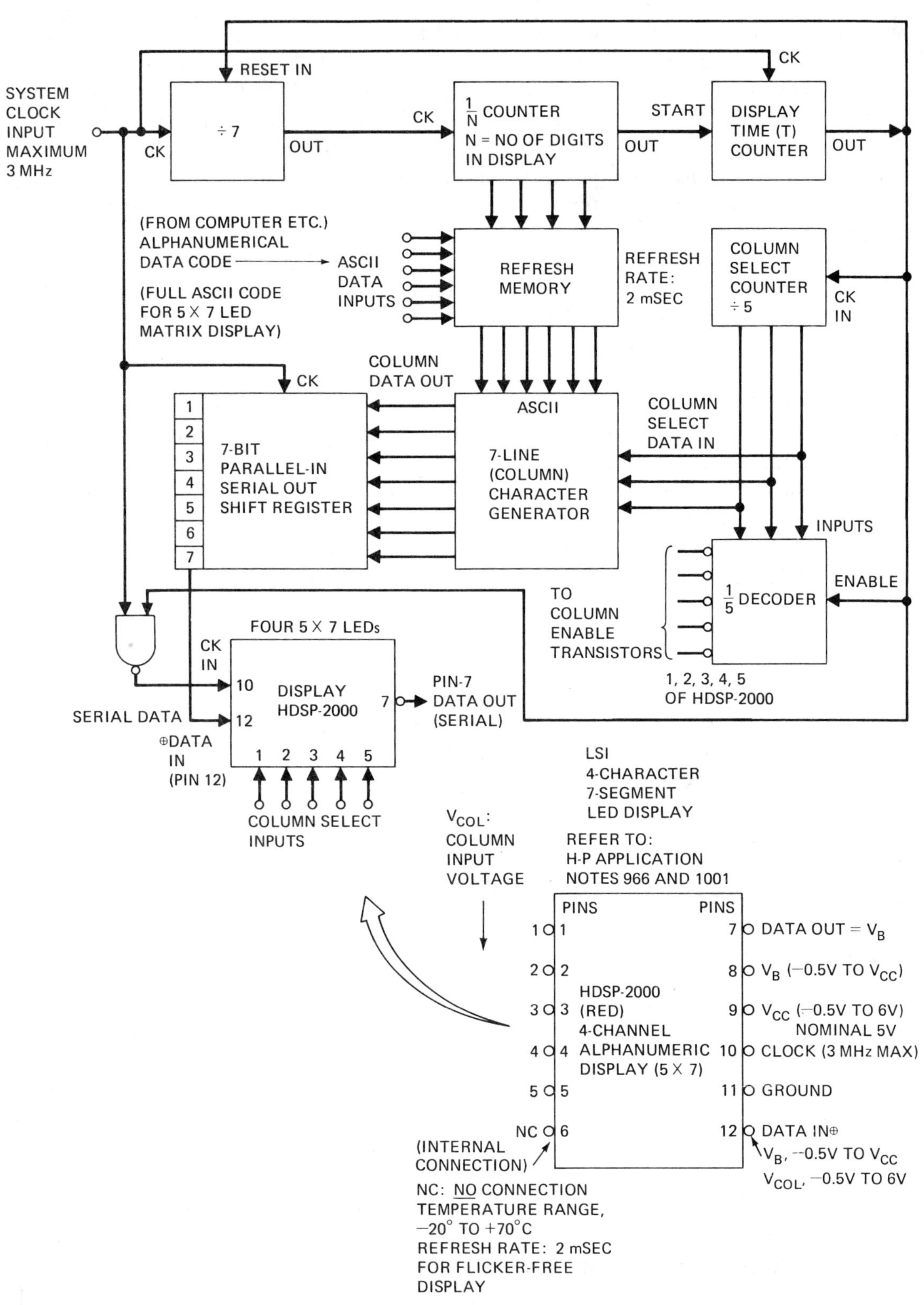

BLOCK DIAGRAM OF A BASIC DISPLAY SYSTEM
(COURTESY OF HEWLETT-PACKARD)

display is an example. Since, unlike LEDs, the LCDs allow continuous display at 1 μW of power consumption especially in digital watch applications, they are being used in applications where power consideration takes priority. Most LCD displays, however, have a light-sensing capability to increase the intensity of the display in bright ambient light, while reducing it in dim light. **Transmissive designs** will have backlighting for viewing in the dark; **reflective designs** will have ambient lighting, and thinner glass-sandwiches will bring the display closer to the face. (Presently, digital watches use the single-chip CMOS or the I^2 L-microprocessor.)

Self-scan bar-graph liquid-crystal display is a new flat-panel display technique from Burroughs Corp., using matrix addressing of individual bar-segments up to 200 at 0.5% resolution. Panel-meter display using this special two-layer LCD technique is an immediate application. The cells are driven by squarewave and are fully saturated at less than 20 V.

Flat-panel liquid-crystal television screen (resolution 175 X 175 and 109 X 82 elements) was demonstrated by Hughes (United States) and Hitachi (Japan). Pocket-television is expected to be a reality during the next 5 years. A/D conversion and digital memory are involved.

Latest DIP alphanumeric, modular type-3947, 0.5″ high, **four-character LCD** PC-board costs $12. Sixteen-segment characters operate on 4 to 17 V rms, requiring all-segments-ON current of 30 μA; 20:1 transmissive contrast ratio (black-characters on clear background or clear characters on black-background), lifetime of 50,000 hrs. Choice of reflective mode is available (HAMLIN Inc., Wisconsin).

13-2.1. Liquid Crystal Displays, 1980. Example: Optel liquid crystal displays (Optel, Refac Electronics Corporation) have low power and low voltage requirements (voltage 2.5 to 15V, maximum power consumption of 5V AC square wave, 30 to 100 Hz, less than 150 μW). They can be viewed in bright sunlight with high contrast-ratio and viewability from all angles. On a flat panel, low-power CMOS circuits can drive them. Sixteen-segment characters allow formation of all numerals and upper-case letters. Fourteen-segment digits allow decimal points in custom-designs of colored display-backgrounds and lighted black-segments; bright digits on black-backgrounds are also available. Life extends to over 50,000 hours in a wide range of temperature, −10° to 80°C. Optel LCDs can be operated in *parallel* in reflective, transmissive, and transflective modes. Type 77000 series alphanumeric displays feature 8 alphanumeric characters with decimal points and type 71000 series stockable displays are available in a range of character and panel sizes.

Due to low power requirements and large size characters, liquid crystal displays are highly popular.

13-2.2. LCD Drivers. LSI decoder chips are available from Hughes Aircraft Company, Solid State Products Division. They can be directly driven from a microcomputer system as shown in the following block-diagram.

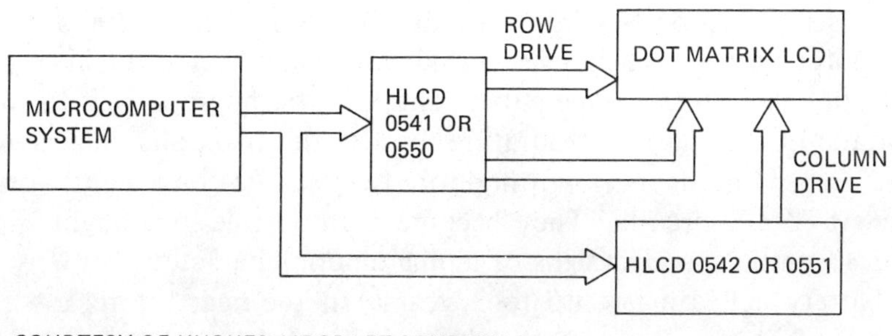

COURTESY OF HUGHES AIRCRAFT COMPANY

Driver	*Capability*
HLCD 0550/1	Up to 32 characters, 5 X 7 dot matrix, includes character encode and refresh.
HLCD 0541/2	5 X 7 dot matrix or 8-row array with arbitrary number of columns, serial or parallel input.
HLCD 0540	Up to 32 X 32 array, 2 circuits are required.
HLCD 0548	Up to 16 X 16 array.
HLCD 0438A	Any LCD, multiplexed or parallel drive, regardless of size.
HLCD 0437	4-digit, 7 segment (for digital voltmeters, etc.)

13-2.3. Liquid Crystal Displays in DPMs. In digital panel meters, $3\frac{1}{2}$ digital display is a common application. The specifications of two types of liquid crystal displays of Datel Intersil Inc. are indicated:

Type DM-3100X:	Input, ±2 V balanced differential Display, 0.6 in. high Battery powered	Case style, short depth Power, 5 V at 6 mA Price, $66
Type DM-3100U2: ($3\frac{1}{2}$ digits: +1.999)	Input, ±2 V balanced differential Display, 0.5 in. high (Input impedance, 1000 megohms, 5 picoamps input bias current)	Case, low profile Power, 115 AC programmable Price, $69

13-2.4. Multiplexing of LCDs. LCDs use minimum power and remain visible in bright sunlight. Hence they are a natural choice for large-area, multiple character application. Multiplexing would halve the number of 7-segment display leads required, simplify drive circuitry, and permit direct interfacing to microprocessors. Limitation in their electro-optic response makes it mandatory to address up to 4 digits sequentially. If each digit could be configured as a matrix, any number of digits could be addressed simultaneously. The displays are wired so that interconnected segments do not share the same symbol backplane.

LCDs used in watches are twisted nematic, field-effect devices. Liquid crystals are sandwiched between front and back planes of thin glass, which are sealed together with plastic or glass to make a plastic or glass case. *Some characteristic features of liquid crystal displays:*

1. Transparent conductor patterns are coated inside glass-planes with a special chemical-film to align liquid-crystal molecules. Outside the glass-plane are laminated polarizers to pass light parallel to the polarizing axis. The light is blocked because the axes are perpendicular to each other.
2. Liquid crystals have properties intermediate to those of liquids and solids within a *finite* temperature range. Their cylinderlike molecules can form in any of 3 meso-phases: smectic, cholesteric, or nematic. The nematic phase is best for display. The twisted nematic LCD imparts a quadrature twist to the two polarizing axes.
3. Voltage and current needs are low; therefore they can be conveniently driven directly by low-current CMOS circuits. They become more legible in sunlight and can reproduce graphics, symbols, and designs of alphanumeric characters. In wristwatch applications, a battery cell can last up to 3 years. In the near future, a whole range of colors may be feasible. Presently liquid crystals can display television pictures; in

future they could perhaps display television in color also. Liquid crystals can be available with or without plastic polarizers. The polarizers attenuate about 50% of the light transmission.

4. A recent technique of activating by means of phosphor coating of radioactive tritium eliminates the need for backlighting in darkness. LCDs are low-voltage devices operating at 3 to 6 volts RMS. With ac, the dc component of the drive signal must be limited to a low millivolt range. (DC may shorten the life of a liquid crystal.)

13-3. MAGNETIC BUBBLE DISPLAYS

In mass-memory applications, the bubbles are assured a place somewhere between CCDs and disks in performance and popularity in the near future. Mullard (Philips) of Great Britain is also using this new technology for display. The magnetic bubbles are cylindrical magnetic domains that have their magnetization reversed with respect to an external bias-field in thin-films of uniaxial magnetic materials. The display is based on a special magnetic material and the faraday-rotation effect to make the bubbles look like a series of mobile light-dots. The bubbles produce a sharp contrast against their background when a linearly-polarized light-beam is directed through the thin-films. The beam's plane of polarization rotates with the direction of magnetization.

A message of, for instance, 100 alphanumeric characters or an outline picture could be sent and stored for later viewing. The display is limited by chip-size to a maximum of 5 mm^2 and needs at least 10X magnification.

The magnetic bubbles display is illustrated in Fig. 13-3.

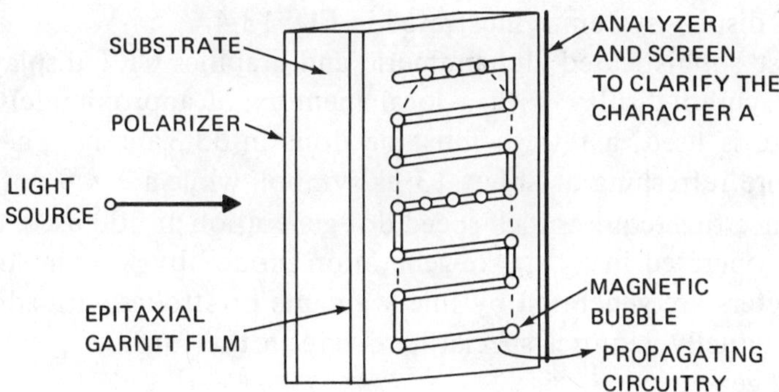

Fig. 13-3. Magnetic bubble displays.

13-4. CRT DISPLAY (GRAPHICS)

The CRT-display has a persistence-time ranging from 0.05 to 95 msec, depending on the phosphor used. For extended phosphor-life, medium persistence and a 60 Hz/sec "refresh" (rewrite) technique are commonly used with phosphor P-31 for minimum flicker. For telephone transmission at a data-rate of 2,400 bauds/sec, a local memory is used to store the data, and drive or refresh the CRT at an increased rate.

The low-cost, fixed-format, limited-symbol, 11-inch diagonal CRT-display provides a fixed number of lines and characters per line (10 to 20 lines, 50 characters/line for a maximum of 1,000 characters, in the absence of the interactive computer Graphics facility). The refresh-memory is a low-cost acoustic or magnetostrictive delay-line, limited to 8,000 bits or 1,000 characters for banking and recordkeeping applications. The characters are displayed and redisplayed each time the memory cycles, and a microprocessor-

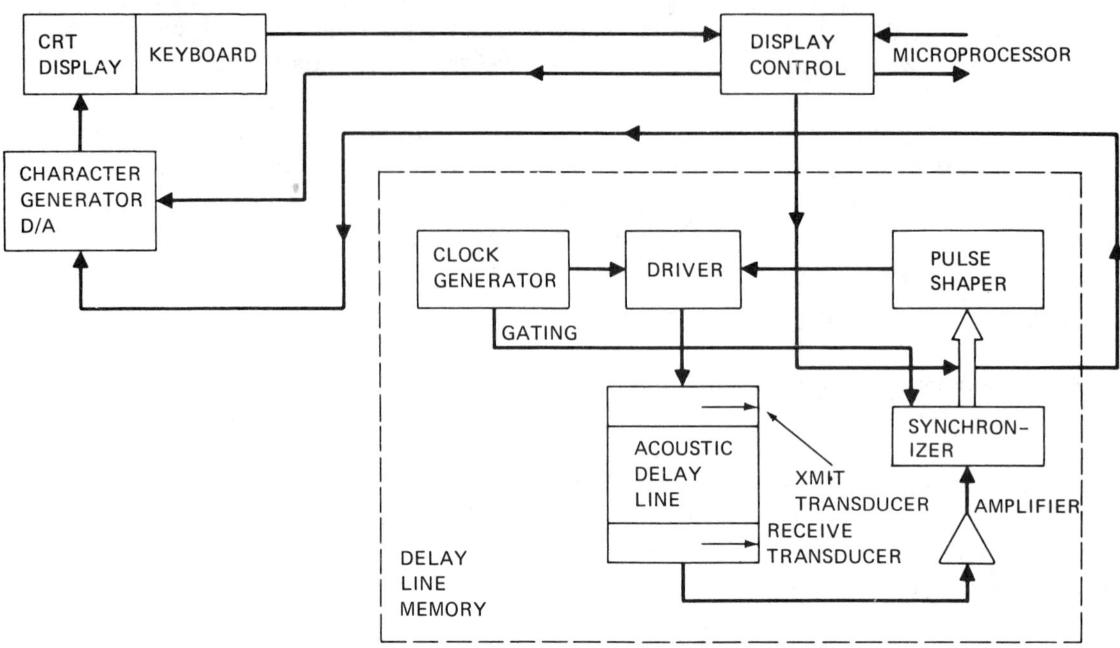

Fig. 13-4. Fixed format refreshed CRT-display system. (*Courtesy of Tektronix Inc.*)

controller interprets input-commands from the associated keyboard and computes for positioning, spacing, line-feed, back-space, rub-out, erase, and cursor. A fixed-format "refreshed" CRT display system is illustrated in Fig. 13-4.

The higher-cost sophisticated alphanumeric and graphics CRT displays use a random-format 50 X 50 symbol-display with a local memory of approximately 64-K bits. If a 30-Hz refresh-rate is used, a refresh must be done in 33.3 msec. The 50 X 50 symbol would then require refreshing at about 13 μs/symbol, while a 7 X 9 dot-matrix generates each symbol. Since this requires high-speed dot-generation at 200 nsec, the large-capacity refresh system is operated in a "stroke-generation mode" by X-Y analog deflection voltages. The characters are generated by line segments or strokes with additional software. This processing actually requires special hardware in the form of a video character generator or a vector generator.

The local memory allows the use of "light-pen" and "selective-erase" modes of operation. The light-pen is a light-sensing device to locate a graphic point on the CRT display and instruct the computer to perform a certain operation at that point. Some light-pen Graphics systems provide an error-sensing feedback mode; the CRT-beam follows the pen movements of simulated "writing." A light-pen system is shown in Fig. 13-5.

A selective-erase system can erase a character from the local memory without affecting the rest of the CRT display. A regular RAM-memory could be used for the local memory. Since the CRT terminal information is sent to the MPU controller (from the keyboard or the line), and not directly to the display, it is called *echoplexing* or *half-duplexing*.

The direct-view nonflicker bistable "storage" CRT display is another low-cost, high-density computer display system. This system also requires the character/vector generator to convert the serial digital data into the required analog format. A dot-character generator and a vector-generator follow the system technique shown in Fig. 13-6.

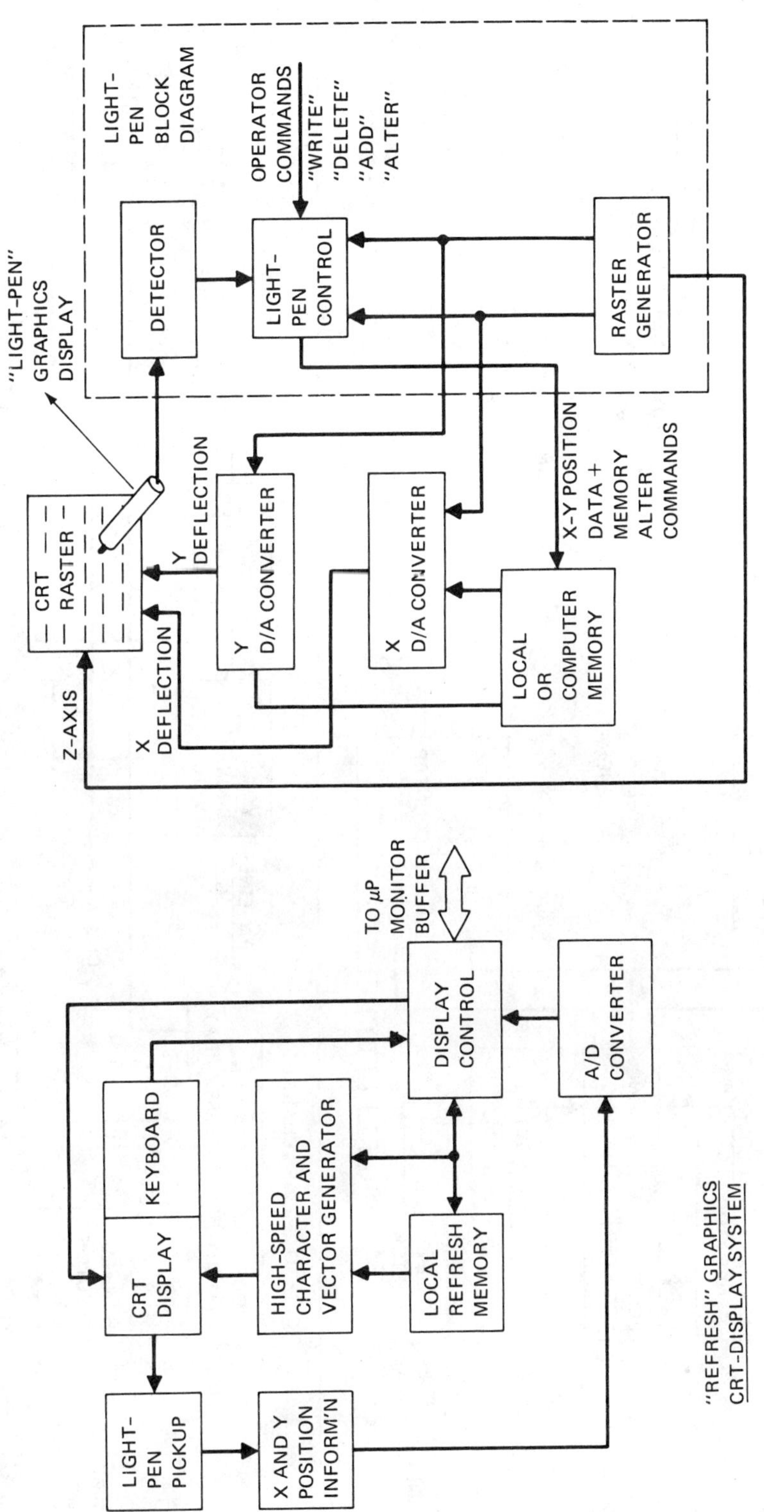

Fig. 13-5. "Refresh" graphics CRT-display system. (*Courtesy of Tektronix Inc.*)

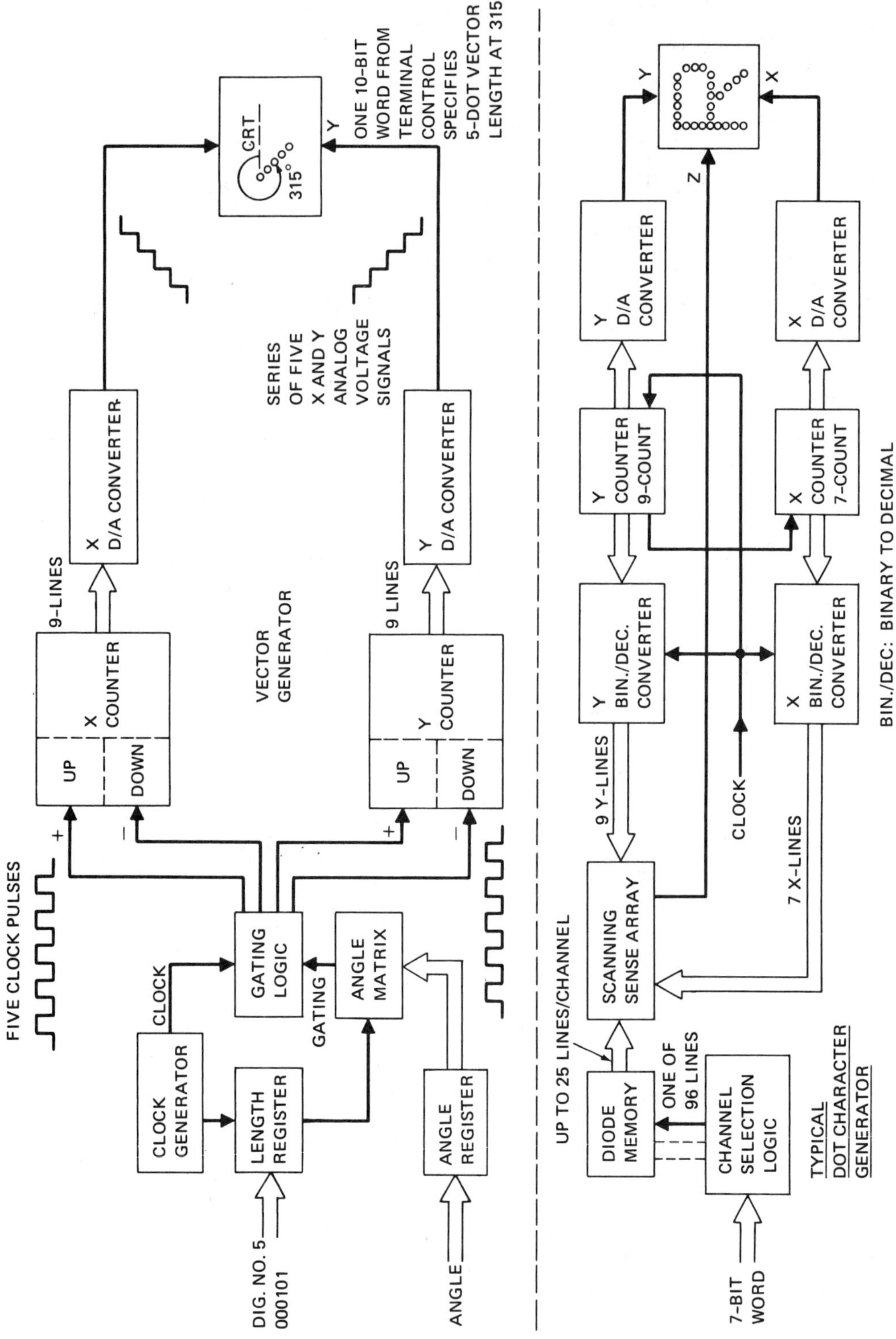

Fig. 13-6. Vector generator and dot-character generator. (*Courtesy of Tektronix Inc.*)

13-5. COMMERCIAL MODELS OF CRT DISPLAY OR VIDEO DISPLAY TERMINAL

A video display terminal (VDT) is commonly used for in-house time-sharing, data entry, inventory control, production control, and planning by the keyboard entry of data and commands. The Texas Instruments 913A keyboard VDT is a typical example, with a 15.5″ (H) X 12.8″ (D) X 19″ (W) display.

Besides the usual display controls, the cursor controls allow access up, down, left, right, and home (the top upper left of the screen). The display terminal includes 14 keys on the keyboard for the entry of the commands. The display characters are formed by a 5 X 7 matrix. Twelve lines and 80 characters/line make the total screen-capacity for using 57 upper-case display characters and 32 control characters of the standard set of ASCII code. The screen can be filled in less than 20 msec. The cursor is positioned by the program written in a built-in ROM memory. The screen refreshes at 50 or 60 frames/sec under the control of the memory located in the controller.

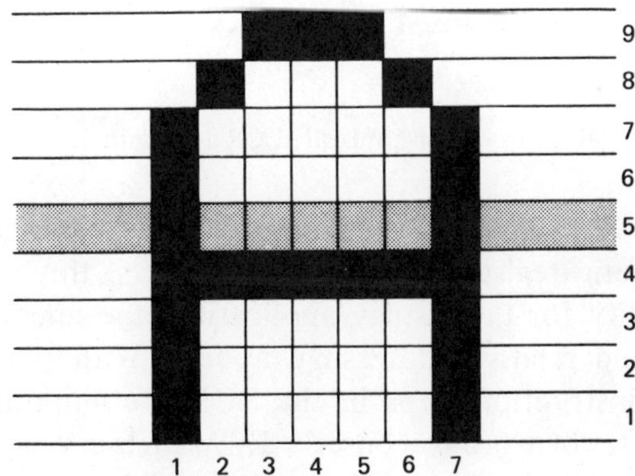

7 X 9 FORMAT—EXAMPLE OF CHARACTER-GENERATION OF ASCII CODE, (A).

13-6. A TYPICAL MICROPROCESSOR-BASED ON-LINE CRT DISPLAY TERMINAL

(Model JK-435, Matsushita; Sol-20, Processor Technology Corp.)

A microprocessor-based CRT terminal can meet the requirements of business, industrial, and scientific applications by the use of EPROMs or by merely plugging in preprogrammed ROMs. The various interface units and peripherals are shown in Fig. 13-7 for this on-line microcomputer system that employs a CRT keyboard display. The complete system is controlled by a single 16-bit microprocessor. The peripherals will of course be supplemented by individual microcontrollers.

I/O data is accepted from the keyboard via its interface or a remote computer via the requisite modem and the communications interface. The microprocessor uses:

1. The external PROM to process the incoming data into 11-bit slices for the display function, and the remaining 5-bit slices for the field-control function.
2. The RAM for temporary storage. The 11-bit data is transferred to the CRT-refresh RAM-memory for the CRT readout. For printout, storage, or transmission, the microprocessor, under the command of the ROM program, picks up the data from the refresh memory to perform the necessary data processing.

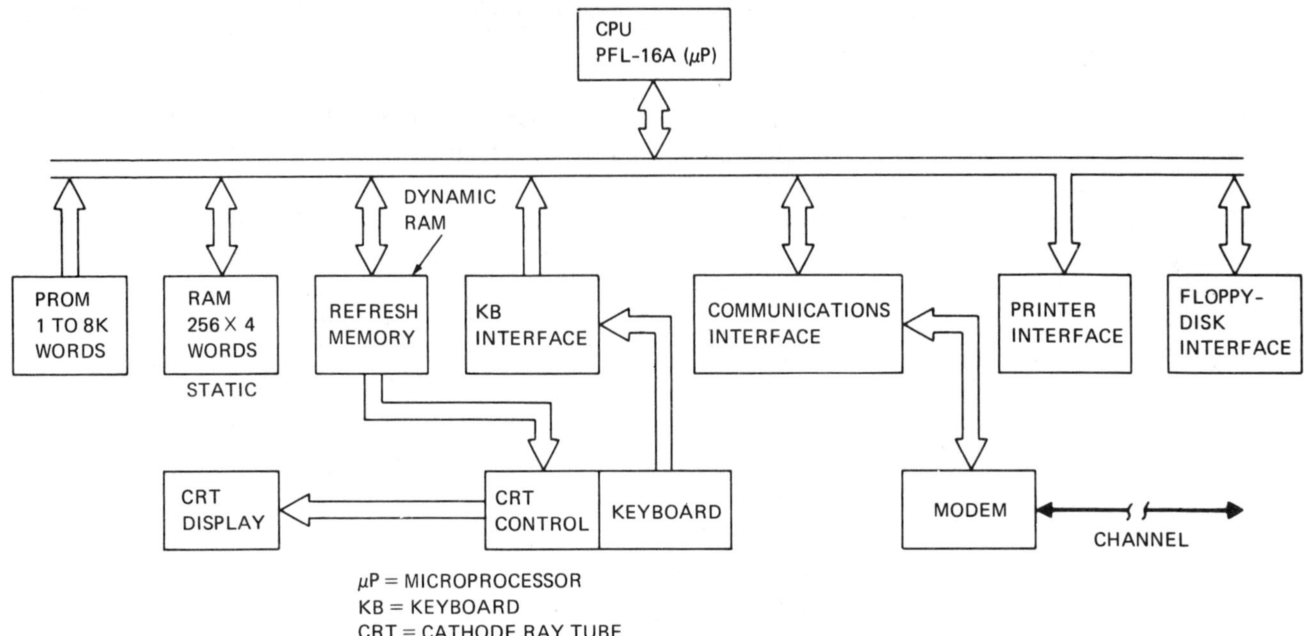

Fig. 13-7. Microprocessor-controlled CRT-Terminal.

The microprocessor PFL-16A has an instruction cycle-time of 3.3 μs, and 33 basic instructions, five arithmetic registers, two index registers, three interrupt levels, and 256 I/O entries. As a facility for the display application, the microprocessor can operate in the direct, indirect, and relative addressing modes. With the index-modifier software used, the number of instruction steps in the ROM are minimized. Besides, the data is manipulated in bit, byte, or word to conserve ROM memory-capacity. Since one instruction corresponds to one word, programming and debugging procedures are simplified.

The ROM and RAM memory capacity can be extended to 8,192 and 4,096 words, respectively. With a P-39 phosphor and its 200-msec persistence, the retrace-rate of 44 Hz is flicker-free. The 14″-high CRT display can display 24/25 lines at 80 characters/line. The 11-bit display-slice consists of 8-bit character-data, 1 memory-protect bit, 1 cursor-display bit, and 1 graph-designation bit. The 128 different characters used in this display system include alphanumerics, punctuation marks, Japanese Katakana characters, and simple graphics.

The field control-data is implemented for the control of the next-field brightness, use of ruled lines, character-blinking, and erasure.

The keyboard has 16 command-function keys for character-insert, character-delete, or data transmission. The modem used in this system has provision for asynchronous data rates of 110, 200, 300, 600, and 1,200 bauds/sec, and synchronous data rates of 2,400, 4,800, 9,600 baud/sec. An optional mini-line-printer, such as Texas Instruments Model 306, and Texas Instruments floppy-disk executive DX-10, can be appropriately interfaced to the PFL-16A. The interfaces in this system are hard-wired, but for dedicated applications, the interface units can be designed with preprogrammed LSI-PLA. An alternative ROM control-memory can be used for the optional printer or disk. The ROM "firmware" will control most of the CRT display functions, e.g., field-protect, field-erase, numeric field-control, tab, backtab, character-insert, character-delete, scrolling, and erase.

If the central computer employs peripherals of other makes, the CRT terminal will modify its firmware to meet the remote peripheral requirements.

Television Video Monitor as Digital CRT Display (Processor Technology Corporation, Emeryville, California). As an alternative to the regular digital CRT display terminals, the low-cost **television video monitor as a CRT display** appears to be the preferred choice in the case of the low-budget microcomputer systems, unless it is an interactive Graphics display system. The characteristic features of a typical low-budget microcomputer are presented to indicate the popularity of the video monitor in microcomputer display applications. (See **Video-RAM**, Section 10-8).

Processor Technology **Sol-20 Keyboard Microcomputer System** in the configuration of a portable typewriter, at a price of $1,495, offers the following built-in facilities for the external peripheral devices. (1) **video monitor**, (2) audio cassette, (3) digital tape system, (4) dual floppy disk, (5) expansion memories, and (6) interfaces not provided in the basic system at the quoted price.

The built-in features of the basic system are:

8080 microprocessor
TTY keyboard and keyboard controller
1,024-character video display circuitry
control PROM memory
1,024 words of static low-power RAM
1,024 words of preprogrammed PROM
cassette interface capable of controlling two recorders
software that includes a preprogrammed PROM module and a data cassette with BASIC-5 language
two sophisticated video games as an attractive feature
the interface to facilitate the use of the external peripherals on a S-100 I/O bus.

13-7. PLASMA-GAS DISPLAY

(Alpha Graphic Display Terminals, Interstate Electronics Corporation)

In plasma display, the gas discharge illuminates any point on the screen under computer control of a sustaining voltage, occurring at a self-refresh rate of 50 kHz/sec, without the use of a storage buffer. The contrast-ratio of plasma gas-discharge display is four times that of a CRT, and it is suitable for high-ambient light-intensity and altitude. With 512 electrodes on each glass-sheet, the flat-display matrix panel provides 262,144, 10-mil dots on a 8.5-in^2 panel. The digital-address nature of the plasma terminal's operation eliminates the need for a D/A converter. Alphanumeric readouts with 0.25″ characters use a 10×14 dot matrix. The wide-view angle image (110°) is flicker-free, and selective edit-erase is feasible. Bulk-erase takes 20 μs. The display-matrix is transparent and is suitable for back-projection images. (Cost: approximately $7,000 to $10,000.)

13.8. OCR PAGE READERS

Optical character recognition peripheral equipment is one of the popular new hardware in information-entry documentation. The OCR page-reader, costing approximately $15,000, is a reliable device, capable of converting typewritten material directly suitable for entry to *word-processing (WP)* CRT systems. The system can handle up to 300 typewritten pages per hour with reliable accuracy, eliminating the need for the time-consuming re-keyboarding of the typewritten page into a word-processing system. This OCR page-reader thus frees the word-processing system to implement the tasks for which it is intended, viz., editing, revision, formatting, assembly, disk-storage, and printing of documents for subsequent distribution. As an advantage, the OCR Readers can be directly interfaced to Telex units for message transmission, along with WP CRT systems and other microcomputer systems. OCR/WP interface-processing is done off-line. There are models that read typewritten and handprinted characters from ordinary documents. The most widespread application for OCR scanners is the reading of turnaround documents prepared by computer line-printers. In some cases, when interfaced to word-processing computers, data that can be optically read are entered via the OCR, while the remaining changes, etc., are keyed by an operator. (These OCR scanners are manufactured by IBM and Computer Data Corporation. IBM OCR equipment is also used for pencil marks on card decks for off-line entry in computers.)

Examples: IBM 3881 optical Mark Reader
IBM 3886 optical character Reader

13-9. STATUS OF CRT/TV AND OTHER DISPLAYS, 1981

1. **Digital color television** for computer terminals and color television is now a feasible proposition at a comparatively lower price tag with minimal assembly time and costs. A large number of components presently required in these display devices are being replaced by a VLSI microcomputer (equivalent to 50,000 gates), and a few data transfer and processor chips for video generator, dot-character generator, RAM memory, multiplexer, deflection and audio. Digitized composite video along chroma and monochrome data paths will use digital filtering techniques. Phase-synchronous demodulation is accomplished by phase-locking the sampling computer clock with the color burst. A deflection processing chip will perform timing and synchronization tasks for horizontal and vertical triggers, and makes the TV/CRT terminal switchable to NTSC, PAL and SECAM color television systems. ITT, West Germany, has developed such a display terminal using, for economy sake, analog RF and intermediate frequency stages.

Along with digital video cassette tape recorders as a parallel development, the box of education and entertainment forecast in Chapter 2 (BOEE) should be a reality before 1985 at a competitive price.

2. **Wordprocessing Display**. Text-processing features such as horizontal and vertical timing margins, tabs, character-highlighting are available with a six hundred dollar BASIC software package of 64-K bytes for a desk-top System/23 IBM, stand-alone, 8085-based personal computer system, using 64-K bytes of main memory, 2.8-M bytes of 8-inch dual-drive disk storage, 112-K bytes of ROM, and a printer at a price under $10K.

3. **Electrochromic Display**. Nippon Kogaku KK, famous for Nikon cameras, has fabricated an experimental low-power consuming electrochromic display (along with variable neutral-density filters), as a possible replacement of LCD displays in a limited number of applications. Two transparent indium tin oxide conducting electrodes, and two electrochromic thin-film layers (colorless tungsten oxide that turns to blue and a metallic hydroxide) are involved in the processing technique, along with an insulating layer on a glass substrate.

14 Reliability of MSI/LSI Microprocessors

14-1. RELIABILITY OF MSI AND LSI MICROPROCESSORS

In the final analysis, the determination of reliability depends upon whether particular MSI or LSI chips, or plug-in CPU cards, or LSI memory components such as a RAM or ROM, are capable of performing their specific functions, without degradation in terms of accuracy or failure, for a specific period of time under the changes in environmental conditions in which they were intended to operate. The reliability engineer is responsible for implementing an adequate program to achieve the reliability objectives under the stresses relating to the operating conditions. The failure analysis devised should be carefully scrutinized and carefully restrained against conditions that would cause catastrophic physical destruction of the device.

The degree of reliability of performance of these newly developed devices will depend on the actual stage in the overall life of the system, when the test for reliability is being made. A typical MTBF (mean time in continuous operating hours before failure) during the three operating stages, during the life of the system-devices, is depicted in Fig. 14-1.

During the early **"shakedown"** period (learning stage), the **MTBF** will be low, since major and minor deficiencies in fabrication will have to be corrected by new techniques or automatic means, when the device is subjected to cycles of changes under various environmental conditions. After shakedown, the feasible maximum degree of reliability would be experienced, during the regular production stage of the device, as a major portion of the life of the device. At the end of the life beyond the generally accepted 7-year period, obsolescence may begin to affect the reliability of performance at an increasing rate. In the case of the solid-state microtechnology, the turnaround time for reintroduction of higher-performance devices, meeting improved specification figures, is much shorter than this period; hence, the obsolescence stage may dictate the replacement of the device by its new improved version, for higher standards of performance,

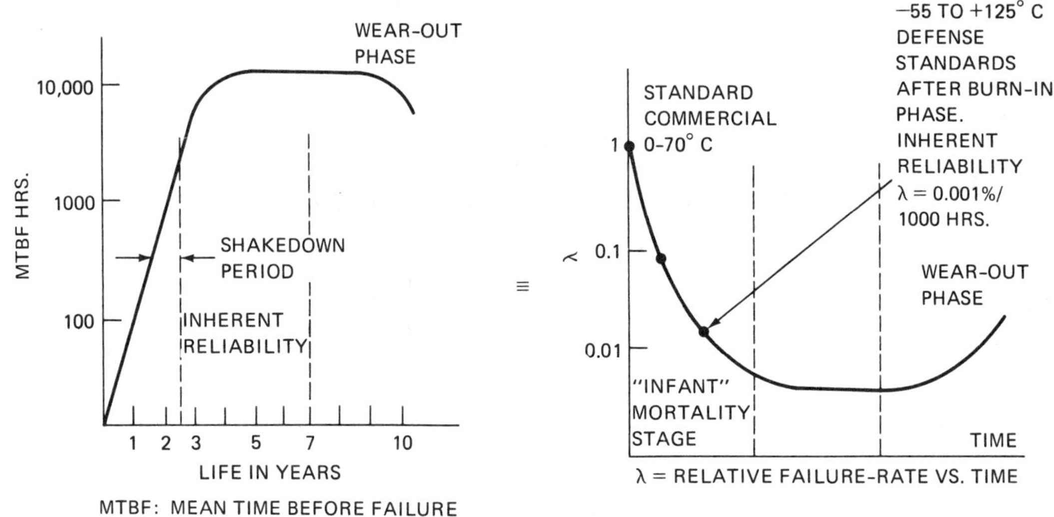

Fig. 14-1. MTBF versus "component life in years."

and not as a result of any increased probability of failure—which is really not so, since the reliability of the MSI/LSI devices is on a continuous ascendancy with the latest improved microcomputer-controlled automatic test procedures (ATP) during fabrication.

At present, the bipolar technology **failure-rates** (inverse of MTBF) for the standard non-prescreened products range from 0.021% to 0.005% per 1,000 hours at 25°C ambient, as calculated at 60% confidence. The corresponding failure-rates for MOS technology are slightly higher, ranging from 0.031% to 0.0035%.

Usually, **life test-data and failure-rates** are organized along the lines of the families of types and the fabrication process-codes in die-processes. Accelerated testing at a junction-temperature above 150°C for prolonged times leads to gold-aluminum intermetallic failure at the bond. However, for this failure mechanism, assessed failure-rates are influenced by random defects related to assembly and packaging, rather than predictable system failures, to which reliability physics could be applied and solutions found on a step-by-step basis during the **"learning" stage.**

Production IC packages (plastic and ceramic) routinely pass the Class B LTPD requirements of MIL-STD-883, method 5005; they also meet **Class A LTPD (limited temperature power dissipation) requirements.** For EPOXY plastic packaging, junction-temperatures must be kept below 150°C to avoid excessive gold-aluminum intermetallic formation as well as bond-wire grain-growth, both contributing to bond failures. Prolonged exposures in extreme environments approaching 85°C ambient and 85% relative humidity should be avoided. They must, however, withstand without failure extended temperature-cycles of 1,000 between -55 to +125°C.

TTL circuits are capable of satisfactory operation during transient gamma **radiation** above 1×10^8 rads/sec, and sustained **neutron-intensity** of $1 \times 10^3/\text{cm}^2$ without permanent damage.

Usually, for the plastic EPOXY-DIP, the concern is **bond-integrity**; for the ceramic CER-DIP, the concern is **hermetic-seal.** For hermeticity, a mass-spectrograph helium leak-detection technique is used. In MSI/LSI microprocessor-unit (MPU) and IC production, approximately 50% of the devices pass the failure-analysis test procedures to output that much **"yield."** Approximately 25% of the devices are damaged by electrical overstress due to incorrect insertion, board-shorts between device-pins, power supply-transients, poor handling, and so on. The remaining 25% are true failures in wafer fabrication, assembly, and packaging. After delivery to a customer, there will be an "infant mortality" phase for the first few months, as shown in the plot of life-versus-MTBF. This phase can be avoided by "burn-in" processing before delivery to the customer at extra cost to meet certain Defense Standards.

14-2. AUTOMATIC TEST PROCEDURES

Automatic test procedures implemented during fabrication are:

1. Monitoring of the wafers by the scanning electron-microscope
2. Die-sort visual acceptance
3. Pre-seal visual acceptance of the die-attach wire-bond
4. Stabilization-bake preconditioning for the plastic-mold packaging or thermal-shock preconditioning for hermetic-seal packaging
5. Centrifugal monitoring and seal-tests for hermetic-seal packaging
6. Complete production electrical testing
7. Hot-rail, high-temperature, and functional testing
8. Outgoing quality control and symbolization
9. Level-B burn-in testing.

14-3. TYPICAL PRODUCTION TEST PROCEDURE

As an example, a typical production test procedure for DEC's LSI-11 microcomputer system is quoted from the vendor's trade literature.

1. The μP chip-set, after visual and gross-leak inspections, is cycled 50 times from -40°C to +150°C.

2. In a thermal intermittent test, it is allowed to cool from 100°C while electrical continuity is checked, and then electrically tested on an automatic Tektronix 3260 test system. It runs 100% functional and electrical tests with every diagnostic that can be run on the chip.

3. Then the 12-volt chip-set is subjected to a short 30-volt stress-test.

4. The chip-set is then assembled on the single-card microcomputer along with the other LSI-memory, I/O and interface chips. The system assembly-and-test facility is run by three PDP-11/40 computers which control the plant via 500 serial-data lines. The automatic product test (APT) system starts with a test sequence from a General Radio-1972 Logic Tester that isolates LSI-11 microcomputer faults to a single line of the card. Such faults are usually caused by imperfect wave-soldering in particular, and can be repaired straight away.

5. The APT diagnostics then verify the cards to check repairs, and the cards go to a bank of temperature chambers, cycling between 0-55°C, while the LSI-11 runs through its instruction set (one full-day test procedure). Thermal cycling is followed by final acceptance tests at quality control before the Microcomputer cards are packaged for OEM shipment. The failure rate is 0.006% in the first six months.

14-4. FMECA (FAILURE MODE, EFFECTS, AND CRITICALITY ANALYSIS—ARP 926)

During the early shakedown period of the electronics system, the Aerospace-recommended design-analysis test procedure, FMECA, aims at achieving a design with high-reliability and high personal safety potential. The method insures the following functions:

1. All conceivable failure-modes and their effects on the operational success of the system are ascertained.
2. A list of the potential failures are ranked according to the magnitude of their effect and probability of occurrence.
3. Initial criteria are formulated for planning test and checkout systems.
4. A basis is found for a quantitative reliability test.
5. A historical documentation is provided as a helpful reference to future field service.
6. The input data are studied for possible trade-offs.
7. Corrective-action priorities are established.
8. Finally, an objective evaluation, relating to available redundancy, failure-detection systems, fail-safe characteristics, and automatic and manual override, is in order.

In the case of the FMEA (Failure-Mode Effects Analysis), failure effects on the subsystem and the overall system, their detection and correction, and Reliability Logic Diagrams where needed for detailed analysis, are particularly important. And, in the case of the FMCA (Failure-Mode Criticality Analysis), a component criticality number is computed for each major component in the system according to the algorithm,

$$C_r = \sum_{n=1}^{j} \beta \alpha K_e K_a \lambda_g t. 10^6,$$

where n = 1, 2, . . . j, α is the failure-mode ratio, β is the probability of failure effects, K_e is the environmental ratio, K_a is the operational ratio, λ_g is the failure-rate or failures per operating cycle, and t is the operating time (hours or cycles: 10).

14.5. NMOS AND BIPOLAR LSI/VLSI DEVICE RELIABILITY

It is well known in 1981 that the *quality control* of LSI/VLSI chips in Japan is superior to that in America because *total quality control* has been meticulously observed in Japan during the last 10 years. According to quality-control experts in Japan, *percentage* of Japanese *device failures* (1) at incoming inspection is 0.11, (2) during equipment assembly, 0.008, and (3) in the field, 0.002. The corresponding figures for imported devices (mostly from America and Europe) are, respectively, 0.54%, 0.11%, and 0.008%; that is, it has been estimated that quality control in Japan results in 4 to 10 times higher reliability in semiconductor devices. Surprisingly, Japan follows the total quality control (TQC) proposed by American experts like W. E. Deming, but the American competition's failure to arrive at similar figures is mainly due to *cost-conscious* quality control and higher labor costs for commercial mass-produced products. The unit of measure used in Japan is percent/10 million hours, while that in America is percent/1000 hours.

The total quality control by automated procedures with automatic test equipment (ATE) are measured as *open-circuit, short-circuit,* and *electrical degradation* during the various stages of mass production of semiconductor devices, on a basis of *successively improved planning programs*. The test procedures of processing, packaging, and usage in the field are described as follows:

1. *Process, Diffusion and Oxidation*: Tested for oxide defects, contamination, surface states and faulty lithographic patterns.
2. *Metallization*: Tested for *open* at oxide step on substrate, corrosion, electromigration, *open* at contact and faulty etching.

3. *Assembly*: Tested for chip-peel, chip-crack, wire cut/peel, intermetallic formation, foreign material, and scratch.
4. *Packaging*: Tested for package-leak, moisture penetration and whisker formations.
5. *Field Usage*: Tested for static electricity and overstress. To screen devices and eliminate potential failures, a *burn-in* at elevated temperatures is commonly used. The effectiveness of burn-in is well-known; the period of burn-in is proportional to decreased failure rates.

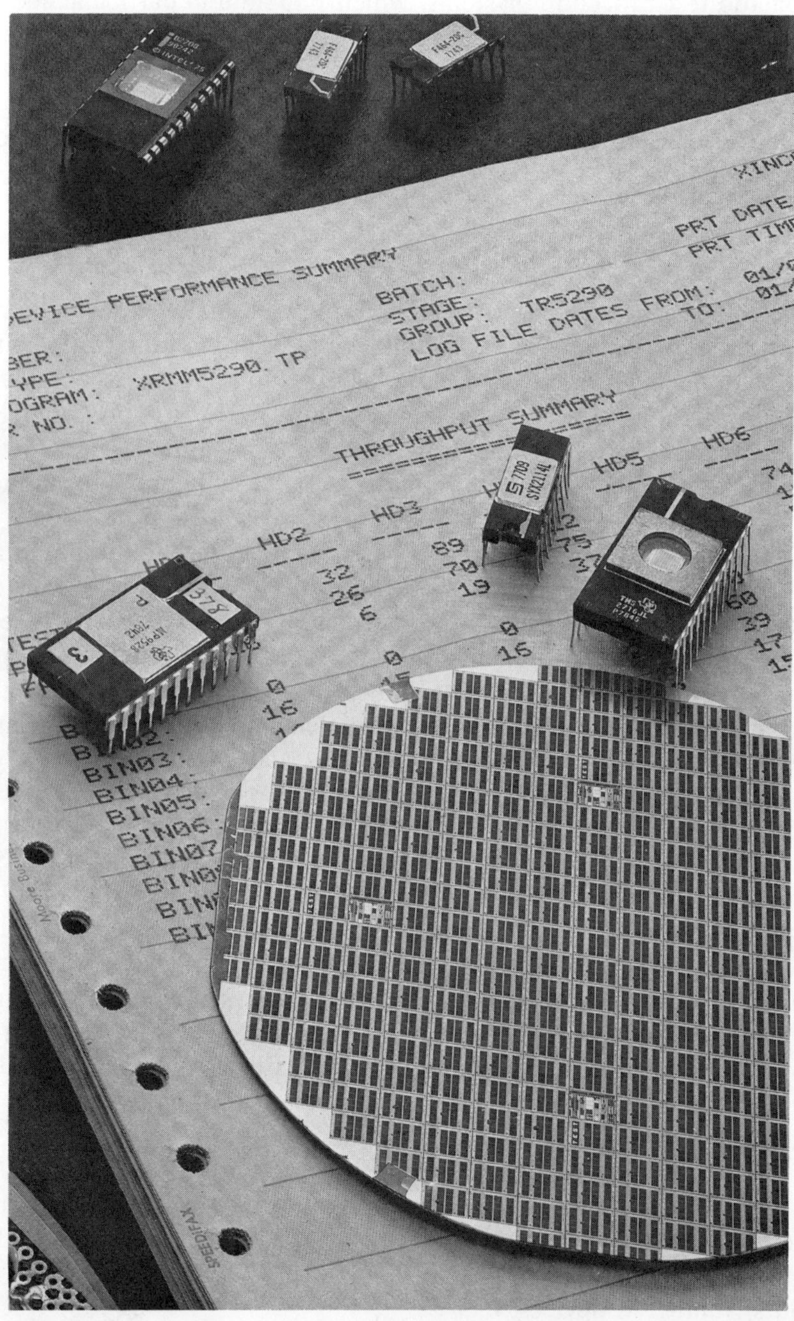

Fig. 14.2 A silicon crystal wafer-disk with hundreds of memory chips on each disk. Each chip is less than 0.2 in.^{2} in area. (*Courtesy of Fairchild Camera and Instrument Corporation*)

14.6. AUTOMATIC TEST PROCEDURE, SOFTWARE XINCOM III

LSI/VLSI memory chips are automatically tested on a distributed architecture basis. XINCOM III software system of Fairchild Camera and Instrument Corporation can accurately test with its 8 satellites up to 32 memory chips such as ROMs, static and dynamic 16-K bit RAMs, and the latest mass-storage magnetic bubble-memory chips. The software involved for the test procedure is identical for the 8 satellite channels. The system enables the checking of the device failure-mechanisms; condensed test-patterns at 12.5 MHz clock-rate permit high throughput production testing.

These automatic test procedure systems, which Fairchild in particular specializes, help reduce the cost of mass-produced LSI/VLSI solid-state memories. There are similar systems of software engineering techniques to test high-density microprocessor chips to minimize their cost by large-scale mass production.

A photograph of the silicon crystal wafer-disk with 100s of memory chips on each disk is shown in Figure 14-2.

14-7. RELIABILITY OF SOLID-STATE LSI INTEGRATED CIRCUITS

At least an order of magnitude in improvement is conventionally expected in reliability of LSI integrated circuits as compared to SSI/MSI ICs used in former minicomputers and hardwired logic. Some manufacturers foresee that, within a few years, complex LSI/VLSI integrated circuits should be able to achieve a failure rate of approximately 0.0001%/1000 hours; the present figures are one or two orders of magnitude below this figure.

The high reliability of fabricating LSI circuits in an all-semiconductor monolithic form is due to the fact that, throughout the various processing stages, production is very closely controlled, and quality assessment is meticulously assured. Reliability is actually built-in. For example, by using the monolithic fabrication, 80% of the connections required for hard-wired logic are eliminated, since the various circuit elements involved are continuous within one bulk material. Mismatches in thermal expansion coefficients are, in principle, minimized; and the use of metal contacts alloyed on the substrate reduces the interface between dissimilar materials. Active and passive elements with negligibly small mass are protected against adverse environmental conditions and damage by shock or vibration fatigue, because the entire circuit is hermetically sealed as a single unit.

Manufacturers subject samples of these LSI/VLSI chips to long-term testing to evaluate, on a statistical basis, their standards of performance and reliability. Some of the tests carried out are as follows: (1) centrifuge at a steady acceleration of 20,000 g, (2) a drop test repeated ten times, (3) a thermal shock of temperature-cycling repeated ten times between 200°C and −65°C (15 minutes at each extreme with no more than a two-minute delay between extremes), and (4) heating the semiconductor junctions to a temperature of 200°C by the application of 20 volts instead of the working voltage of 3 volts in service, and then immersing them in liquid nitrogen at −195°C. The nature of these test procedures on samples validate the ruggedness of the present LSI circuits, especially in defense applications.

Statistical data on reliability is established in practice for a specified *confidence level* such as 60% or 90% according to the following algorithm. Test time/Mean life required = 0.0001 for 60% and 0.001 for 90%. Failure rate = Sample size estimated from special tables/*Sample size actually used × (Test time/Mean life required) × (100 × 1000)/(Element hours/Number of devices*).

15
Conclusion

The microprocessors and microcomputer systems were originally limited to a few stand-alone dedicated applications, because of their low-speed due to the use of the slower PMOS substrate. Now that the faster NMOS microprocessors, and the equally fast mW-power-consuming CMOS and CMOS-on-sapphire microprocessors, and the stand-alone single-chip microcomputers are becoming available, they will start replacing the higher-cost power-consuming minicomputer systems at the low- and mid-end of their application areas, while simultaneously creating at least a tenfold increase in radically new areas of applications. The feasible "add-a-brain" microgadget application possibilities are unlimited–imagination is the limit. The upcoming fast and high-density 16-bit I^2L microprocessors and high-density I^2L memory-LSI provide the system designers with new microprocessing building-blocks for both new and replacement data-processing systems in a truly competitive way. The I^2L concept is applicable to both the linear and digital signals at extremely low-voltages such as 1.5 V and hence at minuscule power consumption. Alternatively, higher voltages can be used for a possible trade-in between speed and power. The bipolar I^2L LSI technique is thus conducive to an unlimited number of linear and digital circuit applications.

Most currently available microprocessors handle 4/8/16 bits in parallel; since 4 bits can represent a decimal digit, these devices can do decimal arithmetic in serial mode and binary arithmetic in parallel mode. The 8-bit devices can handle both binary and alphanumerical data in either 7- or 8-bit form in "intelligent" terminals for processing in the popular Extended Binary Coded Decimal Interchange Code (EBCDIC of IBM) and the American Standard Code for Information Interchange (ASCII) for time-sharing. As emphasized, most units can now handle longer 16-, 18-, 24-, and 32-bit words too by "bit-slice" architectural design approaches.

Microprocessors permit design changes to be made simply by changing the program partly or in totality as a PROM or EPROM or as entirely new ROM plug-in memory. And the change thus involves just a few plug-in components. As compared to hard-wired logic, microprocessors involve implementation of logic in terms of sequences of program steps as microprogramming in the ROMs concerned. This naturally increases instruction time and slows up the execution-time in larger data-processing applications, if the instruction set is limited. In the latest microcomputer systems, even this problem is not a limitation, since new pipelined processing techniques are being introduced to process several instructions in a cycle-time, using additional LSI microprocessor chips if necessary.

As regards the solid-state memory technology applicable to the microcomputer systems in the form of RAMs and ROMs (and the associated bulk software on tape, magbubbles and diskettes), the access-time versus capacity and the cost/bit show an encouraging down trend. The 16-K bit LSI memory chips have arrived, and subminiature 64-K bit CCD memories, accessed on the basis of a word, are announced. The fast-access high-density NMOS and I^2L static and dynamic RAMs have been dominating the memory market; nonvolatile nitride memories and standby-battery–run μW-power-consuming CMOS and I^2L memories will gradually replace the power-consuming CORE memory (if used in these applications).

With the advent of high-speed sophisticated 16-bit microprocessors, the latest trend in aerospace applications in general is gradual substitution of dedicated microcomputer systems (meeting the Defense Standards) in place of the previous minicomputer systems—due to the obvious weight and power considerations. Dedicated microcomputer systems are being successfully implemented for high-class specialized applications like space mission guidance, on-satellite switching systems, synthetic array radars, miniature airborne radar and navigational systems, medical diagnostics, and point-to-point and network data communications.

Developments concerning microprocessors are actually moving faster than forecast. It is not only the former real-time minicomputer systems that are being challenged, but powerful medium-scale general-purpose digital computers of the third generation (using MSI) will be fairly challenged on the basis of the new pipelined architecture which uses several controller-and-task processing LSI chips at relatively lower cost.

Effective user education is one of the principal problems facing the industry here and elsewhere—especially the programming aspects. Industry investment in manuals that explain the details of microcomputer programming and give actual program examples, is one way that is in progress at this time. But this is done on a piecemeal basis; there ought to be some commonality in the aids designed for hardware and software, e.g., by some kind of inexpensive ROM-Translators and Interface-LSI for microprocessor to microprocessor. Documented instructional debug examples on a step-by-step basis, using an ordinary lab-oscilloscope, furnish another method. The present distinction between the software designers and the real-world hardware logic designers would gradually disappear, because the need for specialized hardware designers will be eventually converged in the direction of the LSI and programmable-logic-array (PLA) design houses.

Within the next few years, there is bound to be a new trend of initiation at the high-school science-education level—similar to that of current automobile-driving, first-aid, and auto-maintenance instructions. Microcomputer applications of a limited scope, and instructions in simple programming techniques could be potentially initiated at this stage, because the extremely low cost of the 4-bit microprocessor chips ($5) and a few specially designed high-volume low-speed interface-LSI chips will make the necessary practical instruction feasible on a low-economy budget. Low-cost VRAM-TV monitors and calculator-keyboard-display units will make a fine contribution in this respect. New microcomputer enthusiasts will soon join the ranks of the present-day CB-radio hobbyists.

Finally, it is a justified hope and aspiration of the systems designers of both hardware and software that the industry will in the near future come up with a standard, universally applicable, program-development system that will facilitate in-circuit emulation and software development of several types of microprocessor chips (extending from one to three for a CPU)–to enable a semblance of unity in diversity. A low-cost VRAM-TV and a Graphics light-pen facility would be ideal for low-budget programming capability.

The semiconductor industry, with its latest VLSI technology, has spawned a kind of minirevolution by forcing international large-scale computer manufacturers to compete with newly expanding personal microcomputer companies that specialize in expanding internal and international large-scale markets in low-cost hardware, prewritten software, and services, at comparatively higher standards of reliability, in the following areas:

1. home and personal computers as data network terminals
2. medical diagnosis, decisionmaking, and health care
3. publishing industry
4. educational electronics and audiovisual aids
5. composition of music and art
6. bionics and intelligent prosthetic limbs, and aids for the blind and deaf
7. hand-held language translators
8. worldwide data communications systems via telephone lines, fiber optics, and satellite TDM data communications technology
9. solar photovoltaic energy collection systems that gradually minimize high-cost mechanical machinery around the world
10. safe and foolproof energy generating systems and automatic production equipment
11. high-quality digital voice and display systems
12. interactive computer graphics terminals in color
13. economy word-processing dictation gadgets and office equipment
14. postal mail carried by network data terminals
15. information storage and retrieval systems
16. automatic protection against misuse of computers.

The basic necessities of life at low mass-production costs could be within the reach of the people all over the world if nations coordinate their efforts in this direction. In conjunction with the latest boom in fiber-optics, domestic satellite TDMA, and data communications for telephone traffic, facsimile, educational broadcasting, and digital color television, the highly reliable microcomputer is here to stay and to change the way of life for the better.

A miracle panacea of this unique capability and intelligence is within the reach of every optimistic society. A fully developed world society that takes advantage of modern science/technology and plans, organizes, and observes checks and balances will, perhaps, someday dismiss war (without abusing science/technology) and transform things toward a utopia that most scientists and idealists only dream about.

In conclusion, it is fair to say that the mass-produced, highly reliable economy LSI/VLSI microprocessor is, apparently, about to open a totally new phase of industrial revolution by presenting a novel medium of practical utility and guidance for the benefit of people all over the world.

Appendix A

A Short Introduction to the Field-Effect Transistor and MOSFET—The State-of-the-Art in 1966 and 1977

The following technical report presents a close look at the rapid progress MOS technology has gone through in a little more than a decade. Section A-6 summarizes the latest status of MOS-LSI–VLSI technology.

A-1. FIELD-EFFECT TRANSISTOR

The field-effect transistor (FET), first introduced in 1952 by Shockley and Pearson as a device exhibiting modulation of conductivity by the *field-effect*, has only recently come into regular use in various forms, after the introduction of the *silicon epitaxial-growth* and *planar-diffusion techniques* in the semiconductor processing technology. Sophisticated *thin-film* integrated circuit techniques are currently used to fabricate both field-effect transistors and passive components on a common substrate.

Since not all of the versions of the device involve the use of an **electric field** to control the flow of current, the term *unipolar transistor* is theoretically more appropriate; the current in this device is carried by charges (*majority carriers*) of only one polarity (*either the holes in a P-channel FET or the electrons in an N-channel FET*), as compared to the *bipolar control* of both electrons and holes in conventional junction transistor.

The two basic types of the FET–namely, the hitherto-common junction (J)FET and the insulated-gate (IG)FET (also known as the Metal-Oxide Semiconductor or MOS)–have certain inherent advantages (and hence their increasing popularity): (1) high input-impedance like the original vacuum-tube and unlike the transistor, (2) low noise, (3) high current and power gain, (4) resistance to radiation damage, (5) potentially good high-frequency response, and (6) *the entire absence of a 10 to 200 mV "off-set" voltage-effect for dc chopper applications*, as in the case of the bipolar transistor. The FETs are, therefore, preferred in certain applications at this time, but the types of circuits that can utilize them are as unlimited as those for a vacuum-tube pentode. In fact, like vacuum-tubes, developments toward additional gates do make this device better suitable for special-purpose circuit design.

A-2. JFET

In the extensively used *junction* FET, the control of the current takes place through a bar of N-type semiconductor material, such as silicon, diffused with a P-type semiconductor layer, to make the com-

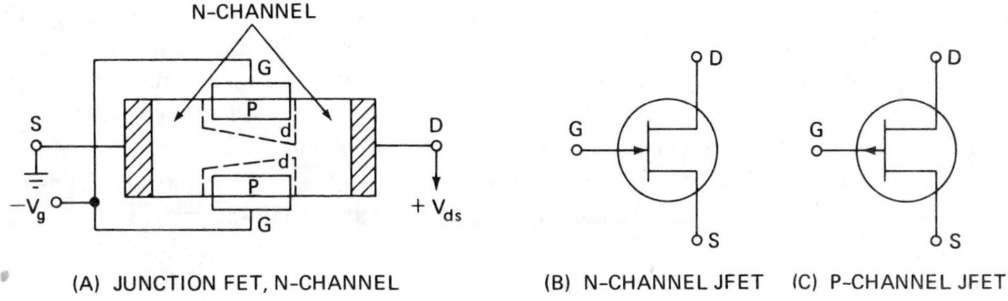

Fig. A-1. Junction FET, N- and P-channel types.

bination a PN-junction. The bar, then termed an *N-channel JFET*, starts to behave like a variable ohmic resistor. (The bar could be, as an alternative, a P-type semiconductor with an N-type layer to make a P-channel JFET.)

Figure A-1 illustrates the substrate and structure of the N-channel junction FET; the symbols of the N-channel/P-channel JFETs are included.

The terminal into which the current is injected is termed the *source*, since the electrons originate from this terminal. The other terminal of the N-channel through which the (majority) carriers flow is called the *drain*. The terminal attached to the diffused P-layer in this N-channel JFET is called the *gate*. The current between the source and the drain is related to the drain-to-source voltage (V_{ds}) by the resistance of the intervening N-channel material. As with any conventional PN junction, a *depletion* region[d] surrounds the junction of the FET *when the junction is reverse-biased.* With increase in reverse voltage, the depletion region extends into the entire N-channel to create an almost infinite resistance between source and drain. **The JFET is said to operate only in the depletion mode**, since the carriers decrease in the channel when a change in gate voltage takes place. The characteristic depletion mode applies to both P- and N-channel JFETs. With zero-gate voltage (V_g), as V_{ds} is increased, the depletion region spreads toward the drain, and a limiting action of drain current (I_d) commences, with a simultaneous increase in channel resistance in the bar or the substrate. The V_{ds} that causes the *current limiting condition* is called the *pinch-off voltage* (V_p), and the **pinch-off region thereon (Fig. A-4) is the region in which the FET operates in the mode of a high-impedance voltage amplifier.** The initial **ohmic region** is the region in which the linear variation, as a function of V_g, makes the device useful as **a voltage-controlled attenuator.** (As an obvious analogy, the terms *source*, *drain*, and *gate* correspond, respectively, to the cathode, plate, and control-grid of a vacuum-tube.)

The input characteristic of a FET is entirely different from that of the bipolar transistor, since, as far

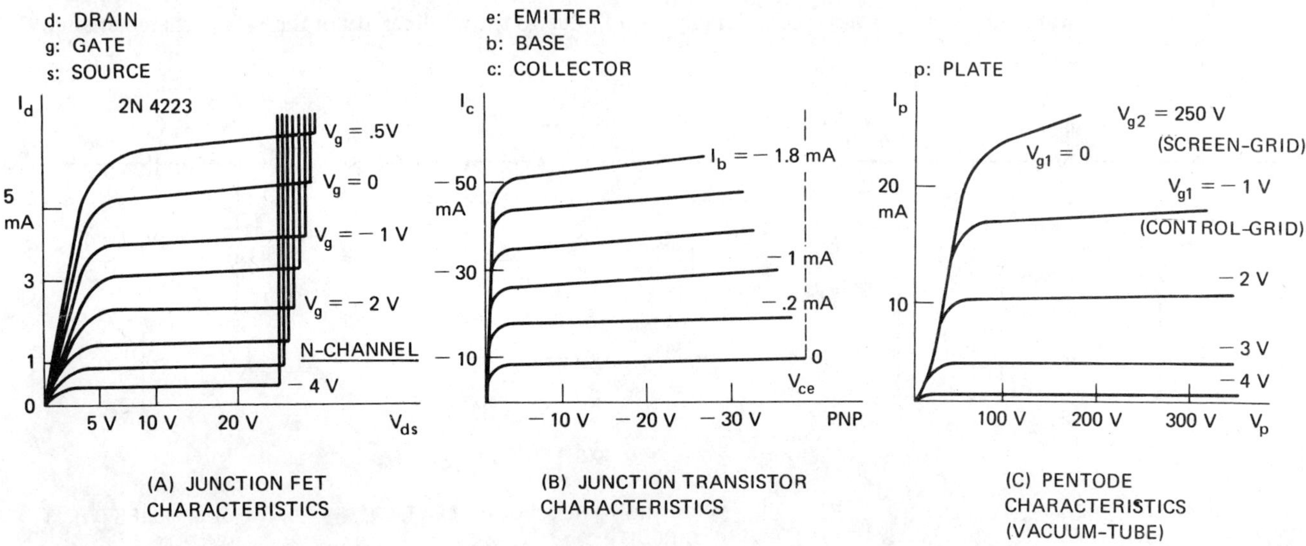

Fig. A-2. Junction FET and transistor characteristics.

as the input terminal is concerned, they act as *reverse- and forward-biased diodes*, respectively. The gate current of the FET is typically a few nanoamperes at a correspondingly high incremental impedance. The minute gate current is exponentially temperature-dependent. However, since a return path is provided for the gate current, the working input resistance is low enough so that, with temperature variation, the potential difference across it is materially insufficient to alter the gate-bias and I_d.

The drain-characteristics of low-voltage JFET are shown in Fig. A-2 as a comparison against the collector-characteristics of an ordinary bipolar junction transistor, and the plate-characteristics of a pentode. The junction transistor saturates at much lower voltages; however, like the transistor, the pentode exhibits, at different control-grid voltage readings, characteristics that run together below their respective saturation points. The pentode thus acts as a fixed resistor. On the other hand, the FET behaves, up to the pinch-off voltage, like a variable ohmic resistance, the value of which is naturally determined by V_g. (The **unijunction transistor or UJT**—also called a **double base diode**—appears similar to the JFET, but the junction in the case of the UJT is biased in the conducting direction to make it behave like the emitter of a transistor. **The UJT exhibits a negative-resistance characteristic** of an open-circuit-stable version at the emitter.)

With the measured and the calculated plots of the characteristics, the low-frequency equivalent circuit can be derived in the more common π-configuration, as shown in Fig. A-3A. A feedback-resistance R_{dg} of the order of the input resistance R_{gs} is a characteristic feature, although the effective feedback-voltage at the low-frequencies is negligble with a relatively low gate-return resistor of approximately 10-M ohm. At high video frequencies, besides the initial rise in admittance, there is a rise in conductance too, since the interterminal capacitances must be considered as being "lossy." The high-frequency equivalent circuit then takes the form shown in Fig. A-3B; a simplified high-frequency version for design purposes is given in Fig. A-3C. The applied-voltage V_{dd} and I_d have only a minor effect on the capacitances shown. Figure A-4A illustrates a "triode" and a "tetrode" connected JFET; Fig. A-4B identifies the "pinch-off" region of one of the V_{DS}/I_D characteristics of the JFET.

If I_{do} is the *saturated drain-current* with zero V_g, and g_m is the *mutual (trans)-conductance in mho* (mA/V), it can be shown that

$$g_m = \frac{\Delta I_d}{\Delta V_{gs}} = KI_{do}/V_p,$$

where K is a constant of value 2 to 3. (Due to its vacuum-tube analogy, the symbol g_m is often used in the place of the forward transadmittance y_{fs}.)

A FET with higher g_m is not necessarily better than that with a lower g_m, since the latter may have such desirable properties as lower input-capacitance and lower leakage-current as advantages in certain applications. With the latest low pinch-off voltage FETs, the drain-current variations with temperature are stabilized in a practical way by the choice of the optimum operating-point, and the appropriate signal-swing; otherwise, g_m varies considerably with I_d due to the nonlinearity of the I_d/V_{gs} characteristic.

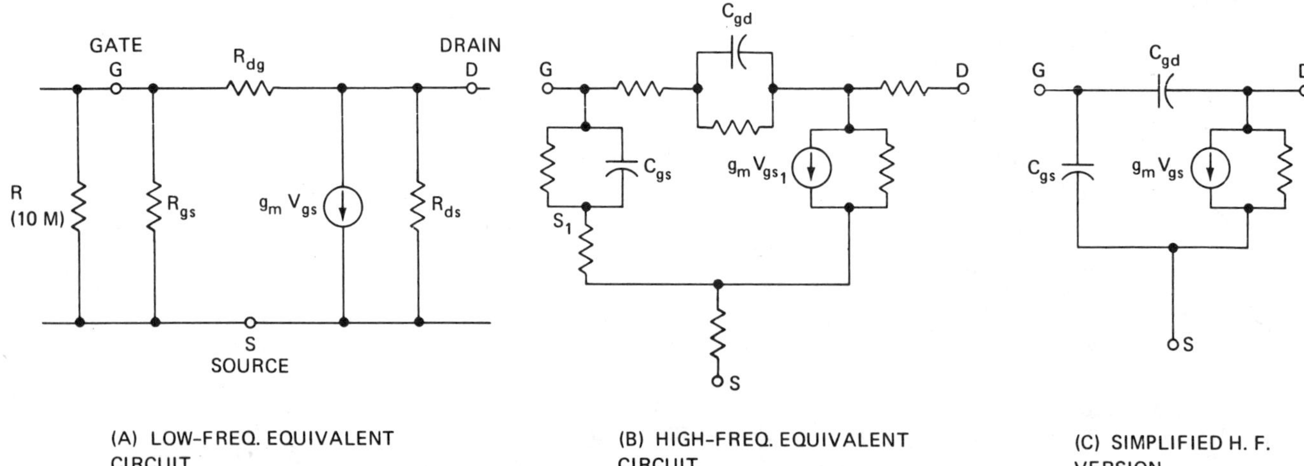

Fig. A-3. Equivalent circuits (low frequency and high frequency).

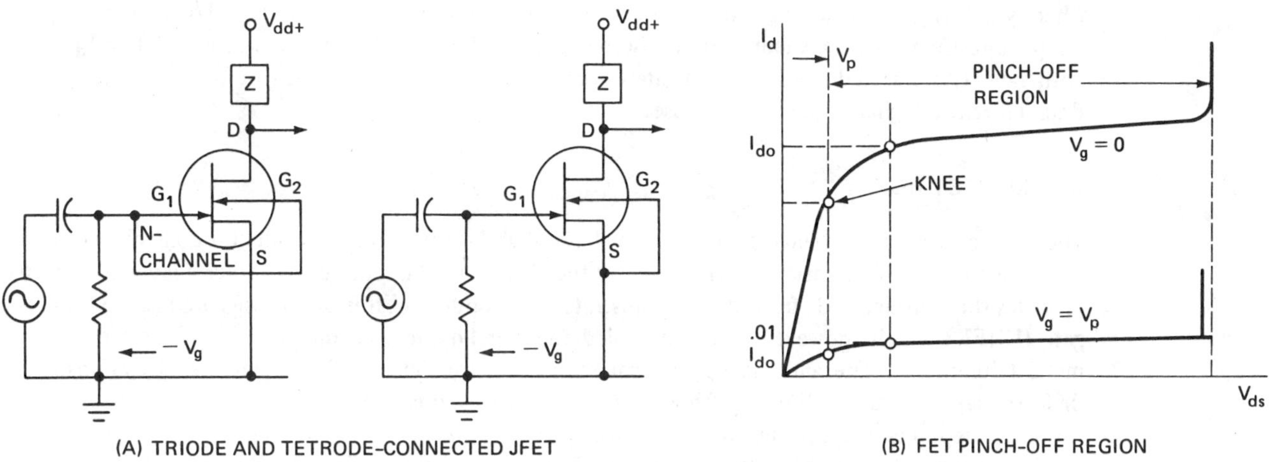

Fig. A-4. Triode and tetrode-connected JFETs; pinch-off.

The general processing technique of the JFET is shown in Fig. A-5. A substrate of P-type silicon makes the common basis for a number of FETs. P-type masked-diffusion is used to form the gates and the separation of the FETs. Since the N-channel lies between an upper and a lower gate of a P-region in this case, the two gates can be separated to make a more versatile device. The use of the upper gate alone allows the FET to be used with lower input-capacitance and gate-leakage, at the expense of some transconductance. With the two gates together, the g_m is increased at the expense of the gain-bandwidth product. Silicon N-channel dual-gate JFETs, having separate gate connections (like Motorola 3N124) are suitable in amplifier applications right from audio to VHF range. They have characteristic features such as high breakdown voltage and low transfer-capacitance, and a noise-figure as low as 2 to 4 dB at a source-resistance of 1 MΩ. Several silicon tetrode JFET numbers are, however, normally available with a common gate terminal only.

For tetrode-connected JFETs, three g_m measurements are usually specified in data sheets, one for the two gates tied together and the other for the two gates individually. For high-frequency devices, an additional g_m figure is specified at the highest frequency of operation. Since g_m (or y_{fs}) has both *real and imaginary components, the data sheets specify a general 1-kHz characteristic as an absolute magnitude* $|y_{fs}|$. The *real part* of y_{fs} is usually considered as a significant *figure-of-merit*. Since the *amplification-factor* μ *has little circuit significance for small-signal applications*, it is not specified.

$$\mu = y_{fs}/y_{os},$$

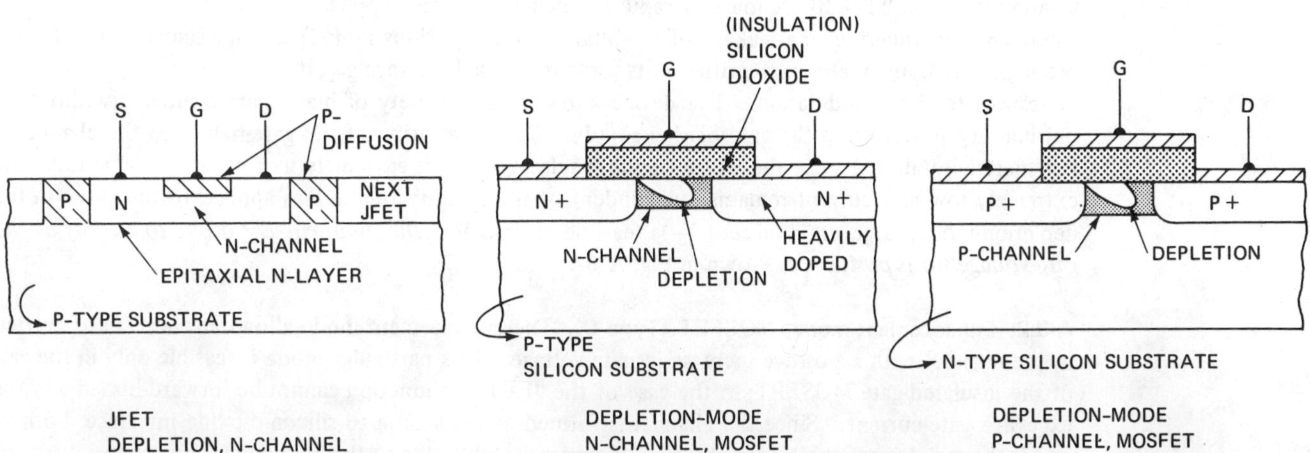

Fig. A-5. JFET, depletion mode—N- and P-channel types.

where $y_{os} = 1/r_d$ is the output-admittance. The output-admittance is analogous to $1/r_p$, the corresponding plate-resistance of the vacuum tube. Some specs of the tetrode-connected JFETs define I_d cutoff, with gate G_1 connected to source, and gate G_2 connected to bias supply; the gate voltage for the flow of drain current is higher in this specific case.

A-3. MOSFET (IGFET)

The second type of the field-effect transistor has a slightly different semiconductor control mechanism, although the current is basically controlled by the electric-field in both cases. **Since a layer of dielectric insulates the gate-electrode from the bar (substrate) semiconductor,** it is often designated as the **insulated-gate (IG)FET**. It is, however, generally called the **metal-oxide semiconductor (MOS)**, since a surface metal (aluminum) plate and the operational semiconductor "channel" are separated by an insulating dielectric-layer of silicon-dioxide. Thus, as the drain and source are in effect isolated by the substrate, the structure is analogous to *two diodes connected back-to-back.*

The structure of a typical **N-channel MOSFET** is shown in Fig. A-5. (The P-channel device will have semiconductor regions of opposite polarity).

In the case of the *junction* (J)FET, the "channel" is structurally present without any application of voltage to the gate, and it operates as a *depletion-mode device only* (normally-ON), since the application of gate-voltage (negative V_{gs}) depletes or decreases the number of carriers in the channel, while the gate acts like a reverse-biased P-N junction. On the other hand, *the MOSFET can have a structure to operate either as a depletion-mode device or as an enhancement-mode device* (normally-OFF). In the latter case, the application of a gate-voltage (positive V_{gs}) increases the number of carriers in the channel. *Unlike the JFET, the MOSFET merely acts like a reverse-biased diode without the initial formation of a "channel" in the absence of the bias* ($V_{gs} = 0$). Being a majority-carrier device in operation (like the JFET), hole-storage effects are not exhibited, as an advantage over the transistor. Since the depletion-mode MOSFET makes use of the same epitaxial techniques to form the "operational" channel, biasing techniques and equivalent circuits are similar to those of the JFET. The frequency response is, as usual, determined by the "dielectric relaxation time" of the semiconductor channel. *The MOSFETs are exceptionally immune to radiation.*

A.3.1. Depletion-mode, MOSFET (Type A). With an exclusive built-in, thin-surface N-layer, the device has characteristics of the form shown in Fig. A-6A. Positive gate-voltage can be used to increase the drain-current, and transconductance g_m (or y_{fs}) is approximately constant over a large range of current readings. Since the biasing and the equivalent circuits of the JFET hold good in this case, it can also be used as a high-impedance voltage-controlled device, exhibiting a general advantage of the *absence of the off-set voltage.*

Since the extremely high gate input-resistance (10^{15}) does not decrease with temperature up to 100°C, it is most suitable as a *high input-impedance device in low-power, small-signal applications.* The depletion-mode MOSFET is the choice in radio-frequency amplifier applications (television receiver, etc.) where *cross-modulation*, the leakage of modulation from spurious radio-frequency signals, is a common problem. With minimal nonlinearities in its forward-transadmittance g_m, it is superior to even a pentode in respect to cross-modulation. The device allows a wide variety of biasing arrangements without requiring any power from the gate biasing supply. The penetration of the gate-field into the channel is not materially altered since the width of the insulating layer is extremely narrow; at the same time, the extremely low gate-current remains independent of the polarity of the bias applied to the gate. In the depletion-mode, large drain-current I_d is feasible at zero V_{gs}; *the drain current drops to cut-off as the gate-voltage turns positive*, as shown in Fig. A-6A.

A-3.2. Enhancement-mode, MOSFET (Type C). The enhancement-mode allows an increase of carriers in the channel with a positive increase in gate-voltage. This particular mode is feasible only in the case of the insulated-gate MOSFET; in the case of the JFET, the junction cannot be forward-biased without excessive gate-current. Since the channel is formed at the silicon to silicon-dioxide interface, both N- and P-channel devices exhibit slightly slower carrier-mobility due to the incomplete crystal structure, unlike that in the case of the depletion-mode device. With an N-channel device, at a zero gate-voltage, since

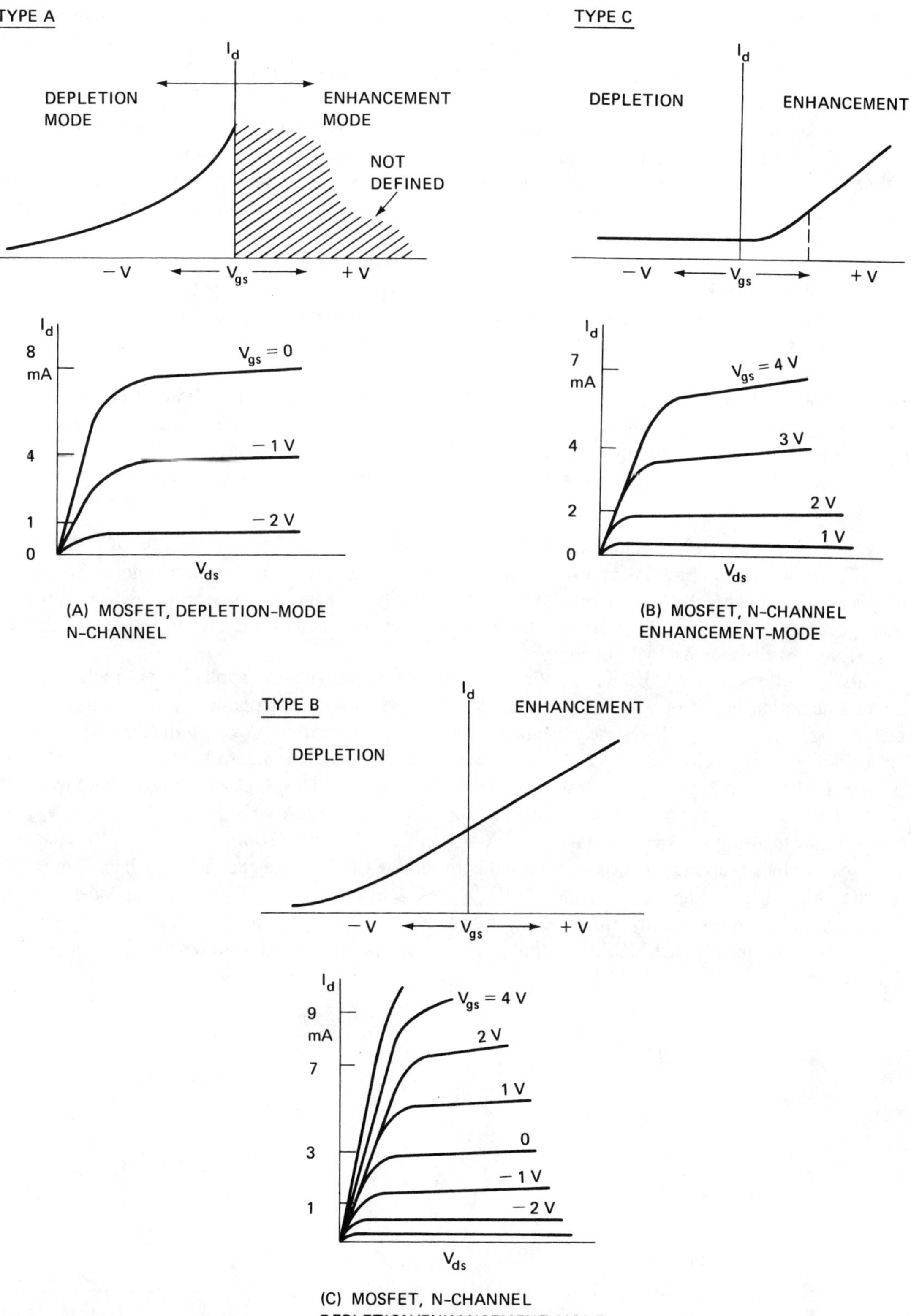

(A) MOSFET, DEPLETION-MODE N-CHANNEL

(B) MOSFET, N-CHANNEL ENHANCEMENT-MODE

(C) MOSFET, N-CHANNEL DEPLETION/ENHANCEMENT-MODE

Fig. A-6. MOSFET. Comparative characteristics–depletion and enhancement modes.

the drain P-N junction is reverse-biased, the drain-current off leakage is extremely low (approximately 0.05 nA); as the gate-voltage is made positive, a negative-charge in the form of the mobile electrons is induced at the surface of the semiconductor. With sufficient gate-voltage, the density of the induced electrons in the device overcomes the initial density of the positive holes in the P-type material to form an N-type channel at the semiconductor surface and allow the flow of current from the source to the drain. The device exhibits the characteristics of a pentode as shown in Fig. A-6B. Since the *enhancement-mode MOSFET* can operate with high-voltage, high-impedance, nonjunction gate characteristics without any off-set voltage, it is the best choice for *chopper or modulator applications.* (Example: Motorola MM2102.)

The gate-voltage required for compensating the surface-layer is known as *"threshold" voltage*; 8 V is a typical value. The threshold is the point at which the channel is completely formed for the flow of current between the source and the drain. For higher gate-voltages beyond this point, the transfer-characteristics are similar to those of the following *type-B, depletion/enhancement-mode MOSFET.*

A.3.3. Depletion/Enhancement-Mode MOSFET (Type B). A special-purpose device that can operate in both depletion and enchancement-modes has been produced; its characteristics are shown in Fig. A-6C. Gate 2 in this device is internally connected to the source terminal. This device exhibits considerable drain-current at zero gate-voltage. In addition, it may have usable forward-characteristics for large gate-voltages.

Note: The depletion and enhancement mode MOSFETs can be described as two distinct forms of the IGFET, as shown in Figs. A-7A and A-7B for the N-channel case, with an N-type channel and an N-type source and drain contacts. The channel is thus identified by the type of source and drain contacts used; this is contrary to the case of the JFET, since its channel is identified by the type of the bar (or the substrate) and not the source and drain contacts.

In the depletion-mode MOSFET, like the JFET, a negative voltage-bias applied to the metal-gate generates a depletion region in a bar of homogeneously doped N-type semiconductor, the extent of the depletion region increasing with the negative-bias. This mode of operation, in which the current due to the electron-flow in an N-channel device decreases with a negative-bias (or due to the hole-flow with a positive-bias in the case of a P-channel), is similar to that of the JFET. The *pinch-off voltage* V_p of the JFET is defined in practice as *the V_{gs} that reduces I_d to 1% of its zero gate-voltage value* (I_{do}), at a V_{ds} that is two times the output "knee"-voltage (Fig. A-4). In the pinch-off region, a portion of the channel is depleted of charge-carriers by the electric field between the gate and the channel; the channel-resistance is hence very high. In the case of the MOSFET, $V_p = V_{ds}$ at the knee itself. If the insulated-gate in this case overlaps source region only, it is referred to as a *half-gate*, or *off-set gate*, or partial-gate MOSFET.

In the enhancement-mode MOSFET, the current from the drain to the source travels in a thin con-

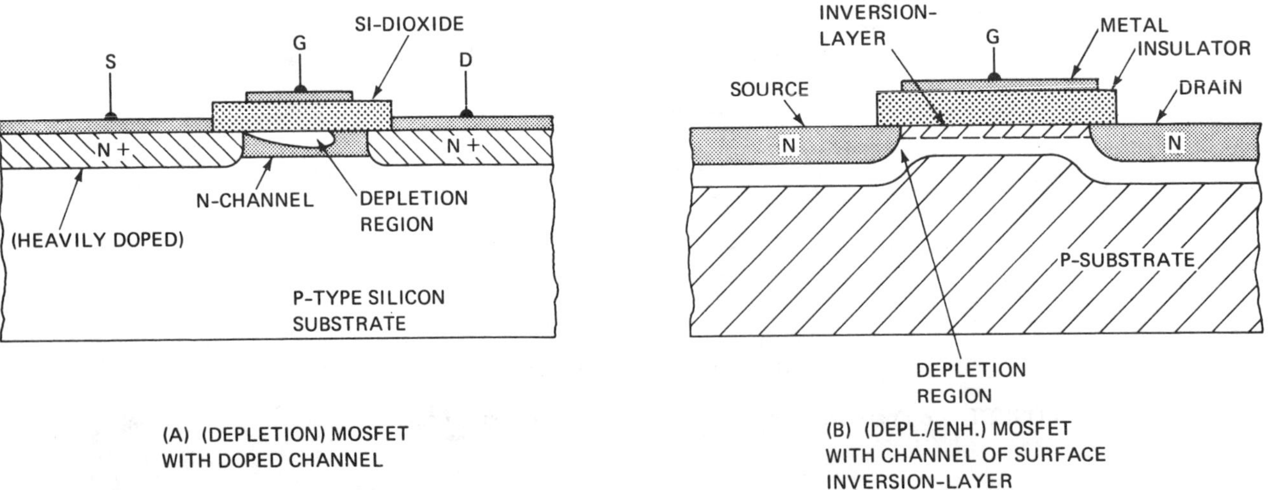

(A) (DEPLETION) MOSFET WITH DOPED CHANNEL

(B) (DEPL./ENH.) MOSFET WITH CHANNEL OF SURFACE INVERSION-LAYER

Fig. A-7. Depletion- and enhancement-mode configurations of MOSFET.

ducting surface-layer called the *surface inversion-layer channel.* This layer is formed in the case of an N-channel device at the surface of a lightly doped N-type semiconductor, as a result of the application of an electric-field that is perpendicular to the surface; the charge may be located either on the gate-electrode or built into the oxide-insulator. The said charge will induce a mobile charge of equal magnitude and opposite polarity on the surface of the semiconductor, and the conducting channel is determined by the built-in charge only. The pinch-off in this case is hence accomplished by an equal amount of the charge of opposite polarity on the gate-electrode. The inversion-layer, in the case of an enhancement-mode device, is thus supplied with an unlimited number of electrons from a highly doped source contact. As mentioned earlier, a combination of the two forms, depletion-cum-enhancement mode, is available for special applications.

A-4. THIN-FILM TRANSISTOR

The vacuum-evaporated, thin-film, insulated-gate, field-effect transistor (TFT) is a microelectronics version parallel to the integrated-circuit type of MOSFET in single-crystal silicon chips. The TFT, however, has the "channel" deposited by vacuum-evaporation as a thin layer (0.04 mil) of polycrystalline cadmium-sulfide (or selenide) semiconductor, with metal electrodes of evaporated gold (0.2 to 2 mils) as the source and drain. Along with a silicon-monoxide insulating-film and an evaporated gold gate-electrode, the TFT consists of just four superimposed layers. The substrate structure is a matter of relatively simple vacuum-evaporation on an inexpensive, inert, insulating substrate such as glass, since the cadmium-sulfide technology will enable the fabrication of both IGFETs and passive components on a common substrate such as glass. An encapsulating nonporous film-deposit of silicon-dioxide (or selenium) makes an overall protective coating against possible contamination. The principle of redundancy, with one FET element replaced by a group of two or four identical elements (if one or two elements become faulty), is a feasible proposition in the case of the FETs only, provided adequate precautions are taken regarding a built-in input-resistance of an appropriate value in the gate-lead. The TFT is used as a diode in integrated-circuits by simply connecting the gate to the drain; the resulting diode-characteristic therefore naturally depends upon the pinch-off voltage.

TFTs operating in enhancement-mode permit direct-coupling between several stages of amplification. Also, complementary-circuits and low-drain flip-flops can be easily fabricated on one and the same substrate by depositing common electrodes for both N- and P-channel cadmium-sulfide cells. Figure A-8 illustrates the semiconductor structure of the TFT, Insulated-Gate FET, and its enhancement-mode and depletion-mode characteristics.

The TFT operates both in enhancement and depletion modes (like the type-B MOSFET), with a relatively large energy-gap (as compared to that of the MOSFET); the induced semiconductor "channel" is due to the injection of electrons (majority carriers) at the source. As a close analogy to the vacuum tube, relatively few thermally generated charge-carriers are present in the semiconductor channel at room temperature. The TFT displays both the high input-impedance and the typical well-saturated pentode-like characteristics of the MOSFET. Except for digital logic, the TFT technology is not applicable to linear circuits yet, since the production of low-noise TFTs is still a research problem. The performance of the more-expensive MOS silicon thinfilm FETs, using a sapphire substrate, is reported to be far superior to the cadmium-sulfide TFTs, which use the inexpensive glass substrate.

The TFTs are, in principle, more radiation-resistant than MOSFETs, because evaporated films are highly disordered, and any damage to crystal structure by radiation should make negligible difference to the operation of the device.

Cadmium-sulfide TFTs, having a gain-bandwidth product of 22 MHz and band-pass resonant characteristics of up to 70 MHz, have been produced; however, the stability of the drain characteristics with aging is still a problem.

A-5. LARGE-SCALE INTEGRATION

The large-scale integration (LSI) of a large number of prefabricated integrated-circuits is accomplished at this time in both experimental and high-technology projects. Both conventional monolithic-silicon transistor circuit-configurations, and MOS/TFT field-effect, transistor circuit-configurations are involved,

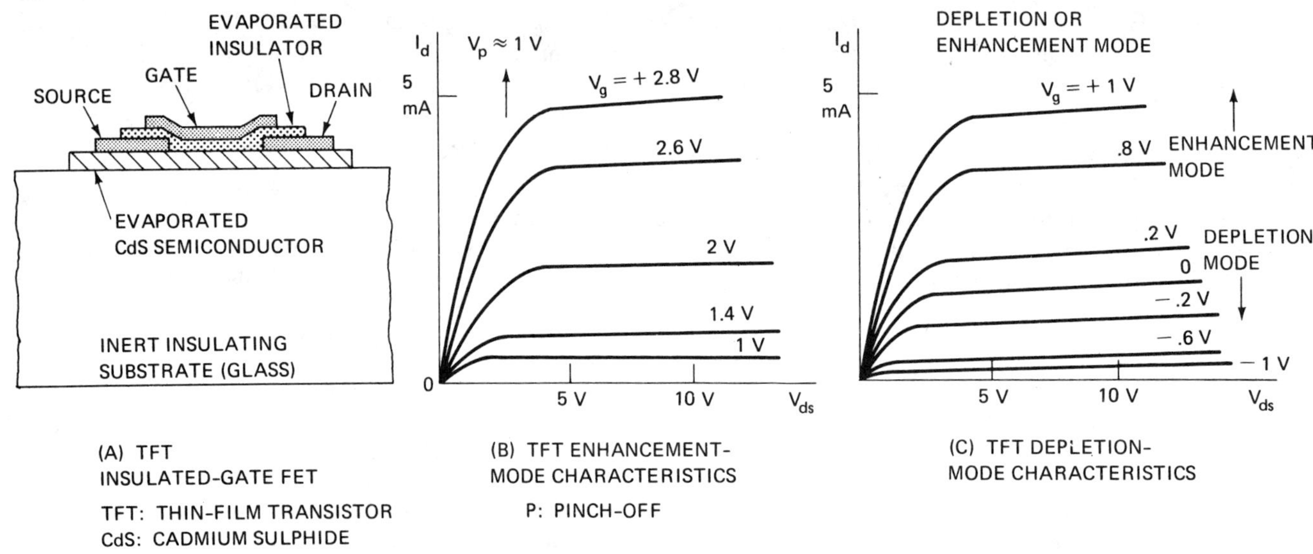

Fig. A-8. Thin-film-transistor MOSFET characteristics.

on a competitive basis, in this latest revolutionary approach in the low-power solid-state microelectronics field. At the moment, complete prefabricated LSI system chips of this character are making their appearance surprisingly novel in computers, avionics, space, and Defense electronics. Since capacitors and resistors, in this order, take relatively more area than the active transistor elements, economical LSI systems require, as a principle, *minimization of the number of passive components*—in contrast to normal discrete component circuit design.

Monolithic-silicon integrated-circuits have the disadvantage of an extra *parasitic-capacitance associated with the substrate, PN isolation diode structure*. Therefore, the latest thin-film transistor (TFT) technology, making use of an inexpensive insulating substrate of virtually unlimited size, scores an advantage, where larger circuit-configurations and higher speeds are required—as in the case of the digital computer. The evaporated polycrystalline cadmium-sulfide TFTs, in particular, provide both enhancement- and

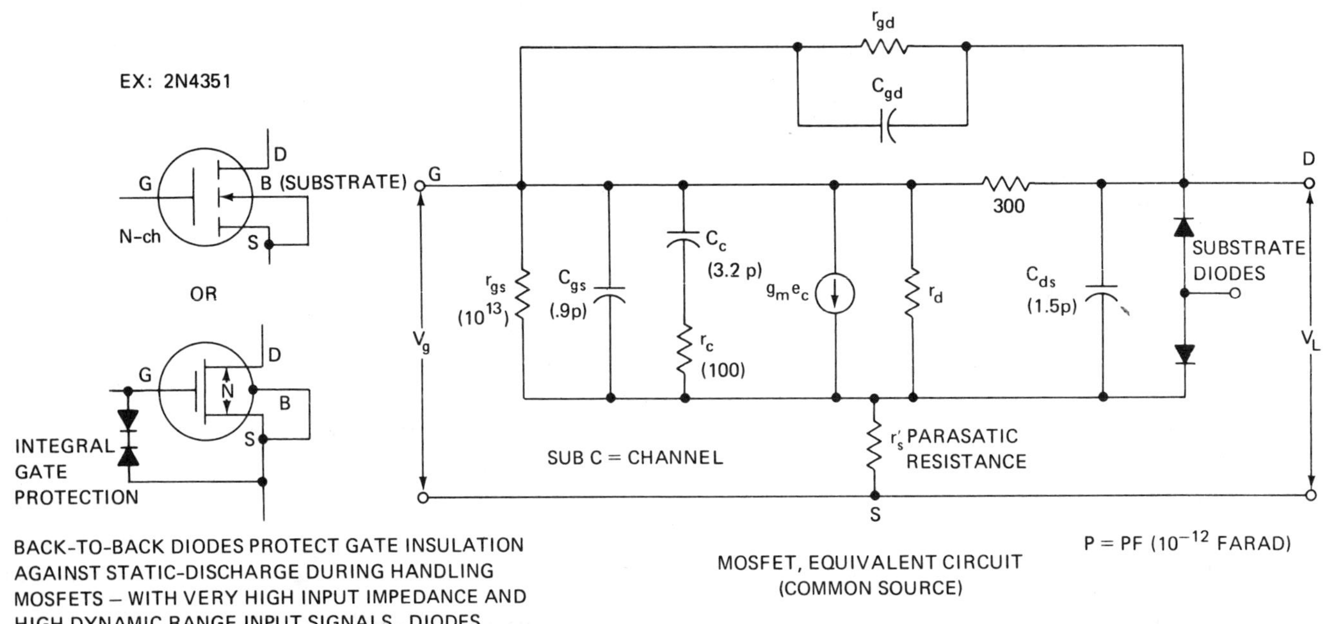

Fig. A-9. MOSFET, equivalent circuit (common source).

depletion-type MOSFETs with high input-impedance and well-saturated vacuum-tube pentode-like characteristics. The enhancement- and depletion-mode characteristics are primarily determined by the process control of V_p, and the gate-voltage required for the pinch-off of the drain-current. Since thin-film MOSFET techniques allow low-cost, low-power, high fan-out, and high noise-immunity operation, they appear to be ideal for LSI in low-speed logic applications.

As an example, to replace the cathode-ray picture tube, experimental thin-film horizontal and vertical scanning circuit-configurations, incorporating several TFTs, have been experimentally processed to operate a solid-state image-panel with photosensitive (or light-emitting) array of diode elements. This is an advance in the direction of a futuristic concept of television.

Nevertheless, there are still several problems associated with stability, speed, and aging in the cadmium-sulfide TFT technology; active research is in progress with silicon thin-film transistors, employing a silicon-layer deposited upon a sapphire single-crystal substrate. This single-crystal technology, with superior performance in solving some of the aforementioned problems, has, however, the demerit of higher cost and limited size for LSI, due to the single-crystal substrate requirement. At present [1966], the scope of the LSI is definitely *limited*, and it is not yet a revolutionary threat to conventional system designs using hybrid transistor-FET-IC circuit-configurations on PC boards (*at least for the next 5 years or so!*). The complexity of an equivalent circuit of a common-source MOSFET is depicted in Fig. A-9. Computer-aided design for analysis and synthesis is conventionally accomplished by way of these equivalent circuits and the effective circuit parameters at the microdimensions involved.

A-6. CURRENT STATUS

In contrast to the premature status of MOS over a decade ago, the current status of NMOS/CMOS technology as LSI/VLSI is an explosive phenomenon in applications. The heavy demand of LSI/VLSI products at this opportune moment is prompting microelectronics manufacturers to production innovation and more and more automation in order to meet the exigencies of competition. Texas Instruments' **Electron-beam lithography** is one of the leading processing techniques. Other common processing steps are X-ray lithography, ion-beam milling, automated diffusion (doping) techniques under mini-or micro-computer control, and **plasma-etched silicon nitride (Si_3N_4) film-deposition for passivation of** 3-to-5-in.-diameter silicon wafers. The previously well-established "contact printing" is giving way to the latest **noncontact "projection printing" from mask to the wafer** for higher yields of memories, microprocessors, and calculators. Etching, ion-implantation, and metallization are to be automated in the near future.

In view of the unlimited scope of the variety of applications, NMOS/CMOS LSI/VLSI technology is put to work by some manufacturers on a **custom basis along several different processing techniques simultaneously**. Depending on the ceiling of costs planned in custom-designed LSI/VLSI, American Microsystems, Inc. (AMI) employs seven parallel MOS LSI/VLSI processing technologies for the applications noted hereafter. The characteristics of the LSI chips processed according to the various approaches are briefly summarized in Table A-1 (using the information available from AMI). Latest VLSI is achieved by scaling down the LSI design and by refining advanced X-ray or electron-beam lithographic processing of silicon "real-estate" (substrate) to 5- to 1-micron dimensions.

The custom designs rarely use the regular off-the-shelf microprocessor types and available interface chips for the custom applications, because this systems approach is more expensive for OEMs who, in the case of microprocessors, deal in quantities of 30 to 40 thousand chips. That is, **the custom LSI designs optimize respective logic, control, ROM/RAM memories, and interface circuits** right on one single chip. Most of the logic design talent and systems innovators are therefore attracted to these custom-design houses. AMI employs a laser interferometer pattern generator to prepare special tooling plates, which shrink the chip circuitry for greater yield per wafer. Custom designs are preferred by a substantial percentage of the OEMs because the application enjoys a high degree of confidentiality between the **Custom Design House (CDH) and the OEM.**

The AMI custom applications, as of the present, belong to the following categories:

1. **Business Equipment**: scientific, printing and business calculators, coin changers, vending machines
2. **Terminal/Peripheral Devices**: fast line printers, keyboard scanners, point-of-sales terminals, code converters, character generators, credit-card verifiers

TABLE A-1. Comparison of MOS/LSI processing techniques (*Courtesy of American Micro Systems, Inc.*)*

1. PMOS–High Voltage, Metal-Gate	2. PMOS–Ion-Implanted Metal-Gate	3. PMOS–Si-Gate	4. CMOS
1. Simplest and most widely used with highest yield. 2. Lowest production cost/wafer. 3. High noise immunity. Best for mechanical equipment generating rf noise. 4. Relatively high power-dissipation with high voltage requirement. 5. Difficult to interface with bipolar TTL circuits. 6. Larger chips acceptable (5″-diameter wafers for higher yields).	1. Used in standard memory products and custom chip applications. 2. Best for flexibility of logic design. 3. Similar to PMOS process-1 with two additional steps. 4. Ion implantation of gate areas reduce device thresholds to low-voltage levels, but high-field thresholds are retained. 5. Second ion implantation in selected areas reduces thresholds to depletion mode. 6. Depletion-mode load transistors increase device speed, noise margins, bipolar interface acceptability. 7. Single unregulated voltage supply.	1. Mostly used for memory applications. 2. Self-aligning fabrication eliminates masking tolerance problems with smaller transistor structures. 3. A third layer of interconnect reduces cell area and interconnections. 4. Self-aligning gate structure minimizes gate capacitance. 5. Circuits faster than PMOS-1. 6. Low voltage device, but much slower than NMOS-7. 7. Simplicity of technique with higher yields.	1. Draw minute static power at low speeds. Power consumed only during switching. At higher frequency logic, power dissipation increases. Best for low power-consumption with single voltage supply. 2. Also best for noise immunity. 3. On-chip clock generation is feasible. 4. Good bipolar compatibility of processors and memories. 5. Best for power-supply variation, 1.5 to 15 V (trade low-voltage level against speed). 6. Good speed per unit area. 7. Silicon-on-Sapphire CMOS is very fast, like Bipolar and I^2L. 8. CMOS ideal (like I^2L) for electronic watches, clocks, memories (rendered nonvolatile with standby battery cells). 9. Best for automotive electronics requiring low standby current and high noise-immunity.
5. NMOS–Si-Gate	**6. NMOS–Ion-Implanted Si-Gate**	**7. NMOS–Ion-Implanted Si-Gate with Depletion Loads**	
1. Faster than PMOS counterparts. 2. Allows high-speed and high-density designs with silicon-gate. 3. Bipolar compatibility ideal, since logic circuit output is positive with respect to ground (as for NPN discrete transistors). 4. Area per logic function minimal, but speed per unit area average. 5. Ideal for high-speed dynamic RAMs.	1. Ion implantation in field areas allows high-field thresholds without thick field-insulating oxides. 2. Gate regions are implanted to establish control of device thresholds. 3. Single voltage supply allowed for highest packing with average performance (NMOS with electron charge-carriers faster than PMOS). 4. Self-aligned feature of process. 5. Ideal bipolar compatibility. 6. Extra layer of interconnect in Si-gate reduces chip interconnect area.	1. High-performance process with complex processing like CMOS. Ideal for microprocessors and memories. 2. Has all the advantages of the inherent NMOS process. 3. Ion-implanted Si-gate process and depletion-load allow best performance with highest speed, minimum area per gate, best flexibility of logic design, and high latitude of single-voltage power supply.	

*See Sections 2-9 and 2-10 for VLSI.
†Double-polysilicon-layer P^2CMOS: See pages 227 and 504.

3. **Government and Defense Work**: security communications links and satellites, lunar landers, Mars Viking landers, inertial guidance microcomputers, sonabuoys.
4. **Industry and Instrumentation**: industrial timers, X-Y plotters, environmental controls, medical monitoring equipment, digital thermometers
5. **Communications and Navigation**: facsimile transmission systems, data modems, switching systems, telephone equipment, police-band radio
6. **Consumer Products**: ignition systems, automotive clock, fuel injection, antiskid braking, oven range-controls, dryer controls, jukeboxes, radio functions, television tuners, hi-fi tuners, citizen's-band radio, video games, garage-door openers, burglar alarms, water-sprinkler controls, sewing machines, etc.

The silicon-on-sapphire CMOS, as anticipated, is currently a successful high-speed LSI technology, using the so-called **local-oxidation** LOS (LOSOS) technique. A total of 300 transistors are packed in each square millimeter on the **sapphire base**, and the processed P- and N-type silicon substrates are packed over the base. A comparatively thick **silicon-nitride layer (involving two "key elements")** is sandwiched between silicon-dioxide layers during processing to minimize leakage contamination and parasitic capacitances and to increase speed. The latest 16-bit, CMOS-on-Sapphire microcomputer chip rivals bipolar devices in performance at an 8-MHz maximum clock-rate. Four LSI chips make a complete Hewlett-Packard microcomputer system with a basic speed of 125 ns and a nominal power-dissipation of 100 mW/chip at 12 V:

1. **16-bit CMOS-on-Sapphire (CPU/MCC) microcomputer chip**
2. 8,192-bit ROM with an access time of 50 ns
3. 2,048-bit static RAM with an access time of 80 ns
4. a single-chip peripheral Interface PHI (consisting of 8000 CMOS transistors) to meet the IEEE-488, 16-line, I/O bus-standard.

The MCC uses a parallel asynchronous bus to directly address up to 65-K memory locations, and 2,048 external I/O registers required for peripheral control. Some 34 groups of instructions require cycle-times from 750 ns to 1.5 μs; 16-bit register-to-register addition takes 875 ns. The RAM requires only 50 μW during battery standby (for nonvolatility of memory).

See Sections 2-9 and 2-10 for information on VLSI. VHSIC—Very high-speed integrated circuits are a further development to apply VLSI technology to Defense requirements.

Appendix B

Original I^2L with Discrete Bipolar Transistors (1960)—and the Latest LSI Bipolar I^2L Technology (1977)

A variation of the concept of the bipolar integrated-injection-logic (I^2L) *was originally developed and used by the author* during the years of his solid-state **discrete-transistor** circuit-design experience. He achieved highly reliable, medium-speed low-power analog/digital signal-processing results in several projects by invariably adapting a variation of this circuit in principle—by cascading PNP and NPN transistor-pairs as basic building blocks. The technique avoided the confrontation of worst-case design problems with both germanium and silicon transistors.

The PNP/NPN transistor-pair is tied to a common negative voltage supply, and the NPN transistor is operated in its forward active or cut-off region to avoid saturation and time-delay (at very low and high pulse-repetition intervals, or PRIs), while the PNP transistor simultaneously functions as a current source to the NPN transistor.

The following design example (Fig. B-1) was also published during 1966 as an incidental part of the author's Ph.D. dissertation to point out its merit as a reliable noise-immune signal-processing technique while he was describing an impulse-immune, medium-speed, digital/analog, phase-lock, high-precision position-control system. He developed this vacuum-guide digital feedback control system for the RCA quadruplex color videotape recorders used in broadcast color television transmission. The following two cascaded pairs had the ability to completely ignore low- or high-PRI periodic or nonperiodic impulse noise at an amplitude, far above 100 times that of the minute input analog error signal actually processed at a rate of 960 Hz/sec. In the discrete PNP-NPN transistor circuit configuration of I^2L technique shown in Fig. B-1, the PNP stage that, in principle, functions as a current source to the following NPN, is simultaneously improvised as a signal handling stage in view of the discrete status of the PNP and NPN transistor pairs. It will be noted that the germanium crystal diodes used in the above circuit serve the same high-speed switching function as the Schottky-diode complements of the present I^2L circuits.

Incidentally, the 2-W output push-pull class-AB transistor power-output stage associated with this digital position servo employs a PNP-NPN series-mode on either arm of an "Avalanche" high-sensitivity low-current power-amp. This circuit, developed also as a "first" of its kind, is shown in Fig. B-2. (The "Avalanche" effect was independently discovered by the author in 1958; he applied the concept to use the back-porch reference subcarrier burst of a color television signal to directly operate a relay by means of one ordinary PNP transistor. It was later learned that a paper was published a few months earlier on the theory of the "delayed collector conduction." The term *Avalanche* was coined during the 1960s.)

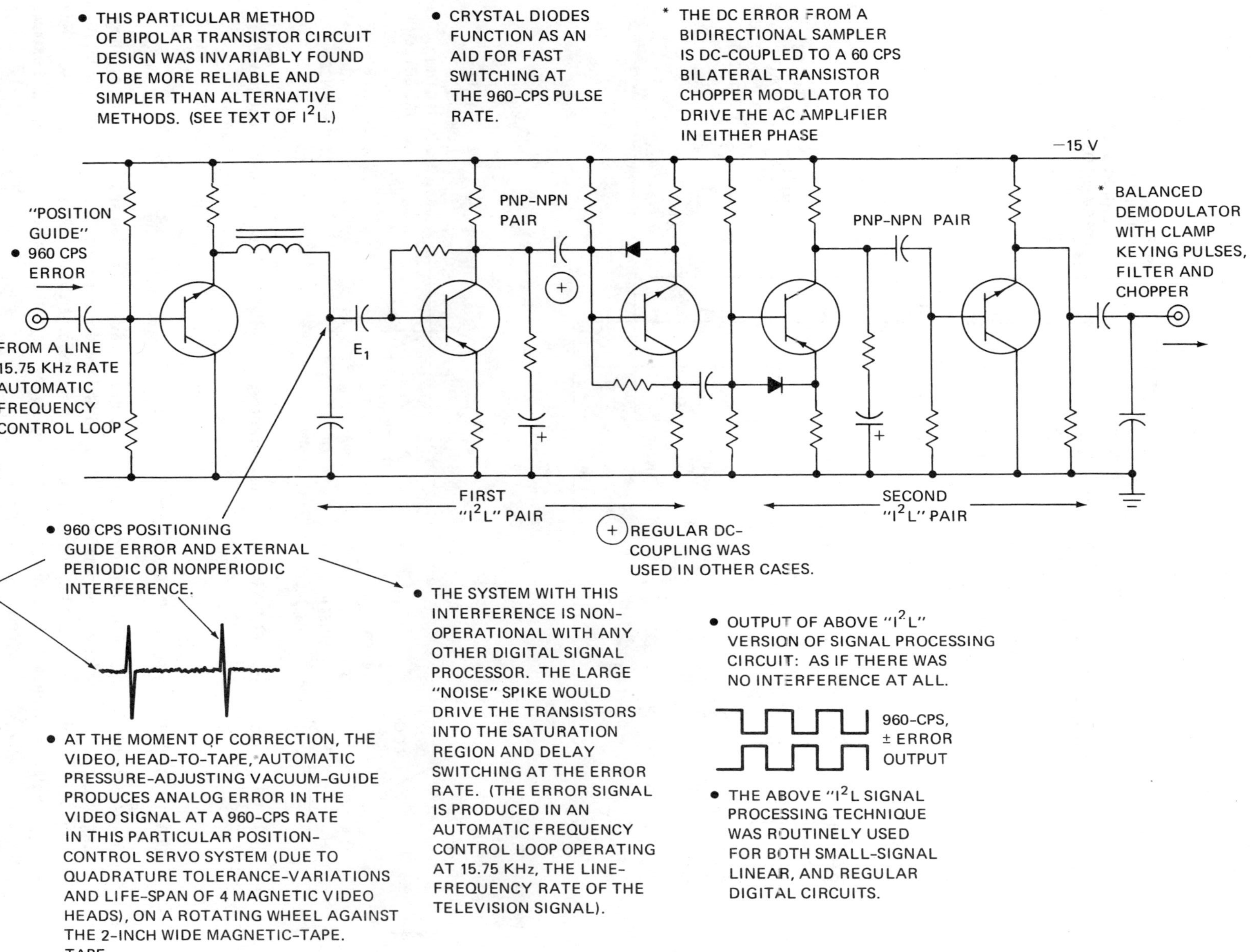
• THIS PARTICULAR METHOD OF BIPOLAR TRANSISTOR CIRCUIT DESIGN WAS INVARIABLY FOUND TO BE MORE RELIABLE AND SIMPLER THAN ALTERNATIVE METHODS. (SEE TEXT OF I²L.)
• CRYSTAL DIODES FUNCTION AS AN AID FOR FAST SWITCHING AT THE 960-CPS PULSE RATE.
* THE DC ERROR FROM A BIDIRECTIONAL SAMPLER IS DC-COUPLED TO A 60 CPS BILATERAL TRANSISTOR CHOPPER MODULATOR TO DRIVE THE AC AMPLIFIER IN EITHER PHASE
−15 V
"POSITION GUIDE"
• 960 CPS ERROR
FROM A LINE 15.75 KHz RATE AUTOMATIC FREQUENCY CONTROL LOOP
E1
PNP-NPN PAIR
PNP-NPN PAIR
* BALANCED DEMODULATOR WITH CLAMP KEYING PULSES, FILTER AND CHOPPER
FIRST "I²L" PAIR
SECOND "I²L" PAIR
+ REGULAR DC-COUPLING WAS USED IN OTHER CASES.
• 960 CPS POSITIONING GUIDE ERROR AND EXTERNAL PERIODIC OR NONPERIODIC INTERFERENCE.
• AT THE MOMENT OF CORRECTION, THE VIDEO, HEAD-TO-TAPE, AUTOMATIC PRESSURE-ADJUSTING VACUUM-GUIDE PRODUCES ANALOG ERROR IN THE VIDEO SIGNAL AT A 960-CPS RATE IN THIS PARTICULAR POSITION-CONTROL SERVO SYSTEM (DUE TO QUADRATURE TOLERANCE-VARIATIONS AND LIFE-SPAN OF 4 MAGNETIC VIDEO HEADS), ON A ROTATING WHEEL AGAINST THE 2-INCH WIDE MAGNETIC-TAPE. TAPE.
• THE SYSTEM WITH THIS INTERFERENCE IS NON-OPERATIONAL WITH ANY OTHER DIGITAL SIGNAL PROCESSOR. THE LARGE "NOISE" SPIKE WOULD DRIVE THE TRANSISTORS INTO THE SATURATION REGION AND DELAY SWITCHING AT THE ERROR RATE. (THE ERROR SIGNAL IS PRODUCED IN AN AUTOMATIC FREQUENCY CONTROL LOOP OPERATING AT 15.75 KHz, THE LINE-FREQUENCY RATE OF THE TELEVISION SIGNAL).
• OUTPUT OF ABOVE "I²L" VERSION OF SIGNAL PROCESSING CIRCUIT: AS IF THERE WAS NO INTERFERENCE AT ALL.
960-CPS, ± ERROR OUTPUT
• THE ABOVE "I²L SIGNAL PROCESSING TECHNIQUE WAS ROUTINELY USED FOR BOTH SMALL-SIGNAL LINEAR, AND REGULAR DIGITAL CIRCUITS.

Fig. B-1. Original discrete PNP-NPN circuit configuration of I^2L signal processing, 1960. (Actual circuit used in the production run of RCA quadruplex color videotape recorders.)

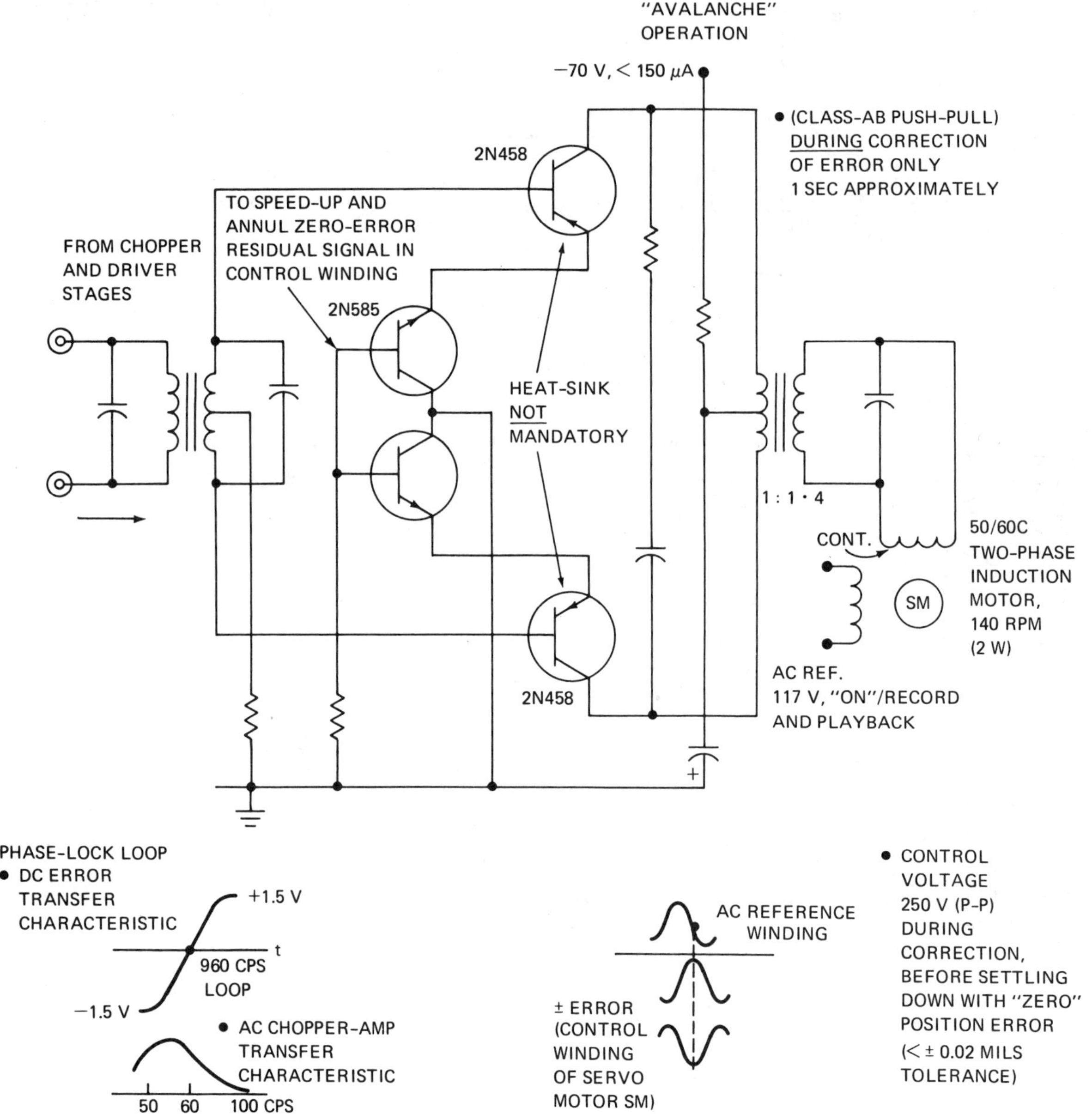

Fig. B-2. "Avalanche" serial PNP-NPN push-pull output stage. High-sensitivity low-current power-output circuit for high-speed position servo.

STATUS OF THE I^2L TECHNOLOGY (1981)

The **preceding reference** to the original discrete transistor version **of the bipolar I^2L circuits, as a beginning,** is just to give an idea of **the simplicity and capabilities of this concept.** The fairly recent revolution in monolithic microelectronics has rediscovered this basic concept afresh—to enable the high-speed low-density bipolar technology to compete and stand on its own against the rapidly developing and expanding high-density NMOS technology.

Actually, I^2L scores an **advantage over NMOS** in two important areas: (1) high-density high-speed applications at significantly lower power-dissipation, and (2) applications that require processing of both analog/linear and digital circuits, "merged" on one and the same chip.

Fairchild Micro Systems has recently applied a **dielectric isolation** technique to I^2L processing to introduce the speed- and density-enhanced **Isoplanar-I^2L** (with its registered trademark, I^3L). This technology attains the performance level of the low-power Schottky TTL with speeds on the order of 5 to 10 ns, at high densities comparable to those of the latest NMOS. By using dielectric-isolation with silicon-dioxide, probably in conjunction with silicon-nitride Si_3N_4. (as in the latest NMOS and CMOS-on-Sapphire technology), Isoplanar-I^2L has scored improvements in power-delay product (from 1 to 0.1 pJ), speed (from over 10 ns to over 5 ns) and density (from 150 to 300 gates/mm^2). In order to enhance the functional density of I^2L, the lateral PNP transistor electron-injector in cascade is presently replaced by a common vertical PNP transistor-injector for several high-speed Schottky I^2L gates (that characteristically limit current-swing as an immunity against impulse noise).

Motorola has a corresponding C^3L/I^2L processing technique (called **complementary constant-current logic**) to meet the same objectives.

Texas Instruments (TI), however, is the first research establishment and manufacturer to market a **16-bit I^2L microprocessor chip** to compete with the recent low-power 16-bit CMOS-on-Sapphire LSI chip at comparable speed, and potentially greater reliability at higher temperatures. TI uses a **nonisolated I^2L version** that can operate at 1 V and draw 500 mA, dissipating just about half-a-watt. The emitter of the NPN and the base of the PNP are tied to the substrate. Thus, TI expects to accomplish **very large-scale-integration (VLSI)** at density levels from 2,000 to 10,000 transistors per chip. However, for greater functional flexibility, TI employs, especially in the case of the memories, a **fully isolated technique** with more complex processing and lower yields. There is a Fairchild Microsystems version also.

In telecommunication applications, I^2L is found to score an advantage over conventional CMOS in operation at 1.75 V, from the viewpoint of reliability at higher temperatures. (CMOS-on-Sapphire may be equally competitive in this respect.) Using dry etching and oxide isolation, TI has recently developed a **"walled-emitter" I^2L** processing technique that uses even less power than the present I^2L versions, to enable 5-ns propagation-delays at very low power-dissipation in 4-K and 16-K bit static RAMs and 16-bit and 32-bit microprocessors.

At this point in time, it is known that in development laboratories, I^2L circuits are operating at clock-rates approaching 20 MHz. And, at this rate of progress in high-density LSI bipolar and MOS technologies, it would not be a surprise if the two coexisting technologies reach the goal of the fastest MECL-III series logic–namely, 1 ns per gate–during the present decade. (See Section 2-10.)

Appendix C

Data Communications via Satellites: Microprocessors Are All Set to Play a Major Role

Within 15 years after the first launch of the Synchronous Satellite, *Early Bird*, in a geostationary equatorial orbit, 35,800 km (22,246 miles) above the Atlantic Ocean, seven Intelsat-IV Satellites launched by Atlas/Centour rockets over the Atlantic, Pacific, and Indian Oceans, are maintaining full-time, global commercial real-time telephone, television-broadcast, and data communications, in conjunction with about 120 Earth Station Terminals located in 75 countries. COMSAT of Washington, D.C., is the Systems Manager for the Intelsat Satellites. The Earth Stations operate under the individual responsibility of the respective nations. The new small Earth Stations hereon will be independently operated by any small-business enterprise. (One day in the future, satellite receivers will be available as consumer products.)

C-1. INTELSAT-IV SATELLITES

The present series of Intelsat-IV (17′ H × 9′ D) built by Hughes Aircraft Co. and weighing 720 kg in orbit, are equipped with 12 Transponders (repeaters) operating FM/FDMA (Frequency Division with Multiple Access) in the 6-GHz band on the receiving *uplink*, and down-converted and amplified to the 4-GHz band on the transmitting *downlink*. The fixed-gain, single down-conversion 12-transponder design is bandwidth-limited to 34 MHz per channel with a 4-MHz guard-band and a total RF-bandwidth of 480 MHz. The solar array, consisting of 4,500 silicon cells and generating about 470 W, enables each 5-W traveling-wave tube amplifier (TWTA) in the effective transponder(s) at any instant to provide about 180 W or 2,500 W (34 dBW) of *effective isotropic radiated power* (e.i.r.p.) on global, and 4.5° spot-beam "despun" transmit dishes, respectively. All transponders receive from a global-beam antenna. By employing TT&C (tracking, telemetry, and command digital attitude control), the global and spot-beam transmit antennas, with a gain of 27 dB, are "despun" or continuously directed toward the pertinent Earth Terminals as the satellite-drum spins slowly. The transponders are rated at about 4,000 telephone circuits or greater on 287 separate links, depending on the number of transponders connected to the spot-beams in the FM/FDMA system in use. At this time, the annual user's cost per telephone circuit is about $1,000. A 33-Mbps PCM digital color-television (DITEC) broadcast channel, along with its digitized audio and 30 telephone channels, will require one full transponder in a single-access mode and replace approximately 960 voice circuits, when a color-television broadcast takes place.

The satellite's receive *gain-temperature ratio* (G/T) is approximately -7 dB/°K, while the Earth Terminal with its 98-ft dish may have a figure like 37 dB/°K. (*Note:* A 35-ft dish may have a noise temperature like 2,610°K, which is equivalent to 1 + 2,610/290 = 10 dB. This equivalent noise-figure will reduce the actual dish-gain by 10 dB, and the resultant G/T figure will represent the effective gain of the antenna along with its equivalent noise-figure. In the case of the smaller dishes, the Kelvin noise-temperature degradation is approximately 0.5 dB; hence, it usually goes unmentioned.)

The present Intelsat IV satellite *telecommunication circuits*, either analog (3KHz) or digital at 9.6 baud/sec, operate on a single carrier per channel as a PCM Multiple-Access Demand Assignment System called SPADE. In multiple-access networks, interference caused by the intermodulation (IM) products may be such that additional power does not significantly improve the bit-error rates in data communications. Therefore, the application of the "forward-acting error coding" (using the error-correcting codes) is practically effective for a threshold bit-error rate (BER) of $1/10^7$ to provide an excellent subjective quality in high carrier-to-IM noise environment. For the bandwidth-limited noncoding systems, and for the maximum likelihood decoding techniques used in the redundant-bit data systems, a BER of $1/10^4$ is a norm that is generally acceptable.

To meet the growing traffic worldwide, the new series of Intelsat IV-A satellites that are being launched at this time will be *three-axis body-stabilized*, as against the *body-spinning* of the present satellites; they employ the satellite-switched, Time-Division Multiple-Access digital techniques (SS-TDMA) using the *frequency-reuse* principle. *In these latest digital systems, the microprocessors could play a highly reliable role.* The new techniques facilitate the establishment of a large number of communications channels (up to 7,000) between multiple destinations, by time-sharing 20 satellite-transponders, operating in two 6/4 and 14/11-GHz up/down-link microwave bands. Redundant 4-phase PSK (phase-shift keying)/ TDMA modems, operating at an input bit-rate of 60.032 Mbps (and an actual transmission bit-rate of 30.016 Mbps), will be used for 36-MHz BW-limited transponders. For a 1.544-Mbps transmission using the four-phase PSK mode, the occupied transmission bandwidth is 926 KHz (1.2 times the symbol rate). For the 1980s, plans are underway to allow from 25 to 50 thousand telephone circuits by time-sharing a larger number of *microprocessor-controlled transponders* in each satellite.

Future Comsat Earth Terminals will use, in place of the present steerable 98-ft parabolas of a highly redundant size, torus antennas that are equivalent to a 30-ft dish; they would provide three independently steerable beams over a 40° synchronous orbital arc.

C-2. DOMESTIC SATELLITE SYSTEMS

Comsat General, Aetna, IBM, RCA, Western Union, American Satellite (Fairchild), and Canadian Telesat are all involved with the FCC's open policy in effect. Presently, Canada's three Domestic Telesat Satelites built by Hughes Aircraft Co. are operative, using an elliptical antenna pattern (3° X 8.5°) that primarily covers the Canadian territory. The 20-K silicon-cell solar-array of the 12-Transponder satellite generates 300 W to provide a minimum e.i.r.p. of 33 dBW at the beam-contour. Each transponder can operate, with TWTA at saturation in a single-access mode, to provide a capacity of 960 voice-circuits or alternatively one color-television channel and two audio circuits. It can also operate at a power backoff on multiple-access FDM/FM/FDMA, to relay telephone, television, data, and facsimile transmission services. Over 50 Earth Terminals using 33-ft dishes are served at a 5.927- to 6.403-GHz up-link (horizontal polarization) and a 3.202- to 4.1786-GHz down-link (vertical polarization); the overall transmission-performance standards achieved are better than those of the terrestrial systems. The transmit e.i.r.p. and receive G/T for these ANIK spacecrafts are 33 dBW/carrier and -7 dB/°K, respectively. Earth Terminals using 98-ft parabola dishes yield a G/T of 37 dB/°K, a figure that includes the effective noise-temperature of the antenna and the noise-figure of the parametric microwave front-end. These larger Earth Terminals use 1.5-KW klystrons to provide an e.i.r.p. of 73 dBW. The Telesat system is the first to introduce the TDMA in the place of the FDMA, and 400 telephone circuits can be handled in place of the 240 FDMA circuits, at an overall transmission rate of 61.248 Mbps and a G/T of 31 dB/°K. The advanced design and operational success of the ANIK spacecraft have resulted in its adoption by other users—the United States' two Western Union Domestic Satellites (Westar) and the Indonesian Domestic Satellite System. The Western Union presently operates five Earth Stations, using 48-ft dishes.

The RCA Corporation has recently established one US-Domsat of its own (Satcom); it is a body-stabilized spacecraft, operating in the 6/4 GHz band, and providing about 15,000 voice circuits by way of 24 transponders, each having a 36-MHz bandwidth on a dual polarization basis. It uses the *frequency reuse* technique for an overall spectrum-bandwidth of 500 MHz. Comsat General, IBM, and Aetna are expected to launch, via NASA Space Shuttle, a new spacecraft of a 10-transponder configuration for an integrated Satellite Business System (SBS) that provides (at 20 W and 14/12 GHz) a "futuristic," *world-wide, long-distance direct-dialing facility* with a bandwidth of 43 MHz. If Congress permits, RCA will probably emphasize low-cost CABLE-TV Systems around the country, devoting a few exclusive transponder channels for coast-to-coast network color-television transmission channels. During the 1980s. rooftop earth terminals will take the place of the present high-cost terminals.

C-3. MOBILE MARISAT SHIP-TO-SHORE COMMUNICATIONS SYSTEM

Telex, telephone, broadcast, and facsimile satellite-communication data-processing facilities, planned for ocean-crossing liners and freighters, will interface with the shoreside, store-and-forward, message-switching computer networks. That is, an end-to-end real-time, one- or two-way connection is set up for each call, using a direct-dialing procedure, which is somewhat similar to the ordinary international telex dialing. As in telex, the called party's terminal need not be manned and 24-hour message deliveries are effective.

An **ATS-6 Applications Technology Satellite**, operating in the L-band 1,600-MHz, fan-beam mode, is used on an experimental basis in conjunction with the United States Maritime Administration's MARAD Earth Station at King's Point, New York, which is presently under the jurisdiction of the NASA/Goddard Space Flight Center, and a NASA Ground Station Earth Terminal at Rosman, North Carolina. Tests were conducted ship-to-shore. The Terminals operate with a G/T of −5 dB/°K and a maximum e.i.r.p. of 36 dBW. A digital frequency synthesizer down-converts 1,559 MHz to a 70-MHz center-frequency for modem interface, and then up-converts to 1,659 MHz for translation to the satellite. The following results assure the potential success of the MARAD project.

1. Using an antenna with a gain of 15 dB and a beam width of 30°, *automatic tracking* was successfully established under all conditions at an elevation above 10° to 12°; under smooth sea conditions, automatic tracking was successful down to an elevation of 4°.
2. Under **multipath conditions** at elevations above 20°, data modem performance was achieved at a BER of $1/10^5$ at 1,200 bps. Below 20°, the modem performance was affected by multipath in accordance with the usual theoretical estimates.
3. **Voice and 1,200-bps digital data** were successfully received simultaneously on a single carrier, demonstrating a new capability that could double the spectrum capability for satellite channels. Radio-frequency interference levels (RFI), on the average, are below thermal-noise levels. Occasionally, noise sources could exceed noise floor by 20 to 30 dB.
4. Differentially-encoded phase-shift keying (DEPSK) was the technique COMSAT used to evaluate **TDM/TDMA** (Time-Division-Multiplex/Time-Domain Multiple-Access) at 1.2 Kbps toward the ship and at 4.8 Kbps toward the shore station.

C-4. MARISAT

Plans are under way for a joint venture to establish **MARISAT**. The European Space Agency (ESA) will have a similar union MAROTS, and both MARISAT and MAROTS systems will perhaps merge into an International Maritime Satellite System.

C-5. AEROSAT

A parallel organization, the **AEROSAT**, under the aegis of the FAA and the ESA, is under way to provide the **ATC facility (aircraft traffic control)** between ocean-crossing aircraft and ground stations, by means of two spaced synchronous satellites. Hard-copy information such as flight-clearance information, position data, fuel management, weather, and telecommunication service to international passengers will be available in the cockpit. Seven AEROSAT satellites (including two polar ones) could furnish a round-the-clock global communications and navigational facility.

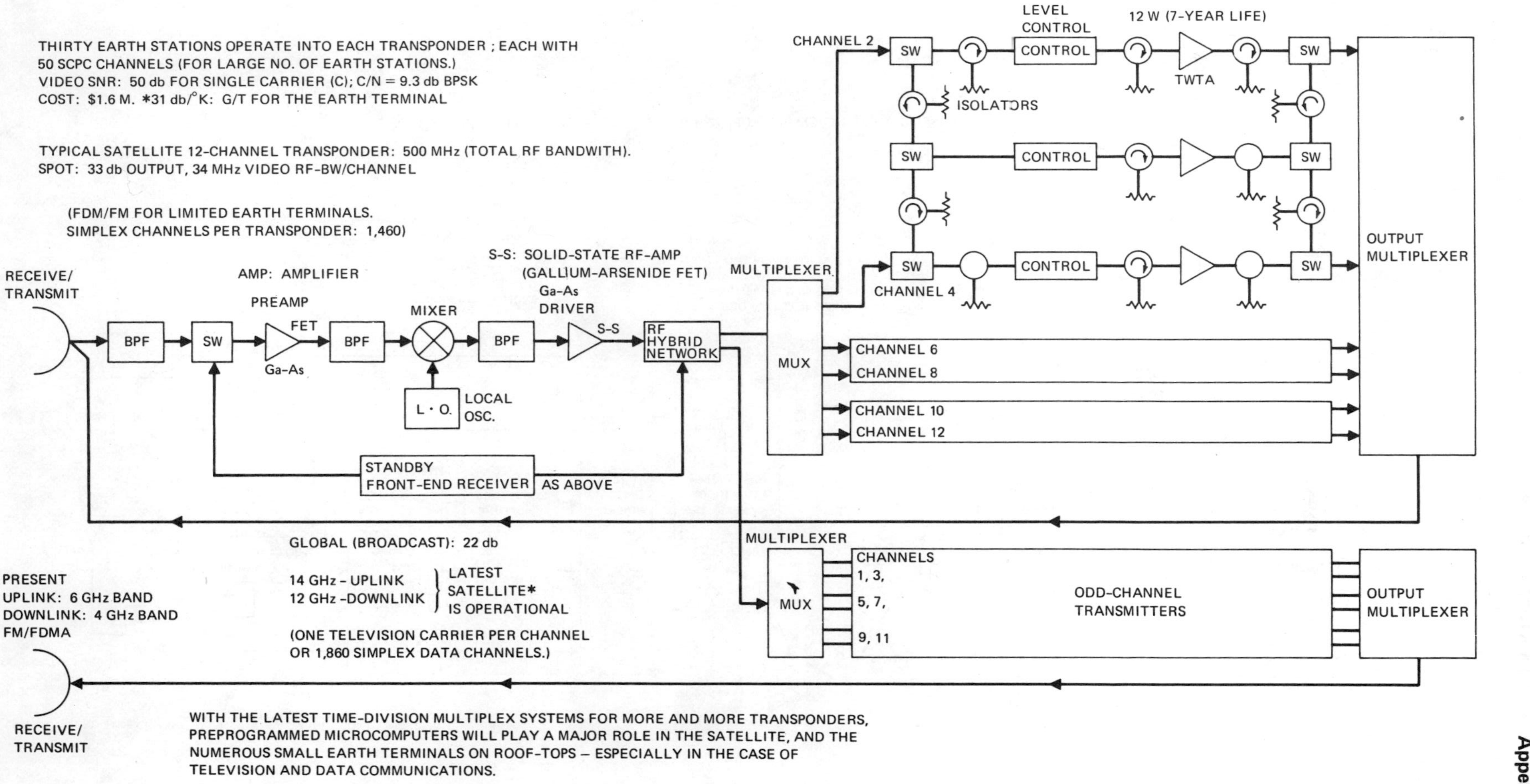

Fig. C-1. Typical 12-channel satellite transponder. (*Courtesy of IEEE, Transactions of Aerospace and Electronics Systems*)

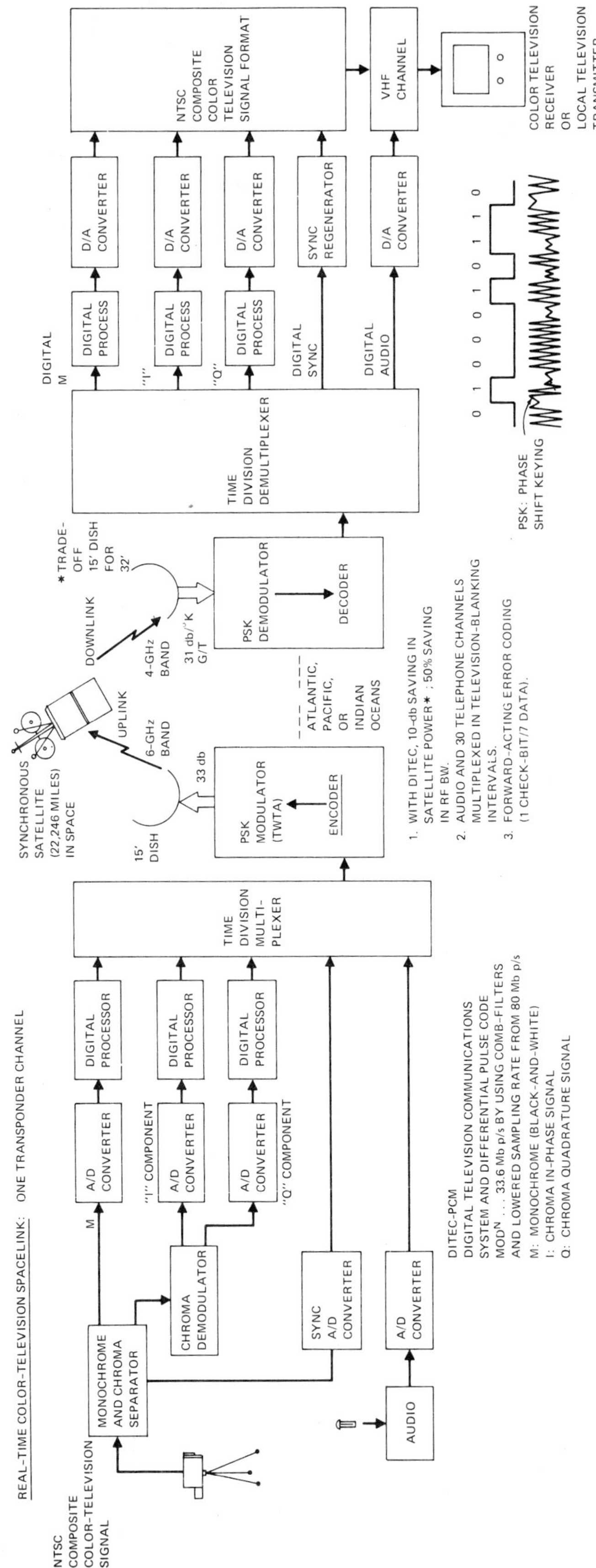

Fig. C-2. Digitized real-time global color-television transmission via satellites.

C-6. SATELLITE ANTENNA SYSTEM

Multi-horn array-feeds in an offset reflector or lens can be used to radiate **multiple-zone beam coverage** from a single aperture. A new technique is presently available for synthesizing a beam coverage of the required cross-section with extremely low side-lobes. This development has important applications for communication satellites, which require multiple-zone beam coverage with sufficient amplitude-isolation between the beams, to permit reuse of a specific frequency spectrum. The technique allows a shelter for the communication satellites that require very low side-lobe beam coverage as a protection against interception and jamming.

C-7. SATELLITE TECHNOLOGY

High-power, body-stabilized, tri-axis gyro-controlled satellites were recently proposed by the General Electric Company Space Systems for significant cost reduction and performance advantage. Technology is presently available to provide a high-power spacecraft that could use a 100-W traveling-wave tube amplifier (TWTA) for **satellite television-broadcasting** (to enable pickup of direct television signals). As an alternative, five 20-W telecommunication channels could be used in the 11.7- to 12.2-GHz band at this time. That is, in future, high-cost Earth Terminals will eventually give way to direct second-generation **Community Antenna Systems** in the place of the presently feasible Cable-TV distribution systems under the first-generation TV-Domsats. This possibility would then create a need for rooftop, small-dish Microwave Television-Receivers for decoded color-television signal distribution in high-rise buildings and apartment complexes where a distant television transmission is desired. Obviously, there is an immediate need for a commercial product of this kind in the developing countries, where **the domestic satellites will shortcut the need for extensive terrestrial microwave links.** In all these new satellite voice and television data-communications systems, the economic, highly reliable LSI microprocessors and the GaAs FET microelectronics will definitely play a dominant role throughout the world.

Fig. C-1 illustrates a typical 12-channel Transponder in a Satellite for a Global Broadcasting Service (GEC). Fig. C-2 illustrates a present real-time space-link for a digitized color-television system; a single full-channel Transponder is required for color or black-and-white television transmission. (COMSAT Laboratories recently demonstrated satellite data transmission of multiplexed, digital, color television signal, audio and 60 telephone channels, using a serial 43-Mbps differential PCM data stream via one of the present Synchronous Domestic Satellites over the United States.)

C-8. LATEST STATUS OF GEOSYNCHRONOUS COMMUNICATIONS SATELLITES

Three Intelsat 4A satellites over the Atlantic, and two Intelsat 4A satellites over the Pacific and Indian Oceans (with backup Intelsat 4 satellites in all oceanic regions) are in service. Three Russian 40-transponder FDMA "statsionar inter-sputnik" satellites with part-time service are in use. The present status of worldwide FDMA and TDMA telecommunications and television broadcasting setup—excluding the latest domestic satellites going up for service in various territorial regions—covers over 75 active communications satellites. The 27-transponder 40/80/240-MHz wide-band, Intelsat-5, fifth-generation satellites are being launched by COMSAT hereon. Canada's three spin-stabilized ANIK-A satellites built by RCA are supplemented by an advanced body-stabilized ANIK-B satellite. American domestic service is also served by two Westar HS-333 satellites of Western Union, two RCA/Americom 14000 voice-circuit Satcom satellites, and three AT&T/GT&E Comstar satellites over the equatorial region in the Western Hemisphere. Most of the new international and domestic satellite systems operate wide-band (43 MHz) at 11/14 GHz and 44 dBW higher effective radiated power; smaller dishes are required for the more economic smaller earth terminals. In order to compensate for attenuation by rain in the higher frequency band, higher power, and more sophisticated "diversity" and special convolution coding techniques are used. American Satellite Corporation operates 21 earth stations of this category with 10-meter unattended antennas on the customer's property. They interface with the customer's PBX's, tie-lines, and microcomputer data terminals such as concentrators in leased private networks.

The latest series of satellites, such as SBS, will use ANIK-C version of pseudonoise (PN) time-division multiple access (TDMA) satellite data communications for both telecommunications and color television

- PN CODE OVERLAY FOR TRAFFIC SECURITY
- TDMA MEETS DEMAND ASSIGNMENT AND PERMITS SIGNIFICANT INCREASE IN ANTIJAM PERFORMANCE WITH PEAK-POWER TRANSMISSION. TDMA PROVIDES FOR BOTH SYNCHRONOUS AND ASYNCHRONOUS INTERFACES FROM 9600 BITS/SEC TO 10 Mb/S, REDUCING EQUIPMENT COSTS (INCLUDES 50 Kb/S AND 1·544 Mb/S RATES)
- TDMA ELIMINATES THE NEED FOR SATELLITE UP-LINK POWER CONTROL AND ALLOWS SATELLITE TO OPERATE AT FULL SATURATED POWER OUTPUT. NETWORK PERFORMANCE IMPROVED BY 4 dB. HENCE, COMPARED TO FDM, TDM ALLOWS SMALL TERMINAL ANTENNA (LOW G/T)
- MODEM FREQUENCY ERROR (IF): ±3500 Hz. AGC: 100 mSEC TIME-CONSTANT
- 15 CHANNELS OF DATA FOR INTEGRAL MULTIPLEXING
- MASTER FRAME: 2^{16} FRAMES, FRAME-RATE: 1200/SEC UNIT INTERVAL: 100 nSEC, XMIT/RECEIVE BITS: 15 DATA, 1 PREAMBLE

CONTROL/ INDICATOR UNIT

5 MHz REFERENCE

QPSK TO TERMINAL

LEVEL: 10 dBm *

BASE-BAND INTERFACE

CH 1 D, C, D, CH 15 C

TRANSMIT BUFFER

MODULATOR (INCLUDES XMIT TIMING FUNCTIONS)

CODE
CLOCK
DOPPLER
MFRP

USC-28 INTERFACE IN TDMA MODE

FOR INTERFACE AND ASYNCHRONOUS DATA-RATE SMOOTHING

−50 to −5 db

CH 1 D, C, D, CH 15 C

PULSE STUFF BUFFER

COMPUTER INTERFACE AND BUILT-IN TEXT EQUIPMENT

BITE

RECEIVE PROCESSOR (INCLUDING RECEIVE TIMING FUNCTIONS)

CODE
CLOCK
DOPPLER
MFRP

- *FROM TRANSMIT BUFFER: STORED FRAME-FORMAT INFORMATION AND SYNCHRONIZED BY EPOCH SIGNALS. BURST MODIFIED BY PREAMBLE, PN-CODE, AND CONVOLUTIONAL CODING.

FEEDBACK CLOCKS 1/CHANNEL

CH 1
CH 15

RECEIVE BUFFER

CONVOLUTION DECODER (VITERBI)

DEMODULATOR

QPSK FROM TERMINAL

FOR K=5 CONVOLUTION CODING

- ±50-ns TIME CORRECTION
- DOPPLER CORRECTED ON XMIT/RECEIVE
- BITE TO TEST DC VOLTS, FREQUENCY, AND TIMINGS
- BITE AND AUTOMATIC PERFORMANCE MONITORING SOFTWARE FOR RAPID FAULT-DETECTION AND ISOLATION OF LINE REPLACEABLE UNIT (LRU)
- INERTIA CHANNELS: 8

POWER: ±5V, +28V, −18V
PN-TDMA: IF AT 700 MHz (PSK) PN CODE COVERAGE 40 Mb/S OPERATES IN 60 MHz BANDWIDTH CHANNELS

PRINTER OR CRT DISPLAY

CENTRAL PROCESSOR (MICROPROCESSOR)

CASSETTE BULK TAPE MEMORY

KEYBOARD

ASR-33 TELETYPE (TTY)

- MFRP: MATCHED-FILTER RECEIVE PROCESSOR FOR UP TO EIGHT REMOTE TERMINALS
- QPSK: QUADRI-PHRASE-SHIFT KEYING OF PHASE-LOCKED CARRIER AT 700 MHz (QPSK BI-PHASE MODULATION MODES)
- EFFICIENCY > 99%. PN: PHASE-NOISE. TDMA: TIME-DIVISION MULTIPLE ACCESS, MULTIPLEX AND ACCESS FOR SATELLITE NETWORKS
- EARTH TERMINALS ASSIGNED TIME-SLOTS IN A FRAME FOR USER TRAFFIC IN BURSTS
- BURST-RATE DETERMINED BY G/T OF DESTINATION EARTH TERMINAL
- BURST-RATE DEPENDS ON BASE-BAND RATE AND BURST-RATE

Fig. C-3. PN-TDMA satellite communications system (*Courtesy of Raytheon Company*)

broadcasting to enable direct interface of economy microcomputer-oriented Cable-Television earth terminals. For a short while, a mix of analog FDMA and digital TDMA is expected for 64-K bit PCM voice circuits with 50-kHz bandwidth.

C-9. A SYSTEM BLOCK-DIAGRAM OF THE LATEST PN-TDMA SATELLITE COMMUNICATIONS SYSTEM IS SHOWN IN FIG. C-3.

The advantages of the small-dish (high G/T) TDMA system include flexible and simplified operational use at full anti-jam peak-power saturated output, and improved network performance on the order of 4 dB at light and heavy traffic loads. TDMA provides for forward-error-correcting FEC Demand Assignment at 9600 bytes/sec to 10 Mb/sec with complexity-wise minimal multiplexing requirements. The digital base-band signals are assigned a fixed time-slot, termed a frame, which is turn is divided into user traffic burst-sequences. A specific burst preamble allows the implementation of the demod-processing in a programmable control unit at the receiving earth terminal without address information. Each terminal generates a burst for each base-band signal to permit nonmultiplexed multiple channels on a common route. Burst-rate is determined by the G/T of the destination terminal, and burst-length by both the base-band rate and the burst-rate. Built-in equipment allows automatic fault detection and isolation. The system provides PN-Code overlay full-security data communications with up to eight 15-channel earth stations.

Input base-band signals go to the Transmit Buffer for retiming (asynchronous data) and storage in a RAM buffer. The order of bit-storage determines the read-out burst-sequence. The PSK Modulator includes transmit-timing according to frame-formatting information and subsequent PN and Convolution Coding. The transmit-burst is supplemented by preamble. The spectrally pure intermediate-frequency (IF) 70-MHz phase-locked carrier is QPSK-modulated (quad phase-shift keyed) and gated to produce the transmit-burst. It is up-converted for transmission at the earth terminal. The received IF signal is processed for gain, AGC, PN-Code removal functions, demodulation, and subsequent conditioning and synchronization under the control of the stored frame-formatting information.

The burst-data is demodulated by means of an inertial carrier and timing-reference system, involving a separate carrier and a phase-reference storage for each independent terminal. Its preamble determines the carrier and time-tracking. Carrier phase and bit-timing are stored from burst to burst in eight sampled phase-lock loops for the eight remote terminals. Bit decision is provided by matched-filter (integrate and dump) detectors, followed by AD Converters to produce a 3-bit "soft" decision for 4.5 dB of coding gain. The burst-data is routed at rate $\frac{1}{2}$, k = 5 Convolutional Coading.

A one-half rate data block-code, implying an efficiency of 50%, has been assumed so that $k = n/2$ when n is the total number of bits transmitted, and k is the number of information bits; then $(n - k)$ stands for the number of redundant bits in a forward error correcting (FEC) system. If these $(n - k)$ redundant bits check information in preceding blocks, the code is called *convolution code*—which is exclusively used in FEC data communications systems. The convolution encoder used in this technique is shown in the accompanying diagram. The decoding algorithm is Viterbi (*maximum likelihood*). The concept of *maximum likelihood* decoding is a sequential decoding procedure; it is extremely powerful and primarily suited for the correction of random errors. The Receiver Buffer-RAM stores the burst-bits in the order received. The base-band signal-readout to a Pulse Stuff Buffer provides the proper interface and data-rate smoothing. The CPU carries out the control and monitoring in conjunction with a CRT-keyboard.

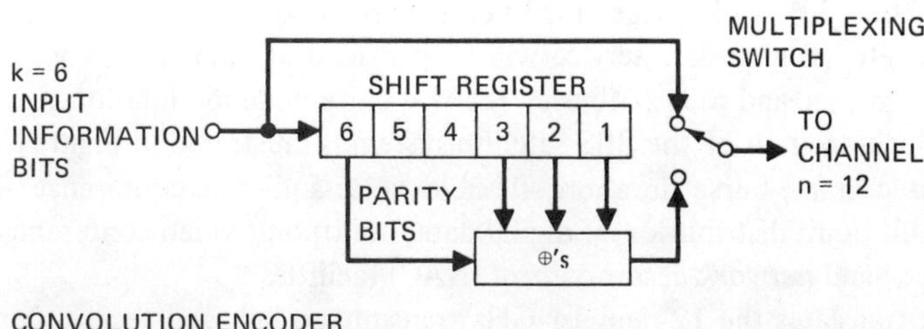

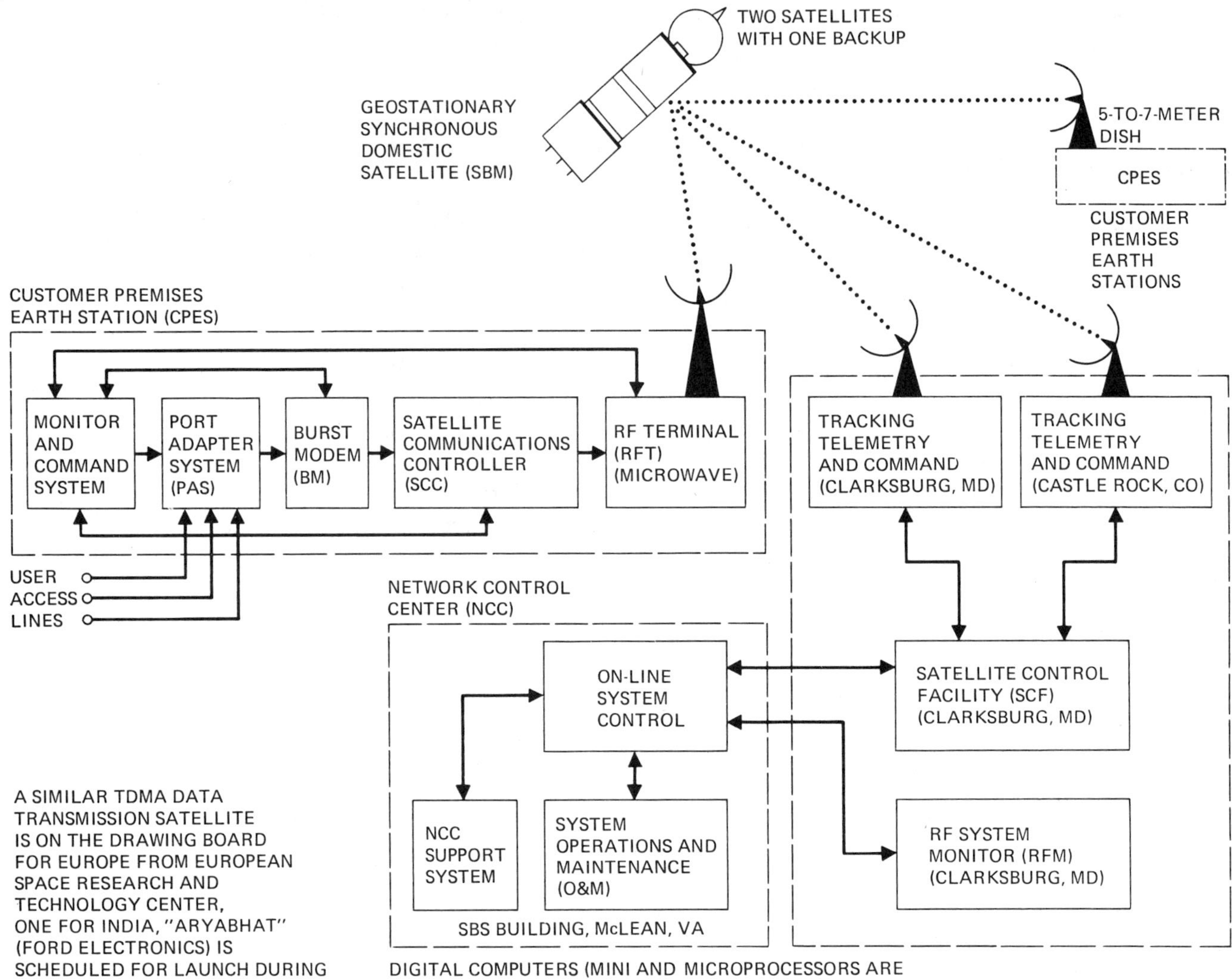

Fig. C-4. Simplified block-diagram of the SBS, TDMA Satellite business Communications System. (*Courtesy of SBS Satellite Systems*)

C-10. SBS DOMESTIC SATELLITE FOR DATA COMMUNICATIONS (1980/81)

The advanced communications service of Satellite Business Systems (SBS) provides time-division multiple access (TDMA) of satellite communications channel in the 12 and 14 GHz bands for fully-integrated voice, data, and image (video-conferencing) traffic to earth stations and independent networks on a *demand assignment* (DA) basis. The system enables efficient utilization of channel capacity by using *voice activity compression* (VAC), with minimal dependence of terrestrial interconnecting facilities. As a contrast to the present Intelsat satellites, the earth stations will be located on customer's premises with 5- and 7-meter parabolic dishes. Interface facilities are provided to customer's PBXs, foreign-exchange lines, data terminals, etc. Digital data service will be provided at data rates from 2.4 Kb/sec to multiplexed PCM at 1.544 Mb/sec and 6.312 Mb/sec. (PCM = pulse-code modulation.)

The simplified block-diagram of the SBS satellite system is illustrated in Figure C-4. The system features include 15-msec frame-burst duration, flexible voice-and-data conference facilities, document distribution from multipoint distribution of digital data, multipoint video conferencing, priority connection facility, and base-band *network-access control* (NAC) facilities.

The RF terminal translates the 12- and 14-GHz transmit up-link and receive down-link frequencies, respectively, to the intermediate 70-MHz interface frequency for the TDMA burst-modem. The burst-modem, besides its mod/demod functions, enables bursts of digital information to be transmitted via each satellite communications channel on a *time-shared* basis. The *satellite communications controller* (SCC), the integrated hardware/software device, consists of a multiprocessor system with functions such as storage, control, TDMA, demand assignment, switching analog-to-digital conversion for voice-grade lines, etc. The *port adapter system* (PAS) provides a compatible interface between the *unattended earth station* (UES) and the customer's network or other data terminals.

Tracking, telemetry and command (TT&C) and *satellite control facility* (SCF) are provided from the *principal control center* (PCC) at Clarksburg, Maryland, and also at Castle Rock, Colorado, for two SBS satellites and a third backup satellite. The transmit command provision is necessary for correcting orbital positions or for switching to redundant satellite components. The system management function includes the *network control center* (NCC) and an *operations and maintenance* (O&M) organization for automated system-diagnostics.

As a TDMA system, the SBS system permits continuous real-time reassignment of the satellite capacity to directly meet the varying requirements of the customer's computer network. Microprocessors in low-cost *small earth stations* (SES) can play a direct role in satellite data communications unlike the previous FDM/FDMA satellites. The Satellite Communications Controller, SCC provides *forward-error-correction* (FEC) coding facility to enable a BER of 1×10^{-7}, 99.5% of the time. With 10 active transponder channels (1-to-2 redundancy ratio) of 43 and 48 Mb/sec bandwidth, or 12,000 to 14,000 voice circuits, the spin-stabilized, 550-kg satellite is manufactured by Hughes Aircraft Company, and placed in orbit by Delta 3910 launch vehicle since the originally planned space shuttle schedules are indefinite. The *domsat* antenna design with a gain of 35 dB consists of a dual-surface offset parabolic antenna using separate receive and transmit multi-beam field arrays. With a total of 16 TWTAs (travelling wave tube amplifier), RF power output of 200 watts, and linear horizontal polarization, the satellite has an e.i.r.p. (effective isotropic radiated power) of 43.7 to 41.2 dBw/transponder, and a receiver G/T of +2 dB/°K to -2.5 dB/°K with linear vertical polarization.

The TDMA burst-modem uses quadri or quaternary phase-shift keying (QPSK) with 2 bits/symbol. The satellite communications control unit (SCC) performs the functions of signaling, call processing, circuit switching, echo suppression, formatting, framing, synchronization, multiplexing, multiple-access control, and demand assignment besides A/D voice conversion, FEC, and VAC.

It was quantitatively shown that video conferencing signals can be efficiently coded by *interframe coding* at the T1 carrier frequency of 1.544 Mb/sec. In conferencing, face-to-face conversation does not generate much differential information due to minimal motion of the picture material from frame to frame. The probability of interframe difference signal over a range of 4 to 246 volts, when controlling

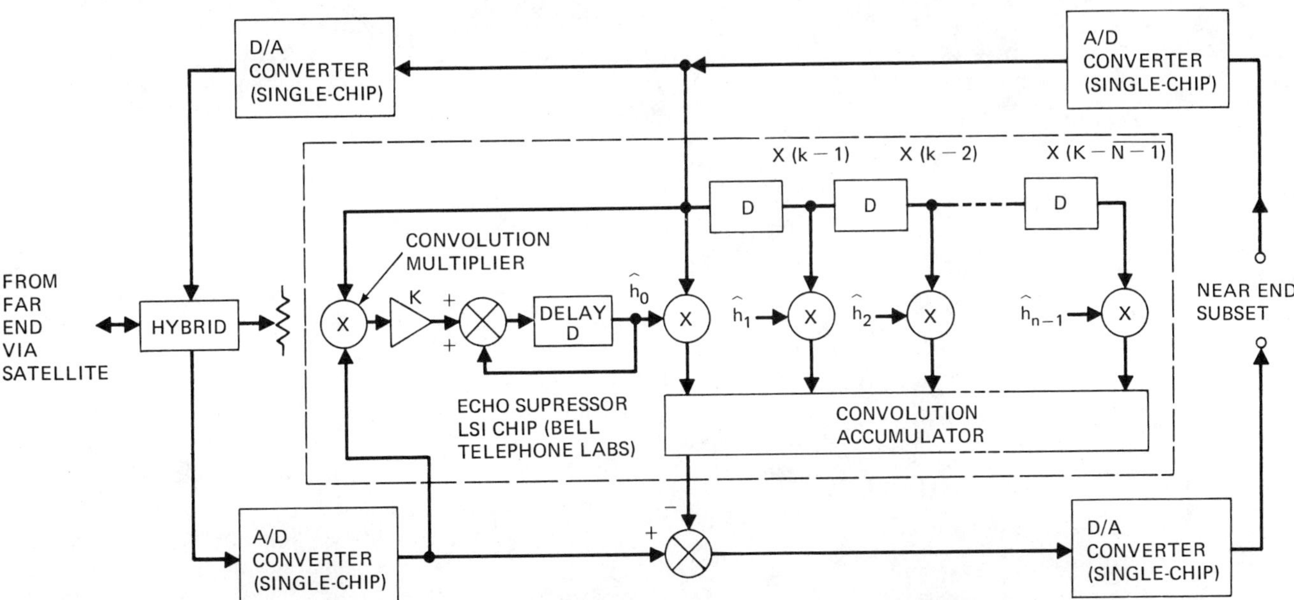

Fig. C-5. LSI Echo Suppressor. (*Courtesy of Bell Telephone Laboratories, Holmdel, N.J.*)

only threshold-level (THL) in a specific mode-control algorithm, is a minimal few percentage points. The change in this probability with time is also less than that of most other signal sources. The degradation of picture-quality tends to be less objectionable if the duration of small moving areas is not continuous during one frame-period (1/30 second). The SBS video conferencing technique is based on this concept, as originated by Nippon Telegraph and Telephone Public Corporation of Japan.*

The signal propagation-time to the satellite and back is approximately 540 msec, and the telephone user waits for the reply of the person he is talking to for this extra delay, if the call goes via satellite in both directions. It is disturbing if the talker hears his voice echoed back to him with the above delay. Normally **echo suppressors** are used for long-distance trunk lines. For satellite applications, Bell Telephone Laboratories have designed a 5-micron channel, 34,397-transistor, NMOS LSI single-chip echo suppressor consisting of a convolution multiplier, convolution accumulator, memory, and miscellaneous logic. A simplified block-diagram of the Echo Suppressor chip is shown in Fig. C-5.

*Transmitting video conferencing signals at 1.544 Mb/sec by interframe coding by Masayuki Inoue, Yukio Kobayashi, National Telecommunications Conference, Vol. 3, IEEE, 1979.

APPENDIX D
Periodic Table of Elements and Electromagnetic Spectrum, and a New Look at Quantum Mechanics, Intergalactic and Intragalactic Modern Cosmology, and Applicable Ancient Philosophy

D-1. MATTER, ENERGY, GRAVITATIONAL FORCE: (MEG—A NATURAL PHILOSOPHY)

Matter, Energy, and Gravitation represent the basic forces of Nature. Present theories to explain the various laws that bind matter, energy, and gravitational force are based on gauge theories deducted from "local" symmetries or regularities apparent mainly in the laws of physics. The *unification* of the various quantum field theories and general theory of relativity* (which Einstein failed to arrive at) is still an unsolvable problem because the nature of quantum fluctuations of space-time continuum in a gravitational field cannot be meaningfully answered. In fact, all known physical theories on this subject follow this pattern of limitation.

For example, according to the science of Quantum Electrodynamics, the gauge symmetry of electromagnetism cannot take into account the electric and magnetic field shifts in the phase of electron wave, since this phase cannot be measured on the basis of quantum theory. However, according to the latest superconductivity theory supporting the Josephson Junction Electron-pair Interferometer (JJI) concept, applicable to the *substantiated*, compact, ultrafast, low-power-consuming computers (microcomputers) working at superconductivity temperatures, the interferometer interference pattern of the bonded electron-pair waves at very low temperatures above Absolute Zero, with the effective cancellation of the opposing momentums of the individual electrons of the pair, is an evolutionary eye-opener toward near-infinite speeds of bonded electron-pair waves at superconductivity temperatures in "matter" (or equally valid intergalactic "space" where such temperatures exist according to the latest discovery of the resonant infrared black-body radiation in space at about 2.9° Kelvin). The JI-Theory breaks the barrier of velocity of light at superconductivity temperatures.

Present theories tend to divide the basic forces of Nature into four separate identities:

1. Electromagnetism covering an infinite spectrum, with the unit of photon as a mass of zero having infinite range
2. Gravitational Force of an unlimited nature, with the mass involved represented as zero
3. Strong Forces that bind protons and neutrons in the nucleus of an atom

TABLE D-1. Revised Periodic Table of Elements—1980 (with Classification of 10 "Key" Elements Including Heavy Hydrogen).

Stable isotope Hydrogen gas ($_1H^1$), high-energy proton ($_1H^1$) with positive charge, and neutron ($_0n^1$) with neutral charge may be classified as the cosmic building blocks of the other elements - in the regenerative process of new solar systems amid dust and gases in space due to "gravitational collapse" and condensation. Atomic Number = Z (Bottom Left); Mass Number = Z+'N' (Top Right); 'N' = $_0n^1$ (neutron); $_1H^2$ = Heavy Hydrogen (HH); 'k' = "key" elements (10). An Element is defined as that possessing protons, neutrons and electrons in a stable state of equilibrium. ('k' stands for an element with equal number of protons and neutrons in nucleus.) HH = Deuterium, D.

PERIOD	GROUP 1	GROUP 2	GROUP 3	GROUP 4	GROUP 5	GROUP 6	GROUP 7	GROUP 8			GROUP 0
1	'k' 2 H-Hydrogen HH-1										'k' 4 Helium He-2
2	3 Lithium Li-2	9 Beryllium Be-4	11 Boron B-5	'k' 12 Carbon C-6	'k' 14 Nitrogen N-7	'k' 16 Oxygen O-8	19 Fluorine F-9				'k' 20 Neon Ne-10
3	23 Sodium Na-11	'k' 24 Magnesium Mg-12	27 Aluminum Al-13	'k' 28 Silicon Si-14	31 Phosphorus P-15	'k' 32 Sulfur S-16	35 Chlorine Cl-17				40 Argon Ar-18
4A	39 Potassium K-19	'k' 40 Calcium Ca-20	45 Scandium Sc-21	48 Titanium Ti-22	51 Vanadium V-23	52 Chromium Cr-24	55 Manganese Mn-25	56 Iron Fe-26	59 Cobalt Co-27	58 Nickel Ni-28	
4B	63 Copper Cu-29	64-68 Zinc Zn-30	69-71 Gallium Ga-31	74-72-70 Germanium Ge-32	75 Arsenic As-33	80-78 Selenium Se-34	79-81 Bromine Br-35				84 Krypton Kr-36
5A	85 Rubidium Rb-37	88 Strontium Sr-38	88-91 Yttrium Y-39	90-94-92 Zirconium Zr-40	93 Niobium Nb-41	98-96-95 Molybdenum Mo-42	99 Technetium Te-43	102,'4,'1 Ruthenium Ru-44	103 Rhodium Rh-45	108,'6,'5 Palladium Pd-46	
5B	107,'9 Silver Ag-47	114,'2 Cadmium Cd-48	115 Indium In-49	120,118 Tin Sn-50	121 Antimony Sb-51	130,128 Tellurium Te-52	127 Iodine I-53				132,129 Xenon Xe-54
6A	133 Cesium Cs-55	138 Barium Ba-56	LANTHANIDE SERIES 57-71	180,178 Hafnium Hf-72	181 Tantalum Ta-73	184,'6,'2 Tungsten W-74	187 Rhenium Re-75	192,'0 Osmium Os-76	193 Iridium Ir-77	195,'4 Platinum Pt-78	
6B	197 Gold Au-79	202,'0,119 Mercury Hg-80	205 Thallium Tl-81	208,'6 Lead Pb-82	209 Bismuth Bi-83	209 Polonium Po-84	210 Astatine At-85				222 Radon Rn-86
7	223 Francium Fr-87	226 Radium Ra-88	ACTINIDE SERIES 89-103								
LANTHANIDE SERIES	139 Lanthanum La-57	140 Cerium Ce-58	141 Praseodymium Pr-59	142,'4,'6 Neodymium Nd-60	145 Promethium Pm-61	152,'4,'7 Samarium Sm-62	153,'1 Europium Eu-63	158,'6,160 Gadolinium Gd-64	159 Terbium Tb-65	164,'2,'3 Dysprosium Dy-66	165 Holmium Ho-67
	166,'8,'7 Erbium Er-68	169 Thulium Tm-69	174,'2 Ytterbium Yb-70	175 Lutetium Lu-71							
ACTINIDE SERIES	227 Actinium Ac-89	232 Thorium Th-90	231 Protactinium Pa-91	238 Uranium U-92	237 Neptunium Np-93	242 Plutonium Pu-94	243 Americium Am-95	247 Curium Cm-96	249 Berkelium Bk-97	251 Californium Cf-98	254 Einsteinium Es-99
	253 Fermium Fm-100	256 Mendelevium Md-101	Nobelium No.102	Lawrencium Lw-103							1-1-1978

4. Weak Forces apparent as decay of particles, or spontaneous disintegration of radioactive elements and isotopes. Strong Forces are in turn represented by (1) Hadrons with the unit *pion* (pi-meson) of mass equivalent to 0.14 Giga-electron volts (GeV), and (2) Quarks with the unit *gluon* of mass equivalent to zero. The Weak Force is represented by the unit *boson*.

Using the various theories, attempts to evolve a Unified (Master) Field Theory to understand Nature and its workings failed dismally. Under these circumstances, philosophically the logical interpretation of Nature as a Unified and Inseparable Trinity of Matter/Energy/Gravitation (or, positive-charge "Hole"/ "Negative-Mass-Electron" Distribution in both matter and space) is ideal from all aesthetic points of view. The author is convinced that no useful purpose is served by splitting the fundamental duality of mutually interchangeable Matter and Energy into three basic forces of nature, with Gravitation as an isolated fourth force. A fresh theory based on three basic forces, as suggested, may lead to a more adequate solution in understanding Nature. It must be realized that, in Nature, the micro- and macrocosmic phases conceptually merge into one another and the distinction between "weak" and "strong" forces is simply relativistic. Nature is inherently characterized in terms of "evolution" and "relativity."* The microcosm of particles and quantum energy packets are merely building-blocks for our limited understanding of the final synthesis of a "macrocosm." The limits of our universe will continue to remain obscure beyond our comprehension. The quasars are obviously not the ultimate distant phenomena; they simply indicate the limits of our instrumentation.

D-2. JOSEPHSON-JUNCTION SWITCH (JJS), SUPERCONDUCTIVITY AND QUANTUM MECHANICS

Most high-performance main-frame Central and Host Large-Scale and Minicomputers in data communications networks have cycle-times on the order of 30 to 50 nsec. The fastest computer in use, Cray-1, has a cycle-time of 12 nsec. The incredibly low-cost VLSI microprocessors as well are breaking the 100-nsec barrier. The next stage of progress is already set for 1-nsec cycle-time for ultrasmart and ultra-compact specialized microcomputer systems, using microamp-pulse switchable magnetic fields.

IBM's Josephson-Junction Switch (JJS), as a 6-picosec processing and memory cell, works on the combined principle of two basic phenomena of quantum mechanics: (1) *tunneling of electron-pairs* across an insulating barrier, and (2) *superconductivity of electron-pairs* by cooling the device to a few degrees above the unattainable absolute zero, -273°C/-459°F, in a bath of liquid Helium (cryogenics). The latter property furnishes the surprise benefit of microwatt power consumption also. That is, a few million JJS-processing and memory cells of a compact microcomputer system will dissipate just a few watts of power! It is expected that the first developmental JJS-Model microcomputer will be a 2 X 3-in. package with a cycle-time on the order of just 2 nsec. A 64 X 64 bit cache memory has been achieved recently. (JJS = Two lead-alloy conductors separated by metal-oxide insulator).

The JJS cells are laid out on a *silicon substrate* by photolithography as **Josephson Junction Interferometers (JI)** (of waves of electron-pairs) in conjunction with appropriate metallic loops. According to quantum mechanics, in a superconducting mechanism, the current is conducted by two electrons, as an electron-pair, with opposite momentum. A single electron or electron wave will have the freedom to move in any direction (if there is a positive-charge "Hole" around), but an electron-pair is restricted to move lockstep in a *coherent* mode at *near-infinite conductivity*, without colliding with the atoms or ions in the crystal-lattice or for that matter in any other medium such as space at superconductivity temperatures. The negative-charge electron of each electron-pair is attracted to the positive charge of the sur-

*The *principle of relativity* asserts that the laws of physics are invariant when determined relative to one inertial system as when determined relative to any other." The *special theory of relativity* is concerned with bodies that are in uniform motion relative to one another in a straight line. And Einstein's postulates state that (1) all motion is relative and it is impossible to determine absolute motion, and (2) the *measured* speed of light in *free space* is constant, independent of motion of the source or the motion of the observer. The author is presently modifying postulate 2 by adding a qualification to *free space–free space "in the environment of a star (sun)."* The *general theory of relativity* extends the principle for application to systems relative to one another. By using a curvilinear space, it leads to the theory of gravitation as a correction to Newton's second law. Effects are observable in large-scale astronomical phenomena such as the bending of a ray of light in the gravitational field of a large massive body like the sun.

TABLE D-2. Electromagnetic Spectrum.

Band Designations, Frequency Bands, Wavelengths, and Natural Manifestation/General use. Velocity c of Electromagnetic waves in stellar environment is constant. There is no absolute vacuum in the living, dynamic, and knowable Universe, operating under the Laws pertaining to Probability and Statistics, Gravitation, Matter, and Energy ($F = G\, m_1 m_2/d^2$; $E = mc^2$, where F stands for Force, m, m_1, and m_2 for Mass, G for Gravitational Constant, d for distance between two animate and/or inanimate objects, and E for Energy). An "absolute" vacuum is nonexistent, since -273° Absolute Kelvin is nonexistent and unattainable, in view of the eternal infrared radiation of $\sim 3^\circ$ Absolute in space. "Hole" distribution in space makes the medium for propagation of radio waves and infrared radiation.

$c \approx 3 \times 10^8$ meters/sec and $\lambda = c/f$, where λ is wavelength in meters (m), cm, mm, μ, and Å; f is frequency in Hertz/sec. Angstrom Å $= 10^{-4}$ micrometers, μ (microns).

No.	Band Designation	Frequency Band	Spectrum	Wavelengths (Center of Band)	Natural Manifestation or General Use
1	Undesignated Low Frequency Band	1–25 Hz/Sec	-	3×10^7 m	Special Applications, Microcomputer/ Asynchronous.
2	ELF (Extra Low Frequency)	25–500 Hz	-	3×10^6 m	High-Voltage 3-Phase Power Transmission at 50/60 Hz/Sec. Music Instruments, Heartbeat, Microcomputer Clock Asynchronous.
3	VF (Voice Frequency)	500 Hz-5 kHz	-	3×10^5 m	Human Voices, Musical Instruments, Computer Clock.
4	VLF (Very Low Frequency)	5–50 kHz	-	3×10^4 m	Music, Radar Omega Navigation, Computer Clock (Synchronous), Supersonic Oceanic Instrumentation, Fixed Services.
5	LF (Low Frequency)	50–500 kHz	-	3×10^3 m	Radio Navigational Aids, Aviation, Maritime Mobile Communications.
6	MF (Medium Frequency)	500 kHz–5 MHz	-	3×10^2 m	Industrial, Relay, Telegraph, Public Safety, Telephone, Land Mobile Communications, Short-Range Broadcast, Short Waves, Amateur, etc., Microcomputer Clock (Synchronous).
7	HF (High Frequency)	5-50 MHz	-	30 m	Aeronautical Communications, Audio and Television Broadcasting, General Mobile, Amateur Citizens Band (CB), Police, etc.
8	VHF (Very High Frequency)	50–500 MHz	-	3 m	Industrial, Railroad, Taxicab, Press Relay, Power Service, Trunk Carriers, CB, Aeronautical Frequencies, Broadcast Television Transmission, etc.
9	UHF (Ultra High Frequency)	500–1500 MHz (1.5 GHz)	-	30 cm	Maritime Mobile Communications, Radio Navigational Aids, Aeronautical Frequencies, Fixed Service Frequencies, Land Mobile Communications, Broadcast Television (Service), FM/AM Television Links, etc.

10	SHF (Super High Frequency	1.5–15 GHz	–	3 cm	Satellite FDMA/TDMA Data Communications, Cable Television, Microwave Links for Color Television, Maritime Mobile Communications, Radio Navigational Aids, Radar Navigation and Countermeasures, Amateur Pocket Radio Network, etc.
11	EHF (Extra High Frequency	15–150 GHz	–	3 mm	Maritime Mobile, High-Resolution Radar, Land-Sat Satellite Terrestrial Photography, Land Mobile, etc. Communications in atmosphere affected by rain, hail, snowfall, and sunspot magnetic disturbances.
12	Infrared Region Commences at 1 THz (1000 GHz)	150 GHz–1.5 THz	–	0.3 mm 300 μ 300×10^4 Å (Angstroms) (micron = micrometer)	Special Applications–Infrared Photography from Aircraft and Satellites, etc.
13	Infrared Region	1.5–700 THz	–	Lowest Wavelength 0.72 μ, 7000 Å (All living organisms hear this "noise" as a cosmic "heterodyne hiss" after rectification in the cerebral fluid that protects the cortex inside the skull.)	Infrared physiological heat waves cover the resonance band of "cosmic noise" ("Life Force"): in conjunction with "Hole" cosmic distribution (Negative-Mass Electron Distribution), responsible for the life of terrestrial (land) and oceanic living orgainsms at ~3° *Absolute Kelvin temperature* (author's conclusion). The "heterodyne hiss" can be heard as a modulation of the "heartbeat," and this is the clock-rate of neutral-logic.[a] The behavior of a "crowd" proves it.[b] *Note*: Cosmologists should use an *infrared suppression filter* for this *resonance band* (from about 3μ to 0.72 μ) and make spectrometer measurements for the light spectrum from the distant galaxies to see whether they still observe Doppler "Red-shift" to red end for the conclusion of an "Expanding Universe."
14	Light (Visible Spectrum)	700–900 THz	–	0.72–0.42 μ, 7000 Å–4200 Å	White light (Physiological Red, Green and Blue Colors), Laser Optical communications (Fiber Optics and Space)
15	Ultraviolet Region	900–10^6 THz	–	0.42 μ–0.3 mμ 4000 Å–3 Å	Physiological action on living organisms is harmful; the Earth's terrestrial atmosphere is a protective agent against this intense radiation from Sun.[c]

Table D-2 (Cont.)

No.	Band Designation	Frequency Band	Spectrum	Wavelengths (Center of Band)	Natural Manifestation or General Use
16	X-Rays (Soft)	50×10^4–10^7 THz	-	15 mμ-30 $\mu\mu$ 150–0.3 Å	Cancer-causing radiation from Sun and X-ray machines that display bone structure on a screen or CRT. If exposure is too intense, X-rays destroy living organisms by dangerously disturbing the bone-marrow mechanism that regenerates the oxygen-carrying red-blood cells for normal vitality.
	X-Rays (Hard)	10^7–10^9 THz	-	Above 0.3 Å or 30 $\mu\mu$	
17	Gamma Rays produced by nuclear explosions and Fission-Reactors. Produced by electron-position annihilations in the environment of cosmic "hole" (negative-mass electron) distribution in space—the environment of Gravitational Forces.	Above 50 Mega-THz	-	Above 0.05 Å or 5 $\mu\mu$	Destroys life as it exists on Earth. (Protective safeguards by way of bulky concrete-lead armor and surrounding leakage-proof water tanks essential in the case of Fission-type nuclear reactors.) . . . *d*, *e*

[a]The synchronization of the "heterodyne" audible "hiss" with the heartbeat is discovered by placing the palm of the right hand on one's heart in a silent environment. The *mirage* that appears on a warm day is a corresponding visual effect of a beat-frequency projection, continuously shifting (and not a socalled optical illusion) in different layers of hot atmosphere. The brain as a "superior computer" could still function asynchronously at a low clock-rate of approximately 50 to 90 cycles/sec, if the heartbeat stops temporarily, and if the blood-circulation (and hence oxygen for the neurons' glial cells) is continued by alternate or artificial means, since the *induced resonant* cosmic infrared "Life-Force" at 3° Absolute temperature is *eternal*.

[b]The automated terminals in a network can synchronously repeat the program of the leading 'host.' (War hysteria and inhumane group behavior of fanatic religious riots work in the same psychological context although every thoughtful *individual* person desires peace.)

[c]The penetrating tropical ultraviolet exposure results in original living species acquiring, as a protection against skin cancer, a tanning pigmentation (melanin), which through generations builds up as dark skin and hair.

[d]*Maxwell's prediction of Electromagnetic waves in space.* Out of Maxwell's equation concerning displacement current, there emerged the surprising result that electromagnetic waves should propagate in space. Maxwell found the velocity of electromagnetic waves as the ratio of electromagnetic and electrostatic units of charge, and concluded that light must be electromagnetic disturbance described by Maxwell's equations. That is how it all began with radio. Hertz was the first to demonstrate the actual propagation of radio waves, and Marconi exploited their use in commercial applications for the first time.

[e]The author's cosmopolitan outlook is based on cosmic infrared radiation, cosmology, and cybernetics. I interpret myself this way: my "body" is hereditarily made up and nurtured by "matter" as carbon and a few "key" elements along with a sprinkle of heavier mineral atoms. They were all created by transmutation in a star of some distant past (mainly during a supernova as a result of eventual Gravitational collapse). India's philosophy interprets the cosmic Gravitational Force as an indescribable Brahman/Nirvana/Sünyatha, Holy Ghost etc . . . As Shakespeare remarked, a rose by any name is equally fragrant. And, my living "self" is made up of an induced quantum of energy of the cosmic eternal infrared electromagnetic radiation that propagates in the medium of the eternal Gravitation (or positive-charge "hole" distribution), which I understand as the Power divine, because it is inseparably involved in the creation of the finitely rejuvenating body and the eternal nonindividualistic "self" as a quantum of infrared "energy" in the Cosmos. As a parallel, the advanced self-programmable microcomputer or a microprocessor-controlled television receiver are developed and produced by us, and when energized, they operate to perform a certain function reliably as long as they silently "tick" under the action of the very same Forces.

TABLE D-3. Concept of "Hole" as "-1."

The concept of "hole" as "-1" or normalized "*negative-mass electron*" is interpreted as the -1 on the negative real axis in feedback control theory of cybernetics and also as gravitation or "hole distribution" of positive-charge in cosmology.

1. *Cybernetics and active/passive networks.* Typical "Nyquist plots' of stability for two closed-loop transfer functions with negative feedback control are illustrated. The Nyquist plot is a conformal mapping of the vertical jω axis in the complex s-plane, where $\omega = 2\pi f$ and f is frequency. A "pole" (a crest to positive ∞) and a "zero" (a trough to negative ∞) cancel to make a point at "-1" on the negative real axis of the Nyquist plot, and -1 is a "hole" or positive-charge negative-mass electron in this interpretation.

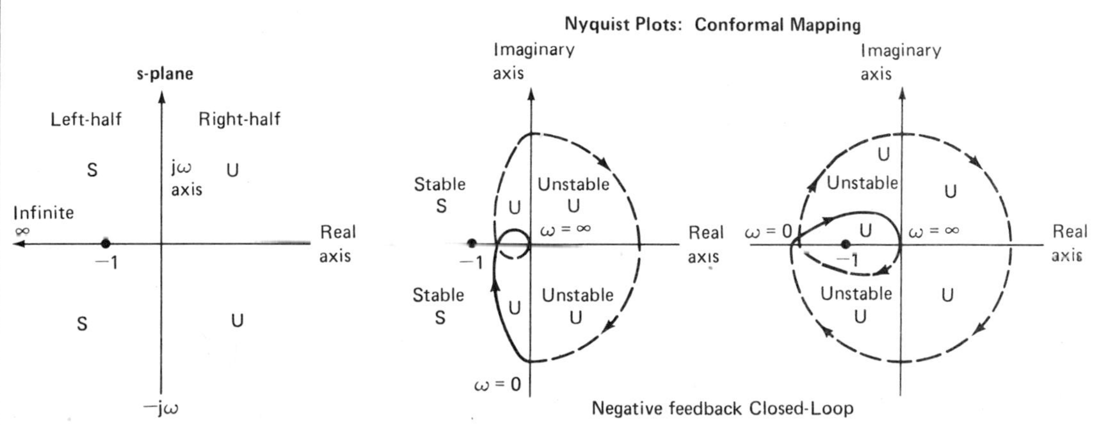

S = Stable region in the negative-half of the plot. The transfer function of the living organism is convergent toward "-1." This phenomenon represents an active, passive, considerate, compassionate, loving, constructive, happy, heavenly, and blissful state of living. Microcomputers and nuclear energy, etc., are put to peaceful constructive use. Negative feedback to oneself is positive feedback to others. "Give, it shall be given to you"; trust, they will trust you . . . . (Give = breathe out as an exercise.)

U = Unstable region of the positive-half. The transfer function or the living organism is divergent from "-1." This phenomenon represents an oscillatory, super-egotistic, self-centered, unhappy state of living. Other characteristics such as uncontrolled emotions or outbursts, depressions, superiority/inferiority complexes, hostility, agression, fear, timidity, and a destructive state of mind are dominant. Science and technology are directed toward destruction. Improper feedback in the left-half of the plot may also result in an unstable condition. Extreme poverty, ignorance, undue fear of survival, and overindulgence are some of the characteristics involved. Intoxicants such as alcohol and narcotic drugs will make a normally stable person with correct judgment subconsciously drift to instability in the positive-half of the s-plane. Greed, inflationary thinking, aggressive saber-rattling, risky cold-war attitudes, extreme left- and right-wing politics, fascist thinking, violence, riots, extreme impatience, etc., belong to this state of mind. Eradication of poverty, ignorance, and prevention of overpopulation are the responsibility of the whole world community, and the United Nations is the proper authority to take up this noble and enterprising commitment unanimously and expeditiously.

2. *Cosmology*. Laws of probability and statistics more or less hold goods on a Cosmic Basis.

S = Solar/planetary stellar inertial space (very small regions of Cosmos) and small cosmic regions of gas and dust. Laws of physics and general theory of relativity, Doppler Effect of frequency-shift hold good. Velocity of light is constant. Inertial space extends to a limited time-period of propagation of light at 3×10^8 meters/sec.

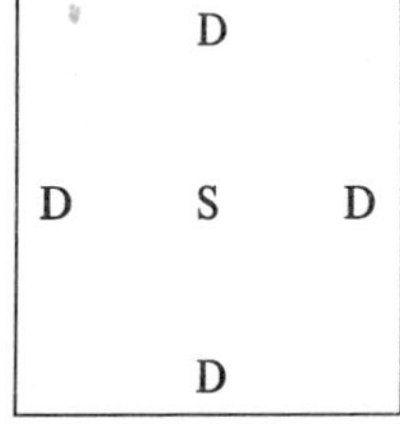

D = Interstellar and intergalactic deep space at superconductivity temperatures around 3° Absolute Kelvin. Cosmic infrared radiation of "nondependent" origin. Cosmic hole (positive-charge negative-mass electron) distribution is interpreted as Gravitation or Gravitational Waves. Mass-less electron-pair waves and photons "tunnel" through deep space. Electron-pairs with cancelled momentums of individual spins propagate under tunnel effect without any barrier of velocity of light. Laws of physics, Doppler Effect, and general theory of relativity do not hold good. Distances in deep space between stars, gas and dust regions, and galaxies (nebula) are immense and colossal. The "tunnel effect" makes the distances immaterial from the propagation point of view. The terms *zero gravity* and *light-year* are not definite and hence inadmissible. The term light-year as a relative unit may be!

3. We use the concept of the positive-charge hole as a "-1" on the real axis in the complex s-plane of feedback control theory, electronics network analysis, and synthesis of both active and passive circuits, and the theory of the complex variables in mathematics. The point "-1" on the negative real-axis (x) is the basic reference for determining the *stability* of a closed-loop feedback control system, represented by poles in the denominator and zeros in the numerator of a system transfer function, with the y-axis as the imaginary $j\omega$ axis, where $j = \sqrt{-1}$, $\omega = 2\pi f$, and f = frequency. The author interprets real number "-1" in the s-plane as representing the positive-charge, a mathematically-defined "negative-mass electron." Black holes of modern cosmology and astronomy can be interpreted as concentrations of collapsed positive-charge "hole distribution" at the centers of galaxies; mathematically speaking, the black holes take their place in the left-half of the s-plane, in which matter and energy converge into a stable region with the black hole at the center. The "-1" = Negative (unit) mass electron with a positive-charge, equivalent to the negative-charge of the positive (unit) mass electron. The positive and "negative" masses of the electrons are normalized as units. The positron is merely an electron that has "flip-flopped" to positive charge in the right-half. The crossing of the imaginary axis is instrumental for this change of mode. This is the case with all *antimatter*—according to the author's interpretation, and hence the scarcity of antimatter in the universe (so that the law of evolution toward something better could be fulfilled). On the same basis, a neutrino could be a mode of the electron itself on the $j\omega$ imaginary axis; and so also is the neutron as a mode of the proton on the imaginary axis, and hence the practical difficulty of capturing these enigmatic particles on nuclear instrumentation. The neutrino, if it does cross over the imaginary axis, may turn into a positron and annihilate an electron to become a gamma-ray in the mode of energy as a replacement of matter. Along the same lines of argument, we may say that a neutron star may be a misnomer for an invisible radio star, which does not possess any substantial form.

The cosmic near-zero gravitation or sparse "hole distribution" or gravitational waves as "hole-pairs" at superconductivity temperatures make the medium feasible for the free propagation of infrared radiation throughout the cosmos (at approximately 3° Absolute Kelvin in deep space) as an eternal phenomenon. Matter in the mode of electron-pair waves can then "tunnel" through without any barriers of the laws of physics and velocity of light at those superconductivity temperatures. In the vicinity of a non-superconductivity environment, the pairing ceases and the laws of physics, as we know, become effective. A very large array (VLA) of 27 antennas, each 82 ft in diameter, spread out in a **Y**-shape along 38 miles of railroad track are linked by underground microwave channels to a central computer at Socorro, New Mexico. They may perhaps reveal a few more secrets about the cosmic infrared radiation and other phenomena, such as quasars, of modern radio astronomy. The space telescope, which NASA is scheduled to launch into orbit in 1985, is expected to reveal more information than any terrestrial-based optical telescopes. As the solar system, at its high temperatures that sustain life on earth, travels through deep space, at a velocity of 155 miles per second, as an inherent part of our spinning galaxy, we are actually space travelers who lack any direct channel of understanding the secrets of a deep-space environment. A future spacecraft may reveal the distance to the superconductivity region.

The positive-charge "hole distribution" is the quintessence of the famous ancient Vedantha/Yoga philosophy of India, as the *Upanishadic* term, *Brahman*, the Reality. The word *holy* is perhaps derived from this original ancient philosophy via Greece and Alexander in the fourth century B.C. The author interprets the term *Brahman* as the Force of Creation, because that (Thath in Sanshrit) provides the eternal medium for the propagation of the life-inducing resonant infrared electromagnetic radiation throughout the Cosmos. The author considers the band of frequencies in this resonant infrared frequency spectrum responsible for the effect of red-shift of distant galaxies, and not the Doppler Effect that holds good in our environment. Hence, this is a dynamic steady-state Universe, *not* an expanding Universe. The term *Yoga* is derived from the Sanserit word *yuga*, meaning infinitely long periods of the dimension of Time in a Cosmos of immeasurable distances between stars, galaxies, and other heavenly objects. As far as deep-space propagation or travel is concerned, the tunnel effect makes the immeasurable distances immaterial. Astronomy and cosmology are not exact sciences, unlike other scientific subjects. We use our knowledge of other subjects to understand and gain a relatively partial knowledge about cosmology. That knowledge in return gives a better perspective to our thinking; a personal philosophy on a psychological basis should follow this criterion.

Inanimate "passive and active" microcomputers such as VLSI integrated circuits can maintain their remarkable stability and reliability in worldwide data communications networks via satellites by using the positive-charge "hole distribution" as an integral part of their makeup and performance. Therefore, we, the "living," *can* also maintain the stability, trust, peace, and progress on a primarily benevolent earth by allowing and enhancing *our* own integral constituent, onmipresent, positive-charge "hole distribution" (the *sūnyatha* of *Madhyamika* philosophy, or the invisible "spiritual force" of life, or for that matter the "kingdom of Heaven or Holy Ghost" of the West) as an insurmountable *stabilizing* force of individual negative feedback control, toward a self-disciplined and harmonious way of life, in arriving at a reasonable understanding of coexistence in the present world context, against idealogical confrontations, and distrusting disagreements of unwarrented "balance of terror" toward self-destruction on this comparatively "heavenly" planet, that sustains life as we know it on a universal basis. In addition, violence is against the gospel of Christ, which the West so openly and proudly professes. Electrons and holes coexist on a thoroughly harmonious basis. Where there is a will, there is a way for coexistence—always. The microcomputer, the revolutionary and outstanding achievement of homo sapiens in the second half of the twentieth century, ticks in absolute silence because of the inherent enigmatic participation of the cosmic "hole distribution." We "live" and survive because of the very "physically-integral, spiritual and moral" dominating factor in all of us. The negative feedback control, universally recurring in electronics technology, is a parallel to the continuous implication of self-discipline in the living organisms of cybernetics.

Those who do not or cannot realize the preceding fundamental truth live a superactive miserable life of psychological outbursts and depressions; the imaginary $j\omega$ axis is the so-called philosophical razor's edge that separates the unstable, oscillatory, destructive, and one-sided, materialistic positive-half, and the meticulously delineated *stable* area about "-1" in the negative-half of the s-plane in feedback control theory. This highly sophisticated mathematics must have originated along with the basics of astronomy in the undocumented prehistoric Near East, and we do not know when or how it started. Was it of extraterrestrial implantation among a few intelligent ancients? This is the author's conjecture based on a thorough historical perspective. It is certainly not a "materialistic" speculation, such as the Big-Bang bandwagon we hear so much about nowadays, which is a downright contradiction to Fred Hoyle and Jayant Narlekar's well-established and mathematically proven "C-Field Steady-State Theory" of the Universe as a systematic and dynamic cyclic continuity in an indefinable Eternity.[a] (As a matter of fact, the speculated "Big-Bang" of 15 billion years ago cannot prove the evolution of the heavy elements in the multigeneration star/supernova, and stellar regeneration in gas cloud systems, nor does it consider the inherent nonlinear characteristic of the Universe with its billions of known nonlinear galactic ingredients.)

The Big Powers have an arduous and glorious task in front of them; they full well know that they must coordinate a genuine and ceaseless effort toward uplifting their fellow humans, irrespective of national aspirations, susceptibilities, and barriers (before it is too late). They must do this in the face of the twin *unstabilizing* forces, poverty and ignorance—which are mainly responsible for population explosion and misery of survival. Satellite data communications with rooftop small earth terminals (SETs), digital color television with enlightening nonideological educational programs, and unlimited use of microcomputers in education and mass-production can make a wonderful contribution to this gigantic task. Science and knowledge are the real look-ahead phenomena of modern times—not the atomic bomb and certainly not the idealogical confrontation; idealogies do not feed the hungry millions nor do the crumbs of charity and foreign aid. As a first priority, modern scientific knowledge, as united effort of the international community, should be oriented on both a cooperative and competitive basis (for quick results) to the giant task of eradicating poverty and ignorance on this our "heavenly" planet. It *can* be done as a crash project once we make a fresh *beginning* with a united front. As one of the major tools in this potential worldwide enterprise the ubiquitous microcomputer gives the needed inspiration! How can computer-aided education feed the hungry? Education emphasizing the proper choice of nutritious food production will certainly play a major role. For example, large-quantity-production protein-rich soybean is 10 times more efficient than beef. Thus, if half the beef production is contributed to the hungry as protein via soybean and directly distributed to the hungry by the United Nations, isn't it a glorious consideration and achievement on the part of the rich nations? Politicians and media might try to divide this world of ours into "three worlds," but it is high time that they realize that this is just a little planet out of billions of such planets in our galaxy. This fact is brought close to our living room by our marvelous space program.

The following tentative plan is suggested for the united effort. The United Nations will initiate, as a crash program, a "Department of International Eradication of Poverty and Ignorance" that is not subject to national, political, or religious barriers. The international community of nations will contribute 50% of their defense budgets. In addition, they will furnish the following facilities and equipment on a contractual basis in order to meet the highest possible standards on a predetermined base of profit for the effort expended. The program will naturally reorient the mass employment of skilled and unskilled labor of the international community on a long-term basis, such as a minimum of four years.

1. The United Nations will manage the installation and maintenance of microcomputer-controlled automated plants in various regions of the world for the mass production of the basic necessities of life. These include prefabricated housing designed to meet the requirements of the climate in the regions

and low-cost protein or synthetic protein products for the prevention of hunger. (These mass-produced basic necessities for the unemployed poor will in no way compete with the regular international business of imports and exports for middle-class people around the world.)

2. Facilities of education as the means of eradication of ignorance:
   - International Education Satellites, geosynchronous (IEDS)
   - International (rooftop) small-earth terminals (SET)
   - Fiber-optic multiplex and digital distribution systems (FODDS)
   - Keyboard television microcomputer terminals (KTMT)
   - Educational Software Systems (ESS) for presenting educational documentary programs (EDPs) and vocational training programs (VTPs) on low-cost all-electronic mass-memory magnetic-bubbles (MMMBs) and electronically erasable programmable read-only memories (EEPROM), etc.

[a]On a bright evening in Rajahmundry, India, the author, then eight years old, and his mother witnessed from the terrace of their home, a spectacular silver-gray, spherical object hovering slowly in the sky over the beautiful river Godavery. At an altitude of about 8000 to 10,000 feet, it appeared to be about as big as the full moon. It hovered for more than 10 minutes, emitting jet-black smoke that swirled slowly up from its bottom. Then, it disappeared from view. This unforgettable spectacle has often bothered the author, because he could not find any explanation for its appearance.

And now, an article in *Scientific American* seems to present some possible explanation to the author's experience. It discusses (1) the property of electron-pairs/waves at superconductivity temperatures, canceling their angular momentums in opposite spins, (2) the "tunneling effect" of electron-pairs in Josephson junction transistors at gate-switching speeds of *picoseconds* as an interferometer effect at superconductivity temperatures (instead of *nanoseconds* at ordinary temperatures), and (3) the recently discovered cosmic infrared radiation at the superconductivity temperature of 3° Abolutes Kelvin. The "tunneling effect" in deep space should beat the barrier of velocity of light. (*Scientific American*, May 1980). The author concludes that these extra-terrestrial deep-space spherical vehicles use "Electron-pair beam" propulsion to "tunnel" through space.

rounding metal ions or holes, and a region of enhanced positive-charge is readily available for attracting the second electron of the pair simultaneously. That is, by the same concept, a "hole-pair" is available as a corresponding phenomena at superconductivity temperatures. The *feeble bonding* of the electron pair is dependent on the "gap-energy"; thermal energy a few degrees above absolute zero is sufficient to provide that feeble energy for the bonded electron-pair. If the magnetic field or current is excessive as at higher temperatures, the electron-pair breaks, and the electrons behave like free individual electrons with usual mobility limitations. Since the electron behaves like both a particle and a wave, superconductivity implies that the electron-pair waves have the same wavelength and the same phase as a coherent phenomenon. Electron-pair waves at two or more junctions follow the same pattern of coherence to minimize or eliminate fan-in and fan-out problems of delay in logic. **The concept of JJI** might one day enable astronauts (cosmonauts) to skip from star to star and galaxy to galaxy at near-infinite speeds beyond the barrier of velocity of light in inertial stellar space.*

So, a JJS cell, according to quantum mechanics, implies that *the tunneling of the electron-pair waves* may take place at near-infinite conductivity (and not at velocity of lights as in the case of the single electrons of the comparatively low-speed regular tunnel diodes. (It is simple to visualize that quantum and classical mechanics merge into one another if the insulating barrier involved is reduced to zero.) If the coherence is feasible in the case of the waves of electron-pairs, it should hold good in the case of other fundamental building-blocks of Matter/Energy, such as photons of light energy and proton and neutron waves too. That is, light waves from distant stars and galaxies "tunnel" through deep space in a short interval of time, and the term "light year" is merely relative, and not an absolute unit of distance.

D-3. MODERN COSMOLOGY

The Universe is a dynamic Cyclic Continuity in Eternity. In a stellar environment, the well-established Laws of Quantum Mechanics and Classical Mechanics for Matter, Energy, and Gravitational Force (or Positive-Charge Hole Distribution) hold good under both steady-state and transient conditions of manifestation. From both the scientific and philosophical points of view, the recent drastic and radical theory of a one-time "Big-Bang" is inadmissible. It is supposed to *originate* from a dimensionless Singu-

*The ultrareliable low-power consuming microcomputers would navigate the space-vehicles, with the astronauts put to sleep at 3° absolute zero! In deep space, JJ-I microcomputers do not need liquid-helium any more, when far away from solar radiations, although they need minimum of battery power in intergalactic short-duration space flights—or the feeble thermal energy of the infrared radiation might be adequate to "tunnel" a spherical space vehicle in deep-space.

larity and a 18-to-15-billion year lifetime of the Universe is estimated by extrapolation—after a short-period (a few days) of blowup to the unknowable dimensions of our present Universe. This "Big-Bang" theory is inadmissible. This radical wild speculation is supposed to be based on (1) "Doppler's Red-Shift" of distant galaxies moving away at velocities approaching velocity of light, and (2) the recent discovery of the cosmic resonant infrared radiation at 2.9° Absolute Kelvin—that this radiation is a "residual effect of the Big-Bang."

Most galaxies, especially those that are spiral in spatial appearance like our Milky Way, assume, depending on their environmental conditions, the attributes of a multidimensional time-frame of billions of "light-years," as *converging phase-portraits* of nonlinear multidimensional control system-complexes with possibly a black-hole at the center of each. (*Black-Holes* might be merely colossal concentrations of positive-charge *Hole Distribution* in space.) On this basis, our Universe, as an overall system of indefinite dimensions, could only converge under the forces of gravitational fields to a stable state-space limit-cycle of significant spatial dimensions (and not a dimensionless Singularity), before it starts diverging again under some catastrophic disturbance, as a cyclic model of inhale-exhale manifestation. The Universe, which is composed of billions of such nonlinear components as our Milky Way, would *never* converge, as linear systems do, to a dimensionless Singularity—which alone could satisfy the plausible conditions for a Big-Bang and instantaneous blowup.

On the other hand, the abovementioned discovery of an eternally pervading infrared radiation at 2.9° above the Absolute-zero in an *eternal* medium of cosmic positive-charge *hole distribution* should provide a relativity-based explanation for the red-shift of distant galaxies in a dynamic but steady-state Universe. New solar systems are born, as we see this evidence amid the gases and dust in space; old stars vanish about 10 billion years or so as radiostars or supernova, etc., depending on their mass classification in any specific galaxy. It seems obvious to the author that the Doppler red-shift phenomena is inoperative in the medium of superconductive deep-space, where the "tunneling" effect is the predominant feature. Doppler effect, like constant velocity of light, holds good in the environment of a star such as our Sun, and not in intra- and inter-galactic deep-space. If Doppler red-shift in an expanding Universe does not apply, an extrapolated "Big-Bang" about 18 billion years ago for the "birth" of our Universe is inadmissible. Also, there could be other Universes besides the one we are aware of!

The matter of red-shift of distant galaxies is further confused by the intricacies involved with the propagation of electron-pair waves in the light of quantum mechanics. At feeble thermal energy levels of 2.9° above Absolute zero, the electron-pair waves maintain their feeble bonding; and the Josephson Interferometer concept of electron-pair waves allows their propagation at near-infinite conductivity in deep-space, considered as a superconducting medium in the environment of a positive-charge hole distribution, unlike the classical propagation of individual electron waves and radio spectrum under the restriction of the velocity of light in the space in the immediate environment of our Sun. Therefore, the red-shift of distant galaxies and their variations as observed in spectrographic measurements is a misnomer under the totally new valid hypotheses of an eternal *resonant* infrared radiation at 2.9° above the Absolute zero and an eternal manifestation of cosmic positive-charge hole distribution in space. As a substantial support to this new proposal in modern cosmology, the "cosmic hole distribution" in the Universe is identified in ancient philosophies of India as Brahman the Reality, Nirvana, *Śūnyathā,* and Cosmic Consciousness, as explained in the following section.

D-4. THE PARALLEL ANCIENT PHILOSOPHY OF ŚŪNYATHĀ

The outstanding and scholarly Nāgārjunā's Mādhyāmikā school of philosophy of the second century A.D., from Andhra, India emphasizes Śūnyathā (the indescribable Absolute) as the Reality. It supports the proposed eternity of cosmic positive-charge hole distribution (or alternatively, Gravitational Force) because, without this background medium or environment, Matter and Energy cannot coexist on a cosmic scale as mutually interchangeable identities. The life processes are especially intertwined with these three basic phenomena. Śūnyathā corresponds to the Nirguna Brahman of India's ancient Upanisads of Vedantha—which merely signifies the phaseout of the earlier Vedas, because they proved to be obsolete in the light of Upanisads. The Buddhist Nirvāna is merely an alternate term because it is more significant for Buddha's interpretations and teachings. Nagarjuna philosophizes (1) *Śūnyathā* as the one and only one "*Relativity-based* Non-origination" (and everything else in the Universe as "Dependent

Originations"), pratitya-samutpada. On this basic foundation, Nagarjuna deals with the other two identities of the Universe on a relative basis (2) as Samvrti, the *phenomenal empirical truth*, which is as *Matter* a *means* at any instant, and (3) as Paramārtha, the *transcendental truth*,* which is as *Energy* an *end result* at any instant. (The recent Transcendental Meditation (TM) of Yoga philosophy is an offshoot of Paramārtha. As one slowly breaths out, uttering a sound such as "ooom," one automatically inhales an extra dose of negative-mass electron/positive-charge "hole" distribution to rejuvenate one's physical and mental faculties–this is the author's interpretation of TM.)

According to historical records, before 450 A.D. India's digital calculating device *Śōrabān* was in usage for manual entry of decimal data and simultaneous display of decimal output data in positive digits. Processing with decimal point was done in a slightly more sophisticated way by finger-manipulated beads, as compared to the Abacus of China. Around this time, India's famous mathematician Aryabhatt wrote the first published treatise on Algebra and Astronomy. In the context of India's subsequent history, there are records to show that 657 sanskrit works were transported to China from India's Nalanda University in the east by monks Yuon Chang and later Fa-hien, and translated into Chinese under the orders of China's emperors. Taxila near Peshaver in present Pakistan in the west, and Amaravathi on river Krishna in Andhra were the two other famous universities of the time. They were actually huge resident and research centers of learning established by the then Buddhist emperors of India. In the year 62 A.D., China's emperor Ming-ti at Shensi invited "monks" from India under the leadership of Kasyapa Matanga. Actually, Buddhist philosophy was first introduced to China in the year 217 B.C. after the dynasty of India's famous emperor, and Buddha's admirer Ashoka. And Bodhidharma from Andhra (Amarabathi) introduced the "Dhyana" school of philosophy (the Zen of modern Japan) to China in the year 470 A.D. The monks were actually considered as scholars (and not Buddhist missionaries in the modern sense.)

The Buddhist philosophy was distorted and subsequently phased out in India, and the historical scriptures and records on processed palm-leaf went up in smoke during the invasions from the Middle-East (with the eventual advent of Islam in India, because large masses of India's citizens lost their human rights as citizens, while the country got socially divided under a rigid caste system). In intellectual circles, the original concepts of philosophy, Matter/Energy/Śūnyathā (or Absolute) were interpreted for the masses by the new schools of philosophy on a symbolic and theological basis of Trinity, as (1) Vishnu, the Lord of the phenomenal world and Preserver of Life, who "assumes" 10 incarnations (*Rama*, Krishna, etc.) in evolutionary time–the Buddha being one of those incranations! (Buddha emphasized Unāthmān philosophy in which there is absolutely no room for reincarnations or rebirth!), (2) Shiva, the Lord of the Transcendental Energy, viz., Shaktī, and (3) Brāhmā, the "unworshipped" Creator or the Absolute, who deputes the "worshipped" Vishnu and Shiva to make the worlds "go" in his all-pervading environment. In the city of Bombay, a gigantic statue of post-Gupta Art in stone, *One Body and Three Heads*, is one of the famous ancient monuments of India. It offers original evidence of the above succeeding or parallel school of philosophy in a country of remarkable religious tolerance up to around A.D. 1000.

In one of the variations of the Mādhyāmikā school of philosophy, the individual "mind" was interpreted as merely another *sense organ* for memory-storage, logic, and judgment (decision). This is the full-fledged brain, without an established soul (*unāthman* or *unātha* in Pali, a version of Sanskrit), since the Buddha originally *emphasized* this aspect, encouraged peace of mind, and disapproved of undisciplined desires, boosted individual ego, and the caste system of modern India. Indeed, cosmic Śūnyathā (or cosmic consciousness/"cosmic soul"/"life-force") as Nirvāna was the supreme foundation for this school of philosophy. Without the positive-charge "Hole-Distribution" as an omnipresent phenomenon (Śūnyathā), and its mobility versus the faster negative-charge electron mobility of quantum theory in our semiconductor physical-chemistry theoretical discussions, it must be recognized that modern, minute but powerful, micron-dimension-oriented, economic, silicon monolithic, very-large-scale integrated microcomputer (as a potential hope of enhanced intercommunication and betterment of humanity) would not have been substantiated as a "miracle" device of outstanding capabilities at the present stage of scientific and technological breakthroughs!

*The *cyclic* sine-wave of the electromagnetic spectrum is a *transcendental* function varying in frequency (between ± infinity)–so is biorhythm (of modern research) at a low-frequency rate.

The subject, the amazing science of the microcomputer systems, is concluded in this final appendix with 10 verses, translated from Pali, from Sir Edwin Arnold's *Light of Asia*, published in 1879 as a reminder of Gautham Buddha's ingenious role as the original philosopher-scientist (563-483 B.C.) of the world status.

OM, AMITHAYA! measure not with words
  Th' Immeasurable; nor sink the string of thought
Into the Fathomless. Who asks doth err,
Who answers, errs. Say nought! . . .

Shall any gazer see with mortal eyes,
  Or any searcher know by mortal mind;
Veil after veil will lift–but there must be
  Veil upon veil behind.

Before beginning, and without an end,
  As space eternal and as surety sure,
Is fixed a Power divine which moves to good,
  Only its Laws endure.

It slayeth and it saveth, nowise moved
  Except unto the working out of doom;
Its threads are Love and Life; and death and pain
  The shuttles of its loom.

It maketh and unmaketh, mending all;
  What it hath wrought is better than hath been;
Slow grows the splendid pattern that it plans
  Its wistful hands between.

This is its work upon the things ye see,
  The unseen things are more; men's hearts and minds,
The thoughts of people and their ways and wills,
  Those, too, the great Law binds.

Unseen it helpeth ye with faithful hands
  Unheard it speaketh stronger than the storm.
The hidden good it pays with peace and bliss,
  The hidden ill with pains.

It knows not wrath nor pardon; utter-true
  Its measures mete, its faultless balance weighs;
Times are as nought, tomorrow it will judge,
  Or after many days.

Such is the Law which moves to righteousness,
  Which none at last can turn aside or stay;
The heart of it is Love, the end of it
  Is Peace and Consummation sweet. Obey! . . .

The Dew is on the lotus!–rise Great Sun!
  And lift my leaf and mix me with the wave.
Ooom! Mäni Pädme Hūm. The Sunrise comes!
  The Dewdrop slips into the shining Sea!"

–Evolution and the Laws of Providence in a Nutshell.

Index

Index